Studies in Latin American Ethnohistory & Archaeology

Joyce Marcus
General Editor

Volume I	*A Fuego y Sangre: Early Zapotec Imperialism in the Cuicatlán Cañada, Oaxaca*, by Elsa Redmond, Memoirs of the Museum of Anthropology, University of Michigan, No. 16. 1983.
Volume II	*Irrigation and the Cuicatec Ecosystem: A Study of Agriculture and Civilization in North Central Oaxaca*, by Joseph W. Hopkins, Memoirs of the Museum of Anthropology, University of Michigan, No. 17. 1984.
Volume III	*Aztec City-States*, by Mary G. Hodge, Memoirs of the Museum of Anthropology, University of Michigan, No. 18. 1984.
Volume IV	*Conflicts over Coca Fields in Sixteenth-Century Peru*, by María Rostworowski de Diez Canseco, Memoirs of the Museum of Anthropology, University of Michigan, No. 21. 1988.
Volume V	*Tribal and Chiefly Warfare in South America*, by Elsa Redmond, Memoirs of the Museum of Anthropology, University of Michigan, No. 28. 1994.
Volume VI	*Imperial Transformations in Sixteenth-Century Yucay, Peru*, transcribed and edited by R. Alan Covey and Donato Amado González, Memoirs of the Museum of Anthropology, University of Michigan, No. 44. 2008.

Frontispiece. A view toward the Urquillos area in the Yucay Valley, Peru. In Inka times, local populations settled near royal estates at the valley floor, establishing their social and economic landscape alongside imperial facilities. Spanish Colonial rule brought changes to indigenous religion, economic organization, and land tenure. Photo by R. Alan Covey.

Memoirs of the Museum of Anthropology
University of Michigan
Number 44

Studies in Latin American
Ethnohistory & Archaeology

Joyce Marcus, General Editor
Volume VI

Imperial Transformations in Sixteenth-Century Yucay, Peru

transcribed and edited by
R. Alan Covey and Donato Amado González

Ann Arbor, Michigan
2008

Printed in the United States of America
ISBN 978-0-915703-67-8

Cover design by Katherine Clahassey

The University of Michigan Museum of Anthropology currently publishes two monograph series, Anthropological Papers and Memoirs, as well as an electronic series in CD-ROM form. For a complete catalog, write to Museum of Anthropology Publications, 4013 Museums Building, 1109 Geddes Avenue, Ann Arbor, MI 48109-1079, or see www.lsa.umich.edu/umma/

Library of Congress Cataloging-in-Publication Data

Imperial transformations in sixteenth-century Yucay, Peru / transcribed and edited by R. Alan Covey and Donato Amado González.
p. cm. -- (Memoirs of the Museum of Anthropology, University of Michigan ; no. 44) (Studies in Latin American ethnohistory & archaeology)
Includes bibliographical references and index.
ISBN 978-0-915703-67-8 (alk. paper)
1. Incas--Peru--Yucay Region--History--16th century--Sources. 2. Incas--Land tenure--Peru--Yucay Region. 3. Incas--Cultural assimilation--Peru--Yucay Region. 4. Yucay (Peru)--History--16th century--Sources. 5. Yucay (Peru)--Colonization. 6. Spain--Colonies--America--Administration. I. Covey, R. Alan, 1974- II. Amado González, Donato, 1962- III. University of Michigan. Museum of Anthropology.
F3429.1.Y83I67 2008
985'.37--dc22

2008020884

The paper used in this publication meets the requirements of the ANSI Standard Z39.48-1984 (Permanence of Paper)

For Sabine MacCormack,
with profound thanks

Contents

PART II

Illustrations

Integrating Ethnohistory and Archaeology

Joyce Marcus

Our understanding of Andean beliefs, practices, and customs is enormously enriched by sixteenth-century Spanish documents. Indeed, if such documents did not exist, we would never have learned details such as (1) the names and deeds of Inka rulers (e.g., Cieza de León 1947[1553a], 1967[1553b]; Cobo 1979[1653a], 1990[1653b]; Guaman Poma de Ayala 1980[1615]; Sarmiento de Gamboa 1906[1572], 2007); (2) the struggles of various ethnic groups to control lands where coca could be grown (e.g., Rostworowski de Diez Canseco 1988); or (3) the Inka custom of keeping brown, black, and white camelids separate from each other (Acosta 1986[1590]).

When the Spaniards reached Peru in AD 1532, they were surprised to learn that the palaces of previous Inka rulers were maintained long after the body of the ruler had been embalmed, and that the new ruler was required to build his own palace and acquire new lands to establish and support his own royal lineage. The embalmed mummies of previous rulers were curated and served by royal attendants, and periodically put on display in the main plaza of Cusco, carefully arranged in the order in which each ruler had reigned (e.g., Pizarro 1978[1571]).

Descendants of each deceased ruler were charged with the task of managing his estates in perpetuity. Such estate management meant that a ruler's property, laborers, and resources were used by his descent group not only to curate the royal mummy, but also to satisfy all of their own needs. The Inka estates were often a series of widely dispersed lands, with associated laborers directed and controlled by the descendants of the ruler (e.g., Niles 1999, 2004; Rostworowski 1962; cf. Rowe 1997).

The Spaniards soon recognized the value of controlling these royal estates, seeking to acquire them as their *encomiendas*. Once the descendants of a ruler understood that the best way to reclaim these estates was to file petitions in the Spanish courts, the latter witnessed a surge in legal actions. Understandably, the descendants of indigenous royalty wanted to hold on to the land and labor to which they had become accustomed.

Royal Estates in the Yucay Valley

The Yucay Valley in the Cusco region, a frost-free area, was not only well suited for the intensification of maize production, but also was a favored locale for Inka rulers to establish their royal estates. Indeed, the Yucay Valley (along with the Sacred Valley of the Inka) appears to have contained the personal landholdings of several Inka rulers, one of whom was Huayna Capac.

Around AD 1500, Huayna Capac ordered that the Yucay Valley be transformed into a place with comfortable facilities for his pleasure and relaxation, as well as for his family. He commissioned his half-brother, Sinchi Roca, to design the necessary buildings. Thousands of laborers were called in from all over the empire to work on this major construction project. One component of the Yucay Valley transformation involved straightening the Urubamba River; another involved the construction of stone terraces for intensive maize cultivation; yet another component was the construction of impressive gardens, palatial residences, and storage facilities.

Huayna Capac also set aside land in the Yucay Valley to maintain the worship and cult of the Sun, to support the families of other dead rulers, and to reward other Inka nobles. After the completion of this huge project, many of the provincial laborers that had been called in were allowed to return to their homes. The remaining local population was, however, joined by 2000 retainers or *yanakuna* (1000 from the part of the empire called Chinsaysuyu and 1000 from the part called Qollasuyu). These *yanakuna* were told to stay and work permanently on the estate.

Huayna Capac—the last Inka ruler to administer a fully unified empire—personally controlled his estate in the Yucay Valley during his lifetime. After he died in Quito (around AD 1525–1528), Huayna Capac was mummified. Specialists removed all his internal organs and dried his body in the sun. After his body was desiccated, attendants dressed him in fine clothing and placed him on a litter adorned with gold and feathers. His mummy was then brought from Quito to Yucay, accompanied by a procession of Inka nobles and people assigned to the service of the dead ruler. His final destination was Quispeguanca, a special structure built in the Yucay Valley to house and protect the mummy. Female ritual specialists were assigned to attend him in perpetuity; these *mamakuna* sang songs recounting Huayna Capac's achievements, using the lyrics to convey the same kinds of information the ancient Maya often recorded on stone monuments.

The Spanish conquest followed shortly thereafter—a conquest aided by the spread of European diseases and facilitated by political turmoil, a by-product of an Inka civil war that took place between AD 1530 and 1532. Although the Yucay estate appears to have remained in Inka hands, an unsuccessful Inka rebellion of 1536 was followed by a re-allocation of royal estate lands and laborers.

By AD 1539, the Spaniard Francisco Pizarro had assigned himself an *encomienda* in the Yucay Valley, taking over what had been Huayna Capac's lands and laborers. Indeed, Pizarro and his allies claimed as their own the Inka's retainers and lands throughout the Cusco region.

After Pizarro's death in AD 1541, his Yucay estate was managed by his brother Gonzalo on behalf of his four children, whose mothers were two Inka princesses. After Gonzalo Pizarro's rebellion against the Spanish Crown was quashed in 1548, Pedro de la Gasca seized the Yucay Valley as a Crown property. This estate had been organized as a system of labor service, but approximately three to five years after the children of Pizarro were exiled, Spanish officials levied a new system of tribute on the Yucay Valley communities. Around AD 1556, a coca tax was imposed; later, personal services and labor in the coca fields of Yucay were replaced by payments of silver (Covey and Elson 2007:309).

In AD 1558, Sayri Tupa, Huayna Capac's grandson, offered his loyalty to the Spaniards and in return was granted the tribute-paying population of the Yucay Valley (Rostworowski de Diez Canseco 1962, 1970).

In AD 1572, Beatriz Clara Coya, the daughter of Sayri Tupa and the great granddaughter of Huayna Capac, was married to Martín García de Loyola. Together, the couple filed legal claims to have the *yanakuna* (retainers, workers, and servants) assigned to them as tributaries. Beatriz Coya and García de Loyola wanted to recoup or extend the base of labor tribute founded on the valley's royal estates, which had been diminishing since the 1530s. They petitioned the Crown to assign them an additional 250 males, men who had been exempt from paying tribute since they were classified as *yanakuna*.

Beatriz Coya claimed these *yanakuna* in the Yucay Valley as part of an *encomienda* to which she was entitled, since she was recognized by the Spanish Crown as the sole and legitimate heir of Sayri Tupa. As noted by Covey and Elson (2007:311), such a claim was a significant departure from Inka practice, which entailed recognizing the corporate or collective claim of the estate, recognizing the legitimate rights of all the other descendants of Huayna Capac in addition to Beatriz Coya.

By the time Beatriz Coya's daughter, Ana María Lorenza García Sayri Tupac de Loyola, finally won her parents' legal case in the early 1600s, the lands and labor system that had once been part of Huayna Capac's estate had been transformed into a Spanish estate called the Marquisate of Oropesa. Fortunately, the Betancur Collection in the Archivo Departamental in Cusco contains a massive archive of documents that were assembled in the eighteenth century to support all the claims being made regarding the holdings of the Marquisate of Oropesa.

In this volume, the editors, R. Alan Covey and Donato Amado González, present an archaeological and historical introduction to the Yucay Valley, as well as the complete transcription of the first volume of documents in the Betancur Collection. In the process of doing this, they show us how and why the lands and resources in the Yucay Valley passed through so many hands.

This book is a major contribution to Andean research because Covey and his colleagues are able to show the disparate and competing interests harbored by diverse people—from Inka emperors to the Spanish Crown, from Colonial period elites to tributary populations—all the while providing the kinds of demographic and ethnic details that archaeologists can only dream about.

Any scholar who recovers, transcribes, analyzes, and publishes key documents is making a major contribution to the Andes, simply by making unpublished information available for so many others to study. Beyond that, the legal documents published in this volume offer unprecedented data on ethnicity, demography, and the history of conflicting claims and interests of all those who worked and lived in the Yucay Valley.

To be sure, many earlier Andeanists—scholars such as John V. Murra, María Rostworowski, Pierre Duviols, Raúl Porras Barrenechea, Waldemar Espinoza Soriano, Franklin Pease, R. Tom Zuidema, Manuel Chávez Ballón, John H. Rowe—paved the way for this kind of volume. Today, however, it is gratifying to see that a whole new generation of scholars, like Covey, Amado González, Bauer, and their many contemporaries, are making enormous progress of their own in what has been a long and remarkable tradition of ethnohistoric scholarship.

References Cited

Acosta, José de

1986[1590] *Historia Natural y Moral de las Indias*, edited by José Alcina Franch. Historia 16. Madrid, Spain.

Cieza de León, Pedro de

1947[1553a] *Primera parte de la Crónica del Perú*. Biblioteca de Autores Españoles, Tomo 26. Madrid, Spain.

1967[1553b] *El Señorío de los Incas, segunda parte de la Crónica del Perú*. Lima, Perú: Instituto de Estudios Peruanos.

Cobo, Bernabé

1979[1653a] *History of the Inca Empire: An Account of the Indians' Customs and their Origin, Together with a Treatise on Inca Legends, History, and Social Institutions*, translated and edited by Roland B. Hamilton. Austin: University of Texas Press.

1990[1653b] *Inca Religion and Customs*, translated and edited by Roland B. Hamilton. Austin: University of Texas Press.

Covey, R. Alan, and Christina Elson

2007 Ethnicity, demography, and estate management in sixteenth-century Yucay. *Ethnohistory* 54(2):303-35.

Guaman Poma de Ayala, Felipe

1980[1615] *El Primer Nueva Corónica y Buen Gobierno*, edited by John V. Murra and Rolena Adorno and translated by Jorge I. Urioste, 3 vols. Mexico City: Siglo Veintiuno.

Niles, Susan A.

1999 *The Shape of Inca History: Narrative and Architecture in an Andean Empire*. Iowa City: University of Iowa Press.

2004 The nature of Inca royal estates. In *Machu Picchu: Unveiling the Mystery of the Incas*, edited by Richard L. Burger and Lucy C. Salazar, pp. 49-68. New Haven, CT: Yale University Press.

Pizarro, Pedro

1978[1571] *Relación del descubrimiento y conquista de los reinos del Perú*, edited by Guillermo Lohmann Villena. Lima, Perú: Pontificia Universidad Católica del Perú.

Rostworowski de Diez Canseco, María

1962 Nuevos datos sobre tenencia de tierras reales en el Incario. *Revista del Museo Nacional* 31:130-64.

1970 El repartimiento de Doña Beatriz Coya en el Valle de Yucay. *Historia y Cultura* 4:153-267.

1988 *Conflicts over Coca Fields in Sixteenth-Century Peru*. Memoirs, no. 21. Museum of Anthropology, University of Michigan. Ann Arbor.

Rowe, John H.

1997 Las tierras reales de los incas. In *Arqueología, antropología e historia: Homenaje a María Rostworowski*, edited by Rafael Varón Gabai and Javier Flores Espinoza, pp. 277-87. Lima: Instituto de Estudios Peruanos.

Sarmiento de Gamboa, Pedro

1906[1572] Segunda parte de la Historia General llamada Indica. . . . In *Geschichte des Inkareiches von Pedro Sarmiento de Gamboa*, edited by Richard Pietschmann. Abhandlungen der Königlichen Gesellschaft der Wissenschaften zu Göttingen, Philologisch-Historische Klasse, neue Folge, vol. 6, no. 4. Berlin: Weidmannsche Buchhandlung.

2007[1572] *The History of the Incas*, translated and edited by Brian S. Bauer and Vania Smith. Austin: University of Texas Press.

Acknowledgments

The present volume was made possible by generous investments of time and material support made by a number of colleagues. Sabine MacCormack initiated the project, obtaining a photocopy of the first 450 folios of the collection published here, as well as funds to support the first stage of the transcription project, which was carried out by Alan Covey from 1999–2002.

Donato Amado joined the project in 2006, taking digital images of the entire volume, completing the transcription of the documents, and checking the transcription against the manuscript at the Archivo Departamental del Cuzco. We thank the staff of the archive for facilitating this research. The final phase of archival work was supported in part by research funds associated with an archaeological survey funded by the National Science Foundation (BCS-0342381) and the National Endowment for the Humanities.

The publication of the manuscript would not have been possible without the support of Joyce Marcus, who encouraged us to submit the work for consideration through her UMMA ethnohistory series, and who helped to motivate the timely completion of the editorial process.

The editorial staff—especially Jill Rheinheimer and Kay Clahassey—turned drafts and copyedits around with surprising speed, and were patient as we worked to edit the manuscript. The introductory chapters to the volume were completed with the help of a number of colleagues. The Calca-Yanahuara Archaeological Project was funded by the Heinz Grant Program for Latin American Archaeology, and was directed by Miriam Araóz Silva. Miriam, Brian Bauer, Jorge Silva, Geaneth Guzmán, and Benigno Zamalloa worked on the 2007 survey project. The second introductory chapter is adapted from a 2007 article co-authored with Christina Elson in *Ethnohistory*. We offer our deepest gratitude to everyone responsible for seeing this project through to completion.

Part I

Chapter 1

Settlement Patterns in the Yucay Valley and Neighboring Areas

R. Alan Covey, Miriam Aráoz Silva, and Brian S. Bauer

The Yucay Valley, defined in the sixteenth century as the stretch of the Vilcanota-Urubamba Valley between Huayoccari and Yanahuara, is a well-documented part of the Inka imperial heartland, one in which the transition from Inka to Spanish rule can be investigated in an interdisciplinary manner (Fig. 1.1). Previous studies of the valley have described its geography and ethnographic populations, as well as many of the monuments constructed in the valley for the Inka elite (e.g., Farrington 1984, 1995; Gade 1975; Niles 1999). Although this volume focuses principally on a significant collection of sixteenth-century documents from the Yucay Valley, the present chapter provides a new body of archaeological evidence from the valley, data we collected in 2007.

The Calca-Yanahuara Archaeological Project involved systematic regional survey designed to determine patterns of prehistoric human occupation in the valley. Survey crews walked all accessible parts of the valley, registering the presence of surface artifacts and architectural remains. In 2007, we covered a region of roughly 100 km^2 and identified more than 150 sites. This new dataset can be used in conjunction with survey results from neighboring areas (e.g., Bauer 1992, 1999, 2004; Bauer and Covey 2002; Covey 2003, 2006a) to reconstruct settlement patterns for the Yucay Valley and to place them in a larger context vis-à-vis broader regional variations and temporal patterns.

Environmental Description and Research Context

The Yucay Valley is located in the Cusco region in the southern Peruvian highlands. The valley floor is approximately 2850 m asl (meters above sea level) in the section we studied in 2007, an area characterized by highly productive maize agriculture and the intensive production of fruits and vegetables (Gade 1975). Glaciated mountains are located to the north of the valley, with a limited number of narrow, steep side valleys and quebradas bringing permanent streams to the Urubamba River (Figs. 1.2, 1.3). The glaciers rise to well over 5000 m asl, and their presence contributes to more marginal environmental conditions at lower elevations than for other parts of the valley (e.g., in the Pisaq area, approximately 40 km upstream).

Two distinct ecological areas lie to the south of the Yucay Valley. The Maras Plain, located at the southwestern margin of the study region, is located just 400 m above the valley floor, and is characterized by the cultivation of European cereals and Andean tubers, as well as limited patches of maize lands. The rolling landscape in the Maras and Chinchero areas contrasts with the steep and arid slopes of the southeastern limits of the Yucay Valley. This area has little productive farmland, and the sides of the valley rise to puna grasslands and mountains that reach 4600 m asl.

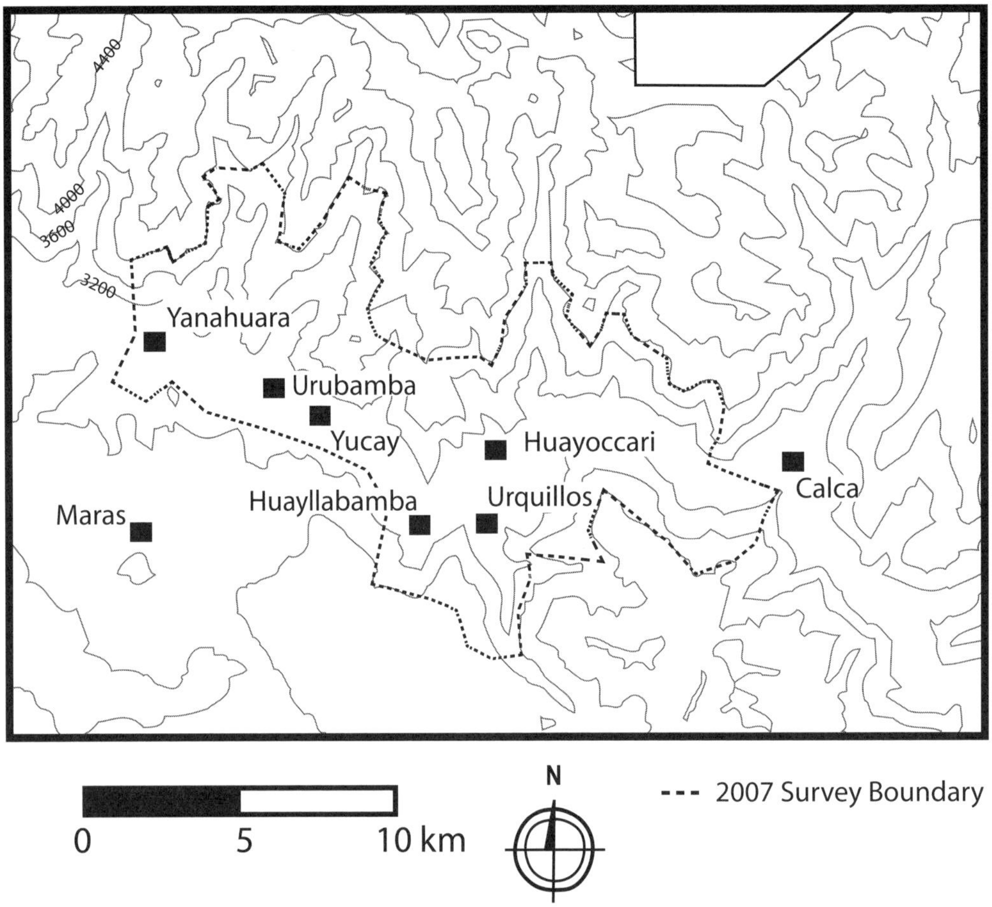

Figure 1.1. The Yucay Valley, showing the boundary of the 2007 survey region and modern towns discussed in the text.

Our 2007 research implemented a full-coverage pedestrian survey in all the accessible parts of the study region that lie below about 3800 m asl, as well as purposive visitation of passable ridges and hillsides above this limit that had potential for human settlement. Large parts of the sides of the valley were too steep to traverse systematically, although steep areas were crossed along existing footpaths whenever possible. The valley bottom presented logistical difficulties not encountered in other survey projects in Cusco. The rapid urbanization of the Yucay Valley and the present partition of prime lands into numerous private plots made full-coverage survey challenging (Fig. 1.4). Areas around Urubamba and Yucay were profoundly disturbed, and information on site sizes and densities is less reliable than would be typical for such a region. Wherever possible, crews of three fieldworkers walked all parts of the study region in lines approximately 50 m apart, registering sites on the basis of surface ceramics and architectural remains. At the edge of urban areas, crews of two went door-to-door, seeking permission of landowners to enter and survey individual plots. Although urban conditions have destroyed important sites and obscured important aspects of the regional settlement pattern, our 2007 research identified archaeological sites representing all known phases of prehispanic and early Colonial settlement.

Preceramic/Aceramic Sites (ca. 5000–2000 BC)

Survey research in the Cusco region has identified two kinds of conclusively identifiable preceramic or aceramic sites: isolated projectile points or stone tools and scatters of such tools in association with debitage (see Bauer 2004, 2007; Covey and Griffis n.d.). Projectile points have been found in almost all surveyed areas, while unmixed lithic scatters are generally seen only in agriculturally marginal areas with no subsequent human population. Stone flakes and tools are found at ceramic sites, but usually cannot be considered to date conclusively to the preceramic

Figure 1.2. The floor of the Yucay Valley in the Huayoccari, Urquillos, and Huayllabamba area. Photo by R.A. Covey.

Figure 1.3. Landscape of the Pumahuanca Quebrada, a side valley draining into the Yucay Valley. Photo by B.S. Bauer.

Figure 1.4. The Yucay Valley around Urubamba. Dense contemporary settlement made it necessary to modify the survey methodology in places. Photo by B.S. Bauer.

period. Carved rocks and cliff paintings are strongly linked to the preceramic occupation of other parts of the Andes, but cannot be considered diagnostic of this period in the Cusco region.

Excavations by Bauer and colleagues at Kasapata have dated the permanent occupation in the Cusco region by nomadic hunter-gatherers by 4500 BC (Bauer 2007), although isolated points similar to Early Archaic tools from the Titicaca Basin suggest that humans were in the region during the Early Archaic period (ca. 9000–7500 BC) (Bauer 2004). Bauer's excavations and the recent identification of a cluster of aceramic sites to the south of Maras (Covey and Griffis n.d.) suggest that foraging movement over time became more localized, relying on stone sources and plant and animal resources within a short distance of a few campsites. Projectile points have been found at higher elevations and at narrow passes between upper valley areas—these locations suggest that early occupants were hunting deer and wild camelids, with some hunting involving ambushing prey as it moved from one grazing area to another.

Despite the abundance of preceramic sites in the Maras Plain, few have been identified in the Sacred Valley proper. A limited number of projectile points were encountered in the 2000 survey of the upper Sacred Valley, and a small scatter of andesite debitage near Pisaq represents the only known artifact scatter from that part of the valley. Our 2007 field season identified a single projectile point in the Urubamba area. In addition, cliff paintings that may be preceramic in date were identified in the San Juan Canyon near Yucay, and a few scattered petroglyphs were encountered in the Urubamba area (Figs. 1.5, 1.6). The side valleys and quebradas of the study region appear to have been conduits for Archaic hunters and gatherers passing between the Sacred Valley and lowland areas such as Lares, and early art may have served to mark these routes. Urban growth in the valley itself has erased any evidence of human settlement for this period.

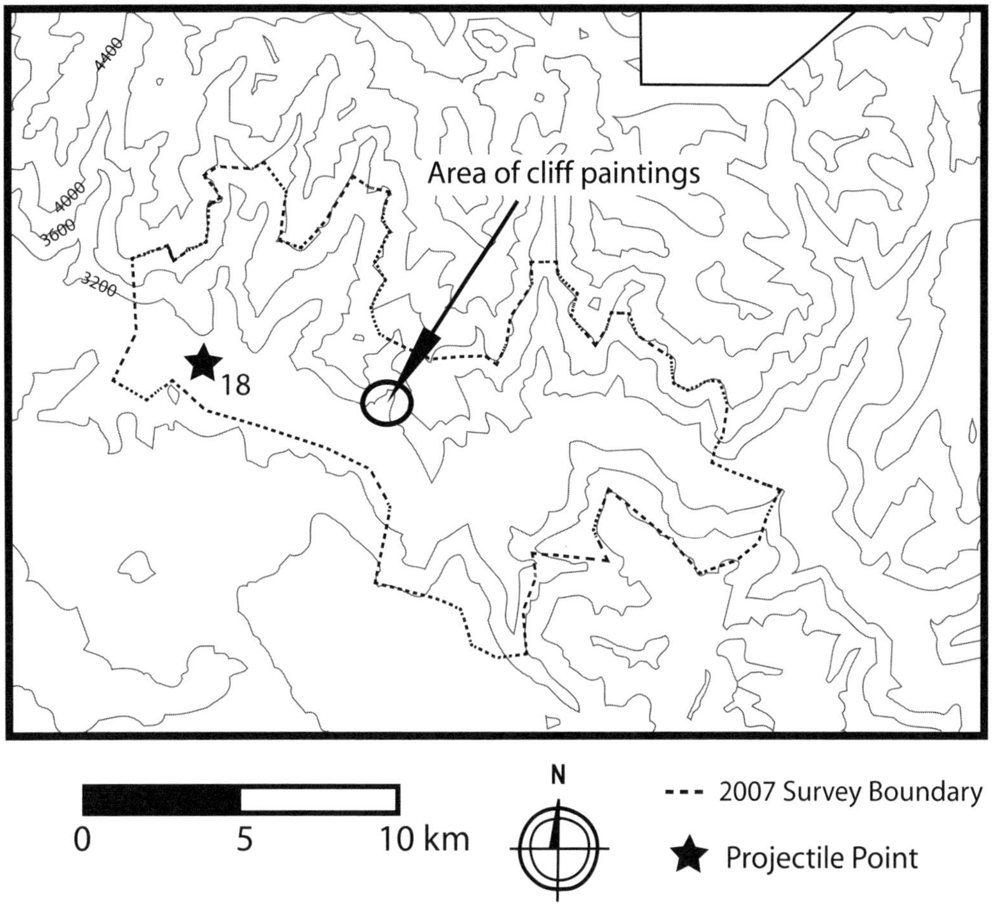

Figure 1.5. Map of Yucay Valley study region with the location of an Archaic projectile point and rock art possibly dating to the preceramic period.

Formative Period Settlement Patterns (ca. 1000 BC–AD 200)

The earliest villages in the Cusco region were established at least by 800 BC, if not before (Chávez 1980, 1981a, 1981b; cf. Bauer 2004). The introduction of agriculture into this region is still an issue of major theoretical importance, and current chronologies leave a gap of 1000 years or more between late broad-spectrum collectors and early agricultural settlements. Early villages were established in all ecozones of the Cusco region, with site locations ranging from below 3000 m to above 4000 m. This vertical span in elevation suggests a corresponding range of economic strategies. Larger villages were established in prominent locations offering good visibility and close access to farming or herding resources. The largest sites had architecture that has been identified as ceremonial (e.g., Bauer 2004; Davis and Covey 2007; Zapata 1998) and these sites appear to have been associated with a regional hierarchy with some degree of economic interdependence by the final centuries of the Formative period. Several large villages have been identified in neighboring areas, in the Xaquixaguana Valley, the Maras Plain, and the Chongo Basin above Pisaq, as well as in the Cusco Basin and Lucre Basin.

Ten Formative sites were identified in the Yucay Valley on the basis of ceramics, with an additional six possible Formative components based on non-diagnostic ceramic identifications. Early villages were established on the low slopes of the valley, as well as on ridges 200–300 m above the valley floor. Sites on the slopes tended to be small (less than 1 ha), while two sites of 1–2 ha were located around 3300 m asl (Fig. 1.7). No evidence of site-size hierarchy was identified for this period, a notable contrast with areas to the south and east of the study region. It is likely that additional Formative settlement lies beneath Inka terracing and modern settlement, but the absence of large valley-

Figure 1.6. Cliff paintings at the entrance to the San Juan Quebrada, above Yucay (Site PACY-139). Photo by R.A. Covey.

bottom settlements in other surveyed regions suggests that this part of the Cusco region simply had a lower population density than neighboring areas at this time.

Early Intermediate Period and Middle Horizon Settlement (ca. AD 200–1000)

The Early Intermediate period (ca. AD 200–600) saw major settlement changes in the Cusco region, with a high percentage of Formative sites abandoned in favor of new settlement locations. The disruption of settlement patterns that had been relatively stable over a millennium or more was not complete—large sites such as Ak'awillay, Chokepukio, and Minaspata continued to be occupied (Bélisle et al. 2007; McEwan et al. 1995)—but in many areas, 70% or more of all Formative sites were abandoned by the Early Intermediate period. The new settlement pattern favored the valley bottoms and was more dispersed, possibly indicating that farmers were shifting to the development of simple irrigation systems. This period is marked by the production of polychrome ceramics (the Qotakalli style) in the Cusco Valley (Bauer 1999; Bauer and Jones 2003).

After AD 600, colonization of Wari settlers from the Ayacucho region affected parts of the Cusco region, especially the Lucre Basin and Huaro area to the southeast of Cusco. Wari populations constructed distinctive architecture, used nonlocal ceramics, and buried their dead in different tomb types than did local populations. The suite of nonlocal traits seen in the Lucre Basin and Huaro area has not been identified elsewhere in the Cusco region, although Cusco Valley populations began to produce a local ceramic style that imitated Wari decorative motifs (the Araway style). Survey research has revealed that the polychrome styles of the Early Intermediate period/Middle Horizon have a restricted distribution outside the Cusco Basin, co-occurring with locally made variants at small sites in the Sacred Valley (near Pisaq and San Salvador), and at sites in the Xaquixaguana Valley (most notably at the large center at Ak'awillay).

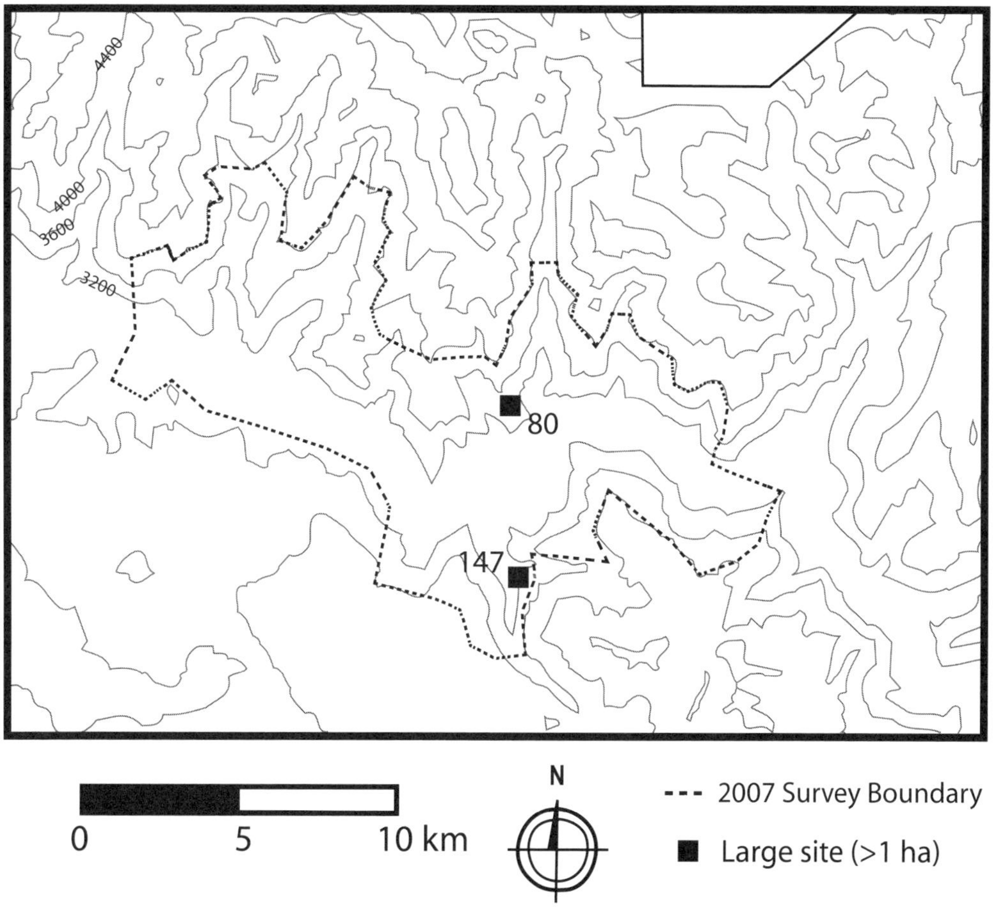

Figure 1.7. Map of important Formative period sites.

The distribution of Cusco Valley ceramics from the Early Intermediate and Middle Horizon times (Qotakalli and Araway) appears to drop off substantially beyond approximately 20 km from Cusco in all directions (e.g., Bauer 1999; Covey 2006a), but it was surprising to find an almost complete absence of these styles in the region we surveyed in 2007. A single Qotakalli sherd was found at one site, and a few possible Araway fragments were found in a site with a Late Intermediate period occupation. The lack of Cusco Valley diagnostics does not necessarily imply that the Yucay Valley was depopulated at this time, but rather more likely that populations residing there were not using decorated pottery that we can currently identify as belonging to these periods.

The lack of clear Early Intermediate period/Middle Horizon components does suggest some interesting patterns for this area. First, despite the presence of excellent farmland for irrigation agriculture, there does not appear to be a regional polity based in this part of the valley from AD 200–1000—such a condition would have been indicated by a local ceramic style, more Cusco Valley pottery, and the presence of more small sites along the lower valley slopes. Second, this part of the valley does not appear to have been colonized by the Wari empire from AD 600–1000, indicating that the Wari occupation of the Cusco region did not target all areas that had a potential for intensive maize agriculture. Instead, Wari colonization was restricted to the Lucre-Huaro area.

Late Intermediate Period Settlement Patterns (ca. AD 1000–1400)

The tenth and eleventh centuries saw major settlement disruption throughout the Cusco region, with a shift away from Early Intermediate period/Middle Horizon patterns in most areas to conditions that prevailed until the Inka imperial reorganization of the region. The final years of the Middle Horizon saw a shift toward the Late Intermediate settlement pattern, and several regional surveys have identified Araway pottery at sites with subsequent Late Intermediate occupations (e.g., Covey 2006a).

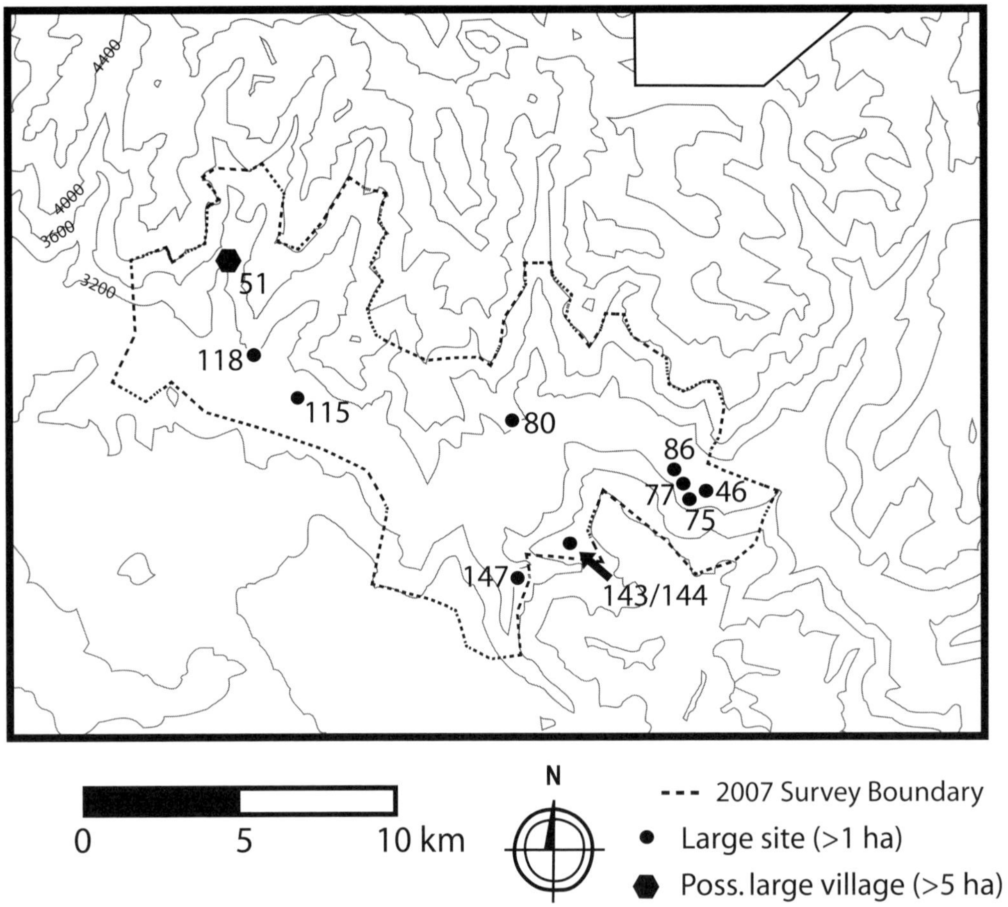

Figure 1.8. Map of important Late Intermediate period sites.

From AD 1000–1400, population in the Cusco region grew and shifted in location, and the picture of regional settlement is too complex to review in detail in this chapter (see Bauer and Covey 2002). A major polity appears to have developed in the Maras area immediately to the south of the Yucay Valley, probably identifiable with ethnohistoric descriptions of the Ayarmaka group (Covey et al. 2006). Survey in the Maras area identified a principal settlement larger than 20 ha, which was surrounded by several large and small villages to create a nucleated settlement system of approximately 120 ha within about 5 km of the principal town. These settlements were located in undefended locations at the margins of quebradas flowing into the Yucay Valley, and there is evidence that maize fields were constructed on terraces close to the largest settlements.

The pattern of Late Intermediate settlement seen near Maras—of hierarchical, nucleated, and undefended settlements in the maize-producing zone—contrasts markedly with settlement patterns in the Sacred Valley, where Late Intermediate settlement shifted to high elevations (more than 4000 m asl) consistent with herding and tuber cultivation (Covey 2006a). These settlements demonstrate only modest hierarchies, and the largest sites before the Inka conquest are 5–6 ha in size. Larger settlements are located on ridgetops and on mountains offering both good views and natural defense; some sites reveal evidence of walls and other defensive works protecting them.

The Late Intermediate settlement of the Yucay Valley appears to be a more modest variant of patterns observed upriver in the Sacred Valley. Ceramics from this period were identified at 66 sites, which spanned all the ecological zones of the study area. Two-thirds of these sites had occupations that continued into Inka times. Only nine sites larger than a hectare were identified—these nine represent small villages located either on the lower valley slopes 50–150 m above the valley floor, or on ridges about 300 m above the valley floor (Fig. 1.8). A regional settlement hierarchy appears to be absent, although a large nucleated site in the Pumahuanca Quebrada measured 5–6 ha. This site consisted of the remains of perhaps 200 stone structures, but the absence of surface ceramics makes it impossible to date the settlement conclusively to the Late Intermediate period. The lack of large settlements in the study region contrasts with the Maras area immediately to the south. Although our 2007 study region does not appear to have had a large or hierarchical population in the centuries prior to Inka expansion, survey results prove that Inka assertions that the valley was sparsely settled and its resources open for Inka development are not accurate.

The Inka Occupation (ca. AD 1400–1535)

The Inka occupation of the Yucay Valley is well documented in published chronicles and archival documents, including the collection published in this volume. As with the Late Intermediate period, the full discussion of settlement patterns for the Cusco region in Inka times lies beyond the scope of this chapter, although fruitful comparisons may be made with the Maras Plain and upper Sacred Valley. In the latter region there is evidence of early Inka expansion into existing communities beginning by the early fourteenth century (Covey 2006a). While many sites continued to be occupied from Late Intermediate to Inka times, settlement patterns indicate a major settlement shift from ridgetops to the valley bottom, where state labor projects developed new agricultural resources that came to be controlled by the families of Inka rulers who had ordered their construction.

The largest Inka sites in the upper Sacred Valley (Calca, Pisaq) were associated with royal estates. Newly established Inka settlements were frequently located at the margins of valley-bottom agricultural terraces, and many of these appear to have been occupied by provincial populations brought to the Cusco region as retainers of the Inka nobility (see Chapter 2; Covey and Elson 2007).

The Maras Plain saw somewhat different processes in its Late Intermediate-Inka transition. The system of nucleated Late Intermediate settlements near Maras has virtually no Inka pottery present, suggesting that it was depopulated before the imperial period. All Late Intermediate sites in the area were abandoned, and documentary sources suggest that local Ayarmaka populations were forcibly resettled in communities located closer to Cusco (e.g., Chinchero, Pucyura, San Sebastián) (Rostworowski 1970). Parts of the Maras Plain were taken for royal estates of Tupa Inca Yupanqui and Huayna Capac—the rulers who developed estate resources in the Yucay Valley—and large parts were set aside as pasture lands for royal herds (e.g., ADC Colegio Ciencias, L. 12, C. 31 [1785]; ADC Urubamba, L. 2, f. 7-8v [1569]; ADC Urubamba, L. 1, f. 1-2v [1594]; AGN Real Audiencia, Causas Civiles, L. 39, C. 150 [1616]; AGN Títulos de Propiedad, L. 1, C. 3 [1557]). Survey evidence and documents indicate that a large Inka settlement was established at the site of the contemporary town of Maras, and that there was investment in nearby salt production facilities and the storage facility at Cheq'oq. These resources were part of the estate of Huayna Capac, and retainers (*yanakuna*) working for this ruler resided in and around Maras.

In the Yucay Valley proper, our 2007 survey indicates patterns of estate development consistent with those occurring in the Maras area, as well as processes of local settlement continuity similar to those seen upriver in the Sacred Valley. Most Late Intermediate sites in the Yucay Valley continued to be occupied in Inka times, although ridgetop sites were abandoned in favor of a settlement shift to the valley bottom. Inka pottery was identified in the 2007 study region at 73 sites, and several other Inka sites were identified on the basis of architectural remains.

The largest Inka sites in our study region tend to be light artifact scatters associated with agricultural terraces and fields; these may represent dispersed occupations of laborers working on the personal estates of Tupa Inca Yupanqui and Huayna Capac, the two Inka emperors who developed lands in the study region (Figs. 1.9, 1.10). Such sites were encountered in close proximity to major terrace groups at the valley bottom in areas with abundant irrigation water from side valleys. It was not possible to determine the size of Inka towns that lie beneath Colonial and contemporary towns (Yucay, Urubamba, Huayllabamba), but it is likely that these settlements had substantial populations in Inka times. While Inka settlement in the Urubamba, Yucay, and Huayllabamba areas appears to have been organized around royal estates, Inka villages in the upper part of the study region show more continuity from Late Intermediate times, and may represent a continued occupation by local populations, especially in the Chimba Calca area.

Inka architecture is pronounced in the study region, with large terrace constructions found near Urubamba, Yucay, and Urquillos (Figs. 1.11, 1.12). These represent a transformation of regional economic production, a shift to more intensive production of crops that is attested to by the presence of several storage complexes on the slopes above the valley floor (e.g., Huaycochea Núñez de la Torre 1994; Niles 1999) (Figs. 1.13, 1.14). The architectural remains of the elite Inka occupation in our study region have been studied by several researchers (e.g., Farrington 1984; Niles 1999; Valencia Zegarra 1982), and our 2007 research registered the locations of these sites, also identifying a pair of apparent religious structures in the upper part of the Pumahuanca Quebrada (Figs. 1.15, 1.16).

The most important elite site is the palace of Huayna Capac at Quispeguanca, a place known to have housed the mummy of the ruler after his death. Royal hunting lodges, pleasure houses, and small shrines have been identified in the Pumahuanca and Chicón Quebradas above the Urubamba and Yucay areas.

During the Inka occupation, parts of the study area were transformed by the development of large Inka estates, which changed the nature of agricultural production and storage and brought new population into the valley. Many people must have lived in towns that lie under Colonial and contemporary towns, while much of the farming population appears to have lived in small villages or hamlets at the margins of royal lands. The population of this part of the valley was augmented by retainers from provincial regions, while areas not developed as estates appear to have been occupied continuously, suggesting that local populations continued to reside there.

(*Upper*) Figure 1.9. Agricultural terraces near the valley floor (Site PACY-6). Note the modest height and rough masonry employed in construction. Photo by M. Araóz Silva.

(*Lower*) Figure 1.10. Abandoned canal associated with Inka terracing (Site PACY-6). Photo by M. Araóz Silva.

Figure 1.11. Aerial view of the terrace complex at Yucay. Photo by R.A. Covey.

Figure 1.12. Terrace construction at Yucay. Terraces at Yucay use cyclopean masonry and drainage systems to construct terraces with retaining walls up to five meters high. Photo by B.S. Bauer.

Figure 1.13. Hillside storage complex in the Yucay Valley (Site PACY-19). Photo by M. Araóz Silva.

Figure 1.14. Hillside storage complex in the Yucay Valley (Site PACY-92). Photo by B.S. Bauer.

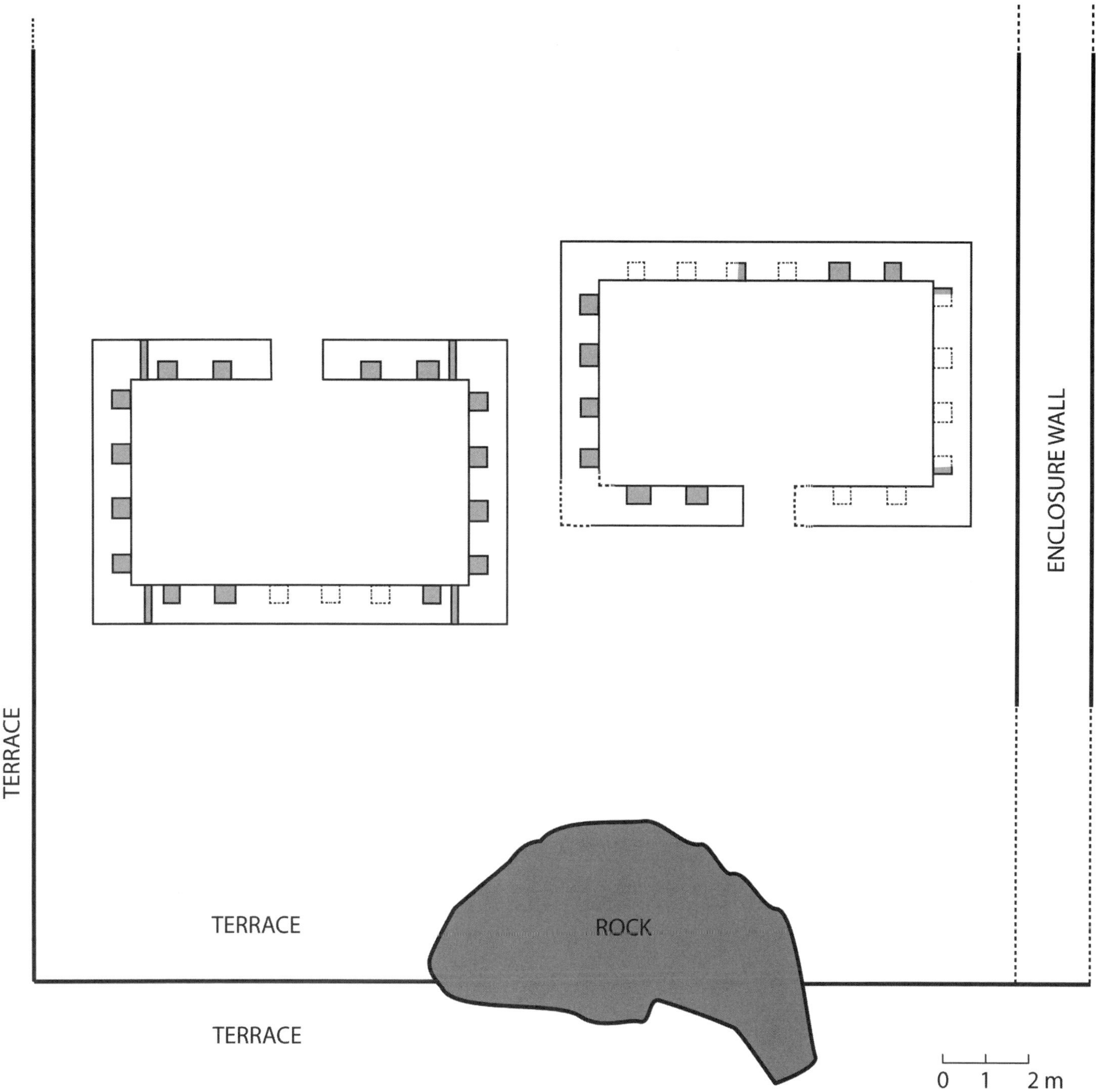

Figure 1.15. Plan of religious complex in the Pumahuanca Quebrada (Site PACY-54).

Figure 1.16. Architectural remains at PACY-54. Photo by B.S. Bauer.

Early Colonial Settlement Patterns

The imperial transformations of the Yucay Valley will be discussed in greater detail in the following chapter, but it is important to provide an archaeological overview of the valley. Colonial pottery was identified at 39 sites, and possibly at one additional site. Almost all of these sites are very small artifact scatters with few diagnostics—of those identified, 28 sites had fewer than five diagnostic sherds collected for laboratory analysis.

As with the Inka period, several Colonial towns (Yucay, Urubamba, Huayllabamba, Urquillos) continue to be occupied today, and the documentary record suggests that the majority of early Colonial settlement would have been in these nucleated Spanish-style towns that had their origins as Inka settlements (Fig. 1.17). Colonial settlement patterns have not been documented for the entire Cusco region, but the Xaquixaguana Plain Archaeological Survey did register the location of Colonial pottery, noting the presence of a significant number of small scatters. As with the Yucay Valley, it appears that Colonial settlement was concentrated in the Spanish-style towns of the area, but that there was considerable dispersal from these towns, either as small hamlets and herding stations or as temporary activity areas in use for specific activities in the agropastoral calendar. Survey work in the Qoricocha *puna* grasslands has revealed a proliferation of small corral complexes with Colonial pottery, suggesting that transhumant pastoralism may have increased as an informal part of local economies (Covey and Yager 2005).

Settlement Patterns and Documents

Archaeological settlement patterns provide the only source of data on the first 4000 or more years of human occupation in the Yucay Valley of the Cusco region. After AD 1000, the reconstruction of the past involves the study of Colonial period documents, and the relationship between archaeological data and documentary accounts changes by time period. Late Intermediate period settlement pattern data can be augmented by general observations

Figure 1.17. Inka wall remains in the Colonial center of Yucay. Photo by B.S. Bauer.

of narratives of the deeds of pre-imperial rulers, but these have little to say about local populations or their interactions with the developing Inka state. The Inka imperial transformation of the Yucay Valley and nearby areas is narrated in much greater detail by chroniclers such as Juan de Betanzos and Pedro Sarmiento de Gamboa, as well as in information provided in a wide range of administrative documents. For the period after AD 1400, archaeological and architectural studies of monumental constructions in the Yucay Valley have added significant information regarding the elite occupation of the valley, while new settlement pattern data help to contextualize retainer and commoner settlements as part of a regional estate system. Such perspectives add to the important data on Yucay Valley *yanakuna* published in this volume. The final phase of historical archaeology in the Yucay Valley is the early Colonial period. Interruptions in archaeological chronology and a lack of fine-grained studies of Colonial artifacts and settlement relegate archaeology to a more indirect role in reconstructing regional processes from the 1530s on. The documentary record for this period is also fragmentary, but provides a great deal of information on how this part of the Inka imperial heartland was transformed into a peripheral part of the Spanish empire. This narrative is reconstructed in brief in the chapter that follows.

Chapter 2

Imperial Transformations in the Yucay Valley in the Fifteenth and Sixteenth Centuries

R. Alan Covey

By the time the Inka state began to expand its territory in the Cusco region, the Yucay Valley had a modest native population that was distributed throughout the range of ecological zones in the valley (see preceding chapter). (For a more complete discussion of the documentary evidence, see Covey and Elson 2007; Niles 1999; Rostworowski 1970; and Villanueva 1971.)

The Yucay Valley—with its frost-free climate and abundant irrigation water from side valleys—was an ideal area for maize production, and the annexation of this valley by the Inka state was followed by major investments in production intensification that concentrated land and water resources in the hands of the Inka elite. By the time of the European invasion, a system of royal estates dominated the political economy of the Inka heartland, especially along the Sacred Valley and Yucay Valley, where at least six Inka rulers are said to have established personal landholdings (Fig. 2.1). Interestingly, despite its rich agricultural potential, the Yucay Valley was one of the later areas of estate construction in that valley, while areas upriver and downriver are said to have been developed by the earlier rulers Yahuar Huaccac (Paullu/Qhapaqkancha/Lamay), Viracocha Inca (Caquia Xaquixaguana/Calca), and Pachacutic Inca Yupanqui (Pisaq and Ollantaytambo) (e.g., Covey 2006a; Niles 1999; Rowe 1997). Although some buildings are said to have been constructed in the Yucay Valley by Pachacutic Inca Yupanqui, it was under his son and grandson that the valley was transformed.

Inka Estates in the Yucay Valley

The first ruler to develop estate resources in the Yucay Valley was Tupa Inca Yupanqui, who had an impressive complex of agricultural terraces and irrigation works built for him at the mouth of the Urquillos Canyon (e.g., Villanueva 1971). This ruler had a country palace built at Chinchero, a picturesque spot located on a high elevation plain between Cusco and the Yucay Valley (Alcina Franch 1976; Sarmiento de Gamboa 1965[1572]; cf. Nair 2003).

The area surrounding Chinchero produced potatoes and other high elevation crops, and had good herding resources nearby, but it was only through the development of lands at the bottom of the nearby Yucay Valley that Tupa Inca Yupanqui's estate could produce maize for the sustenance of his household and descendants. The terraces at Urquillos (called Urcos in early Colonial documents) were probably built in the second half of the fifteenth century. The remains of these constructions are two to three meters high and are faced with fitted polygonal masonry (Figs. 2.2, 2.3).

While Tupa Inca Yupanqui brought provincial herders and other retainers to the Cusco region to serve him, the residents of Urquillos in early Colonial times appear to have been Inka (Rostworowski 1990), suggesting that the emperor drew this body of retainers from existing local populations. Our 2007

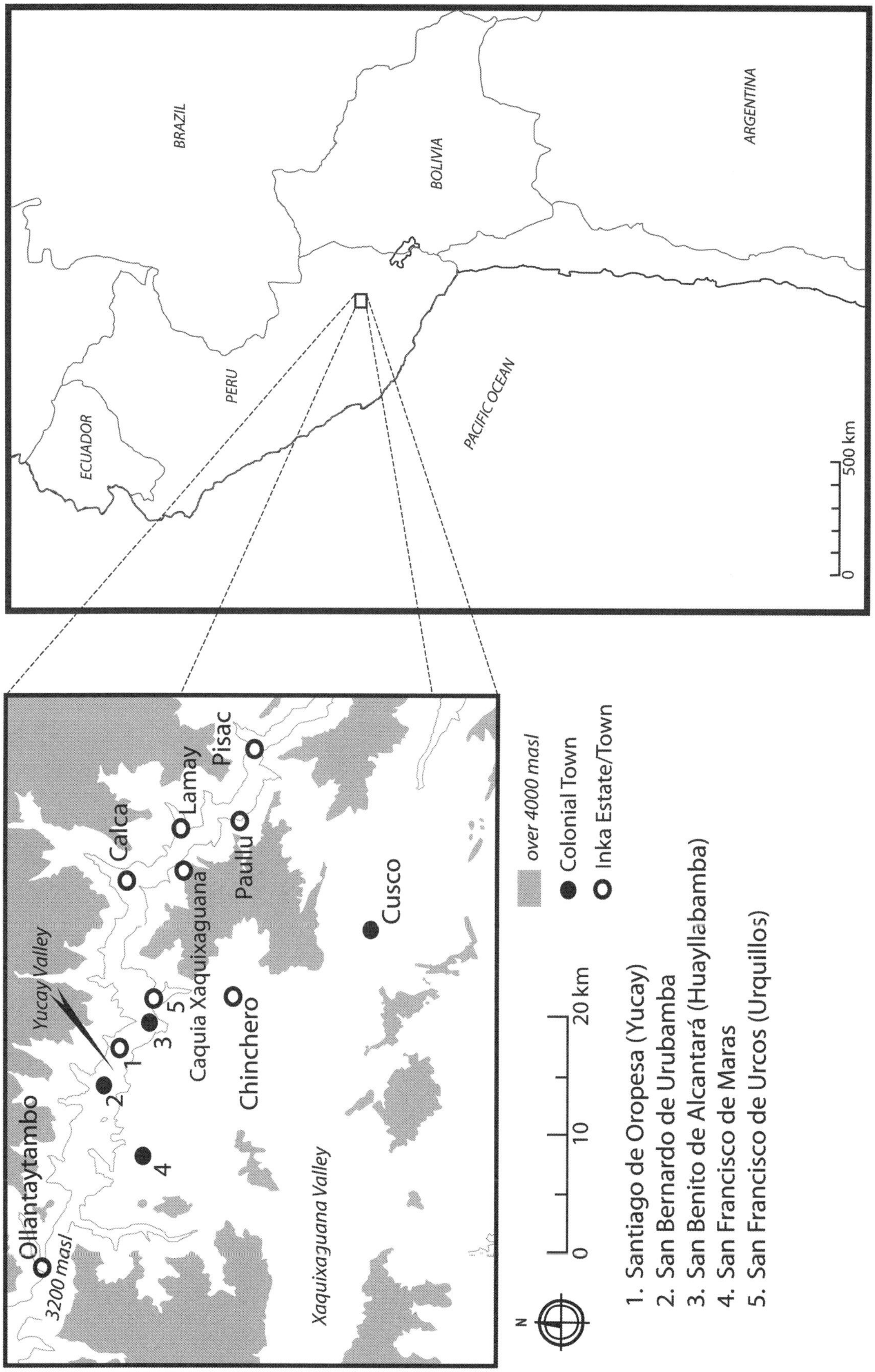

Figure 2.1. The Cusco region, showing Inka estates and Colonial towns in the Sacred Valley and Yucay Valley.

Figure 2.2. Aerial view of the terrace system built for Tupa Inca Yupanqui at the mouth of the Urquillos Canyon. Photo by R.A. Covey.

Figure 2.3. Close-up of terrace masonry at Urquillos. Stones tend to be of modest size, worked to fit together closely without mortar, and terrace height is modest. Photo by R.A. Covey.

Figure 2.4. The Yucay Valley. River canalization and terrace construction improved large tracts of well-watered land for the estate of Huayna Capac. Photo by R.A. Covey.

archaeological survey of the Yucay Valley encountered a dense scatter of Late Intermediate period ceramics at the edge of the contemporary town of Urquillos, which appears to have been the center of settlement for the side valley through Inka and Colonial times as well. This pattern of continued local occupation contrasts markedly with the estate of Huayna Capac, the penultimate Inka ruler.

Before setting off for an extended campaign on the northern frontiers of his empire, Huayna Capac sent his half-brother, Sinchi Roca, to the Yucay Valley to build a country palace where he and his family could relax and enjoy themselves (see f. 165, 174v, 424; Betanzos 1999[1551-1557: pt. 1, ch. 43]; Murúa 1987[1590-1611: bk. 1, ch. 30]; Sarmiento de Gamboa 1965[1572: ch. 58]). A provincial labor force numbering in the thousands was assembled in the Yucay Valley for this task. The laborers straightened the course of the meandering Urubamba River and shaped productive parts of the valley floor by hauling boulders and earthen fill and constructing terraces that are five meters high in some places (Fig. 2.4).

Huayna Capac was the owner of these new lands and facilities, and while he and his family retained ownership of most of the best lands, he gave plots of land in the Yucay and Urubamba area to the cult of the Sun, to members of the Inka nobility, and to the families of his royal ancestors (f. 123v, 129, 165, 174v, 424; see Betanzos 1999[1551-1557: pt. 1, ch. 43]; Niles 1999). In addition to the improvement of large tracts of farmland, the labor force constructed a palace complex at the site of Quispeguanca, as well as gardens, fountains, storage, and other recreation facilities for the ruler and his family (Figs. 2.5, 2.6).

After the principal construction work was finished, the temporary provincial labor force left the valley and a permanent staff was assigned to the estate. Two thousand retainers (*yanakuna*) were drawn from the Qollasuyu and Chinchaysuyu provinces (one thousand from each) and they were resettled in the Yucay Valley, living alongside the local population (f. 139, 145, 149v, 165, 174v). Retainers lived in villages of different sizes in and near the valley and provided a variety of services to the royal family, including agricultural labor (cultivating maize, chile pep-

Figure 2.5. Remains of the palace of Huayna Capac at Quispeguanca. The emperor's body was kept here with a contingent of retainers to serve it. Photo by B.S. Bauer.

pers, and fruits), maintenance of estate architecture, and personal services (f. 123v, 154v, 160v, 165; Betanzos 1999[1551-1557: pt. 1, ch. 43]; Villanueva 1971:37, 39). In the early Colonial period, witnesses in Yucay declared themselves (or their forebears) to be agricultural specialists (Toledo 1940[1571b]:108-12), masons (Toledo 1940[1571c]:126-33), salt producers (Toledo 1940[1571b]:108-12), soldiers (Toledo 1940[1571b]:108-12, 112-18; 1940[1571c]:158-67), and overseers of local laborers (Toledo 1940[1571b]:108-12).

The Yucay Valley Estates in the 1530s

At the time of the European invasion, the Yucay Valley estates of Tupa Inca Yupanqui and Huayna Capac still served their founders, but in a different manner than at the time of their construction. The mummies of the founding rulers remained the nominal owners of estate resources; it was their descendants who oversaw ritual duties for the royal mummies and who benefited from the facilities and products of the estates. Although little is known of the maintenance of Tupa Inca Yupanqui's mummy, the documents presented in this volume contribute to a detailed account of how Huayna Capac's body was brought back from the northern frontier with a retinue of servants, and how it was curated at Quispeguanca (e.g., f. 100, 114v, 115v, 121, 126v-127, 132, 137v, 148, 157v-158, 275v, 283v-284; see Betanzos 1999[1551-1557: pt. 2, ch. 1]; Niles 1999; Villanueva 1971).

Royal estates were shaped by the Inka descent groups that held them in the name of their founding ancestors. The diverging fortunes of the descent groups of Tupa Inca Yupanqui and Huayna

Figure 2.6. Remains of a guard tower at Quispeguanca. Photo by B.S. Bauer.

Capac led to different trajectories for the Yucay Valley estates after the European invasion. Before the Pizarro expedition ever reached Cusco, the descendants of Tupa Inca Yupanqui had been decimated by Atahuallpa as punishment for their support of his rival half-brother Huascar in the Inka civil war (Sarmiento de Gamboa 1965[1572: ch. 67]). The weakening of this royal lineage left the estate of Tupa Inca Yupanqui vulnerable. By the 1550s, Chinchero was abandoned, the *cabildo* of Cusco had allocated a number of garden plots in the Urquillos Canyon to Spaniards, and local *encomenderos* were using the absence of Inka owners to extend the lands on which their native laborers worked (e.g., f. 415v, 417v, 418-418v, 419, 419v, 420).

By contrast, Huayna Capac's Yucay Valley estate appears to have remained in the hands of his descent group until Francisco Pizarro awarded himself a sizeable *encomienda* from its retainer population sometime in the later 1530s (Rostworowski 1970:254, 257). This award was one of a series of grants made to the surviving Pizarro brothers (Francisco, Gonzalo, and Hernando) following the Inka uprising of 1536, which mapped the Pizarro family onto many of the estate resources of Huascar, Huayna Capac, Pachacutic Inca Yupanqui, and Viracocha Inca (Covey 2006a; Julien 2001; Rowe 1990; Varón Gabai 1997, 1998). Even though he resided in the new coastal city of Los Reyes, Francisco Pizarro took the Casana, Huayna Capac's palace in Cusco, as well as coca and maize lands in the Cusco region that had belonged to that ruler (f. 89v, 97, 102v, 107v, 112v, 118, 124, 129v, 134v, 140, 145v, 150, 155, 161, 166, 175; see Rivera Serna 1965[1534]:33; Varón Gabai 1997). Pizarro was present in the Yucay Valley in 1538–1539 (Betanzos 1999[1551-1557: pt. 2, ch. 32]; Lohmann Villena 1986:128-30, 132, 353, 369), but the overall management of the former Inka estate was entrusted to his *mayordomo* Diego de Gumiel, who supervised the native tributary population of the valley (f. 171-171v, 175v; Espinal 1959[1539]:364). Pizarro's reassignment of Inka retainers to his *encomienda* involved a shift in native administration, with the local Inka lord (Gualpa Tupa) replaced by Francisco Chilche, a Cañari noble who pledged early loyalty to the Spaniards and supported them during the Inka uprising (f. 90, 156v-157, 171v-172; see Heffernan 1995; Varón Gabai 1997). The early years of the transition from Inka estate to Spanish *encomienda* saw few significant changes in the kinds of services given. Indeed, Inka *yanakuna* continued to labor in the fields of Yucay, to maintain its production infrastructure, and to provide personal service.

The Transition to Crown Control in the 1540s and 1550s

During the 1540s, Charles V began to assert increasing crown authority over Peru, with limits set on the scope of the *encomienda* system. Francisco Pizarro's Yucay Valley *encomienda* provides an example of these processes. After Pizarro was assassinated in 1541, his possessions and estates were managed on behalf of his children (he had fathered four children with two Inka princesses and had taken different kinds of action to make them legitimate; see, for example AGI Patronato 90A, N. 1, R. 9 [1537]). His young son Gonzalo inherited the Yucay *encomienda*, while another son (Francisco) also appears to have been supported with its income after Gonzalo died in 1546 at age nine (f. 271v-272; see Hemming 1970:270; Varón Gabai 1997:90-107). The announcement of the New Laws (1542) imposed new limits on *encomiendas* and led to an uprising of Peruvian *encomenderos* under the *conquistador* Gonzalo Pizarro (the uncle of the two boys just mentioned). After Pedro de la Gasca suppressed this rebellion in 1548, he exiled the Pizarro children to Spain, asserting Crown authority over the Yucay *encomienda* while supporting the children with income from the valley and from other Crown holdings (AGI Patronato 90B, N. 1, R. 51 [1551]; Calvete de Estrella 1964[1565-1567: bk. 4, ch. 8]:36; Gutiérrez de Santa Clara 1963[ca. 1600: bk. 5, ch. 47]; Hemming 1970:284). The Yucay Valley became a royal trust managed by officials in Cusco.

In its transformation from *encomienda* to royal holding, the Yucay Valley and its native population moved away from a system of labor service that had been similar to the original Inka practices of Huayna Capac's estate, in which native descent groups and administrative units sent their members to cultivate maize and coca, to gather firewood and herbs, and to provide personal services, food, and drink (f. 130, 232).

By the early 1550s, royal officials imposed a *tasa* on the population of the Yucay Valley, requiring a payment of tribute in kind as specified by a royal inspection (118v-119, 135-135v, 150v, 155v-156, 161-161v, 175v). The new tribute demands retained service requirements in the maize and coca fields, but eliminated personal services. Around AD 1556, payments of coca leaf were included in the *tasa*, and it was not until several years later that labor service related to coca cultivation was replaced by payments of silver (f. 155v-156; see f. 116, 121v-122, 127v-128).

Despite the fact that coca leaf could not be cultivated in the Yucay Valley (it was grown on improved plots in nearby lowland areas owned by Huayna Capac), royal officials administering the native population of the Yucay Valley initially focused their attention on maintaining coca production, while indirectly administering other aspects of the local economy (f. 89v-90v). By the 1550s, coca consumption had become a vital part of the early Colonial economy, particularly in mining regions. The Crown tended to assume ownership of Inka coca lands (using the argument that they were exclusive royal possessions in Inka times), while leaving local agricultural production under native management. The indirect administration of the Yucay Valley and the question of how Inka estates and Colonial *encomienda* grants translated into land ownership led Inkas, Cañaris, and Spaniards to move onto plots of land in the valley and to establish their retainers and tributary laborers there.

Several descendants of Huayna Capac managed to have tributary laborers assigned to them in the Yucay Valley, as did a small number of other Inka elites. These legal grants were often augmented with service by *yanakuna*—natives who either served the Inka nobility before the European invasion or who sought Inka patronage afterward (f. 90-91v). Cañari elites, who had prospered in their administrative positions under the Pizarro family, had accumulated their own tributary laborers and *yanakuna*; they opposed the erosion of their privilege through legal protest and illegal activities (including, allegedly, hiding tributary labors from administrators) (e.g., f. 90-92).

Spaniards were attracted to the rich farmland in the Yucay Valley, and they sought out vacant plots where they could establish their own *yanakuna* and workers from nearby *encomienda* grants. The terraced lands formerly belonging to Tupa Inca Yupanqui at Urquillos were parceled out to prominent Spaniards by Cusco's *cabildo*, and many Spaniards began to build country houses and orchards in the valley (f. 415v; see AGI Patronato 29, R. 16 [1561]; Villanueva 1971).

Strategic Allocations of Crown Resources

The transition to Crown administration of most of the Yucay Valley involved a shift in economic emphasis from personal service and labor management to annual payments in staples, commercial goods and silver. Some of this income was sent to Spain, but Crown resources in Peru also went to supporting local priests and royal officials, as well as providing support for loyal subjects. The rebellions of the 1540s and 1550s sped up the royal absorption of *encomienda* grants, but also created a new set of obligations to reward prominent Spaniards who remained faithful to the Crown. Rather than grant new *encomiendas*, the Crown opted to reward exceptional loyalty with income from its administered resources. The case of Gómez Arias Dávila illustrates how the Yucay Valley played a role in this process.

During the 1553–1554 uprising of Francisco Hernández Girón, royal officials in Cusco following a royal mandate offered an income of 2000 pesos to the Spaniard who captured the rebel leader or brought back his head (Fernández 1963[1571: pt. 2, bk. 2, ch. 58]). Dávila, a citizen of León de Huánuco, fought on the royal side and was credited with capturing Hernández Girón, and in 1556 the viceroy issued a provision for the 2000 pesos in income to be paid from the *encomienda* formerly belonging to Hernández Girón (the Xaquixaguana Valley and Guayla, Quipa, and Pucara) (f. 35-35v; cf. Murúa 1987[1590-1611]). Dávila was to play no part in the administration of the tributary laborers, but would receive an annual income that would be passed down to his legitimate heir after his death (f. 35; see f. 2).

As officials in Cusco were arranging to pay Gómez Arias Dávila the income from former Inka estates, the Marqués de Cañete, viceroy of Peru, was using the same resources as an incentive to secure the loyalty of Sayri Tupa Manco Capac Yupanqui Inca, the grandson of Huayna Capac. Sayri Tupa was the son and heir of Manco Inca, the Inca prince who had come to power as an ally of the Spaniards, but who led a regional uprising against them in 1536 after it became clear that the days of Inca rule were not to return under Spanish overlords. After failing to take Cuzco in 1536, Manco Inca retreated to the Yucay Valley, and then withdrew downriver, first to Ollantaytambo, and then farther into the jungle, where he established a small kingdom in Vilcabamba (see Hemming 1970 for a general overview). After Manco Inca was assassinated by Spaniards in 1544, his son Sayri Tupa assumed the Inca title in Vilcabamba. The persistence of an autonomous Inca nobility in Vilcabamba was problematic for the Spanish crown in a practical and a philosophical sense.

The Inka kingdom was blamed for raids on Spanish towns and highways, as well as for fomenting native resistance to Spanish rule. On a philosophical level, the continued existence of an independent Inka dynasty challenged the legitimacy of the Spanish Crown in the Americas at a time when Spain was anxious to retain the resources needed to take the lead in the counter-Reformation in Europe, as well as challenges to Ottoman expansion in the circum-Mediterranean region (e.g., Covey 2006b). To defuse the situation, the viceroy sent messengers (including Inka nobles and Dominican friars) to Vilcabamba to parlay with Sayri Tupa, offering amnesty to him and his captains if they would leave the jungle, accept baptism, and swear loyalty to the Spanish king. In return for these considerations, Sayri Tupa demanded the estates of his grandfather, and after extended negotiations, a deal was struck in 1557. Sayri Tupa emerged from Vilcabamba, fulfilled his obligations to the Crown, and was awarded the Yucay Valley, as well as the *encomiendas* of Hernández Girón and parts of those once belonging to Hernando Pizarro (Betanzos 1999[1551-1557: pt. 2, ch. 33]; see also Fernández 1963[1571: pt. 3, ch. 4]; Guaman Poma 1980[1615: f. 439-43]; Marúa 1987[1590-1611]; Titu Cusi Yupanqui 1992[1570]:62-63) (Fig. 2.7).

Sayri Tupa was given papal dispensation to marry his full sister María Cusi Guarcay (Cobo 1964[1653: bk. 12, ch. 21]; cf. Guaman Poma de Ayala 1980[1615: f. 443-44]; Murúa 1987[1590-1611]). Their daughter Beatriz Clara Coya was still an infant when Sayri Tupa died unexpectedly in 1561. She inherited his belongings and *repartimientos*, which were managed for her by Tilano de Anaya (f. 1v, 84, 534v), a leading citizen of Cusco. As a young child, Beatriz Coya was placed in the convent of Santa Clara in Cusco, to be raised there until a suitable marriage could be arranged for her (Burns 1999:27-31; Hemming 1970; Rostworowski 1970:153-58). She was removed from the convent by her mother at age eight and lived in the house of Arias Maldonado. While there, she was raped by Cristóbal Maldonado, who subsequently attempted to marry her for her inheritance and engaged in a lengthy legal battle to claim a legal right to her estate (e.g., f. 451, 490; AGI Indiferente 426, L. 25, f. 161r-161v [1572]; AGI Justicia 657, N. 2 [1566-1568]; AGI Patronato 3, N. 25 [1578]).

The death of Sayri Tupa reversed the effects of diplomatic efforts and royal grants aimed at securing the cooperation of the Vilcabamba Inkas. Sayri Tupa's half brother Titu Cusi Yupanqui had remained in Vilcabamba, and he assumed the title of Inka when news of Sayri Tupa's demise reached him. Realizing that his kingdom could not completely shut out Spanish influence, Titu Cusi permitted Augustinian priests to enter Vilcabamba, received baptism, and sought royal favor as a subject of the Spanish crown. Over time, new negotiations were initiated with the Vilcabamba Inkas in which marriage to Beatriz Coya would provide the basis for access to rich estates, and in 1571, Philip II obtained a papal dispensation for Beatriz Coya to marry her cousin Quispe Titu (Titu Cusi Yupanqui's son) (Hemming 1970:420; Ocampo 1999[1610]).

While negotiations were underway, Titu Cusi Yupanqui died suddenly, and some Inkas blamed a Spanish priest and the Inka's mestizo secretary for poisoning him (Hemming 1970:417-18). The alleged conspirators were killed, and Vilcabamba was closed off to the outside world. When communication was broken with Vilcabamba, Beatriz Coya's representative Tilano de Anaya was selected as an emissary to try to convince the Inka to leave Vilcabamba. He was murdered by the Vilcabamba Inkas, a provocation serious enough to provoke war. Hemming (1970:423) notes that "Anaya was the first Spaniard known to have been killed by the Vilcabamba regime since the renegades who assassinated Manco [Inca] over a quarter century earlier. And Anaya was no ordinary victim. He was a prominent citizen, a friend and business associate of the Inca, and a sympathetic expert on native affairs. Worse still, he had been murdered while on an official embassy bearing grants and letters from the Pope, the King, and the Viceroy." This act led the viceroy Francisco de Toledo to send a Spanish expedition into Vilcabamba with orders to destroy the kingdom and capture the Inka (Cobo 1964[1653: bk. 12, ch. 21]; Ocampo 1999[1610]; Villar 1906[1589]:185).

In 1572, after the conquest of Vilcabamba and the capture and execution of Tupa Amaro (another half brother of Sayri Tupa,

Figure 2.7. Architectural remains identified as the palace of Sayri Tupa in Yucay. Photo by M. Araóz Silva.

who assumed the Inka title for a short time following the death of Titu Cusi Yupanqui), Toledo used Beatriz Coya's estates to reward Martín García de Loyola for capturing the Inka (e.g., AGI Patronato 118, R. 9 [1572]; AGI Lima 1, N. 3 [1576]; Murúa 1987[1590-1611]). The couple was betrothed, and García de Loyola enjoyed the benefits of Beatriz Coya's estates for many years, first while she was still too young to marry, and later as legal cases were resolved to allow them to marry. (The couple attempted to marry in 1580, but Cristóbal Maldonado's claim to be Beatriz Coya's legal husband postponed the wedding for nearly a decade as the case moved through the legal system.)

The Toledan *Reducciones* and Reclassification of Yucay *Yanakuna*

As the final Inka resistance to Spanish colonial rule was eliminated, alliances and negotiations involving the designation of Yucay Valley lands and labor tribute were conducted with the approval of the viceroy Francisco de Toledo. Toledo's mandate included the administrative consolidation of Peru, as well as the collection of new historical narratives and accounts of indigenous cultural practices that would reinforce Spanish imperial authority. While Toledo was involved in rewriting Inka history, he was also attempting to transform the Andean landscape by reducing native populations to Spanish-style towns. The Toledan *reducciones* altered the composition of the retainer and tributary populations of the Yucay Valley, and set the stage for a prolonged legal battle

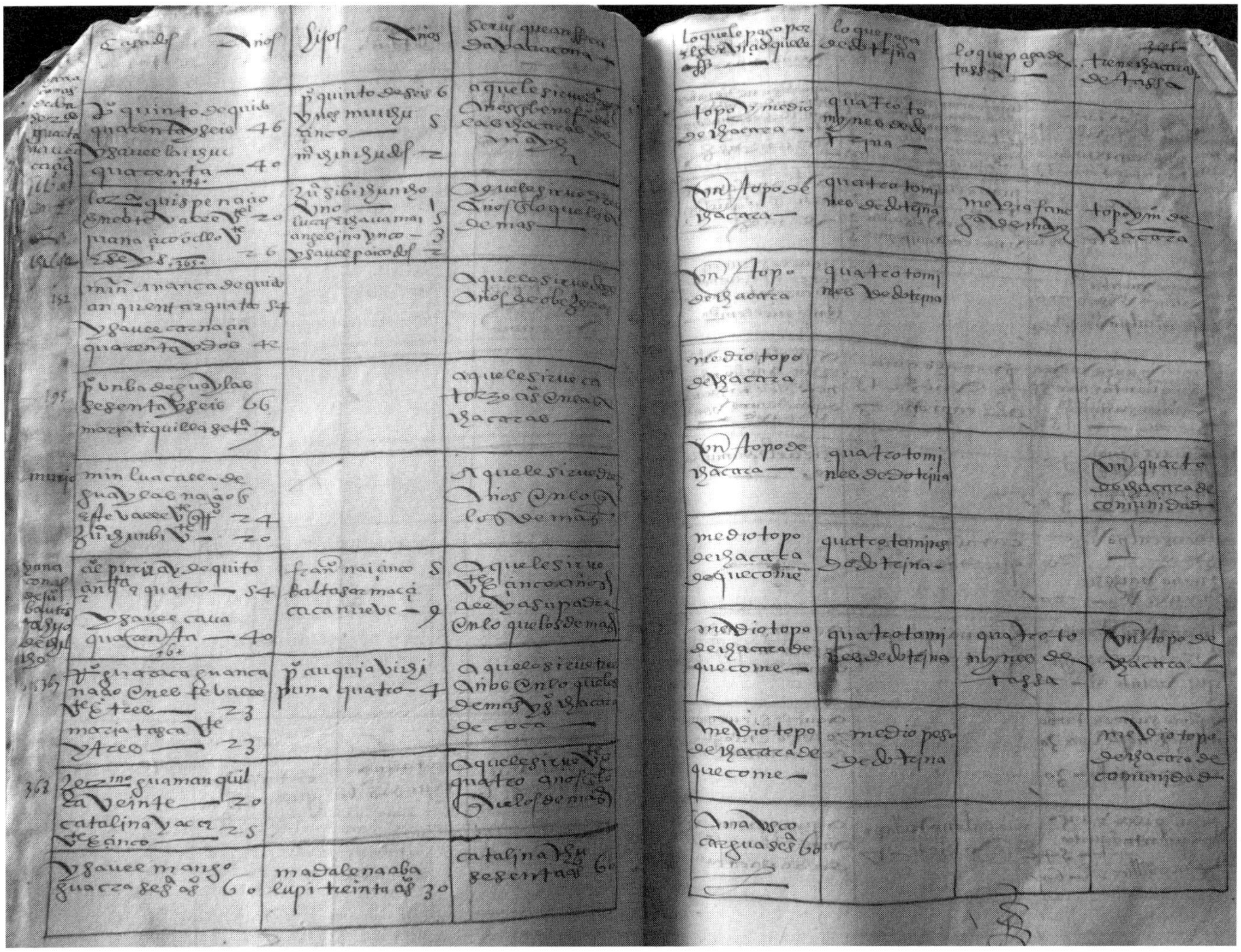

Figure 2.8. Example of household survey data copied from Diego de Escudero's notebook. Photo by D. Amado González.

between Beatriz Coya (and her husband) and other landowners and masters of *yanakuna* in the valley. These included representatives of Gómez Arias Dávila, who was promised an income from the estate as his reward for service in the Peruvian civil wars; Cristóbal Maldonado, who claimed to be the legal husband of Beatriz Coya; as well as other Spaniards and Andeans who had tributary laborers and retainers in the Yucay Valley.

In 1569, Diego Escudero, the parish priest in the Yucay Valley, registered the names of the tributary and non-tributary population of the valley (Fig. 2.8). When Pedro Gutiérrez Flores visited the valley in 1571 to initiate the Toledan *reducción* program, he used Escudero's notebook as a reference and reduced the *yanakuna* of the valley into towns with the tributaries (f. 91-91v). The surveys consist of household-level data from more than 800 families (more than 2300 individuals) in four communities in the Yucay Valley: Santiago de Oropesa (f. 319v-352), San Bernardo (f. 352v-387), San Benito de Alcantará (f. 387v-406), and San Francisco de Maras (f. 406v-409v). These lists were presented by Beatriz Coya and her husband in legal proceedings to have native labor added to their *repartimiento* (Fig. 2.9).

Legal Proceedings and the Yucay Valley

The allegations regarding labor tribute made by Beatriz Coya and Martín García de Loyola required legal action to resolve, and as the couple entered into these proceedings, they also engaged in an attempt to maximize the size of the labor pool in their native *repartimiento* in the Yucay Valley. As described already, the Yucay Valley was transformed over time from an Inka estate

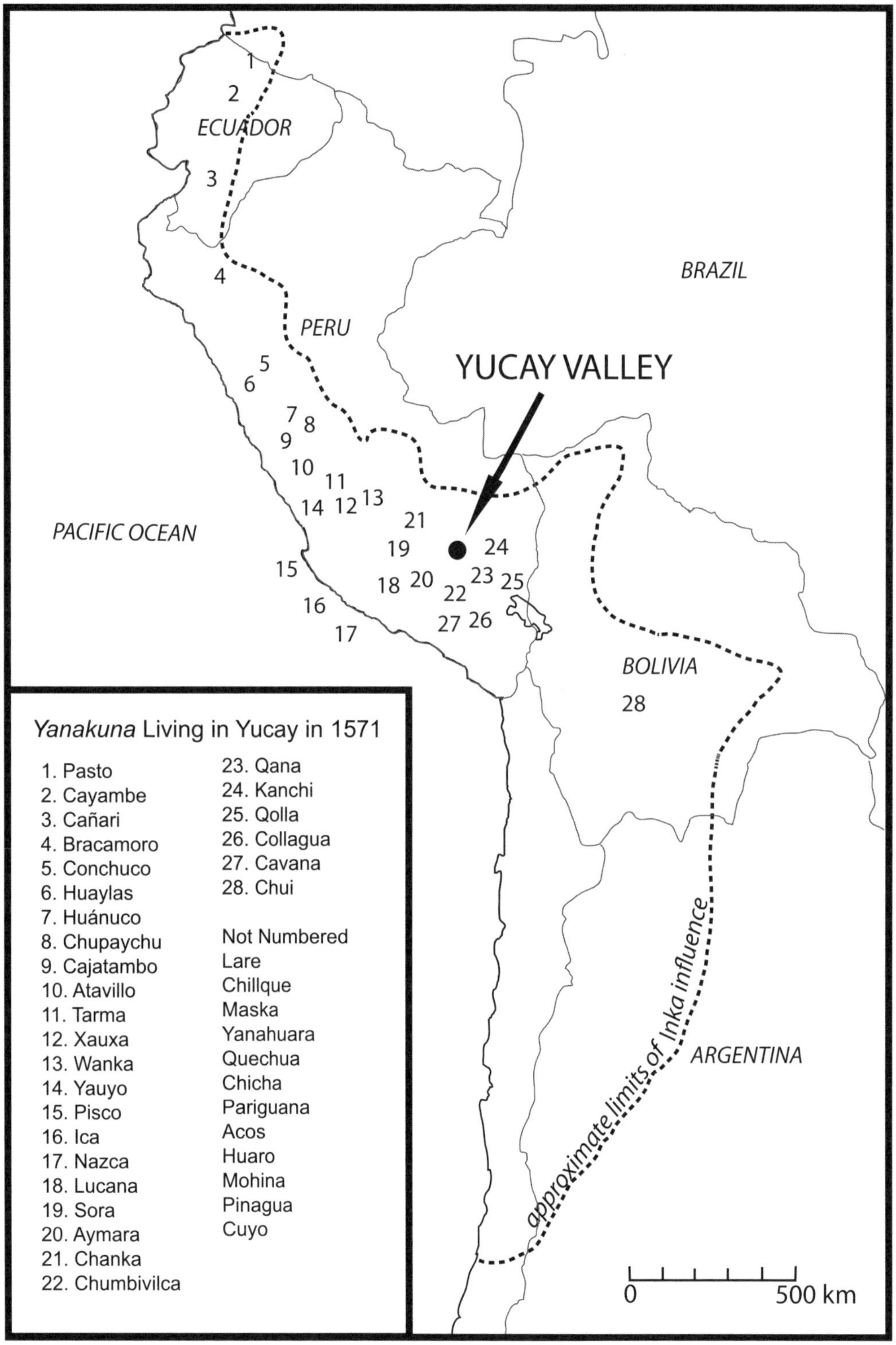

Figure 2.9. Ethnic identities of *yanakuna* residing in the Yucay Valley in 1571. Male heads of house came primarily from dozens of ethnic groups in the Andean highlands, with a few individuals coming from coastal regions.

system to a Spanish system of *repartimientos* and native villages were subject to annual tax levies (*tasa*). The restructuring of the Yucay Valley occurred during a period of rapid demographic decline, and native Inkas and provincial retainers were faced with the opportunities and costs of remaining in the Yucay Valley or establishing themselves elsewhere on the developing Colonial landscape. Adding to the administrative complexity of this process was the division of the great Inka estates into plots of productive land granted to Spaniards and Andean elites and worked for them by retainers using the Quechua title "*yanakuna*." As Spanish administrators attempted a more direct control over land and labor in the Yucay Valley (through *tasas* and *reducciones*), individual Spaniards and Andeans exploited changing social conditions to pursue their own ends.

The legal claim pursued by Beatriz Coya and her husband centered on the reallocation of tributary labor during the Toledan *reducciones* (see Rostworowski 1970; Villanueva 1971). Their estate included the tributary laborers in the Yucay Valley, but Beatriz Coya and her husband requested that approximately 250 men living in the valley and categorized as tribute-exempt *yanakuna* be added to their estate on the grounds that their retainer status dated to Inka times (f. 180v-182v, 200v-232). The couple claimed that Gutiérrez Flores' 1571 administrative visit to the Yucay Valley had not been conducted with proper notification and had improperly designated tributary laborers as *yanakuna* (f. 2-2v). The principal claim of the court case involved tributary laborers in four communities (Yucay, Urubamba, Huayllabamba, and Maras), but it also exposed how retainership exploited fault lines in the administrative structure of the valley.

The Marquisate of Oropesa and the Betancur Collection

The eventual recategorization of many of the Yucay Valley *yanakuna* as tributary natives led to their assignment to Beatriz Coya's *repartimiento*, although her legal victory did not affect all *yanakuna* living in the valley (e.g., f. 423v-424). Spanish and Andean masters continued to enjoy the services of retainers at the end of the sixteenth century, but by this time the agricultural lands and labor base that were most clearly tied to Huayna Capac's estate had been restructured as a hereditary Colonial estate, the Marquisate of Oropesa.

As the descendants of Beatriz Coya and Martín García de Loyola were established as Colonial nobility, the documentation of the process became important for demonstrating their status and privileges. The legal documents published in this volume offer unprecedented details regarding how royal Inka resources were transformed in the early Colonial years, with surprising insight into the intersection of individual interests with local and imperial government.

The documents not only yield a chronological narrative of the Yucay Valley throughout the sixteenth century, but also an incredibly detailed portrait of the native population of the valley at the time of the Toledan administrative consolidation. The various questionnaires and excerpted documents reveal several classes of information that were brought to bear on legal claims at this time, including the use of tributary records, witness interviews, and excerpts of Crown-approved histories of Peru.

Chapter 3

The Marquisate of Oropesa and the Preservation, Collection, and Study of Its Documents

R. Alan Covey and Donato Amado González

The Constitution and Inheritance of the Marquisate of Oropesa

The marriage of Martín García de Loyola and Beatriz Clara Coya produced one daughter, Ana María Lorenza García Sayri Tupac de Loyola, who was born in Chile in 1593 and was still a young child when her mother died in 1600 (her father had been killed while fighting the Araucanians in Chile in 1598) (see Hemming 1970:458-61, 464-72, 506 for an overview of the dates and genealogical information provided in this section).

Ana María was sent to Spain in 1603, where she was raised at court by a distant cousin of her father, Don Juan de Borja y Castro. She married Juan Enríquez de Borja y Almansa—the nephew of her protector, and a man chosen for her by Philip III—in 1611. A year earlier, a tribunal had brought resolution to the long court case brought by Beatriz Coya and her husband regarding the tributary labor of the Yucay Valley. The court ruled in favor of Ana María and returned the tributaries, giving her the title of Marquesa de Oropesa and a large pension, and eventually (in 1614) granting her sovereignty over a hereditary estate comprising the four towns in the Yucay Valley. Ana María and her husband traveled to Peru in 1615 and resided in Yucay until 1627, when they returned to Madrid. The remaining Marquises of Oropesa resided in Spain and had their fiefdom managed for them.

Following the death of the first Marquesa in 1630, the estate passed to the eldest of the couple's eight children, Juan Enríquez de Almansa Inca y Loyola, who lived to 1675 and passed the estate to his daughter Teresa-Dominga, the eldest child of his second marriage (to Juana Teresa de Velasco y Guzmán, Duque de Frías).

Teresa-Dominga died in 1711, and her estate passed first to her son Pascual Enríquez de Almansa y Borja, and then to his younger sister María de la Almudena Enríquez de Cabrera when he died in 1739 leaving no children. María lived for two more years before she, too, died (in 1741) without leaving an heir to the estate.

Estate Claims in Eighteenth-Century Cusco

Upon the death of María de la Almudena Enríquez de Cabrera in 1741, the Marquisate of Oropesa reverted to the Spanish Crown. The next year saw the beginning of a series of claims made on the estate in an unsuccessful attempt to have the title reassigned. In the decades that followed, the claimants participating in this genealogical fight included Juan de Bustamante Carlos Inca, Diego Felipe Betancur Tupa Amaro, and José Gabriel Condorcanqui Tupa Amaro.

One interesting aspect of these legal claims is that they were based on Inka descent from Huayna Capac rather than close kinship with the recent descendants of the Marqueses de Oropesa. The Peruvian legal pursuit of the Oropesa estate involved the presentation of documentation of the genealogy of each claimant relative to descent from Huayna Capac's sons Paullu Inca and Manco Inca. The tailoring (or outright falsification) of one's ancestry was part of this process, and claims of fraudulent documentation were common responses from rival parties (e.g., Cahill 2004).

Don Juan de Bustamante Carlos Inca

Don Juan de Bustamante Carlos Inca began his fight for the Marquisate of Oropesa in 1742 (see AGI Lima 472 for a collection of documents from this process). His claim to the title was based on descent from the Inka line—he claimed that his ancestry followed Huayna Capac's lineage, through Paullu Inca and his descendants Carlos Inca and Melchor Carlos Inca (see Hemming 1970:511). Although the pursuit of his claim failed to convince the Crown to grant him the title and estate, Bustamante did manage to receive a minor title, an annual income, and a travel subsidy (Cahill 2004:144). This modest success surely stimulated other Peruvians aspiring to receive royal support.

Diego Felipe Betancur Tupa Amaro

While the claim of Bustamante had run through the lineage of Paullu Inca, that of Diego Felipe Betancur Tupa Amaro traced descent through Manco Inca and his son Tupa Amaro, who was captured in the 1572 expedition to Vilcabamba and executed in Cusco. Beginning in 1751, he claimed that a son of Tupa Amaro (Don Juan Titu Tupac Amaro) had survived the destruction of Vilcabamba, and this Inka was alleged to have been the great-great grandfather of the claimant (Cahill 2004:140, 151; Garrett 2005:203; Hemming 1970). The claim of descent from Tupa Amaro appeared to have convinced royal officials. By 1765, the viceroy recognized Betancur's descent in a provision that was reconfirmed in 1777 (Cahill 2004:147). As Cahill notes (2004:141), however, the claim to the Oropesa estate made little headway in the twenty-five years after it was first made. In 1776, the presentation of a rival petition for the estate appears to have invigorated Betancur's defense of his claim, although it seems that much of the energy and motivation came from Betancur's ambitious grandson-in-law, Vicente José García, who continued with the case after Betancur's death in 1778.

José Gabriel Condorcanqui Tupa Amaro

The claim of Betancur was contested by José Gabriel Condorcanqui Tupa Amaro, who also claimed descent from Tupa Amaro. Starting around 1776, he claimed that Tupa Amaro had fathered a daughter (doña Juana Pilco Huaco) in Vilcabamba, rather than a son, and that this daughter had married his great-great grandfather, Felipe Condorcanqui (Cahill 2004:148-49; Garrett 2005:203; Hemming 1970:507). Condorcanqui came from minor nobility in the province of Canas y Canchis (see Stavig 1999), and his claim to the Oropesa estate was part of an unsuccessful attempt to be accepted by the Inka nobility in Cusco (Cahill 2004). The legal proceeding between Betancur and Condorcanqui lasted for five years and has been most comprehensively reviewed by Cahill (2004; see also Rowe 1982; Valcárcel 1970). Having failed to secure Crown favor, Condorcaqui invested in fighting the Colonial system as the most visible leader of the Great Rebellion.

The Assembly of the Betancur Collection and Allegations of Fraud

Competing claims to the Oropesa estates and the subsequent assembly of the Betancur Collection documents occurred as the Spanish Colonial order was crumbling, a time when Inka identity was asserted as an essential element of Colonial society in Cusco as well as a revolutionary alternative to that society (see Cahill 2006; Garrett 2005; Stern 1987). The Inka contestation of the Oropesa estate should be placed into context, that is, among other claims of royal Inka descent being alleged at this time. It is important to note that fraud and forgery were common practices, as well as common claims leveled against one's legal opponents, as citizens of Cusco contended for prominence on a fading Colonial landscape.

As noted above, Vicente José García provided the energy behind the late push by Betancur to claim the Oropesa estate. García, a former army officer and lawyer who was married to one of Betancur's granddaughters, pursued the Betancur claim in the Spanish courts with a zeal that was matched by his willingness to alter and even falsify the documents that were used to substantiate his case. He secretly gathered the documents and titles of nobility of the Twenty-four Electors (elected representatives of the royal Inka lineages in Colonial Cusco) with the intent of using them to support Betancur's claims. García reproduced parts of these documents, altering their content in places to favor the descent of Betancur. Even after Betancur's death, García continued to gather (and, at times, falsify) documents to shore up the standing of his wife's family; for example, he doctored the documentary record so that Diego Felipe Betancur appeared as a deceased member of the electors of the *alférez real*.

In 1785, the election of Inka officials for the city of Cusco (*alférez real*) was prohibited through García's intervention. At the time, he was in possession of the documentary archive of titles of Inka nobility, and the noble Inka aspirants to the positions of *alférez real* were forced to pursue their legal claims under his representation (Amado 2004). By the end of the eighteenth century, García had accumulated an impressive body of documents pertaining to noble Inka descent.

The Betancur Collection during the Rise of Contemporary Historiography in Cusco

The collection of documents published in the present volume bears the signature of Vicente José García, who completed the index for his volume in June, 1795. The story of the collection does not end with García, however, but rather winds its way to Ángel Vega Enríquez, a lawyer and avocational historian in Cusco in the first half of the twentieth century (Amado 2004). Ángel Vega Enríquez was the great-great-great-great grandson of Diego Felipe Betancur Tupa Amaro, and was considered to be of Inka descent not only because of his descent from Betancur, but also because of assumed links to Garcilaso de la Vega.

Vega inherited the Betancur Collection documents from his mother and aunt, and he scrutinized the collection, removing many that he considered to be suspect or false. When drafting his will in 1931 at age 55, Vega noted that he had no children, making him the final descendant of a family tree reaching back to Inka emperors (ADC Protocolo Notarial, Basilio Cevallos [1931]). In that document, he described the collection of documents as including "twelve volumes richly filled with the imperial descent of the Inkas" that he suggested might be sold to an American university or to the government of Argentina in order to fund an institute called the Centro Nacional de Arte e Historia (ADC Protocolo Notarial, Basilio Cevallos [1931]: f. 447). This sale never transpired, and the documents were ultimately donated to the Universidad Nacional San Antonio Abad del Cusco, eventually joining the collections of the regional archive housed at the university.

A Brief Note on the Authenticity of the Present Collection

The documents published in this volume have a remarkable history, but one that has been tainted by the known and alleged doctoring of the documentary record in the late eighteenth century. As Cahill (2004) notes, sympathy for José Gabriel Condorcanqui Tupa Amaro led to the rise of the "hagiographic" interpretation that the erstwhile Inka noble and eventual rebel leader was unfairly dispossessed of the Oropesa estate through the machinations of Vicente José García (this is seen particularly in Valcárcel 1970 and Rowe 1982).

Cahill concludes that the allegations of wholesale fraud by García overstate the reality, and Amado (n.d.) observes that García spent the final decades of the eighteenth century accumulating a vast archive of original documents pertaining to the Inka nobility. Presumably, the documents that García altered or forged were those most directly related to the descent of Tupa Amaro, and many of these were identified and removed from the collection by Ángel Vega Enríquez.

Because of potential skepticism regarding the authenticity of the present collection, a few brief remarks should be made. The documents do not pertain to the descent of Tupa Amaro, but rather to the legal proceedings of the Yucay Valley in the years prior to the creation of the Marquisate of Oropesa. The handwriting of the documents is consistent with late sixteenth-century manuscripts, and copied documents in the collection include the scribe's testimony to their accuracy and validity. The documentary record published here speaks to the transformation of an Inka estate during the sixteenth century, providing valuable and detailed information that previous scholars have considered of reliable provenance (e.g., Rostworowski 1970; Villanueva 1971).

Part II

Documents from the Betancur Collection, Archivo Departamental del Cusco

ARCHIVO REGIONAL DEL CUZCO
DOCUMENTOS DE LA DIRECCION
GENEALOGIA DE D. DIEGO SAIRE Y ESTADO DE OROPESA
LIBRO NO.4 (30)
Este libro originalmente esta signado
Como el "Libro "2do"

<u>Genealogia</u>
De la Casa Ascendencia y Descendencia de
Dn Diego Sairitupac Mango Capac Yupangui Ynga
<u>Desde</u>
Antes y Despues de la Feliz Conquista y Pacificaz^on^
Del Reyno del Peru
<u>Asta</u>
El dia 31 de Julio de 1741 en q^e^ termino por fallecimiento
<u>De la Exma S^ra^</u>
Dª Maria Henrriquez de Cabrera Duquesa de
Medina de Rioseco Marq^sa^. de Alcañizas y de Santiago de
Oropesa
<u>Libro 2°</u>
Comprende el Qua.^no^ 1° de los Autos a q^e^ se contrae
en fox^s^. 553 numeradas de 1^a^ h^ta^. 553 inclusas 10 rayadas
en bl^co^
<u>Con los Ynstrum^tos^.</u>
Calificatibos de las Rentas y Merceds. concedidas a el estado y Mayorazgos de Oropesa fundados
vajo de los llama-
mientos qe. los instituidos en Castilla con facultad R^l^.
<u>Formado</u>
Por
D^n^. Vicente Jose Garcia Capitan graduado de los R^s^. Extos.
Ten^te^. Coronel y comandante del Regim^to^ de Dragones de Cota-
bambas residente en Madrid. Año de 1795.

<u>Quaderno 1°</u>
De los autos Originales seguidos en la Real
Audiencia de la Ciudad de Lima Reyno del Peru:
<u>Por:</u>
El Comendador Martin Garcia Oñaz de Loyola
del Orden de Calatraba como Marido y conjunta persona
de la Coya Dª Beatriz hija legitima unica y unibersal
heredera de D^n^. Diego Sairitupac Mango Capac Yupan-
gui Ynga y de la Coya D^a^. Maria Cusiguarcay su hermana
y mujer legitima in facie ecclesie:
<u>Con:</u>
El Señor Fiscal de dha Real Audiencia
<u>Sobre:</u>
La Restitucion de los 531 Yndios Yanaconas que
del Valle de Yucay propios del mayorazgo de dha Da. Bea-
triz saco el Señor Virrey D^n^. Francisco de Toledo y los in-
corporo en la Corona Real mandando que su tributo des-
de 20 de septiembre de 1572 fuese para la Real Ha-
cienda:

<u>En cuyos Autos</u>
Yncide la mutua Demande que puso dho Senor Fiscal
a la referida D^a^. Beatriz sobre todos los Yndios de los Repar-
timientos de su Mayorazgo y restitucion de lo que la hu-
viesen rentado.

/f.1/ Libro 2
Qno. 1°
Muy poderoso Señor

En M[d]. A 20 noviembre 1596 se trajo este pleito de palo
Empezado aver por los Ss. Benavente Olmedilla Don Fran[co]. Texada Don Juan Villagomez en 24 de março 60.

Martin Garcia de Loyola Cauallero del auito de Calatraua como marido y conjunta persona de doña Beatriz Coya hija legitima y unibersal heredera de don Diego Saire Topa y de doña Maria Coya su mujer y nietos de Guaina Capac Señor que fue destos rreinos en la mejor bia que forma que a lugar de dr[o] con licencia que para ello pido a V. Alt[a] pongo action y demanda a V rreal Hacienda y digo que passa assi que hauiendo su mag[d]. del emperador don Carlos ntro Señor hecho ynstancia y mando a los bissoreyes don Antonio de Mendoza marques de Cañete y a otros sus gobernadores que procurasen a traer de paz a su obediencia y servicio a Mango Ynga hijo del dho Guainacapac y su legitimo subçesor abuelo de la dha doña Beatriz y a su padre questauan rreuelados en Bilcabamba causando muchas ynquietudes y perterbando la paz y sosiego deste rreino les dio comission que para en segun la salida de los dhos yngas husasen de los medios que conbiniesen para atraello de paz a conocimiento de la sancta fee catolica y de su rreal servicio dandoles para esto comissiones bastantes y particulares para asentar con el dho ynga los medios y conciertos con que tubiese efecto su salida y ofreciendo como por ellas su mag[d]. ofrescia al dho don Diego todas las tierras que auia poseydo Mango Ynga su padre que balian a la sazon mas de cinquenta mill pessos de rrenta cada año que son las tierras que fue ocupado la fundacion del Cuzco y balle de Yucay y otras partes y para ello el dho marques de cañete embio por sus mensajeros a Fray Melchor de Los Reyes y a Francisco de Arrona de la Horden de Santo Domingo para que en su n[e] tratasen con el dho ynga don Diego mi suegro que a la sazon hera biuo y auia subcedido al dho Mango Ynga su padre que saliese a este rreino a dar la obediencia a su mag[d]. y al dho marques de Cañete en su n[e] ofresciendole de su parte en n[e] de su mag[d] mucha merced mediante lo qual el dho ynga correspondiendo al desseo que tenia del servicio de su mag[d]. despacho sus capitanes dando auisso al dho marques de la llegada de los dhos mensajeros y para informarse del que merçedes se le avian de hazer al dho ynga y habiendo el dho marques ofrescidoles lo que auia de hazer y particularmente se le encomendaria para si y para sus hijos y descendientes y subcesores perpetuamente para siempre jamas por bia de mayorazgo el repartimiento que era //
/f.1v/ encomienda Fr[co]. Hernandez Giron y el valle de Yucay que tubo encomendado don Francisco Arias del Marques don Fr[co] Piçarro que estaban bacos con todo lo a ellos subjeto segun poseen y poseyeron los dhos don Fr[co] Piçarro y Fran[co] Hernandez Giron que a la sazon rrentaban veinte mill pessos de plata ensayada para que los tuviesse y gozasse enteramente sin pinsion alguna y que se le darian perdon de las muertes daños y rrobos que se auian caussado y se le darian tierras y solares y otras cossas con que se pudiesse sustentar su persona mujer cassa y estado y que se le daria titulo de Señor y se le arian otras muchas merçedes en el entre tanto que su mag[d] le azia otras mayores con que el dho ynga saliese dentro de seis meses y biniesse ante el dho marques a dar la dha obediencia y basallaje en cumplimiento de lo qual el dho ynga aviendo entendido el dho ofrescimiento y que se cumpliria con el salio ante el dho marques en el dho tr[no] dexando como dexo toda la provincia de Bilcabamba que tenia y gozava y en ella mas de cinco mill yndios tributarios sin las provincias de los Mañaries y Pilcoçones que tenia debaxo de su obediencia e basallaje que son mas de quinze mill yndios y el dho marques le hizo rrescevir muy honrrosamente significando ser este el mayor servicio que avia hecho a su magd. para la pacificacion destos rreinos y seguridad de su rreal conçiencia y le ospedo y festejo y el dho ynga dio la ovediencia y basallaje a su mag[d] y al dho marques en su rreal nombre el qual en birtud de los poderes que de su mag[d] tenia y cumpliendo el pacto y asiendo que con el dho ynga avia thomado y con los dhos capitanes y rreligiosos dio titulos al dho don Diego de adelantado del dho balle de Yucay y de la dha encomienda de los dhos repartimientos con titulo de mayorazgo como por el consta por birtud del qual el dho don Diego Saire Topa en su bida tomo la posesion de los dhos repartimientos y titulo de adelantado y los tubo y poseyo quieta y pacificamente llevando y gozando los tributos de los dhos yndios segun el titulo de la dha encomienda y despues de su muerte subcedio en todo lo suso dho la dha doña Beatriz mi mujer y siendo la suso dha menor y estando debaxo de la tutoria y curadoria de Tilano de Anaya y estando el dho Tilano de Anaya ausente de la ciudad del Cuzco por mandado de don Francisco de T[do] vuestro bissorey que fue destos rreinos en las montañas de Bilcabamba el dho vuestro vissorrey cometio la bissita del dho valle de Yucay al doctor fray Pedro Gutierrez el qual sin çitar a la dha doña Beatriz ni a su curador y sin hacer con ellos otra ning[a] diligencia ni emplaçami[to] de las que de dr[o] se requiren fue al dho valle y lo vissito y aviendo allado por la visita que del hizo mucho numero de yndios tributarios que tenian nombre de yanaconas desde el tpo del ynga por ser muchos de ellos yndios mitimaes adbenidizos y averlos hecho benir al dho valle el dho ynga para su servicio por ser aquel balle de que es rrecamara y recreacion suya sin otra averiguacion ni informacion ofreciendole que en esto azia servicio a V alt[a] en virtud de un capitulo de su instruccion en que se rrefiere //
/f.2/ que los yndios bagamundos que no estubiesen vissitados ni tributasen los ponga en la Caxa Real el dho frai Pedro Gutierrez declaro y numero por yndios bagamundos tenidos en esta memoria que presento que son demas y allende de otros que en horden numero por yanaconas e yndios bagamundos sobre que tengo puesto debido pleito en esta real audi[a] a vuestra real hacienda siendo como los dhos yndios y sus padres an sido tributarios assi al dho ynga en su tiempo como a don Fr[co] Piçarro y a su hijo don Fr[co] Piçarro y a V alt[a] estando bacos por muerte de los dhos Piçarro antes del pacto que se tomo el dho don Diego mi suegro y en su vida y despues de su muerte y constando por la visita y numeracion que dellos hizo que pagavan y ayudavan a pagar la tassa general del dho repartimiento y gozavan de las tierras y aprovechamiento del dho balle como yndios tributarios y naturales y si algunos dexaban de contribuir para la dha tassa hera por averlos rreservado don Garcia Quispe Capi caçique principal de los naturales del dho balle y don Fr[co] Chilche caçique principal de los mitimaes del dho repartimi[to] que el uno y el otro a porfia los reservavan de la dha tassa cargando a los yndios pobres la que ellos devian pagar por servirse dellos en sus chacaras y aprovechamientos y por ser padres y hermanos y deudos de yndias con quien ellos fueron cassados y amançevados y que respeto desto y por otras causas los reservavavan de la dha tassa y la cargavan a los demas con

la qual color y por darles a entender el dho visitador que siendo yanaconas no avian de pagar tassa y por quedarse con ellos los dhos caçiques dieron a entender al dho visitador que eran anaconas [*sic*] el qual sin atender al dho concierto y a los dhos yndios heran de la dha encomienda que se avia hecho en el dho mi suegro por titulo onorosso y sin hacer diligencia ninguna hizo la dha numeracion y declaravan mediante la qual el dho vuestro bisorrey puso y aplico a. V. rreal corona los dhos dozientos treynta y un yndios questos y los demas de que tengo movido pleyto sobre quinientos y sesenta y tres yndios y aplico los tributos dellos para los gastos de la fortaleça del Cusco tassandolos por si y desde le dha declaraçion y tassacion yo y la dha mi mujer avemos estado y estamos desposeydos de los dhos yndios y tassa que de ellos fue hecha pertenesciendonos como nos pertenesçen y que los tributos en que fueron tassados y los tributos con que se nos acude por los demas yndios del dho repartimiento no monta lo uno y lo otro la mitad de los veinte mill pessos que el dho marques de Cañete dio al dho ynga entendio que se le davan y avian de sustentar a el y a sus hijos y descendientes perpetuamente del dho concierto. Demas de que de los tributos que los dhos yndios nos dan somos conpelidos injustamente a pagar dos mill pessos de pinssion en cada un año a don Juan Arias Davila en lo que la dha mi mujer e yndios y //
/f.2v/ avemos resivido e ressivimos notorio daño e agravio y V alt[a] los debe rremedio mandando cumplir el dho concierto y haciendo las demas mercedes que al dho ynga se le ofrecieron y como herederos del dho Guaynacapac.

Por que pido y suplico a V. Alteza que dando por ninguna la numeracion hecha por frai Pedro Gutierrez en nuestro perjuizio y el auto proveido por el dho vuestro bissorrey en que la confirmo y puso en vuestra real caveza el numero de los dhos indios declare pertenecer al dho nuestro repartimiento por el dho titulo y nos los mande volver y restituir con todos los tributos que an rentado y podido rentar y rentaren asta la real restitucion condenando en todos ellos A.V Real Hazienda y pues injustamente fuimos desposeidos de los dhos indios sin oirnos ni citarnos ni preçeder auiriguacion ninguna y mande que con la facilidad que fuimos desposeydos en tiempo que la dha doña Beatriz hera menor con essa mesma seamos restituidos y pido justicia y juro a Dios y a esta que es cruz que esta demanda no proçede de malicia y que agora nuevamente ha venido a mi noticia que este numero de indios que pido es de mas numero de indios que por el dho pleyto pendiente tengo pedidos

Y para que que lo suso dho tenga efecto como negocio que nuevamente avenido a mi noticia apelo de lo proveido y hecho por el dho vuestro bissorrey don Fr[co] de T[do] y del dho Frei Pedro Gutierrez y me presento ante V. Alteza para que esta Real Audiencia a que particularmente esta cometido el rremedio de los agravios que se hizieren vuestro Bissorrey y gobernadores desaga esta y pido justicia. Ba henmendado treynta sesenta vala y estando de mas de que de los tributos que los dhos indios nos dan no vala.

Llin[do] Myn garcia Loyola (rubrica)
Falcon. (rubrica)

En la ciudad de Los Reyes en diez e nueve dias del mes de jullio de mill quinientos e ochenta e cinco años ante los Señores presidente e oidores y estando en audiencia publica que presento esta peticion

Y por los dhos Señores vista mandaron dar treslado al fiscal de su majestad.

P Montoya (rubrica)

/f.3/ **YNDIOS DE ESTE 2º PLEITO**

1v Agustin Marca—
2v Agustin Pariguana—
3v Alonso Sitpulla—
4v Alonso Canagua—
5v Alonso Pachai—
6v Alonso Puruai—
7v Andres Guamalli—
8v Alonso Caque—
9v Alonso Pota—
10v Alonso Yuare—
11v Alonso Marca Quichua—
12v Andres Ponpoma—
13v Alonso Cassi—

14v Alonso Trapa—
15v Alonso Guaco puquis—
16v Alonso Yanai poma—
17v Alonso Cuchillailas—
18v Alonso Chunguiparia—
19v Alonso Vilcaparia—
20v Alonso Condur Quichua—
21v Anton Anco Aros—
22v Alonso Suco—
23v Alonso Siuipuclla—
24v Alonso Cuyochin—
25v Alonso Aros Ylepoma—
26v Agustin Chuquiapar—
27v Alonso Calchipulla—
28v Agustin Atao suyo—
29v Alonso Quispillalli—
30v Anton Quispi—
31v Alonso Supantaiom—
32v Alonso Talmaguan—
33v Alonso Pacaguano—
34v Andres Condur—
35v Alonso Condur—
36v Alonso Caguia—
37v Andres Quispe—
38v Agustin Sulca—
39v Alonso Condori—
40v Alonso Marca—
41v Alonso Tincas—
42v Andres Cannic—
43v Agustin Guamanca—
44v Andres Masquies—
45v Alonso Camasyanas—
46v Andres Caxavilca—
47v Andres Guaman Pullaca—
48v Alonso Yupangui—
49v Alonso Billa—
50v Agustin Llaguachicha—
51v Agustin Calaquipan—
52v Alonso Guarta Soca—
53v Alonso Chaca—
54v Antonio Saqui—
55v Alonso Ynga Tomao—
56v Alonso Tuiro Cheque
57v Alonso Pariguan
58v Alonso Marca
59v Usco Desora
60v Andres Caruyanac
61v Vicente Chico
62v Bartolome Guaman
63v Baltasar Anas
64v Baltasar Angas
65v Diego Maran
66v Diego Quispe
67v Diego Sicha
68v don Pedro Guari Tito
69v Diego Pomacunca
70v don Luis Tito
71v Diego Acotom
72v Diego Gamini
73v Domingo Pumaruco
74v Diego Machacaua
75v Diego Alpa Uqui
76v Diego Gualpa Cunca
77v Diego Auquigualpa
78v Diego Cai
79v Diego Chaton
80v Diego Puma Supaico
81v Diego Conde Gualpa
82v Diego Puma Canche
83v Diego Laimi
84v Diego Guanca Colla
85v Domingo Casmai
/f.3v/ 86v Francisco Tacuri
87v Francisco Cautanala
88v Felipe Cocha Charca
89v Francisco Manco Guayacondo
90v Francisco Quispe
91v Felipe Cañari
92v Francisco Quipaca
93v Francisco Rimache
94v Francisco Yana
95v Francisco Cassa Quinaman
96v Francisco Cuxo
97v Francisco Marcas
98v Francisco Taipe Taipe
99v Francisco Cutiquella
100v Francisco Anluzila
101v Felipe Quino
102v Francisco Chuca Guaman
103v Francisco Condor Supa
104v Garcia Tiqueilla Chaupis
105v Garci Gual Guari
106v Gregorio Guailba Chumbi
107v Garcia Chara
108v Hernando Guntat Nauca
109v Hernando Estaula
110v Hernando Ville Colla
111v Hernando Lancaina
112v Hernando Yaupa
113v Juan Ynga Paucar
114v Juan Atau Suno
115v Juan Cusi Guaman
116v Juan Toto
117v Juan Tacuri

118v Juan Sulca
119v Juan Canan
120v Juan Cayo
121v Juan Calpac
122v Juan Chucalla
123v Juan Calco
124v Juan Suno
125v Juan Auca Gualpa
126v Juan Tupa Yupnagui
127v Juan Uchpilco
128v Juan Caya
129v Juan Aupo
130v Juan Conduri
131v Juan Gualpa Toca
132v Juan Yslema
133v Juan Culpo
134v Juan Perca Colla
135v Juan Tuto
136v Juan Paucar Cusi
137v Juan Achuqui Buldi
138v Juan Paucar Atavillo
139v Juan Corna Cuna
140v Juan Cochachi
141v Juan Aysma
142v Juan Condori
143v Lucas Cucu Savit
144v Luis Quispe Guaman
145v Lucas Yaque
146v Luis Tupa Yupangui
147v Lucas Quispe
148v Martin Sicha
149v Martin Cuacalla
150v Miguel Paucar
151v Martin Cura Pinagua
152v Martin Amanca
153v Martin Curiguaman
154v Martin Sulca Guaillas
155v Martin Ynga Sono
156v Martin Guari Paucar
157v Marcos Puri
158v Martin Casi Tancar
159v Martin Cuco
160v Martin Sulca
161v Martin Guaman
162v Martin Amai
163v Martin Chichui
164v Martin Bilinaula sastre
165v Mateo Ataganca
166v Martin Llacai
167v Miguel Mataguairi
168v Martin Tuta Niali
169v Martin Naupa de Caicai
170v Marcos Auqui
171v Martin Carua Yana
172v Miguel Tiquilla
173v Martin Guarta Puca
/f.4/ 174v Miguel Nina Carua
175v Martin Yaro Vilca
176v Martin Cura Colla
177v Martin Rimabo
178v Martin Callupa
179v Marcos Chilque
180v Martin Tacoxi Conde
181v Miguel Guaracunca
182v Martin Tona
183v Matheo Chucuru
184v Martin Quispi Guanca
185v Miguel Llocolla
186v Matheo Auris
187v Auris
187v Martin Guanaco
188v Martin Malta
189v Martin Bilca
190v Martin Paucar Arba
191v Miguel Quispi
192v Pedro Marin
193v Pedro Puruan
194v Pedro Quinto
195v Pedro Unba
196v Pedro Acha Yauyo
197v Pedro Guasco Cayanbi
198v Pedro Chuquicondor
199v Pedro Caucana
200v Pedro Guaua sastre
201v Pedro Caque
202v Pedro Anta
203v Pedro Pariguana
204v Pedro Guanca Capoma
205v Pedro Auqui
206v Pedro Pacha
207v Pedro Paucar Chaupa
208v Pedro Machaguai
209v Pedro Raimachua
210v Pedro Curi
211v Pedro Caita
212v Pedro Caparamoco
213v Pedro Uma
214v Pedro Chinco
215v Pedro Rimache
216v Pedro Yauquipau
217v Pedro Cauana
218v Pedro Asto Paucar
219v Pedro Alca Monricolla
220v Pedro Pullo
221v Pedro Guantalla
222v Pedro Chumbi
223v Santiago Pacha
224v Sebastian Una Pau
225v Sebastian Cacha
226v Simon Llanco
227v Xpobal Cona Gualpa
228v Simon Ylla Topa
229v Xpobal Maeta
230v Xpobal Gualpa
231v Xpobal Sulca Naui
Martin Garcia e Loyola (rubrica).

/f.4v/ /en blanco/

/f.5/ Muy poderoso señor

dice que puso otra vez esta
demanda y se remitio con
a la de malinas al consejo

El L^{do} Alvr^{o} de Carvajal vro fiscal respondiendo a cierta pets^{on} / o demanda puesta por Myn Garcia de Loyola como marido e conjunta persona de doña Beatriz Coya en que pide ciertos yanaconas digo que la dha demanda no se debe admitir ni proçederse ni hazer pleito sobre ella porque estos mysmos yanaconas e yndios tiene pedido en esta Rreal Audiencia y se proçedio en la causa por la orden dada en vra rreal provs^{on} dada en Malinas y se rremytio la causa conforme a ella a vro rreal consejo de Yndias y se a llevado el proçeso alla y asi le obta la ececion de la cosa juzgada o litis pendençia

A Vuestra al^{t} pido y suply^{co} declare no deuerse admitir la dha demanda ni proçederse sobre ella o lo que mas convenga al dr^{o} de vro real fisco pido justicia y costas y el real of^{o} ymploro.

Otro sy a vuestra al^{t} pido y suplico mande se trayga el proçeso de la causa que asi siguio el dho Myn Garcia de Loyola para verse juntam^{te} con esta demanda que esta ante el presente escri^{o} de Camara y se me de un testimonio de ella con el estado e relacion de la causa que todo lo presentara e pido justicia.

Licenciado Alv^{o} de Caravajal (rubrica)

/f.5v/ En la ciudad de Los Reyes en v^{te} e siete dias del mes de agosto de mill e qui^{o}s e ochenta y cinco a^{o}s ante los señores presidente e oidores en audiencia publica se presento esta peticion

E por los dhos señores vista mandaron dar treslado a la otra pte e que pa la proxima aud^{a} responda e con lo que dixiecen o no se traigan los autos y el processo que esta peticion dice.

Montoya (rubrica)

/f.6/ Muy Poderoso Señor
Respondiendo a la dilatoria que
Yanaconas que ahora pido
diferentes en numero y especie

Jhoan Ss de los Rios en n^{e} de Martin Garcia de Loyola en la causa con vro fiscal sobre los yanaconas que de nuevo pide respondiendo a la dilatoria de contrario alegada en que en efecto dize que sobre estos mismos yanaconas esta pleito pendiente y remite. Digo que sin embargo dello sea de proceder en esta causa y azer segun por mi parte esta pedido por que los yanaconas que de nuevo que son otros diferentes en num^{o} y especie de los que tenga pedidos y assi parecera por el proceso el qual con su mandato que se traiga como el fiscal lo dize para que se vea y proceda y se aga a mi parte justicia la que pido y para ello

El Licenciado Falcon (rubrica) Martin Garcia de Loyola (rubrica)

/f.6v/ En la ciudad de Los Reyes en veinte dias del mes de ag^{to} de mill qui^{o}s y ochenta y cinco años ante los Señores presidente y oidores estando en audiencia publica se presento esta peticion

E por los dhos señores vista mandaron traer los autos para proveer justicia
Montoya (rubrica)

Va en provision al rr S^{e} a esçibirse esta caussa prueba al rreal se le devuelve y registra .
(rubrica)

Que responde derechamente. El fiscal.

En la ciudad de Los Reyes en tres dias del mes de setiembre de mill y quinientos y ochenta y cinco años los señores presidente y oidores desta Rreal Audiencia visto esta caussa en provision con la causa principal mandaron que el fiscal de su majestad responda derechamente a ella y ansi lo proveyeron e mandaron

Ante mi Joan de Montaya (rubrica)

/f.7/ Muy poderoso Señor
Suplica de mandar responder directamente al demanda

El L[do] Alvaro de Carvajal vro fiscal en la causa con Martin Garcia de Loyola e doña Beatriz Coya su mujer sobre los yn[o]s yanaconas digo: que en esta dha causa se proveyo auto en que se me manda que responda derechamente a la demanda puesta por los suso dhos lo qual hablando con el acatamiento devido no se devio proverse por que yo tengo respondido juridica derechamente a la dha dem[da] puesta por la dha doña Beatriz y alegando la eleccion de la cosa juzgada o litis pendencia la qual impide de el litis yngreso mayorm[te] constantando por los autos que en esta rreal audiencia sean tratado y ante todas cosas se a ade determinar sobre esto por que siendo como es asi que es sobre esto mesmo sea hecho e tratado pleito en esta Rreal Audiencia y concluso rremytido a vuestro Rreal Consejo de Indias no se debe permitir ni dar lugar aque sobre lo mesmo se haga otro pleyto pues ningun hefecto puede tener mas de en embarazar con pesas yndividas e impertinentes estos rreales estrados y los de vuestro Rreal Consejo de Indias
A vuestra Al[t] pido y suplico sin enbargo del dho auto haga segun que pedido y suplicado tengo y si es necesario suplicar del suplico pido justicia y costas en real oficio ynploro

El Lic[do] Alv[o] de Caravajal (rubrica)

/f.7v/ En la ciudad de Los Reyes a doce del mes de septiembre de mill quinientos y ochenta y cinco a[o]s ante los señores presidentes e oidores de esta Rreal Audiencia estando haziendo audiencia publica se presento esta pet[on]

E por los dhos señores vista mandaron dar treslado a la otra parte e que por la pr[te] audiencia responda pressente Joan Sanches de Los Rrios a quien se notifico
Montoya (rubrica)
Que se confirma

En la ciudad de Los Reyes en treze dias del mes de setiembre de mill y quinientos y ochenta y cinco años los señores presidente y oidores de esta Rreal Audiencia vista esta causa en provision confirmaron el autos por los dhos señores en ella proveido en que mandaron que el fiscal de su majestad responda derechamente a ella sin embargo de la suplicacion interpuesta por el dho fiscal y ansi lo proveyeron e rubricaron

(tres rubricas)

/f.8/ Muy P[o] Señor

Joan Sanches de los Rrios en nombre de doña Beatriz Coya en la caussa con vro fiscal sobre los yanaconas que mi parte pide respondiendo a la suplicacion de contrario presentado en que en efecto dize sea de revocar el auto de vro presidente e oidores que le mandaron respondiese derechamente a la dha demanda digo que sin embargo de lo en ella se a de confirmar el dho mauto por lo que tengo dho y alegado y por que como por las demandas parece es diferente cossa lo que agora pide mi parte en numero y espeçie de indios y si vuestro fiscal ubiera visto atentamente la visita y demanda por mi parte presentadas no se hubiera dho lo que dize

Por que pido y supp[co] a Vuestra Alteza confirme el dho auto y sobre pido justicia y para ello etc
El lic[do] Falcon. (rubrica)

En la ciudad de Los Reyes en treze dias del mes de setiembre de mill y quinientos y ochenta y cinco años estando los señores presidente y oidores de la Real Audiencia en audiencia publica se presento esta peticion
Por los dhos señores vista mandaron llevar los autos a la sala para proveer

Montoya (rubrica)

/f.8v/ (margen) Auto de Prueba
En la ciudad de Los Reyes en veinte y quatro dias del mes de septiembre de mill y quinientos y ochenta y cinco años los señores presidente y oidores de esta Real Audiencia aviendo visto este procenso y autos dexeron que las dhas partes y a cada una de ellas dentro de noventa dias puestos siguientes pressenten las escrituras y testigos de que se entienden aprovechar con que ninguna dellas pressente mas de doze testigos con apercebimiento que el dho termino passado con lo que huvieren fecho sin les admitir otra provança alguna se rremitira a su majestad y a su rreal consejo de Indias conforme a la hordenança y asi lo proveyeron y rubricaron

Ante mi Jhoan de Montoya
(Al margen) Martin de Loyola

En los Reyes en veinte Nueve dias del mes de noviembre del mill y quinientos y ochenta y cinco años yo escrivano Juan de Montoya notifique elauto arriba proveido por los señores presidente y oidores de esta Real Audiencia a Martin Garcia de Loyola en su persona y de ello doy fee

Jhoan de Montoya

/f.9/ Muy poderoso s^{r}

Myn Garcia de Loyola por mi procu^{or} en el pleito nuevo con vro fiscal sobre los otros indios en que fue sin oirme desposeido digo que vro fiscal alegado que estos indios de esta dem^{da} nueva dize que son los mesmos de la dem^{da} y pleito viejo ya pa que el Licenciado Vizcarra Relator a hecho el cotejo en presencia de M^{or} de Castillo solicitador y procurador del fisco y a vysto el memoria de los indios de la demanda vieja y cotejados con la memoria de la demanda nueba se ve claramente son diferentes los unos y los otros que el numero hedad y nombres y que estos de la demanda nueba no se comprenden ni estan en l demanda vieja conviene a mi derecho en el dho relator lo declare y lo de firmado de su nombre por mando de vuestro presidente y oidores

Pido y suplico a V. Alt^{a} lo mande al dho relator y que lo de el escripto y firme el de su nombre y se ponga en esta provision pa que en toda parte y lugar conste dello y fallo etc

Martin Garcia de Loyola (rubrica)

/f.9v/ En Los Reyes en onze dias del mes de octubre de mill e quenientos e ochenta e cinco años ante los señores y presidente e oidores estando en audiencia publica se presento esta peticion

E los dhos señores mandaron della al fiscal de su majestad y que para la primera audiencia responda alguacil que estava presente se lo notifique

Montoya (rubrica)

/f.10/ Muy Poderoso Señor

Martin Garcia de Loyola Por my procu^{or} en el pleyto con vuestro fiscal sobre los ys^{o} que se me quitaron en el Valle de Yucay ago pres^{cion} del ttr^{do} del titulo de g^{or} que vuestro fiscal me dio de las provincias del Rio de la Plata y Paraguay

A V alt^{a} suplico aya por pres^{do} y se paga por proceso por prueba de my dr^{o}

Myn Garcia de Loyola (rubrica)

En la Ciudad de Los Reyes en onze dias del mes de noviembre de mill y quinientos ochenta y cinco años ante los señores press^{te} e oydores desta real audiencia estando en audiencia publica presento esta peticion e leydo en ella.

E por los dhos señores vista mandaron dar treslado a la otra parte e que para la primera audiencia responda presente el l^{do} Alvaro de Carvajal fiscal de su mag^{td} al qual se notifico e que se ponga en el proceso. Montoya (rubrica)

/f.10v/ /en blanco/

/f.11/ Don Phelipe por la Gracia de Dios Rey de Castilla de Leon de Aragon de las dos Cecilias de Jerusalen de Portugal de Navarra de Granada de Toledo de Valencia de Galicia de Mallorca de Sevilla de Cerdeña de Cordova de Corcega de Murcia de Jaen de los Algarves de Algeçira de Occidentales Islas y tierras firme del Mar Oceano Archiduque de Austria Duque de Borgona de Brauante y Milan Conde de Habspurgo de flandes de tirol y de Barcelona Señor de Vizcaya y de Molina etc. Por quanto por haber fallecido el adelantado Joan Ortiz de Çarate nro Gobernador y Capt Gen^{al} que era de las provincias del Rrio de la Plata proveymos en su lugar a Don Basco de Guzman entre tanto que se veya y determinava si avia de subceder en el dho cargo la persona que caso con la hija y heredera del dho adelantado y otra cosa proveyamos y el dho don Basco a puesto algunos inconvenientes por los quales no haze ni ade hazer el viaje y asi conviene a vuestro servicio proveer persona que gobierne las dhas provincias y por ende acatando lo que voz Martin Garcia de Loyola Caballero de la orden de Calatrava y residente en las Provincias del Piru nos aveis servido y por la satisfeccion que tenemos de vuestra prudencia abilidad y otras buenas partes tenemos por bien y es nuestra merced que seais nuestro gobernador y Capitan General de las dhas provincias del dho Rrio de La Plata en lugar del dho adelantado Juan Ortiz de Çarate entre tanto que se vea y determinado si lo hade ser la persona que caso con la dha su hija y heredera y otra cosa proveamos y que como tal nuestro gobernador y capitan general de las dhas provincias vos y no otra persona alguna useis los dhos cargos en los casos y cossas a ellos anexas y concernientes por vos y vuestros lugar tenientes y oficiales asi en lo civil como en lo criminal en todas las ciudades villas y lugares que estan y obladas y se poblaren en los dhos provinçias guardando y cumpliendo y haziendo fundar y cumplir las ordenanças e instrucciones cedulas y provincias que estan dadas y se dieren para las dhas provincias segun y de la manera que podia usar y exercer el dho adelantado Joan Ortiz de Çarate y lo usaron y pudieron usar los otros gobernadores capitanes generales que antes fueron de las dhas provincias y por esta nuestra carta o por su traslado signado de escrivano publico mandamos a los consejos justicias regidores caballeros escuderos officiales y hombres buenos de todas las ciudades villas lugares que estan poblados y se poblaren en las dhas provincias y a los nuestros officiales de nuestra hazienda dellas que luego como con ella fueren ressividos sin esperar otra nuestra nuestra carta segunda ni terceza jusion tomen y reciban de vos el dho Martin Garcia de Loyola el juramento y con la solenidad que en tal casso se requiere //
/f.11v/ y deveis hazer el qual por vos asi hecho os ayan reciban y tengan por tal nuestro gobernador y capitan general de los dhos provincias entre tanto que como dhos es se ven y determinen lo suso dho y proveamos otra cossa y os deseen libremente oyr y librar y conocer de todos los pleytos y causas asi ceviles como criminales que en los dhos provincias oviere y de vos devieredes y pudieredes conocer como tal nuestro gobernador y capitan general de ellas y proveer todas las otras cossas que podian proveer el dho adelantado Juan Ortiz de

Çarate y los otros gobernadores que fueron de las dhas provincias y tomar e rrecevir todas y quales quier pesquisas e ynformaciones en lexrasos [*sic*] y cosas de dr^{o} permisas que entendieredes que a nro servis^{o} y execucion de nra justicia y buena governacion de las dhas provincias convenga y llevar y lleveis vos y vros lugartenientes y oficiales los derechos a los dhos oficios anexos y pertenescientes y en persona los usar y exercer cumplir y executarse conforme con vos con sus personas y gentes y os obedezcan y den y hagan dar todo el fabor y ayuda que les pidieredes y menester ovieredes y en todo os acaten y obedezcan y cumplan vros mandamientos y de vros lugartenientes y que en ello ni en parte dello embargo ni contr^{o} alguno no expongan ni consientan poner que nos por la presente os resivimos y avemos por rresevido a los dhos oficios y al uso y exercicio dellos y os damos poder e ffacultad para los usar y exercer caso que por ellos o alguno dellos a ellos no seais recevido. Y otro si por esta nuestra carta mandamos a qualesquier perssonas que tienen o tuvieren el govierno de las dhas provincias y la administracion de nuestra justizia que luego que por vos fueren requeridos os den y entreguen y hagan dar y entregar las varas de nuestra justizia y no usen mas de sus oficios en manera alguna so las penas en que caent yncurren las personas que ussan de oficios publicos y reales por nra que no tienen poder por el presente los suspendemos y avemos por suspendidos de sus oficios y os mandamos que las penas y condenaciones pertenescientes a nuestra camara y ffisco que vos y los dhos vro lugar tenientes y las otras justicias hizieredes las executeis y hagais executar y dar y entregar a los nuestros oficiales de las dichas provincias. Otro si es nuestra mrd que si vos el dho Martin Garcia de Loyola entendieredes ser cumplidero a nuestro servs^{o} y a la execucion de nuestra justizia que quales quier personas que agora estan y adelante estuvieren en las dhas provincias //

/f.12/ salgan y no entren mas en ellas y se vengan ante nos e vos se lo podais mandar de nuestra parte y los hagais salir dellas conforme a la pragmatica que sobre ello habra dando a la persona que asi desterrades la causa por que le desterrais y si os paresciere que sea secreta se la dareis cerrada y sellada y un traslado della nos enviareis por dos vias para que seamos informados dello pero aveis de estar advertido que quando ovieredes de desterrar algunos no sea sin muy gran caussa para qual todo que dho es os damos poder cumplido con todas sus yncidencias y dependencias anexidades y conexidades y mandamos que ayais y lleveis de salario cada un año con los dhos cargos todo el tpo que los sirvieredes dos mil ducados y otros dos mil de ayuda de costa que por todo sean quatro mil ducados que valen un ciento y quinientos mill mrs como los tenia el dho adelantado de las rentas y provechos que tubieremos en las dhas provincias del dho Rio de la Plata porque no aviendo las dhas rentas no avemos de ser obligado a pagaros de otra parte el dho salario y ayuda de costa y asi mandamos a los nuestros oficiales de las dhas provincias que las dhas rentas y provechos que en ellos tuvieremos y ffueren a su cargo os dent y paguen el dho salario y ayuda de costa de los dhos quatro mil ducados cada año por los tercios del desde el dia que por testim^{o} signado de escrivano les constare que salieredes de las dhas provincias del Peru para yr a servir los dhos cargos en adelante el tpo que como dicho es los sirvieredes que son vras cartas de pago y treslado signado de esta nra provs^{on} y el dho testimonio mandamos se le resziba y pase en cuenta lo que assi os vieren y pagaren sin otro recaudo alguno. y asimesmo les mandamos que asienten esta nra provisi^{on} en los nuestros libros que tuvieren y asentado la buelban originalm^{te} a vos el dho Myn Garcia de Loyola para que la tengais por vro titulo. dada en Lisboa a treze dias de nobiembre de mill e qui^{o}s y ochenta y un años. yo el Rey. Yo Antonio de Erazo secretario de su mag^{t} catolica la fize escrevir por su mandado y a las espaldas de la dha real cedula estan las firmas siguientes. El licen^{do} Gasca de Salazar. El licen^{do} Al^{o} Myres Espadero. El licen^{do} don Diego de Çuñiga. El licen^{do} Henao. El licen^{do} Hinojossa.
Registrada Pedro de Ledesma canciller Sant Joan de Sardaneta.
Fecho y sacado originalmente e concertado fue este treslado con la dha provis^{on}

/f.12v/ Rese orign^{al} questava firmada de una firma que dize yo El rrey refrendada de Ant^{o} de Eraso y a las espaldas de Ella estavan cinco firmas del tenor s^{e} el licen^{do} Gasca de Salazar el licen^{do} Al^{o} Myres Espadero el licenciado Diego de Çuñiga el licen^{do} Henao el licen^{do} Hinojosa y registrada por P^{o} de Ledesma y por canciller Sant Joan de Sardaneta segun por ella parecia en la ciudad de los Reyes del Piru en cinco dias del mes de henero año del señor de mill e quinientos y ochenta y tres años siendo testigos a lo ver sacar corregir e concertar con la dha provi^{on} original Mingo [*sic*] de Valencia y Leandro de Sanctiago y Fran^{co} Mynes estantes en esta dha ciudad.

E yo Al^{o} de Valencia escrivano de su mg^{t} publico del num^{o} desta ciudad de los Reyes intervino con los dhos tg^{os} al sacar corregir e concertar este traslado que la dha probysyon [ilegible] y la expidio de pedimento del capitan Martin Garcia de Loyola gobernador de la dha Provincia del Rio de la Plata e fize e signe este my signo en testimonio de verdad.

Al^{o} de Valencia (rubrica)
Escrivano Pu^{o}

Nos los escrivanos de su mag^{t} publicos del numero desta ciudad de los reyes que aqui firmamos nros nombres damos fee que Alonso de Valencia de quien ba signada y firmada esta escriptura es escrivano de su mag^{t} publico del numero desta ciudad de los reyes y a sus escripturas y autos que ante el an pasado y pasan se les ha dado y da entera fee y creditos huicios [*sic*] y fuera del y para que dello conste dimos esta en la ciudad de los reyes a cinco dias del mes de henero de mill e quin^{o}s y ochenta y tres años.

Pedro Ochoa (rubrica)	(ilegible)	Estevan (ilegible)
Escrivano Publico	Escrivano publico	Escrivano publico

/f.13/ Muy P^{o} señor

Suplica sea recebido prueba que se cosa este con el otro.

El llic^{o} Alvar^{o} de Carvajal vro fiscal en la causa que segunda vez trata Martin Garcia de Loyola e doña Beatriz Coya su mujer sobre los ynd^{o}s yanaconas con vro rreal fisco lo qual esta vaya remytida y enbiada a vro real consejo de las Yndias. Digo que a mi not^{a} ha venido

que en ella se a dado por vro pres^{te} e oydores auido en que se rescibio a prueba con noventa dias de ter^{no} conforme a la acordada de Malinas el qual dho auto ha obedecido con el acatamy^{to} deuido no se pudo ni devio dar y el ninguno y ynjusto y mui agraviado contra vro rreal fisco y como de tal salvo el dr^{o} de la nulidad del suplico por el qual se a de anular y rebocar por lo que desto auto y consta por los quales consta qye sobresto mismo esta hecho pleito y recibido a prueba por la misma orden de la acordada de Malinas y rremytido a vro rreal consejo y enviado alla el proceso y asi lo tengo alegado y siendo la mysma causa onimodam^{te} no se puede ny deve hazer otro proceso ni aqui pudo la parte contraria pedir la cosa alguna sobre lo mysmo ny se debe proceder en la causa y en qualquier manera que esta excepcion se oponga o por via de ynpedir el yngreso del pleito o por via de perentoria sea de absolver la pte de vro rreal fisco y declarar no deverse procedera otro auto hasta que sobre esto se de thermino pues siendo //
/f.13v/ asi como el y consta evidentem^{te} de los mismos autos que esta es la misma causa sobre que se a hecho proceso y remytido no se puede ny se debe hazer otro proceso en ella misma y lo que se hiziere contrariam^{te} ypso jure nulo y mayorm^{te} esto a lugar en el caso presente en el qual no se a de determinar difinitivam^{te} en esta real audi^{a} porque si en ella se ovierase de terminar difinitivamente pudiera en la difinitiva remediar y rreparar lo qual no se puede hazer aora porque este auto quando a esta rreal aud^{a} el difinitivo y asi siendo la ecepcion perentoria se a de proveher sobre ella para no dar lugar a pleitos impertinentes.

A V al^{t} pido y suplico anule e reboque el dho auto en quanto es contra la pte de vro rreal fisco haziendo en ello como por el esta pedido e pido justizia y costas y el real oficio imploro.

Otro sy. Digo que como e dho este mismo es el mysmo que antes esta hecho y rremitido a vro real consejo a V. Al^{t} pido y suplico mande que este se cosa y junte con el pues es el mismo o en defeto desto se acumule originalm^{te} pues esta ante un mismo escrivano que si necesario es hago del otro rresentacion para esta causa o si lo uno u otro no oviere lugar se me de un traslado autorizado /para lo tachado/ deto se vean junto y el uno no se vea syn el otro porque haziendose asy constara evidentemente ser tdo uno y sobre una misma cossa e pido justizia.

El Lis^{do} Alu^{o} de
Caravajal (rubrica)

/f.14/ En los Reyes veinte e seys dias noviembre de myll e quinientos e ochenta e cinco as^{o} ante los señores presidente e oydores en audi^{a} pub^{a} se pres^{to} esta pet^{on}.

E los dhos señores mandaron dar t^{do} de todo a la otra parte e que para la proxima aud^{a} responda.

Montero (rubrica)

/f.14v/ /en blanco/

/f.15/ Loyola sobre los Yn^{s} de la Coya Presenta escriptura
Yanaconas

Muy P^{o} Señor

Martin Garcia de Loyola por procurador en el pleyto con vro fiscal sobre los yndios qye se me quitaron con so color de yanaconas del Repartimiento de doña Beatriz Coya mi mujer del valle de Yucay hago presentacion de los papeles y los recaudos siguientes.

Un treslado autoriçado de una provision de V. Al^{a} en que perdona los rrobos y saltos que mi suegro y sus capitanes hizieron despachada por el Presidente Gasca.

Otro traslado autoriçado del dho presidente Gasca en que le encomienda los yndios en ella contenidos y veinte y tres o veinte y quatro leguas de tierra para el y sus hijos.

Otra provision real hemanada por esta rreal audiencia en que le ofrecen lo propio.

Un traslado autoriçado del /encima: una rreal provision/ titulo de adelantado del marques de Canete vro visorey dio al dho mi suegro.

Otro traslado autoriçado de otra provision rreal en que por ella se le perdona al dho ynga todos los rrobos y saltos que hizo.

Otro traslado autoriçado de la mrd que el dho marques de Canete en vro rreal nombre hizo de los yndios del valle de Yucay y Xaquexaguana y los demas contenidos en la dha provision para loe gozase el y sus hijos y subcesores perpetuam^{te} libre de pinsion.

Va entre renglones una real prov^{on}

/f.15v/ Una provision original en que el dho marques de Canete declara que ha de gozar el dho mi suegro y sus herederos y sucesores los dhos repartimientos libres de pinsion la qual se me buelba quedando un traslado.

A V. Al^{a} pido y sup^{co} aya por presentados los dhos recaudos para en prueba de mi dr^{o} y pido just^{a}.

Myn Garcia de Loyola (rubrica)

En la ciudad de los Reyes a quinze dias del mes de n^{o} mill e quinientos e ochenta e cinco años ante los ss^{e} pres^{te} e oidores de esta rreal audi^{a} estando haziendo audi^{a} pub^{ca} se pres^{to} esta pet^{on}.
E por los dhos señores vista lo hubieron por presentada e mandaron dar traslado a la otra p^{te} y estando presentes el fiscal de su mag^{d} se le notifico.

Montoya (rubrica)

Ba restado guard.

/f.16/ Perdon

Don Carlos por la Divina clemencia enp^{or} sen per [*sic*] Augusto rrey de Alemania doña Juana su madre y el mismo don Carlos por la gracia de dios Reyes de Castilla de Leon de Aragon de las dos Çesilias de Jerusalen de Navarra de Granada de Toledo de Valencia de Galicia de Mallorca de Sevilla de Çerdeña de Cordova de Murcia de Jaen de los Algarves de Algezira de Gibraltar de las yslas de Canaria de las Yndias yslas e tierra firme del mar oceano condes de Flandes e de Tirol e yo por quanto somos ynformados que vos Xayre Topa hijo de Mango Ynga Yupangue natural de los nros rreynos y provinçias del Piru que al presente residis en la provinçia de los Andes de los dhs nuestros reynos aviendo entendido el deseo que hemos tenydo y tenemos de que vos y todos los demas naturales de los dhos nuestros reynos seays bien tratados faborecidos y anparados para que bibays en vras casas con vras mujeres e hijos gozando de los que teneys y que por ninguna via seays maltratados y molestados por que con mejor gana os inclineis e atraigais a las cosas de la santa fee catholica e bibays como los otros nuestros subditos y vasallos que en los nuestros reynos de España tenemos y que para que se haga y cunpla ansi lo hemos sienpre encargado y mandado a las personas que en nuestro nombre han llebado nuestras vezes y nros reales poderes a los dhos nuestros reynos e provincias algunos de los quales no lo han puesto en execucion con el calor y deseo que han conoscido de nos e con que les fue encargado y mandado antes han tratado asperamente de vras cosas por cuya causa el dho Mango Ynga vro padre se rretraxo a bibir con algunos deudos y amigos suyos a la dha provincia de los andes donde fallescio desta presente vida e os dexo a vos como su hijo en su lugar encargado a Poma Xupa vro curador y agora avos y el dho vro curador entendido como dho es que el licen^{do} Pedro de la Gasca del nro consejo de la santa y general //
/f.16v/ inquisicion presidente de los dhos nuestros rreynos e provinçias como zeloso de nro servicio y de cumplir y poner en efeto lo que de nos cerca de lo susodho teneys y le fue mandado a procurado y procura por todas las vias el buen tratamiento y conservacion de los dhos naturales le enbiastes vros mensajeros a manifestar que queriades saliros con vros amigos y deudos de donde estays retraidos a bybir e asentar en la ciudad del Cuzco de los dhos nros reynos e les enbiastes a pedir que en nro os diese y señalase asiento tierras e otras cosas para vra bibienda e mantenimyento y que porque durante en tiempo que el dho vro padre estubo retraido hasta que murio con vos y con los naturales que consigo tenia hizo guerra a los españoles que estuvieron en el Cuzco y despues diversas vezes yvan contra el y en las dhas guerras obo muertes de hombres de una parte y de otra y se cometieron otros delitos se vos diese a vos y a los dhos naturales nra carta y provision real de perdon de lo susodho y de seguro y anparo para que por virtud del podays salir de donde estays e bibir como dho es en la dha ciudad del Cuzco entre los demas nros subditos y vasallos todo lo qual usando como en este caso usamos de nro poderio real absoluto perdonamos a vos el dho Xayre Topa e Poma Xupa vro curador e a todos qualesquier vros deudos capitanes e amigos e naturales ansi que residieron con el dho Mango Ynga vro padre como a los que agora esten con vos de todos e qualesquier delitos crimines y excesos guerras y muertes que en vida del dho vro padre cometyeron e agora si alguno aveys cometido para que por razon dellos ny de alguno dellos no seays ny sean punidos ny castigados e vos tomamos //
/f.17/ a vos y a ellos debaxo de nuestra proteçion y anparo e mandamos a todas y qualesquier nuestras justiçias mayores e menores de todos los dhos nros reynos e provincias del Peru [*sic*] e a cada uno e qualquier dellos que no procedan contra vos ny contra nynguno de los susodhos vros amigos y deudos y capitanes que con el dho vro padre anduvieron y con vos estan por razon de los dhos delitos ny por alguno dellos de oficio ny a pedimento de parte antes les mandamos y mucho encargamos a ellos e a todos los demas nuestros subditos e vasallos de los dichos nuestros reynos que vos traten bien y no consientan que por nynguna via seays ny sean molestados ny maltratados so pena de caer e yncurrir en las penas en que caen e yncurren los que no cumplen ny obedescen nuestras cartas y mandamyentos reales porque desde agora como dho es vos ponemos debaxo de nuestra proteccion y anparo el qual dho perdon vos e damos y hazemos contando que dentro de quatro meses de la data desta nra carta vos salgais todos de la dha provincia de los nades donde estays y vengais y vengan antel dicho nuestro presidente o antel muy reberendo yn Xpo padre don fray Gr^{mo} de Loaysa arçobispo de los Reyes que en cosas de nuestro servicio a de estas entendiendo en la dha ciudad del Cuzco e si alli no estuviere antel licençiado Cianca que alli en nro nombre esta con las vezes del dho nuestro presidente a darle en nuestro nombre la obidiencia que como nros subditos teneys e si ansi no lo hizieredes sea en si nenguno este dho perdon y no tenga fuerça alguna. De lo qual mandamos dar y dimos la pres^{te} sellada con nuestro real sello. Dada en el asiento de Guaynarima a diez e ocho dias del mes de agosto de myll e quinyentos e quarenta e ocho años. E yo Pero Lopez escrivano de camara //
/f.17v/ de su cesarea catholica magestad la fize escrevir por su mandado con acuerdo de su presidente registrada Pero Lopez por chanciller Juan de Aulestia e a las espaldas de la dha real provision estava señalada una firma que dize el licen^{do} Gasca.

En el Cuzco en veinte dias del mes de noviembre de myll e qui^os^ e setenta e dos años yo Geronimo de Quesada escrivano publico del n^o^ de la dha ciudad hize sacar este tr^do^ de la provision original del y que es cierto y verdadero el qual exhibio ante mi p^a^ el dho efecto la presente del capitan Martin Garcia de Loyola y doña Beatriz Coya su mujer y fueron testigos Miguel de Zalcedo y Alv^o^ de Zalcedo y Gomez de Duran y lo fize escrivir y fize aqui my signo.

Gr^mo^ de Quesada
Scriu^o^ pu^co^

/f.18/ /en blanco/

/f.18v/ V. Alteza perdona a Mango Ynga Saire Topa y a sus capitanes qualesquier delitos que hubieren cometido a viniendo a la hubidiencia de V. Altz^a^ y que se le proveran de yndios en avancay e volveran las casas e tierras que su pdre dexo en el Cuzco y se le entregaran tierras en que pueblo los yndios q tuvo.

/f.19/ Don Carlos por la divina clemencia enp^r^ senp Augusto rrey de Alemania doña Juana su madre y el mismo don Carlos por la misma gracia Reyes de Castilla de Leon de Aragon de las dos Çeçilias de Jerusalen de Navarra de Granada de Toledo de Valencia de Galicia de Mallorca de Sevilla de Çerdeña de Cordova de Murcia de Jaen de los Algarves de Algezira de Gibraltar de las yslas de Canaria de las Yndias yslas e tierra firme del mar oceano condes de Flandes e de Tirol por quanto dona Veatriz Yupangui mujer legitima de D^o^ Hernandez vezino del Cuzco y tia de Xairitopa rrevelado contra nro rreal serv^o^ por una peticion que presente ante el presidente e oidores de la nra rreal audiencia e chancilleria q' por nro mandado rreside en los nros rreinos del Piru nos hizo rrelacion diciendo q' vien saviamos como el dho Mango Ynga Sairitopa a dias q' andan rrevelado contra nro rreal serviz^o^ y fuera de nra rreal huvidiencia e q' por nos servir tiene voluntad de procurar e dar horden como venga de paz a nra rreal huvidiencia para cuyo efeto enbiara al dho su marido e a un hijo suyo e algunos tios suyos el al dho Sairitupa y para le dar a entender lo mucho q' le conbiene hazelo para su descanso e para q' sea dotrinado en las cossas de nra santa fe catolica e nos pidio e suplico q' pues ella tenya voluntad de q' esto tuviese efeto le hiziesemos md de q' el dho Sairitopa e Poma Supa natural del Cuzco e Raime natural de Charca e Vasqui natural de Quito e tanpais natural de Mayos e Tarpuntay natural de Cayuy Cachi capitanes myos fueren perdonados de los delitos q' hubiesen cometido en qualquier manera e a los yndios que consigo tienen hasta el dia que viniesen de paz y q' asimesmo q' viniendo a nra rreal huvidiencia le hicieremos md de yndios en avancay y de le volver las casas e tierras que su padre dexo en esta ciudad del Cuzco y le señalemos tierra en que poblase los yndios que en su compañia tiene o como la nra md fuese lo qual visto por el dho presidente e oidores fue acordado que deviamos mandar dar esta nra carta para vos en la dha rrazon e nos tovimoslo por bien por la qual perdonamos al dho Mango Ynga Xairitopa e a los dhos capitanes e yndios q' consigo tuviere todos e qualesquier robos e delitos q' huvieren cometido hasta el dia q' venga a nra rreal huvidiencia e viniendo a ella rremytimos qualquier pena en q' aya yncurrido por rrazon de los aver cometido e prometemos q' viniendo como dho es le seran dados yndios en la provincia de avancay y le mandaremos volver las tierras e casas q' su padre dexo e tenia en la ciudad del Cuzco y haremos prover de tierras en q' pueblen los yndios q' en su compañia tienen e teniendo efeto su venida mediante la diligencia e cuidado que vos la dha doña Veatriz Yupangui e Diego Hernandez vro marido e vro hijo tomasen mandamos que seos gratifiq' y por la presente mandamos a los caçiques e indios de los repartimientos por donde fueren q' les den todo buen aviamiento favor e ayuda q' les pidiere etc. Dada en la ciudad del Cuzco a nueve dias del mes de noviembre de mill e qui^os^ e cinquenta e quatro años.

Yo P^o^ de Avendaño escrivano de camara de sus cesareas e catolicas magestades la fize escribir por mandado con acuerdo del su presidente e oidores.
Toca a Mango Ynga

/f.19v/ Geronimo de Xarava (rubrica) El Licenciado Fernando de Santillan (rubrica)

El Licenciado Marcos de Peñalosa (rubrica)

Secretario Avendaño.

/f.20/ Este es un treslado bien y fielmente sacado de una cedula y provision original del muy excelente señor don Hurtado de Mendoza marques de Cañete visorrey de estos reinos y cedula de encomienda de yndios hecha a don Diego Ynga conciertos autos de posesion y contradicciones que su tenor es como se sigue:

Don Hurtado de Mendoza marques de Cañete guarda mayor de la ciudad de Quenca visorrey y capitan general en estos reinos y provincias del Peru por su majestad etc. Por cuanto su magestad por sus provisiones y costas reales tiene mandado que se procure por las buenas maneras y que ser pudieren traer de paz a su obediencia y servicio real al ynga pa que viniesen el y los naturales que con el anduviesen en conocimento de nuestra Santa Fe catolica y la rrecibiesen pa su salvacion y en cumplimiento dello luego como llegue a estos dhos reinos porque cesasen los grandes daños e inconvinientes que a causa de andar alçado y de guerra en los andes Sayre Topa Mango Capa Yupangui Ynga hijo de Mango Ynga y nieto de Guayna Capa señor natural que fue de estos reinos por los muchos saltos muertes y robos que ordinariamente se hacian por sus capitanes y gente en los caminos reales a españoles y naturales y la cantidad de naturales que llevaba y recoxia a los dhos andes donde andava de los questan pacificos y debaxo de la obidiencia y desasosiego ynquietud y que con el dho ynga tenian los naturales de los repartimientos de yn^os^ q' sirven a los vez^nos^ //

/f.20v/ de la ciudades del Cuzco y Huamanga provey que religiosos y mensajeros fuesen a hablarle de p[te] de su magestad y de la mia en su real nombre pa que viniese de paz a su real obediencia y servicio y le enbie perdones de las muertes despañoles y naturales que hubiese hecho y de otros qualequier criminales y delitos que hubiese cometido ofreciendole que viniendo de paz y a lo suso dho dentro de cierto termino que le fue señalado se le hazian mrd en su rreal nombre de los rrepartimy[o]s de yndios de Yucai questuvo encomendado en don Fran[co] Piçarro menor hijo del marques don Fran[co] Piçarro difuntos y de Xaquixaguana Guaylla Quipa y Pucarra que estuvo encomendado en don Francisco Hernandes Giron vecino del Cuzco difunto que estan vacos con todo lo a ello sujeto y que demas de lo suso dho le serian hechas otras mercedes de tierras y solares y otras cosas contenidas en las provisiones que de ello se mandaron dar y enviar lo qual habiendole tratado los dhos religiosos y mensajeros con el dho ynga lo aceto y salio y vino de paz y entro en esta ciudad de Los Reyes y corte vispera de la fiesta de los Reyes de este presente año de quinientos y cincuenta y ocho y dio a su magestad e a mi en su real nombre la obediencia debida y prometio de siempre servirle como un bueno y leal vasallo debe y es obligado a hacer y porque habiendo hecho lo suso dho es justo que se tenga cuenta con su persona y se le cumplan las dhas mercedes pa con que se sustente y su mujer y casa y familia y de nuevo se le hagan otras porque se aficione y obligue mas al servicio de su magestad y tenga voluntad de se convertir y convierta a nuestra santa fe catolica pa que //
/f.21/ se salve y obligue y anime a los demas naturales de estos dhos reinos a que hagan lo mismo ques lo que principalmente su magestad ha pretendido y pretende y por lo que importa a la quietud y sosiego de estos dhos reinos por la presente en su real nombre y por virtud de su real poder que para ello tengo que su tenor del qual es el que se sigue.

Don Carlos por la divina clemencia emperador semper agusto rrey de Alemania doña Juana su madre y el mismo don Carlos por la misma gracia reyes de Castilla de Leon de Aragon de las dos Secilias de Jerusalen de Navarra de Granada de Toledo de Toledo [*sic*] de Valencia de Galicia de Mallorcas de Sevilla de Cerdeña de Cordoba de Corcega de Murcia de Jaen de los Algarvies de Algezira de Gibraltar de las islas de Canaria de las islas Yndias y tierra firme del mar y oceano condes de Flandes y de Tirol. Etc. E pa todos los consejos regidores caballeros escuderos oficiales y omes /hombres/ buenos de todas las ciudades villas y lugares de las provincias de la Nueva Castilla llamada Peru y de la Nueva Toledo y las otras provincias e islas sujetos y comprendidas en el distrito y juridiccion de la nuestra audiencia y chancilleria real de las dhas provincias del Peru y otras qualesquier personas eclesiasticos y seglares de qualquier estado y condicion preeminencia y dignidad que sean o ser puedan vecinos estantes y habitantes en las dhas provincias y en cada una de ellas a quien toca y atañe y pueda tocar y atañer lo en esta nra carta contenido y a cada uno y qualquier de vos salud y gracia de pades [*sic*]. Que nos aviendo entendido las alteraciones y casos acalcidos en esas dhas

Entre renglones dize entendido

/f.21v/ provincias del Peru depues que Fran[co] Hernandez Xiron con otros muchos que con el se juntaron y alzaron con la ciudad del Cuzco y prendieron a Gil Ramirez Davalos mi corregidor que era en la dha ciudad y deseando como deseamos que esas dhas provincias se pongan en toda paz sosiego y quietud pa que ellas se hagan el servicio de dios mi señor y su santa fe catolica sea aumentada pa este efeto y que nos seamos servidos y esas dhas provincias vayan en todo crecimiento y noblecimiento y los pobladores de ellas bivan en todo contentamiento habemos acordado de enviar a ellas una persona de autoridad y confianza pa que entienda en ello y por el gran concepto que tenemos de la persona de don Hurtado de Mendoza marques de Cañete de habemos elegido y señalado por mi visorrey de esa tierra y por presidente de la audiencia real que en ella reside pa que haga y administre justicia igual a todos nuestros subditos y vasallos y para que asimismo entienda en hacer y ordenar todo lo que convenga pa el sosiego quietud y noblecimiento de esa tierra como dho es por la presente de nuestro propio motivo y deliberada voluntad elegimos constituimos y señalamos pa ello al dho marques de Cañete y le damos y otorgamos todo nuestro poder cumplido libre e llenero y bastante con libre y general administracion segun y tan cumplidamente que lo nos habemos y de hecho y derecho mas y mejor puede y debe pa que por nos y en nuestro nombre y como nuestras mismas personas pueda entender y entienda en la pacificacion y sosiego de esas dhas provincias y administracion de justicia //
/f.22/ en ellas y provea en todas las cosas que ocurrieren asi consermientes a la dha administracion y execucion de la mia justicia como de la buena gobernacion y defensa de esas dhas provincias y noblecimiento de ellas y gratificacion de los pobladores nuestros subditores y vasallos que los ha ido a poblar y bien y buen tratamiento y conservacion de los naturales de ellas y buen recaudo de mi hacienda y en todas las otras cosas y negocios de qualquier calidad y condicion que sean y se ofrezcan lo que le perteneciere y viere que conviene y se debe hacer y provea en nombre nombre [*sic*] y como nos mismos hacer y prover todos los oficios y cargos ansi de justicia y de gobernacion como de otra qualquier manera y de esas dhas provincias y de cada una de ellas que conforme a derecho nos podemos y debemos proveer y hacer en nuestro nombre gracias y mercedes de qualesquier tenencias alcaydias regimientos escrivanos y otros qualesquier oficios y casos de qualquier calidad que sean ansi por renunciaciones como por vacacion y en otra qualquier manera y pa que siendo menester para defension de esas provincias y bien y utilidad de ellas pueda apercebir de guerra y y llamar y convocar a las ciudades villas y otros pueblos y a los perlados gobernadores justicias caballeros y otras personas de esas provincias y estantes en ellas pa que vengan donde fueron necesarios con la gente que por el les fuere mandado y sobre ello hacer todas las otras provisiones y mandamientos //
/f.22v/ que al caso convengan y le pareciere y finalmente pueda hacer y proveer y provea todo aquello que nosotros mismos podiamos hacer y proveer de qualquier calidad y condicion que sea y ser pueda en esas dhas provincias. Porque vos mandamos a todos y cada uno de ellos como dho es que lo que ansi por el dho marques de Cañete fuere proveido y ordenado y mandado en qualesquier casos y cosas que sean o ser puedan en esas provincias lo guardeis y cumplais y executeis y hagais guardar y cumplir y executar y le obedezcais y acateis como una persona que tiene nuestras veces y que representa nuestras personas reales y hagais y cumplais sus mandamientos segun y de la manera quel lo dijere y mandare de nuestra persona por escrito y por palabra y fuere contenido en las dhas sus cartas y provisiones y mandamientos sin poner en ello excusa ni dilacion alguna y sin dar a ello otro entendimiento ni interpretacion ni declaracion y sin nos mas

requerir ni consultar ni esperar sobre ello otro nuestro mandado bien asi como si por mias mismoas personas y por nuestras cartas firmadas de nuestros nombres lo dixesemos ordenasemos y mandasemos lo qual vos mandamos que asi lo hagais y cumplais so pena de caer en mal caso y de las otras penas en que caen e incurren los que no obedescen las cartas y mandamientos de sus reyes y señores naturales y so las penas que por el vos fueren puestas comos por la presente le damos y concedemos y otorgamos pa ello y pa todo lo a ello

restado dize mand no bala

/f.23/ consermiente en qualquier manera vuestro poder cumplido y bastante con todas sus incidencias y dependencias y mergencias anexidades y conexidades y queremos que este dho poder tenga tanta fuerza como si fuera hecho y otorgado en cortes generale y decimos y otorgamos que todo cuanto el dho marques de Cañete en nuestro nombre hiciere y ordenare y mandare conforme a este dho poder en esas dhas provincias que lo abremos por firme estable y valedero pa siempre jamas de lo qual mandamos dar la presente firmada de mi el rey y sellada con nuestro sello dada en la villa de Bruçelas a diez dias del mes de marzo de mill y quinientos y cincuenta y cinco años yo el rrey. e yo Francisco de Herado secretario de sus cesarias y catolicas magestades la fize escribir por su mandamiento registrada Ochoa de Luyando chanciller Martin de Rramoyn el marques el Licenciado Tello de Sandoval el Licenciado don Juan Sarmiento el Doctor Vasquez el Licenciado Villagomez.

Hago merced al dho Sayre Topa Mango Capa Yupangue Ynga de los dhos repartimientos de yndios de Yucay Xaquixaguana Guallaquipa y Pucara que son en terminos de la ciudad del Cuzco y estan vacos por muerte de los dhos don Fran^{co} Piçarro menor y Francisco Hernandez Xiron con todos los yndios y estancias y sus terminos caciques principales e yndios de ellos y a ellos sujetos y pertenecientes segun y como los tenian y poseian tuvieron y poseyeron y gozaron de ellos los suso dhos y cada uno de ellos pa que los tenga e posea haya goze y cobre todos los tributos que son //
/f.23v/ o fueron obligados a dar y dieron den de primero de este presente mes de enero y año de mill y quinientos y cincuenta y ocho años en adelante conforme a las tasas que estan hechas y se hicieren y pa que por su fin y muerte subcedan perpetuamente en el dho repartimiento de yndios sus hijos descendientes y sucesores que tuviere como se pueda y debe suceder en los mayorazgos que se hacen con licencia de su magestad en los reinos de España y con las condiciones apelido [*sic*] y armas que el dho ynga quisiere y ordenare que para ello le doy licencia y facultad pa que vaya en crecimiento su honrra y linaje y estado y descendientes descendiendo como desciende de linaje de los yngas y principales de estos dhos reinos del Peru y porque haya memoria e renombre de quien tuvo principio de esta merced y porque permanezca y mejor se aficione al servicio de dios mio señor y ensalçar nuestra santa fee catolica y a servir a su magestad pa honrra y defensa de su linaje casa y estado con que por si ni por interpositas personas no se sirva de servicio personal de los dhos yndios en su casa ni en otras obras y granjerias so las penas contenidas en las provisiones y cedulas reales que acerca de ello estan dadas y con que los trate bien y procure su conservacion y multiplicacion y tenga cuidado de que en el dho repartimiento haya clerigo o religiosos que dotrinen a los naturales en las cosas de nuestra santa fe catolica y por la presente mando al licenciado Muñoz corregidor de la dha ciudad del Cuzco que luego y por parte del dho Sayre Topa Mango Capa Yupangue Ynga fuere pedida posesion del dho repartimiento de indios //
/f.24/ se la de y metido el y las demas justicias de su magestad le amparen y defiendan en ella y no consientan q' della sea despojado sin primero ser oido y vencido por fuero y juicio lo qual asi hagan y cumplan so pena de cada dos mill pesos de oro pa la camara y fisco de su majestad. Fecho en Los Reyes a trece dias del mes de enero de mill y quinientos y cincuenta y ocho años el marques por mandado de su excelencia Juan Muñoz Puco [*sic*].

En la gran ciudad del Cuzco cabeza de estos reinos e provincias del Peru a veinte y un dias del mes de Março año del nacimiento de nuestro salvador Jesucristo de mill y quinientos y cincuenta y ocho años ante el muy mag^{co} señor licen^{do} Bautista Muñoz correg^{or} y just^{a} mayor en esta dha ciudad y su juridiccion por su mag^{d} y en presencia de mi Fran^{co} de Barrientos escrivano de su magestad y escrivano pu^{co} del numero de la dha ciudad y de los ts^{o} de yuso escriptos parecio presente doña Beatriz Mango Capa Yupangue mujer de Diego Hernandez vezino de la dha ciudad en nombre de Sayre Topa Mango Capa Yupangue y por virtud del poder que del tiene de que hizo presen^{on} signado del escrivano de su magestad y en el dho nombre presento esta provicion y cedula de encomienda del muy ex^{te} señor marques de Cañete visorrey destos reinos y pidio y requirio al dho señor corr^{or} que conforme a ella en el dho nombre le de la posesion corporal autual velcasi de los caciques e yns^{o} de los dhos repartimys^{o} de que por su mag^{d} y su excelencia del dho señor visorrey en su real nombre fue y esta fecha

Restado dize press.

/f.24v/ merced al dho Sayre Topa Mango Capa Yupangue Ynga la qual dha posesion le de en don Francisco Chilche cacique principal del repartimy^{o} de Yucay e don Pedro e don Lucas principales del dho repartimiento y en don Xpoval Chotas e don Diego Caguata caciques principales de Xaquixaguana y don Alonso Callena cacique de Quilluay que presentes estavan repartimys^{o} encomendado por su X^{a} en nombre de su magestad en el dho Sayre Topa Mango Capa Yupangue Ynga su parte como por la dha provision de su excelencia consta y parece sobre que pidio just^{a}.

Y el dho señor corr^{or} tomo en sus manos la dha provision de su excelencia y la obedecio con el acatamiento debido y en quanto al cumplimiento de ella dixo questa presto de hacer y cumplir lo que por ella le hera man^{do} y haziendola y cumpliendola tomo por las manos al dho don Fran^{co} Chilche cacique principal de Yucai e don P^{o} y don Lucas principales del dho repartimy^{o} y don Xpoval Chotas y don Diego Caguata caciques principales de Xaquixaguana y don Al^{o} Collena cacique de Quillauay y en señal de posesion los entrego por las manos a la dha doña Beatriz Mango Capa Yupangue Ynga en nombre del dho Sayre Topa Mango Capa Yupangue Ynga su parte en nombre de los demas caciques principales e yns^{o} naturales de los dhos repartimientos y pueblos dellos.

E luego la dha doña Beatriz Capa Yupangue en el dho nombre tomo por las manos a los dhos caciques y //
/f.25/ principales e los dhos pueblos de suso nombrados en señal de posesion propiedad y señorio como subjetos y vasallos del dho Sayre Topa Mango Capa Yupangue Ynga su parte conforme a la dha provision de su Exª la qual dha provision dixo que tomaba y tomo en el dho nombre en los dhos caciques y principales de suso nombrados por ellos y en voz y en nombre de todos los demas principales yndios e yndias a ellos sujetos y de como tomaba y tomo la dha posesion quieta y pacificamente sin contradiccion de persona alguna la dha doña Beatriz en el dho nombre lo pidio por testimonio signado pa en guarda de su drº y el dho señor corr^{or} se lo mando dar lo qual todo segun y como de suso se contiene la dha doña Beatriz dixo y le fue dada a entender por lengua de Pº de Nicasio ladino en lengua de yndio siendo presentes por tsº a lo que dho es Gaspar de Sotelo alcde hordinario de la dha ciudad y Diego de Truxillo y Miguel Sanches y Antonio de Marchena vezinos de la dha ciudad y el dho señor corr^{or} lo firmo aqui de su nombre el licen^{do} Muñoz paso ante mi Fran^{co} de Barrientos.

El tenor del qual dho poder del dho Sayre Topa Mango Capa Yupangue y signado de escrivano es el que se sigue.

Sepan cuantos esta carta de poder vieren como yo Sayre Topa Mango Capa Yupangue otorgo y conozco por esta presente carta que doy e otorgo todo mi poder cumplido libre e llenero y bastante segun que lo yo e y tengo //
/f.25v/ y el drº mas puede y debe valer a vos doña Beatriz Mango Capa Yupangue my tia que sois ausente pa que por mi y en mi nombre representando mi propia persona podais tomar y tomeis la posesion de los ynsº que su excelencia me ha hecho merced y los tener en administracion cobrando dellos los tributos de las tasas que son obligados a me dar y pagar y pa que podais entrar en juizios sobre ello ante todas qualesquier justizias e juezes de su mag^{d} y hazer todo aquello que yo haria siendo presente e si los oficiales de su mag^{d} ovieren cobrado de los dhos mis yndios algunos tributos desde el dia del año nuevo a esta parte deste presente año de cinquenta e ocho años los podais cobrar de los dhos oficiales de su magestad conforme a la merced que su excelencia me tiene hecha y pa que podais tomar evados [*sic*] pa el benefº de las dhas mis haciendas dandoles los salarios que os parecieren y pa que podais pedir en el cabildo desta ciudad en mi nombre qualesquier tierras y mercedes o titulos de las tales tierras que asi os hicieren merced donde yo soy vecino y pa recibir y cobrar ansi en juizio como fuera del todos los psº de oro que me debieren por esciptura o por otra qualquier via e razon que sea y de lo que recibieredes y cobraredes podais dar y deis vuestras cartas de pago y de finiquito las quales valan y sean tan firmes bastantes e valederas como si yo mismo las diese y a ellas pres^{e} fuese y general pa pleitos y causas con poder //
/f.26/ de jurar y sostituir en Diego Hernandez vezino vuestro marido y el dho Diego Hernandez y vos podais sostituir un procurador o dos o mas y los revocar cuando quisieredes y aver otros de nuevo quedando en vos este poder principal a los quales y a vos relievo segun forma de drº y obligo mi persona y bienes muebles y raices habidos y por haber so espresa oblig^{on} que pa ello hago de la dha mi persona y bienes en forma con libre y general administracion que tiene por bueno lo que por virtud de este poder en mi nombre hicieredes y de las rentas dispongais como a vos os pareciere y quisieredes con todas sus incidencias dependencias anexidades y conexidades e vos relievo en forma a vos y a los por vos sostuidos como dho es e quan cumplido y bastante poder que yo e y tengo otro tal y ese mismo vos doy y cedo y trespaso en vos la dha doña Beatriz Mango Capa Yupangue mi tia en testimonio de lo qual otorgue esta carta ante el presente escrivano y tsº de yuso escriptos y quiero y es mi voluntad que por falta de este poder y no ir en el especificado quiero en esta lo que por vos la dha mi tia hicieredes questa e aya estado como cosa vuestra propia y dispongais en ello como quisieredes que es fecha e otorgada en Umaca termino y jur^{on} de la ciudad de Guamanga en tres dias del mes de Março de mill y quinientos y cincuenta y ocho años //
/f.26v/ siendo tsº Juan de Cardenas y Pº de Busto y Juan Serra y al dho Juan Sierra rogo el dho Sayre Topa Mango Capa Yupangue firmase por el en el registro desta carta a los quales yo el presente escrivano doy fe que conozco Juan Serra de Leguiçamo e yo Juan Lopez de Ydiaques escrivano de su magestad presente fui en uno con los dhos tsº y con el dho otorgante y lo escribi e fize leer y por ende fize aqui este mi signo ques a tal en testimonio de verdad Juan Lopez de Ydiaquez escrivano de su majestad.

E despues de lo suso dho en la dha ciudad del Cuzco a veinte e dos dias del mes de Marzo de mill y quisº y cinquenta e ocho años ante el dho señor corr^{or} y en presencia de mi el dho Francisco de Barrientos testigo parecio presente Fran^{co} Perez procurador en nombre de don Fran^{co} Piçarro hijo del marques don Fran^{co} Picarro difunto y por virtud del poder e sostitucion que tiene ante mi el dho escrivano y presento el testimonio del tenor siguiente

contradiçion de la poss^{on} por don Fran^{ço} Pizarro hijo del marques Fran^{ço}.

Muy magnifico señor. Fran^{co} Perez en nombre de don Fran^{co} Piçarro hijo del marques don Fran^{co} Piçarro difunto digo que a mi notª es venido que por parte de Sayre Topa Ynga de los ynsº de Yucai encomendados en el dho don Fran^{co} mi parte por virtud de cierta encomy^{da} que dizen aver hecho en el dho Sayre Topa de los dhos ynsº segun que mas largamente se contiene en el dho pedimyº sobre ello hecho por parte del dho Sayre Topa cuyo tenor repetido digo que Vmd no deve hazer //
/f.27/ cosa alguna de lo pedido por el dho Sayre Topa en razon de la dha posesion por lo siguiente.

Porque la dha posesion no es pedida por parte bast^{e} y los recaudos por virtud de los quales se pide la dha posesion no son bastantes pa que por ellos se le puede dar.

Lo otro porque su mag^{d} y el licen^{do} Gasca presidente que fue destos reinos en su real nombre encomendaron en el dho don Fran^{co} mi pte los dhos ynsº por virtud de la qual dha encomy^{da} el dho mi parte ha estado y esta en posesion de los dho yndios y goza de los tributos y aprovechamy^{o}s que los dhos ynsº son obligados a dar en cada un año a su encomendero de mas de diez años a esta parte como es notorio y por tal lo alego y estando como los dhos yns^{o} estan encomendados en el dho don Fran^{co} no ay causa ny razon bastante pa que el dho Sayre Topa se le de posesion en ellos.

Lo otro porque puesto caso que al dho Sayre Topa se le ouiese hecho merced y nueva encomienda de los dhos yns^{o} como vacos q' dicen estar por muerte del dho don Fran^{co} y se le aya dado provision de la dha encomyenda de la dha merced y encomyenda no debe ni puede aver hefeto porque el dho don Fran^{co} no es muerto en tal se averiguara y hasta tanto que este averiguado el dho don Fran^{co} ser muerto los dhos yndios no se an de tener por vacos ny se pueda hazer la dha encomy^{da} //
/f.27v/ tenyendo como la tiene el dho don Fran^{co} por su mag^{d} y en su real nombre por todos los dias de su vida.

Por tanto a Vmd pido y suplico si necesario es hablando con el debido acatamiento que debo requiero las vezes que de dr^{o} soy obligado no haga cosa alguna de lo pedido por parte del dho Sayre Topa en rrazon de la dha posesion antes defienda y ampare al dho mi parte en la que tiene de los dhos yns^{o} y de gozar de los tributos y aprovechamientos dellos pa lo qual el of^{o} de Vmd imploro y pido just^{a} y si es necesario espresamente contradigo la posesion por parte del dho Sayre Topa pedida y suplico de la dha provision y nueva encomienda en el hecha de los dhos yndios y pido testimonio de todo.

Otro si digo que si la dha posesion se oviere dado al dho Sayre Topa o a otra persona en su nombre asimismo espresamente lo contradigo y protesto no pare por juiz^{o} al dho mi parte y si necesario es me ofrezco a dar informacion de como el dho don Fran^{co} esta vivo en los reinos de España pa lo qual etc.

Otro si pido a Vmd mande queste scripto y la contradiccion se ponga con la posesion que se oviere tomado o tomare por parte del dho Sayre Topa sobre que pido justicia pa lo qual etc.

Y asi presentado el dho scripto el dho señor corregidor m^{do} dar treslado a la otra parte y mando que se ponga en la dha posesion ts^{o} que fueron presentes Benito //
/f.28/ de la Pena escrivano publico y Miguel Martinez y Andres de Ybarra residentes en la dha ciudad.

E despues de lo sobre dho en la dh ciudad del Cuzco el dho dia y año sobre dho yo el dho escrivano notifique lo sobre dho a la dha doña Beatriz en el dho nombre del dho Sayre Topa su parte presente Diego Hernandez su marido y Gonzalo Rodriguez procurador.

E despues de lo sobre dho en la dha ciudad del Cuzco en veinte e seis dias del mes de Abril del dho año de mill e quis^{o} y cinquenta e ocho años ante el dho señor licen^{do} Muñoz corregidor en la dha ciudad y por ante mi el dho escrivano y de los ts^{o} de yuso escriptos parecio presente Sebastian de Bacca procurador en nombre y como curador adliten del dho Sayre Topa Mango Capa Yupangue segun que la dha curaduria le fue y esta discernida por su mrd por ante Benito de la Pena escrivano pub^{co} de la dha ciudad y dixo que no embargante en nombre del dho su parte estaba tomada la posesion de los repartimientos e yns^{o} de la encomienda que por el señor visorrey le fue hecha en nombre de su mag^{d} que agora pa mayor abundamy^{to} y corroboracion pedia e pidio la de al dho Sayre Topa Mango Capa Yupangue que esta presente y a el en su nombre y añadiendo fuerça a fuerça y si neces^{o} era tomada y tomo en los ys^{o} del dho repartimy^{o} que presentes estava y pidio a su mrd le ampare y defienda en ella y de como //
/f.28v/ lo dezia y dixo lo pidio por testimonio

E luego el dho señor corre^{dor} estando presentes don Fran^{co} Chilche cacique de Yucai y don Luis de la parcialidad de don Garcia y el dho don Garcia y don Gaspar cacique de Quipa e Condor Guamani cacique de Pucara e Chagua cacique de Gualla e don Martin cacique de Xaquixaguana y don Baltasar principal del pueblo de Hequeco y don Al^{o} cacique de Quilluay caciques e principales de los repartimientos encomendados en el dho Sayre Topa por ellos y por los demas yndios a ellos subjetos en cumplimiento de la provision de sus excelencia les tomo por la mano corporalmente y en señal de posesion les dio y entrego al dho Sayre Topa el qual presente su curador dijo por lengua de P^{o} de Nicasio ladino que continuando la dha posesion que los dhos caciques e yns^{o} tenia y les estaba dada aniendo [*sic*] fuerza a fuerza si necesario hera la tomaba y tomo en los dhos caciques e yndios los quales en señal de posesion tomo por la mano y en voz y en nombre de los demas principales e yns^{o} de los dhos repartimientos a ellos subjetos y lo pidio por testimonio.

E luego parecio presente el dho Fran^{co} Perez en el dho nombre del dho don Fran^{co} Piçarro y dixo que contradezia y contradixo la dha posesion y protesto no le pare perjuicio alguno al derecho del dho su parte y lo pidio por testimonio.

Y luego el dho señor corr^{dor} sin embargo de la dha contradiccion dixo que daba la posesion de los //
/f.29/ dhos yndios al dho Sayre Topa y al dho Sebastian de Bacca su curador en su nombre por los dhos caciques y principales que presentes estavan por ellos y en voz y en nombre de los demas yndios a el encomendados conforme a la dha provision de su Excelencia y se lo mando dar ansi por testimonio en pu^{ca} forma siendo presentes por testigos a lo que dho es Juan Alvarez Mal^{do} y Juan de Betanços vezinos de esta dha ciudad y Benito de la Pena escrivano pu^{co} de la dha ciudad el Licen^{do} Muñoz e yo Fran^{co} de Barrientos escrivano de su magestad y escrivano publico del numero de la dha ciudad del Cuzco presente fui a lo que dho es en uno con los dhos ts^{o} del dho pedimy^{to} y mandamy^{to} del dho señor corr^{dor} que aqui firmo su nombre lo fizescribir segun que ante mi paso y por ende fize aqui este mio signo que va tal en testimonio de verdad. Fran^{co} de Barrientos.

Hecho y sacado corregido y concertado ffue este dho treslado de la dha cedula y titulos originales y posesion y demas autos que de suso van ynsertos de pedimiento del dho P° de Çarate administrador de los bienes de doña Beatriz menor hija del dho don Diego Ynga difunto y de mandamy[to] del muy mag[co] señor Licen[do] Polo corr[dor] e just[a] mayor en esta dha ciudad del Cuzco a diez dias del mes de henero de mill y quinyentos y sesenta años siendo presentes por testigos a los ver e corregir con el dho original Juan Balça y Her[do] de Salzedo y Fran[co] Hernandez estantes en esta dha ciudad.
Y yo Sancho Ortiz de Orue vecino y escribano //
/f.29v/ pu[co] y del cavildo de esta dha ciudad del Cuzco lo fize sacar y corregir e fizo a este mio signo que es a tal en testimonio de verdad.

Sancho de Orue
Escry° Pu[co] y Cab°

/f.30/ Perdon
Don Carlos por la Divina clemencia enp[or] sen per [*sic*] Augusto rrey de Alemania doña Juana su madre y el mysmo don Carlos por la mysma gracia de dios Reyes de Castilla de Leon de Aragon de las dos Sezilias de Jerusalen de Navarra de Granada de Toledo de Valencia de Galicia de Mallorcas de Sevilla de Çerdeña de Cordova de Corcega de Murcia de Jaen de los Algarves de Algezira de Gibraltar de las yslas de Canaria de las Yndias yslas e tierra firme del mar oceano condes de Flandes e de Tirol etc. A vos Sayre Topa Ynga sabed que nos somos ynformados que por algunos malos tratamyentos que los españoles de los nros reynos del Piru hizieron a Mango Ynga Yupangui vro padre se alço y andubo alçado haziendo algunos daños e que muerto el quedastes vos e que aveys andado y andays /alçado tarjado/ tambien alçado y destraido de nuestro real servicio e de la conversaçion de los Xpianos e que traeys en vra compañia algunos caçiques e yndios capitanes de vro padre haziendo algunos daños como lo han hecho de poco tiempo a esta parte quemando las puentes de Apurima y Abancay y por otra parte tenemos relaçion que estays pro supuesto de venyr de paz y estar debaxo de nra real obidiençia y señorio y consyderado esto y el deseo que tenemos de vro bien y salvaçion y quanto nro señor y nos seremos servidos de que vos y los que en vra compañya andan vengais de paz porque esperamos que sera causa para que mas presto los naturales de los dhos nros reynos vengan en conoscimy° de nuestra sante fee catolica y vysto por don Hurtado de Mendoça marques de cañete nro visorrey de los dhos nuestros reynos fue acordado de dar esta nuestra carta para vos en dha rrazon //
/f.30v/ E nos tuvimos por bien por la qual vinyendo como dho es vos el dho Sayre Topa Ynga e los caziques e yndios que con vos andan alçados de paz e a bibir y estar debaxo de nro rreal serviçio y obidiençia vos perdonamos ansi el dho alçamy[to] como qualesquier daños e muertes robos e otras cosas que ayays fecho y cometido desde el dia que os alçastes hasta que como dho es vengais de paz e vos prometemos e aseguramos que agora ny en nynguna tiempo a vos ny a los caziques y yndios que con vos vinyeren de paz ny vros subcesores ny deudos no sereys enajenados de nuestra real corona e que vos sera fecho todo buen tratamiento e que las chacaras e casas que tenya el dho Mango Ynga vro padre al tiempo que se alço se os bolveran y restituyran y se os señalara parte e lugar donde hagais vros pueblos y bibays y si quisieredes estar en las tierras y provincias donde andays lo podays hazer bybiendo de paz y en nro real serviçio e amystad de los españoles donde se proveera que hagan yglesias y se os predique el sagrado evangelio y enseñen las cosas de nuestra santa fee catolica e que en todo se os guardara y cumplira lo contenydo en esta nuestra real provision e que se yra contra ello ny contra parte dello advirtiendo os a que sy no deliberays e determynays a lo ansi hazer y todavia quisieredes estar en vra pertinancia mandaremos que el dho nro vysorrey os envie a capturar con el rigor que se requiere. Dada en la ciudad de los rreyes a primero dia del mes de henero de myll e quis° y zinquenta e siete años. el marques. E yo Pedro //
/f.31/ de Avendaño escribano de camara de sus cesareas e catolicas mag[des] la fize escrivir por su mandado con acuerdo del su vysorrey. Registrada Ant° Hervallejo por chanciller. Fran[co] Hortigosa.

En el Cuzco en veynte dias del mes de nov[e] de myll e qui°s y setenta y dos anos yo Geronimo de Quesada escribano pu[co] y del num° desta dha ziudad hize sacar y saque este dho treslado de la provision original del que ante my ysivio [*sic*] /exhibio/ para el dho efeto la parte del capitan Martin Garcia de Loyola y doña Beatriz Coya su mujer y va çierto y verdadero. Testigos Miguel de Salzedo y Alvaro de Salzedo y Juanes Durana y Alv° Diaz y lo firmo aqui el señor Alcalde Valdes y lo fize ver y aqui my signo.

Ger[mo] de Quesada
Scriv° Pu°

/f.31v/ /en blanco/

/f.32/ /parte superior incompleto/ Titulo de adelantado …guanas Guaylaquipas Pucara.

Don Phelipe por la gracia de Dios rey de Castilla de Leon de Aragon de Ynglaterra de Francia de las dos Sizilias de Jerusalen de Navarra de Granada de Toledo de Valencia de Galicia de Mallorcas de Sevilla de Çerdeña de Cordova de Corcega de Murcia de Jaen de los Algarves de Algezira de Gibraltar de las yslas de Canaria de las Yndias yslas e tierra firme del mar oceano conde de Barcelona señor de Viscaya e de Molina Duque de Athenas y de Neopatria marques de Oristany de Goçiano archiduque de Austria duque de Borgoña y de Bravante y Milan conde de Flandes y de Tirol etc. Por quanto por nras cartas y provisiones reales tenemos proveydo que en los dhos nros reynos del Piru que es en las nras yndias del mar oceano se procure por las vias que ser pudieren traer de paz y a nra obidiencia y servicio real al Ynga hijo del Ynga señor que fue de los dhos nros reynos del Piru que andava alçado para que vinyesen el y los que con el anduviesen de paz y en conoszimy[to] de nra Santa fee catolica y las rrescibiesen para su salvaçion y en cumplimy° dello. Don Hurtado de Mendoça marques de Cañete guarda mayor de la çiudad de Cuenca nro vysorrey e capitan general de los dhos nros rreynos y porque çesacen los grandes daños e ynconvynientes que a

causa de andar alçado y de guerra en los Andes Sayre Topa Mango Capa Yupangui Ynga hijo de Mango Ynga y nieto de Guayna Capa señor natural que fue de los dhos nros reynos por los muchos saltos muertes y rrobos que hordinariamente se hazian por sus capitanes y gentes en los caminos reales a españoles y naturales y la cantidad de naturales que llebaba y rrecogia a los dhos Andes donde //
/f.32v/ andava de los que estan pazificos y debaxo de nra rreal obidiençia y el desasosiego y ynquietud que con el dho ynga tenian los naturales de los repartimi^{o}s de yndios que sirven a los vezinos de la ciudad del Cuzco e Guamanga proveyo que religiosos y mensajeros le fuesen a hablar de nra parte para que viniese de paz y a nra rreal obidiençia y servicio y les enbio perdones de las muertes de españoles y naturales que obiese echo y de otros qualesquier crimynes delitos que obiese cometido ofresciendole que vyniendo de paz dentro de cierto termino que le fue señalado de nra parte se le harian merçedes de los repartimyentos de yndios de Yucay que tubo en nro nombre encomendado don Fran^{co} Piçarro menor hijo del marques don Fran^{co} Piçarro difuntos y de Xaquixaguana Guayllaquipa y Pucara que estubo encomendado en Fran^{co} Hernandez Giron vezino del Cuzco difunto que estan vacos con todo lo a ello subjeto y que les serian echas otras mercedes de tierras e solares e otras cosas contenydas en las provisiones q' dello se mandaron dar y enbiaron lo qual aviendolo tratado los dhos religiosos y mensajeros con el dho Ynga lo açepto y salio y vino de paz y entro en nra corte y chancilleria que rreside en la ciudad de los rreyes de los dhos nros reynos del Piru vyspera de la fiesta de los reyes deste presente años de myll e quinientos y cinquenta y ocho años e dio al dho Marques de Cañete y nro visorrey en nro real nombre la obidiençia devida e prometio de siempre nos servir como //
/f.33/ bueno y leal vasallo de veyes [*sic*] obligado de hazer y porque aviendo echo lo suso dho es justo que se tenga quenta con su persona y se le cumpla lo q' se le ofrescio para con que se sustente e su mujer casa e famylia y de nuevo se le hagan otras mercedes porque se aficione y obligue mas a nro rreal servicio y tenga voluntad de se convertir y convierte a nra santa fee catolica para que se salve y obligue y anime a los demas naturales de los dhos nuestros reynos a que hagan lo mysmo que es lo que principalmente avemos pretendido y pretendemos y por lo que ynporta a la quietud y sosiego de los dhos nuestros reynos vysto por el dho marques de Cañete nuestro visorrey paresçio que deviamos hazer mrd al dho Ynga de le nombrar y hazer nro adelantado de los dhos repartimy^{o} de yndios de suso declarados y pueblos a ellos subjetos y que deviamos mandar dar esta nra carta y titulo dellos en la dha razon y nos tovimoslo por bien por ende por hazer bien y merced a vos el dho Sayre Topa Mango Capa Yupangui Ynga acatando lo suso dho y los servicios que esperamos que nos hareis de aqui adelante es nra mrd y voluntad que agora y de aqui adelante y en el entretanto que por nos otra cosa se provee seays nro adelantado de los dhos repartimy^{o}s e pueblos de yndios de Yucay e Xaquixaguana Guayllaquipa e Pucara e pueblos y estancias a ellos subjetos y pertenescientes y por esta nuestra carta o por su treslado sygnado de escribano publico encargamos al Ylustrisimo principe de España nro muy caro e muy amado hijo y mandamos a los ynfantes perlados duques marqueses //
/f.33v/ condes rricos homes [*sic*] maestros de las hordenes priores comendadores y subcomendadores alcaydes de los castillos y casas fuertes y llanas y a los del nro consejo presidente e oydores de las nras audiencias y a los nros vysorreyes governadores y capitanes generales y otros nros mynistros y oficiales y a todoas y qualesquier nuestras justiçias e juezes y a los conçejos justiçias regidores veinte e quatros cavallerosjurados escuderos oficiales y homes buenos de todas las ciudades villas y lugares asi de los nros reynos y señorios de la corona de Castilla como de los dhos reynos del Piru y de las otras provincias que tenemos en las dhas Yndias del mar oceano que al presente estan descubiertas y pobladas y adelante se descubrieren y poblaren y a otras qualesquier personas de qualquier estado preheminencia o dignidad que sean y a cada uno y qualesquier dellos en sus lugares y jurisdiçiones que os ayan e tengan por nro adelantado del dho repartimy^{to} pueblo y estançias de suso declarados y usen con vos en el dho cargo y oficio en todos los casos y cosas a ella anexas y pertenesçientes y os guarden y hagan guardar todas las honrras graçias merçedes franquezas y libertades esençiones premynençias y todas las otras cosas y cada una dellas que por razon del dho oficio deveys a ver y gozar y os deven ser guardadas segun que mejor y mas cumplidam^{te} se an guardado y devido guardar a los otros nros adelantados que han sido y son en las otras provinçias de las dhas Yndias de todo bien y cumplidam^{te} en guisa que vos non mengue [*sic*] en de cosa //
/f.34/ alguna y que en ello ny en parte dello enbargo ni contr^{o} alguno vos no pongan ny consientan poner canos [*sic*] por la presente vos rrescibimos y avemos por rrescibido al dho cargo y oficio de adelantado y al uso y exerçiçio del y os damos poder y facultad para lo usar y exerçer caso que por los suso dhos o por alguno dellos a el no seays reszibido contando que por razon del dho oficio e cargo no lleveys ny gozeys por el pres^{te} hasta que nos mandemos otra cosa de nyngun salario ny dr^{o}s de los que pertenescen o podian pertenescer al dho off^{o} y cargo y los unos ny los otros no fagades ni fagan en de al [*sic*] por alguna manera so pena de la nra mrd y de myll pesos de oro para la nra camara a cada uno que lo contr^{o} hiziere. Dada en la ciudad de los Reyes doze dias del mes de henero de myll e quinientos y zinquenta y ocho años. el Marques. Yo Joan Muñoz Rrico secretario de camara de su cesarea y catholica mag^{t} la fize escribir con acuerdo y por mandado de su visorrey.

En el Cuzco en veynte dias del mes de novi^{e} de myll e qui^{o}s y setenta y dos a^{o}s yo Geronimo de Quesada escriv^{o} pu^{co} del num^{o} de esta dha ciudad hize sacar y saque este dho treslado de la provisyon original del que ante my esivio para el dho efeto la parte del capitan Martin Garcia de Loyola y doña Beatriz Coya su mujer y va cierto y verdadero y lo firmo el s^{or} alcalde de (ilegible) testigos Myguel de Salzedo y Alv^{o} de Salzedo y lo fize escribir y aqui my signo.

Gr^{mo} de Quesada
Scriv^{o} Pu^{co}

/f.34v/ /en blanco/

/f.35/ Capitulacion de los 2000 ps que se pagaban a Gomez Arias Davila.

Don Hurtado de Mendoça marques de Cañete guarda mayor de la Cibdad de Cuenca Visorrey e capitan general en estos reynos e provincias del Peru por su mag^{t} etc. A vos los oficiales de la rreal hazienda de la cibdad del Cuzco que al presente sois e por tpo fueredes bien sabeis e deveis saber como en dias pasados por cabsas [*sic*] que me movieron mande dar e di una mi provision para que de los tributos que se cobrasen del repartimiento de yndios que tuvo encomendado Fran^{co} Hernandez Giron o de otro qualquier vacante se diesen a Gomez Arias de Avila vezino de Leon de Guanuco dos myll pesos de renta en cada un año por dos vidas como abreis visto e vereis por la provision que desto le fue dada el tenor de la qual es el q' se sigue.

/Al margen: Provision/ Don Hurtado de Mendoça marques de Cañete guarda mayor de la cibdad de Cuenca visorrey e capitan general en estos reinos e provincias del Peru por su magestad etc. A vos los oficiales que al presente sois e por tpo fueredes de la rreal hazienda en la cibdad del Cuzco e a cada uno e qualquier de vos sabed que Gomez Arias Davila vezino de la cibdad de Leon de Guanuco ppr una peticion que ante mi presento me hizo relacion diziendo que de mas de aver tpo de diez e ocho años que ha que paso a Yndias y aver servido en ellas y en estos dhos reynos a su mag^{t} con cargo de capitan y sin el en lo que sea ofrecido particularmente sirvio en el castigo de Fran^{co} Hernandez Giron con sus armas e cavallos como es notorio desde que se alço hasta que en la provincia de Pucara fue vencido e desbaratado y despues en su seguimiento hasta que en el valle de Xauxa fue preso y de alli traydo a esta cibdad de los rreyes donde se hizo justicia y que hera asi que despues que el dho Fran^{co} Hernandez fue desbaratado en la dha prov^{a} de Pucara y se fue huyendo con cierta gente de su opinion camino de la costa probeyeron en el Cuzco los oydores de la rreal audiencia e chancilleria que por mandado de su magestad reside en esta cibdad de los Reyes capitanes e gente que fuesen en su seguimiento e busca e mandaron por un auto que qualquier persona que truxese bivo al dho Fran^{co} Hernandez o syu cabeça se le darian dos myll pesos de rrenta en cada un año y perdonarian qualesquier delitos que hasta entonces oviese cometido e que el dho Gomez Arias fue en su seguimiento con los dempas que a ello se enviaron hasta que en Xauxa lo encontraron y tuvieron con el cierto encuentro y en el el dho Gomez Arias Davila le rindio e prendio e tomo las armas que tenia e con que se defendio el lo llevo a las ancas de su cavallo a su toldo y fue en traerle a esta dha cibdad como dixo que parescia por una ynformacion de que hizo presentacion la qual por mi vista y la confision del dho Fran^{co} Hernandez por donde confiesa aver sido el dho Gomez Arias la primera persona que le prendio y tomo las armas e atento lo probeido por la dha rreal abdiencia por la presente en nombre de su magestad e por virtud de su rreales provisiones que para ello tengo hago md al dho Gomez Arias Davila de dos myll pesos de rrenta en cada un año //
/f.35v/ de valor cada uno de a quatrocientos e cinquenta maravedies los quales vos mando que de los pesos de oro que ovieren sido o fueren a vro cargo de cobranças de tributos vacos del rrepartimiento que el dho Fran^{co} Hernandez tuvo encomendado en la dha cibdad del Cuzco o de otras qualesquier vacantes que ha avido e oviere se los deis y pagueis a el o a quien su poder para ello tuviere en cada un año por todos los dias de su vida e de un hijo o hija suyo legitimo qual el señalare que comiençe a correr desde el dia de la fecha desta en adelante que dandoselos y pagandoselos y tomando la rrazon deste titulo en los libros de la rreal hazienda y un traslado del para que se le buelva al dho Gomez Arias este original y su carta de pago en cada año de los que se los pagaredes mando que vos sean rrescibidos e pasados en cuenta para vros descargos lo que asi en virtud desta mi provision le dieredes y pagaredes segund en la forma arriba dha sin que sea obligado a servir mas vezindad de la que fue en la dha cibdad de Guanuco donde es vezino ny que por rrazon desta provision le compelan a otra cosa. Fecho en los Reyes a veinte e un dias del mes de agosto de mill e quinientos e cinquenta y seis años. El Marques. Por mandado de su excelencia Pedro de Avendaño. Y en ansi que despues de hcha la dha md por mi orden fueron mensajeros a los Andes con provisiones e recaudos para que Sayre Topa Mango Capa Yupangue Ynga que estava alçado con gente de guerra vyniese a la obidiencia e servicio de su mag^{t} y para q' todo el dho rrepartimiento de yndios que fue de Fran^{co} Hernandez para con que se sustentase el qual en cumplimiento dello vino a esta corte y se le hyzo md del dho rrepartimiento e dio titulo del y por que el dho Sayre Topa use libremente de la dha md conforme al titulo que della le fue dada y se le prometio y goze de los tributos que oviere de dar por la presente en nombre de su mag^{t}. Alço e quito la rrenta de los dhos dos myll pesos que fueron señalados al dho Gomez Arias Davila contenidos en la provision de suso incorporada en el dho rrepartimiento e mando que desde primero dia de henero deste presente año de quinientos e cinquenta e ocho en adelante que es desde quando el dho Sayre Topa Ynga a de gozar de los tributos del dho rrepartimiento no se acudan ny hagan acudir al dho Gomez Arias Davila ny a otra persona alguna con los dhos dos mill pesos de los tributos en que estan tasados o se tasaren el rrepartimiento de yndios que fue del dho Fran^{co} Hernandez Giron y que den de en adelante se guarde y cumpla con el dho Gomez Arias de Avila la provision e md de suso incorporada de la cobrança que es y fuere a cargo de vos los dhos oficiales de qualesquier tributos de rrepartimientos de yndios vacos que ay o oviere en terminos de la dha cibdad como en ella se contiene en el entretanto que se le señala un rrepartimiento particular sobre que se cobre la //
/f.36/ dha renta conforme al dho titulo suso encorporado y de lo que oviere corrido de la md del dho Gomez Arias Davila hasta el dho dia primero de henero deste año de cinquenta e ocho y de lo que corriere adelante en los dhos tributos vacos terneis [*sic*] cuidado de que le cobren los dhos ocho mil pesos que al dho Gomez Arias de Avila se prestaron por mi orden para ayuda a los gastos que hizo para el descubrimiento y poblacion que fue a hazer de la governacion de Rupa Rupa y se metan en la caxa de tres llaves como os esta mandado y cobrados le acudiereis o a quien su poder oviere con la dha renta de los dhos dos mil pesos al tenor e forma de la dha md. fecho en los Reyes a dos dias del mes de hebrero de mil e quinientos e cinquenta e ocho años.

Mendoza (rubrica)

Por mandado de su Ex.

Ioan Illmoz Rico (rubrica)

Para que los oficiales reales del Cuzco no acudan a Gomez Arias de Avila ni a quien su poder tuviere de los tributos del repartimiento de yndios que fue de Fran^{co} Hernandez Giron con los dos mil pesos que en el se le hizieron md al tenor de la provision aqui ynserta y que le cumplan la dha md de otros tributos de repartimientos de indios vacos atento que Sayri Topa a de gozar de los tributos del dho repartimiento libremente desde el dho dia en adelante conforme a la md que dello le fue fecha y que de lo corrido y de lo que corriere de la dha md del dho Gomez Arias de Avila se acabe de cobrar los ocho mil pesos que por mandado de Vra excelencia se le prestaron pa la poblacion de Rupa Rupa.

/f.36v/ /en blanco/

/f.37/ Joan S^{e}s de los Rios en n^{e} de Martin Garcia de Loyola y doña Beatriz Coya su mujer en la causa con vro fiscal sobre los indios que les quitaron diziendo ser yanaconas digo que para presentar en esta causa tengo necesidad de las escripturas siguientes:

Las provisiones y cedulas de Vra real persona en que mando traer de paz a Mango Ynga y Sayre Topa Ynga y las mrds que les mando hazer por que biniesen de paz.

Yten la cedula de vra real persona en que mando que el marques de Cañete cumpliese y ejecutase las cedulas y provisiones que avia dado dirigidos a don Antonio de Mendoça y a los demas visorreyes.

Yten un testimonio de la platica que frey Pedro Gutierrez hizo a los yndios del valle de Yucay quando empeço a hazer la bisita del y de si ay en la dha bisita citacion hecha a la dha doña Beatriz Coya o alguna persona por ella y de los capitulos de la ynstruccion por catorze y sesenta y siete en que don Fran^{co} de Toledo vro visorrey dava el horden que se avia de thener en declarar por indios tributarios o no a los yndios forasteros o yanaconas.

Yten que se saque de la coronica [*sic*] destas partes de las Yndias que compuso Diez Hernandez el capitulo quarto libro tr^{o} en que trata de la horden y subcesion de los Yngas y del capitulo quarto de dho libro en que trata del horden que el dho marques tubo en sacar al dho Sayre Topa Ynga de paz y lo que en fecho con las provisiones de V. Alt^{a} para para en premien //
/f.37v/ /manchado/ consta quel Conde de Nieva y los comisarios escrivieron a V. real persona sobre el sacar de paz el Ynga a pedimento de Ju^{o} Sierra de Leguiçamo.

A V. Alt^{a} pido y sup^{co} mande a los escribanos de camara en cuyo poder estan los procesos y cedulas de yuso conthenidas me den un treslado de todo ello en publica forma sacado con citacion de vro fiscal para lo presentar en esta causa sobre que pido justicia y para ello es.

Martin Garcia Loyola Joan Sanchez.

En la ciudad de los Reyes en ocho dias del mes de N^{e} de myll e qui^{o}s y ochenta y cinco años ante los señores presidente e oidores desta Real Audiencia pu^{a} se presento esta peticion.

E por dhos señores vista mandaron que se le de a cada parte. Presente el Llz^{do} a Luis de Carvajal fiscal de su mag^{d}. Montoya a quien se notifico //
/f.38/ Martin Garcia de Loyola por mi procurador en el pleito con vro fiscal sobre los yndios que doña Beatriz Coya mi mujer e yo estamos desposeidos en el balle de Yucay diziendo que son yanaconas digo que al dr^{o} de mi parte conbiene presentar un testimonio de dia en que se bautizo la dha doña Beatriz mi mujer la qual esta presentada en el pleito matrimonial que tratamos con Xpoval Mal^{do} e yo ante Fran^{co} de Alarcon notario apostolico residente en esta ciudad.

A V Alt^{a} suplico mande dar su compulsorio para que me den un treslado autorizado y para ello es.

Otro si digo que en pleito biejo de los demas yndios de questamos la dha mi mujer e yo desposeidos que con el dho vro fiscal tratamos en vro real consejo de Yndias esta un auto proveido por don Fran^{co} de T^{o} bisorrey que fue destos reinos en que el puso los dhos yn^{o}s sobre que agora se trata pleito en vra corona real sin averse notificaco a la dha mi mujer ni a su curador.

A V. Alt^{a} pido y sup^{co} mande se ponga en este proceso un treslado del dho auto y de como no consta averse notificaco a la dha mi mujer ni a su curador.

Martin Garcia de Loyola (rubrica)

/f.38v/ En la ciudad de los Reyes en quinze dias del mes de N^{e} de myll e qui^{o}s e ochenta e zinco años ante los señores pres^{te} e oydores desta Audiencia estando haziendo audiencia se presento esta pet^{on}.

E por los dhos señores vista mandaron que se les de con citacion de la otra parte y estando pres^{te} el fiscal de su mag^{d} se le notifico.

Montoya (rubrica)

/f.39/ Muy P^{o} S^{r}

Martin Garcia de Loyola por mi proc^{or} digo que pa prueba de mi dr^{o} en el pleito que trato con vro fiscal sobre los y^{o}s de Yucay tengo necesidad de que el secretario de camara ante quien paso saque del proceso viejo de los dhos y^{o}s los dhos de P^{o} Diaz Baldeon y don Fran^{co} Chilche dif^{o}s cuyas certificaciones y se me resciban razon como los suso dhos son dif^{o}s.

A V. Alt^{a} sup^{co} asi que provea y m^{de} y aya las dhas declaraciones por pres^{dos} y pido justicia. Etc.

Martin Garcia de Loyola

/f.39v/ En la ciudad de los Reyes en doze dias del mes de Nov^{e} de myll e qui^{o}s y ochenta y cinco años ante los señores presidente e oydores desta Real Audiencia estando en audiencia publica se presento esta peticion.

E por los dhos señores vista mandaron que se le den con citacion de la parte contraria y estando presente el l^{do} Alvaro de Carvajal fiscal de su mag^{d} al qual se notifico y que se le resciba la informacion que ofreze.

Montoya (rubrica)

/f.40/ Muy P^{o} S^{r}

Pide que se pongan en este proceso ciertos recaudos con citacion de fiscal.

Joan Sanchez de los Rios en n^{e} de doña Beatriz Coya en el pleito con vro fiscal digo que al dr^{o} de mi parte conbiene que se ^{me} saquen y se pongan en este proceso los recaudos siguientes

Un treslado de la tassa que vro bisorrey don Fran^{co} de T^{do} hizo de los yndios sobre ques este pleito.

Un treslado de dos capitulos del libro llamado Republicas del Mundo que son del primero y quinze capitulos del titulo llamado Republica de los Yndios Occidentales con la licencia de V. Alt^{a} que para que enpremir el dho libro 460.

Yten un treslado del capitulo doze de un libro intitulado El Descubrimiento y Conquista del Peru hecha por Agustin de Zarate contador de V. Alt^{a} impreso con licencia de V. Alt^{a}

Suplico a V. Alt^{a} mande al secret^{o} que saque los dhos recaudos con citacion de vro fiscal y los ponga en este proceso que desde luego yo en n^{e} de mi parte hago presentacion dellos para en prueva de su just^{a} la qual pido y para ello es.

El Liz^{do} Alonso. (rubrica)

/f.40v/ En la ciudad de los Reyes en v^{te} y dos dias del mes de noviembre de myll e qui^{o}s y ochenta y cinco años estando los señores presidente e oydores desta Real Audiencia en audiencia publica se pres^{to} esta peticion.

Por los dichos señores vista mandaron que se le de.

/f.41/ Muy P^{o} S^{r}

Responde a /roto/ de aberse rezebido a prueba

Martin Garcia de Loyola por mi procurador en la causa con vro fiscal sobre os yndios que por mi y en n^{e} de doña Beatriz Coya mi mujer pido de nuevo respondiendo a la peticion ultima en que vro fiscal suplica de averse rescivido esta causa a prueba digo que sin embargo de lo en ella contenido se a de ir por la causa adelante y azerse segun que pedido tengo porque por autos de bista y rebista con vro fiscal se admitio esta nueva demanda y se le mando respondiese derechamente y se recibio la causa a prueva y asi no tiene que aser sino en el termino della alegar y provar lo que biere que le combiene y para le convencer yo consiento que se haga la cumulacion del pleito primero que el pide.

Por que pido y suplico a V. Alt^{a} asi lo provea y m^{de} sin dar lugar a nuevas dilaciones sonre que pido just^{a} y para ello es.

El Ll^{do} Falcon

En la ciudad de los Reyes a veinte y nueve dias del mes de noviembre de mill e qui^{o}s y ochenta y cinco años ante los señores presidente y oydores de esta Real Audiencia estando en audiencia publica se presento esta peticion.

Y por los dichos señores visto mandaron llevar los autos a la sala para proveer.

Montoya.

/f.41v/ Que se confirma sin embargo en 6 de di^{e} 1585 años. Los señores su excelencia de Castro //
/f.42/ En la causa del comendador Martin Garcia de Loyola por doña Beatriz Coya su mujer con el fiscal de su mag^{d} sobre ls yndios yanaconas que el virrey don Francisco de Toledo mando poner en la corona real.

En la ciudad de los Reyes en seis dias del mes de diziembre de myll e quinientos e ochenta e cinco años. Los señores Presidente e Oydores de esta Real Audienzia vista la dha causa en provi^{on} confirmaron el auto por los dhos señores en ella proveido en veinte quatro dias del mes de set^{e} deste presente año en que las dhas partes dentro de noventa dias presentasen las escrituras y testigos de que se entienden aprovechar con aperzevimiento quel dho tr^{no} /termino/ pasado con lo que ovieren fecho sin se les admitir otra provanza alguna se remitira a su magestad e a su Real Consejo de Yndias conforme a la hordenanza el qual mandaron sea llebado a devida ex^{on} con efeto sin embargo de la sup^{on} ynterpuesta por el dho fiscal e ansi lo proveyeron e rubricaron.

/siguen rubricas/

Pronunciose este auto ante los señores presidente e oydores desta real audiencia en dho dia mes y año en el contenido.

Jhoan de Montoya (rubrica)

/f.42v/ En los Reyes en diez dias del mes de diciembre de myll e qui^{o}s y ochenta y seis [*sic*] años notifique este auto al señor Llz^{do} Alvaro de Carvajal fiscal de su mag^{d} en su persona e dello doy fe.

Jhoan de Montoya (rubrica)

/f.43/ Muy P^{o} s^{r}

Que se le prorrogue por otros nobenta dias.

Prorrogacion por otros tres meses.

Jhoan S^{e}s de los Rios en n^{e} de Martin Garcia de Loyola y la coya doña Beatriz su mujer en el pleito con vro fiscal sobre los y^{o}s del balle de Yucay que estan mis partes desposeidos digo que siendo terminado los tres meses que se dio pa hazer las probanças mis partes no an podido azer por no averse podido /ilegible/ pa yr desta corte.

A V. Alt^{a} sup^{co} se le ponga el dho termino y otros tres meses mas y pido justicia.

Martin Garcia de Loyola (rubrica)

En la ciudad de los Reyes veinte y ocho dias de mes de henero mill e qui^{o}s y ochenta y seis años estando los señores presidente y oydores de esta Real Audiencia en audiencia publica se presento esta peticion.

E por los dhos señores vista prorrogaron otros tres meses mas de termino comunes a las partes. Presentes el Lic^{do} Alvaro de Carvajal a quien se notifico.

Montoya (rubrica)

/f.43v/ /en blanco/

/f.44/ Yo Jhoan de Montoya escri^{o} de camara de la audiencia real que por mandado de su mag^{d} reside en esta ciudad de los Reyes destos reynos e provincias del Piru doy fe que estando los señores presidente e oydores de la dha Real Audiencia en audiencia pu^{ca} en la ciudad de los Reyes en ocho dias del mes de noviembre de mill e quinientos y ochenta y cinco años en la causa que pende ante los dhos señores ente el comendador Martin Garcia de Loyola y doña Beatriz Coya su mujer con el lic^{do} Alvaro de Caravajal fiscal de su mag^{d} sobre los y^{o}s que le quitaron diziendo ser yanaconas por parte del dho Martin Garcia de Loyola se press^{to} una peticion y un capitulo della es del tenor siguiente.

Yten un testimonio de la platica que fray Pedo Gutierrez dijo a los yn^{o}s del valle de Yucay quando empeço a hazer la visita del y de si ay en la dha visita citacion fecha a la dha doña Beatriz Coya o a alguna persona por ella y de los capitulos del a ynstruccion primero catorce y setenta y siete en que don Fran^{co} de Toledo vro visorrey dava el horden que se avia de tener en declarar por yndios tributarios e no a los yndios forasteros e yanaconas.

E presentada la dha peticion e por los dhos señores vista mandaron que Jhoan Ramos de Gauna u otra qualquiera persona en cuyo poder este la dha visita e recaudo que en la dha peticion se haze mencion al dho Martin Garcia de Loyola un treslado signado en publica forma de la dha platica y lo demas que en el dho capitulo de la dha visita se contiene citada la parte del dho fiscal pa lo qual //
/f.44v/ fue citado el licenciado Alvaro de Caravajal fiscal de su mag^{d} en forma e para que dello conste de pedimento de la parte del dho Martin Garcia de Loyola di el presente en los Reyes en veinte y un dias del mes de henero de mil e qui^{o}s y ochenta y seis años.

Jhoan de Montoya (rubrica)

En cumplimiento de lo qual yo Jhoan Ramos de Gauna en cuyo poder esta la dha visita que de suso se haze mension que el de los indios del balle de Yucay hecha por el dotor fray Pedro Gutierrez Flores hize sacar un treslado del parlamento que en dho compulsorio se haze minsion que es del tenor siguiente.

Despues de lo suso dho en el dho balle de Yucay a veynte y seis dias del mes de julio de mil y quinientos y setenta y dos años el dho señor visitador por ante mi el dho escrivano hizo parecer ante si personalmente a don Fran^{co} Chilche y a don Garcia Quispecapi caciques principales deste repartimiento y a don Lucas y a don Hernando Guartanaula y a Lope Martin Condemayta y a otros muchos principales e indios //
/f.45/ atun lunas naturales del dho repartimiento encomendados en la dha doña Beatriz de Mendoça menor e por lengua del dho Hernando de Morales ynterprete les dixo y dio a entender otra vez lo de suso referido e que su mrd quiere començar mañana la bisita de ñps dhos yndios para saber los yn^{o}s que ay en este repartimiento que todos esten juntos e apercevidos para lo suso dho como les tiene mandado la qual quiere començar por los caciques principales deste repartimiento y por los yndios a ellos subjetos que tienen en el circuito deste asiento y balle de Yucay y la horden que a de tener en ella para que la sepan y entiendan es que se an de visitar y escrevir todos distinta e apartadamente por sus pueblos ayllos e parcialidades ansi xptianos como ynfieles si los obiere e para ello se començara por los dichos caciques asentandolos con sus mujeres e hijos legitimos e bastardos con sus nombres y hedades e bienes y luego se an de començar a escrevir los yndios de su parcialidad y ayllo por la dha horden asentando por casado al que lo fuere con los hijos que tubiere y acavado de escrevir y bisitar los casados con sus mujeres hijos e aziendas se començaran a escrevir todos los yn^{o}s biudos e solteros de hedad para tributar con sus hijos y luego se escreviran y bisitaran los muchachos que hubiere huerfanos y luego los yndios biejos tullidos mancos ciegos e ympedidos para tributar y luego las yndias biudas e solteras con sus hijos e haziendas y les hizo saver que los yndios que de otro repartimiento estuvieren en este repartimiento de diez años a esta parte que an de quedar //
/f.45v/ por tributarios para que tributen y sirvan como los demas que para ello se junten todos por la mañana e se començaran a escrevir e bisitar por la horden retro escripta que por ninguna bia ni manera encubran ningun yndio ni yndia biejo ni moço que por el libro del bautismo y demas averiguaciones que hiziere lo a de benir a saver y los castigara con gran rigor que miren bien lo que hazen e se pongan todos por sus ayllos y parcialidades destintos e apartados como les tiene dho para los escrevir e bisitar que en esta forma a de hazer la dha bisita y lo firmo juntamente con el dho ynterprete testigos Juan Enriquez y Pedro Sanchez. El Ll^{do} frey Pedro Gutierrez Flores ante mi Pedro Diaz Baldeon escribano.

Y no parece por la dha visita citacion ning^{a} hecha para ella a la dha dona Beatriz Coya en el treslado de suso del dho parlamento que ba corregido con el original de la dha visita a que en todo me refiero. Fecho en los Reyes a v^{te} y siete dias del mes de hen^{o} de myll e quinientos y ochenta y seis años.

Joan Ramos de Gauna (rubrica).

/f.46/ Muy P^{o} S^{r}

Martin Garcia de Loyola por su procu^{or} en el pleito con vro fiscal sobre los yn^{o}s del balle de Yucay digo que yo tengo necesidad de pres^{tar} un tr^{do} de la md que el bisorrey don Fran^{co} de T^{o} me hizo de mill e qui^{o}s pesos de renta por dos vidas en la ciudad de Arequipa questa en poder de los secretarios de gobernacion.

A V. Alt^{a} suplico se me de lo que solicito y sacar el dho traslado como demostracion del dho sobre y de pase en el proceso. Pido justicia.

Martin Garcia de Loyola

En la ciudad de los Reies a veinte y cinco dias del mes de febrero de mill e qui^{o}s y ochenta y seis años estando los señores presidente e oydores desta Real Audiencia en audi^{a} P^{ca} se presento esta peticion.

Y por los dhos señores vista mandaron que se le de el compulsorio que pide.

Montoya.

/f.46v/ /en blanco/

/f.47/ Muy P^{o} señor.

Que se ponga en la carzel a Juan Sanchez

El licenciado Alvaro de Caravajal vro fiscal en la causa con Martin Garcia de Loyola sonre la çituacion digo que a mi pedimento y por mandado de vra alteza se notifico a Ju^{o} Sanchez de los Rios que trujese este pleito para que se determinase y no lo a hecho.

A Vra Alteza pido y suplico mande poner en la carcel al dho Ju^{o} Sanchez de los Rios hasta que lo buelva y pido justicia.

En la ciudad de los Reyes en siete dias del mes de março de mill e qui^{o}s y ochenta y seis años ante los señores pr^{e} y oydores desta Real Audiencia estando en audi^{a} publica se presento esta peticion.

E por los dhos señores vista mandaron que Ju^{o} Sanchez de los Rios lo buelba.

Montoya

/f.47v/ /en blanco/

/f.48/ Jhoan S^{e}s de los Rios en n^{e} de doña Beatriz Coya en el pleito con vro fiscal sobre los yn^{os} de Yucay digo que a mi dr^{o} conviene presentar una provision que vro bisorrey Marques que Cañete despacho para don Diego Sayre Topa Ynga padre de la dha mi parte por la qual en vro real n^{e} le prometio que saliendo de paz a dar la obediencia a V. Alt^{a} le aria mrd de dar los repartimientos que al presente tiene y titulo de adelantado para el y sus hijos y herederos y subcesores perpetuamente por bia de mayorazgo en el entretanto que su mag^{d} le azia otras y mejores mercedes la qual dha provision se envio con fray Melchor de los Reyes y fray Pedro de Moreno (¿) de la horden de Santo Domingo.

A V. Alt^{a} pido y suplico me de su compulsorio para que los secretarios de gobernacion y desta Real Aud^{a} en cuyo oder estuviere el original me de un treslado con çitacion de vro fiscal y pido justicia y para ello es.

Otro si digo que para la ynfor^{on} que boy haziendo tengo necesidad de un treslado de los nombres de los yn^{o}s del pleito biejo questa remitido a V. real juicio y de los nombres de los yn^{o}s sobre ques este pleyto.

A V. Alt^{a} suplico mande al secret^{o} de la causa se me y para ello es.

Jhoan Sanchez.

/f.48v/ En la ciudad de los Reyes en veinte y nueve dias del mes de abril de mil e qui^{o}s y ochenta y seis años ante los señores presidente e oydores en audiencia pu^{ca} se presento esta pet^{on} el lic^{do} en nombre de su parte.

Y los dhos señores vista mandaron que se le de con citacion del fiscal presente el lic^{do} Alvaro de Caravajal fiscal de su mag^{d} a quien se notifico.

Montoya

/f.49/ Muy P^{o} S^{r}

Presento escriptura

S^{o} Montoya

Martin Garcia de Loyola por mi procu^{or} en el pleito de los y^{o}s de Yucay con vro fiscal ago pres^{on} desta provis^{on} de vro visorrey don F^{co} de Toledo sacado con los procesos de Vra Alt^{a}

Pido y suplico aya por pres^{do} y se ponga en el proceso y pa ello es.

Martin Garcia de Loyola (rubrica)

En la ciudad de los Reyes en tres dias del mes de junio de mill y qui^{o}s y ochenta y seis años estando los señores presidente e oydores desta Real Audiencia en audiencia pu^{ca} se presento esta peticion.

E por los dichos señores vista mandaron dar traslado a la otra parte e se bieron por presentada los dhos recaudos. press^{te} el fiscal de su mag^{d} a quien se notifico.

Montoya (rubrica)

/f.49v/ /en blanco/

/f.50/ Yo Joan de Montoya escribano de camara desta Real Audiencia que por mandado de su majestad reside en esta ciudad de los Reyes destos reinos e provincias del Piru doy fee questando los señores presidente e oydores de la dha real audiencia en audiencia publica en veynte e cinco dias del mes de febrero de myll e quinientos e ochenta e seis a^{o}s Martin Garcia de Loyola por peticion pidio y sup^{co} a los dhos señores le mandasen dar compulsorio para que el secretario de governacion le de un treslado autorizado de la mrd que el bisorrey don Françisco de Toledo le hizo de myll e quinientos p^{o}s de renta or dos vidas en la ciudad de Arequipa para presentarlo en el pleito que trata con el fiscal de su majestad sobre los yanaconas e por los dhos señores vista le mandaron darle dho compulsorio e para que dello conste de pedimento del dho Martin Garcia de Loyola di el presente en los Reyes en tres dias del mes de março de myll e qui^{os} e ochenta e seis años. Juan de Montoya.

En cumplimiento de lo qual yo Melchor Perez de Maridueña escrivano de su majestad e mayor de la governacion destos reynos del Piru fize sacar y saque un traslado del registro de la provi^{on} de mrd questa en el quaderno de consultas de mercedes hechas por el Exmo don Fran^{co} de Toledo visorrey que fue destos dhos reinos //
/f.50v/ ante Alvaro Ruiz de Navamuel su secretario que su tenor del dho registro de mrd es como se sigue.

Don Fran^{co} de Toledo e por quanto aviendo entendido visto e pra/c/ticado la ynport^{a} que hera para el servicio de nuestro señor e verdadera conversion de los naturales deste reyno e provincias a el comarcanas e para la seguridad e pacificacion temporal destos reynos de la majestad del rey nro señor de que pendia poder el sancto evangelio ser propagado e adelantado como su santidad lo pretendio e quiso quando dio el titulo destas tierras e provincias de la corona real de Castilla ser tan particular remedio para estos buenos efectos quitar un daño tan grande de como hazia a la tirania de los yngas que avian quedado conservados en la provincia de Vilcabamba donde despues de averse levantado contra el servi^{o} de su majestad Mango Ynga a quien sus ministros dieron la borla de Ynga por la fidelidad que presto a su majestad por el e por sus hijos que por no lo aver guardado vinieron tan grandes daños universales en todo este reyno e se retruxo a la dha provincia de Vilcabamba donde con la libertad de su traicion e ydolatrias llevo todos los yndios para conservar en los yndios que quedavan en este reyno la esperança de livertad //
/f.51/ que podian levantar y bolver a sus ritos e cultos de sus ydolatrias conservandoloes en la del ydolo Punchao del sol con los demas que llevo de la ciudad del Cuzco con el qual se quedavan en ella las leyes e cultos de religion ydolatrias a todo el reyno e queriendo evitar el daño questa hazia de no poderse ynfundir en los naturales por esta causa la doctrina del santo evangelio por los metropolitanos obispos y eclesiasticos e religiones que en el a vido e ay cp xpiano zelo del emperador e rey don Felipe nuestro señor que para obreros desta plata los an enviado aviendo tenido experiencia del daño que avian causado para este reyno todos los medios que los visorreyes governadores e ministros pasados avian tomado e con lass ocasiones tan grandes e justificadas que dieron en my tiempo para les hazer la guerra de las muertes e daños e trayziones que avian hecho e tratavan acorde de mandar hazer la guerra a los sucesores del dho Mango Ynga aviendolos primero prevenido con todos los medios posibles e uno de los instrumentos entre otros que para la execucion de la dha guerra tome fue al capitan Martin Garcia de Oñaz e Loyola cavallero de la horden de la milicia y cavalleria de Calatrava que con la gente de mi casa y allegados della tuvo conducta de capitan por mi para seguir la guerra en servicio de dios y //
/f.51v/ e de la majestad del rey don Phelipe nuestro señor el dho capitan Martin Garcia de Loyola se hallo en la vanguardia en el primer encuentro e guaçabara que los capitanes e yndios de guerra de la provincia salieron a dar al campo de su majestad e peleando por su persona e las de sus soldados el y el maese de campo que con el yva hasta llegar a los braços con los dhos yndios ynfieles no embargante el daño que avia hecho ellos antes que llegasen a los braços el arcabuzeria los hicieron retraer con perdida de cinco capitanes e otros yndios principales e aviendo llegado despues de algunos dias al fuerte principal de Guayna Pucara que los dhos Yngas avia tantos dias que hazian fortificar y donde pensaron e salieron a hazer su defensa tocando al dho capitan Garcia de Loyola aquel dia la banguardia y estando Quispi Tito hijo de Tito Cusi Ynga a la defensa del dho fuerte con sus capitanes e soldados el dho Martin Garcia de Oñaz e Loyola tomo los altos de la montaña para venir encima de los enemigos que hera lo que ellos temian sin lo qual no parescio ser posible combatilles [*sic*] el fuerte por lo bajo por donde yba el campo e subio la dha montaña por donde no parecia posible poderlo hazer con armas e arcabuzeria e una pieza de artilleria e ganados los //
/f.52/ dichos altos e visto por los dhos yndios questavan perdidos desampa/ra/ron el dho fuerte e por esta causa se gano la provincia e ciudad de Vilcabamba tomandose la posesion della por su majestad dia de San Joan Baptista año pasado de myll e qui^{os} e setenta y dos y siendo tan aspera y dificultosa la montaña e aviendose huydo por ella toda la mayor parte de los yndios con los Yngas capitanes e caveças e no paresciendo que tenia seguridad la posesion de su majestad ny la poblacion que en la dha provincia yo pretendia e queria hazer de españoles sin limpialla de todos los Yngas e caveças principales que en ella avido perseverando en la dha guerra e alçamiento de aquella provincia el dho Martin Garcia de Oñaz e Loyola con animo codicioso del real servicio de su majestad e queriendose particularizar en esto pidio a Martpin Hurtado de Arbieto my lugarteniente que con los soldados de su compañia le dexase ir al Capacati en seguimiento de Topa Amaro provincia mas aspera y mal acreditada de enferma que hera ynavitable sino de algunos mitimaes a quien el Ynga enviava para guarda de sus ydolos e guacas e cosas particulares que en ella queria conservar e aviendole el dho Martin Hurtado dado licencia fue a ella y llego al pueblo de Panquisa donde hizo prision de dos hermanos del dho Topa Amaro e una hija suya e quatro sobrinos e del capitan Curi Paucar principal agresor de la dicha guerra e de //
/f.52v/ de cantidad de indios capitanes e de particulares e de ynsignias e adereços del dho Ynga con los quales dio la buelta a la ciudad del Vilcabamba desando de proseguir mas adelante por entender de algunos yndios que el dho Topa Amaro avia tomado otra derrota con la nueva de su yda e aviendose entendido en Vilcabamba por cartas que yo avia escripto a mi lugarteni^{e} e al dho capitan Loyola lo mucho que ymportava al servicio de su majestad el aver a las manos al dho Ynga e capitanes y el contentamiento que en esto me daria por no poder tener seguridad ni plantar la fee de nuestro señor en la provincia en tanto que el quedase en ella aunque al presente se ofrecian otras jornadas donde avian noticia de mucho ynteres e tono a pedir al dho mi lugarteniente le dexase con su compañia yr a la provincia de los Manaris adentro a donde tenia noticia avia portado el dho Amaro Ynga e aviendole dado la dicha licencia e partido el dho capitan Loyola con algunos soldados en su busca llegado al embarcadero de los Guambos que es en el rio grande que baxa a los Manaries hallo de la otra parte del rio ocho o diez yndios manaries amigos del Ynga que enbiava a buscar a Gualpa Yupangui su general y el resto de la gente que con el venia de los quales prendio los ocho y dellos supo que el dho Topa Amaro estava en un lugar //
/f.53/ que llama Momori en tierra de los Manaries con seguridad que alla no yvan xpianos tras el ansi por la aspereza de la tierra como por la dificultad de baxar por el rio a causa de las muchas corrientes e raudales que tiene e tambien entendio dellos que por tierra tardarian

muchos en llegar e que dos yndios que avian escapado llegarian mucho antes e ternia lugar de meterse el dho Amaro la tierra dentro donde no hera posible hallarle lo qual visto por el dho capitan Loyola con la determinacion que llebava de no dexar de buscarle con tanta presteza como se requeria en el mismo dia hizo cinco balsas y se echo rio avajo y se determino de seguirle con sus soldados e armas sin otro impedimyento teniendo por cierto que qualquiera era de dilacion le hera muy perjudicial e aviendo llegado al dho lugar de Momori con toda la priesa [*sic*] y diligencia que llebava avia ya tenido el dho Ynga aviso de su yda e se avia retirado con su gente la tierra dentro y entrando el dho capitan Loyola en la tierra al pasar de un rio caudaloso le salio de guerra en cacique e yn^{os} de Momori con quien se dio tan buena maña que hizo de ellos amigos y le dixeron a donde podian aver el general Gualpa Yupangui al qual hallaron en una montaña tan aspera y fragosa que sin este aviso hera //

/f.53v/ cosa ymposible toparle al qual quedo a las manos camynando de noche con sus soldados por la dha montaña aspera con lumbre e tambien le avisaron del camino que avia llevado el dho Ynga Topa Amaro a quien yendo siguiendo el dho Martin Garcia de Loyola muy necesitado de comida a causa de averse perdido el el rio donde se le zozobraron las balsas le vino a topar casi a vista de los Guambos amigos que benian a socorrerle y le prendio y a el e a Gualpa Yupangui e los demas yndios que con el avian entrado truxo e metio en la provincia de Vilcabamba e de alli por horden e mandado mio recoxiendo a todos los yndios e capitanes presos bivos e muertos enbalsamados e ydolos y entregado dellos el dho capitan Loyola y el maese de campo Joan Alvarez Maldonado los truxeron a la ciudad del Cuzco donde los metio y me los entregaron presos encadenados e alli se hizo justicia dellos y el dho capitan Martin Garcia de Loyola me pidio e sup^{co} le diese licencia e facultad para que juntamente con las armas e ynsignias de la antigüedad y nobleza de su linaje pudiese poner la cabeça del dho Ynga que avia aprezado lo qual yo le concedi y porque de la grandeza y benignidad de la majestad del rey don Felipe nuestro señor le es muy propia la gratificacion a los que bien y llanam^{te} //

/f.54/ le sirven e para que se animen a hazerlo los que son fieles y leales a su real servicio e por aver yo prometido en su real nombre prometido por bandos publicos quando mande publicar la dha guerra que qualquier español que prendiese al Ynga se le darian mill pesos de renta por dos vidas en yndios vacos por ende atento a lo suso dho e por constarme ser verdad e por la informacion que a pedimento del dho capitan yo la mande tomar al dotor Graviel [*sic*] de Loarte alcalde de corte de su mag^{d} y en pago de lo bien que en la dha guerra e conquista e poblacion dela ciudad de San Francisco de la Vitoria el dho capitan a servido con tanto riesgo e peligro de su persona e gasto de su hazienda sin aver sido ayudado de la caxa real e por que su majestad por particular comision me mandava que diese a Titu Cusi Ynga que en la dha provincia de Vilcabamba estava alguna cantidad de p^{o}s de oro para que se consiguiese el allanamiento de aquella provincia en servi^{o} de Dios e de su majestad e que lo que ansy le diese prefiriese a qualesquier cedulas e mercedes que su majestad tuviese mandadas hazer en este reyno e porque con la dha guerra e servicio particular que el dho Martin Garcia de Loyola en ella hizo a su majestad se consiguio el dho allanamiento con mayor aumento //

/f.54v/ y seguridad para el servicio de dios e suyo e las demas causas suso dhas e acordado e tengo or bien en cumplimiento de la promesa que mande hazer antes de la dha guerra para este efeto e jornada de hazer mrd al dho capitan Martin Garcia de Loyola en nombre de su majestad e por birtud de los poderese comisiones que de su majestad tengo que por su notoriedad no van aqui insertas de le encomendar como por la presente le encomiendo los primeros yndios que en estas provincias y reyno del Piru vacaren por dos vidas segun y como su majestad lo tiene permitido con myll e quinientos pesos de plata ensayada e marcada de renta en cada un año por las dhas dos vidas libres de diezmo e doctrina sin embargo de otras qualesquier cedulas e provisiones que de su majestad estan dadas en el entretanto que su majestad no le haze mayor mrd en estos reynos fuera dellos respecto de los dhos sus servicios e de lo que las informaciones de ellos le constara que merecen e mando que esta mrd se cumpla e anteceda a todos como su majestad queria e mandaba se hiziese para el allanamiento de la dha provincia con el dho Tito Cusi e por todas las dichas causas le balga al dho Martin Garcia de Loyola esta mrd aunque sea por muerte mia e quealesquiera justicias le pueda meter e meta //

/f.55/ en la posesion de los dhos indios con los dhos myll e quinientos p^{o}s de renta sobre ellos sin embargo de las provisiones que por estan dadas ynsertas otras de su majestad para que ninguna justicia pueda meter en poss^{on} de indios a ninguna persona sin mi horden e poder que yo para este efeto se le doy quedando en su fuerça y vigor la dha provision para los demas e ansi dadas e amparado y defendido en la dha posesion de la qual mando que no sea desposeýdo sin ser primero oydo e vencido conforme a derecho e que de la demasia de lo montaren los tributos de los dhos yndios que ansi vacaren pagados los dhos mill e quinientos p^{o}s ensayados como dho es en cada un año por las dhas dos vidas se pague diezmo e dotrina e lo demas quede en vacaçion para proverlos a quien paresciere que mas convenga los quales dichos yndios con los dhos myll e quinientos p^{o}s de renta el dho capitan Loyola los tenga goze e posea por todos los dias de su vida e despues subceda en ellos su hijo o hija my^{or} legitimos e no los aviendo su legitima mujer conforme a las cedulas e provisiones que su majestad tiene dadas çerca de la subcesion de los yndios e con tanto que no lleve a los dhos yndios mas tributos de los dhos myll e quinientos p^{o}s so las penas contenidas //

/f.55v/ en las cedulas y provisiones de su mag^{d} que sobre ello disponen en las quales incurra lo contrario haziendo demas que se cobrara la tal demasia de su persona e bienes con todo rigor e con que trate bien a los dhos yndios e los haga doctrinar en las cosas de nuestra santa fee catholica ley natural e buena pulicia y si en ello algun descuydo tuviere cargue sobre su conciencia y no sobre la de su majestad ni mia a que en su real nombre se los encomiendo e la dha doctrina a de ser en que yo o los visorreyes e governadores qye por tpo fueren señalaremos comparecer del horden^{o} que se deve dar a los dhos yndios la qual sea de pagar de lo que mas rentare el dho repartimiento con que no se sirva de ningun servicio personal en su casa obras haziendas ni granjerias que tuviere por si ny por ynterpositas [*sic*] personas ni comutar ninguna cosa de las que tuviere obligados a dar conforme a la tasa por servicio personal ny por otra cosa rescibiendo sus tributos en las mysmas cosas en que estuvieren tasados conforme a lo por su majestad proveydo proveydo [*sic*] e hordenado e con que no pueda tener ni tenga con los dhos yndios tratos ny granjerias ni consienta que los tengan los frayles ny clerigos que //

/f.56/ los dotrinaren y que sea obligado a defenderlos e ampararlos que no sean apremyados ni agraviados de sus caciques ni curacas so pena que por cada vez que quebrantare qualquiera de las dhas condiciones por la primera pierda los tributos de un año demas de la satisfacion de la parte e por la segunda de dos años e por la tercera de privacion de la dha encomienda e con que por razon del dho feudo de mas de la oblig^{on} que tiene de servir a su majestad como a su rey y señor natural le sera fiel y leal e a los reyes subcesores de la corona de

Castilla e Leon señores destos reynos e acudira siempre a su real servicio y boz e a sus visorreyes e governadores justicias mayores e menores que agora son en nombre de su majestad en estos reynos cada que fuere menester e cumplirla su real servicio llamado o no llamado e se metera devajo del estandarte y enseña real con su familia armas y cavallos e peleara por el real servicio de su majestad en defensa destos reynos contra todos los hombres del mundo a su costa y si uviere en esta tierra guerras bullicios o levantamientos en qualquier manera que venga a su noticia la pratica e trato dellos avisara a los visorreyes e governadores //
/f.56v/ y otras justicias por su persona de palabra e por cartas e con el nombre e apellido de su majestad defendera e amparara la justicia e pendon real so pena de caer en mal caso y en aquellas penas en que caen e yncurren los hijosdalgo que no guardan la fee y omenaje que deven e prometen a sus reyes e señores naturales lo qual a de jurar de guardar e cumplir ansy ante my e porque respecto del servicio que hizo merece de mi gratificacion que al presente esta casado con mujer que tenia yndios en la ciudad del Cuzco si los yndios que se le encomiendan con los dhos myll e quinientos p^{o}s por dos vidas no fueren en terminos de la dha ciudad del Cuzco sino de otra ciudad mando que no sea obligado a residir ni hazer vezindad sino en una de las dichas dos partes qual mas quisiere y en ella todas las vezes que por el virrey governador e justicias os fuere mandado hazer reseña o alarde saldreys a ello y no le ausentareys de la dha ciudad sin licencia del dho visorrey e gobernador e que si salieredes del por el tiempo que estuviere del ausente se le poner e ponga por el dho visorrey e governador persona que por vos asista en la dha ciudad y acuda a las cosas questays obligado señalandole el salario que mereciere //
/f.57/ e paresciere que conviene de los reditos de la dha encomienda e los unos ny los otros no dexeis de lo ansi cumplir por alg^{a} manera so pena de cada myll p^{o}s de oro para la camara de su majestad. Dada en la villa Ymperial de Potosi a diez dias del mes de febrero de myll e quinientos y setenta y tres años. don Fran^{co} de Toledo por mandado de su Exc^{a} Albaro Ruiz de Navamuel.

El qual treslado fue correg^{do} y concertado con el dho registro original que queda en mi poder a que me refiero y para que dello conste di el presente testimonio que es fecho en los Reyes a diez y ocho dias del mes de abril de mill e qui^{o}s y ochenta y seis años siendo testigos a lo ver corregir Diego Fernandez Aceituno y Diego de Norena y Antonio Peña residentes en esta corte. Va tachado /a pagar/ contratos.

Por ende fize aqui este mi signo ques a tal en testimonio de verdad.

Melchor Perez de Maridueña. (rubrica)

Tiene ocho fojas con esta di^{o}s tres pesos y medio.

/f.57v/ /en blanco/

/f.58/ Muy P^{o} Señor

Responde a las peticiones otro si pone demanda otro si pide compulsorio.

El Lldo Alvaro de Caravajal vro fiscal en la causa que segunda vez trata Martin Garcia de Loyola e doña Beatriz Coya su mujer sobre los yndios yanaconas con vro real fisco. Respondi^{en}do a tres peticiones e testimonios con ellas presentados por la parte contraria digo que demas de que no son autenticos ni hazen fee ny aprovechan para el negocio. En quanto al titulo de mrd de los dhos repartimientos fecho por el Marques de Cañete vro visorrey del mismo consta e paresce que es ninguno porque dize que le hare mrd de los repartimientos a Sayre Topa Mango Capa Yupangui Ynga padre de la dha doña Beatriz para si e para sus subcesores perpetuamente para que en el subcedan por via de mayorazgo como subçeden en vros reynos de España lo qual es cosa clara e notoria que no pudo hazer el dho marques ny nyngun visorrey destos reynos a tenido tal poder ni aun tal a hecho porque enagenar los bienes de vra real corona lo qual ny aun vra real persona es servido de hazer y el poder questa ynserto en el mismo titulo no es para esto ni a ello se puede estender.

Yten. El titulo o encomienda de don Fran^{co} de T^{do} vro visorrey que fue que presenta de myll e qui^{o}s p^{o}s es ansymismo ninguno porque en el dize que es encomienda los primeros yndios que vacaren que renten hasta en la dha cantidad lo qual no pudo hazer el dho visorrey porque no puede dar espectativas para lo que no a vacado y solamente puede encomendar lo questa vaco como expresamente los poderes lo dizen de mas de que si el dho Martin Garcia de Loyola //
/f.58v/ estava casado con la dha doña Beatriz no se le pudo hazer la dha encomienda pues poseya otra y si fue antes hecha al tpo que se caso avia de elegir la que queria lo qual protesto digo yn perjuizio de lo que tengo alegado en el capitulo antes deste sobre que no tiene titulo ni derecho al repartimiento que fue dado a Sayre Topa.

A V. alt^{a} pido y sup^{co} sin embargo de los dhos testimonios haga segun que por partes de vro real fisco esta pedido e justizia la qual pido y el real favor imploro.

Otro si digo que por la via que mejor de derecho aya lugar por via de nueva conbencion o reconvencion pongo demanda a los dhos Martin Garcia de Loyola e doña Beatriz su mujer y digo que los suso dhos detentan y poseen ynjustamente los dhos repartimientos de Yucay e Xaquixaguana Guallaquipa y Pucara que son en los terminos de la ciudad del Cuzco y sin tener titulo legitimo para ello porque como esta dho y consta del instrumento que presentado tienen el titulo que dizen le dio el Marques de Cañete es ninguno notoriamente y contra todo derecho de vras reales leyes como dado por quien no tubo facultad ny poder alguno para lo dar y asi los dhos repartimi^{o}s e yn^{o}s son e pertenecen a vra real corona con todos los reditos y frutos que an rentado.

A Vra Alt^{a} pido y sup^{co} que avida esta mi relacion por bastante e la p^{te} que baste condene a los dhos Martin Garcia de Loyola e doña Beatriz su mujer a que buelban e restituyan a vra alteza los dhos repartimientos con todos los frutos reditos e tributos que an dado rentado y podido dar e rentar dende que los suso dhos y cada uno de ellos y el dho Sayre Topa su padre los detentan //
/f.59/ e ynjustamente poseen y an llevado y podido llevar y llebaren hasta la real entrega e restitucion lo qual se liquidara en la prosecucion desta causa e por las tasas que dellos estan hechas y si otro mas e mejor pedimi^{o} es necesario hazer lo hago y pido justicia y costas y el real favor ymploro.

Otro si digo que al derecho de vro real fisco conviene se me de un traslado autorizado de la mrd que don Fran^{co} de Toledo hizo al dho Martin Garcia de Loyola de la situacion de myll e qui^{o}s p^{o}s en cumplimi^{to} del titulo que presenta en esta causa.

A Vra Alt^{a} pido y sup^{co} mande al escriv^{o} de govierno me de el dho traslado e testimonio de lo que sobre esto ay e parece por los libros de governacion e pido just^{a}

Ll^{do} Alv^{o} de Caravajal (rubrica)

En la ciudad de los Reyes en v^{te} dias del mes de junio de mill y qui^{o}s y ochenta e seys a^{o}s estando los señores presidente e oydores desta Real Aud^{a} estando en aud^{a} pu^{ca} se presento esta pet^{on}.

E por los dhos señores vista mandaron dar ttr^{do} a la otra parte y que se de el compulsorio que pide. Presente Juan Sanchez de los Rios procurador a quien se notifico.

Montoya (rubrica)

/f.59v/ /en blanco/

/f.60/ Muy P^{o} Señor

El Ll^{do} Albaro de Caravajal vro fyscal en la causa que seg^{da} vez trata Martin Garcia de Loyola e doña Beatriz Coya su mujer sobre los yndios yanaconas con vro real fisco la qual estava ya remytida y enviada a vro real consejo de Yn^{a}s digo que por otras e pedido e suplicado se cosa este seg^{do} proceso con el primero pues es todo uno o en defeto desto se acomule a el o en defeto de los uno o de lo otro se me de un traslado autorizado de todo el dho proceso en forma sacado con citacion de la parte contraria para lo presentar en este y aunque se a dado traslado a la otra parte y no lo a contradho no sea proveydo aunque devieron los autos y porque en el dho proceso esra el derecho de vro real fisco y el fundamento del y como digo este y el otro es todo una misma cosa y ansi conviene al derecho de vro real fisco se haga lo que pedido tengo.

A V. Al^{a} pido y sup^{co} lo haga y provea asy como pedido tengo y si es necesario lo buelvo a pedir y digo que lo que en el dho proceso tengo alegado alego agora de nuevo y todo lo en el presentado presento en este y pido just^{a} y costas y el real favor imploro.

Ll^{do} Alv^{o} de Caravajal (rubrica).

/f.60v/ En la ciudad de los Reyes en v^{te} dias del mes de junio de mil y qui^{o}s y ochenta e seis a^{o}s estando los señores presidente e oydores desta Real Audiencia estando en aud^{a} Pu^{ca} se presento esta peticion.

E por los dhos señores vista mandaron llevar estos autos a la saca para proveer.

Montoya.

/f.61/ Muy P^{o} S^{r}

Joan Sanchez de los Rios digo que del secretario Juan de Montoya me notifico del pedimento e dem^{da} que vro fiscal presento contra el cap^{t} Martin Garcia de Loyola sobre unos yndios yanaconas y esto se a de notificar en España al dho Martin Garcia de Loyola por el nuevo pedimento.

A V. Al^{a} sup^{co} m^{de} se notifique en persona el dho pedimento e demanda al dho Martin Garcia de Loyola questa en Guamanga. Etc.

Joan Sanchez (rubrica)

/f.61v/ En la ciudad de los Reyes en veinte y siete dias del mes de junio de mill y qui^{o}s y ochenta y seis años ante los ss^{es} pre^{e} y oydores desta Real Aud^{a} estando en audi^{a} publica se presento esta peticion.

E por los dhos señores vista mandaron dar ttr^{o} al fiscal de su mag^{d} al qual testado estando pres^{te} se le notifico /no bala/

Montoya

El ll[do] Caravajal vro fiscal respondiendo a esta peticion digo es a lugar de se hazer lo que pide y pido lo pedido y justicia.

Que se leuo 12 fs q sy /ilegible/ y se acomulen ambos pleitos.

Autos

En 16 de agosto

En la ciudad de los Reyes en treynta e un dias del mes de junio de mill y quinientos y ochenta y seis años estando los señores presidente e oydores desta real audiencia en aud[a] publica se pres[to] esta p[on] porl el fiscal de su mag[d]

E por los dhos señores vista mandaron llevar los autos a la sala para proveer.

Jhoan de Montoya (rubrica)

Ba restado estando presente se le notifico.

/f.62/ En la causa del comendador Martin Garcia de Loyola por si y como conjunta persona de doña Beatriz Coya su mujer con el licenciado Alvaro de Caravajal fiscal de su mag[d] sobre los yndios yanaconas que don Fran[co] de Toledo visorrey que fue destos reynos mando poner en la corona real en los terminos de la ciudad del Cuzco en el articulo de la acomulacion pedida por el dicho fiscal del pleyto biejo questa remitido a los reynos de España con este y sobre si se a de notificar en persona la nueva dem[da] que el dho fiscal pone al dho comendador Martin Garcia de Loyola de los repartimi[o]s de yndios de Yucay y Jaquijaguana

En la ciudad de los Reyes en diez y seis dias del mes de agosto de mill y quinientos y ochenta y seis años los señores presidente e oidores desta Real Audiencia vista la dha causa en los dhos articulos mandaron que el pleyto que se remitio a los reynos de España que el dho fiscal pide se acomulen con este atento al consentimy[o] que dello haze el dho Martin Garcia de Loyola y que la demanda y reconvencion nuevamente puesta en esta causa por el dho fiscal al dho Martin Garcia de Loyola sobre los dhos repartimi[o]s de yndios se notifique en persona al dho Martin Garcia de Loyola y doña Beatriz Coya su mujer y para ello se de enplazamiento al dho fiscal y ansi proveyeron e rubricaron.

/f.62v/ Pronunciose este auto ante los señores presidente e oydores desta Real Audiencia el dho dia mes y año en el contenido.

Jhoan de Montoya

En diez y nueve dias del mes de agosto de mill y quinientos y ochenta y seis a[o]s yo el presente secretario de camara notifique el auto de atras proveydo por los señores pr[e] e oydores desta real au[a] al licenciado Alvaro de Caravajal fiscal de su mag[d] en su persona y dello doy fee.

Jhoan de Montoya

En los Reyes el dho dia mes y año yo el dho secretario de camara notifique el dho auto de atras proveido por los señores pr[e] e oydores a Joan Sanchez de los Rios como a procurador del comendador Martin Garcia de Loyola e dello doy fee.

Jhoan de Montoya

/f.63/ Muy P[o] S[or]

Jhoan Sanchez de los Rios en nombre de Martin Garcia de Loyola y de doña Beatriz Coya su mujer en la causa con vuestro fiscal sobre los yanaconas que les quitaron respondiendo a la peticion ultima del licenciado Albaro de Caravajal vuestro fiscal en que en efeto dize que mis partes poseen los repartimi[o]s que tienen de qual vuestro real nombre les hizo merced en marques de Cañete sin titulo bastante porque el Marques de Cañete no tubo poder para se los encomendar perpetuos e por bia de mayorazgos y la situacion de los mill e qui[o]s p[o]s que mi parte tiene dijo que no la puede tener por que se le dio antes que bacase y que es a que la tubiera baco por tener los dhos yndios e aver de escoger uno de los repartimi[o]s pide se le quiten con los tributos que a llevado por via de reconvencion segun mas largamente en la dha peticion se contiene con su thenor repetido digo que V. Alt[a] no la deve admitir ni dar lugar a semejantes peticiones ni conbiene a vuestro real servi[o] que dello se trate por lo general que he aqui por espreso.

Porque siendo como la dha mrd es hecha a decendiente de los Yngas que es notorio y vuestra real persona lo tiene muchas bezes dho e confesado por muchas cedulas y provisiones que fueron señores destos reinos e como a tales les ofrecio e sus gobernadores muy mayores mercedes e mando que se les hiciesen no se deva de admitir ni tratar de les quitar lo poco que tienen.

Y porque aunque esto no hubiera ni vuestra real persona hubiera mandado hazerles las dhas mrdes ni el dho Marques de Cañete que se las hizo tubiera poder para ello estando como estavan de guerra y para efeto de que cesase qualquiera cap[on] tenia de dr[o] poder para ofrecer y dar lo que el dho vuestro visorrey dio para que la guerra cesase y vuestra real pers[a] fue y es obligado a lo cumplir

Va enmendado de que en lo.

/f.63v/ En quanto a la encomienda que a mi parte hizo don Fran^{co} de Toledo por lo que sirvio en Bilcapampa la pudo muy bien hazer de lo que no estubiese baco pues la hizo por justa causa y notoria aunque verdaderam^{te} fuera encomienda que no fue pues no señalo repartimi^{o} y el que puede dar puede prometer que es menos en especial con tan justa causa y lo que el fiscal dize pudiera aver lugar quando encomendaria particularm^{te} los yndios que otro tenia por el peligro de procurarle la muerte y lo uno y lo otro no ha lugar en este caso por que mi parte no el encomienda sino situacion la qual no esta proybida tener con repartimi^{o} ni esta obligado el que la tiene a elegir quando se casa con mujer que tenga encomienda en especial que como esta dho la que la dha doña Beatriz Coya tiene no es encomienda que se acava sino mayorazgo perpetuo.

Por lo que pido e supp^{co} a V Al^{a} declare no aver lugar lo en contrario pedido e m^{de} que mi parte e sus subcesores sean amparados en la posesion de las dhas mercedes que tiene y hazer en la causa principal segun que tengo pedido sobre que pido justicia e para ello es.

El ll^{do} Falcon (rubrica) Jhoan Sanchez (rubrica)

En la ciudad de los Reyes en catorce dias del mes de nobiembre de mill y qui^{o}s y ochenta y seis años. ante los s^{e}s pr^{e} e oydores desta real audi^{a} estando en audi^{a} publica se presento esta peticion

E por los dhos señores vista mandaron dar ttr^{do} a la otra parte y que para la primera audiencia y estando presente el fiscal de su mag^{d} a quien se notif^{co}

/f.64/ Muy P^{o} Señor

Respuesta

El ll^{do} Alvaro de Caravajal vro fiscal en la causa con Martin Garcia de Loyola e doña Beatriz de Mendoça su mujer sobre los yanaconas y reconvencion y demanda que tengo puesta respondiendo a la respuesta por su parte dada cerca de la dha reconvencion digo que sin embargo della y afirmandome en lo que dho tengo concluyo.

A Vra Al^{a} pido y sup^{co} aya la causa por conclusa e pido justicia y costas y el real oficio imploro

LL^{do} Alv^{o} de Caravajal (rubrica)

En la ciudad de los Reyes en diez y ocho dias del mes de nobienbre de mill y qui^{o}s y ochenta y seis a^{o}s ante los señores presidente y oydores desta real aud^{a} en aud^{a} publica se presento esta peticion.

E por los dhos señores vista hubieron esta causa por conclusa en forma e mandaron llevarlos ante el procurador Joan Sanchez de los Rios procurador contrario a quien se notifico.

Montoya

/f.64v/ El auto hordi^{o} s^{e} todo y corrala por el desde agora. En 21 de nob^{re} de 1586 a^{o}s.

/f.65/ Otra vez se recibe apru^{a} sobre la reconvencion

En la causa de la nueva demanda y reconvencion puesta por el licenciado Alvaro de Caravajal fiscal de su mag^{d} al comendador Martin Garcia de Loyola y doña Beatriz Coya su mujer en el pleito y causa que se trata entre las dhas partes sobre los indios yanaconas que don Fran^{co} de Toledo visorrey que fue destos reynos mando poner en la corona real en los terminos de la ciudad del Cuzco y la dha nueva demanda del dho fiscal sobre la posesion de los repartimientos de yndios de Yucay e Jaquixaguana Guallaquipa y Pucara en los terminos de la dha ciudad del Cuzco.

En la ciudad de los Reyes en veinte y un dias del mes de noviembre de myll y quinientos y ochenta y seis años los señores presidente e oydores desta real audiencia vista la causa en provision mandaron que las dichas partes dentro de noventa dias primeros siguientes digan y aleguen y prueven lo que les convenga y presenten las escrituras y recaudos y testigos y provanças que a su derecho conbenga con que no presenten mas de hasta doze testigos y se les aperabe [*sic*] que con lo que en el dho termino hubieren alegado y provado remitiran la dha causa a su mag^{d} en su real consejo de las Yndias conforme a la provision real dada en Malinas y declaraciones della que trata acerca del conocimiento de las causas sobre repartimientos de yndios y mandaron citar las dhas partes en forma para sus provanças con que el dho termino de los dhos noventa dias se entiendan ansimismo en la causa que tratan los suso dhos sobre los dhos yanaconas el qual corra y comience a correr desde oy dia y ansi lo proveyeron e rubricaron.

Pronunciose este auto ante los ss pre^{e} e oydores desta real audiencia el dho dia mes y año en el contenido. Presentes el licen^{do} Alv^{o} de Caravajal y Ju^{o} Sanchez de los Rios a quienes se notifico.

Jhoan de Montoya (rubrica)

/f.65v/ Notificacion. En la ciudad de los Reyes del Piru en veinte y un dias del mes de noviembre de mill y quinientos y ochenta y seis años yo Joan de Montoya escriv^{o} de camara de su mag^{d} catolica notifique este auto e lo proveido al licenciado Alvaro de Caravajal fiscal de su mag^{d} en su persona el qual dixo que lo oya siendo testigos el s^{or} Molina y el relator Viscarra e yo que de le doy fee.

Jhoan de Montoya

Notificacion. En los Reyes el dho dia mes y año arriba dho yo el dho escrivano de camara notifique este auto y lo en el proveydo por los señores presidente e oydores desta real audiencia a Joan Sanchez de los Rios como a procurador de el comendador Martin Garcia de Loyola el qual dijo que lo oya t^{os} los suso dhos.

Jhoan de Montoya

Ban restados los tres renglones de arriba.

/f.66/ Poder de Martin Garcia de Loyola y doña Beatriz Coya su mujer.

En la villa de Oropesa en catorce dias del mes de diziembre de mill y quinientos y ochenta y seis a^{o}s ante mi el escri^{o} e t^{os} los muy ilustres s^{e}s Martin Garcia de Loyola cavallero del abito de Calatrava y corregidor desta villa y doña Beatriz Coya su mujer con licencia y autoridad y consentimi^{o} que la dha s^{ra} doña Beatriz pidio y demando al dho señor comendador y correg^{or} y el se la dio y concedio para hazer y otorgar esta escrip^{a} y poder y usando della ambos a dos dixeron y otorgaron que daban y dieron su poder cumplido bastante qual conbenga y sea neces^{o} a Juan Sanchez de los Rios y Miguel Ruiz y Ju^{o} de Sant Elias procuradores de causas de la real audi^{a} de los Reyes a todos tres juntos mancomunado y a cada uno dellos por si ynsolidun y con que lo que el uno començase lo pueda el otro o los otros mediar y acavar y con ratificacion y aprobacion de qualesquiera autos y peticiones y otras dilige^{as} que en su nom^{e} ayan fecho dado y presentado los quales aprueban y aprobaron y ratifican y los dan por firmes y valederas y les dan y otorgan este poder a los suso dhos ynsolidum para que en qualesquier pleitos y demandas que los tenga puesto el fiscal de su mag^{d} sobre qualesquier casos y cosas y en otros qualesquier causas y pleitos que les toquen y lo a ello anexo y consequentemente puedan los suso dhos o qualquier dellos parescer y parescan ante qualesquier juezes y justi^{a}s de su mag^{d} y hazer y poner y presentar qualesquier demandas y reconvenciones y pedim^{o}s requerimi^{o}s citaciones protestaciones emplazamientos y presentar t^{o}s y provanças escriptos y escripturas y otro genero de prueva y pedir y sacar de poder de qualesquier secretarios escrivanos y otras pers^{a}s qualesquier escripturas testim^{o}s y otros recaudos y usar dellos y les //
/f.66v/ presentar donde conbengan y fazer juramentos de calunia y desagravio y recusar juezes y escrivanos y letrados y dar las causas de las recusaciones siendo neces^{o} y las provar y averiguar pedir y oir qualesquier sentencia o sentencias y las que fueren en su favor consentir y de las que fueren en su favor consentir y de las en contr^{o} apelar y suplicar y seguir la tal apelas^{on} y supp^{on} donde conbenga en todos los grados e instancias y tachar y contradecir todo lo fecho y que rehazer de contr^{o} y en efecto puedan fazer y fagan en todos sus pleitos y causas que tienen y tubiesen en qualesquier manera los demas autos y dilig^{as} conbenientes en su ayuda y defensa que tal poder qual para ello es neces^{o} y dieron y otorgaron a los dhos Ju^{o} S^{e}s de los Rios y Miguel Ruiz y Ju^{o} de Sant Elias y a cada uno ynsolidum con sus incidencias y anexidades y los relevaron en forma de dr^{o} y a la firmeça y cumplimi^{o} oblig^{on} sus personas y bienes avidos y por aver y lo firmaron de sus nombres a quien yo el presente escriv^{o} doy fee que conozco siendo presentes por tg^{os} Fran^{co} de Yrrarazabal y Ju^{o} Mz Descorca y Alonso de Tobar estantes en esta villa. Martin Garcia de Loyola Coya doña Beatriz. Ante mi Fran^{co} de Bascones escriv^{o} publico.

Ba fuera del margen La Coya.

Yo Fran^{co} de Bascones escriv^{o} de su mag^{t} y pu^{co} desta villa de Oropesa lo fize escribir y fize mi signo en testimonio de verdad.

Fran^{co} de Bascones
Escriv^{o} Pu^{co}

/f.67/

Muy P^{o} S^{or}

Acusar a la citatoria

El l^{do} Albaro de Caravajal vro fiscal en la causa con Martin Garcia de Loyola e doña Beatriz su mujer sobre la demanda que les tengo puesta hago presentacion desta citacion en cit^{on} hecha a los suso dhos en sus personas.

A Vra Al^{a} pido y sup^{co} la mande poner en la causa y si es necesario le acuso la rebeldia y pido justicia y costas y el real efecto imploro.

En la ciudad de los Reyes en veinte e siete dias del mes de henero de mil y quinientos y ochenta y siete años ante los señores presidente e oydores desta real audiencia estando en audiencia publica se presento esta peticion

E por los dhos señores vista mandaron dar tr^{do} a la otra parte y que para la primera audiencia responda y que se ponga citatoria en el proceso.

Montoya

/f.67v/ /en blanco/

/f.68/ El Licen^{do} Ramos de Cartagena (rubrica) El D^{or} Arteaga (rubrica) J^{o} H^{o} Criado de Castilla

Montoya Sn^{o} fiscal (rubrica)

Enplazamiento por nueva demanda en forma de pedimento del fiscal de su mag^{d} contra el capitan Martin Garcia de Loyola.

Con^{de} (rubrica)

/f.68v/ DON PHELIPE POR la gracia de dios Rey de Castilla de Leon de Aragon de las dos Cicilias de Jherusalem de Portugal de Navarra de Granada de Toledo de Valencia de Algeria de Gibraltar de las Islas de Canaria de las Yndias Orientales y Occidentales islas y tierra firme de mar oceano archiduque de Borgoña Bravante y Milan conde de Abepurgo y de Barcelona señor de Vizcaya de Molina etc a vos el capitan Martin Garcia de Loyola cavallero de la horden de Calatrava y doña Beatriz Coya vra mujer y a cada uno de vos salud y gracia bien saveis el pleito y causa que en la dha audiencia esta pendiente entre el licenciado Alvaro de Caravajal nro procurador fiscal en la nra corte y chancilleria ante el presidente e oydores de la nra audiencia que por nro mandado esta y reside en la ciudad de los Reyes del Piru de la una parte con vos el dicho Martin Garcia de Loyola y la dicha vra mujer de la otra sobre los yn^{o}s yanaconas que se pusieron en nra real corona en la ciudad del Cuzco y su jurisdiccion a que pretendeys tener derecho y sobre las demas causas y razones en el proceso del dho pleyto contenidas en el qual dicho pleyto el dicho licenciado Alvaro de Caravajal nro fiscal por un capitulo de una peticion que presento o expuso una demanda del tenor siguiente: Otro si digo que por la via que mejor de derecho aya lugar por via de nueva conbencion o reconbencion pongo demanda a los dichos Martin Garcia de Loyola y doña Beatriz su mujer digo que los suso dhos detentan y poseen injustamente los dichos repartimi^{o}s de Yucay y Xaquixaguana Guallaquipa y Pucara que son en los terminos de la ciudad del Cuzco y sin tener titulo legitimo para ello porque como esta dicho y consta del testimonio que presentado tiene el titulo que dicen le dio el Marques de Cañete es ninguno notoriamente y contra todo derecho de vras reales leyes como dado por quien no tubo facultad ni poder alguno para lo dar y ansi los dhos reparti^{o}s e yn^{o}s son y pertenecen a vra real corona con todos los reditos y frutos que an rentado a vra Al^{a} pido y supp^{co} que avida esta mi relacion y por bastante o la parte que baste condene a los dhos Martin Garcia de Loyola y doña Beatriz su mujer a que buelvan y restituyan a V. Al^{a} los dichos repartimi^{o}s con todos los frutos reditos y tributos que an dado rentado y podido dar y rentar dende que los suso dhos y cada uno dellos y el dho Sayre Topa su padre los detentan ynjustamente poseyan llevado y pido llevar y llevaren hasta la real reparticion lo qual se liquidara en la prosecucion desta causa e por las tasas que dellos estan hechas y si otro mas o mejor pedimi^{o} es neces^{o}s hazer lo hago y pido justicia y costas y el real oficio imploro. Otro si digo que al dr^{o} de vro real fisco conviene se me de un traslado autorizado de la mrd que don Fran^{co} de Toledo hizo al dicho Martin Garcia de Loyola de la situacion de mill y quinientos p^{o}s en cumplimiento del titulo que presenta en esta causa. A Vra Al^{a} pido y suplico mande al escriv^{o} de governacion y pido justicia. El licenciado Alvaro de Caravajal. Y presentada la dha peticion y demanda y por los dhos nro presidente e oydores vista por autos de vista y revista se mando que la dha peticion y demanda se notificase en vras personas y por los dhos nro presidente e oydores fue acordado que deviamos mandar dar esta nra carta para vos en la dha razon y nos tuvimos por bien porque vos mandamos que del dia que vos fuere leyda y notificada en vras personas y pudiendo ser avidos y sino ante las casas de vras moradas //
/f.69/ diciendolo o haziendolo saber a alguno o algunos de vros criados e vecinos mas cercanos para que os lo digan e hagan saver por manera que venga a vra noticia y dello no podays pretender ignorancia hasta treinta dias primeros siguientes bengays o envieis a la dha nra audiencia antes los dhos nro presidente e oidores della a tomar copia y traslado de la dha demanda y a ponerse contra ella vras exenciones y defensiones y a dezir y alegar lo que dezir y alegar quisieredes que si binieredes o enviaredes segun dho es los dhos nro pr^{e} e oydores vos e yran e guardaran en todo vro derecho e justi^{a} en otra manera en vra ausencia y rebeldia avida por presencia haran y determinaran en el dho pleyto y causa lo que hallaren por justicia sin os mas citar ni llamar sobre ello que nos por la presente vos citamos llamamos y enplazamos perentoriamente y os señalamos los estrados de la dha nra audiencia donde os seran fechos y notificados los dhos autos y os pararan el perjuizio que de derecho hubiere lugar y mandamos a qualquier escriv^{o} publico o al que para ello fuere llamado que de al que vos mostrare testimonio signado con su si/g/no por que nos sepamos en como se cumple nro mandado. Dada en los Reyes a diez y nueve dias del mes de nobr^{e} de myll y qui^{o}s y ochenta y seis años.

E yo Juan de Montoya scr^{o} de cam^{a} de su Mt Catholica la fize escribir por su m^{do} con acuerdo del su pr^{e} e oydores.

Joan de Sagastigueta (rubrica) Chanciller Ju^{o} de Aliaga (rubrica)

/f.69v/ Yo Juan de Montoya escriv^{o} de cam^{a} desta Real audiencia que por m^{do} de su mag^{d} reside en esta ciudad de los Reyes del Piru doy fee que el pleyto y causa conteni^{do} en esta p^{on} dada de su mag^{d} y entre la presente que en ella se declara esta recivido a prueva con ter^{no} de noventa dias pasado siguienes y corren y se quentan desde veynte y un dias del mes de n^{e} deste presente año de qui^{o}s y ochenta seys a^{o}s y para que dello conste del pedime^{to} del lic^{do} Alvaro de Caravajal fiscal de su mag^{d} di el presente en la ciudad de los Reyes a tres de diciembre de mill e qui^{o}s y ochenta y seis a^{o}s

Jhoan de Montoya (rubrica)

En la villa de Oropesa a veinte y nueve dias del mes de diziembre de mill y qui^{o}s y ochenta y seis a^{o}s yo el presente escriv^{o} de su mag^{d} e pu^{co} desta dha villa ley e notifique esta provision real como en ella se contiene a los muy ilustres s^{e}s Martin Garcia de Loyola cavallero del avito de Calatrava y la Coya doña Beatriz su mujer en sus personas e sus mds dijeron que lo oyan testigos Juan de Villegas e Xpoval de Hern^{des}

Fran^{co} de Bascones
Scriv^{o} Pu^{co}

/f.70/ Muy P^{o} S^{or}

Representa los ynterr^{o}s y provanças en esta causa

Jhoan Sanchez de los Rios en n^{e} del capitan Martin Garcia de Loyola y doña Beatriz Clara Coya su mujer en la causa con vro fiscal sobre los yanaconas y lo demas en el articulo de la reconvencion e nueva demanda que vro fiscal puso a mi pte hago presentacion de las escrituras e provanças hechas en esta causa por mi pte y presentadas y del ynterrogatorio por mi parte presentado y pa hazer mas probança

Pido e sup^{co} a V. Al^{a} me mande dar receptoria en persona ynsertas en ellas el dho ynterrogatorio con citacion de vro fiscal e pa ello es.

Otro sy sup^{co} a V. Al^{a} mande que por ques esta causa es de tanta cantidad e calidad e las provanças se an de hazer en todas las partes deste reyno que el ter^{no} de los nov^{ta} dias //
/f.70v/ se prorrogue por otros tres meses mas e pa ello esl juro a Dios en forma que no la pido de malicia.

El lldo Falcon (rubrica) Jhoan Sanchez (rubrica)

En la ciudad de los Reyes en treynta dias del mes de henero de mill y quinientos y ochenta y siete años ante los señores desta real audi^{a} en aud^{a} pu^{ca} se presento esta peticion

E por los dhos señores vista le prorogaron el termino por otros tres meses mas comunes a las partes y que se le de recepetoria pres^{te} el licenciado Alvaro de Caravajal a quien se notifico. Ba restado mandaron

Jhoan de Montoya (rubrica)

/f.71/ Muy P^{o} S^{or}

Pide a cumplimiento y de los seis meses

Jhoan Sanchez de los Rios en n^{e} del cap^{t} Martin Garcia de Loyola en el pleito con vro fiscal sobre los y^{o}s e yanaconas digo que asta la fecha se recibio a prueba con el ter^{no} ordinario.

A V. Al^{a} sup^{co} se me conceda a cumplimyento de los seys meses conforme al alegato.

Joan Sanchez

En la ciudad de los Reyes en treinta dias del mes de septiembre de mill e quinientos e ochenta e siete años ante los señores presidente e oydores en audiencia publica se presento esta peticion

E por los dichos señores vista le prorrogaron eñ termino probatorio a cumplimiento a seis meses presente el licen^{do} Alvaro de Caravajal fiscal de su mag^{d} e Joan Sanchez de los Rios a quien se notifico.

Montoya

/f.71v/ /en blanco/

/f.72/ Muy P^{o} S^{or}

Pide /roto/

El L^{do} Alvaro de Caravajal vro fiscal en la causa con Martin Garcia de Loyola y doña Beatriz su mujer sobre los repartimi^{o}s de Yucay y Xaquixaguana y Guallaquipa y Pucara y la situacion de mill e qui^{o}s p^{o}s que hizo vro visorrey don Fran^{co} de T^{do} al dho Martin Garcia de Loyola e Ju^{o} Sanchez de los Rios por ellos digo que al derecho de vro fisco conviene poner en esta causa traslado autorizado de las tasas de los tributos que dan los yn^{o}s de los dhos repartimi^{o}s para averiguacion de los aprovechamientos e rentas que dellos an tenido y llebado y asimismo el traslado autorizado de la situacion y mrd que el dho visorrey don Fran^{co} de Toledo hizo al dho Martin Garcia de Loyola.

A V. Al^{a} pido y sup^{co} mande al escriv^{o} de governacion o a otro en cuyo poder estuviere me den los dhos traslados autorizados para el dho efeto con cit^{on} de la pte contraria y pido justicia y el real efecto ymploro.

El Ll^{do} Caravajal (rubrica)

En la ciudad de los Reyes en nueve dias del mes de octubre de mill y quinientos y ochenta y siete a^{o}s estando los señores presidente e oydores desta real audiencia en audiencia publica se presento esta p^{on}

E por los dichos señores vista mandaron que se le de el compulsorio que pide con citacion de la parte contr^{a} press^{te} Joan Sanchez de los Rios a quien se cito p^{a} ello.

Montoya (rubrica)

/f.72v/ /en blanco/

/f.73/ Muy P^{o} S^{or}

Que corran de los 3 meses

Jhoan Sanchez de los Rios en nombre del cap^{t} Martin Garcia de Loyola y doña Beatriz Coya su mujer en el pleito con vro fiscal sobre los yanaconas digo que esta causa se recibio a prueva con el auto hordinario y enbie a mi parte la receptoria e ynterrogatorio y se perdio en en camyno porque no a parezcido e asy a dexado de hazer la probança y se le va pasando todo el termy^{no}

A V. Al^{a} suplico se me concedan otros tres meses mas de termyno pa que hagan sus probanças e que corran desde oy e juro a dios en persona mia y de mi pte que no lo pido de malicia.

Jhoan Sanchez (rubrica)

En la ciudad de los Reyes en nueve del mes de octubre de mill y quinientos y ochenta y siete a^{o}s estando los señores presidente e oydores desta real audiencia en audiencia pu^{ca} se presento esta peticion.

E por los dhos señores vista mandaron dar ttr^{do} al fiscal de su mag^{d} al qual estando presente se le notifico.

Montoya (rubrica)

/f.73v/ /en blanco/

/f.74/ Muy P^{o} S^{or}

Respuesta contradize la prroroga del termino

El L^{do} Alvaro de Caravajal vro fiscal en la causa con Martin Garcia de Loyola e doña Beatriz su mujer sobre los repartimi^{o}s de Yucay e los demas e Ju^{o} Sanchez de los Rios por ellos respondiendo a la peticion de la parte contraria en que pide se le prorrogue el ter^{no} de los tres meses en ques fue r^{do} a prueba conforme a la de Malinas por otros tres meses mas digo que no a lugar de se hazer por que ya esta prorrogado el dho ter^{no} de tres meses y no puede aver mas de una prorrog^{on} conforme a vra real provision de mpas de que a mas de un año que se concedio.

A Vra Al^{a} pido y sup^{co} declare no aver lugar lo por la parte contraria pedido y hazer en todo segun que tengo pedido y justicia la qual y costas pido y el real efecto imploro.

Ll^{do} Alv^{o} de Caravajal (rubrica)

En los Reyes en treze de otr^{e} de mill e quin^{o}s y ochenta y siete a^{o}s estando los señores pres^{te} e oydores desta real aud^{a} en aud^{a} publica se pres^{to} esta p^{on}

E por los dhos señores vista mandaron llebar los autos a la sala para proveer.

Montoya

Restado a seys

/f.74v/ /en blanco/

/f.75/ Muy P^{o} S^{or}

Responde a la contra del fiscal y pide restitucion

Joan Sanchez de los Rios en nombre del cap^{t} Martin Garcia de Loyola e doña Beatriz Coya su mujer en el pleito con vro fiscal sobre los yndios digo que sin embargo de la contradizion de vro fiscal se me an de conceder la prorrogacion de los tres meses del ter^{no} por quanro durante el primer termino y cosas recpetorias e ynterrogatorios e los enbie al dho cap^{t} que estava en Guamanga y se perdio y dare ynform^{on} de como lo habre e por carta que escrivio el dho cap^{t} consta que no fueron los recaudos a su poder e asy se perdieron e aquy a avido legitimos ny justos y a pedimento por donde mi pte no a podido hazer su probança e al impedido no le corre termino por donde los tres meses pedidos por my peticion de nueve de Oct^{e} se me an dado por la clausula general e por la via que mejor de dr^{o} ny a lugar e juro a dios en persona e anima de mi parte que no lo pido de malicia e aunque sea ter^{no} legal se puede prorrogar e dar nuevo termy^{no} pues es termyno que se a de dar con ministerio de juez especialm^{te} e mayorm^{te} que la materia de probanças no se a de entregar sino alargar e aviendose de remityr a vro real consejo de Yndias en España corre mayor razon pa que no se me deniegue ter^{no} e por falta del perezca la justicia de mi parte y dexe de hazer sus defensas e provanças.

Pido e sup^{co} a V. Al^{a} mande que se me //

/f.75v/ concedan los dhos tres meses pedidos de nueve de Oct^{e} deste año o a lo mas que los tres meses concedidos por mi pet^{on} de treynta de set^{e} corran desde el dho dia nueve de oct^{e} que di la dha pet^{on} por la justa causa de la perdida e pido justicia.

Otro si pido que el secretario Montoya declare como saque la receptoria e ynterrogatorio y me ofresco a dar ynformacion de como se enbio y de como no lo recibio el dho mi pte no obligandome a diligencia demasiada.

/ilegible/ Fajardo Jhoan Sanchez

En los Reyes en v^{te} y siete de oct^{e} de mill e qui^{o}s y ochenta y siete a^{o}s estando los señores pres^{te} e oydores en audiencia publica se pres^{to} esta p^{on}

E por los dhos señores vista mandaron dar traslado a la otra p^{te} e para la prim^{a} aud^{a} responda e con lo que dixere uno se traigan los autos a la sala para probeer pres^{te} el licen^{do} Als^{o} de Caravajal fiscal de su mag^{t} a quien se not^{o}

Montoya

/f.76/ Muy P^{o} S^{or}

Rr^{a} a la restitucion

Joan Sanchez de los Rios en nombre del cap^{t} Martin Garcia de Loyola y doña Beatriz Coya su mujer en el pleito con vro fiscal sobre los yndios digo que del escrito que pres^{te} en que pedia e restituyan se dio traslado a vro fiscal e e se le notifico e no responde yo le acuso la rebeldia.

A V. Al^{a} pido e puvlico aya la causa porque sobre esto articulo e justicia.

Joan Sanchez

En la ciudad de los Reyes a treynta dias del mes de Oct^{e} de myll e qui^{o}s y ochenta y siete años los s^{e}s Pre^{e} e oydores desta real audi^{a} en audiencia publica se presento esta peticion.

E por los dhos señores vista mandaron llevar e auto a la sala pa proveer.

Montoya

/f.76v/ En proviss^{on} al S^{or} xii /ilegible/

Que se le notifique este auto que se le concedio a Ju^{o} Sanchez

En la ciudad de los Reyes en tres dias del mes de nobiembre de myll e qui^{o}s y ochenta y siete años los señores pr^{e} e oydores desta real audiencia a vista la dha causa.

/f.77/ En la causa del comendador Martin Garcia de Loyola y doña Beatriz Coya su mujer con el Lic^{do} Albaro de Carbajal [*sic*] sobre los /y/ anaconas que se pusieron en la corona real y reconvencion puesta por el dho fiscal de los repartimientos que tiene en encomienda en el articulo del termino que pide la pte del dho Martin Garcia de Loyola para hazer su probança y restitucion por su pte pedida.

En la ciudad de los Reyes en tres dias del mes de nobiembre de myll e qui^{o}s y ochenta y siete años los señores pr^{e} e oydores desta real audiencia vista la dha causa mandaron quel termino de los nobenta dias que se concedieron e prorrogaron conforme a la hordenança en treynta dias del mes de henero deste año de ochenta y siete a la pte del dho Martin Garcia de Loyola se notifiquen a su procurador para que le corran de oy dho dia atento a que no les tan notificados y ansi lo proveyeron e rubricaron. Ba enmendado este.

/f.77v/ Pronunciose este auto ante los señores pr^{e} e oydores desta real audiencia que en ella firmaron sus nombres estando en audi^{a} publica el dho dia mes y año en el contenido presentes el licen^{do} Alv^{o} de Caravajal fiscal de su mag^{d} y Joan Sanchez de los Rios a quien se notifico.

Jhoan de Montoya (rubrica)

/f.78/ Muy poderoso señor

Responde y que se entienda con la pr^{a}

Martin Garcia de Loyla cavallero del avito de Calatrava por mi procurador como marido y conjunta persona de la Coya doña Beatriz mi legitima mujer en el pleito con el licenciado Albaro de Carvajal vro fiscal sobre los yndios yanaconas y reconvencion del mayorazgo. Allegando mas de mi justicia digo que se a de azer en esta causa segun y como tengo pedido y suplicado por todo lo que dho y alegado tengo e aqui por repetido y por lo siguiente lo uno por lo general lo otro por que estando en posesion quieta y pacifica Mango Ynga Yupangui abuelo de la dha doña Beatriz deste reino y aviendole coronado por tal rey y tomado la borla del Ynga quera la ynsignia dello en la casa del sol de la ciudad del Cuzco con toda las solenidades cerimonias y requisitos de juramento y estando presente el sumo sacerdote y todos sus hermanos y los demas Yngas deste reino le dieron la obediencia a esta sazon entro en este reino don F^{co} Piçarro y dexo por su lugar theniente en la dha ciudad del Cuzco a Hernando Piçarro su hermano en qual demas de los malos tratamientos que le hizo que tengo alegados le hizo otros muchos asi de palabra como de hobra y obligandole que por fuerça cada domingo le diese cinco costales de oro y cinco de plata y esto duro tiempo de dos año que a justa y comun estimacion serian mas de cinco millones de pesos de oro y plata sin el resgate que de la plata que pertenecia al dho Mango Ynga le tomaron por fuerça y tiranicamente los secuazes de Atabalipa que se avia pretendido llevantar [*sic*] con este reino si les pertenecer para resgatar al dho Atabalipa //
/f.78v/ en Caxamalca como se resgato anque despues le mato el dho Francisco Piçarro questo fue mas de ocho millon de plata y no solo el dho Hernando y F^{co} Piçarro quito lo susodho al dho Mango Ynga sino otras muchas joyas de oro y sus casas reales que por sucesion de sus abuelos le pertenecian queran en la plaça de la dha ciudad del Cuzco y continuamente le apremiavan echandole prisiones y dandole tormentos asta que le dio todo el oro y plata que para el servicio de su casa e yndios tenia sin quedarse con cosa alguna todo a fin de redimir las dhas molestias y bexaciones y aunque el dho F^{co} y Hernando Piçarro entendian que el dho Mango Ynga no les podia dar mas oro y plata de lo que les avia dado por le molestar y aflixir le pedian mas plata cosas queran imposible podellas dar y en esto le hizieron tanta fuerça con amenazas que cada dia le azian que le obligaron contra su voluntad a que se retirase a la provincia de Bilcabamba donde todos los yndios del reino le tubieron por tal su rey y señor y como a tal le obedecian y retirado en la dha provincia el dho don F^{co} Piçarro y los demas españoles entraron en todas sus tierras y balles que abia eredado de su padres y abuelos en el balle de Yucay y balle de Maras y otras muchas partes las quales pertenescen a la dha doña Beatriz Coya como su huniversal heredera las quales protesto pedir ante quien biere que me conviene.

Lo otro por que demas de todas las dhas cosas de que despojaron al dho Mango Ynga despojaron ansimismo al dho don Diego Saire Topa hijo legitimo del dho Mango Ynga y padre de la dha doña Beatriz que a la sazon hera señor de todos los yndios y heredamientos casas minerales que Topa Ynga Yupangui metio en un mayorazgo que hizo e instituyo en Mango Ynga su nieto padre del dho don Diego para que lo tubiese y poseyese por el dho titulo de mayorazgo apartandolo y separandolo del señorio y corona per- /Ba restado al dho Herna^{do} abia/ //
/f.79/ tenecientes al reino como muchos de los Yngas le hizieron por todo lo qual y lo que mas ase en mi favor y tengo alegado y en esta peticion se contiene.

A V. Alt^{a} pido y suplico mande proveer en esta causa a favor de la dha doña Beatriz Coya segun y como tiene pedido y suplicado y en esta peticion se contiene y para ello es. Vuestro real oficio imploro y pido justicia y costas.

Martin Garcia de Loyola El Lldo Ruiz de la Torre

Otro si supp^{co} a V. Alt^{a} m^{de} que la sent^{a} de prueba se entienda con lo que en esta pet^{on} y alega della y pido just^{a} y pa ello es.
Jhoan Sanchez

En la ciudad de los Reyes en v^{te} y nueve dias del mes de hen^{o} de myll e qui^{o}s y ochenta y ocho a^{o}s estando los ss^{res} presidente e oydores desta real audiencia en audiencia pu^{ca} se pres^{to} esta peticion.

E por los dhos señores vista mandaron dar treslado a la otra parte para la prim^{a} aud^{a} responda e que se entienda en la sent^{a} de prueba. pres^{te} el licen^{do} Alv^{o} de Caravajal fiscal de su mag^{t} a quien se not^{o}.

Montoya (rubrica)

Ba restado que.

/f.79v/ /en blanco/

/f.80/ Muy P^{o} S^{or}

Pide el traslado de unas cedulas

Jhoan Sanchez de los Rios en n^{e} del com^{or} Martin Garcia de Loyola y doña Beatriz Coya su mujer digo que en el pleito y causa que los dhos mis partes tratan con vro fiscal sobre los yanaconas estan presentados por mis partes dos cartas una del emperador nro s^{or} de gloriosa memoria y otra de vuestra alteza y otra asymesmo del emperador en que perdona al Ynga padre y suegro de mis partes todos los robos y muertes que hizo estando en Vilcabamba y otra probision en que le mandan salirse de paz y se le daryan las chacaras y casas de los que les tiene necesidad el dho mi parte para en guarda de su dr^{o}.

A V. Al^{a} pido y suplico mande al pres^{te} secret^{o} me de un traslado dellas en pu^{ca} forma y manera que haga fee para el dho efeto y pido justicia y para ello es.

Jhoan Sanchez (rubrica)

Ba restado S. dos y enmendado es

/f.80v/ En los Reyes a siete dias del mes de jullio de mil e qui^{o}s y ochenta e nuebe a^{o}s ante los ss^{es} presidente e oydores desta real aud^{a} en aud^{a} publica se presento esta peticion

Y por los dichos s^{e}s vista mandaron que se le de como lo pide.

Montoya (rubrica)

En cumplimiento de lo qual yo Juan de Montoya scv^{o} de camara desta real audiencia doy feeque en el pleyto e causa que en esta real aud^{a} esta pendiente entre el fiscal de su mag^{d} de la una parte e don Martin Garcia de Loyola cavallero del avito de Calatrava y doña Beatriz Coya su mujer sobre los yanaconas que se pusieron en la corona real y los yndios de su encomienda y sobre las demas causas e razones en el proceso del dho pleyto contenidas estan las provisiones que por las dhas peticiones se piden e demandan de las quales hize sacar y saque un treslado ques del tenor sig^{te}.

/f.81/ Muy P^{o} S^{or}

Martin Garcia de Loyola por mi procu^{or} en el pleito con vro fiscal sobre los yanaconas del balle de Yucay digo que a mi dr^{o} conbiene sacar un testimonio de lo q an sentenciado los dhos señores en octubre del año de setenta y uno que don F^{co} de T^{o} los puso en la corona real hasta pte dia.

A V. Alt^{a} pido y sup^{co} se me de compulsorio pa que los escrivanos reales de la ciudad del Cuzco en cuyo poder a estado y le remita me los de y sea con citacion que de fee y pido justicia.

Martin Garcia de Loyola

/f.81v/ En los Reyes a prim^{o} de ag^{to} de myll e qui^{o}s y ochenta y nueve a^{o}s est^{do} los ss^{es} presidente y oydores en aud^{a} pu^{ca} se pres^{to} esta peticion.

Y por los dhos s^{e}s vista mandaron que se citada la pte. Presente el fiscal de su mag^{d}.

Montoya (rubrica)

/f.82/ Muy P^{o} señor

Pide el proceso

El licenciado Alvaro de Caravajal vro fiscal en la causa con doña Beatriz Clra Coya y Martin Garcia de Loyola su marido sobre la demanda que les tengo puesta de los yndios que les dio el Marques de Cañete vro bisorrey que fue destos reinos digo que estando esta causa conclusa conforme a la de Malinas fue hecha remision della por vro presidente e oydores a vro real consejo de las Yndias.

A vra Alt^{a} pido y suplico mande a Ju^{o} de Montoya escrivano de camara ante quien pasa me de y entregue el proceso del dho pleito para que lo enbie a vro real consejo y pido justicia y el real oficio imploro.

En la ciudad de los Reyes en diez dias del mes de noviembre de mill y quinientos y ochenta y nueve a^{o}s ante los señores presidente e oydores desta real audi^{a} en audi^{a} pu^{ca} se presento esta peticion.

Y por dichos s^{e}s vista mandaron llevar los autos a la sala para proveer.

Montoya (rubrica)

Ba restado encomendo y entre renglones dio.

/f.82v/ /en blanco/

/f.83/ este falta por sacar.
Pleito acumulado por el auto de 16 de agosto de 1586.

Muy poderoso señor - Juan de Arrandolaça en nombre de Doña Beatriz Coya me presento ante vtra alteza en grado de apelacion nulidad e agravio con este proceso e testimonios de çierta sentencia e autos dados e pronunçiados por el Visitador del partido de Yucay en terminos de la çiudad del Cuzco en que en efeto le quito ciertos y^{o}s yanaconas.

Pido e sup^{co} a vra alteça me aya por presentado en el dho grado e se me de pa alegar de la justicia de mi parte e para ello es. El dotor Juan de Herr^{a} Arrandolaça.

V En la ciudad de los Reies en veinte dias del mes de julio de mil e qui^{o}s e setenta e quatro años ante los señores Presidentes e oydores estando en audiencia publica Juan de Arrandolaça en nombre de su parte presento esta peticion con el dho proceso e testimonios.

V Y los dhos señores lo hubieron por presentado en el dho grado quanto a lugar de derecho e mandaron que se le de el proceso Francisco de Caravajal.

V En la gran ciudad del Cuzco cabeça destos reinos y provincias del Piru a onze dias del mes de henero de mil e qui^{o}s e setenta y quatro años ante el Yll^{e} señor dotor don Gabriel de Loarte del consejo de su m^{t} y su alcalde de corte en estos reinos corregidor e justiçia m^{or} por su m^{t} en esta dha ciudad e su jur^{on} e por ante Pero Diaz Baldeon escriv^{o} de su mag^{td} publico e del numero desta dha ciudad parecio presente el capitan Martin Garcia Oñaz y de Loyola vz^{o} desta dha ciudad pres^{to} la peticion y provision memorial e ynterrogatorio de preguntas siguientes.

V En la ciudad del Cuzco a onze dias del mes de henero de mill e qui^{o}s y setenta e quatro años //
/f.83v/ ante el YIl^{e} señor dotor Gabriel de Loarte del Consejo de su Magestad e justicia mayor de esta ciudad del Cuzco y su jur^{on} la presento el contenido.

V YIl^{e} señor Martin Garcia de Loyola por mi y como conjunta persona de doña Beatriz mi mujer cuyos son los y^{o}s del valle de Yucay hago ante V. M. presentacion de esta provision del Ex$^{mo.}$ señor Virrey destos reinos por la qual manda se reciba ynformacion sobre lo en ella contenido.

V A V. M. pido mande recibir ynformacion de todo ad perpetuam rrei memoriam y los testigos que presentare se exsaminen por estas preguntas que presento y fecha la dha informacion se me de un treslado o mas en manera que haga fee para en guarda de mi dr^{o} y pido justicia. Martin Garcia de Loyola.

V Don Francisco de Toledo mayordomo de su mag^{t} y su bisorrey y gobernador y capitan general destos reinos e provincias del Piru e Tierra Firme etc. Por quanto el capitan Martin Garcia de Oñez y Loyola cavallero de la orden de Calatrava por su peticion me hizo relacion que Juan Fernandez Coronel con poder suyo en su nombre y de doña Beatriz su mujer pres^{to} ante Diego Barrantes besitador del valle de Yucay una peticion y memorial de ciertos y^{o}s los quales en todas las visitas pasadas se an visitado los que an manifestado los caciques y se an podido aver por yndios tributarios del dho valle encomendados en la dha su mujer hasta la ultima visita que por mi mandado hizo el Licenciado Frei Pedro Gutierrez Flores en la qual los dhos y^{o}s fueron visitados por yanaconas como me constava por una peticion presentada //
/f.84/ ante el dho Diego Barrantes por los caçiques principales del dho valle como pretendiendo ellos reservarlos de tributo por servirse de los dhos y^{o}s como lo an fecho antes de aora y porque al tiempo que se hizo la numeracion y visita del dho valle estaba Atilano de Anaya curador que era de la dha doña Beatriz por mi mandado ocupado en la jornada del Ynga no se pudo hallar persona que asistiese a la dha visita en nombre de la dha su mujer y que aora ha venido a su noticia que los oficiales reales del Cuzco les piden a los dhos y^{o}s y les molestan a que paguen el tributo que yo les tase poniendolos en la corona real y que pues es de su mag^{td} y de mi en su real nombre dar a cada uno lo ques suyo hizo y los y^{o}s contenidos en la pet^{on} que por su parte se presento ante el dho visitador son y pertenecen a su encomienda porque si yo tuve relacion que no lo heran fue por las causas suso dhas y por yntereses particulares de los dhos caciques me pidio y sup^{co} mandase que los dhos y^{o}s y los demas que pareciere que le pertenecen no paguen ni acudan a su mag^{td} ni a otra persona con tributos antes ayuden a los demas y^{o}s del dho valle a la paga de su tasa pues son suios y le pertenecen como me constara por ynformacion cierta y verdadera questa presto y aparexado de dar y pa la hazer mandase al dho Diego Barrantes o a otra persona que reciban los testigos que por su parte se presentaren para que me conste de ello y asi mesmo obiese por presentadas las peticiones y memorial y lo en ellas contenido que por su parte fueron presentadas ante el dho visitador //
/f.84v/ cerrado y sellado como se presento y me pidio justicia y por mi visto juntamente con otra peticion que sobre lo suso dho ante mi presento acorde de dar y di la presente por la qual mando al dotor Gabriel de Loarte alcalde de corte de su m^{t} y justicia maior de la dha ciudad del Cuzco que luego questa mi provision le fuere mostrada reciba la ynformacion quel dho capitan Loyola le diere sobre el pleito de los yanaconas del dho valle de Yucay en que dize y pretende aver sido engañado y defraudado y fecha la dha informacion le mande dar un treslado autoriçado en publica forma y manera que haga fee para en guarda de su dr^{o} y no dexe de lo asi cumplir. Fecha en la Plata a dos dias de diziembre de mil e qui^{o}s y setenta y tres años. ba emendado fui. Don Francisco de Toledo por mandado de su Exª. Alvaro Ruiz de Navamuel.

Memoria de los y^{o}s que dixeron los caciques y viejos deste valle de Yucay que siendo de tasa andavan fuera della con nombre de yanaconas

	Años	
	30 V	Cristobal Paucartica de treinta años tiene hijos
	50 V	Don Diego Rimachi de cinq^{ta} años tiene hijos
	30 V	Pedro Machaguai de treinta años tiene hijos
	30 V	Mateo Curas de treinta años tiene hijos
	57 V	Alonso Chauca de cinq^{ta} e siete años
	30 V	Miguel Vilca Condor de treinta años tiene hijos
	26 V	Martin Pomacondor de v^{te} e seis años tiene hijos
	16 V	Simon Cusiminga de diez y seis años tiene hijos
	6 V	Juan Churimache de seis años guerfano
	30 V	Mateo Curu de treinta años
	48 V	Alonso Quispe de quarenta y ocho años
	20 V	Francisco Quispi de veinte años tiene hijos
	47 V	Francisco Llancari de quarenta y siete años
	20 V	Juan Quiquinyanac de veinte años
	7 V	Xp^{o}bal Caquipay de siete años guerfano
/f.85/	20 V	Mateo Ricra de beinte años guerfano
	3 V	Pedro Machaguai guerfano de tres años
	18 V	Diego Asto Camasca de diez y ocho años
	40 V	Pedro Alcamari de quarenta años
	18 V	Diego Cunis Malma de diez y ocho años tiene hijos
	35 V	Agustin Camasca de treinta y cinco años tiene hijos
	23 V	Fran^{co} Rampa Yupangui de veinte e tres años tiene hijos
	18 V	Juan Yanac Camasca de diez y ocho años
	60 V	Agustin Chuquiapac de sesenta años
	60 V	Antonio Caquiguari de sesenta años
	20 V	Andres Duibus de veinte años
	38 V	Alonso Quispi de treinta y ocho años tiene hijos
	25 V	Marcos Chilli de veinte y cinco años tiene hijos
	16 V	Diego Laymi de diez y seis años guerfano
	10 V	Martin Ynancila de diez años guerfano
	38 V	Juan Bautista Manchi de treinta y ocho años
	25 V	Miguel Jimri Naula de veinte e cinco a^{o}s ti^{e} hijos
	10 V	Pedro Tini Lalbai de diez años guerfano
	30 V	Francisco Mivancila de treinta años tiene hijos
	18 V	Andres Tinimaza de diez y ocho años tiene hijos
	9 V	Mateo Llivi Putlla de nueve años guerfano
	20 V	Andres Cazad Naula de veinte a^{o}s tiene hijos
	26 V	Francisco Biznaisila de veintiseis años tiene hijos
	17 V	Mateo Palchi Biznay de diez y siete años
	8 V	Francisco Yumbu de ocho años guerfano
	55 V	Alonso Caquicuya de cinq^{ta} y cinco a^{o}s tiene hijos
	30 V	Yngas Chilli Guaman de treinta años tiene hijos
	28 V	Xp^{o}bal Nazpi de v^{te} e ocho años
	33 V	Martin Caçitamha de treinta y tres años tiene hijos
	37 V	Martin Bilitamha de treinta y siete años tiene hijos
	13 V	Lucas Sangai Limpay de treze años
	26 V	Andres Quiri Viznay de veinte y seis años tiene hijos
	53 V	Agustin Alao de cinquenta y tres a^{o}s
	20 V	Yngas Bili Dunbay de v^{te} a^{o}s
	33 V	Pedro Guaman Achi de treinta y tres años tiene hijos
	27 V	Pedro Sulca de veinte e siete años tiene hijos
	7 V	Juan Bautista Acu de siete años guerfano
	26 V	Agustin Tolagua de veintiseis años tiene hijos
	17 V	Pedro Guasiviznay de diecisiete años
	27 V	Pedro Quilano de veintisiete años tiene hijos
/f.85v/	65 V	Pedro Millic de sesenta y cinco años

20 V Pedro Langaizaca de veinte años tiene hijos
38 V Cristobal Guamanaisi de treintiocho años tiene hijos
35 V Juan Usco de treinticinco años tiene hijos
20 V Cristobal Uscotoma de veinte años tiene hijos
39 V Antonio Gualpar de treintinueve años tiene hijos
49 V Martin Malqui de cuarentinueve años tiene hijos
20 V Francisco Guachalla de veinte años tiene hijos
22 V Pedro Atla de veintidos años tiene hijos
58 V Hernando Lalnay de cincuentiocho años
20 V Domingo Libipuchai de veinte años tiene hijos
58 V Cristobal Sumansanai de cincuentiocho años
30 V Juan Bautista Samanpuslla de treinta años tiene hijos
30 V Cristobal Araranca de treinta años
34 V Hernando Pasto de treintiquatro años
30 V Rodrigo Tacuri de treinta años tiene hijos
27 V Juan Bautista Cacpaipai de veintinueve años tiene hijos
13 V Benito Rimachi de treze años huerfano
18 V Francisco Gualpa de dieciocho años tiene hijos
20 V Juan Pasto de veinte años
27 V Agustin Llachua de veintisiete años
14 V Benito Llachua de catorze años huerfano
38 V Juan Sicsi de treintiocho años tiene hijos
33 V Diego Tanta de treintitres años tiene hijos
33 V Diego Uscohuaman de treintitres años tiene hijos
8 V Pedro Paucarlloclla de ocho años huerfano
12 V Martin Supaico de doze años huerfano
20 V Juan Guasi de veinte años tiene hijos
25 V Jeronimo Cuyo de veinticinco años tiene hijos
45 V Cristobal Juchinaizay de cuarenticinco años tiene hijos
57 V Pedro Jinincila de cincuentisiete años tiene hijos
20 V Benito Guartalangnai de veinte años
28 V Pedro Ninlasaca de veintiocho años tiene hijos
52 V Pedro Burban de cincuentidos años
23 V Martin Marcauichay de veintitres años
35 V Alonso Biliviznai de treinticinco años tiene hijos
/f.86/ 30 V Pedro Salina de treinta años tiene hijos
40 V Alonso Urcunlalai de quarenta años tiene hijos
30 V Goncalo Tanbuiputlla de treinta años tiene hijos
53 V Martin Sabai de cincuentitres años
18 V Alonso Jivisputlla de dieciocho años
18 V Juan Juainguarin de dieciocho años
60 V Sebastian Tenicela de sesenta años
10 V Juan Cazasnaula de diez años huerfano
30 V Rodrigo Lalchiviznai de treinta años tiene hijos
25 V Hernando Chaco de veinticinco años tiene hijos
54 V Alonso Tocro de cincuentiquatro años
58 V Alonso Cartam de cincuentiocho años
30 V Cristobal Tamay de treinta años tiene hijos
48 V Pedro Ayachagua de cuarentiocho años
40 V Simon Yllatupa de quarenta años
43 V Juan Vichupanta de cuarentitres años tiene hijos
10 V Felipe Condor de diez años huerfano
18 V Agustin Tacopuma de dieciocho años
40 V Cristobal Sulcanahui de quarenta años
17 V Pedro Paucar Cumaza de diecisiete años tiene hijos
20 V Pedro Vilea Cajhia de veinte años tiene hijos
19 V Agustin Halanda de diecinueve años
43 V Toribio Arimana de cuarentitres años tiene hijos
10 V Martin Titogualpa de diez años huerfano
17 V Cristobal Huisacahuana de diecisiete años

	50 V	Alonso Marcagualpa de cinquenta años tiene hijos
	24 V	Cristobal Chalcuri de veintiquatro años tiene hijos
	48 V	Alonso Acosi de cuarentiocho años tiene hijos
	60 V	Martin Tunzila de sesenta años
	16 V	Francisco Chaquicumsa de dieciseis años
	65 V	Cristobal Cusiguaman de sesenticinco años
	43 V	Antonio Urcracosi de cuarentitres años
	64 V	Juan Guacal de sesentiquatro años
	25 V	Pedro Sulca Guacal de veinticinco años tiene hijos
	33 V	Alonso Ginamamay de treintitres años tiene hijos
	30 V	Pedro Cuzcuc de treinta años tiene hijos
	18 V	Benito Garchinaula de dieciocho años tiene hijos
	27 V	Juan Bautista Diagul de veintisiete años tiene hijos
/f.86v/	38 V	Martin Nina Puma de treintiocho años tiene hijos
	23 V	Cristobal Tomailla de veintitres años tiene hijos
	18 V	Juan Chuquicanchi de dieciocho años
	19 V	Lucas Chuquicondor de diecinueve años tiene hijos
	15 V	Juan Carnajanca de quinze años huerfano
	30 V	Lorenzo Quispe de treinta años tiene hijos
	60 V	Pedro Urimba de sesenta años
	23 V	Rodrigo Guacara de veintitres años tiene hijos
	20 V	Jeronimo Guamanquilca de veinte años
	V	Hasta aqui eran de don Francisco Chilche y su hijos
	-38-	
	40 V	Diego Guaman de quarenta años'
	20 V	Alonso Cordorsupa de veinte años
	14 V	Paulo Pumacordor de catorze años huerfano
	28 V	Agustin Sulcatocas de veintiocho años
	24 V	Juan Malqui de veintiquatro años
	16 V	Juan Bautista Aillaguaco de dieciseis años
	25 V	Juan Rimachi de veinticinco años
	33 V	Domingo Apasa de treintitres años
	50 V	Francisco Llacsayupari de cinquenta años tiene hijos
	50 V	Alonso Usco de cinquenta años tiene hijos
	23 V	Francisco Guauyausco de veintitres años tiene hijos
	42 V	Pedro Tinta de cuarentidos años
	18 V	Francisco Quispeyupa de dieciocho años tiene hijos
	25 V	Alonso Comicyupari de veinticinco años tiene hijos
	43 V	Agustin Condori de cuarentitres años
	20 V	Andres Caruapisco de veinte años tiene hijos
	20 V	Mateo Atauchuco de veinte años
	65 V	Alonso Muqui de sesenticinco años
	19 V	Andres Auquis Yupari de diecinueve años tiene hijos
	25 V	Martin Atragua de veinticinco años
	18 V	Juan Manta de dieciocho años
	7 V	Cristobal Cuyatupa de siete años huerfano
	50 V	Alonso Pilpi de cinquenta [*sic*]
	30 V	Martin Quispe de treinta años tiene hijos
	60 V	Martin Guanaco de sesenta años
	30 V	Pedro Rimahuaman de treinta años tiene hijos
	56 V	Juan Aisma de cincuentiseis años
/f.87/	18 V	Domingo Pumaruon de dieciocho años
	60 V	Juan Bautista Tanaupachi de sesenta años tiene hijos
	37 V	Cristobal Siuinta de treintisiete años tiene hijos
	20 V	Juan Vilcas Pariguana de veinte años tiene hijos
	17 V	Alonso Guaman de diecisiete años
	50 V	Martin Mayta de cinquenta años tiene hijos
	16 V	Juan Camachaira de dieciseis años
	56 V	Cristobal Panallussu de cincuentiseis años
	36 V	Alonso Pana de treintiseis años. tiene hijos

	19 V	Alonso Aucaypuru de diecinueve años tiene hijos
	40 V	Domingo Vilca de quarenta años tiene hijos
	25 V	Francisco Visahuaman de veinticinco años tiene hijos
	6 V	Alonso Aruco de seis años huerfano
	39 V	Juan Cochachin de treintinueve años tiene hijos
	27 V	Pedro Hanampa de veintisiete años tiene hijos
	23 V	Domingo Yarovilca de veintitres años
	28 V	Francisco Yanac de veintiocho años
	8 V	Domingo Cuspa de ocho años huerfano
	60 V	Diego Amaro de sesenta años
	26 V	Alonso Condormachaguay de veintiseis años
	64 V	Martin Cavascanco de sesentiquatro años
	24 V	Alonso Coca Vascanco de veintiquatro años tiene hijos
	22 V	Martin Vica de veintidos años
	26 V	Cristobal Tupa Yupangui de veintiseis años tiene hijos
	30 V	Alonso Gualpasucsu de treinta años tiene hijos
	32 V	Cristobal Rasmi de treintidos años
	19 V	Hernando Ataocana de diecinueve años tiene hijos
	45 V	Don Juan Ailambo de cuarenticinco años tiene hijos
	V	Hasta aqui eran de don Alonso Tito Ataoche que son 55
	39V	Juan Malcopariguana de treintinueve años tiene hijos
	50 V	Pedro Guancapuma de cinquenta años tiene hijos
	42 V	Juan Aucagualpa de cuarentidos años tiene hijos
	23 V	Pedro Mallaocui de veintitres años tiene hijos
	20 V	Diego Machaca de veinte años tiene hijos
	50 V	Pedro Conca de cinquenta años
	43V	Diego Gualpacuiquis de cuarentitres tiene hijos
	19V	Pedro Auquis de diecinueve años tiene hijos
	32 V	Santiago Yanac de treintidos años tiene hijos
/f.87v/	32 V	Pedro Pacha de treintidos años tiene hijos
	23 V	Martin Carhuayanac de veintitres años
	18 V	Francisco Llacsahuaman de dieciocho años
	10 V	Benito Guaman de diez años huerfano
	15 V	Goncalo Pumagualpa de quinze años
	38 V	Sebastian Cusiyhuara de treintiocho años tiene hijos
	11 V	Jeronimo Pilco Yucra de diecisiete años
	32 V	Juan Ancay de treintidos años tiene hijos
	23 V	Felipe Paguaman de veintitres años
	45 V	Cristobal Muti Yupangui de cuarenticinco años tiene hijos
	18 V	Diego Tupa Yupangui de dieciocho años tiene hijos
	14 V	Domingo Turus de catorze años huerfano
	25 V	Alonso Quispe de veinticinco años
	8 V	Alonso Sulcamaivasca de ocho años huerfano
	10 V	Alonso Guanasca de diez años huerfano
	20 V	Agustin Atas Suyuiquina de veinte años tiene hijos
	46 V	Pedro Paucar de cuarentiseis años
	21 V	Juan Guandapi de veintiun años tiene hijos
	10 V	Alonso Aucatuma de diez años huerfano
	8 V	Diego Calani de ocho años huerfano
	10 V	Juan Gualca de diez años huerfano
	18 V	Domingo Guaman de dieciocho años
	18 V	Pedro Yucra de dieciocho años tiene hijos
	20 V	Andres Guamalli de veinte años tiene hijos
	56 V	Cristobal Guamalli de cincuentiseis años
	40 V	Martin Alonso Muru de quarenta años tiene hijos
	43 V	Diego Cusipuru de cuarentitres años
	20 V	Agustin Cusipaucar de veinte años tiene hijos
	24 V	Martin Pusaguaman de veintiquatro años
	11 V	Alonso Cusirimachi de onze años huerfano
	30 V	Martin Guamanhuisa de treinta años

	44 V	Martin Quicana de cuarentiquatro años tiene hijos
	35 V	Juan Asacacha de treinticinco años tiene hijos
	35 V	Goncalo Suyucaisi de treinticinco años
	38 V	Cristobal Guartaitusu de treintiocho años tiene hijos
	30 V	Antonio de Quiñones Janampa de treinta años tiene hijos
/f.88/	34 V	Diego Ninaricsa de treintiquatro años tiene hijos
	26 V	Domingo Sulca de veintiseis años tiene hijos
	23 V	Hernando Carhuavanca de veintitres años
	54 V	Salvador Llachuasto de cincuentiquatro años
	25 V	Luis Sulcallachua de veinticinco años tiene hijos
	20 V	Vicente Chiguan de veinte años tiene hijos
	12 V	Francisco Chiguan de doze años huerfano
	30 V	Juan Bautista Ranaiacchac de treinta años tiene hijos
	55 V	Hernando Pumacondor de cincuenticinco años
	17 V	Cristobal Chuquicondor de diecisiete años
	20 V	Antonio Pumacondor de veinte años tiene hijos
	28 V	Juan Chichi de veintiocho años tiene hijos
	18 V	Francisco Pumachinchi de dieciocho años
	30 V	Francisco Sulcacondor de treinta años tiene hijos
	2 V	Francisco Guaypar de dos años huerfano
	20 V	Ambrosio Pillaca de veinte años tiene hijos
	16 V	Hernando Gualparimachi de dieciseis años
	14 V	Martin Gualparoco de catorze años huerfano
	49 V	Martin Rimachi Yupangui de cuarentinueve años tiene hijos
	28 V	Juan Tupa Yupangui de veintiocho años tiene hijos
	40 V	Martin Ataucusi de quarenta años
	18 V	Diego Pisana de dieciocho años tiene hijos
	35 V	Don Carlos Gualpa Roca y treinticinco años tiene hijos
	37 V	Miguel Minagualpa de treintisiete años tiene hijos
	26 V	Cristobal Chacchimarca de veintiseis años
	55 V	Pedro Vilcaruna de cincuenticinco años
	22 V	Martin Rimachi de veintidos años tiene hijos
	24 V	Don Alonso Tupacusigualpa de veintiquatro años tiene hijos
	30 V	Felipe Manchapa de treinta años
	20 V	Agustin Pactiz de veinte años
	28 V	Alonso Pariango de veintiocho años
	15 V	Cristobal Parinanga de quinze años huerfano
	V	Pedro Villa de quinze años
/f.88v/	28 V	Alonso Capo de veintiocho años tiene hijos
	40 V	Juan Alonso Auca Tupa de quarenta años tiene hijos
	50 V	Martin Guartatpuslla de cinquenta años
	37 V	Felipe Putllacila de treintisiete años
	33 V	Martin Puchuna de treintitres años tiene hijos
	26 V	Agustin Gualutu de veintiseis años tiene hijos
	47 V	Diego Llamuca de cuarentisiete años
	18 V	Agustin Aroni de dieciocho años
	28 V	Alonso Guaman Cusi de veintiocho años tiene hijos
	20 V	Juan Carhuaruna de veinte años tiene hijos
	50 V	Goncalo Tongoragua de cinquenta años
	66 V	Martin Auti de sesentiseis años
	24 V	Martin Santa de veintiquatro años
	30 V	Hernando Casivilca de treinta años
	27 V	Pedro Pollancachuc de veintisiete años
	52 V	Hernando Carhuati de cincuentidos años
	50 V	Martin Marca de cinquenta años
	22 V	Pedro Quispe de veintidos años tiene hijos
	50 V	Sebastian Sulca de cinquenta años
	18 V	Francisco Curi de dieciocho años
	35 V	Lucas Rimasca de treinticinco años tiene hijos
	50 V	Pedro Llahua de cinquenta años tiene hijos

	20 V	Pedro Quipi de veinte años tiene hijos
	37 V	Alonso Mucac de treintisiete años tiene hijos
	8 V	Sebastian Maibasca de ocho años huerfano
	48 V	Juan Picarro Cusi Ataoche de cuarentiocho años tiene hijos
	19 V	Lorenzo Guari Tupa de diecinueve años
	26 V	Martin Luay de veintiseis años
	20 V	Lorenzo Quispe Guaman de veinte años tiene hijos
	28 V	Domingo Tupa Cusigualpa de veintiocho años tiene hijos
	33 V	Alonso Caquicuya de treintitres años tiene hijos
	10 V	Cristobal Cirasviznai de diez años huerfano
	19 V	Francisco Guartasnaula de diecinuve años tiene hijos
/f.89/	59 V	Fabian Cuchillo de cincuentinueve años tiene hijos
	32 V	Pedro Quispe de treintidos años
	59 V	Felipe Yupangui de cincuentinueve anos tiene hijos
	32 V	Martin Pinaula de treintidos años tiene hijos
	45 V	Miguel Mitnaguarai de cuarenticinco años
	30 V	Pedro Chururana de treinta años tiene hijos
	30 V	Alonso Tabras de treinta años tiene hijos
	50 V	Pedro Condori de cinquenta años tiene hijos
	60 V	Marcos Puri de sesenta años tiene hijos
	17 V	Domingo Gualparimachi de diecisiete años
	30 V	Francisco Chucuna de treinta anos
	20 V	Alonso Napanga de veinte años
	28 V	Pedro Ricra de veintiocho años
	55 V	Luis Sulca de cincuenticinco años tiene hijos
	39 V	Martin Arcaipaucar de treintiocho años tiene hijos
	23 V	Juan Bautista Chuquipaucar de veintitres años tiene hijos
	60 V	Agustin Paco de sesenta años
	30 V	Marcos Chalco Yupangui de treinta años tiene hijos
	43 V	Alonso Yuipar de cuarentitres años tiene hijos
	10 V	Diego Llamac de diez años huerfano
	33 V	Juan Yaris de treintitres años tiene hijos
	33 V	Alonso Aihua de treintitres años tiene hijos
	18 V	Juan Yugapaucar de dieciocho años tiene hijos
	55 V	Hernando Villi de cincuenticinco años
	40 V	Francisco Carhua Mango de quarenta años.

v Lo qual se deve presuponer para entender la justicia que el capitan Loyola tiene para pedir los yºs que siendo yºs de tasa en el valle de Yucay estan agora en nombre de Yanaconas e fuera de tasa.

v Lo primero que en tiempo de Guayna Capac ynga este valle de Yucay fue como recamara suya y asi los yºs que en el vivian ansi na- //
/f.89v/ turales como mitimas no eran de ninguno de los quatro suyos en que todo el Piru esta repartido para los servicios de guerra e otras cosas sino solamente estos eran yanaconas del Ynga que le servian aqui a el e a sus hijos e deudos e les beneficiavan sus chacaras que aqui tenian e le heran camayos de muchas cosas aqui.

v E quando el marques don Françisco Piçarro entro en esta tierra tomo pa si este valle entre otras cosas y empeçose a servir de los yºs del de yanaconas e por tributo como no se llevava otro entonzes mandavales beneficiar e coxer e plantar las chacaras de coca que el dho marques tenia en los andes que eran Tono Canauire Paucarbamba Yanatai e otras de maiz en este valle y en el Cuzco otra que tenia el mesmo que se decia Tiopampa de maiz y en que le diesen mitayos e le hiciesen camarico de yerba leña como entonzes se usava.

v Despues del marques Piçarro subcedio en estos yºs en encomienda don Gonçalo Piçarro su hijo al qual le tributaron siempre que bibio en lo mismo que a su padre y en el benefº de las mismas chacaras acudiendo con todo a su mayordomo.

v Despues del dho don Gonçalo Piçarro vinieron a ser estos yºs de su magestad e ni mas ni menos le tributavan a su mag^{td} en el benefº de las dhas chacaras de coca acudiendo con el fruto dellas a Garçia de Melo como su tesorero.

v Despues de todo el marques de Cañete visorrey destos reynos los dio a estos yºs en encomienda e con perpetuidad e mayorazgo a don Sairi Topa Ynga nieto de Guayna //
/f.90/ Capac e hijo de Mango Ynga cuya hija y heredera es doña Beatriz Coya mujer del capitan Loyola como los avia tenido el marques Piçarro.

v Y agora de saver que en todo lo mas del tiempo de la vida del marques y que tuvo estos y^{os} e de su hijo hasta que vino don Diego Sayri Topa de Bilcabamba mandava e mando estos y^{os} como curaca principal puesto por el marques Piçarro el qual quito a Gualpa Topa que antes lo hera por ciertas causas don Françisco Chilche que oy bive y este don Françisco Chilche mandava a todos los y^{os} que ban en la memoria que constava y a los padres de los mozos que en ella ban cuyos hijos viven e a los demas deste valle como tributarios de los quales muchos eran de tiempo de Guaina Capac e otros binieron despues con Chalcochima capitan de Atagualipa Ynga e de otras partes e se quedaron en este valle tributando como los demas en lo dho al marques e a su hijo y subcesores.

v Despues de todo esto un yndio de la deçendencia de los Yngas que se dice don Garçia Quispicapi puso demanda al don Fran^{co} Chilche del mando e cacicazgo diciendo que a el le pertenecia por ser hijo e nieto de los que avian mandado este valle y los y^{os} del el qual pleito se fenecio con que se conzertaron el dho don Françisco Chilche y don Garçia Quispicapi en quel mismo fuese cacique de los naturales del dho valle y el otro lo fuese de los mitimas y advenedizos a el.

v En este tiempo de las disensiones e p^{tos} destos dos y^{os} como en reino deviso e como no tenian tasa particular de plata ni otras cosas señaladas sino solo el benef^{o} de las chacaras dhos y^{os} se le hazian los pobres e los que poco podian empessaronse a salir de la tasa //
/f.90v/ muchos y^{os} por su boluntad favoreçiendose unos de el un cacique y otros del otro e como no tenian amo que les resistiese porque en este tiempo estavan por su mag^{td} e sus oficiales contentavanse con que se les diese su coca a que tenian obligacion e no curavan de otra cosa vinieron a quedarse muchos fuera de la obligacion del benef^{o} de las chacaras como le tenian mucho antes como mitimas de este valle$^{/encima/}$ e otros de los naturales deste valle se salieron de la tasa diziendo que en tiempo del Ynga Guaina Capac abvan servido a hijos e hijas e parientes del dho Guaina Capac e que querian servir a sus decendientes e como no tenian contradicion pudieron hazer su voluntad.

v Despues de esto subzedio la visita de Damian de la Bandera hizo general por comision del marques de Cañete en la qual empadrono muchos destos que se avian esimido de la tasa y porque no tubo noticias de todos dexo algunos fuera de su visita porque los caciques se los encubrieron y entonzes empadrono a los y^{os} que don Alonso Tito Atauche dize que son sus yanaconas por merzed e les mando tasasen y tributasen como los demas y ellos lo avian fecho y estos y^{os} que entonzes se les mando tributar e oy son yanaconas de Tito Atauche en secreto sin ser entendidos eran guardas e yanaconas del cuerpo de Guaina Capac aunque en lo publico eran y fueron en tiempo del marques Piçarro y sus subcesores y^{os} tributarios como los demas e coxian las dhas chacaras de coca a estos pidio don Alonso Tito Atauche que era curaca e cacique dellos e nieto de Guaina Capac al governador que era de su mg^{t}d con //
/f.91/ falsa relacion diciendo que en Yucay avia ciertos yanaconas e guardas de su abuelo que le hiziese mezced dellos para sus yanaconas porque ya el cuerpo se avia llevado a Rimac e asi por esta sola relacion se le hizo la merzed siendo como dho es y^{os} de tasa son estos y de los antiguos e hijos de los muertos los que biven cinquenta e cinco sin los hijos e mujeres.

v Despues de todo esto vino a visitar este valle Garçia de Melo e la tasa de coca la reduxo a plata en el qual tiempo e bisita se escondieron algunos de los que en la de Damian de la Bandera se avian visitado e no menos de los que se avian salido en las pasiones e pleitos de los curacas que dho tengo y don Fran^{co} Chilche demas de que de los de antes se avian salido de la tasa tenian muchos consigo con color de yanaconas desta ultima besita saco veinte e cinco diziendo que el pagaria sus tasas e les daria tierras de las tierras suyas e que le sirviesen a el de Yanaconas e ansi se an estado e pagavan lo que les cabian e quando yo Diego Escudero vine a este valle a dotrinar que aura cinco años como no halle padrones ni claridad de cuales eran tributarios ni yanaconas tube neçesidad pa empadronarles de informarme de los caciques e ansi los que me decian que eran yanaconas puselos en un libro por si e los de tasa en otro.

[f.91v] v E quando el Licenciado Frel Pedro Gutierrez Flores visito este valle de Yucay y por el visorrey mi señor la visita de los yanaconas se hizo por mi padron e libro sin preguntar a los y^{os} ni a otra persona si avian sido de tasa o no porque no avian sospecha de tal cosa entonzes e los y^{os} como se les dezia entonzes que avian de ser libres y ellos lo entendian ansi dixeron todos que eran yanaconas llanamente ansi los que al principio se salieron de la tasa como los que avia Tito Atauche pedido de merzed como los que en la visita de Melo avian dho que pagando su tasa servirian a don Francisco Chilche e asi se quedaron unos y otros por yanaconas.

v Despues visto que les mandavan tributar e que no tenian tantas chacaras como los demas tributarios ellos por una parte y los caciques por otra viendo que ya no se podian servir de ellos an declarado los que eran e an sido y^{os} de tasa e los hijos de los muertos que oy biven cuyos padres salido de la tasa e ansi vinieron a lo dezir algunos e yo por mas satisfazerme hize parecer ante mi a don Françisco Chilche e a don Garcia Quispicapi caciques principales deste valle e a don Juan Xilambo cacique principal de los yanaconas del e a Marcos Puri cacique ansi mismo de cien yanaconas e uno de los que salio con los demas quando //
/f.92/ las pasiones de los dos caciques e a Lope Martin Condemaita e a don Hernando Chiritupa e a don Pedro Cocharchin e don Alonso Tuparimache e Juan Bautista Gualpa Rucana e Garçia Paucar Suillu e Martin Yupangui e Martin Yanac e Alonso Raimi todos y^{os} viejos del tpo del Ynga unos de los quales son de los naturales deste valle e otros de los mitimas del e otros de los yanaconas antig/u/os del e a todos sin dexar uno les pregunte en particular si era verdad lo sobre dho e todos dixeron que si y estando juntos todos estos dhos caciques e viejos les leey [*sic*] uno por uno todos los yanaconas deste valle e diziendo todos de cada uno que se les preguntaba como y quando avian venido a este valle se hallo que los que van en la siguiente memoria que con estava eran e avian sido yndios de tasa e avian tributado como arriba se dixo e que se le avian salido afuera por las ocasiones contadas.

v Por las preguntas siguientes siguientes [*sic*] se an exsaminados los testigos que se presentaren por parte del cap^{t} Martin Garcia de Loyola y de doña Beatriz Coya su mujer en la informacion que hacen por provision de su Exª sobre los y^{os} del valle de Yucay que siendo y^{os} tributarios y de tasa se bisitaron por y^{os} yanaconas.

1 v Primeramente sean preguntados si conocen a las partes e si tiene noticia de los dhos y^{o}s contenidos en la dha vi- //
/f.92v/ sita y puestos por y^{o}s yanaconas siendo tributarios y de tasa que son los contenidos en este memorial que pide se muestre a los testigos.

2 v yten si saven e conocen que en tiempo de Guaina Capac Ynga señor que fue destos reinos el dho valle de Yucai fue como recamara del dho Ynga y los y^{o}s del dho valle asi los naturales del como los mitimas servian al dho Ynga y a sus hijos y mujeres y parientes y les beneficiavan sus chacaras que tenian en el dho valle y eran asimismo camayos suyos en muchas cosas que en el dho valle tenia digan e conocen y eran sus yanaconas e tenian este nombre e con el le servian.

3 v Yten si saven e conocen que al tiempo que se conquistaron estos reinos por los españoles el marques don Françisco Piçarro luego como entro en esta tierra tomo pa si e para su servi^{o} todo el dho valle de Yucai e y^{o}s del ansi naturales como mitimaes que en el estavan todos los quales saven los testigos que sirvieron siempre al dho marques en todo lo que les mandava y le beneficiavan coxian e plantaban las chacaras de coca que tenia en los andes nombradas Tono Canabire Paucarbamba Yanatay y otras que tenia de maiz en este valle y en el Cuzco y le davan y^{o}s mitayos de servi^{o} para leña y yerba y otros servi^{o}s y le acudian siempre con camarico digan e conocen.

4 v Yten si saven e conocen que en aquel tiempo todos los y^{o}s deste reino no tenian tasa //
/f.93/ y que en lugar de tributo davan a sus encomenderos servi^{o} personal y le beneficiavan sus chacaras de coca y maiz y les daban y^{o}s camaios y servi^{o} pa casa y camarico y otras cosas y que lo mesmo que los demas y^{o}s deste reino davan a sus encomenderos davan asi mesmo los y^{o}s del valle de Yucai al dho marques don Fran^{co} Piçarro como yndios tributarios.

5 v Yten si saven e conocen que despues desto el dho valle de Yucay y todos los y^{o}s del ansi naturales como mitimaes encomendados en don Gonçalo Piçarro hijo del dho marques don Françisco Piçarro el qual se sirvio dellos y le tributaron y le acudieron con todas las cosas y con el mesmo servi^{o} que davan al marques su padre y le beneficiavan sus chacaras y le servian y a sus mayordomos en su nombre como lo solian hazer con el dho su padre.

6 v Yten si saven e conocen que por ausencia y muerte del dho don Gonçalo Piçarro los dhos y^{o}s del dho valle de Yucai vinieron a estar en cabeza de su m^{t} y los oficiales reales desta ciudad del Cuzco todo el tiempo que estuvieron bacos se sirvieron dellos en el benef^{o} de las chacaras y acudiendoles los dhos y^{o}s con el fruto dellos y con los demas servi^{o}s y cosas que solian dar al dho don Françisco Piçarro [*sic*] y al dho marques su padre.

7 v Yten si saven e conocen que despues de todo esto el dho valle de Yucai y todos los y^{o}s del ansi naturales como mitimaes fueron encomendados por el marques de Cañete visorrey que fue destos reinos con //
/f.93v/ titulo de mayorazgo y perpetuidad en don Diego Sayri Tupa Ynga hijo de Mango Ynga y nieto de Guaina Capa para que los tubiese y se sirviese dellos como lo avian fecho los demas sus antepasados y por muerte del dho don Diego Sayri Topa subcedio en la dha encomienda doña Beatriz Coya su hija legitima y unibersal heredera mujer que es del capitan Loyola digan e conocen.

8 v Iten si saven e conocen que en todo el dho tiempo los dhos y^{o}s questavan en el dho valle al tiempo que entraron en esta tierra los españoles estuvieron siempre subjetos juntamente con todos los y^{o}s contenidos en la memoria presentado en esta causa e sirvieron a don Fran^{c}isco Chilche cañari que fue cacique principal de todo el dho valle puesto por el marques don Françisco Piçarro y mando siempre a todos los dhos y^{o}s y haziendo que sirviesen y tributasen al dho marques y a los demas sus encomenderos digan e conocen.

9 v Yten si saven e conocen que despues desto el dho don Françisco Chilche fue puesto pleito por don Garcia Quispicapi descendiente de los y^{o}s diziendo perteneçelle a el el cacicazgo del dho valle los quales se conzertaron quel dho don Françisco fuese cacique de los y^{o}s mitimaes y adbenedizos del dho valle y el dho don Garcia lo fuese de los naturales del y ansi se an quedado y sido caciques hasta este tiempo digan e conocen.

10 v Yten si saven e conocen que desde aquel tiempo algunos de los dhos y^{o}s se favorecieron de los dhos caciques y no acudian al servi^{o} que se hazia a sus encomenderos haziendo que se cargase todo el benef^{o} de las chacaras a los y^{o}s pobres del dho valle y como sus //
/f.94/ encomenderos no tenian mas quenta de que les diesen su servi^{o} y les beneficiasen sus chacaras no fueron a la mano a los dhos y^{o}s para que sirviesen con los demas digan.

11 v Iten si saven e conocen que no embargante que los dhos y^{o}s no servian con los demas siempre estavan subjetos a los dhos caciques y les obedecian y que si dexaban de servir o tributar hera por quererlo asi los dhos sus caciques y por tener en ellos favor y que siempre avian servido y tributado a todos sus encomenderos como los demas y^{o}s tributarios del dho valle digan.

12 v Iten si saven e conocen que al tiempo que Damian de la Vandera por mandado del marques de Cañete visito el dho valle de Yucai puso por y^{o}s tributarios la mayor parte de los dhos y^{o}s que avian dexado de servir y tributar y los mando que sirviesen y tributasen y que si dexo de tributar algunos de los dhos y^{o}s por tributacion fue porque los dhos caciques los escondieron.

13 v Iten si saven e conocen que muchos de los dhos y^{o}s a quien el dho Damian de la Vandera mando tributar y servir y algunos otros de secreto heran guardas del cuerpo de Guaina Capa e que no embargante esto eran y^{o}s tributarios y servian como los demas del dho

valle a todos los dhos sus encomenderos y que don Alonso Tito Atauche que era curaca y mandon dellos pidio se hiziese merzed de ellos pa sus yanaconas y que no embargante que se le hizo merzed de los dhos y^{o}s por yanaconas la verdad es que eran yndios tributarios y avian servido y servian como los demas del dho valle.

/f.94v/ 14 v Yten si saven e conocen que al tiempo que el tesorero Garcia de Melo visito este valle de Yucai e conmuto la tasa de coca y servi^{o} personal que davan a plata por mandado y orden de los dhos caciques se escondieron todos los y^{o}s o la mayor parte dellos que Damian de la Vandera avia visitado por tributarios y otros muchos y^{o}s que antes por orden de los caciques se avian exsemido del servi^{o} e que demas de los quel dho don Françisco Chilche escondio y de otros que el tenia consigo so color de yanaconas saco en esta dha visita otros v^{te} e cinco diziendo que le servian de yanaconas y les daria tierras y pagaria por ellos su tasa y declaren que y^{o}s son y como se llaman.

15 v Iten si saven e conocen si saven que al tiempo que el Padre Diego Escudero vino por cura del valle de Yucai que avia cinco años poco mas o menos queriendo empadronar los y^{o}s que eran tributarios y los que eran yanaconas se informo de los dhos caciques y le informaron que eran yanaconas los quellos quisieron y les parecio y ansi puso por yanaconas los quellos dixeron digan.

16 v Iten si saven e conocen que al tiempo que el Lic^{do} frei P^{o} Gutierrez Flores visito el valle por mandado de su Ex^{a} puso por yanaconas todos los que tenian puestos el dho Padre Diego Escudero en su libro sin hazer sobre ello otra diligencia ni pesquisa sobre si avian tributado o no e que los y^{o}s por entender que avian de quedar libres sin tributar dixeron ser yanaconas y que los tales saven que todos los y^{o}s que el dho frei P^{o} Gutierrez puso por yanaconas siempre an sido y^{o}s tributarios deste valle y subjetos a sus caciques del y an servido y tributado como todos los demas y^{o}s del dho valle y que si alguna bez se an exsedido //
/f.95/ de servir e tributar ha sido por el favor que ha tenido en los dhos caciques y por averles escondido como esta dho en las preguntas antes desta y no porque no fuesen y^{o}s tributarios.

17 v yten si saven e conocen que al tiempo quel dho Lic^{do} frei Pedro Gutierrez visito el dho valle todos los dhos yndios que puso por yanaconas servian y tributaban pa la tasa la parte que se les repartia por los caciques y asi se aberiguo en la dha visita por el dho visitador como por ella parecera e que no embargante que algunas bezes avian dexado de acudir a servir por causa de los dhos sus caciques eran y^{o}s tributarios y ansi tributaron al tiempo de la dha bisita e mas diez años e mucho tiempo atras siempre eçepto las vezes que los dhos caciques por sus fines los essemian de la tasa e servi^{o}s digan.

18 v Iten si saven e conocen todos los y^{o}s del dho valle questan puestos por yanaconas en la visita del dho frei Pedro Gutierrez despues aca an benido a declarar como heran y^{o}s tributarios y siempre avian servido y tributado y que si save a dho /si se avia dho/ que eran yanaconas avia sido por entender que avian de quedar libres del tributo e que el Padre Diego Escudero ha fecho aberiguacion con todos los caciques y principales del dho valle asi naturales como mitimaes y con los dhos que se dizen yanaconas y sus principales e que son todos ellos aberiguo que todos los y^{o}s contenidos en el dho memorial que esta presentado que pido se muestre a los testigos heran y son y^{o}s tributarios e que si avian dexado algun tiempo de servir y tributar fue por las razones contenidas en las preguntas antes desta

/f.95v/ 19 v Y saven que todo lo suso dho es publico y notorio. El Licenciado Pedraza.

El señor dotor en cumplimiento de la provision de su Exª visto lo pedido por el dho cap^{t} Martin Garcia de Loyola mando quel suso dho presente los tg^{os} de que en esta causa se entiende aprovechar y se reciba la informacion dellos como su Exª lo m^{da} por la dha provision y se le de por testim^{o} todo como lo pide en su pedimento ante mi Pero Diaz Valdeon escriv^{o}

v En la ciudad del Cuzco a onze dias del mes de henero de mil qui^{o}s e setenta e quatro años antel dho señor dotor por ante mi el dho escri^{o} el dho capitan Martin Garcia de Loyola presento por testigos en esta causa a don Pedro Cochachi e a Sebastian Tinaicha e a Juan Batavina e a don Diego Casatambo y a Martin Yupangui y a Martin Yana y a Lucas Chico e a Martin Caritopa e a don Garcia Paucar y a Miguel Chura Suca e a Martin Condemaita e a Martin Sauni; todos y^{o}s naturales e mitimas del dho valle de los quales y de cada uno dellos el señor dotor por lengua de Pero Miguel tomo juramento en forma jurando por Dios e por Santa Maria su madre y por la señal de la Cruz que cada uno hizo con su mano derecha que como buenos xpianos guardando sus conciencias diran verdad en este negocio de que son presentados por tg^{s} y si asi lo hizieren Dios les ayude e lo contrario se le demande como a malos xpianos e cada uno dellos dixo si juro e amen. tg^{os} Alonso de Valdes e don Jer^{mo} Marañon alguazil mayor vz^{o}s desta ciudad. Pero Diaz Valdeon escrivano.

v En la ciudad del Cuzco a diez dias del mes de febrero de mil e qui^{o}s y setenta e //
/f.96/ quatro años ante el dho señor dotor y por ante mi el dho escribano Alonso de Valdes en nombre del dho capitan Martin Garcia de Loyola presento por t^{gos} en esta causa a Diego Escudero clerigo presvit^{o} cura e vic^{o} del valle de Yucai del qual el señor dotor tomo juramento en forma segun orden sacerdotal e prometio de dezir verdad so pena de perjuro t^{gos} Rodrigo de Cespedes e don Jer^{mo} Marañon Pero Diaz Valdeon escrivano.

v En el Cuzco en treze dias del mes de febr^{o} de mil e qui^{o}s e setenta e quatro años ante el dho señor dotor e ante mi el dho escriv^{o} el dho Alonso de Valdes en el dho nombre presento por t^{go} pa en esta causa a Marcos Cayo Gualpa yndio del qual el dho señor dotor por lengua del dho Pedro Miguel ynterprete tomo e recibio juramento en forma de dr^{o} por Dios nuestro s^{or} e por la señal de la cruz a tal como esta † el qual prometio de dezir verdad e a la fuerça e conclusion del dho juramento dixo si juro e amen t^{gos} los dhos Pero Diaz Baldeon escrivano.

v E despues de lo suso dho en la dha ciudad del Cuzco a diez y nueve dias del mes de febr^{o} de mil e qui^{o}s y setenta e quatro años antel dho señor dotor Loarte e ante mi el dho escri^{o} el dho Alonso de Valdes en el dho nombre presento por t^{o} para en la dha razon a Alonso Chauca yndio del qual el dho señor dotor por el dho ynterprete suso dho tomo e recibio juramento en forma de dr^{o} segun que a los demas t^{gos} de suso e a la fuerça e conclusion del dho juram^{to} dixo si juro e amen t^{go} Juan Bautista procurador e Fran^{co} Perez Pero Diaz Valdeon escrivano.

/f.96v/ v E despues de lo suso dho en la dha ciudad del Cuzco en diez dias del mes de março de mil e qui^{o}s e setenta e quatro años antel dho señor dotor e ante mi el dho escri^{o} el dho Alonso de Valdes en el dho nombre presento por testigo para en la dha causa a Pedro Chinanzila yndio cañar y a Hernando Tociacalla de los quales el señor dotor por el dho ynterprete tomo e recibio juram^{to} en forma segun a los demas t^{o}s de suso y a la conclusion del dho juramento dixeron si juro e amen t^{gos} los dhos. Pero Diaz Valdeon escri^{o}.

v E lo que los dhos t^{gos} e cada uno dellos dixeron e depusieron es como se sigue. Pero Diaz Valdeon escrivano.

El dho don Pedro Cochachin natural del valle de Yuca yndio mitima del dho valle de Yuca vz^{o} de la villa de Santiago de Oropesa presentado por el dho capitan Martin Garcia de Loyola aviendo jurado y siendo preg^{do} dixo lo siguiente:

i A la primera preg^{ta} dixo que conoce a las partes tiene noticia de los dhos y^{o}s yanaconas porqueste t^{o} lo vio visitar. De las generales dixo ques de hedad de mas de setenta años e no concurre en ninguna dellas mas de estar encomendado en el dho capitan Martin Garcia de Loyola y no por eso dexara de dezir verdad.

ij A la pregunta dos dixo queste testigo es yndio mitima del dho valle de Yucay y le puso en el dho valle un capitan de Guaina Capa e quel dho valle de Yucay se llamaba la casa del Ynga y todos los mitimaes e naturales que en el dho valle avian servian al dho Ynga y a sus hijos e mujeres e parientes e les beneficiavan //
/f.97/ las chacaras que tenian y le servian de yanaconas e camayos como y^{o}s que los tenia el dho Ynga en el dho valle ocupados en el servi^{o} de su casa y edeficios y sementeras que en el dho valle hazia y esto save e vio desta pregunta.

iij A la pregunta tres dixo que al tiempo quel marques don Françisco Piçarro y los demas cristianos que con el venian entraron en esta ciudad del Cuzco este t^{o} era ya ombre de treinta años poco mas o menos porque tenia hijos y luego el dho marques don Françisco Piçarro tomo pa si los y^{o}s del dho valle de Yucai como cosa mas principal de la tierra e por ser y^{o}s que avian servido al Ynga y estar todos ellos en titulo y boz de yanaconas porque los y^{o}s que servian al Ynga en las cosas que tiene dha en la pregunta antes desta los tenia por sus yanaconas que quiere dezir en lengua española criados de su servi^{o} e asi todos los y^{o}s del dho valle mitimas e naturales heran yanaconas del Ynga y sirvieron todos desde luego al dho marques don Françisco Piçarro en las cosas contenidas en la dha preg^{ta} y en todo lo demas que les mandavan el y sus mayordomos y servian todos en lo suso dho en esta ciudad y en el dho valle de Yucai y en los andes y en otras partes sin reservar a ninguno so color de dezir que eran yanaconas del Ynga o de sus hijos porque todos ellos se llamaban y^{o}s del marques don Fran^{co} Piçarro y le sirvieron hasta que murieron y esto save e vio desta pregunta.

iiij A la pregunta quatro dixo que luego quel marques don Françisco Piçarro entro en esta ciudad y tomo todos los y^{o}s miti- //
/f.97v/ mas e naturales del dho valle pa si ellos y los demas y^{o}s del reino no tenian tasa y todos en lugar de tributo davan a las personas que los thenian el servi^{o} y demas cosas que la pregunta dize e lo mesmo dieron e hizieron al dho marques don Fran^{co} Piçarro y esto vio este t^{o} por tratar en aquel tiempo mas en particular que otro ninguno y esto save e dixo a esta pregunta.

v A la pregunta cinco dixo que luego quel marques don Françisco Piçarro murio subcedieron en don Gonçalo Piçarro hijo del dho marques don Françisco Piçarro e se sirvio dellos y le tributaron acudiendolo con todas las cosas y servi^{o} personal segun e como avian fecho al dho marques don Françisco Piçarro y sus mayordomos y esto save e vio desta pregunta.

vj A la pregunta seis dixo que save e vio este t^{o} que despues quel dho don Gonçalo Piçarro se fue a los reinos despaña [*sic*] y murio subcedieron luego en su magestad y acudieron con el tributo a los oficiales reales desta ciudad en que le davan el tributo de maiz y trigo y papas e y^{o}s pa las chacaras de coca por la forma e orden que lo avian dado y davan al dho Gonçalo Piçarro y al dho don Fran^{co} Piçarro su padre pa lo qual contribuyan todos los y^{o}s mitimaes e naturales del dho valle porque ningun yndio del dho valle so color de dezir que eran yanaconas ni en otra forma se llamavan de otros ni servian a ninguna otra persona y esto dixo a esta preg^{ta}.

vij A la pregunta siete dixo que estando en cabeza de su m^{t} todos los y^{o}s mitimas y naturales del dho valle como tiene declarado //
/f.98/ en la pregunta antes desta el marques de Cañete visorrey que fue destos reinos los encomendo a todos ellos asi naturales como mitimas en don Diego Sayre Topa Ynga hijo de Mango Ynga y nieto de Guaina Capac para el efeto contenido en esta pregunta y se los dio con titulo de mayorazgo como la pregunta lo dize y parecera por el titulo que dellos tiene y como tales sus y^{o}s todos ellos le acudian con el tributo que por la tasa que el Lic^{do} Gasca Presidente que fue destos reinos dio a los oficiales reales desta ciudad se les mandava diesen e muerto el dho don Diego Sayre Topa subcedieron luego todos en doña Beatriz Coya su hija legitima mujer legitima que al pres^{te} es del dho capitan Martin Garcia de Loyola a la qual y a sus curadores en su nombre hasta que se caso dieron el tributo que por la tasa se les mandava y antes que fuesen encomendados en el dho don Diego Sayre Topa fueron exsimidos del dho servi^{o} en tiempo del Presidente Gasca los y^{o}s de Coto que dio al Padre de don Alonso Ucosicha y se los dio y saco del dho repartimiento siendo todos

ellos yos tributarios del dho repartimiento y anexos a el e mitimas puestos por el Ynga por yanaconas del sol engaño y suvreticia [*sic*] relacion que en ella hizo al dho Presidente Gasca y porque los caciques principales del dho valle por saver la verdad no se los quitasen el padre del dho don Alonso y el dho don Alonso de Ucosicha tenia por vien de que todos ellos ayudasen a pagar el tributo y hazer el benefo de coca y demas servios que por la tasa estavan obligados a pagar al dho don Diego Sayre Topa y a la dha doña Beatriz Coya su hija e si esto no hicieran los dhos caciques por ser yos //
/f.98v/ del dho repartimiento los uvieran sacado por pleito e como contribuian con el tributo que les cabia los dexaban servir al padre del dho don Alonso y al dho don Alonso Ucusicha su hijo y esto save e vio desta pregunta.

viij A la pregunta ocho dixo despues de averle leido todos los nombres de los yos contenidos en el dho memorial que save e vio este to que todos ellos de los que eran yos para poder servir y tributar en tiempo del dho marques y del dho Gonçalo Piçarro su hijo y el tiempo que estuvieron en cabeza de su magestad e despues que fueron encomendados en don Diego Sayre Topa padre de la dha doña Beatriz Coya mujer del dho capitan Martin Garcia de Loyola siempre estuvieron todos subjetos al dho repartimito como yos tributarios del e lo estuvieron hasta que Damian de la Vandera e Garcia de Melo los visito que en el tiempo que Damian de la Vandera los besito algunos dellos aunque pocos quedaran por yanaconas de don Françisco Chilche cacique principal del dho repartimito e don Alonso Tito Ataoche e de otros yos e yndias Yngas naturales desta ciudad del Cuzco e por ser yos del dho repartimito y anexos a el como los demas e que como tales goçaban del fruto de las tierras del e porque los demas yos atun lunas [*sic*] del dho repartimiento no reclamasen sobre ello e les hiciesen bolver al dho repartimiento para estar subjetos a el como todos los demas que contribuyan y an contribuido siempre //
/f.99/ todos con el tributo que les cavia y el cacique e caciques y principales del dho valle les repartia e asi save que todos son yos tributarios del dho repartimiento e los que son al presente moços de los yos contenidos en el dho memorial son hijos de los yos tributarios del dho repartimiento e asi todos como tales tributarios an pagado y pagaron el dho tributo e contribuyeron con los demas servios que los demas yos atun lunas del dho repartimiento han hecho y hazen en el hasta quel licenciado frei Po Gutierres Flores los visito y puso por yanaconas de lo qual este to y los demas yos an recebido agravio porquel tributo que pagavan los yos contenidos en el dho memorial lo pagavan agora todos los yos del dho repartimiento demas del que solian dar para cumplir la que por la tasa estan obligados y esto save e ha visto desta pregunta.

ix A la pregunta nueve dixo quel marques don Françisco Piçarro sirviendose de los yos nombro por cacique principal de todos ellos asi de los mitimas como de los naturales al dho don Françisco Chilche y lo fue e uso del dho cargo hasta que estando todos en la cabeza de su mt don Garcia Quispicapi pidio ante la justicia desta ciudad que atento a quel era cacique principal de todo el dho repartimiento se le diese el cacicazgo e asi por concierto que entre ellos ubo y por sentencia que en la causa se dio mediante el concierto quedaron por caciques principales //
/f.99v/ de todos los yos del dho repartimito los dhos don Françisco Chilche e don Garcia Quispicapi en que el dho don Francisco Chilche fuese cacique de los yos mitimas y el dho don Garcia Quispicapi cacique de los yos naturales del dho valle e ansi lo an sido y usado de los dhos cargos hasta agora.

x A la pregunta diez dixo que despues que el dho don Françisco Chilche e don Garcia Quispicapi por el dho concierto fueron ambos caciques principales del dho repartimiento hubo division entre los dhos yos en que favoreciendose de los caciques en especial del dho don Françisco Chilche no acudian al servio que se hazia a sus encomenderos ni con todo el tributo que le avian de dar e todo lo que se quitava a estos se cargava a los demas yos tributarios del dho repartimiento y lo hizieron asi los dhos caciques hasta quel dho licdo frei Pedro Gutierrez los bisito por yos yanaconas e los reservo de todo el tributo del dho repartimiento y esto save desta pregunta.

xj A la pregunta onze dixo que save e vio este testigo que aunque los dhos yos contenidos en el dho memorial que asi le fue leido e mostrado no servian como los demas yos tributarios del repartimito por ser todos ellos yos tributarios siempre estuvieron subjetos a los dhos caciques y les obedecian en todo lo que les mandavan asi en el pagar del tributo que les repartian como en todo lo demas segun y como la pregunta lo dize y declara y esto save de ella.

/f.100/ xij A la pregunta doze dixo que save e vio este to que al tiempo que Damian de la Vandera visito los yos del dho valle visto la disulucion que avia en que los caciques reservavan a unos de tributos mas que a otros so color e diciendo que eran sus yanaconas pa que no ubiese tantos yos del repartimiento de tributo reservado ni que dexasen de pagar lo que les cavia el dho Damian de la Bandera mando a la mayor parte de los yos contenidos en el memorial que pagasen su tributo como los demas del dho repartimito y asi lo pagaron e an pagado hasta que el dho licdo frei Pedro Gutierrez los visito y esto save desta pregunta.

xiij A la pregunta treze dixo que muerto Guaina Capa en la Provincia de Quito traxeron su cuerpo al dho valle de Yucai y para guarda del dho cuerpo los capitanes tomaron de los yos mitimas del dho valle quarenta yos a los quales pusieron por guarda del dho cuerpo y para que tuviesen quenta con el e le diesen de comer e beber y le beneficiasen chacaras de maiz para este efeto y en las fiestas principales que hazian tenian cargo de sacar el dho cuerpo en unas andas a ellos y de que le ofreciesen todos alli y no obstante esto siempre pagavan su tributo y hazian el servio personal que los demas yos del repartimiento y don Alonso Tito Atauche al tiempo que murio un yno que se llamaba Atau Rimache que tenia //
/f.100v/ a cargo los dhos quarenta yos dexo en su lugar al dho don Alonso Tito Atauche e asi por fin e muerte del dho Atau Rimache el dho don Alonso Tito Atauche subcedio en ser mandon de los dhos quarenta yos en el qual en la visita de Damian de la Vandera se visito por yos del repartimito del dho valle de Yucay e por caciques de los dhos quarenta yos que asi guardavan el cuerpo del dho Guaina Capa y despues de visitados los dhos quarenta yos pagavan y pagaron su tributo al encomendero segun y por la orden quel cacique se lo repartia

y lo pagaron todos y los que dellos deçendieron hasta que por yanaconas los visito el dho Lic^{do} frei Pedro Gutierrez y los exsimio del dho repartimiento y esto save desta pregunta.

xiiij A la pregunta catorze dixo que al tiempo que Damian de la Vandera visito los dhos y^{o}s que llamo a don Françisco Chilche cacique principal de ellos pa que le declarase e manifestase los y^{o}s que del dho repartimiento y encomienda avia en el dho valle encomendados en el dho don Diego Sayre Topa el dho don Françisco Chilche cacique por sus fines e intereses dexo de manifestar al dho Damian de la Vandera todos los y^{o}s contenidos en el dho memorial los unos porque los avia el quitado del dho repartimiento e los tenia so color e diziendo que eran sus yanaconas y los otros porque guardavan el cuerpo de Guayna Capa y los otros por tenerlos a cargo el dho don //
/f.101/ Alonso Ucusicha asi al tiempo que el dho Damian de la Vandera los vesito el dho don Françisco Chilche no le encubriera los dhos y^{o}s e le declarara la verdad el dho Damian de la Vandera los dexara por y^{o}s tributarios del dho repartimiento con los demas que en el avia y esta fue la causa que el dho Damian de la Vandera no los declaro a todos por y^{o}s tributarios del dho repartimiento e asi bista la gran disulucion que en ello avia mando que contribuyesen muchos de ellos con tributo como lo tiene declarado este t^{o} en la pregunta.

Y save e vio este testigo que quando Garcia de Melo visito los y^{o}s del dho repartimi^{to} el dho don Françisco Chilche demas de los y^{o}s que dexo de manifestar ante Damian de la Vandera tomo de los y^{o}s del dho repartimi^{to} otros muchos y^{o}s que no los manifesto ni declaro al dho Garcia de Melo por y^{o}s tributarios del dho repartimi^{to} y todos estos despues de averlos visitado el dho Garcia de Melo pagavan tributo en el dho repartimi^{to} aunque no estavan visitados por y^{o}s tributarios del a causa de que los y^{o}s atun lunas del dho repartimiento no reclamasen e se descubriesen la verdad y los y^{o}s que ultimamente escondio y dexo de manifestar el dho don Fran^{co} Chilche en la visita del dho Garcia de Melo los nombres dellos este t^{o} no se acuerda mas de que save que son de los contenidos en el dho memorial que le fue leido y mostrado y esto save desta pregunta.

xv A la pregunta quinze dixo que es verdad lo contenido en la dha pregunta porquel dho Diego Escudero en la visita que de los dhos //
/f.101v/ hizo puso por yanaconas los y^{o}s quel dho don Françisco Chilche y los demas caciques e principales del dho valle le manifestaron.

xvj A la pregunta diez y seis dixo que quando se visitaron los y^{o}s yanaconas del dho valle de Yucai se visitaron por el libro del dho Diego Escudero e si dexaron de manifestarse por y^{o}s tributarios fue entendiendo que se avian de evadir del excesivo trabajo que tenian los demas y^{o}s del dho repartimiento y todos los y^{o}s que asi se dexaron de bisitar e se visitaron por yanaconas de los contenidos en el dho memorial heran tributarios del dho repartimiento como tiene dho y como tales an servido y tributado como todos los demas e si alguna bez se exsemian del dho trib^{o} y servi^{o} hera por el favor que tenian con los caciques y por avellos escondido el dho don Françisco Chilche como tiene dho y esto save y vio desta pregunta.

xvij A la pregunta diez y siete dixo ques verdad todo lo contenido en la dha preg^{ta} porque este testigo a visto de mas de treinta años a esta parte ser y pasar asi en el dho repartimiento con los y^{o}s contenidos en el dho memorial y no ha bisto ni oydo cosa en contrario.

xviij A la pregunta diez y ocho dixo que si los y^{o}s que del dho repartimi^{to} se visitaron por yanaconas entendieran que no avian de pagar tributo como al presente lo pagan no se visitaran por yanaconas sino por y^{o}s atun lunas del dho repartimi^{to} como lo eran de antes y lo mesmo los caciques y entendieran que no se avian //
/f.102/ de quedar con los dhos yanaconas pa se servir dellos como de antes no los manifestaran por yanaconas y declararan ser y^{o}s tributarios del dho repartimiento como en la realidad de verdad lo son y esto save desta preg^{ta}.

xix A la pregunta diez y nueve dixo que lo que dho y declarado tiene por lengua de los dhos ynterpretes es verdad so cargo del dho juramento e siendole tornado e dado a entender que los dhos ynterpretes se afirmo y ratifico en ello por ser verdad e no firmo porque dixo que no savia e lo firmaron los ynterpretes va testado /o lo mas/ /suyo dis/ y esto save de esta pregunta a la pregunta quinze dixo que entre renglones de Melo. Hernardo de Morales Felipe Sayre Martin Palacios ante mi Pero Diaz Valdeon escri^{o}.

Testigo. El dho Sebastian Tenazela natural del valle de Yucay indio cañar aviendo jurado en forma y siendo preg^{do} por las preguntas del dho interro^{o} dixo lo siguiente:

j A la primera preg^{ta} dixo que conoze a las partes e tiene noticia de los yanaconas porque a este testigo siendo yn^{o} de la dha encomienda le hizieron visitar por yanaconas.

De las generales de la ley dixo ques de hedad de mas de setenta años e no concurre en ninguna de las generales.

ij A la pregunta dos dixo que al tiempo que los españoles entraron en esta ciudad del Cuzco entro este t^{o} en el valle de Yucay que venia por soldado de Chalcho- //
/f.102v/ chima y Quizquiz capitanes de Atagualpa e se quedo por yndio tributr^{o} en el dho valle con otros y^{o}s cañares que con el vinieron e vio que en aquel tiempo todos los y^{o}s del dho valle se llamaban del Ynga y que eran dos parcialidades la una de mitimas que quiere dezir y^{o}s advenediços e la otra de naturales e todos servian al Ynga e a sus hijos e mujeres e parientes e les beneficiavan las chacaras que tenian y le servian todos de Yanaconas como y^{o}s que los tenia el dho Ynga ocupados en el servi^{o} de su casa y edeficios de sementeras que hazia en el dho valle y esto save desta pregunta.

iij A la pregunta tres dixo que luego que el marques don Françisco Piçarro y la demas gente que con el venia entraron en esta ciudad del Cuzco e se apoderaron en ella luego el dho marques tomo para si los yºs del dho valle de Yucai por ser yºs que avian servido al Ynga y estar todos en titulo de yºs yanaconas del Ynga que quiere dezir criados del Ynga y mando que le sirviesen y asi le comenzaron a servir todos en las cosas contenidas en la dha pregunta como los demas yºs del dho valle e yban al benefº de las chacaras de coca que el dho marques tenia en los Andes e todos sin quedar ninguno se llamaban yºs del marques e le servian a el y a sus mayordomos en todo lo que les mandava como se declara en la pregunta y esto save della.

iiij A la pregunta quatro dixo que luego quel marques don Françisco Piçarro tomo pa si los yºs del valle de Yucay le comen- //
/f.103/ çaron a servir como dho tiene y entonzes ellos y los demas yºs del dho reino no tenian tasa de tribuº que avian de pagar asi y en lugar de tribuº servian por la forma y orden que se declara en la dha pregta e sirvieron al dho marques don Françisco Piçarro dandole por tributo todo lo que la pregunta dice a el y a sus mayordomos porque este tº lo vio ser y pasar asi por servir y tributar con ellos al dho marques como los demas yºs del dho valle y esto save desta pregunta.

v A la pregunta cinco dixo que save e vio este tº que por fin e muerte del dho marques don Françisco Piçarro subcedieron todos los yºs del dho valle en el dho don Gonçalo Piçarro su hijo e le sirvieron e tributaron segun e de la forma y manera que servian y tributaban al dho marques don Franco Piçarro su padre y a sus mayordomos y esto save e vio desta pregunta.

vj A la pregunta seis dixo que save e vio este tº que despues de muerto el dho don Gonçalo Piçarro subcedieron luego en su magestad y acudieron luego con el tributo a los oficiales reales desta ciudad en que le daban el tributo de maiz y trigo y papas e yºs pa las chacaras de coca por la forma y orden que lo avian dado y davan al dho don Gonçalo Piçarro y al dho don Françisco Piçarro su padre para lo qual contribuian todos los yºs del dho valle sin que ningun yndio de los que en el vivian se llamase de otra persona español ni Ynga con nombre de yanaconas ni de otra manera y esto dixo a esta pregunta.

vij A la pregunta siete dixo que estando en cabeza de su mt todos los yºs mitimas //
/f.103v/ y naturales del dho valle como tiene declarado en la pregunta anterior desta el marques de Cañete visorrey que fue destos reinos los encomendo a todos ellos asi naturales como mitimas en don Diego Sayre Topa Ynga hijo de Mango Ynga y nieto de Guaina Capac para el efeto contenido en esta pregta y se los dio con titulo de Mayorazgo como la pregunta lo dize y como parecera por el titulo e provision que dellos tiene y despues de ser encomendados en el dho don Diego Sayre Topa Ynga padre de la dha doña Beatriz de Mendoça el dho don Francisco Chilche junto los yºs principales del dho valle e les dixo quel licdo Baca de Castro le avia dado para si e por sus yºs los yºs cañares que vinieron al dho valle con Chalcochima y Quizquiz capitanes de Atagualpa e que el los queria quitar e sacar del dho repartimiento e que no tributasen al dho don Diego Sayre Topa e asi quito e tomo del repartimito treinta yºs cañaris e de alli adelante los reservo de tributo del dho repartimito y el tributo que davan lo repartian por los yºs tributarios del dho repartimito y algunas bezes porque los yºs atun lunas del dho repartimiento no se quexasen de lo suso dho ayudaban los dhos treinta yºs con alguna cosa pa el tributo de la tasa y demas destos treinta yºs el dho don Françisco Chilche tomo e saco en vezes de los yºs mitimas tributarios y advenediços que avian benido en tiempo de la conquista que todos heran ya encomendados y del dho repartimiento cinquenta yºs tributarios //
/f.104/ e los tomo pa su serviº y estos esento asimismo del tributo de la tasa aunque algunas vezes porque no ubiese quexas y se descubriese esto el dho don Françisco Chilche hazia que ayudasen con algun tributo para la tasa e saven lo suso dho don Diego Casitumbai e Lope Martin Condemaita y Lucas Chico y otros yºs viejos. Y muerto el dho don Diego Sayre Topa subcedieron luego en la dha doña Beatriz Coya su legitima hija mujer legitima del dha capitan Martin Garcia de Loyola a la qual y a sus curadores en su nombre dieron el tributo que por la tasa estavan obligados a dar e para ello ayudavan e contribuian los yºs quel dho don Françisco Chilche avia tomado del dho repartimiento aunque poca cosa y este tº es uno de los yºs que el dho don Franco tomo e saco del dho repartimito para si diziendo que el licdo Vaca de Castro se los avia dado y demas de los yºs quel dho don Franco Chilche saco del dho repartimito save este tº que se exsentaron del dho repartimito los yºs de Coto que serian quarenta yºs poco mas menos diziendo Ucusicha padre de don Alonso Ucusicha que el Presidente Gasca e el licdo Baca de Castro se los avia dado para si y a esta causa los tomo e saco del dho repartimito y estando en poder del dho don Alonso Ucusicha no save si pagaron tributo para el dho repartimiento mas de que save que los tomaron e quitaron de los yºs del dho repartimiento y esto save desta pregunta.

viij A las ocho preguntas dixo aviendole leido el memorial de yºs presentado en esta causa que este tº es uno de los //
/f.104v/ contenidos en este memorial e save e vio este tº que todos ellos de los que heran yºs para poder servir y tributar entre en poder del marques e del dho don Gonçalo Piçarro su hijo y el tiempo que estuvieron en cabeza de su magestad y despues que fueron encomendados en el dho don Diego Sayre Topa padre de la dha doña Beatriz Coya e despues que subcedieron en la dha doña Beatriz Coya mujer del dho capitan Martin Garcia de Loyola siempre estuvieron subjetos al dho repartimito como yºs tributarios del y obedecian al dho don Françisco Chilche como a su cacique principal y estuvieron asi subjetos hasta que Damian de la Bandera e Garcia de Melo los bisitaron y en el tiempo que Damian de la Vandera los bisito que fue antes que Garcia de Melo los visitase el dho don Franco Chilche no quiso manifestar ante el dho Damian de la Vandera a los dhos ochenta yºs que asi thenia sacados e quitados del dho repartimito y quedaron esentos de la dha visita los dhos yºs y los yºs de Coto e otros yºs como fueron los yºs que don Alonso Tito Ataoche saco diziendo que eran sus yanaconas siendo como heran todos del dho repartimiento e asi save que todos son yºs tributarios del dho repartimito y los que son al presente moços de los contenidos en el dho memorial son yºs hijos de los yºs tributarios deste repartimiento e asi todos como tales tributarios e subjetos al dho repartimito pagavan tributo para ayuda a la tasa hasta que el Licdo frei Pº Gutierrez Flores los visito e puso por yanaconas de lo qual //
/f.105/ este tº y los demas se admiraron que los sacasen del dho repartimito y los pusiesen en la corona real y esto respondio a esta pregunta.

ix A la pregunta nueve dixo que save este testigo lo contenido en la dha pregunta porque lo vio ser y pasar asi como en ella se contiene y an usado de los dhos cacicazgos como la pregunta lo declara.

x A la pregunta diez dixo que los yndios mitimas an sido subjetos al dho don Fran^{co} e los naturales al dho don Garcia Quispicapi e todos ellos an andado por la forma e orden que los caciques lo an querido ocupar en su servi^{o} y en lo demas que les mandavan.

xj A la pregunta honze dixo que save e vio este t^{o} que los yndios contenidos en el dho memorial que le fue leido e mostrado por ser todos y^{o}s tributarios del dho repartimi^{to} y encomienda siempre an estado y estuvieron subjetos a los caciques del dho repartimi^{to} e contribuian con algun tributo pa la tasa y no en tanta cantidad como los demas a efeto que los demas del repartimi^{to} no se quexasen e pidiesen su justicia sobre ellos y esto hizieronhasta que el lic^{do} frei P^{o} Gutierrez Flores los bisito en el valle de Yucay que los visito por yanaconas siendo y^{o}s tributarios del dho repartimiento y esto save desta pregunta.

xij A la pregunta doze dixo que los dhos don Françisco Chilche e don Garcia Quispicapi e don Alonso Tito Atauche y otros principales del dho valle de Yucai dexaron de mani- //
/f.105v/ festar muchos y^{o}s tributarios del dho repartimiento que los tenian y avian tomado e sacado del dho repartimiento pa servirse dellos y visto por Damian de la Vandera la disolucion que en ello avia mando a los dhos caciques que no se sirviesen de los dhos y^{o}s so color de dezir que eran yanaconas e que tributasen en el dho repartimi^{to} como los demas tributarios pues heran todos tributarios e naturales del repartimi^{to} e sin embargo desto no lo quisieron hazer e se sirvieron dellos y asi lo exsentaron del dho repartimiento siendo tributarios del y por que los y^{o}s atun lunas no reclamasen sobre esto pagavan los y^{o}s contenidos en el dho memorial alguna cosa del dho tributo y esto save della.

xiij A la pregunta treze dixo que save e vio este testigo que los y^{o}s que se llamaban apo yanaconas que quiere dezir criados del cuerpo de Guaina Capa estos tenian cargo de guardar el cuerpo de Guaina Capa e hazer sacreficios e otros servi^{o}s segun su rito antigüo y eran todos ellos y^{o}s tributarios del dho repartimiento de los mitimas que en el avia y si se exsentaron de tributo en alguna manera fue porque los caciques lo consentian e consintieron por la dha razon e siempre pagaron tributo para ayuda a la tasa hasta que el dho lic^{do} frei P^{o} Gutierrez los visito por yanaconas e los esento del tributo de la dha tasa y esto save desta pregunta.

/f.106/ xiiij A la pregunta catorze dixo que quando Garcia de Melo bisito los dhos y^{o}s averiguo bastantemente como el dho don Françisco Chilche avia tomado e sacado para si de los y^{o}s cañares mitimas del dho repartimiento mucha cantidad de y^{o}s e dellos bisito e restituyo al repartimiento veintiocho y^{o}s e se quedo con los demas y esto save vio desta pregunta.

xv A la pregunta quinze dixo ques verdad lo contenido en la dha pregunta porque el dho Diego Escudero en la visita que hizo de los y^{o}s del dho valle pa su dotrina puso por y^{o}s yanaconas los y^{o}s que dho don Françisco Chilche e los demas y^{o}s principales le manifestaron por yanaconas sin hazer mas aberiguacion e asi puso tantos yanaconas en el dho libro.

xvj A la pregunta diez y seis dixo que quando el licenciado frei P^{o} Gutierrez Flores visito los dhos yanaconas los visito por el libro de yanaconas quel dho Diego Escudero tenia e como los sacaron y escrivieron por el dho libro no se hizo aberiguacion de como los caciques los avian tomado de los y^{o}s tributarios del dho repartimiento y esto save desta pregunta.

xvij A la pregunta diez y siete dixo ques verdad lo contenido en la dha preg^{ta} por queste t^{o} vio que fue paso asi como en ella se declara.

xviij A la pregunta diez y ocho dixo que todos los y^{o}s contenidos en el dho memorial //
/f.106v/ an sido y son y^{o}s tributarios del dho valle y repartimiento como tiene dho y si se an exsentado del dho repartimi^{to} fue por los caciques averlos sacado del y servidose de ellos so color de yanaconas no siendo yanaconas sino y^{o}s tributarios del repartimiento e que agora visto que los caciques no consienten que los y^{o}s y yanaconas gocen de las tierras e aprovechamientos del repartimiento como antes gozaban les a pesado a todos por no aver declarado la verdad para se visitar por y^{o}s tributarios del dho repartimi^{to} y esto responde a esta preg^{ta}.

xix A la pregunta diez y nueve dixo que lo que dho tiene por lengua de los dhos ynterpretes es verdad so cargo del dho juramento e siendole leydo se afirmo e ratifico en ello e lo firmaron los ynterpretes. Hernando de Morales Felipe Saire. Ante mi Pero Diaz Valdeon escri^{o}.

Testigo. Este dia juro el dho Juan Bautista Rucana presentado en esta causa por el dho capitan Martin Garcia de Loyola yndio natural del valle de Yucai y aviendo jurado y siendo preguntado por el tenor del dho interr^{o} dixo lo siguiente:

j A la primera pregunta dixo que conoce a las partes e tiene noticia de los yanaconas porqueste t^{o} es natural del dho valle y save que los yanaconas contenidos en esta causa son de los tributarios contenidos en el dho repartimiento.

/f.107/ De las generales dixo ques de hedad de noventa años poco mas o menos e que no concurre en nynguna dellas mas de estar encomendado en el dho capitan Martin Garcia de Loyola.

ij A la pregunta dos dixo queste t^{o} es natural del dho valle de Yucai e vio que en tiempo de Guaina Capa Ynga senor que fue destos reinos el dho Guaina Capac tenia el dho valle y asiento de Yucai como casa suya por ser apacible y asi hizo los hedeficios y casas que en el dho valle avia pa su recreacion e bibienda y en el dho valle tenia muchos y^{o}s mitimas e yanaconas que quiere dezir y^{o}s pa su servi^{o} los quales avia traido o recogido al dho valle de muchas partes deste reino e todos ellos servian al dho Ynga y a sus hijos e mujeres e parientes e les beneficiavan sus chacaras y les servian de camayos e como sus yanaconas y esto save e vio desta pregunta porque en aquel tiempo hera este testigo moço de hedad que se acuerda bien de lo que paso.

iij A la pregunta tres dixo queste t^{o} save que luego que los españoles entraron en esta ciudad del Cuzco el marques don Françisco Piçarro tomo para si el valle de Yucay y todos los y^{o}s que en el avia asi mitimas como naturales camaios e yanaconas del Ynga los quales vio este t^{o} que le beneficiaban para el dho marques todas las chacaras que en el dho valle //
/f.107v/ avia del Ynga y le traian el maiz que de ellas se coxian y asi mismo le beneficiavan otras chacaras en esta ciudad a do dizen Tiobamba y las chacaras de coca que el dho marques thenia en Tono y Paucarbamba y le servian en su casa de dalle yerba e leña e y^{o}s de servi^{o} para mitaios sin que ningun yndio de los del dho valle fuesen de otra persona alguna todo lo qual save este t^{o} porque lo vio y sirvio siempre que le cupo de servirle que ya en aquel tiempo hera ombre de mas de quarenta años y esto save y vio desta pregunta.

iiij A la pregunta quatro dixo que save que mucho tiempo despues que los españoles entraron en esta ciudad y al tiempo que entraron los y^{o}s todos de este reino no pagavan tributo por tasa como al presente lo pagan solo daban servi^{o} personal a los españoles y le beneficiavan chacaras de coca y de maiz asi los y^{o}s de Yucai sirvieron al dho marques en las cosas que dho tiene como y^{o}s tributarios y esto save e vio desta pregunta.

v A la pregunta cinco dixo que luego como murio don Françisco Piçarro subcedio en los y^{o}s del valle de Yucay don Gonçalo Piçarro hijo del dho marques don Françisco Piçarro al qual sirvieron todos los y^{o}s mitimas e naturales camayos e yanaconas que fueron de los yangas /yungas/[*sic*] en todas las cosas //
/f.108/ que servian al dho marques su padre como dho tiene e le sirvieron todos ellos como y^{o}s tributarios e de su repartimiento y encomienda sin reservar ninguno porque aunque los y^{o}s que en el dho valle de Yucai avia en tiempo del Ynga dellos eran naturales y dellos mitimas y dellos yanaconas fueron todos encomendados en el dho don Gonçalo Piçarro sin reservar ninguno e asi le tributaron y sirvieron todos como en la preg^{ta} se dize y declara y esto save e vio desta preg^{ta}.

vi A la pregunta seis dixo queste t^{o} save e vio que por fin e muerte del dho don Gonçalo Piçarro subcedieron todos los y^{o}s del dho repartimiento segun e como los tenia e poseya el dho don Gonçalo Piçarro en cabeza de su magestad y por estar todos ellos en cabeza de su m^{t} los oficiales reales desta ciudad cobraron los tributos de todos los y^{o}s del dho repartimiento conforme a la tasa que tenian y a del Presidente Gasca sin que se reservasen por y^{o}s yanaconas los y^{o}s contenidos en el dho memorial porque todos ellos pagavan tributo mitimas e naturales e yanaconas a su m^{t} como encomienda que avia subcedido en su magestad por fin e muerte del dho don Gonçalo Piçarro y esto save desta pregunta.

vij A la pregunta siete dixo que este testigo save e vio questando todos los y^{o}s del dho valle de Yucai en cabeza de su mag^{td} y que pagavan el tributo a los oficiales reales el marques de Cañete bisorrey que fue destos reinos encomen- //
/f.108v/ do los dhos y^{o}s de todo el valle de Yucai en don Diego Sayre Topa Ynga y que no save el titulo que dellos le dio que si alguno tubo se remite al dho titulo o titulos el que dellos se le dio y este t^{o} save e vio que los dhos y^{o}s del valle de Yucay le servian todos asi naturales como mitimas pagandole tributo y sirviendole como los demas y^{o}s de la comarca desta ciudad hazian a los demas y^{o}s en quienes estavan encomendados ecepto los y^{o}s del pueblo de Coto que servian a don Alonso Ucusicha a quien los dexo Ucusicha su padre que hera un yndio principal de los cañares el qual saco los dhos y^{o}s del dho repartimiento por dezir que se lo avia dado el Presidente Gasca le dio titulo dellos porque el dho Ucusicha le ynformo falsamente que eran yanaconas suyos y no anexos al dho repartimiento siendo como son mitimas puestos en el dho valle por el Ynga por camaios del Sol y que como y^{o}s del dho repartimi^{to} sirvieron al dho marques con los demas camayos e yanaconas que ubo en el dho valle y que por muerte del dho don Diego Sayre Topa subcedio en los dhos y^{o}s doña Beatriz Coya su hija legitima y universal heredera a quien los y^{o}s del dho valle de Yucai an servido y pagando su tributo y a sus curadores en su nombre hasta que se caso con el dho capitan Martin Garcia de Loyola a quien pagan tributo los y^{o}s del dho valle ecepto los y^{o}s cuyos nombres se a leido a este t^{o} que siendo del dho repartimi^{to} y que sirvieron e tributaron a los antecesores del dho don Diego Sayre Topa y algunos a el se le an salido de ser tributarios al dho capitan Loyola so color //
/f.109/ de dezir que son yanaconas de muchas personas a quien se an arrimado aunque no estan ni an estado exsemidos de pagar tasa en el dho repartimi^{to} porque los yanaconas de Coto que asi saco del dho repartimiento Ucusicha y los que despues saco don Alonso Tito Atauche siempre an ayudado a pagar tributo a los y^{o}s del repartimiento aunque no en tanta cantidad como an pagado los demas y^{o}s y las personas que los an so sacado lo an consentido porque no se los saquen los caciques del repartimi^{to} por pleitos y esto save e vio desta pregunta.

viij A la pregunta ocho dixo que save y a visto este testigo que save e ha visto este testigo que todos los y^{o}s contenidos en el memorial que le fue leido fueron y^{o}s tributarios del dho repartimi^{to} y algunos moços de poca hedad questan en el memorial son hijos de y^{o}s asi mesmo tributarios en el dho repartimi^{to} y que estuvieron subjetos a don Françisco Chilche y^{o} cañar cacique principal del dho repartimiento a quien servieron y obedecieron en todo lo que les mandava en las cosas tocantes al servi^{o} del marques don Françisco Piçarro y a los demas sus encomenderos y de acudir a todas aquellas cosas y tributo que le davan e todos sirvieron al dho don Fran^{co} Chilche como a su cacique principal y a los dhos sus encomenderos antes que tuviesen tasa y despues que la tuvieron hasta las visitas que dellos hizo Damian de la Bandera y Garcia de Melo donde el dho don Fran^{co} Chilche saco muchos y^{o}s cañares y de otras naciones del dho repartimi^{to} y no los manifesto en las dhas visitas por dezir que eran y^{o}s advenediços y //

/f.109v/ que el los avia juntado pa yanaconas suios y otros yos e yndias Yngas naturales desta ciudad sacaron algunos de los yos del dho memorial en las dhas visitas por dezir que fueron camayos de sus padres y antepasados no embargante lo qual todos los dhos yos ayudaron a tributar a los yos del dho repartimito en poca cantidad hasta que el licdo frei Pedro Gutierrez Flores visitando los yos del dho repartimiento bisito los yos contenidos en el dho memorial por yos yanaconas y desde que se hizo la dha visita los dhos yos no an contribuido con aquella parte que antes de la dha visita contribuian de lo qual este to y los demas yos del dho repartimiento son agraviados porque cargan el tribuo que ellos avian de dar en este to y en los demas yos del dho repartimiento.

ix A la pregunta nueve dixo que el marques don Françisco Piçarro sirviendose de los dhos yos nombro por cacique principal de todos ellos asi de los mitimas como de los naturales a el dho don Françisco Chilche y lo fue e uso del dho cargohasta que estando todos en la cabeza de su mt don Garcia Quispicapi cacique pidio ante la justicia desta ciudad que atento a que era cacique principal del dho repartimito se le diese el cacicazgo e asi por concierto que entre ellos hubo y por sentencia que en la causa se dio mediante el concierto quedaron por caciques principales de todos los yos del dho repartimito los dhos don Franco Chilche e don Garcia Quipspicapi en que el dho don Françisco Chilche fuese cacique de los yos mitimas y el dho don Garcia Quispicapi cacique de los yos naturales del dho valle e ansi lo han sido hasta agora e usado de los dhos cargos.

x A la pregunta diez dixo que despues quel dho don Françisco Chilche y don Garcia Quispicapi //
/f.110/ por el dho concierto fueron ambos caciques principales del dho repartimito hubo division entre los dhos yos en que favoreciendose de los caciques en especial del dho don Franco Chilche no acudian al servio que se hazia a sus encomenderos ni con todo el tributo que avian de dar e todo lo que se quitava destos se cargava a los demas yos tributarios del repartimito y lo hizieron asi los dhos caciques hasta quel dho licdo frei Pedro Gutierres los besito por yos yanaconas e los reservo de todo el tributo del dho repartimito y esto save desta pregunta.

xi A la pregunta honze dixo que save e vio que aunque los yos contenidos en el dho memorial que le fue leido y mostrado no servian como los demas yos tributarios del dho repartimito por ser todos ellos yos tributarios siempre estuvieron subjetos a los dhos caciques y les obedecian en todo lo que les mandavan asi en el pagar del tributo que les repartian como en todo lo demas segun e como la pregta lo dize y esto save y vio desta pregunta.

xij A la pregunta doze dixo que save e vio que quando Damian de la Vandera visito los yos del dho valle de Yucai hallo el dho visitador muchos yos questavan exsemidos de pagar tributo en el dho repartimiento como fueron yos questavan en nombre de yanaconas que avian servido al marques don Franco Piçarro y otros que tenian en guarda el cuerpo de Guayna Capa y otros muchos quel dho don Françisco Chilche avia ocultado y los visito por el dho repartimito y mando que tributasen y se dexo de visitar algunos yos de los dhos en la dha memoria fue porque los escondieron los dhos caciques y esto responde a esta pregunta.

/f.110v/ xiij A la pregunta treze dixo que como dho tiene el dho Damian de la Vandera hallo que en el dho valle avia mas de treinta yos en guarda del cuerpo de Guaina Capa los quales estavan exsemidos de pagar por entero el tributo por razon de la ocupacion que tenian lo qual consentian los caciques y el dho Damian de la Vandera los visito por del dho repartimiento y les mando que tributasen por entero en la dha visita nombro por cacique de ellos a don Alonso Tito Atauche el qual dixo al dho visitador que avia sido siempre cacique de los dhos yos e despues de cierto tiempo oyo dezir este to quel dho don Alonso los avia pedido de merzed en la audiencia real de la ciudad de los Reies e que se los avia dado no embargante lo qual los dhos yos siempre lo an ayudado a pagar la tasa a todos los encomenderos que an sido del dho repartimito hasta agora que los pagan por ser yos mitimas del dho repartimito y esto save e vio desta pregta.

xiiij A las catorce preguntas dixo que save e vio que quando el tesorero Garcia de Melo visito los yos del dho valle de Yucay y conmuto la tasa de coca y servio personal que davan a plata los caciques escondieron los yos que avian escondido en la visita de Damian de la Vandera y por pesquisa quel dho Garcia de Melo hizo hallo algunos dellos y aberiguando ser yos tributarios de dho repartimito los besito entre los demas yos del y mando que tributasen con los yos del dho repartimito y demas de muchos yos quel dho don Franco Chilche tenia escondidos pidio al dho Garcia de Melo que declarase ser suyos otros veinte e cinco yos que saco del dho repartimito que los unos y otros estan en el dho memorial que le fue leido y esto save y vio desta pregunta.

/f.111/ xv A la pregunta quinze dixo ques verdad lo contenido en la pregunta por quel dho Diego Escudero en la visita que de los dhos yos hizo puso por yanaconas los yos que el dho don Françisco Chilche y los demas principales le dixeron y manifestaron siendo yos del repartimito tributarios como docho tiene en las preguntas antes desta.

xvj A la pregunta diez y seis dixo queste to save e vio que quando el licdo Gutierrez visito los yos del dho valle de Yucai los visito por el libro del dho Diego Escudero guardando la orden que en el avia y asi visito por yanaconas todos los yos que los dhos caciques le avian manifestado por tales yanaconas sin hazer otra pesquisa ni aberiguacion sobre ello y que como dho tiene los yos contenidos en el memorial que se le a leido fueron yos tributarios del dho Valle de Yucay y que nunca dexaron de tributar en poca o en mucha cantidad hasta que por la visita del dho licdo Gutierrez se exsentaron de lo hazer por quedar visitados por yanaconas y divisos de los yos tributarios y que demas de que este to lo a oydo muchas bezes a los principalesde los dhos ya/na/conas a entendido que se dexaron visitar por yanaconas entendiendo que no avian de pagar tasa mas de servir a las personas a quien se avian arrimado por orden de los dhos caciques.

xvij A la pregunta diez y siete dixo que ha oydo dezir que muchos de los dhos yanaconas e yos contenidos en el dho memorial an benido a dezir que son yºs tributarios del dho valle y que lo fueron sus padres y que se dexaron visitar por yanaconas por las razones que dho tiene y esto save e vio desta pregunta.

/f.111v/ xviij A la pregunta diez y ocho dixo que si los yºs del dho repartimiento se visitaron por yanaconas fue por entender que no avian de pagar tributos como al preste lo pagavan no se visitaron por yanaconas sino por yºs atun lunas como lo heran de antes porque despues que se visitaron por yanaconas a bueltas de los demas que ay en el dho valle son impididos [*sic*] en las tierras y aprovechamientos del de questan muy arrepisos los caciques si entendieran que no se avian de quedar con los dhos yanaconas para se servir dellos como de antes no los manifestaran por yanaconas y declararan ser yºs tributarios del dho repartimito como en realidad de verdad lo son y esto save desta pregunta.

xix A la pregunta diez y nueve dixo que lo que dho e declarado tiene por los dhos ynterpretes es verdad so cargo del dho juramento e siendole leido y dado a entender por lengua de los dos ynterpretes se afirmo y ratifico en ello por ser verdad e no firmo porque dixo que no sabia e lo firmaron con los ynterpretes. Va testado emprendas a la pregunta dos/ dixo pase por testado y entre renglones y a los demas sus encomenderos. Hernando de Morales. Felipe Saire. Ante mi Pero Diaz Valdeon escrivano.

Testigo. El dho don Diego Lastumbay natural del valle de Yucay yndio cañar vzº de la villa de Santiago de Oropesa del dho valle presentado por el dho capitan Martin Garcia de Loyola y preguntado por el tenor del dho interrº dixo e depuso lo siguiente.

j A la primera pregunta dixo que conosce a las partes e tiene noticia de los yanaconas sobre ques este pº porque a mas de quarenta años que los conoce y conocio a los //
/f.112/ padres de los yºs moços contenidos en el memorial que se le a leido y save que fueron yºs tributarios en el por que los vio servir y tributar juntamte con este tº y los demas yºs naturales e mitimas del dho valle.

De las generales dixo ques de hedad de ochenta años poco mas o menos e no concurre en ninguna dellas mas destar encomendado en el dho capitan Martin Garcia de Loyola e no por eso dexara de dezir verdad.

ij A la pregunta dos dixo que en el tiempo de Guascar Ynga y Atahualpa hijos de Guaina Capac tuvieron diferencias y guerras sobre el señorio deste reino este tº vino con Chalcochima y Quizquiz capitanes de Atagualpa Ynga questava en Quito y se quedo en el dho valle que a mas de quarenta años y en el dho tiempo y despues aca siempre aa savido e oydo dezir a yºs muy antiguos del dho valle y desta ciudad del Cuzco como el dho valle de Yucae hera casa de Guayna Capa Ynga y que el dho Ynga mando hazer los edeficios casas y andenes que ay en el dho valle donde puso muchos yºs de diversas partes deste reino por mitimas camayos e yanaconas de su serviº de mas de los yºs naturales que avia en el dho valle los quales todos estuvieron ocupados en los reparos de la dhas casas y edeficios y sementeras que el dho Ynga y sus mujeres e hijos tenian en el dho valle y esto save desta pregunta.

iij A la pregunta tres dixo que al tiempo que el marques don Françisco Piçarro y los españoles que con el vinieron a esta ciudad entro en ella este tº bibia en el valle de Yucai entre los yºs cañares mitimas que en el avia de la parcialidad de Palchichapla principal de los //
/f.112v/ dhos yndios cañares y servian en el benefº de las chacaras del Ynga y las demas cosas que a esta parcialidad cavia de servir y asi vio que luego quel dho Marques Piçarro entro en esta ciudad tomo pa su serviº todos los yºs del valle de Yucai y los quales le sirvieron en el benefº de las chacaras de coca que tenia en los Andes de Tono Paucarbamba y Anatai y en otras de maiz que tenia en esta ciudad donde dizen Tiobamba y las chacaras que avia en el dho valle de Yucay del Ynga y le acudian con el fruto dellas todos los yºs naturales mitimas e camaios que el Ynga tenia en el dho valle sin que ningun yndio de todos ellos se llamase de otra persona mas que del dho marques y queste tº y otros diez yºs cañares que vinieron con los dhos Chalcochima y Quisquis en el tiempo que tiene dho le sirvieron y tributaron no embargante que como dho tiene vinieron casi en el mismo tiempo que entraron los españoles en este reino y todos asi mismo le servian en su casa de darle yerva e leña e yºs pa su serviº y esto save y vio desta pregunta.

iiij A la pregunta quatro dixo que save e vio en esta ciudad del Cuzco que despues que los españoles entraron en el y repartieron entre si los yºs deste reino y mucho tiempo despues nunca los dhos yºs pagaron tributo por tasa como al presente lo pagan sino que servian de beneficiar las chacaras de coca e maiz e labraban minas de oro e plata e servian personalmente en las casas de sus encomenderos e asi en el dho tiempo los yºs del valle de Yucai sirvieron al dho marques en las cosas que tiene como yºs tributarios y esto save e vio desta pregunta.

/f.113/ v A la pregunta cinco dixo que luego como murio don Françisco Piçarro subcedio en los yºs del valle de Yucai don Gonçalo Piçarro hijo del dho marques don Françisco Piçarro al qual sirvieron todos los yºs mitimas e naturales camayos yanaconas que fueron de los Yngas en todas las cosas que servian al dho marques su padre como dho tiene e le sirvieron todos ellos como yºs tributarios sin que ninguno se exsiviese dello por ninguna razon y esto save e vio desta pregunta.

vj A la pregunta seis dixo que save e vio que por fin e muerte de don Gonçalo Piçarro hijo del dho marques don Françisco Piçarro subcedieron los yºs todos del dho valle de Yucay en cabeza de su mt e pagaron tributo por tasa que les dieron del presidente Gasca todo el tiempo que estuvieron bacos a los oficiales reales desta ciudad del Cuzco sin que eximiesen por yanaconas de pagar tributo los yºs contenidos en el dho memorial porque todos ellos pagavan tributo mitimaes e naturales e yanaconas a su magtd como encomienda que avia subcedido con su magestad por fin e muerte del dho don Gonçalo Piçarro y esto save e vio desta pregunta.

vij A la pregunta siete dixo que save e vio questando todos los y^{o}s del dho valle de Yucay en cabeça de su magestad e que pagavan el tributo a los oficiales reales el marques de Cañete bisorrey que fue destos reinos encomendo los dhos y^{o}s de todo el dho valle de Yucai en don Diego Sayre Topa Ynga y que no save el titulo que dellos le dio y que si alguno tuvo se remite al titulo o titulo que de los dhos y^{o}s le dio y este t^{o} save que de los dhos y^{o}s del valle de Yucay de servian todos //
/f.113v/ asi naturales como mitimas pagandole el tributo e sirviendole como los demas y^{o}s deste reino hazian a los demas y^{o}s y españoles en quienes estavan encomendados ecepto los y^{o}s de Coto que servian a don Al^{o} Ucusicha a quien los dexo Ucusicha su padre que era un yndio principal de los y^{o}s cañares el qual dho Ucusicha saco los y^{o}s del dho repartimi^{to} por dezir que se los avia dado el presidente Gasca y ha oydo dezir que el dho presidente Gasca le dio titulo dellos porquel dho Ucusicha le ynformo falsam^{te} al dho presidente Gasca diziendo ser yanaconas suyos e no anexos al dho repartimi^{to} siendo como son y^{o}s mitimas puestos por el Ynga pa camayos del sol y que como y^{o}s del dho repartimi^{to} servian al dho marques como los demas camayos e yanaconas que hubo en el dho valle e que por muerte del dho don Diego Sayre Topa subcedio en los dhos y^{o}s doña Beatriz su hija legitima y su huniversal heredera a quien los y^{o}s del dho valle de Yucay an servido y pagado su tribu^{o} y a sus curadores en su nombre hasta que se caso con el dho capitan Martin Garcia de Loyola a quien pagan los tributos los y^{o}s del dho valle eçepto los y^{o}s cuyos nombres no se le leyeron a este t^{go} que siendo del dho repartimiento y que sirvieron y tributaron a los antecesores del dho don Diego Saire Topa y alg^{o}s a el se han salido de ser tributarios al dho capitan Loyola so color de dezir que son yanaconas de muchas personas a quien se an arrimado aunque no estan esemidos de pagar tasa en el dho repartimi^{to} porque los yanaconas de Coto que asi saco del dho repartimiento Ucusicha y los que despues saco don Alonso Tito Ataoche y muchos y^{o}s cañares que don Françisco Chilche tenia so color de dezir que heran yanaconas suyos an contribuido a la //
/f.114/ tasa del dho repartimi^{to} con poca o mucha cantidad aunqueste t^{o} se acuerda que solo un yn^{o} de los yanaconas de Coto contribuian a la tasa del dho repartimi^{to} y los demas estavan exsemidos de los pagar de todo punto porque servian al dho don Alonso Ucusicha y que los dhos don Alonso Tito Ataoche e don Françisco Chilche an consentido pagar tributo los dhos yanaconas porque los demas caciques del dho repartimi^{to} no se los sacavan por pleitos y esto responde a esta pregunta.

viij A la pregunta ocho dixo que save e vio que al tiempo que los españoles entraron en esta ciudad y los y^{o}s del valle de Yucay fueron del marques don Fran^{co} Piçarro todos los dhos y^{o}s naturales mitimas e camayos del dho valle fueron subjetos a don Fran^{co} Chilche yndio cañar a quien el dho marques puso por cacique principal del dho valle sin que nyngun yndio estuviese fuera de su subjecion y mando por razon alguna de ser yanaconas camayos ni de otra manera y todos los hazian lo quel les mandava tocante al servi^{o} de sus encomenderos como al tributo que avian de pagar y otras cosas que la justicia desta dha ciudad del Cuzco mandava que hiziesen los y^{o}s del dho valle y los y^{o}s contenidos en el dho memorial sirvieron y contribuyeron con aquella parte que les cavia en las parcialidades y ayllos donde estavan poblados y sirvieron al dho don Françisco Chilche como a su cacique principal hasta la bisita que dellos hizo Damian de la Vandera donde el dho don Françisco Chilche escondio muchos y^{o}s de los contenidos en el dho memorial publicando que eran yanaconas suyos y el dho Damian de la Bandera aberiguo aver algunos y^{o}s entre los quel dho don Françisco Chilche dezia ser //
/f.114v/ suyos que eran y^{o}s tributarios del dho valle e por tales los visito y asimysmo visito por y^{o}s tributarios y otros treinta o quarenta yndios que por ser guardas e yanaconas del cuerpo de Guayna Capa no pagavan por entero la tasa lo qual se hazia por orden y consentimi^{to} de los caciques y les mando que tributasen como los demas y^{o}s del dho repartimi^{to} y asi mesmo en la visita que dellos hizo Garcia de Melo aberiguo el dho bisitador tener ocultados el dho don Françisco Chilche muchos y^{o}s del dho repartimi^{to} y en las averiguaciones que sobre ello hizo restituio al dho repartimi^{to} veinte e ocho y^{o}s y les mando que de alli adelante tributasen con los demas y^{o}s del y esto save e vio desta pregunta.

ix A la pregunta nueve dixo que save e vio lo contenido en la pregunta ser y pasar como en ella se contiene y hasta que don Garcia Quispicapi puso pleito al dho don Françisco Chilche sobre el cacicazgo siempre el dho don Fran^{co} fue cacique principal de todos los y^{o}s del dho valle y esto save y vio desta pregunta.

x A la pregunta diez dixo que despues que don Françisco Chilche y don Garcia Quispicapi por conciertos fueron ambos caciques del dho repartimi^{to} hubo division entre los y^{o}s dhos en que favoreçiendose de los caciques en especial del dho don Françisco Chilche no acudian con el servi^{o} que se hazia a sus encomenderos ni con todo el servi^{o} e tasa que avian de dar e todo lo que se quitava a estos y^{o}s que favorecian los dhos caciques se cargava y lo pagavan los demas y^{o}s tributarios del dho repartimi^{to} y asi lo hizieronlos dhos caciques hasta quel visitador frei P^{o} Gutierrez los visito por y^{o}s yanaconas e los reservo de todo el tribu^{o} del dho repartimi^{to} y esto save desta preg^{ta}.

/f.115/ xj A la pregunta honze dixo que save e a bisto que los y^{o}s contenidos en el dho memorial aunque andavan exsemidos en alguna manera de pagar tasa como los demas y^{o}s siempre anduvieron subjetos a los caciques principales del dho valle y an fecho siempre lo que les an mandado y si no an pagado por entero el tributo a sido por favorecer los dhos caciques y save que antes que los dhos caciques diesen en ocultarlos siempre sirvieron los dhos y^{o}s a los encomenderos que an sido del dho valle y les pagaron tributo y esto save e vio desta pregunta.

xij A la pregunta doze dixo que save e vio que en la visita que Damian de la Bandera hizo de los y^{o}s del dho valle de Yucay el dho visitador averiguo que ciertos y^{o}s que tenian a cargo de guardar el cuerpo de Guayna Capa no pagavan por entero la tasa como los demas y^{o}s e asimesmo otros y^{o}s que don Françisco Chilche tenia favorescidos y los bisito por y^{o}s tributarios y mando que de alli adelante siempre pagasen por entero la tasa como los demas y^{o}s y que demas de los y^{o}s que el dho visitador averiguo que el dho don Françisco Chilche sacava por yanaconas suyos del dho repartimi^{to} y el dho visitador le restituyo y quedaron otros que no se visitaron y quedaron por yanaconas del dho don Françisco y esto save y vio desta pregunta.

/f.115v/ xiij A la pregunta dixo que como dho tiene el dho Damian de la Vandera visitando los y^{o}s del dho valle de Yucai hallo cinq^{ta} y^{o}s questavan ocupados en guarda y servir el cuerpo muerto de Guaina Capac y le hazian sacrefiçios segun su rito antiguo y por esta razon los caciques prinçipales del dho valle los tenian reservados de pagar por entero la tasa aunque contribuyan a ella con poca cosa porque los demas y^{o}s del dho repartimiento no se quexasen de que anduviesen los dhos y^{o}s reservados de pagar toda la tasa y los besito por y^{o}s tributarios del dho repartimiento y hizo cacique de ellos a don Alonso Tito Ataoche el qual siendo cacique de ellos por nombrami^{to} del dho visitador a oydo dezir este t^{o} que fue a la ciudad de los Reies y pidio de merzed los dhos y^{o}s diz^{do} que heran yanaconas suyos y vio que por virtud de una provision que sobre ellos gana pidio en esta ciudada la justicia della le entregasen los dhos y^{o}s y les de entonzes aca que abra ocho años o siete poco mas o men^{os} se an llamados yanaconas del dho don Alonso los veinte y^{o}s dellos e los unos y los otros estan en el memorial que al presente se le a leido y save que no embargante que los dhos veinte yndios se an llamados yanaconas del dho don Alonso Tito Ataoche nunca an dexado de tributar en el dho repartimi^{to} como de antes sirvieron y tributaron a los demas encomenderos del dho repartimiento y esto save e vio desta preg^{ta}.

/f.116/ xiij A la pregunta catorze dixo que save que en la visita que Garcia de Melo hizo en el valle de Yucay de los y^{o}s del dho repartimiento hizo ciertas averiguaciones de que el dho don Françisco Chilche dexava de vesitar muchos y^{o}s tributarios por dezir que si visitaban muchos y^{o}s los tasarian en mucho dinero de la comutacion que hizo a plata del servi^{o} personal que davan pa el benef^{o} de coca hasta entonzes y^{o}s los visito el dho Garcia de Melo por y^{o}s del dho repartimiento y el dho don Françisco Chilche se ofrecio de pagar el tribu^{o} que cupiese a veinte e cinco y^{o}s de los que avia vesitado por y^{o}s tributarios y les daria tierras donde se sustentasen todo porque le sirviesen a el y asi mesmo visito otros y^{o}s que por favor de los caciques no se ponian en el numero de y^{o}s del dho repartimi^{to} y que antes de la dha visita no pagavan por entero la tasa los quales dhos y^{o}s todos estan en el memorial que le fue leido y esto save desta pregunta.

xv A la pregunta quinze dixo que save que luego quel dho Diego Escudero fue por cura del valle de Yucai visito los y^{o}s del por la declaracion y orden que los caciques del dho valle le quisieron dar y asi visito por y^{o}s tributarios los y^{o}s que los dhos caciques manifestaron y por yanaconas muchos y^{o}s del dho repartimiento tributarios que son los contenidos en el dho memorial y esto save e vio desta pregunta.

/f.116v/ xvj A la pregunta diez y seis dixo queste t^{o} save y vio que quando el lic^{do} Gutierres visito los y^{o}s del dho valle de Yucai los visito por el libro del dho Diego Escudero guardando la orden que en el dho libro avia y asi visito por yanaconas todos los y^{o}s que los dhos caciques avian manifestado al dho Diego Escudero por tales yanaconas sin hazer otra pesquisa ni averiguacion sobre ello e que como dho tiene los y^{o}s contenidos en el memorial que se le ha leido fueron y^{o}s tributarios del dho valle de Yucai y que nunca dexaron de tributar en poca o mucha cantidad hasta que por la visita del dho lic^{do} Gutierrez se exsentaron [*sic*] de lo hazer por quedar visitados por yanaconas y divisos de los y^{o}s tributarios y que demas de que este t^{o} lo a oydo muchas vezes a los principales de los dhos yanaconas a entendido que se dexaron visitar por yanaconas entendiendo que no de pagar tasa mas de servir a las personas a quien se avian arrimado por orden de los dhos caciques y esto save e vio desta pregunta.

xvij A la pregunta diez y siete dixo que save que muchos de los y^{o}s quel dho lic^{do} Gutierrez visito por yanaconas por la orden que dho tiene an dho publicamente en las diferencias que los y^{o}s tributarios del dho valle han thenido con ellos sobre que los y^{o}s tributarios ha pedido que los yanaconas no an de goçar de tierras ningunas del dho valle sino solos los y^{o}s tributarios quellos son y^{o}s tributarios y lo fueron sus padres y demas de haber oydo a muchos de los dhos y^{o}s que asi se visitaron por yanaconas que se visitaron por entender que avian //
/f.117/ de quedar exsemidos de pagar tasa este t^{o} lo a entendido asi por las dhas diferencias que an thenido sobre los aprovechamientos del dho repartimi^{to} y esto save desta pregunta.

xviij A la pregunta diez y ocho dixo que como dho tiene los y^{o}s que el dho lic^{do} frei P^{o} Gutierrez por yanaconas que son los contenidos en el dho memorial fueron y^{o}s del dho repartimi^{to} y los vio tributar en el aunque los demas dellos por favor de los dhos caciques y las demas razones que dha tiene no tributaron por entero la qual dha orden se tuvo y guardo hasta que por la visita que el lic^{do} Gutierrez hizo dellos y los declaro por yanaconas que lo dexaron de hazer y esto save desta preg^{ta}.

xix A la pregunta diez y nueve dixo que lo que dho tiene e declarado por los dhos ynterpretes es verdad so cargo del dho juram^{to} y siendole leido y dado a entender por lengua de los dhos ynterpretes se afirmo e ratifico en ello por ser verdad e no firmo porque no supo e lo firmaron con los ynterpretes va testado a la pregunta dos dixo. Hernando de Morales Felipe Saire ante P^{o} Diaz Valdeon escri^{o}.

Testigo el dho Martin Yupangui natural del valle de Yucai vz^{o} desta villa de San Bernardo de Urobamba t^{go} presentado por el dho capitan Martin Garcia de Loyola aviendo jurado e siendo preguntado dixo lo siguiente.

j A la primera pregunta dixo que conoce a las partes y tiene noticia de los yanaconas sobre que es este pleito porque a mas de quarenta e cinco años que los co- //
/f.117v/ noce y conocio a los padres de los y^{o}s moços contenidos en el memorial que se a leido y save que fueron tributarios en el dho valle por que los vio servir y tributar juntamente con este t^{o} ques yn^{o} tributr^{o} de los mitimas que el Ynga puso en el dho repartimi^{to}.

De las generales dixo ques de hedad de sesenta años poco mas o menos e no concurre en ninguna de ellas mas de estar encomendados en el dho cap^{t} Loyola y no por eso dexara de dezir verdad.

ij A la pregunta dos dixo que Gu/a/ina Capa Ynga puso por mitima en el dho valle a su padre deste t^{o} que se llamava Yupangui y era natural desta ciudad del Cuzco para que tuviese quenta con el reparo de los edefiçios y casas quel dho Ynga tenia en el dho valle y despues de cierto tiempo que el dho su padre bibio en Yucay nacio este t^{o} en el y desde que se supo acordar vio y entendio que todo el valle de

Yucay se llamaba entre los y^{o}s casa del dho Guayna Capa y no tierra ni pus^{o} a ninguna provincia de quatro en questava repartido este reino subjeto y como es notr^{o} el dho Guayna Capa tenia sus casas hechas en el dho valle con todos los oficios de su servi^{o} y despensas y depositos en que le ençerravan los frutos de las chacaras que el dho Ynga tenia hechas pa benef^{o} de lo qual save e vio este t^{o} que el dho Ynga tenia en el dho valle muchos y^{o}s mitimas e camayos traidos de diversas partes deste reino y ellos y los naturales del dho valle que son los pueblos de Cachepaca y Chicho y Chauca sirvieron de //
/f.118/ camayos e yanaconas al dho Ynga repartiendo entre si los oficios reales en que le avian de servir asi en benef^{o} de chacaras como reparos de casas y edeficios y esto save desta pregunta.

iij A la pregunta tres dixo que save e vio que luego quel marques don Françisco Piçarro entro en esta ciudad haciendo la conquista deste reino tomo para su servi^{o} todo el valle e y^{o}s de mitimas e naturales porque le dixeron ser valle apaçible e que estava en el dho valle las casas y hedeficios de Guayna Capa con muchos y^{o}s que tenian cargo de reparallo e beneficiallo y asi los y^{o}s todos mitimas e naturales como los tubo Guaina Capac sin faltar ninguno le sirvieron en su casa dandole yerva y camarico y beneficiandole las chacaras que tenian esta ciudad en Tiobamba y en el valle de Yucay todas las que avia del dho Ynga y asimesmo le beneficiavan las chacaras de coca de Tono Paucarbamba y Yanatai sin que ningun yndio de los que vivian en el dho valle se llamase de otra persona yndio ni español y esto responde a esta preg^{ta}.

iiij A la pregunta quatro dixo que save e vio este to que hasta algunos años despues que los españoles entraron en esta ciudad del Cuzco todos los y^{o}s deste reino no tributavan a los españoles que los tenia en encomienda por el orden que agora tributan mas de que le servian personalmente dandoles y^{o}s de servi^{o} y paxa yerva y leña y les beneficiavan las chacaras de maiz e o de coca a cada uno lo que tenia y algunos españoles los ocupavan en //
/f.118v/ buscar minas de oro e p^{ta} e asi los y^{o}s del dho valle de Yucai no tributavan de otra manera al dho marques sino como dho tiene beneficiandole de todo benef^{o} las chacaras de coca e maiz que tiene dho hasta entregarle los frutos dellos y de servirle en su casa con el camarico y servi^{o}s que tiene dho como y^{o}s tributarios y esto save desta pregunta.

v A la pregunta cinco dixo queste t^{o} save e vio que luego como murio el marques don Françisco Piçarro en la ciudad de los Reies subcedio en todos los y^{o}s del dho valle de Yucay mitimas e naturales camayos e yanaconas de Guayna Capac asi como los tenia el dho marques don Françisco Piçarro don Gonçalo Piçarro su hijo a quien todos los dhos y^{o}s sirvieron y tributaron con todas las cosas que tiene dhas sin faltar en cosa ninguna ni haber y novacion en los dhos y^{o}s ni parte dellos al qual dho don Gonçalo Piçarro y a sus mayordomos en su nombre entregaron el maiz coca servi^{o} personal y camaricos que daban al dho marques antes que muriese y esto save desta pregunta.

vj A la pregunta seis dixo queste t^{o} save que por fin e muerte de don Gonçalo Piçarro hijo del dho marques don Françisco Piçarro subcedieron los y^{o}s del dho valle de Yucai en cabeça de su m^{t} y acudieron con el fruto de las chacaras de coca que el dho marques tenia en Tono y Paucarbamba y con el maiz y papas que coxian de las chacaras de Yucay al tesorero Garcia de Melo //
/f.119/ por la orden que lo pagavan al dho marques y a don Gonçalo su hijo aunque de ay a dos o tres años lo pagavan conforme a la tasa que les vino del presidente Gasca sin que en aquel tiempo fuese reservado de lo pagar e contribuir ningun yndio de los contenidos en el memorial hasta que en las visitas que se han fecho del dho valle desde la visita de Damian de la Vandera a esta parte los caciques con cautela los an ydo asentando por sus fines y esto save desta pregunta.

vij A la pregunta siete. dixo que save e vio que estando el repartimi^{to} e y^{o}s del valle de Yucay en cabeça de su magestad e que pagavan tributo a los oficiales reales siendo bisorrey deste reyno el marques de Cañete vino a esta ciudad don Diego Sayre Topa Ynga que avia salido de Vilcabamba a dar la obebiencia a su m^{t} tomo posesion de los caciques e principales todos mitimas e naturales e camayos y les dixo que el dho visorrey se los avia dado perpetuos para que le sirviesen y tributasen a el y a sus hijos y deçendientes y que se remite a los titulos e provisiones que sobre ello le dio a que se remite y que desde entonzes todos los dhos caciques y los y^{o}s a ellos subjetos con los y^{o}s contenidos en el memorial que se le ha leido le sirvieron y tributaron sin faltalle en cosa ninguna de lo que hasta entonzes avian tributado a los demas sus encomenderos y save que por fin y muerte del dho don Diego Sayri Topa Ynga subcedio en los dhos y^{o}s del valle de Yucay en doña Beatriz Coya su hija legitima y universal here- //
/f.119v/ dera mujer que al pres^{te} es del capitan Martin Garcia de Loyola a quien sirven y tributan los y^{o}s del dho valle mitimas e naturales eçepto los y^{o}s del pueblo de Coto que servian a don Alonso Ucusicha a quien los dexo Ucusicha su padre que era un yn^{o} principal de los cañares que bivian en esta dha ciudad del Cuzco el qual saco los dhos y^{o}s del dho repartimiento por dezir se los avia dado el Presidente Gasca y ha oydo dezir que el dho Presidente Gasca le dio titulo dellos en el asiento de Guainarima donde le informo el dho Ucusicha falsamente que eran yanaconas suyos y no anexos al dho repartimiento de Yucay siendo como son y^{o}s mitimas puestos en el dho valle de Yucai por camayos del sol y que como y^{o}s del dho repartimi^{to} sirvieron al dho marques en todas las cosas que dho tiene que sirvieron los y^{o}s del dho repartimi^{to} como camayos e yanaconas que huvo en el dho valle y esto save y vio desta pregunta.

viij A la pregunta ocho dixo que como dho tiene todos los y^{o}s mitimas naturales e camayos del valle de Yucay sirvieron y tributaron al marques don Françisco Piçarro sin que ningun yndio del dho valle se llamase de otra persona yndio ni español por razon de dezir que era camayo ni por otra manera alguna e sirvieron asimesmo a don Gonçalo Piçarro hijo del dho marques en el qual dho tiempo fue cacique principal de todos los dhos y^{o}s don Françisco Chilche yndio cañar a quien el dho marques Piçarro nombro y elij/i/o por tal cacique e vio que todos los dhos y^{o}s mitimas e naturales con los en el memorial //
/f.120/ contenidos y los padres de los que en el dho memorial son moços fueron subjetos y sirvieron al dho don Françisco Chilche y el se servia de todos ellos y les hazia tributar y servir a sus encomenderos y esto save desta pregunta.

ix A la pregunta nueve dixo que save que abra quinze años poco mas o m^{o}s que estando el dho don Françisco Chilche en el cacicazgo del dho valle de Yucay por orden del marques Piçarro don Garcia Quispicapi de la deçendencia de los Yngas puso p^{to} al dho don Françisco Chilche sobre el cacicazgo del dho repartimi^{to} ante la justicia m^{or} (mayor) desta ciudad del Cuzco donde por concierto concluyeron que el dho don Françisco Chilche tuviese el cacicazgo de todos los y^{o}s mitimas que avia en el dho repartimiento y el dho don Garcia Quispicapi los naturales del e asi lo an sido hasta agora cada uno en su parcialidad y esta save desta pregunta.

x A la pregunta diez dixo que save que despues que el cacicazgo del dho repartimi^{to} se dividio por la orden que dho tiene cada uno de los dhos caciques hizieron de los y^{o}s de su parcialidad lo que quisieron aprovechandose de muchos dellos por yanaconas y a otros favoreciendo por parientes como fue tomar el dho don Françisco Chilche los y^{o}s mitimas cañares de Chicon que fueron mas de cinq^{ta} publicando entre los demas y^{o}s a el subjetos que aquellos heran yanaconas suyos que se los avia dado el rey y favoreciendo a otros diez o doze que se llamavan yanaconas que avian sido del marques don Françisco Piçarro y el dho don //
/f.120v/ Garcia Quispicapi otros diez o doze yndios tributarios del dho repartimiento que los traya en su servicio y la parte que a todos estos y^{o}s cabia de trabajar en el benef^{o} de las chacaras y tributos que tiene dho cargavan los dhos caciques en los demas de sus parcialidades de que eran agraviados los y^{o}s pobres y como nunca an tenido encomendero que los aya visitado e ynquirido el tratamiento y orden que los caciques deben tener en los y^{o}s mas de para cobrar los tributos que los dhos caciques han fecho en esto lo que an querido aunque por respeto que no se quexasen los principales e y^{o}s entendidos en negocios a las justicias del dho agravio los dhos caciques demacia los ocupavan en algunas cosas pocas del servi^{o} y tributos que an dado a sus encomenderos de manera que nunca an dexado de tributar y estar subjetos a los dhos caciques hasta que el lic^{do} frei Pedro Gutierrez los visito por yanaconas y los declaro por y^{o}s yanaconas y no anexos al dho repartimi^{to} y esto save desta pregunta.

xi A la pregunta onze dixo que este t^{o} dize lo que dho ti^{e} en la preg^{ta} antes desta.

xij A la pregunta doze dixo que save e vio que en la visita que Damian de la Vandera hizo de los y^{o}s del dho valle de Yucai en el asiento de Mohina el dho visitador aberiguo que se avian ocultado algunos y^{o}s los quales visito por y^{o}s tributarios del dho repartimiento y dexo de bisitar todos los y^{o}s cañares de Chicon que el dho don Françisco Chilche avia sacado del dho reparti- //
/f.121/ miento por que dixo al dho visitador que eran yanaconas suyos e los avia el traydo al dho valle y que asimesmo visito el dho Damian de la Vandera cinquenta y^{o}s que averiguo que por razon de guardar el cuerpo muerto de Guayna Capa no tributaban por entero como los demas y^{o}s del dho repartimi^{to} y les mando el dho visitador que de alli adelante tributasen y sirviesen con los demas del dho valle y asimesmo visito por y^{o}s tributarios diez o doze y^{o}s que vivian en el dho valle so color de dezir que eran yanaconas que avian sido del marques Piçarro y que se dexaron de visitar en la dha visita muchos y^{o}s que los dhos caciques dexaron de manifestar al dho visitador diziendo ser yanaconas adqueridos por ellos y no del repartimi^{to} los quales y los dexaron de manifestar en la visita que despues hizo dellos Garcia de Melo vz^{o} desta ciudad estando en el dho memorial que le a sido leido y esto responde a esta preg^{ta}.

xiij A la pregunta treze dixo que save e vio que el dho Damian de la Vandera hizo principal de los dhos cinq^{ta} y^{o}s que guardavan el cuerpo de Guayna Capa que se llaman apoyanaconas y Tumibamba que quiere dezir criados principales de señor y don Alonso Tito Atauche y asi los dhos y^{o}s con el dho su principal a bisto este testigo que pagavan el tributo //
/f.121v/ que les cavia por los yndios que heran en el dho repartimiento y como dho tiene antes de la dha visita contribuian como y^{o}s tributarios aunque no en tanta cantidad como los otros por la razon que dho tiene y estando los dhos y^{o}s en costumbre de pagar la tasa y tribu^{o} como dho es don Alonso Tito Atauche de ser principal dellos avra ocho años poco mas o menos que el dho don Alonso publico averle fecho merzed el Audiencia Real de veinte y^{o}s de los que se le avian encargado en la dha visita para que fuese cacique dellos y que la justicia desta ciudad se los avia entregado y asi el dho don Alonso se servia de los dhos veinte y^{o}s aunque nunca los veinte y^{o}s an dexado de contribuir y tributar con los demas y^{o}s del repartimiento y esto save desta pregunta.

xiiij A la pregunta catorze dixo que save que en la visita que Garcia de Melo vz^{o} desta ciudad del Cuzco hizo del valle de Yucai e comuto el benef^{o} de coca que hazian a plata el dho don Fran^{co} Chilche escondio muchos y^{o}s que son todos todos los contenidos en el dho memorial y otros quel dho visitador descubrio por averiguaciones que hizo sobre ello y asi averiguo el dho visitador que los veinte e cinco y^{o}s contenidos en el dho memorial heran yndios mitimas del dho repartimiento e los visito y m^{do} que tributa- //
/f.122/ sen de alli adelante como los demas y^{o}s del dho repartimiento aunque el dho don Françisco Chilche pidio que se los dexase declarados por yanaconas suyos que el pagaria la tasa que aquellos y^{o}s cupiese y les daria chacaras de que sustentasen aunque le quedavan muchos mas que no se visitaron que como dho tiene los unos y los otros estan en el dho memorial y esto save desta preg^{ta}.

xv A la pregunta quinze dixo que save que quando el dho Diego Escudero fue al dho valle de Yucay por cura del visito los y^{o}s todos e hizo padron dellos por la orden de los caciques se los quisieron manifestar de manera que hizieron empradronar por yanaconas e y^{o}s distintos del repartimiento todos los y^{o}s contenidos en el dho memorial e otros muchos que en el dho valle ay de españoles e y^{o}s e los demas restantes por yndios tributarios mitimas y naturales y esto save desta pregunta.

xvj A la pregunta diez y seis dixo que save e vio este testigo quel lic^{do} frei P^{o} Gutierrez Flores que en esta visita general visito el valle de Yucay en la visita que hizo de los y^{o}s del no hizo averiguaciones ni pesquisa con los caciques ni principales sino que los visito por la orden que el dho Clerigo thenia en su padron y asi bisito por yanaconas todos los y^{o}s del dho memorial aviendo sido como dho tiene yndios tributarios //

/f.122v/ del dho repartimiento y que los dhos y^{os} se dexaron visitar por yanaconas por entender que avian de quedar libres de pagar tributo y no avia de hazer mas de servir aquellas personas en cuyo servicio declaravan estar e que save este t^{o} que todos los y^{os} contenidos en el memorial que el dho lic^{do} frei P^{o} Guterrez visito por yanaconas fueron y^{os} tributarios y tributaron siempre en poca o mucha cantidad y si fueron relevados de tributar por entero fue por favor que tenian de los dhos caciques y por averlos escondido en las visitas que dho tiene y esto save desta pregunta.

xvij A las diez y siete preguntas dixo que a oydo dezir muchas veces a los mas de los y^{os} en el memorial contenidos que son y^{os} tributarios y lo fueron sus padres lo qual an dho en las diferencias que an tenido los y^{os} tributarios del dho repartimi^{to} con los dhos yanaconas sobre dezir que los dhos ya/na/conas no an de tener chacaras ni aprovechamientos en el dho valle e que demas de esto se a fecho averiguacion con todos los principales del dho repartimi^{to} y este t^{o} presente ser todos los y^{os} en el dho memorial contenidos y^{os} tributarios del dho repartimiento y lo an confesado asi los principales de los pachacas dellos y esto save desta preg^{ta}.

xviij A la pregunta diez y ocho dixo que dize lo que dho tiene en las preguntas antes desta y esto responde a esta preg^{ta}.

/f.123/ xix A la pregunta diez y nueve dixo que lo que dho e declarado tiene por lenguas de los dhos ynterpretes es la verdad so cargo del dho juramento e siendole leido y dado a entender por los dhos lenguas y se afirmo y ratifico en ello por ser verdad e publico y notorio entre los dhos yndios e no firmo porque no supo y lo firmaron los ynterpretes Hernando de Morales Felipe Saire ante mi Pero Diaz de Baldeon escrivano.

Testigo el dho Martin Yana natural de Guayllas yndio mitimae en el valle de Yucai vz^{o} del pueblo de San Bernardo del asiento de Viobamba presentado por el dho capitan Martin Garcia de Loyola aviendo jurado e siendo preguntado dixo y depuso lo siguiente.

A la primera pregunta dixo que conoce a las partes e tiene noticia de los yanaconas sobre que es este pleito desde que se save acordar porque nacio en el dho valle de Yucai y conoce y conocio a todos los y^{os} contenidos en el memorial que le fue leido y save que an sido y son tributarios del dho repartimiento y los vio servir y tributar juntamente con este testigo y los demas y^{os} mitimas e naturales del dho valle y esto save e vio desta pregunta.

De las generales dixo ques de hedad de mas de sesenta años e no concurre en ninguna dellas mas de estar encomendado en el dho capitan Martin Garcia de Loyola y no por eso dexara de dezir verdad.

/f.123v/ ij A la pregunta dos dixo que antes que los españoles entrasen en este reino algunos años hera muerto Guayna Capa Ynga en Quito e desde queste testigo se supo acordar y entender negocios entre yndios oyo dezir a su padre e a otros yndios antiguos mitimas e naturales residentes en el dho valle de Yucai como el dho Guayna Capa avia fecho las casas estancias y edeficios que en el ay y asi llamava casa del Ynga y no pueblos ni tierra anexa a ninguna de las quatro provincias en queste reino estava repartido de y^{os} tributarios que el dho Ynga tuvo en el valle de Yucay muchos y^{os} mitimas traidos de muchas partes deste reino para el reparo y beneficio de las dhas chacaras y casas edeficios y chacaras que en el dho valle tenia y asi despues que este t^{o} se supo acordar que fue mas de seis años antes que los españoles entrasen en este reino vio ser y pasar lo que avia oydo dezir a los dhos y^{os} antiguos acerca de ser de Guayna Capa el dho valle de Yucai porque vio que todos los y^{os} mitimas y naturales que en el dho valle bibian sirvian de camayos yanaconas del dho Ynga cada uno en el of^{o} en que le avia puesto y dexado e que acudian con el fruto de las tierras e chacaras que beneficiavan a los depositos que para ello estavan fechos por el dho Ynga e nunca ningun yndio de los del dho valle mitima //
/f.124/ ni natural se conto con los suyurunas que quiere dezir gente tributaria hasta que los españoles entraron en este reino y esto save y vio desta pregunta.

iij A la pregunta tres dixo que save e vio que luego como el marques don Françisco Piçarro entro en esta ciudad luego tomo pa su servicio todos los y^{os} del valle de Yucay y las chacaras del Ynga y las chacaras del Ynga [*sic*] que en el dho valle avia por ser muchas y muy buenas y asi desde luego sirvieron al dho marques todos los y^{os} que en el dho valle avia mitimas e naturales camayos y yanaconas de Guayna Capa sin faltar ninguno dandole servi^{o} de leña y yerva en su casa e mitayos e beneficiandole las chacaras que thenia en esta ciudad del Cuzco en Tiobamba y en el dho valle de Yucai todas las chacaras que avia del dho Ynga y asi mismo le beneficiavan las chacaras de coca que el dho marques tenia en el valle de Tono Paucarbamba y Yanatai sin que ningun yndio de los que avia en el dho valle se dixese ser de otra persona yndio ni español y esto save desta preg^{ta}.

iiij A la pregunta quatro dixo que save lo contenido en la pregunta porque lo vio ser y pasar asi entre los y^{os} todos de la comarca desta ciudad y asi este testigo y los demas y^{os} mitimas e naturales del dho valle de Yucay sirvieron al dho marques Piçarro en beneficialle sus chacaras de coca y de maiz y dalle servicio de leña y yerva e y^{os} para mitaios y no por tasa como agora tributan todos y esto save e vio desta pregunta.

/f.124v/ v A la pregunta cinco dixo que este testigo save que por muerte del marques don Françisco Piçarro subcedio en los yndios del valle de Yucay don Gonçalo Piçarro su hijo a quien sirvieron e tributaron todos los y^{os} del dho valle sin que ninguno se exsimiese de servir y tributar asi como lo hazian al dho marques Piçarro y le acudian a el y a sus mayordomos con el fruto de las chacaras de coca e maiz que dho tiene que beneficiavan al dho marques e con el demas servi^{o} personal que tiene dho y esto save e vio desta pregunta.

vi A la pregunta seis dixo que save que por ausencia e muerte de don Gonçalo Piçarro hijo del dho marques don Françisco Piçarro quedaron los y^{o}s del valle de Yucai en cabeça de su magestad e pagaron el tributo a los oficiales reales segun y como lo pagavan al dho marques y don Gonçalo Piçarro su hijo los primeros tres o quatro años y despues les vino tasa fecha por el presidente Gasca de las cosas que avian de dar de tribu^{o} y asi de alli adelante tributaron por la dha tasa en las mismas cosas que antes que fue el benef^{o} de coca e de maiz que avia en el valle de Yucai y no davan el servi^{o} personal ni camarico para lo qual contribuian todos los y^{o}s del dho valle de Yucay //
/f.125/ mitimas e naturales eçepto los y^{o}s de Coto que servian a don Alonso Ucusicha a quien los dexo su padre Ucusicha que hera un yndio principal de los cañares que avia en esta ciudad del Cuzco el qual ha oydo dezir este testigo que informo al presidente Gasca que tenia unos yanaconas en Yucai que le avia adquerido y juntado y alcanço con la dha relacion falsa titulo y merzed dellos y desde entonzes se servio de ellos y los traia fuera del dho repartimiento con boz de yanaconas suyos que se los avia dado el dho presidente siendo como eran y^{o}s tributarios del dho valle e que los avia puesto por mitimas el dho Ynga por camayos del sol y que avian tributado al dho marques don Françisco Piçarro y a don Gonçalo Piçarro su hijo y esto save y vio desta pregunta.

vij A la pregunta siete dixo que estando en cabeça de su magestad los dhos y^{o}s de Yucay como dho tiene el marques de Cañete visorrey destos reinos los encomendo en don Diego Saire Topa Ynga hijo de Mango Ynga y nieto de Guayna Capa que salia de la provincia de Vilcabamba a dar la obedencia a su m^{t} el qual tomo posesion de los caciques principales de todos los y^{o}s del valle de Yucay mitimas e naturales del dho valle y les dio a entender como el dho visorrey se los avia dado a todos ellos para que le sirviesen y tributasen //
/f.125v/ a el y a sus hijos y deçendientes y asi desde luego que esto paso le sirvieron tributaron y reconocieron por tal encomendero eçepto los dhos y^{o}s de Coto que como dho tiene andavan fuera del dho repartimiento y sujeçion de los caciques del y por fin e muerte del dho don Diego Saire Topa subcedieron todos los dhos y^{o}s del valle de Yucay /en/ doña Beatriz Coya su hija heredera mujer que al presente es del cap^{t} Martin Garcia de Loyola su marido a quien pagan tributo al presente y esto save y vio desta pregunta.

viij A la pregunta ocho dixo que este testigo save y vio que desde luego que el marques don Françisco Piçarro tomo para si los dhos y^{o}s de Yucay y le sivieron todos como dho tiene mitimas e naturales con los y^{o}s de Coto y demas contenidos en el memorial que le a sido leido y asimismo sirvieron a don Gonçalo Piçarro y a los oficiales reales de su magestad sino fueron los y^{o}s de Coto que como dho tiene servian al dho Ucusicha por las razones que dhas ti^{e} y los y^{o}s contenidos en el memorial sirvieron hasta que en la visita de Damian de la Vandera y Garcia de Melo por orden y maña de los caciques y principales se fueron saliendo y exsentando de ser tributarios del dho valle con color de que eran yanaconas de los dhos caciques y no por eso dexaban de contribuir en el benef^{o} de las chacaras de tasa //
/f.126/ y otros servi^{o}s que han hecho en el dho repartimiento por que de otra manera los caciques de las otras parcialidades del dho repartimi^{to} los huvieran fecho tributar por entero dando parte a las justicias de su magestad dello y desde que el dho marques don Françisco Piçarro entro en esta ciudad y nombro por cacique principal de todos los y^{o}s del valle de Yucay mitimas e naturales hasta que estuvieron en cabeça de su magestad siempre el dho don Françisco Chilche tuvo y mando y señorio sobre ellos y los dhos yndios le obedecieron y sirvieron en todo lo que les mandava y por su orden y mandado sirvieron y tributaron al dho marques y a don Gonçalo su hijo y a los oficiales reales y esto responde a esta pregunta.

ix A la pregunta nueve dixo que save e vio que estando el dho don Françisco Chilche en posision de ser cacique principal de todos los y^{o}s del dho valle mitimas y naturales por orden y nombramiento del dho don Françisco Piçarro le puso p^{to} sobre el dho cacicazgo don Garcia Quispicapi de la desendencia de los Yngas los quales se convinieron que el dho don Françisco Chilche fuese cacique de todos los y^{o}s mitimas y el dho don Garcia Quispicapi de los naturales del dho valle y ansi lo an sido caciques hasta agora cada uno en su parcialidad y esto save desta pregunta.

x A la pregunta diez dixo que save lo contenido en la pregunta y lo vio muchas veces ser y pasar ansi y en especial lo hazia don Françisco Chilche con muchos y^{o}s //
/f.126v/ cañares a unos por servirse dellos y a otros por favorecellos y save que los encomenderos que an tenido no an tenido quenta en saver los agravios que los dhos caciques an fecho a sus y^{o}s mas de en cobrar dellos el tributo y por esto la parte del tribu^{o} y servicios que cavian de hazer a los dhos y^{o}s favorecidos se cargava entre los demas y^{o}s que tributavan por entero en el repartimiento y esto save desta pregunta.

xj A la pregunta honze dixo que save que todos los dhos y^{o}s mitimas y camayos con los en el memorial contenidos siempre fueron subjetos y obedecieron a los a los [*sic*] caciques e principales del dho repartimi^{to} aunque no pagavan por entero el tributo y servicio como los demas por las razones que dho tiene y porque en las visitas que se han fecho del dho repartimi^{to} los an escondido los dhos caciques y dexado de manifestar a los dhos visitadores dando a entender a los demas y^{o}s que se los avian dado los dhos visitadores y esto responde a esta pregunta.

xij A la pregunta doze dixo que save e vio que el dho Damian de la Bandera quando visito la tierra por provision del marques de Cañete visorrey que fue destos reinos visito los y^{o}s del valle de Yucai e aberiguo que avia diez o doze y^{o}s que so color de dezir que avian sido yanaconas del marques Piçarro bibian en el dho valle de Yucai sin pagar tributo los quales visito por y^{o}s tributarios y les mando que de alli adelante siempre tributasen como las demas y^{o}s del dho repartimiento y asimesmo visito otros cinquenta //
/f.127/ yndios por razon de que sirvian el cuerpo de Guayna Capa no servian ni tributaban por entero en el dho repartimi^{to} sino que ayudavan al benef^{o} de las chacaras de donde pagavan la tasa e aviendolos visitado los mando asimesmo que de alli adelante sirviesen y tributasen por entero e no embargante esto quedaron muchos y^{o}s tributarios del dho repartimi^{to} que no se visitaron por averlos dexado de manifestar el dho don Garcia Quispicapi y don Françisco Chilche diciendo ser yanaconas suyos que son los mas y^{o}s de los en el dho memorial contenidos y esto save e vio desta pregunta.

xiij A la pregunta treze dixo que save e vio quel dho Damian de la Bandera al tiempo que bisito los dhos y^{o}s del valle de Yucay hizo principal de los dhos cinquenta y^{o}s que guardaban el cuerpo muerto de Guayna Capac que se llaman apoyanaconas y Tumibamba que quiere dezir criados principales del señor a don Alonso Tito Atauche y asi los dhos y^{o}s con el dho su principal a visto este t^{o} que pagavan el tributo que les cavia por los y^{o}s que eran en el dho repartimi^{to} y como dho tiene antes de la visita contribuian como yndios tributarios aunque no en tanta cantidad como los otros por la razon que dho tiene y asi estando los dhos y^{o}s en costumbre de pagar la tasa y tribu^{o} como dho es y el dho don Alonso Tito Atauche de ser principal de ellos avra siete años poco mas o menos queste testigo oyo dezir publicamente en el valle de Yucai a muchos y^{o}s del quel dho don Alonso Tito Atauche tenia provi^{on} de la Audiencia Real de los Reies en que //
/f.127v/ le hazian merzed de veinte y^{o}s de los que se avian encargado en la dha visita para que fuese cacique de ellos y que la justicia de esta ciudad se los avia entregado y dadole la posesion dellos y asi el dho don Alonso se servia de los dhos veinte y^{o}s aunque nunca los dhos y^{o}s an dexado de contribuir y tributar con los demas y^{o}s del dho valle y repartimi^{to} de Yucai y esto save y vio desta pregunta.

xiiij A la pregunta catorze dixo que save y vio que en la visita que Garcia de Melo hizo de los y^{o}s del dho valle donde el dho visitador comuto a dinero el servi^{o} personal que davan e hazian de beneficiar la coca el dho visitador por declaracion y dho de don Garcia Quispicapi hallo quel dho don Françisco Chilche tenia sacados de los y^{o}s mitimas tributarios del dho valle veinte y cinco y^{o}s so color de dezir que eran yanaconas suyos y aviendolos visitado los restituyo al dho repartimi^{to} y les mando que de alli adelante pagasen tribu^{o} a lo qual al dho don Françisco Chilche por dar color a su malicia dixo al dho visitador rogandole que se los dexase declarados por yanaconas suyos que el pagaria el tributo que les cupiese y les daria tierras de donde comiesen no embargante lo qual por no aver quien advirtiese en otros muchos y^{o}s que el dho don Françisco Chilche dexo de manifestar en la dha visita se quedaron por yanaconas suyos que son muchos de los contenidos en el memorial que le a sido leido siendo y^{o}s tributarios como dho tiene que lo fueron desde el tiempo del Ynga del dho repartimiento //
/f.128/ hasta las dhas visitas y esto save e vio desta pregunta.

xv A la pregunta quinze dixo que save que avra cinco años poco mas o menos que Diego Escudero clerigo que los dotrina hizo padron dellos para las cosas tocantes a la dotrina guardando la orden que los caciques tuvieron en manifestarselos por aver demas de los y^{o}s tributarios del dho repartimi^{to} muchos y^{o}s que servian algunos españoles yndios e yndias Yngas desta ciudad de Yanaconas asi el dho clerigo los acepto en el dho su padron por yanaconas a todos los y^{o}s que los dhos caciques e principales le dixeron que lo eran siendo y^{o}s tributarios del dho repartimi^{to} como dho es y que los dhos caciques los avian escondido en las visitas pasadas y esto save e vio desta preg^{ta}.

xvj A la pregunta diez y seis dixo que save e vio que el lic^{do} frei P^{o} Gutierrez Flores quando visito los y^{o}s del dho valle de Yucai los visito por orden quel dho Diego Escudero tema en su padron y asi sin hazer otra pesquisa ni aberiguacion alguna visito por yanaconas todas los y^{o}s que hallo en el dho padron con este nombre de yanaconas e que los dhos y^{o}s se dexaron visitar asi por entender que avian de quedar libres de pagar tributo quedando en el servi^{o} de las personas de quien se nombraban ser yanaconas aviendo sido siempre y^{o}s tributarios del dho repartimi^{to} y que aunque los dhos caciques los avian escondido y favorecido nunca avian dexado de tributar en poca o en mucha cantidad como dho tiene y esto save y vio desta pregunta.

/f.128v/ xvij A la pregunta diez y siete dixo que save e a visto que muchos de los y^{o}s quel dho lic^{do} frei P^{o} Gutierrez visito por yanaconas en el dho valle an dho muchas vezes que son y^{o}s tributarios en el dho repartimiento y lo fueron sus padres y avian tributado en el dho valle hasta que por mandado del dho frei P^{o} Gutierrez les hazen pagar tributo a su m^{t} demas de lo qual en la aberiguaciones que se an fecho sobre este negocio lo an confesado ser y pasar ansi todos los principales del dho repartimiento y los principales que estan nombrados de los dhos yanaconas an declarado que todos los yndios en el dho memorial conthenidos avian sido y^{o}s tributarios del dho valle y esto save y vio desta pregunta.

xviij A la pregunta diez y ocho dixo que dicze lo que dho tiene en las preg^{tas} antes desta.

xix A las diez y nueve preguntas dixo que lo que dho tiene y declarado tiene por lenguas de los dhos ynterpretes es la verdad so cargo del dho juramento y siendole leido y dado a entender por los dhos lenguas dixo que se afirmo e ratifico por ser la verdad y publico y notorio y no firmo porque no supo y lo firmaron los dhos ynterpretes Hernando de Morales Felipe Saire. Ante mi Pero Diaz Valdeon escriv^{o}.

Testigo: El dho Lucas Chico mitima en el valle de Yucai vz^{o} del pueblo de San Benito de Alcantara del asiento de Guaillabamba presentado por el dho capitan Martin Garcia de Loyola e aviendo jurado e siendo preg^{do} dixo e depuso lo siguiente:

j A la primera pregunta dixo que este t^{o} conoze a las partes y tiene noticia de los yanaconas sobre ques este pleito desde que se save acordar porqueste t^{o} nacio //
/f.129/ en el dho valle de Yucai e conosce e conocio todos los y^{o}s contenidos en el memorial que le fue leido y save que son y an sido tributarios del dho repartimi^{to} y los vio servir y tributar juntamente con este t^{o} y los demas y^{o}s mitimas camayos e yanaconas del dho valle y esto save desta pregunta.

De las generales dixo que es de hedad de mas de setenta años e que no concurre en ninguna dellas mas de estar encomendado en el dho capitan Martin Garcia de Loyola y no por eso dexara dezir verdad de lo que supiere y le fuere preg^{do}.

ij A la pregunta dos dixo que save e vio que Guayna Capa Ynga tenia sus casas de recreacion en el valle de Yucay el qual dho valle y la tierra de el nunca en el dho tiempo se tenia por parte ni anexo a ninguna de las quatro provincias en queste reino estava repartido e

asi el dho Ynga como cosa suya propia hizo limpiar e cultivar toda la tierra que en el dho valle avia de manera que fuese de provecho pa sementeras haciendo muchos andenes y edeficios y hinchiendolos con tierra traida a mano de otras partes pa suyo benef^{o} y reparo oyo dezir este testigo a Canari su padre y a otros y^{o}s antiguos que el dho Ynga los avia traido de sus tierras a ellos y a los demas y^{o}s mitimas y despues queste testigo se savia acordar y tenia fuerzas para trabajar vio que todos los y^{o}s que avia en el dho valle mitimas y naturales sirvieran al dho Ynga y a sus mujeres e hijos beneficiandoles las chacaras que tenian en el dho valle en el reparo de las casas y edeficios que en el tenia donde este testigo servia en aquello quel dho Ynga //
/f.129v/ tenia repartido a su padre que hera beneficiar chacaras y esto save desta pregunta.

iij A la pregunta tres dixo que save e vio que luego que el marques don Françisco Piçarro entro en esta ciudad con los españoles que con el venian a la conquista deste reino el marques tomo pa si el repartimiento e y^{o}s del valle deYucai y las chacaras del Ynga que en el avia y asi todos los y^{o}s mitimas y naturales camayos e yanaconas del dho Guayna Capac que bibian en el dho valle le sirvieron y tributaron con beneficialle las chacaras de coca que tenia en Tono Paucarbamba y Yanatai y otras chacaras de maiz que tenia en el valle de esta ciudad y las chacaras del Ynga que avia en el dho valle de Yucai demas de lo qual le davan yndios de servi^{o} en su casa y leña e yerva e camarico pa lo qual todo contribuyan los dhos y^{o}s sin que ninguno lo dexase de hazer por ninguna razon y esto save y vio desta pregunta.

iiij A la pregunta quatro dixo que save e vio lo contenido en la pregunta y que en lugar del tribu^{o} que le avian de pagar servian los yndios deste reino a sus encomenderos en benef^{o} de sus chacaras de coca y maiz y los que no las tenian los ocupavan en buscar y labrar minas de oro y plata y se servian dellos en sus casas y en que les diesen yerva y leña y ansi en el dho tiempo los y^{o}s de Yucay no tributaron en mas del servi^{o} camarico y benef^{o} de chacaras que tiene dho al dho marques don Françisco Piçarro y esto save e vio desta pregunta.

/f.130/ v A la pregunta cinco dixo que save y vio que por fin e muerte del dho marques don Françisco Piçarro subcedio en los y^{o}s del dho valle de Yucay don Gonçalo Piçarro su hijo a quien todos los dhos y^{o}s mitimas e naturales sirvieron e tributaron en las mismas cosas e de la manera que sirvieron y tributaron al dho marques don Françisco Piçarro su padre sin que en el numero de los y^{o}s ni en cosa alguna de los dhos servicios le faltase acudiendole con el fruto de las dhas chacaras y que asi le beneficiaban a el y a sus mayordomos en su nombre y esto save y vio desta pregunta.

vj A la pregunta seis dixo que save que por muerte de don Gonçalo Piçarro quedaron los y^{o}s del dho valle de Yucai en cabeça de su magestad y ansi entregavan los tributos que pagavan al dho marques y al dho don Gonçalo Piçarro su hijo a Garcia de Melo tesorero de la real hacienda de su magestad y los dhos y^{o}s mitimas e naturales contribuian por sus parcialidades e ayllos para el benef^{o} de las dhas chacaras de coca y maiz ecepto que los y^{o}s del pueblo de Coto andaban exsemidos de contribuir para lo suso dho por dezir Ucusicha indio cañar principal de los cañares que bibian en esta ciudad que se lo dio de merzed el presidente Gasca e que oyo dezir este t^{go} que el dho Ucusicha informo al dho presidente que heran yanaconas suyos que los avia adquerido e juntado por su trabajo la qual dha relacion que asi hizo el dho Ucusicha save este t^{o} que fue falsa porque los dhos y^{o}s fueron y^{o}s mitimas puestos en el dho valle en el dho asiento de Coto por camayos del sol y por causa de las gue- //
/f.130v/ rras que en aquel tiempo hubo no hubo cacique ni yndio que fuese contra la voluntad del dho Ucusicha y desta manera quedaron los dhos y^{o}s por su fin e muerte en don Alonso Ucusicha su hijo y apartados del dho repartimiento solo por no aver tenido el dho repartimiento quien aya procurado juntarlos ni defenderles en las demasias que les han fecho en esto y en otras cosas y aviendo dos o tres años que los dhos y^{o}s pagavan al dho tesorero el tributo por la orden que lo pagavan al marques les vino tasa fecha por el presidente Gasca por la qual pagaron el maiz papas y coca en ella contenida y no daban servi^{o} personal ni camarico al dho thesorero y esto save e vio desta preg^{ta}.

vij A la pregunta siete dixo que save y vio que estando en cabeça de su magestad todos los dhos y^{o}s del valle de Yucai pagando el tributo como dho tiene los encomendo el marques de Cañete visorrey que fue destos reinos en don Diego Saire Topa Ynga hijo de Mango Ynga y nieto de Guayna Capac el qual teniendo juntos todos los caciques principales y los demas y^{o}s del dho valle mitimas e naturales dixo que tomava posesion dellos porque se los avia dado el dho visorrey pa el y sus deçendientes e asi los caciques principales le obedecieron por tal encomendero y desde luego le sirvieron y tributaron todos los y^{o}s mitimas e naturales del dho valle eçepto los y^{o}s de Coto que por las razones dhas estavan apartados y fuera del dho repartimi^{to} e que no save el titulo que dellos le dio el dho visorrey al dho don Diego Saire Topa Ynga y que si alguno le dio parecera por el que se remite e por fin e muerte del dho //
/f.131/ don Diego Saire Topa Ynga subcedio en los dhos y^{o}s doña Beatriz Coya su hija legitima y universal heredera a la qual y a sus curadores en su nombre todos los y^{o}s del dho valle mitimas y naturales le an tributado y servido hasta agora que se caso con el capitan Martin Garcia de Loyola a quien de presente pagan sus tributos y esto save e vio desta pregunta.

viij A la pregunta ocho dixo que save e vio que desde que los españoles entraron en este reino hasta mas de veinte años despues aca todos los y^{o}s del dho valle de Yucai mitimas e naturales fueron subjetos a don Fran^{co} Chilche que por nombramiento del dho marques don Fran^{co} Piçarro fue cacique principal en el dho repartimi^{to} al qual todos los dhos y^{o}s con los en el memorial que se le a leido contenidos sirvieron y obedecieron juntam^{te} con los de Coto hasta que en el tiempo que tiene dhos los saco el dho Ucusicha y asi el dho don Fran^{co} Chilche indio cañar los hazia servir y tributar al dho marques y a los mas sus encomenderos en el tiempo que como dho tiene fue cacique principal de todos los dhos y^{o}s y esto save e vio desta pregunta.

ix A la pregunta nueve dixo que save que en tiempo que los y^{o}s del dho valle de Yucai estavan en cabeça de su magestad hubo pleito sobre el cacicazgo del dho valle en que don Garcia Quispicapi de la descendencia de los Yngas le pidio pertenecerle a el el cacicazgo del dho valle por averlo tenido su padre del dho don Garcia sobre lo //

/f.131v/ qual se conçertaron en que el dho don Fran^{co} Chilche fuese cacique principal de los y^{o}s mitimas que bivian en el dho valle y el dho don Garcia Quispicapi de los y^{o}s naturales del y ansi lo an sido hasta agora cada uno en su parcialidad y esto save desta pregunta.

x A la pregunta diez dixo que save e vio ser y pasar lo contenido en la preg^{ta} como en ella se contiene e especialmente vio que lo hazia el dho don Fran^{co} Chilche trayendo consigo muchos y^{o}s desocupados de tributar y de acudir al benef^{o} de las chacaras a questavan obligados los y^{o}s del dho repartimiento y la parte que a estos cavia se cargava en los demas y^{o}s de su parcialidad y esto responde desta pregunta.

xj A la pregunta honze dixo que save que los y^{o}s que ansi andavan esentos de tributar por favor de los dhos caciques todos obedeçian a sus principales e caciques y servian en algunas cosas tocante a los tributos y servicios de su encomendero que no save este t^{o} que los dhos y^{o}s favorecidos y que servian a los dhos caciques dexasen y obligaciones del dho repartimi^{to} en tiempo alguno y esto save desta pregunta.

xij A la pregunta doze dixo que save que en la visita que hizo Damian de la Vandera de los y^{o}s del dho valle aberiguo que muchos y^{o}s del dho repartimiento andavan exsemidos de tributar por orden y boluntad de los caciques y los bisito y mando que de alli adelante tributasen como los demas especialmente se acuerda este t^{o} que paso //
/f.132/ lo suso dho con unos y^{o}s que bevian en el dho valle sin tributar por dezir que avian sido yanaconas del marques don Françisco Piçarro y otros y^{o}s que eran favoreçidos de los dhos caciques y con todo esto save este testigo que el dho don Françisco Chilche dexo de manifestar muchos y^{o}s que son todos los contenidos en el dho memorial que se le ha leido los quales aunque no se manifestaron en la dha visita nunca dexaron de acudir al beneficio de las chacaras de tasa aunque no tan por entero como los otros y esto save desta pregunta.

xiij A la pregunta treze dixo que este t^{o} save que entre los y^{o}s que el dho Damian de la Bandera visito y mando tributar porque aberiguo que los dhos caciques los reservavan de tributar fueron cinq^{ta} y^{o}s questavan ocupados en el servi^{o} e guarda del cuerpo muerto de Guayna Capac y en hazelle sacrificios y ofrecimi^{o}s segun sus ritos antiguos y por esta razon estavan descargados en la mayor parte del benef^{o} de las chacaras de coca y maiz e otros servi^{o}s que los y^{o}s del dho repartimi^{to} hazian a sus encomenderos y les mando el dho bisitador que alli adelante pagasen cada uno dellos por entero la tasa conforme a como la pagavan los demas y^{o}s del dho repartimiento y nombro por cacique dellos a don Alonso Tito Atauche y dende a dos años que paso lo suso dho oyo dezir este testigo que el dho don Alonso avia pedido de merzed en la ciudad de los Reies veinte y^{o}s de los que se le avian encar- //
/f.132v/ gado pa que fuese cacique y desde entonzes hasta agora a oydo dezir que el dho don Alonso y su mujer se an servido dellos no embargante lo qual a visto este t^{o} que los dhos veinte y^{o}s y los otros treinta que se encargaron al dho don Alonso siempre an beneficiado las chacaras de la tasa como y^{o}s tributarios e que no save como se le hizo la merzed de los dhos y^{o}s siendo como son y^{o}s mitimas del dho repartimi^{to} y esto save e vio desta pregunta.

xiiij A la pregunta catorze dixo que save e vio que en la visita que Garcia de Melo hizo de los y^{o}s del dho repartimiento de Yucai escondieron los caciques principales de los mitimas todos los y^{o}s contenidos en el dho memorial que se le a leido y por aviso de don Garcia Quispicapi aberiguo el dho visitador que el dho don Françisco Chilche thenia so color de yanaconas suyos veinte y cinco y^{o}s mitimas y los visito por y^{o}s del dho repartimiento y les mando que tributasen y el dho don Françisco Chilche dixo al dho visitador que se los dexase declarados por yanaconas suyos que el les daria chacaras de donde comiesen y pagava por ellos la tasa que les cupiese de pagar que los dhos y^{o}s estan en el memorial que se le a leido que algunos dellos son de los primeros que se nombran en el dho memorial y esto save y vio desta pregunta.

xv A la pregunta quinze dixo que este t^{o} save e vio que despues que Diego Escudero clerigo fue al dho repartimiento a dotrinar //
/f.133/ los y^{o}s del avra cinco años poco mas o menos dixo a los caciques que el queria hacer un libro de todos los y^{o}s del valle que le diesen orden de como se bisitasen por si los y^{o}s que eran yanaconas apartados de los y^{o}s tributarios y asi el dho clerigo hizo su padron por la orden que los dhos caciques le manifestaron los y^{o}s yanaconas e tributarios y pusieron por yanaconas todos los y^{o}s contenidos en el dho memorial aviendo sido y^{o}s tributarios y que como dho tiene son mitimas puestos en el dho valle por Guayna Capa Ynga y esto save e vio desta pregunta.

xvj A la pregunta diez y seis dixo que este testigo save e vio que quando el lic^{do} frei Pedro Gutierrez Flores visito los y^{o}s del valle de Yucay no hizo el dho visitador pesquisa ni averiguacion ninguna de las cosas que cerca de la orden que los y^{o}s tenian en el dho valle y si estavan apartados y enanexados algunos dellos mas de que llamava a los y^{o}s pa vesitallos por la orden que el dho clerigo tema en su padron e asi visito por yanaconas todos los y^{o}s contenidos en el dho memorial y desde entonzes los dhos y^{o}s no an tributado en el dho repartimiento por la horden que hasta la dha visita lo avian fecho que era acudir y reconocer en algunas cosas y cargas del dho repartimi^{to} a sus caciques y que se dexaron visitar por yanaconas por ser y^{o}s pereçosos y holgacanes que entendieron que siendo yanaconas no a- //
/f.133v/ vian de tributar y esto save e vio desta pregunta.

xvij A la pregunta diez y siete dixo que ha oydo dezir lo contenido en la pregunta e que se hizieron las dhas aberiguaciones en el valle de Yucai en ausencia deste testigo que no save quienes declararon en las dhas averiguaciones ni lo que cada uno dixo mas de que ha oydo dezir que los dhos yanaconas avian dho que eran y^{o}s mitimas en el dho valle e y^{o}s tributarios y esto responde a esta pregunta.

xviij A la pregunta diez y ocho dixo que este testigo dize lo que dho tiene en las preguntas antes desta y esto responde a esta pregunta.

xix A la pregunta diex y nueve dixo que lo que dho e declarado tiene por lenguas de los dhos ynterpretes es verdad so cargo del dho juramento y siendole leido e dado a entender por lengua de los dhos ynterpretes se afirmo e ratifico en ello por ser verdad e no firmo porque no supo e lo firmaron los dhos ynterpretes. Va testado de las generales dixo que es de edad de sesenta aºs que no bala pase por testado. Hernando de Morales Felipe Sayre. Ante mi Pero Diaz Baldeon escrivano publico.

Testigo: El dho Martin Cutipa yndio mitima en el pueblo de San Benito de Alcantara del valle de Yucay presentado por el dho capitan Martin Garcia de Loyola el qual aviendo jurado e siendo //
/f.134/ por el tenor del dho interrogatorio dixo y depuso lo siguiente—

j A la primera pregunta dixo que conoze a las partes y tiene noticia de los yanaconas sobre ques este pleito contenidos en este memorial se le a leido

De las generales dixo que es de hedad de setenta años poco mas o menos e no concurre en ninguna dellas mas de estar encomendado en el dho capitan Martin Garcia de Loyola e no por eso dexara de dezir verdad.

ij A la pregunta dos dixo que este testigo save y vio que el dho valle de Yucai comunmente entre los yºs deste reino se tenia por casa del Ynga y no tierra ni pueblos anexos a ninguna provincia de los en que esta este reino repartidas y que la mayor parte de los yºs que avia en el dho valle heran yºs mitimas traydos por el dho Ynga de muchas partes deste reino para que le sirviesen en su casa reparos de edeficios y chacaras que el dho Ynga e sus mujeres e hijos tenian y los dhos yºs mitimas y los que en el dho valle avia naturales en el que son los yºs de los pueblos de Cachi Chauca y Paca todos fueron yanaconas y camaios del dho Ynga y no suyo runas que qiere dezir gente tributaria y en los dhos oficios de camaios e yanaconas le sirvieron siempre y esto save e vio desta pregunta.

iij A la pregunta tres dixo que save que despues que el marques don Fran^{co} Piçarro entro en esta ciudad haziendo //
/f.134v/ la conquista deste reino luego tomo pa si todos los yºs del valle de Yucay mitimas e naturales y este testigo con los demas mitimas del dho valle le sirvieron dende luego beneficiandole las chacaras de coca que tenia en los Andes de Tono Paucarbamba e Yanatai y las chacaras de maiz que tenia en esta ciudad y en el valle de Yucai y le acudieron con el fruto dellas y demas desto le servian con camarico y yºs mitayos y de dalle yerva y leña en su casa como yºs de su encomienda tributarios sin que ningun yndio mitima ni natural ni yanacona del Ynga estuviese exsemido de servir o tributar al dho marques en lo que tiene dho por ninguna razon y esto save e vio desta pregunta.

iiij A la pregunta quatro dixo que save e vio que algunos años despues que los españoles entraron en esta ciudad del Cuzco se servian los españoles a quien cavia tener yºs en el benefº de sus chacaras de coca y maiz y en labrar en minas de oro y de que les diesen yerva y leña y serviº de yºs pa en su casa lo qual este testigo vio muchas bezes en esta ciudad y que ningunos yºs de la comarca della tributavan en otra manera e asi los yºs todos del valle de Yucai sirvieron al dho marques en las cosas que tiene dho y no en otra cosa y esto save e vio desta pregunta.

v A la pregunta cinco dixo que por fin y muerte del marques don Françisco Piçarro subcedio en los yºs del valle de Yucai don //
/f.135/ Gonçalo Piçarro su hijo a quien sirvierony trivutaron todos los yºs naturales y mitimas con los yºs en el memorial que se le a leido contenidos residentes en el dho valle sirviendole e tributandole en las cosas que dho tiene que sirvieron al dho marques sin que en el numero de yºs ni en la manera y tributo huviese inovacion alguna acudiendole el y a sus mayordomos en su nombre con el fruto de las chacaras e servicios que tiene dho y esto save e vio desta pregunta.

vj A la pregunta seis dixo queste testigo save e vio que luego que se dixo el dho don Gonçalo Piçarro hijo del dho marques hera muerto acudieron con el tribuº que davan al dho marques Piçarro y a su hijo don Gonçalo Piçarro a Garcia de Melo thesorero de su magestad que era en esta ciudad por aver quedado en cabeça de su magestad los yºs del dho valle mitimas e naturales asi como los avian thenido el dho marques e don Gonçalo Piçarro su hijo y dende a tres años poco mas o menos que tributavan por la orden que dho tiene les vino tasa del presidente Gasca por donde pagaron y tributaron al dho tesorero todos los dhos yºs mitimas y naturales eçepto los yºs de Tono [*sic*] que servian a don Alonso Ucusicha a quien los dexo Ucusicha su padre que era un ynº principal de las cañares que avia en esta ciudad del Cuzco el qual ha oydo dezir este tº que ynformo al presidente Gasca que el thenia unos yanaconas en Yucai //
/f.135v/ que el avia adquerido y juntado y alcanço con la dha falsa relacion titulo de merzed dellos y desde entonzes se sirvio dellos y los traia fuera del dho repartimiento con boz de yanaconas suyos que se los avia dado el dho presidente Gasca siendo como heran yºs tributarios del dho valle y que los avia puesto por mitimas el dho Ynga pa camayos del sol y que avian tributado al dho marques don Françisco y a don Gonçalo Piçarro su hijo y esto save y vio desta preg^{ta}.

vij A la pregunta siete dixo que save e vio questando como dho tiene los yºs del dho valle de Yucay en constumbre de pagar el tribuº a Garcia de Melo thesorero de su magestad se encomendaron todos los dhos yºs del valle de Yucay mitimas e naturales en don Diego Sayre Topa Ynga hijo de Mango Ynga y nieto de Guaina Capac que salio de Bilcabamba a dar la obidencia a su magestad el qual luego que bino a esta ciudad junto todos los caciques y yºs prinçipales del dho valle mitimas e naturales con los en el memorial conthenidos e sus caciques por ellos en theniendolos juntos tomo posesion dellos y les dixo que el marques de Cañete visorrey que fue a la sazon hera en estos reinos se los avia dado pa que ellos y los yºs a ellos subjetos le sirviesen y tributasen a el y a sus hijos e deçendientes y que no save que los titulos que el dho visorrey le dio dellos y asi desde luego todos los dhos yºs mitimas e naturales le sirvieron y tributaron eçepto los dhos yºs de Coto que por no haber tenido //
/f.136/ encomendero particular que procurase y supiese los yºs que avia en el dho valle de la dha encomienda fueron sacados del dho repartimiento y porque el dho don Diego Saire Topa murio un año despues que vino a esta ciudad y despues aca siempre los an tenido a cargo los

curadores e mayordomos que a thenido doña Beatriz Coya hija ligitima y universal heredera del dho Ynga que subcedio en ellos los quales dhos curadores e mayordomos nunca procuraron de saver si el dho repartimi^{to} estaba enterado en los y^{o}s qee le an sido anexos y pertenecientes mas de en cobrar los tributos que los dhos y^{o}s an pagado y como dho tiene por fin e muerte del dho don Diego Saire Topa subcedio en los dhos y^{o}s de Yucai la dha doña Beatriz Coya su hija y a sus curadores en su nombre an pagado el tributo hasta agora que se caso con el capitan Martin Garcia de Loyola y esto save y vio desta pregunta.

viij A la pregunta ocho dixo que save e vio que despues que el marques don Fran^{co} Piçarro entro en esta ciudad y tomo para si el dho repartimi^{to} de Yucay nombro por cacique principal de todos los y^{o}s del a don Fran^{co} Chilche yndio cañar a quien estuvieron subjetos todos los y^{o}s del dho valle de Yucay mitimas e naturales el qual los haçia servir y tributar a todos los encomenderos que tuvieron sin que ningun yndio mitima ni natural estuviese fuera de su subjecion y mando e a el le sirvieron en el benef^{o} de sus chacaras y en todo lo que les mandava todos los y^{o}s //
/f.136v/ del dho repartimiento con los del memorial contenidos que todos heran y^{o}s tributarios porque no avia otro cacique si el solo no en todo el dho repartimiento y esto save desta pregunta.

ix A la pregunta nueve dixo que estando en posesion el dho don Françisco Chilche en el cacicazgo principal del valle de Yucai en el tiempo que estuvieron los y^{o}s del dho repartimiento en cabeça de su magestad don Garcia Quispicapi de la desendencia de los Yngas le puso pleito sobre el cacicazgo e siguiendose la causa ellos se conzertaron en que el dho don Françisco Chilche fuese cacique principal de los y^{o}s mitimas y el dho don Garcia cacique principal de los y^{o}s naturales del dho valle y ansi an tenido cada uno el cacicazgo de la parte que le cupo y los yndios que en el memorial que se le a leido estan escriptos son de los y^{o}s mitimas que cupo al dho don Fran^{co} Chilche por cuya orden y maña se avian exsemido de ser y^{o}s tributarios en las visitas que de los dhos y^{o}s de Yucai hizieron Damian de la Bandera y Garcia de Melo aunque despues de hechas las dhas visitas contribuyan a algunos beneficios de la tasa en poca cosa porque los demas y^{o}s no se quexasen y declarasen ante la justicia el agravio que se le hazia relevando el dho don Françisco Chilche a los dho y^{o}s y esto save y vio desta pregunta.

x A la pregunta diez dixo que save e a visto que despues que se hizo la particion del //
/f.137/ cacicazgo de los y^{o}s del dho valle de Yucay por la orden que dho tiene muchos y^{o}s de los mitimas se favorecieron con don Françisco Chilche unos por dezir que eran parientes suyos y otros porque se servia dellos el dho don Françisco Chilche e asimesmo lo hizo el dho don Garcia Quispicapi aunque no en tanta cantidad de y^{o}s como el dho don Françisco a cuya causa andavan relevados de servir y tributar en muchas cosas de la tasa lo qual se cargava entre los demas y^{o}s de las parcialidades donde an sido los dhos yndios favorescidos lo qual an fecho los dhos caciques sin que aya avido quien les aya ydo a la mano en ello por las razones que tiene dho en la pregunta siete y esto save y vio desta pregunta.

xj A la pregunta honze dixo que dize lo que dho tiene en las preguntas antes desta y esto dixo a esta pregunta.

xij A la pregunta doze dixo que save e vio que en la visita que Damian de la Vandera hizo de los y^{o}s del dho valle de Yucai averiguo aver en el dho valle de Yucai muchos yndios que favorecerlos los caciques principales andavan relevados de muchas cosas del servi^{o} y tribu^{o} a que heran obligados todos los y^{o}s del dho repartimi^{to} y los visito por del dho repartimi^{to} y mando que de alli adelante tributasen por entero los quales dhos y^{o}s estan en el memorial que le a sido leido los quales aunque an sido favorescidos y relevados nunca se dexaron de servir y contribuir en algunas cosas como dho tiene y esto save e vio desta pregunta

/f.137v/ xiij A la pregunta treze dixo que save e vio que mas de treinta y^{o}s de los quel dho Damian de la Vandera hallo relevados de pagar por entero la tasa heran yndios que tenian a cargo y en guarda al cuerpo muerto de Guayna Capa y por esta razon los dhos caciques los relevavan de la dha visita en algunas cosas de las que le cavian de tributar y servir rata por cantidad de los y^{o}s que eran hasta que por la dha visita consto de lo suso dho y el dho visitador les mando que tributasen y les dio por cacique dellos a don Alonso Tito Atauche el qual acepto el dho cacicazgo y estando en costumbre los dhos y^{o}s de tributar por entero por orden del dho Damian de la Vandera dende a dos años oyo dezir que el dho don Alonso avia pedido en la Audiencia Real de los Reies titulo de veinte y^{o}s de los que le avian dado pa que fuese cacique dellos por dezir que avian sido de su abuelo Guayna Capa y despues que oyo dezir lo susodho a esta parte siempre a visto que los dhos veinte y^{o}s an servido al dho don Alonso Tito Atauche y no an pagado tribu^{o} al dho repartimi^{to} y que como dho tiene desde quel marques entro en esta ciudad hasta la visita que hizo el dho Damian de la Vandera siempre los bio tributar aunque no por entero como los demas y^{o}s del dho valle y despues de la visita del dho Damian de la Bandera los vio tributar por la horden que el dho visitador les dio y esto save e vio desta pregunta.

/f.138/ xiiij A la pregunta catorze dixo que vio la visita que Garcia de Melo hizo de los y^{o}s del dho valle de Yucai y la comutacion que hizo del benef^{o} de la coca de Tono e Paucarbamba a plata e que no save ni entendido los y^{o}s que el dho don Françisco Chilche ni los demas principales escondieron mas de que se acuerda quel dho Garcia de Melo aberiguo quel dho don Françisco Chilche dexaba de manifestar muchos y^{o}s mitimas del dho valle por dezir que eran yanaconas suyos y despues de haber fecho las dhas averiguaciones el dho visitador visito veinte y cinco y^{o}s de los que el dho don Françisco Chilche tenia escondidos y y les mando que de alli adelante tributasen con los y^{o}s del dho repartimi^{to} los quales tributaron y sirvieron en todos los quales cupo tocante a la tasa hasta que bisito el lic^{do} frei P^{o} Gutierrez los y^{o}s del dho valle y entre muchos y^{o}s que visito por yanaconas visito los dhos veinte y cinco y^{o}s por yanaconas del dho don Francisco Chilche y esto save desta pregunta.

xv A la pregunta quinze dixo que save y vio que despues que Diego Escudero clerigo los fue a dotrinar que a mas de cinco años el dho clerigo hizo libro y padron de los y^{o}s que avia en la dha dotrina a los y^{o}s tributarios por si y a los yanaconas e y^{o}s questavan con este nombre por si pa saver el numero que avia de los unos y de los otros y mando a los caciques del dho repartimi^{to} se los diesen por la dha orden y asi el dho don Frannisco Chilche e los demas principales le dieron por yanaconas en todos los contenidos en el dho //
/f.138v/ memorial y el dho clerigo los escribio en el dho padron por yanaconas y distintos de los y^{o}s tributarios del dho repartimiento siendo como antiguamente fueron todos yndios mitimas e tributarios del dho valle puestos por Ynga y que avian tributado a los encomenderos que an sido del dho repartimiento hasta las dhas visitas y esto save y vio desta pregunta.

xvj A la pregunta diez y seis dixo que save e vio que el licenciado frei P^{o} Gutierrez Flores que visito los dhos y^{o}s del valle de Yucay no hizo pesquisa ni aberiguacion alguna en la numeracion y quenta que hizo de los dhos y^{o}s sino que siguiendo el horden que el dho clerigo thenia en su padron los llamaba por sus parcialidades y los escrivia por la dha orden y asi visito por yanaconas todos los y^{o}s en el dho memorial contenidos porque los hallo con este nombre de yanaconas en el dho padron siendo y^{o}s tributarios y subjetos a los dhos don Françisco Chilche e don Garcia Quispicapi caciques principales y que an servido y tributado en el dho repartimiento en poca o mucha cantidad conforme a como los dhos an querido y esto save desta pregunta.

xvij A la pregunta diez y siete dixo que ha oydo dezir que los principales y muchos y^{o}s del dho repartimi^{to} y los mas de los yanaconas contenidos en el memorial an dho que todos los dhos y^{o}s de este memorial son y^{o}s tributarios mitimas del dho valle queste testigo entiende que los dhos y^{o}s se dexaron bisitar por yanaconas por en- //
/f.139/ tender que los dexarian por yanaconas libres de tributo y no porque no son tributarios y lo fueron sus padres como dho tiene y esto save desta pregunta.

xviij A las diez y ocho preguntas dixo que dize lo que dho tiene en las preguntas antes desta y esto dixo a esta preg^{ta}.

xix A las diez y nueve preguntas dixo que lo que dho e declarado tiene por los dhos lenguas es la verdad so cargo del dho juramento y siendole leido y dado a entender por los dhos lenguas se afirmo e retefico en ello por ser verdad e publico e notorio entre los dhos y^{o}s e no firmo porque no supo e lo firmaron los ynterpretes Hernando de Morales Felipe Saire. Ante mi Pero Diaz Valdeon escrivano.

Testigo: El dho don Garcia Paucar natural del pueblo de Paca del valle de Yucay vz^{o} del pueblo de Santiago de Oropesa presentado por el dho capitan Martin Garcia de Loyola aviendo jurado y siendo preguntado por el tenor del dho interrogatorio dixo e depuso lo siguiente.

j A la primera pregunta dixo que conoce a las partes y tiene noticia de los yanaconas sobre ques este p^{to} que son los contenidos en el memorial que se le a leido.

De las generales dixo ques de hedad de setenta años poco mas o menos e que no le toca ninguna dellas mas de estar encomendado en el cap^{t} Martin Garcia de Loyola y no por eso dexara de dezir verdad.

ij A la pregunta dos dixo que save e vio quel valle de Yucay hera casas y //
/f.139v/ chacaras del dho Ynga donde tuvo muchos y^{o}s camayos e yanaconas que puso en el dho valle traidos de muchas partes deste reino demas de otros que avia naturales del dho valle que los unos y los otros sirvieron al dho Ynga en el benef^{o} de sus chacaras y reparos de las casas que en el dho valle tenia y otros beneficios de recreacion que el dho Ynga tenia en el dho valle e a oydo dezir a muchos y^{o}s antiguos en esta ciudad del Cuzco que antes que el dho Guayna Capa hiciese las dhas sus casas y hedeficios en el dho valle de Yucay no avia y^{o}s mitimas camayos ni yanaconas en el tiempo de los demas Yngas antecesores del dho Guayna Capa mas de los y^{o}s naturales del dho valle que son los y^{o}s de los pueblos de Paca Chauca y Cache del dho valle e despues que este testigo se supo acordar que fue antes que fuese el dho Guayna Capa fuese a la conquista de Quito vio que todos los dhos y^{o}s mitimas e naturales sirvieron al dho Guayna Capa y a sus mujeres e hijos en los of^{o}s que les tenia repartidos el dho Ynga y sus capitanes en lo qual sirvieron hasta que los españoles entraron en esta ciudad y esto save desta pregunta.

iij A la pregunta tres dixo que save e vio que despues que los españoles entraron en esta ciudad quando conquistaron este reino el marques don Françisco Piçarro tomo pa su servi^{o} los y^{o}s del dho valle de Yucay mitimas y naturales y camayos que fueron del dho Guayna Capac la quales todos sirvieron y tributaron al dho mar- //
/f.140/ ques don Françisco Piçarro beneficiandole las chacaras de coca que tenia en los yngas de Tono Paucarbamba e Yanatai y las chacaras de maiz que tenia en esta ciudady en el valle de Yucay y asimesmo le daban y^{o}s de servi^{o} en su casa e yerva y leña e camarico y esto save y vio desta pregunta.

iiij A la pregunta quatro dixo que save e vio en esta ciudad que todos los y^{o}s de la comarca della no tributaban por tasa como agora mas de en beneficiar las chacaras de coca y maiz e minas de oro e plata a los españoles en quien estavan encomendados y de darles leña y yerva e y^{o}s de servi^{o} en su casa y asi los dhos y^{o}s del valle de Yucay sirvieron al dho marques en las cosas que dho tiene como y^{o}s tributarios y no save ni vio que tributasen en otra cosa en el dho tiempo y esto save desta pregunta.

v A la pregunta cinco dixo que save que por fin e muerte del dho marques don Françisco Piçarro subcedio en todos los dhos y^{o}s del valle de Yucay mitimas y naturales don Gonçalo Piçarro hijo del dho marques a quien los dhos y^{o}s sirvieron y tributaron segun e de la manera que al dho marques sin que en numero de y^{o}s ni en la cantidad de servicios y beneficios de chacara que al dho marques hazian hiziesen falta acudiendole con los frutos de coca y maiz que se coxia de las chacaras al dho don Gonçalo Piçarro y a sus mayordomos en su nombre y esto save desta pregunta.

/f.140v/ vj A la pregunta seis dixo que luego que se dixo que el dho don Gonçalo Piçarro hera muerto en el camino yendo para España acudieron con los frutos de las dhas chacaras de coca e maiz que beneficiaban a Garcia de Melo tesorero de su magestad pa lo qual contribuian todos los dhos y^{o}s del valle de Yucay mitimas e naturales eçepto los y^{o}s de Coto que servian a don Alonso Ucusicha a quien los dexo Ucusicha su padre que eran un indio principal de los cañares que avia en esta ciudad del Cuzco el qual a oydo dezir este t^{o} que ynformo al presidente Gasca que tenia unos yanaconas en el valle de Yucai que el avia adquerido y juntado y alcanzo con la dha falsa relacion titulo e merzed dellos y desde entonzes se sirvio dellos y los traya fuera del dho repartimi^{to} con boz de yanaconas suyos que se los avia dado el dho presidente Gasca siendo como heran yndios tributarios del dho valle y que los avia puesto por mitimas el dho Ynga pa camayos del sol y que avian tributado al dho marques don Françisco Piçarro y a don Gonçalo Piçarro su hijo y esto save y vio desta pregunta.

vij A la pregunta siete dixo que estando los dhos y^{o}s del valle de Yucay en cabeça de su m^{t} y pagando todos los mitimas e naturales el tributo al tesorero Garcia de Melo por tasa que les vino del presidente Gasca dos //
/f.141/ o tres años despues que tributaban por la orden que avian tributado al marques don Françisco Piçarro el marques de Cañete visorrey que fue destos reinos del Piru encomendo todos los dhos y^{o}s del dho valle de Yucay en don Diego Saire Topa Ynga y nieto de Guayna Capac que salio de la provincia de Bilcabamba a dar la obidiencia a su magestad el qual tomo posesion de todos los caciques y principales de todos los y^{o}s del dho valle de Yucay mitimas e naturales y les dixo y dio a entender como el dho marques de Cañete visorrey se los avia dado y fecho merzed dellos pa que le sirviesen y tributasen a el y a sus hijos y deçendientes y asi luego questo vieron le sirvieron y tributaron y reconocieron como a tal encomendero todos los dhos y^{o}s eçepto los y^{o}s del pueblo de Coto que como dho tiene andavan fuera del dho repartimi^{to} y subjecion de los caciques del por no aver tenido encomenderos que procurasen recoger los y^{o}s que andavan fuera del dho repartimiento mas de cobrar los tributos que los dhos y^{o}s heran obligados a dalles y por fin e muerte del dho don Diego Saire Topa subcedieron todos los dhos y^{o}s del valle de Yucay en doña Beatriz Coya su hija legitima y universal heredera mujer que al presente es del capitan Martin Garcia de Loyola su marido a quien pagan el tributo al presente todos los dhos y^{o}s y esto save y vio desta pregunta.

/f.141v/ viij A la pregunta ocho dixo que save que al tiempo que los españoles entraron en este reino muchos años despues hasta las visitas que Damian de la Vandera y Garcia de Melo hizieron de los y^{o}s del dho valle siempre los y^{o}s en el memorial contenidos fueron subjetos a don Françisco Chilche con los demas y^{o}s mitimas e naturales del dho valle de Yucai y le obedecian por averlo nombrado por tal cacique principal del dho valle el marques don Françisco Piçarro poco despues que tomo el dho repartimi^{to} de Yucay para si el qual dho don Francisco los hazia servir y tributar a todos los dhos y^{o}s mitimas e naturales del dho valle que todos le servian e obedecian al dho don Françisco Chilche por tal cacique principal y esto save desta preg^{ta}.

ix A la pregunta nueve dixo que save e vio lo contenido en la pregunta e a visto sobre/ que guardando el concierto que entre los dhos caciques hizieron sobre el cacicazgo del dho valle cada uno dellos an thenido el cacicazgo de los y^{o}s que a cada uno cupo sin que en ellod haya avido ynovacion ni diferencia alguna de manera que el dho don Fran^{co} Chilche tiene el cacicazgo de los y^{o}s mitimas y advenedizos al dho valle y el dho don Garcia de los y^{o}s naturales del y esto save y vio desta preg^{ta}.

x A la pregunta diez dixo que save que despues que por el dho concierto se dividieron los dhos y^{o}s del valle de Yucay en dos caciques por la orden que //
/f.142/ dho tiene muchos de los y^{o}s en el memorial contenidos favoreciendose del dho don Françisco Chilche y de los demas principales de las parcialidades andavan relevados de muchas cosas del servi^{o} y benef^{o} de chacaras que hazian de que tributavan hasta que en la visita que de los dhos y^{o}s de Yucay hizo Damian de la Vandera por maña y horden del dho don Fran^{co} Chilche se dexaron de bisitar muchos de los y^{o}s conthenidos en el memorial y se quedaron por dezir que eran y^{o}s yanaconas de particulares los quales antes de la dha visita e despues aunque se exsentaron del nombre que tenian de y^{o}s tributarios por las dhas razones nunca dexaron de acudir a los servicios y beneficios de chacaras aunque en poca cantidad y la parte questos dexaban de travajar save este testigo que se cargava a los demas y^{o}s pobres del dho repartimi^{to} porque como dho tiene en la setima pregunta ninguno de los mayordomos y curadores que an tenido a cargo de cobrar los tributos de los dhos y^{o}s nunca procuraron de saver ni entender lo que conbenia a los y^{o}s del dho repartimi^{to} ni el tratamiento que los caciques les hazian mas de cobrar los tribu^{o}s dellos y esto save desta pregunta.

xj A la pregunta honze dixo que save que todos los y^{o}s en el dho memorial contenidos aunque andavan relevados de algunas cosas del servi^{o} e tribu^{o}s //
/f.142v/ que avian de hacer por favorezerlos el dho don Françisco y demas principales nunca dexaron los dhos y^{o}s de obedezer al principal a quien siempre fueron subjetos y haciendo aquellas cosas que les an mandado tocantes al servi^{o} y tribu^{o}s que an pagado a sus encomenderos e que muchas vezes que lo dexaron de pagar fue por averlos encomendado los caciques a quien an sido subjetos y como dho tiene antes de las dhas visitas siempre avian tributado y servido al dho marques Piçarro y a los demas encomenderos que tuvieron hasta la dha visita y esto save e vio desta preg^{ta}.

xij A la pregunta doze dixo que save que hasta la visita quel dho Damian de la Bandera hizo de los y^{o}s del dho valle de Yucay andavan diez u doze y^{o}s so color de dezir que avian sido yanaconas del marques don Françisco Piçarro sin tributar en el dho repartimiento y

otros quarenta yºs asimesmo que por haber guardado el cuerpo muerto de Guayna Capac y haziendole sacrificios segun su rito antiguo dexaban de tributar por orden y boluntad de los caciques del dho repartimi^{to} y no acudian mas de al benefº de las chacaras de maiz que hazian en el dho valle para tributar a los quales y a otros que asimesmo aberiguo que andavan favorecidos de los caciques los visito por del dho repartimi^{to} y les mando que tributasen de alli adelante como los demas y dexo de bisitar mas //
/f.143/ de cinquenta yºs cañares que bivian en la quebrada de Chicon mitimas puestos por el dho Guayna Capa porque el dho don Françisco Chilche los escondio y dio a entender a los demas yºs del dho repartimi^{to} que heran yºs yanaconas que se los avia dado su magestad aviendo sido yºs tributarios y que iban al benefº de las chacaras de coca por sus mitas juntamente con este tº muchas vezes los quales dhos yºs estan escriptos en el memorial que se le ha leido y esto save y vio desta pregunta.

xiij A la pregunta treze dixo que save lo han tenido en las preguntas como en ella se contiene y vio que el dho Damian de la Bandera nombro por cacique de los dhos yºs que guardavan el cuerpo muerto de Guayna Capa a don Alonso Tito Atauche aviendolos visitado por yºs tributarios del dho valle y dende a dos o tres años despues de las dhas visitas oyo dezir este testigo que el dho don Alonso Tito Atauche avia pedido de merzed veinte yºs de los que asi le entregaron pa que fuese cacique dellos informando en el Audiencia Real que eran yºs tributarios yanaconas suyos y que se le avia dado titulo de ellos siendo los dhos veinte yºs mitimas en el dho valle y que avian tributado a todos los encomenderos que an tenido el dho repartimiento en aquella parte que tiene dho de benefº de chacaras por orden y boluntad de los dhos caciques e aunque el dho don Alonso publicava ser los dhos veinte yºs yanaconas suyos por merzed que dellos le hizo el Audiencia Real de los Reies y se servia //
/f.143v/ dellos por esta razon los dhos veinte yºs nunca dexaron de acudir al beneficio de las chacaras de la tasa y servicio del dho repartimi^{to} hasta que los visito el lic^{do} frei Pedro Gutierrez e los declaro por yanaconas e despues aca no han fecho el dho serviº y esto save desta preg^{ta}.

xiiij A la pregunta catorze dixo que save e vio que el tesorero Garcia de Melo visitando los yºs del dho repartimiento del valle de Yucay aberiguo que don Françisco Chilche le dexaba de manifestar muchos yºs mitimas por dezir que eran yanaconas suyos de que resulto que el dho Garcia de Melo visito veinte y /arriba/ cinco yºs de los que el dho don Françisco Chilche tenia por yanaconas suyos por averiguar que heran yºs mitimas del dho valle que avian sido tributarios no embargante lo qual el dho don Françisco Chilche escondio muchos yºs que vivian en Chicon que se llamavan la parcialidad de los yºs cañares de Panpallata los quales aunque el dho don Fran^{co} Chilche los escondia y dexaba de manifestar en las dhas visitas por yºs tributarios los dhos yºs no dexaban de acudir al beneficio de las chacaras de tasa y otros servicios hasta que tambien por visita y declaracion del dho frei Pº Gutierrez quedaron por yanaconas y esto save y vio desta pregunta.

xv A la pregunta quinze dixo que save y vio que al principio que Diego Escudero clerigo fue a dotrinar los yºs del dho valle que avia cinco años poco mas o menos el dho clerigo hizo juntar todos los yºs que bivian en el dho valle y por ver que avia //
/f.144/ mucha cantidad de yºs en nombre de yanaconas dixo al dho don Françisco Chilche y demas caciques del valle que le diesen por si a besitar los yºs tributarios y por si los yanaconas que en el dho valle bivian y asi el dho clerigo escrivio en el dho padron los yºs que el dho don Françisco Chilche y principales mitimas le señalaron por yanaconas todos los yºs en el dho memorial contenidos que son yºs mitimas del dho valle y que an sido tributarios a los encomenderos que antes de las dhas visitas han tenido sin que uviese ninguna persona que fuese a las manos a los dhos caciques sobre el visitallos por yanaconas y esto save desta pregunta.

xvj A la pregunta diez y seis dixo que save y vio que el licenciado frei Pero Gutierrez Flores de la orden y cavalleria de Alcantara quando hizo la visita de los yºs del dho repartimiento no hizo aberiguacion ni pesquisa alguna acerca del que avia pasado en el valle en bisitar los dhos yºs por yanaconas sino que siguiendo la orden que el dho clerigo tenia en su padron los llamaba por sus parcialidades e ayllos e los empadrono por esta orden de manera que los dhos yºs en el memorial contenidos quedaron visitados e declarados por yanaconas e los dhos yºs que asi bisito el dho lic^{do} frei Pº Gutierrez por yanaconas se dexaron visitar por tales entendiendo que quedavan libres de pagar tributo y de los demas serviºs que los yºs tributarios del dho valle hazen y no porque //
/f.144v/ no aya sido tributarios ellos y sus padres y esto save y vio desta pregunta.

xvij A la pregunta diez y siete dixo que save y a visto que todos los yºs en el memorial contenidos que el dho licenciado frei Pº Gutierrez visito por yanaconas y el cacique principal y los principales de pachacas que el dho visitador nombro por mandones de los dhos yºs an declarado y dho que son yºs tributarios nacidos en el dho valle hijos de yºs mitimas y esto save y vio desta pregunta.

xviij A las diez y ocho preguntas dixo que dize lo que dho tiene en las preguntas antes desta.

xix A las diez y nueve preguntas dixo que todo lo que dho y declarado tiene por lengua de los dhos ynterpretes es la verdad pa el juramento que tiene fecho y siendole leydo y dado a entender dixo que se afirma e ratifica en ello por ser verdad y porque no supo firmar lo firmaron los ynterpretes Hernando de Morales Felipe Saire. Ante mi Pero Diaz Valdeon escrivº.

Testigo: El dho Miguel Chirisuca mitima en el valle de Yucay vzº del pueblo de San Benito de Alcantara del dho valle presentado por parte del capitan Martin Garcia de Loyola el qual aviendo jurado e siendo preguntado por el tenor del dho pedimiento dixo e depuso lo siguiente.

j A la primera pregunta dixo que conoze a los en ella contenidos y tiene noticia de los yanaconas sobre ques este pleito que son los yºs contenidos en el memorial que se la a leido.

/f.145/ De las generales dixo ques de hedad de sesenta años poco mas o menos e que no concurre en ninguna dellas mas de estar encomendado en el dho capitan Martin Garcia de Loyola e que no por eso dexara de dezir verdad.

ij De la segunda pregunta dixo que save que antes que los españoles entrasen en este reino el dho valle de Yucay y los yºs que en el bivian se llamaba publicamente casa de Guayna Capac y los yºs y yanaconas y camayos del serviº de su casa chacaras y edeficios y asi lo vio desde que este testigo se supo acordar e que ningun yndio natural ni mitima se contaba ni hera anexo a los yºs suyu runas que quiere dezir gente tributaria ni la tierra del dho valle se entendia ser ninguna de las quatro provincias en que este reino esta repartido sino como dho tiene casas y edeficios del dho Guayna Capac el qual puso en el dho valle muchos yºs mitimas para los servicios que dho tiene y a oydo dezir a yºs muy antiguos en el dho valle que antes que el dho Guayna Capac hiziese las casas y edeficios y chacaras en el dho valle no avia yºs mitimas sino los yºs naturales del dho valle que son los puºs de Paca y Chauca y Cache los quales juntamente con los yºs mitimas sirvieron al dho Guayna Capa en las cosas que dho tiene al dho Ynga y a sus mujeres e hijos y esto save desta pregunta.

iij A la pregunta tres dixo que save e vio que luego que los españoles entraron en esta ciudad tomo pa si el marques don Françisco Piçarro el valle de Yucay y los yºs que en el avia mitimas //
/f.145v/ e naturales y desde luego los dhos yºs sin eçeptar ninguna por ninguna razon le sirvieron en su casa dandole yerva e leña e camarico en el benefº de las chacaras de coca que tenia en los Andes de Tono Paucarbamba e Yanatai y las chacaras de de maiz que tenia en esta ciudad y otros que tenia en el dho valle de Yucay y le acudieron con el fruto de todas ellas y esto save e vio desta pregunta.

iiij A la pregunta quatro dixo que save e vio en esta ciudad muchas vezes muchos años despues que los españoles entraron en este reino todos los yºs de la comarca desta ciudad servian personalmente a los españoles en quien estavan encomendados beneficiandoles sus chacaras de coca e maiz e los que no las tenian los ocupavan en labrar minas de oro e plata e demas desto le servian en sus casas dandoles yerva leña e camarico y no pagavan tasa en las cosas e orden que agora se haze e asi los yºs del dho valle de Yucay mitimas e naturales como dho tiene servian al dho don Françisco Piçarro como yºs tributarios en las cosas y servicios que dho tiene y esto save desta pregunta.

v A la pregunta cinco dixo que la save como en ella se contiene porque despues que el dho don Françisco Piçarro murio este testigo y los demas yºs mitimas e naturales del dho valle sirvieron y contribuyeron en los dhos servicios en benefº de chacaras al dho don Gonçalo Piçarro hijo del dho marques //
/f.146/ sin aver exsçetacion ni falta de como sirvieron al dho marques y esto save desta pregunta.

vj A la pregunta seis dixo que save que por muerte del dho don Gonçalo Piçarro quedaron los dhos yºs de Yucai en cabeça de su magestad e acudieron con el fruto de las dhas chacaras que asi beneficiavan al tesorero Garcia de Melo que fue en esta ciudad por su magestad sin que faltase en cosa ninguna de lo que tributavan al dho marques y a su hijo don Gonçalo Piçarro ni en numero de yºs eçepto los yºs de Coto quedavan esemidos de contribuir pa lo susodho por dezir Ucusicha yndio cañar principal de los cañares que bivian en esta ciudad que se los dio de merzed el presidente Gasca e que a oydo dezir este tº que el dho Ucusicha ynformo al dho presidente Gasca que heran yanaconas suyos que los avia adquerido e juntado por su trabajo cacique la qual dha relacion que asi hizo el dho Ucusicha save este tº que fue falsa porque los dhos yºs fueron yºs mitimas puesto en el dho valle en el dho asiento de Coto por camayos del sol y por causa de las guerras que en aquel tiempo hubo no hubo cacique ni ynº que fuese contra la voluntad del dho Ucusicha y desta manera quedaron los dhos yºs por su fin e muerte en don Alonso Ucusicha su hijo y apartados del dho repartimi[to] solo por no aver thenido el dho repartimiento quien aya procurado juntarlos ni de entenderlos en las demasias que les han fecho //
/f.146v/ en esto y en otras cosas y aviendo dos o tres años que los dhos yºs pagavan al dho tesorero el tributo por la horden que lo pagavan al marques les vino tasa fecha por el presidente Gasca por la qual pagaron el maiz papas y oca en ella contenido y no davan serviº personal ni camarico al dho tesorero y esto save y vio desta pregunta.

vij A la pregunta siete dixo que estando como dho tiene los yºs del valle de Yucai mitimas e naturales en cabeça de su majestad despues que salio don Diego Saire Topa Ynga hijo de Mango Ynga del valle de Bilcabamba a dar la obidencia a su magestad hizo en esta ciudad a los caciques principales y mandones de las parcialidades y ayllos de yndios del dho repartimiento mitimas y naturales y les dixo que tomava posesion de ellos porque se los avia dado el marques de Cañete visorrey destos reinos para que le sirviesen y tributasena el y a sus hijos y deçendientes e asi los dhos caciques principales con todos los yºs a el los subjetos sirvieron y obedecieron por tal su encomendero y le pagaron los tributos que por la tasa estavan obligados a pagar y que no save el titulo o titulos que el dho visorrey le dio al dho Ynga de los dhos yºs y por fin y muerte del dho Ynga Saire Topa Ynga save este testigo que subcedio en todos los yºs del dho repartimiento doña Beatriz Coya su hija ligitima y universal heredera a quien an //
/f.147/ pagado los tributos y son obligados a pagar los yºs del dho repartimiento e a sus curadores e mayordomos en su nombre hasta que se caso la dha Coya con el capitan Martin Garcia de Loyola a quien al presente tributan y esto save desta pregunta.

viij A la pregunta ocho dixo que save la pregunta como en ello se contiene e que todos los yºs del dho valle mitimas e naturales con los en el dho memorial contenidos fueron subjetos a don Françisco Chilche yndio cañar que por nombrami[to] del marques don Françisco Piçarro fue cacique principal del dho repartimi[to] hasta que por pleito que pusieron al dho don Fran[co] sobre el dho cacicazgo se dividieron los dhos yºs en dos caciques y questo save desta pregunta.

ix A la pregunta nueve dixo que como dho tiene ubo pleito sobre el dho cacicazgo en que pidio don Garcia Quispicapi yndio de la desendencia de los Yngas pertenecerle a el el cacicazgo del dho repartimi[to] y en el dho pleito se conzertaron en que el dho don Garcia

Quispicapi tuviese el cacicazgo de los y^{o}s naturales del dho valle y el dho don Fran^{co} Chilche todos los y^{o}s mitimas e advenedizos que bivian en el y asi cada uno a estado en el cacicazgo que le cupo en el dho concierto hasta agora y esto save desta pregunta.

x A la pregunta diez dixo que save que por haber dos caciques en el dho repartimiento cada uno en su parcialidad tenia algunos y^{o}s favorecidos por que servian dellos a los quales releva- //
/f.147v/ ron de muchas cosas y servicios del dho repartimi^{to} lo qual hera en gran daño de los y^{o}s pobres porque se cargava la parte de que relevan los dhos caciques a los y^{o}s que favorecian en los dhos y^{o}s pobres aunque en efeto siempre los dhos y^{o}s se ocupavan en el benef^{o} de las chacaras que avia en el dho valle de donde pagavan tasa y algunos otros servicios porque nunca el dho repartimiento an tenido encomendero que aya procurado de saver e ynquerir el tratamiento que los dhos caciques han fecho a los y^{o}s pa remediar lo susodho y recoxer los y^{o}s que los dhos caciques sacavan del so color de yanaconas de su servi^{o} y esto responde a esta pregunta.

xj A la pregunta honze dixo que como dho tiene aunque los dhos y^{o}s en el memorial contenidos y otros muchos que andaban favorecidos de los dhos caciques no por eso dexaban de ocuparse en el beneficio de las chacaras de la tasa y otros servicios del dho repartimi^{to} por orden y mandado de sus caciques a quien siempre han estado subjetos hasta que por la visita que frei P^{o} Gutierrez Flores hizo de los y^{o}s del dho repartimi^{to} que los declaro y bisito por yanaconas a cuya causa dexaron de obedecer sus caciques antiguos del dho repartimiento y esto responde a esta preg^{ta}.

xij A la pregunta doze dixo que save e vio que en la visita que hizo Damian de la Vandera de los y^{o}s del dho valle averiguo //
/f.148/ el dho visitador que muchos y^{o}s de los que en el vivian no pagavan tributo por entero por dezir que avian sido yanaconas del marques Piçarro y por estas razones que con favor de los dhos caciques eran creidos e los bisito por y^{o}s del dho repartimiento y mando que de alli adelante siempre tributasen igualmente con los demas del dho repartimi^{to} no embargante lo que el dho don Fran^{co} Chilche escondio y dexo de manifestar en la dha bisita mas de cinquenta y^{o}s cañares mitimas de la parcialidad de Panpallata que bivian en la quebrada de Chicon por orden y mandado de Guayna Capa y que avian tributado a los encomenderos que avian tenido el dho repartimi^{to} hasta la dha visita los quales dhos y^{o}s se numeraron y declaran en el memorial que se le ha leido y esto save desta pregunta.

xiij A la pregunta treze dixo que save que el dho Damian de la Vandera visito mas de cinq^{ta} y^{o}s por del dho repartimi^{to} que por tener a cargo el cuerpo muerto de Guayna Capac andavan relebados en muchas cosas en que los demas y^{o}s del dho repartimiento tributavan e servian y el dho visitador mando a los caciques principales de los y^{o}s mitimas que de alli adelante hiziesen tributar y servir a los dhos y^{o}s como a los demas del dho repartimi^{to} y les nombro por cacique y mandon dellos a don Alonso Tito Ataoche e despues dos años que paso la dha visita oyo dezir este testigo //
/f.148v/ que el dho don Alonso avia pedido en la ciudad de los Reies veinte de los dhos yanaconas que asi avia tenido a cargo y desde entonzes se dezia que los dhos veinte yndios servian al dho don Alonso no embargante qual este testigo vio que los dhos veinte yndios beneficiavan las chacaras de donde tributavan los y^{o}s del dho repartimiento a la dha doña Beatriz Coya y que en efeto este testigo save que los dhos veinte y^{o}s con los otros treinta a cumplimiento de cinquenta que se encargaron al dho don Alonso son y^{o}s mitimas del dho repartimiento y esto save y vio desta pregunta.

xiiij A la pregunta catorze dixo que save e vio que en la visita que hizo Garcia de Melo del dho repartimi^{to} el dho don Françisco escondio muchos y^{o}s de los contenidos en el dho memorial y el dho Garcia de Melo aberiguo que el dho don Fran^{co} Chilche dexava de manifestar en la dha visita veinte y^{o}s por dezir que eran yanaconas suyos y por constalle ser y^{o}s mitimas del dho repartimi^{to} los visito e mando que tributasen e sirviesen como los demas y^{o}s del y esto save desta pregunta.

xv A la pregunta quinze dixo que save e vio lo contenido en la pregunta y que paso como en ella se contiene y el dho clerigo escrivio en el dho su padron todos los y^{o}s que los dhos caciques le dieron por yanaconas y esto save desta pregunta.

xvj A la pregunta diez y seis dixo que save y vio que el licenciado frei P^{o} Gutierrez //
/f.149/ que bisito los y^{o}s del dho repartimiento no hizo pesquisa ni averiguacion alguna en cosas tocantes a los y^{o}s que yncubrian y dexavan de visitar mas de dezirselo de palabra que no escondiesen ningun yn^{o} so pena de ser castigados gravemente y los visito por la orden que el dho clerigo tenia en su padron y asi quedaron visitarlos por yanaconas todos los quel dho don Fran^{co} Chilche y otros principales avian manifestado al dho clerigo por yanaconas siendo yndios tributarios mitimas en el dho valle y que aunque andavan favorecidos de los dhos caciques porque se servian dellos save este testigo que servian y tributavan en poca o mucha cantidad aunque heran relevados de algunas cosas de la tasa y servicios del dho repartimi^{to} y andavan subjetos a los principales de las parcialidades donde estavan poblados y esto save desta pregunta.

xvij A la pregunta diez y siete dixo que save a visto que los y^{o}s quel dho licenciado frei P^{o} Gutierrez besito por yanaconas todos an dho que ellos son y^{o}s mitimas del dho repartimiento e que lo fueron sus padres y don Françisco Chilche los aver fecho visitar por yanaçonas y este t^{o} entiende que los dhos y^{o}s no manifestaron lo que pasava acerca desto al dho visitador por entender que avian de quedar libres de tributar lo qual asimesmo an confesado los caciques que el dho visitador nombro de los dhos yanaconas y que como dho tiene los y^{o}s del dho memorial contenidos siempre fueron subjetos a los principales del dho repartimiento y hazian aquellas cosas que //
/f.149v/ mandava en el beneficio de las chacaras de tasa y esto save desta pregunta.

xviij A la pregunta diez y ocho dixo que dize lo que dho tiene en las preg^{tas} antes desta.

xix A la pregunta diez y nueve dixo que todo lo que dho tiene por lengua de los dhos ynterpretes es la verdad para el juramento que hizo y no firmo porque dixo que no supo y lo firmaron los ynterpretes Hernando de Morales Felipe Saire. Ante mi P^{o} Diaz Baldeon escriv^{o}.

Testigo: El dho Lope Martin Condemayta testigo presentado por el capitan Martin Garcia de Loyola vz^{o} de la villa de Santiago de Oropesa del valle de Yucai yndio mitima en el dho valle natural desta ciudad el qual aviendo jurado y siendo preguntado por las preguntas del ynterrogatorio dixo e depuso lo siguiente:

j A la primera pregunta dixo que conoce a los en ella contenidos y tiene noticia de los yanaconas sobre que es este pleito.

De las generales dixo que es de hedad de sesenta años poco mas o menos y que no concurre en ninguna dellas mas de estar encomendado en el capitan Martin Garcia de Loyola.

ij A la pregunta dos dixo que oyo dezir a Paucar Tito padre deste testigo e a otros y^{o}s antiguos lo contenido en la pregunta e que dezian los dhos y^{o}s que antes que el dho Guayna Capa hiziese sus casas edeficios y chacaras en el dho valle no avia en el ningunos y^{o}s mitimas de los y^{o}s naturales del dho valle que son los que bivian en los pueblos de Paca Chauca y Cachi e despues //
/f.150/ que el dho Ynga hizo las dhas casas y hedeficios puso por mitimas en el dho valle muchos y^{o}s de diversas partes deste reino los quales todos juntamente con los y^{o}s naturales del dho valle que dho tiene sirvieron de camayos y yanaconas al dho Ynga en el benef^{o} de las dhas chacaras reparos de sus edeficios que tenia y asi este testigo despues que se save acordar lo a visto ser y pasar asi antes que los españoles entrasen en este reino.

iii A la pregunta tres dixo que save y vio que luego que los españoles entraron en esta ciudad tomo el marques don Francisco Piçarro para si los y^{o}s del valle de Yucay y desde luego los dhos y^{o}s todos mitimas y naturales camayos y yanaconas del dho Guayna Capa le sirvieron como y^{o}s tributarios beneficiandole las chacaras de coca que tenia en Tono Paucarbamba Yanatai y otras de maiz que tenia en esta ciudad y en el dho valle de Yucay e le sirvieron en su casa de mitayos proveiendo en ella la yerva leña y paxa que les pedian para su servicio.

iv A la pregunta quatro dixo que save e vio en esta ciudad que todos los y^{o}s de la comarca della algunos años despues que los españoles vinieron no tributaban por tasa a los españoles en quien estaban encomendados ni les daban tributo en las cosas que agora lo pagan hasta que los visitaron y tasaron y asi los y^{o}s del dho valle de Yucay no tributaban en otra cosa mas de beneficiar de todo benef^{o} las chacaras de coca e mayz que tiene dho y le sirvieron en su casa y dieron //
/f.150v/ camarico como y^{o}s tributarios y esto save desta pregunta.

v A la pregunta cinco dixo que save lo contenido en la pregunta como en ella se contiene y que los y^{o}s del dho valle mitimas e naturales sirvieron e tributaron al dho don Gonçalo Piçarro hijo del dho marques en las cosas que tributaron al dho don Francisco Piçarro su padre sin que ningun yndio del dho valle mitima ni natural ni yanacona del Ynga se reservase entonzes por razon alguna de acudir a los servicios y beneficios de chacaras que los y^{o}s del dho repartimi^{to} hacian.

vi A la pregunta seis dixo que despues que se dixo que el dho don Gonçalo Piçarro hijo del dho marques era muerto acudieron con el fruto de las dhas chacaras de coca y maiz a Garcia de Melo tesorero que fue en esta ciudad por su magestad y asi oyo dezir este testigo que avia quedado en cabeza de su magestad por muerte de Gonçalo Piçarro y pagaron el tributo del beneficio de las dhas chacaras hasta que les vino tasa por el presidente Gasca dende a quatro o cinco años que tributaban con el fruto de las dhas chacaras y esto save desta pregunta.

vii A la pregunta siete dixo que estando el repartimi^{to} e y^{o}s del dho valle de Yucay en cabeça de su magestad como dho tiene vino a esta ciudad don Diego Saire Ynga aviendo salido a dar la obidiencia a su magestad y junto todos los caçiques e principales del dho repartimiento de Yucay mitimas e naturales y les dixo que tomava posesion dellos pa que de alli adelante //
/f.151/ le tributasen a el y a sus hijos e deçendientes por averselos dado el visorrey que estaba en la ciudad de los Reies e que no save de que manera se los dio el titulo o titulos del dho repartimiento que por ellos constaria y asi los dhos caciques y principales con los y^{o}s a ellos subjetos mitimas y naturales le sirvieron y tributaron al dho don D^{o} Saire Topa segun y de la manera que lo avian fecho a los oficiales reales por la tasa que tenian del presidente Gasca y por fin y muerte del dho don Diego Saire Topa subcedio en los dhos y^{o}s del dho repartimiento doña Beatriz Coya su hija legitima y universal heredera a quien an pagado los dhos tributos y a sus encomenderos curadores en su nombre hasta que se caso con el capitan Martin Garcia de Loyola a quien al presente tributan y esto save desta preg^{ta}.

viii A la pregunta ocho dixo que save e vio que todos los y^{o}s del dho valle de Yucay mitimas y naturales con los en el memorial contenidos fueron y^{o}s tributarios del dho repartimi^{to} todos ellos subjetos a don Francisco Chilche yndio cañar a quien el marques don Françisco Piçarro nombro por caçique principal del dho repartimiento el qual tubo mando y señorio mucho tiempo sobre los dhos y^{o}s mitimas y naturales y todos ellos le obedecieron y sirvieron y por orden y mandado sino tributavan e servian a sus encomenderos y esto save desta preg^{ta}.

ix A la pregunta nueve dixo que save que los y^{o}s del dho repartimiento en cabeça de su magestad que abra diez y seis o diez y //
/f.151v/ siete años estando el dho don Fran^{co} Chilche en posesion del caçicazgo de los y^{o}s del dho valle le puso pleito don Garcia Quispicapi de la desendencia de los Yngas diziendo pertenecerle a el el dho caçicazgo y siguiendose el dho pleito ellos se conzertaron en que el

dho don Françisco Chilche quedase por caçique prinçipal de todos los yos mitimas y advenediços que bivian en el dho valle y el dho don Garcia Quispicapi fuese cacique principal de los yos naturales del dho valle y asi despues aca siempre han estado cada uno en el caciçazgo que por el dho concierto les cupo y esto save desta pregunta.

x A la pregunta diez dixo que save que despues que uvo division en el dho cacicazgo en la manera que dho tiene el dho don Francisco Chilche comenzo a favoreçer algunos yos de los mitimas que le cupieron de que avia de ser caçique a unos por servirse dellos y a otros por parentesco y asi como no avia quien le fuese a la mano los rrelevava de la tasa en cosas de mucho trabajo y solo los que ocupava en algunas façiles de hazer y asi lo que dexavan de travajar estos yos se cargava en los yos pobres de aquella parcialidad y ninguno de los encomenderos que an tenido han procurado de quitar y castigar las bexaciones que los caciques an fecho a los yos de saver como sacavan los yos del dho repartimito los caciques por yanaconas a cuya causa el dho don Françisco Chilche los //
/f.152/ a ydo sacando en cada bez que sean bisitado los yos del dho repartimito y esto save desta pregunta.

xj A la pregunta honze dixo que como dho tiene en la pregunta antes dha los yos en el dho memorial contenidos aunque por favor del dho don Franco Chilche andavan reservados de algunas cosas de la tasa nunca dexaron de acudir al benefo de las chacaras de tasa e algunos servicios a que los yos del dho repartimiento estan obligados y siempre an estado subjetos a los principales de las parcialidades donde an estado y en las cosas que dexaron de tributar por favor de los dhos caciques como dho tiene se cargava a los yos de la parcialidad donde estavan poblados y esto save desta pregunta.

xij A la pregunta doze dixo que save e vio que en la visita que Damian de la Vandera hizo de los yos del dho repartimiento el dho visitador aberiguo que muchos yos de los que bivian en el dho valle no pagavan tasa por voluntad de los caciques del dho repartimiento y los visito por yos tributarios y mando que de alli adelante tributasen cada uno dellos igualmente con los demas yos del dho repartimiento demas desto que el dho visitador averiguo andar los dhos yos reservados de tributar save este testigo que el dho don Franco Chilche escondio y dejo de manifestar al dho bisitador mas de treinta yos cañares mitimas del dho valle que bivian //
/f.152v/ en la quebrada de Chicon por orden del Ynga los quales estan nombrados y declarados en el memorial que se le a leido y esto save y vio desta pergunta.

xiij A la pregunta treze dixo que save e vio que muchos de los yos que el dho Damian de la Bandera visito y mando que tributasen en el dho repartimito eran yos que estavan ocupados en guardar el cuerpo muerto de Guayna Capa y le hazian ofrecimyento segun su rito antiguo y despajes de averlos visitado hizo dellos y de otros veinte yos mitimas una parcialidad de cinquenta yos y los encargo a don Alonso Tito Ataoche a quien nombro por prinçipal dellos y dende a un año poco mas o menos oyo dezir este testigo publicamente en esta ciudad a muchas personas que el dho don Alonso Tito Ataoche avia pedido en la ciudad de los Reies que le hiziese merzed de veinte yos por dezir que eran yanaconas suios y que se los avia dado y asi el dho don Alo se servia dellos de manera que en la visita que hizo Garcia de Melo de los yos del dho repartimito dejo de visitar el dho visitador los dhos veinte yos e con todo eso antes de la dha visita e despues aca siempre beneficiaron las chacaras que en el dho valle ay de donde pagan los yos del dho repartimiento su tasa hasta que por la visita que el licenciado Frei Pedro Gutierrez hizo del dho repartimiento donde los declaro por //
/f.153/ yanaconas que despues aca no an contribuido con nada en el dho repartimito e queste testigo save que los dhos veinte yos son yos mitimas del dho repartimito que fueron yanaconas de Guayna Capa y esto save desta pregunta.

xiiij A la pregunta catorze dixo que save que el dho don Françisco Chilche escondio en la visita que hizo del dho repartimiento Garcia de Melo los yos de Panpallata que avian escondido en la visita de Damian de la Bandera y como dho tiene los los [*sic*] veinte yos que don Alonso Tito Ataoche pidio de merzed diciendo ser yanaconas suyos se dejaron asimesmo por visitar en la dha visita aunque como dho tiene son yos tributarios de lo quall dio noticia don Garcia Quispicapi al dho visitador y por las averiguaciones que sobre ello hizo le consto que veinte e cinco yos de los quel dho don Francisco Chilche dezia ser yanaconas suyos y no yos tributarios heran yos mitimas del dho valle puestos por el Ynga y que avian tributado a los encomenderos pasados y asi los visito por yos tributarios del dho repartimiento y mando que de alli adelante tributasen y sirviesen igualmente con los demas yos del dho repartimiento y el dho don Francisco Chilche dixo al dho visitador que se los dexase declarados por yanaconas suyos quel pagaria la tasa por ellos y les daria chacaras donde comiesen de las suyas y esto save desta pregunta.

/f.153v/ xv A la pregunta quinze dixo que save y vio que despues que Diego Escudero clerigo fue al dho repartimiento a dotrinallos [*sic*] mando juntar todos los caçiques e yos del dho valle pa los visitar y empadronar y porque hallo muchos yos que se llamaban yanaconas de particulares yos y españoles mando a los dhos caçiques que le diesen quenta de los yos tributarios del dho repartimiento por si y todos los yanaconas por si y los dhos caçiques manifestaron y dieron por yanaconas todos los contenidos en el dho memorial y otros muchos que en el dho valle ay de españoles siendo como dho tiene los yos del dho memorial yos mitimas siendo tributarios del dho valle y esto save desta pregunta.

xvj A la pregunta diez y seis dixo que save y vio que el licenciado Frei Po Gutierrez Flores que en la visita que hizo de los repartimitos del dho valle no hizo averiguaciones ni pesquisa alguna sobre si avia algunos yos del dho repartimito fuera de servir y tributar con los yos que en el avia mas de apercivilles [*sic*] que no le escondiesen yndio ninguno so pena de ser castigados y los visito por la horden que el dho clerigo tenia y tiene por su padron llamandolos por sus ayllos y los yanaconas e yos tributarios que por el dho libro y padron le constaron y asi visito por yanaconas todos los yos en el dho memorial contenidos siendo mitimas del valle como dho tiene y los yos del //

/f.154/ dho memorial se dexaron visitar por yanaconas entiendo que quedarian libres de pagar tributo y no ternyan [*sic*] mas travajo de servir a las personas por cuyos se escrevian y no porque no dejasen de ser y^{o}s del dho valle subjetos a los principales en cuya parcialidad avia estado y de aver contribuido al benef^{o} de la chacara de la tasa que hay en el dho valle y esto save desta pregunta.

xvij A la pregunta diez y siete dixo que save e a visto que todos los y^{o}s en el memorial contenidos que son los y^{o}s que ^{el} licenciado Frei Pedro Gutierrez visito por yanaconas siendo como dho tiene y^{o}s tributarios del dho valle de Yucay y en esta ciudad que ellos son y^{o}s mitimas del dho repartimiento y que lo fueron sus padres y como tales tenian sus chacaras y casas en el dho valle que por haberlos manifestado los caciques por yanaconas los avian visitado por tales y que este testigo entiende que si los dhos caciques y principales entendieron que en esta visita general que avia de obligar a los yanaconas a tributar que ellos los visitaron por y^{o}s tributarios a ellos subjetos y no por yanaconas y esto save desta pregunta.

xviij A la pregunta diez y ocho dixo que dize lo que dho tiene en las preguntas antes desta.

xix A la pregunta diez y nueve dixo que todo lo que dho tiene por lengua de los dho interpretes es la verdad y lo que save desta caso para el juramento que //
/f.154v/ hizo y porque no supo firmar lo firmaron los interpretes Hernando de Morales Felipe Saire. Ante mi Pedro Diaz de Valdeon escrivano.

Testigo: El dho Martin Sauni vz^{no} de la villa de Santiago de Oropesa del valle de Yucay yndio mitima en el dho valle testigo presentado por el capitan Martin Garcia de Loyola aviendo jurado y siendo preguntado por las preguntas del ynterrogatorio dixo e depuso lo siguiente:

j A la primera pregunta dixo que conoce a los en ella contenidos y que tiene noticia de los yanaconas sobre que es este pleito contenidos en el memorial que se ha leydo.

De las generales dixo que no save dezir la hedad que tiene mas de que en el tiempo que Atagualpa y Guascar Ynga tuvieron guerras sobre el señorio deste rreino el hera ya ombre y que andava en la guerra y parecio por su aspeto de mas de cinq^{ta} a^{o}s.

ij A la pregunta dos dixo que ha oydo dezir a Xulca padre deste testigo que fue mitima en el dho valle e otros y^{o}s antiguos que el dho Guayna Capa avia fecho sus casas en el dho valle de Yucay con todos los edeficios andenes y chacaras que en el ay para reparo y benef^{o} de las dhas chacaras casas y edeficios puso en el dho valle muchos y^{o}s mitimas de diversas ptes deste reino los quales estavan repartidos en lo que avian de entender y beneficiar y despues queste testigo se supo acordar algunos años antes //
/f.155/ que biniesen los españoles vio que todos los y^{o}s que bivian en el dho valle mitimas e naturales entendian como dho tiene en el reparo y benef^{o} de las dhas chacaras y casas por del dho Guayna Capa Ynga y esto save desta pregunta.

iij A la pregunta tres dixo que save y vio que despues que los españoles entraron en esta ciudad del Cuzco algunos dias el marques don Françisco Piçarro tomo para si el dho valle de Yucay con todos los y^{o}s que en el avia naturales y mitimas los quales todos con los camayos e yanaconas que avia del Ynga le sirvieron y beneficiaron las chacaras que tenia de coca en Tono Paucarbamba y Yanatai y las chacaras de maiz que tenia en esta ciudad y en el valle de Yucay y le dieron ansimismo en su casa yerba y leña y camarico sin que ningun y^{o} de los que en el dho valle avia fuese reservado de eso y esto save y vio desta pregunta.

iiij A la pregunta quatro dixo que save y vio en esta ciudad que los y^{o}s de la comarca desta ciudad no pagavan tributo por la orden e tasa que agora lo pagan sin que solamente sirvian a sus encomenderos de darles yerba leña y camaricoeen su casa y le beneficiavan sus chacaras de coca e maiz y los que no los thenian les buscaban minas de oro y plata los y^{o}s de //
/f.155v/ quencomienda e asi los y^{o}s del dho valle de Yucay sirvieron al dho como y^{o}s tributarios al dho marques en las cosas que dho tiene y esto save desta pregunta.

v A la pregunta cinco dixo que save que despues que murio el marques don Françisco Piçarro en la ciudad de los Reie subcedio en los y^{o}s del dho repartimiento de Yucay al qual sirvieron todos los dhos y^{o}s naturales y mitimas segun y como sirvieron al dho marques su padre acudiendole con los frutos de las dhas chacaras de coca y maiz y con el camarico y demas servicios personales que hazian al dho marques Piçarro y esto save desta pregunta.

vj A la pregunta seis dixo que save e vio que despues que se dixo en esta ciudad que el dho don Gonçalo Piçarro hijo del dho marques hera muerto subcedio en todos los y^{o}s del dicho repartim^{to} su magestad e asi acudieron con los frutos de las dhas chacaras de coca y maiz a Garcia de Melo que hera tesorero por su magestad e acudian al benef^{o} de las dhas chacaras de coca e maiz todos los y^{o}s del dho repartimiento de Yucay mitimas y naturales sin que ningun yndio se reservase dello por razon alguna y desde algunos años que los dhos y^{o}s acudian con el fruto de las dhas chacras de coca //
/f.156/ e maiz al dho tesorero les vino tasa fecha por el presidente Gasca de lo que avian de tributar e dos años e dos años [*sic*] poco mas o menos despues que tributaban por la dha tasa a su magestad se encomendaron los dhos y^{o}s en don Diego Saire Topa Ynga y esto save desta pregunta.

vij A la pregunta siete dixo que como dho tiene estando los y^{o}s del dho valle de Yucay en cabeza de su magestad vino a esta ciudad don Diego Saire Topa Ynga y nieto de Guayna Capa hijo de Mango Ynga y hizo juntar los caciques e y^{o}s principales del dho repartim^{to} mitimas

e naturales y les dixo que tomaba posesion dellos pa que de alli adelante le avian de tributar y servir a el y a sus hijos e deçendientes por averselos dado su mag^{t}d y asi este testigo oyo dezir en esta ciudad que se los avian dado porque salio de Bilcabamba a dar la obidiencia a su magestad y desde luego que esto paso todos los y^{o}s del dho repartimiento mitimas e naturales y que vivian en el dho valle con nombre de camayos e yanaconas del Ynga le sirvieron y tributaron ecepto los y^{o}s del pueblo de Coto que por no aver tenido encomendero particular que procurase y supiese los y^{o}s que avia en el dho repartimiento de la dha encomienda fueron sacados por Ucusicha //
/f.156v/ yndio cañar que fue cacique de los y^{o}s canares desta ciudad el qual los dexo a don Alonso Ucusicha su hijo e asi quando los dhos y^{o}s estuvieron en cabeza de su magestad los y^{o}s de Coto servian al dho don Alonso Ucusicha y no tributavan con los del repartimiento como heran obligados por ser y^{o}s mitimas del dho valle e que este testigo save que el Ynga los puso en al ansiento de Coto por camayos del sol e despues que se encomendaron los dhos y^{o}s de Yucay en el dho don Diego Saire Topa sirvieron ansimismo los dhos y^{o}s de Coto al dho don Alonso Ucusicha y el dho no los procuro ni pidio porque despues que se le encomendaron los dhos y^{o}s desde a un año murio y despues por fin e muerte del dho Ynga subcedio en ellos doña Beatriz Coya su hija legitima siempre estuvieron los dhos y^{o}s a cargo de los curadores y mayordomos que tenia los quales nunca procuraron el bien de los y^{o}s ni de saver lo que en este caso los caciques hazian mas de cobrar dellos los tributos que pagavan hasta que se caso la dha doña Beatriz Coya con el cap^t Martin Garcia de Loyola a quien tributan y sirven al presente y esto save y vio desta pregunta.

viij A la pregunta ocho dixo que save que despues que el dho marques Piçarro tomo para si los dhos y^{o}s del valle de Yucay //
/f.157/ y dende a dos años poco mas o m^{o}s nombro por cacique principal de todos los y^{o}s del dho valle mitimas e naturales a don Francisco Chilche e asi este testigo y los demas y^{o}s del dho repartimiento mitimas e naturales e camayos e yanaconas del Ynga le fueron subjetos y le obedecieron en todo lo que les mandava asi en el benef^o de las chacaras de coca y maiz en que tributaban como en el servirle a el que era su cacique principal con los y^{o}s contenidos en el memorial que se le ha leido que son mitimas del dho valle y esto save desta pregunta.

viiij A la pregunta nueve dixo que la save como en ella se contiene y que despues que el dho don Francisco Chilche y don Garcia Quispicapi se conzertaron en la forma contenida en la dha pregunta hasta agora han estado cada uno en su cacicazgo y esto save desta pregunta.

x A la pregunta diez dixo que save que despues que se dividio el dho caçicazgo en los y^{o}s contenidos en la pregunta antes desta por el dho concierto don Francisco Chilche yndio cañar a quien cupieron los y^{o}s mitimas y advenedizos que vivian en el dho valle favoreciendo a muchos y^{o}s cañares e otras naciones so color de dezir que avian sido yanaconas del marques y de que eran parientes suios e a otros porque le servian los traya /traia/ relevados de la tasa y de benef^o de las chacaras de maiz y coca a questan obligados //
/f.157v/ todos los y^{o}s del dho repartimiento y aquella parte en que estos andaban relevados se cargava en los y^{o}s en cuya parcialidad y aillo bivian aunque en algunas cosas del serv^o que se hazia en el dho repartimi^{to} al sacerdote que los dotrinaba y otros servicios faciles acudian y obedecian en esto a los principales dellos aillos del dho repartimi^{to} y esto es lo que save desta pregunta.

xj A la pregunta honze dixo que dize lo que dho tiene en las preguntas antes desta.

xij A la pregunta doze dixo que save y vio que en la visita que hizo Damian de la Vandera de los y^{o}s del dho repartimiento se aberiguo como andaban muchos y^{o}s en el dho repartimiento que no tributavan y los y^{o}s pobres andavan agraviados y reçibian vexacion de contribuir y servir en los que avia de hazer a los dhos y^{o}s que por favor de los caciques andavan relevados y los visito por y^{o}s tributarios del dho repartimiento que de alli adelante los hiziesen tributar ygualmente con los demas y^{o}s del dho repartimiento y esto save y vio desta preg^{ta}.

xiij A la pregunta treze dixo que save y vio que entre los y^{o}s que el dho Damian de la Vandera aberiguo que andavan relevados de pagar tributo avia çinquenta y^{o}s de las parcialidades de Apo yanaconas y Tomebamba //
/f.158/ que quiere dezir criados del señor que por razon de que guardavan el cuerpo muerto del dho Ynga y le hazian sacrificios segun su rito antiguo andavan relevados de pagar por entero el tribu^o aunque acudian al benef^o de las chacaras que ay en el dho valle de donde pagavan tasa y despues de averlos numerado el dho visitador mando que tributasen en el dho repartimiento por entero como y^{o}s mitimas que se aberiguo ser y nombro por cacique dellos a don Alonso Tito Atauche que hasta entonzes avia sido mandon dellos en la guarda del dho cuerpo muerto de Guayna Capa y dende a un año que se hizo la dha bisita oyo dezir que el dho don Alonso avia pedido en la Audiencia Real de la ciudad de los Reies que le hiziesen merzed de veinte y^{o}s diziendo ser yanaconas suyos e que avia traido provision a la justicia desta ciudad para que se los diese e despues que se dixo esto que dho tiene no que los dhos veinte y^{o}s le servian en el dho valle de Yucay y en esta ciudad no embargante lo qual los dhos y^{o}s benficiavan las chacaras que ay en el dho valle de dondep gan tributo los y^{o}s a su encomendero e save que los dhoz veinte y^{o}s son mitimas del dho valle puestos por el Ynga y lo fueron sus padres y no yanaconas adqueridos por el dho don Alonso y esto save desta pregunta.

xiiij A la pregunta catorze dixo que save que en la visita que Garcia de Melo hizo //
/f.158v/ del dho repartimi^{to} el dho don Fran^{co} Chilche escondio los dhos y^{o}s cañares de Chocon (Chicon) y otros muchos de lo qual dio noticia al dho visitador don Garcia Quispicapi y por las averiguaciones que sobre ello le hizo le consto que dexaba de manifestar por y^{o}s mitimas tributarios en la dha visita veinte y^{o}s mitimas e los visito por del dho repartimiento y mando que de alli adelante tributasen igualmente con los demas y^{o}s del dho repartimiento e dexo de visitar los dhos y^{o}s de Chicon de la parcialidad de Panpallata por no haver quien lo dijese al dho visitador y esto save desta pregunta.

xv A la pregunta quinze dixo que save que abra quatro años poco mas o menos que Diego Escudero clerigo que avia ido a dotrinarlos hizo juntar todos los y^{o}s del dho repartimi^{to} pa los empadronar e visitar e mando a los caciques e principales del dho repartimiento mitimas e naturales que le diesen todos los y^{o}s e yndias que avia tributarios en el dho repartimi^{to} por si y los y^{o}s yanaconas que avia ansimesmo de por si por sus aillos y parcialidades porque asi los avia de excebir por si y los dhos caciques mitimas por horden del dho don Francisco Chilche manifestaron al dho clerigo por yanaconas todos los y^{o}s en el memorial contenidos entre otros muchos que hay despañoles en el dho valle y esto save desta pregunta.

/f.159/ xvj A la pregunta diez y seis dixo que save y vio que el licenciado Frei P^{o} Gutierrez Flores que bisito los y^{o}s del dho repartimiento no hizo averiguaciones ni pesquisa alguna de los y^{o}s que avia en el dho valle mas de llamarlos por sus aillos segun la orden que hacen por el padron del dho clerigo e asi visito por yanaconas todos los contenidos en el dho memorial siendo como son y^{o}s tributarios y mitimas puestos por el Ynga y que han tributado en el dho repartimi^{to} en poca o en mucha cantidad por la orden que dho tiene estando subjetos a los principales de los ayllos donde an estado como los demas y^{o}s tributarios aunque por favor de los dhos caciques han sido relevados de algunas cosas de tributos y servicios que an fecho los y^{o}s del dho repartimiento y esto save desta pregunta.

xvij A la pregunta diez y siete dixo que avia dos meses poco mas o menos que todos los y^{o}s contenidos en el dho memorial questan visitados por yanaconas y sus caciques declararon en ciertas averiguaciones que sobre esto se hizo que ellos eran mitimas y lo fueron sus padres y como tales tenian sus casas y chacaras por orden del Ynga y entiende este testigo dellos que se dexaron visitar por yanaconas entendiendo que avian de quedar libres de tributar y no ternian otra ocupacion mas de servir a las personas por cuyos se avian escripto en la dha visita.

/f.159v/ xviij A la pregunta diez y ocho dixo que dize lo que dho tiene en las preguntas antes desta.

xix A la pregunta diez y nueve dixo que lo que dho e declarado tiene por lengua de los dhos interpretes es la verdad pa el juramento que tiene fecho e porque no supo firmar lo firmaron los interpretes Hernando de Morales Felipe Saire. Ante mi Pedro Diaz de Valdeon escrivano.

Testigo: El dho Diego Escudero clerigo presbitero cura del valle de Yucai presentado en la dha razon por parte del dho capitan Martin Garcia de Loyola el qual aviendo jurado y siendo preguntado por el tenor del dho interro^{o} dixo y depuso lo siguiente.

j A la primera pregunta dixo que conoce a los en ella contenidos y tiene noticia de los yanaconas sobre que es este pleito que son los contenidos en el memorial que se le ha leido.

De las generales dixo que es de hedad de cinquenta años poco mas o menos y que no concurre en ninguna dellas.

ij A la pregunta dos dixo y a todas las demas preguntas del dicho interro^{o} dixo que ha cinco años que este testigo esta y dotrina en el valle de Yucai donde estan y residen los yanaconas contenidos en las dhas preguntas y muchas vezes este testigo ha oido a muchos dellos yanaconas viejos e mozos quexandose de los caciques que avian sido y eran que los avian fecho yanaconas no lo siendo porque ellos avian sido y eran y^{o}s tributarios del dho valle y sus padres siempre lo //
/f.160/ fueron y como tales avian comido las tierras del dho valle y que agora por nombrarse yanaconas no tienen tierras de donde comer y quexandose desta suerte a este testigo le dezian que se diese orden como se aclare la verdad para que ellos pudiesen ser y^{o}s de la dha encomienda como antes lo avian sido ellos y sus padres y asi este t^{o} a pedim^{to} de muchos de los dhos y^{o}s hizo una relacion a manera de informacion con muchos viejos del dho valle todos los quales sin descrepar ninguno dijeron todo lo contenido en todas las preguntas del dho interrogatorio que dho tiene es la verdad y no save otra cosa para el juramento que tiene fecho y lo firmo de su nombre. Diego Escudero ante mi Pedro Diaz Valdeon escrivano.

Testigo: El dho Marco Cayo Gualpa natural del valle de Yucai vez^{no} del pueblo de San Vernardo del ansiento de Huribamba [*sic*] en el dho valle presentado por pte del capitan Martin Garcia de Loyola el qual aviendo jurado e siendo preguntado por las preguntas del interogatorio dixo y depuso lo siguiente:

j A la primera pregunta dixo que conoce a los en ella contenidos e tiene noticia de los yanaconas sobre que es este pleito que son los contenidos en el memorial que se le ha leido.

De las generales dixo que es de hedad de ochenta años poco mas o menos y no le tocan ninguna dellas.

ij A la pregunta dos dixo que save y vio en tiempo de Guina [*sic*] Capa que fue antes poco quel dho Ynga fuese a la conquista de //
/f.160v/ de Quito que el dho valle de Yucai comunmente se llamava entre los y^{o}s casas y chacaras del dho Ynga y asi vio este testigo que todos los y^{o}s del dho valle mitimas e naturales y otros muchos forasteros andavan ocupados en el benef^{o} y reparos de las dhas casas y edeficios del Ynga y oyo dezir a su padre de este testigo que se llamaba Gualpa que antes quel dho Guayna Capa hicieze las dhas chacaras y casas en el dho valle de Yucay no avia y^{o}s mitimas ni los dhos edeficios quel dho Guayna Capa avia traido todos los y^{o}s mitimas que avia en el dho valle de muchas partes de este reino a quienes y los y^{o}s naturales del dho valle tenia repartidos los servicios que le avian de hazer e asi unos tenian nombres de yanaconas y otros de camayos que quiere dezir oficiales y criados del Ynga y despues que el dho Ynga se fue y murio en la provincia de Quito hasta que binieron los españoles a este reino siempre vio que los dhos y^{o}s del valle de Yucai mitimas e naturales entendian en los dhos reparos y beneficios de las dhas chacaras que avia en el dho valle por del dho Ynga Guayna Capa y sus hijos y esto save desta pregunta.

iij A la pregunta tres dixo que save y vio que luego que el marques don Francisco Piçarro entro en esta ciudad tomo para si el valle de Yucai con todos los y^{o}s mitimas y naturales yanaconas y camayos que en el vivian por orden del dho Ynga y asi los dhos y^{o}s todos le sirvieron en su casa de mitimas dandole yer- //
/f.161/ va y leña e camarico y le beneficiavan las chacaras de coca que tenia en el valle de Tono Paucarbamba e Yanatai en los Andes y las chacaras de maiz que tenia en esta ciudad y en el dho valle de Yucay.

iiij A la pregunta quatro dixo que save y vio que en todo el tiempo que este testigo y los demas y^{o}s del dho valle de Yucai fueron del dho marques todos los y^{o}s de la comarca desta ciudad servian a los españoles en quien estavan encomendados beneficiandole sus chacaras de maiz y de coca y otros en labrar minas de oro e plata y en el servi^{o} de sus casas dandoles yerva y leña e otros camaricos y no por tasa ni en las cosas que agora tributan los dhos y^{o}s e asi los y^{o}s del dho valle de Yucai sirvian al dho marques don Fran^{co} Piçarro en las cosas que dho tiene y esto save desta preg^{ta}.

v A la pregunta cinco dixo que por fin e muerte del dho marques don Françisco Piçarro subcedio en los dhos y^{o}s de todo el valle de Yucai don Gonçalo Piçarro hijo del dho marques a quien sirvieron y tributaron todos los y^{o}s del dho valle en las cosas que sirvian e tributaban al dho marques don Fran^{co} Piçarro su padre y a sus mayordomos en su nombre y esto save desta pregunta.

vj A la pregunta seis dixo que save y vio que por fin y muerte de Gonçalo hijo del dho marques Piçarro los y^{o}s del dho valle de Yucay mitimas y naturales camayos e yanaconas que en el vivian acudieron con el servi^{o} y frutos de las dhas chacaras de coca y maiz a Garcia de Melo thesorero que era por su magestad e oyo dezir que eran del Rey los dhos y^{o}s y dende a tres o quatro años poco mas o menos que tri- //
/f.161v/ butaban por la orden que dho tiene les vino tasa por el presidente Gasca por donde avian de tributar y en que cosas y asi los dhos y^{o}s mitimas e naturales del dho valle tributaron por ella ecepto los y^{o}s del pueblo de Coto que por no aver thenido encomendero particular que procurase y supiese los y^{o}s que avia en el dho repartimiento de la dha encomienda fueron sacados por Ucusicha yndio cañar que fue cacique de los y^{o}s cañares desta ciudad el qual los dexo a don Alonso Ucusicha su hijo e asi los dhos y^{o}s estuvieron en cabeza de su magestad los y^{o}s de Coto sirvian al dho don Alonso Ucusicha y no tributaban con los del repartimiento como heran obligados por ser y^{o}s mitimas del dho valle y que este testigo save que el Ynga los puso en el ansiento de Coto por camayos del sol e despues que se encomendaron los dhos y^{o}s de Yucay en don Diego Saire Topa sirvieron ansimesmo los dhos y^{o}s de Coto al dho don Alonso Ucusicha y el dho Ynga no los procuro ni pidio porque despues que se los encomendaron los dhos y^{o}s desde a un año murio y despues que por fin e muerte del dho Ynga subcedio en ellos doña Beatriz Coya su hija ligitima siempre estuvieron los dhos y^{o}s a cargo de los curadores y mayordomos que tenia los quales nunca procuraron el bien de los y^{o}s hasta que se caso la dha doña Beatriz Coya con el capitan Martin Garcia de Loyola a quien tributaron y sirvieron al presente y esto save desta preg^{ta}.

vij A la pregunta siete dixo que estando en cabeza de su magestad los y^{o}s del dho //
/f.162/ valle de Yucay vino a esta ciudad don Diego Saire Topa Ynga de la ciudad de los Reies de aver dado la obidiencia de su magestad y salido de la provincia de Bilcabamba de donde estaba rebelado e hizo juntar los caciques e principales del dho valle de Yucay mitimas y naturales y teniendolos juntos les dixo que de alli adelante avian de ser suios y pagarle tributo a el y a sus hijos y deçendientes porque asi se los avia dado el Rey e que los tenia juntos para tomar posesion dellos e de alli adelante los dhos caciques e y^{o}s del dho valle de Yucai todos le sirvieron y tributaron por la dha tasa hasta que como dho tiene murio e por su fin e muerte subcedio en ellos doña Beatriz Coya su hija ligitima y universal heredera a quien y a sus curadores en su nombre an tributado hasta que se caso con el capitan Martin Garcia de Loyola y esto save desta pregunta.

viij A la pregunta ocho dixo que save e vio que dos o tres años despues que el dho marques Piçarro tomo pa si los y^{o}s del dho valle de Yucai nombro por cacique principal de todos ellos mitimas e naturales a don Francisco Chilche yndio cañar a quien todos los dhos y^{o}s sirvieron y obedecieron en todo lo que les mandava tocante al benef^{o} de las dhas chacaras de donde tributaban y demas servi^{o}s que hazian a sus encomenderos como en servir al dho Chilche en el benef^{o} de sus chacaras y servi^{o} de su casa con los y^{o}s contenidos en el dho memorial sin que ninguno estuviese reservado de su subjecion por razon alg^{a} y esto save desta pregunta.

/f.162v/ ix A la pregunta nueve dixo que en el tiempo que como dho tiene tributaban a su magestad estando en posesion del cacicazgo de todo el valle de Yucay el dho don Françisco Chilche que avra diez y ocho años poco mas o menos le puso pleito sobre el dho cacicazgo don Garcia Quispicapi de la desendencia de los y^{o}s por dezir que le pertenecia el cacicazgo del dho valle como a subcesor del cacique que avia sido del dho valle antes que viniesen los españoles y siguiendo el dho pleito se conzertaron entranbos [*sic*] en que el dho don Françisco Chilche tuviese el cacicazgo de los mitimas y y^{o}s advenedizos que avia en el dho valle y el dho don Garcia de los y^{o}s naturales del dho valle y esto save y vio desta preg^{ta}.

x A la pregunta diez dixo que save e a bisto que despues quel cacicazgo del dho valle de Yucay en los dhos don Françisco Chilche e don Garcia Quispicapi el dho don Françisco Chilche favoreçiendo a muchos y^{o}s cañares e de otras naciones que le cupo en su caçicazgo los traia exsemidos de pagar tasa e de hazer algunos servicios de los a que estan obligados los y^{o}s del dho valle lo qual se cargava a los demas y^{o}s de las parcialidades de donde eran los dhos y^{o}s favorecidos por los caciques y como no han tenido los dhos y^{o}s encomendero particular que aya procurado el bien dellos nunca avido quien lo remediase y fuese a la mano al dho Chilche y esto save desta pregunta.

xj A la pregunta onze dixo que aunque los dho y^{o}s andavan exsemidos de algunas cosas de la dha tasa siempre vio este testigo //
[f.163] que los dho y^{o}s acudian al beneficio de las chacaras de maiz que en el valle hay señaladas para pagar el maiz que por la tasa estan

obligados y asi los dhos y^{o}s favorecidos siempre anduvieron subjetos a los principales a quien estuvieron subjetos antes que por favor del dho don Françisco Chilche los esimiese de tributar por entero y lo que dexaban de tributar y servir los dhos yndios hera porque como dho tiene lo queria asi el dho don Françisco Chilche y no porque no fuesen y^{o}s mitimas del dho repartim^{to} desde el marques don Françisco Piçarro hasta que estuvieron en cabeça de su magestad y esto save y vio desta preg^{ta}.

xij A la pregunta doze dixo que vio en la visita que Damian de la Vandera hizo a los y^{o}s del dho repartimi^{to} que el dho visitador averiguo que abia muchos y^{o}s en el dho valle que andavan reservados de muchas cosas del tribu^{o} y servicios a que estavan obligados los dhos y^{o}s del dho repartimi^{to} por boluntad e orden de sus caciques e despues de averlos numerado entre los demas y^{o}s que se manifestaron del dho repartimi^{o} les mando que de alli adelante tributasen y sirviesen todos los dhos y^{o}s igualmente e algunos y^{o}s que despues de la dha visita dexaban de pagar tributo en el dho repartimiento fueron los y^{o}s cañares de la parcialidad de Panpallata que bivian en la quebrada de Chicon por averlos escondido el dho don Françisco Chilche por dezir que heran yanaconas suyos y esto save y vio desta pregunta.

/f.163v/ xiij A la pregunta treze dixo que save que entre los y^{o}s que el dho Damian de la Bandera aberiguo que avian andado reservados a tributar en el dho repartimiento se hallo que ciertos y^{o}s que se llamaban apoyanaconas que quiere dezir criados del señor lo andavan por razon de que guardavan el cuerpo muerto de Guayna Capa y le hazian ofrecimientos segun su rito antiguo de los quales y de otros yndios de la parcialidad de Tomebamba hizo el dho visitador una parcialidad de cinquenta y^{o}s y nombro por principal dellos a don Alonso Tito Ataoche e dende a tres o quatro años este testigo oyo dezir a los principales del dho repartimi^{to} de Yucai como el dho don Alonso Tito Ataoche avia pedido en la Audiencia Real de los Reies le hiciesen merzed de veinte yndios diziendo ser yanaconas suyos e que avia traido provision para ello y por virtud de ella le dieron veinte yndios de los que el dho Damian de la Bandera le avia encargado pa que fuese cacique dellos y los dhos y^{o}s fueron de los que se nombravan apoyanaconas los quales este testigo save que son mitimas en el dho repartimiento y los vio beneficiar las chacaras e maiz que en el dho valle ay de donde an pagado el tribu^{o} los y^{o}s del dho repartimiento antes de la visita y despues de ella y despues quel dho don Alonso Tito Atauche se sirvio de los dhos y^{o}s hasta que los bisito el licenciado Gutierrezque los declaro por yanaconas y esto save desta pregunta.

xiiij A la pregunta catorze dixo que save que en la visita que Garcia de Melo del dho repartimiento escondieron los principales //
/f.164/ de los ayllos de los y^{o}s mitimas del dho repartimi^{to} muchos y^{o}s por orden y mandado de don Françisco Chilche de lo qual dio noticia don Garcia Quispicapi y en las averiguaciones que el dho visitador hizo sobre ello hallo que el dho don Françisco Chilche tenia con nombre de yanaconas suyos veinte e cinco y^{o}s mitimas del dho repartimiento y los visito e mando que de alli adelante pagasen el tribu^{o} como los demas y^{o}s del dho repartimiento igualmente e por no haber quien diese noticia de los demas yndios quel dho don Francisco Chilche thenia escondidos quedaron por visitar por el del dho repartimiento los y^{o}s cañares de Panpallata y otros muchos que se contiene en el memorial que se le ha leido y esto save desta pregunta.

xv A la pregunta quinze dixo que avia quatro años poco mas o menos que fue a dotrinar los y^{o}s del dho repartimiento Diego Escudero clerigo el qual dende cierto tiempo despues que fue al dho valle hizo juntar todos los y^{o}s mitimas e naturales del dho repartimi^{to} y les dio a entender que los queria visitar y empadronar que le diese de por si los y^{o}s tributarios del dho repartimiento y todos los yanaconas por si porque asi los avia descrevir apartados los unos de los otros y por orden del dho don Françisco Chilche manifestaron al dho clerigo por yanaconas todos los dhos y^{o}s en el dho memorial contenidos que como dho tiene este testigo los conoce todos por y^{o}s mitimas del dho repartimiento con otros muchos yanaconas de españoles que ay en el dho valle y asi el //
/f.164v/ dho clerigo los escribio por yanaconas y esto save desta pregunta.

xvj A la pregunta diez y seis dixo que save y vio que el licenciado Frei Pero Gutierrez Flores en la visita que hizo de los y^{o}s del dho repartimiento no hizo pesquisa ni averiguacion alguna de los y^{o}s que avia en el dho repartimi^{to} y los que estaban ausentes mas de apercivilles que no le escondiesen yndio ninguno so pena de ser gravemente castigados e hizo la numeracion e visita por la orden que el dho clerigo tenia por su padron llamandolos por sus parcialidades y ayllos y asi visito por yanaconas todos los y^{o}s en el dho memorial contenidos los quales se dexaron visitar por yanaconas entendiendo de quedar libre de pagar tributo y este t^{o} save como dho tiene que todos los dhos y^{o}s son mitimas y lo fueron sus padres y avian tributado al marques don Fran^{co} Piçarro y el tiempo que anduvieron sin pagar entero la tasa fue por las razones que dho tiene y esto responde a esta pregunta.

xvij A la pregunta diez y siete dixo que save y vio que abra tres meses poco mas o menos que los mas de los y^{o}s en el memorial contenidos dexaron en el valle de Yucay en ciertas averiguaciones que se hizieron sobre este negocio que ellos heran y^{o}s mitimas del dho repartimi^{to} y lo fueron sus padres y como tales tenian sus casas y chacaras en el dho valle por orden del Ynga lo qual lo declaron ansimismo a los caciques que el dho licenciado Gutierrez nombro de los dho yanaconas y como dho tiene se dexa- //
/f.165/ ron visitar los dhos y^{o}s por yanaconas pensando quedar libres de pagar tribu^{o} y esto save desta pregunta.

xviij A la pregunta diez y ocho dixo que dize lo que dho tiene en las preguntas antes desta.

xix A la pregunta diez y nueve dixo que lo que dho y declarado tiene por lengua de los dhos interpretes es la verdad para el juram^{to} que tiene fecho y porque no supo firmar lo firmaron los interpretes Hernando de Morales Felipe Saire. Ante mi Pedro Diaz de Valdeon escriv^{o}.

Testigo: El dho Alonso Chauca yndio mitimae vecino del pueblo de San Bernardo del valle de Yucay de nacion Guaylas mitima en el dho valle del qual fue tomado e recevido juram^{to} en forma e siendo preguntado dixo y depuso lo siguiente:

j A la primera pregunta dixo que conoce a los en ella contenidos y tiene noticia de los yanaconas sobre que es este pleito.

De las generales dixo que era de edad de ochenta años parecio por su aspeto de edad de mas de sesenta años y no le toca ninguna de ellas.

ij A la pregunta dos dixo que despues que este testigo se supo acordar que fue diez años poco mas o menos antes que viniesen los españoles a este reino vio que todas las chacaras que avia en el valle de Yucay se beneficiavan para Guayna Capa de maiz y axi y otras legumbres y ansimesmo vio muchas casas y edeficios de recreaciones que el dho Guayna Capa tenia en el dho valle y que se edificaban y reparaban cada año por del dho Ynga oyo dezir //
/f.165v/ a su padre que se llamaba Malcaca Yapac y a otros yndios viejos que antes que el dho Guayna Capa hiciese las chacaras e andenes y casas que ay en el dho valle todo hera tierra valdia y de poco provecho y avia muy pocos yndios en el dho valle naturales del que son los y^{o}s de los pueblos de Paca y Chauca y Cache y Chimo e que despues que el dho Guayna Capa hizo las dhas casas y edeficios puso por mitimas en el dho valle muchos yndios traidos de diversas partes deste reino que serian mas de dos mill y^{o}s los quales todos andaban ocupados en hazer los dhos edeficios y reparallos en el beneficio de las chacaras que el dho Ynga tenia en el dho valle unos con nombre de yanaconas que quiere dezir criados otros con nombre de camaios que quiere dezir oficiales o que tienen a su cargo algunas obras que hazer e no se contaban los dhos y^{o}s mitimas ni naturales del dho valle con los y^{o}s de las provincias de gente tributaria que ellos llamaban suyorunas y esto responde a esta pregunta.

iij A la pregunta tres dixo que save e vio que despues que los españoles entraron en esta ciudad en la conquista de este reino tomo el marques don Françisco Piçarro para si todo el valle de Yucay con los yndios que en el avia mitimas e naturales camayos e yanaconas los quales todos le sirvieron sin que ningun yndio o yndios que en el dho valle bivian quedasen reservados del dho servi^{o} por razon alguna sino que todos le beneficiavan las chacaras de coca que tenia en el //
/f.166/ valle de Tono Yanatai e Paucarbamba y chacaras de maiz que tenia en el valle desta ciudad y en Yucai a lo qual este testigo acudia siempre que le cabia su mita que quiere dezir su vez y en las dhas vezes vio que todos los dhos yndios mitimas e naturales camayos e yanaconas del dho valle acudian al benef^{o} de las dhas chacaras e a los servicios que en su casa hazian al dho marques proveyendole de yerva leña e paja e otros camaricos y esto save desta pregunta.

iiij A la pregunta /quatro/ dixo que save e vio que despues que los españoles entraron en esta ciudad y repartieron entre si los y^{o}s de la comarca de ella hasta que les visitaron los dhos yndios no tributaban a los españoles en quien estaban encomendados por orden de tasa como lo hacen agora ni les davan las cosas en que agora estan tasados mas de servirles en sus casas de darles yerva y leña e camarico de beneficiarles las chacaras de coca y maiz que tenia en este valle e algunos en labrar minas de oro e plata e asi en el dho tiempo este testigo y los demas y^{o}s del dho valle mitimas e naturales camayos e yanaconas sirvieron al dho marques en las cosas que dho tiene y no mas y esto save desta pregunta.

v A la pregunta cinco dixo que save y vio que por fin e muerte del dho marques don Françisco Piçarro subcedio en los y^{o}s del dho valle de Yucai don Gonçalo Piçarro su hijo a quien los y^{o}s del dho valle de Yucay y todos sirvieron en las cosas que avian servido al dho marques su padre sin que en el num^{o} //
/f.166v/ de los y^{o}s ni en los servi^{o}s y beneficios de chacaras le faltasen en cosa alguna a el y a sus mayordomos en su nombre como los demas yndios tributarios de la comarca desta ciudad lo hazian con sus encomenderos y esto save desta pregunta.

vj A la pregunta seis dixo que save e vio que despues que en esta ciudad se dixo que el dho don Gonçalo Piçarro hera muerto acudieron todos los y^{o}s del dho valle de Yucay con el fruto de las dhas chacaras de coca y maiz que beneficiavan a Garcia de Melo tesorero de su magestad que fue a la sazon y dende algun tiempo que este testigo no se determina quantos años que los dhos y^{o}s tributaban con el benef^{o} solo de las dhas chacaras les vino tasa de lo que avian de pagar y asi todos los y^{o}s del dho repartimiento mitimas e naturales tributaron por ella exepto los y^{o}s de Coto que servian a don Alonso Ucusicha a quien los dexo Ucusicha su padre que hera un yndio cacique de los cañares que vivian en esta ciudad del Cuzco el qual este testigo oyo dezir que les pidio al presidente Gasca informandole que eran yanaconas suyos que tenia en el valle de Yucai e los avia adquerido e juntado el dho Ucusicha por su trabajo e con esta relacion alcanzo titulo y merzed dellos y desde el dho tiempo e antes el dho Ucusicha se sirvio dellos y los traya distintos de los yndios del dho repartimiento con nombre de yanaconas suyos que se le avia dado el dho presidente Gasca e por esta razon los dhos y^{o}s se enaxeron del dho repartimi^{to} y por fin e muerte del dho Ucusicha sirvie- //
/f.167/ ron y an servido al dho don Alonso su hijo siendo como son y^{o}s mitimas del dho valle puestos por el Ynga por camayos del sol en el dho valle y queste testigo los vio tributar y servir al dho marques y a su hijo y esto save desta pregunta.

vij A la pregunta siete dixo que despues de ocho o nueve años que los y^{o}s del dho repartimi^{to} acudian con los tributos al dho tesorero Garcia de Melo y se llamaban y^{o}s de su magestad acudieron con los dhos tributos a don Diego Sayre Topa Ynga hijo de Mango Ynga y nieto de Guayna Capa que salio de Bilcabamba donde estava rebelado contra el servi^{o} de su magestad y oyo dezir a muchos y^{o}s del dho repartimi^{to} que el dho Ynga avia tomado posesion dellos y dijoles a los caciques principales que de alli adelante avian de ser suyos y de sus hijos y deçendientes que asi se los avia dado su magestad como dho tiene este testigo y los demas y^{o}s del dho repartimiento exepto los y^{o}s de Coto le sirvieron y tributaron todo el tiempo de su vida e por su fin e muerte subcedio en ellos doña Beatriz Coya su hija legitima y universal heredera a quien y a sus curadores en su nombre hasta que se caso con el capitan Martin Garcia de Loyola han tributado y esto save y vio desta pregunta.

viij A la pregunta ocho dixo que save e vio que dos o tres años despues que los y^{o}s del dho repartimiento de Yucay servian y tributaban al dho marques don Françisco Piçarro el dho marques nombro por cacique principal de todos mitimas e naturales camayos e yanaconas y^{o}s del dho valle a don Françisco //
/f.167v/ Chilche yndio cañar por cuyo nombramiento los dhos y^{o}s sirvieron y obedeçieron al dho cacique todo el tiempo que fueron del dho marques y don Gonçalo Piçarro su hijo y algunos años despues que estuvieron en cabeça de su magestad y por su orden y mandado sirvieron a los dhos sus encomenderos y acudian al benef^{o} de las dhas chacaras por su orden hasta que don Garcia Quispicapi de la desendencia de los Yngas puso plaeito al dho don Françisco Chilche sobre el cacicazgo y en el dho pleito se conzertaron en que el dho don Garcia Quispicapi tuviese el cacicazgo de los y^{o}s naturales del dho valle y el dho don Fran^{co} Chilche todos los y^{o}s mitimas y advenedizos que avia en el y asi cada uno ha estado en el cacicazgo que le cupo en el dho concierto hasta agora y esto save desta pregunta.

ix A la pregunta nueve dixo que dize lo que dho tiene en la pregunta antes desta y esto responde a esta pregunta.

x A la pregunta diez dixo que save e a visto que despues que se dividio el cacicazgo del dho repartimiento por concierto entre los dhos don Françisco y don Garcia el dho don Françisco favoreciendo a muchos de los y^{o}s mitimas a el subjetos a unos por parentesco y a otros porque le servian los traia y ha traido relevados de pagar por entero la tasa y de acudir al benef^{o} de las chacaras de maiz que ay en el dho valle de donde pagan su tasa ocupandolos en muy poca parte de ella y cargandole en los demas yndios de su parcialidad lo qual ha fecho el dho don Françisco Chilche y sus principales por no haber avido persona que los haya tenido en encomienda //
/f.168/ que procurase el bien de los y^{o}s y de yr a la mano a los dhos caciques en los agravios que hazen y han fecho a los y^{o}s del dho repartimiento porque cansi siempre despues que dexaron de ser del marques don Fran^{co} Piçarro los y^{o}s del dho repartimiento an andado a cargo de mayordomos y curadores de los en quien an estado encomendados e las tales personas nunca an tenido quenta con mas de cobrar dellos los tributos y de que beneficiasen las chacaras de coca y maiz que en tiempos pasados solian beneficiar y esto save desta pregunta.

xj A la pregunta honze dixo que save e a visto que los y^{o}s que el dho don Françisco Chilche a traido reservados en alguna manera de tributar en el dho repartimiento que son los contenidos en el memorial que se le ha leido nunca an dejado de ser subjetos a los principales de las parcialidades donde an estado segun la orden orden antigua que en esta an tenido y los dhos principales los an ocupado en algunas cosas del dho tribu^{o} o servicios que an fecho los y^{o}s del dho repartimi^{to} porque como dho tiene a sido la dha ocupacion en cosas leves e de poco trabajo y porque ellos an entendido siempre que son indios mitimas del dho repartimiento e antes que hubiese division en el dho cacicazgo los vio tributar y servir igualmente con los demas y^{o}s del dho repartimiento y esto save desta pregunta.

xij A la pregunta doze dixo que oyo dezir lo contenido en la pregunta a muchos y^{o}s del dho valle e que este testigo no fue //
/f.168v/ al ansiento de Mohina donde el dho Damian de la Vandera hizo la visita ques ocho leguas del dho repartimiento de Yucai por ser y^{o}s viejos e que despues que se hizo la dha visita vio que tuvieron en el dho repartimiento muchos yndios de los que el dho don Francisco Chilche tenia reservados de pagar por entero la tasa y esto save desta pregunta.

xiii A la pregunta treze dixo que oyo dezir a muchos y^{o}s del dho valle de Yucay mitimas especialmente a los del pueblo de Coto en donde este testigo ha resedido que son este testigo y los yndios que dho tiene parte de los quel dho don Alonso Ucusicha saco del dho repartimi^{to} como dho tiene los quales dhos y^{o}s de Coto dijeron a este testigo que el dho Damian de la Vandera avia visitado por yndios tributarios del dho repartimiento los apoyanaconas que tenian en guarda el cuerpo muerto de Guayna Capa y que avia fecho dellos y de otros y^{o}s que llaman la parcialidad de Tomebamba una parcialidad de cinquenta y^{o}s y nombrado por cacique dellos a dbn Alonso Tito Atauche e que no save ni a oydo dezir que el dho don Alonso pidiese los veinte y^{o}s que la pregunta dize ni si los dhos y^{o}s an dejado de tributar en el dho repartimiento mas de que save que los dhos yndios apoyanaconas y^{o}s de Tomebamba son mitimas puestos por Guayna Capa Ynga en el repartimiento y esto save desta pregunta.

/f.169/ xiiij A la pregunta catorze dixo que save e vio que el tesorero Garcia de Melo en la visita que hizo del dho repartimiento visito por yndios tributarios del v^{te} e cinco y^{o}s quel dho don Françisco Chilche dexo de manifestar en la dha visita por dezir que eran yanaconas suyos y el dho visitador averiguo ser y^{o}s mitimas del dho repartimiento por averlo manifestado asi don Garcia Quispicapi y les mando que de alli adelante tributasen por entero con los demas yndios del dho repartimiento y que no save ni a oydo dezir lo demas contenido en la dha pregunta y esto responde a esta pregunta.

xv A la pregunta quinze dixo que luego que Diego Escudero clerigo fue a dotrinar los yndios del dho repartimiento dende a quatro o cinco mese oyo dezir este testigo que el dho clerigo los mandaba juntar para visitallos y empadronallos y que mandaba que le diesen de por si las yanaconas que en el dho valle avia de yndios y españoles y ansimesmo los y^{o}s tributarios porque los avia de tener visitados distintos los unos de los otros e asi parece que el dho don Françisco Chilche hizo visitar por yanaconas todos los y^{o}s contenidos en el dho memorial que se le ha leido que este testigo save que son yndios mitimas del dho repartimi^{to} y que tributaron al marques y a su hijo y por el dho memorial parece ansimismo este testigo estar //
/f.169v/ nombrado en el a la quinta partida del donde dize Alonso Chauca de hedad de cinquenta y siete años y a Matheo Curas su hijo deste testigo que esta en la quarta partida del dho memorial de hedad de treinta años siendo como el y el dho su hijo y^{o}s mitimas en el dho valle este testigo por camayos de una chacara de alli que el dho Guayna Capa tenia en el dho ansiento de Coto y al dho Mateo Curas como hijo suyo y esto save desta pregunta.

xvj A la pregunta diez y seis dixo que save e vio que en la visita prostera [*sic*] que del dho valle se a fecho que la hizo el licenciado Frei Pedro Gutierrez capellan de su Exª del señor visorrey don Françisco de Toledo el dho visitador hizo la dha visita por el padron que el dho clerigo tenia fecho de los dhos y^{o}s mitimas e naturales y de los yanaconas como dho tiene llamandolos por sus parcialidades y nombre que en el dho libro estavan escriptos sin hazer otra pesquisa ni averiguacion alguna mas de apercivir los caciques que no le escondiesen y^{o}s so pena que seran castigados por ello y asi le parece a este testigo que como el dho clerigo tenia escriptos en el dho padron a este testigo y a su hijo Mateo Curas y a los demas en el dho memorial contenidos por yanaconas los escribio el dho licenciado Frei Pedro Gutierrez sin que este testigo supiese questaba besitado en el numero de los yanaconas y que no save si lo supieron los demas yanaconas y dexaron de manifestar //
/f.170/ ser y^{o}s tributarios por lo que la pregunta dize y que no lo a visto ni oido dezir mas de que save como dho tiene que todos los dhos y^{o}s en el memorial contenidos y este testigo y su hijo son y^{o}s mitimas puestos por el Ynga en el dho valle y que tributaron siempre en el dho repartimi^{to} en poca o mucha cantidad estando subjetos a sus principales como dho tiene y esto save desta preg^{ta}.

xvij A la pregunta diecisiete dixo que avia quatro o cinco meses que el dho Diego Escudero clerigo hizo juntar todos los y^{o}s en el memorial contenidos y les hizo ciertas preguntas a que todos los yndios le respondieron ser y^{o}s mitimas del dho repartimi^{to} e que avian tributado al marques Piçarro y a su hijo y al dho Tesorero Garcia de Melo por su magestad y que como tales y^{o}s mitimas tienen sus chacaras y casas segun como se las dio y repartio el Ynga lo qual asimesmo declararon los caciques e principales que el dho visitador dejo nombrados pa el gobierno de los dhos y^{o}s que estava visitados por yanaconas y esto responde a esta pregunta.

xviij A la pregunta diez y ocho dixo que dize lo que dho tiene en las preguntas antes desta.

xix A la pregunta diez y nueve dixo que todo lo que dho y declarado tiene por lenguas de los dhos interpretes es la verdad pa el juramento que fecho tiene y porque no supo firmar lo firmaron los dhos interpretes Hernando de Morales Felipe Saire. Ante mi Pero Diaz Valdeon escrivano publico.

Testigo: El dho Pedro Chinanzila yndio cañar residente en el pueblo de Santiago de Oropesa //
/f.170v/ del valle de Yucay encomendado en el capitan Martin Garcia de Loyola testigo presentado por parte del dho capitan Loyola e aviendo jurado y siendo preguntado por el thenor del dho interogatorio dixo lo siguiente:

j A la primera pregunta dixo que conoce a las partes e tiene noticia de los yanaconas sobre que es este pleito.

De la generales dixo que es de hedad de mas de ochenta y cinco años y que no le toca ninguna de ellas mas de estar encomendado en el dho capitan Martin Garcia de Loyola mas que por ello no dejara de dezir la verdad.

ij A la pregunta dos dixo que este testigo vino de Tomebamba que es en la provincia de Quito en el tiempo que Chalcochima y Quisquis capitanes de Atagualpa Ynga vinieron a prender a Guascar Ynga questava en esta ciudad y en el dho tiempo vio en el valle de Yucay muchos y grandes edeficios de casas fuentes y otras recreaciones e oyo dezir publicamente en el dho valle de Yucay y en esta ciudad a yndios antiguos que el dho el dho [*sic*] valle de Yucay todo era de Guayna Capa Ynga el qual hizo su casa e chacaras en el dho valle y puso en el mas de mil y^{o}s mitimas traidos de muchas partes deste reino e que estaban repartidos en los servicios que avian de hazer al dho Ynga en el dho valle y asi quando este testigo vino como dho tiene al dho Ynga en el dho valle la primera vez fue poco tiempo antes que viniesen los españoles a este reino vio los dhos y^{o}s mitimas juntamente con los natu- //
/f.171/ rales del dho valle que servian en el beneficio de chacaras reparo de edeficios que avia en el dho valle unos con nombre de yanaconas que quiere dezir criados y otros con nombre de camayos que quiere dezir oficiales y esto responde a esta pregunta.

iij A la pregunta tres dixo que save que despues que los españoles entraron en esta ciudad cuando vinieron a la conquista deste reino el marques don Françisco Piçarro tomo pa si los y^{o}s del valle de Yucay los quales vio este testigo que le servian en su casa de mitayos dandole camarico e leña e yerva en su casa y ansimismo vio que le daban y^{o}s para el beneficio de la coca en los Andes y le beneficiavan chacaras de maiz en el dho valle de Yucay y que no save en que provincia de los yungas les beneficiavan la dha coca porque este testigo vivia en esta ciudad con los y^{o}s cañares que en ella hay y no fue al dho valle en aquellos quatro años y que lo que dho tiene lo vio asi muchas vezes en casa del dho marques.

iiij A la pregunta quatro dixo que no lo save porque este testigo y los demas cañares que avia en esta ciudad siempre andaban ocupados en las cosas de la guerra e no tenian tiempo pa saver lo que se le pregunta

v A la pregunta cinco dixo que save y vio que por fin e muerte del dho marques don Françisco Piçarro acudian con el fruto de las dhas chacaras de coca e maiz los dhos yndios de Yucay mitimas e naturales a un español que se llamaba el ma- //
/f.171v/ estre sala Gumiel e oyo dezir este testigo publicamente que todos los dhos y^{o}s de Yucai mitimas e naturales eran de don Gonçalo Piçarro hijo del dho marques por quien el dho Gumiel cobraba los dhos tributos e los dhos yndios todos le sirvian al dho Gumiel como lo hazian en casa del dho marques Piçarro cuando era vivo y esto responde a esta pregunta.

vj A la pregunta seis dixo que en el tiempo que dho tiene que los y^{o}s del dho valle de Yucai mitimas e naturales avian quedado por fin e muerte del dho marques en don Gonçalo Piçarro su hijo don Fran^{co} Chilche cacique principal del dho Valle envio a este testigo al valle de Sairechaca en los andes para que alli le sirviese en el beneficio de su coca asi este testigo no vio lo contenido en la pregunta mas de que oyo dezir que todos los dhos yndios de Yucai mitimas e naturales acudian con el tributo que pagavan al tesorero Garcia de Melo y esto responde a esta pregunta.

vij A la pregunta siete dixo que oyo dezir lo contenido en la pregunta estand este testigo en el dho valle de Sairechaca e que los dhos yndios de Yucai mitimas e naturales servian y tributaban al dho don Diego Saire Topa Ynga y esto responde a esta pregunta.

viij A la pregunta ocho dixo que save e vio que dos o tres años despues que el dho marques don Françisco Piçarro tenia los yndios del dho valle de Yucai el dho marques nombro por cacique principal del dho valle de Yucay al dho don Fran^{co} //
/f.172/ Chilche yndio cañar al qual todos los y^{o}s del dho valle mitimas e naturales y yanaconas e camayos obedecieron y sirvieron como a su cacique principal y por su orden y mandado servian al dho marques y a los demas encomenderos que tuvieron el dho valle e porque como dho tiene en la sesta pregunta deste su dho en el tiempo que los y^{o}s del dho valle de Yucai fueron de don Gonçalo Piçarro hijo del dho marques el dho don Françisco Chilche cacique principal puso a este testigo en el valle de Sairechaca como a yndio advenedizo pa que alli le sirviese en el beneficio de la coca que tenia donde estuvo treinta años poco mas o menos hasta que abra tres años que se volvio a vivir en el dho valle de Yucay e asi no save los y^{o}s en el memorial que se le ha leido contenidos tributaron en algun tiempo ni si an sido siempre yanaconas e que se acuerda que muchos dellos dhos y^{o}s del memorial que oy son vivos fueron subjetos al dho don Françisco Chilche con los demas y^{o}s mitimas e naturales del dho valle y estos siempre sirvieron de camayos que quiere dezir oficiales que tenia cargo de beneficiar unos axi y otros madera y otros maiz de lo que se coxe temprano antes de la cosecha del maiz que generalmente todos los beneficiavan el qual dho maiz axi yervas y otras cosas beneficiavan para dar de presente a españoles e a sus encomenderos e muchos dellos en el dho memorial contenidos no los conoce este testigo algunos que conoce dellos demas de los que arriba tiene dho vio que Garcia de Melo visitado los yndios del dho valle de Yucai los visito por indios //
/f.172v/ tributarios del dho repartimiento aunque le dixo don Françisco Chliche que eran yanaconas suyos y por esto vio que el dho Garcia de Melo dixo que aunque los visitaba por yndios del dho repartimi^{to} los dhos yndios que asi bisitaba no abian de hazer en el mas de pagar el dinero que les cupiese de la tasa y no otra cosa y esto responde a esta pregunta.

ix A la pregunta nueve dixo que abra quinze años poco mas o menos que saliendo este testigo del valle de Sairechaca con fruta e presentes al dho don Françisco Chilche vio en el dho valle de Yucai que un fraile de la orden de Santo Domingo que se llamava frei Domingo trataba en el dho valle de Yucai el cacicazgo de los y^{o}s del pertenecia a don Garcia Quispicapi de la desendencia de los Yngas y tratandose del negocio vio este testigo que quedaron çonzertidos los dhos don Garcia Ynga y el dho don Françisco Chilche cañar por orden del dho fray Domingo en que el dho don Garcia fuese cacique de los yndios naturales del dho valle y el dho don Francisco Chiche de los yndios mitimas y advenedizos que en el vivian e luego otro dia de como esto paso este testigo se volvio al dho valle de Sairechaca donde vivia y no bio lo demas que en este negocio paso y esto responde a esta pregunta.

x A la pregunta diez dixo que dize lo que dho tiene en las preguntas antes desta e que no save que el dho don Françisco Chilche favoreciendo a algunos yndios los reservase de servir y tributar ni que los sacase del dho repartimiento.

xj A la pregunta onze dixo que dize lo que dho tiene.

/f.173/ xij A las doze preguntas dixo que en el tiempo que Damian de la Bandera visito los y^{o}s del valle de Yucai este testigo salio a dar fruta al dho don Françisco Chilche del dho valle de Sayrechaca donde estaba e vio que el dho Damian de la Bandera visito los yndios del dho repartimiento por la orden que los caciques se los manifestaba y estandose haziendo la dha visita doña Ynes Coya mujer del dho don Fran^{co} Chilche dio una peticion al dho visitador en que le pidio que el dho su marido tenia muchos yndios yanaconas de su servi^{o} que se los visitase por suyos y asi el dho visitador se los dexo todos por suyos que entre y^{o}s e yndias e muchachos serian mas de cien personas y tornandole a leer el dho memorial con apercibimiento que se acordase bien de si vio que el dho Damian de la Bandera los visitase por y^{o}s tributarios del dho repartimiento leyendole primero los nombres de yndios que en el dho memorial se dize ser de don Françisco Chilche dixo que no conoce a los mas de los que asi se leyeron y los que dixo que conocia fueron setenta e quatro y^{o}s y preguntado si los visito el dho Damian de la Vandera por del dho repartimi^{to} dixo que los y^{o}s que tiene declarado que conoce del dho memorial son que el dho Damian de la Vandera declaro ser yanaconas del dho don Francisco Chilche y entre ellos esta este testigo con dos hijos que tiene que son los que en el dho memorial se nombran Pedro Ximinzila de hedad de cincuenta e siete años y Benito Guarta Languai de //
/f.173v/ veinte años y Pedro Niulazara de veinte e ocho siempre este testigo con los demas que dho tiene an servido de yanaconas al dho don Françisco Chilche y nunca han tributado en el dho repartimiento y leyendole los nombres de yndios que en el memorial se dize heran de don Alonso Tito Atauche dixo que conocia a seis yndios dellos y no mas e save que estos siempre vivian en el dho valle con nombre de yanaconas de Guayna Capa con otros yndios de la parcialidad de apoyanaconas e que siempre oyo dezir que eran yanaconas del Ynga y no tributarios e no save si el dho Damian de la Bandera los visito por el dho repartimi^{to} y esto responde.

xiij A la pregunta treze dixo que dize lo que dho tiene en las preguntas antes desta.

xiiij A la pregunta catorze dixo que no save de lo contenido en la dha preg^{ta} mas de que oyo dezir que el dho don Garcia de Melo visito por yndios del dho repartimiento algunos yanaconas de los de don Françisco Chilche y no save este testigo quantos fueron y esto responde a esta pregunta.

xv A la pregunta quinze dixo que a oido dezir lo contenido en la preg^{ta} e que estan visitados por el dho clerigo los yanaconas por si y los y^{o}s tributarios por si dixo que save y vio que cuando el licenciado frei P^{o} Gutierrez Flores visito los yndios del dho valle de Yucay el dho visitador junto todos los caciques del dho repartimi^{to} mitimas e //
/f.174/ naturales y los apercibio muchas bezes que le manifestasen todos los y^{o}s que avia en el dho repartimi^{to} y los y^{o}s que con nombre de yanaconas bivian en el dho valle poniendo muy grandes penas a los caciques e principales de las parcialidades que escondiesen algunos y^{o}s e asi los visito por la horden que los dhos caciques e principales tenian por sus parcialidades e a los yanaconas con el nombre cuyos dezian ser que las tales personas que tenian yanaconas en el dho valle y^{o}s y españoles los tenian en sus estancias cada uno como podia que unos tenian muchos y otros pocos e no vio este testigo que el dho visitador los bisitase por el libro del dho clerigo aunque algunas vezes thenia el dho visitador un libro sobre la mesa en que estaba bisitando e no bio este testigo que el licenciado Gutierrez visitase ningunos yndios tributarios del dho repartimiento por yanaconas sino que los y^{o}s que visito por yanaconas este t^{o} los avia visto andar con el dho nombre de yanaconas sirviendo a sus amos y no save que tributasen en ningun tiempo y esto responde a esta preg^{ta}.

xvij A la pregunta diez y siete dixo que no lo save.

xviij A las diez y ocho preguntas dixo que dize lo que dho tiene en las preg^{tas} antes desta.

xix A la pregunta diez y nueve dixo que lo que dho y declarado tiene por lengua de los dho interpretes es la verdad y lo que save por el juramento que hizo y en ello se afirmo y ratefico y no firmo poque no supo y lo firmaron los dhos ynterpretes //
/f.174v/ enmendado serian y testado cinquenta y ocho indios. Felipe Saire Hernando de Morales. Ante mi Pero Dia Valdeon escrivano.

Testigo: El dho Fernando Caocalla yndio mitima residente en Santiago de Oropesa del valle de Yucai presentado por pte del capitan Martin Garcia de Loyola el qual aviendo jurado y siendo preguntado por las preguntas del dho interr^{o} dixo y depuso lo siguiente:

j A la primera pregunta dixo que conoce a las partes e tiene noticia de los yanaconas sobre que es este pleito.

De las generales dixo que es de hedad de sesenta e un años poco mas o menos e que no concurre en ninguna dellas mas de ser encomendado en el dho capitan Martin Garcia de Loyola pero que no dexara por eso de dezir verdad.

ij A la pregunta dos dixo que desde que este testigo se save acordar que a mas de quarenta e cinco años vio en el valle de Yucay muchas casas y edeficios de fuentes y andenes y otras cosas de recreacion e oyo dezir a su padre deste testigo que se llamaba Coata que era mitima en el dho valle que las dhas casas y edeficios avian sido de Guayna Capa Ynga e que para su cuerpo muerto se beneficiavan las chacaras que avia en el dho valle y se repararian y aderezarian siempre los dhos edeficios e casas que para el dho Guayna Capa en su vida avia puesto en el dho valle dos mil y^{o}s mil de Chintaisuyo [*sic*] y mil de Collasuyo que son dos provincias de este reino los quales y //
/f.175/ los yndios naturales del dho valle que son los y^{o}s de los pueblos de Chaucai Pacai Cache tuvieron a cargo el benef^{o} de los dhos edeficios y chacaras hasta que entraron los españoles en este reino y esto responde.

iij A la pregunta tres dixo que save e vio que despues que los españoles entraron en esta ciudad cuando conquistaron este reino el marques don Françisco Piçarro tomo luego para si el dho valle de Yucay e asi de los y^{o}s mitimas e naturales e yanaconas del Ynga sirvieron al dho marques beneficiandole las chacaras de coca que tenia en el valle de Tono Paucarbamba e Yanatai y otras chacaras de maiz que tenia en esta ciudad y en el dho valle de Yucay y le sirvieron en su casa con camarico de yerba y leña y le acudian con los frutos de las dhas chacaras de coca y maiz y esto responde a esta pregunta.

iiij A la pregunta quatro dixo que save e vio que en el tiempo susodho y algunos despues todos los y^{o}s de la comarca desta ciudad no tributaban a los españoles en quien estaban encomendados por orden de tasa como lo han fecho despues aca que solamente los servian personalmente beneficiandoles sus chacaras y sirviendoles en sus casas de mitaios con camarico de leña yerba como dho tiene que lo hazianlos dhos y^{o}s de Yucai con el marques don Françisco Piçarro y esto hazian todos los dhos y^{o}s en lugar de los tributos que despues an dado a sus encomenderos y esto responde a esta pregunta.

/f.175v/ v A la pregunta cinco dixo que save que por fin y muerte del dho don Françisco Piçarro todos los dhos y^{o}s del dho valle de Yucay mitimas e naturales acudian con el fruto de las dhas chacaras de coca e maiz y el servi^{o} personal de la manera que dho tiene que los hazian al dho marques y al maestre sala Gumiel y este testigo oyo dezir en el dho tiempo que los y^{o}s del valle de Yucai eran de don Gonçalo Piçarro hijo del dho marques que estaba en la ciudad de los Reies por quien recibia el dho tribu^{o} el dho Gumiel y esto responde a esta preg^{ta}.

vj A la pregunta seis dixo que algunos años despues que acudian con el fruto de las dhas chacaras de coca y maiz los dho y^{o}s de Yucai a los mayordomos del dho don Gonçalo Piçarro los dhos y^{o}s de Yucai mitimas e naturales davan los dhos frutos a Garcia de Melo thesorero de su magestad porque se dixo que el dho don Gonçalo Piçarro era muerto e por su fin e muerte avia subcedido en ellos su magestad y no save que los dhos y^{o}s de Yucay sirviesen al dho Garcia de Melo como sirvian al dho maestre sala Gumiel y esto responde.

vij A la pregunta siete dixo que save e vio que diez o doze años despues que los dhos yndios de Yucai mitimas e naturales pagavan trib^{o} a su magestad por tasa del presidente Gasca se encomendaron los dhos y^{o}s en don Diego Saire Topa Ynga hijo de Mango Ynga que avia estado retirado en la montaña de Bilcabamba contra el servicio de su magestad //

/f.176/ por aver salido de la dha montaña dando la obediencia a su magestad le dieron todos los dhos y^{o}s de Yucai mitimas e naturales ecepto los yndios del pueblo de Coto que serian quinze o diez y seis los quales andavan despernados [*sic*] e divisos del dho repartimiento desde el tiempo que los y^{o}s del dho valle de Yucay tributaban a don Gonçalo Piçarro hijo del marques Piçarro por averlos sacado Ucusicha yndio cañar principal de los cañares que bivian en esta ciudad por consentimi^{to} de los caciques e principales del dho valle de Yucai. El qual los dejo a don Alonso Ucusicha su hijo que por fin e muerte del dho su padre se ha servido dellos hasta que en esta visita general quedaron declarados por y^{o}s tributarios de su mag^{td} por no haber avido quien diese noticia de los que a pasado acerca de los dhos y^{o}s e de como son y^{o}s mitimas del dho valle de Yucai puestos por camayos de las chacaras del sol e los demas yndios del dho valle mitimas e naturales sirvieron y tributaron al dho don Diego Saire Topa el qual ha oido dezir este testigo que teniendo juntos todos los caciques e principales del dho repartimiento de Yucay les dixo que su magestad se los avia dado a el para que le sirviesen y tributasen pa siempre a el y a sus hijos y descendientes y por fin e muerte del dho don Diego Saire Topa Ynga subcedio en los dhos y^{o}s de Yucay doña Beatriz Coya su hija legitima y heredera a quien y a sus curadores en su nombre han servido y tributado hasta agora que se caso //
/f.176v/ con el capitan Martin Garcia de Loyola a quien todos los yndios sirven y tributan al presente y esto responde a esta pregunta.

viij A la pregunta ocho dixo que save e vio que en el tiempo que los yndios del dho valle de Yucai mitimas e naturales tenian por cacique principal a don Françisco Chilche por orden y nombramento del marques don Françisco Piçarro todos los dhos yndios con los queste testigo conoce de los en el dho memorial contenidos que seran hasta ciento y setenta yndios todos servian y obedecian al dho don Françisco Chilche e por su orden y mandado servian y tributaban al dho marques don Françisco Piçarro y a los demas sus encomenderos que los an tenido e que los demas y^{o}s que dho tiene que no conoce por los nombres si los viese diria si son yndios antiguos en el dho valle mitimas advenedizos y que como dho tiene todo el tiempo que el dho don Fran^{co} Chilche tuvo el solo el cacicazgo del dho valle de Yucai todos los yndios que bivian en el le servian y ovedecian sin que ninguno estuviese reservado de tributar y servir a los dhos encomenderos y esto save desta pregunta.

ix A la pregunta nueve dixo que lo save como en ella se contiene porque tratandose pleito sobre el cacicazgo del dho repartimiento entre el dho don Françisco Chilche y don Garcia Quispicapi Ynga los conzerto un fraile dominico que se llamava fray Domingo en que el dho don Fran^{co} Chilche fuese cacique principal de los y^{o}s //
/f.177/ mitimas y advenedizos que ay en el dho valle y el dho don Garcia Quispicapi lo fuese de los yndios naturales del e asi cada uno dellos ha sido cacique en la parte que a cada uno cupo en el dho concierto hasta agora y esto save desta pregunta.

x A la pregunta diez dixo que save que despues que el dho don Françisco Chilche quedo con el cacicazgo de los dhos yndios mitimas y advenedizos el dho don Fran^{co} traya relevados de pagar tasa muchos yndios cañares y otros y^{o}s mitimas por dezir que eran yndios advenedizos y no mitimas del dho valley se sirvia dellos en el benef^{o} de sus chacaras y granjerias e asi los dhos yndios quedaron con nombre de yanaconas del dho don Françisco no embargante lo qual los mas de los dhos indios que ansi andaban relevados de tributar no dexaban de beneficiar las chacaras de maiz y coca que se beneficiavan para pagar el tribu^{o} que devian a sus encomenderos y en otros servicios leves del dho repartimiento y las demas cosas en que avian de andar ocupados los dhos y^{o}s se cargava en los yndios de las parcialidades de donde hera los dhos y^{o}s relevados y los dhos y^{o}s que ansi andaban cargados no osavan pedir cosa alguna en este negocio por respeto del dho don Françisco Chilche y esto responde a esta pregunta.

xj A la pregunta honze dixo que dize lo que dho tiene en la pregunta antes desta y que los dhos yndios que don Fran^{co} Chilche tenia por yanaconas suyos siempre //
/f.177v/ anduvieron subjetos a los principales de sus parcialidades y al dho don Françisco Chilche como su cacique principal y las cosas en que andavan relevados no la dexaban de hazer por no ser yndios del dho repartimiento si no porque asi lo queria y ordenaba el dho don Françisco Chilche y esto save desta pregunta.

xij A la pregunta doze dixo que oyo dezir que el dho Damian de la Vandera quando visito los y^{o}s del dho repartimiento de Yucai mitimas e naturales visito por y^{o}s de dho repartimiento cinquenta yndios que son de las parcialidades de apoyanaconas y Tomebamba que hasta la dha visita no pagavan tasa porque heran yanaconas del cuerpo muerto de Guayna Capa e ansimismo oyo dezir que el dho don Françisco Chilche dejo de manifestar en la dha visita muchos y^{o}s que fueron los que dho tiene que traya relebados de tributar y otros y^{o}s cañares mitimas del dho valle que bivian en la quebrada de Chicon del dho repartimi^{to} dando a entender a los y^{o}s tributarios del dho repartimiento que los y^{o}s que asi dexava de visitar se los avia dado el visitador por yanaconas suyos y esto save desta pregunta.

xiij A la pregunta treze dixo que dize lo que dho tiene que en la visita que hizo Garcia de Melo de los y^{o}s del repartimi^{to} oyo dezir que don Alonso Tito Atauche le avian dado en la audiencia real de los Reies veinte yndios de la parcialidad de apoyanacona de que fue cacique //
/f.178/ en la visita que de los dhos yndios hizo Damian de la Bandera que asi vio que el dho Garcia de Melo los visito a los dhos v^{te} yndios por yanaconas del dho don Alonso Tito Atauche e que save que los dhos veinte indios de la parcialidad de apoyanaconas que asi saco el dho don Alonso Tito Atauche son yndios mitimas del dho valle y lo fueron sus padres y esto save desta pregunta.

xiiij A la pregunta catorze dixo que no save lo en la pregunta contenido porque despues que el dho Melo estava visitando estando enfermo e asi no vio lo que la pregunta dize mas de que oyo dezir despues que se hizo la dha visita quel dho Garcia de Melo avia bisitado unos yanaconas de don Françisco Chilche por y^{o}s tributarios del dho repartimiento e no save quantos y esto save desta pregunta.

xv A la pregunta quinze dixo que al tpo quel dho Diego Escudero clerigo visito y empadrono los y^o^s del dho valle este testigo estava en esta ciudad por ayarico e oyo dezir que el dho clerigo avia fecho la dha visita de la manera que la pregunta dize e que hizo bisitar don Françisco Chilche muchos yndios mitimas del dho repartimiento por yanaconas suyos y esto save desta preg[ta].

xvj A la pregunta diez y seis dixo que save y vio que el licenciado frei P[o] Gutierrez que visito los y[o]s del dho valle en esta visita general que por orden del señor bisorrey don Françisco de Toledo se a fecho el dho licenciado frei Pedro Gutierrez visitava los y[o]s del dho valle por el libro e padron del dho clerigo guardando la orden que en el abia e asi bisito //
/f.178v/ por yanaconas todos los yndios que por el libro del dho clerigo estavan visitados con este nombre sin hazer aberiguacion ni pesquiza sobre si algun yndio de los que davan a visitar por yanaconas oviesen sido yndios tributarios del dho repartimiento y los dhos yndios de la parcialidad de Pampallata que bivian en la quebrada de Chicon que son algunos de los queste t[o] conoce del dho memorial con otros y[o]s del dho valle que seran los ciento y setenta y[o]s que dho tiene que conoce del memorial quedaron visitados por yanaconas siendo y[o]s mitimas del dho valle y que como dho tiene en poca o en mucha cantidad avian servido con los demas y[o]s del dho repartimi[to] y avian andado subjetos a los principales de las parcialidades donde antiguamente fueron ellos y sus padres y esto save de la pregunta.

xvij A la pregunta diez y siete dixo que oyo dezir lo contenido en la pregunta a muchos yndios del dho valle y esto responde a esta pregunta.

xviij A la pregunta diez y ocho dixo que dize lo que dho tiene en las preguntas antes desta.

xix A la pregunta diez y nueve dixo que todo lo que dho tiene es la verdad pa el juramento que tiene fecho y en ello se afirmo y ratifico y lo firmaron los ynterpretes Hernando de Morales Felipe Saire. Ante mi Pero Diaz Valdeon escrivano.

En el Cuzco a primero dia de abril de mil y qui[o]s y setenta e quatro años ante el Ilustre Señor dotor Gabriel de Loarte del consejo de Su Magestad y justicia m[or] //
/f.179/ en esta ciudad la presento el contenido en el dho nombre del capitan Martin Garcia de Loyola por el poder que tiene de que doy fee que es bastante presento el escripto siguiente:

Il[e] Señor Alonso de Valdes en nombre del capitan Martin Garcia de Loyola digo que mi parte tiene dada la informacion que por la provision de su Ex[a] se mando recivir sobre los yanaconas del valle de Yucai de la encomienda de mi parte de la qual mi parte tiene neçesidad pa guarda de su dr[o]

Pido a V.M. le mande dar un treslado o dos o mas de ella pa en guarda de su dr[o] interponiendo en ella V.M. su autoridad y decreto judicial y pa ello es y pido justicia. Alonso de Baldes.

El señor dotor mando se le de un treslado o mas de la dha provança pa el efeto que la pide a lo qual ynterpuso su autoridad e decreto judicial pa que balga y haga fee do quier que fuere presentado y lo firmo el Dotor Loarte ante mi Pero Diaz Valdeon escrivano. Va entre renglones o diz no diez e despues que subcedieron en la dha doña Beatriz Coya poca caciq' por ser muchas y muy buenas y asi desde luego sirvieron al dho marques todos los y[o]s que en el dho valle avia se Piçarro que vino a esta çiudad y despues e vio que abra tres meses poco mas o menos no. Y enmendado/ o diz cinquenta diez y ocho el/ o d buta/ paga y[o]s/ dho Ynga unos con bala y testado/ o diz/ V/ H/ po/ ros/ z/ ras/ testigos/ mu/ es/ que los/ en/ p/ do/ z/ s/ e/ q q/ v/ de/ de/ e/ y/ caciquez/ te/ v/ dhos vto/ repartimi[to] no bala. Yo Pero Diaz Baldeon escri[o] de su magestad publico e del numero de la dha ciudad del Cuzco fuy presente a todo lo suso dho e hize aqui mi signo es testimonio de verdad. Pero Diaz de Baldeon escri[o] Pu[co].

/f.179v/ En la villa de Santiago de Oropesa a veinte e ocho dias del mes de mayo de mill qui[o]s y setenta y tres años ante el Yll[e] señor Diego Barrantes Perero Visitador General por su magestad en este valle de Yucay parecio presente Juan Fernandez Coronel y presento la peticion siguiente.

Yll[e] señor Juan Fernandez Coronel en nombre del capitan Martin Garcia de Loyola vez[no] de la ciudad del Cuzco y de doña Beatriz Clara Coya su mujer digo que en la visita que el señor licenciado frei Pedro Gutierrez antecesor de V. M. hizo en este valle de Yucay de la encomienda de mis ptes uvo yerro contra mis partes en cantidad de mas de docientos cinquenta y[o]s los quales son e an sido y[o]s de tasa e lo fueron en tiempo del marques don Françisco Piçarro su primero encomendero e despues del fueron de su hijo don Françisco [*sic*] Piçarro y ansimismo le tributaron con lo que entonzes se usava e tenian que despues de esto fueron encomendados en don Diego Saire Tupa Ynga padre de la dha doña Beatriz Coya mi pte por el marques de Cañete con titulo de mayorazgo losquales les encomendaron al dho don Diego bien y como lo avia tenido e poseido el dho marques e su hijo don Françisco y los dhos y[o]s an sido bisitados con los demas por tales y[o]s de tasa deste dho repartimiento por Juan de Berrio y Pero Alonso Carrasco por mandado del Presidente Gasca e ansimismo fueron muchos dellos visitados por Damian de la Vandera e los que entonzes no se visitaron por tales yndios de tasa fue que los escondieron algunos caciques e yndios y españoles de la dha visita y despues fueron visitados por Garcia de Melo aunque tan- //
/f.180/ bien le escondieron muchos dellos en todas las quales visitas los dhos yndios o los mas dellos por tasa como lo son e como tales siempre ellos e sus hijos an ayudado en las tasas e servicios hordinarios de este repartimiento e ayudan hasta agora y los que no lo han fecho ni pagado a sido por ser la dha doña Beatriz mi parte menor e no tener ni aver tenido quien mirase por su hazienda a cuya causa muchos caciques e y[o]s y españoles tomavan y[o]s de la dha encomienda pa sus servicios llamandoles yanaconas e ansi se an quedado con este nombre hasta agora por no tener dueño que los recojese e los contradixese a los tales e ansi el dho señor lic[do] Gutierrez los bisito por

yanaconas poniendolos fuera de la bisita de los demas tributarios de la encomienda de mis ptes sin citar a la dha doña Beatriz ni a sus curadores ni la dha ni su curador ansistio a la dha visita ni a parte della de lo qual an recivido e reciben mis partes notorio agravio y agora es venido a mi noticia que los oficiales reales de la ciudad del Cuzco piden la tasa a los dhos yndios por les haber su Exª puesto en cabeza de su magestad como si fueran yanaconas e y^{os} no desta encomienda de que mis ptes y los dhos y^{os} reciben mucho agravio.

A V. M. pido reciba mi informacion en lo susodho la qual me profiero de dar luego e bastante e verdadera e siendo asi como lo es V. M. declare los dhos y^{os} con sus mujeres e hijos y descendientes por y^{os} que son de tasa de los dhos mis partes e a ellos encomen- //
/f.180v/ dados e como tales bisitados en muchas bisitas los quales y^{os} son los que se contienen en esta memoria de que hago presentacion con mas sus mujeres e hijos que aqui no ban puestos e si otro pedim^{to} mas queste fuere nezesario protesto en nombre de mis partes de lo hazer como mas a su dr^{o} conbenga e pido a V. M. mande a los dhos y^{os} no paguen ni acudan con tasa alguna a los dhos oficiales reales ni a otra persona que en su nombre lo pidan si no fuere a mis partes que lo an de aver con protestacion que hago que sea ninguna en si lo que en contr^{o} se mandare e no pare perjui^{o} a mis partes y que lo cobrare de Vra. Md. e de su persona e bienes e de me quexar a su magestad e a donde de dr^{o} soy obligado e de como lo digo pido e requiero al presente escrivano me lo de por testimonio e pido justicia etc. Juan Fernandez Coronel.

V Los yndios que son de tasa e de la encomienda de Martin Garcia de Loyola e de doña Beatriz Coya su mujer en este valle de Yucay e Guayllabamba los quales por yerro se bisitaron por yanaconas por el licenciado frei Pedro Gutierrez Flores son los siguientes:

v Don Diego Rimache
v Pedro Machaguai
v Andres Cazatnaula
v Francisco Biznaiçila
v Matheo Atras
v Alonso Chauca
v Mateo Curu
v Alonso Quispi
v Francisco Quispi
v Pedro Guatalla
v Francisco Leancari
v Juan Quiquinyanac
v Mateo Ricra
v Goncalo Canchari
v Diego Asto Camasca
v Pedro Alcamari
v Diego Cunis Malma
v Agustin Camasca
/f.181/ v Francisco RanpaYupangui
v Juan Yanac Camasca
v Miguel Bilcacondor
v Simon Cusiminga
v Antonio Çaquiguari
v Andres Duibus
v Alonso Quispi
v Marcos Chilli
v Juan Bautista Manchi
v Miguel Zinglinaula
v Francisco Mibancila
v Andres Tinianagua
v Mateo Lliui Juytlla
v Mateo Palchiviznay
v Alonso Zaquiarya
v Cristobal Guamancondor
v Lucas Chillilliguaman
v Agustin Alao
v Lucas Bilidunbay
v Pedro Guamanaisi
v Paulo Aisiguaorao
v Pedro Millic
v Pedro Languirisaca
v Martin Malqui
v Francisco Guachalla
v Pedro Alla
v Cristobal Zimansanay
v Fernando Pasto
v Rodrigo Tacuri
v Juan Bautista Zapaipay
v Benito Rimachi
v Francisco Hualpa
v Alonso Canagua
v Agustin Llachua
v Benito Llachua
v Juan Sicsi
v Diego Tanta
v Diego Uscoguaman
v Martin Supaico
v Alonso Pinchay
v Jeronimo Cuyo
v Cristobal Chuquinachay
v Pedro Zinincila
v Benito Guartalanguay
v Pedro Nivlazca
v Pedro Buruan
v Martin Marcavichay
v Alonso Biliviznay
v Pedro Salina
v Alonso Vihunlalay
v Juan Taubuiputlla
v Martin Sabar
v Alonso Jiviputlla
v Juan Zucunguazin
v Sebastian Tenezela
v Juan Cazatnaula
v Hernando Charo
v Simon Illatupa
v Agustin Tucapuma
v Cristobal Sulcanaui
v Pedro Paucar Aymara
v Pedro Vilcacarsia
v Agustin Salanda
v Toribio Cirimana
v Cristobal Visacauana
v Alonso Aransi

v Francisco Chuquiconsa
v Alonso Vinanabay
v Pedro Cuzcuc
/f.181v/ v Juan Bautista Duizul
v Martin Ninapuma
v Cristobal Tomaylla
v Juan Chuquicancha
v Lucas Chuquicondor
v Juan Caruabanca
v Rodbrigo Guaraca
v Jeronimo Guamanquilla
v Domingo Apasa
v Francisco Llacsaiyupari
v Alfonso Usco
v Francisco Guayausco
v Pedro Tinta
v Francisco Quispiyupa
v Alfonso Conucyupari
v Agustin Conduri
v Andres Caruapisco
v Alonso Muqui
v Andres Auquisyupari
v Juan Manta
v Alonso Pilpi
v Martin Quispi
v Martin Guanaco
v Pedro Pumaguaman
v Juan Cusma
v Juan Bautista Naupachi
v Cristobal Sivinta
v Juan Vilcaspariguana
v Alonso Guaman
v Martin Nayta
v Juan Camacsayza
v Cristobal Pañallucu
v Alonso Paña
v Alonso Ancaypuru
v Domingo Vilca
v Francisco Vichaguaman
v Juan Cochachin
v Domingo Yarovilca
v Alonso Condurmachaguay
v Martin Cavascanco
v Alonso Cocabascanco
v Alonso Gualpacuacu
v Cristobal Raymi
v Hernando Ataocava
v Don Juan Aylanbo
v Diego Uñapaucar
v Anton Cabana
v Martin Callacana
v Felipe Tomaylla.
v Juan Malcopariguana
v Francisco Chizua
v Pedro Guancapuma
v Juan Supnoyupangui
v Juan Aucagualpa
v Juan Tupa Yupangui
v Pedro Mallovauri
v Diego Machaca
v Cristobal Supno
v Pedro Canica
v Pedro Uscagualpa
v Cristobal Martin TupaYupangui
v Diego TupaYupangui
v Domingo Turue
v Alonso Quispe
v Alonso Guanasca
v Pedro Paucar
v Cristobal GualpaYupangui
v Juan Guandapi
v Domingo Guaman
v Pedro Yunaira
/f.182/ v Pedro QuispitupaYupangui
v Andres Gugmalli
v Cristobal Guamalli
v Martin Cunumuru
v Diego Cusipuro
v Agustin Cusipaucar
v Martin Punjaguaman
v Martin Guamanjucha
v Pedro Siuipaucar
v Martin Quicaña.
v Juan Pumayanac
v Goncalo Suyucachi
v Miguel Guaranga
v Cristobal Yaurichagua
v Francisco Paucar
v Cristobal Guartaytuyu
v Antonio de Quiñones Janampa
v Diego Ninaricza
v Domingo Sulca
v Hernando Caruabanca
v Salvador Llaguasto
v Luis Sulca Llacgua
v Vicente Chiguan
v Francisco Chiguan
v Hernando Pumacondor
v Cristobal Chuquicondor
v Antonio Pumacondor
v Juan Chichi
v Francisco Pumachinchi
v Ambrosio Pillaca
v Hernando Gualparimachi
v Martin Rimachi Yupangui
v Juan TopaYupangui
v Martin Ataocusi
v Miguel Ninagualpa
v Cristobal Yachimarca
v Pedro Vilcaruna
v Martin Rimachi
v Alvaro Parinango
v Pedro Villa
v Juan Alonso Aucasupe
v Felipe Putllacila
v Martin Pichuna
v Agustin Gualuto
v Diego Llamuca
v Agustin Aroni
v Alonso Guamancusi

v Juan Caruaruna
v Goncalo Ungaragua
v Martin Sanca
v Pedro Pallanchu
v Martin Marca
v Pedro Quispe
v Sebastian Sulca
v Lucas Rimasca
v Pedro Llacgua
v Diego Acota
v Redro Quispi
v Alonso Mucac
v Sebastian Maybasca
v Juan Picarro Cusiataoche
v Lorenzo Guaritupa
v Diego Cristobal Tupacusigualpa
v Alonso Caquicuya
v Francisco Guartatnaula
v Fabian Cuchillo
v Pedro Quispi
v Felipe Yupangui
/f.182v/ v Miguel Nutnaguarai
v Pedro Chuquitana
v Alonso Tabrac
v Pedro Condori
v Marcos Puri
v Domingo Gualparimachi
v Alonso Cansinti
v Francisco Chuaina
v Martin Zucaipaucar
v Alonso Guaypar
v Alonso Napanga
v Diego Llamac
v Juan Yaris
v Alonso Cipa
v Juan Ingapaucar
v Andres Casabilca

Y demas de los suso dhos pido los que mas con verdad parecieren ser de tasa desta dha encomienda de Yucay - Juan Fernandez Coronel.

Sepan quantos esta carta vieren como yo Martin Garcia de Loyola comendador del abito de Calatrava vez^{o} desta gran ciudad del Cuzco y capitan de la guarda del ex^{mo} señor don Francisco de Toledo virrey destos reinos e yo doña Beatriz Coya su ligitima mujer con licencia y expreso consentimi^{to} que pido e demando al dho señor capitan mi marido para otorgar esta escriptura como en ello fuere contenido la qual dha licencia yo el dho capitan le doy e conçedo quan firme y bastante de derecho se require y me obligo de la aver por firme y lo que por virtud della fuere fecho y otorgado en esta escriptura so obligacion que para ello hago de mi persona e bienes avidos e por aver e usando della e ambos a dos juntos e ynsolidun otorgamos e conocemos que damos y otorgamos nuestro poder cumplido qual de dr^{o} se require a Alonso de Baldez y a Juan Fernandes Coronel a ambos a dos //
/f.183/ juntamente e cada uno dellos ynsolidun especialmente pa que por nos y en nuestro nombre tenga el benef^{o} y administracion los tribu^{o}s e y^{o}s de nuestra encomienda e los defiendan e anparen como mas y mejor convenga a los dhos y^{o}s y les ponga dotrina suficiente e pague lo que se deviere pagar a los sacerdotes que los dotrinasen y los ponga en buena puliçia e siga e los defienda en todos sus pleitos e causas que tuvieren asi y de la manera que nosotros lo podriamos hazer e pa que pidan reciban y cobren de los dhos yndios de nuestra encomienda todos los tribu^{o}s y haziendas que son y fueren obligados a nos dar y pagar de tasa en cada un año e lo que pareciere devernos de las mitas pasadas y de resto de quentas y en otra qualquier manera y de otras qualesquier personas qualesquier maravedis y pesos de oro plata joyas esclavos ganados mercadurias e otras cosas qualesquier que nos devan y devieren por escripturas y recaudos y en otra qualquier manera y del recibo dellos den y otorguen sus cartas de pago finiquito e casto y cancelacion y los demas autos que conbengan y balgan como si nos e cada uno de nos las diesemos y otorgasemos e para que pidan e tomen quenta a los dhos yndios y otras qualesquier personas que nos las devan dar en qualquier manera y les hagan cargos y reciban descargos y las adicionen y nombren terceros contadores y adbitradores [*sic*] y les den y señalen ter^{no} /termino/ e facultad pa ello //
/f.183v/ y hagan alcanzes e los reciban y cobren y den e otorguen carta de pago e finiquito dello segun de suso se contiene y siendo necesario renuncien la exsecucion y leies del entrego paga e prueba della e del engaño como en ellas se contiene e para que puedan vender nuestros bienes y tribu^{o}s y arrendar qualquier casas y chacaras y otros vienes raizes por el precio o precios que les pareciere de contado o fiado al tiempo que quisieren y recevir el precio dello obligandonos a la evicion y saneamiento de lo que asi vendieren y arrendaren en la forma que les fuere pedido y bien visto y para que puedan pagar e paguen de nuestros bienes y hazienda a qualesquier personas la deudas que pareciere deverles por escripturas conocimientos y quenta corriente y en otra manera y recivan los recaudos de pago y finiquito que convengan y si yo el dho capitan Martin Garcia de Loyola enbiare a los dhos Alonso de Baldez y Juan Fernandez Coronel algunas cartas y memorias firmadas de mi nombre las cunplan qualquier dellos y hagan y compren y vendan y paguen y concierten lo que por ella les dixere como convenga y vieren ser nezes^{o} y pa recevir y salariar qualesquier mayordomos e criados que entiendan en el benef^{o} y aumento de nuestras haziendas el fruto de las quales reciban y cobren y vendan e beneficien como lo demas de suso contenido y les tomen quenta y salarien letrados y procuradores y solicitadores para nuestros pleitos e causas y los despidan y a los dhos criados //
/f.184/ o a los que de presente tenemos y les señale y nombre salarios y se los den y paguen de nuestros bienes e reciban medicos e cirujanos y los salarien y paguen segun dho es e para que hagan otorguen y efetuen con qualesquier personas qualesquier compañias y conciertos transaciones sueltas quiebras quitas en poca o mucha cantidad y por el precio y tiempo y en la forma o manera que les pareciere e pongan de nuestra parte los puestos y posturas y condiciones necesarias y que les parecieren y den y paguen de contado lo que concertaron o fiado a los plazos que en las escripturas fuere contenidos para que puedan comprar e compren de qualesquier personas qualesquier bienes y haziendas muebles e raizes ropa mercadurias esclavos e otras cosas que les pareciere de contado o fiado y lo paguen o nos obliguen a que los daremos y pagaremos a los plazos que se concertaren y sobre todo suso dho e cada cosa e parte de ello hagan e otorguen las escripturas de pago finiquito cancelacion obligacion poderes transaciones conciertos ventas compromisos arrendamientos salarios e demas escrituras que sean necesarias con las firmezas e vinculos obligaciones renunciaciones sumisiones poder a las justicias e demas firmezas

que pa su balidacion se requieran que asi y de la manera que ellos las hicieren y otorgaren nos las otorgamos aprovamos corroboramos e confirma^{os} como en ellas fuere contenido las quales avemos aqui por ynsertas y especificadas y las cumpliremos y pagaremos y para //
/f.184v/ que parescan ante qualquier juezes y tribunas y presenten y pidan qualesquier cedulas e provisiones e las que yo les enviare y diere y pidan cumplimento dellas e tomen e aprehendan posision de los y^{o}s de nuestra encomienda conforme a la provision y provisiones que para ello tenemos e la amparen defiendan y contradigan y usen del efeto de las dhas provisiones como y donde convenga y sobre lo suso dho y cada cosa y parte de ello siendo neces^{o} parezcan en jui^{o} y en el y fuera del pidan demanden respondan nieguen conozcan contradigan aleguen satisfagan juren prueven tachen presenten recusen abonen y se aparten de las recusaciones pidan e hagan ex^{nes} /execuciones/ prisiones ventas de bienes y remates dellos y presenten qualesquier escripturas y otros recaudos y usen dellos en juicio e fuera del e hagan todos los demas autos e diligencias judiciales y estrajudiciales que convengan e nosotros hariamos quel poder que pa todo lo que dho es necesario y se requiere se lo damos y otorgamos con sus yncidencias e dependencias e conexidades y libre y general administracion e con facultad que lo puedan sustituir e revocarlos e poner otros de nuevo a los quales y a ellos relevamos en forma de dr^{o} e para lo ansi cumplir e lo que por virtud del fuere fecho obligamos nuestras personas y bienes avidos e por aver e damos poder a qualesquier juezes e justicias de qualesquier partes ante quien esta carta pareciere para que por todo rigor de dr^{o} e via exsecutiva nos compelan apremien a los ansi cumplir como por //
/f.185/ sentencia pasada en cosa juzgada y renunciamos qualesquier leies fueros y dr^{os} en nuestra favor e la que dize que renunciacion de leies fecha en general no bala e yo la dha doña Beatriz renuncio las leies de los emperadores Justiniano y Veliano y el senatus consulto y leies de toro fuero e partida e leies segundas nuncias y todo augilto [*sic*] y remedio de buen baron y las demas que son en favor de las mujeres de cuyo efeto e remedio fui avisada por el presente escr^{no} e asi las renuncio e otorgamos esta carta en el Cuzco en treinta e un dias del mes de otubre de mill y qui^{o}s y setenta e dos años. Testigos Juan de Çianca y Francisco Perez procurador y Domingo de Garro y lo firmaron los otorgantes a los quales yo el escri^{no} conozco. Martin Garcia de Loyola doña Beatriz Coya ante mi Geronimo de Quesada escrivano publico. yo Ger^{mo} de Quesada escrivano publico del numero del Cuzco ante quien paso los suso dho lo hize escribir y aqui mi signo. Ger^{mo} de Quesada escr^{no} pu^{co}.

Don Hurtado de Mendoza marques de Cañete guarda mayor de la ciudad de Quenca visorrey e capitan general en estos reinos e provincias del Piru por su majestad. E que por cuanto su magestad por sus provisiones y cartas reales tiene mandado que procure por las buenas maneras que ser pudiere traer de paz y a su obidencia y servi^{o} real al Ynga pa que viniesen el y los naturales que con el anduviesen en conocimiento de nuestra santa fee catolica y la reciviesen pa su salvacion y en cumplimiento //
/f.185v/ dello luego como llegue a estos dhos reinos porque cesasen los grandes daños e ynconvenientes que a causa de andar alçado y de guerra en los Andes Saire Topa Mango Capa Yupangui Ynga hijo de Mango Ynga y nieto de Guayna Capa señor natural que fue de estos dhos reinos por los muchos saltos muertes e robos que hordinariamente hazian con sus capitanes y gente en los caminos reales a españoles y naturales que llevaba y recogia a los dhos Andes donde andava de los questaban pacificos y debaxo de la obidencia de Su Magestad y el desasosiego e ynquietud que con el dho Ynga tenian los naturales de los repartimientos de y^{o}s que sirven a los vez^{o}s de la ciudad del Cuzco e Guamanga provei que religiosos y mensajeros fuesen a hablarle de parte de Su Magestad y de la mia en su real nombre pa que biniese de paz y a su real obidencia y servi^{o} y le enbie perdones de las muertes de españoles y naturales que obiese echo y de otros qualesquier crimenes delitos que obiese cometido ofreciendole que biniendo de paz e a lo suso dho dentro de cierto termino que le fuesen dado se le harian merzedes en su real nombre de los repartimientos de y^{o}s de Yucay que tuvo encomendado don Françisco Piçarro hijo del marques don Françisco Piçarro [*sic*] dif^{os} y de Xaquixaguana Guayllaquipa e Pucara questuvo encomendado en Francisco Hernandez Giron vz^{o} del Cuzco difunto que estan bacos con todo lo a ellos subjeto y que demas de lo suso dho le serian fechas otras merzedes de tierras y solares y otras cosas contenidas en la provisiones que dello se mandaron dar y enbiaron lo qual aviendolo tra- //
/f.186/ tado los dhos religiosos e mensajeros con el dho Ynga lo acepto y salio y vino de paz y entro en esta ciudad de los Reies y corte bispera de la fiesta de los Reies deste presente año de qui^{o}s e cinquenta y ocho y dio a Su Mag^{td} y a mi en su real nombre la obidencia devida e prometio de siempre servir como su bueno e leal vasallo deve y es obligado hazer y porque aviendo fecho lo suso dho el justo que se tenga quenta con su persona y se le cumplan las dhas merzedes para con que se sustente e su mujer e casa e familia y de nuevo se le hagan otras porque se aficione y obligue mas al servicio de Su Magestad y tenga boluntad de se convertir y convierta a nuestra santa fee catolica para que se salve y obligue y anime a los demas naturales destos dhos reinos a que hagan lo mismo que en lo que principalmente Su Magestad a pretendido y pretende y por lo que importa a la quietud e sosiego de estos dhos reinos por la presente en su real nombre y por virtud de su real poder que para ello tengo su tenor del qual es el que se sigue. Don Carlos por la divina clemencia emperador semper Augusto Rei de Alemania doña Juana su madre y el mismo don Carlos por la misma gracia Reies de Castilla de Leon de Aragon de las dos Seçilias de Jerusalen de Navarra de Granada de Toledo de Valencia de Galicia de Mallorca de Sevilla de Cerdeña de Cordoba de Corcega de Murcia de Jaen de los Algarbes de Algecira de Gibraltar de las islas de Canaria de las Indias Islas y tierra firme del Mar Oceano Conde de Flandes e de Tyrol etc. A todos los consejos regidores caballeros escuderos y oficiales y homes /hombres/ buenos de todas las ciudades villas e lugares de las provincias de la Nueba Castilla llamada Piru y de la nueva Toledo //
/f.186v/ y de las otras provincias e islas subjetas y comprehendidas en el distrito y juridicion de la nuestra audiencia y chançilleria real de las dhas provincias del Peru y otras qualesquier personas eclesiasticas y seglares de qualquier estado condicion preminencia e dignidad que sean o ser puedan vz^{o}s estantes y abitantes en las dhas provincias y en cada una de ellas a quien toca y atañe y puede tocar y atañer lo en esta nuestra carta contenido y cada uno y qualquier de vos salud e gracia. sepades que nos aviendo entendido las alteraciones y cosas acaecidas en las dhas provincias del Piru despues que Françisco Hernandez Giron con otros muchos que con el se juntaron se alzaron con la ciudad del Cuzco y prendieron a Gil Ramirez de Abalos nuestro corregidor que hera en la dha ciudad y deseando como deseamos quesas provincias se pongan en toda paz sosiego y quietud para que en ellas se haga el serv^{io} de Dios nuestro Señor y su santa fee catolica sea aumentada y para este efeto y que nos seamos servidos y esas dhas provincias vayan en todo crescimi^{to} y noblecimiento y los pobladores de ellas bivan en todos contentamiento habemos acordado de inviar a ellas una persona de autoridad y confianza para

que entienda en ello y por el gran conzepto que te/ne/mos de la persona de don Hurtado de Mendoça marques de Cañete le abemos elegido y señalado por nuestro visorrey desa tierra y por presidente de la audiencia real que en ella reside para que haga y administre justicia igual a todos mas subditos y vasallos y para que ansimismo entienda en hazer y ordenar todo lo que convenga para el sosiego y quietud y noblecimi^{to} desa tierra como dho es por la presente de nuestro propio //

/f.187/ motivo e deliberada voluntad elegimos constituimos y señalamos para ello al dho marques de Cañete y le damos y otorgamos todo nuestro poder cumplido libre y llenero y bastante con libre e general administracion segun e tan cumplidamente que lo nos avemos y de fecho y dr^{o} mas y mejor puede y debe valer pa que por nos y en nuestro nombre e como nuestras mismas personas pueda entender y entienda en la pacificacion y sosiego desas dhas provincias y administracion de justicia en ellas y provea en todas las cosas que occurieren ansi concernientes a la dha administracion y ex^{o}n de la nuestra justicia como de la buena governacion y defensa desas dhas provincias y noblecimi^{to} dellas e gratificacion de los pobladores nuestros subditos y vasallos que los an ydo a poblar y bien e buen tratami^{to} y conservacion de los naturales della y buen recaudo de nuestra hazienda y en todas las otras cosas y casos e negocios de qualquier calidad e condicion que sean y se ofrezcan lo que le pareciere y viere que conviene y se deve hazer y provea en nuestro nombre y como nos mysmos lo podriamos hazer y proveer todos los oficios y cargos asi de justicia y de governacion como de otra qualquier manera de esas dhas provincias y de cada una de ellas que conforme a dr^{o} nos podemos y devemos proveer y hazer en nuestro nombre gracias merzedes de qualquier tenencia alcaydias regimi^{to}s escrivanias y otros qualesquier oficios y cosas de qualquier calidad que sean ansi por renunciacion como por vacacion y en otra qualquier manera y para que siendo menester para defension desas provincias y bien y utilidad de ellas pueda apercevir de guerra y llamar y convocar a las ciudades e villas //

/f.187v/ e otros pueblos y a los perlados governadores justicias cavalleros y otras personas desas provincias y estantes en ellas para que vengan donde fuere necesario con la gente que por el les fuere m^{do} y sobre ello hazer e proveer y prove a todo aquello que nosotros mismos podriamos hazer y proveer de qualquier calidad y condicion que sea o ser pueda en esas dhas provincias porque nos mandamos a todas e cada uno de vos como dho es que lo que ansi por el dho marques de Cañete fuere proveido hordenado y mandado en qualesquier casos y cosas que sean o ser puedan en esas provincias lo guardeis y cumplais y exsecuteis y hagais guardar e cumplir y exsecutar y le obedezcais y acateis como persona que tiene nuestras personas reales e hagais e cumplais sus mandamientos segun y de la manera que lo dixere y mandare de nuestra parte por escripto e por palabra y fuere contenido en las dhas sus cartas e provisiones e mandamientos sin poner en ello esarsa [*sic*] ni dilacion alguna y sin dar a ello otro entendimiento ni interpretacion ni declaracion y sin nos mas requerir ni consultar ni esperar sobre ello otro mandado bien asi como si por nuestras personas y por nuestras cartas firmadas de nuestros nombres lo dixesemos hordenasemos e mandasemos lo qual vos mandamos que ansi hagais e cumplais so pena de caer en mas caso y de las otras penas en que caen e yncurren los que no obedecen las cartas e mandamientos de sus reies e señores naturales y solas penas que por el os fuere puestas canos [*sic*] por la presente le damos y conçedemos y otorgamos //

/f.188/ para ello y para todo lo a ello conçerniente en qualquier manera nuestro poder cumplido y bastante con todas sus incidencias y dependencias anexidades e conexidades e queremos que este dho poder tenga tanta fuerza como si fuera fecho y otorgado en cortes generales e dezimos e otorgamos que todo quanto el dho marques de Cañete en nuestro nombre hiziere ordenare e mandare conforme a este dho poder en esas dhas provincias que le abremos y avemos por firme estable y valedero para siempre jamas de lo qual mandamos dar la presente firmada de mi el Rei y sellada con nuestro sello dada en la villa de Bruselas a diez dias del mes de março de mill y qui^{o}s e cinquenta e cinco años. Yo el Rey. Yo Francisco de Herazo secretario de sus cesareas y catolicas magestades la hize escribir por su mandado registrada. Ochoa de Luyando chanciller Martin de Ramuin el marques el licenciado Tello de Sandoval licenciado don Juan Sarmiento el doctor Bazquez el licenciado Villa Gomez. Hago merzed al dho Saire Topa Mango Capa Yupangui Ynga de los dhos repartimi^{o}s de y^{o}s de Yucay e Xaquixaguana e Guayllaquipa y Pucara que son en terminos de la ciudad del Cuzco y estan bacos por muerte de los dhos don Françisco Piçarro menor y Françisco Hernandez Giron con todos los pueblos y estancias y sus terminos caciques principales y y^{o}s dellos e a ellos subjetos y pertenecientes segun e como los thenian e poseyan tuvieron e poseyeron y goçaron dellos los suso dhos y cada uno dellos para que los tenga y posea aya e goze y cobre todos los tributos que son o fueren obligados a dar o dieren desde primero deste presente //

/f.188v/ mes de henero e año de mill e qui^{o}s e cinquenta e ocho años en adelante conforme a las tasas que estan fechas e se hizieren y para que por su fin y muerte subcedan perpetuamente en el dho repartimi^{to} de y^{o}s sus hijos e desçendientes y susçesores que tuviere como se puede y debe subceder en los mayorazgos que se hacen con licencia de su magestad en los reinos de España y con las condiciones apellido y armas que el dho Ynga quisiere y ordenare que para ello le doy licencia e facultad porque baia en acrecentami^{o} su honra linaje y estado de sus hijos y deçendientes deçendiendo como deçiende de linaje de los Yngas y principal destos dhos reinos del Piru y porque aya memoria y renombre de quien tuvo principio desta merzed y porque permanezca y mejor se aficione al servi^{o} de Dios nuestro Señor y ensalçar nuestra santa fee catolica y a servir a su magestad pa honra y defensa de su linaje caso y estado con que por si ni por interpositas no se sirva de servi^{o} personal de los dhos y^{o}s en su casa ni en otras obras e granjerias so las penas contenidas en las provisiones y cedulas reales que cerca de ello estan da dadas [*sic*] y con que los trate bien y procure su conservacion y multiplicacion y tenga cuydado de que en el repartimi^{to} aya clerigos e religiosos que dotrinen a los naturales en las cosas de nuestra santa fee catolica y por la presente mando al licençiado Muñoz corregidor de la dha ciudad del Cuzco que luego que por pte de los dhos Saire Topa Mango Capa Yupangui Ynga fuere pedida posesion del dho repartimiento de y^{o}s se la de y metido el y las demas justicias de su magestad le amparen //

/f.189/ y defiendan en ello y no consientan que de ella se ha despojado sin primero ser oido y vencido por fuero y jui^{o} lo qual asi hagan e cumplan so pena de cada dos mil p^{o}s de oro pa la camara y fisco de su majestad. fecho en los Reies a treze dias del mes de enero de mil e qui^{o}s e cinq^{ta} e ocho años el marques por mandado de su exelencia Juan Muñoz Rico.

V En la gran ciudad del Cuzco cabeça destos reinos y provincias del Peru a v^{te} e un dias del mes de março año del nacimi^{to} de nuestro salvador Jesu Cristo de mil e quini^{o}s y cinquenta e ocho años ante el muy mag^{co} señor lic^{do} Juan Bautista Muñoz corregidor e justicia m^{or} en la dha ciudad e su juridicion por su magestad en presencia de mi Francisco de Barrientos escriv^{o} de su mag^{td} e escriv^{o} publico del

numero de la dha ciudad y de los tg^{os} yuso escriptos parecio presente doña Beatriz Mango Capa Yupangui mujer de Diego Hernandez vecino de la dha ciudad en nombre de Saire Topa Mango Capa Yupangui e por virtud del poder que del tiene de que hizo presentacion signado de escr^{o} de su magestad en el dho n^{e} presento esta provision e cedula de encomienda del muy ex^{te} señor marques de Cañete visorrey destos reinos e pidio e requirio al dho señor corregidor que conforme a ella en el dho nombre le de la posesion corporal autual velcansi de los caciques e y^{o}s de los dhos repartimientos de que por su majestad y su Exª del dho señor visorrey en su real nombre fue y le an fecho merzed al dho Saire Topa Mango Capa Yupangui Ynga la qual dha posesion le de en don Françisco Chilche cacique principal del repartimi^{to} de Yucay e don Pedro e don Lucas principales //
/f.189v/ del dho repartimiento y en don Xp^{o}bal Chotas e don Diego Caguatai caciques e principales de Xaquixaguana y don Alonso Callena cacique de Quilloa que presentes estavan repartimi^{o}s encomendados por su Exª en nombre de su magestad en el dho Saire Topa Mango Capa Yupangui Ynga su parte como por la dha provision de su Exª constava e parecia sobre que pidio justicia.

v El dho señor corregidor tomo en sus manos la dha provision de su Exª y la obedecio y con el acatami^{to} debido y en quanto al cumplimiento della dixo questaba presto de hazer y cumplir lo que por ella le hera mandado y haziendolo y cumpliendolo lo tomo por las manos al dho don Françisco Chilche cacique principal de Yucai e don P^{o} e don Lucas principales del dho repartimiento y don Xp^{o}bal Chotas e don Diego Caguatai caciques e principales de Xaquixaguana e don Alonso Callena cacique de Quilloa y en señal de posesion los entrego por las manos a la dha doña Beatriz Mango Capa Yupangui en nombre del dho Saire Topa Mango Capa Yupangui Ynga su parte en nombre de los demas caciques e principales y y^{o}s naturales de los dhos repartimi^{o}s e pueblos dellos e luego la dha doña Beatriz Capa Yupangui en el dho nombre tomo por las manos a los dhos caciques e principales de los dhos pueblos de suso nombrados en señal de posesion propiedad e señorio como subjetos e vasallos del dho Saire Topa Mango Capa Yupangui Ynga su parte conforme a la dha provision de su Exª la qual dha posesion dixo que tomaba y tomo en el dho nombre en los dhos caciques e principales de //
/f.190/ suso nombrados por ellos y en boz y en nombre de todos los demas principales e y^{o}s y y^{a}s a ellos subjetos e de como tomaba e tomo la dha posesion quieta e pacificamente sin contradicion de persona alguna e yo el dho escrivano viese y oyese de que yo doy e fago fee que paso ansi sin contradicion alguna a la dha doña Beatriz en el dho nombre lo pidio por testimonio signado y pa en guarda de su dr^{o} y el dho señor corregidor se lo mando dar lo qual todo segun y como de suso se contiene la dha doña Beatriz dixo e le fue dado a entender por lengua de Pedro de Nicansio ladino en lengua de yndio siendo presentes por testigos a lo que el dho es Gaspar de Sotelo alcalde hordinario de la dha ciudad e Diego de Truxillo e Miguel Sanchez e Antonio de Marchena vz^{o}s de la dha ciudad y el dho señor corregidor lo firmo aqui de su nombre el licenciado Muñ^{oz} paso ante mi Francisco de Barrientos.

v El tenor del qual dho poder del dho Saire Topa Mango Capa Yupangui signado de escrivano es el siguiente.

v Sepan quantos esta carta de poder vieren como yo Saire Topa Mango Capa Yupangui otorgo e conozco por esta presente carta que doy e otorgo todo mi poder cumplido libre llenero bast/an/te segun que yo he y tengo y de d^{ro} mas puede y deve valer a vos doña Beatriz Mango Capa Yupangui Ayta que soys ausente pa que por mi y en mi nombre representando mi propia persona podais tomar e tomeis la posesion de los y^{o}s que su excelencia me ha fecho merzed e los tener en administracion cobrando dellos los tribu^{o}s de las tasas que son obligados a me dar e pagar e para que podais entrar en jui^{o} /juicio/ sobre ellos //
/f.190v/ ante todas y qualesquier justicias e juezes de su magestad e hazer todo aquello que yo haria siendo presente y los oficiales de su mag^{td} uvieren cobrado dellos dhos mis y^{o}s algunos tributos desde el dia de año nuevo a esta parte deste presente año de cinq^{ta} e ocho años los podais cobrar de los dhos oficiales de su magestad conforme a la merzed que su Exa me tiene fecha e pa que podais tomar criados pa el benef^{o} de las dhas merzedes haciendas dandoles los salarios que os parecieren e para que podais pedir en el cabildo desta ciudad en mi nombre y pa mi qualesquier tierras e merzedes e titulos de las tales tierras que ansi os hicieren merced donde yo soy vz^{o} e pa recibir e cobrar ansi en jui^{o} como fuera del todos los p^{o}s de oro que me devieren por escripturas e por otra qualquier via e razon que sea e de lo que recibieredes y cobraredes podais dar e deis vuestras cartas de pago e de finiquito las quales valan y sean firmes bastantes e balederas como si yo mismo las diese y a ellas pres^{te} fuese e general pa pleitos e causas con poder de jurar y sostituir en Diego Fernandez vuestro marido y el dho Diego Fernandez y vos podais sostituir un procurador e dos e mas e los revocar cuando quisieredes y hazer otros de nuevo quedando en vos este poder principal a los quales y a vos relievo segun forma de dr^{o} e obligo mi persona e bienes muebles e raizes avidos e por aver su espresa obligacion que para ello hago de la dha mi persona e bienes en forma con libre e general administracion que terne por bueno lo que por virtud deste poder en mi nombre hizieredes e para que en todas mis haziendas rentas dispongais //
/f.191/ como a vos os pareciere e quisieredes con todas sus yncidencias e dependencias anexidades e conexidades e vos relievo en forma a vos e a los por vos sostituidos como dho es e quan cumplido bastante poder segun que lo yo y tengo otro tal y ese mismo vos doi cedo y traspaso en vos la dha doña Beatriz Mango Capa Yupangui Aytia en testimonio de lo qual otorgue esta carta antes el pres^{te} escriv^{o} y testigos de yuso escriptos y quiero y es mi boluntad que por falta deste poder y no ir en el es pacificado [*sic*] quiero que bala lo que por vos la dha mi tia hizieredes vala e ayais en todo como cosa propia y dispongays en ello como quisieredes ques fecha y otorgada en Vinaca termino e jurisdicion de la ciudad de Guamanga en tres dias del mes de marzo de mil y qui^{o}s y cinq^{ta} y ocho años siendo testigos Juan de Cardenas y Pedro de Bustinça e Juan Sierra e al dho Juan Sierra rogo el dho Saire Topa Mango Capa Yupangui firmase por el en el registro desta carta a los quales yo el presente escr^{o} doy fe que conozco Juan Sierra de Leguisamo e yo Juan Lopez de Ydiaquez escrivano de su magestad presente fui en uno con los dhos testigos y con el dho otorgante y lo escribi e hize escrebir e por ende hize aqui este mi signo que es a tal en testimonio de verdad Juan Lopez de Ydiaquez escrivano de su magestad.

v Despues de lo sobre dho en la dha ciudad del Cuzco a v^{te} e dos dias del mes de março de mil e qui^{o}s y cinq^{ta} y ocho años ante el dho señor corregidor y en presencia de mi Francisco de Barrientos escri^{o} parecio presente Fran^{co} //

/f.191v/ Perez procurador en nombre de don Fran^{co} Piçarro dif^{o} hijo del marques don Françisco Piçarro dif^{o} e por virtud del poder e sostitucion que tiene ante mi el dho escri^{o} e pres^{to} el escripto del tenor siguiente.

v Muy magnifico señor Françisco Perez en nombre de Fran^{co} Piçarro hijo del marques don Fran^{co} Piçarro dif^{o} digo que a mi noticia es venido que por parte de Saire Topa Ynga de los y^{o}s de Yucai encomendados en el dho don Françisco Piçarro mi parte por virtud de cierta encomienda que dizen averse fecho en el dho Saire Topa de los dhos de los dhos [*sic*] y^{o}s segun que mas largam^{te} se contiene en el pedim^{to} sobre ello fecho por parte del dho Saire Topa cuyo tenor repetido digo que vuestra merced no deve de hazer cosa alguna de lo pedido por el dho Saire Topa en razon de la dha posesion por lo siguiente.

v Porque la dha posesion no es pedida por parte bastante e los recaudos por virtud de los quales se pide la dha posesion no son bastantes pa que por ellos se le pueda dar.

v Lo otro porque su magestad y el licenciado Gasca presidente que fue destos reinos en su real nombre encomendaron en el dho don Françisco mi parte los dhos y^{o}s por virtud de la qual dha encomienda el dho mi parte ha estado y esta en posesion de los dho y^{o}s e goza de los tributos y aprovechamientos que los dhos y^{o}s y goza de los tributos y aprovechamientos que los dhos y^{o}s estan encomendados en el dho don Fran^{co} no /ha/y causa ni razon bastante pa que el dho Saire Topa se le de posesion dellos.

v Lo otro porque puesto caso que al dho Saire Topa se le oviese fecho merzed e nueve encomienda de los dhos y^{o}s como bacos que dizen es- //
/f.192/ tar por muerte del dho don Fran^{co} que se le aya dado provision de la dha encomienda la dha merzed no deve ni puede aver efeto porque el dho don Françisco no es muerto ni tal se aberigua y hasta tanto que este averiguado el dho don Françisco ser muerto los dhos y^{o}s no se an de tener por bacos ni se puede hazer la dha encomienda theniendo como la tiene el dho don Françisco por su magestad y en su real nombre por todos los dias de su vida.

v Por tanto a vuestra magestad pido e sup^{co} y si es nezes^{o} hablando con el acatami^{to} que devo requiero las vezes que de dr^{o} soy obligado no haga cosa alguna de lo pedido por parte del dho Saire Topa en razon de la dha posesion antes defienda y ampare al dho mi parte en la que tiene de los dhos y^{o}s e de goçar de los tribu^{o}s e aprovechami^{o}s dellos pa lo qual el oficio de V. M. imploro y pido justicia y si es nezesario espresamente contradigo la posesion por parte del dho Saire Topa pedida e sup^{co} de la dha provision e nueva encomienda en el fecha de los dhos y^{o}s y pido testimonio de todo.

v Otro si digo que si la dha posesion se uvieren dado al dho Saire Topa e a otra persona en su nombre ansimismo espresamente la contradigo e protesto pare perjui^{o} al dho mi parte y si es neces^{o} me ofresco a dar informacion de como el dho don Francisco esta vivo en los reinos de España para lo qual es.

v Otro si pido a V. M. mande que este escripto y contradicion se ponga en la posesion que se oviere tomado e tomare por parte del dho Saire Topa sobre que pido justicia para lo qual es.

v E ansi presentado el dho escripto el dho señor corregidor mando dar treslado del a la parte //
/f.192v/ e mando que se ponga en la dha posesion testigos que fueron presentes. Benito de la Peña escriv^{o} pu^{co} e Miguel Martinez e Andres de Ybarra residentes en la dha ciudad.

v Despues de lo suso dho en la dha ciudad del Cuzco el dho dia mes e año sobre dhos yo el dho escriv^{o} notefique lo sobre dho a la dha doña Beatriz en el dho nombre del dho Saire Topa su parte presente Diego Hernandez su marido e Gonçalo Reyes procurador.

v Despues de lo sobre dho en la dha ciudad del Cuzco a veinte e seis dias del mes de abril de mil y qui^{o}s y cinq^{ta} y ocho años ante el dho señor licenciado Muñoz corregidor en la dha ciudad e por ante mi el dho escriv^{o} y de los testigos de yuso escriptos parecio presente Sebastian de Balça procurador en nombre e como curador ad liten del dho Saire Topa Mango Capa Yupangui segun que de la dha curaduria le fue y esta discernida por su merzed por ante Benito de la Peña escrivano publico desta ciudad dixo que no embargante en nombre del dho su parte estava tomada la posesion de los repartimi^{o}s e y^{o}s de la encomienda que por el señor bisorrey le fue fecha en nombre de su magestad que agora para mayor abundami^{to} e corroboracion pedia e pidio a su merzed de al dho Saire Topa Mango Capa Yupangui questa presente y a el en su nombre a midiendo fuerza a fuerza y si necesario era la tomava e tomo en los y^{o}s del dho repartimi^{to} que pres^{te} estavan e pido a su merzed le ampare y defienda en ella y de como lo dezia e dixo lo pido por testimonio.

v E luego el dho señor corregidor estando pres^{te} don Françisco Chilche cacique de Yucay y don Luys de la parcialidad de don Garcia y el dho //
/f.193/ don Garcia y don Gaspar caciques de Quipa e Condor Guaman cacique de Pucara e Chagua cacique de Gualar e don Martin cacique de Xaquixaguana y don Baltasar principal del pu^{o} de Equeco y don Alonso cacique de Yquilloay caciques e principales de los repartimi^{o}s encomendados en el dho Saire Topa por ellos y los demas y^{o}s a ellos subjetos en cumplimiento de la provision de su Exª les tomo por la mano corporalmente y en señal de la posesion les dio y entrego al dho Saire Topa el qual presente el dho su curador dixo por la lengua de P^{o} Nicansio ladino que continuando la posesion que de los dhos caciques e y^{o}s tenian y les daba dada añidiendo [*sic*] fuerza

si necesario hera la tomava e tomo en los dhos caciques e y^{o}s los quales en señal de posesion tomo por la mano por ellos y en voz y en nombre de los demas principales e y^{o}s de los dhos repartimi^{o}s a ellos subjetos e lo pidio por testim^{o}.

v E luego parecio pres^{te} el dho Francisco Perez en el dho nombre del dho Françisco Piçarro hijo del dho marques don Françisco Piçarro e dixo que contradecia e contradixo la dha posesion y protesto no pare perjui^{o} alguno al dr^{o} del dho su parte e lo pidio por testimonio.

v Y luego el dho señor corregidor sin embargo de la dha contradiccion dixo que dava e dio la posesion de los dhos y^{o}s al dho Saire Topa y al dho Sebastian de Balça su curador en su nombre por los dhos caciques e principales que presentes estavan por ellos y en voz y en nombre de los demas y^{o}s a el encomendados conforme a la dha provision de su Exª e se lo mando dar asi por testim^{o} y en forma siendo pres^{tes} por testigos a lo que dho es Juan Alvarez Maldonado y Juan de Betanços vecinos de la dha ciudad y Benito de la //
/f.193v/ Peña escrivano publico de la dha ciudad el Lli^{do} Muñoz e yo Francisco de Barrientos escrivano de su magestad y escrivano publico del numero de la ciudad del Cuzco presente fui a lo que dho es en uno con los dhos testigos del dho pedimiento e mandam^{o}s del dho señor corregidor que aqui firmo su nombre lo hize escribir segun que ante mi paso por ende hize aqui este mio signo ques a tal en testim^{o} de verdad Fran^{co} de Barrientos.

v En el pueblo de San Francisco de Maras de la encomienda de P^{o} de Ure vz^{o} del Cuzco a tres dias del mes de junio de mil e qui^{o}s y setenta y tres años ante el dho señor visitador lo pres^{to} don Fran^{co} Chilche y don Françisco Guarta Naula.

v Yll^{e} señor don Françisco Chilche e don Garcia Quispicapi e don Her^{do} Guartat Naula caciques principales del valle de Yucai por nos y en nombre de los demas y^{o}s e principales encomendados en el cap^{t} Martin Garcia de Loyola dizimos que en la visita que hizo el señor licenciado frei Pedro Gutierrez antecesor de V.Md. visito muchos y^{o}s del dho valle y encomienda que tenian nombre de yanaconas los quales an sido e son siempre y^{o}s de tasa de la dha encomienda e nos an siempre ayudado a pagar la tasa y en los demas servi^{o}s que emos fecho a nuestros encomenderos e si algunos an faltado de nos ayudar en estos servi^{o}s e tasa a sido por la desorden general que a abido en todos los repartimi^{o}s e mas en este por haber estado muchos años sin amo que bolviese por nosotros los quales dhos y^{o}s se contienen en la memoria que a V.M. dio Juan Fernandez Coronel a que nos remitimos y los dhos y^{o}s fueron visitados por yanaconas solo por el nombre que tenian //
/f.194/ y por no saver lo que de la visita avia de suceder no replicamos en el negocio cosa alguna y los dhos y^{o}s quisieron ser bisitados por tales yanaconas entendiendo que por esta via si ysimirian [*sic*] de la tasa e /a/gora es venido a nuestra noticia que su Exª los tiene puestos en cabeza de de su magestad y mandado acudan con la tasa a sus oficiales de lo qual a nosotros y los demas y^{o}s de nuestro repartimiento se nos sigue notorio agravio perjui^{o} e daño asi por quitarsemos los dhos nuestros yndios como por cargarse la tasa suya sobre los pocos que quedamos.

v A V.M. pedimos debare los dhos y^{o}s por yndios de tasa como lo son del dho repartimiento e no permita acudan con tasa alguna a los oficiales reales sobre que pidimos justicia e pa ello es. Don Francisco Chilche por testigo de Hernando y a ruego Alonso Gutierrez e/n/mendado z/je/bre/testado/ dos entre renglones fago acudan vala.

v En el Cuzco a diez y siete dias del mes de setiembre de mil e qui^{o}s y setenta e quatro años ante el señor visitador la presento el contenido.

v Yll^{e} señor Alonso de Baldez en nombre del comendador Martin Garcia de Loyola marido y conjunta persona de doña Beatriz Coya hija legitima de don Diego Saire Topa Ynga y su heredera digo que a mi noticia es venido que V.M. quiere tomar ciertas tierras deste valle de Yucay pa las dar a ciertos yndios yanaconas y a ciertos españoles y otras personas y afirmandome en la contradicion fecha por Juan Fernandez Coronel en nombre del dho comenda- //
/f.194v/ dor Loyola digo que no a lugar de se repartir las dhas tierras ni darse a persona alguna ni V.M. se deve entremeter en ello por lo general y por lo que esta dho y alegado y porque todas las tierras y estancias deste valle de Yucai son del dho mi parte que las tiene y posee por merzed que dellos le hizo su magestad y el marques de Cañete visorrey que fue destos reinos en su nombre y por virtud de sus poderes reales que pa ello tuvo como parece por los recaudos que ante V.M. estan presentados la qual merzed le fue fecha al dho don Diego Saire Topa Ynga cuyo heredera fue la dha doña Beatriz mujer del dho comendador Loyola y la dha merzed se hizo con titulo de mayorazgo y con las condiciones con que su magestad suele conzeder los dhos mayorazgos y asi las dhas tierras y estancias deste dho valle no se pueden enagenar ni sacar del dho mayorazgo conforme al dho titulo y merzed ni aunque mi parte las quisiese vender ni enagenar no podria y asi no se pueden dar a persona alguna demas de que conforme a dr^{o} a ninguno se le puede tomar su hazienda ni compelerle a que la venda y la instruccion que V.M. tiene pa dar tierras a los y^{o}s que llaman yanaconas se entiende de las tierras que antiguamente eran del Ynga o dedicadas al sol y estan bacas lo qual no ay en este dho valle porque si algunas a habido que fuesen del Ynga o del sol esta fecha merzed dellas a mi parte e no se le pueden quitar y si algunas tierras sobrasen a la comunidad de los y^{o}s deste valle son ansimesmo del dho mi parte //
/f.195/ por el dho titulo y merzed.

v A V.M. pido y si es necesario requiero no se entremeta a quitar a mi parte tierras algunas del dho valle ni a dar las ni a repartirlas a españoles ni a y^{o}s ni a otra persona alguna y si algunas V.M. uviere dado repartido o dado posesion de algunas a qualquier persona por qualquier titulo o color que sea V.M. lo reponga y de todo por ninguno y las buelva e restituya a mi parte amparandole en la posesion de todo de las dhas tierras en lo qual V.M. hara justicia y de lo contrario lo recibo por agravio y con el acatami^{to} debido apelo de todo ello y de qualquier auto o autos que V.M. uviere proveido o proveyere en perjui^{o} de mi parte pa ante la real audi^{a} de los Reies y protesto no pare perjui^{o} a mi mas dha mi parte y todo lo demas que protestar me conviene y pidolo por testimonio y justicia y en lo necesario etc. Alonso de Valdez el licençiado Pedraça el señor visitador dixo que lo vera y proveera. Pero Diaz Baldeon escriv^{o}. Yo Pero Diaz Baldeon escrivano de su mag^{td} publico y del numero de la dha ciudad del Cuzco fui presente y lo hize escrevir segun que ante mi paso en fe de lo qual hize aqui mi signo en testimonio de verdad Pedro Diaz Valdeon escriv^{o} pu^{co}.

v En el pueblo de Yucaybamba ques el valle de Yucay y juridicion de la ciudad del Cuzco a veinte dias del mes de henero de mil e qui^{o}s y setenta e dos años el YIl^{e} señor lic^{do} frei Pedro Gutierrez Flores de la orden y cavalleria de Alcantara visitador general por su magestad e por el Exmo señor don Fran^{co} de Toledo bisorrey destos reinos en su //
/f.195v/ real nombre en el dho valle de Calca Quiquixana y su distrito como consta por la provision que pa ello tiene de su Exª ques la que se sigue.

v Don Francisco de Toledo mayordomo de su mg^{td} su visorrey y gobernador y ca^{t}p general en estos reinos e provincias del Piru presidente de la audiencia real y reside en la ciudad de los Reies etc. Por cuanto su mg^{td} tiene dadas muchas cedulas cartas e provisiones e ynstituciones sobre la orden que se debe tener en la visita de los y^{o}s naturales destos reinos y en la averiguacion y tasacion de los tributos que an de dar a sus encomenderos como pa sus caciques e principales tambien esta proveido lo que los dhos caciques y encomenderos an de cumplir con sus y^{o}s y los yndios con ellos que se reduzgan [*sic*] a pueblos y que se nombren entre ellos alcaldes y regidores y alguaziles pa que tengan republicas fundadas y ansimismo estan dadas por su mg^{td} otras muchas cartas e provisiones pa el buen gobierno e polecia de los y^{o}s demas de lo qual las audiencias reales destos reinos y los governadores que en ellos a abido an proveido y ordenado otras muchas cosas tocantes al buen tratami^{to} y conservacion de los dhos naturales pa la ex^{on} y cumplimi^{to} de las quales se an dado algunos medios pa que con menos costa e vexacion de los dhos naturales se pudiese poner en ex^{on} y ultimamente se cometieron algunas de las dhas cosas a personas particulares quales por ser muchas y de diversos pareceres //
/f.196/ y opiniones han traido varios efetos lo qual a sido causa de muchos ynconvinientes y especialmente que los excesos que algunos encomenderos y caciques han fecho y hacen con sus y^{o}s son grandes aviendo de ser ellos los que avian de procurar su bien y conservacion y para remediar lo suso dho y dar ansiento entre los dhos naturales en otras cosas que son muy necesarias y que los que estan muy cargados en los tribu^{o}s que pagan sean relevados y descargados y se de orden como de aqui adelante los tributos sean fijos y se tasen los yndios en particular y cada uno sepa lo que ha de pagar y no le puedan pedir mas y sean dotrinados en las cosas de nuestra santa fee catolica y mantenidos en paz e justicia y que biban descansadamente y bisto que todo lo suso dho no parecia que se podia executar y poner en efeto por la orden y traza que su magestad me manda en las dhas sus instituciones y poderes pa el ansiento universal destos reinos en lo espiritual e temporal dellos sin que procediese la visita general esperando de ello tan grande bien e frutos acordado aviendose pa ello fecho junta de las personas mas graves de estos reinos en conformidad de todos que se haga en todos estos reinos la visita general por tanto confiando de vos el licenciado frei P^{o} Gutierrez Flores clerigo de la orden de Alcantara y de vuestra prudencia y abilidad y espirencia y que soys persona en quien concurren las calidades necesarias pa la dha visita //
/f.196v/ y que entendereis en ello como convenga al servi^{o} de Dios nuestro Señor y de su magestad y bien e conservacion de los dhos naturales y de la real conciencia y mia por la presente que de su magestad y por virtud de sus reales poderes y comisiones e instituciones que pa ello tengo os proveo elixo e nombro por visitador de los repartimientos de yndios que estan en todo el valle de Yucay para que vos sin visitador lego atento a que yo ansisto y e de ansistir algunas temporadas en el dho valle y entender por mi ps^{a} /persona/ en algunas cosas tocantes a la dha visita para que vos vais al dho valle y visiteis personalmente los y^{o}s naturales de los repartimientos del y sus pueblos contandolos y saviendo las hedades que an y sus tratos e granjerias y pusibilidades [*sic*] que tienen y la calidad y grosedad de la tierra y donde estan poblados y los tributos que daban en el tiempo del Ynga y los que dan agora y los que seria bien que den adelante. Otro si vos mando que precedais contra los encomenderos caciques y principales y otras personas que uvieren excedido de las tasas que hasta aqui an tenido o tuvieren fecho comutaciones sin licencia en qualquier manera y procediendo contra ellos haciendo las ynformaciones y averiguaciones necesarias pa saver y averiguar la verdad conociendo e determinando qualesquier pleitos de yndios que ante vos se pusieren como no sean criminales porque destos y malos //
/f.197/ tratamientos y agravios que se hubieren fecho a los y^{o}s me abisareis pa que yo probea lo que convenga y ansimismo proveereis y dareis horden como los dhos yndios se reduzgan a pueblos pa sus republicas fundadas y goviernen entre si dandoles ordenanças y manera de bivir guardando cerca de todo lo suso dho y de las dhas bisitas y casos la institucion firmada de mi nombre que con estas entregara en todo y por todo como en ella se contiene haziendo las demas aberiguaciones e ynformaciones y diligencias que por ella se vos cometen y mandan guardando y cumpliendo y haziendo guardar y cumplir y executar las cedulas e provisiones que por su mg^{td} estan dadas para el buen gobierno y policia tratamiento bien y conservacion de los dhos indios. Otro si vos doy poder e facultad pa que podais conocer y conozcais de todas las causas y negocios ceviles que se ofrecieren y acaecieren por las partes e lugares donde anduvieredes visitando del distrito que se los señala asi entre yndios como españoles en qualquier manera haziendo en ello justicia e sentenciando las causas conforme a dr^{o} y executando las sentencias que en ellos dieredes en los casos que conforme a dr^{o} y a la dha institucion se pueden y deben executar y por la presente mando al corregidor y alcaldes ordinarios y a otras qualesquier justicias de la dha ciudad del Cuzco y su distrito y su jur^{on} del dho distrito y a todos los vz^{o}s y moradores de la dha ciudad e jur^{on} e a otras qualesquier //
/f.197v/ personas de qualquier calidad e condicion que sean y a los caciques e principales e yndios de los dhos repartimientos que vos ayan e tengan por tal bisitador y os obedezcan y acaten y tengan e parezcan a vros llamamientos y emplaçamientos y cumplan y executen los mandamientos e comisiones que pa ello dieredes en cumplimiento y ex^{on} de lo contenido en esta mi provision y en la dha mi instrucion y en las demas comisiones que se vos diere en qualquier cosa e parte dello y que contra ello no bayan ni pasen ni consientan yr ni pasar en manera alg^{a} so las penas que de parte de su m^{t} les pusieredes en las quales yo desde agora les doy por condenados lo contrario haziendo y las executareis en la personas y bienes de los que remisos e ynobidientes fueren que pa entender en lo suso dho y en todo lo demas en la dha ynstrucion y demas cosas contenidos fuera de los dhos negocios criminales vos doy poder cumplido con todas sus incidencias y

dependencias anexidades e conexidades y ansimismo vos doy el dho poder para que en el entre tanto que bais al dho valle y despues en las ausencias que hizieredes podais nombrar la persona que vos pareciere para que entienda en la dha visita y reduçion pa que no pueda aver dilacion en ella pues es cosa que ymporta tanto y vos mando que useis desta provision sin que sea necesario presentaros con ella en el cabildo de la dha ciudad que yo por la presente os recibo y he por recibido al uso y exercicio de lo e- //
/f.198/ n ella contenido e mando que en todo lo suso dho vos ocupeis todo el tiempo que fuere necesario hasta aver visitado y reducido todos los dhos repartimiºs y aver cumplido en la dha mi ynstrucion y comisiones contenido en lo que no fuere contra esta mi comision que acabada la dha visita se vos mandara gratificar el trabajo y ocupacion que en ello tuvieredes por la orden que para ello esta dada y por ques necesario que lleveis un alguazil que execute vros mandamientos y un escrivano ante quien se haga la dha visita y las informaciones y averiguaciones y demas autos que se uvieren de hazer por la presente nombre por alguazil a Juan Enriquez y por el escrivº a Pero Diaz Baldeon escrivº de su magestad y por lengua o ynterpretacion pa los yndios a Hernando de Morales los quales ayan de salario por cada un dia de los que en lo suso dho se ocuparen y con vos andubieren que se quente desde el dia que con vos salieren desta ciudad en adelante el dho alguazil quatro pesos y el dho escriº tres pesos y la dha lengua un peso todo en plata ensayada e marcada de balor cada un peso de a quatro cientos y cinqta maravedies los quales salarios an de haber de las penas e condenacionesque hiçieredes a los que hallaredes culpados en lo suso dho las quales hareis cobrar dellos e de sus bienes sin embargo de qualquier apelacion que de ello ynterpongan y el dho escriº demas del dho salario aya y lleve de todo lo que ante el pasare sus dros conforme al aranzel de la real audiencia de la ciu- //
/f.198v/ dad de los Reies que se le manda que lleve con que en lo que toca a los dros que a de llevar a los yºs guarde lo que sobre ello esta proveido y demas del dho salario que aveis de llevar vos y los dhos oficiales los yºs de los repartimientos que visitaredes vos an de dar la comida que por otra mi provision que llevais se les manda que vos den pa en cada un dia sin que por ella seais obligado a les hazer cosa alguna atento que la dha visita general se haze pa su benefº y utilidad dellos e los unos y los otros no dexeis ni dexen de lo asi cumplir por alguna manera so pena de mil pºs de oro a cada uno que lo contrº hiziere. Fecha en la ciudad del Cuzco a treinta dias del mes de julio de mil e quiºs y setenta e un años. Don Françisco de Toledo por mandado de su Exª Diego Lopez de Herrera.

v En la ciudad del Cuzco a diez y siete dias del mes de agosto de mil y quiºs e setenta e un años el ilustre señor liçenciado frei Pedro Gutierrez Flores de la orden y cavalleria de Alcantara pidio a mi el preste escriº le de por testimonio como oy dho dia en cumplimiento desta provision que tiene del muy Exe señor don Franco de Toledo visorrey de estos reinos se parte a hazer la visita y reducion de pueblos que por ella manda su Exª y para ello lleva por alguazil mayor a Juan Enriquez e por escrivano de la dha visita a mi el presente escriº e por lengua a Hernando de Morales y pa que conste de ello y del dia en que el dho señor bisitador se partio con la dha gente a hazer la dha //
/f.199/ visita di la presente. testigos Bartolome de Arana e Xpºbal Ximenez. El licenciado frei Pedro Gutierrez Flores Pero Diaz Baldeon escrivano publico.

v Dixo que por cuanto su merzed en cumplimiento de lo que su mt y de lo que su Exª en su real nombre manda a benido a este valle de Yucay a entender en la dha visita y el informado que en el ay muchos yºs que no tributan ni estan encomendados en persona alguna so color de dezir que son yanaconas y pa saver la cantidad dellos y a quien se allegan y en que entienden y se les de orden como lo an de hazer conviniese bisiten pa lo qual mando se junten todos y estando juntos la mayor parte dellos por lengua de Hernando de Morales ynterprete general de la dha visita las dixo e dio a entender el bien que se les a seguido de abellos reduzido a pueblos formados como lo estan pa que sean xpianos /cristianos/ y biban publicamente e que su magestad como tan cristianisimo principe siempre ha tenido y tiene zelo de su buen tratamiento y que sean mantenidos en paz y justicia y que nadie los maltrate ni injurie e que si uviere de pagar algun tributo sea moderado en tal manera que en las tasas y de ello se les diere se ha de tener consideracion a que despues de aver pagado su tribuº les quede con que se sustentar ellos e sus mujeres e hijos e tengan haziendas y granxerias con que se aprovechen y se bayan enriqueciendo e no empobreciendo y que sepan y entiendan que por ser xpianos y estar debaxo de la obidencia de su mt an de vivir mas relevados y descargados //
/f.199v/ que en tiempo de los Yngas que pa este efeto su magestad manda hazer esta visita general e que su Exª del dho señor bisorrey se dispuso a venir a ello en persona todo este reyno como an bisto para ver los agravios que les an fecho para que sean desagraviados y biban en todo pulicia y xpianda/d/ e que movido con este buen zelo a venido a la dha visita como les dixo en la pratica que les hizo cuando les mando reduzir e para ello los quiere visitar y saver que dotrina an tenido y ques lo que se les ha pagado por el servicio que an hecho y que de aqui adelante tengan dotrina bastante para que mejor bengan en conocimiento de nuestra santa fee catolica y se conserven en ella y para que con mas facilidad se haga todo conviene saver el numero de los yndios que son para lo qual les mando se bengan a manifestar todos ante el dho señor visitador con sus mujeres y hijos para que //
/f.200/ se asienten y escrivan en la dha visita con la edad de cada uno y hazienda que tuviere en tal manera que no quede nynguno y les apercibio que haziendo lo contrario el que se dejare de escrevir y manifestar le castigara sobre ello por todo rigor como a personas que no quieren thener dotrina ni bivir en justicia y el yndio que los descubriere le hara cacique y principal de los dhos yanaconas y despues de haberles hecho muchos apercibimientos tocante a lo suso dho y a los demas que les conbenia para su salvacion dixeron questavan prestos de lo ansi hazer e cumplir y se hizo la visita y numeracion dellos por la orden que adelante pareze de que doy fee tgos Diego de Escudero e Xpºbal Holgado Pero Diaz Valdeon escrivano.

/f.200v/

	casados—años	*hijos—años*	*servicio que ha hecho cada yanacona*
	Don Diego Rimache natural del Cuzco quarenta y ocho años—48 Isabel Cusi Inquilla cinquenta años—50	Teresa Pata doce 12 Lucas Tito cinco—5 Miguel Mayunc quatro años—4 Juan Bautista Pilla dos—2	a treinta años que le sirve en el beneficio de las chacaras
	Pedro Machaguay Guanca de treinta años—30 Catalina Asto de treinta y tres años—30	Juana Mulmusaso trece 13 Diego Yarinlluclla quatro—4 Ana Pachua dos años—2 Agustin Yarolluclla seis años—6	a diez y ocho años que sirve en lo que los demas
	Mateo Curisgual veinte y ocho años—28 Teresa Tocto Ocllo de veinte y tres años—23	Ana Llapi dos—2 Lucia Nachac uno—1 Madalena Anas quatro—4 Luysa Nacha de tres años—3	a doce años sirve en lo que lo demas
	Mateo Curo Quichua nacio en este valle veinte y ocho años—28 Maria Yanapuco veinte y seis años—26	Maria Machi de tres años—3	a quince años que sirve en lo que lo demas
	Francisco Quispi yunga de diez y siete años—17 Francisca Paigua diez y seis años—16		a un año que sirve en en el beneficio de las chacaras y yerba y leña
	Francisco Llancari quarenta años—40 Inez Anguaytuco cinquenta años—50	Catalina Puchisque diez y ocho años—18 Francisca Chucaschilqui quatro años—4	a treinta e seis años que le sirve en lo que los demas
	Juan Quiquinyana Chanca veinte años—20 Beatriz Llamilla diez y seis años—16		a tres años que le sirve en lo que los demas
246 282	Cristobal Cacaquiguay huerfano Juanbautista Cura huerfano	+248+ Pedro Machaguay huerfano	Juan Ycherimache huerfano +240+

/f.201/

lo que le paga de servicio	*lo que paga de dotrina*	*lo que paga de tasa*	*tiene chacaras de comunidad*
dos topos y medio de chacaras	dos tomines de dotrina	quatro tomines de tasa	
medio topo de chacara	dos tomines de dotrina	quatro tomines de tasa	tres topos de chacara de la comunidad
medio topo de chacara	dos tomines de dotrina	quatro tomines de tasa	dos topos y medio de chacara
medio topo de chacara	dos tomines de dotrina	un peso de tasa	dos topos y cuarto de chacara
medio topo de chacara	dos tomines de dotrina	quatro tomines de tasa	topo y medio de chacara
medio topo de chacara	dos tomines de dotrina	quatro tomines de tasa	dos topos y medio de chacara
medio topo de chacara	dos tomines de dotrina	quatro tomines de tasa	
Diego Laime huerfano	Martin Yabacala huerfano +261+	Pedro Tomilasbay huerfano	Francisco Yambo huerfano

/f.201v/

	casados—años	*hijos—años*	*servicion que ha hecho cada yanacona*
	Pedro Alcamari Colla nacio en este valle quarenta años—40 Inez Tatachuqui cinquenta—50	Juan Pumallalla simple siete años—7	a diez años que le sirve en lo que los demas
	Diego Cuainismalma Chanca veinte años—20 Inez Pachua treinta y quatro años—34	Madalena Chisqui quatro años—4 Ana Cusla dos—2 Mencia Yanachisqui uno 1 Juan Guaman siete—7 Alonso Paucar cinco—5	a ocho años que le sirve en el beneficio de las chacaras
	Agustin Casmahuido— Catalina Chisqui treinta y cinco años—35	Juan Yanacasma +254+ diez años—10 Pedro Guamanarcos seis—6 Ana Chisqui tres años—3	a diez años que le sirve en lo que lo demas
253	Francisco Ranpa Yupanqui veinte y dos años—22 Leonor Cicamocho diez y ocho años—18	Francisca Tapara de un años—1	
	Martin Malqui natural de la provincia de Quito cincuenta años—50 Inez Toto treinta años—30	Diego Alchayan ocho años—8 Juan Bautista Curi tres años—3	treinta y cinco años de darle yerba y leña y beneficio de las chacaras por sus mitas
	Francisco Pachalla nacio en este valle de diez y ocho años—18 Catalina Paca Ocllo veinte años—20		a un año que le sirve esto que le manda no le paga nada
294	Pedro Alla nacio en este valle veinte años—20 Leonor Mato veinte y dos años—22	Francisco Quinanta tres años—3	a que le sirve tres años en lo que le manda
295	Hernando Lanbai natural de Yuain esta provincia de Quito treinta y seis años—36 Isabel Bulazamay sesenta años—60		a que le sirve treinta años de beneficiar de las chacaras por sus mitas no le da nada por ello.

/f.202/

Lo que le paga del servicio	*lo que paga de dotrina*	*lo que paga de tasa*	*tiene chacaras de comunidad*
dos topos de chacara	dos tomines de dotrina	quatro tomines de tasa	
un topo de chacara	dos tomines de dotrina	dos tomines de tasa	
medio topo de chacara	dos tomines de dotrina	quatro tomines de tasa	un topo de chacara
un cuarto de chacara de que come	quatro tomines de dotrina		
topo y medio de chacara de que come de treinta y cinco años a esta parte que a que le sirve	seis tomines de tasa	seis tomines de dotrina	
sustentase de las chacaras de su padre	medio peso de dotrina		
un topo de chacara de que come el dicho que le sirve	quatro tomines de dotrina	seis tomines de tasa	
sustentase de un topo de chacara que es de su mujer			

/f.202v/

casados—años	*hijos—años*	*servicio que ha hecho cada yanacona*
Cristobal Suman Sanad natural de Tomebamba sesenta años—60 Leonor Angay sesenta años—60		a que sirve al dicho don Francisco treinta y cinco años en beneficiarle las chacaras
Juan Bautista Duman Puclla nacio en este valle treinta años—30 Catalina Churai treinta años—30	Alonso Tininpaua de nueve años—9 Martin Caquia cinco—5 Jorge Tanbulbizna tres 3 Inez Luachuc ocho—8 Juana Chalan dos—2	A que sirve diez y seis años esto que los demas
Domingo Libi Puchai nacio en este valle veinte y dos años—22 Inez Caxana de veinte años—20	Teresa Chaicho de dos años	A ocho que le sirve de beneficias de las chacaras de maiz y coca por sus mitas
Cristobal Yararan natural de Pasto treinta años—30 Beatriz Ocllo quarenta años—40	Miguel Pasto seis años 6 Diego Pasto un año—1 Inez Tata cinco—5 Ana Chinbo tres—3 Juan Llaclla diez años—10	A que le sirve diez y ocho años en beneficias de las chacaras de maiz y coca y darle yerba y leña huevos y aves por sus mitas
Rodrigo Tacuri nacio en este valle treinta y cinco años—35 Beatriz Nacuchuc treinta años—30	Lucas Sisac tres—3 Maria Juichu cinco años—5 Margarita Zucho de un año—1	A que le sirve diez y ocho años en lo que le manda
Juan Bautista Cacpaipa nacio en este valle treinta años—30 Isabel Tuca veinte y seis años—26	Catalina Batichuc de tres años—3	A que le sirve diez y ocho años en beneficias de las chacaras de maiz y coca
Francisco Gualpa nacio en este valle diez y seis años—16 Ana Lapachuc veinte años—20		Sirve de dos años a esta parte en lo que le manda
Juan Sicsi nacio en este valle treinta y cinco años—35 Francisca Chinbo treinta y quatro años—34	Juan Toto Yaure diez—10 Isabel Cumia siete—7 Francisco Guaman Capacha—5 Inez Cunia un año—1	A que le sirve diez y ocho años en lo que es de arriba

/f.203/

Lo que le paga de servicio	*Lo que paga de dotrina*	*Lo que paga de tasa*	*Tiene chacaras de comunidad*
quitole medio topo de chacara de que se sustentaban despues que le sirve que a seis años	tres tomines de dotrina		
medio topo de chacara de que se sustenta	quatro tomines de dotrina	quatro tomines de tasa	un topo y medio de chacara no paga tributo della
no le da nada porque come con su padre	quatro tomines de dotrina	quatro tomines de tasa	
da le por ello topo y medio de chacara de que come	seis tomines de tasa	quatro tomines de dotrina	
da le un topo de chacara de que come	quatro tomines de dotrina	seis tomines de tasa	medio topo de chacara no paga tributo della
dale un topo de chacara de que come por el servicio que le hace	quatro tomines de dotrina	seis tomines de tasa	
da le un topo de chacara de que se sustenta	seis tomines de dotrina		
da le un topo de chacara de que se sustenta	quatro tomines de dotrina	paga un peso para la tasa	

/f.203v/

Casados—años	*Hijos—años*	*servicio que ha hecho cada yanacona*
Diego Tanta nacio en este valle treinta y quatro años—34 Inez Tonso treinta y cinco años—35	Martin China Quispi ocho años—8 Isabel Aimias siete—7 Francisco Guaman Capiga—5 Inez Aimia un año 1	A que le sirve veinte años en lo que lo demas
Diego Uscos Guaman nacio en este valle treinta años—30 Isabel Chisqui treinta y seis años—36	Madalena Asto Caquia catorce años—14 Cristobal Usco Guaman ocho años—8 Juan Usco Ancumpa cinco 5 Angelina Caquiapa dos—2	A que le sirve quince años en que es de arriba
Juan Guari veinte años—20 Inez Cagai Chucmano diez y nueve—19		
Diego Marin nacio en este valle veinte y tres años—23 Inez Chinbo treinta años—30	Maria Coca tres años—3 Agustin Pilzuchic un año—1	A que le sirve cinco años en curar la mula y caballo
Geronimo Cuyo veinte y nueve años—29 Beatriz Llacssa veinte y quatro años—34	Agustin Mitima quatro años—4 Maria Yupati de un año—1	
Pedro Suni Zilaca Cañar nacio en Tomebamba cincuenta y cinco años—55 Catalina Angai cincuenta años—50	Alonso Bilidunbai simple diez y ocho años—18 Benito Guanta Languai de diez y seis años—16 Juan Casa doce años—12 Martin Muxanaulao ocho—8 Isabel Zachuc dos—2	A que le sirve veinte y ocho años esto y sus hijos en beneficias de sus chacaras y hace el la mita de yerba
Pedro Niulazaca Cañar nacio en este valle veinte y ocho años—28 Isabel Caba treinta y ocho años—38	Sebastian [Alasala] siete años Diego Tarnianzaca cinco años—8 Francisco Dunian tres años—3	A que le sirve doce años en beneficias de las chacaras y da le yerba y leña por sus mitas
Pedro Puavan Cañar de Tomebamba cincuenta y dos años—52 Isabel Chanchu cincuenta y ocho años—58	Leonor Citchuc diez y ocho años—18 Martin Guanbrupulla de diez y nueve años—19	A que le sirve treinta años en beneficias de sus chacaras y dar por su mita yerba y leña

/f.204/

Lo que le paga de servicio	*Lo que paga de dotrina*	*Lo que paga de tasa*	*Tiene chacaras de tasa*
da le tres cuartos de chacara de que come	quatro tomines para la dotrina	quatro tomines en la tasa	medio topo de chacara no paga tributo
da le un topo de chacara de que come	quatro tomines de dotrina		
da le medio topo de chacara de que come			
da le un topo de chacara de que come	quatro tomines de dotrina	quatro pesos de tasa	
	quatro tomines de dotrina		

/f.204v/

Casados—años	*Hijos—años*	*Servicio que ha hecho cada yanacona*
Martin Marcabuchai cañar nacio de este valle veinte y tres años—23 Leonor Zuburchue catorce años—14		A que le sirve dos años en beneficiar las chacaras de maiz y coca y hazeles mita de yerba y leña
Alonso Bilibijuaican nacio en este valle treinta y cinco años—35 Madalena Guayanchuc treinta y ocho años—38	Inez Llanchuc seis años—6 Maria Tanchuc quatro años—4	A que le sirve veinte años en todo lo que los demas
Pedro Salina Cañar nacio en este valle treinta años—30 Leonor Yanauzic veinte y dos años—22	Isabel Cuchuc 4 Felipe Yabichai 3 Madalena Nurchu 1 Ana Murabichoc quatro 4	A que le sirve doce años en lo que los demas
Alonso Uchunlalai Cañar nacio en este valle quarenta y cinco años—45 Catalina Caba treinta y ocho años—38	Martin Lazancuila siete años—7 Sebastian Marcabichuai cinco años—5 Juan Bautista Bilidunbai dos—2	A que le sirve treinta años en todo lo que los demas
Benito Lartalanguay veinte y dos años—22 Leonor Lamaichuc veinte y tres años—23		
Gonzalo Tambru Pulla nacio en este valle treinta años—30 Isabel Cava veinte y cinco años—25	Francisco Guartanaula quatro años—4 Gonzalo Quipulla un año—1	A que le sirve veinte años en el beneficio de las chacaras
Martin Sabar Cañar de Tomebamba cincuenta y quatro años—54 Catalina Caba treinta y ocho años—38	Inez Durchuc veinte años—20	A que le sirve veinte años en beneficio de las chacaras de maiz y de hacele mita de yerba y leña
Alonso Sibipulla Cañar nacio en este valle veinte años—20 Maria Zinbai veinte y cinco años—25	Madalena Batichuc tres años—3	A que le sirve en lo que le manda y en beneficio de las chacaras de maiz veinte años.

/f.205/

Lo que le paga de servicio	*Lo que le paga de dotrina*	*Lo que le paga de tasa*	*Tiene chacaras de tasa*
	Quatro tomines de dotrina		Un topo y cuarto de chacara no paga tributo de ella
Medio topo de chacara de que se sustenta	Quatro tomines de dotrina	Seis tomines para la tasa	Un topo de chacara no paga tributo de ella
	Quatro tomines de dotrina		Tres cuartos de chacara
Un topo de chacara de que come	Quatro tomines de dotrina		Un topo de chacara
Un topo de chacara de que come	Quatro tomines de dotrina		Tres cuartos de chacara
Un cuarto de chacara de que come	Quatro tomines de dotrina		
	Quatro tomines de dotrina		Tres cuartos de chacara
Medio topo de chacara de que come	Quatro tomines de dotrina		Un cuarto de chacara

/f.205v/

	Casados—años	*Hijos—años*	*Servicio que ha hecho cada yanacona*
536	Rodrigo Laschi Viznay Cañar nacio en este valle treinta años—30 Maria Chuco veinte y ocho años—28	Francisco Chimcho ocho años—8 Isabel Zitonchuc siete 7 Juan Bautista Chaluzac tres años—3	A que le sirve veinte años en lo que le manda y en beneficiarle las chacaras de maiz
	Hernando Chara Cañar nacio en este valle veinte y quatro años—24 Maria Cuyun de treinta y quatro años—34	Alonso Avisucha seis años—6 Juan Damancaca tres—3 Gaspar Sumansana dos años—2 Ana Yugatocto cinco años—5	
	Hernando Pasto nacio en este valle treinta y seis años—36		A que sirve a don Francisco Chilche en beneficiarle las chacaras ocho años
	Benito Rimache nacio en este valle diez y seis años—16		Comenzo a servir ahora
305	Juan Pasto nacio en este valle veinte años—20		Comenzo a servir ahora
340	Cristobal Sulcanaui Cañar nacio en este valle treinta y seis años—36 Isabel Chunbi quarenta años—40	Juana Cusichinbo quince años—15	Sirviole diez años en lo que los demas
	Pedro Vilcacaquia Collagua nacio en este valle treinta y seis años—36 Isabel Chunbi quarenta años—40	Juana Cusichinbo doce años—12	Sirviole diez y ocho años en lo que los demas
	Pedro Paucar Aymara de Anta nacio en este valle veinte años—20 Inez Toto treinta años—30		

/f.206/

Lo que le paga de servicio	*Lo que paga de dotrina*	*Lo que paga de tasa*	*Tiene chacaras de comunidad*
Topo y medio de chacara	Dos tomines de dotrina	Tres tomines de tasa	
Dos topos y medio de que come	Quatro tomines de dotrina	Seis tomines para la tasa	
Un topo de chacara	Seis tomines de dotrina	Dos pesos de tasa	
Un topo de chacara	Quatro tomines de dotrina	Dos pesos de tasa	

/f.206v/

	Casados—años	*Hijos—años*	*Servicio que ha fecho*
	Agustin Halanta Collagua veinte años—20 Francisca Chinbo Urma diez y nueve años—19	Inez Carua un año—1	Sirviole en beneficiar la chacara de maiz
	Toribio Arimana Collagua quarenta años—40 Inez Vilca Cargua quarenta años—40	Madalena Ingaillay de diez años—10 Catalina Quispe nueve—9 Pedro Suacalla quatro—4 Isabel Auio uno—1	Sirviole veinte años en lo que los demas
	Rodrigo Cuzco Cañar nacio en este valle treinta y seis años—36 Isabel Zemchuc treinta y quatro años—34	Cristobal Zumbaizila tres años—3 Martin Chunbai un año—1 Leonor Machuc cinco años—5	Sirviole quatro años en lo que los demas
	Francisco Llassayupan Guanca cincuenta años—50 Inez Marchullassa quarenta años—40	Madalena Antaicaba seis años—6 Pedro Primaynpari cinco—5 Lucas Sulcai quatro—4 Ana Carancarua dos—2	A quatro años que le sirve en lo que los demas
	Rodrigo Guaraca Guanca nacio en este valle veinte y tres años—23 Maria Tasca veinte y tres años—23	Pedro Anquiyachi quatro años—4	A que le sirve tres años en lo que los demas y en la chacara de coca
	Geronimo Guamanquilca veinte años—20 Catalina Yachi veinte y cinco años—25		A que le sirve quatro años en lo que los demas
423	Don Juan Airanbo quarenta y dos años—42 Catalina Cusichinbo treinta y tres—33	Maria Chirchiclli cinco años—5 Luis Guamantito diez—10 Juan Guamancu Tanbo—1 Felipe Guamanpuco—7 Juan Guaman Airanbo tres—3 Pedro Cusi Culanbo seis—6 Catalina Cusichinbo—8	A que le sirve diez años de manda sus yanaconas de don Alonso Tito Atauche y las haciendas
	Cristobal Sino de Tambo nacio en este valle de treinta años—30 Costanza Pinta de treinta años—30		A que le sirve quince años en lo que ha mandado

/f.207/

Lo que le paga de servicio	*Lo que paga de dotrina*	*Lo que paga de tasa*	*Tiene chacaras de tasa*
Tres cuartos de chacara	Quatro tomines de dotrina		
Medio topo de chacara			Un cuarto de chacara de comunidad
Dos topos de chacara de que come	Seis tomines de dotrina	Tres cuartillas de maiz de tasa	
Medio topo de chacara de que come	Quatro tomines de dotrina	Quatro tomines de tasa	Un topo de chacara
Medio topo de chacara de que come	Medio peso de dotrina		Medio topo de chacara de la comunidad
Declaro don Juan Airambo que todas las tierras que estan repartidas a el y a los yanaconas de don Alonso Tito Atauche son chacaras de las que comian los indios que guardaban el cuerpo de Guayna Capac			Medio topo de comunidad
Tres cuartos de chacara			

/f.207v/

Casados—años	*Hijos—años*	*Servicio que ha hecho cada yanacona*
Domingo Guaman Eschui nacio en este valle diez y nueve años—19 Beatriz Guarcai veinte y cinco años—25		A dos años que le sirve en lo que los demas
Pedro Yucura de Guaro nacio en este valle diez y ocho años—18 Catalina Chunbe veinte años—20		
Diego Cusipuro de Maras quarenta años—40 Isabel Yunga cincuenta años—50		A que le sirve diez y siete años en lo que los demas
Agustin Cusipaucar de Maras veinte y dos años—22 Luisa Cusichinbo veinte y cinco años—25	Isabel Sillacoca de tres años—3	A que le sirve tres años en lo que los demas
Martin Pungaguaman de Xaquixaguana veinte y cinco años—25 Isabel Virca veinte y dos años—22		A que le sirve cinco años en lo que los demas
Martin Guamani Hochi treinta años—30 Beatriz Uizucnanco veinte y quatro años	Inez Chinbo uno—1 Isabel Cusinnaca siete años—7 Diego Chiquillaca quatro años—4	A que le sirve cinco años en lo que los demas
Pedro Siuipaucar de Xaquixaguana quarentacinco años—45 Inez Chipi quarenta y cinco años—45	Ana Cocaquipi cinco años—5 Alonso Guamanyucra siete años—7	A que le sirve diez y ocho años en beneficio de las chacaras
Martin Quiquicana Quechua cincuenta y quatro años—54 Catalina Yupullai treinta años—30	Beatriz Cusiynguillay—17 Isabel Cayotiquilla—7 Maria Pacarsuyo quatro—4 Juan Asiquillo dos años—2 Pedro Chamaicumara un año—1	A que le sirve diez y siete años en lo que los demas

/f.208/

Lo que le paga de servicio	*Lo que le paga de dotrina*	*Lo que le paga de tasa*	*Tiene chacaras de comunidad*
Medio topo de chacara de que come	Quatro tomines de dotrina		
Medio topo de chacara	Quatro tomines de dotrina		
Medio topo de chacara	Quatro tomines de dotrina		
Medio topo de chacara	Quatro tomines de dotrina		
Medio topo de chacara			
Medio topo de chacara	Quatro tomines de dotrina		
Medio topo de chacara	Quatro tomines de dotrina		

/f.208v/

	Casados—años	*Hijos—años*	*Servicio que ha hecho cada yanacona*
	Cristobal Guamalli de sesenta años—60		A diez y siete años que le sirve en beneficio de aji
Yanaconas de doña Maria Ramirez	Antonio de Quiñones de Hananpa treinta años—30 Juana Ayalpo de treinta años—30	Alonso Carnapilla ocho años—8 Martin Cura seis años—6	A que le sirve tres años de ortelano y de beneficiarles las chacaras
Coxo 472	Diego Ninaricza de Guayllas treinta y quatro años—34 Maria Cocanco treinta y dos años—32	Catalina Yncri quince 15 Juan Machacuai ocho 8 Isabel Yancas seis 6 Lucas Hanampa cinco 5 Alonso Sulcaguaman tres—3	A que le sirve tres años en lo ques de arriba.
	Domingo Sulca Guayllas de veinte y seis años—26 Maria Aba veinte y nueve años—29	Domingo Llaguas seis años—6 Juanbautista Sulca tres años—3 Ana Quipa dos años—2	A tres años que le sirve en lo que los demas
	Hernando Carua Auanca de Guayllas veinte y tres años—23 Inez Libiachuquc veinte años—20	Ana Carnayucre tres años—3	A tres años que le sirve en lo que los demas
Yanaconas de Pedro de Bustinza	Salvador Laqueasto Quichua cincuenta y quatro años—54 Cecilia Aquipi cincuenta años—50		A que le sirve cinco años de ortelano
	Luis Sulca Llaqua Quichua veinte y quatro años—24 Isabel Pullo treinta años—30	Catalina Ypuco cinco años—5 Catalina Chunbe tres—3 Ana Llachuapuco uno—1	A seis años que le sirve de ortelano
477	Vicente Chiqua de Chicho de este valle de veinte años—20 Inez Paucarocllo veinte y ocho años—28	Juan Chiguangualpa tres—3	A que le sirve tres años en lo que los demas

/f.209/

Lo que le paga de servicio	*Lo que paga de dotrina*	*Lo que paga de tasa*	*Tiene chacaras de tasa*
Un topo de chacara			
Medio topo de chacara	Quatro tomines de dotrina		Dos topos de chacara
Medio topo de chacara	Quatro tomines de dotrina		Topo y medio de chacara
Tres cuartos de chacara	Quatro tomines de dotrina		
Medio topo de chacara	Quatro tomines de dotrina		Medio topo de chacara
Tres cuartos de chacara	Quatro tomines de dotrina		Un cuarto de chacara
	Quatro tomines de dotrina		Un topo de chacara
Medio topo de chacara	Quatro tomines de dotrina		Un cuarto de topo de chacara

/f.209v/

	Casados—años	*Hijos—años*	*Servicio que ha hecho cada yanacona*
	Juan Ataosuno de Pacaritambo de treinta y seis años—36 Ana Suca veinte y ocho años—28	Costanza Paico quatro años—4 Francisco Guaipar dos años—2	Sirve a don Carlos Guaparoca en beneficiarle las chacaras y dales leña
556	Alonso Biua de Mohina treinta y tres años—33 Catalina Chinbourma treinta y tres años—33	Pedro Paucarguaman quatro años—4 Madalena Ailanpilla un año—1	A que le sirve quatro años de ortelano y de beneficiar las chacaras
315	Cristobal Dachino Cañar treinta y dos años—32	Alonso Puri de veinte años—20	A que le sirve dos años de ortelanos y de beneficiar las chacaras
	Juan Malco Pariguana treinta y nueve años—39 Inez Cusichinbo de cincuenta años—50		
257	Andres Duibus Cañar nacio en este valle diez y ocho años—18 Catalina Yachi diez y ocho años—18		A dos años que le sirve en el beneficio de las chacaras de maiz
	Alonso Quispe Cañar nacio en este valle treinta y ocho años—38 Isabel Caba cincuenta años—50	Maria Cacinchuc diez y siete—17	A que le sirve diez y siete años en lo que los demas
	Marcos Chillic Cañar nacio en este valle veinte y cinco años—25 Madalena Ciminchuc veinte y cinco años—25	Beatriz Abizaba quatro años—4 Catalina Chuc dos años—2	A que le sirve diez años en lo que los demas
	Juanbautista Manchi Cañar nacio en este valle treinta y ocho años—38 Catalina Galinchuc veinte y dos años—22		A diez años que le sirve en lo que los demas

/f.210/

Lo que le paga de servicio	*Lo que paga de dotrina*	*Lo que paga de tasa*	*Tiene chacaras de tasa*
Medio topo de chacara	Seis tomines de dotrina		Dos topos de las chacaras de la comunidad
Un topo de chacara			
Un cuarto de topo de chacara			Un cuarto de topo de chacara
Un topo de chacara de que come	Quatro tomines de dotrina	Dos pesos de tasa	
	Quatro tomines de dotrina	Dos pesos de tasa	Un topo de la chacara de la comunidad
	Dos tomines de dotrina	Quatro tomines de tasa	Topo y medio de chacara
	Dos tomines de dotrina	Quatro tomines de tasa	Topo y medio de chacara

/f.210v/

	Casados—años	*Hijos—años*	*Servicio que ha hecho cada yanacona*
	Miguel Guiguinaula Cañar nacio en este valle veinte y cinco años—25 Isabel Ynchicaua veinte años—20	Isabel Carnichuc cinco años—5 Juanbautista Cuaipulla dos años—2	A diez años que sirve en lo que los demas
Yo quedo aqui	Francisco Miunzilaca Cañar nacio en este valle treinta y cinco años—35 Madalena Mano treinta años—30	Elvira Nahaschuc cinco años—5 Rodrigo Tinanyanba quatro—4 Beatric Macichuc dos años—2	A que les sirve diez y ocho años en todo lo que los demas
265	Andres Tinimaci Cañar nacio en este valle diez y nueve años—19 Costanza Poco veinte y tres años—23	Elvira Nazcho un año—1	A quatro años que le sirve en lo que los demas
	Andres Casanaula Cañar nacio en este valle veinte años—20 Madalena Puluchuc veinte años—20	Madalena Angai dos años—2 Nazirinchuc un año—1	A ocho años que le sirve de cumbicamayo y beneficiales las chacaras y mita de yerba y leña
	Francisco Biznaicila Cañar nacio en este valle veinte y quatro años—24 Mencia Caba veinte y dos años—22	Gonzalo Ybanzicha tres años—3 Geronimo Acuzaba un año—1 Madalena Cacacho dos—2	A diez años que le sirve de lo que le mandan
	Mateo Palchobiznai Cañar nacio en este valle quince años—15 Madalena Yugantuco quince años—15		A un año que le sirve de beneficiarle las chacaras
	Alonso Quiquia Cañar nacio en este valle cincuenta y quatro años—54 Luisa Yngaotoco cincuenta y cinco años—55		A treinta años que le sirve en lo que los demas
	Lucas Chilliguaman Ynga nacio en este valle quarenta años—40 Beatriz Yllanchuc treinta y seis años—36	Lucas Quispe siete años—7 Isabel Toco cinco años—5	A veinte años que le sirve en lo que los demas

/f.211/

Lo que paga de servicio	*Lo que paga de dotrina*	*Lo que paga de tasa*	*Tiene chacaras de tasa*
Topo y cuarto de chacara	Quatro tomines de dotrina	Un peso de tasa	
Dale medio topo de chacara	Quatro tomines de dotrina	Un peso de tasa	
Dale medio topo de chacara	Quatro tomines de dotrina	Quatro tomines de tasa	
Dale un topo de chacara de que come	Quatro tomines de dotrina	Quatro tomines de tasa	
	Quatro tomines de dotrina	Un peso de tasa	Topo y medio de chacara de comunidad
Medio topo de chacara	Quatro tomines de dotrina	Quatro tomines de tasa	
	Quatro tomines de dotrina	Un peso de tasa	Medio topo de chacara
Dos topos de chacara	Quatro tomines de dotrina	Dos pesos de tasa	

/f.211v/

	Casados—años	Hijos—años	Servicio que ha hecho cada yanacona
	Cristobal Nazpi Cañar nacio en este valle veinte y ocho años—28 Maria Machui veinte y ocho años—28	Catalina Muchuc siete años—7	A diez años que le sirve en lo que los demas
	Martin Tacitanga Cañar de Tomebamba treinta y tres años—33 Inez Colque treinta años—30	Anton Bilivichizi quatro años—4 Hernando Caquimaca un año—1	A veinte años que le sirve en lo que los demas
	Martin Bilantanga Cañar treinta y siete años—37 Inez Caba treinta y cinco años—35	Lucas Sangailipai quince años—15 Luisa Guallachi tres—3 Madalena Yzmichico un año—1	A veinte años que le sirve en lo que los demas
	Andres Quiribiznai Cañar nacio en este valle veinte y siete años—27 Catalina Caua veinte y ocho años—28	Juan Cacitpulla quatro años—4 Beatriz Batichuc un año—1	A doce años que le sirve en lo que los demas
	Agustin Alao Cañar cincuenta y quatro años—54 Catalina Culcaichimi cincuenta y dos años—52	Inez Aviara seis años—6	A veinte años que le sirve en lo que los demas
	Pedro Guamancusi de Xaquixaguana nacio en este valle treinta y tres años—33 Inez Chuco treinta y siete años—37	Pedro Vianchi seis años—6 Felipe Pomaquico tres años—3	A quince años que le sirve en lo que los demas
355	Pedro Sulca Yauyo nacio en este valle veinte y siete años—27 Francisca Macha veinte y ocho años—28	Juanbautista Cañarvilca nacio en este valle cinco años—5 Alonso Caruayanca tres años—3 Hernando Lasapucma uno—1	A diez años que le sirve en loq ue los demas
283	Agusto Laua Chicha nacio en este valle veinte y seis años—26 Catalina Mulloocllo treinta y cinco años—35		A veinte años que le sirve en lo que los demas

/f.212/

Lo que paga de servicio	Lo que paga de dotrina	Lo que paga de tasa	Tiene chacaras de tasa
Un topo y un cuarto de chacara	Dos tomines de dotrina	Quatro tomines de tasa	
Topo y medio de chacara	Dos tomines de dotrina	Quatro tomines de tasa	
Topo y medio de chacara	Dos tomines de dotrina	Quatro tomines de tasa	
Topo y medio de chacara	Dos tomines de dotrina	Quatro tomines de tasa	
Un topo de chacara	Quatro tomines de dotrina	Quatro tomines de tasa	
Topo y medio de chacara	Dos tomines de dotrina	Quatro tomines de tasa	
Topo y medio de chacara	Quatro tomines de dotrina	Un peso de tasa	
Un topo de chacara	Dos tomines de dotrina	Quatro tomines de tasa	

/f.212v/

	Casados—años	*Hijos—años*	
	Lucas Bilidunbai Cañar nacio en este valle veinte y dos—22 Ana Lunchar catorce años—14		
	Pedro Quicana de los Canches veinte y siete años—27 Inez Chimima treinta años—30	Pedro Condurquicalla cinco—5 Leonor Guacapuco tres—3 Alonso Conduri un año—1 Isabel Chinbourma ocho años—8	A ocho años que sirve de los que los demas
	Diego Rimache natural del Cuzco quarenta y ocho años—48 Isabel Cusiynguilla cincuenta años—50	Teresa Pata doce años—12 Lucas Tito cinco años—5 Miguel Mayun quatro años—4 Juanbautista Pilla dos—2	A treinta años que le sirve en el beneficio de las chacaras
	Pedro Machaguai Guanca treinta años—30 Catalina Asto treinta y seis años—36	Juana Mulmucazo trece—13 Diego Yarinlliclla quatro—4 Ana pachua dos años—2 Agustin Yarolluclla seis años—6	A diez y ocho años que sirve en lo que los demas
235	Mateo Curis Guayllas veinte y ocho años—28 Teresa Tocto Ocllo de veinte y tres años—23	Ana Llapi dos—2 Lucia Nachac uno—1 Madalena Anas quatro—4 Luysa Nacha de tres años—3	a doce años sirve en lo que lo demas
	Mateo Curo Quichua nacio en este valle veinte y ocho años—28 Maria Yanapuco veinte y seis años—26	Maria Machui de tres años—3	a quince años que sirve en lo que lo demas
	Francisco Quispi yunga de diez y siete años—17 Francisca Pachua diez y seis años—16		a un año que sirve en el beneficio de las chacaras y yerba y leña
	Francisco Llancari quarenta años—40 Inez Angaituco cinquenta años—50	Catalina Pucochisque diez y ocho años—18 Francisca Chucaschisque quatro años—4	a treinta y seis años que le sirve en lo que los demas

/f.213/

Lo que le paga de servicio	*Lo que paga de dotrina*	*Lo que paga de tasa*	*Tiene chacaras de tasa*
Topo y medio de chacara	Dos tomines de dotrina	Quatro tomines de tasa	
Dos topos de chacara	Dos tomines de dotrina	Quatro tomines de tasa	
Medio topo de chacara	Dos tomines de dotrina	Quatro tomines de tasa	Tres topos de chacara de la comunidad
Medio topo de chacara	Dos tomines de dotrina	Quatro tomines de tasa	Dos topos y medio de chacara
Medio topo de chacara	Dos tomines de dotrina	Un peso de tasa	Dos topos y medio de chacara
Medio topo de chacara	Dos tomines de dotrina	Quatro tomines de tasa	
Medio topo de chacara	Dos tomines de dotrina	Quatro tomines de tasa	Dos topos y medio de chacara

/f.213v/

	Casados—años	*Hijos—años*	*Servicio que ha hecho cada yanacona*
	Juan Quiquinyana Chanca veinte años—20 Beatriz Llamilla diez y seis años—16		A tres años que le sirve en lo que los demas
247	Mateo Ricratavillo veinte y dos años—22 Teresa Mullo veinte años—20	Diego Chaupiscondur un año—1	A quatro años que le sirve en lo que los demas
332	Alonso Tairo Chilque cincuenta y quatro años—54 Isabel Panpa cincuenta y quatro años—54	Inez Guacrococa cinco años—5	Sirviole veinte años en lo que el de arriba
	Pedro Alcamari Colla nacio en este valle quarenta años—40 Inez Tatachuqui cincuenta años—50	Juan Pumallulla simple siete años—7	A diez años que sirve en lo que los demas
	Miguel Vilcacondur Conchucos treinta años—30 Costanza Guachisamuc treinta y tres años—33	Beatriz Llassa seis—6 Cristobal Vilcagua quatro años—4 Catalina Vilsil tres años—3 Diego Vilcamanco dos—2	A veinte años que sirve en lo que los demas
	Simon Cusiminga de Xaquixaguana quince años—15 Maria Xaspa diez y ocho años—18		A quatro años que sirve en lo que los demas
	Martin Pomacondur treinta años—30	Juan Vilcamango quatro años—4	
256	Anton Saquiguara sesenta años—60		A diez y ocho años que sirve en lo que los demas

/f.214/

Lo que le paga de servicio	*Lo que paga de dotrina*	*Lo que paga de tasa*	*Tiene chacaras de tasa*
Medio topo de chacara			Un topo y cuarto de chacara
Medio topo de chacara	Dos tomines de dotrina	Quatro tomines de tasa	Dos topos y medio de chacara
Medio topo de chacara	Dos tomines de dotrina	Quatro tomines de tasa	
Un topo de chacara	Dos tomines de dotrina	Quatro tomines de tasa	Topo y medio de chacara
Medio topo de chacara	Dos tomines de dotrina	Quatro tomines de tasa	Dos topos de chacara de comunidad
Medio topo de chacara	Dos tomines de dotrina	Quatro tomines de tasa	

/f.214v/

	Casados—años	*Hijos—años*	*Servicio que ha hecho cada yanacona*
	Alonso Cartan de Quito sesenta años—60 Inez Aco cincuenta y ocho años—58		Sirviole diez y ocho años de ortelano
	Cristobal Mai de Quito de treinta años—30 Inez Cata de veinte y ocho años—28	Juan Aulavisaic cinco años—5 Leonor Ganaiui quatro años—4	Sirviole diez y seis años en lo que los demas
375	Pedro Yachagua de Tauillo cincuenta años—50 Luisa Tiquilla de treinta y ocho años—38		Sirviole diez y ocho años de ortelano y viñadero y servicio de chacaras
	Simon Yllatopa Cuzco quarenta y dos años—42 Madalena Caua treinta y dos años—32	Inez Coa veinte años—20 Juan Yllatopa quatro años—4 Felipe Tupa cinco años—5 Angelina Toto cinco—5	Sirvile diez años en hacer sus negocios como su hermano que es—
	Juan Uchopanta de Quito quarenta y cinco años—45 Isabel Coca Chilque quarenta años—40	Catalina Ocanchinquel diez y seis años—16 Felipe Condus ocho—8 Ana Unanchis seis años—6 Leonor Chiuacanchi quatro años—4	Sirviole veinte años en lo que los demas
348	Alonso Marcaguallpa Chilque cincuenta años—50 Maria Suchuc quarenta y seis años—46	Francisco Toroguallpa diez y ocho años—18 Francisca Chilquechuc seis años—6 Gonzalo Marca dos—2	Sirviole diez y seis años en lo que los demas
25	Alonso Arose de Pomacanche cincuenta años—50 Isabel Chichacarua quarenta y tres años—43	Isabel Puco diez y ocho años—18 Francisco Chuquiconsa quince—15 Ana Guairo quatro años—4 Inez Toma dos años—2 Maria Guaromalqui nueve—9 Martin Condos seis años—6 Mencia Toto tres—3	Sirviole diez años en el beneficio de las chacaras
350	Martin Tutaniali Cañar sesenta años—60 Catalina Sichuc sesenta años—60	Isabel Caba veinte años—20	Sirviole diez año en lo que los demas

/f.215/

Lo que le ha pagado de servicio	*Lo que paga de dotrina*	*Lo que paga de tasa*	*Tiene chacaras de tasa*
Medio topo de chacara	Dos tomines de dotrina		
Un topo de chacara	Quatro tomines de dotrina		
Medio topo de chacara	Quatro tomines de dotrina	Medio peso de tasa	Medio topo de chacara de comunidad
Medio topo de chacara Otro topo de don Francisco Chilche	Medio peso de dotrina		
Un topo de chacara	Dos tomines de dotrina	Dos tomines de tasa	
Topo y cuarto de chacara	Dos tomines de dotrina	Quatro tomines de tasa	
Topo y medio de chacara	Dos tomines de dotrina		
Medio topo de chacara de don Francisco Chilche			

/f.215v/

	Casados—años	*Hijos—años*	*Servicio que ha hecho cada yanacona*
	Cristobal Cusiguaman de Maras setenta años—70 Isabel Ynguillai cincuenta años—50		Sirvieronle veinte años en lo que los demas
	Cristobal Chaucuri Chilque veinte y cinco años—25 Madalena Yrinchu treinta y dos años—32	Andres Churigualpa cinco años—5 Isabel Sacacoca tres años—3	Sirvieronle diez y seis años en lo que los demas
	Agustin Chuquiapa setenta años—70	Maria Yuquilla treinta años—30	A veinte años que le sirve en el beneficio de las chacaras
Yanaconas de don Hernando Guartananla	Juanbautista Diusul Cañar nacio en este valle veinte y siete años—27 Leonor Caba veinte y ocho años—28	Francisco Yachi cinco años—5 Agustin Ninabla quatro años—4 Teresa Chunbai dos años—2	A diez años que le sirve en el beneficio de las chacaras de maiz y papas
	Martin Ninapoma Caricha quarenta años—40 Beatriz Colqui treinta años—30	Diego Nacuri tres años—3	A que le sirve trece años en el beneficio de las chacaras de maiz y papas
	Cristobal Tomailla Canche nacio en este valle veinte y seis años—26 Beatriz Chucho treinta años—30	Felipa Titanzila seis años—6 Maria Machuc dos años—2	A once años que le sirve en lo que los demas
	Lucas Chuquicondur Yanacondur veinte años—20 Leonor Ocllo veinte años—20		A diez años que le sirve en lo que los demas
	Juan Chuquicarochi nacio en este valle y diez y seis años—16 Costanza Chinbo quince años—15		Esta con su padre y come comer

/f.216/

Lo que le paga de servicio	*Lo que paga de dotrina*	*Lo que paga de tasa*	*Tiene chacaras de tasa*
Tres cuartos de chacara			
Topo y medio de chacara			
Medio topo de chacara	Quatro tomines de dotrina		
Topo y medio de chacara	Quatro tomines de dotrina		
Topo y medio de chacaras	Quatro tomines de dotrina		
Un topo de chacara de que come	Quatro tomines de dotrina		
Un topo de chacara de que come	Quatro tomines de dotrina		

/f.216v/

	Casados—años	*Hijos—años*	*Servicio que ha hecho cada yanacona*
371	Alonso Condor Quichua nacio en este valle veinte años		A cinco años que le sirve en las chacaras y en lo demas que le ocupo
	Francisco Quispeyupa diez y ocho años—18 Madalena Asto diez y ocho años—18	Juanbautista Vilcarache un año—1	
	Agustin Sulcatocas Chonchabuyo veinte y ocho años—28 Catalina Nachuqui Tinta quarenta años		A diez años que le sirve en lo que los demas
	Juan Malqui de Lanco nacio en este valle veinte y quatro años—24 Isabel Chinbococa veinte y nueve años—29		A diez años que le sirve en lo que los demas
	Francisco Llasayupanguaca cincuenta años—50 Inez Machullasa quarenta años—40	Madalena Antaicarua seis años—6 Pedro Pumayupari—5 Lucas Sulcai quatro—4 Ana Carancarua dos—2	A quatro años que le sirve en lo que los demas
	Francisco Guayavisco natural de Sora de veinte y tres años—23 Inez Sachachunbi diez y nueve años—19	Juan Usco uno—1 Madalena Aucas dos años—2 Isabel Puco un año—1	A diez años que le sirve en lo que los demas
	Alonso Usco de Sora de cincuenta años—50 Leonor Gallanachuc cincuenta años—50	Martin Payausco diez—10 Isabel Chunbi siete—7 Alonso Quispe seis años—6 Miguel Llamuca cinco años—5 Madalena Asib diez y ocho años—18	A quince años que le sirve en lo que los demas
	Pedro Tinta de Quito nacio en este valle quarenta y dos años—42 Inez Pachua treinta años—30	Lucas Pitan tres años—3	A diez y seis años que le sirve en lo que los demas

/f.217/

Lo que le paga de servicio	*Lo que paga de dotrina*	*Lo que paga de tasa*	*Tiene chacaras de tasa*
Tres topos de chacara	Seis tomines de dotrina		
Tres topos de chacara	Seis tomines de dotrina		
Dos topos de chacara	Seis tomines de dotrina	Tres cuartillas de maiz de tasa	
Dos topos de chacara	Seis tomines de dotrina	Tres cuartillas de maiz	
Medio topo de chacara de que come	Seis tomines de dotrina	Tres cuartillas de mais	
Un topo de chacara de que come	Tres tomines de dotrina	Tres cuartillas de maiz	Un topo de chacara de comunidad
Topo y medio de chacara de que come	Seis tomines de dotrina	Tres cuartillas de maiz	

/f.217v/

	Casados—años	*Hijos—años*	*Servicio que ha hecho cada yanacona*
	Alonso Conoyupari Guanca nacio en este valle veinte y cinco años—25 Catalina Yacocarua veinte y quatro años—24	Maria Caruachapi quatro años—4 Catalina Uno dos—2 Ana Chaycatanta un año—1	A diez años que le sirve en lo que los demas
	Agustin Conduri Guanca nacio en este valle quarenta y dos años-42 Ana Yache quarenta años—40	Felipe Condurcochachi dos años—2	A veinte años que le sirve en lo que los demas
	Andres Caruapisco Guanca nacio en este valle quarenta y dos años—42 Leonor Murmuchuc diez y siete años—17		A diez años que le sirve en lo que los demas
386	Mateo Atachuc Guanca nacio en este valle veinte años—20 Juana Ciqui veinte y dos años—22	Marcos Nayanchuc dos años—2	A que le sirve cinco años en lo que los demas
	Alonso Muquiguaya Condor sesenta años—60 Maria Sachunbi cincuenta años—50		A diez años que le sirve en lo que los demas
	Andres Auquisyupari diez y nueve años—19 Maria Llaimibamba veinte y un años—21	Ana Chaicotanta un año—1	A tres años que le sirve en lo que los demas
	Martin Caragua de Sora veinte y cinco años—25 Leonor Quispe veinte y dos años—22		A nueve años que le sirve en lo que los demas
	Alonso Pilpe de Atavillo cincuenta años—50 Leonor Cullquillasa cincuenta años—50		A diez años que le sirve en lo que los demas

/f.218/

Lo que le paga de servicio	*Lo que paga de dotrina*	*Lo que paga de tasa*	*Tiene chacaras de tasa*
Topo y medio de chacara de que come	Seis tomines de dotrina	Tres cuartillas de maiz	
Un topo de chacara de que come	Seis tomines de dotrina	Tres cuartillas de maiz	Un topo de chacara
Tres cuarto de topo de chacara	Seis tomines de dotrina		
Medio topo de chacara de que come	Seis tomines de dotrina		
Un topo de chacara de que come		Cinco cuartillas de maiz	
	Quatro tomines de dotrina	Tres cuartillas de maiz	Media chacara de comunidad
Topo y medio de chacara de que come	Quatro tomines de dotrina	Tres cuartillas de maiz	
Tres topos de chacara de que come	Seis tomines de dotrina	Tres cuartillas de maiz	

/f.218v/

	Casados—años	*Hijos—años*	*Servicio que ha hecho cada yanacona*
	Martin Quispi Guanca nacio en este valle treinta años—30 Teresa Yache veinte y cinco años—25	Madalena Yarotanta quatro años—4 Juana Mirañoquispe dos años—2 Lucas Parin uno—1	A diez años que le sirve en lo que los demas
	Martin Guanaco Yanaguara sesenta y nueve años—69 Juana Binat cincuenta y seis años—56		A diez años que le sirve en lo que los demas
396	Juan Cusma Cuncara sesenta años—60 Inez Quispe sesenta y seis años—66		A diez años que le sirve en lo que los demas
73	Domingo Pumaruco diez y seis años—16 Leonor Tiquillamaca diez y seis años—16		
	Pedro Pomaguaman Yanaguara nacio en este valle treinta años—30 Inez Parinquilico treinta años—30	Agustin Pomaguana—6 Inez Caquiapuco—6 Juan Ancoquilaco quatro—4 Isabel Carua tres—3 Isabel Guamachuqui—3	A diez años que le sirve en lo que los demas
	Juanbautista Naupachiguay Condor sesenta años—60 Costanza Puyanchucho cincuenta y seis años—56	Catalina Panyac veinte años—20 Juanbautista Chuquimanco quince años—15	A quince años que le sirve en lo que los demas
399	Cristobal Siuinta de Condesuyo treinta y siete años—37 Francisca Cocachinbo treinta y seis años—36	Lucia Ayache tres—3 Isabel Stasus seis—6 Francisca Comachinbo dos años—2 Cristobal Siuinta ocho—8	A cinco años que le sirve en lo que los demas
	Juan Vilcas Pariguana yunge veinte años—20 Francisca Usica veinte años—20	Isabel Cayoquispe un año—1	A un año que le sirve en lo que los demas

/f.219/

Lo que le paga de servicio	*Lo que paga de dotrina*	*Lo que paga de tasa*	*Tiene chacaras de dotrina*
Un topo de chacara de que come	Seis tomines de dotrina	Tres cuartillas de maiz	
	Quatro tomines de dotrina	Una cuartilla de maiz	Un topo de chacara de comunidad
	Seis tomines de dotrina	Tres cuartillas de maiz	Topo y medio de chacara de comunidad
Un topo de chacara de que come	Seis tomines de dotrina	Tres cuartillas de maiz	Dos topos de chacara de comunidad
	Seis tomines de dotrina	Tres cuartillas de maiz	Tres topos y medio de chacara de comunidad
Topo y medio de chacara	Seis tomines de dotrina	Tres cuartillas de maiz	
	Seis tomines de dotrina	Tres cuartillas de maiz	Un topo de chacara de comunidad

/f.219v/

	Casados—años	Hijoa—años	Servicio que ha hecho cada yanacona
512	Alonso Guaman de Xaquixaguana diez y ocho años—18 Catalina Sulcaymandor diez y ocho años—18	Juan Cussiyinguillay un año—1	A quatro años que le sirve en lo que los demas
402	Martin Mayta del Cuzco quarenta y ocho años—48 Isabel Asto cincuenta años—50	Juanbautista Pascamayta diez años—10	A que sirve diez y seis años en lo que los demas
	Juan Camanchairac Quichua veinte años—20 Maria Ropo diez y nueve años—19		A dos años que sirve en lo que los demas
	Cristobal Paynalluco de Xaquixaguana cincuenta años—50 Ana Yache cincuenta y quatro años—54		A diez años que sirve en lo que los demas
	Alonso Pana de Xaquixaguana treinta y seis años—36 Madalena Quispi treinta años—30	Pedro Pucaraimara tres—3 Alonso Pana uno—1 Francisca Cusichinbo diez y ocho—18 Juanbautista Guolpauro—7	A diez años que le sirve en lo que los demas
	Alonso Ucaipuro de Xaquixaguana veinte y dos años—22 Isabel Cocachinbo veinte y dos años—22	Lucia Chinbo Urma dos años—2 Juan Nataullaico un año—1	A dos años que sirve en lo que los demas
	Domingo Vilca Collagua quarenta años—40 Lucia Cocanco treinta y tres años—33	Juanbautista Pangui un año—1 Miguel Guaguaiyanqui cinco años—5 Simon Chara diez años—10	A diez y seis años que sirve en lo que los demas
	Francisco Uchaguaman Quichua veinte y cinco años—25 Ana Chunbihuida	Juan Llasachunbi uno—1	A diez años que sirve en lo que los demas

/f.220/

Lo que le paga de servicio	Lo que paga de dotrina	Lo que paga de tasa	Tiene chacaras de tasa
Dos topos de chacara	Seis tomines de dotrina		
	Seis tomines de dotrina	Tres cuartillas de maiz	Tres topos de chacara de la comunidad
	Seis tomines de dotrina		
	Seis tomines de dotrina	Tres cuartillas de maiz	Tres topos de chacara de la comunidad
	Seis tomines de dotrina	Tres cuartillas de maiz	Tres topos de chacara de la comunidad
	Seis tomines de dotrina		Medio topo de chacara
	Seis tomines de dotrina	Tres cuartillas de maiz	Dos topos y medio de chacara
	Seis tomines de dotrina	Tres cuartillas de maiz	Dos topos y medio de chacara

/f.220v/

	Casados—años	*Hijos—años*	*Servicio que ha hecho cada yanacona*
410	Juan Cochachin Guanca nacio en este valle quarenta años—40 Isabel Ocllo quarenta y seis años—46	Cristobal Naupari siete años—7 Juan Cochachin cinco años—5	A diez y seis años que le sirve en lo que los demas
	Pedro Hanbo Guayllas nacio en este valle veinte y ocho años—28 Leonor Cuya treinta años—30	Juan Limahananpa dos años—2	A diez años que le sirve en lo que los demas
	Domingo Arovilca Yanca nacio en este valle veinte y tres años—23	Angelina Cussiocllo cinco años—5	Un topo de chacara de que come
	Francisco Yanac de Tauillo nacio en este valle veinte y cinco años—25 Inez Chunbi treinta y cinco años—35	Domingo Cospa hijo de ella ocho años—8	A diez años que sirve en lo que los demas
414	Diego Amar de Lari sesenta años—60 Leonor Hachama sesenta años—60		Un cuarto de topo de chacara
415	Alonso Condormachaguai de los Conchucos nacio en este valle veinte y cinco años—25 Francisca Caliz veinte y quatro años—24	Pedro Caruayana de un año—1	A diez años que le sirve en lo que los demas
418	Martin Bilca Ancara nacio en Vilcabamba veinte y quatro años—24 Maria Cocango veinte y tres años—23	Agustin Yaulicopa cinco años—5 Pedro Guache uno—1	
	Francisco Rimache quarenta años—40 Juana Chaquna quarenta años—40	Maria Curimaiqua seis años—6	

/f.221/

Lo que le paga de servicio	*Lo que paga de dotrina*	*Lo que paga de tasa*	*Tiene chacaras de tasa*
	Seis tomines de dotrina	Tres cuartillas de maiz	Dos topos y medio de chacara
Medio topo de chacara	Seis tomines de dotrina	Tres cuartillas de maiz	Medio topo de chacara
	Seis tomines de dotrina		
Topo y medio de chacara	Seis tomines de dotrina	Tres cuartillas de maiz	
	Dos tomines de dotrina		
Un topo de chacara	Seis tomines de dotrina	Tres cuartillas de maiz	Dos topos de chacara
Quatro tomines de dotrina	Media fanega de maiz		Topo y medio de chacara
	Quatro pesos de plata		

/f.221v/

	Casados—años	Hijos—años	Servicio que ha hecho cada yanacona
426 Yanaconas de don Felipe Ylla Topa	Pedro Guanca Pomaguayando cincuenta y quatro años—54 Isabel Yuyo quarenta y cinco años—45	Isabel Lasto seis años—6 Pedro Guancapoma quatro años—4	A que le sirve quarenta años en lo que le manda y en el beneficio de las chacaras
427	Juan Aucagualpa de Canche quarenta y dos años—42 Catalina Chinbococa treinta y dos años—32	Domingo Guallapa cinco años—5 Lucas Chuchaguaman quatro años—4 Juan Aucagualpa dos—2	A que le sirve veinte años en el beneficio de las chacaras y en lo que los demas
428	Pedro Mallaocuri Guanca veinte y siete años—27 Maria Cocaguarimi quarenta años—40		A quatro años que le sirve en lo que los demas
432	Diego Alpa Uqui de Maras quarenta y tres años—43 Inez Sumaicoca quarenta años—40	Catalina Jumaichinbo—7 Costanza Chinbo cinco—5 Maria Coca tres años—3 Isabel Yuyochinbo dos años—2 Juana Cocaynguilla once—11	A treinta años que le sirve en el beneficio de las characras y de dalle yerba y leña
433	Pedro Auqui de Maras veinte años—20 Lucia Yanguiguaro veinte y seis años—26	Angelina Caca tres años—3	
	Santiago Yanac de Guanuco treinta y cinco años—35 Inez Cochao treinta y cinco años—35	Inez Malla quatro años—4 Martin Yaque un año—1	A veinte años que le sirve en lo que los demas
435	Pedro Pacha de Xaquixaguana treinta y dos años—32 Leonor Cusichinbo treinta y siete años—37	Angelina CusiYnguillay quatro años—4 Inez Sumaiquilla dos años—2 Alonso Pachatauca enfermo cinco años—5	A veinte años que le sirve en lo que los demas
436	Martin Caruayana de Guayllas veinte y quatro años—24 Inez Cusichinbo veinte años—20	Juana Chapa un año—1	A quince años que le sirve en lo que los demas

/f.222/

Lo que le paga de servicio	Lo que paga de dotrina	Lo que paga de tasa	Tiene chacaras de tasa
Un topo de chacara	Quatro tomines de dotrina		
Un topo de chacara	Quatro tomines de dotrina		
Tres cuartos de chacara	Seis tomines de dotrina		
Seis topos de chacara	Seis tomines de dotrina		
Tres topos de chacara	Seis tomines de dotrina		
Cinco topos de chacara	Seis tomines de dotrina		
Quatro topos de chacara	Seis tomines de dotrina		
Tres topos y medio de chacara	Seis tomines de dotrina		

/f.222v/

	Casados—años	*Hijos—años*	*Servicio que ha hecho cada yanacona*
437	Francisco Cassaguaman de Atavillos diez y ocho años—18 Madalena Cassacarua diez y nueve años—19		A cinco años que le sirve en lo que los demas
	Sebastian Cusiyucra de Xaquixaguana treinta y ocho años—38 Inez Yaro quarenta años—40	Inez Cocaynguillay ocho—8 Catalina Chuquiynguillai quatro—4 Francisca Chapo uno—1 Catalina Cusiynguillai seis—6	A treinta años que le sirve en lo que los demas
441	Geronimo Pilcoyucra de Xaquixaguana diez y ocho años—18 Maria Cussichinbo diez y seis años—16		
442	Juan Ancai de Tambococha treinta y tres años—33 Maria Coca treinta y cinco años—35	Catalina Coca siete—7 Juan Anari seis—6 Maria Chinbourma—4 Ana Cocatasmi quatro años—4	A diez y ocho años que le sirve en lo que los demas
439	Gonzalo Pomagualpa de Xaquixaguana diez y seis años—16 Inez Toto catorce años—14		
	Felipe Guamanagara veinte y tres años—23 Francisca Sasi veinte y siete años—27	Teresa Yuyococa quince—15 Isabel Cisaocllo siete—7 Lucia Toctoocllo quatro—4 Lucas Titoyupangui dos—2 Cristobal Quispicuri uno—1 Catalina Curicimai ocho años—8	A quatro años que le sirve en el beneficio de las chacaras
	Cristobal Mutitupa Yupangui Cuzco quarenta y cinco años—45 Inez Malqui treinta y ocho años—38		
	Diego Topa Yupangui del Cuzco diez y ocho años—18 Catalina Yache veinte y seis años—26	Pascual Cutigual un año—1	A dos años que le sirve en el beneficio de las chacaras

/f.223/

Lo que le paga de servicio	*Lo que paga de dotrina*	*Lo que paga de tasa*	*Tiene chacaras de tasa*
Quatro topos de chacara	Quatro tomines de dotrina		
Tres topos y medio de chacara	Seis tomines de dotrina		
Tres topos y medio de chacara	Seis tomines de dotrina		
Cinco topos de chacara	Seis tomines de dotrina		
	Quatro tomines de dotrina		
Un topo de chacara			
Un topo de chacara			

/f.223v/

	Casados—años	*Hijos—años*	*Servicio que ha hecho cada yanacona*
	Alonso Quispi Yunga veinte y tres años—23 Catalina Guininchu quince años—15	Felipa Rajo pariona de veinte y cinco años—25 Sobre si se ha de sacar	A quatro años que le sirve en lo que los demas
450	Agustin Ataosuyoquina Quichua veinte y quatro años—24 Madalena Cuyaurma treinta años—30		A diez años que le sirve en el beneficio de las chacaras
	Pedro Paucar Chauca quarenta y seis años—46 Isabel Chacho cincuenta y siete años—17		A quince años que le sirve en lo que los demas
470	Cristobal Guantapi quarenta años—40 Mitima que nacio en este valle	Agustin Guantapi de veinte años—20	
	Pedro Yajarimay setenta años—70 Juan Anguallapi quarenta y siete años—47 Inez Chuquitinta quarenta años—40	Luisa Culpo doce años—12	
	Cristobal Guamancusi nacio en este valle treinta y ocho años—38 Inez Cocaynguilla treinta y seis años—36	Francisca Ynguilla tres años—3 Juan Totocri un año—1 Francisco Aite trece—13 Juan Cayo ocho años—8 Inez Chinbococa—6	A que le sirve veinte años en el beneficio de las chacaras de maiz y coca y serviole leña e yerba
	Cristobal Uscotuma de Andaguayllas nacio en este valle veinte años—20 Isabel Sasa veinte años—20	Francisco Chisque dos años—2	A que le sirve tres años en el beneficio de las chacaras y dalle demas que le manda
	Antonio Guaspar natural de Pasto nacio en este valle treinta años—30 Francisca Pusan veinte y ocho años—28	Juanbautista Guanbo seis años—6	A que le sirve diez y ocho años en lo que los demas

/f.224/

Lo que le paga de servicio	*Lo que paga de dotrina*	*Lo que paga de tasa*	*Tiene chacaras de tasa*
Topo y medio de chacara			
Medio topo de chacara	Quatro tomines de dotrina		
Un topo de chacara	Quatro tomines de dotrina		
Tres cuartos de chacara de que come	Quatro tomines de dotrina	Quatro tomines de tasa	
Dos topos y medio de chacara	Quatro tomines de dotrina		
Topo y medio de chacara	Quatro tomines de dotrina	Seis tomines de tasa	

/f.224v/

	Casados—años	*Hijos—años*	*Servicio que ha checho cada yanacona*
353	Anton Urcoaros de Xaquixaguana nacio en este valle quarenta años—40 Juana Ana quarenta y dos años—42	Francisco Gualcaltanta un año—1 Maria Tantacallai tres años—3	Sirviole quatro años en lo que los demas
De don Alonso Tito Atauche	Alonso Suco del Cuzco nacio en este valle treinta y ocho años—38 Maria Yache treinta años—30	Juan Quispeauro seis años—6 Francisco Maita cinco años—5 Ana Chuquicisa un año—1 Lucas Suco dos años—2 Inez Paico diez años—10	A diez años que le sirve en el beneficio de las chacaras de maiz y en mita de yerba y leña
421 murio	Cristobal Raime Colla treinta y dos años—32 Juana Mullaca veinte y ocho años—28		A diez años que le sirve en lo que los demas
	Hernando Atauca nacio en este valle diez y nueve años—19 Isabel Tuta diez y nueve años—19	Gonzalo Guamantao un año—1	
479	Juanbautista Unayachac Yauyo treinta años—30 Costanza Atacarua treinta y dos años—32	Miguel Chuchoyauri—8 Alonso Runayache cinco—5 Hernando Yaunyanac dos años—2 Maria Misocarua tres años—3	A que le sirve quatro años en el beneficio de las chacaras
	Antonio Pumacondori veinte y dos años—22 Catalina Cusichinbo veinte años—20	Pedro Pumacondori dos años—2	A que sirve seis meses de ortelano
	Cristobal Chuquicondori de Cajatambo nacio en este valle veinte años—20 Maria Yacosuyo diez y nueve años—19		A que sirve seis meses de ortelano
	Cristobal Maitayupangui del Cuzco nacio en este valle veinte y seis años—26 Ana Tococto veinte y quatro años—24	Domingo Quinoyupangui siete años—7 Angelina Yupo cinco años—5	A que le sirve doce años de ortelano

/f.225/

Lo que le paga del servicio	*Lo que paga de dotrina*	*Lo que paga de tasa*	*Tiene chacaras de tasa*
Un topo de chacara	Quatro tomines de dotrina		
Topo y medio de chacara de que come	Medio peso de dotrina		
Un topo de chacara	Medio peso de dotrina		
Un cuarto de topo de chacara	Quatro tomines de dotrina	Dos tomines a don Garcia	
Tres cuartos de chacara			
Tres cuartos de chacara			
Un topo de chacara			

/f.225v/

	Casados—años	Hijos—años	Servicio que ha hecho cada yanacona
	Lorenzo Quispeguaman nacio en este valle veinte años—20 Lucia Toto diez y ocho años—18	Beatriz Cancharma dos años—2	A que le sirve siete años en las chacaras
De don Alonso Tito Atauche	Domingo Apasa Colla treinta y seis años—36 Angelina Cocaquipi treinta años—30		A que le sirve quince años
469	Gonzalo Suyocache Guanca quarenta años—4		A mas de quin [*sic*] años que le sirve
	Pedro Lauazaca Cañar treinta años—30 Maria Suchu veinte y seis años—26	Isabel Racaichuco un año—1	A mas de quince años que le sirve
	Pedro Quispil treinta y tres años—36 Inez Aclla quarenta y seis años—46	Juan Ramos	Sirve en lo que le manda
	Lorenzo Quispe nacio en este valle veinte años—20 Juana Cicoacllo veinte y seis años—26	Juana Asiuichinbo un año—1 Lucas Chauamai cinco—5 Angelina Ynco tres—3 Isabel Pauco dos años—2	A que le sirve diez años en lo que los demas
431	Pedro Canca Quichua cincuenta y quatro años—54 Isabel Yache cincuenta y quatro años—54	Ana Yuco diez y siete años—17	A que le sirve en el beneficio de sus chacaras diez años
	Felipe Yupangui del Cuzco cincuenta y quatro años—54 Leonor Guarcai quarenta años—40	Alonso Yupangui nueve años—9 Francisca Tocto Ocllo ocho años—8	No sirve a nadie

/f.226/

Lo que le paga de servicio	Lo que paga de dotrina	Lo que paga de dotrina	Tiene chacaras de tasa
Un cuarto de topo de chacara			
Un topo de chacara	Quatro tomines de dotrina	Media fanega de maiz	Topo y medio de chacara
Medio topo de chacara			
	Seis tomines de dotrina		Dos topos de las chacaras de la comunidad

/f.226v/

	Casados—años	*Hijos—años*	*Servicio que ha hecho cada yanacona*
	Ambrosio Pillaca de Guaro veinte años—20 Costanza Ciza Ocllo de veinte años—20	Ana Chuco Ocllo de un año—1	Sirve en lo que le manda
	Hernando Gualparimache diez y seis años—16 Isabel Ciza veinte y cinco años—25	Juana Cichuc de un año—1	A que le sirve quatro años en lo que los demas
	Juan Tupa Yupangui del Cuzco veinte y ocho años—28 Madalena Ciza veinte y nueve años—29		A que sirve tres años en el beneficio de las chacaras y dalle leña
	Martin Ataocusi de Xaquixaguana quarenta y dos años—42 Costanza Chinbocalis veinte y nueve años—29		A que sirve diez años en lo que los demas
	Diego Picaña de Pasto diez y ocho años—18 Ana Chinbococa diez y seis años—16		A quatro años que sirve a sus hijas de Gualpa Roca
	Don Carlos Gualparo nacio en este valle treinta y cinco años—35 Catalina Ciza Ocllo treinta y dos años—32		
huerfanos	Martin Gualpa Roca quince años—15	Juana Pata diez y ocho años—18	
De doña Ana Quispe	Cristobal Yachimarca Ynnga veinte y seis años—26 Inez Cullapullo veinte y quatro—24		A que le sirve diez y ocho años en beneficialle las chacaras y dalle leña

/f.227/

Lo que le paga de servicio	*Lo que paga de dotrina*	*Lo que paga de tasa*	*Tiene chacaras de tasa*
Medio topo de chacara	Seis tomines de dotrina		
			Un cuarto de topo de chacara
Tres cuartos de chacara	Seis tomines de dotrina		
Tres cuartos de topo	Seis tomines de dotrina		
Medio topo de chacara	Seis tomines de dotrina		

/f.227v/

	Casados—años	*Hijos—años*	*Servicio que ha hecho cada yanacona*
	Pedro Uilcovina Ynca cincuenta años—50 Inez Carua quarenta años—40	Leonor Callas simple de cinco años—5	A que le sirve treinta años en lo que los demas
	don Alonso Tupacusi Gualpa Ynga veinte y cinco años—25 Leonor Totociza veinte y dos años—22	Madalena Sarpai dos años—2 Juana Quispeciza un año—1	
	Martin Limache de Xapie veinte y tres años—23 Francisca Caua diez y nueve años—19	Alonso Rimache cinco años—5 Juan Yanguigualpa dos—2 Maria Urmacoca uno—1	A que sirve al suso dicho diez años en beneficiarles las chacaras y darles leña
499	Felipe Manchapa de Guayocondo treinta años—30 Maria Guallima veinte y nueve años—29	Beatriz Cussi un año—1	
	Alonso Pariangocayanbi veinte y ocho años—28 Leonor Cucha veinte y cinco años—25		A que le sirve quince años en beneficialle las chacaras y dalle leña
	Alonso Sosapo veinte y ocho años—28 Catalina Chimbo veinte años—20	Juan Bilcachamo dos años—2	
	Agustin Partia veinte años—20 Isabel Chulo veinte años—20		A diez años que sirve en beneficio de las chacaras
Yanaconas de Diego de Mercado	Martin Pichuna de Quito treinta años—30 Catalina Yapoyachi treinta años—30	Luisa Chuma quatro años—4 Ana Caima trea años—3	A que le sirve seis años en beneficialle las chacaras de maiz y coca

/f.228/

Lo que la paga de servicio	*Lo que paga de la dotrina*	*Lo que paga de tasa*	*Tiene chacaras de tasa*
Medio topo de chacara	Seis tomines de dotrina		
Tiene nueve topos de chacaras suios y setenta pies de arboleda	Seis tomines de dotrina		
	Seis tomines de dotrina	Media fanega de maiz de tasa cada año	
Tres cuartos de chacara	Quatro tomines de dotrina	Una cuartilla de maiz	
Medio de chacara de que come	Quatro tomines de dotrina	Una cuartilla de amiz	
Un topo de chacara			

/f.228v/

	Casados—años	Hijos—años	Servicio que ha hecho cada yanacona
	Juan Guamancusi de Tambococha veinte y ocho años—28 Costanza Coca veinte y seis años—26	Marcos Cusipuma seis años—6 Lucia Cocatazun quatro años—4 Juan Cusiguaman uno—1	A que sirve quatro? Años en darles leña alejo y en lo demas que le manda
	Diego Llamaoca Conde quarenta y siete años—47 Juana Chuimacin quarenta y cinco años—45	Agustin Arom diez y ocho años—18	A que le sirve cinco años en el beneficio de chacaras y dalle leña
	Sebastian Sulca Guanca quarenta y siete años—47 Ana Chunbi cincuenta años—50	Catalina Culpo diez y siete años—17	A que sirve veinte y cinco años en lo que los demas
	Francisco Acu nacio en este valle diez y seis años—16 Madalena Yuyo veinte años—20		A que le sirve tres años en lo que los demas
	Lucas Remasca nacio en este valle veinte y quatro años—24 Catalina Cocachinbo treinta años—30	Gonzalo Astoananca quatro años—4 Martin Mutima tres años—3 Juan Aucanco dos años—2 Inez Poco uno—1	
525	Pedro Llachua chanca de cincuenta años—50 Catalina Puco cincuenta y cinco años—55	Leonor Cunia nueve años—9 Arcospuntaulla ocho años—8	A que le sirve siete años en el beneficio de las chacaras y dalle leña
	Pedro Quispe nacio en este valle veinte años—20 Leonor Paicochinbo veinte y dos años—22	Catalina Yapuma tres años—3 Juana Cota dos años—2	A que le sirve un año en beneficialle las chacaras
526	Diego Cota nacio en este valle de quarenta y nueve años—49 No tiene mujer	Francisco Tarisca doce años—12	A que le sirve treinta años en lo que los demas

/f.229/

Lo que le paga de servicio	Lo que le paga de dotrina	Lo que paga de tasa	Tiene chacaras de tasa
Un cuarto de topo de chacara	Seis tomines de dotrina		
Medio topo de chacara	Seis tomines de dotrina		
Un topo y un cuarto de chacara	Quatro tomines de dotrina		
Un topo y un cuarto de chacara			
Un topo de chacara	Quatro tomines de dotrina		
Un topo de chacara	Quatro tomines de dotrina		

/f.229v/

	Casados—años	*Hijos—años*	*Servicio qu ha hecho cada yanacona*
De don Cristobal Vilca Topa	Pedro Condurimayan cincuenta años—50 Francisca Yache cincuenta y tres años—53	Maria Cocachinbo veinte años—20 Isabel Chapo diez—10 Cristobal Cusicondur ocho—8 Catalina Quillai seis años—6 Beatriz Coca quatro—4 Petronilla Cusichinbo uno—1	A que sirve veinte años en el beneficio de las chacaras
De Marcos Puri	Marcos Puri de Moyobamba sesenta años—60 Catalina Ciza Ocllo quarenta y ocho años—48	A Catalina Acrai diez y nueve años—19 Isabel Paico diez y siete años—17	
	Francisco Chuquna nacio en este valle treinta años—30 Isabel Chinbo treinta años—30		A que le sirve veinte años en lo que los demas
	Martin Cuzupaucar treinta y ocho años—38 Isabel Paico quarenta años—40	Diego Gualpa siete años—7 Tomas Cusigualpa cinco años—5	A que le sirve cinco años en el beneficio de las chacaras y servicio de leña
138	Juan Ynga Paucar nacio en este valle quince años—15 Juana Urmas quince años—15		A que le sirve dos años en el beneficio de las chacaras
543	Pedro Churucana treinta y seis años—36 Inez Cica Ocllo veinte y ocho años—28	Cristobal Quica siete años—7 Ana Quinbo tres años—3	
489 de don Francisco Cayo Topa	Martin Rimache Yupangui de Potosi diez y siete años—17 Catalina Cassa diez y seis años—16		A que le sirve nueve años en beneficio de las chacaras y servicio de leña
	Domingo Topacusi Gualpa nacio en este valle veinte y ocho años—28 Isabel Paicocaca veinte y siete años—27	Ana Chinboquipi cinco años—5 Maria Cusirimai tres años—3 Juana Guaro Ocllo un año—1	

/f.230/

Lo que le paga de servicio	*Lo que paga de dotrina*	*Lo que paga de tasa*	*Tiene chcacaras de tasa*
Medio topo de chacara	Seis tomines de dotrina		
Tiene tres topos y medio de chacara suyos y docientos pies de arboleda			
	Seis tomines de dotrina		
	Quatro tomines de dotrina		
Topo y medio de chacara			

/f.230v/

	Casados—años	*Hijos—años*	*Servicio que ha hecho cada yanacona*
	Francisco Guartanaula Cañar nacio en este valle diez y nueve años—19 Catalina Ciuichuc veinte años—20		
	Fabian Cuchillo Cañar cincuenta y nueve años—59 Juana Utra treinta y ocho años—38	Francisca Yngaitoco doce—12 Maria Quischu nueve—9 Alonso Canuispuclla cinco—5 Cristobal Marcaspulla dos—2	
429 de don Felipe Topa	Diego Machacaua Colla veinte años—20 Madalena Quillaichinbo veinte años—20	Juan Machao un año—1 Catalina Chinbo Ocllo quatro años—4	A diez años que le sirve en beneficio de las chacaras
	Diego Gualpa Cunsa de Acos veinte y tres años—23 Madalena Coca veinte y ocho años—28	Maria Tinta un año—1	A que le sirve tres meses
De don Francisco Pacanaula 506	Martin Guartapulla Cañar cincuenta años—50 Madalena Sirita cincuenta años—50	Francisca Mischo de diez y seis años—16	A que le sirve en el beneficio de las chacaras treinta años y de darles leña
549	Pedro Viera de Chinchaysuyu nacio en este valle veinte y siete años—27 Francisca Panpasuna veinte y cinco años—25		A seis años que le sirve de ortela y labrador
	Juan Yaris Guanca nacio en este valle quarenta años—40 Leonor Uccic treinta años—30	Juan Murmu quince—15 Pedro Yarinlloylla seis—6 Lucas Punallulla cinco—5 Martin Yarolloc tres años—3 Isabel Pachua uno—1	A siete años que le sirve de ortelana y labrador
De don Luis Quisana	Felipe Pullaciala Cañar treinta y siete años—37		A que le sirve veinte años en el beneficio de las chacaras

/f.231/

Lo que le paga de servicio	*Lo que paga de dotrina*	*Lo que paga de tasa*	*Tiene chacaras de tasa*
Come dos topos y medio			
Un topo de chacara			
Medio topo de chacara	Quatro tomines de dotrina		
Medio topo de chacara			
Un topo de chacara	Seis tomines de dotrina		
Un topo de chacara			
	Quatro tomines de dotrina		Medio topo de chacara

/f.231v/

	Casados—años	*Hijos—años*	*Servicio que ha hecho cada yanacona*
	Gonzalo Tangoraua yunga cincuenta años—50 Isabel Lilzo sesenta años—60		A que le sirve quince años en el beneficio de las chacaras
560	Hernando Villi Colla nacio en este valle treinta y ocho años—38 Francisca Pocotiquilla quarenta y ocho años—48		A que sirve veinte años en el beneficio de las chacaras
554	Marcos Chilqui Yupangui de Cuzco treinta años—30 Luisa Chinbo treinta y dos años—32	Martin Topa doce años—12 Juan Muyun quatro—4 Diego Mayuntopa tres—3 Inez Ciza ocho—8	A que le sirve siete años que sirve en lo que los demas
	Agustin Paca nacio en este valle cincuenta y seis años—56 Juana Payco Ocllo cincuenta y ocho años—58		A que le sirve veinte años en el beneficio de las chacaras
532	Martin Luai de Atavillo treinta años—30 Juana Ypanpra quarenta y cinco años—45		A que le sirve diez y ocho años en el beneficio de las chacaras
	Juan Carnalaura de diez y ocho años es Guanca—18 Catalina Caxa veinte años—20	Juana Yaurichinbo dos años—2	A cinco años que le sirve
	Los indios huerfanos que hay en esta visita de los con— Martin Garcia de Loyola diciendo ser—		
 311 329	Benito Llachua— Pedro Paucarllo Colla— Martin Supaico— Juan Casanaula—	Felipe Condor—338 Martin Tito Gualpa 345 364 Juan Caruaguaman Pablo Pomacondur 372	Cristobal Cuyatopa—391 Alonso Aruco—409 Benito Guaman—438 Domingo Turos—446

/f.232/

Lo que le paga de servicio	*Lo que paga de dotrina*	*Lo que paga de tasa*	*Tiene chacaras de tasa*
Medio topo de chacara		Quatro tomines de tasa Media fanega de maiz	
Medio topo de chacara			
Medio topo de chacara			
Un topo de chacara			
Un cuarto de topo de chacara			
tenidos en el memorial que se dieron al dicho capitan de su encomienda son los siguiente			
Alonso Xulca 236 Pedro Maiuasca Alonso Guanasca Alonso Aucatoma	455 456 Juan Gualza— Diego Calam— Alonso Cusirimache +464+	Francisco Chiguan 478 Martin Gualparoca— 400	Francisco Guaipa Cristobal Parinanco— 502

/f.230v/ En los demas yndios que faltan del memorial contenido en la ynformacion que sobre los yanaconas se hizo no se hallaron en la bisita de los dhos yndios yanaconas. Pedro Diaz Valdeon escrivano—

En la ciudad del Cuzco a honze dias del mes de enero de mil e qui^{o}s e setenta e quatro años ante el YIl^{e} Señor Dotor Graviel de Loarte corregidor e justicia mayor en esta ciudad por su magestad e por ante mi el escrv^{o} ynfraescripto el capitan Martin Garcia de Loyola como conjunta persona de doña Beatriz Coya su mujer pres^{to} el escripto siguiente.

v YIl^{e} señor Martin Garcia de Oñaz y Loyola por mi y como conjunta persona de doña Beatriz Coya cuyo son los y^{o}s del valle de Yucay digo que a mi noticia es venido que en la bisita que hizo del dho valle por mandado de su Exª el liçenciado frei Pero Gutierrez visito por yanaconas ciertos y^{o}s contenidos en la dha visita que eran hasta trescientos y treinta poco mas o menos e por dezir que heran y^{o}s que nunca avian tributado su Exª del señor bisorrey los puso en cabeça de su magestad y los taso y mando pagasen sus tributos a la caxa real desta ciudad en lo qual yo y la dha mi mujer emos sido notoriamente agraviados porque los dhos y^{o}s no son de los que su magestad manda se pongan en su cabeça porque todos ellos son y an sido siempre y^{o}s tributarios y subje- //
/f.231/ tos a los caciques principales del dho repartimiento y siempre an servido y tributado y acudido a las cosas de la comunidad como los demas y^{o}s tributarios del dho valle y siendo como son mios y de la dha mi mujer los y^{o}s del dho valle de Yucay no se pudo proveer lo que se proveyo en la dha visita ni ponerse en cabeza de su magestad los dhos y^{o}s y en se aver fecho nosotros fuimos agraviados y agora que viene a mi noticia parezco ante V.M. como Justicia mayor desta ciudad y como persona que tiene provision general su Ex^{a} pa definir y acabar y que se prosigan ante V.M. todos los negocios tocantes a las visitas deste distrito y por haber ya acabado su of^{o} el dho licenciado frei Pedro Gutierrez ante V.M. salvo el dr^{o} de la nulidad apelo con acatamiento devido de todo lo fecho y autuado por el dho licenciado frei Pedro Gutierrez la dha visita en mi perjui^{o} y de la dha mi mujer y de se aver puesto los dhos yndios en cabeça de su mag^{t} para ante la real audiencia de la ciudad de los Reies haga ante quien e con dr^{o} deva y pida e me otorgue esta mi apelacion ynformacion y testimonio y lo neces^{o}. etc. Martin Garcia de Loyola. El Licenciado Pedraça.

v El Señor Dotor dixo que lo oyo. Pedro Diaz Valdeon escrivano.

v En la ciudad del Cuzco a onze dias del del [*sic*] mes de henero de mil e qui^{o}s y setenta y quatro años ante el Señor Doctor la pres^{to} el contenido:

/f.231v/ v yIl^{e} Señor Martin Garcia de Loyola por mi y en nombre y como marido y conjunta persona de doña Beatriz Coya me pres^{to} ante Vra Al^{a} en grado de apelacion nulidad e agravio como en la mejor via e forma que de dr^{o} aya lugar de ciertos autos en mi perjui^{o} de la dha mi mujer fechos por el licenciado frei P^{o} Gutierrez en la visita que hizo en el valle de Yucai jur^{on} de la ciudad del Cuzco en que visito ciertos y^{o}s mios e de la dha mi mujer y de cierto proveimiento en prosecucion de lo fecho por don Fran^{co} de Toledo vro visorrey en que en efeto puso los dhos y^{o}s en vra Corona Real y los taso e mando acudir con los tribu^{o}s a vra Caxa Real de la dha ciudad del Cuzco.

v A Vra Alteza pido y suplico me aya por pres^{do} en el dho grado y protesto espresar mis agravios contra los dhos autos y proveimientos conforme a vra real ordenança y pa ello es. Martin Garcia de Loyola. El Llic^{do} Pedraça.

v El Señor Dotor lo uvo por presentado en el dho grado de apelacion en quanto a lugar de dr^{o}. Pero Diaz Valdeon escriv^{o}.

v En el Cuzco a onze dias del mes de henero de mill e qui^{o}s y setenta e quatro años ante el Señor Dotor la pres^{to} el cont^{do}:

v Muy poderoso señor Martin Garcia de Oñaz y Loyola por mi y en nombre y como conjunta persona de doña Beatriz Coya espresando agravios de ciertos autos fechos por el licenciado frei P^{o} Gutierrez en la visita que hizo del valle de Yucai en que en efeto bisito por yanaconas ciertos y^{o}s //
/f.232/ contenidos en la dha visita siendo como heran y^{o}s tributarios propios mios y de la dha mi mujer y de cierto proveymi^{to} fecho por don Fran^{co} de Toledo vro visorrey en que en ef^{to} puso en vra corona real los dhos y^{o}s digo que Vra Al^{a} deve emendar y revocar los dhos autos y proveimi^{to} y declarar ser propios mios y de la dha mi mujer y nos pertenecer los dhos y^{o}s por lo general que aqui se suele dezir y alegar e porque de todos los y^{o}s del dho valle de Yucay le fue fecha merzed por el marques de Cañete visorrey que fue destos reinos a don Diego Saire Topa Ynga como por el titulo dello parece al qual subcedio la dha doña Beatriz mi mujer como su hija ligitima y universal heredera y ansi todos los yndios del dho valle pertenecen a la dha mi mujer y a mi en su nombre y todos los y^{o}s que por el dho licenciado frei P^{o} Gutierrez fueron visitados por yanaconas eran y^{o}s tributarios y lo an sido siempre y an servido y tributado a los encomenderos que an sido del dho valle de Yucay como fue el marques don Fran^{co} Piçarro que luego que entro en esta tierra a la Conquista y pacificacion della tomo pa su servicio los y^{o}s del dho valle de Yucay y le sirvieron siempre con el servi^{o} personal que en aquel tiempo acostumbrava a dar por no aver otra cosa y le davan siempre camarico de maiz y otras cosas y le beneficiavan sus chacaras ansi las de coca que tenian en los Andes como las de maiz que tenia en esta ciudad del Cuzco y valle de Yucai y despues desto los y^{o}s del dho valle de Yucai fueron encomendados en don Fran^{co} Piçarro hijo del dho marques al qual ansimismo sirvieron todos //
/f.232v/ los dhos yndios que agora se dizen yanaconas y sus antepasados y le acudieron siempre con el mismo servi^{o} personal e benef^{o} de chacaras camarico y demas cosas que acostumbraban dar al dho su padre e despues desto tuvieron a su cargo los y^{o}s del dho valle de Yucay los oficiales reales de la dha ciudad del Cuzco por estar bacos por ausencia del dho don Fran^{co} Piçarro que fue a Castilla y murio en ellas y los dhos oficiales reales cobraron siempre de los dhos y^{o}s que se dizen yanaconas el mismo servi^{o} y tributo y lo mismo hizo el dho don Diego Saire Topa Ynga a quien fue fecha md dellos por el dho marques de Cañete bisorrey que fue destos reinos y siempre los dhos y^{o}s

estuvieron subjetos a los caciques principales del dho valle de Yucai y acudian siempre a las cosas de la comunidad y demas servi^{o}s que hazian los demas y^{o}s tributarios del dho valle y ansi no se pudieron poner en cabeça de su magestad los dhos y^{o}s pues no son estos los de que habla la cedula real ni la instruccion del dho vro bisorrey la qual claramente habla en los y^{o}s antiguos que no an estado ni estan subjetos a caciques lo qual no ay en los dhos y^{o}s que se bisitaron por yanaconas en el dho valle de Yucai pues como tengo dho siempre an tributado y servido y acudido a las cosas de la comunidad con los demas y^{o}s tributarios y an estado subjetos a sus caciques y no importa en nombre que dizen tener los dhos y^{o}s de yanaconas porque no se ha de mirar al nombre sino al eff^{to} y a lo dispuesto por la dha vra cedula real instruccion del dho vro bisorrey y en el tpo de los Yngas señores que fueron destos reinos todos los yndios del dho valle //
/f.233/ de Yucay heran yanaconas y servian al Ynga y a sus mujeres hijos e parientes en les beneficiar sus chacaras y en otros servicios y cosas que le mandavan y no por eso se ponen todos los y^{o}s del dho valle en la corona real porque como tengo dho siempre an estado subjetos a caciques y ansi siempre an sido encomendados por los governadores destos reinos y el mismo derecho ay en los y^{o}s que agora se an visitado por yanaconas los quales si alguna vez an dexado de tributar ha sido por culpa de los dhos caciques que disimulaban con ellos y los sacaban del servi^{o} del encomendero pa servirse dellos y el dho servicio cargaban en los yndios pobres del dho valle lo qual no ha de parar perjui^{o} a mi ni a la dha mi mujer pues como tengo dho los dhos y^{o}s nunca an estado fuera de la subjecion de los caciques ni dexado de servir ni tributar lo qual claramente consta por la misma visita que el dho lic^{do} frei P^{o} Gutierrez hizo por la qual se aberiguo que los dhos yndios cada uno dellos pagava la parte que se les repartia pa el tributo por los dhos caciques y ansi injustamente los dhos yndios se me quitavan pues consta ser propios mios y de la dha mi mujer y el mismo dr^{o} ai en los y^{o}s que se pusieron en cabeça de su m^{t} por yanaconas que eran los que servian a don Alonso Tito Atauche los quales ansimismo fueron yndios tributarios juntamente con el dho don Alonso subjetos a los caciques principales del dho valle y ansimismo me an de ser adjudicados a mi y a la dha mi mujer como los demas y si al tiempo que se hizo la visita //
/f.233v/ del dho valle se dejo de alegar y contradezir lo susodho fue por ser la dha mi mujer menor de hedad y estar debaxo de la curadoria de Tito Cusi Yupangui questava rebelado contra el servicio de Dios e de su m^{t} y Tilano de Anaya que tenia su poder y entendia el benef^{o} de las haziendas de la dha doña Beatriz por mandado de vro bisorrey y en aquel tiempo entro en la provincia de Bilcabamba a traer de paz al dho Tito Cusi donde el dho Tilano de Anaya murio y ansi la dha doña Beatriz mi mujer quedo indefensa sin tener quien volviese por ella ni hiziese sus negocios y ansi todo lo hecho y actuado contra ella en la dha visita es ninguno y por tal pido se declare y en caso que alguno sea por ser la dha doña Beatriz menor y aver sido lega y danificado en ello le conpete benef^{o} de restitucion pa que todo ello sea puesto en el punto y estado que estava antes y al tiempo que se hiciese la dha visita la qual restitucion pido en la mejor forma y via que de dr^{o} aya lugar y si alguna negligencia o descuydo a vido en los curadores de la dha doña Beatriz por no hazer que tributasen todos los dhos y^{o}s que agora se dizen yanaconas en caso que sean nesçesario pido ansimesmo la dha restitucion yn yntregun

v A Vra Al^{a} pido y sup^{co} de por ning^{o} todo lo fecho y actuado por el dho frei P^{o} Gutierrez en la dha visita y lo reboque juntamente con el proveymi^{to} del dho vro visorrey en que puso en vra corona real los dhos y^{o}s declarando ser propios mios y de la dha mi mujer y pertenezernos todos ellos y no ampare en la //
/f.234/ posesion dellos y en caso que sea necesario me conçeda la dha restitucion en n^{e} de la dha mi mujer en la mejor via forma que de dr^{o} aya lugar sobre que pido justicia y costas para lo necesario es y pido sea relevado a prueva. Martin Garcia de Loyola. El liçenciado Pedraza.

v Y los yndios yanaconas que se bisitaron en el dho valle de Yucai asi los aqui cont^{dos} como los demas que en el se hallaron su Ex^{a} los taso pa que pagasen tributo a su magestad por la forma y orden que se declara en la tasa que dellos hizo que es la que se sigue.

Don Francisco de Toledo mayordomo de su magestad su visorrey y governador y capitan general destos reinos e provincias del Peru y tierra firme y presidente de la real audiencia y chancilleria que reside en la ciudad de los Reies etc. A vos los caciques principales que sois o fueredes del pueblo de San Benito de Alcantara y del pueblo de Santiago de Oropesa y del pueblo de San Bernardo que agora nuevam^{te} se an señalado y reducido por el liçenciado frei P^{o} Gutierrez del abito de Alcantara y visitador general por mi nombrado en el valle de Yucai e a los caciques de pachacas principales e y^{o}s de los dhos pueblos a quien lo quede y uso en esta mi provi^{on} sera contenido toca y atañe y a guardar y cumplir y a cada uno y qualesquier de vos save que aviendo bisto la visita numeracion y averiguacion de los y^{o}s quel dho visitador allo en el dho valle de Yucay que no estavan encomendados a ningun encomendero ni an pagado ni pagan tributo parece por //
/f.234v/ la dha visita y fee que della se dio que los dhos y^{o}s que no pagaban tributo ni estavan encomendados hallo y redujo en el dho pueblo de San Benito de Alcantara setenta e cinco yndios casados de hedad de diez y ocho años hasta cinquenta y ocho yndios solteros de los dhos de los dhos [*sic*] diez y ocho hasta cinq^{ta} años y en el pueblo de Santiago de Oropesa ciento y sesenta y ocho y^{o}s casados de diez y ocho hasta cinq^{ta} años y catorce y^{o}s solteros de las dhas hedades y en el dho pueblo de San Bernardo ciento y treinta y seis yndios casados de la dha hedad de diez y ocho hasta cinq^{ta} años y ocho y^{o}s solteros de las dhas hedades y en el pueblo de San Francisco de Maras poblo y reduxo otros nueve y^{o}s de las dhas hedades los quales dexo subjetos a vos el dho cacique principal del pueblo de San Bernardo que son por todos los dhos y^{o}s que ansi se reduxeron a los dhos pueblos por la forma y orden y dha es quatrocientos y diez y ocho y^{o}s tributarios de los que como esta dho no estavan encomendados ni pagavan tributo y aviendo visto ansimismo el parecer que el dho visitador dio de los tribu^{o}s que debriades y podriades [*sic*] pagar a su m^{t} en cada un año en cuya cabeça y corona por un auto mio esta ympuestos y por la presente os pongo siendo nezes^{o} aplicando como aplico los tributos provision y bastim^{to} del castellano y personas que an de quedar en esta ciudad y asistir en la fortaleça della para que mejor pa que mejor [*sic*] se pueda conservar y sustentar en el servicio de su magestad segun que de yuso yra declarado e ynformandome de personas celosas de vro bien y teniendo consideracion a que nuevamente se bos manda pagar este tributo y //
/f.235/ a los gastos y trabajos que abeis tenido en la reduçion de los dhos pueblos ydeficios de la yglesia me apareceis de proveer y mandar como por la pres^{te} proveo y mando que desde el dia que os fuere noteficado esta mi provision en adelante pagueis vos el dho cacique y los dhos

vros pachacas principales e y^{o}s de los dhos pueblos que como dho es no estan encomendados a persona alguna ni aveis pagado tributo hasta agora en cada un año de seis y seis meses la mitad a su m^{t} y a sus oficiales reales que residen en la ciudad del Cuzco pa los efetos susodhos en que por la pres^{te} aplico los tribu^{o}s que aveis de pagar mil e docientos y cinq^{ta} y quatro pesos de plata ensayada e marcada de valor cada uno de quatrocientos y cinq^{ta} maravedis que sale razonado por cabezas cada yndio tributario de la dha hedad de los dhos quatrocientos y diez y ocho y^{o}s que ansi quedan reducidos y poblados en los dhos pueblos a tres pesos de p^{ta} ensayada y marcada aunque respeto de lo que pagan los demas yndios a sus encomenderos y de los ressates oficios y aprovechamientos que por estar tan cerca de la ciudad del Cuzco teneis y de benef^{o} quede yncorporaros en la corona real se echase podriades pagar mucho mas los quales dhos tribu^{o}s vos los dhos caciques aveis de cobrar cada uno por lo que le toca de repartiendolo ygualm^{te} e sin agravio de ning^{o} de los dhos y^{o}s y pagarlo a los dhos oficiales reales para los dhos efetos a los plazos susodhos en la forma y orden siguiente:

/f.235v/ Doscientos hanegas de trigo puestas en la dha ciudad del Cuzco en poder de los dhos oficiales reales y tasadas y moderadas a dos p^{o}s de p^{ta} corriente que es el precio a que comun/men/te valen en la dha ciudad suman y montan quatrocientos pesos de /al margen: II cientos pesos/ p^{ta} corriente y entre tanto que no tuvieren tierras pa dar el dho trigo la paguen en plata al dho precio pa que los dhos oficiales reales les compren de harina para la dha fortaleça y no se pueda gastar en otra cosa.

v Doscientos hanegas de maiz puestas ansimismo en la dha ciudad del Cuzco en poder de los dhos oficiales reales que tasados y moderados a los dhos dos p^{o}s de p^{ta} corriente cada una ques al precio a que comunmente valen en esta dha ciudad montan otros /al margen II cientos pesos/ quatrocientos p^{o}s de p^{ta} corriente.

v Quatrocientas cargas de leña del topo de la ciudad del Cuzco que tasados y moderados a tomin cada una ques el precio a que comunmente balen montan cinquenta /al margen: II Lv/ y seis p^{o}s y dos tomines de plata corriente.

v Que todo lo suso dho suma /al margen: VDciilvip^{o}sv/ y monta ochocientos y cinquenta y seis p^{o}s y dos tomines de la dha plata corriente.

v Y lo demas restante pagado todo lo susodho en el dho trigo maiz y leña a cumplimien- //
/f.236/ to de los dhos mil e doscientos e cinquenta y quatro pesos de la dha plata ensaiada e marcada lo aveys de dar y pagar a los dhos oficiales reales en la dha plata ensayada so pena de privacion de vros cacicazgos si ansi no lo hicieredes y cumplieredes y cobrado y repartiendo a los y^{o}s mas tribu^{o}s de los que conforme a lo que dho es les cupiere y siendo nos o qualquier de nos negligente en la cobrança y pago de los dhos tributos a los plazos se ponia en vro lugar otro cacique que mejor lo cobre y haga conforme a lo que dexo ordenado a los dhos oficiales reales en la ynstruccion que les mande dar y an de ser ansimesmo a vro cargo tener quenta que no se derramen los dhos y^{o}s de los pueblos por que aunque alegueis que se os ayan ydo y muerto no se os aya de recevir descuento alguno pues en lugar de los que se mueren yran entrando otros en la dha hedad de diez y ocho a^{o}s y pagaran tasa que agora son menores y no se les reparte tribu^{o} y de los que en adelante fueren naciendo ni tampoco se vos ha de pedir mas tribu^{o} de lo que aqui se os manda pagar a que de los dhos y^{o}s menores de los diez y ocho años baian entrando en edad de tributar mas de los fueren saliendo y tampoco por razon de los ausentes se os a de descontar nada pues esta a vro cargo el recoxerlos y conservarlos por la obligacion de vros oficios y porque la conciencia de su m^{t} se descargue de la obligacion que tiene de daros dotrina //
/f.236v/ mando a los dhos oficiales reales que de los dhos tributos que asi aveis de dar y pagar en plata en cada un año den y paguen por los tercios del como fueren cobrando de vosotros al sacerdote o sacerdotes que estan presentados o adelante se presentaren a los cargos y dotrinas de los dhos pueblos para que os administren los sacramentos de la santa yglesia y enseñe y dotrine en las cosas de nra santa fee catolica el salario que rata por cantidad cupiere y se deviere pagar por razon de los dhos quatrocientos y diez y ocho yndios del salario questuviere señalado o señalare en las dotrinas de los dhos pueblos y porque mejor se puedan cobrar los dhos tribu^{o}s y conservar y recoxer los y^{o}s en los dhos pueblos mando al dho visitador os entreguen a vos los dhos caciques principales un treslado autentico de la numeracion de todos los y^{o}s que de los dhos pueblos se hiciere ansi varones como hembras por sus ayllos y cacicazgos y principales y mando al corregidor y alc/al/des ordinarios y otras justicias qualesquier de la dha ciudad del Cuzco y de otras qualesquier villas y lugares destos reinos ante quien pidieredes cumplimi^{to} de justicia que os entreguen y hagan dar y restituir los y^{o}s contenidos en la dha numeracion y los hijos y nietos que adelante tuvieren que se ausentaren y ovieren ausentado de los dhos pueblos haziendo os acudir con los tribu^{o}s que por esta tasa se mandan pagar a cada yndio //
/f.237/ del tiempo que huvieren estado ausentes y los unos ni los otros no deseeis ni deseen de lo ansi cumplir y hazer so las dhas penas puestas a vos los dhos caciques principales y de cada mill pesos de oro para la camara de su majestad. Fecha en la ciudad del Cuzco a veinte dias del mes de setiembre de myll e qui^{o}s y setenta y dos años. don Francisco de Toledo por mandado de su Exª Albaro Ruiz de Navamuel.

En la ciudad del Cuzco a veinte y siete dias del mes de setiembre de mill e qui^{o}s e setenta e dos años yo el dho secretario notefique esta tasa y provision de su Exª a Miguel Sanchez contador de la real hazienda desta ciudad y al fator Juan Perez de Prado en sus personas y dello doy fee. t^{gos} Felipe de Leon y Ger^{mo} Diez y lo firmaron Miguel Sanchez Juan Perez de Prado. Alvaro Ruiz de Navamuel.

En la ciudad del Cuzco a treinta dias del mes de setiembre de mill e qui^{o}s e set^{a} e dos años por ynterpretacion de Mateo Hernandez yo el escrivano publico notefique esta tasa y comutacion a don Ju^{o} Xiranbo cacique principal de los yanaconas e y^{o}s en esta tasa contenidos y a Pedro Guayan Condor y a don Juan Palana caciques de los pachacas. T^{gos} Marcos Mellado y P^{o} de Ribera y ansimismo notifique esta tasa a otros y^{o}s de los en esta tasa contenidos que vinieron con los dhos caciques. t^{gos} los dhos Sebastian de Musica escrv^{o} pu^{co} Miguel Sanchez Juan Perez de Prado.

Y en capitulo de la ynstruccion que su Exª dio para sitar los yºs yanaconas sacado de la instruccion de su Exª es el que se sigue

/f.237v/ v Yten porque por una cedula de su m^{t} esta proveydo que los yºs yanaconas antiguos que no estan subjetos a caciques no tributen a encomenderos ni personas particulares y questos se reduzgan a pueblos y si ubieren de tributar sea solo a su m^{t} os informareis que yanaconas ay en vro distrito y si fueren numero bastante pa reducirlos a puºs lo hareis y sino reducirlos a los demas pueblos de yºs y traireis relacion particular dellos pa que bista se provea lo que convenga y conforme al dho capitulo fueron visitados los dhos yanaconas de que yo el presento escrivº doy fe. Pero Diaz Valdeon escrivº.

v Y por el Señor Dotor visto lo susodho remitio este negocio a la real audiencia de los Reies y el pa que en ella los señores presidente e oydores della provean lo que fueren servidos y lo firmo el Dotor Loarte ante mi Pero Diaz Valdeon escrivº. va entre renglones que diz/ de/visto/ y e m^{do} /ta/bala y testado o/x/lo que/qua/g g d d no vala. Yo Pero Diaz Valdeon escrivº de su magestad publico y del numero de la dha ciudad del Cuzco fui presente a lo suso dho e fize escrevir segun que ante mi paso en fee de lo qual fize aqui mi signo en testimº de verdad. Pero Diaz Valdeon escrivº.

v En la ciudad de los Reies en tres dias del mes de agosto de mil e quiºs y setenta y seis años los señores presidente y oydores desta real audiencia aviendo visto esta causa mandaron dar treslado al licenciado Caravajal fiscal desta real audiencia de los agravios pasados por doña Beatriz y ansi lo mandaron presente el dho fiscal. Albaro Ruiz de Nabamuel.

v Muy poderoso señor el licenciado Albaro de Caravajal vro fiscal respondiendo a cierto peticion de agravios y apelacion ynterpuesta //
/f.238/ por parte de doña Beatriz Coya de aver puesto don Francisco de Toledo vro visorrey en vra real corona ciertos yºs yanaconas que estan en el valle de Yucai terminos de la ciudad del Cuzco y de otras cosas en ella contenidas digo que la dha peticion no devia ser admitida en juiº en la dha apelacion a lugar de se admitir ni sobre ello en esta vra real audiencia se puede conozer porque conforme a vras reales leies cedulas y provisiones de las encomiendas fechas por vro bisorrey asi cerca de vra real corona como en particulares no a lugar apelacion y no obstante ellas se an de executar y si las partes algun drº pretenden lo an de seguir y pedir por la orden que se da en vra real provision dada en Malinas y en este caso por los autos y confesion de la parte consta aver el dho vro visorrey puesto los dhos yanaconas en vra real corona y asi no a lugar lo por la parte contraria pedido.

v A Vra Alª pido y sup^{co} declare no aver lugar lo de contrº pedido y si es necesario absuelva y de por libre a vro real fisco dello declarando no se dever admitir la dha apelacion ny seguirse en esta real audiencia lo qual pido por la via y orden que mejor aya lugar de drº y convenga a vra real hazienda y pido justicia e costas y el real ofº ymploro. Va testado en la causa. El lic^{do} Albaro de Caravajal.

v En los Reies a veinte y uno de agosto de mil e quiºs y setenta y seis años ante los señores presidente e oydores en audiª publica se presento esta peticion por el licenciado Alvaro de Caravajal fiscal de su m^{t}.

v Y los dhos señores ovieron esta causa por conclusa en forma. Navamuel.

v En la causa de doña Beatriz Coya y Juan de Arrandolaça su pr^{or} con el licenciado Albaro //
/f.238v/ de Caravajal fiscal de su magestad sobre el despojo de los yºs del repartimi^{to} de Yucai de su encomienda que por yanaconas no tributarios se pusieron en la corona real.

v En la ciudad de los Reies v^{te} y ocho dias del mes de setiembre de mil e quiºs e setenta e seis años los señores presidente y oydores desta real audiª aviendo visto esta causa declararon no aver lugar lo pedido por parte de la dha doña Beatriz Coya y mandaron que siga su justicia como viere que le conviene y asi lo proveieron y rubricaron.

v Pronunciaron este auto los señores presidente y oydores estando haziendo audiencia publica en el dho dia mes y año en el contenido presente Juan de Herrandolaça pr^{or} de la dha doña Beatriz Coya a quien se notefico y ansimismo estando presente el licenciado Caravajal fiscal de su m^{t}. Albaro Ruiz de Navamuel.

v Muy poderoso señor Juan de Hernandolaça en nombre de doña Beatriz Coya mujer legitima del capitan Martin Garcia de Loyola vzº de la ciudad del Cuzco premisa la benia y licencia que entre caso de drº se require digo que teniendo y poseiendo la dha mi parte en encomienda y por justos y dr^{os} titulos yºs del valle de Yucai ques en termino de la ciudad del Cuzco que son don Diego Rimache y don Pedro Meloguay y los demas que el licenciado frei Pedro visito contenidos en la memoria que esta en este proceso y teniendolos ansi encomendados por virtud de vros reales poderes y comisiones del marques de Cañete visorrey que fue destos reinos tuvo y teniendolos ansimesmo poseydo en encomienda Gonçalo Piçarro hijo del marques don Fran^{co} Piçarro y despues abellos ansimismo encomendados don Diego Saire Topa yndio padre de la dha mi parte la qual //
/f.239/ estando en la dha su quieta y pacifica posesion de los dhos yºs sin contradiccion de persona alguna el licenciado frei Pedro Gutierrez Flores por una manera de visita que hizo por mandado de vro visorrey don Francisco de Toledo de los dhos yndios que el dho licenciado y el dho visorrey quitaron y despojaron a la dha mi parte de la dha posicion y el dho vro visorrey sin guardar la orden de dr^{os} puso y m^{do} poner en vra real corona los dhos yºs y mando desposeer y desposeio a la dha mi parte y le desposeio dellos sin le oir de que a reçebido notorio agravio en el despojar de hecho de la dha a su posision que de los dhos yºs del dho valle de Yucai tenia y de los tribuºs y cosas que como a su verdadero y legitimo heredero le acudian y contribuyan.

v A V. Al^{a} pido y suplico ante todas las cosas mande reyntegrar y bolver a mi pte en la antigua y quieta posesion en que estava de los dhos yndios del dho valle de Yucai declarando no aver podido ser despojada ni desposeida de los dhos y^{o}s y pertenecerle y dever goçar de la dha su encomienda revocando todo fecho y autuado por vro bisorrey sobre que pido justicia y costas y pa ello es. El Dotor Juan de Herrera Arrandolaça.

v En la ciudad de los Reies en diez y seis dias del mes de otubre de mil e qui^{o}s y setenta y seis años ante los señores presidente y oydores estando en audiencia publica fue presentada esta peticion por Juan de Her^{do} Laça en nombre de su parte.

v Y por los dhos señores fue mandado dar treslado al licenciado Carvajal fiscal de su mag^{t} y que pa la primera audi^{a} responda presente el dho fiscal—Navamuel—

/f.239v/ v Muy poderoso señor el Lic^{do} Alvaro de Carvajal vro fiscal respondiendo a vra demanda puesta por parte de doña Beatriz de Mendoza Coya de unos y^{o}s que no declara de que dize fue despojado y puestos en vra corona real como se contiene en la dha demanda a que me refiero digo que la dha demanda no procede ni avia de ser recibida o a lo menos vro fisco y real hazienda se avia de dar por libre della por lo que della consta y parece y por lo siguiente.

v Lo primero por no ser puesta por parte ni entrego ni en forma ni contener cierta relacion ni verdadera la qual niego como en ella se contiene.

v Lo otro porque hablando con el acatamiento devido de la dha demanda y negocio conforme a vras reales cedulas y provisiones no se puede conocer en esta real audiencia antes se debe remitir a vra real persona y consejo.

v Lo otro porque puesto que lo arriba dho cessara que no cessa a la dha doña Beatriz Coya no tiene ningun dr^{o} ni accion a lo que pide ni por vro bisorrey y le fue fecho agravio alguno porque los dhos y^{o}s que dize fueron puestos en vra real corona por el dho vro visorrey fue fecho justicia y juridicamente porque conforme a vras reales cedulas todos los y^{o}s e yanaconas que no estan encomendados ni pagavan tributos esta mandado se pongan en vra real corona y se tasen y den tributo a vra real hazi^{da} de los quales eran y son los yndios que la parte contraria pretende como parece por la visita que dellos hizo el licenciado frei Pedro Gutierrez Flores que por comision de vro visorrey los bisito conforme a la qual constando ser tales yanaconas vro bisorrey los puso en vra real corona y por la misma visita parece //
/f.240/ que aunque los dhos yanaconas vivian en el dho valle de Yucay nunca fueron tributarios ni pagavan tributo a los encomenderos del dho valle ni aun a los Yngas lo pagaron sino solamente le servian de yanaconas y asi nunca fueron contados ni tenidos por tributarios con lo qual se excluie la posesion que dize la parte contraria que tuvo ella y sus predecesores encomenderos del dho valle porque como dho es nunca estuvieron en posicion de tributar aunque vivian en el dho valle.

v A Vra Alteza pido y suplico mande no se admita la dha demanda y se repele deste juicio o en defeto desto absuelva y de por libre a vro real fisco y hazienda de lo en ella contenido poniendo perpetuo silencio e la parte contraria condenandole en las costas e yntereses de las quales pido justicia y el real off^{o} ymploro. El Llic^{do} Albaro de Carvajal.

v En la ciudad de los Reies en primero dia del mes de diziembre de mil e qui^{o}s y set^{a} y seis años ante los señores presidente y oydores fue presentada esta peticion estando en audiencia pu^{ca} y por los dhos señores fue mandado dar treslado a la otra pte y que para la primera audiencia responda presente Juan de Her^{do} Laça pr^{or} Yr^{o} a quien se notifico. Navamuel.

v Muy poderoso señor Juan de Arrandolaça en nombre de doña Beatriz Coya en el pleito con vro fiscal sobre los y^{o}s de la encomienda de mi pte digo que al dho fiscal se dio treslado de mi demanda e no la a contestado ni alegado aunque son pasados todos los terminos.

v Pido y sup^{co} a Vra Al^{a} la mande aver por conclusa la causa y se reciba a prueva con el auto //
/f.240v/ hordinario conforme a la de Malinas e pido justicia e para ello es. Arrandolaça.

v En los Reies en treze de noviembre de mil e qui^{o}s y setenta y seis años ante los señores presidente e oydores en audiencia pu^{ca} la presento Juan de Arrandolaça en nombre de su parte.

v Y por los dhos señores vista mandaron dar treslado al dho fiscal y que para la primera audiencia responda no estaba presente Navamuel.

v Muy poderoso señor Juan de Arrandolaça en nombre de Martin Garcia de Loyola y de doña Beatriz Coya su mujer en el pleito con vro fiscal sobre los y^{o}s del valle de Yucai que llama yanaconas digo que a mas de un mes que se le notefico al dho fiscal la demanda por mi pte puesta sobre los dhos y^{o}s y aunque han pasado a muchos dias no a respondido ni quiere responder de que mi parte recive notorio agravio por dilatarse la causa y pasarse el tiempo de la flota en que a de yr el proceso y estar despojado de sus yndios.

v A V. Al^{a} suplico mande en su reveldia aver la causa por conclusa y recevirla a prueva conforme a la ordenança pues en todo tiempo puedo alegar lo que viere que le esta bien pa su justicia la qual pido y para ello es. Arrandolaça.

v En la ciudad de los Reies en veinte e siete dias del mes de nobiembre de myll e qui^{o}s y setenta y seis años ante los señores pres^{e} y oydores estando en audi^{a} pu^{ca} fue presentada esta peticion y por los dhos señores vista mandaron que para la primera audiencia el dho fiscal responda y concluya Navamuel.

v Muy poderoso señor Juan de Arrandolaça en nombre del capitan Loyola y doña Beatriz Coya su mujer en el pleito con vro fiscal sobre los y^{o}s del valle de Yucai de la encomienda de mi pte que visito el lic^{do} frei Pedro Gutierrez //
/f.241/ sobre que es este pleito digo que sin embargo de lo dho y alegado por el dho vro fiscal se a de hazer lo que tengo pedido en mi demanda porque yo soy parte y lo es el dho capitan Loyola y la dha doña Beatriz su mujer y este pleito como ha sido despojo autual de los y^{o}s que los dhos mis ptes tenian e poseian asi sea y deve con la misma facilidad bolver a reintegrar a mi pte en su posesion y vro presidente e oydores han y deven conocer del dho despojo y quando por alguna via se hubiese de remitir a vro real consejo de Yndias pa que Vra real persona conociese della avia ya de ser aviendo ante todas cosas buelto a mi parte en la quieta y pacifica posesion que tan antigua de los dhos y^{o}s de su encomienda ha tenido y tiene por virtud de la encomienda que dellos ha tenido y tiene y tuvieron sus predecesores para que la paguen y tribu/t/en en todo y por todo como como hasta agora lo an fecho y tributado lo qual consta ebidentem^{te} por los titulos de su encomienda y a lo que esta provado y los yanaconas quel dho vro fiscal dize questa mandado por vra persona real a vro visorrey poner en vra real corona son los que no estaban encomendados e que bivian de por si y los que a mi pte se le quitaron y despojaron le estavan encomendados y los tenia y poseyeron y les tributavan a los otros sus predecesores contenidos en mi demanda y en la dha posesion de tributar han estado y asi no se pudo ni devio hazer el dicho despojo.

v A V. Al^{a} pido y sup^{co} haga en todo como por mi parte esta pedido en la dha su demanda y ansi lo pido y sup^{co} sin embargo de lo dho y alegado por el dho fiscal sobre que pido just^{a} y costas y para ello es. Arrandolaça. //
/f.241v/ El Dotor Juan de Herrera.

v En los Reies quatro de diziembre de mill e qui^{o}s y setenta y seis años ante los señores presidente e oydores desta real audi^{a} estando en audiencia pu^{ca} Juan de Arrandolaça en nombre de su parte pres^{to} esta pet^{on}.

v Y los dhos s^{e}s mandaron dar treslado a la otra parte y que para la primera audiencia responda estuvo presente al licenciado Carvajal fiscal de su mag^{t}. Navamuel.

v Muy poderoso señor Juan de Arrandolaça en nombre de Martin Garcia de Loyola e doña Beatriz Coya su mujer en el pleito con vro fiscal sobre los y^{o}s de Yucai digo que el dho vro fiscal llevo termino pa venir diziendo e concluyendo pa e aunque se le notifico no dize cosa alguna.

v A V. Al^{a} pido y sup^{co} mande aver por conclusa la causa e se haga el auto ordinario conforme a la de Malinas y pido justicia y para ello es. Arrandolaça.

v En los Reies siete dias del mes de diziembre de mill e qui^{o}s y setenta y seis años ante los señores presidente e oydores desta real audi^{a} estando en audi^{a} pu^{ca} Juan de Arrandolaça en nombre de su parte presento esta peticion y por los dhos señores vista mandaron traer los autos. Navamuel.

v En la causa de doña Beatriz Coya mujer del capitan Martin Garcia de Loyola y Juan de Herrandolaça su pr^{or} en su nombre y el lic^{do} Albaro de Carvajal fiscal de su m^{t} sobre el despojo de los yndios del repartimiento de Yucai de su encomienda que por yanaconas no tributarios se pusieron en la corona real de su m^{t}.

/f.242/ v En la ciudad de los Reies a onze dias del mes de diziembre de mil y qui^{o}s y setenta y seis años los señores presidente y oydores desta real audiencia aviendo visto el proceso de la dha causa dixeron que las dhas partes y cada una dellas dentro de noventa dias primeros siguientes presenten las escripturas y t^{o}s de que se entienden aprovechar con que ninguna dellas presenten mas de doze testigos con apercibimi^{to} quel dho termino pasado con lo que ovieren fecho sin les admitir otra provança alguna se remitira a su magestad y a su real consejo de Yndias conforme a la ordenança y ansi lo pronunciaron y mandaron y señalaron.

v El qual dho auto fue proveido por los señores presidente y oydores en el dho dia mes y año en el contenido presente Herrandolaça a quien se notefico y ansimismo estava presente el dho fiscal. Alvaro Ruiz de Navamuel.

v Muy poderoso señor el licenciado Alvaro de Carvajal vro fiscal en la causa con doña Beatriz Coya sobre los yanaconas digo que yo pedise me diese un treslado autoriçado de la cedula de vra real persona por donde se provee y manda que todos los yanaconas o naborias [*sic*] se tasen y paguen a vra alteza en cuya corona se pongan y ansimismo del auto por donde vro visorrey puso los dhos naborias en vra real corona lo qual no se me a dado tengo necesidad dello para hazer ynterr^{o} e presenta en la dha causa.

v A V. Al^{a} pido y sup^{co} mande se me de luego pa el dho efeto para lo qual es.

v Otro si digo que en la dha causa corre el ter^{no} de los noventa dias y como he dho para hazer interr^{o} tengo necesidad de lo susodho.

v A Vra Alteza pido y suplico mande y provea que hasta que se me de no me corra ter^{no} para lo qual el real //
/f.242v/ oficio ymploro e pido justicia. El licenciado Alvaro de Carvajal.

v En los Reies en primero de març̧o de mil e qui^{o}s y setenta y siete a^{o}s ante los señores presidente e oydores estando en audiencia publica fue presentada esta peticion por el dho fiscal y por los dhos señores vista en lo primero mandaron se le de lo que pide y en lo segundo que se oye. Navamuel.

v En la ciudad de los Reies nueve dias de maio de mil e qui^{o}s e setenta y siete años notefique el dho probeymiento al secretario Alvaro Ruiz de Nabamuel el qual dixo que el no tiene la dha cedula t^{gos} Ant^{o} Bautista de Salazar e Juan Sierra Juan Gutierrez de Molina.

v Muy poderoso señor Juan de Arrandolaça en nombre de doña Beatriz Coya en el p^{to} con vro fiscal sobre los yndios contradigo el ter^{no} pedido por el dho fiscal e digo que no a lugar de se le conçeder porque los noventa dias de la prueva son pasados y el se dho paso y pasa en el Cuzco y asi no se le deve prorrogar ter^{no} alguno y la cedula de su magestad en que declara que se prorrogue el termino por vros oydores se entiende pasando el hecho en los Charcas o Chile o Quito y no para donde basto el ter^{no} hordinario pa el Cuzco y el dho fiscal lo haze a fin que el proceso no se pueda ir en esta flota.

v Por tanto a V. Al^{a} pido y suplico se le deniegue y mande hazer el auto de remision en forma citandose pa ello las partes e pido justicia e pa ello es.

v Otro si digo que Castillo solicitador del dho vro fiscal no quiere traer el proceso aunque se le a mandado pido e sup^{co} a vra alteza mande que un alguazil le ponga preso hasta que lo vuelva. Etc. Arrandolaça.

/f.243/ v En los Reies en cinco dias del mes de Março de mil e qui^{o}s e setenta e siete años ante los señores presidente e oydores en audiencia publica presento esta peticion Juan de Arrandolaça en nombre de su pte.

v Y los dhos señores mandaron que se guarde lo proveido. Navamuel.

v Muy poderoso señor Licenciado Alv^{o} de Carvajal vro fiscal en la causa con doña Beatriz Coya sobre los yanaconas del valle de Yucay que pide digo que la dha causa esta recibida a prueva con el ter^{no} de los noventa dias conforme a la provision de Malinas en el qual ter^{no} no puedo ni he podido hazer la probança tocante a vro fisco porque se a de hazer fuera e lexos desta ciudad y asi tengo neçesidad de que se prorroguen otros noventa dias mas con forme a la dha provision y ordenanças.

v A V. Al^{a} pido y suplico mande se me den y prorroguen los dhos noventa dias mas despues de cumplidos los otros noventa con que fuimos recividos a prueva pa lo qual es. El licenciado Alvaro de Carvajal.

v En los Reies en cinco dias del mes de março de mill e qui^{o}s e setenta e siete años ante los señores presidente e oydores en audiencia pu^{ca} se leyo esta peticion.

v Y los dhos señores dixeron que prorrogaban y prorrogaron los dhos noventa dias mas de termino comunes a las ptes ps^{tes} el dho fiscal de su magestad y Juan de Arrandolaça pr^{or} contrario a quien se notifica Navamuel.

v Muy poderoso señor Juan de Arrandolaça en nombre de doña Beatriz Coya mujer del cap^{t} //
/f.243v/ Loyola en la causa con vro fiscal sobre los y^{o}s del valle de Yucay que se llama yanaconas digo que a pedimiento del dho fiscal se prorrogo el termino probatorio por otros noventa dias mas y pa que conste dello tengo necesidad de un testimonio.

v A V. Al^{a} suplico mande al secretario Navamuel me de testimi^{o} y fee de la dha prorrogacion y que se cite a vro fiscal pa la ratificacion de los testigos que mi pte oviere presentado y esaminacion de los que de nuevo presentare y si quisiere nombrar escriv^{o} de su parte nombre y pa ello es. Arrandolaça.

v En los Reies en quinze de março de mill e qui^{o}s y setenta y siete años ante los señores presidente e oydores en audi^{a} pu^{ca} la pres^{to} Juan de Arrandolaça en nombre de su pte.

v Y por los dhos señores fue mandado se le de lo que pide citando al fiscal de su mag^{t}. Navamuel.

v En la ciudad de los Reies en diez y ocho dias del mes de marzo de mil e qui^{o}s y set^{a} y siete años ley e notefique la peticion desta otra parte escripta y lo a ella proveido por los señores desta real audiencia al s^{or} licenciado Alvaro de Carvajal fiscal de su mag^{t} del dho real audiencia en su persona todo lo en ella contenido y especialmente le cite pa ver presentar jurar y conocer los testigos que en esta causa se presentaren y para la ratificacion de los que se huvieren presentado en forma de dr^{o} y su md dixo que la dha citacion hera ympertinente que bastava la noteficacion del auto de prorogacion que esto dava y //
/f.244/ dio por su respuesta t^{o} Melchor de Castillo y dello doy fee testado para Juan Ramos de Gauna escrivano real.

v Muy poderoso señor el licenciado Alvaro de Carvajal vro fiscal en la causa con doña Beatriz Coya sobre los yanaconas digo que por otras tengo pedido se me de un treslado de la cedula de vra real persona e capitulo de carta por la qual se mando que los y^{o}s yanaconas o navorias se pongan en vra real corona y se les tassen los tribu^{o}s que an de dar y no sirvan ni tributen a p^{a}s particular que aunque se mando se me diese no se me ha dado ni da e sin della yo no puedo hazer ynterr^{o} en la causa ni alegar lo que a vro derecho convenga y el tiempo de la prueva corre.

v A V. Al^{a} pido y sup^{co} mande se me de el dho treslado y en el entre tanto que no se me da no me corra el ter^{no} porque asi conviene a vro real servi^{o} y que aya la dha cedula consta por un capitulo de la ynstruccion dada por vro visorrey al licenciado frei P^{o} Gutierrez visitador que fue del valle de Yucay que esta en este mismo proceso y pido justicia y pa ello es. El licenciado Alvaro de Carvajal.

v En los Reies a veinte e dos dias del mes de março de mill e qui^{o}s e setenta e siete años ante los señores presidente e oydores est^{do} haziendo audiencia pu^{ca} pres^{to} esta peticion el fiscal de su magestad y por los dhos señores vista fue mandado se le de lo que pide y en el entretanto no corra el termino de prueva. Navamuel.

v Muy poderoso señor Juan de Arrandolaça en nombre de doña Beatriz Coya en el pleito //
/f.244v/ con vro fiscal sobre los y^{o}s digo que al dho fiscal se a mandado por dos apercibimi^{o}s que responda a una peticion por mi presentada e no responde cosa alguna e se dilata la causa.

v Pido y sup^{co} a Vra Al^{a} mande aver por conclusa la causa en este articulo e se traygan los autos para proveer e para ello es. Arrandolaça.

v En la ciudad de los Reies a diez y seis dias del mes de abril de mil e qui^{o}s y set^{a} y siete años ante los señores presidente e oydores desta real audi^{a} estando haziendo audi^{a} pu^{ca} Juan de Arrandolaça pres^{to} esta peticion en nombre de su pte e por los dhos señores vista dijeron que avian e ovieron esta causa por conclusa y que se lleven los autos a la sala. Navamuel.

v Muy poderoso señor Juan de Arrandolaça en nombre de doña Beatriz Coya mujer del cap^{t} Martin Garcia de Loyola en el pleito con vro fiscal sobre los y^{o}s digo que el dho fiscal llevo ter^{no} pa responder a mi suplicacion del auto que se pronuncio que no le corra el ter^{no} provatorio y no dize cosa alguna aunque se le notefico.

v Pido y sup^{co} a Vra Al^{a} mande aver por conclusa en el dho articulo e mande se traygan los autos para proveer justicia. Arrandolaça.

v En los Reies en treinta de marzo de mil e qui^{o}s y setenta y siete a^{o}s ante los señores presidente e oydores estando en visita general de carzel fue presentada esta peticion por el contenido.

v Y por los dhos señores vista mandaron que con lo que dixere o no la pte contr^{a} para la primera audiencia ovieron esta causa por conclusa en forma pres^{te} el fiscal de su magestad. Navamuel.

v En v^{te} e quatro dias de marzo de mil e qui^{o}s y setenta e siete años Juan de Arrandolaça en nombre de su pte presento esta peticion //
/f.245/ con protestacion de la ratificar. Juan Gutierrez de Molina.

v Muy poderoso señor Juan de Arrandolaça en nombre de doña Beatriz Coya en el p^{to} con vro fiscal sobre los y^{o}s que se llaman yanaconas digo que vros oydores proveyeron que se diese a vro fiscal cierta cedula o capitulo de ynstruicion de su m^{t} en que dize que los yanaconas se pongan en vra real corona y en el entretanto que no se le dava no le corriese el ter^{no} que a su pedimi^{to} se le dio y por questo es dilatar la causa lo qual no se puede ni deve hazer pues mi pte no ti^{e} la dha cedula ni esta obligado a la traer y el fiscal la deve de traer y la a de presentar y mi pte esta despojada de su hazienda y querer que por otra parte dilatar su just^{a} es hazerle notorio agravio.

v A V. Al^{a} pido y sup^{co} reponga el dho auto e si nezes^{o} es para este efeto suplico del y pido segun de suso e sobre todo justicia e pa ello es. El licenciado Falcon. Arrandolaça.

v En los Reies en veinte e seis dias del mes de março de mil e qui^{o}s e setenta y siete años antes los señores presidente e oydores estando en audi^{a} pu^{ca} fue presentada esta peticion por Her^{do}laça en nombre de su pte y por los dhos señores fue mandado dar treslado al fiscal de su magestad y que pa la primera audi^{a} responda presente el fiscal de su magestad. Navamuel.

v Muy poderoso señor el lic^{do} Alvaro de Carvajal vro fiscal en el pleito con doña Beatriz Coya sobre los yanaconas respondiendo a la suplicacion por la pte contraria ynterpuesta de averse proveido por vro presidente e oydores que no me corriese el ter^{no} provatorio hasta que se me diese cierta vra real //
/f.245v/ cedula para conforme a ella articular lo que a vro real dr^{o} convenga digo que sin embargo de lo por la parte contr^{a} pedido y alegado se a de confirmar por lo que resulta de los autos y porque yo no puedo hazer los articulos y preguntas sin ver la dha vra real cedula la qual esta en poder del escrivano de governacion como consta de los mismos autos donde della haze mincion y asi estoi justamente impidido y sin culpa y ansi de dr^{o} y sin que espresam^{te} se proviera corria termino y lo esto se satisfize a lo por la pte contraria dho.

v A Vra Alteza pido y sup^{co} confyrme lo mandado sin embargo de lo por la parte contrario dho y pido justicia y el real of^{o} imploro. El licenciado Alvaro de Carvajal.

v En los Reies a veinte y seis dias del mes de abril de mil e qui^{o}s e setenta y siete años ante los señores presidente y oydores la presento el licenciado Alvaro de Carvajal fiscal de su magestad y por los dhos señores vista se uvo la causa por conclusa en forma. Navamuel.

v En la causa de doña Beatriz Coya mujer del cap^{t} Martin Garcia de Loyola con el fiscal de su magestad sobre los yanaconas sobre el ter^{no}.

v En la ciudad de los Reies a quatro dias del mes de mayo de mil e qui^{o}s y setenta y siete años los señores presidente y oydores desta real audi^{a} aviendo visto esta causa mandaron que el dho fiscal dentro de diez dias primeros siguientes presente los recaudos que en esta causa tiene que presentar y no los presentando en el dho termino corra el termino de la prueva como corre y ansi lo proveyeron y señalaron. Juan Gutierrez de Molina.

/f.246/ v En la ciudad de los Reies a siete dias del dho mes y año notefique [*sic*] el dho auto al licenciado Carvajal fiscal de su magestad en su persona. Albaro Ruiz de Navamuel.

v Muy poderoso señor el licenciado Alvaro de Carvajal vro fiscal en la causa con doña Beatriz Coya sobre los yanaconas o naborias que pide digo que pa presentar en la dha causa tengo necesidad se me de un treslado de la visita e reducion que hizo el lic^{do} frei P^{o} Gutierrez de los y^{o}s que hallo yanaconas en el valle de Yucai y San Francisco de Maras en los pu^{o}s de San Benito de Alcantara Santiago de Oropesa San Bernardo San Francisco de Maras que estan en el quaderno de las visitas que el dho licenciado Frei Pedro hizo de los repartimi^{o}s de y^{o}s del termino de la ciudad del Cuzco que comiença a fojas setecientas y sesenta y siete y acava en ochocientas y sesenta e tres.

v A V. Al^{a} pido y sup^{co} mande al secretario Alvaro Ruiz de Navamuel saque un treslado de la dha visita y me la de pa el dho efeto citada la pte contraria pa lo qual es.

v Otro si a V. Al^{a} pido y sup^{co} mande dar su carta y provision real para que los oficiales de vra real hazienda de la ciudad del Cuzco me den un treslado del auto que vro visorrey y proveyo por donde puso los dhos yanaconas o naborias en vra real corona e la tasa que dellos hizo que entrego a los dhos vros oficiales reales para el dho efeto y con la dha citacion pa lo qual es. El licenciado Alvaro de Carvajal.

v En los Reies en veinte e uno de junio de mil e qui^{o}s y setenta y siete años ante los señores presidente e oydores en audi^{a} //
/f.246v/ publica se presento esta peticion por el licenciado Alvaro de Carvajal fiscal de su magestad e por los dhos señores vista mandaron se le de todo lo que pide con citacion de la parte contraria pres^{te} Juan de Her^{do}laca pr^{or} a quien se notefico y cito. Navamuel.

v Muy poderoso señor el licenciado Alvaro de Carvajal vro fiscal en la causa con doña Beatriz Coya sobre los yanaconas que estan en vra real corona digo que a mi pedim^{to} V. Alt^{a} mando que el termino de los noventa dias que se me prorogaron no corriese hasta que se me diese un treslado de la cedula por la qual manda vra real ps^{a} se pongan todos los yanaconas deste reino en su real corona pa poder hazer ynterr^{o} la qual nunca se me a dado y despues por otro auto se m^{do} que dentro de diez dias yo presentase los recaudos que tenia que presentar en la dha causa donde no que el dho ter^{no} corriese como corria y porque el dho auto no esta noteficado a la parte contr^{a} ni el secretario me despacha la receutoria por dezir que no save desde quando ha de correr el dho ter^{no} de la prorrogacion.

v A V. Al^{a} pido y sup^{co} mande que se me de luego la dha receutoria y se declare corra el dho termino desde oy lo qual se notefique ansi luego a las partes para lo qual es. El licenciado Alvaro de Carvajal.

v En los Reies en quatro dias del mes de julio de mil e qui^{o}s y setenta y siete años ante los señores presidente y oydores estando en la audi^{a} de relaciones fue presentada esta peticion y por los dhos señores vista mandaron que el dho termi^{o} //
/f.247/ corra desde oy proveyo se presente Juan de Her^{do}laça parte de la dha doña Beatriz a quien se notefico y ansimismo estuvo presente el fiscal de su magestad. Navamuel.

v Muy poderoso señor Juan de Arrandolaça en nombre de doña Beatriz Coya mujer del capitan Martin Garcia de Loyola en el pleito con vro fiscal sobre los yanaconas digo que el termino probatorio es pasado.

v Pido e sup^{co} a V. Al^{a} mande hazer publicacion en la causa e para ello es. Arrandolaça.

v En los Reies en ocho dias del mes de otubre de mil e qui^{o}s e setenta e siete años ante los señores presidente e oydores estando en audiencia publica la presento Juan de Arrandolaça en nombre de su pte.

v Y los dhos señores vista mandaron dar treslado a la otra pte y que responda pa la primera audiencia. Navamuel.

v Muy poderoso señor Juan de Arrandolaça en nombre de doña Beatriz Coya en el pleito con vro fiscal sobre los yanaconas digo que la parte contraria llevo ter^{no} pa venir diciendo porque no se debe hazer la publicacion por mi pedida y aunque se le notefico no dizo cosa alguna.

v A V. Al^{a} pido y sup^{co} la mande hazer e para ello es.

v Otro si pido y suplico a Vra Al^{a} pues todos los terminos se an pasado mande se haga el auto de remision en forma y se citen las partes en forma e pa ello es. Arrandolaça.

v En la ciudad de los Reies en onze dias del mes de otubre de mil e qui^{o}s e setenta y siete años ante los señores presidente e oydores en audiencia publica Juan de Arrandolaça en nombre de su parte pres^{to} esta pet^{on}

/f.247v/ /al margen: Provança de doña Beatriz. Estava puesto o de abajo en la margen desta hoja del proceso orig^{a}l la provança que se hizo por esta rrecep^{a} real se tornaron a retificarlos por la prorrog^{on} al termy^{o} que vino a pedimi^{o} del s^{or} fiscal por su citacion questa a nobenta y cinco fojas la prorro^{on} cita con las retificaciones de a mas adelante con el testim^{o} de dos y^{o}s que por ser muertos no se ratificaron/

v Y por los dhos señores vista en lo primero ovieron por fecha la publicacion de testigos con el termino de la ley y en lo demas mandaron que se haga el auto de remision en forma pres^{te} el dho Juan de Arrandolaça a quien se notefico y ansimismo estava pres^{te} el fiscal de su magestad. Navamuel.

v Don Felipe por la gracia de Dios Rey de Castilla de Leon de Aragon de las dos Secilias de Jerusalen de Navarra de Granada de Toledo de Valencia de Galicia de Mallorcas de Sevilla de Cerdeña de Cordoba de Corcega de Murcia de Jaen de los Algarves de Algecira de Gibraltar de las islas de Canaria de las Indias islas e tierra firme del Mar Oceano conde de Flandes y de Tirol etc. A vos el nuestro corregidor y alcaldes ordinarios y otras nuestras justicias ansi de la ciudad del Cuzco de los nuestros reinos del Peru como de todas las demas ciudades villas de los dhos nuestros reinos y a cada uno y qualquier de vos en vros lugares y juridiciones a quien esta nuestra carta fuere mostrada y pedido cumplimi^{to} salud e gracia. Sepades que en la nuestra corte y chancilleria real que reside en la ciudad de los Reies ante el nuestro presidente y oydores della se trata y esta pendiente p^{to} entre doña Beatriz Coya mujer de Capt Loyola vz^{o} de la dha ciudad y Juan de Arrandolaça su pr^{or} en su nombre y de la otra el licenciado Carvajal nro fiscal en la dha nuestra audiencia sobre el despojo del repartimiento de yndios de Yucay que dize ser de su encomienda que dize pusieron en nuestra real corona por yanaconas no tributarios y las demas causas y razones en el proceso del dho p^{to} contenidas en el qual aviendo las //
/f.248/ dichas partes dho y alegado de su justicia la causa fue recibida a prueva con terno de noventa dias y por parte de la dha doña Beatriz Coya nos fue pedido que porque los t^{o}s de que se entendia aprovechar estaban en esa dha ciudad y otras ptes le diesemos nuestra carta y provision real receptoria pa hazer su probança en ella o que sobre ello proveyesemos como la nuestra md fuese lo qual visto por el dho nro pres^{e} y oydores fue acordado que deviamos mandar dar esta nra carta para vos en la dha razon e nos tuvimoslo por bien por la qual vos mandamos que ante vos pareciere la parte de la dha doña Beatriz dentro de los dhos noventa dias que corren y se quenta desde onze dias del mes de diziembre deste presente año hagais venir y parecer ante vos a todas las personas que por testigos dixeren se entienden aprovechar como no pasen de doze t^{o}s de los quales y de cada uno dellos recibireis juramento y sus dhos y depusiciones preguntandoles por el conocimi^{to} de las partes y preguntas generales de la ley y por las del ynterr^{o} que ante vos sera presentado firmado del secretario infraescripto y al testigo que dixere que save la pregunta le preguntareis como y porque la save y al que lo oyo dezir a quien y como y quando de manera que den razon suficiente de sus dhos y depusiciones y lo que los dhos t^{o}s dixeren y depusieren escripto en limpio firmado de vro nombre y del escrivano ante quien //
/f.248v/ pasaren nombrando por parte de la dha doña Beatriz cerrado y sellado en manera que haga fe lo dad y entregad a la parte de la dha doña Beatriz para que lo traiga y presente ante nos en el dho pleito y causa pagando al escriv^{o} los dr^{os} que oviere de haber lo qual ansi cumplid aviendo citado el dho nro fiscal pa que si quisiere nombre escriv^{o} de su parte ante quien pase y se haga la dha provança y no lo nombrando dentro de terzero dia pase y se haga ante el escrivano solo nombrado por parte de la dha doña Beatriz y no fagades en de al so pena de la ntra md y de qui^{o}s p^{o}s para la nuestra camara. Dado en los Reies a veinte dias del mes de diziembre de mill e qui^{o}s y setenta y seis años. Don Fran^{co} de Toledo el lic^{do} don Albaro Ponce de Leon el lic^{do} Sanchez Paredes yo Alvaro Ruiz de Navamuel escrivano de camara de su magestad catolica la fize escrevir por su mandado con acuerdo de su presidente e oydores registrada Juan de Murga chanciller Lor^{zo} de Aliaga los t^{gos} que fueren presentados por parte de doña Beatriz Coya mujer legitima del capitan Martin Garcia de Loyola su marido vz^{o} de la ciudad del Cuzco y en nombre del dho capitan en el pleito con la real hazienda y fisco de su magestad y con el licenciado Carvajal fiscal desta real audiencia sobre los yndios de que ha sido despojada la dha doña Beatriz que fueron y son de su encomienda en el valle de Yucay ques ter^{no} de la dha //
/f.249/ ciudad del Cuzco sean preguntados por las preguntas siguientes:

j v Primeramente si conozen a las partes y si tienen noticia e conocimiento de los y^{o}s del dho repartimiento de la dha doña Beatriz que son en el dho valle de Yuca y que a tenido y poseido y en que subzedio por titulo de encomienda que son trescientos y treinta y un yndios de visita contenidos en una memoria que ba referida a esta pregunta con este ynterrogatorio que comienza Xpobal Paucartica y acaba Francisco Cairomarca que sea a mostrado a los testigos para que digan lo que saven.

ij v Iten si saven que los dhos y^{o}s contenidos en la dha memorial referida en la preg^{ta} antes desta que son en el dho valle de Yucay y ter^{no} de la dha ciudad del Cuzco los tuvo y poseio y ha tenido y poseido la dha doña Beatriz Coya por titulo de encomienda y sucesion como yndios tributarios que le fueron encomendados en quien subcedio como hija legitima de don Diego Saire Topa y de doña Maria Manrique su madre en quien los encomendo como y^{o}s tributarios y los deposito el marques de Cañete bisorrey que fue destos reinos por virtud de los reales poderes que de su m^{t} tubo digan lo que saven y para el dho efeto se les muestre a los testigos la encomienda que el dho marques en el dho don Diego Sayre Topa hizo.

iij v Iten si saven que el dho don Diego Saire Topa Ynga podra aver diez y nueve años //
/f.249v/ poco mas o menos que se caso y belo segun orden de la santa madre yglesia con doña Maria Manrique Coya y como tales legitimos marido y mujer como lo manda la santa madre yglesia de Roma hicieron vida maridable de sufrano [*sic*] y del dho matrimonio huvieron e procrearon por su hija ligitima a la dha doña Beatriz Coya a que al presente esta casada con el dho capitan Martin Garcia de Loyola y por tal su hija legitima le trataron y nombraron y fue abida e tenida y comunmente reputada digan lo que saven.

iiij v Iten si saven que los dhos don Diego Saire Topa y la dha doña Maria Manrique no tuvieron otro hijo ni hija legitima sino fue a la dha doña Beatriz Coya la qual subcedio en todos sus bienes y hazienda en el repartimiento de y^{o}s que le fueron encomendados y si tuvieran otros hijos barones los t^{o}s lo supieran y no pudiera ser menos por el mucho trato e comunicacion que con ellos tuvieron digan lo que saven.

v Iten si saven e conocen que antes que el dho marques de Cañete encomendase y diese como dio por via de mayorazgo los dhos y^{o}s contenidos en la dha memoria de que se haze mincion en la primera pregunta al dho don Diego Saire Topa tuvo los mesmos yndios en encomienda el marques don Fran^{co} Piçarro y se sirvio dellos y le tributavan en las cosas que en aquella saçon acostumbravan a contribuir pagar y servir y de la mesma manera los tuvo //
/f.250/ y poseio Gonçalo Picarro su hijo y por tales yndios que se an encomendado fueron y son avidos y tenidos de diez y veinte y muchos mas años a esta parte digan lo que saven y como tributavan y hazian las sementeras y chacaras de coca y Tono y Paucarbamba y las demas que tenia que eran en aquella sazon a manera de tributar que avia.

vj Iten si saven que antes que el dho marques don Françisco Piçarro entrase en estos reinos tuvo y poseyo Guayna Capac Ynga señor que fue deste reino en el dho valle de Yucay los dhos contenidos en la dha memoria y ansi de los naturales como de los mitimas se sirvia dellos y de sus hijos y mujeres y le beneficiavan sus chacaras que hera el tributo que en aquella sazon se dava digan lo que saven.

vij Iten si saven que la tasa que se dava en tpo del dho marques don Françisco Piçarro en lugar de tributos como agora se dan por tasa era en aquella sazon beneficiar la chacara y hazer servi^{o} personal digan lo que saven y de la manera que lo pagavan e sirvian.

viij Iten si saven e conocen que los dhos yn^{o}s cont^{do}s en la dha memoria de la misma manera que an servido y tributado a los dhos Guayna Capa y don Françisco Piçarro y Gonçalo Piçarro y don Diego Saire Topa an servido y beneficiado las chacraas de las demas personas que los a thenido y poseido digan lo que saven de la manera que les an bisto tributar y servir asi a don Françisco Chilche cañare como a los demas

/f.250v/ ix Iten si saven que algunos de los dhos y^{o}s contenidos en la dha memoria se favorecieron del dho don Françisco Chilche y de don Garcia Quispicapi y procuraron de no acudir a hazer el servi^{o} y dar el tributo que heran obligados procurando de que cargase sobre los y^{o}s pobres y asi los escondian y escondieron ansi en la visita que hizo Damian de la Vandera el qual expresamente mando que tributasen y pagasen el tributo como los demas y asi lo mando el tesorero Garcia de Melo y la otra bisita que hizo a los dhos y^{o}s y los comuto la tasa de coca y servicio personal que lo pagasen en plata y por esta relacion se escondieron en dineros y ocultaron muchos de los dhos y^{o}s que el dho Damian de la Vandera visito y numero digan lo que saven.

x Iten si saven que queriendo poner por memoria y y empadronar los yndios que habia tributarios en el dho valle de Yucai el padre Diego Escudero cura que fue en el dho valle los caciques del por favorecer los dhos y^{o}s contenidos en la dha memoria escondieron a entender que eran algunos dellos yanaconas y que no pagavan tributos ni hazian servi^{os} ni chacaras lo qual fue al contrario de la verdad porque siempre los dhos y^{o}s an tributado y fecho los dhos servicios y chacaras digan lo que saven.

xj Iten si saven que el licenciado frei P^{o} Gutierrez Flores visitador que fue del dho valle de Yucay en la visita que hizo en los dhos yndios por sola la rela- //
/f.251/ cion que tuvo de lo que el dho padre Diego Escudero hizo de los y^{o}s que asi empadrono declaro por yanaconas a los dhos yndios contenidos en la dha memoria los quales saven los testigos que no son tales y^{o}s yanaconas sino yndios tributarios y subjetos a sus caciques todos los trescientos y treinta y un yndios contenidos en la dha memoria digan lo que saven.

xij Iten si saven que los dhos y^{o}s contenidos en la dha memoria con el favor de los dhos sus caciques y por entender que no avian de pagar tributo publicavan que heran yanaconas y despues que el dho licenciado frei P^{o} Gutierrez hizo la dha bisita an dho y declarado la verdad como eran yndios tributarios y que siempre an servi^{do} y trivutado digan lo que saven y les an oido dezir y publicar.

xiij Iten si saven e conocen que la dha doña Beatriz Coya y el dho capitan Martin Garcia de Loiola su marido an sido despojados y desposeidos de los dhos sus y^{o}s contenidos en la dha memoria por el dho frei P^{o} Gutierrez y por su Exª del señor bisorrey don Francisco de Toledo y an sido y son agraviados en les aver quitado la posesion que tenian de los dhos yndios contenidos en la dha memoria y de los tribu^{o}s que les davan como y^{o}s de su encomienda en que subcedio la dha doña Beatriz Coya digan lo que saven.

xiiij Iten si saven que todo lo susodho es pu^{co} y notorio y pu^{ca} voz y fama. El Dotor Juan de Herrera Arrandolaça. Alvaro Ruiz de Navamuel.

/f.251v/ v En la ciudad del Cuzco a diez y seis dias del mes de febr^{o} de mil e qui^{o}s y setenta y siete años antes el Yll^{e} señor don Gabriel Paniagua de Loaysa cavallero de la orden de Calatrava corregidor y justicia mayor por su magestad en esta ciudad y su jur^{on} y por ante mi Pero Diaz Valdeon escriv^{o} de su magestad publico y del numero desta dha ciudad del Cuzco parecio presente Domingo Lopez de Larrinaga y en nombre del capitan Martin Garcia de Loyola y de doña Beatriz Coya su mujer y en virtud del poder que dellos tiene presento esta provision real de su magestad emanada de la real audiencia de los Reies e interr^{o} de preguntas y pidio al señor corregidor mande se exsaminen los testigos que presentare en esta causa por las preguntas del dho interr^{o} y por el señor corregidor visto obedecio la real provision con el acatamiento devido y en quanto al cumplimiento mando que el dho Domingo Lopez de Larrinaga en el dho nombre presente los testigos de que se entienda aprovechar ese exsaminaran como su magestad lo manda por la dha real provision y lo firmo testigos el licenciado Gabriel de Pedraza y Sancho de Verdugo alguacil m^{or} don Gabriel Paniagua de Loaysa. Ante mi Pero Diaz Valdeon escrivano.

v Memoria de los yndios que tiene en encomienda doña Beatriz Coya mujer del capitan Martin Garcia de Loyola en el valle de Yucay de los quales despojo el licenciado frei Pedro Gutierrez Flores por mandado de su Exª //
/f.252/ del señor visorrey don Francisco de Toledo que van referidos a la primera pregunta del ynterrogatorio que se pres^{to} por parte de la dha doña Beatriz en este pleito que trataron el fiscal de su magestad sobre el despojo de los dho yndios.

v Xp^{o}bal Paucartica de treinta a^{o}s tiene hijos
v don Diego Mache de cinq^{ta} a^{o}s tiene hijos
v P^{o} Machaguay de treinta a^{o}s tiene hijos
v Mateo Airas de treinta años tiene hijos
v Al^{o} Chauca de cinq^{ta} a^{o}s digo cinq^{ta} y siete años
v Miguel Vilcacondur de treinta años tiene hijos
v Martin Pomacondur de v^{te} e seis a^{o}s tiene hijos
v Simon Aisiminga diez y seis años tiene hijos
v Juan Churimache de seis años huerfano
v Mateo Airo de treinta a^{o}s
v Alonso Quispe de quarenta y ocho años
v Fran^{co} Quispe de veinte años tiene hijos
v Francisco Llancari de quarenta y siete años
v Juan Quiquin Yanac de veinte a^{o}s
v Xpobal Cacaquipa de siete años huerfano
v Mateo Ricra de v^{te} a^{o}s huerfano
v P^{o} Machaguay huerfano de tres años
v Diego Asta Camasca de diez y ocho años
v P^{o} Alcamari de quarenta años
v Diego Aysmalma de diez y ocho a^{o}s tiene hijos
v Agustin Camasca de treinta y cinco a^{o}s tiene hijos
v Fran^{co} Ranpa Yupangui de v^{te} e tres a^{o}s tiene hijos
v Juan Yanaq Camasca de diez y ocho años
v Agustin Chuquiapac de sesenta años
v Ant^{o} Caquia Guari de sesenta años
v Andres Duibus de veinte años
v Alonso Quispe de treinta y ocho años tiene hijos
v Marcos Chili de veinte e cinco a^{o}s tiene hijos
v Diego Laimi de diez y seis años huerfano
v Martin Yncancila de diez a^{o}s huerfano
/f.252v/ v Juan Bautista Manchi de treinta y ocho a^{o}s
v Miguel Timri Naula de v^{te} e cinco a^{o}s tiene hijos
v P^{o} Tini Balbai de diez a^{o}s huerfano
v Fran^{co} Mito Ancila de treinta a^{o}s tiene hijos
v Andres Tinimaza de diez y ocho a^{o}s tiene hijos
v Mateo Llivipuilla de nueve a^{o}s huerfano
v Andres Cazadnaula de v^{te} a^{o}s tiene hijos
v Fran^{co} Vinaicila de v^{te} y seis años tiene hijos
v Mateo Palchito Yznai de diez y siete años
v Fran^{co} Ymibri de ocho años huerfano
v Al^{o} Caquiaiya de v^{te} e cinco años tiene hijos
v Lucas Chilaguaman de treinta a^{o}s tiene hijos
v Xp^{o}bal Nazpi de v^{te} y ocho años
v Martin Cacitancha de treinta e tres a^{o}s tiene hijos
v Martin Vilitancha de treinta e siete a^{o}s tiene hijos
v Lucas Sangai Linpai de treze años
v Andres Quiri Biznai de v^{te} e seis a^{o}s tiene hijos
v Agustin Alao de cinquenta y tres años
v Lucas Bili Dumbai de veinte años
v P^{o} Guaman Aisi de treinta e tres años tiene hijos
v Pedro Sulca de veinte y siete años tiene hijos
v Ju^{o} Bautista Curo de siete años huerfano
v Agustin Tolagua de veinte y seis años tiene hijos
v P^{o} Zucai Toyznai de diez y siete años
v P^{o} Quicana de veinte e siete a^{o}s tiene hijos
v P^{o} Milli de sesenta e cinco a^{o}s
v Pedro Langayza de veinte años tiene hijos
v Xp^{o}bal Guaman Cusi de treinta y ocho a^{o}s tiene hijos
v Ju^{o} Tosco de treinta e cinco años tiene hijos
v Xp^{o}bal Uscotoma de v^{te} a^{o}s tiene hijos
v Antonio Guaspar de treinta e nueve a^{o}s tiene hijos
v Martin Malque de quarenta y nueve años tiene hijos
/f.253/ v Francisco Guachalla de v^{te} años tiene hijos
v P^{o} Alla de v^{te} e dos a^{o}s tiene hijos
v Her^{do} Llalbai de cinq^{ta} y ocho años
v Domingo Libi Puchai de v^{te} años tiene hijos
v Xp^{o}bal Suman Ausauay de cinq^{ta} y ocho años
v Juan Bautista Duman Pudlla de treinta años tiene hijos
v Xp^{o}bal Araranca de treinta a^{o}s
v Her^{do} Pasto de treinta e quatro a^{o}s
v R^{o} Tacuri de treinta años tiene hijos
v Juan Bautista Cacpaipay de veinte e nueve años tiene hijos
v Benito Rimache de treze años huerfano
v Francisco Gualpa de diez y ocho a^{o}s tiene hijos
v Ju^{o} Pasto de veinte a^{o}s
v Agustin Llaccohua de veinte y siete años
v Benito Llacchila de catorze a^{o}s huerfano
v Juan Sisi de treinta y ocho años tiene hijos
v Diego Tanta de treinta y tres años tiene hijos
v Diego Usco Guaman de treinta e tres años tiene hijos
v P^{o} Paucar Lloclla de ocho años huerfano
v Martin Supaico de doze años huerfano
v Juan Guari de veinte años tiene hijos
v Jer^{mo} Cuyo de veinte y cinco años tiene hijos
v Xp^{o}bal Diachi Nachay de quarenta e cinco a^{o}s tiene hijos
v Pedro Zinmala de cinquenta y siete a^{o}s tiene hijos
v Benito Guartailanga de veinte años
v P^{o} Lazaca de v^{te} y ocho años tiene hijos
v Pedro Buran de cinq^{ta} y dos a^{o}s
v Martin Marca Vichay de v^{te} e tres años

v Al^{o} Bili Viznay de treinta e cinco a^{o}s tiene hijos
v P^{o} Salina de treinta años tiene hijos
/f.253v/ v Al^{o} Uchunlalay de quarenta años tiene hijos
v Gonçalo Tanbay Putlla de treinta años tiene hijos
v Martin Sabay de cinquenta y tres años
v Al^{o} Zunit Putlla de diez y ocho años
v Juan Amguarin de diez y ocho años
v Sebastian Tenicela de sesenta años
v Juan Caçad Naula de diez años huerfano
v R^{o} Lalchi Viznai de treinta años tiene hijos
v Her^{do} Oharo de veinte e cinco a^{o}s tiene hijos
v Al^{o} Toyro de cinquenta y quatro años
v Al^{o} Cartam de cinquenta y ocho años
v Xp^{o}bal Tamay de treinta años tiene hijos
v P^{o} Ayachagua de quarenta y ocho años
v Simon de YllaTopa de quarenta años
v Ju^{o} Uchopanta de quarenta y tres a^{o}s tiene hijos
v F^{e} Condor de diez a^{o}s huerfano
v Agustin Tacopa de diez y ocho años
v Xp^{o}bal Sulca Pomanabi de quarenta años
v P^{o} Paucar Aymara de diez y siete años tiene hijos
v P^{o} Bilca Cachia de veinte años tiene hijos
v Agustin Alaya de diez y nueve años
v Toribio Curimana de quarenta y tres años tiene hijos
v Martin Titogualpa de diez años huerfano
v Xp^{o}l Ucha Cauana de diez y siete años
v Al^{o} Marcagualpa de cinq^{ta} años tiene hijos
v Xp^{o}bal Chalcuri de veinte e quatro años tiene hijos
v Al^{o} Arosu de quarenta y ocho a^{o}s tiene hijos
v Martin Tutunicilla de sesenta años
v Fran^{co} Chuquimissa de diez y seis a^{o}s
v Xp^{o}bal Cusiguaman de sesenta e cinco años
v Ant^{o} Urco Arossi de quarenta y tres a^{o}s
/f.254/ v Juan Guacal de sesenta y quatro a^{o}s
v P^{o} Sulca Guacal de veinte y cinco años tiene hijos
v Alonso Vinamamai de treinta e tres a^{o}s tiene hijos
v Rodrigo Cuzcuc de treinta años tiene hijos
v Benito Garchinaula de diez y ocho a^{o}s tiene hijos
v Juan Bautista Duysul de veinte e siete años tiene hijos
v Martin Ninapuma de treinta y ocho años tiene hijos
v Xp^{o}bal Tomaylla de v^{te} e tres a^{o}s tiene hijos
v Juan Chuquicanche de diez y ocho a^{o}s
v Lucas Chuquicondur de diez y nueve a^{o}s tiene hijos
v Juan Caroaguarca de quince años huerfano
v Lor^{co} Quispe de treinta años tiene hijos
v P^{o} Rinba de sesenta a^{o}s
v R^{o} Guaraca de veinte e tres a^{o}s tiene hijos
v Jer^{mo} Guaman Guilca de veinte a^{o}s
v hasta aqui eran de don Fran^{co} Chilche y sus hijos
—138—
v Diego Guaman de quarenta años
v Al^{o} Condursupa de v^{te} a^{o}s
v Paulo Poma Condor de catorze años huerfano
v Agustin Sulca Tocas de veinte e ocho a^{o}s
v Juan Malqui de veinte y quatro años
v Juan Bautista Culla Gua^{co} de diez y seis años
v Juan Rimache de veinte e cinco años
v Domingo Apassa de treinta e tres años
v Fran^{co} Llacssa Yupari de cinq^{ta} años tiene hijos
v Al^{o} Usco de cinq^{ta} años tiene hijos
v Francisco Guayua Usco de veinte e tres a^{o}s tiene hijos
v P^{o} Tinta de quarenta y dos a^{o}s
v Francisco Quispi Yupa de diez y ocho a^{o}s tiene hijos
v Al^{o} Cunye Yupari de veinte e cinco a^{o}s tiene hijos
v Agustin Condori de quarenta y tres años
v Andres Caroa Pisco de veinte años tiene hijos
v Mateo Ataochuco de veinte años
v Alonso Muqui de sesenta y cinco años
/f.254v/ v Andres Cuquis Yupari de diez y nueve a^{o}s tiene hijos
v Martin Curagua de veinte e cinco años
v Juan Manta de diez y ocho años
v Xpobal Cuyatupa de siete años huerfano
v Alonso Pilpi de cinq^{ta} años
v Martin Quispi de treynta años tiene hijos
v Martin Guanaco de sesenta años
v P^{o} Pumaguaman de treinta años tiene hijos
v Juan Cusma de cinquenta y seis años
v Domingo Pumaruon de diez y ocho años
v Ju^{o} Bautista Naupachi de sesenta años tiene hijos
v Xpobal Siumta de treinta y siete años tiene hijos
v Ju^{o} Bilcas Pariguana de v^{te} a^{o}s tiene hijos
v Alonso Guaman de diez y siete años
v Martin Mayta de cinq^{ta} a^{o}s tiene hijos
v Ju^{o} Camachaira de diez y seis años
v Xpobal Pana Lucri de cinquenta y seis a^{o}s
v Al^{o} Puma de treinta e seis años tiene hijos
v Al^{o} Ancaypuro de diez y nueve años tiene hijos
v Domingo Bilca de quarenta a^{o}s tiene hijos
v Fran^{co} Uchaguaman de v^{te} e cinco años tiene hijos
v Al^{o} Aruco de seis años huerfano
v Juan Cochochin de treinta y nueve años tiene hijos
v P^{o} Ananpa de veinte y siete años tiene hijos
v Domingo Yarobilca de v^{te} e tres años
v Fran^{co} Yanac de veinte y ocho años huerfano
v Diego Amaro de sesenta años
v Al^{o} Condormachaguay de veinte e seis años
v Martin Cauas Canco de ses^{a} e quatro años tiene hijos
v Alonso Coca Bascanco de v^{te} e quatro a^{o}s tiene hijos
v Martin Bica de v^{te} e dos años
v Xp^{o}bal Topa Yupangui de v^{te} e seis a^{o}s tiene hijos
v Al^{o} Gualpa Cuzco de treinta años tiene hijos
v Xp^{o}bal Rasni de treinta y dos años
/f.255/ v Her^{do} Ataocaba de diez y nueve a^{o}s tiene hijos
v don Juan Aylanbo de quarenta e cinco años tiene hijos
v hasta aqui eran de don Alonso Tito Atauche que son cinq^{ta} e cinco.
v Juan Malco Pariguana de treinta e nueve años tiene hijos.
v Pedro Guancapuma de cinquenta años tiene hijos
v Juan Ancagualpa de quarenta y dos años tiene hijos
v P^{o} Mallaocubi de v^{te} e tres años tiene hijos
v Diego Machaca de v^{te} años tiene hijos
v Xp^{o}bal Supao de veinte e seis años
v P^{o} Camca de cinq^{ta} años
v Diego Gualpa Auquis de quarenta y tres años tiene hijos
v P^{o} Auquis de diez y nueve años tiene hijos
v Santiago Yanac de treinta y dos a^{o}s tiene hijos
v P^{o} Pacha de treinta e dos años tiene hijos
v Martin Caroayanac de veinte y tres años
v Fran^{co} Lasac Guaman de diez y ocho años
v Venito Guaman de diez y ocho años huerfano
v Gonçalo Pumagualpa de quinze años
v Sebastian Cusi Yucra de treinta y ocho años tiene hijos
v Jer^{mo} Pilco Yucra de diez y siete años

v Juan Ancay de treinta y dos años tiene hijos
v Ff^{e}Guaman de v^{te} e tres años
v Xpobal Muti Yupangue de quarenta e cinco años tiene hijos
v Diego Tupa Yupangue de diez y ocho años tiene hijos
v Domingo Turus de catorze años huerfano
v Al^{o} Quispi de v^{te} e cinco años
v Al^{o} Sulca Myuasca de ocho años huerfano
v Al^{o} Guanasca de diez a^{o}s huerfano
v Agustin Atao Suyuiquina de v^{te} años tiene hijos
v P^{o} Paucar de quarenta y seis años
v Juan Guandapi de veinte e un años tiene hijos
/f.255v/ v Al^{o} Aucatuma de diez años huerfano
v Diego Calami de ocho a^{o}s huerfano
v Juan Gualca de diez años huerfano
v Domingo Guaman de diez y ocho años
v P^{o} Yucara de diez y ocho años tiene hijos
v Andres Guamolli de veinte años tiene hijos
v Xpobal Guamalli de cinquenta y seis a^{o}s
v Martin Alonso Muru de quarenta años tiene hijos
v Diego Cusipuro de quarenta y tres años
v Agustin Cusipaucar de v^{te} a^{o}s tiene hijos
v Martin Puriga Guaman de veinte e quatro a^{o}s
v Al^{o} Cusirimache de onze años huerfano
v Martin Guamanchucha de treinta años
v P^{o} Sibipaucar de quarenta y siete años
v Martin Quicana de quarenta y quatro a^{o}s tiene hijos
v Juan Asto Capcha de treinta e cinco años tiene hijos
v Gonçalo Sumcachi de treinta e cinco años
v Xpobal Guarta Ytuip de treinta y ocho a^{o}s tiene hijos
v Ant^{o} de Quiñones Ananpa de treinta a^{o}s tiene hijos
v Diego Nina Ricra de treinta y quatro años tiene hijos
v Domingo Sulca de v^{te} e seis años tiene hijos
v Her^{do} Carua Vanca de veinte e tres años
v Salvador Llachu Asto de cinq^{ta} e quatro años
v Luis Sulca Llachua de v^{te} e cinco años tiene hijos
v Vicente Chiguan de veinte años tiene hijos
v Fran^{co} Chiguan de doze años huerfano
v Juan Bautista Rauayache de treinta años tiene hijos
v Her^{do} Pumacondor de cinquenta e cinco años
v Xpobal Chucondor de diez y seis años
v Ant^{o} Pumacondor de v^{te} años tiene hijos
v Juan Chiche de veinte e ocho años
/f.256/ v Fran^{co} Puma Chinche de diez y ocho años
v Francisco Sulcacondor de treinta años tiene hijos
v Ambrosio Pillaca de años [*sic*] tiene hijos
v Her^{do} Gualparimache de diez y seis años
v Martin Gualparoca de catorce a^{o}s huerfano
v Martin Rimache Yupangue de nueve años tiene hijos
v Juan Tupa Yupangue de veinte y ocho años tiene hijos
v Martin Ataocusi de qu^{ta} a^{o}s
v Diego Picana de diez y ocho años tiene hijos
v don Carlos Gualpa Roca de treinta e cinco años
v Miguel Ninagualpa de treinta e siete a^{o}s tiene hijos
v Cristobal Yacchimarca de veinte e seis años
v P^{o} Bilcarima de cinquenta e cinco años
v Martin Rimache de veinte e dos años tiene hijos
v don Al^{o} Tupa Cusi Gualpa de v^{te} e quatro años tiene hijos
v Ff^{e} Manchapa de treinta a^{o}s
v Agustin Pactir de v^{te} años
v Al^{o} Pariango de v^{te} e ocho años
v Xpobal Pariango de quinze años
v Pedro Villo de quinze a^{o}s
v Alonso Capo de veinte y ocho años tiene hijos
v Juan Alonso Aocasupa de quarenta a^{o}s tiene hijos
v Martin Guartat Puclla de cinquenta años
v F^{e} Putllacilla de treinta y siete años
v Martin Puchuna de treinta y tres a^{o}s tiene hijos
v Agustin Gualuto de v^{te} e seis años tiene hijos
v Diego Llamuca de quarenta y siete años
v Agustin Arone de diez y ocho años
v Alonso Guamancusi de v^{te} e ocho a^{o}s tiene hijos
v Juan Caroaruna de v^{te} años tiene hijos
v Goncalo Tongoragua de cinquenta años
v Martin Cuti de sesenta y seis años
v Martin Sanca de veinte e quatro años
v Her^{do} Casavilca de treinta años
v P^{o} Pallanchuc de veinte e siete años
v Her^{do} Caruati de cinquenta y dos años
v Martin Marca de cinquenta años
/f.256v/ v Pedro Quispe de veinte e dos años tiene hijos
v Sebastian Sulca de cinquenta años
v Francisco Curi de diez y ocho años
v Lucas Rimasca de treinta e cinco años tiene hijos
v P^{o} Llachua de cinq^{ta} años tiene hijos
v Diego Acata de quarenta años tiene hijos
v P^{o} Quispe de v^{te} a^{o}s tiene hijos
v Al^{o} Mucac de treinta e siete años tiene hijos
v Sebastian Maybasca de ocho años huerfano
v Juan Piçarro Cusi Ataochi de quarenta y ocho años tiene hijos
v Lor^{ço} Guaritupa de diez y nueve años
v Martin Luay de veinte y seis años
v Lor^{ço} Quispeguaman de veinte a^{o}s tiene hijos
v Domingo Topa Cusigualpa de v^{te} e ocho años tiene hijos
v Alonso Caquicuya de treinta e tres a^{o}s tiene hijos
v Xpobal Ara Viznay de diez y ocho años huerfano
v Francisco Guartad Naula de diez y nueve a^{o}s tiene hijos
v Fabian Chachillo de cinq^{ta} e nueve años tiene hijos
v P^{o} Quispe de treinta y dos años
v Ff^{e} Yupangue de cinq^{ta} e nueve años tiene hijos
v Martin Piri Naula de treinta e dos años tiene hijos
v Miguel Nitnaguaray de quarenta y cinco años
v P^{o} Churocana de treinta a^{o}s tiene hijos
v P^{o} Condori de cinq^{ta} a^{o}s tiene hijos
v Marcos Puri de ses^{a} a^{o}s tiene hijos
v Domingo Gualparimache de diez y siete años
v Fran^{co} Chucuna de treinta años
v Alonso Napanga de v^{te} a^{o}s
v P^{o} Ricra de v^{te} y ocho años
v Luis Sulla de cinq^{ta} e cinco a^{o}s tiene hijos
v Martin Cucco Paucar de treinta y ocho a^{o}s tiene hijos
v Juan Bautista Chuquipaucar de veinte e tres a^{o}s tiene hijos
v Agustin Paco de sesenta años
v Marcos Chalco Yupangue de treinta a^{o}s tiene hijos
v Alonso Guaypa de quarenta y tres años tiene hijos
v Di^{o} Llamas de diez a^{o}s huerfano
v Ju^{o} Yaris de treinta e tres a^{o}s tiene hijos
v Alonso Vina de treinta e tres años tiene hijos
v Juan Ynga Paucar de diez y ocho años tiene hijos
v Her^{do} Villi de cinquenta e cinco años
v Francisco Caro Mango de quarenta años

v El Dotor Herrera Arrandolaça

/f.257/ Sepan quantos esta carta vieren como yo Fray Domingo de Loyola vico provincial de la orden de los predicadores y yo el capitan Francisco de Barrasa que al presente residimos en esta ciudad de Arequipa del Peru en voz y en nombre del Capitan Martin Garcia de Onaz y Loyola y por virtud de su poder que paso ante el escrivo desta carta cuyo tenor sacado del original es este que se sigue.

v Sepan quantos esta carta de poder vieren como yo el capitan Marti Garcia de Loyola de Onaz y de Loyola vzo de la ciudad del Cuzco del Peru comendador de la orden de Calatrava que al presente resido en esta ciudad de Arequipa de camino para los reinos de España otorgo e conozco por esta carta que doy y otorgo mi poder cumplido libre llenero baste de dro se requiere y mas puede y debe valer al muy reverendo padre Fray Domingo de Loyola de la orden de los predicadores vico provincial desta provincia del Peru questa presente y al capitan Martin Dolmos vecino de la ciudad del Cuzco y al fator Juan de Salas y a don Jermo de Figueroa y a Franco de Barrasa y Alonso de Valdez ausente como si fuesen presentes a todos juntamente e cada uno e qualquier dellos por si ynsolidun pa que en mi nombre representando mi propio persona puedan tener y tengan a su cargo e administracion el repartimiento de yos que yo tengo y poseo en terminos de la ciudad del Cuzco y la renta e situacion que tengo en esta dha sobre repartimito de yos que yo tengo y poseo en terminos de la ciudad del Cuzco y la renta e situacion que tengo en esta dha sobre el repartimito de yos de Puquma que fueron encomendados en Diego Hernandez de Mendoça y otros qualesquier haziendas que al presente tengo //
/f.257v/ e adelante tuviere en este reino en qualquier manera e puedan pedir e demandar recibir y cobrar en juio y fuera del de los caciques principales e yos de los dhos repartimientos e de otras personas de quien e con dro devan ansi los dhos tribuos rentas y aprovechamios de mis haziendas como todos y qualesquier maravedis y pesos de oro plata ropa mercadurias esclavos ganados e otros bienes muebles raizes y se movientes deudas dros e acciones que me deven e devieren de aqui adelante por obligaciones conocimientos quentas ceçiones y traspasos e por otras escripturas o sin ellas en qualquier manera e que qualesquier personas lo ayan rescibido e cobrado en mi nombre con mi poder o sin el a los quales e a otras personas que an tenido a su cargo e administracion mis bienes y haziendas puedan pedir e tomar quenta con pago e les hazer cargos e recibir sus descargos e poner adiciones e nombrar terzeros contadores que hagan y liquiden las dhas quentas y las aprovar y cobrar los alcanzes y de lo que ansi recivieren y cobraren den cartas de pago lasto e finiquito con renunciacion de la exepon de la ynnumerata pecunia e leies de prueva e paga sino fuere ante escrivo que della de fe y balga como si las otorgase estando presente e pa que puedan vender y vendan qualesquier mis tribuos bienes muebles raizes y semovientes que tengo e tuviere y me pertenecen en qualquier manera e que les paresciere vender a las personas //
/f.258/ e por los precios de maravedis y pos de oro e otras cosas de contado o fiado o los tocar e cambiar por las cosas que les pareciere o los arrendar por el tiempo e precio que les pareciere e puedan hazer qualesquier sueltas y esperas en poca o en mucha cantidad y por el tiempo que les paresciere y hazer qualesquier conciertos en esto e convenencias con mis deudores y acrehedores y con otras personas y con promenter qualesquier mis pleitos e deudas en manos y poder de terzeros y juezes arbritos arbritadores e amigables con componedores e prorogar en ellas entera juron e puedan dar e tomar a censo qualesquier quentas de pesos de oro posesiones e otros bienes y ceder e trespasar qualesquier mis bienes con mis dros e acciones e otorgar e acetar ceciones y traspasos e puedan comprar en mi nombre y para mi esclavos y otros bienes y haziendas por el precio que les pareciere de contado o fiado y para que puedan fletar qualesquier recuas de carnero pa las partes y lugares que bien bisto les fuere y tomar criados y los asalariar por tiempo y precio y aquellos despedir y tomar otros y pagarles los salarios e lo mesmo a letrados e procuradores y puedan pedir minas y estacas y demasias y ternos pa las labrar y poblar y dellas y de otros qualesquier bienes puedan tomar e aprehender la posesion con las solenidades que se requiere e puedan revocar e revoquen qualesquier //
/f.258v/ poder e poderes que yo he dado a qualesquier personas pa que no usen dellos desde el dia que les fuere revocados demas de lo qual les doy mi poder pa que me puedan obligar a mi persona bienes e haziendas avidos e por aver en la cantidad de maravedis o pesos de oro que fueren menester y nezesarios pa el benefo e aumento e acrecentamito de bienes y haziendas e otorguen escripturas de obligacion con las fuerças que pa su balidacion se requieran e aquellos pagar de los dhos mis bienes y haziendas y puedan vender qualesquier haziendas mias adelantadas y obligarme al entrego dellos y enviarme partadas de oro e plata e otras cosas a los reinos de España por la orden y forma que les pareciere a mi costa e riesgo registrados o por registrar con la facultad e condiciones que quisieren y por vien tuvieren y para que puedan hazer compañias con qualesquier personas y en qualesquier bienes y generos e con las condiciones tiempos posturas y penas que por vien tuvieren e aquellos o las que yo tengo fechas puedan deshazer anular e chancelar cerca de todo lo qual puedan hazer e otorgar escripturas de pago venta e compra arrendamito y de censo çesiones y traspasos y de sueltas y esperas e compromisos pactos e conveniencias trueque e cambio e obligaciones e las demas que en la dha razon y pa todo lo dho en general e para cada cosa dello en particular convengan e sean nezesarios con obligacion de mi persona //
/f.259/ e bienes poder a las justicias sumisiones renunciaciones de leies y de fuero y con las demas fuerças e firmeças que pa su balidacion se requieran que siendo por los dhos a quien doy este poder e por qualquier dellos fechas e otorgadas yo desde agora las otorgo y e por otorgadas y me obligo de las cumplir como en ellas y en cada una dellas se contuviere e so la pena e penas que sobre mi e mis bienes pusieren e finalmente les doy este dho mi poder pa que puedan hazer e hagan en mi ne todo e que ello que mi propia persona podra e puede hazer aunque aqui no baya espacificado porque yo por espresos y espacificado aqui las clausulas que para ello pareciere faltar e fuere necesarios de manera que para todo tenga libre e general administracion sin eçetacion alguna con que el dho Alonso de Valdez actualmente tenga a su cargo e administracion los dhos mis bes y haziendas e rentas y entienda en el benefo y ministerio dellas por si e por personas que pa ello pusiere atento quel dho Alonso de Valdez es la persona que a de tener quenta e razon de las dhas mis haziendas y bienes y de lo que cobrare y pagare al qual dho Alonso de Valdez en particular doy poder pa que pueda pagar e gastar de mis bienes lo que yo le dexare por instrucion y memoria firmada de mi nombre y le escriviere por mis cartas misivas y de lo que ansi pagare y gastare se le reçiva y pase en quenta por fin e //
/f.259v/ muerte del dho Alonso de Valdez o por justo ympedimito caso que çubceda puedan los demas contenidos en este poder todos o los tres dellos juntamente nombrar persona que en lugar del dho Alonso de Valdez rixa y administre las dhas mis haziendas y use deste poder como si a la tal persona rezara. Otro si doy este dho mi poder a los dhos Domingo de Loyola y capt Martin Dolmos y factor Juan de

Salas y don Jer^{mo} de Figueroa y a Francisco de Barrasa e Alonso de Valdez e a qualquier dellos ynsolidun como dho es con que no puedan responder a nueva demanda que se me ponga sin que primero se me notefique en persona generalmente pa todos mis pleitos causas y negocios civiles y criminales movidos e por mover quantos tengo y tuviere con qualesquier personas y sus bienes e las tales e otras qualesquier los an e tienen y esperan aver y tener contra mi en qualquier manera e pa que asi demandando como defendiendo puedan parezer y parezcan ante su magestad e su presidente e oydores de sus reales audiencias y chancillerias e ante otras justicias y seglares de qualesquier ptes que sean ante los quales e cada uno y qualquier dellos siendo actos o reos puedan hazer e poner qualesquier demandas pedimi^{o}s requirimi^{o}s autos protestaciones presentaciones de testigos escriptos y escripturas y hazer en mi anima qualesquier juram^{o}s de calunia y de asocio e ymliten y dad decir //
/f.260/ e los difirir en las partes contrarias y poner articulos e pusiciones e absolver a los que contra mi fueren puestos negando o confesando e ver presentar jurar e conozer los testigos que contra mi se presentaren e los tachar e contradezir en dhos y en personas e abonar mis testigos e lo por mi parte fecho y sacar qualesquier escripturas procesos y testimonios que me convengan de poder de escrivanos e secretarios e otras personas en cuyo poder esten e hazer provanças e pedir testimonios e quartos plazos ordinarios e ultramarinos e hazer las diligencias nezesarias e ganar provisiones en mi favor e contradezir las que de contrario se quisieren ganar y hazer recusaciones de juezes escriv^{o}s e acompañados jurarlas e se apartar dellas si vieren que conviene e pedir costas tasacion e paga della y pedir embargos ex^{on}es ventas y remates de vienes e concluyr e oyr sentencias interlocutorias e difinitivas e las consentir o apelar dellas y seguir y dar quien siga las apelaciones y suplicaciones y en el ef^{to} hazer y hagan por todos grados e ynstancias todos aquellos y demas autos y diligencias judiciales y estrajudiciales que convengan e yo haria e podria hazer estando presente aunque pa ello se requiera mi mas especial poder e presencia personal porque yo se la doy e otorgo con sus yncidencias e dependencias anexidades e conexidades e con libre e general administracion con facultad que lo puedan //
/f.260v/ sustituyr en todo en la pte que del quisieren en una o mas personas e aquellos revocar e sostituir de nuevo las vezes e cuando quisieren e los relevo en forma de dr^{o} e de lo que deven ser relevados e pa lo aver por iorme obligo mi ps^{a} e bienes avidos e por aver doy poder a las justicias de su magestad de qualesquier ptes que sean a cuya jur^{on} me someto y renuncio mi propio fuero e juridiccion domicilio y vezindad e la ley sit convenerit de juridicionen onium judicum pa que me apremien al cumplimiento de lo que dho es ese contuviere en las escripturas que es virtud deste poder se otorgaren como por sentencia pasada en cosa juzgada en testimi^{o} de lo qual otorgue esta carta ante el scriv^{o} pu^{co} y t^{gos} yuso escriptos en cuyo registro firme mi nombre e yo el presente escriv^{o} doy fe que conozco al dho otorgante desta carta que es fecha en Arequipa a v^{te} e dos dias del mes de henero año del señor de mill e qui^{o}s y setenta y quatro años testigos que fueron presente a lo que dho es Juan Guizelmo y Fran^{co} de Baraona y Bautista Alvares residentes en esta ciudad Martin Garcia de Loyola. Paso ante Juan de Vera scriv^{o} pu^{co} del numero desta ciudad de Arequipa por su mag^{t} fui pres^{te} al otorgamiento desta carta y fize aqui mi signo que es a tal en testimonio de verdad Ju^{o} de Vera escrivano publico.

/f.261/ Otorgamos e conocemos que ante todas cosas revocamos el poder que el dho cap^{t} Loyola dio y otorgo a Pedro de San Juan pa que no use del en manera alguna e pedimos le sea noteficada esta revocacion dexandole como le dexamos en su onrra y buena vida y fama y debaxo de la dha revocacion sostituimos el dho poder suso yncorporado segun y como en el se contiene sin excetar ni reservar del cosa alg^{a} en Juan Ruiz de Leon y en Domingo Lopez de la Reinaga y en qualquier dellos ynsolidun en el dho Juan Ruiz de Leon para las cobranças quel dho capitan Loyola tiene en esta ciudad de su situacion y otras cobranças que en esta ciudad y sus ter^{nos} ocurieren y para los pleitos e causas movidos e por mover al dho cap^{t} tocantes en qualquier manera y en al dho Domingo de la Reinaga pa todo lo en que en el dho poder cont^{do} sin limitacion excetacion alguna y por quanto Alonso de Valdez contenido en el dho poder es muerto nombramos al dho Domingo Lopez de la Rinaga pa el uso del dho poder y para que entienda en la administracion de las haziendas y tribu^{o}s del dho capitan Loyola segun y como el dho Alonso de Valdez lo podia e pudo hazer de manera que en su lugar çuceda en el uso del dho poder el dho Domingo Lopez de la Rinaga y los relevamos como somos relevados e para lo aver por firme obligamos la persona y bienes del dho cap^{t} Loyola y lo otorgamos ante el scriv^{o} pu^{co} y testigos yuso es- //
/f.261v/ critos en cuyo registro firmamos nuestros nombres. Fecho en Arequipa a diez y nueve de otubre de mil e qui^{o}s y setenta e cinco años testigos que fueron presente a lo que dho es. Juan de Çianca y Fran^{co} de Reinosa y Pedro de Murguia residentes en esta ciudad y doy fe que conozco a los dhos otorgantes fray Domingo de Loyola Fran^{co} de Barrasa paso ante mi Juan de Vera scriv^{o} pu^{co}. Yo Ju^{o} de Vera escrivano pu^{co} del numero desta ciudad de Arequipa y su jur^{on} por su mag^{t} fuy pres^{te} al otorgamiento desta carta e fize aqui mi signo ques a tal en testim^{o} de verdad. Ju^{o} de Vera scriv^{o} pu^{co}.

Don Hurtado de Mendoça marques de Cañete guarda maior de la çiudad de Cuenca bisorrey e capitan general en estos reinos e provincias del Piru por su m^{t} etc. por quanto su m^{t} por sus provisiones y cartas reales tiene mandado que procure por las buenas maneras que ser pudiere traer de paz y a su obdiencia y servi^{o} real al Ynga pa que biniesen el y los naturales que con el anduviesen en conocimi^{to} de nra santa fee catolica y la recibiesen pa su salvacion y en cumplimi^{to} dello luego como llegue a estos dhos reinos porque cesasen los grandes daños e ynconvenientes que a causa de andar alçado y de guerra en los Andes Saire Topa Mango Capac Yupangue Ynga hijo de Mango Ynga nieto de Guayna Capac señor natural que fue destos dhos reinos por los muchos saltos e muertes y robos que ordinariamente hazian por sus capitanes y gente en los caminos //
/f.262/ reales a españoles y naturales y la cantidad de naturales que llevava y recogia a los dhos Andes donde andava de los questavan paçificos y debaxo de la ovidencia de su m^{t} y el desasosiego e ynquietud que con el dho Ynga tenian los naturales de los repartimientos de y^{o}s que sirven a los vz^{o}s de las ciudades del Cuzco e Guamanga provei que religiosos y mensajeros fuesen a hablarle de pte de su magestad y de la mia en su real nombre pa que viniese de paz y a su real obidencia y servi^{o} y le envie perdones de muerte de españoles y naturales que obiese fecho y de otros qualesquier crimines y delictos que uviese cometido ofreciendole que biniendo de paz e a lo susodho dentro de cierto termi^{o} que le fue señalado se le hazian merzedes en su real nombre de los repartimi^{o}s de y^{o}s de Yucay questuvo encomendado don

Fran^{co} Piçarro menor hijo del marques don Françisco Piçarro dif^{o} y de Xaquixaguana Guayllaquipa y Pucara que estuvo encomendado en Francisco Hernandez Giron vz^{o} del Cuzco dif^{to} que estan vacos con todo lo a ello subjeto y que demas de los susodho le serian fechas otras mercedes de tierras y solares y otras cosas contenidas en las provisiones que dello se mandaron dar y enviaron lo qual aviendolo tratado los dhos religiosos y mensajeros con el dho Ynga lo acepto y salio y vino de paz y entro en esta ciudad de los Reies y corte vispera de la fiesta de los Reies deste presente año de qui^{o}s y cinq^{ta} y ocho y dio a su m^{t} y a mi en su real nombre la obidiencia devida y prometio de siempre servirle como su bueno y leal vasallo debeis obligado //
/f.262v/ hazer y porque aviendo fecho lo suso dho es justo que se tenga quenta con su persona y se cumplan las dhas merzedes pa con que se sustente e su mujer e casa e familia y de nuevo se le hagan otras porque se aficione y obligue mas al servi^{o} de su mag^{t} y tenga voluntad de se convertir y convierta a nra santa fee catolica pa que se salve y obligue y anime a los demas naturales destos dhos reinos a que hagan lo mismo ques lo que principalm^{te} su m^{t} a pretendido y pretende destos dhos reinos por la pres^{te} en su real nombre y por virtud de su real poder que pa ello tengo su tenor del qual es este que se sigue.

v Don Carlos por la divina clemencia emperador semper agusto rey de Alemania doña Juana su madre y el mismo don Carlos por la misma gracia Reies de Castilla de Leon de Aragon de las dos Ceçilias de Jerusalen de Navarra de Granada de Toledo de Valencia de Galicia de Mallorcas de Sevilla de Cerdena de Cordova de Corcega de Murcia de Jaen de los Algarves de Algecira de Gibraltar de las Islas de Canaria de las Yndias islas e tierra firme del mar oceano conde de Flandes e de Tirol etc. A todos los conçejos regidores cavalleros escuderos y oficiales y omes buenos de todas las ciudades villas e lugares de las provincias de la Nueva Castilla llamada Piru y de la nueva Toledo y de las otras provincias e yslas subjetas y comprehendidas en el distrito y juridicion de la nuestra audiencia y chancillerias real de las dhas provincias del Piru e otras qualesquier personas eclesiasticas y seglares de qualquier estado condicion preminencia e dignidad que sea o ser pue- //
/f.263/ dan vz^{o}s estantes y abitantes en las dhas provincias y en cada una dellas a quien toca e atañe y puede tocar y atañer lo en esta carta contenido y a cada uno y qualquier de vos salud e gracia. Sepades que nos aviendo entendido las alteraciones cosas acaeçidas del Peru despues que Francisco Hernandez Giron con otros muchos que con el se juntaron se alçaron en la ciudad del Cuzco y prendieron a Gil Ramirez Davalo nro corregidor que era en la dha ciudad deseando como deseamos que esas provincias se pongan en toda paz sosiego y quietud para que en ellas se haga el servi^{o} de Dios nuestro s^{or} y su santa fee catolica se aumentada y para este efeto e que nos seamos servidos y esas dhas provincias vayan en todo crecimi^{to} y noblecimi^{to} y los pobladores dellas biban en todo contentami^{to} avemos acordado de enviar a ellas una persona de autoridad de confiança pa que entienda en ello y por el gran conzepto que tenemos de la persona de don Hurtado de Mendoça marques de Cañete le avemos elexido y señalado por nro bisorrey desa tierra y por presidente en la audi^{a} real que en ella reside pa que haga y administre justicia igual a todos nros subditos y vasallos y para que ansimismo entienda en hazer y ordenar todo lo que convenga pa el sosiego quietud y noblecimiento desa tierra como dho es por la presente de nro propio motuo y deliverada voluntad eleximos constituymos y señalamos pa ello al dho marques de Cañete y le damos y otorgamos //
/f.263v/ todo nuestro poder cumplido libre llenero bast^{e} con libre e general administracion segun e tan cumplidam^{te} que lo nos avemos y de dr^{o} y de hecho mas puede y deve valer para que por nos y en nro nombre y como nras mysmas personas pueda entender y entienda en la pacificacion y sosiego desas dhas provincias y administracion de justicia en ellas e provea en todas las cosas que ocurrieren ansy conçernientes a la dha administracion y ex^{on} de la nuestra justicia como de la buena governacion y defensa desas dhas provincias y noblecimi^{to} dellas y gratificacion de los pobladores nuestros subditos y vasallos que los an ydo a poblar y bien e buen tratami^{to} y conservacion de los naturales della y buen recaudo de nra hazienda y en todas las otras cosas e casos e negocios de qualquier calidad e condicion que sean y se ofrezcan lo que le pareciere y biere que conviene y se deve hazer e provea en nro nombre y como nos mismos lo podriamos hazer y proveer todos los ofi^{o}s e cargos ansi de justicia y de governacion como de otra qualquier manera desas dhas provincias e de cada una dellas que conforme a dr^{o} nos podemos y devemos proveer e hazer en nro nombre gracias merzedes de qualesquier tenencias y alcaidias regimientos escrivanias e otros qualesquier oficios y cosas de qualquier calidad que sean ansi por renunciacion como provacion y en otra qualquier manera y para que /roto/ siendo menester para defension desas dhas provincias y bien y utilidad dellas //
/f.264/ pueda apercivir de guerra y llamar y convocar a las ciudades e villas e otros pu^{o}s y a los prelados governadores justicias cavalleros y otras personas desas provincias y estantes en ellas pa que bengan donde fuere neçes^{o} con la gente que por el les fuere mandado y sobre ello hazer todas las otras provisiones y mandami^{o}s que al caso convengan y le pareciere y finalmente pueda hazer y proveer todo aquello que nosotros mismos podriamos hazer y proveer de qualquier calidad y condicion que sea y ser pueda en esas dhas provincias porque vos mandamos a todos y a cada uno de vos como dho es de lo que asi por el dho marques de Cañete fuere proveido ordenado y mandado en qualesquier caso y cosas que sean e ser puedan en esas provincias lo guardeis y cumplais executeis y le obedezcais e acatais como persona que tiene nuestras vezes y que representa nra p^{a}s real y hagais y cumplais sus mandami^{o}s segun e de la manera que el lo dixere y mandare de nra parte por escripto e por palabra y fuere contenido en las dhas sus cartas y provisiones y mandami^{o}s sin poner en ello escusa ni dilacion alguna e sin dar a ello otro entendimiento ni ynterpretacion ni declaracion y sin vos mas requerir ni consultar ni executar para ir sobre ello otro mandado bien asi como si por nras personas e por nas cartas firmadas de nros nombres lo dixesemos ordenasemos e mandasemos lo qual mandamos que asi hagais y cumplais so pena de caer en mas caso y de las otras penas en que caen e yncurren los que no obedeçen las cartas //
/f.264v/ y mandami^{o}s de sus Reies e señores naturales y so las penas que por el os fueren puestas canos [*sic*] por la presente le damos y conçedemos y otorgamos para ello y pa todo lo a ello conçerniente e qualquier manera nro poder cumplido y bastante con todas sus incidencias y dependencias anexidades e conexidades e queremos que este dho poder tenga tanta fuerça como si fuera fecho y otorgado en cortes generales e decimos e otorgamos que todo quanto el dho marques de Cañete en nutro nombre hiziere hordenare e mandare conforme a este dho poder en esas dhas provincias que le abremos por firme estable y valedero para siempre jamas de lo qual y sellada con nro sello. Dada en la villa de Bruselas a diez dias del mes de março de mill e qui^{o}s e cinquenta e cinco años. Yo el rey. Y a Fran^{co} de

Eraso secretr^{o} de su cesarea y catolica m^{t} la fize escrevir por su mandado registrada Ochoa de Luyando chanciller Martin de Ramuin el marques el liçenciado Tello de Sandoval el liçenciado don Juan Sarmiento el Dotor Vazquez el liçenciado Villa Gomez. Hago merzed al dho Saire Topa Mango Capa Yupangue Ynga de los dhos repartimi^{o}s de y^{o}s de Yucay e Xaquixaguana Yllaquipa y Pucara que son en terminos de la ciudad del Cuzco y estan bacos por muerte de los dhos don Françisco Piçarro menor y Françisco Hernandez Giron con todos los pueblos y estancias y sus terminos caciques principales e y^{o}s dellos y a ellos subjetos y pertenecientes segun y como lo tenian y poseian tuvieron e poseyeron y goçaron dellos los susodhos y cada uno dellos //
/f.265/ para que los tenga y posea el y goze y cobre todos los tributos que son o fueren obligados a dar y dieren desde primero deste presente mes de henero e año de mil e qui^{o}s y cinq^{ta} y ocho años en adelante conforme a las tasas que estan fechas e se hiçieren e para que por su fin e muerte çubcedan perpetuam^{te} en el dho repartimi^{o} de y^{o}s sus hijos e deçendientes e subcesores que tuviere como se puede çubceder en los mayorazgos que se hazen con licencia de su m^{t} en los reinos de España y con las condiciones apellido y armas que el dho Ynga quisiere y ordenare que para ello le doy licencia y facultad porque vaya en acrecentamiento su onrra e linaje y estado de sus hijos e deçendientes deçendiendo como deçienden de linaje de los Yngas y principales destos dhos reinos del Piru e porque aya memoria y renombre de quien tuvo este principio desta md e porque permanezca y mejor se aficione al servi^{o} de Dios nro señor y ensalçar nra santa fee catolica y servir a su m^{t} pa onrra y defensa de su linaje casa y estado con que por si ni por ynterpositas no se sirva de servi^{o} personal de los dhos y^{o}s en su casa ni en otras obras y granjerias so las penas contenidas en las provisiones y cedulas y con que los trate bien y procure su conservacion y multiplicacion y tenga cuidado de que en el repartimi^{to} aya clerigos e religiosos que dotrinen a los naturales en las cosas de nra santa fee catolica y por la presente mando al licenciado Muñoz corregidor de la dha ciudad del Cuzco que //
/f.265v/ luego que por parte de los dhos Saire Topa Mango Capa Yupangue Ynga fuere pedida posesion del dho repartimiento de y^{o}s se la de y metido el y las demas justicias de su magestad le amparen y defiendan en ella y no consientan que della sea despojado sin primero ser oydo e vencido por fuero y jui^{o} lo qual ansi hagan e cumplan so pena de cada dos myll pesos de oro pa la camara y fisco de su majestad. Fecha en los Reies a treze dias del mes de henero de myll e qui^{o}s e cinq^{ta} e ocho años. El marques por mandado de su Exª Ju^{o} Muñoz Rico.

v En la gran ciudad del Cuzco cabeça destos reinos e provincias del Piru a veinte e un dias del mes de março año del nacimi^{to} de nro salvador Jesuxpo de myll y qui^{o}s e cinq^{ta} y ocho a^{o}s ante el muy mag^{co} señor licenciado Bautista Muñoz corregidor e justicia mayor en la dha ciudad y su jur^{on} por su magestad y en presencia de mi Fran^{co} de Barrientos scriv^{o} de su magestad e escriv^{o} pu^{co} del numero de la dha ciudad y de los testigos de yuso escriptos parecio presente doña Beatriz Mango Capac Yupangue mujer de Diego Hernandez vz^{o} desta dha ciudad en nombre de Saire Topa Mango Capa Yupangue y por virtud del poder que del tiene de que hizo presentacion signado de scriv^{o} de su m^{t} en el dho nombre presento esta provision cedula de encomienda del muy Ex^{e} señor marques de Cañete bisorrey destos reinos e pidio e requirio al dho señor corregidor que conforme a ella en el dho nombre le de la posesion corporal actual belcasi [*sic*] de los caciques e y^{o}s de los dhos repartimi^{o}s de que por su m^{t} y su Exª del dho señor bisorrey en su real n^{e} //
/f.266/ fue e le an fecho md al dho Saire Topa Mango Capa Yupangue Ynga la qual dha posesion le de en don Francisco Chilche cacique principal del repartimiento de Yucay e don Pedro e don Lucas principales del dho repartimiento y en don Xpobal Chotas y don Diego Caguata y caciques e principales de Xaquixaguana y don Alonso Callina Arca de Quilleua que presente estavan repartimi^{o}s encomendados por su Exª en nombre de su m^{t} al dho Saire Topa Mango Capac Yupangue Ynga su primo como por la dha provision de su Exª constava y parecia sobre que pidio justicia.

v El dho señor corregidor tomo en sus manos la dha provision de su Exª e la obedecio y con el acatami^{to} devido y en quando al cumplimiento della dixo questava presto de hazer e cumplir lo que por ella le hera mandado e haziendolo y cumpliendola tomo por las manos al dho don Fran^{co} Chilche cacique principal de Yucay e don Pedro e don Lucas principales del dho repartimi^{to} e don Xpobal Chotas y don Diego Caguatay caciques e principales de Xaquixaguana e don Alonso Calleña cacique de Quillua y en señal de posesion los entrego por las manos a la dha doña Beatriz Mango Capa Yupangue en nombre del dho Saire Topa Mango Capa Yupangue su parte en nombre de los demas caciques e principales de los dhos repartimi^{o}s e pueblos dellos e //
/f.266v/ luego la dha doña Beatriz Capa Yupangue en el dho nombre tomo por las manos a los dhos caciques e principales de los dhos pueblos de suso nombrados en señal de posesion propiedad e señorio como subjetos e vasallos del dho Saire Topa Mango Capa Yupangue Ynga su parte conforme a la dha provision de su Exª la qual dha posesion dixo que tomava e tomo en el dho nombre en los dhos caciques e principales de suso nombrados por ellos y en voz y en nombre de todos los demas principales e yn^{o}s e yndias a ellos subjetos y de como tomava e tomo la dha posesion quieta y pacificamente sin contradiccion de persona alguna que yo el dho scriv^{o} viese ni oyese de que yo doy fee que paso ansi sin contradiccion alguna e la dha doña Beatriz en el dho nombrelo pidio por testimonio signadopara en guarda de su dr^{o} y el dho señor corregidor se lo mando dar lo qual todo segun e como de suso se contiene la dha doña Beatriz dixo y le fue dado a entender por lengua de Pedro de Nicasio ladino en lengua de de yn^{o} siendo presentes por testigos a lo que dho es Gaspar de Sotelo alcalde ordinario de la dha ciudad e Diego de Trux^{o} e Miguel Sanchez e Antonio de Marchena vz^{o}s de la dha ciudad y el dho señor corregidor lo firmo aqui de su nombre el licenciado Muñoz paso ante mi Francisco de Barrientos.

/f.267/ v El tenor del qual dho poder del dho Saire Topa Mango Capa Yupangue signado de escrivano es el siguiente.

v Sepan quantos esta carta de poder vieren como yo Saire Topa Mango Capa Yupangue otorgo e conozco por esta presente carta que doy e otorgo todo mi poder cumplido libre e llenero e bastante segun que lo yo he y tengo e de dr^{o} mas puede e deve valer a vos doña Beatriz Mango Capa Yupangue Ayta [*sic*] que soys ausente para que por mi y en mi nombre representando mi propia persona podais tomar e tomeis la posesion de los yndios que su Exª me a fecho merced en los tener con administracion cobrando dellos los tributos de las tasas que son obligados a me dar e pagar e para que podais entrar en jui^{o} sobre ellos ante todas e qualesquier justicias jueces de su magestad e hazer todo aquello que yo haria siendo pres^{te} e si los oficiales de su magestad obieren cobrado de los dhos mis yn^{o}s algunos tribu^{o}s desde el dia de año nuevo a esta pte deste presente año de cinq^{ta} e ocho años los podais cobran de los dhos oficiales de su magestad conforme a la md que su Exª me tiene fecha e pa que podays tomar criados pa el benef^{o} de las dhas mis haziendas dandoles los salarios que os parecieren y para que podais pedir en cabildo de la ciudad en mi nombre e para mi qualesquier tierras e merzedes e titulos de las tales //

/f.267v/ tierras que ansi os hizieren md donde yo soy vz^{o} e para recebir y cobrar ansi en jui^{o} como fuera del todos los pesos de oro que me devieren por escripturas e por otra qualquier via e razon que sea e de lo que reçibiere del e cobraredes podais dar e deis vras cartas de pago e de finiquito las quales balan y sean firmes e bastantes e balederas como si yo mismo las diese y a ellas presente fuese general pa pleitos y causas con poder de jurar y sustituir con Diego Hernandez vro marido el dho Diego Hernandez y vos podais sustituir un procurador o dos o mas y los revocar quando quisieredes y hazer otros de nuevo quedando en vos este poder principal a los quales y a vos relievo segun forma de dr^{o} e obligo mi persona e bienes muebles e raizes avidos e por aver so espresa obligacion que para ello hago de la dha nuestra ps^{a} e bienes en forma con libre e general administracion que terne por bueno lo que por virtud deste poder en mi nombre hicieredes pa que en todas mis haziendas rentas dispongais como a vos os pareciere y quisieredes con todas sus incidencias e dependencias anexidades e conexidades e vos reliebo en forma a vos e a los por vos sustuidos como dho es y quan cumplido bastante poder segun que lo yo e y tengo otro tal y ese mismo bos doy cedo y trespaso en vos //

/f.268/ la dha doña Beatriz Mango Capa Yupangue Ayna en testimonio de lo qual otorgue esta carta ante el presente scriv^{o} e t^{gos} de yuso escriptos e quiero y es mi voluntad que por falta deste poder y no ir en el especificado quiero que valga lo que por vos la dha mi tia hiçieredes bala y ayais en todo como cosa vra propia y dispongais en ello como quisieredes que es fecha e otorgada en Viñaca terminos e jur^{on} de la ciudad de Guamanga en tres dias del mes de março de mil e qui^{o}s y cinq^{ta} e ocho años siendo tg^{os} Juan de Cardenas e Pedro de Bustinça e Juan Sierra. E al dho Juan Sierra rogo el dho Saire Topa Mango Capa Yupangue firmase por el en el registro desta carta a los quales yo el presente scriv^{o} doy fe que conozco Juan Sierra de Leguizamo e yo Juan Lopez de Ydiaquez scriv^{o} de su magestad presente fui en uno con los dhos tg^{os} e con el dho otorgante e lo escrevi y fize escrevir y por ende fize aqui mio signo que es a tal en testimonio de verdad Juan Lopez Ydiaque scriv^{o} de su m^{t}.

v E despues de los suso dho en la dha ciudad del Cuzco a v^{te} e dos dias del mes de março de mil e qui^{o}s y cinquenta y ocho años ante el dho señor corregidor y en presencia de mi el dho Francisco de Barrientos escriv^{o} pu^{co} presente Francisco Perez pr^{or} en nombre de don Fran^{co} Piçarro hijo del marques don Fran^{co} Piçarro difunto e por virtud del poder e sustitucion que tiene ante mi el dho scriv^{o} e presento el escripto del tenor sig^{te}.

/f.268v/ v Muy mag^{co} señor Fran^{co} Perez en nombre de Françisco Piçarro hijo del marques Françisco Piçarro difu^{o} digo que a mi noticia es venido que por parte de Saire Topa Ynga de los y^{o}s de Yucay encomendado en don Fran^{co} Piçarro mi parte por virtud de cierta encomienda que dizen averse fecho en el dho Saire Topa de los dhos y^{o}s segun que mas largamente se contiene en el pedimi^{to} sobre ello hecho por parte del dho Saire Topa cuyo tenor repetido dho que vra md no debe de hazer cosa alguna de lo pedido por el dho Saire Topa Ynga en razon de la dha posesion por lo siguiente.

v Porque la dha posesion no es pedida por parte bastante y los recaudos por virtud de los quales se pide la dha posesion no son bastantes pa que por ellos de les pueda dar.

v Lo otro porque su m^{t} y el licenciado Gasca presidente que fue destos reinos en su real nombre encomendaron en el dho don Fran^{co} mi parte estando y esta en posesion de los dhos yndios e goça dellos tribu^{o}s e aprovechami^{o}s que los dhos y^{o}s estan encomendados en el dho don Françisco no ay causa ni razon bastante pa que el dho Saire Topa se le de posesion dellos.

v Lo otro porque puesto caso que el dho Saire Topa se le oviese fecho md e nueva encomienda de los dhos y^{o}s como bacos que dize estan por muerte del dho don Françisco e se le ha dado provision de la dha encomienda no deve ni puede aver ef^{cto} por que el dho don Fran^{co} no es muerto ni tal se aberigua //

/f.269/ e hasta tanto que sea averiguado el dho don Françisco ser muerto los dhos y^{o}s no se an de tener por vacos ni se puede hazer la dha encomienda teniendo como la tiene el dho don Françisco por su magestad y en su real nombre por todos los dias de su vida.

v Por tanto a V.M. pido e sup^{co} e si es nezes^{o} hablando con el acatami^{to} que devo requiero las vezes que de dr^{o} soy obligado no haga cosa alguna de lo pedido por parte del dho Saire Topa en razon de la dha posesion antes defienda e ampare al dho mi pte en la quel tiene de los dhos y^{o}s e de gozar de los tribu^{o}s y aprovechami^{o}s dellos pa lo qual el of^{o} de vra md imploro y pido justicia y si es nezes^{o} espresamente lo contradigo la posesion por parte del dho Saire Topa pedida y sup^{co} de la dha provision y nueva encomienda en el fecha de los dhos yndios e pido testimi^{o} de todo.

v Otro si digo que si la dha posesion se oviere dado al dho Saire Topa e a otras personas en su nombre ansimismo espresamente la contradigo e protesto no pare perjui^{o} al dho mi parte y si es nezes^{o} me ofresco a dar ynformacion de como el dho don Françisco esta vivo en los reinos de España para lo qual.

v Otro si digo a V.M. mande que este escripto y contradiccion se ponga en la posesion que se oviere tomado e tomare por parte del dho Saire Topa sobre que pido justicia paralo qual es.

v Y ansi presentado en dho escripto el dho señor corregidor mando que se ponga en la //
/f.269v/ dha posesion testigos que fueron presentes Benito de la Peña escrivano pu^{co} e Miguel Martinez e Andres de Ybarra residentes en la dha ciudad.

v E despues de la dha ciudad del Cuzco el dho dia mes y año sobre dho yo el dho scriv^{o} notefique lo sobre dho a la dha doña Beatriz en el dho nombre del dho Saire Topa su pte presente Diego Hernandez su marido e Gonçalo Rodriguez pr^{or}.

v E despues de lo sobre dho en la dha ciudad del Cuzco a veinte e seis dias del mes de abril del dho año de mil e qui^{o}s y cinq^{ta} y ocho años ante el dho señor lic^{do} Muñoz corregidor en la dha ciudad e por ante mi el dho scriv^{o} y de los testigos de yuso escriptos parecio presente Sebastian de Balça pr^{or} en nombre e como curador ad liten del dho Saire Topa Mango Capa Yupangue segun que de la dha curadoria le fue y esta discernida por su md por ante Benito de la Peña escriv^{o} pu^{co} desta ciudad e dixo que no embargante en nombre del dho su parte esta tomada la posesion de los repartimi^{o}s e y^{o}s de la encomienda que por el señor bisorrey le fue fecha en nombre de su magestad que agora pa m^{or} abundamiento e corroboracion pedia e pidio a su md la de al dho Saire Topa Mango Capa Yupangue que esta presente y a el en su nombre añadiendo fuerça a fuerça y si es nezes^{o} hera lo tomaba e tomo en los y^{o}s del dho repartimiento que presentes estavan y pidio a su md le ampare y defienda en ella e de como lo decia e dixo lo pidio por testimonio.

/f.270/ v E luego el dho señor corregidor estando presentes don Françisco Chilche cacique de Yucay y don Luis de la parcialidad de don Garcia y el dho don Garcia y don Gaspar cacique de Quipa e Condor Guaman cacique de Pucara y Chagua cacique de Gualar e don Martin cacique de Xaquixaguana y don Baltasar cacique del pueblo de Eculco e don Al^{o} cacique de Quilloa y caciques e principales de los repartimi^{o}s encomendados en el dho Saire Topa por ellos e los demas y^{o}s a ellos subjetos e cumplimiento de la provision de su Exª les tomava por la mano corporalmente y en señal de posesion los dio y entrego al dho Saire Topa el qual presente el dho su curador dixo por lengua de P^{o} de Nicasio ladino que continuando la posesion que de los dhos caciques e y^{o}s tenia y le estava dada añadiendo fuerça si nezes^{o} hera la tomava e tomo en los dhos caciques e y^{o}s los quales en señal de posesion tomo por la mano por ellos y en boz y en nombre de los demas principales e y^{o}s de los dhos repartimi^{o}s a ellos subjetos e lo pidio por testimonio.

v E luego parecio presente el dho Fran^{co} Perez en el dho nombre del dho Fran^{co} Piçarro e dixo que contradezia e contradixo la dha posesion y protesto no pare perjuicio alguno al dr^{o} del dho su parte e lo pidio por testimi^{o}.

v E luego el dho señor corregidor sin embargo de la dha contradicion dixo que dava e dio la posesion de los dhos y^{o}s al dho Saire //
/f.270v/ Topa y al dho Sebastian de Balça su curador en su nombre por los dhos caciques e principales que presentes estavan por ellos y en voz y en nombre de los demas yndios a el encomendados conforme a la dha provision de su Exª y se lo mando dar ansi por testim^{o} y en pu^{ca} forma siendo presentes por testigos a lo que dho es Juan Albarez Maldonado vz^{o} de la dha ciudad y Benito de la Peña scriv^{o} pu^{co} de la dha ciudad el lic^{do} Muñoz e yo Fran^{co} de Barrientos scriv^{o} del numero de la ciudad del Cuzco presente fui a la que dho es en uno con los dhos testigos del dho pedimi^{to} e mandamientos del dho señor corregidor que aqui firmo su nombre lo fize escrevir segun que ante mi paso por ende fize aqui este mio signo que es a tal en testim^{o} de verdad Fran^{co} de Barrientos sacose del original en el Cuzco a siete dias del mes de diz^{e} de mil e qui^{o}s y setenta e tres años siendo tg^{os} a ver corregir con el original Miguel de Bitorino y Diego Hernandez y Her^{do} de Morales en fee de lo qual fize aqui mi signo en testimonio de verdad Pero Diaz Valdeon escrivano.

v En la ciudad del Cuzco a diez y nueve dias del mes de febr^{o} de mil e qui^{o}s e setenta e siete años ante el dho señor corregidor e por ante mi el dho scriv^{o} parecio presente el dho Domingo Lopez de la Rinaga y en el dho nombre presento por testigo en esta causa a Garcia de Melo vecino desta ciudad del qual fue tomado juramento en forma jurando por Dios e por Santa Maria su madre e por la señal de la cruz guardando conciencia dira verdad en este negocio e si asi lo hizie- //
/f.271/ re Dios le ayude y lo contr^{o} se lo demande dixo si juro e amen. tg^{o} Diego de Torres v^{o} e alcalde ordinario desta dha ciudad y el tesorero Gregorio Lopez de Unçueta yernos de Garcia de Melo Pero Diaz Valdeon scriv^{o}.

v En el pueblo de Santiago de Oropesa del valle de Yucay en veinte e tres dias del mes de febr^{o} de mil e qui^{o}s e setenta e siete años el dho Domingo Lopez de la Rinaga en nombre de los dhos capitan Martin Garcia de Loyola e doña Beatriz Coya su mujer presento por testigo en esta causa a don Francisco Chilche cacique principal de los y^{o}s del valle de Yucay y a Marcos principal de los dhos y^{o}s yanaconas de pachaca y Alonso Bermudez poblador en este reino residente en el dho valle de los quales e de cada uno dellos fue tomado juramento en forma segun que del dho Garcia de Melo e prometieron de dezir verdad so pena de perjuro testigos Her^{do} de Morales e Martin Palacios Pero Diaz Valdeon escrivano.

v En la ciudad del Cuzco a veinte e cinco dias del mes de febr^{o} de mil e qui^{o}s e setenta y siete años ante el dho señor corregidor por ante mi el dho escrivano parecio presente el dho Domingo Lopez de la Rinaga y en el dho nombre presento por tg^{o} en esta causa Bachicabo [*sic*] vz^{o} desta ciudad del qual fue tomado juramento en forma segun que de los demas testigos e prometio de dezir verdad so pena de perjuro tg^{os} Agustin de Madrid e Diego de Torres vz^{o} e alcalde hordinario desta ciudad. P^{o} Diaz Valdeon scriv^{o}.

/f.271v/ v En el Cuzco a veinte e seis dias del mes de feb^{ro} de mil e qui^{o}s y setenta y siete años el dho Domingo Lopez de la Rinaga en el dho nombre presento por testigo en esta causa a Pedro de Bustinça vz^{o} desta ciudad del qual fue tomado juramento en forma segun que de los demas testigos e prometieron de dezir verdad so pena de perjuro testigos Rodrigo de Villalobos e Martin de Bustinça. Pero Diaz Baldeon escrivano.

v E lo que cada uno de los dhos testigos dixo y depuso secreta y apartadamente es como se sigue. Pero Diaz Valdeon scriv^{o}.

Provanca del cap^{t} Loyola e de doña Beatriz su mujer en segunda instançia.

Testigo: El dho Garcia de Melo vz^{o} desta ciudad del Cuzco aviendo jurado y preguntado dixo lo siguiente.

j A la primera pregunta dixo que conoce a las partes e tiene noticia deste repartimi^{o} y conoce mucha parte de los y^{o}s del por averlos visitado este testigo en la visita que ultimamente e hizo dellos antes de la bisita general e no conoce al fiscal de su m^{t} contenido en esta preg^{ta}.

De las generales dixo que es de hedad de sesenta y siete años poco mas o m^{o}s e que no concurre en ninguna de las generales.

ij A la pregunta dos dixo queste testigo save quel marques de Cañete visorrey que fue destos reinos encomendo a don Diego Saire Topa Ynga padre de la dha doña Beatriz todos los y^{o}s del valle de Yucay que abia tenido en encomienda don Gonçalo //
/f.272/ Piçarro y por su muerte goço de los tributos don Françisco su hermano por merzed que le hizo el licenciado Gasca y este testigo como curador del dho don Françisco cobro los tribu^{o}s de los dhos y^{o}s todo el tiempo de su vida e save e bio que todos los y^{o}s que estavan en el dho valle de Yucay subjetos al dho repartimiento de que eran caciques don Françisco Chilche y don Garcia Quispicapi ansi mitimas como naturales y otros y^{o}s advenediços que se yntitulavan yanaconas tributavan todos en los tribu^{o}s que davan por su tasa al dho encomendero como y^{o}s que tenian en el dho valle tierras e que se sustentavan repartidas por los caciques y comunidad y asi save este testigo que las tienen de presente y an tenido y que este testigo visito los dhos yndios como tiene dho en la primera pregunta e les hizo la tasa que de sus tribu^{o}s avian de dar fue la que tenian antes de la ultima que se le hizo por la visita general que de presente tienen e todos los y^{o}s mitimas e yanaconas y naturales que avian en el dho valle se bisitaron en la visita queste testigo hizo por yndios tributarios desta encomienda ecepto ciertos y^{o}s yanaconas de don Fran^{co} Chilche que eran allegados con el dho don Fran^{co} cacique del dho valle e se sustentavan en las tierras del dho cacique serian como treinta yndios poco mas o m^{o}s e los yanaconas questavan en las guertas e otros que eran de Diego de Trux^{o} //
/f.272v/ do doña Maria de Betanços que serian los que ellos de presente tienen que son fuera de los sobre ques este pleito e save que despues que se le encomendaron los yndios del dho valle de Yucai en el dho don Diego Saire Topa los tuvo el dho don Diego Saire Topa en la dha encomienda e le tributaron juntamente sin que oviese division de yanaconas e save que lo mismo hicieron a la dha doña Beatriz su hija porqueste t^{o} lo vio ser y pasar asi como la preg^{ta} lo dize porqueste testigo fue coadjutor del curador de la dha doña Beatriz Coya siendo menor e vio que los tribu^{o}s lo pagavan todos como y^{o}s tributarios como la pregunta lo dize y lo mismo lo pagavan en el tiempo que no estuvieron encomendados porqueste testigo siendo tesorero de la real hazienda cobro los tribu^{o}s de los dhos y^{o}s con loas demas oficiales de la real hazi^{da} sin que oviese division de yanaconas ningunos porque si la uviera este t^{o} lo supiera por la que dho tiene y esto sabe desta pregunta.

iij A la pregunta tres dixo ques asi como la pregunta lo dize porqueste t^{o} vio al dho don Diego Saire Topa tener por su legitima mujer a la dha doña Maria Manrique e hazer vida maridable con ella e vio que tenian por su hija legitima avida de legitimo matrimonio a la dha doña Beatriz mujer que al presente es del dho capitan Marti Garcia de Loyola y //
/f.273/ como tal su hija ligitima subcedio en los dhos y^{o}s como parecera por los titulos que de la dha encomienda tiene a que refiere.

iiij A la preg^{ta} quatro dixo queste t^{o} no sabe que tuviese el dho don Diego Saire Topa ni la dha doña Maria Manrique su mujer otro hijo ni hija mas que la dha doña Beatriz Coya mujer del dho cap^{t} Loyola e si lo tuvieran este testigo lo supiera y en lo demas dize lo que dho tiene en la pregunta antes desta.

v A la pregunta cinco dixo que sabe lo contenido en esta preg^{ta} por lo que dho tiene en la pregunta dos y lo a bisto ser y pasar asi como lo dize esta pregunta sin que obiese division de los dhos y^{o}s yanaconas contenidos en la pregunta a los demas tributarios en el tiempo que los tuvo en encomienda el marques don Fran^{co} Piçarro e despues sus hijos como dho tiene en las demas preguntas.

vj A la preg^{ta} seis dixo que es pu^{co} y notr^{o} lo contenido en esta pregunta y por tal pu^{co} e notorio este testigo save que el dho Guaynacava tenia el dho valle de Yucay como recamara suya e todos los y^{o}s que en el dho valle vivian heran como criados e yanaconas de los quales esta entendido que los que al pres^{te} ay son proçedidos deste que dho tiene y ansi se a de entender lo que tiene dho en el principio desta preg^{ta} porqueste testigo no pudo saver ni ver lo que paso en tpo //
/f.273v/ del dho Guayna Capa mas de como dho tiene esta entendido que los y^{o}s yanaconas sobre que es este pleito son procedidos de los que en el dho valle tenia el dho Guayna Cava puestos por mitimas del e por criados suyos y ques pu^{co} e notorio y por tal este t^{o} lo sabe que hazian al dho Guayna Caba los dhos y^{o}s el servi^{o} que la preg^{ta} dize.

vij A la pregunta siete dixo que save que antes que oviese hecha tasa a los dhos yn^{o}s no tributavan mas cosas de lo contenido en esta pregunta.

viij A la pregunta ocho dixo queste t^{o} save como dho tiene que en tiempo que no abia fecha tasa de los y^{o}s tributaban los yndios sobre ques este pleito juntamente con los demas del dho valle a los encomenderos en quien estavan encomendados y a los caciques del dho valle que eran don Fran^{co} Chilche y don Garcia Quispicapi porque al tiempo que este t^{o} visito como dho tiene no avia division de yanaconas sino que todos eran una cosa y asi lo aberiguo este t^{o} en la dha visita que dellos hizo.

ix A la pregunta nueve dixo queste testigo es el tesorero Garcia de Melo contenido en esta pregunta e bisito los dhos y^{o}s como en ella se contiene y entendio haziendo la dha visita que los dhos caciques tenian algunos de los dhos y^{o}s fechos sus yanaconas y se servian dellos sin repartiles ningun tribu^{o} porque la comunidad de los demas se quexaron dello a este testigo y le pidieron los mandase tributar como //
/f.274/ de antes lo hazian y este testigo quito a los dhos caciques los y^{o}s que berifico tener del dho repartimi^{to} sacados por sus yanaconas e mando que todos ellos tributasen con los demas y^{o}s tributarios y asi ellos como los dhos caciques dijeron que era muy bien fecho asi pues todos se sustentavan de las tierras del dho repartimi^{to} y eran del.

x A la pregunta diez dixo queste testigo ha oydo dezir lo contenido en esta preg^{ta} a muchas personas que residen en el dho valle de Yucay.

xj A la pregunta onze dixo queste t^{o} a oydo dezir que el dho Diego Escudero clerigo trato con el dho frei P^{o} Gutierrez visitador de los dhos y^{o}s empadronase por y^{o}s yanaconas a los que la pregunta dize y en lo demas dize lo que dho tiene en las demas preguntas.

xij A la pregunta doze dixo que se remite a lo que los y^{o}s an dho sobre este negocio despues de la visita general.

xiij A la pregunta trece dixo queste testigo sabe que el dho Martin Garcia de Loyola y doña Beatriz Coya su mujer an sido despojados en las visita general de los dhos yndios y queste testigo parece an sido agraviados en ello porque este t^{o} como dho tiene nunca supo ni entendio antes de la visita general que obiese dibision de los dhos y^{o}s sobre ques este p^{to} de los demas tributarios del dho repartimiento.

xiiij A la preg^{ta} catorze dixo que lo que dho ti^{e} es verdad so cargo del dho jurame^{o} e la firmo siendole leido su dho. Melo. Ante mi P^{o} Diaz Valdeon scriv^{o}.

/f.274v/ Testigo: El dho Marcos Puri principal de los y^{o}s deste valle aviendo jurado y preguntado dixo lo siguiente.

j A la primera pregunta dixo que conoze a las partes e no conoze al señor fiscal de la real audiencia y conoce a todos los y^{o}s deste valle de Yucay en quien çubcedio la dha doña Beatriz Coya y el cap^{t} Martin Garcia de Loyola su marido por el titulo de mayorazgo que dellos tienen.

De las generales dixo que es de hedad de mas de sesenta años e que no concurre en ninguna de las generales.

ij A la pregunta dos dixo que save y es verdad que todos los y^{o}s contenidos en la dha memoria que le fue leida y mostrada son y an sido de la encomienda de la dha doña Beatriz Coya e del dho capitan Martin Garcia de Loyola y save y vio este t^{o} que los caciques que los an tenido a cargo como a sido don Fran^{co} Chilche e otros los an ido sacando y tomando para si so color de dezir que son sus yanaconas y que los avian recoxido siendo al contrario de la verdad porque eran todos de la dha encomienda de los y^{o}s que puso en este valle el dho Guayna Caba y quando se encomendaron por el marques de Cañete los y^{o}s deste valle en don Diego Saire Topa padre de la dha doña Beatriz Coya tributavan e tributaron mucho tiempo al dho don Diego Saire Topa y antes a su m^{t} despues de muerto el dho don Di^{o} Saire Topa tributaron todos a la dha doña Beatriz Coya su hija y a sus curadores en su nombre hasta que el dho don Françisco Chilche cacique deste repartimiento los disipo y saco de la dha encomienda //
/f.275/ para los tener por sus yanaconas tuviendolos sacados porque los y^{o}s deste repartimiento no diesen noticia dello les hazian tributar e contribuir con alguna cosa para ayuda a la tasa e asi sabe este testigo e vio que eran todos desta encomienda y fueron sacados della por la orden que dho tiene.

iij A la preg^{ta} tres dixo que save y es verdad que don Diego Saire Topa Ynga y doña Maria Manrique fueron casados y belados en faz de la santa madre yglesia porque este testigo en tiempo del licenciado Bautista Muñoz siendo corregidor de la ciudad del Cuzco los vio casar y belar e sabe que durante su matrimonio tuvieron por su hija legitima avida de legitimo matrimonio a la dha doña Beatriz Coya mujer que al presente es del dho capitan Martin Garcia de Loyola en quien çubcedieron los dhos yndios por no tener otro hijo baron ni hija y por tal su hija legitima la trataron y nombraron y fue avida y tenida y comunmente reputada y respetada entre todos los y^{o}s por Coya hija del dho Ynga y de la dha doña Maria Manrique su mujer y esto sabe e vio desta pregunta.

iiij A la preg^{ta} quatro dixo que es verdad lo contenido en esta pregunta e no ay cosa en contr^{o} dello e si lo uviera este t^{o} lo supiera e no pudiera ser menos.

v A la preg^{ta} cinco dixo que sabe e vio este testigo que todos los dhos yndios y antecesores dellos de donde descienden los cont^{dos} en la dha memoria que asi le fue leida //
/f.275v/ y mostrada e muchos dellos que son los viejos sirvieron al dho marques don Fran^{co} Piçarro y los tuvo a todos ellos en encomienda el dho Gonçalo Piçarro su hijo y despues fueron todos encomendados en el dho don Diego Saire Topa y el tiempo que estuvieron bacos tributavan todos a su m^{t} como y^{o}s anexos y pertenecientes a esta encomienda y hazian e hizieron lo que la preg^{ta} dize porque asi lo vio este testigo como yndio antiguo deste valle.

vj A la pregunta seis dixo ques verdad lo contenido en esta pregunta porque este testigo quando vino de la provincia de Quito a este valle de Yucay vio que traxeron el cuerpo de Guayna Capa a este valle y este testigo vino con los y^{o}s que lo trayan pa le poner en el dho valle como cosa suya que era e que tenia todos los y^{o}s y tierras como la pregunta lo dize y declara y todos o la mor pte de los yndios contenidos en la memoria fueron de los que traxeron el cuerpo de Guaynacava a este valle que venian como suyos acompañando el cuerpo.

vij A la pregunta siete dixo que es verdad lo contenido en esta pregunta porque ansi lo bio este testigo ser y pasar y dar y pagar el dho tributo y no pagaban mas de lo que la pregunta dize de tribu^{o}.

viij A la pregunta ocho dixo que sabe e vio este testigo que todos los dhos y^{o}s contenidos en la dha memoria con los demas deste valle fueron y son desta encomienda y sirvieron y tributaron a todos los encomenderos contenidos en esta pregunta que los ha tenido en //
/f.276/ encomienda desde Guayna Capa hasta don Diego Saire Topa a quien los encomendo todos el marques de Cañete y estuvieron todos juntos y le sirvieron y tributaron hasta la visita de Damian de la Vandera que tomo los y^{o}s pa si el dho don Fran^{co} Chilche porque aunque el visitador hizo sobre ello mucha diligencia se quedo el dho don Fran^{co} Chilche con mucha parte de los dhos y^{o}s contenidos en la dha memoria que los escondio aunque y los restituyo algunos dellos y asi los disipo y dividio del dho repartimiento y consintio que don Alonso Tito Atauche y otros y^{o}s e yndias del Cuzco sacasen muchos y^{o}s deste repartimi^{to} por yanaconas e de donde se hizieron los yanaconas a los españoles que no tenian encomienda y^{o}s fue y ha sido de los y^{o}s que an estado en encomienda que se huyen de los repartimientos y otros que se van a servir a españoles y como les sirven se quedan por yanaconas y asi se salen del repartimi^{to} y los tienen menos el encomendero y desta manera se dividieron los y^{o}s deste repartimiento cont^{dos} en la dha memoria siendo todos desta encomienda como dho tiene.

ix A la preg^{ta} nueve dixo ques verdad lo contenido en esta preg^{ta} porque los dhos Garcia de Melo e Damian de la Vandera como visitadores restituyeron muchos y^{o}s de los que ansi tenian escondidos y usurpados los caciques y mandaron que tributasen como los demas y esto save desta preg^{ta}.

x A la pregunta diez dixo que es verdad lo cont^{do} en esta preg^{ta} porqueste t^{o} lo vio ser y pasar asi todo e despues que el dho Diego Escudero los //
/f.276v/ visito por yanaconas se quedaron exsentos del repartimito y vino a ser con ellos todo lo contenido en esta pregunta.

xj A la pregunta honze dixo que save y es verdad todo lo contenido en esta preg^{ta} porque este testigo lo vio ser y pasar asi se hallo pres^{te} en la dha visita todo ello y si los y^{o}s cont^{dos} en la dha memoria en en esta pregunta entendieron que avian de pagar tributo no se bisitaran por yanaconas sino por y^{o}s desta encomienda como lo son e la causa por donde se visitaron por yanaconas dividiendose de su encomienda fue por la numeracion que dellos tenia fecho el dho Diego Escudero que los habia dividido deste repartimi^{o} con nombre de yanaconas y asi los visito el dho lic^{do} frei Pedro Gutierrez por yanaconas siendo desta encomienda sin hazer otra diligencia en ello.

xij A la preg^{ta} doze dixo que dize lo que dho tiene en las preguntas antes desta porque es notorio ser ansi lo cont^{do} en esta preg^{ta}.

xiij A la preg^{ta} treze dixo que es verdad lo contenido en esta preg^{ta} porque los dhos cap^{t} Martin Garcia de Loyola y doña Beatriz Coya su mujer an sido desposeidos de los dhos yndios contenidos en la dha memoria y/n/dibididamente y recivido notorio agravio en les aver quitado la posesion de los dhos y^{o}s y la causa desto a sido por no aver tenido la dha doña Beatriz Coya persona que aya procurado por los dhos y^{o}s hasta agora.

xiiij A la pregunta catorce dixo que lo que dho tiene es verdad so cargo del dho juramento por lengua de los dhos ynterpretes y siendole tornado a dar a entender otra vez se afirmo e ratifico en ello y lo firmaron los yn- //
/f.277/ terpretes Hernando de Morales Martin Palacios. Ante mi Pero Diaz Valdeon escrivano.

Testigo: El dho don Francisco Chilche cacique principal de los y^{o}s del valle de Yucay repartimiento y encomienda aviendo jurado y preguntado por las preg^{tas} del dho ynterogatorio dixo lo siguiente.

j A la primera preg^{ta} dixo que conoce a las partes e tiene noticia de todos los y^{o}s contenidos en esta pregunta y memoria y no conoce al señor fiscal.

De las generales dixo que es de hedad de mas de ochenta años e que no concurre en ninguna de las generales que dira verdad en el negocio.

ij A la pregunta dos dixo queste testigo es cacique principal de los yndios del valle de Yucay deste repartimi^{to} y encomienda y aviendole leido y dado a entender todos los y^{o}s contenidos en la dha memoria dixo que los conoce a todos ellos e save que son todos y^{o}s deste repartimi^{to} y encomienda porque binieron los y^{o}s mitimas sus antepasados y anteçesores destos por yanaconas de los Yngas a este valle de Yucay y ansi fueron todos encomendados en don Diego Saire Topa Ynga padre de la dha doña Beatriz y esto sabe desta pregunta.

iij A la preg^{ta} tres dixo que save e vio este testigo que los dhos don Diego Saire Topa Ynga e doña Maria Coya su mujer fueron casados y belados segun orden de la santa madre yglesia y como tales marido y mujer les vio este testigo hazer vida maridable durante su matrimonio uvieron por su hija legitima a la dha doña Beatriz Coya mujer //
/f.277v/ del dho capitan Martin Garcia de Loyola y por tal su hija legitima la an tenido e tiene este t^{o} y es avida e tenida y comunmente reputada en este reino.

iiij A la pregunta quatro dixo ques verdad lo contenido en esta preg^{ta} porque este t^{o} save e vio que no tuvieron mas hijos ni hija que a la dha doña Beatriz Coya la subcedio en los bienes y haziendas de los dhos sus padres y en el repartimi^{to} de y^{o}s que tenia el dho don Diego Saire Topa que son los y^{o}s deste valle de Yucay e los demas que tiene en encomienda en el titulo de mayorazgo que dellos tiene y si otra cosa fuera este t^{o} lo supiera y oviera visto.

v A la pregunta cinco dixo que sabe y vio que los y^{o}s deste valle asi los contenidos en la dha memoria como los demas que al pres^{te} estan bisitados por desta encomienda y avia en el dho valle todos ellos los tuvo e poseyo el marques don Françisco Piçarro y estuvieron subjetos a este testigo como cacique principal que era de todos ellos y asi subçedieron en la encomienda del dho Gonçalo Piçarro su hijo y lo mismo en tpo que tributaron a su magestad por estar bacos y despues fueron encomendados por el marques de Cañete visorrey que fue destos reinos en el dho don Diego Saire Topa Ynga y Pero Alonso Carrasco y Juan de Berrio visitaron a todos los y^{o}s contenidos en la dha memoria por yndios tributarios deste repartimi^{to} con los demas que en el avia al tiempo que se visitaron y esto sabe y vio desta pregunta e todos ellos tributaban por tribu^{o} y tasa en las cosas que la pregunta dize porque hazian las semen- //
/f.278/ teras y chacaras de coca y servi^{o} personal que en aquella sazon se acostumbrava a dar y hazer.

vj A la pregunta seis dixo que es muy notorio lo contenido en esta pregunta e que fue y paso como en ella se dize.

vij A la preg^{ta} siete dixo que es verdad lo contenido en la dha pregunta porque en tiempo del dho marques don Françisco Piçarro los y^{o}s deste repartimi^{to} no pagavan su tributo sino es lo que la pregunta dize y esto fue hasta que el presidente Gasca los taso.

viij A la pregunta ocho dixo que dize lo que dho tiene.

ix A la pregunta nueve dixo que la causa por donde se dividieron los y^{o}s deste repartimi^{to} y se convertieron de y^{o}s de encomienda en y^{o}s yanaconas fue por la diferencia que ubo entre este t^{o} y el dho don Garcia Quispicapi porque como estavan diferentes el uno con el otro por aver dividido y partido entre ellos el cacicazgo cada uno sacava los y^{o}s del dho repartimi^{to} que querian y los escondian y se servian dellos como de y^{o}s yanaconas siendo todos y^{o}s tributarios deste repartimiento y encomienda dando y pagando tasa todos ellos como tributarios que heran desta encomienda.

x A la preg^{ta} diez dixo ques verdad que como por las razones que dho tiene en la preg^{ta} antes desta se avia exsentado muchos y^{o}s deste repartimi^{to} y encomienda y estavan ya puesto como por yanaconas el dho //
/f.278v/ Diego Escudero como cura deste repartimiento hizo division entre ellos poniendo unos por yanaconas como se los nombraron los principales y declara en esta preg^{ta}.

xj A la preg^{ta} honze dixo que save y es verdad que el lic^{do} frei P^{o} Gutierrez visitador que fue deste valle hizo la visita de los dhos yanaconas segun como se declara en esta pregunta e todos a efeto de que pagasen tribu^{o} a su m^{t} e no al dho encomendero y ansi quito deste repartimiento veinte e cinco y^{o}s que Garcia de Melo avia adjudicado a este repartimi^{to} quando los visito que los quito a este t^{o} que los tenia por yn^{o}s yanaconas a causa de visitallos por el padron del dho Diego Escudero a buelta de otras yanaconas que a este t^{o} quedaron de la bisita del dho Garcia de Melo sin hazer distincion de unos ni de otros sino todo por adquerir en esta visita mucho numero de yanaconas y esto sabe y vio desta preg^{ta}.

xij A la pregunta doze dixo que la causa que fue visitar los dhos yndios por yanaconas y no por y^{o}s tributarios deste repartimi^{to} y encomienda como lo son fue por sacarlos del padron que el dho Di^{o} Escudero tenia fecho y asi por sacarlos el dho visitador de alli se bisitaron por yanaconas e no por yndios tributarios.

xiij A la pregunta treze dixo que save y es verdad que la dha doña Beatriz Coya y el cap^{t} Martin Garcia de Loyola su marido an sido desposeidos de los dhos y^{o}s individamente a causa de no aver tenido quien los recoxiese //
/f.279/ y mirase por ellos en lo qual an sido muy agraviados porque se les quito el tributo que habia de haber de los dhos yndios siendo suyos dellos.

xiiij A la pregunta catorce dixo que lo que dho ti^{e} por lengua de los dhos ynterpretes es la verdad so cargo del dho juram^{to} y tornandoselo a dar a entender se afirmo y ratifico en ella por ser verdad so cargo del dho juram^{to} y lo firmaron los dhos ynterpretes y este testigo don Fran^{co} Chilche Hernando de Morales Martin Palacios ante mi Pero Diaz Valdeon escrivano.

Testigo: El dho Alonso Bermudez residente en este valle de Yucai aviendo jurado y preguntado por las preg^{tas} del dho ynterrogatorio dixo lo siguiente.

j A la primera preg^{ta} dixo que conoce a los contenidos en esta preg^{ta} e que no conoce al señor fiscal.

De las generales dixo que es de hedad de mas de cinquenta años e que no concurre en ninguna dellas.

ij A la pregunta dos aviendo bisto el memorial de los dhos y^{o}s dixo queste t^{o} que reside en este valle de Yucai mas de v^{te} e çinco años y save que los y^{o}s deste valle con los contenidos en este memorial fueron encomendados en el dho don Diego Saire Topa Ynga padre de la dha doña Beatriz Coya y por su fin y muerte subçedieron en la dha doña Beatriz Coya como hija legitima del dho don Diego Saire Topa e de la dha doña Maria Manrique su mujer por la encomienda que en ellos hizo el marques de Cañete bisorrey que fue destos reinos.

/f.279v/ iij A la preg^{ta} tres dixo ques verdad lo cont^{do} en esta pregunta porqueste t^{o} save que el dho don Diego Saire Topa y doña Maria Manrique su mujer fueron casados y velados como se declara en la preg^{ta} y durante el matrim^{o} huvieron y procrearon por su hija ligitima a la dha doña Beatriz es avida e tenida y la tiene este testigo.

iiij A la preg^{ta} quatro dixo que es notorio lo que la pregunta dize e si tuvieran otros hijos o hija este t^{o} lo supiera y no pudiera ser menos por aver residido en el valle tanto tiempo e asi por no tener otro hijo save e vio este t^{o} que la dha doña Beatriz Coya como hija ligitima de los dhos don Diego Saire Topa y doña Maria Manrique subcedio en los dhos y^{o}s y en los bienes y hazienda de los dhos sus padres.

v A la preg^{ta} cinco dixo que save y vio este testigo quel marques don Fran^{co} Piçarro tuvo todos los y^{o}s deste valle y despues subçedieron por via de encomienda todos ellos en el dho Gonçalo Piçarro su hijo y por su fin y muerte quedaron en su magestad y fueron todos ellos como y^{o}s bacos encomendados en el dho don Diego Saire Topa en la dha doña Beatriz Coya su hija.

vj A la preg^{ta} seis dixo que este testigo por que esta en este reino quarenta y dos años y sabe ques asi como se declara en esta pregunta y esto fue muy notorio porque quando los españoles entraron en este reino el dho Ynga thenia y poseia los y^{o}s deste valle y se servia de todos dellos como la preg^{ta} dize y esto es muy notr^{o}.

vij A la preg^{ta} siete dixo que es verdad lo contenido en esta pregunta porque asi lo vio este t^{o} ser y pasar en tpo del dho marques.

/f.280/ viij A la pregunta ocho dixo ques verdad que los dhos y^{o}s an servido y tributado siempre en el benef^{o} de las chacaras deste valle como los demas tributarios del.

ix A la preg^{ta} nueve dixo ques verdad que los yndios yanaconas contenidos en la dha memoria que deste repartimi^{to} se an sacado a sido causa los caciques porque ellos mesmos se servian dellos y otras personas y asi se yban exsentando pa no pagar tribu^{o} que una de las causas por donde se an fecho yanaconas a sido esto que todos eran desta encomienda sino que como se yban a servir a otros se quedavan por yanaconas y se exsentaban deste repartimi^{to}.

x A la pregunta diez dixo queste testigo vio que el padre Diego Escudero como cura de los y^{o}s deste repartimi^{to} empadrono los y^{o}s deste valle a unos por tributarios y a otros por yanaconas por la razon que la preg^{ta} dize.

xj A la preg^{ta} onze dixo queste testigo vio hazer la dha visita al dho lic^{do} frei P^{o} Gutierrez e procuro por todas vias de que los dhos y^{o}s fuesen yanaconas e no desta encomyenda como lo heran y esto sabe e vio desta preg^{ta}.

xij A la preg^{ta} doze dixo que los dhos y^{o}s antes que el dho frei Pedro Gutierrez los bisitase por yanaconas andavan libres como gente que se avian exsentado y salido de los demas y^{o}s deste repartimi^{to} y si ellos entendieran que bisitandose por yanaconas avian de pagar tribu^{o} como al pres^{te} lo pagan no se bisitaran por yanaconas sino por y^{o}s desta encomienda.

/f.280v/ xiij A la pregunta treze dixo que es notorio lo que la pregunta dize y en ello a visto este testigo que esta agraviada la dha doña Beatriz Coya y el dho cap^{t} Martin Garcia de Loyola su marido por el dho despojo que de los dhos y^{o}s se les a hecho.

xiiij A la pregunta catorze dixo que lo que dho tiene es verdad y lo que deste caso sabe su cargo del dho juramento y siendole tornado a leer se afirmo e ratifico en ella y lo firmo. Alonso Bermudez. Ante mi P^{o} Diaz Baldeon escrivano.

v Testigo. El dho Her^{do} bachicabo vz^{o} desta ciudad del cuzco auiendo jurado y preguntado dixo lo siguiente

j A la primera preg^{ta} dixo que conoze a las partes e no conoçe al señor fiscal y conoçe a muchos de los yndios contenidos en el memorial

E de las generales dixo que es de hedad de quarenta y tres años poco mas o m^{o}s e que no concurre en ninguna de las generales

ij A la preg^{ta} dos dixo auiendole mostrado el titulo de encomienda que save y es verdad que la dha doña Beatriz Coya tubo y poseio todos los y^{o}s del valle de yucai en encomienda asi los de la memoria como los demas del dho valle y este t^{o} vio a muchos de los y^{o}s contenidos en la dha memoria estando encomendados como los demas en la dha doña Beatriz Coya que yban a benefiçiar la coca del valle de Tono que davan de tassa a la dha doña Beatriz y lo mismo benefiçiavan las chacaras de maiz en el dho valle de yucay y save que el Marques de Cañete //
/f.281/ bisorrey que fue destos rreinos encomendo todos los dhos yndios en don Diego Saire Topa padre de la dha doña Beatriz Coya como pareçe por el titulo de mayorazgo que dellos le dio pareçe a que se rremite.

iij A la preg^{ta} tres dixo ques verdad lo cont^{do} en la dha preg^{ta} porqueste t^{o} vio casar a los suso dhos en esta ciudad y este t^{o} con otros vz^{os} desta ciudad jugaron cañas en el rregocijo que se hizo en sus bodas y les vio como marido y muger a los dhos don Diego Saire

Topa e doña Maria Manrique hazer vida maridable en uno como la pregunta lo dize e uvieron por su hija ligitima avida de legitimo matrimonio a la dha doña Beatriz Coya que al pres^{te} esta casada con el dho cap^{t} Martin Garcia de Loyola y por tal su hija legitima fue avida y tenida y la tiene este testigo.

iiij A la preg^{ta} quatro dixo que save y es verdad que los dhos don Di^{o} Saire Topa e doña Maria Manrique no tuvieron ningun hijo ni hija ligitima mas de la dha doña Beatriz Coya muger del dho cap^{t} Martin Garcia de Loyola por que otra niña que tuvieron menor que la dha doña Beatriz se murio siendo de leche y este testigo se hallo en su entierro y por esto save que no uvo mas de la dha doña Beatriz Coya de los dhos don Di^{o} Saire Topa e doña Maria Manrique que asi subçedio en los bienes y herençia de los dhos sus padres y en los yndios del valle de Yucay y los demas del dho titulo de mayorazgo segun y como el dho su padre los tenia y poseya po el dho titulo.

/f.281v/ v A la preg^{ta} cinco dixo que es muy notorio que los y^{o}s del valle de Yucay los tuvo todos ellos el marques don Fran^{co} Piçarro governador que fue destos rreinos como la preg^{ta} lo dize e por su fin e muerte çubçedieron todos los dhos y^{o}s en Gonçalo Piçarro su hijo despues los tuvo en encomyenda a todos ellos don Diego Saire Topa y el tienpo que estuvieron bacos cobravan de todos ellos los oficiales rreales los tribu^{o}s y esto save desta pregunta.

vj A la preg^{ta} seys dixo que es notorio lo que la preg^{ta} dize e a oydo este t^{o} a y^{o}s muy antiguos ser ansi lo contenido en esta preg^{ta} porque era rrecamara del Ynga el dho valle de Yucay y esto save desta preg^{ta}.

vij A la preg^{ta} siete dixo que save y es verdad que la tassa que acostunbravan a dar hera de las cossas contenidas en la dicha pregunta.

viij A la preg^{ta} ocho dixo que save y a visto este testigo que por tassa del presidente Gasca y por otras que despues dellas se hizieron antes de la bisita general los y^{o}s del valle de Yucai pagauan su tributo en las cossas que la preg^{ta} dize y en coca y maiz aves y carvon y en lo demas que tenian de su cosecha.

ix A la pregunta nueve dixo que este t^{o} save que los caciques se sirvian de los y^{o}s tributarios del rrepartimi^{to} y de los que se sirvian es notorio que ellos mesmos los rreservavan de tributo y cargavan este tribu^{o} que a estos quitavan a los demas tributarios del dho rrepartimyento y esto save desta pregunta.

/f.282/ x A las diez preguntas dixo que lo cont^{do} en esta pregunta lo oyo dezir este testigo al dho Diego Escudero.

xj A la preg^{ta} honze dixo ques muy notr^{o} lo contenido en esta pregunta y entiende y cree este testigo por cossa muy cierta que si Diego Escudero clerigo cura del dho valle entendiera que los y^{o}s del dho valle subçedieran como an subçedido con el cap^{t} Martin Garcia de Loyola no se enpadronaran por yanaconas los y^{o}s del dho memorial por ser como hera del dho rrepartimi^{to} y si se enpadronaron fue por no tener quien a la sazon volviese por ellos y por dar a entender que avia muchos yanaconas en el dho valle y esto save desta preg^{ta}.

xij A la preg^{ta} doze dixo que save y es verdad que si los dhos y^{o}s entendieran que avian de pagar tribu^{o} quando se visitaron por yanaconas no se visitaran por yanaconas ny los caçiques del dho valle lo consintieran syno que se visitaran todos por y^{o}s tributarios como lo eran y se visitaron los demas.

xiij A la preg^{ta} treze dixo que en averse quitado al dho capitan Martin Garcia de Loyola y a la dha doña Beatriz Coya su muger an sido agraviados en ello y como tales be que piden su Justiçia en este casso por cobrar dellos los oficiales rreales el dho tributo y no el dho capitan Martin Garcia de Loyola y esto save desta pregunta.

xiiij A la preg^{ta} catorze dixo que lo que dho tiene es verdad so cargo del dho juram^{to} y lo firmo y siendole leydo su dho se afirmo e rratifico en ello Her^{do} Bachicao ante mi P^{o} Diaz Valdeon escribano.

/f.282v/ T^{o} El dho Pedro de Bustinça v^{o} desta çiudad presentado por el dho Domingo Lopez de Larrinaga aviendo jurado y preg^{do} dixo lo siguiente.

j A la primera pregunta dixo que conoçe las partes y que no conoze al señor fiscal e conoçe a todos los y^{o}s en el memorial o a la mayor pte dellos como persona que los a thenido a cargo como curador que a sido de la persona y bienes de la dha doña Beatriz de Mendoça muger que al pres^{te} es del dho cap^{t} Martin Garcia de Loyola.

De las generales dixo ques de hedad de mas de treinta e ocho años e que no concurre en ninguna de las generales

ij A la pregunta dos dixo que es verdad todo lo contenido en esta pregunta por que este testigo como curador que fue de la persona y bienes de la dha doña Beatriz Coya vio que todos los dhos y^{o}s contenidos en la dha memoria con los demas y^{o}s tributarios del dho valle los tuvo en encomienda don Diego Saire Topa padre de la dha doña Beatriz Coya y subçedio en todos ellos como hija heredera del dho don Diego Saire Topa e de doña Maria Manrique su muger y save que se los encomendo el marques de Cañete por via de mayorazgo como pareçe por el titulo que le dio como bisorrey que hera destos rreinos y este testigo a bisto el titulo dellos porque lo a tenido en su poder como tal curador y esto save desta preg^{ta}.

iij A la pregunta tres dixo que save y es verdad que los dhos don Diego Saire Topa y doña Maria Manrique su muger fueron cassados y velados segun orden de la santa madre yglesia y este testigo les vio cassar y velar //
/f.283/ en esta ciudad y save que durante el matrimonio que entre ellos huvo hubieron por su hija ligitima avida de ligitimo matrimonio a la dha doña Beatriz Coya muger del dho cap^{t} Martin Garcia de Loyola y al tienpo que se cassaron contenida en esta preg^{ta} e por tal su hija ligitima a sido y es avida y thenida y comunmente rreputada y la tiene por tal este testigo.

iiij A la pregunta quatro dixo que save y es verdad que el dho don Diego Saire Topa y la dha doña Maria Manrique su muger no tuvieron otro hijo baron mas de la dha doña Beatriz Coya muger del dho capitan Martin Garcia de Loyola y por tal su hija ligitima subçedio en todos sus bienes y haziendas y en el rrepartim^{to} de y^{o}s que fueron encomendados en el dho don Diego Saire Topa perpetuos por el dho marques de Cañete como bisorrey destos rreinos y una hija que tuvieron despues de la dha doña Beatriz syendo niña de leche se les murio y este testigo la vio enterrar porque se hallo en su entierroy asi save que no tuvieron otro hijo ni hija mas de la dha doña Beatriz Coya muger del dho cap^{t} Martin Garcia de Loyola.

v A la pregunta cinco dixo que es muy notr^{o} lo contenido en esta pregunta porque este testigo como curador que fue de la dha doña Beatriz supo lo contenido en la dha pregunta por cossa muy çierta e que todos los y^{o}s del dho valle avian subçedido en el dho Gonçalo Piçarro hijo del //
/f.283v/ dho marques don Fran^{co} Piçarro y por tales y^{o}s encomendados an sido avidos e tenidos desde queste testigo se acuerda y despues por fin y muerte del dho Gonçalo Piçarro estuvieron los dhos y^{o}s sobre ques este pleito y los demas del dho valle en cabeça de su magestad hasta que el dho marques de Cañete los encomendo a todos ellos en el dho don Di^{o} Sayre Topa e doña Maria Manrique su muger padres ligitimos de la dha doña Beatriz y este testigo como tal curador vio que todos ellos tributavan y an tributado por de la dha encomienda en hazer sementeras en las chacaras de coca de Tono y Paucarbanba y en otras cossas que en su tierra tenian como constara por la tassa antigua y esto save desta pregunta.

vj A la pregunta seis dixo que es muy notorio la contenido en esta pregunta porque este testigo siendo curador de la dha doña Beatriz como persona que a nacido y criadose en este rreyno se ynformo de cosas de antiguedades y supo por muy çierto que el dho Guayna Capa Ynga señor que fue destos rreinos tuvo todos los y^{o}s del dho valle asi mitimas como naturales y se sirvio dellos en lo que la pregunta dize porque este testigo supo por muy çierta que tuvo y posseyo todos los dhos y^{o}s el dho Ynga y que tenia el dho valle e y^{o}s del como rrecamara hizo como sepultura como señor deste rreino donde se avia de enterrar //
/f.284/ y por tenerla fecha y ser dedicado todo ello pa el dho Ynga aunque murio en Quito le traxeron el cuerpo al dho valle de Yucay y lo pusieron los y^{o}s del dho valle en la sepoltura que tenia alli fecha en el asiento de Quispeguanca y por esto save y entiende ques verdad todo lo contenido en la dha preg^{ta}.

vij A la preg^{ta} siete dixo ques asi como la pregunta lo dize porqueste testigo siendo como dho tiene curador de la dha menor supo que los dhos y^{o}s dauan al marques don Françisco Piçarro de tributo las cossas que la pregunta dize.

viij A la pregunta ocho dixo ques verdad lo contenido en la dha pregunta por que todos los y^{o}s del dho valle y sus açendientes y deçendientes que an subçedido en las tierras y chacaras del dho valle y otros y^{o}s que an venido a el todos ellos an trivutado y pagado su tribu^{o} segun y como la pregunta lo dize hasta que su Exª del Exmo señor don Françisco de Toledo bisorrey destos rreinos los taso en esta visita general que por mandado de la rreal m^{t} hizo en este rreino y esto save desta preg^{ta}.

ix A la preg^{ta} nueve dixo que siendo este testigo curador de la dha doña Beatriz Coya muger que al presente es del dho capitan Martin Garcia de Loyola visto en los dhos don Fran^{co} Chilche y don Garçia Quispicapi caçiques principales de los dhos y^{o}s por sus fines y aprouecham^{tos} que tenian con los y^{o}s de la dha encomienda que sacauan cada dia y^{o}s del dho rrepartimyento se sirvian dellos y cargava el tribu^{o} //
/f.284v/ sobre los demas que quedauan en el dho rrepartimyento y que los y^{o}s que ansi tomavan y sacavan dellos hazian yanaconas y los exentavan de tributos y que se yba disipando el rrepartimi^{to} y que cargava todo el tributo sobre los demas tributarios que en el quedavan y que aunque Damian de la Vandera como visitador mando que pagasen todos tributo los caçiques no querian por servirse dellos como yanaconas pidio este testigo provision en la rreal audiencia de los Charcas que a la sazon estava subjeta esta ciudad a ella pa que se bisitasen e tributasen todos e no se sirviesen dellos los caçiques y la gano y en virtud della Garçia de Melo a quien bino cometida la dha visita asistio en ella y la hizo con asistençia deste testigo como tal curador porque se le notificose hallase pres^{te} a la dha visita pa que ynquiriese y supiese los y^{o}s que avian escondido y ocultado los dhos caçiques y otras personas y entre otros muchos y^{o}s que se hallo escondidos y ocultados hallo solo en poder de don Françisco Chilche mas de ciento y çinq^{ta} y^{o}s que avia tomado e osurpado del dho rrepartimi^{to} y el dho Garçia de Melo mando pagar tribu^{o} y por esto save que los y^{o}s contenidos en la dha memoria sobre que es este pleito son y^{o}s tributarios del dho rrepartimi^{to} y no yanaconas.

x A la pregunta diez dixo ques asi como la pregunta lo dize porque este t^{o} supo por cossa çierta que el dho Diego Escudero como cura del dho valle hizo lo contenyido en esta pregunta.

/f.285/ xj A la pregunta honze dixo que es verdad que el dho liçenciado frei Pedro Gutierrez como visitador general que fue del dho valle hizo lo que la pregunta dize por las causas y rrazones en ella contenidos.

xij A la pregunta doze dixo que save es verdad que los y^{o}s sobre que es este p^{to} los caçiques entendiendo que no avian de pagar de tribu^{o} los visitaron por yanaconas y consintieron que otras personas los visitassen por yanaconas so color de servirse y aprovecharse dellos e que si entendieran que avian de pagar tributo e ponerlos en la corona rreal como los puso su Exª no los visitaron por yanaconas syno por y^{o}s tributarios del dho rrepartimiento como lo son y esto save desta pregunta.

xiij A la preg^{ta} treze dixo que save y es verdad que los dhos capitan Martin Garçia de Loyola y doña Beatriz Coya su muger contenidos en la dha memoria yndividamente por las causas y rrazones que dho tiene y en ello an sido muy agraviados porque siendo como son todos ellos desta encomienda y rrepartimyento los visitaron por yanaconas y a esta causa entendiendo su Exª que lo heran los mando tassar por yanaconas y entran los tribu^{o}s en la rreal caxa y no los cobra su encomendero de que rreçibe notorio agravio y esto save desta preg^{ta}.

xiiij A la pregunta catorze dixo que lo que dho tiene es la verdad y lo que deste caso.

/f.285v/ save so cargo del dho juram^{to} e siendole leido se afirmo e rratifico en ello y lo firmo Pedro de Bustinça ante mi Pero Diaz Valdeon escribano.

Ratificacion de los t^{o}s que se exsaminaron en la provança que hizo el cap^{t} Martin Garcia de Loyola vz^{o} de la çiudad del del [*sic*] Cuzco sobre los y^{o}s que so color de yanaconas le quitaron del rrepartimi^{to} de los y^{o}s del valle de Yucai que ti^{e} en encomienda

v En el dho pueblo de Santiago de Oropesa del valle de Yucay a veinte e dos dias del mes de hebr^{o} de myll e qui^{o}s e set^{a} e siete años pa exsaminar los t^{o}s que se rratifican en esta prouança por dos ynterpretes que el señor corregidor nonbro pa este ef^{o} el uno fue Her^{do} de Morales ynterprete de la gran çiudad del cuzco y el otro Martin Palaçios entendido en la lengua de los naturales y abil para exsaminar los t^{o}s anbos a dos juraron por dios e por Santa Maria su madre e por la señal de la cruz que cada uno dellos hizo con su mano dr^{a} que como buenos xpianos guardando su conçiençia usaran del dho of^{o} de ynterpretes fielmente syn quitar ni añadir cossa alguna a su saver y entender diran y declaran todo lo que los dhos testigos dixeren y declararen en estas rretificaçiones y en los demas y^{o}s que se presentaren en la provança a cunplimyiento de los doze t^{o}s que su m^{t} mandase exsamynen por cada preg^{ta} del dho ynterr^{o} y si ansi lo hizieren dios les ayude y lo contr^{o} se lo demande y lo firmaron Hernando de Morales Martin Palaçios ante mi Pero Diaz Valdeon scriv^{o} pu^{co}.

/f.286/ En el dho pueblo de Santiago de Oropesa a veinte e dos dias del mes de hebr^{o} de myll e qui^{o}s e setenta e siete a^{o}s el dho Domingo Lopez de la rrinaga pres^{to} por t^{o} para le rratificar en este plenario jui^{o} a don Pedro Cochachi natural deste valle de Yucai yndio mitima del dho valle vz^{o} del dho p^{o} de Santiago de Oropesa del qual fue tomado juram^{to} en forma jurando por Dios e por Santa Maria su madre y por la señal de la cruz que hizo con su mano dr^{a} que como buen xpiano guardando su conçiençia dira verdad en este negoçio y si asi lo hiziere dios le ayude y lo contr^{o} se lo demande y siendo preguntado por las preg^{tas} del dho ynterr^{o} dixo que este testigo tiene dho su dho en esta causa en la provança que sobre este negoçio se hizo el dho cap^{t} Martin Garcia de Loyola donde dixo y declaro todo lo que sauia y siendole leido y dado a entender el dho que dixo en esta causa en onze dias del mes de hen^{o} del año de myll e qui^{o}s y setenta y quatro años ante el Dotor Loarte y ante mi el dho escr^{o} dixo que ansi como le fue leido y dado a entender lo dixo y declaro segun y como los dhos ynterpretes se lo dixeron y dieron a entender y en ello se afirmo y rretifico por ser verdad so cargo del dho juramento y torno a dezir y declarar que en este plenario jui^{o} y lo firmaron los ynterpretes e dixo e dixo [*sic*] ques de hedad de //
/f.286v/ mas de setenta e dos años e que no concurre en ninguna de las generales Her^{do} de Morales Martin Palaçios ante mi P^{o} Pero [*sic*] Diaz Valdeon escribano.

v En el pueblo de Santiago de Oropesa en veinte e dos dias del mes de hebr^{o} de myll e qui^{o}s e setenta e siete años el dho Domingo Lopez de Larrinaga en el dho nonbre pres^{to} por t^{o} en esta causa a Sebastian Tenaçella natural del valle de yucay yn^{o} cañar del qual fue tomado juram^{to} en forma segun que del primero t^{o} y preg^{do} por las preguntas del dho ynterrogatorio dixo que este t^{o} tiene dho su dho en esta causa en la provança que hizo el cap^{t} Martin Garcia de Loyola en el qual dixo todo lo que sauia deste neg^{o} que siendole mostrado e leydo y dado a entender el dho que dixo en la dha prouança en onze dias del mes de henero del dho año de setenta e quatro años ante el dho Dotor Loarte e por ante mi el dho scriv^{o} despues de averlo oydo y entendido tado por los dhos ynterpretes dixo que asi como le fue leido y dado a entender lo dixo y declaro y en ello se afirmo e rratifico por ser verdad y lo torno a dezir de nuebo en este plenario jui^{o} e dixo ques de hedad de mas de setenta e tres años e que no concurre en ninguna de las generales y lo firmaron los ynterpretes Her^{do} de Morales Martin Palaçios ante mi P^{o} Dias Valdeon scriv^{o}.

/f.287/ v En este dho dia en el dho Santiago de Oropesa el dho Domingo Lopez de Larrinaga en el dho nombre pres^{to} por testigo en esta causa a Juan Bautista rucana natural del dho valle de Yucay del qual fue tomado juramento en forma segun que de los demas t^{o}s y preg^{do} por las preguntas del dho ynterrogatorio dixo que este t^{o} tiene dho su dho en esta causa en la provança que hizo el cap^{t} Martin Garçia de Loyola sobre este negocio donde dixo y declaro todo lo que savia y siendole leido y dado a entender el dho que dixo en la dha provança en onze dias del mes de henero de myll e qui^{o}s e setenta e quatro años/ ante el Dotor Loarte y ante mi el dho scriv^{o} dixo que asi como le fue leido y dado a entender por los dhos ynterpretes lo dixo y declaro y en ello se afirmo y rratifico y lo torno a dezir y declarar de nueuo en este plenario jui^{o} por ser verdad so cargo del dho juramento y dixo que es de hedad de mas de noventa años y que no concurre en nyngunas de las generales mas destar encomendado en el cap^{t} Martin Garçia de Loyola y que por esto no a dexado de dezir uerdad y lo firmaron los ynterpretes Hernando de Morales Martin Palaçios ante mi Pero Diaz Baldeon escribano.

v En este dho dia mes y año dho en el dho pueblo de Santiago de Oropessa el dho Domingo Lopez de Larrinaga en el dho nonbre pres^{to} por testigo en esta causa a don Diego Lachintunbay natural del dho valle de Yu- //
/f.287v/ cay yndio cañar vz^{o} del dho pueblo de Santiago de Oropesa del qual fue tomado juramento en forma segun que de los demas testigos preguntado por las preguntas del dho ynterr^{o} dixo que este t^{o} tiene dho su dho en esta causa en la provança que hizo el cap^{t} Martin Garçia de Loyola sobre este negoçio donde dixo y declaro todo lo que savia y siendole leido y dado a entender el dho que dixo en la dha provança en quinze dias del mes de henero de myll e qui^{o}s e setenta e quatro años ante el Dotor Loarte y ante mi el dho scriv^{o} dixo que asi como le fue leido y dado a entender por los ynterpretes lo dixo e declaro y en ello se afirmo y rratifico y lo torno a dezir y declarar de nueuo en este plenario jui^{o} por ser verdad so cargo del dho juramento dixo ques de hedad de ochenta años y que no concurre en ning^{a} de las generales mas de ser encomendado en el dho cap^{t} Martin Garçia de Loyola y sin enbargo desto a dho verdad y lo firmaron los ynterpretes Hernando de Morales Martin Palaçios ante mi Pero Diaz Baldeon escribano.

v En este dho dia mes y año dho en el dho pu^{o} de Santiago de Oropesa el dho Domingo Lopez de Larrinaga en el dho nonbre presento en esta causa a Martin Yupangue natural del dho valle de Yucai vz^{o} del pueblo de San Bernardo de Urobanba del qual fue tomado juram^{to} en forma segun que de los //
/f.288/ demas t^{o}s e preguntado por las preguntas del dho ynterr^{o} dixo queste t^{o} tiene dho su dho en esta causa en la prouança que hizo el cap^{t} Martin Garçia de Loyola sobre este negoçio donde dixo y declaro todo lo que savia y siendole leido y dado a entender el dho que dixo en la dha provança en onze dias del mes de henero de myll e qui^{o}s e set^{a} y quatro años ante el Dotor Loarte y ante mi el dho escrivano dixo asi como le fue leido y dado a entender por los dhos ynterpretes lo dixo y declaro y en ello se afirmo y rratifico y lo torno a dezir y declarar de nuevo en este plenario jui^{o} por ser verdad so cargo del dho juram^{to} e dixo ques de hedad de mas de sesenta años e que no concurre en nyinguna de las generales mas de ser encomendado en el dho cap^{t} Martin Garçia de Loyola e sin enbargo desto a dho verdad e lo firmaron los ynterpretes Her^{do} de Morales Martin Palaçios ante mi P^{o} Diaz Valdeon scriv^{o}.

v En el dho pueblo de Santiago de Oropesa este/ d[ic]ho dia mes e año dho el dho Domingo Lopez de Larrinaga en el dho nonbre pres^{to} por t^{o} en esta causa a Martin yanacona natural Guaylas yndio mitima en el valle de Yucai vz^{o} del pueblo de San Bernardo del asiento de Urobanba del qual fue tomado juram^{to} en forma segun que de los demas t^{o}s e preguntado por las preg^{tas} del dho ynterr^{o} dixo queste testigo tiene dho su dho en esta causa en la provança que hizo el cap^{t} Martin Garçia de Loyola sobre este negoçio donde dixo y declaro todo lo que savia y siendole leido y dado a entender //
/f.288v/ el dho que dixo en la dha provança en onze dias del mes de henero de myll e qui^{o}s y setenta y quatro años ante el /doctor/ Gabriel de Loarte y ante mi el dho escrivano dixo que asi como le fue leido y dado a entender por los dhos ynterpretes lo dixo y declaro y en ello se afirmo y rratifico y lo torno a dezir y declarar de nuevo en este plenario jui^{o} por ser verdad so cargo del dho juramento y dixo ques de hedad de mas de sesenta y dos años y que no concurre en nyinguna de las generales mas destar encomendado en el d[ic]ho cap^{t} Martin Garçia de Loyola e que a dho verdad como tiene declarado y lo firmaron los ynterpretes Hernando de Morales Martin Palaçios ante P^{o} Diaz Valdeon escribano.

v Este dho dia mes y año en el dho pu^{o} de Santiago de Oropesa el dho Domingo Lopez de Larrinaga en el dho nonbre pres^{to} por t^{o} en esta causa a Her^{do} Coa Colla yndio mytima rresidente en el dho pu^{o} de Santiago de Oropesa del qual fue tomado juram^{to} segun que de los demas t^{o}s e preguntado por las preguntas del dho ynterr^{o} dixo que este t^{o} tiene dho su dho en esta causa en la provança que hizo el cap^{t} Martin Garçia de Loyola sobre este negoçio donde dixo y declaro lo que savia y siendole leido y dado a entender el dho que dixo en la provança en diez dias del mes de março de mill e qui^{o}s e set^{a} e quatro años ante el Dotor loarte y ante mi el dho escrivano dixo que asi como le fue leido y dado a entender por los dhos ynterpretes lo dixo y declaro y en ello se afyrmo y rratifico y lo torno a dezir y declarar de nuevo //
/f.289/ en este plenario jui^{o} por ser verdad so cargo del dho juramento e dixo ques de hedad de mas de sesenta años e que no concurre en nynguna de las generales mas destar encomendado en el dho cap^{t} Martin Garçia de Loyola e sin enbargo desto a dho uerdad y lo firmaron los ynterpretes por cuya lengua lo declaro Her^{do} de Morales Martin Palacios ante mi P^{o} Diaz Valdeon escriv^{o}.

v Este dho dia mes y año dho el dho Domingo Lopez de Larrinaga en el dho nonbre pres^{to} por testigo en esta causa a Lucas Checo natural del pu^{o} de San Benito de Alcantara de Guayllabanba del qual fue tomado juramento segun que de los demas t^{o}s y preg^{do} por las preguntas del dho ynterr^{o} dixo que este t^{o} tiene dho su dho en esta causa en la provança que hizo el cap^{t} Martin Garcia de Loyola sobre este negoçio donde dixo y declaro todo lo que savia y siendole leydo y dado a entender el dho que dixo en la provança en onze dias del mes de hen^{o} de myll e qui^{o}s y setenta e quatro a^{o}s ante el Dotor loarte y ante mi el dho escri^{o} dixo que asi como le fue leido y dado a entender por los dhos ynterpretes lo dixo y declaro y en ello se afyrmo y rratifico y lo torno a dezir y declarar de nuebo queste plenario jui^{o} por ser verdad so cargo del dho juram^{to} e dixo que es de hedad de mas de setenta e çinco años y que no concurre en ninguna de las generales mas destar encomendado en el dho Martin Garçia de Loyola e sin enbargo desto a dho verdad y lo firmaron los ynterpretes Her^{do} de Morales Martin Palaçios ante mi Pero Diaz Valdeon scriv^{o}

/f.289v/ v Este dho dia mes e año en el dho pu^{o} de Santiago de Oropesa Domingo Lopez de Larrinaga en el dho nonbre pres^{to} por testigo a Martin Cutipa yn^{o} mitima natural del dho pu^{o} de San Benito de Alcantara del qual fue tomado juram^{to} en forma segun que de los demas t^{gos} y preg^{do} por las preguntas del dho ynterr^{o} dixo que este t^{o} tiene dho su dho en esta causa en la provança que hizo el capitan Martin Garcia de Loyola sobre este negoçio donde dixo y declaro lo que sauia y siendole leydo y dado a entender el dho que dixo en la dha provança en onze dias del mes de hen^{o} de mill e qui^{o}s y setenta e quatro a^{o}s ante el Dotor Loarte y ante mi el dho scriv^{o} dixo que asi como le fue leydo y dado a entender por los dhos ynterpretes lo dixo y declaro y en ello se affirmo y rretifico y lo torno a dezir y declarar de nuebo en este plenario jui^{o} por ser verdad so cargo del dho juram^{to} e dixo ques de hedad de mas de setenta e dos años y que no concurre en ninguna de las generales mas de ser yndio encomendado en el dho cap^{t} Martin Garçia de Loyola e sin enbargo desto a dho verdad y lo firmaron los ynterpretes Her^{do} de Morales Martin Palaçios. Ante mi P^{o} Diaz Valdeon escribano.

v Este dho dia mes y año el dho domingo Lopez de Larrinaga en el dho nonbre pres^{to} por testigo a Martin Sauca yndio natural del dho pu^{o} de Santiago de Oropesa del qual fue tomado juramento en forma segun que los demas/ y preg^{do} por las preguntas del dho ynterr^{o} dixo queste t^{o} tiene dho en esta causa en la provança que hizo el capitan Martin Garcia de Loyola sobre este negoçio donde dixo y //
/f.290/ declaro todo lo que savia e siendole leido y dado a entender el dho que dixo en la dha prouança en onze dias del mes de hen^{o} de mill e qui^{o}s e setenta y quatro a^{o}s antel Dotor Loarte y ante mi el dho scriv^{o} dixo que asi como le fue leydo y dado a entender por los dhos ynterpretes lo dixo y declaro y en ello se afirmo y rratifico y lo torno a dezir y declarar de nueuo en este plenario jui^{o} por ser verdad so cargo del dho juramento e dixo ques de hedad de mas de sesenta años e que no concurre en ninguna de las generales mas de ser yndio encomendado en el cap^{t} Martin Garçia de Loyola e sin enbargo desto a dho uerdad y lo fyrmaron los ynterpretes Her^{do} de Morales Martin Palaçios ante mi Pero Diaz Valdeon escri^{o}.

v t^{o} Este dho dia el dho Domingo Lopez de Larrinaga en el dho nonbre pres^{to} por testigo en esta causa a don Garçia Paucar natural del pu^{o} de Paca del valle de Yucay y del qual fue tomado juram^{to} en forma segun que de los demas t^{o}s e preguntado por las preg^{tas} del dho ynterr^{o} dixo queste t^{o} tiene dho en esta causa en la provança que hizo el cap^{t} Martin Garcia de Loyola en este negoçio donde dixo y declaro todo lo que savia y siendole leido y dado a entender el dho que dixo en la provança en onze dias del mes de hen^{o} de myll e qui^{o}s y setenta e quatro a^{o}s ante el Dotor Loarte y ante mi el dho scriv^{o} dixo que asi como le fue leido y dado a entender por los d]hos ynterpretes lo dixo y declaro y en ello se afyrmo y rratifico y lo torno a dezir y declarar //
/f.290v/ de nuebo en este plenario jui^{o} por ser verdad so cargo del dho juram^{to} e dixo que es de hedad de setenta e dos años poco mas o menos e que no concurre en ninguna dellas mas destar encomendado en el dho Martin Garçia de Loyola e no por esto a dexado de dezir la verdad y lo firmaron los ynterpretes Her^{do} de Morales Martin Palaçios ante mi Pero Diaz Valdeon escribano.

v t^{o} Este dho dia mes y año el d]ho Domingo Lopez de Larrinaga en el dho nonbre pres^{to} por t^{o} en esta causa a Miguel Chirisuca yndio mitima en este valle de Yucai vz^{o} del pueblo de San Benito de Alcantara del qual fue tomado juramento en forma segun que de los demas testigos y preg^{do} por las preguntas del dho ynterr^{o} dixo que este t^{o} tiene dho su dho en esta causa en la provança que hizo el capitan Martin Garcia de Loyola sobre este negoçio donde dixo y declaro todo lo que savia y siendole leydo y dado a entender el dho que dixo en la dha provança en onze dias del mes de hen^{o} de myll e qui^{o}s y set^{a} y quatro a^{o}s ante el Dotor Loarte y ante mi el dho escrivano dixo que asi como le fue/ leydo y dado a entender por los dhos ynterpretes lo dixo y declaro todo y en ello se afirmo y rratifico y lo torno a dezir y declarar de nuevo en este plenario jui^{o} por ser verdad so cargo del dho juram^{to} e dixo ques de hedad de mas de sesenta e dos años poco mas o menos y que no concurre en nynguna de las generales mas destar encomendado en el dho cap^{t} Martin Garçia de Loyola e que no por esto a dexado de dezir verdad y lo firmaron los ynterpretes Her^{do} de Morales Martin Palaçios ante mi P^{o} Diaz Valdeon scriv^{o}.

/f.291/ v Este dho dia v^{te} e dos del mes de hebr^{o} de myll e qui^{o}s e setenta e siete a^{o}s el dho Domingo Lopez de la rrinaga en el dho nonbre presento por t^{o} en esta causa a P^{o} Olunanzela yndio cañar rresidente en el pueblo de Santiago de Oropessa del qual fue tomado juram^{to} en forma segun que de los demas t^{o}s y preg^{do} por las preguntas del dho ynterr^{o} dixo queste t[estig]o tiene d[ic]ho su dho en esta causa en la prouança que hizo el cap^{t} Martin Garcia de Loyola sobre este negoçio donde dixo y declaro todo lo que savia y siendole leido y dado a entender el dho que dixo en la prov^{a} en diez dias del mes de março de myll e qui^{o}s y setenta e quatro años ante el Dotor Loarte y ante mi el dho escrivano dixo que asi como le fue leido y dado a entender por los dhos ynterpretes lo dixo y declaro todo y en ello se afymo y rratifico y lo torno a dezir y declarar de nuevo queste plenario jui^{o} e por ser verdad so cargo del dho juram^{to} dixo ques de hedad de mas de ochenta años e que no concurre en ninguna de las generales mas destar encomendado en el dho cap^{t} Loyola e por esto no a dexado de dezir verdad e lo firmaron los ynterpretes Her^{do} de Morales Martin Palaçios ante mi P^{o} Diaz Valdeon scriv^{o}.

v En el pueblo de Oropesa a veinte e tres dias del mes de hebr^{o} de myll e qui^{o}s e setenta y siete a^{o}s el dho Domingo Lopez de Larrinaga en el dho nonbre pres^{to}.

/f.291v/ por t^{o} en esta causa a Marcos Cayo Gualpa natural del valle de Yucai vz^{o} del pueblo de San Bernardo del asiento de Urobanba del qual fue tomado juram^{to} en forma segun que de los demas testigos y preguntado por las preguntas del dho ynterr^{o} dixo que este t^{o} tiene dho su dho en esta causa en la provança que hizo el capitan Martin Garcia de Loyola sobre este negoçio donde dixo y declaro lo que savia y siendole leydo y dado a entender el dho que dixo en la dha provança en treze dias del mes de hebr^{o} de myll e qui^{o}s y setenta y quatro años ante el Dotor Loarte y ante mi el dho escrivano dixo que asi como le fue leido y dado a entender por los dhos ynterpretes lo dixo y declaro y en ello se afirmo e rratifico y lo torno a dezir y declarar de nuebo en este plenario jui^{o} por ser verdad so cargo del dho juramento e dixo ques de hedad de mas de ochenta años e que no concurre en ninguna de las generales y lo firmaron los ynterpretes Her^{do} de Morales Martin Palaçios ante mi P^{o} Diaz Valdeon escri^{o}.

v En el pueblo de Santiago de Oropessa en v^{te} e tres dias del mes de hebr^{o} de myll e qui^{o}s e setenta y siete años el dho Domingo Lopez de Larrinaga en el dho nonbre pres^{to} por testigo en esta causa a Alonso chauca yndio mitima vz^{o} deste dho pueblo de San Bernardo deste valle //
/f.292/ del qual ffue tomado juram^{to} en forma segun que de los demas t^{o}s y preg^{do} por las preguntas del dho ynterr^{o} dixo que este t^{o} tiene dho su dho en esta causa en la provança que hizo el capitan Martin Garcia de Loyola sobre este negoçio donde dixo y declaro todo lo que savia y siendole leydo y dado a entender el dho que dixo en la dha provança en diez y nueve dias del mes de hebr^{o} de myll e qui^{o}s y

setenta y quatro años ante el dho Dotor Loarte y ante mi el dho escrivano dixo que asi como le fue leido y dado a entender por los dhos ynterpretes lo dixo y declaro y en ello se afyrmo y rratifico y lo torno a dezir y declarar de nuebo en este plenario jui^{o} por ser verdad so cargo del dho juram^{to} y dixo ques de hedad de mas de ochenta años e que no concurre en ninguna de las generales y lo ffyrmaron los ynterpretes Her^{do} de Morales Martin Palaçios ante mi P^{o} Diaz Valdeon escribano.

v En el dho pueblo de Santiago de Oropessa a veinte e tres dias del mes de heb^{o} de myll e qui^{o}s y setenta y siete a^{o}s el dho Domingo Lopez de Larrinaga en el dho nonbre pres^{to} en esta causa a Diego Escudero clerigo presvitero cura de los y^{o}s del rrepartimyento deste valle de Yucay del qual fue tomado juram^{to} en forma segun orden saçerdotal e prometio de dezir verdad e siendo preguntado dixo lo siguiente.

/f.292v/ j A la primera preg^{ta} dixo que conoze a las partes y a los y^{o}s contenidos en el dho memorial e que conoçe al señor liç^{do} Carvajal fiscal de la rreal audiencia.

De las generales ques de hedad de mas de çinquenta años e que no concurre en ning^{a} dellas.

ij A la pregunta dos dixo queste testigo tiene dho su dho en esta causa en diez dias del mes de hebr^{o} de myll e qui^{o}s y sententa y quatro años ante el Dotor Loarte y ante my el dho escrivano donde dixo y declaro y se afirmo e rratifico en ello y lo torno a dezir de nuebo en este plenario jui^{o} por ser verdad so cargo del dho juram^{to} Diego Escudero ante mi P^{o} Diaz Valdeon scriv^{o}.

v En el cuzco a veinte e ocho de hebr^{o} de myll e qui^{o}s y setenta y siete años ante el señor corregidor la pres^{to} el contenido.

v Yll^{e} señor Domingo Lopez de Larrinaga en nonbre del capitan Martin Garçia de Loyola y doña Beatriz Coya su muger en la causa de la ynformaçion que ante Vra merzed e fecho por rreçeutoria de la rreal audiençia de los Reies digo que yo tengo acavada de hazer la dha ynformaçion y no tengo mas t^{o}s que presentar al presente.

v Pido a V. M. mande dar la dha ynformaçion ynterponiendo V. M. en ella su autoridad y decreto judiçial y para ello es. Domingo Lopez de Larrinaga.

v El señor corregidor mando se de al dho Domingo Lopez de Larrinaga en el dho n^{e} un treslado de la dha provança como //
/f.293/ su mag^{d} lo manda por la dha provision rreal a lo qual ynterpuso su autoridad y decreto judiçial para que balga e haga ffee e lo firmo t^{gos} Diego de torres alcalde ordinario desta çiudad e Jer^{mo} de Quesada e Juan de Castañeda escrivanos don Gabriel Paniaga de Loaysa ante mi P^{o} Diaz Valdeon scriv^{o}.

v En la çiudad del cuzco a veinte e un dias del mes de mayo de myll e qui^{o}s y setenta y siete años ante el Yll^{e} señor don Gabriel Paniagua de Loaysa cavallero de la orden de calatrava corregidor e justiçia mayor en esta dha çiudad y su jur^{on} e por ante my el dho escrivano el contenido presento la petiçion con el testimonio siguiente.

v Yll^{e} señor Domingo Lopez de la Rrinaga en nonbre del comendador Martin Garçia de Loyola y doña Beatriz Coya su muger en la causa de la ynformaçion que ante V. M. hago por rreçeptoria de la rreal audi^{a} de los Reies hago ante Vra Md presentaçion este testimonyo de prorrogaçion de otros tres meses de termino conçedidos en esta causa.

v Pido a V. M. lo mande poner con la dha rreçeptoria y que durante el dho termino se me rreçiban todos los testigos de ynformaçion que diere y atento que para la primera provança que hize no estava çitado el fiscal agora lo esta por el dho testimi^{o} pido a V. M. se me tornen a rretefficar y todo se me de en publica forma como lo tengo pedido y pido justicia y pa ello es. El liçençiado Pedraça Domingo Lopez de Larrinaga.

v Yo Alvaro Ruiz de Nabamuel escrivano de camara de su m^{t} en su audi^{a} rreal de los //
/f.293v/ Reies doy fee quel lic^{do} Alvaro de Carvajal fiscal de su magestad en la dha rreal audiençia ante los señores presidente e oydores della pres^{to} una petiçion del tenor sig^{te}. Muy poderosso señor el liçençiado Albaro de Carvajal vro fiscal en la causa con doña Beatriz Coya sobre los yanaconas del valle de Yucay que pide digo que la dha causa esta rreçibida a prueva con termino de los noventa dias conforme a la provision de Malinas en el qual dho termino no puedo ny he podido hazer la provança tocante a vro fisco porque se a de hazer fuera y lexos desta çiudad y asi tengo nezesidad de que se prorroguen otros noventa dias conforme a la dha provision y ordenanças.

v A Vra Al^{a} pido y sup^{co} mande se me den y prorroguen los d[ic]hos noventa dias mas despues despues de cumplidos los otros noventa con que fuimos rreçibidos a prueva para lo qual es. Alvaro de Caruajal.

v En los Reies en çinco dias del mes de março de myll e qui^{o}s y setenta y siete años ante los señores presidente e oydores en audiençia pu^{ca} se leyo esta petiçion y los dhos señores dixeron que prorrogavan y prorrogaron los dhos noventa dias mas de termino comunes a las partes presente el dho fiscal de su magestad y Juan de Herrandolaça pr^{or} contrario a quien se noteffico. Nabamuel.

v Y ansi mysmo doy fee que ante los d]hos señores presidente e oydores el dho Ju^{o} de Arrandolaça en nonbre de la dha doña Beatriz Coya pres^{to} otra petiçion del tenor siguiente.

/f.294/ Muy poderoso señor Juan de Arrandolaça en nonbre de doña Beatriz Coya muger del capitan Loyola en la causa con vro fiscal sobre los y^{o}s del valle de Yucay que le llama yanaconas digo que a pedimi^{o} del dho fiscal se prorrogo el termino provatorio por otros nobenta dias mas pa que conste dello tengo neçesidad de un testim^{o}.

v A Vra Al^{a} sup^{o} mande al secretr^{o} Nauamuel me de testimi^{o} y fee de la dha prorrogaçion de los t^{o}s que mi pte ouiere presentado y exsaminaçion de los que de nuevo presentare y que si quisieren nonbrar scriv^{o} de su parte nonbre y pa ello es. Hernandolaça.

v En los Reies en quinze dias de março de myll e qui^{o}s y setenta y siete años ante los señores presidente e oydores en audiençia publica la presento Juan de Her^{do} Laça en nonbre de su parte.

v Y por los dhos señores fue mandado se le de lo que pide çitado el fiscal de su majestad. Nabamuel.

v En la çiudad de los Reies en diez y ocho dias del mes de março de myll e qui^{o}s y setenta y siete años ley y notefique la petiçion desta otra pte escripta y lo a ella proveydo por los señores desta rreal audiençia al señor liç^{do} Alvaro de Carvajal fiscal de su m^{t} de la dha rreal audiençia en su persona todo lo en ella contenido y espeçialm^{te} le çite pa ver presentar jurar y conoçer los t^{gos} que en esta causa se presentaren y para la rretificaçion de los que sea presentado //
/f.294v/ en forma de dr^{o} y su md dixo que la dha çitaçion hera ynpertinente que bastava la notificaçion del auto de la prorrogaçion questo dava e dio por su rrespuesta t^{o} Juan Ramos de Gauna escrivano receptor.

v Segun consta y pareçe por las dhas petiçiones proueimyentos y çitaçion en ellas puestas a que me rrefiero y para que dello/ conste de pedimyento de la parte de la dha doña Beatriz di el pres^{te} fecho en los Reies a v^{te} e tres dias de março de myll e qui^{o}s y setenta y siete años testado a que entre rrenglones puedo mi e fize aqui my signo en testimonio de verdad Aluaro Ruiz de Nauamuel.

v El señor corregido lo obo por pres^{do} y mando los t^{gos} que presentare se exsamynen por las preguntas del dho ynterr^{o} presentado en esta causa P^{o} Diaz Valdeon escrivano.

v En la çiudad del Cuzco a v^{te} e dos dias del mes de mayo de myll e qui^{o}s e setenta y siete años ante el Yll^{e} señor corregidor e por ante mi el dho escrivano pareçio pres^{te} el dho Domingo Lopez de Larrinaga y en el dho nonbre presento por testigo en esta causa a Pedro de Bustinça vz^{o} desta çiudad del qual tomo juramento en forma por dios nro señor e por Santa Maria su madre e por la señal de la cruz que hizo con su mano dr^{a} que como buen xpiano dira verdad y si asi lo hiziere dios le ayude y de lo contrario se lo demandase y dixo si juro e amen t^{o} Jer^{mo} de Quesada y Roman de Baños y Diego de Mercado. //
/f.295/ Pero Diaz Valdeon escribano.

v En la çiudad del cuzco a veinte e tres dias de mayo del dho año ante el dho señor corregidor y por ante mi el pres^{te} escrivano parecio presente el dho Domingo Lopez de Larrinaga y pres^{to} por testigo en esta causa a Martin Cutipa yn^{o} mytima cay [*sic*] y a Miguel Chiresusa mitima del dho valle de los quales y de cada uno dellos por lengua de Her^{do} de Morales el señor corregidor tomo juramento en forma segun que de los demas testigos e prometieron de dezir verdad so pena de perjuros t^{gos} Br^{me} Baez e Di^{o} de Mercado. P^{o} Diaz Valdeon escribano.

v En la çiudad del cuzco a v^{te} e quatro dias del mes de mayo de myll e qui^{o}s y setenta y siete años ante el dho señor corregidor e por ante mi el dho escrivano parecio presente Domingo Lopez de Larrinaga y pres^{to} por t^{o} en esta causa a Her^{do} Bachicabo vz^{o} desta çiudad del qual fue tomado juramento en/ forma segun que de los demas tg^{os} y prometio de dezir verdad so pena de perjuro t^{gos} Agustin de Madrid y Juan Bautista y Lazaro de Resinero. P^{o} Diaz Valdeon escribano.

v En la çiudad del cuzco a veinte e çinco dias del mes de mayo de myll e qui^{o}s y setenta y siete años ante el dho señor corregidor y por ante mi el dho escrivano Domingo Lopez de Larrinaga y pres^{to} en esta causa a don Françisco Chilche caçique prinçipal de los y^{o}s del valle de Yucay y del qual el señor corregidor tomo juramento en forma segun que de los demas t^{o}s y prometieron de dezir verdad so pena //
/f.295v/ de perjuros el qual dixo juramento se le tomo por ynterpretaçion de Her^{do} de Morales ynterprete Pero Diaz Valdeon escribano.

v En la çiudad del cuzco a veinte e çinco dias de mayo de myll e qui^{o}s y setenta y siete años ante el dho señor corregidor y por ante mi el dho escrivano el dho Domingo Lopez de Larrinaga para la dha prouança pres^{to} por testigo al tesorero Garçia de Melo vz^{o} desta çiudad del qual se tomo e rreçibio juramento segun que los demas el qual lo hizo bien y cunplidamente y prometio de dezir verdad de lo que supiere e a la conclusion del dho juramento dixo si juro e amen tg^{os} los dhos. Pero Diaz Valdeon escribano.

v En la çiudad del Cuzco a veinte e seis dias de mayo de myll e qui^{o}s e setenta y siete años /ante/ el dho señor corregidor e por ante mi el dho escrivano el dho Domingo Lopez de Larrinaga dixo que le tenia en el valle de yucay muchos tgos que digan e declaren sus dhos en esta causa pidio al señor corregidor mande que yo el pres^{te} escrivano tome juram^{to} dellos en forma y digan sus dhos ante mi y por el señor corregidor visto dio comision a mi el dho escrivano pa que los tg^{os} que el dho Domingo Lopez de Larrinaga en el dho nonbre presentare juren y declaren ante mi e por ante dos ynterpretes sus dhos y para ello me dio poder y comision en forma y lo firmo. Br^{me} Baez y Gonçalo Quixada ante mi P^{o} Diaz Valdeon escrivano.

v En la çiudad del Cuzco a veinte e seis dias de mayo del dho mes y año el dho señor corregidor nonbro //
/f.296/ por ynterpretes en esta causa con quien se esxamynen los testigos a Herdo de Morales y a Martin Quispe Topa entendidos en la lengua de los naturales y aviles pa exsamynar los tgos ambos a dos juraron por dios e por santa Maria su madre e por la señal de la cruz que cada uno dellos hizieron con si mano dera que como buenos xpianos guardando su conçiençia usaran del dho ofo de ynterpretes fielmente y sin quitar ni añadir cossa alguna a su saver y entender diran y declaran todo lo que los dhos tos dixeren y declararen en estas rretificaçiones y en los demas yos que se presentaren en la provança a cunplimyento de los doze tos que su mt manda se exsaminen por cada pregunta del dho ynterro y si asi lo hiziere dios le ayude y lo contrario se lo demande y lo firmaron Hernando de Morales Martin Quispe Topa. Po Diaz Valdeon escrivano.

v En el valle de Yucay a vte e nuebe dias del mes de mayo de myll y quios y seta y siete años ante mi el dho scrivo el dho Domingo Lopez de Larrinaga en el dho nonbre presto por testigo en esta causa a Diego Escudero cura y vico del dho valle del qual fue tomado juramento en forma segun orden saçerdotal y prometio de dezir verdad tos Alonso Bermudez y Herdo de Morales Po Diaz Valdeon escrivo.

v En el valle de Yucay a vte e nueve dias del mes de mayo de myll y quios y setenta y siete años el dho Domingo Lopez de Larrinaga presto por testigo en esta causa a Alonso Bermudez del qual fue tomado //
/f.296v/ juramento segun que de los demas tos y prometio de dezir verdad so pena de perjuro tgos Andres Sanchez y Diego Escudero Pero Diaz Valdeon scrivo.

v En el valle de Yucay a veinte e nueue dias del mes de mayo de myll e quios e setenta e siete años ante mi el dho scrivo el dho Domingo Lopez de Larrinaga en el dho nonbre presento por testigo en esta causa a don Diego Cusitumbay y a don Pedro Cochachi y a Juan Bautista Rucana y Martin Yana y a Pedro Chinanjelo y a Herdo Coacalla y a Marcos Puri y a Martin Yupangue y a Lucas Checo y a Martin Sauni y a don Garçia Paucar y a Alo Chaoca y a don Antonio Caquinbay y a Juan Guaçual de los quales y de cada uno dellos por lengua de Herdo de Morales y de Martin Quispe Topa ynterpretes fue tomado juramento por Dios y por Santa Maria su madre y por la señal de la cruz que cada uno dellos hizo con su mano dera que como buenos xpianos guardando sus conçiençias diran verdad en este negoçio y si ansi lo hizieren dios les ayudase y de lo contro se lo demandase y cada uno dellos dixo si juro e amen y prometieron de dezir verdad so pena de perjuros tos Andres Sanchez y Xpobal Holgado y Diego de Mercado. Po Diaz Valdeon escribano.

v En la çiudad del cuzco a treinta e uno de mayo de myll e quios e setenta e siete años el dho Domingo Lopez de Larrinaga presto por tos a Pero Diaz Valdeon scrivo puco desta dha çiudad y a Herdo de Morales ynterprete de los quales y de cada uno dellos se tomo e reçivio juramento en forma //
/f.297/ por Dios nuestra señor y por Santa Maria su madre y por la señal de la cruz que hizieron con su mano dera y prometieron de dezir verdad y si ansi lo hiziesen dios les ayudase y de lo contro se lo demandase e dixeron si juro e amen to Franco Minez de Linpias e Diego de Salzedo y Juan Bautista. Pero Diaz Baldeon escrivano.

to El dho Pedro de Bustinça vzo desta çiudad del cuzco aviendo jurado y siendo pregdo por las preguntas del ynterro dixo lo sigte.

j A la primera pregta dixo que conoze a las ptes.

De las generales dixo ques de hedad de mas de treinta y ocho años y que no yncurre en nynguna de las generales.

ij A la pregunta y a las demas preguntas del dho ynterro dixo que este testigo tiene d]ho su dho en esta causa en la ynformacion que se hizo por la d]ha rreçeptoria el qual dixo y declaro en veinte e seis dias del mes de hebro deste presente año donde dixo y declaro todo lo que sauia abiendolo bisto oydo y entendido dixo que asi como le fue leido y mostrado lo dixo y declaro y si es nezeso lo torno a dezir de nuevo en este plenario juiçio en lo qual se afirmo e rratifico por ser uerdad so cargo del dho juramto y lo firmo de su nonbre Pedro de Bustinça ante mi Po Diaz Valdeon scrivo

to El dho Martin Cutipa yndio mytima Colla en el pueblo de San Benito de Alcantara del valle de Yucay presentado por pte del dho capt Martin Garçia de Loyola aviendo jurado y siendo preguntado por las pregtas del dho ynterro dixo lo siguiente.

/f.297v/ j A la primera pregunta dixo que conoçe a las partes y tiene notiçia de los yos yanaconas sobre que es este pto.

De las generales dixo ques de hedad de mas de setenta e dos años e que no concurre en ninguna de las generales mas de ser de la encomienda del capitan Martin Garçia de Loyola y que sin enbargo dira verdad.

ij A la pregunta dos y a las demas pregas del ynterro dixo queste to tiene dho su dho en esta causa en la prouança que hizo el capitan Martin Garçia de Loyola sobre este negoçio donde dixo y declaro todo lo que savia y siendole leydo y dado a entender el dho que dixo en la dha provança en onze dias del mes de heno de myll e quios e setenta e quatro años ante el Dotor Loarte e ante mi el dho escrivano en lo qual dixo que se rretifico otra bez en el valle de Yucay en veinte e dos dias del mes de hebro deste preste año e que asi como le fue leido y dado a entender por los dhos ynterpretes lo dixo e declaro y en ello se afyrmo e rratifico y lo torno a dezir y declarar de nuevo en este plenario juio por ser verdad so cargo del dho juramto e no firmo porque dixo que no savia y lo firmaron los dhos ynterpretes Herdo de Morales Martin Quispe Topa.

v t^{o} El dho ^{Miguel} Chirisuca yn^{o} mitima en el valle de Yucai vz^{o} del pueblo de San Benito de Alcantara presentado por pte del dho Martin Garçia de Loyola aviendo jurado y siendo preg^{do} por las preguntas del dho ynterr^{o} dixo lo siguiente.

j A la primera preg^{ta} dixo que conoze a las partes y tiene notiçia de los y^{o}s yanaconas sobre ques este p^{to}.

/f.298/ de las generales dixo ques de hedad de mas de sesenta e dos años e que no concurre en ninguna de las generales mas de ser de la encomienda del dho cap^{t} Martin Garçia de Loyola e que sin enbargo desto dira verdad.

Ij A la pregunta dos y a las demas del dho ynterr^{o} dixo qyeste t^{o} tiene dho su dho en esta causa en la provança que hizo el cap^{t} Martin Garçia de Loyola sobre este negocio donde dixo y declaro todo lo que savia y siendole leydo y dado a entender el dho que dixo en la dha provança en onze dias del mes de henero de myll e qui^{o}s e setenta e quatro años ante el dotor Loarte y ante mi el dho escrivano en lo qual dixo que se ratefico otra bez en el valle de Yucay en v^{te} e dos dias del mes de hebr^{o} deste pres^{te} año e que asi como le fue leido y dado a entender por los dhos ynterpretes lo dixo e declaro y en ello se afirmo e ratifico y lo torno a dezir e declarar de nuevo en este plenario jui^{o} por ser verdad so cargo del dho juram^{to} e no firmo por que no supo firmar e lo firmaron los dhos ynterpretes Her^{do} de Morales Martin Quispe Topa ante mi Pero Diaz Baldeon. scriv^{o}.

t^{o} El dho Her^{do} Bachicabo vz^{o} desta ciudad del Cuzco aviendo jurado y siendole preg^{do} dixo lo siguiente.

i A la primera pregunta dixo que conoze a las partes.

De las generales dixo ques de hedad de mas de quarenta y tres años poco mas o menos y que no concurre en ninguna dellas.

Ij la pregunta dos y a las demas del ynterr^{o} dixo queste t^{o} tiene dho su dho //
/f.298v/ en esta causa en la ynformacion que se hizo por la dha rreçeptoria de qual dixo y declaro en veinte e cinco dias del mes de hebr^{o} deste pres^{te} año donde dixo e declaro todo lo que savia y aviendolo visto oydo y entendido dixo que asi como le fue leido y mostradolo dixo y declaro y si necesario es lo torno a dezir de nuebo y declararlo en este plenario jui^{o} en lo qual se afirmo e ratifico por ser verdad so cargo del dho juram^{to} e ratifico por ser verdad so cargo del dho juramento e lo firmo de su nombre. Her^{do} Bachicao. Ante mi Pero Diaz Baldeon escrivano.

t^{o} El dho Fran^{co} Chilche cacique principal de los y^{o}s del valle de Yucay aviendo jurado en esta ciudad del Cuzco y siendo preg^{do} por las preg^{tas} del dho ynterr^{o} dixo lo siguiente.

De las generales dixo ques de hedad de mas de ochenta años e que no concurre en ninguna de las generales e que dira verdad en este negocio.

Ij A la preg^{ta} dos y a las demas del ynterr^{o} dixo queste testigo tiene dho en esta causa en veinte e tres dias del mes de hebr^{o} de mill e qui^{o}s y setenta y site años donde dixo e declaro todo lo que savia e siendole leydo dado a entender por los dhos ynterpretes dixo que asi como le fue leydo y dado a entender lo dixo y declaro y en ello se afirmo y ratifico por ser verdad so cargo del dho juramento y lo firmaron con los dhos ynterpretes. Her^{do} de Morales Martin Quispe Topa ante mi P^{o} Diaz Baldeon escrivano.

/f.299/ t^{o} El dho tesorero Garcia de Melo vz^{o} desta ciudad del Cuzco aviendo jurado y siendo ciudad del Cuzco aviendo jurado y siendo preguntado dixo lo siguiente.

i A la primera pregunta dixo que conoce a las ptes.

De las generales dixo ques de hedad demas de sesenta y siete años e que no concurre en ninguna dellas.

ij A la pregunta dos y a las demas preg^{tas} del ynterr^{o} dixo queste t^{o} declaro su dho en esta causa en veinte e tres dias del mes de hebr^{o} deste pres^{te} año y aviendolo leido oydo y entendido dixo que asi como esta escripto e lo leyo e vio lo dixo y declaro y en ello se afirmo y ratifico y lo torno a dezir de nuebo en este plenario jui^{o} por ser verdad so cargo del dho juram^{to} y lo firmo de su nombre. Melo. Ante mi Pero Diaz Baldeon. scriv^{o}

t^{o} El dho mui reverendo padre Diego Escudero cura vicario del valle de Yucai aviendo jurado segun orden saçerdotal y preguntado dixo lo siguiente.

ij A la pregunta dos y a las demas preg^{tas} del ynterr^{o} dixo queste t^{o} declaro su dho en esta causa en veinte e tres dias del mes de hebr^{o} deste presente año dondo dixo lo que savia e siendole mostrado despues de averlo leydo dixo que asi como le fue leido y mostrado lo dixo y declaro y en ello se afirmo e ratifico por ser verdad so cargo del dho juram^{to} e lo firmo de su nombre. Di^{o} Escudero ante mi Pero Diaz Baldeon scriv^{o}.

t^{o} El dho Alonso Bermudez residente en esta valle de Yucai aviendolo jurado y siendo preg^{do} dixo lo siguiente.

i A la primera preg^{ta} dixo que conoce a las ptes.

De las generales dixo ques de hedad de mas de cinq^{ta} e siete años y que no concurre en ninguna dellas.

/f.299v/ ij A la preg^{ta} dos y a las demas preg^{tas} del ynterrogatorio dixo queste t^{o} declaro su dho en esta causa en veinte e tres dias del mes mes de hebr^{o} de myll e qui^{o}s y setenta y siete años donde dixo todo lo que savia y siendole mostrado despues de averlo leido dixo que asi como le fue leido y mostradolo dixo y declaro y en ello se afirmo e ratifico por ser verdad so cargo del dho juram^{to} e lo firmo. Alonso Bermudez ante mi P^{o} Diaz Valdeon escrivano.

t^{o} El dho don Diego Cusi Tunbai natural deste de Yucai indio cañar aviendo jurado y siendo preguntado dixo lo siguiente.

i A la primera preg^{ta} dixo que conoce a las partes.

De las generales dixo que es de hedad de mas de ochenta años e que co concurre en ninguna dellas mas de estar encomendado en el cap^{t} Martin Garcia de Loyola e que no por esto dexara de dezir verdad.

ij A la pregunta dos y a las demas del ynterrogatorio dixo queste t^{o} tenia dho su dho en esta causa en la provança que hizo el capitan Martin Garcia de Loyola sobre este negocio dondo dixo y declaro todo lo que savia y siendole leido y dado a entender el dho que dixo en la dha provança en onze dias del mes de henero de mill e qui^{o}s y setenta y quatro años ante el dotor Loarte y ante mi el dho scriv^{o} en lo qual dixo lo que savia y se retifico en ello otra bez en este valle de Yucai en v^{te} e dos dias del mes de hebr^{o} deste pres^{te} año dixo que asi como le fue leydo y dado a entender lo uno y lo otro por los dhos ynterpretes lo dixo y declaro y en ello se afirmo y ratifico y lo torno a dezir y declarar de nuevo en este plenario jui^{o} por ser verdad so cargo del dho juram^{to} //
/f.300/ e no firmo porque dixo que no savia y lo firmaron los dhos ynterpretes. Hernando de Morales Martin Quispe Topa ante mi Pero Diaz Baldeon escrivano.

t^{o} El dho don P^{o} Cochachina natural deste valle de Yucay mitima aviendo jurado y preguntado dixo lo siguiente.

i A la primera preg^{ta} dixo que conoze a las partes e que no conoce al señor fiscal.

De las generales dixo ques de hedad de mas de setenta y dos años y que no concurre en ninguna dellas.

ij A la preg^{ta} dos y a las demas preguntas del ynterr^{o} dixo queste t^{o} declaro su dho en esta causa en la provança que sobre este negocio hizo el cap^{t} Martin Garcia de Loyola donde declaro todo lo que savia lo qual dixo en onze dias del mes de hen^{o} del año de myll e qui^{o}s y setenta y quatro años ante el dotor Loarte y ante mi el dho scriv^{o} en lo qual se ratifico otra bez en este valle de Yucai en veinte e dos dias del mes de hebr^{o} deste pres^{te} año de set^{a} y siete siendole leydo y dado a entender por los dhos ynterpretes anbos dhos dixo que asi como le fueron leidos y dados a entender los dixo y declaro y en ello se afyrmo y ratifico y lo torno a dezir y declarar todo de nuevo en este plenario jui^{o} por ser verdad so cargo del dho juramento y no firmo por que no supo y lo firmaron los dhos yntepretes Her^{do} de Morales Martin Quispe Topa ante mi Pedro Diaz Valdeon escriv^{o}.

t^{o} El dho Juan Bautista Rucana natural deste valle de Yucai aviendo jurado y siendo preguntado dixo lo siguiente.

/f.300v/ i A la primera preg^{ta} dixo que conoce a las partes e que no conoce al señor fiscal.

De las generales dixo que es de hedad de mas de noventa años e que no concurre en ninguna de las generales mas de estar encomendado en el dho capitan Martin Garcia de Loyola e que sin embargo desto dira verdad.

ij A la pregunta dos y a las demas preg^{tas} del ynterr^{o} dixo queste t^{o} declaro su dho en esta causa en la provança que sobre este negocio hizo el dho cap^{t} Martin Garcia de Loyola donde declaro todo lo que savia lo qual dixo en onze dias del mes de henero de myll e qui^{o}s y setenta y quatro años ante el dotor Loarte e ante mi el dho escrivano en lo qual se ratifico otra bez en este valle de Yucai en v^{te} e dos dias del mes de hebr^{o} deste pres^{te} año de setenta y siete años siendole leydo y dado a entender por los dhos yntepretes anbos dhos dixo que asi como le fueron leidos y dados a entender los dixo y declaro y en ello se afirmo y ratifico y lo torno a dezir y declarar todo de nuevo en este plenario jui^{o} por ser verdad so cargo del dho juram^{to} e no firmo por que no supo lo firmaron los dhos yntepretes. Her^{do} de Morales Martin Quispe Topa ante mi P^{o} Diaz Baldeon escriv^{o}.

t^{o} El dho Martin Yana natural Guayllas yn^{o} mitima en el valle de Yucai vz^{o} del pueblo de San Bernardo del asiento de Uropampa aviendo jurado y siendo preguntado dixo lo siguiente.

i A la primera preg^{ta} dixo que conoce a las ptes y que no conoce al señor fiscal.

/f.301/ De las generales dixo ques de hedad de mas de setenta e dos años e que no concurre en ninguna de las generales mas de estar encomendado en el dho cap^{t} Martin Garcia de Loyola e que syn enbargo desto dira verdad.

ij A la prg^{ta} dos y a las demas preg^{tas} del ynterr^{o} dixo queste t^{o} declaro su dho en la dha provança que sobre este negocio hizo el cap^{t} Martin Garcia de Loyola en onze dias del mes de henero de myll e qui^{o}s e setenta e quatro años ante el dotor Loarte e ante mi el dho escrivano en lo qual se ratifico otra bez en este valle de Yucai en v^{te} e dos dias del mes de hebr^{o} deste pres^{te} año de setenta y siete años donde dixo y declaro en anbos dhos todo lo que savia y siendole leydo y dado a entender anbos dichos lo uno y lo otro por los dhos ynterpretes dixo que asi como le fueron leidos y dados a entender anbos dichos dixo y declaro y en ello se afirmo y ratifico y lo torno a dezir de nuevo en este plenario jui^{o} por ser verdad so cargo del dho juramento e lo firmaron los yntepretes. Her^{do} de Morales Martin Quispe Topa ante mi P^{o} Diaz Valdeon escriv^{o}.

t^{o} El dho P^{o} Chinanzella yn^{o} cañar vz^{o} del pueblo de Santiago de Oropesa aviendo jurado y siendo preg^{do} dixo lo siguiente.

i A la primera preg^{ta} dixo que conoce a las partes e que no conoce al s^{or} fiscal.

De las generales dixo que es de hedad de mas de ochenta y dos años e que no concurre en nyng^{a} dellas mas de ser enco- //
/f.301v/ mendado en el dho capitan Martin Garcia de Loyola e que sin embargo desto dira verdad.

ij A la pregunta dos y a la demas del ynterr^{o} dixo que este testigo declaro su dho en este negocio en la provança que hizo el cap^{t} Martin Garcia de Loyola en diez dias del mes de março de myll e qui^{o}s y setenta y quatro años ante el dotor Loarte y ante mi el dho escrivano en lo qual se retifico otra bez en este valle de Yucai en veinte e dos dias del mes de hebr^{o} deste pres^{te} año de setenta y siete donde dixo y declaro en anbos dhos todo lo que savia e siendole leido y dadole a entender todo ello por los dhos ynterpretes dixo que asi como le fueron leidos y dados a entender anbos dhos los dixo y declaro y en ello se afirmo y ratifico y lo torno a dezir y declarar de nuevo en este plenario jui^{o} por ser verdad so cargo del dho juram^{to} y no firmo por que dixo que no savia y lo firmaron los dhos ynterpretes. Her^{do} de Morales Martin Quispe Topa ante mi P^{o} Diaz Valdeon escriv^{o}

t^{o} El dho Her^{do} Coacalla mitima vz^{o} del pueblo de Santiago de Oropesa aviendo jurado y siendo preg^{do} dixo lo siguiente.

i A la primera preg^{ta} dixo que conoce a las partes y que no conoce al señor fiscal.

De las generales dixo ques de hedad de mas de setenta y dos años y que no concurre en ninguna de las generales mas de ser de la encomienda del cap^{t} Martin Garcia de Loyola que sin embargo desto dira verdad.

/f.302/ ij A la pregunta dos y a las demas pre^{gtas} del ynterr^{o} dixo queste t^{o} declaro su dho en este negocio en la ynformacion que hizo el cap^{t} Martin Garcia de Loyola en diez dias del mes de março del año de myll e qui^{o}s y setenta y quatro años ante el dotor Loarte e ante mi el dho escriv^{o} en lo qual se retifico en esta villa de Yucay en v^{te} e dos dias del mes de hebr^{o} deste pres^{te} año y en anbos dhos dixo y declaro todo lo que savia y siendole leido y dado a entender por los dhos ynterpretes anbos dhos dixo que asi como le fueron leidos y dados a entender los dixo y declaroy en ello se afirmo e ratifico y lo torno a dezir todo de nuevo en este plenario jui^{o} por ser verdad so cargo del dho juram^{to} e no firmo por que no supo y lo firmaron los dhos yntepretes. Her^{do} de Morales Martin Quispe Topa ante mi P^{o} Diaz Valdeon escrivano.

t^{o} El Dho Marcos Puri aviendo jurado y preguntado dixo lo siguiente.

i A la primera preg^{ta} dixo que conoce a las partes e que no conoce al señor fiscal e que conoce a las y^{o}s en la memoria presentada en esta causa.

De las generales dixo que es de hedad de mas de setenta años e que no concurre en ninguna dellas por ques principal de los y^{o}s yanaconas que antes heran desta encomienda sobre que se trata este pleito e que dira verdad en este negocio.

ij A la preg^{ta} dos y a las demas preg^{tas} del dho ynterr^{o} dixo queste t^{o} tiene dho su dho en esta causa en veinte y tres dias del mes de heb^{ro} deste pres^{te} año de set^{a} //
/f.302v/ y siete donde dixo y declaro lo que savia y siendole leido y dadole a entender por los dhos yntepretes dixo que asi como le fue leido y dado a entender lo dixo y declaro y en ella se afirmo e ratifico por ser verdad so cargo del dho juram^{to} e lo torno a dezir de nuevo en este plenario juizio y no firmo por que no supo y lo firmaron los ynterpretes. Her^{do} de Morales Martin Quispe Topa ante mi P^{o} Diaz Valdeon escriv^{o}

t^{o} El dho Martin Yupangue natural deste dho valle y vz^{o} del pueblo de San Bernardo de Uropampa aviendo jurado y preguntado dixo lo siguiente.

i A la primera preg^{ta} dixo que conoce a las partes y que no conoce al señor fiscal.

De las generales dixo ques de hedad de mas de setenta años e que no concurre en ninguna dellas mas de ser de la encomienda del capitan Loyola e que sin embargo desto dira verdad.

ij A la preg^{ta} dos y a las demas preguntas del ynterr^{o} dixo queste t^{o} declaro su dho en esta causa en la provança que sobre este negocio hizo el cap^{t} Martin Garcia de Loyola donde declaro todo lo que savia lo qual dixo en onze dias del mes de hen^{o} de myll e qui^{o}s y setenta

y quatro años ante el dotor Loarte y ante mi el dho escrivano en lo qual se ratifico otra bez en este valle de Yucai en v^{te} e dos dias del mes de hebr^{o} deste presente año de set^{a} e siete años y siendole leido y dado a entender por los dhos yntepretes anbos dhos dixo que asi como le fueron leidos y dados a entender los dixo y declaro //
/f.303/ y en ello se afirmo y ratifico y la torno a dezir y declarar todo de nuevo en este plenario jui^{o} por ser verdad so cargo del dho juram^{to} e no firmo porque dixo que no savia y lo firmaron los dhos ynterpretes. Her^{do} de Morales Martin Quispe Topa ante mi P^{o} Diaz Valdeon escrivano.

t^{o} El dho Lucas Checo yndio natural del pueblo de San Benito de Alcantara de Guayllapampa aviendo jurado y preg^{do} dixo lo siguiente.

i A la primera pregunta dixo que conoce a las partes y a los y^{o}s contenidos en el dho memorial e que no conoce al s^{or} fiscal.

De las generales dixo que es de hedad de mas de setenta y cinco años y que no concurre en ninguna de las generales.

ij A la pregunta dos y a las demas preg^{tas} del dho ynterr^{o} dixo queste t^{o} declaro su dho en esta causa en la provança que sobre este negocio hizo el cap^{t} Martin Garcia de Loyola donde declaro todo lo que savia lo qual dixo en onze de henero de mill e qui^{o}s y set^{a} y quatro años ante el dotor Loarte y ante mi el dho escriv^{o} en lo qual se ratifico otra vez en este valle de Yucay en veinte e dos dias del mes de hebr^{o} deste pres^{te} año de setenta y siete siendole leido y dado a entender por los dhos ynterpretes ambos dhos dixo que ansi como le fueron leidos y dados a entender los dixo y declaro y en ello se afirmo y ratifico y lo torno a dezir y declarar todo de nuevo en este plenario jui^{o} por ser verdad so cargo del dho juramento e no firmo porque //
/f.303v/ dixo que no savia y lo firmaron los dhos yntepretes. Her^{do} de Morales Martin Quispe Topa ante mi Pero Diaz Baldeon escrivano.

t^{o} El dho don Gonçalo Paucar vz^{o} del pueblo de Paca aviendo jurado y siendo preg^{do} dixo lo siguiente.

i A la primera preg^{ta} dixo que conoce a las partes y a los yndios contenidos memorial [*sic*] y no conoce al señor fiscal.

De las generales dixo ques de hedad de mas de setenta y dos años y que no concurre en ninguna dellas mas de ser de la encomienda del capitan Martin Garcia de Loyola e que sin embargo desto dira verdad.

ij A la primera preg^{ta} dos y a las demas del ynterr^{o} dixo queste t^{o} tiene dho su dho en esta causa en la provança que hizo el cap^{t} Martin Garcia de Loyola donde declaro lo que avia y siendole mostrado el dho que dixo en onze dias del mes de hen^{o} de myll e qui^{o}s e setenta y quatro años ante el dotor Loarte y ante mi el dho escrivano y la retificacion que del hizo en este valle a v^{te} e dos dias del mes de hebr^{o} deste pres^{te} año dixo que asi como le fueron leidos y mostrados anbos dhos los dixo y declaro y en ello se afirmo e ratifico e lo torno a dezir y declarar todo de nuevo en este plenario jui^{o} por ser verdad so cargo del dho juramento e no firmo porque dixo que no savia e lo firmaron los dhos yntepretes Her^{do} de Morales Martin Quispe Topa ante mi Pedro Diaz Valdeon escrivano.

/f.304/ t^{o} El dho Alonso Chauca yndio mitima vz^{o}del pueblo de San Bernardo de Urobanba aviendo jurado y siendo preguntado dixo lo siguiente.

i A la primera preg^{ta} dixo que conoce a las partes y a los y^{o}s contenidos en el dho memorial y no conoce al señor fiscal.

De las generales dixo que es de hedad de mas de ochenta años e no concurre en ninguna dellas.

ij A la preg^{ta} dos y a las demas preg^{tas} del ynterrogatorio dixo queste t^{o} declaro su dho en esta causa en la provança que sobre este negocio hizo el cap^{t} Martin Garcia de Loyola en onze dias del mes de henero de myll e qui^{o}s y setenta y quatro años ante el dotor Loarte y ante mi el dho escrivano en lo qual se ratifico otra vez en este valle de Yucai en veinte e tres dias del mes de hebr^{o} de myll e qui^{o}s y setenta y siete años donde dixo y declaro en anbos todo lo que savia y siendole leido y dado a entender lo uno y lo otro por los dhos ynterpretes dixo que asi como le fueron leidos y dados a entender anbos los dixo y declaro y en ello se afirmo e ratifico y lo torno a dezir de nuevo en este plenario jui^{o} por ser verdad so cargo del dho juram^{to} y no firmo por que dixo que no savia y lo firmaron los dhos ynterpretes. Her^{do} de Morales Martin Quispe Topa ante mi Pedro Diaz Valdeon escrivano.

t^{o} El dho don Ant^{o} Caquivari yndio cañar vz^{o}del pu^{o} de San Bernardo de Urobanba natural deste valle de Yucai aviendo jurado y siendo preg^{do} dixo lo sig^{te}

/f.304v/ i A la primera preg^{ta} dixo que conoce a las partes e a todos los contenidos en el memorial presentado en esta causa e que no conoce al señor fiscal.

De las generales dixo que es de hedad de mas de setenta años porque conocio a Guayna Capac e quando el dho Guayna Capa murio hera este t^{o} hombre y que no concurre en ninguna de las generales porqueste t^{o} es de los y^{o}s yanaconas que de antes heran tributarios deste repartimiento y encomienda de doña Beatriz Coya mujer del capitan Martin Garcia de Loyola e de los contenidos en el dho memorial que agora tributa a su majestad.

ij A la preg^{ta} dos dixo queste t^{o}save e vio que los y^{o}s viejos y ombres de hedad contenidos en el dho memorial que le fue leido y mostrado a este testigo y eran todos desta encomienda y lo mismo los dellos deçendientes y todos ellos como tales y^{o}s desta encomienda a tributado los que an sido de hedad a la dha doña Beatriz Coya y a don Diego Saire Topa su padre y a los demas encomenderos sus antecesores porqueste testigo como yndio antiguo tributario dellos e yn^{o} mitima deste valle lo ha visto con ellos hasta esta visita general que los bisitaron por y^{o}s yanaconas siendo tributarios deste repartimi^{to} y encomienda y^{o}s mitimas desde el tiempo de Yngas y la causa por que se hizieron todos los y^{o}s contenidos en el dho memorial yanaconas y se entraron de la dha encomienda porque servia dellos don Fran^{co} Chilche cacique principal deste //
/f.305/ valle y mandose visitase por yanaconas a fin de servirse dellos como de antes se sirvia y pa que el visitador se los dexase por suyos en la bisita y esto save desta pregunta.

vi A la pregunta seis dixo que save e vio este testigo que todos los y^{o}s contenidos en el dho memorial sus padres y aguelos e los que dellos tienen hedad fueron de Guayna Capac Ynga señor que fue destos reinos e los puso por y^{o}s mitimas deste valle pa camayos como y^{o}s yanaconas que desde entonzes se llamaban yanaconas que quiere dezir criados de su casa e haziendas e como tales les servian e le sirvio este t^{o} con los demas ancianos contenidos en el dho memorial en los oficios y cosas que el dho Guayna Caba [*sic*] les ocupava y los y^{o}s moços e muchachos de los cont^{dos} en el dho memorial son y proceden de los y^{o}s camayos e yanaconas antiguos que el dho Guayna Capa tuvo y asi servia dellos e de sus hijos y mujeres y les beneficiavan sus chacaras y le hazian los edeficios e casas que tenian en este valle y esto save e vio este t^{o}.

vii A la preg^{ta} siete dixo que save este testigo que luego que el marques don Françisco vino a este reyno tomo los y^{o}s deste valle asi los mitimas como camaios e naturales e yanaconas e de todos ellos se sirvio en las cosas que la preg^{ta} dize y este t^{o} como uno de los dhos y^{o}s le sirvia e sirvio en todo y le contribuian por tributo todos ellos en las cosas que la pregunta dize de beneficialle chacaras //
/f.305v/ de coca e maiz y en lavor de minas y hazelle otros servicios personales y esto save desta pregunta.

viii A la preg^{ta} ocho dixo que save y vio este t^{o} que despues del marques don Fran^{co} Piçarro tuvo en encomienda todos los dhos y^{o}s Gonçalo Piçarro su hijo y despues subcedieron en su majestad e cobro los tributos dellos cierto tiempo el tesorero Garcia de Melo hasta que se encomendaron en don Diego Saire Topa padre de la dha doña Beatriz mujer del capitan Martin Garcia de Loyola y todos ellos an tributado y tributavan a los dhos encomenderos y a su majestad y al dho don Diego Saire Topa e a la dha doña Beatriz su hija hasta que en la visita de Damian de la Vandera don Fran^{co} Chilche cacique los reservo tomandolos por sus yanaconas para servirse dellos y asi los fue sacando e tomando de la dha encomienda siendo todos ellos y^{o}s tributarios y desta encomienda y los save por lo vio ser y pasar asi.

ix A la preg^{ta} nueve dixo ques y pasa asi como la pregunta lo dize y declara y los save este t^{o} porques uno de los y^{o}s que el dho don Fran^{co} Chilche escondio e restituyo en la visita que el dho Damian de la Bandera al dho repartimi^{o} con los demas del dho memorial y los que dellos quedaron de restituir en la visita que hizo Garcia de Melo los restituyo al dho repartimi^{o} e mando que todos ellos tributasen a sus encomenderos y lo hizieron asi hasta que en esta visita general los torno a sacar e quitar //
/f.306/ de la dha encomienda el dho don Fran^{co} Chilche y los visito el licenciado frei P^{o} Gutierrez por yndios yanaconas y ase exsentaron del dho repartimi^{to} y los hicieron yanaconas y esto save e vio este t^{o} como yndio antiguo que es en este valle y deste repartimi^{o}.

xiij A la preg^{ta} treze dixo que save que la dha doña Beatriz Coya y el dho capitan Martin Garcia de Loyola su marido an sido y son despojados de todos los y^{o}s cont^{dos} en el dho memorial por las razones que en el dho memorial por las razones que dho tiene en lo qual son agraviados los dhos cap^{t} Martin Garcia de Loyola e doña Beatriz Coya su mujer por les aver quitado de la dha encomienda los dhos y^{o}s y esta es la verdad y lo que deste caso save so cargo del dho juram^{to} e no declaro en las demas preguntas por que no fue presentado para en mas y se afirmo y ratifico en todo y no firmo por que no e lo firmaron los dhos yntepretes. Her^{do} de Morales Martin Quispe Topa ante mi P^{o} Diaz Valdeon escriv^{o}

t^{o} El dho Juan Guacac vz^{o} del pueblo de San Benito de Alcantara de los y^{o}s yanaconas sobre que se trata este p^{to} aviendo jurado y siendo preguntado dixo lo siguiente.

i A la primera preg^{ta} dixo que conoce a las partes y conoce a la mayor parte de los y^{o}s contenidos en el dho memorial e que no conoce al señor fiscal.

De las generales dixo que es de hedad de mas de setenta años e que no concurre en ninguna dellas por ques de los y^{o}s yanaconas que de antes heran desta encomienda y al presente despues de la visita //
/f.306v/ general aca sean puesto en la corona real de su majestad e que dira verdad en este negocio.

Ij A la pregunta dos dixo queste t^{o} save e vio que los y^{o}s viejos y onbres de hedad contenidos en el dho memorial que le leydo y mostrado son y eran todos desta encomienda y los mismo los deçendientes dellos y ansi an tributado a la dha doña Beatriz Coya mujer del cap^{t} Martin Garcia de Loyola y a don Diego Saire Topa padre de la dha doña Beatriz Coya y a los demas encomenderos sus antecesores por queste testigo como indio antiguo y tributario que hera desta encomienda lo save e vio ser y pasar asi siendo todos ellos y^{o}s tributarios deste repartimi^{to} y encomienda se hicieron yanaconas e los reservaron de la dha encomienda a causa de sacarlos don Fran^{co} Chilche y los demas caciques por yanaconas y servirse dellos y esto save y vio desta pregunta.

v A la preg^{ta} cinco dixo queste testigo fue unos de los dhos y^{o}s que fueron encomendados en el dho don Diego Saire Topa Ynga padre de la dha doña Beatriz Coya y fueron todos los que tuvo e poseyo el marques don Françisco Piçarro con los demas y^{o}s deste valle y repartimiento y todos los del dho memorial de los anaconas con los demas de la dha encomienda pagavan y davan el tribu^{o} que la pregunta dize.

vi A la preg^{ta} seis dixo que save e vio este testigo que el dho Guayna Capac tuvo y poseyo todos los y^{o}s deste valle de //
/f 307/ Yucay y dellos deçendieron los contenidos en el dho memorial y se sirvian dellos como de mytimas naturales deste valle a causa de que los tenia para su servi^{o}

vij A la pregunta syete dixo que es verdad lo contenido en la dha pregunta por que este t^{o} vio ser y pasar asi y vio que como tales tributarios pagavan y davan todos el tributo que la preg^{ta} dize.

viij A la preg^{ta} ocho dixo ques verdad lo cont^{do} en la dha pregunta porque de la mesma manera que tributaron a los dhos Guaina Capa y a don Fran^{co} Piçarro y Gonçalo Piçarro an servido y tributado al dho don Diego Saire Topa y a la dha doña Beatriz Coya su hija hasta la visita general y hasta que tuvieron tassa tributaron en lo que la pregunta dize.

ix A la preg^{ta} nueve dixo que save e vio que los dhos sobre que es este pleito los dhos son Fran^{co} Chilche y don Garçia Quispicapi caçiques tomaron y sacaron los dhos y^{o}s deste repartimiento y encomienda para servirse dellos y de otros que se sirviesen otros deudos y amigos suyos visto la disoluçion que en esto avia Damian de la Vandera Visitador que fue de los dhos y^{o}s m^{do} que tributasen como los demas tributarios del dho repartimi^{to} pues todos ellos heran deste repartimi^{to} y lo mysmo m^{do} Garçia de Melo en la segunda visita que dellos hizo y esto save e vio desta preg^{ta}.

x A la preg^{ta} diez dijo que save e vio este t^{o} que fue e paso ansi como la preg^{ta} lo dize y declara y el dho don Fran^{co} Chilche les //
/f.307v/ dixo e dio a entender que si se bisitauan por yanaconas no avian de pagar tribu^{o} e asi se visitaron por yanaconas syendo todos ellos y^{o}s desta encomienda y repartimi^{to} y engañaron en ello al visitador y esto save desta preg^{ta}.

xj A la preg^{ta} onze dixo ques verdad quel liçençiado frei P^{o} Gutierrez los visito por yanaconas por la rrelaçion que dello le dieron e que si le dixeran verdad los visitara por y^{o}s tributarios deste repartimiento y encomienda como siempre lo avian sydo y lo heran al presente que por no le dezir ny tratar verdad los visito por yanaconas y los saco del repartimi^{to} y los puso en la corona real y esto save y vio desta pregunta.

xij A la pregunta doze dixo que es verdad lo contenido en la preg^{ta} por las causas y razones que dho tiene.

xiij A la pregunta treze dixo que save e vio este t^{o} que la dha doña Beatriz Coya y el capitan Martin Garçia de Loyola su marido an sido desposeidos de los dhos y^{o}s contenido en el dho memorial que por las causas y razones que dho tiene en lo qual an sido y son muy agraviados en les aver quitado de la posesion que tenia de los dichos y^{o}s y tribu^{o} que les davan como yn^{o}s que eran todos deste repartimi^{to} y encomyenda y esto save desta preg^{ta}.

xiiij A la preg^{ta} catorze dixo que lo que dho ti^{e} es la verdad so cargo del dho juram^{to} y en ello se afirmo y ratifico y no firmo porque dixo que no savia y lo firmaron los ynterpretes //
/f.308/ Hernando de Morales Martin Quispe Topa ante mi P^{o} Diaz Valdeon escribano.

T^{o} El dho Hernando de Morales ynterprete general desta çiudad aviendo jurado y siendo preguntado dijo lo siguiente.

j A la primera pregta dixo que conoçe a las partes y conoçe a algunos de los y^{o}s cont^{dos} en el memorial que le fue mostrado e a oydo dezir que los dhos y^{o}s son y^{o}s mitimas tributarios en el repartimi^{to} de Yucay lo qual oyo dezir este testigo a los y^{o}s que asi conoçe a los de la dicha memoria e a otros y^{o}s del dho valle de Yucai asi por auer esaminado alguno dellos como ynterprete desta çiudad por t^{o} en esta causa como por auerse hallado presente en algunas platicas que sobre este pleito an tenido los caçiques e y^{o}s principales del dho repartimi^{to} y los que a examinado este testigo en este p^{to} an dho y declarado que son y^{o}s mytimas en el dho repartimi^{to} puestos por Guaina Capa y como tales avian servido y tributado al marques Piçarro y demas encomenderos que an tenido el dho repartimi^{to} hasta el Ynga don Diego Saire Topa que asimysmo los tuvo en encomienda como mas largamente consta de sus dhos a que se refiere este testigo.

De las generales dixo ques de hedad de treinta e nueue años e que no le tocan nynguna de las generales de la ley.

xj A la pregta onze dixo que lo que della save es que este t^{o} fue ynterprete en la visita que el liç^{do} frei Pedro Gutierrez Flores visitador general hizo de los y^{o}s del //
/f.308v/ repartimiento de Yucai e asi vio este testigo que el dho visitador hizo la visita de los dhos y^{o}s de Yucai y asi vio este testigo que el dho uisitador hizo la visita de los dhos y^{o}s de Yucai [*sic*] por el padron que Diego Escudero clerigo cura del dho valle de Yucay thenia fecho pa su dotrina y asi visito todos los y^{o}s que hallo nombrados por el dho padron diviendolos a los unos en nombre de yanaconas y a los otros por y^{o}s tributarios del rrepartimiento de yucai e no hizo el dho visitador pesquisa ni aberiguaçion ninguna açerca de que los dhos y^{o}s que asi bisito por yanaconas fuesen tales yanaconas o no ni ubo persona nynguna de parte del encomendero del dho repartimiento que advirtiese al dho visitador se governo por el dho padron por entender que de aquella manera no le ocultarian y^{o}s ningunos y despues desa

la dha visita a çierto tienpo vio este t^{o} en el valle de Yucai en esta çiudad tratar a muchos españoles e y^{o}s que por orden de los caçiques del dho repartimi^{to} de Yucai avian visitado por yanaconas y^{o}s tributarios a su M^{t} mas de treçientos y^{o}s del dho repartimi^{to} de Yucay y que eran mitimas y lo avian sido sus padres y aguelos y asi en este pleito lo an declarado todos/ los t^{os} queste testigo a exsaminado/ en este p^{to} los quales todos avian sido y al pres^{te} heran subjetos a los caçiques del dho repartimi^{to}.

xij A la preg^{ta} doze dixo que dize los que dho tiene en la pregunta antes desta y por lo que a este t a entendido de los dhos y^{o}s e caçiques entiende que los dhos y^{o}s que asi se vi- //
/f.309/ sitaron por yanaconas e lo hizieron por escusarse de ser tributarios en el dho repartimi^{to} y los caçiques lo hizieron por servirse de los dhos y^{o}s por todo lo qual este t^{o} y entiende que cautelosamente usurparon los dhos y^{o}s que ansi se visitaron por yanaconas y les quitaron del dho repartimi^{to} y encomienda el cap^{t} Martin Garçia de Loyola y esto es lo que saue y entiende deste negoçio y es la verdad para el juramento que tiene fecho y no declaro en mas preg^{tas} porque no fue presentado para mas y lo firmo de su nombre Her^{do} de Morales. Ante mi Pero Diaz Valdeon escribano.

T^{o} El dho P^{o} Diaz Valdeon escrivano pu^{co} desta çiudad presentado por el dho Domingo Lopez de Larrinaga para la dha provança el qual aviendo jurado e siendo preguntado dixo lo siguiente.

j A la primera preg^{ta} dixo que conoçe a las ptes.

De las generales dixo ques de hedad de çinquenta años e que no concurre en nynguna dellas.

ij A la pregunta dos dixo que este t^{o} verifico en la visita general que ante el se hizo de los y^{o}s del dho valle que muchos de los y^{o}s contenidos en el dho memorial pagavan tributo a la dha doña Beatriz Coya y lo avian dado a los demas encomenderos y es de creer y tener por cosa muy çierta que sino fueron todos de la dha encomienda que no pagaran tribu^{o} a los dhos encomenderos e si se bisitaran por yanaconas fue por el padre Diego Escudero que los dotrinaba por thenerlos yntitulados en lugar de yanaconas y como su Ex^{a} avia mandado que todos los y^{o}s yanaconas se enpadronasen por si entendiendo que en ellos se hazia //
/f.309v/ servi^{o} se hizo asi y su uviera al tiempo que se enpadronaron quien procurara por ellos por parte de su encomendero se berificava bastantem^{te} ser de la dha encomienda y se visitaran todos por de la dha encomienda porque pagando tribu^{o} al encomendero hera de creer que heran todos de la dha encomienda y esto rresponde a esta pregunta y a las demas preg^{tas} del dho ynterr^{o} e dixo que es verdad so cargo del dho juram^{to} y lo firmo Pedro Diaz Baldeon escrivano.

/al margen: fee de como solos dos yn^{o}s no ratificaron por averse muerto primero/
Yo Pedro Diaz Baldeon escrivano pu^{co} y del numero desta çiudad del cuzco doy fee que no se ratificaron en esta provança Marcos Cayo Gualpa y Sebastian Tenançela que tienen dho sus dhos en esta causa a causa de ser muertos e aver pasados esta vida y con todo lo suso dho por el libro que se tiene en el valle de Yucai de los que mueren y naçen conforme a una ordenança fecha por su Exª y para que conste dello di esta fee de lo qual fijze aqui my signo en testimonio de verdad. Pedro Diaz Baldeon escrivano.

v En la çiudad del Cuzco a diez y siete dias del mes de julio de mill e qui^{o}s e setenta e siete años ante el Yll^{e} señor don Gabriel Panyagua de Loaysa cavallero de la orden de Calatrava corregidor e justiçia mayor en esta dha çiudad e su jur^{on} por su m^{t} e pa que por ante mi el dho escrivano la presento el cont^{do}.

v Yll^{e} señor Domingo Lopez de Larrinaga en nonbre del cap^{t} Loyola en la causa con su m^{t} sobre los yanaconas de Yucay digo que en la dha rrazon yo presente reçeptoria de su m^{t} pa hazer mi provança e la tengo fecha.

v Pido a V. M. mande que el presente escribano me de un treslado de la dha provança en pu^{ca} //
/f.310/ forma e manera que haga fee ynterponiendo a ella vra md su autoridad en forma para lo qual es. Domingo Lopez de Larrinaga.

v El señor corregidor mando se de al dho Domingo Lopez de Larrinaga en el dho nonbre un treslado de la dha provança como su m^{t} lo manda al qual ynterpuso su autoridad y decreto judiçial y lo firmo t^{os} Juan de Castañeda y Juan de Quiroz don Gabriel Paniagua de Loaysa ante mi P^{o} Dias Baldeon escribano.

va testado Beatriz/ dhos/ huerfano por el les fuere/ mandado y sobre ello/ doze/ dho/ nombrado/ su Her^{do}/ de Morales/ de Cañete no bala/ ba emendado/ bore/ cortes/ Mango/ tener/ en los/ bala/ entre renglones Andres Puamalli de v^{te} a^{o}s tiene hijos/ Quiñones Ananpa de treinta años tiene hijos/ veinte e/ quales/ nro/ a la dha doña Beatriz/su muger/ Min Palaçios vala. Don Gabriel Paniagua de Loaysa yo Pedro Diaz Baldeon escrivano de su magestad pu^{co} del numero de la dha çiudad del Cuzco fuy pres^{te} e fize aqui my signo en testimonio de verdad P^{o} Diaz Baldeon escribano.

v Muy poderoso señor. El Liç^{do} Alvaro de Carvajal vro fiscal en la causa con doña Beatriz Coya sobre los yanaconas digo que yo saque en tienpo rreceptorio pa hazer la provança en la çiudad del Cuzco donde estan los dhos yanaconas y la ynbie a vro corregidor de la dha çiudad con los demas recaudos neçesarios para hazer la provança por pte de vro real fisco y por caso fortituido o por negoçiaçion de la parte contraria o colusion de los que lo llevaron o otra personas la dha receptoria y recaudos no se reçivio por el dho vro corregidor hasta el mes de otubre proximo pasado //

/f.310v/ quando ya hera pasado el tr^{no} provatorio que se avia dado como pareçe por esta carta de don Gabriel Paniagua vro corregidor de la dha çiudad del Cuzco y asi no se a fecho la dha provança en tienpo y asi vra real haz^{da} e fisco es lesa e dañificada porque a el conviene que se haga la dha prouança espeçialmente no aviendo otra ynstançia por se aver de ynbiar a vro Real Consejo de Yndias conforme a la acordada de Malinas.

v A Vra Alteza pido y sup^{co} por via de prorrogaçion o quarto plazo o por la via que mejor oviere lugar de dr^{o} se me den otros noventa dias del tr^{no} para hazer la dha provança e para que aya efeto si es necesario pido restitucion yn yntregun e juro en forma que no lo pido de malicia sino porque asi conviene a vro real dr^{o} e no se pierda por falta de la dha provança pa lo qual y en lo nezesario el real of^{o} imploro e pido justicia por la via e forma que mas conviene a vro real fisco. El Licenciado Alvaro de Carvajal.

En los Reyes en ocho dias del mes de noviembre de myll e qui^{o}s e setenta e siete años ante los señores presidente e oydores en audiencia pu^{ca} la presento el fiscal y por los dhos señores vista mandaron dar treslado a la otra parte e con lo que dixere o no para la primera audi^{a} se traygan los autos. Navamuel.

Yll^{e} señor. Dos pliegos de V. M. de treze y veinte y ocho de junio recivi juntos en quatro de otubre por manera que era ya pasado el termino pa hazer las provanças y sin embargo de eso se hazen por ser //
/f.311/ cosa de su magestad el que me las traxo dize las tomo a un yndio questava enfermo en el camino todos los demas recaudos que venian se entregaron a los ofiçiales reales como V. M. lo mando y se tomo por fee el dia del entrego por averse tardado tanto y por que de presente no se ofreçe cosa de nuevo que suplicar a V. M. no dire en esta mas de que V. M. sea aver de siempre de mandarme como a tan verdadero servidor nro señor la Yll^{e} p^{a}s de V. M. guarde estado acreçiente etc. Del Cuzco catorze de otubre de myll e qui^{o}s e setenta e siete años Yll^{e} señor besa las manos a V. M. su servidor don Gabriel Paniagua de Loaysa al Yll^{e} señor Liçençiado Albaro de Caruajal fiscal de su magestad etc. mi señor.

v Muy Poderoso señor Juan de Arrandolaça en nombre de doña Beatriz Coya en el pleito con vro fiscal sobre la posesion de los y^{o}s contradiziendo el termino de contrario pedido digo que no a lugar de se le conceder por que demas que de otra vez se le conçedio sin causa ligitima y aviendo de tener solos tres meses pa provar e aver presentado la provança a tenido mas de diez e onze meses y por mi pte no se a ynpedido antes sea procurado que se haga y de contr^{o} se pretende dilaçion por estar como mi pte esta despojado aviendo de ser restituida sin admitir provança Alguna lo qual pido que se haga ante todas cosas y protesto que lo que sea pedido e alegado çerca de la propiedad solo se entienda pa Justificar la posesion e no pretendo litigar sobre ello hasta que my pte sea restituida.

/f.311v/ v en su posision por que pido y sup^{co} a Vra Al^{a} aya por contradho el dho termino y/ mande hazer el auto de remysion como esta mandado hazer sobre que pido Justicia y para ello es.

v Otro si digo que para convencer y con protestaçion que no sea bisto consentir que se de ter^{no} alguno y para que en vro real consejo se tenga consideraçion a las provanças hechas por vro fiscal en lo que ubiere lugar de dr^{o} e no en mas quiero e consiento que se le conçeda la mytad del ter^{no} que pide con que se haga dende luego el auto hordinario y al fin del dho termyno se ynbie el proçeso con lo que el dho fiscal uviere traido o no para lo qual es. El Licenciado. Falcon. Arrandolaça.

v En los Reies en doze dias del mes de noviembre de myll e qui^{o}s e setenta e siete a^{o}s ante los dhos señores presidente e oydores en audiençia pu^{ca} Arrandolaça presento esta petiçion en nonbre de su parte.

v Y por los dhos señores vista en lo primero ouieron esta causa por q^{a} en forma y en lo segundo mandaron dar treslado a la otra parte y que para la primera audi^{a} responda y con lo que dixere o no se traygan los autos presente El liçençiado Carvajal fiscal de su mag^{t}. Navamuel.

v Muy poderoso señor el lic^{do} Alvaro de Carvajal vro fiscal en la causa con doña Beatriz Coya sobre los yanaconas respondiendo a la ultima peticion dada por la pte contraria en que contradize el ter^{no} por mi pte pedido y dize lo consentira con //
/f.312/ ciertas condiciones digo que sin embargo dello por la parte contr^{a} dho se a de hazer lo por mi pte pedido y dar el dho ter^{no} por las razones que dhas tengo y la forma en que la pte contr^{a} dize que consentira el dho termino no es conviniente a vra real hazienda por que es neces^{o} todo el ter^{no} de los tres meses pa hazerse la provança en el Cuzco donde estan los dhos yanaconas y en otras partes y no es justo ny aun conforme a razon que la parte contr^{a} ponga leies y condiçiones en lo que tan justamente se pide por pte de vro real fisco.

v A Vra Al^{a} pido y sup^{co} mande proveer segun que pedido tengo para lo qual es.

v En la ciudad de los Reies en quinze dias del mes de nobienbre de myll e qui^{o}s y setenta e siete años ante los señores presidente e oydores estando en audi^{a} pu^{ca} fue presentada esta peticion y por los dhos señores vista ovieron esta causa por q^{a} en forma. Juan Gutierrez de Molina.

v En la causa de doña Beatriz Coya muger del cap^{t} Martin Garcia de Loyola y Juan de Her^{do}laça su pr^{or} en su nombre y el liç^{do} Alvaro de Carvajal fiscal sobre el despojo de los y^{o}s del repartimi^{to} de Yucai que por yanaconas no tributarios se pusieron en la corona real en el articulo de la restituçion pedido por el fiscal del ter^{no} de prueva que pide se le conceda.

v En la ciudad de los Reies en diez y nueve dias del mes de nobienbre de myll e qui^{o}s //
/f.312v/ e setenta y siete años los señores presidente y oydores desta real audiençia vista la dha causa en el dho articulo conçedieron al dho

fiscal la dha restituçion y mandaron que los dhos noventa dias del ter^{no} ultimo que se dieron al dho fiscal corran desde oy y ansi lo proveyeron y señalaron pres^{te} Ju^{o} de Arrandolaça pr^{or} de la dha doña Beatriz questava pres^{te} a quien se notefico y ansi mysmo el fiscal de su mag^{t} ante my Juan Gutierrez de Molina.

v Muy poderoso señor Juan de Arrandolaça en nombre del capitan Martin Garçia de Loyola y dona Beatriz Coya su muger en la causa con vro fiscal sobre los y^{o}s digo que abiendose pasados todos los terminos que se dieron a las ptes se mando por Vra Al^{a} hazer el auto hordinario de remision pa vro Real Consejo de Yndias y estando en este estado ultimam^{te} se dieron al dho vro fiscal otros noventa dias de ter^{no} el qual es pasado y de la dilaçion mis ptes an reçibido y reçiven gran daño.

v Pido y sup^{co} a Vra Al^{a} mande que se haga el dho auto de remision e se firme y se me de el proçeso pa que se enbie en el primer nabio e para ello es. Arrandolaça.

v En la çiudad de los Reies en v^{te} e un dias del mes de hebr^{o} de mill e qui^{o}s y set^{a} y ocho años ante los señores presidente e oydores de la audi^{a} real de su mag^{t} en pu^{ca} audiençia se pres^{to} esta pet^{on}.

v los dhos señores mandaron dar treslado al fiscal y que se traygan los autos con lo que dixere o no a la prim^{a}. Navamuel.

/f.313/ v Muy poderoso señor el liç^{do} Alvaro de Carvajal vro fiscal en la causa con doña Beatriz Coya muger de Martin Garçia de Loyola sobre los yanaconas del valle de Yucay que pide respondiendo a la petiçion dada por la pte contraria en que pide se haga el auto de remision por dezir ser pasado el termino de los noventa dias digo que no a lugar de se hazer por que las provanças hechas por pte de vro fisco en esta causa por algunas causas y cosas hasta agora no an benido aunque por mi pte se an fecho todas las diligençias neçesarias y estan fechas dentro del ter^{no} y cada dia las espero como pareçe por estas cartas del correg^{or} e alguazil mayor de la ciudad del Cuzco donde se an fecho e no es justo que por culpa agena vaya el dho proçeso sin las provanças tocantes al dr^{o} de vro fisco.

v A V. Al^{a} pido y sup^{co} mande sobre ser el dho auto y enbiada del dho proçeso hasta que bengan las dhas provanças y pido just^{a} e para ello es.

v En la ciudad de los Reies en v^{te} e ocho dias del mes de hebr^{o} de mill e qui^{o}s y setenta e ocho años ante los señores presidente e oydores de la audi^{a} real de su m^{t} en pu^{ca} audi^{a} el liç^{do} Alvaro de Caravajal ffyscal de su magestad pres^{to} esta pet^{on}

v E vista por los dhos señores presidente e oydores mandaron traer los autos y dar treslado a la otra parte de lo que presenta y luego ante los dhos señores Juan de Arrandolaça pr^{or} contr^{o} concluyo sin embargo y por los dhos señores fue abida esta causa por conclusa en forma Juan Gutierrez de Molina.

/f.313v/ v Yll^{e} señor la de V. M. reçibi con el despacho para los ofiçiales reales en que venia la preg^{ta} añadida en el negoçio de doña Beatriz Coya açerca de los yanaconas de Yucay y sobre ello se hazen las ynformaçiones con toda diligençia asi mesmo reçiui la provision contra Pedro Banegas y sobre este mesmo por una provision de su m^{t} en que manda que los ministros de la santa cruzada/ thesoreros y reçedores [*sic*] usando los dhos ofiçios no se le conpela a yr a España a hazer vida con sus mugeres por tiempo de seis años y por esto me a pareçido suspender el uso de la provision hasta que pareçe que para conpelerle a que baya sera menester provision en que se mande que sin embargo de lo dho vaya bienes que poderle tomar en lo que toca a Sancho de Luro el no a llegado a esta ciudad que se quedo en Guamanga segun me dizen en lo que toca al auto que los señores proveyeron en lo de Fran^{co} Martin por la muerte de su muger aca nos espanto a todos por que lo mas en su favor que los que hazian sus negoçios esperavan era que mandasen asoluer y o yr de nuevo para que aquellas ynformaçiones fechas ante el provisor se dixera contra ellas y se verificara pero el ba ya con dios que para mi fue gran md quitarme la ocasion de ahorcarle y pareçeme fuera justo biniera algo en execucion de no aver cunplido la provision rreal pues yo no fize exorvitançia en sacarle con la yn- //
/f.314/ formaçion questava ante mi y pareçer de dos letrados en delito tan atroz y ansi an quedado tan bitoriosos que proçeden contra mi sin que yo que tenga reparo que no me queste mi hazienda el aver fecho el dever escarmentaremos pa otro dia yo deseo mucho me venga suçesor asi asi [*sic*] por las causas que a su Ex^{a} escripto como porque me pareçe conviene por que como en esta ciudad es tan pu^{co} averse proveido ya no ay alguazil que trate sino de hazer amigos y con los escrivanos va todo a fuerça de braços y en efeto en estando en este estado no se puede cunplir con la justiçia sup^{co} a V. M. de mucha priesa pa que con brevedad se haga que çierto conviene nro señor la Yll^{e} ps^{a} de V. M. guarde con tanto acreçentami^{to} destado como sus servidores deseamos del Cuzco veinte e uno de henero de mill e qui^{o}s y setenta y ocho años. Yll^{e} señor besa las manos a V. M. su servidor don Graviel Panyagua de Loaysa. Al Yll^{e} señor liçençiado Alvaro de Caravajal fiscal de su magestad etc. mi señor.

v Yll^{e} señor a vro ocho dias rreçivi una de su M. juntam^{te} con los despachos para que se haga la ynformaçion sobre aquel negoçio de la muger de Loyola los quales tienen los ofiçiales reales y en ello se haze todo lo que es posible y asi se hara y despachara con la mas brevedad que pueda ser por que aunque yo estoy excomulgado y por esta causa ynpedido para poder entender en ello por alla fuera el soliçitar con el testimonio //
/f.314v/ que tome los tg^{os} y lo demas a mi posible lo hago con mucho cuydado y asi hare todo lo que V. M. siempre me enbiare a mandar los despachos que V. M. dize enbio con Sancho de Luro ni el ni ellos no an aportados por aca esto se concluyra con la mas brevedad

posible y se despachara asi mesmo la causa de mi excomunion ya creo V. M. alla la sabra por que la ynformaçion que hizo el alcalde ques el que conoçe de la causa se enbio a su Exª y a esa real audiençia dirigida al secreº Alvaro Ruiz de Navamuel y por ella abra visto V. M. la desverguença que tuvo aquel hidalgo conmigo a v. m. sup^{co} me la haga de que en lo que ouiere lugar se me haga md como yo estoy confiado V. M. me la hara en todo con esta va una ynformaçion que se a fecho sobre el avito que traya Durana el que tuvo el descomidimi^{to} conmigo por la qual pareçe no balerle la corona conforme a las leies de su m^{t} sera neçesario V. M. buelva por la jur^{on} real pues por aca se mete tanto en ella la eclesiastica y esto es de suerte que nos traen tan acobardados que no osamos menearnos al alcalde que conoçe desta causa que _________ en ella y se la rremyitio el procu^{or} en lo que a mi tocava le excomulgaron diziendo no conoçiese en lo que tocava a Durana por ser de grados y corona y asi mismo que no conoçiese de la causa de un esclavo mio que se hallo conmigo quando subzedio el negoçio y el no hizo mas de echar mano a la espada y andarse tras mi y quieren hazer diferente la causa del negro y la mia syendo toda una. A V. M. sup^{co} no lo permita y sea servido de en ello hazerme merzed y en todo lo que en este negoçio se ofreçiere como a tal servidor cuya Yll^{e} persona nro señor guarde y en aquel estado a- //
/f.315/ creçiente que puede y V. M. desea del cuzco y de henero veinte e tres de setenta y ocho años Yll^{e} señor besa las manos a V. M. su muy servidor Sancho Verdugo al Yll^{e} señor liç^{do} Alvaro de Carauajal fiscal de la real audiençia de los Reies etc. mi señor—

v muy poderoso señor Juan de Arrandolaza en nonbre de Martin Garçia de Loyola y doña Beatriz Coya su muger en la causa con vro fiscal sobre los yºs digo que yo pedi e suplique a Vra Alª mandase se hiziese el auto de remysion pa Vro Real Consejo por se aver pasado los noventa dias que ultimam^{te} se le dieron y se le dio treslado de la dha petiçion e aunque a ocho dias que lo tiene en su poder no quiere responder y de la dilaçion mis ptes an reçiuido e resçiuen gran daño pido y sup^{co} a Vra Alª mande quel dho auto de remision se haga e se me de el proçeso porque el tiempo no da lugar a mas largas ni dilaçiones que en esta causa a avido e para ello es.

v otro si pido y sup^{co} a V^{ra} Alª le mande con pena a Castillo soliçitador del dho vro fiscal que luego trayga el proçeso que lleuo con la peticion etc. Arrandolaça.

v En la çiudad de los Reies en v^{te} e ocho dias del mes de hebrº de mill e quiºs e setenta e ocho años ante los señores presidente e oydores de la audiençia rreal de su magestad en pu^{ca} audiençia Juan de Arrandolaça procurador en nonbre de su parte pres^{to} esta peticion.

v E vista por los dhos señores mandaron quel dho fiscal y soliçitador traiga el proçeso so pena de seis pºs pres^{to} el dho fiscal y Castillo su soliçitador Molina.

/f.315v/ v muy poderoso señor el liçençiado Alvaro de Carauajal vro fiscal en la causa con el cap^{t} Loyola y doña Beatriz su muger sobre los yºs yanaconas hago presentaçion desta prouança fecha por carta receutoria cerrada y sellada.

v A V Alª pido y sup^{co} la aya por presentada y mande poner en el proçeso y pido justiçia

v otro sy hago presentaçion deste testimº sacado de la visita que se hizo de los dhos yanaconas. A Vra Alª sup^{co} lo aya por presentado y el real ofº ynploro.

v en la çiudad de los Reies en ocho dias del mes de abril de myll e quiºs y setª y ocho años ante los señores presidente e oydores en audiª pu^{ca} fue presentada la petiçion y testimº y prouança y por los dhos señores vista fue mandado en la primero que se haga como lo pide y en lo demas dar tr^{do} a la parte contraria y que para la primera audiençia responda y se ponga la dha provança asi mysmo en el proçeso. pres^{te} Juan de Arrandolaça pr^{or} contrario a quien se notefico. Navamuel.

En el pueblo de Yucaybamba ques en el valle de Yucai juridiçion de la ciudad del Cuzco a v^{te} dias del mes de henero de mill e quiºs y setenta y dos años el Yll^{e} señor liç^{do} frei Pedro Gutierrez Flores de la orden y cavalleria de Alcantara visitador gen^{al} por su m^{t} y por el Exmo señor don Francisco de Toledo visorrey destos reinos del Piru en su real nonbre en el dho valle Calca y su distrito como consta por la provision que para ello tiene de su Exª ques la que se sigue.

Don Fran^{co} de Toledo mayordomo de su mag^{t} su visorrei e governador y cap^{t} general en estos reinos y provinçias del Piru presidente del audiençia real que reside en la çiu- //
/f.316/ dad de los Reies etc. Por quanto su m^{t} tiene dadas muchas çedulas cartas provisiones e ynstruçiones sobre la orden que se deve tener en la visita de los yºs naturales destos reinos y en la averiguacion y tasacion de los tributos que an de dar a sus encomenderos como pa sus caçiques y prinçipales tanbien esta proveido lo que los dhos caçiques y encomenderos an de cunplir con sus yºs y los yºs con ellos y que se rreduzgan a pueblos y que se nonbren entrellos alcaldes y regidores y alguaçiles para que tengan republicas fundadas y ansimesmo estan dadas por su m^{t} otras muchas çedulas y provisiones pa el buen govierno y puliçia de los yºs demas de lo qual las audiençias reales de los reinos y los governadores que en ellos a avido an proveido y ordenado muchas cosas tocantes al buen tratamiento y conservaçion de los dhos naturales para la ex^{on} y cumplimi^{to} de las quales se an dado algunos medios para quqe con menos costa y bexacion de los dhos naturales se pudiesen poner en ex^{on} y ultimamente se cometieron algunas de las dhas cosas a personas particulares las quales por ser muchas y de diversos pareçeres y opiniones an traido barios efetos lo qual a sydo causa de muchos ynconvinientes espeçialmente que los eçesos que alg^{os} encomenderos y caçiques an echo y hazen con sus yºs son grandes aviendo de ser ellos los que avian de procurar su bien y conservaçion y para remediar lo suso dho y dar asiento entre los dhos naturales en otras cosas que son muy neçesarias y que

los que estan muy cargados en los tributos que pagan sean relevados y descargados y se de or- //
/f.316v/ den como de aqui adelante los tribu^{os} sean fijos y se tasen los y^{os} en particular y cada uno sepa lo que an de pagar y no le puedan pedir mas y sean dotrinados en las cosas de nra santa fee catolica y mantenidos en paz y justiçia y que biuan descansadam^{te} y bisto que todo lo suso dho no pareçia que se podia executar y poner en efeto por la orden y traça que su mag^{t} me manda en las dhas sus ynstruçiones y poderes para el asiento uniuersal de los reinos en lo/ espiritual y tenporal dellos sin que proçediese la visita general esperando dello tan grande bien y fruto he acordado aviendose para ello fecho junta de las personas mas graves destos reinos la visita general por tanto confyando de vos el liç^{do} frei Pedro Gutierrez clerigo de la orden de Alcantara y de vra prudençia y abilidad y esperiençia y que soys persona en quien concurren las calidades neçesarias para la dha visita y que entendereis en ello como convenga al servi^{o} de dios nro señor y de su m^{t} y bien y conversion de los dhos naturales y de la real conçiencia y mia por la pres^{te} en nonbre de su magestad y por virtud de sus reales poderes y comisiones ynstruçiones que para ello tengo os proveyo elijo y nonbro por visitador de los repartimi^{os} de y^{os} questan en todo el valle de Yucay pa que vos sin bisitador lego atento a que yo asisto y he de asistir algunas temporadas en el dho valle y entender por mi persona en algunas cosas tocantes a la dha visita para que vos bais al dho valle y visiteis personalmente los y^{os} naturales de los repartimi^{os} del y sus pueblos contandolos y saviendo las hedades que an y sus tratos y grangerias //
/f.317/ y posibilidades que tienen y la calidad y grosedad de la tierra y donde estan poblados y los tribu^{os} que davan en tiempo del ynga y los que da agora y los que seria bien que den adelante otro si vos mando que proçedais contra los encomenderos caçiques y prinçipales y otras personas que huvieren eçedido de las tasas que hasta aqui an tenido o tuvieren echo comutaçiones sin liç^{a} en qualquier manera y proçediendo contra ellos haçiendo las ynformaçiones y aberiguaçiones neçesarias para saver y averiguar la verdad conoçiendo y determinando qualesquier pleitos de y^{os} que ante vos se pusieren como no sean criminales por que destos y de malos tratami^{os} y agravios que se uvieren fecho a los y^{os} me abisareis pa que yo provea lo que conbenga y ansi mesmo proveereis y dareis orden como los dhos y^{os} se rreduzgan a pueblos para sus republicas fundadas y se goviernen entre si dando las ordenanças y maneras de biuir guardando çerca de todo lo suso dho y de las dhas visitas y casos la ynstruçion firmada de mi nonbre que con esta se vos entregara en todo y por todo como en ella se contiene haziendo las demas averiguaciones ynformaciones y diligençias que por ella se vos cometen/ y mandan guardando y cunpliendo y haziendo guardar y cunplir y executar las çedulas y provisiones que por su m^{t} estan dadas para el buen govierno y puliçia tratami^{to} bien y conservaçion de los dhos y^{os}. Otro si vos doy poder y facultad para que podais conoçer y conozcais de todas las causas y negoçios çebiles que se ofreçieren y acaeçieren //
/f.317v/ Por las partes y lugares donde anduvieredes visitando del destrito que se bos señala ansi entre y^{os} como españoles en qualquier manera haziendo en ella justiçia y sentençiando las causas conforme a dr^{o} y executando las suyas que en ellos dieredes en los casos que conforme a dr^{o} y a la dha ynstruçion se pueden y deven executar y por la pres^{te} mando al corregidor y alcaldes ordinarios y otras qualesquier justicias de la dha çiudad del cuzco y su distrito y jur^{on} del dho distrito y a todos los vz^{os} y moradores de la dha çiudad y juridiçion y otras qualesquier personas de qualquier calidad y condiçion que sean y a los caçiques y principales e y^{os} de los dhos repartimi^{os} que vos ayan y tengan por tal visitador y os obedezcan y acaten y tengan y parezcan a vros llamados y enplazami^{os} y cunplan y executen los mandamientos y comisiones que para ello dieredes en cunplimi^{to} y ex^{on} de lo cont^{do} en esta mi provision y en la d[ic]ha mi ynstruçion y en las demas comisiones que se vos dieren y de qualquier cossa y parte dello y que contra ello no bayan ni pasen ni consientan yr ni pasar en manera alguna so las penas que de pte de su m^{t} les pusieredes en las quales yo desde agora les doi por condenados lo contrario haziendo y las executareis en las personas y bienes de los que remisos e ynobedientes ffueren que para entender en lo suso dho y en todo lo demas en la dha ynstruçion y demas cosas contenidas fuera de los dhos negoçios criminales vos doy poder cunplido con todas sus ynçidençias y depen- //
/f.318/ dençias anexidades y conexidades y ansimismo vos doy el dho poder pa que en el entretanto que vais al dho valle y despues en las ausençias que hizieredes podais nonbrar la persona que os pareçiere para que entienda en la dha visita y reduçion para que no pueda aver dilaçion en ella pues es cosa que ynporta tanto y vos mando que usere desta provision sin que sea neçesario presentaros con ella en el cabildo de la dha ciudad por que yo por al pres^{te} bos resçivo y e por resçivido al uso y exerçiçio de lo en ella contenido y mando que en todo lo suso dho vos ocupeis todo el tpo que fuere neçesario hasta auer besitado y reduçido todos los dhos repartimientos y aver cunplido lo en la dha mi ynstruçion y comisiones contenido en lo que no fuere contra esta mi comision que acavada la dha visita se vos mandara gratificar el trabajo y ocupaçion que en ella tuvieredes por la orden que pa ello esta dada y por ques neçesario que lleveis un alguazil que execute vros mandamientos y un escrivano ante quien se haga la dha visita y las ynformaçiones y averiguaçiones y demas autos que se uvieren de hazer por la presente nonbro por alguazil a Juan Enriquez y por escrivano a Pero Diaz Valdeon escrivano de su m^{t} y por lengua e ynterprete para los y^{os} a Her^{do} de Morales los quales ayan de salario por cada un dia de los que en lo suso dho se ocuparen y con vos anduvieren que se quenten desde el dia que con vos salieren desta ciudad en adelante el dho alguazil quatro p^{os} y el dho es^{no} tres p^{os} y la dha lengua un peso todo en plata ensayada y marcada //
/f.318v/ de valor cada peso de quatroçientos y çinquenta maravedis los quales salarios an de aver de las penas y condenaçiones que hizieredes a los que hallaredes culpados en lo suso dho las quales hareis cobrar dellos y de sus bienes sin enbargo de qualquier apelaçion que dello ynterpongan y el dho es^{no} de mas del dho salario aya y lleue de todo lo que ante el pasare sus dr^{os} conforme al aranzel de la real audi^{a} de la çiudad de los Reies que se le m^{da} que lleve con que en lo que toca a los dr^{os} que a de llevar a los y^{os} guarde lo que sobre ello esta proveido y demas del dho salario que aveis de llevar vos y los dhos ofiçiales los y^{os} de los repartimi^{os} que visitaredes vos an de dar la comida por esta mi provision que llevais se les manda que vos den para en cada un dia sin que por ella seays obligado a les pagar cosa alguna atento a que la dha visita general se haze para su benef^{o} y utilidad dellos y nos unos ny los otros no dexeis ni dexen de lo ansi cunplir por alguna manera so pena de mill p^{os} de oro a cada uno que lo contr^{o} hiziere. Fecha en la ciudad del Cuzco a treinta dias del mes de jullio de mill e qui^{os} y setenta y un años. don Fran^{co} de Toledo por mandado de su Exª Diego Lopez de Herrera.

En la ciudad del Cuzco a diez y siete/ dias del mes de agosto de mill e qui^{os} e setenta e un años el Yll^{e} señor liç^{do} frei P^{o} Gutierrez Flores de la orden de Alcantara pidio a mi el es^{no} ynfraescripto lo de por testimonio como oy dho dia en cumplimiento desta provision que

tiene del muy Ex^{e} señor don Francisco de Toledo //
/f.319/ visorrei destos reinos de parte a hazer la bisita y reduçion de pueblos que por ella manda su Exª y para ello lleva por alguazil mayor a Ju^{o} Enriquez y por escri^{o} de la dha visita a mi el pres^{te} escri^{o} y por lengua a Her^{do} de Morales y para que conste dello del dia que el s^{or} visitador partio con la dha gente pa hacer la dha visita di la pres^{te} tg^{os} Br^{me} de Arana y Xpobal Ximenez el liç^{do} frei P^{o} Gutierrez Flores. P^{o} Diaz Baldeon escr^{o} pu^{co}.

Dixo que por quanto su md en cunplimi^{to} de lo que su m^{t} y de lo que su Ex^{a} en su real nonbre manda a venido a este valle de Yucai a entender en la d[ic]ha visita y es ynformado que en el ay muchos y^{o}s que no tributan ni estan encomendados en persona alguna so color de deçir que son yanaconas y pa sauer la cantidad dellos y a quien se allegan y en que entienden y se les de orden de lo que an de hazer conviene se visiten pa lo qual m^{do} se junten todos y estando juntos la mayor pte dellos por lengua de Her^{do} de Morales ynterprete general de la dha visita les dixo e dio a entender el bien que se les a seguido de avellos reduçido a pueblos formados como lo estan pa que sean cristianos y biban pulidicam^{te} y que su m^{t} como tan cristianisimo principe siempre a tenido y tiene solo su buen tratami^{to} e que sean mantenidos en paz y en justiçia y que nadie los maltrate ni ynjurie y que si uvieren de pagar algun trib^{o} sea moderado en tal manera de las tasas que dello se les diere se a de tener consideraçion a que despues de aver pagado les quede con que se sustentar dellos y sus mugeres e hijos y tengan haziendas y grangerias con que se aprovechen y se baian enriqueçiendo y no enproveçiendo y que sepan y entiendan que por ser cristianos y estar debajo de la ovidiençia de su m^{t} an de biuir mas relevados y descargados que en tpo de los Yngas y que pa este efeto su m^{t} mando hazer esta uisita gen^{al} y que su Exª del dho señor bisorrey se dispuso a benir a ello en p^{a} por todo este reino como an bisto pa ver los agravios que les an fecho para que sean desagraviados y biban en toda puliçia y cristiandad y que movido con este buen zelo a venido a la d[ic]ha visita como les dixo en la pratica que les hizo quando los m^{do} reduçir y pa ello los quiere bisitar y sauer que dotrina an tenido y que es lo que se les a pagado por el servi^{o} que an fecho y que de aqui adelante tengan dotrina bastante para que mejor bengan en conoçimi^{to} de nra santa fee y se conserven en ella y pa que con mas facilidad se haga todo conviene saver el numero de los y^{o}s que son pa lo qual les mando se vengan a manifestar todos ante el dho s^{or} visitador con sus mugeres e hijos pa que se asienten y escrivan en la dha visita con la hedad de cada una e hazienda que tuviere en tal manera que no quede nynguno y les aperçivio que haziendo lo contr^{o} //
/f.319v/ el que se dexare descrevir y manifestar le castigara sobre ello por todo rrigor como a personas que no quieren entender dotrina ni biuir en justiçia y el yndio que los decubriere le hara caçique prinçipal de los dhos yanaconas y despues de averles fecho muchos aperçiuimi^{o}s tocante a lo suso dho y a lo demas que les convenia pa su saluaçion dixeron questavan prestos de lo ansi hazer y cunplir y se hizo la bisita y numeraçion dellos por la orden que adelante pareçera de que doy fee tg^{os} Diego Escudero y Xpobal Holgado. P^{o} Diaz Baldeon ss^{o}.

A de entender quien esta visita viere a la larga de ambas planas el yn^{o} que tiene y en la primera casa ban los çera [*sic*] el servi^{o} que a fecho cada yanacona servio en la quinta lo que paga de tasa las chacaras que tiene.

los y^{o}s yanaconas quel señor bisitador vio hallo fundado en este valle de Yucai son los flores ante mi Pero Diaz Baldeon.
Estos yndios son yanaconas de don Fran^{co}.

	Casados Años	*Hijos Años*	*Servi^{o} que a fho cada yanacona a su amo*
292	Martin Malqui natural de Lata de la prouinçia de Quito çinq^{ta}—50 Ynes Toto treinta—30	Diego Alchayan ocho—8 Juan Bautista Curi—3	treinta e çinco a^{o}s de darle yerva y leña y beneficiarle las chacaras por sus mytas
293	Fran^{co} Guachalla naçio en este valle diez y ocho—18 Catalina Paca Ocllo veinte—20		a un año que le sirve en lo que le manda no le pago nada
219	P^{o} Alla naçio en este valle veinte—20 Leonor Macto veinte e dos—22	Fran^{co} Quicantai tres—3	a que le sirve tres años en lo que manda
111	Her^{do} Lancaina natural de Yuconi en la provincia de Quito treinta y seis—36 Ysavel Bulaçamai sesenta—60		a que le sirve treinta a^{o}s de beneficiarle las chacaras por sus mytas no le da nada por ello.

/f.320/ Re[on] que cada casa de raya a rraya el renglon casado viudo soltero con sus hijos y hazienda casados en la Segunda los hijos en la ter[a] a su amo en la quarta lo que le paga por el en la sesta lo que paga de dotrina en la setima.

sitio y poblo en la villa de Santiago de Oropesa de yuso contenidos y lo firmo. frei P[o] Gutierrez. scriv[o].
Chilche caçique deste valle.

Lo que le a pagado por el serv[o] que le a fecho.	Lo q' paga de tasa pa ayudar a dar a pagar el trib[o] a los y[o]s de doña Beatriz de Mendoça menor por qstan en su trr[a]	La dotrina que tienen la pagan los mesmos yanaconas.	Las chacaras de comunidad que tienen son estas.
topo y m[o] de chacara que como de treinta e cinco a[o]s a esta pt que le sirve	seis tomines de tassa—	seys tomines de dotrina—	
sustentase de las chacaras de esa p[e]		medio pesso de dotrina—	
un topo de chacara de que come el tpo que le sirve	quatro tomines de tassa	quatro tomines de dotrina—	
sustentase de un topo de chacara que tiene su mujer			

/f.320v/

	Casados Años	*Hijos Años*	*Serviçio*
	Xpobal Xuman Sanai natural de Tomebamba sesenta años—60 Leonor Angai sesenta—60		q' sirve al dho don Francisco en benefiçiarle las chacaras de coca no sirve ya por ser uiejo
298	Ju^{o} Bautista Suman Puclla naçio en este valle treinta años—30 Catalina Churay de treinta—30	Al^{o} Tininpa de nueue—9 Martin Caqui Cura de çinco—5 Jorge Tanbul Bizmai de tres—3 Ynes luichu de ocho—8 ju^{o} achalan de dos—2	a que sirve diez y seis años en lo que los demas
296	Domingo Libipuchai naçio en este valle de v^{te} e dos—22 Ynes Cargua de v^{te}—20	Teresa Echaicho de dos—2	A ocho años q' le sirve en beneficiarle las chacaras de maiz y coca por sus mytas
299	Xpobal Chararanca natural de Pasto de treinta a^{o}s—30 Beatriz Ocllo de quarenta—40	Miguel Pasto de seis—6 Di^{o} Pasto de uno—1 Ynes Tuta de çinco—5 Ana Chinbo tres—3 Ju^{o} Llacllea diez—10	a que le sirve diez y ocho a^{o}s en benefiçiarle las chacaras de maiz y coca y darle yerva y leña y aves miros
301	R^{o} Gota Curi naçio en este valle treinta e dos—32 Beatriz Nacuchuc treinta—30	Lucas Asac tres—3 Maria Juichu çinco—5 Margarita Chuj uno—1	a que le sirve diez y ocho años en lo ques de arriba
murio 66	Diego Quispe enfermo de los andes quarenta—40 Juana Myra çin^{ta} e çinco—55	Juan Quispi siete—7	a que le sirve tres años en lo que los demas
02	Ju^{o} Bautista Tacac Paipai naçio en este valle treinta—30 Ysavel Tusa v^{te} e seis—26	Cat^{a} Batichuc tres—3	a que le sirve diez y ocho años en benefiçiarle las chacaras de maiz y coca
04	Fran^{co} Gualpa naçio en este valle diez e seis—16 Ana Lapachu v^{te}		sirve de dos años a esta pte en lo que le manda
4	Al^{o} Canagua natural del pu^{o} de Tinta en los Quichuas quarenta e seis—46 Cat^{a} Caqui Achiculla quarenta e quatro—44	Fran^{co} Guaraca siete—7 Maria Caquiapuc seys—6	aque le sirve treinta a^{o}s en benefiçiarle las chacaras de coca y maiz y darle yerva y leña por sus mytas

/f.321/

Paga del servi^{o}	*tasa pa el encomendero deste repartimiento*	*paga de dotrina el mesmo yndio cada año*	*tiene chacaras de tassa*
Quitole m^{o} topo de chacara de q' se sustentava despues que no sirve que a seis años		tres tomines de dotrina	
Medio topo de chacara de que sustenta	quatro tomines para la tassa	quatro tomines de dotrina	un topo y m^{o} de chacara no paga tributo della
No le da nada por que come con su padre	quatro tomines para la tassa	quatro tomines de dotrina	
Dale por ello topo y medio de chacara en que come	seys tomines de tassa	quatro tomines de dotrina	
Dale un topo de chacara en que come	seys tomines pa la tassa	quatro tomines de dotrina	medio topo de chacara no paga tribu^{o} della
medio topo de chacara de que come			
Dale un topo de chacara de que come por el servicio que le haze	seys tomines pa la tassa	quatro tomines de dotrina	
Dale un topo de chacara de que se sustenta		seys tomines de dotrina	
tiene un topo de chacara de que come		quatro tomines de dotrina	

/f.321v/

306	Agustin Llachua naçio en este valle v^{te} e siete años—27 Maria Chinbo Coca quarenta—40		a que le sirve diez años en benefiçiarle las chacaras de maiz y coca y en todo lo que los demas por sus mytas
308	Ju^{o} Selsi naçio en este valle treinta e çinco—35 Françisca Chinbo treinta e quatro—34	Ju^{o} Toto Yaure diez 10 Ysavel Cumia siete 7 P^{o} Guaman Capcha çinco—5 Ynes Conya uno—1	a que le sirve diez y ocho a^{o}s en el ofiçio de lo que de los de arriba
309	Diego Tanta naçio en este valle treinta e quatro—34 Ynes Tonso treinta e çinco—35	Martin China Quispe ocho—8 P^{o} Chusa çinco—5 Beatriz Yapa qt^{o}—4	a que le sirve v^{te} a^{o}s en todo lo que los demas
310	Di^{o} Usco Guaman naçio en este valle treinta—30 Ysavel Chisque treinta e seis—36	Madalena Asto Cargua catorze—14 Xpobal Uscoguaman ocho—8 Ju^{o} Uso Hananpa çinco—5 Angelina Caquiapaq 2	a que le sirve doze años en todo lo que de los de arriba
313	Juan Guari v^{te}—20 Ynes Casay Chucmano diez y nueue—19		
65	Di^{o} Marin naçio en este valle v^{te} e tres—23 Ynes Chinbo treinta—30	Maria Caca tres—3 Agustin Chiuchi uno—1	a que le sirve cinco años en curalle la mula y caballo.
192	P^{o} Marin natural de Nicaragua çinquenta e seis—56 Françisca Quispe quarenta—40	Agustin Suchi diez y ocho—18 Costança Paica doze—12 Maria Tuzmu ocho—8 Luçia Chinbo Urma dos—2	a que le sirve ve^{te} y çinco a^{o}s en benefiçiarles sus chacaras
315	Al^{o} Puchai natural de Tomebamba çinq^{ta} e dos—52 Ynes Ynanchuc çinq^{ta} y seis—56		a que le sirve v^{te} e çinco años en benefiçiarle la chacara de maiz y en otras cosas
314	Jer^{mo} Cuyo v^{te} e nueue años—29 Beatriz Llacxa v^{te} e quatro—24	Agustin Mitima quatro—4 Maria Yupati uno—1	

/f.322/

Dale un topo y medio de chacara de que come	quatro tomines pa la tasa	quatro tomynes a la dotrina	medio topo de chacara no paga tribo della
Dale un topo de chacara de que se sustenta	paga un peso para la tassa	quatro tomines a la dotrina	
Dale tres quartos topo de chacara de que come	quatro tomines pa la tassa	quatro tomines pa la dotrina	medio topo de chacara no paga trib^{o} della
Dale un topo de chacara de que come		quatro tomines de dotrina	
Dale medio topo de chacara de que come			
Dale por el servi^{o} m^{o} topo de chacara de que come		quatro tomines de dotrina	
Dale por este servi^{o} tres quartos de chacara		quatro tomines a la dotrina	

/f.322v/

108	Her^{do} Gartai Nauca cañar naçio en el Cuzco quarenta—40 Ynes Caba cuarenta y ocho—48	Benito Quituizac catorze—14 Catalina Murchuc diez—10	a que le sirve quinze años en lo que le manda
148	Martin Sicha cañar naçio en este valle v^{te} e dos 22 Leonor Camaichuc treinta—30	Ysavel Pulbechu siete—7 Xpobal Xinguinaulas seis—6	a que le sirve tres años en todo que los de arriba ecepto en las chacaras de coca
316	P^{o} Zinilizila cañar naçio en Tomebanba çinq^{ta} e çinco—55 Cat^{a} Angai çinq^{ta}—50	Al^{o} Bilidunbai sinple diez y ocho—18 Benito Guartat Languay diez y seis—16 Ju^{o} Calla doze—12 Martin Murat Naula ocho—8 Ysavel Suchuc dos—2	a que le sirve v^{te} e ocho a^{o}s el y sus hijos en benefiçiarle sus chacaras y hazer la myta de yerva y leña
318	P^{o} Nivlazaca cañar naçio en este valle v^{te} e ocho—28 Ysavel Caua treinta y ocho—38	Sebastian Alasaca siete—7 Di^{o} Manzaca çinco—5 P^{o} Duman tres—3	a que se sirve doze a^{o}s en benefiçiarle las chacaras y yerva y leña por sus mytas
193	P^{o} Puruan cañar de Tomebanba çinq^{ta} e dos—52 Ysavel Sanchuc çinq^{ta} y ocho años—58	Leonor Ritchuc diez—10 Martin Guambui Puclla diez y nueue—19	a que se sirve treinta a^{o}s en benefiçiarle sus chacaras y dar por su myta yerva y leña
320	Martin Marcauichai cañar naçio en este valle v^{te} e tres—23 Leonor Zubaicchuc catorze—14		a que le sirve doze años en benefiçiarle las chacaras de maiz y coca y hazelle myta de yerva y leña
321	Al^{o} Bilibisnai cañar naçio en este valle treinta e çinco—35 Madalena Guayanachuc treinta e ocho—38	Ynes Llanchuc 6 Maria Tatanchuc quatro—4	a que le sirve v^{te} a^{o}s en todo lo que los demas
322	P^{o} Salina cañar naçio en este valle treinta—30 Leonor Yanamzuc veinte e dos—22	Ysavel Zuichuc quatro—4 Felipe Maiabincha tres—3 Madalena Nucho uno—1 Ana Muro Urchu q^{tro}—4	a que le sirve doze a^{o}s en todo lo que los demas
323	Al^{o} Uchuilolan cañar naçio en este valle quarenta e çinco—45 Catalina Caua—38	Martin Cazatnaulo siete—7 Sebastian Mauravichai çinco—5 Ju^{o} Bautista Bilidu—2	a que le sirve treynta años en todo lo que los demas

/f.323/

un quarto de chacara de que come			
Dale un topo de chacara de que come		quatro tomines a la dotrina	
Dale un topo de chacara de que come	quatro p^{o}s de tassa	quatro tomynes de dotrina	dos topos y un quarto
Comen en casa don Françisco		quatro tomines de dotrina	
		quatro tomines de dotrina	un topo y qr^{to} de chacara no paga tributo della
medio topo de chacara de que se sustenta	seis tomines pa la tassa	quatro tomines de dotrina	medio topo de chacara
		quatro tomines de dotrina	tres quartos de chacara
un topo de chacara de que come		quatro tomines nes de dotrina	un topo de chacara

/f.323v/

317	Benito Guartalangua veinte e dos—22 Leonor Lamaichuc veinte e tres—23		
324	Gonçalo Tanbuipulla naçio en este valle treinta—30 Ysavel Caba v^{te} e çinco—25	Fran^{co} Guartanaul v^{te} e quatro—24 Gonçalo Guipulla uno—1	a que le sirve v^{te} a^{o}s en benef^{o} de las chacaras de maiz y hazelle myta de leña y paja
325	Martin Sauar cañar de Tomebanba çinq^{ta} e quatro—54 Cat^{a} Cauatre treinta e ocho—38	Ynes Durchai veinte—20	a que le sirve v^{te} a^{o}s en benefiçiarle las chacaras de maiz y hazelle myta de yerva y leña
3	Al^{o} Sitpulla cañar naçio en este valle v^{te}—20 Maria Zinbai v^{te} e çinco—25	Madalena Batichul tres—3	a que le sirve en lo que le manda y en benef^{o} de las chacaras de maiz v^{te} a^{o}s
157	Marcos Puri yunga sesenta—60 Ysavel Chunbi quarenta—40	Fran^{co} Mahecocho ocho—8	a que le sirve en beneficio de las chacaras de maiz quinze años
330	R^{o} Lalchibisnai cañar naçio en este valle treinta—30 Maria Zucchuc veinte e ocho—28	Fran^{ca} Chincha ocho 8 Ysavel Zitinchuc siete—7 Ju^{o} Bautista Chaluzai—3	a que le sirve v^{te} años en lo que le m^{da} y en beneficiarle las chacaras de maiz
331	Her^{do} Charo cañar nacio en este valle v^{te} e quatro—24 Mª Cuyun treinta e q^{tro} 34	Al^{o} Avesicha seis—6 Ju^{o} Dumancaca tres—3 Gaspar Sumangana 2 Ana Yusatoco çinco 5	
biudas	Costança Asco çinquenta—50	Benito Llaqua 16 +307+	sirve le en lo que le manda
3	Juana Pilcoquipi çinquenta 50	Martin Supaico diez y seis años 16	sirve le en lo que les manda

/f.324/

un topo de chacara de que come		quatro tomines de dotrina	tres quartos de chacara
un quarto topo de que come		quatro tomines de dotrina	
		quatro tomines de dotrina	tres quartos de chacara
medio topo de chacara de que come			
medio topo de chacara de que come		quatro tomines de dotrina	un quarto de chacara
topo y mi^{o} de chacara	tres tomines de tassa	dos tomines de dotrina	

/f.324v/

	Maria Cuyo de çinquenta—50	Maria Toto quinze—15	sirve le en lo que le manda mas de quinze a^{o}s
	Catalina Piala çinquenta 50	Catalina Punatupo veinte 20	a quinze a^{o}s que le sirve en lo que le manda
	Ynes Quanay quarenta—40	Juana Tillea diez años 10	a quinze años que le sirve en lo que le manda
	Catalina Lanoschul de treinta 30	Pedro Quispe dos—2	a que le sirve mas de diez a^{o}s en los que le manda
biejas	Ysavel Chunchu çinquenta	Juana mulata sesenta 60	Maria Contipa tiene sesenta – 60
300	Her^{do} Pasto naçio en este valle treinta e seis—36		A que le sirve a don Fran^{co} Chilche en beneficiar sus chacaras diez y ocho años
303	Benito Rimache naçio en este valle diez y seis 16		començo a servirle agora
305	Ju^{o} Pasto naçio en este valle valle v^{te} 20		començo a servirle agora
67	Diego Sicha cañar de Tomebanba quarenta e nuebe—49	Simon Chun diez y 6—16 Ysavel Cabo ocho 8 Bartolome Sicha 5 Cat^{a} Yngao—4	a que le sirve v^{te} quatro años en las chacaras de maiz

/f.325/

Catalina Aguanay ses^{a} 60	Catalina Yupati ses^{a} 60	Ynes Camucho çinq^{ta}—50	Françisca Anayu çinquenta—50
dos topos y medio de que come	seis tomines de tassa	quatro tomynes pa la dotrina	
		dos tomines de dotrina	un topo de chacara

/f.325v/

	Casados Años	*hijos Años*	*servi^{o} que tiene cada yanacona*
	Elvira Cocachuqui quarenta—40	Juan Yaca tres años—3	A que le sirve mas de v^{te} años en en benefiçio de las chacaras
	Ysavel Cava treinta y siete—37	Maria Durcho doze—12 Ana Sichu seis—6	a que le sirve v^{te} años en benefiçio de las chacaras
	Juana Chinbo quarenta—40		a que le sirve veinte años en lo que los demas
527	Pedro Quispie treinta e tres—33 Ynes Acella quarenta y seis—46	Juan Ramos	sirveles en lo que le manda
	Catalina Micay çinq^{ta} e çinco—55	Ana Bispa 7	sirve le en lo que le manda
	Catalina Caua cañar sesenta—60		sirve le en lo que le manda
	Ysavel Langabai sesenta—60	Maria Pilcheturo veinte	a que sirve v^{te} en el beneficio de las chacaras y en lo que las demas viejas
	Ynes Raimetiquilla treinta e siete—37	P^{o} Nynayaris çinco años—5 Ynes Pacho q^{o} 4	a que le sirve mas de diez a^{o}s en beneficiarle las chacaras de maiz
	Pedro Pullo sesenta años—60		sirve le en lo que le manda

/f.326/

Lo que le paga por el servi^{o} que le a fecho	*lo que paga de tassa*	*lo que paga de dotrina*	*tiene chacara de tassa*
dos topos de chacara			
Tiene de suyo tres quartos de chacara		dos tomines de dotrina	
			un quarto de chacara
medio topo de chacara	dos hanegas de mays		

/f.326v/

	Casados Años	*hijos Años*	*serv^{o} que tiene cada yanacona*
yanaconas de doña Ynes muger de don Fran^{co} Chilche	Agustin Tacopoma naçio en este valle diez y nueve 19 Ynes Yllanchucuc treinta e çinco—35 +339+		serviole çinco años en lo que los demas
	Xpobal Sulcanabi cañar naçio en este valle—36 Ysavel Chunbi quarenta—40 +231+	Juan Cusi Chinbo quinze—15	sirviole doze? años en lo que los demas
48	Alonso Yupangui veinte e çinco—25 Maria Angay veinte e seis—26	Costança Riocho uno 1	
342	P^{o} Bilcaquia collagua naçio en este valle 36 Isabel Chunbi—40	Juana Cusi Chinbo doze 12	sirviole diez y ocho años en lo que los demas
207	P^{o} Pauca aymara de Anta naçio en este valle—20 Ynes Totio treinta—30		
	Agustin Alanta collagua veinte a^{o}s—20 Fran^{ca} Chunbiurma diez y nueve—19	Ynes Carua un año—1	sirviole en benefiçiar las chacaras de mays
344	Toribio Arimana collagua naçio en este valle quarenta—40 Ynes BilcaCarua qu^{ta}—40	Madalena Ynguillai diez—10 Cat^{a} Quispe nueve—9 P^{o} Guacallo quatro—4 Ysavel Aujo uno—1	sirviole veinte años en lo que los demas
357	R^{o} Cuzco cañar naçio en este valle treinta e seis—36 Ysavel Zezenchuque treinta e quatro—34	Xpobal zunbaichila tres años—3 Martin Chunbai uno—1 Leonor malchud çinco—5	sirviole quinze a^{o}s en lo que los demas
103	Fran^{co} Condori ses^{a} y seis—66		

/f.327/

lo que le paga en el servi^{o} que a fecho	*lo que paga de tassa*	*lo que paga de dotrina*	*tiene chacaras de tasa*
topo y medio de chacara	tres tomines de tassa	dos tomines de dotrina	
un topo de chacara	seys tomines de tassa	dos p^{o}s de dotrina	
un topo de chacara	dos p^{o}s de tassa	quatro tomines de dotrina	
tres quartos de chacara	quatro tomines de tassa		
tres quartos de chacara		quatro tomines de dotrina	
medio topo de chacara			un quarto de chacara de comunidad

/f.327v/

	Casados Años	hijos Años	servi° que a fecho cada yanacona
6	Simon Llanco de los bracamoros sesenta 60	Ynes Yacro diez y siete—17	sirviole un año en el benef° de la chacara de mays
la muger de don Françisco	Catalina Machac sesenta—60		sirviole en el benef° de las chacaras v^te^ años
San Bernardo	Catalina Yboacasa treinta e çinco—35	Agustin Pintosalo ocho años 8 Leonor Ninanco seis 6	sirviole dos años en lo que le mando
viejas	Ynes Yan çin^ta^ 50	Xpobal Uchacauana catorze su hijo—14 346	
San Bernardo	Ysavel Chinbococa de qu^ta^ e çinco 45	Baltasar Tacuri su hijo quatro 4	
	Ana Bicho sesenta años 60	Ysavel Pay çinquenta 50	Ynes Guayuchuc treinta
	Leonor Chinbourma veinte—20	guerfanos Madalena Maichuc seis años 6	Ysavel Chuchu siete años 7

/f.328/

lo que le paga por el servi° que a fecho	lo que paga de dotrina	lo que paga de tassa	tiene chacaras de tassa
un quarto de topo de chacara de que come			
medio topo de chacara de que come			
medio topo de chacara de que come			
Leonor Chuquina ses^a^ 60	Catalina chuc ses^a^ 60	Catalina Yngulla ses^a^ 60	

/f.328v/

	Casados Años	*hijos Años*	*serui[ci]o que an fecho cada yanacona*
yanaconas de don Her^{do} Guartanaula cacique /ilegible/ don F^{co} Chilche	P^{o} Quinto de Quito quarenta y seis 46 Ysavel Laichuc quarenta—40 +194+	P^{o} Quinto de seis 6 Ynes Muichu çinco—5 Mª Chinchu dos—2	a que le sirve diez años en benef^{o} de las chacaras de mays
	Lor^{ço} Quispe naçio en este valle v^{te} 20 Juana çico Ocllo v^{te} e seys—26 +365+	Ju^{a} Sibichuncho uno—1 Lucas Echauamai 5 Angelina Ynco—3 Ysavel Paico dos 2	a que le sirve diez años en lo que los demas
152	Martin Ananca de Quito cinquenta e quatro 54 Ysavel Carnaçin quarenta e dos 42		a que le sirve dos años de obejero
195	P^{o} Unba de guaylas sesenta e seis 66 Maria Tiquilla set^{a} 70		a que le sirve catorze a^{o}s en las chacaras
Murio	Martin Luacalla de guaylas naçio en este valle v^{te} e quatro 24 Juana Chunbi v^{te} 20		a que le sirve diez años en lo que los demas
yanaconas de Ju^{o} Bautista hijo de Chilche	Al^{o} Puruay de Quito çinq^{ta} e quatro—54 Ysavel Caua quarenta—40 +6+	Fran^{co} Nai çinco 5 Baltasar Macçicaca nueve—9	a que le sirve v^{te} e çinco años a el y a su padre en lo que los demas
367	R^{o} Guaraca guanca naçio en este valle v^{te} e tres—23 Maria Tasca v^{te} y tres—23	P^{o} Auquia Vichipuna quatro—4	a que le sirve tres años en lo que los demas y^{o}s chacara de coca
368	Jer^{mo} Guamanquilca veinte—20 Catalina Yacce v^{te} e çinco—25		a que le sirve v^{te} e quatro años en lo que los demas
	Ysavel Mangoguacra ses^{a} a^{o}s 60	Madalena Abalupi treinta a^{o}s 30	Catalina Chu sesenta a^{o}s 60

/f.328/ [*sic*]

lo que le pago por serviçio que le a hecho	*lo que paga de dotrina*	*lo que paga de tassa*	*tiene chacaras de tassa*
topo y medio de chacara	quatro tomynes de dotrina		
un topo de chacara	quatro tomines de dotrina	media fanega de mayz	topo y m^{o} de chacara
un topo de chacara	quatro tomines de dotrina		
medio topo de chacara			
un topo de chacara	quatro tomines de dotrina		un quarto de chacara de comunidad
medio topo de chacara de que come	quatro tomines de dotrina		
medio topo de chacara de que come	quatro tomines de dotrina	quatro tomynes de tassa	un topo de chacara
medio topo de chacara de que come	medio peso de dotrina		medio topo de chacaras de comunidad
Ana Uscocargua ses^{a} 60			

/f.328v/ [*sic*]

	Casados Años	*hijos Años*	*serviº que a fecho cada yanacona*
de don Alº Titu Atauche 422	don Juº Ayranbo quarenta y dos 42 Catª Cusichunbo treinta e tres 33	Luis Guamantito diez—10 Juº Guamantanbo uno—1 Felipe Guamanpuco ocho—8 Juº Guamanairanbone—3 Pº Cusiailanbo seis—6 Catª OcusiChinbo ocho—8 Maria Chuichillay çinco—5	a que le sirve diez años de mandar los yanaconas de don Alonso Tito Atauche y las haziendas
379	Alonso Ua sesª 60 Catalina Cola sesª 60	Juana Lusa Ynguillear tres—3 Ynes Coca Ynguilla 3 Ynes Cocaquipe çinco 5	a v^{te} años que le sirve en lo que los demas
yanaconas de Diº truxo	Diego Yuribicha Yunga v^{te} e seis 26 Fran^{ca} Culpo v^{te} e qtº 24		a que le sirve catorze años los çinco en su casa y los demas en lo que le mando
	Martin Yunga de Yca çinquenta e çinco 55 Ysavel Saçi çinq^{ta} y dos—52	Pº Yanoche quinze años 15 Alº Capi ocho 8	a que le sirve v^{te} e dos años en beneficio de la chacara de garbanços y de mayz
34	Pº Machaguai treinta e dos 32 Juª Punachiqui treinta—30		sirvele de muchacho
	Lucas Calpa v^{te} e çinco—25 Juana Yache su muger v^{te}—20	Catalina Chisque dos años 2	
	Juº Unalari v^{te} e ocho 28 Ysavel Sasichuqui veinte aºs—20	Juana Quispe quatro años 4	a que le sirve diez y seis años en lo que le manda
	Xpobal Suno de tanbo naçio en este valle 30 Costança Pita—30		a que le sirve quinze años en lo que le a mandado
	Fran^{co} Pisco Yunga çinquenta e quatro—54 Ynes Billico sesª—60	Madalena Chillaya diez y siete—17	a que le sirve diez años en el beneficio de las chacaras

/f.329/

lo que le paga por servº que le a hecho	*lo que paga de dotrina*	*lo que paga de tassa*	*tiene chacaras de tassa*
declaro don Juº Aylanbo que todas las tierras estan repartidas a el y a los yanaconas de don Alonso Tito Atauchi son chacaras de las que tenian los yºs que guardavan el cuerpo de Guaina Caba			medio topo de comunidad
			medio topo de chacara de comunidad
topo y mº			
tres quartos de chacara			
tres quartos de chacara			
un topo de chacara			

/f.329v/

	Casados Años	*hijos Años*	*serviçio que a fecho cada yanacona*
	Pº Cucocari veinte e siete—27 Catª Ynga Tocto veinte e quatro 24	Diego Cuco ocho 8 Maria çazi seis 6	a que le sirve diez años en el benefiçio de las chacaras
	Martin Bilcayavio sesª y nueve—69 Costança Carua 65		a que le sirve quinze años en el beneficio de las chacaras
	Alº Malcula de Lari naçio en este valle veinte e ocho—28 Ynes Tarpo—38	Felipe Uno tres—3 Luis Asi uno—1	a que le sirve v^{te} años en lo que les manda
	Pº Conca Quichua çinq^{ta} e quatro—54 Ysavel Yachi çinquenta e quatro—54	Ana Yuco diez y siete 17	a que le sirve diez años en el benefº de sus chacaras
	Pº Uscaguamanchauca diez y ocho—18 Ysavel Ocllo—20	Ynes Sasi 3	
	Alº Casau de Lari çinquenta y nueve natural de Lari—59	Juan Pazna veinte e çinco 25	a que le sirve veinte años
	Ana Yuyo v^{te} e ocho—28	Gonçalo Pilca ocho aºs 8 Rº Bilcamanco—6 Ynes Tanpai qtrº—4 Domingo Manco tres—3 Diego Manco dos—2	
viejas	Luya Toto sesª 60	Leonor Chinbo sesª 60	Françisca Tuipai sesenta 60
de Alº de Tapia	Lucas Vilcacuri Yauyo quarenta e quatro—44 Ysavel Curisasa 44	Alonso Casabilca ocho años 8 Gonçalo Chaucasancho çinco—5 Tomas Sulcapoma—3	a que le sirve dos aºs y medio en guardar ganado y en benefº de una chacara

/f.330/

lo que le paga por serviçio que le a fecho	*lo que paga de dotrina*	*lo que paga de tassa*	*tiene chacaras de tassa*
medio topo de chacara			
un quarto de topo			
medio topo de chacara			
medio topo de chacara			
un quarto de chacara			
Constança Chubi sesenta 60			
un topo de chacara			

/f.330v/

	Casados Años	*hijos Años*	*servi^{o} que fecho cada yanacona*
539	P^{o} Quispa Chupaicho treinta—30 Madalena Cusi Asarpai v^{te} e çinco—25		
yanaconas de don Jer^{mo} Quispe Capi caçique	P^{o} Acha Yauyo treinta e ocho—38 Beatriz Urmacoca veinte e çinco—25		a que le sirve veinte años en el benefiçio de las chacaras y de dalle leña
	Ju^{o} Gandapi quichua veinte e dos—22 Maria Pio v^{te} e dos—22 +452+	Petronilla Sumaya tres—3 Madalena Guarcaichunbe uno—1	
456	Domingo Guaman Eschui naçio en este valle diez e nueue 19 Beatriz Guarcai veinte e çinco—25		a dos años que le sirve en lo que los demas
457	P^{o} Yucurca de guaro naçio en este valle diez y ocho—18 Cat^{a} Chunbi—20		
	Angelina Quichui sesenta—60		a que le sirve v^{te} años en el benefiçio de las chacaras
	Catalina Coca Anco setenta—70		sirviole v^{te} e çinco años en el benefiçio de las chacaras
	Leonor Ynguilla sesenta—60		sirviole nueve años en lo que los demas
	Costança Caguaso sesenta—60	Alonso Aucatoma diez—10	

/f.331/

lo que le paga de servi^{o} que le a fecho	*lo que paga de dotrina*	*lo que paga de tassa*	*tiene chacaras de tassa*
un topo de chacara	quatro tomynes de dotrina		
medio topo de chacara	quatro tomynes de dotrina		
medio topo de chacara de que come			
medio topo de chacara			
medio topo de chacara			
medio topo de chacara	seys tomines de dotrina		

/f.331v/

	Casados Años	*hijos Años*	*servi^{o} que a fecho cada yanacona*
	Ynes Yachi quarenta e quatro—44	Juana Gualca diez +455+ —10 Diego Calami siete 7 +454+	a que sirve quatro años en lo que los demas
	Luis Piscoma quarenta y siete	Catalina Tupo Anpana quinze 15 Ynes Caria quatro 4 Leonor Entima dos 2	a que sirve quatro años en lo que los demas
	Ysavel Puco çinq^{ta} y çinco—55	Ysavel Urma Chinbo tollido v^{te}—20 Maria Chinbo onze—11	a diez años que le sirve en lo que los demas
	Ysavel Yspa sesenta 60		a quatro años que le sirve en lo que los demas
	Ynes Toto Ocllo çinquenta y ocho 58	Xpobal Nanpa veinte e tres—23 Ysavel Rimaichunbo v^{te} e çinco—25 Teresa Cumai—15	a que sirve tres meses
	Catalina Guaito sesenta—60	Martin Tusan tullido veinte e quatro—24	
	Ynes Cupi ses^{a} y nueue—69	Xpobal Yngaroca Mancono quarenta es para tassa—40	
	Ysavel Chuquinquilla treinta e dos—32	Benito Anai doze—12 Cat^{a} Carua nueve 9 Angelina Chucha çinco—5	sirve en el benefiçio de las chacaras y en su cassa
viejas	Ynes Carua ses^{a} 60	Elena Chinbo set^{a} 70 Maria Colla Chubi 60	Maria Anyu—60
	Leonor Yucy ses^{a}—60 P^{o} Quispetupe doze 12	Maria Chinbo doze—12	Ysavel Ysas Chinbo veinte—20

/f.332/

lo que le paga por el servi^{o}	*lo que paga de dotrina*	*lo que paga de tassa*	*tiene chacaras de tassa*
medio topo de chacara de que come			
un quarto de topo de chacara			
un quarto de topo de chacara			
un topo de chacara de que come			
un quarto de chacara de que come			
tres topos de chacara suyos			
medio topo de chacara			
Ysavel Coca Chinbo ses^{a}—60	Fran^{ca} Carua ses^{a} 60	Fran^{ca} Pita 50	Barbola Chunbi sesenta 60

/f.332v/

	Casados Años	*hijos Años*	*servi^{o} que a fecho cada yanacona*
de doña Maria Cusi Guaycay 7	Andres Guamalli Ynga veinte e tres 23 Ynes Sasi veinte 20		a que le sirve tres años en beneficio de las chacaras
460	Martin Al^{o} Muro Yunga quarenta—40 Costança Tasai quarenta—40	Fran^{co} Airin diez 10 Martin Pachabillun 4 Domingo Martino seys—6	a que le sirve catorze años en beneficio de agi
8	Al^{o} Caque Guaillas çinquenta e çinco 55 Ana Raho çinq^{ta} 50	Alonso Sucacacque diez 10 Mateo Andacaque onze a^{o}s 11	a que le sirve seis años en el beneficio de las chacaras
418	Martin Bilca Guaraz de Guanuco naçio en este valle v^{te} e dos 22 Madalena Yao diez y seis—16		a que le sirve diez años en lo que los demas
462	Agustin Cusipaucar de Maras veinte e dos 22 Luçia CusiChinbo—25	Ysavel Sillacoca tres—3	a que le sirve tres años en lo que los demas
	Diego Cusipuri de Maraz quarenta 40 Ysavel Yunga çinquenta—50		a que le sirve diez y siete años en lo que los demas
463	Martin Pungaguaman de Xaquixaguana veinte e çinco—25 Ysavel Birca v^{te} e dos 22		a que le sirve çinco años en lo que los demas
465	Martin Guamanyochi treinta—30 Beatriz Zurunanco veinte e quatro—24	Ynes Chinlo uno—1 Ysavel Asinaca siete años 7 Diego Chuquillara quatro 4	a que le sirve çinco años en lo que los demas
	P^{o} Sibipaucar de Xaquixaguana quarenta e çinco—45 Ynes Quipi qu^{ta} e çinco—45	Ana Cocaquipi çinco—5 Al^{o} Guaman Ycra siete años—7	a que le sirve diez y ocho a^{o}s en beneficio de las chacaras

/f.333/

que paga de servi^{o}	*lo que paga de dotrina*	*lo que paga de tassa*	*tiene chacaras de tassa*
	seys tomines de dotrina		medio topo de chacara de comunidad
	quatro tomines de dotrina		un topo y tres quartos de chacara de comunidad
medio topo de chacara	quatro tomines de dotrina		
medio topo de chacara	quatro tomines de dotrina		
medio topo de chacara	quatro tomines de dotrina		
medio topo de chacara	quatro tomines de dotrina		
medio topo de chacara	quatro tomines de dotrina		
medio topo de chacara			
medio topo de chacara	quatro tomines de dotrina		

/f.333v/

	Casados Años	*hijos Años*	*serviº que a fecho cada yanacona*
de doña Mª Cusi Guarcai 458	Andres Guamalli Ynga vte e tres 23 Ynes Sasi vte—20		a que le sirve tres años an beneficio de las chacaras
460	Martin Alº Muro Yunga quarenta—40 Costança Tasai quarenta—40	Franco Airin diez 10 Martin Pachabillen quatro—4 Domingo Muro seis 6	a que le sirve catorze años en beneficio de agi
	Alº Caqui Guayllas çinquenta e çinco 55 Ana Raho çinqta 50	Alonso Sucaq diez—10 Mateo Andacaque onze aºs 11	a que le sirve onze años en el beneficio de las chacaras
	Martin Bilca Guaraz de Guanuco naçio en este valle vte e dos 22 Madalena Yao—16		a que le sirve en el beneficio de las chacaras diez años
461	Diego Cusipuro de Maraz quarenta 40 Ysavel Yunga çinquenta 50		a que le sirve diez y siete años en lo que los demas
	Agustin Cusipaucar de Maras vte e dos 22 Luçia Cusi Chinbo veinte e çinco 25	Ysavel Sillacoca tres 3	a que le sirve tres años en lo que los demas
463	Martin Punga Guaman de Xaquixaguana veinte e çinco—25 Ysavel Birar vte e dos 22		a que le sirve çinco años en lo que los demas
465	Martin Guamani Chochi treinta—30 Beatriz Niruinanco vte e quatro—24	Ynes Chinbo uno 1 Ysavel Asinasca siete años—7 Diº Chuquillara qtº 4	a que le sirve çinco años en lo que los demas
	Pº Sibipaucar de Xaquixaguana quta e çinco 45 Ynes Quipi quta e çinco 45	Ana Cocaquipi çinco—5 Alº Guaman Yncrasi siete aºs 7	a que le sirve diez y ocho años en beneficialle las chacaras

/f.334/

lo que le paga por el serviº	*lo que paga de dotrina*	*lo que paga de tassa*	*tiene chacaras de tassa*
	seis tomines de dotrina		medio topo de chacara de comunidad
	quatro tomines de dotrina		un topo y tres quartos de chacara de comunidad
medio topo de chacara	quatro tomines de dotrina		
medio topo de chacara	quatro tomines de dotrina		
medio topo de chacara	quatro tomines de dotrina		
medio topo de chacara	quatro tomines de dotrina		
medio topo de chacara	quatro tomines de dotrina		
medio topo de chacara			
medio topo de chacara	quatro tomines de dotrina		

/f.334v/

	Casados Años	*hijos Años*	*servi^{o} que a fecho cada yanacona*
tullido	Br^{me} Guamany Cuyo veinte e seis a^{o}s 26 Angelina Tabat treinta—30	Maria Sacsachunbi tres—3 Fran^{ca} Yacochuqui uno—1	a que le sirve çinco años en lo que los demas
197	P^{o} Guasco Cayanbi sesenta y çinco—65 Maria Cuslaco quarenta y seis 46	Catalina Andago diez 10 P^{o} Suachalla ocho 8 Ynes Coca Anco q^{o} 4	a que le sirve diez y siete a^{o}s en lo que los demas
467	Martin Quicana quichua çinq^{ta} e quatro 54 Cat^{a} Yupallay—30	Beatriz Cusiynquilla diez y siete—17 Ysavel Caiotiella siete—7 Maria Pacarsayo—4 Ju^{a} Siquilla dos—2 P^{o} Chamaicumara uno 1	a que le sirve diez y siete a^{o}s en lo que los demas
	Sebastian Cusipacha de Xaquixaguana quarenta—40 Ysavel Quepo quarenta e çinco 45		a que le sirve quinze años en lo que los demas
459	Xpobal Guamalli sesenta—60		a diez y siete años que le sirve en el beneficio de agi
9	Alonso Pota çinq^{ta} y ocho—58		a diez y siete años que le sirve en lo que le mandan
	Ysavel Ynacando veinte e dos 22		a seis años que le sirve de ortelana
	Frantçisca Toto çinquenta e çinco 55	Fran^{co} Cusirimache doze—12	a doze a^{o}s que le sirve en benefiçiarle las chacaras
	Maria Ynacasa treinta y quatro	Juan Bautista quinze—15 Mª Rucumuco quatro—4	a que sirve doze años en lo que los demas

/f.335/

lo que paga por el servi^{o}	*lo que paga de dotrina*	*lo que paga de tassa*	*tiene chacaras de tassa*
medio topo de chacara quatro	quatro tomines de dotrina		
	quatro tomines de dotrina		dos topos y m^{o}
	quatro tomines de dotrina		dos topos y m^{o}
medio topo de chacara	quatro tomines de dotrina		
un topo de chacara			
un quarto topo de chacara			
un quarto topo de chacara			
medio topo de chacara			

/f.335v/

	Casados Años	*hijos Años*	*servi°* *que a fecho cada yanacona*
	Ysavel Chulco treinta 30	Myguel Usco seys—6	a que sirve çinco años en lo que los demas
	Leonor Cava v[te] e quatro—24		
	Catalina Ysla veinte e ocho 28	Ysavel Zica treze 13	
	Madalena Mastichul quarenta e çinco 45	Ynes Nacho nueue—9 Domingo Naucha tres—3	a diez a°s que sirve en lo que le manda
	Catalina Coca sesenta 60	Fran[ca] Coca Ynquillai diez y ocho 18 Fran[co] Chingua doze 12 +476+	
viejos	Catalina Asto sesenta 60	Ynes Chinbo Rimai—60	Ysavel Colque setenta 70
yanaconas de doña M[a] Ramirez	Anton de Quiñones de Ananpa treinta—30 Juana Yalpo treinta 30 +471+	Al° Carnapillao ocho—8 Martin Curas seys 6	a que le sirve tres años de ortelano y en beneficialle las chacaras
coxo	Domingo Naricara de Guaillas treinta e quatro 34 Maria Cocanco treinta e dos—32	Cat[a] Yuco quinze 15 Juan Machaguai ocho 8 Ysavel Chauca seis 6 Lucas Ananpo çinco 5 Al° Sulcaguaman tres 3	a que le sirve tres años en lo que es de arriba
	Domingo Sulca Guaillas veinte e seis—26 Maria Aba v[te] e nueue 29	Domingo Llaguas seis—6 Ju° Bautista Sulca tres 3 Ana Quipa dos—2	tres años a que syrue en lo que los demas

/f.336/

lo que paga de servi°	*lo que paga de dotrina*	*lo que paga de tassa*	*tiene chacaras de tassa*
medio topo de chacara			
un topo de chacara			
medio topo de chacara			
Ynes Santao setenta—70			
medio topo de chacara	quatro tomines de dotrina		dos topos de chacara
medio topo de chacara	quatro tomines de dotrina		topo y medio de chacara
tres quartos de chacara	quatro tomines de dotrina		

/f.336v/

	Casados Años	*hijos Años*	*servi^{o} que a fecho cada yanacona*
474	Her^{do} Carua Abanca de G Ynes Libiachuqui veinte—20	Ana Caruayuco tres—3	a tres años que le sirve en lo que los demas
	Juan Ancos guayllas çinquenta—50	Madalena Puma Carua diez 10	a quatro años que le sirve de hortelano
viejas	Leonor Yme ses^{a}—60	Catalina Chuqui sesenta 60	
viejos	Juan Ancos çinquenta e quatro—54	Madalena Poma Carua diez—10	
yanaconas de P^{o} de Bustinça	Salvador Llaqua Asto Quichua çinqta e quatro 54 Ciçilia Quispi çinq^{ta} 50 +475+		a que le sirve doze años de hortelano
476	Luis Sulca Llaqua Quichua veinte e quatro 24 Ysavel Pullo treinta 30	Cat^{a} Ypuco çinco—5 Cat^{a} Chunbi tres—3 Ana Llaguapuco uno 1	a seis años que le sirve de hortelano
227	Xpobal Canagualpa de Xaquixaguana quarenta—40 Mª Ynquillai treinta e çinco 35		a que le sirve treze años de ortelano y de benefiçialle las chacaras
61	Viçente Chucho deste valle veinte—20 Ynes Paucar Ocllo veinte e ocho—28	Juan Chiguan Gualpa tres 3	a que sirve seis años en lo que los demas

/f.337/

lo que le paga por servi^{o}	*lo que paga de dotrina*	*lo que paga de tassa*	*tiene chacaras de tassa*
tres quartos de chacara	quatro tomines de dotrina		medio topo de chacara
un quarto de topo de chacara			
medio topo de chacara	quatro tomines de dotrina		un quarto de chacara
	quatro tomines de dotrina		un quarto de chacara
medio topo de chacara	quatro tomines de dotrina		
medio topo de chacara	quatro tomines de dotrina		un quarto de topo de chacara

/f.337v/

	Casados Años	*hijos Años*	*servi^{o} que a fecho cada yanacona*
Viejas	Ysavel Cusla ochenta 80	Ysabel Lastopo ochenta 80	
Yanaconas de Guapo y Rocayro y sus hermanos	Felipe Yupangui del Cuzco çinq^{ta} e quatro 54 Leonor Guarcai 40 +540+	Al^{o} Yupangui nueue—9 Fran^{ca} Toto Ocllo ocho—8	no sirve a nadie
114	Juan Ataosuno de Pacaritambo treinta y seys—36 Ana Suca veinte e ocho—28	Costança Paico quatro—4 Fran^{co} Guaipar dos 2	sirve a don Carlos Gualpa Roca en beneficialle las chacaras de de dalle leña
486	Anbrosio Pillaca de Guaro veinte 20 Costança çica Ocllo v^{te} e çinco 25	Ana Chucobello un año 1	sirve en lo que los demas
487	Her^{do} Gualparimache diez y seis—16 Ysavel çica v^{te} e çinco 25	Juan Chicohuc uno—1	a que le sirve quatro años en lo que los demas
153	Martin Curiguaman aymara v^{te} e quatro 24 Fran^{ca} Yauritanta quarenta y seis—46	Catalina Caquia ocho—8 Ynes Supaoqui seis años—6	A que le sirve v^{te} a^{o}s en lo que los demas
2	Agustin Pariguana Aymara naçio en este valle veinte—20 Madalena Tuta v^{te} 20		A que sirve tres años en beneficio de las chacaras y de dalle leña
126	Juan Tupa Yupangui del Cuzco veinte e ocho—28 Madalena Cica veinte e nueve—29		A que sirve diez años en lo que los demas

/f.338/

lo que le paga por el servi^{o}	*lo que paga de dotrina*	*lo que paga de tassa*	*tiene chacaras de tassa*
	seis tomines de dotrina		dos topos de las chacaras de comunydad
medio topo de chacara	seys tomines de dotrina		
medio topo de chacara	seys tomines de dotrina		
			un quarto de topo de chacara
medio topo de chacara	seys tomines de dotrina		
medio topo de chacara	seys tomines de dotrina		
tres quartos de chacara	seys tomines de dotrina		

/f.338v/

	Casados Años	*hijos Años*	*serui[ci]o q[ue] a fecho cada yanacona*
491	Martin Ataucusi de Xaquixaguana quarenta e dos 42 Costança Chinbocalisi veinte e nueve 29		a que le sirve veinte años en lo que los demas
492	Di^{o} Picana de Pasto diez y ocho—18 Ana Chunbicoca diez y seis 16		a quatro años que sirve a sus hijos de Gualparoca
493	don Carlos Gualparoca naçio en este valle treinta e çinco—35 Cat^{a} çica ocllo treinta e dos 32		
viejas	Teresa Muramo sesenta 60	Juana Coca sesenta 60	Luysa Toto Ocllo sesenta 60
	Maria Yuyo çinquenta 50	Catalina Chuqui Urma diez 10	
huerfanos 488	Myguel Pauca quinze años 15	Juana Pata diez y ocho 18	
yanaconas de don Ju^{o} Sona	Martin Sulca Guayllas çinquenta—50 Ynes Quipi çinq^{ta} y ocho—58 +160+		a que le sirve veinte años en benefiçialle las chacaras y dalle leña
115	Juan Cusiguaman de Xaquixaguana quarenta y ocho—48 Mª Cusla çinq^{ta}—50		a que le sirve dos años de llevalle leña al Cuzco
viejas	Ynes Coca çinq^{ta} y seys—56	Ynes Quila sesenta 60	

/f.338/

lo que le paga por el servi^{o}	*lo que paga de dotrina*	*lo que paga de tassa*	*tiene chacaras de tassa*
tres quartos de topo	seys tomynes de dotrina		
Leonor Chinbo Urma ses^{a} 60	Ysavel Toto sesenta 60		
un quarto topo de chacara	quatro tomynes de dotrina		
un quarto topo de chacara	quatro tomynes de dotrina		

/f.338v/

	Casados Años	*hijos Años*	*servi^{o} que a fecho cada yanacona*
don Guari Tito enfermo no paga tribu^{o}	don P^{o} Guari Tito Ynga del Cuzco no paga tributo—38 Madalena Cuinpo 33 +68+		
de doña Ana Quispe	Xpobal Yachimarca Yunga veinte e seis 26 Ynes Cullapullao veinte e quatro 26 +495+	Juana Paicoçica tres—3	
496	P^{o} Bilcaruna Ynga çinquenta a^{o}s—50 Ynes Carua quarenta años—40		a que le sirve diez y ocho a^{o}s en benefiçialle las chacaras y dalle leña
69	Diego Pumacunia veinte años—20 Teresa Yaroquilpo veinte e dos 22	Leonor Calco sinple de çinco 5	a que le sirve treinta años en lo que le manda
yanaconas de Al^{o} Topa Cusi Gualpa	don Al^{o} Tulpo Cuxi Gualpa Ynga veinte e çinco—25 Leonor Totoçica 22 +498+	Madalena Tuto dos—2	
	Martin Lunache de Xapie veinte e tres—23 Fran^{ca} Cauidisyo 19	Madalena Sarpai dos—2 Ju^{a} Quispiçica uno 1	
499	Felipe Manchapa de Guayocondo treinta—30 Mª Guallima—29	Al^{o} Rimache çinco—5 Ju^{o} Yanquigualpar 2 Mª Urmacoca uno 1	a que le sirve al suso dho diez años en benefiçialle las chacaras y dalle leña
501	Al^{o} Parinango Cayanbi veinte e ocho—28 Leonor Cucha v^{te} e çinco—25	Beatriz Cusi un año 1	
			a que le sirve quinze años en benefiçialle las chacaras

/f.339/

lo que le paga por el servi^{o}	*lo que paga de dotrina*	*lo que paga de tassa*	*tiene chacaras de tassa*
un quarto de chacara			
dos topos de chacara doç^{os} treinta pies de arboleda			
medio topo de chacara	seys tomines de dotrina		
tiene nueve topos de chacara doç^{os} y set^{a} pies de arboleda	seys tomines de dotrina		
	seys tomines de dotrina	media fanega de tassa cada año de maiz	
tres quartos de chacara	quatro tomines de dotrina	una quartilla de maiz	

/f.339v/

	Casados Años	*hijos Años*	*servi^{o} que a fecho cada yanacona*
504	Al^{o} Sapo v^{te} e ocho 28 Catalina RimaiChinbo veinte 20	Juan Bilcachema dos 2	
500	Agustin Patic v^{te} 20 Ysavel Chulo v^{te} 20		a diez años que sirve en beneficio de las chacaras
155	Martin Ynga Songo v^{te} e dos—22 Ynes Sangaina veinte e ocho—28		
156	Martin Guaripaucra çinquenta y ocho 58	Juan Guacoychuco veinte e seis—26	sirven sus hijos y el en lo que les mandan
viejas	+502+ Ynes Cacrapa çinquenta 50 +503+	Xpobal Parinango quinze a^{o}s—15 P^{o} Bilca quinze a^{o}s 15 sus hijos anbos de un bientre	sirven en lo que les mandan
	Ysavel Toto çinq^{ta} 50	Maria Muhotanta çinq^{ta} 50	Leonor Pilco Tanta çinquenta 50
yanaconas de Di^{o} … mer…do	Martin Pichuna de Quito treinta—30 Catalina chapoyachi treinta—30	Luya Chuma quatro—4 Ana Cayma tres 3	a que le sirve seis años en beneficialle las chacaras de mayz
9	Agustin Gualuto de Quito naçio en este valle v^{te} e quatro 24 Ynes Caruaviche veinte e seis—26	Lor^{ço} Chunbana seys—6 Mª Cunicana tres 3	a que le sirve seis años en lo que es arriba
	Martin Nynadechuro Viuibilca quarenta 40 Fran^{ca} Cumin caña veinte e dos años—22	Madalena Caquia Ama seis a^{o}s—6 Ana Chuquipaque 4 Costança Bilcama 2	a que le sirve seis años en lo que los demas

/f.340/

lo que le paga por el servi^{o}	*lo que paga de dotrina*	*lo que paga de tassa*	*tiene chacaras de tassa*
medio topo de chacara de que come	quatro tomines to dotrina	una quartilla de maiz	
medio topo de chacara	quatro tomines de dotrina		
tres quartos de topo	tres tomynes de dotrina	una quartilla de maiz	
tres quartos de topo	dos tomines de dotrina	una quartilla de maiz	
un topo de chacara			
un topo de chacara			
un topo de chacara			

/f.340v/

	Casados Años	*hijos Años*	*servi^{o} que a fecho cada yanacona*
	Martin Taipe Aymara veinte e çinco—25 Fran^{ca} Vellamaybai veinte e dos a^{o}s 22	Diego Guainaori uno—1	a que le sirve çinco años en lo que los demas
vieja	Maria Caquiama çinquenta a^{o}s 50		
De don Ju^{o} Tupa Cuzco 510	Diego Llamocaconde quarenta e siete 47 Juana Chumia—55	511+ Agustin Aromi diez y ocho 18	a que le sirve v^{te} e çinco años en beneficio de chacaras y dalle leña
401	Alonso Guamancusi de Tanbococha veinte e ocho 28 Costança Coca v^{te} e seis 26	Marcos Cusipoma seis—6 Luçia Caquiasun—4 Ju^{o} Cusiguaman—1	a que le sirve cinco años en llevalle leña al Cuzco y demas que le manda
vieja	Beatriz Paque setenta 70		
de don Ju^{o} Ailanbo	Al^{o} Yaure Rucana quarenta e çinco 45 Elvira Guanai çinquenta—50	Ysavel Muramochunbo uno 1	a que le sirve tres años en benefiçialle las chacaras y dalle leña
11	Al^{o} Marca Quichua çinquenta—50 Leonor Pitai çinq^{ta} e çinco—55		a que le sirve çinco a^{o}s en benefiçialle la chacara y dalle leña
de Di^{o} Sanchez	Ju^{o} Caiguan quarenta e quatro—44 Leonor Chiguacai çinquenta e dos 52	Ju^{a} Chuquibichu nueve—9 Fran^{co} Guaman Quispi siete—7	A que le sirve siete años en lo que le mandan
	Diego Carianaula cañar naçio en este valle diez y siete—17 Ysavel Chicchuco—18		a que sirve siete a^{o}s de buscar y^{o}s para los andes

/f.340/

lo que le paga por el servi^{o}	*lo que paga de dotrina*	*lo que paga de tassa*	*tiene chacaras de tassa*
medio topo de chacara	seys tomines de dotrina		
un quarto de topo de chacara	seis tomines de dotrina		
medio topo de chacara			
medio topo de chacara	quatro tomynes de dotrina		
un topo de chacara	quatro tomynes de dotrina		
	quatro tomynes de dotrina		un quarto de topo de chacara de comunidad

/f.340v/

	Casados Años	*Hijos Años*	*servicio que a fecho cada yanacona*
De Lucas Moreno	Al^{o} Curi Quechua v^{te} e dos años—22 Costança Toto Ocllo veinte e dos—22	Agustin Tacuri quatro—4 Simon Cabana uno 1	a que sirve onze a^{o}s en beneficio de las chacaras y en su cassa
	Martin Causi de Cuanycondor quarenta y seis 46 Elvira Anbio treinta—30	Fran^{co} Musun tres—3	a que le sirve v^{te} e quatro a^{o}s y a v^{te} que salio de su tierra
519	Her^{do} Carnate yunga çinquenta 50	Domingo Carnate ocho 8	a que le sirve dos años y v^{te} e quatro que salio de su tierra
vieja	Ysavel Puco sesenta		
520 de doña Beatriz Cucul	Martin Marca yunga naçio en este valle quarenta e çinco 45 Costança Chinbo Urmo çinq^{ta} e çinco—55		a que le sirve v^{te} e çinco a^{o}s en beneficialle las chacaras y de leña
	P^{o} Quispi yunga naçio en este valle v^{te}—20 Maria Siquilla veinte e çinco 25	Xpobal Marca uno—1	a que le sirve tres años en beneficiarle las chacaras
	Sebastian Sulca guanca quarenta e siete 47 Ana Chunbi çinq^{ta} 50	Catalina Culpo diez y siete 17	a que sirve v^{te} e çinco años en lo que los demas
	Fran^{co} Curi naçio en este valle diez y seis 16 Madalena Yuyo v^{te}—20		a que sirve dos años en lo que los demas
	Lucas Rimasca naçio en este valle v^{te} e quatro 24 Cat^{a} Chinbo Coca treinta—30	Gonçalo Asto Ananca quatro—4 Martin Mutama tres—3 Ju^{o} Aucataco dos—2 Ynes Poco uno—1	a diez años que le sirve en lo que los demas

/f.341/

lo que le paga de servicio	*lo que paga de dotrina*	*lo que paga de tassa*	*tiene chacaras de tassa*
medio topo de chacara			
un topo de chacara			
un topo de chacara			
un topo de chacara	quatro tomynes de dotrina		
un topo de chacara	quatro tomynes de dotrina		
un topo y quarto de chacara	quatro tomynes de dotrina		
un topo y quarto de chacara			

/f.341v/

	Casados Años	*Hijos Años*	*servicio que ha fecho cada yanacona*
viejas en San Benito	Ynes Sangaiche treinta e ocho 38	Baltasar Tupa seis 6	a que sirve v^{te} años en lo que se le manda
116	Juan Toto $çinq^{ta}$ 50	Luis Acaloma quatro 4	a veinte $a^{o}s$ que le sirve en el beneficio de las chcacaras
	Ysavel Yuyo veinte e çinco 25	Ynes Puco dos—2	
	Madalena Yuyo diez y nueve 19		
de don P^{o} Cochachi	P^{o} Llagua Auca de çinquenta 50 Catalina Apuco çinquenta e çinco 55	Leonor Cumia nueve—9 Ju^{o} Arcospunta Ylla ocho—8	a que le sirve siete años en el beneficio de chacaras y de dalle leña
151	Martin Curo Pinagua naçio en este valle çinquenta e çinco 55 Costança Cusi Chinbo 55	Martin Aucallalli mudo diez y seys—16	a que sirve çinco años en beneficio de las chacaras y de dalle leña

/f.342/

lo que le pagan por el servicio	*lo que paga de dotrina*	*lo que paga de tassa*	*tiene chacaras de tassa*
un topo de chacara de que come			
tres quartos de topo de que come			

/f.342v/

	Casados Años	*Hijos Años*	*servicio que ha fecho cada yanacona*
de don Ant^{o} Nari Gualpa	P^{o} Quispe naçio en este valle v^{te}—20 Leonor Paico Chinbo veinte e dos—22	Catalina Ya Puma tres—3 Juana Cota dos 2	a que le sirve un año de benefiçialle las chacaras
tullido 528	Al^{o} Muca de Guaro de treinta e siete 37 Madalena Chuquitanta treinta—30	Maria Paico siete 7 P^{o} Muca tres—3 Ju^{o} Yanquerimache un año 1	a que le sirve diez años en lo que los demas
71	Di^{o} Acotan naçio en este valle de quarenta e nueve—49 no tiene muger	Fran^{co} Tarisca doze—12	a que le sirve treinta años en lo que los demas
	Madalena Chunbi çinquenta a^{o}s 50	+529+ Sebastian Maybasca ocho 8	a diez años que syrve en las chacaras
viejas	Madalena Chinbo çinquenta—50	Sebastian Mayusca doze—12	
	Leonor Colequi de çinquenta—50		
544 de don Xpobal Sulla Tupa	P^{o} Condurimayan çinquenta—50 Françisca Yachi çinquenta e tres 53	Mª Chinbo Coca v^{te}—20 Ysavel Chapo diez 10 Xpobal Cusicondor ocho 8 Cat^{a} Ynquillai seis—6 Beatriz Coca quatro 4 Petronilla Cusi Chinbo uno 1	a que sirve v^{te} años en beneficio de las chacaras
vieja	Ynes Culpa çinq^{ta} 50		a çinco años que syrve de guardar obejas
de don Garçia Rima Topa	Andres Ponpanaqui quichua v^{te} e ocho—28 Leonor Sulca Chunbi treynta—30	Juan Quispe Nanca çinco—5 Petronilla Marca Chinbo uno 1	a que le sirve v^{te} años en el benef^{o} de las chacaras

/f.343/

lo que le paga por el servicio	*lo que paga de dotrina*	*lo que paga de tassa*	*tiene chacaras de tassa*
un topo de chacara	quatro tomynes de dotrina		
un topo de chacara	quatro tomynes de dotrina		
un topo de chacara	quatro tomynes de dotrina		
dale de comer			
medio topo de chacara	seys tomynes de dotrina		
medio topo de chacara			
medio topo de chacara	quatro tomynes de dotrina		un quarto de topo de chacara de comunydad

/f.343v/

	Casados Años	*Hijos Años*	*servicio que ha fecho cada yanacona*
Huerfanos	Costança Chinbo Tiquilla onze años		
157 de Marcos Puri	Marcos Puri de Moinabanba sesenta 60 Catalina Ciça Ocllo quarenta y ocho—48	Catalina Acray diez y nueue 19 Ysavel Paico diez y siete 17	
546	Domingo Gualpa Rimache hijo del dho Marcos Puri—15 Leonor çichu catorze 14		
13	Al^{o} Casi treinta e dos 32 Madalena Yuyo quarenta e çinco 45	Fran^{co} Tasin seis 6 Ju^{o} Casiti tres 3 Leonor Yanqui siete—7	
86	Fran^{co} Tacuri naçio en este valle diez y ocho 18 Ynes Ypi veinte—20		a que le sirve dos años en beneficio de las chacaras y leña
547	Fran^{co} Chucuna naçio en este valle treinta 30 Ysavel Chinbo treinta—30		a que le sirve veinte años en lo que los demas
vieja	Maria Tiquilla de sesenta a^{o}s 60 Ju^{o} Gualo treinta—30		
+555+ de Ju^{o} de Pancorbo	Al^{o} Guaipa de Chauca quarenta e tres 43 Ysavel Rupo—45	Ynes Toto quinze—15 Costança Chinbo seis 6 Xpobal Guaipar çinco 5 Ana Sillo Chinbococa tres 3 Ana Chinbo dos—2	a que le sirve diez años en beneficialle las chacaras
222 de G^{o} Martin	Pedro Chunbillo Yauyo quarenta—40 Juana Curma treinta e siete—37	Domingo Llama diez y seis 16 Ynes Maiban quinze 15 Xpobal Chunbillo onze 11 Alonso Guaçio ocho—8 Maria Suyochunbi seis 6 Ju^{o} Tilla çinco—5 Ju^{o} Bilca quatro—4	a diez años que sirve de hortelano

/f.344/

lo que le paga por el servicio	*lo que paga de dotrina*	*lo que paga de tassa*	*tiene chacaras de tassa*
tiene tres topos y medio de tierra suyos y doçientos pies de arboleda			
medio topo de chacara			
un quarto de topo	quatro tomynes de dotrina		
un quarto de topo			
medio topo de chacara			
ha le pagado por servicio en obejas vestidos plata y un quarto de chacara			

/f.344v/

	Casados Años	*Hijos Años*	*servicio que ha fecho cada yanacona*
548	Alonso Napaga naçio en este valle es Yauyo de veinte—20 Maria CusiChinbo veinte e dos—22		a tres años que sirve de ortelano
viejas	Juana Llasa cinq^{ta} y siete 57 Ysavel Colque 50	Catalina Chinbo Coca doze—12 Diego Llana doze 12 +556+	sirve en lo que le manda
de Bermudez	Ju^{o} Tacuri Ancara veynte—20 Ynes Rinchu çinquenta 58		a que sirve dos años en lo que le mandan
397	Martin Quipi Yanaguara treinta e siete—37 Fran^{ca} Pachu—30		a nueve a^{o}s que sirve en lo que del arriba
viejas	Costança çibis çinq^{ta} y ocho a^{o}s 58	Agustin Costa ocho—8 Andres Yupo diez y seis 16	a diez años que le sirve
	Fran^{ca} Laura çinq^{ta} y çinco años—55		
de ju[an] ortiz	Al^{o} Bica treinta—30 Ysavel Chisca treinta—30	Ynes Puma Chisque dos—2	
	Andres Pariguaman v^{te} e çinco 25 Cat^{a} Sulca Chinbo veinte—20	Pedro Cunas dos—2	

/f.345/

lo que le paga por el servicio	*lo que paga de dotrina*	*lo que paga de tasa*	*tiene chacaras de tassa*
le ha pagado su servicio en bestidos y plata y come un pedaço de tierra			
un quarto de chacara	pagale la dotrina		
pagale su servicio			
pague su servicio en bestidos y coca			
	seys tomines de dotrina		
dale de comer y de bestir	pagale la dotrina		

/f.345v/

	Casados Años de Martin de Meneses	*Hijos Años*	*servicio que ha fecho cada yanacona*
	Alonso Puchana de Quito naçio en este valle veinte—20 Cat^{a} Ciça Ocllo—20		a que le sirve quatro años de labrador
	P^{o} Yunbo de Quito naçio en este valle veinte—20 Cat^{a} Ciça Ocllo v^{te} 20		
	P^{o} Sicha cañar naçio en este valle diez y ocho—18 Ynes Yngao diez y seis—16	Elvira Caychucar uno—1	a que le sirve dos años en lo que le manda
viejas	Maria Coca Aca çinquenta a^{o}s 50	Ju^{o} Lumequano diez 10 Ana Papami Chinbo 16 Ynes Pachachina quinze 15 Cat^{a} Paico v^{te} e çinco 25 Mençia Parachi çinco a^{o}s 5	
de Damian de la Bandera	P^{o} Quispi Yupangui del Cuzco treinta e ocho 38 Madalena Chisquia quarenta—40	Felipe Quico çinco a^{o}s—5 P^{o} Quispe Yupangui quatro años 4 Alonso Tito tres 3	a que sirve cinco años en el beneficio de las chacaras
558	Al^{o} Biba de Moyna treinta e tres 33 Catalina Chinbo Urma lo mesmo 33	P^{o} Paucar Guaman quatro—4 Madalena Aylan Pila uno—1	a que le sirve quatro años de ortelano y de beneficialle las chacaras
	Myguel Aromi Aymara naçio en este valle treinta 30 Costança Paico 40	Mª Tasca onze—11 Martin Cochi Aran ocho 8 Ju^{o} Chisque seis—6 Damian Tupia Condur quatro anos 4	a que le sirve cinco años en lo que los demas
203	P^{o} Pariguana Quichua veinte e quatro—24 Juana Paico v^{te} 20		a ocho años que sirve a una yndia vieja
murio	P^{o} Cavana Condesuyo çinq^{ta} años 50 enfermo de los andes	Fran^{co} Pallasca diez—10 Juana Paque çinco—5	a que sirve quatro años en ayudar en la guerta

/f.346/

lo que le paga por el servicio	*lo que paga de dotrina*	*lo que paga de tassa*	*tiene chacaras de tassa*
medio topo de chacara es medio suyo			
medio topo de chacara			
topo y m^{o} de chacara			
un topo de chacara			
un topo de chacara			
un topo de chacara			

/f.346v/

	Casados Años	*Hijos Años*	*servicio que a fecho cada yanacona*
vieja	Ysavel Cocanbo setenta a^{o}s 70		
de Di^{o} Lopez de Ayala 408	Fran^{co} Pacha Guaman de Guanuco treinta y ocho—38 Maria Sumai qu^{ta}—40	Leonor Chunbicarba ocho—8 Fran^{co} Pita quatro—4 Br^{me} Cacha tres—3	a que le sirve ocho años de guardalle ganado y beneficialle la chacara de coca
274	Martin Casitancar cañar veinte e seis 26 Ynes Sired v^{te} e dos 22	Catalina Sirinchu un año—1	
	Xpobal Duchina cañar treinta e dos—32	Al^{o} Purit v^{te} e dos—22	a que le sirve dos años de ortelano y de beneficialle la chacara
	Al^{o} Llamoca de treinta e seis 36 Ana Bincho quarenta—40		
yanaconas de don Garçia Ynguel Topa	Martin Cuco Paucar treinta e ocho—38 +159+ Ysavel Paico quarenta—40	Diego Gualpa siete años—7 Tomas Cusigualpa çinco—5	a que le sirve çinco años en el beneficio de las chacaras y servicio personal
103 559	Juan Ynga Paucar naçio en este valle quinze—15 Juana Urma quinze 15		a que le sirve dos años en beneficio de las chacaras
14	Alonso Trapa treinta e çinco 35 Madalena Yaro Guato—30	Cat^{a} Ynguillai seys—6 P^{o} Mylla CusiChinbo dos—2	
199	P^{o} Chunu Cana treinta y seis—36 Ynes çiza v^{te} e ocho 28	Xpobal Quizo siete—7 Ana Quinbo tres 3	

/f.347/ *en el original /355/*

lo que le paga por el servicio	*lo que paga de dotrina*	*lo que paga de tassa*	*tiene chacaras de tassa*
un quarto de chacara			
un quarto de topo de chacara			un quarto de topo de chacara
	seys tomines de dotrina		quatro topos de chacara de comunidad
	quatro tomines de dotrina		

/f.347v/ en el original s.f.

	Casados Años	*Hijos Años*	*serviº que a fecho cada yanacona*
164	Martin Bilinaula Cañar naçio en este valle treinta e dos—32 Catalina Tocto Chinbo treinta e dos 32		
200	Pº Guaba Condor sastre quarenta—40 Maria Caua treinta e dos—32		
90	Fran^{co} Quispe treinta e çinco—35 Ynes Aca Ocllo veinte e çinco—25		come un topo de tierra
sirve a Xpobal de Ojeda	Juº Guaman Cana a onze aºs que salio de su tierra—30 Juana Yngilla 28		un año de serviçio
yanaconas de don Carlos Ynga	Alº Guaco Puquis quarenta—40 +15+ Leonor Anchuc quarenta e tres—43	Leonor Chululcu diez—10 Gaspar Guaso seys—6	a que sirve catorze años en lo que puede
91	Felipe Cañari quarenta—40 Ynes Maco treinta—30	Juan Guarcai Unguilla tres años 3	a diez y seis años que e en el

/f.347/ [*sic*]

blanca
un topo de chacara

/f.347v/ [*sic*]

	Casados Años	*Hijos Años*	*servicio que a fecho cada yanacona*
	Ynes Colca de sesenta—60	Catalina admoso çinq[ta]—50	Juana Cusi Rimai ses[a] 60
de don Fran[co] Cayo Topa	Martin Rimache Yupangui diez y 7 17 Catalina Casa—16 +497+		A que le sirve nueve años en el beneficio de las chacaras
no tienen amos 530	Juan Piçarro Cusi Atauchi Ynga naçio en este valle—55 Ju[a] Chunbo qu[ta]—40	Leonor Toto Chinbo quinze—15 Ana Chuqui—1	
531	Lor[ço] Guaretopa naçio en este valle diez e nueue—19 Françisca çiza—17		
534	Domingo Topa Cusigualpa naçio en este valle v[te] e ocho—28 Ysavel Paico Coca—20	Ana Chinbo Quipi—5 M[a] Cusirimai tres 3 Ju[a] Guaco Ocllo uno 1	
70	don Luis Tito çinq[ta] y ocho—58 Luysa Paico Ocllo—58		
271 535	Alonso Caquiaya Cañar naçio en el Cuzco 33 Ju[a] Caua treinta e dos 32	Luisa Naulchi seis 6 Her[do] Coacui Pulla tres 3 Ju[o] Bautista quatro 4 Madalena Birnuc 1 Agustin Yngao seis 6	come topo y m[o] de don Francisco Chilche
87	Fran[co] Cautanaula naçio en este valle treinta e nueve—39 Cat[a] Auchuc—20		
	Fauian Auylo cañar çinquenta e nueue 59 Juana Utca—38	Fran[co] Ynga Toco 17 M[a] Quichu nueve 9 Alonso Canbis Pulla 5 Xpobal Marca 2	come dos topos y medio

/f.348/

lo que le paga por el servicio	*lo que paga de dotrina*	*lo que paga de tassa*	*tiene chacaras de tassa*
come quatro topos de chacara			
come medio topo de chacara			
topo y m[o] de chacara			

/f.348v/ /en blanco/

/f.349/

lo que le paga por el servicio	*lo que paga de dotrina*	*lo que paga de tassa*	*tiene chacaras de tassa*

/f.349v/

	Casados Años	*Hijos Años*	*servicio que a fecho cada yanacona*
201	Pº Caque Guallas çinquenta—50 Françisca Ylla Corva çinquenta—50	Alonso Taicache veinte 20	A que le sirve diez y ocho aºs en mandar los yanaconas
154	Martin Sulca Guallas villa veinte—20 Catalina Rupai Carua diez y nueue	Juan Caqui uno—1	a que le sirve dos años en beneficio de las chacaras
	Juº Sulca Libia de Guaylas treinta e dos 32 Ana Tocto treinta 30		a que le sirve doze años en el beneficio de las chacaras
	Agustin Marca Guaman naçio en este valle catorze—14 Catalina Cusi Ynguillai—17		sirve en lo que le manda
	Myguel Guaman Libia Guaylas v^{te} e q^{tro} 24 Catª Toto v^{te}—20		a que le sirve doze años en lo que los demas
16	Alº Yanacpoma Guailas veinte e ocho 28 Costança Guaca Condo veinte e seis 26	Lucas Rimay Condor çinco aºs 5 Diº Tuquicuchi dos años—2	a que sirve diez años en lo que los demas
17	Alº Cochillaillas çinquenta—50 Ynes Coca Chinbo çinquenta—50		a diez años questa con el
112	Her^{do} Yarpa Guayllas veinte e nueue 29 Leonor Colque Cucho 28	Andres Poma Cusi quatro aºs 4 Diego Guara Puma dos años—2	a que le sirve v^{te} aºs en el beneficio de las chacaras y servicio personal
202	Pº Antaguayllas veinte e nueve aºs 29 Ysavel Pacho v^{te} e quatro—24	Juan Caque uno 1	a doze años syrue de hortelano

/f.350/

lo que le paga por el servicio	*lo que paga de dotrina*	*lo que paga de tassa*	*tiene chacaras de tassa*

/f.350v/

	Casados Años	*Hijos Años*	*servicio que a fecho cada yanacona*
19	Alonso Chunchi Paria Guayllas veinte años—20 Teresa Cayso v[te]—20		a questa con el desde niño
162	Martin Amay Guaillas veinte años 20 Ysavel Yapuche diez y ocho—18		a questa con el desde niño
163	Martin Chuichu Guaillas diez y ocho—18 Madalena Chaucas quinze—15		a questa con el seys años
19	Alonso Bilca Paria setenta 70		a veinte años que le sirve en lo que le manda
	Maria Condor Colqui çinquenta e quatro—54	Ysavel Colque Cunsa doze—12 Ju[o] Poma Yana diez—10	sirve en lo que le mandan
	Madalena Carua Colque çinq[ta] e quatro—54	Juana Carua Casa quinze 15	sirve en lo que le mandan
	Ana Tiquilla quarenta a[o]s 40	Diego Quispe çinco años 5	
	Fran[ca] Liuia Caruia treinta 30	Ynes Carua casa tres 3	sirve en lo que mandan
viejas	Maria Puco çinq[ta] 50	Ynes Chapa çinq[ta] 50	Ysavel Puro cinq[ta] 50
	Alonso Libia diez y ocho 18	Martin Carua yana diez y ocho 18 +171+	Baltasar Nauia enfermo de los andes quarenta—40

/f.350?/

lo que le paga por el servicio	*lo que paga de dotrina*	*lo que paga de tasa*	*servicio que a fecho cada yanacona*
Ara Vischo çinq[ta] 50 Ynes Poma diez y seis 16	Catalina Ynguilla çinquenta 50	Catalina Paico çinq[ta] e çinco 55	

/f.350v?/

	Casados Años	*Hijos Años*	*servicio que a fecho cada yanacona*
yanaconas de doña Maria Diez de Betanços	Diego Vira Paucar treinta e ocho—38	Ju^{o} Toto catorze a^{o}s—14 Çeçilia Chunchoca ocho—8 Lucas Rimache dos—2 Baltasar Calla Caua tres—3	
	Anton Cauana quarenta y ocho 48 Costança Rupo quarenta e tres 43	Anton Cusi Yunga seys—6 Diego Paico quatro—4	
	Martin Calla Caua sesenta—60 Ynes Chuquirimay sesenta—60		
	Felipe Tomayllo çinq^{ta} e quatro 54 Ysavel Paico çinquenta—50		
374 425	Ju^{o} Malco Pariguana treinta e nueve 39 Ynes Cusichimbo çinquenta 50	Fran^{co} Chirua v^{te} e siete—27	
	Fran^{co} Chirua veinte e siete—27 Ynes Mullicorocha v^{te} e çinco a^{o}s 25	Martin Quilli—3 Felipe Tacuri uno 1	
	Ysavel Carua quarenta—40 Maria Llasa ses[ent]a—60	Juan Quicana syete 7	
yn^{a}s e yn^{o}s sin amos	Ysavel Quipe treinta años 30	Ynes Chinbo seis 6 Juan Bautista Yupangui çinco 5	
	Ynes Sanya sesenta a^{o}s 60	Beatriz Murmoaco treinta—30 Alonso Puma diez y nueue—19	

/f.351/

lo que le paga por el servicio	*lo que le paga de dotrina*	*lo que paga de tassa*	*tiene chacaras de tassa*

/f.351v/

	viejas Años		
	Ynes Chinbo ses^{a} 60	Ju^{a} Cusirimai çinquenta e ocho—58	Xpobal Sapana quinze—15
	Ynes Cayachi ses^{a} 60	Maria Anas quarenta y ocho 48	Ynes Aca Ocllo veinte e çinco—25
	Ju^{a} Cusirimai ses^{a} 60		Fran^{co} Yngai …
huerfanas	Leonor Niquichuc doze 12	+536+ Xpobal Sirabisnai diez años—10	

El Yll^{e} señor liç^{do} frei P^{o} Gutierrez Flores de la orden y cavallero de alcantara visitador general por su m^{t} y por el ex^{mo} señor don Fran^{co} de Toledo bisorrey destos rreinos en su rreal nonbre en los valles de Yucai Amaybanba Quiquixana y su distrito aviendo bisitado los yndios yanaconas que poblan la villa de Santiago de Oropessa que fundo en el valle de Yucay y hizo dellos el resumen siguiente

clxiiij yndios casados de diez y ocho años a çinquenta para poder tributar çiento y sesenta y quatro

xvi y^{o}s solteros de diez y ocho a cinquenta años pa poder tributar diez y seis.

v son los y^{o}s yanaconas tributarios que biuen en este pueblo de Santiago de Oropesa çiento y ochenta
CLXXX

yndios de doze a diez y ocho años quinze	xv
muchachos de doze a^{o}s abaxo çiento y çinq^{ta} e dos	clii
viejos casados de çinquenta años arriba treinta e siete	xxxvii
viejos solteros de çinquenta años arriba diez	x
tullidos y enfermos çinco	v

/f.352/

Catalina Muchuca çinq[ta] 50	Madalena Nasmay sesenta y seis 66	Costança Tiquilla ses[a] e tres 63	Ysavel Çica Ocllo treinta 30

huerfanos tres iij
mugeres viudas y solteras de diez y ocho años a çinquenta años treinta e dos xxxij
moças de doze años a diez y ocho veynte xx
muchachas de doze años abajo çiento y çinquenta y ocho clviij
mugeres viejas de çinquenta años çiento c
huerfanas çinco v

Es toda la gente que bibe en este pueblo de Santiago de Oropesa de los y[o]s yanaconas entre casados y solteros e de otras hedades ochoçientas y setenta y seis personas Dccc Lxx Vi

E para que conste a su Ex[a] de lo suso dho se hizo el dho resumen e lo firmo el dho señor bisitador el liçençiado frei Pedro Gutierrez Flores ante my P[o] Diaz Valdeon escrivano—

/f.352v/ los y[o]s yanaconas que se poblaron en este valle de yucay en el pueblo de San Bernardo son los siguientes/

	Casados Años	*Hijos Años*	*servicio que a fecho cada yanacona*
	Martin Tina cañar natural deste valle quarenta—40 M[a] Chinbo quarenta 40		a que le sirve diez y seis en el beneficio de las chacaras
257	Andres Durbui cañar naçio en este valle diez e ocho 18 Cat[a] Yachi—18		a dos años que sirve en el beneficio de las chacaras de maiz
	Al[o] Quispi cañar naçio en este valle 48 Ysavel Caua—50	Maria Caçinchuc diez e siete 17	a que le sirve diez y ocho en lo que los demas
	Marcos Echilli cañar naçio en este valle veinte e çinco a[o]s 25 Madalena Aninchuc—15	Beatriz Abicaba quatro años 4 Cat[a] Chuc dos 2	a que le sirve diez años en lo que los demas
	Ju[o] Bautista Manchi cañar naçio en este valle treinta e ocho 38 Cat[a] Galinchuc—22		a diez años que sirve en lo que los demas
	Miguel Guinginaula cañar naçio en este valle veinte e çinco 25 Ysavel Ynchicaua—20	Ysavel Casinichuc çinco—5 Juan Bautista Cucupulla—2	a diez años que sirve en lo que los demas

/f.353/

lo que le paga por el servicio	*lo que le paga de dotrina*	*lo que paga de tassa*	*tiene chacaras de tassa*
Dale un topo de chacara de que come	quatro tomines de dotrina	paga quatro tomines de tassa	
un topo de chacara	quatro tomines de dotrina	dos pesos de tassa	
	quatro tomines de dotrina	dos p[o]s de tassa	un topo de chacara de la comunidad
	quatro tomines de dotrina	quatro tomines de tassa	topo y m[o] de chacara
	dos tomines de dotrina	quatro tomines de tasa	topo y m[o] de chacara
topo y quarto de chacara	quatro tomines de dotrina	un peso de tassa	

/f.353v/

	Casados Años	*Hijos Años*	*servicio que a fecho cada yanacona*
	Fran^{co} Anbuzilaca cañar naçio en este valle treinta e çinco—35 Madalena Mano treinta—30	Eluira Naaschu çinco—5 R^{o} Tinanchai ocho—8 Beatriz Machichuc 2	a que le sirve diez y ocho años en lo que los demas
265	Andres Tinimaçi cañar naçio en este valle diez e nueue 19 Costança Ooco v^{te} e tres 23	Eluira Nascho uno 1	a quatro años que le sirve en lo que los demas
267	Andres Casanaula cañar naçio en este valle veinte a^{o}s 20 Madalena Pullacucho veinte—20	Madalena Angai dos—2 Mazirinchuc uno 1	a ocho a^{o}s que le sirve de cunbicamayo y beneficialle las chacaras y dalle yerva y leña
268	Fran^{co} Bisnaiala cañar naçio en este valle v^{te} e quatro 24 Mençia Carua v^{te} e dos 22	G^{o} Ybanzucha tres—3 Ger^{mo} Acusaca—1 Madalena Cacacho dos 2	a diez a^{o}s que sirve de lo que le mandan
269	Matheo Palcho Biznai cañar naçio en este valle—15 Madalena Yugaitoco 15		a un año que le sirve en beneficialle las chacaras
	Al^{o} Caqui Cuya cañar naçio en este valle çinquenta e quatro 54 Luisa Ygaotoco—55		a treinta años que sirve en lo que los demas
272	Lucas Chilliguaman naçio en este valle quarenta—40 Beatriz Yllanchuc—36	Lucas quispe siete a^{o}s—7 Ysavel Toto çinco años—5	a v^{te} años que sirve en lo que los demas
273	Xpobal Naspi cañar naçio en este valle veinte e ocho—28 Mª Machi v^{te} e ocho—28	Catalina Muchuc siete años 7	a diez años que sirve en lo que los demas
158	Martin Taçitanga cañar Tomebanba treinta e tres—33 Ynes Colque treinta 30	Anton Billibichai quatro a^{o}s 4 Her^{do} Caquimaca uno—1	a v^{te} años que sirve en lo que los demas

/f.354/

lo que le paga por el servicio	*lo que paga de dotrina*	*lo que paga de tassa*	*tiene chacaras de tassa*
Dale medio topo de chacara	quatro tomines de dotrina	un peso de tassa	
Dale medio topo de chacara	quatro tomines de dotrina	un peso de tassa	
Dale un topo de chacara de que come	quatro tomines de dotrina	quatro tomines de tassa	
	quatro tomines de dotrina	un peso de tassa	topo y m^{o} de chacara de comunidad
medio topo de chacara	quatro tomines de dotrina	quatro tomines de tassa	
	quatro tomines de dotrina	un peso de tassa	medio topo de chacara
dos topos de chacara	quatro tomines de dotrina	dos pesos de tassa	
un topo y un quarto de chacara	dos tomines de dotrina	quatro tomines de tassa	
topo y medio de chacara	dos tomines de dotrina	quatro tomines de tassa	

/f.354v/

	Casados Años	*Hijos Años*	*servicio que a fecho cada yanacona*
275	Martin Bilitangar cañar treinta e siete a^{o}s Ynes Caua treinta e çinco—35	Lucas Sangailipai quinze a^{o}s 15 Luisa Guallachi tres 3 Madalena Yzunchu 1	a v^{te} años que sirve en lo que los demas
277	Andres Quiribisnai cañar naçio en este valle v^{te} e siete 27 Catalina Caua 28	Ju^{o} Casitipulla quatro años 4 Beatriz Beatichu uno—1	a doze años que sirve en lo que los demas
	P^{o} Bingluimiba cañar naçio en este valle veinte e quatro 24 Mª Calacho v^{te} e tres 23		a diez años que sirve en lo que los demas
278	Agustin Alao cañar çinquenta e q^{tro} 54 Cat^{a} Lucache çinq^{ta} e dos—52	Ynes Abira seys años 6	a veinte años que sirve en lo que los demas
280	P^{o} Guaman Cusi de Xaquixaguana naçio en este valle treinta e tres—33 Ynes Chuco—37	P^{o} Guarichi seis a^{o}s 6 Felipe Pomaquico tres—3	a diez años que sirve en lo que los demas
281	P^{o} Sulca Yauyo naçio en este valle v^{te} e siete—27 Fran^{ca} Muchaua—28	Ju^{o} Bautista cañar Bilca çinco años 5 Al^{o} Caruayana tres 3 Her^{do} Llasopucma 1	a diez años que sirve en lo que los demas
50	Agustin Lasuachicho naçio en este valle veinte e seis—26 Cat^{a} Mullo ocllo treinta e çinco—35		a veinte años que sirve en lo que los demas
279	Lucas Bilidunbai cañar naçio en este valle veinte e dos—22 Ana Lunchuc catorze 14		
185	Miguel Llocolla Conchuco treinta e quatro—34 Luisa Caua treinta 30	D^{go} Sulca quatro—4 Got^{a} Aguamyn tres 3 Ju^{o} Sulcachaico uno—1 Ynes NinaCarua doze 12 Leonor Caruacolqui nueve—9	a diez y ocho años que sirve en lo que los demas

/f.355/

lo que le paga por el servicio	*lo que paga de dotrina*	*lo que paga de tassa*	*tiene chacaras de tasa*
topo y medio de chacara	dos tomines de dotrina	quatro tomines de tassa	
topo y m^{o} de chacara	dos tomines de dotrina	quatro tomines de tassa	
dos topos de chacara	dos tomines de dotrina	quatro tomines de tassa	
un topo de chacara	dos tomines de dotrina	quatro tomines de tassa	
topo y medio de chacara	dos tomines de dotrina	quatro tomines de tassa	
topo y medio de chacara	quatro tomines de dotrina	un peso de tassa	
un topo de chacara	dos tomines de dotrina	quatro tomines de tassa	
topo y quarto de chacara	dos tomines de dotrina	quatro tomines de tassa	

/f.355v/

	Casados Años	*Hijos Años*	*servicio que a fecho cada yanacona*
285	Pº Quicana de los Canches veinte e siete 27 Ynes Chimima treinta—30	Pº Condor Quicallo çinco—5 Leonor Guacapuco—3 Alº Condori uno—1 Ysabel Chinbo—8	a ocho años que sirve en lo que los demas
181	Felipe Quino cañar de Tomebamba quarenta e ocho 48 Leonor Chimo Urma çinquenta e dos—52	Mª Sumachel diez y nueve—19 Anbrosio Subala 9 Lucas Nauca çinco 5	a treinta años que sirve en lo que los demas
23	Alº Sibipula cañar diez y siete—17 Catalina Toto—15	Teresa Pata doze—12 Lucas Tito çinco—5 Myguel Mayun 4 Juº Bautista Pilla 2	
233	don Diº Rimache natural del Cuzco quarenta e ocho—48 Ysavel Cusi Ynguilla çinquenta—50	Juª Mullmuca catorze—14 Diº Yarinlluclla q^{tro} 4 Ana Pachua dos 2 Agustin Yarulluclla 6	a treinta años que le sirve en beneficio de las chacaras
	Pº Machaguai guanca treinta—30 Catalina Asto treinta e tres 33	Ana Llapi dos—2 Luçia Nachac uno 1 Madalena Anas—4 Luisa Chac tres 3	a diez y ocho años que sirve en lo que los demas
186	Matheo Auris Guaillas v^{te} e ocho—28 Teresa Tocto Ocllo 23	Maria Machui tres—3	a doze años que sirve en lo que los demas
183	Matheo Chuquru Quichua naçio en este valle v^{te} e ocho 28 Mª Yanapuco—26	Françisca Zica veinte—20	a quinze años que le sirve en lo que los demas
258	Alº Quispe Yunga quarenta y ocho 48 Catalina Paico Ocllo çinquenta 50		a treinta años que le sirve en lo que los demas
382	Fran^{co} Quispe Yunga diez y siete aºs—17 Fran^{ca} Pachua—16		a un año que le sirve en beneficio de las chacaras

/f.356/

lo que le paga por el serviº	*lo que paga de dotrina*	*lo que paga de tassa*	*tiene chacaras de tassa*
topo y medio de chacara	dos tomines de dotrina	quatro tomines de tasa	
un topo de chacara	quatro tomines de dotrina	quatro tomines de tassa	
dos topos y mº de chacara	dos tomines de dotrina	quatro tomines de tasa	
medio topo de chacara	dos tomines de dotrina	quatro tomynes de tassa	tres topos de chacara de la comunidad
medio topo de chacara	dos tomines de dotrina	un peso de tassa	dos topos y medio de chacara
medio topo de chacara	dos tomines de dotrina	un peso de tassa	dos topos y medio de chacara
medio topo de chacara	dos tomines de dotrina	quatro tomines de tassa	topo y medio de chacara
medio topo de chacara	dos tomines de dotrina	quatro tomines de tassa	

/f.356v/

	Casados Años	*Hijos Años*	*servicio que a fecho cada yanacona*
167	Miguel Mataguarai quarenta 40 Ynes Rruchuc çinquenta e çinco 55		
221	P^{o} Guatalla Yunga quarenta e ocho—48 Maria Puma quarenta—40	Costança Nysuma seys—6 Diego Sulca q^{tro} 4 P^{o} Mandi dos—2	a catorze años que le sirve en lo que los demas
244	Fran^{co} Llancari quarenta—40 Ynes Angaituco çinquenta—50	Catalina Puco Chisque diez e ocho 18 Fran^{ca} Chucas Chisque quatro—4	a treinta años que le sirve en lo que los demas
245	Ju^{o} Quiquin Yanacancha veinte—20 Beatriz Llamilla diez y siete—17		a tres años que le sirve en lo que los demas
241	Matheo Rira Atavillo veinte e dos 22 Teresa Mullo veinte—20	P^{o} Macha quatro 4	a diez años que le sirve en lo que los demas
	Gonçalo Chancari de Xauxa v^{te} e çinco 25 Ysavel Chuqui 20	P^{o} Macha quatro 4	a diez años que le sirve en lo que los demas
250	P^{o} Allamari colla naçio en este valle quarenta 40 Ynes Tatachinqui çinquenta—50	Juan Prima Llulla siete 7	a diez años que le sirve en lo que los demas
251 enferma de los andes	Diego Cumismalmacha v^{te} e ocho—28 Ynes Pachua treinta e quatro 34	Madalena Chisq qtr^{o} 4 Ana Cusla dos—2 Mençia Yanachisque 1 Ju^{o} Guaman siete—7 Al^{o} Paucar çinco—5	a ocho años que le sirve en beneficio de las chacaras
84	Di^{o} Guanca colla çinquenta y ocho 58 Maria Mullo çinq^{ta} 50		a diez y seis años que le sirve en beneficio de las chacaras

/f.357/

lo que le paga por el servicio	*lo que paga de dotrina*	*lo que paga de tassa*	*tiene chacaras de tassa*
medio topo de chacara	quatro tomines de dotrina	un peso de tassa	un topo de chacara de comunidad
medio topo de chacara	dos tomines de dotrina	quatro tomines de tassa	dos topos y mi^{o} de chacara
medio topo de chacara			un topo y quarto de chacara
medio topo de chacara	dos tomines de dotrina	quatro tomines de tassa	dos topos y medio de chacara
medio topo de chacara	dos tomines de dotrina	quatro tomines de tasa	dos topos de chacara
dos topos de chacara	dos tomines de dotrina	quatro tomynes de tassa	
un topo de chacara	dos tomines de dotrina	dos tomines de tassa	
	quatro tomines de dotrina	quatro tomines de tasa	un topo de chacara

/f.357v/

	Casados Años	*Hijos Años*	*servicio que a fecho cada yanacona*
252	Agustin Camasca huydo— Catalina Chisque treinta e çinco—35	Ju^{o} Yanacamasca diez—10 P^{o} Guaman Arcos seis—6 Ana Chisque tres 3	a diez años que le sirve en lo que los demas
98	Fran^{co} Ranpa Yupangui veinte e dos—22 Leonor Zizamoho diez y ocho—18	Fran^{ca} Tapara uno—1	
	Miguel Bilcacondor Conchuco treinta 30 Costança Guchasonuc treinta e tres—33	Beatriz Llasa seis—6 Xpobal Bilcagua q[ua]tro 4 Catalina Bisnil tres 3 Di^{o} Bilcamanco dos—2	a v^{te} años que le sirve en lo que los demas
239	Simon Cusimyngo de Xaquixaguana—15 Maria Xarpa diez y ocho—18		a quatro años que le sirve en lo que los demas
245	Di^{o} Asto Camasca veinte años—20 Ju^{a} Murmocaco diez y ocho—18		
238	Martin Pomacondor treinta—30	Juan Bilcamango quatro a^{o}s 4	
84	Domingo Lalmabi çinquenta—50		a mas de quinze años que le sirve en el beneficio de las chacaras
52	Alonso Guartasaca sesenta 60		a mas de quinze años que le sirve en lo que los demas
53	Alonso Chaca sesenta años 60		sirvele mas de v^{te} años en lo que los demas

/f.358/

lo que le paga por el servicio	*lo que paga de dotrina*	*lo que paga de tassa*	*tiene chacaras de tassa*
medio topo de chacara	dos tomines de dotrina	quatro tomines de tasa	un topo de chacara
un topo de chacara de que come digo quatro de chacara	quatro tomines de dotrina	quatro tomines de tassa	
un topo de chacara	dos tomines de dotrina		topo y medio de chacara
Medio topo de chacara	dos tomines de dotrina	quatro tomines de tasa	dos topos de chacara
Medio topo de chacara	dos tomines de dotrina	quatro tomines de tassa	
Medio topo de chacara	dos tomines de dotrina	quatro tomines de tassa	
Medio topo de chacara	dos tomines de dotrina	quatro tomines de tassa	

/f.358v/

	Casados Años	*Hijos Años*	*servicio que a fecho cada yanacona*
	Pedro Chunbi çinquenta e seis—56		a doze años que le sirve en el beneficio de las chacaras
54	Antonio Saquiguari ses^{a} años 60		a diez y ocho años que le sirve en lo que los demas
55	Alonso Yngatoma ochenta a^{o}s 80		a mas de veinte años que le sirve en lo que los demas
	Ysavel Yuyo quarenta e çinco 45	P^{o} Sucobisnai diez y ocho 18 Fran^{ca} Quispechuc diez—10	a mas de doze años que le sirve en el beneficio de las chacaras
	Ynes Mullo treinta e siete años—37	Xpobal Llama Mynga ocho 8 Chuqurimache 4	a mas de ocho a^{o}s que le sirve en el beneficio de las chacaras
	Catalina Mucho çinquenta 50	Fran^{co} Ynnbayoca seis 6 Ysavel Alchuc—5 Mª Chupa diez y 7 17 Ynes Larchu nueue 9 Ynes Chucha tres 3	a mas de diez años que le sirve en lo que le mandan
	Ysavel Baichuc sesenta a^{o}s 60	Matheo Bilitana veinte años 20	a mas de diez años que le sirve en lo que los demas
	Ysavel Arai quarenta a^{o}s 40	Matheo Libilla diez—10 Mª Yngao nueue 9	a mas de ocho años que le sirve en lo que los demas
	Françisca Chuquitinta treinta a^{o}s 30	P^{o} Sibicnaul diez 10 Felipe Gasti dos—2 Ynes Latuchuc—3 Xpobal Sannay uno 1	a mas de seis años que le sirve en el beneficio de las chacaras

/f.359/

lo que le paga por el servicio	*lo que paga de dotrina*	*lo que paga de tassa*	*tiene chacaras de tassa*
medio topo de chacara	dos tomines de dotrina	quatro tomines de tassa	
medio topo de chacara	dos tomines de dotrina	quatro tomines de tassa	
medio topo de chacara	dos tomines de dotrina	quatro tomines de tasa	
medio topo de chacara	dos tomines de dotrina	quatro tomines de tasa	
medio topo de chacara	dos tomines de dotrina	quatro tomines de tasa	
medio topo de chacara	dos tomines de dotrina	quatro tomines de tasa	
un topo de chacara	dos tomines de dotrina	quatro tomines de tassa	
un topo de chacara	dos tomines de dotrina	quatro tomines de tasa	
medio topo de chacara de que come	dos tomines de dotrina	quatro tomines de tassa	

/f.359v/

	Casados Años	*Hijos Años*	*servicio que a fecho cada yanacona*
	Madalena Mollopata çinquenta 50	P^{o} Timbal ocho 8 +263+	a mas de doze años que le sirve en el beneficio de las chacaras
	Beatriz Yanai sesenta 60	Eluira Quitre treinta 30 D^{go} Yunas Sucho q^{tro} 4 Ynes Raimetiquilla—3 P^{o} Nina Yaris çinco 5 Ynes Pachua q^{tro} 4	sirve en lo que los demas
huerfanos	Ynes Yupucho çinquenta e çinco 55	Beatriz Ynacassa v^{te} años 20	a mas de diez años que le sirve en lo que le manda
	Ynes Sinchil seis 6	Maria Chibil tres años—3	Diego Laime diez y ocho 18
	Maria Guaçiçe çinquenta—50	Ynes Totozizo v^{te} e çinco 25 Her^{do} Pama dos 2 Ju^{o} Libia Carua tres 3	a mas de doze años que le sirve en lo que los demas
	Maria Caba sesenta 60	Leonor Urma diez y siete 17	a mas de quinze años que le sirve en lo que los demas
viejas	Ysavel Abicaua çinquenta e çinco 55	Ynes Paico quarenta 40	Ynes Agua çinquenta 50
	Catalina Caua sesenta a^{o}s 60	Ynes Anay çinquenta 50	Maria Ysmuchuc cinq^{ta} 50
	Leonor Pilanai sesenta años	Catalina Timinchuc ochenta 80	Leonor Quispe çinquenta 50

/f.360/

lo que le paga por el servicio	*lo que paga de dotrina*	*lo que paga de tassa*	*tiene chacaras de tassa*
medio topo de chacara	dos tomines de dotrina		
medio topo de chacara	quatro tomines de dotrina		
medio topo de chacara	quatro tomines de dotrina		
Martin Yznan quinze 15			
medio topo de chacara	quatro tomines de dotrina		
medio topo de chacara	dos tomines de dotrina		
Madalena Taipi çinquenta 50	Ynes Upiai sesenta y seis 66		
Ynes Yupucho çinquenta y çinco 55	Juana Culincaua ses^{a} 60	Ysavel Durchu sesenta 60	Ysavel Nacamuco ses^{a} 60
Leonor Tantichuc çinquenta y çinco 55	Ysavel Ynguilla quarenta 40	Leonor Guasuma çinquenta 50	Fran^{ca} Carua çinquenta 50

/f.360v/

	Casados Años	*Hijos Años*	*servicio que a fecho cada yanacona*
	Ynes Pachisque sesenta años 60	Costança Toto çinquenta 50	Ysavel Guairo Bispo çinquenta y seis 56
yanaconas de doña Ynes muger de don Fran^{co} Chilche	Martin Guanaco naçio en este valle v^{te} e çinco 25 Ana su mg v^{te} e q^{tro} 24 +187+	P^{o} Toyro tres 3 Fran^{ca} Punpa uno—1	siruiole diez y ocho años en las chacaras de coca y leña
56	Al^{o} Toyro Chilque çinq^{ta} e quatro—54 Ysavel Ponpa—54	Ynes Gaitococa çinco años 5	siruiole veinte años en lo que esta arriba
333	Alonso Cartan de Quito sesenta a^{o}s 60 Ynes Oco çinq^{ta} e ocho 58		siruiole diez y ocho años como hortelano
57	Alonso Pariguan quichua—40 Costança Udco—30	Rodrigo Patabanba un año 1	Siruiole doze años en lo que los demas
361	Xpobal Tomay de Quito treinta—30 Ynes Cata de v^{te} e ocho—28	Ju^{o} Naulabiza çinco—5 Leonor Ganaibi 4	siruiole diez y seis años en lo que los demas
335	P^{o} Yachagua de Atabilo—50 Luçia Tiquilla treinta e ocho—38		siruiole diez y ocho años de ortelano y viñadr^{o} y serv^{o} de chacaras
	P^{o} Pariguana v^{te} e çinco 25 Mª Guaro Malqui diez y seis—16		dos topos de chacara
122	Ju^{o} Chucalla Yunga de Chari setenta—70 Ysavel Tanco sesenta y seis 66		siruiole dos años en beneficialle las chacaras de mays

/f.361/

lo que le paga por el servicio	*lo que paga de dotrina*	*lo que paga de tassa*	*tiene chacaras de tassa*
Juana Paico quarenta 40			
medio topo de chacara	quatro tomines de dotrina	quatro tomines de tassa	
medio topo de chacara	dos tomines de dotrina	quatro tomines de tassa	
medio topo de chacara	dos tomines de dotrina		
un topo de chacara	dos tomines de dotrina	quatro tomines de tassa	
un topo de chacara	quatro tomines de dotrina		
medio topo de chacara	quatro tomines de dotrina	medio peso de tassa	medio topo de chacara
	quatro tomines de dotrina		
come un topo de chacara de maiz de don Françisco Chilche	dos tomines de dotrina		

/f.361v/

	Casados Años	*Hijos Años*	*servicio que a fecho cada yanacona*
228 336	Ximon Ylla Topa Cuzco quarenta e dos 42 Madalena Caua treinta a°s—30	Ynes Coa v^te 20 Ju° Ylla Topa q^tro 4 Felipe Tupa çinco 5 Angelina Toto çinco 5	siruiole diez a°s en hazerle como sus neg°s como su heredero ques
337	Ju° Uchupanta de Quito quarenta e çinco—45 Ysavel Coca Chilque—40	Cat^a Chingul diez y seis 16 Felipe Condor ocho 8 Ana Ucanchi seis 6 Leonor quatro 4	siruiole v^te años en lo que los demas
24	Al° Cuyochin natural de Lari—54 Maria Tanta çinquenta e çinco 55		siruiole diez y ocho años en las chacaras de maiz
58	Al° Marca Gualpa Chilque—50 Maria Zuchuc quarenta e seis 46	Fran^ca Torogualpa diez y ocho—18 Fran^co Chilquechuc 6 Gonçalo Marca dos—2	siruiole diez y seis años en lo que los demas
349	Al° Arosllepoma çinquenta—50 Ysavel Chucha Carua quarenta e tres 43	Ysavel Puco diez y ocho 18 Fran^co Chuquiconsa—15 Ana Guairo quatro 4 Ynes Toma dos—2 M^a/ 5 / Martin/ 6/ Mençia 3	siruiole diez años en el beneficio de las chacaras
168	Martin Tutamali cañar sesenta 60 Ysavel Ynguillai çinquenta—50	Ysavel Caua veinte 20	siruiole diez años en lo que los demas
352	Xpobal Siguaman de Maras set^a 70 Ysavel Ynguillai 58		siruiole v^te años en lo que le manda
348	Xpobal Chaucari Chilque v^te e çinco 25 Madalena Yunchu treinta e dos—32	Andres Churiagualpa çinco—5 Ysavel Sacacoca tres 3	Siruiole diez y seis años en lo que los demas
	Costança Malqui diez y ocho—18	siruiole de china diez años	

/f.362/

lo que le paga por el servicio	*lo que paga de dotrina*	*lo que paga de tasa*	*tiene chacaras de tasa*
medio topo de chacara otro topo de don Francisco Chilche	medio peso de dotrina		
un topo de chacara	dos tomines de dotrina	dos tomines de tassa	
un topo de chacara			
topo y quarto de chacara	dos tomines de dotrina	quatro tomines de tassa	
topo y medio de chacara	dos tomines de dotrina		
medio topo de chacara de don Fran^co Chilche			
tres quartos de chacara			
topo y medio de chacara			
medio topo de chacara de que come			

/f.362v/

	Casados Años	*Hijos Años*	*servicio que a fecho cada yanacona*
565	Maria Quato sesenta—60		Siruiole en el benefº de las chacaras
	Ysavel Rimai çinquenta—50		Siruiole veinte años en lo que los demas
	Maria Ruconanbo sesenta años 60		siruiole veinte años en lo que los demas
	Beatriz Yngastoco quarenta—40	Ysavel Colqueyaco 17 Martin Casa siete—7 Juº Andiauca çinco 5	siruiole vte años en el beneficio de las chacaras
	Leonor Yncassa çinqta y seis aºs 56		siruiole vte años en el benefiº de las chacaras
	Ynes Urmacoca treinta e quarto 34	Franco Pauchaqui Tinta quarto—4 Lucia Ochochuco tres—3	siruiole un año en lo que le mando

/f.363/

lo que le paga por el servicio	*lo que paga de dotrina*	*lo que paga de tassa*	*tiene chacaras de comunydad*
medio topo de chacara			
un topo de chacara			
tres quartos de topo			
mº topo de chacara			
tres quartos de topo			
un topo de chacara de don Franco Chilche			

/f.363v/

	Casados Años	*Hijos Años*	*servicio que a fecho cada yanacona*
26	Agustin Chuquiapa de sesenta años 60	Maria Chuquilla de treinta 30	a v^{te} años que le sirve en el beneficio de las chacaras
viejas	Ysavel Nacai sesenta años 60	Maria Milanc Pucta sesenta a^{o}s 60	Maria Yuyo çinquenta 50
yanaconas de don Her^{do} Guartanaule	Ju^{o} Bautista Duisu cañar naçio en este valle v^{te} e siete—27 Leonor Caba v^{te} e ocho 28 +359+	Fran^{co} Zachi çinco a^{o}s 5 Agustin Nylasia—4 Teresa Chubai—2	a diez años que le sirve en el beneficio de las chacaras
360	Martin Ninapoma Acanche quarenta—40 Beatriz Colqui treinta 30	Diego Nacuri tres 3	a que le sirve treze años en el benef^{o} de las chacaras de maiz
123	Ju^{o} Calco de Nasca çinquenta e seis 56 Cat^{a} Achara treinta e seis—36	Bautista Callapilla tres a^{o}s 3	a v^{te} años que sirve a a padre y a hijo en todo lo que le mandan
334	Xpobal Tomaillacancha naçio en este valle veinte e seis—26 Beatriz Chicho treinta 30	Felipe Tutanzila seis años—6 Maria Machuc dos—2	a onze años que le sirve en lo que los demas
363	Lucas Chuquicondor Yayocondor veinte 20 Leonor Ocllo veinte 20		a diez años que le sirve en lo que los demas
362	Ju^{o} Chuquicaroche naçio en este valle diez y seis—16 Costança Chinbo—15		esta con su padre y come con el
viejas	Ana Yachin çinq^{ta} a^{o}s 50	Françisco Chimche Sinple diez y ocho años—18 +404+	a mucho tiempo que sirve a el y a sus padres

/f.364/

lo que la paga por el servicio	*lo que paga de dotrina*	*lo que paga de tassa*	*tiene chacaras de tassa*
medio topo de chacara	quatro tomines de dotrina		un topo de chacara de comunidad
Maria Suaychu çinquenta e çinco 55	Leonor Guanai sesenta—60		
Topo y m^{o} de chacara de que come	quatro tomines de dotrina		
Topo y medio de chacara de que come	quatro tomines de dotrina		
un topo de chacara de que come	quatro tomines de dotrina		
un topo de chacara de que come	quatro tomines de dotrina		
un topo de chacara de que come	quatro tomines de dotrina		

/f.364v/

	Casados Años	*Hijos Años*	*serviº que a fecho cada yanacona*
	Ynes Guanpa çinquenta aºs 50	Juª Caruamaca catorze años—14 Ysabel Chuquitanta siete 7	a ocho años que le sirve en las chacaras
	Ana Malqui quarenta y ocho 48	Juª Caruamaca catorze años—14 Ysabel Chucotanta—7	a ocho años que le sirve en lo que los demas
	Ana Altay sesenta aºs 60	Juana Carbabanca—15	a diez años que le sirve en lo que los demas
	Catalina Quinque çinquenta e quatro 54	Maria Chuquirima Sinple diez y nueve 19	a diez años que le sirve en el benefº de las chacaras
	Leonor Guallimachi çinquenta—50	Catalina Chirchuc quinze—15	a diez años que le sirve en lo que los demas
viejas	Catalina Poco sesenta años—60	Elvira Chupai setenta 70	
huerfanos	Miguel Chiles de seys años 6	Paulo Pomacondor quinze 15 +372+	Fran^{co} Maytapangui ocho 8
72 yanaconas de don Alº Tito Atauche	Diº Gamini Quito quarenta años 40 Beatriz Pilcochuc çinquenta e dos 52		a que le sirve v^{te} e quatro años en las chacaras de maiz y Coca
39	Alonso Condor Quichua naçio en este valle 20		a çinco años que le sirve en las chacaras y en lo demas que le ocupa

/f.365/

lo que le paga por el servicio	*lo que paga de dotrina*	*lo que paga de tassa*	*tiene chacaras de tassa*
medio topo de chacara			
un quarto de chacara de que come			
medio topo de chacara de que come			
Xpobal Cuyo Topa seys 6	Alº Tomayauri ocho—8 +10+	Angelina Yuyococo çinco—5	
dos topo y medio de chacara	seys tomines de dotrina		medio topo de chacara de comunidad
tres topos de chacara	seys tomines de dotrina		

/f.365v/

	Casados Años	*Hijos Años*	*servicio que a fecho cada yanacona*
92	Fran^{co} Quipaya diez y ocho años—18 Madalena Asto 18	Ju^{o} Bautista Bilcarache uno—1	
373	Agustin Sulcatocas Chinchaysuyu v^{te} e ocho 28 Cat^{a} Nachuquitinta quarenta—40		a diez años que le sirve en lo que los demas
	Ju^{o} Malqui Delanco naçio en este valle v^{te} e q^{tro} 24 Ysabel Chinbo Coca—29		A diez años que le sirve en lo que los demas
378	Fran^{co} Llasa Yupan Guanca çinquenta—50 Ynes Machullasa quarenta—40	Madalena Antaycarua seis—6 P^{o} Puma Yupan—5 Lucas Sulcai—4 Ana Caran Carua dos—2	A quatro años que le sirve en lo que los demas
380	Fran^{co} Guayausco natural de Sora v^{te} e tres 23 Ynes Sasachinbi diez y nueve—19	Ju^{o} Usco uno—1 Madalena Auca dos 2 Ysabel Poco uno—1	a diez años que le sirve en lo que los demas
59	Alonso Usco de Sora de çinquenta—50 Leonor Gallanachu çinquenta—50	Martin Paya Usco diez 10 Ysabel Chunbi siete 7 Al^{o} Quispi seis—6 Miguel Llamoca—5 Madalena Asto—18	a quinze años que le sirve en lo que los demas
381	P^{o} Tinta de Quito naçio en este valle quarenta e dos—42 Ynes Pachua—30	Lucas Paitan tres—3	a diez y seis años que le sirve en lo que los demas
383	Alonso Cono Yupari Guanca naçio en este valle v^{te} e çinco—25 Catalina Yacocarua v^{te} e q^{tro} 24	Maria Carua Chapia quatro—4 Cat^{a} Una dos—2 Ana Chaicotanta uno 1	a diez años que le sirve en lo que los demas
384	Agustin Condori Guanca naçio en este valle quarenta y seis—46 Ana Yachi—40	Felipe Condorcochachi dos a^{o}s 2	a veinte años que le sirve en lo que los demas

/f.366/

lo que le paga por el servi^{o}	*lo que paga de dotrina*	*lo que paga de tassa*	*tiene chacaras de tassa*
tres topos de chacara	seys tomines de dotrina		
dos topos de chacara	seys tomines de dotrina		
dos topos de chacara de que come	seys tomines de dotrina	tres quartillas de mays de tassa	
medio topo de chacara de que come	seis tomines de dotrina	tres quartillas de maiz	
un topo de chacara de que come	tres tomines de dotrina	tres quartillas de maiz	un topo de chacara de comunidad
topo y medio de chacara de que come	seis tomines de dotrina	tres quartillas de mayz	
topo y medio de chacara de que come	medio peso de dotrina	peso y medio de tassa	
un topo de chacara de que come	seys tomines de dotrina	tres quartillas de mayz	un topo de chacara

/f.366v/

	Casados Años	*Hijos Años*	*servicio que a fecho cada yanacona*
60	Andres Caruapisco guanca naçio en este valle v^{te} e dos—22 Leonor Murmochoo diez y siete—17		a diez años que le sirve en lo que los demas
165	mateo Ataganca naçio en este valle v^{te} 20 Ju^{a} Aque v^{te} e dos 22	Marcos Mayanchuc dos—2	a que le sirve cinco años en lo que los demas
387	Al^{o} Muquiguaya Condor sesenta e dos 62 Maria Sacachunbi çinquenta—50		a diez años que le sirve en lo que los demas
388	Andres Auquis Yupari diez e nueve 19 Maria Llamimayba veinte e uno—21	Ana Chaicotanta uno 1	a tres años que le sirve en lo que los demas
389	Martin Curagua de Sora veinte e çinco—25 Leonor Quispe v^{te} e dos 22		a nueve años que le sirve en lo que los demas
392	Alonso Pilpe ~~guande naçio en este valle~~ de Atabilo çinquenta 50 Leonor Culquilla $çinq^{ta}$ 50		a diez años que le sirve en lo que los demas
	Martin Quispi Guanca naçio en este valle treinta—30 Teresa Yachi v^{te} e çinco 25	Madalena Ayarotanta—4 Ju^{o} Mirano Quispe dos 2 Lucas Yaropari—1	a diez años que le sirve en lo que los demas
394	Martin Guanaco Yanaguara sesenta e nueve 69 Juana Uma $çinq^{ta}$ e seis 56		a diez años que le sirve en lo que los demas
	Juan Aysma Ancara sesenta—60 Ynes Quispe de sesenta y seis 66		a diez años que le sirve en lo que los demas

/f.367/

lo que le paga por el servicio	*lo que paga de dotrina*	*lo que paga de tassa*	*tiene chacaras de tassa*
tres quartos de topo de que come	seis tomines de dotrina		
medio topo de chacara de que come	seys tomines de dotrina		
un topo de chacara de que come		çinco quartillas de mayz	
	quatro tomines de dotrina	tres quartillas de mayz	media chacara de comunidad
topo y medio de chacara de que come	quatro tomines de dotrina	tres quartillas de maiz	
tres topos de chacara de que come	seys tomines de dotrina	tres quartillas de maiz	
un topo de chacara de que come	seys tomines de dotrina	tres quartillas de mayz	
	quatro tomines de dotrina	una quartillas de maiz	un topo de chacara de comunidad
	seys tomines de dotrina	tres quartillas de mayz	topo y medio de chacara de comunidad

/f.367v/

	Casados Años	*Hijos Años*	*servicio que a fecho cada yanacona*
392	Domingo Pumaruco diez y seis años—16 Leonor Tiquillamaca diez y seis—16		
395	P^{o} Poma Guaman Yanaguara naçio en este valle treinta—30 Ynes Parinquisco—30	Agustin Pumaguara seis 6 Ynes Caquiapuco seis 6 Ju^{o} Aucocalaco quatro—4 Ysabel Carua tres 3 Ysabel Guamanchuqui 3	a diez años que le sirve en lo que los demas
398	Juan Bautista Naupa Chigoya Condur ses^{a} 60 Costança Puyanchuco çinquenta y seis 56	Catalina Panya v^{te} 20 Juan Bautista Guachiquinanco 15	a quinze años que le sirve en lo que los demas
	Xpobal Binta de Condesuyo veinte e siete 27 Françisca Coca Chinbo 36	Luzia Ayache tres—3 Ysabel Santasul—6 Françisca Machinbo dos—2 Xpobal Sibinta—8	a çinco años que le sirve en lo que los demas
400	Juan Bilcas Pariguana yunga veinte a^{o}s 20 Françisca Causica—20	Ysabel Yayo Quispe uno 1	a un año que le sirve en lo que los demas
	Alonso Guaman de Xaquixaguana diez y ocho—18 Cat^{a} Sulcayman diez y ocho 18	Juana Cusiyuguilla uno 1	a quatro años que le sirve en lo que los demas
188	Martin Malta del Cuzco quarenta y ocho a^{o}s 48 Ysabel Lasto çinq^{ta}—50	Juan Bautista Pascamaira diez 10	a que le sirve diez y seis años en lo que los demas
403	Ju^{o} Camachairac quichua veinte—20 Maria Ropo diez y nueve 19		a dos años que le sirve en lo que los demas
404	Xpobal Painalluco de Xaquixaguana çinqu^{ta} 50 Ana Yachi çinq^{ta} e q^{tro} 54		a diez años que le sirve en lo que los demas

/f.368/

lo que le paga por el servicio	*lo que paga de dotrina*	*lo que paga de tassa*	*tiene chacaras de comunidad*
un topo de chacara de que come			
un topo de chacara de que come	seys tomines de dotrina	tres quartillas de mayz	dos topos de chacara de comunidad
	seys tomines de dotrina	tres quartillas de maiz	tres topos y m^{o} de chacara de comunidad
topo y medio de chacara	seys tomines de dotrina	tres quartillas de maiz	
	seys tomines de dotrina	tres quartillas de maiz	un topo de chacara de comunidad
dos topos de chacara	seys tomines de dotrina		
	seys tomines de dotrina	tres quartillas de maiz	tres topos de chacara de comunidad
	seys tomines de dotrina		
	seys tomines de dotrina	tres quartillas de maiz	tres topos de chacara de comunidad

/f.368v/

	Casados Años	*Hijos Años*	*serviº que a fecho cada yanacona*
405	Alº Pana de Xaquixaguana treinta e seis 36 Madalena Quispi treinta—30	Gº Paucar Aymara—3 Alº Para uno—1 Fran^{co} Cusi Chinbo—18 Juan Bautista Gualpa Urco—17	a diez años que le sirve en lo que los demas
406	Alº Aycaipuro de Xaquixaguana v^{te} e dos 22 Ysabel Coca Chinbo veinte e dos—22	Luzia Chinbo Urma dos—2 Juº Atallaico uno—1	a dos años que le sirve en lo que los demas
407	Domingo Bilca Collagua quarenta—40 Luzia Cocanco treinta e tres—33	Juº Bautista Pangui treinta y siete 37 Miguel Guagayanque—5 Ximon Chara diez 10	a diez años que le sirve en lo que los demas
102	Fran^{co} Chuchaguaman Quichua v^{te} e çinco—25 Ana Chin viuda—	Juan Llasa Chunbi uno—1	a diez años que le sirve en lo que los demas
140	Juº Cochachi Guanca naçio en este valle quarenta—40 Ysabel Ocllo quarenta y seis—46	Xpobal Naupari siete—7 Juan Cochachin çinco—5	a diez y seis años que le sirve en lo que los demas
411	Pº Ananba Guaylas naçio en este valle v^{te} e ocho 28 Leonor Cuya treinta 30	Juº Libia Ananpa dos—2	a diez años que le sirve en lo que los demas
412	Domingo Arobilca Yunga naçio en este valle veinte e tres 23 Juª Chinbo Urma qua^{ta} 40	Angelina Cusi Ocllo çinco—5	un topo de chacara de que come
413	Fran^{co} Yanac de Atabillo naçio en este valle veinte e çinco—25 Ynes Chunbi treinta e çinco 35	Domingo Cospa hijo della—8	a diez años que le sirve en lo que los demas
414	Diº Amaro de Lari sesª 60 Leonor Chachama sesenta—60		un quarto de topo de chacara

/f.369/

lo que le paga por el servicio	*lo que paga de dotrina*	*lo que paga de tassa*	*tiene chacaras de comunidad*
	seys tomines de dotrina	tres quartillas de maiz	tres topos de chacara de comunidad
	seys tomines de dotrina		medio topo de chacara
	seys tomines de dotrina	tres quartillas de mayz	Dos topos y mº de chacara
	seys tomines de dotrina	tres quartillas de mayz	dos topos y medio de chacara
	seys tomines de dotrina	tres quartillas de maiz	dos topos de chacara
medio topo de chacara	seys tomines de dotrina	tres quartillas de maiz	medio topo de chacara
	seys tomines de dotrina		
topo y medio de chacara	seys tomines de dotrina	tres quartillas de maiz	
	dos tomines de dotrina		

/f.369v/

	Casados Años	*Hijos Años*	*servicio que a fecho cada yanacona*
35	Al^{o} Machaguai de los Conchucos veinte e çinco—25 Frančisca Liz v^{te} e q^{tro} 24	P^{o} Caruayana uno—1	a diez años que le sirve en lo que los demas
416	Martin Cabascanco de Quito setenta—70 Ysabel Cusla ses^{a} 60	Al^{o} Cocabascanco veinte e çinco tullido—25	a diez y seis años que le sirve en lo que los demas
189	Martin Bilca Ancara naçio en ~~este valle~~ Vilcabanba v^{te} e quatro 24 Mª Coca Anco v^{te} e tres 23	Agustin Yabeicopa çinco—5 P^{o} Guacache uno 1	
viejas	Beatriz Ganache çinquenta—50	Ynes Ayquipa sinple diez y seis—16	a v^{te} años que le sirve en el benef^{o} de las chacaras
	Ynes Santo çinquenta 50		a diez años que le sirve en el benef^{o} de las chacaras
	Leonor Yarutiqui sesenta—60	Juan Manta diez y ocho—18	a nueve años que le sirve en lo que los demas
	Maria Yuyococo çinquenta—50		tiene quatro topos de chacaras suyos
	Ysabel Usica sesenta y seis 66	Ysabel Bispacallo quarenta 40	a que le sirve quinze años en lo que los demas
	Costança Tanco sesenta y q^{tro} 64	Catalina Yacolqui v^{te} 20	a quinze años que le sirve en lo que los demas

/f.370/

lo que le paga por el servicio	*lo que paga de dotrina*	*lo que paga de tassa*	*tiene chacaras de comunidad*
un topo de chacara	seys tomines de dotrina	tres quartillas de maiz	dos topos de chacara
	quatro tomines de dotrina	media fanega de maiz	tres topos y quarto de chacara
	quatro tomines de dotrina	media fanega de maiz quatro p^{o}s en plata	topo y m^{o} de chacara
medio topo de chacara de que come			
un topo de chacara de que come			
un topo de chacara de que come			
			m^{o} topo de chacara de comunydad
			m^{o} topo de chacara de comunydad

/f.370v/

	Casados Años	*Hijos Años*	*servi^{o} que a fecho cada yanacona*
	Ana Tito Acan sesenta—60		a çinco años que le sirve en lo que los demas
	Ysabel Paico çinquenta e çinco años—55		a que sirve quinze años en lo que los demas
	Catalina Chinbo çinquenta e çinco a^{o}s 55	Catalina Quipi veinte e seis—26 Juliana Tiquillameta quatro—4	a que sirve quinze años en lo que los demas
93	Françisco Rimache quarenta—40 Juana Chuquna quarenta—40	Maria Curimalqui seis años—6	
172	Myguel Tiquilla chaupas ses^{a} a^{o}s 60	Juan Rimache veinte e çinco 25 Juan Bautista Collagua diez y ocho 18	a que le sirve quinze años en el benef^{o} de las chacaras y en lo demas que le manda
94	Fran^{co} Ynara çinq^{ta} e quatro—54		
viejas	Fran^{ca} Ynacasa çinquenta—50	Ysabel Chuqui çinquenta—5	Ysabel Chinbo sesenta—60
	Ana Mancopachua setenta 70	Madalena Murmo quinze—15	Ysabel Lasto çinquenta—50
	Beatriz Maibai çinquenta e çinco 55	Ynes Maca sesenta e çinco 65	

/f.371/

lo que le paga por el servicio	*lo que paga de dotrina*	*lo que paga de tasa*	*tiene chacaras de tassa*
un topo de chacara de que come			
medio topo de chacara de que come			
medio topo de chacara de que come			
Un topo de chacara			
Luzia Chimchu sinple v^{te} e dos 22	Beatriz Chuqui Ocllo çinq^{ta} 50	Ynes Tallei çinquenta 50	Leonor Carua çinquenta e çinco—55
	Ysabel Guacoma çinquenta e çinco 55	Ynes Carua çinquenta 50	Leonor Murmo çinq^{ta} e çinco 55
Ynes Binas sesenta 60	Ana Culpo sesenta 60	Costança Tuta sesenta 60	Ynes Toto Coca cinq^{ta} 50

/f.371v/

	Casados Años	*Hijos Años*	*servicio que a fecho cada yanacona*
	Ynes Urma Coca sesenta 60	Françisca Chan çinquenta 50	Ynes Quillaco sesenta—60
yanaconas del canonigo Juº de Beres	Juº Calas quarenta 40 Ynes Libia Chimbi çinquenta e tres 53	Domingo Carvache uno—1	a tres meses que le sirve sirvio a doña Angelina veinte aºs en las chacaras
	Xpobal Guarco Yauyo çinquenta e seis 56 Leonor Andicarua çinquenta e çinco 55		el mesmo servicio quel de arriba
	Felipe Mullo Guanaco de Sora treinta e ocho 38 Maria Mancocaco 30	Beatriz Billachima 6 Pº Ancasguarcai 4 Diego Sulcamullo Guanaco tres aºs 3	el mesmo servicio quel de arriba
376	Juº Asturimache de Sora diez y ocho—18 Juana Paico Ciça veinte e dos—22		tres meses de serviºs al canonigo nueve años a Betanços
	Diego Guancare de Sora veinte—20 Leonor Chinbo Coca diez y nueve—19	Maria Asto Guayla uno 1	tres meses al dho canonigo y ocho de serviº a Betanços
	Alº Llasaguaman Guaca quarenta 40 Luisa Yuyo treinta e dos—32	Leonor Yariquispa catorze—14 Catª Murmo Quispa quatro—4 Sebastian Gualca Guaman 2	tres meses de serviº al canonigo diez y ocho años a doña Angelina y a su hijo
	Diego Chapas Guanca veinte e çinco—25 Ynes Chinbo Coca veinte e quatro 24	Ynes Chunbi quatro—4 Diº Llasaguaman uno 1	el mesmo serviº que el de arriba
176	Martin Curo del Cuzco quarenta—40 Barbola Tacamo treinta e seis 36	Juº Yupangui quatro—4 Luzia Toto çinco 5 Madalena Aca uno 1	el mesmo serviº que los demas

/f.372/

lo que le paga por el serviº	*Lo que paga de dotrina*	*lo que paga de tassa*	*tiene chacaras de comunidad*
Ysabel Sora Toto sesenta 60	Ysabel Tiquillase sesenta 60		
medio topo de chacara	medio peso de dotrina		un quarto de chacara de comunidad
medio topo de chacara	dos tomines de dotrina		
medio topo de chacara	quatro tomines de dotrina		un topo de chacara
medio topo de chacara		quatro tomines de dotrina	medio topo de chacara
medio topo de chacara	quatro tomines de dotrina		
medio topo de chacara	quatro tomines de dotrina		
medio topo de chacara	medio peso de dotrina		
medio topo de chacara	quatro tomines de dotrina		

/f.372v/

	Casados Años	*Hijos Años*	*servi^{o} que a fecho cada yanacona*
	Martin Carua Sulca sesenta años 60 Ysabel Chaupi Carua quarenta e çinco—45	Françisca Carua Yana nueve—9	el mesmo servicio que los demas
viejas	Ynes Ninachinbi sesenta 60	Elena Carua Chuqui sesenta 60	Leonor Coya ochenta—80
yanaconas de don Felipe Ylla topa 204	P^{o} Guanca Capoma Yanacondo cinq^{ta} e quatro—54 Ysabel Yuyo quarenta e çinco—45	Ysabel Asto seys—6 P^{o} Guancapoma q^{tro} 4	a que le sirve quarenta años en lo que le manda
124	Ju^{o} Suno Yupangui del Cuzco diez y seis 16 Cat^{a} Chinbo Coca—32		esta con el desde que naçio
125 427	Ju^{o} Aucagualpa de Canche quarenta e dos—42 Cat^{a} Chinboco—32	Domingo Gualpa—5 Lucas Chuchaguaman quatro 4 Ju^{o} Abeagualpa dos 2	a que le sirve v^{te} años en el benef^{o} de las chacaras y en lo que le manda
490	Ju^{o} Topa Yupangui del Cuzco quarenta e çinco 45 Costança Purichinbo veinte e seis—26		a que le sirve quatro años en lo que los demas
286	P^{o} Mallai Curi Guanca v^{te} e siete—27 Maria Coca Guauni quarenta—40		a quatro años que sirve en lo que los demas
169	Martin Naupo de Caicai sesenta—60 Leonor Aulasanto sesenta—60		
	Catalina Toto Ocllo çinquenta y ocho 58	Ysabel Paico Ocllo treinta años 30	a mucho tiempo que le sirve en lo que le manda

/f.373/

lo que le paga por el servicio	*lo que paga de dotrina*	*lo que paga de tassa*	*tiene chacaras de tassa*
medio topo de chacara	quatro tomines de dotrina		
un topo de chacara	dos tomines de dotrina		
un topo de chacara	quatro tomines de dotrina		
un topo de chacara	quatro tomines de dotrina		
un topo de chacara	quatro tomines de dotrina		
un topo de chacara	quatro tomines de dotrina		
tres quartos de chacara	seys tomines de dotrina		
un topo de chacara			

/f.373v/

	Casados Años	*Hijos Años*	*servi° que a fecho cada yanacona*
	Maria Sasa sesenta años 60	Ju° Machac uno 1 Catalina Chinbo Ocllo quatro 4	
de don Felipe Topa 74	Diego Machacaua Colla v^te^ años 20 Madalena Naquilla Chinbo veinte 20		a diez años que le sirve en el beneficio de las chacaras
	Ynes Yaurichinbi çinquenta a°s 50	Ana Gualli siete—7	
yanaconas de Di° de Truxillo	don Diego Paucar Calpa de Lari çinq^ta^ 50 Costança Guacalli quarenta e çinco 45	Costança Gualli uno—1 P° Paucar Quispe dos a°s 2	a treinta a°s que le sirve de azerrar madera
341	P° Paucar de Lari naçio en este valle 18 Leonor Gualcayachaca diez y ocho—18	Alonso Quispe çinco 5 Martin Mucha q^tro^—4 Diego casados dos—2	
397	Martin Quispe Yunga treinta e çinco—35 Beatriz Aybi treinta e çinco—35		
	Al° Punacuca de Lari çinq^ta^ e siete—57 Ynes Chinbo treinta e tres—33		
	G° Tomailla Quichua çinquenta e çinco 55 Costança Ninti çinquenta y seis—56		a quinze años que le sirve en llevalle leña

/f.374/

lo que le paga por el servicio	*lo que paga de dotrina*	*lo que paga de tassa*	*tiene chacaras de comunidad*
un topo de chacara	quatro tomines de dotrina		
			tres topos y medio de chacara de la comunidad en llamac
			topo y medio de chacara en llamac
			dos topos de chacara de comunidad
			dos topos de chacara de la comunidad
			topo y medio de chacara de la comunidad

/f.374v/

	Casados Años	*Hijos Años*	*servi^{o} que a fecho cada yanacona*
	Martin Pariguana quichua quarenta e q^{tro} 44 Ynes Chunbi—40	Fran^{ca} Quispi /borroso/—8 Ana Bilca Chunbi—5 Al^{o} Asto Rima—4 Cat^{a} Ysla—20 Luzia Chunbi diez y ocho 18	a veinte años que le sirve de darle leña
	Miguel Pungo Lari sesenta—60 Ysabel Ana Chuqui çinquenta y ocho—58	Ana Sasi sinple nueve a^{o}s 9	a doze años que le syrue en lo que los demas
	Diego Yana de Guailas quarenta y ocho—48 Maria Tiquilla Chinbo—30	Angelina Carua Llaosa çinco—5 Maria Quiquin Carua uno—1	
79	Diego Chatan de Quito treinta—30 Mª Gualli v^{te} e dos—22	Domingo Chinba tres 3 Madalena Uco uno—1	
	Ju^{o} Quicana Quichua veinte e ocho—28 Ana Pachulla treinta 30		a tres años que le syrue de darle leña y en lo demas que le manda
551	Martin Usco Quichua çinquenta e ocho—58 Costança Carua ses^{a} 60		a quatro años que le sirve en lo que los demas
viejos	Isabel Carua ses^{a} 60	Costança Condor Chisque seis 6	a que le sirve quinze años en lo que los demas
	Ysabel Malqui quarenta e q^{tro} 44		a que le sirve diez años en lo que la manda
	Beatriz Zacha çinq^{ta} 50	Fran^{ca} Sasa Chunbi seis 6	a que le sirve quinze años en lo que le manda

/f.375/

lo que le paga por el servicio	*lo que paga de dotrina*	*lo que paga de tassa*	*tiene chacaras de comunidad*
			dos topos de chacara de comunidad
			un topo de chacara de la comunidad
			dos topos de chacara de la comunydad
			dos topos de chacara de la comunidad
			un topo de chacara de la comunidad
			un topo de chacara de la comunidad
			dos topos de chacara
			un topo de chacara

/f.375v/

	Casados Años	*Hijos Años*	*servicio que a fecho cada yanacona*
de don Felipe 64	Baltasar Ancas sesenta—60	Maria Tiquilla diez y seis—16 Pº Mibichuc diez 10	a veinte años que le sirve en lo que le manda
de don Diego Acamaqui 29	Alonso Quispi çinquenta—50	Maria Callinbo treinta—30	a dos años que le sirve de guardar ganado
127	Juan Uchapilco sesenta e çinco 65	Ynes Astollasa ocho—8	a que le sirve de salinero treinta años
de don Alº Ucusicha 198	Pº Chuqui Condur Guaylla naçio en este valle—30 Ynes Caba—30	Catª Sumai Chinbo siete 7 Costança Chinbo çinco 5 Ana Chinbo Coca quatro 4 Mª Coca tres—3 Ysabel Yuya Chinbo dos—2 Juª Coca Ynguilla onze—11	a veinte años que le sirve en el beneficio de las chacaras
75	Diego Alpauqui de Maras quarenta e tres 43 Ynes Sumaycoca—40	Angelina Coca tres—3	a treinta años que le sirve en el beneficio de las chacaras y de dalle yerua y leña
205	Pº Auqui de Maras veinte años 20 Luzia Yanqui Guairo vte e tres 23	Angelina Chinbo Coca treinta e seis 36	
170	Marcos Auqui de Maras ochenta—80 Maria Coca setª 70	Ynes Mallco quatro—4 Martin Yanac uno—1	a treinta años que le sirve en el beneficio de las chacaras
434	Santiago Yanca de Guanuco treinta e çinco—35 Ynes Cocha treinta e çinco 35		a veinte años que sirve en lo que los demas
206 435	Pº Pacha de Xaquixaguana treinta e dos—34 Leonor Cusi Chinbo 37	Angelina Cusi Ynguillai quatro—4 Ynes Sumai Quilla dos 2 Alonso Pachatauca enfermo çinco—5	a veinte años que le sirve en lo que los demas

/f.376/

lo que le paga por el servicio	*lo que paga de dotrina*	*lo que paga de tassa*	*tiene chacaras de comunidad*
un quarto de topo de chacara			
cinco topos de chacara			
seys topos de chacara	seys tomines de dotrina		
tres topos de chacara	seys tomines de dotrina		
dos topos y mº de chacara	seys tomines de dotrina		
çinco topos de chacara			
quatro topos de chacara	seys tomines de dotrina		
	seys tomines de dotrina		

/f.376v/

	Casados Años	Hijos Años	servi° que a fecho cada yanacona
171	Martin Carua Yana de Guaillas—24 Ynes Cusi Chinbo veinte—20	Juª Chapa uno 1	a quinze años que le sirve en lo que los demas
385	Andres Carua Yanac çinquenta 50 Ana Quipi quᵗᵃ e dos 42		a diez años que le sirve en lo que los demas
95	Franᶜᵒ Casaqnaman de Atabilos diez e ocho 18 Madalena Casa Carua diez e nueve—19		a çinco años que le sirve en lo que los demas
440	Sebastian Cusi Yncca de Xaquixaguana treinta e ocho—38 Ynes Yaro—40	Ynes Coca Ynguillai 8 Catalina Chuque Ynguillay qᵗʳᵒ 4	a treinta años que le sirve en lo que los demas
	Jerᵐᵒ Yucra Pilco de Xaquixaguana diez e ocho—18 Maria Cusi Chinbo 16		
120	Ju° Cai de Tanbocochа treinta e tres—33 Maria Coca treinta e çinco—35	Catalina Coca siete 7 Ju° Cay seis—6 Mª Chunbo Urma 4 Ana Coca Tasmi 4	a diez y ocho a°s que le sirve en lo que los demas
439	G° Pomagualpa de Xaquixaguana diez y seis—16 Ynes Toto catorze 14		
443	Felipe Guaman Angara veinte e tres 23 Françisca Sasi veinte e siete 27		
27	Alonso Calchipulla Cañar treinta e ocho—38 Madalena Aucabo quarenta—40	Franᶜᵃ Naschu—5 Leonor Durcho 4 Ana Sulla Sumachuc uno—1	a dos años que le sirve en el benef° de las chacaras y mas de leña

/f.377/

lo que le paga por el servicio	lo que paga de dotrina	lo que paga de tassa	tiene chacaras de comunidad
tres topos y medio de chacara	seys tomines de dotrina		
por questa enfermo le quito la chacara que le dio.	medio peso de dotrina	un peso y una fanega de maiz	topo y medio de chacara
quatro topos de chacara	quatro tomines de dotrina		
tres topos y m° de chacara	seys tomines de dotrina		
tres topos y medio de chacara	seys tomines de dotrina		
çinco topos de chacara	seys tomines de dotrina		
	quatro tomines de dotrina		
	quatro tomines de dotrina		

/f.377v/

	Casados Años	*Hijos Años*	*servi° que a fecho cada yanacona*
	Catalina Tiquilla Yaro quarenta y seis—46	Benito Guaman ocho—8 Catalina Llasa onze—11	
	Angelina Tanta quarenta e nuebe 49		Sirve en el beneficio de las chacaras
	Ana Panpai treinta y ocho—años 38		a que le sirve diez años en el beneficio de las chacaras
viejas	Ynes Bispa sesª 60	G° Macho bobo y tonto [*sic*] vᵗᵉ e dos 22	
	Ynes Sana çinquenta e çinco 55	Maria Carua setenta años 70	Ynes Capa çinquenta 50
	Ynes Chinbo sesª 60 Agustin Sanbo Vayocondor sesenta e çinco—65 Catª Pasna sesenta 60	Leonor Poma Carua ochenta a°s 80	
yanaconas de Al° de Tapia 444	Xpobal Mutitu Yupangui Cuzco quarenta e çinco 45 Ynes Malqui 38	Teresa Yuyo Coca 15 Ysabel Sicallo 7 luzia Toto Ocllo—4 Lucas Tito Yupangui 2 Xpobal Quispi—1 Catª Cusibimai—8	a quatro años que le sirve en el beneficio de las chacaras
445	Diego Tupa Yupangui del Cuzco diez y ocho 18 Catalina Yacho vᵗᵉ y seis 26	Pascual Cutigualpa uno—1	a dos años que le sirve en el beneficio de las chacaras
292	Al° Quispi Yunga veinte e tres 23 Catª Siminchuc quinze—15	Felipe Raopariona de veinte e çinco 25 sobre si se a de sacar	a quatro años que le sirve en lo que los demas

/f.378/

lo que le paga por el servicio	*lo que paga de dotrina*	*lo que paga de tasa*	*servi° que a fecho cada yanacona*
topo y medio de chacara			
Madalena Mitata sesª años 60	Ynes Chinbo sesenta 60	Leonor Ytao sesenta 60	Ysabel Yurique sesª—60
un topo de chacara			
un topo de chacara			
topo y m° de chacara			

/f.378v/

	Casados Años	*Hijos Años*	*servi^{o} que a fecho cada yanacona*
viejas	Maria Quilla çinquenta a^{o}s 50	Alonso Sulca Maybasca ocho—8 Beatriz Yapo 6 +448+	a que le sirve dos años y medio en lo que los demas
	Ynes Panguia sesenta años 60	Domingo Turoys diez—10	a que le sirve dos y medio en lo que los demas
	Costança Cocay Chinbo çinquenta y dos años 52	Alonso Guanasca ocho—8 +449+	a que le sirve tres años en el benef^{o} de las chacaras
	Catalina Cusi Bispa çinquenta años 50 de don G^{a} Quispe Capi cacique		
	Fran^{co} Condursupa Quichua quarenta e çinco años—45 Leonor Casapun çinq^{ta} 50		a que le sirve veinte años en el benef^{o} de las chacaras
28	Agustin Atausuyo Quino Quichua v^{te} e quatro 24 Madalena Aya Urma treinta—30		a diez años que le sirve en el benef^{o} de las chacaras
454	P^{o} Paucar Chauca quarenta y seis 46 Ysabel Chapo çinq^{ta} y seis—56		a quinze años que le sirve en lo que los demas
104	Garçia Tiquilla Achaupis Guanca ses^{a} y seis—66 Costança Pichu ses^{a} 60		
76	Diego Gualpa Cunsa de Acos veinte e tres 23 Madalena Coca veinte e ocho—28	Maria Tinta uno 1	a que le sirve tres meses

/f.379/

lo que le paga por el servicio	*lo que paga de dotrina*	*lo que paga de tassa*	*tiene chacaras de tassa*
medio topo de chacara			medio topo de chacara
topo y medio de chacara			
medio topo de chacara			
Ana Ypoi cinq^{ta} e cinco			
topo y medio de chacara	quatro tomines de dotrina	media fanega de maiz	
medio topo de chacara	quatro tomines de dotrina		
un topo de chacara	quatro tomines de dotrina		
medio topo de chacara			

/f.379v/

	Casados Años	*Hijos Años*	*servi^{o} que a fecho cada yanacona*
	Ysabel Chunbi quarenta y ocho 48	Ju^{a} Marca diez—10 Leonor Cocacama 8 Maria Chunbi Pillo—5	a que le sirve tres meses
	Ysabel Chuqui Ynquillai treinta e tres 33	Benito Amacas 10 Cat^{a} Carua—8 Angelina Chucha quatro—4	
230 huerfanos	Xpobal Gualpa Yupangui diez y seis 16		
de Caçalla	Al^{o} Quispi Llalli treinta e quatro 34 Costança Quipi treinta e çinco 35	Bautista Buama Yalli tres—3 Mª Marca Chilla—5 Ju^{a} Chinbo uno—1	
vieja	Leonor Guacay de çinquenta e çinco 55		
yanaconas de doña Mª Cusi Guarcoy	Sebastian Cacha de Guanuco treinta e nueve—39 Mª Tiquilla—48 +225+	Ysabel Chaya Mumada diez 10	a v^{te} años que le sirve de salinero
	Lucas Quispi Angara veinte e çinco—25 Ynes Tarpo çinq^{ta} 50		a tres años que le sirve en el benef^{o} de las chacaras
viejas	Teresa Cana quarenta y seis—46	Ynes Canchuma sesenta 60	
yanaconas de Beatriz de Mendoça	Ju^{o} Asto Cacha de Guanuco treinta e çinco—35 +468+	Felipe Tiquilla Chaupis quatro 4	a seys años que le sirve en el benef^{o} de las chacaras

/f.380/

lo que le paga por el servicio	*lo que paga de dotrina*	*lo que paga de tassa*	*tiene chacaras de tassa*
		una fanega de maiz	un topo de chacara de comunidad
	quatro tomines de dotrina	media fanega de maiz un p^{o} en plata	un topo y tres quartos de chacara
	quatro tomines de dotrina		dos topos de chacara

/f.380v/

	Casados Años	*Hijos Años*	*servi^{o} que a fecho cada yanacona*
de don Ju^{o} Sona 223	Santiago Capcha de Tarma quarenta e ocho 48 Luysa Yalpo quarenta e çinco 45	Ju^{o} Rupaicacha quinze 15 R^{o} Pomacacha seis—6 Antonio Bilcacacha—4 Alonso Pumacalla dos 2 Andres Caquepoma 10	a que le sirve v^{te} e çinco años en el beneficio de las chacaras y en dalle yerua y leña
145 de Guari tito	Lucas Yaque Sabilchinque v^{te} e ocho 28 Ysabel Cusi Ynquillai veinte e seis 26		a diez y seis años que le sirve en el beneficio de las chacaras
Vieja	Catalina Coca sesenta—60		
huerfano enfermo de los andes	Françisco Cuxo de veinte años 20 +96+		
de don Fran^{co} Paca Naula 173	Martin Guartapuca Cañar çinquenta 50 Madalena Sirit çinquenta—50	Fran^{co} Mischo de diez y seis 16	a que le sirve treinta años en el beneficio de las chacaras y de dalle leña
de Miguel Codicula 143	Lucas Lucusibit Cañar naçio en este valle çinquenta—50 Leonor Guallachuc 55		a que le sirve v^{te} e çinco años de dar serviçio de leña
yanaconas de Martin de Meneses	Santiago Condur Carua naçio en este valle veinte e çinco 25 Ysabel Pumapaqui veinte e tres 23		a que le sirve doze años de labrador
	Françisca Gualcari Cana naçio en el Cuzco treinta e ocho—38 Elvira Chinbo—30	a diez años que le sirve de cavallerizo y en lo demas que le manda	
549	P^{o} Riquira de Chinchaisuyo naçio en este valle—27 Fran^{ca} Paupasucha 25		a siete años que le sirve de ortelano y labrador

/f.381/

lo que le paga por el servicio	*lo que paga de dotrina*	*lo que paga de tassa*	*tiene chacaras de tassa*
dos topos de chacara	seis tomines de dotrina		
un topo de chacara	quatro tomines de dotrina		
m^{o} topo de chacara	seys tomines de dotrina		
	quatro tomines de dotrina		
un topo de chacara			
medio topo de chacara			
un topo de chacara			

/f.381v/

	Casados Años	*Hijos Años*	*servi° que a fecho cada yanacona*
557	Ju° Yaris Guanca naçio en este valle quarenta 40 Leonor Utico treinta e tres—33	Ju° Murmo quinze 15 P° Yaringaillo 16 Lucas Pumallulla—5 Martin Yarollos—3 Ysabel Pacha uno—1	a siete años que le sirve de ortelano y labrador
	Ju° Surca Guamanmarca treinta—30 Luzio Yllachunbo veinte e tres—23	Juan Sulga Guaman dos—2	a que le sirve quatro años de ortelano y labrador
	P° Urco Naupa Quichia naçio en este valle treinta—30 Ana Uchotinta treinta 30	P° Pumaupa uno 1	a que le sirve nueve años de labrador y demas que le manda
	Juan Cordorcauana sesenta—60	Ju° Quispe v^te y ocho 28 Ysabel Chuquispa diez y ocho—18 Sebastian Caquia Conduri siete	a que le sirve diez años de ortelano
	Maria Coca çinquenta e çinco 55	Ana Cumapancha 10 P° Learinelossela quinze—15 Ju° Camiguano diez 10	a que sirve diez años de lo que le manda
	Catalina Usco treinta e ocho—38	Juana Mayacai tres—3	a diez años que le sirve en lo que le manda
	Ana Jama treinta y seis—36	Ana Tinba sinco—5 P° Chaupe ocho 8	a diez años que le sirve de ortelano
	Costança Tasa çinquenta años 50	Marcos Guaman veinte e dos 22 Ju° Machaguai dos 2	a que le sirve ocho años de ortelano
	Fran^co Chacara Chinbe çinquenta—50	P° Chalpa diez y seis—16	a diez años que le sirve en la guerta

/f.382/

lo que le paga por el servicio	*lo que paga de dotrina*	*lo que paga de tassa*	*tiene chacaras de tassa*
un topo de chacara			
tres quartos de topo de chacara			
un topo de chacara			
un topo de chacara			
			medio topo de chacara de comunidad
medio topo de chacara			
un topo de chacara			
un topo de chacara			
un topo de chacara			

/f.382v/

	Casados Años	*Hijos Años*	*servi^{o} que a fecho cada yanacona*
	Catalina Motolla de çinquenta 50	Beatriz Astopuca diez y siete—17 Fran^{ca} Villama siete 7 Catalina Guallama quatro—4	a diez años que le sirve en lo que los demas
	Juana Supo de Chinchaisuyo çinquenta—50		a que le sirve catorze años en lo que los demas
bibe sobre si	Juan Aupo de Chinchaisuyo ses^{a} y seis 60 +129+		a ocho años que le sirve a los caciques bibe sobre si
de P^{o} Miguel 237	Miguel Bilca treinta e q^{tro} 34 Ynes Mango Chinca 30	Alonso Curo Bobo diez y ocho 18	
de don Felipe Saire Topa	Myguel Nina Carua quarenta 40 +174+	Xpobal Guaipatapi siete años—7 Ysabel Chunbo Carua diez—10 Angelina Paco Tinta—4	
90	Fran^{co} Quispe treinta e çinco—35 Fran^{ca} Yache treinta e seis—36		
vieja	Beatriz Aca Ocllo çinquenta años 50		
208	P^{o} Machaguai quarenta—40 Ysabel Guachuc quarenta e dos 42	Beatriz Curochinbo seys—6 Costança Popo Carua quatro—4 Leonor Murmo dos 2	a diez y ocho años que le sirve en el beneficio de las chacaras e de dalle yerva y leña
yanaconas de la çiudad del Cuzco que guardan la madera	Lucas Cusi de Xaquixaguana treinta 30 Ysabel Pulla Coca diez y ocho—18		a diez años que le sirve en guardar la arboleda de madera

/f.383/

lo que le paga por el servicio	*lo que paga de dotrina*	*lo que paga de tassa*	*tiene chacaras de tassa*
medio topo de chacara			
un topo de chacara			
tiene un topo y un quarto de chacara			
Medio topo de chacara	quatro tomines de dotrina		
un topo de chacara	seys tomines de dotrina		

/f.383v/

	Casados Años	*Hijos Años*	*serviº que a fecho cada yAnacona*
505	Juº Alº Auca Supa Quichua quarenta—40 Ynes Colla vte e ocho 28	Juº Naupa Hananpa ocho—8 Juº Culpo tres 3	a que le sirve treze años en lo ques de arriba
	Juº Cusicondo de Xaquixaguana treinta e çinco—35 Leonor Chinbo—37	Juº Bautista Pomacondor seis—6 Alº Cusipaucar ocho—8	a que le sirve nueve años en beneficiar la madera
118	Juº Sulca Yauio treinta—30 Ynes Aca treinta e çinco—35		a que sirve seis años en el beneficio de la madera
	Alº Pilco de Xaquixaguana quarenta e çinco—45 Ynes Galli—36	Franco Toto Ynquilla siete—7 Domingo Puma çinco 5 Mª Suma Ynquillai tres 3 Catª Cusi uno—1	a nueue años que sirve en el beneficio de la madera
	Pº Oscollo quarenta—40		a nueve años que sirve en beneficiar la madera de la çiudad
	Elvira Bilca quarenta aºs 40	Catª Cusi Urma quinze—15 Ynes Cusi Chinbo siete 7 Juan Cusi Aymara 6	a que sirve diez años en beneficio de la madera
	Ysabel Ynacapa sesenta aºs 60		
	Xpobal Guantapi quarenta mytima que naçio en este valle 40	Agustin Guantapique naçio en este valle—20	
de don Luis Quisna	Felipe Pullasila Cañar treinta e siete 37 +507+		a que le sirve vte años en el beneficio de las chacaras

/f.384/

lo que le paga por el servicio	*lo que paga de dotrina*	*lo que paga de tassa*	*tiene chacaras de comunidad*
topo y mº de chacara	seys tomines de dotrina		
un topo de chacara	quatro tomines de dotrina		
un topo de chacara	seis tomines de dotrina		
un topo de chacara	quatro tomines de dotrina		
un topo de chacara	quatro tomines de dotrina		
un topo de chacara			
			dos topos de chacara
	quatro tomines		medio topo de chacara

/f.384v/

	Casados Años	*Hijos Años*	*servi^{o} que a fecho cada yanacona*
San Benito	Ynes Maca treynta años 30		
		Domingo Ubia ocho 8 Ju^{o} Chasca Chunbi quatro—4 Lazaro Cari tres 3	a que le sirve ocho años en el beneficio de las chcaras
	Catalina Tiquilla çinquenta—50	Leonor Manca siete—7	a veinte a^{o}s que le sirve en lo que los demas
de don Fran^{co} Chilche	Anton Yaquiguari Cañar naçio en este valle sesenta—60 +256+		a que le sirve v^{te} años en el beneficio de las chacaras

/f.385/

lo que le paga por el servicio	*lo que paga de dotrina*	*lo que paga de tassa*	*tiene chacaras de comunydad*
un topo de chacara			
medio topo de chacara			
dos topos de chacara	dos tomines de dotrina	quatro tomines de tasa	

/f.385v/

	Casados Años	*Hijos Años*	*servi^{o} que a fecho cada yanacona*
255	Agustin Chuqui Aparcana naçio en este valle sesenta—60		a que le sirve veinte años en el beneficio de las chacaras
	Catalina Guanay sesenta—60		sirvele en las chacaras de maiz
	Costança Acasuma çinquenta—50	Benito Llama catorze—14	sirve su hijo en lo que le manda
de don Felipe Cari Topa 419	Xpobal Topa Yupangui Sanoyto veinte e dos 22 Ysabel Chinbo Ocllo 20		siruiole dos años
77	Diego Auqui Gualpa quarenta y seis 46 Catalina Toto quarenta—40		tiene cargo de la puente de Paca
de Ju^{o} Enrriquez	Sebastian Cacanuta quarenta y siete 47 Françisca Toto—36	Di^{o} Sachaquibai diez 10 Fran^{co} Archinta—4 Ysabel Tincho doze 12 Madalena Supiso—9 Ju^{a} Yachu siete—7 Costança Ziucha—2	
	P^{o} Pairimai—70 Juan Angallapi quarenta y siete 47 Ynes Chuquitinta 40	Luisa Culpo doze—12	natural de Xaquixaguana
131	Ju^{o} Gualpa Topa v^{te} e seys—26 Mª Coca Quipi v^{te} e tres 23		
de don Ju^{o} Ayranbo 78	Diego Cay çinq^{ta} y çinco—55 Madalena Coca quarenta—40	Ju^{o} Pacollo diez 10 Martin Raime dos 2 Catalina Urma onze—11	

/f.386/

lo que le paga por el servicio	*lo que paga de dotrina*	*lo que paga de tassa*	*tiene chacaras de tassa*
dos topos de chacara			
un topo de chacara			
			m^{o} topo de chacara de comunidad
dos topos y m^{o} de chacara			
un topo de chacara que tiene de suyo			

/f.386v/ El Yll^{e} señor liçençiado frei P^{o} Gutierrez de la orden y cavalleria de Alcantara visitador general por su magestad y por el Exmo señor don Fran^{co} de Toledo visorrey destos rreinos del Piru en los valles de Yucay Tanbo Amaybanba Quiquixana y su distrito aviendo bisitado los y^{o}s yanaconas del valle de Yucay que se reduxeron al pueblo de San Bernardo que se fundo en el dho hizo dellos el resumen siguiente—

c xl vij yndios casados de diez y ocho a^{o}s a çinq^{ta} para poder tributar çiento y quarenta y siete—

x vij yndios solteros de diez y ocho años a çinquenta para poder tributar diez y siete—

c lx iiij son los y^{o}s tributarios questan en este pueblo de San Bernardo çiento y sesenta e quatro tributarios entre casados y solteros—

yndios de doze a^{o}s para diez y ocho seis	vj
muchachos de doze años abaxo çiento y çinquenta y tres	c l iij
yndios viejos casados de çinq^{ta} años arriba treinta e nueve	xxxix
viejos solteros de çinq^{ta} a^{o}s arriba treze	x iij
tullidos y enfermos casados çinco	v
mudos y tontos dos	ij
huerfanos nueue	ix
mugeres biudas y solteras de diez y ocho a çinquenta años quarenta y una	xl j

/f.387/ moças de diez y ocho a doze a°s veinte e çinco xx v
muchachas de doze años abaxo çiento y çinquenta y ocho c l viij
biejas de çinquenta años arriba çiento y catorze c x iiij
huerfanos dos ij

Es toda la gente que biue en este pueblo de San bernardo
entre casados y solteros nueue çientas y siete personas dcccc vij

y para que conste a su Ex[a] dello se hizo el dho resumen/ y lo firmo el dho señor visitador frei P[o] Gutierrez Flores ante mi P[o] Diaz Valdeon escrivano—

/f.387v/ los yndios quel señor visitador visitto de San Benito de Alcantara del valle

	Casados Años	*Hijos Años*	*servi° que a fecho cada yanacona*
288 yanaconas de don Fran[co] Chilche	Xpobal Guaman Cusi naçio en este valle treinta e ocho—38 Ynes Coca Ynguillai treinta y seis 36	Fran[co] Ynguilla tres 3 Ju[o] Totoco uno—1 Fran[co] Ayti treze 13 Ju[o] Cayo Ocho—8 Ynes Chinbo Caua seis 6	a que le sirve v[te] años en el beneficio de las chacaras de maiz e Coca y servi[o] de yerva
97	Fran[co] Marcas natural de Andaguailas treynta e seis—36 Ynes Condor Chunbe v[te] 20		a que le sirve quinze años en lo ques de arriba
	Ju[o] Usca naçio en este valle treinta e seis 36 Ynes Chisque treinta y siete—37	P[o] Sulca Cosca çinco 5 Ynes Chisque ocho 8 G[o] Ariusco quatro 4 Ynes Cuia uno 1 Martin Anaymarcas 18	a que le sirve v[te] e çinco años en lo que los demas
88	Felipe Copachacca naçio en este valle veinte e ocho—28 Ysabel Chirao v[te] e ocho 28	Hernando tres 3 Myguel Purca uno 1	a que le sirve veinte años en lo que los demas
190	Martin Parcar Arba de Chacaxa treinta e dos 32 Beatriz Chisqui treinta 30	Maria Nuca Ynguillay çinco 5 Ana CusiChinbo tres 3 Ju[a] Coya dos—2	a que le sirve v[te] años en lo que los demas
290	Xpobal Uscotoma de Andaguailas nacio en este valle v[te]—20 Ysabel Sese veinte 20	Fran[ca] quisque dos—2	a que le sirve tres años en el benef[o] de las chacaras y lo demas que le manda

/f.388/ por yanaconas e los reduxo y poblo en el pueblo de Yucay son los siguientes

~~lo que le paga por el servicio~~			
lo que paga por el servicio	lo que paga de dotrina	lo que paga de tassa	tiene chacaras de comunidad
tres topos de chacara de que come	quatro tomines de dotrina	quatro tomines de tassa	
dos topos de chacara de que come			
dos topos de chacara de que come	quatro tomines de dotrina		
dos topos de chacara de que come	quatro tomines de dotrina	quatro tomines de tasa	
dos topos y m° de chacara	quatro tomines de dotrina		

/f.388v/

	Casados Años	*Hijos Años*	*serviº que a fecho cada yanaconas*
	Catalina Yracas quarenta aºs 40	Agustin Piltoca diez—10 Leonor Luqui seys—6	
	Françisca Cutima sesenta años 60	Juana Chinbo Erma çinquenta 50	Ynes Suanuco çinquenta 50
huerfano 119	Juan Puca çinco 5		
de doña Ynes muger de don Fran^{co} Chilche	Juº Cañari naçio en este valle treinta 30 Beatriz Chisque veinte e ocho 28	Teresa Caba quatro—4 Juª Culucha dos 2	sirviole dos años y mº en el beneficio de las chacaras de mayz
21	Anton Acco Aros de Xaquixaguana naçio en este valle quarenta 40 Juª quarenta e dos—42	Fran^{ca} Gualcatanta uno—1 Maria Tantacallay tres 3	sirviole quatro años en lo que los demas
128	Juº Cuyo naçio en este valle quinze 15 Catalina Tanta 15		sirviole de paje
132	Juº Yslima de Quito sesenta y seis 66 Catalina Taco sesenta y siete—67		sirviole en las chacaras mas de veinte años
49	Alº Billamabai de Quito naçio en este valle veinte e ocho 28 Beatriz Sumaytos treinta—30	Leonor Cullat seys—6 Diº Masi tres—3 Fran^{co} Tinichaca—1	sirviole seis años en lo que los demas
121	Juº Lalpal de Quito naçio en este valle veinte e quatro 24 Maria Chisqui quarenta 40		sirviole como los demas

/f.390/

lo que le paga por el servicio	*lo que paga de dotrina*	*lo que paga de tassa*	*tiene chacaras de comunydad*
Catalina Cauro sesª 60			
dos topos de chacara de que come			
un topo de chacara	quatro tomines de dotrina		
topo y medio de chacara	medio peso de dotrina	medio peso de tassa	
un topo de chacara	dos tomines de dotrina		

/f.390v/

	Casados Años	*Hijos Años*	*servi° que a fecho cada yanaconas*
	Beatriz Paico çinquenta a°s 50	Juan Paucho ocho años 8	sirviole tres años en el beneficio de las chacaras
133	Juan Culpo treinta e çinco—35	P° Gualla tres 3 Fran^{co} Mumano uno—1	sirviole dos años en el beneficio de las chacaras
	Madalena Chuquirimay sesenta 60		
	Leonor Suro çinquenta 50	Catalina Chivi siete 7	
	Ynes Rata çinquenta 50	Leonor Chinbo sesenta 60	Juan Gucal sesenta 60 +359+
de Ju° Bautista Tulpulla 51	Agustin Calaquipar naçio en este valle treinta e çinco—35	Ysabel Asa Ocllo treinta e seys—36	a que le sirve doze años en el beneficio de las chacaras
32	Alonso Tacma Guanca treinta—30 Elvira Yaro quarenta y seis—46	Leonor Colochu Caua diez y ocho 18	a que le sirve quinze años en lo ques de arriba y en la chacara de coca
de Lucas Anda Bisnai 175	Martin Yarobilcay treinta y seis 36 Ynes Yabaocaua veinte e çinco 25	Domingo Guari Poma quatro 4 Ysabel Año tres 3	a que le sirve el suso dho y a su padre veinte años
de don Al° Tito Atauchi 22	de don Al° Titu Atauchi Al° Suco del Cuzco naçio en este valle—38 Maria Yache—30	Ju° Quispiuao seis—6 Fran^{ca} Maita—5 Ana Chuqui Ciça—1 Lucas Cuco dos—2 Ynes Paico diez—10	a diez a°s que le sirve en benefiçiarle las chacaras de maiz y mita de yerva y leña

/f.391/

lo que le paga por el servicio	*lo que paga de dotrina*	*lo que paga de tassa*	*tiene chacaras de tasa*
dos topos de chacara de que come		pasa por entero la tassa al encomendero	
dos topos y m° de chacara de don Françisco Chilche			
dos topos de chacara	quatro tomines de dotrina		
topo y medio de chacara de que come	medio peso de dotrina		

/f.391v/

	Casados Años	*Hijos Años*	*servi^{o} que a fecho cada yanacona*
Murio	Xpoball Rayme Colla treinta años ~~e dos~~ 30 Juana Molloca veinte e ocho—28		a diez años que le sirve en lo que los demas
109	Her^{do} Astaula naçio en este valle diez y nueve 19 Ysabel Tuta 19	G^{o} Guamantao uno—1	
viejas	Ysabel Sutullai sesenta—60	Leonor Sac sesenta a^{o}s 60	Leonor Tanbo sesenta 60
yanaconas de don G^{a} Taina caçique de Urcos	Diego Pama Supaico treinta e dos—32 +80+ Juana Paico Ocllo veinte años—20	Martin Yanapa dos—2	a que le sirve seis años en el beneficio de las chacaras
	Juan Bautista Unayachoc Yauyo treinta 30 Costança Atacarua treinta e dos—32	Miguel Chuayaure ocho 8 Al^{o} Runayache çinco 5 G^{o} Yaunyanaque dos 2 Maria Mysa Carua tres—3	a que le sirve quatro años en el beneficio de las chacaras
211	P^{o} Caito de Parinacocha treinta e seis 36 Ynes Quispima 23	Maria Canacayo ponia tres años 3 P^{o} Lluqui uno—1 Al^{o} Cutira mudos 3	a que le sirve tres años en lo que los demas
viejos	Ynes Muopoco sesenta años	Leonor Tiquilla sesenta—60	
de Xpobal Apassa 514	Gonçalo Tongoraba Yunga çinquenta—50 Ysabel Lilco sesenta—60		a que le sirve quinze años en el beneficio de las chacaras

/f.392/

lo que le paga por el servicio	*lo que paga de ~~tassa~~ dotrina*	*lo que paga de ttassa*	*tiene chacaras de comunidad*
medio topo de chacara	medio peso de dotrina		
Fran^{ca} Topalla sesenta—60			
medio topo de chacara	medio peso de dotrina		
un quarto de topo de chacara	quatro tomines de dotrina	dos tomines a don Garçia	
medio topo de chacara	quatro tomines de dotrina		
medio topo de chacara		quatro tomines de tassa m^{a} fanega de maiz	

/f.392v/

	Casados Años	*Hijos Años*	*servi° que a fecho cada yanacona*
	Martin Cura Colla sesenta y seis 66 Maria Abi çinq[ta] e q[tro] 54	Luzia Millo diez—10	a que le sirve v[te] años a el y a sus padres
134	Juan Pirca Colla sesenta—60 Ysabel Canaguaco çinquenta—50		no sirve por ser viejo
de don Al° Tupa Rimache	Al° Pacaguano de Quito sesenta—60 +33+ Leonor Quillaco sesenta—60	P° Caparamoco enfermo de los andes v[te] e seis 26 +212+	a que le sirve seis años en el beneficio de las chacaras
de doña Mençia Toto	Diego Condegualpa de Chuco v[te] e siete 27 +81+ Catalina Ocllo—30	Alonso Arotongo uno—1	a doze años que le sirve de beneficio de chacaras
viejas	Costança Alma çinquenta—50	Pedro Ahalla siete—7	a que le sirve diez años en su cassa e chacara
	Leonor Guayancho çinquenta y ocho		a que le sirve diez años en su casa y lo que le manda
	Maria Coyuc sesenta—60	Catalina Paico diez y ocho 18	a que le sirve diez años en su cassa
de Pablo de Carauajal	Xpobal Pariguaman Caxatanbo naçio en este valle—30 Maria Coca veinte e quatro—24	Ger[mo] Curilanca—4 Luçia Guarmequilla 6 Paulo Pita tres 3 Alonso Misco doze 12	a que le sirve diez años de ortelano y lo que le manda
	Martin Tomaylla Quichua veinte e ocho—28 Leonor Chinbo Coca veinte e dos 22	Juan Pumanaupo quatro—4 Diego Guache uno 1	a que le sirve quatro años de ortelano y lo que le mandan

/f.393/

lo que le paga por el servicio	*lo que paga de dotrina*	*lo que paga de tassa*	*tiene chacaras de comunidad*
un topo de chacara			
medio topo de chacara			
medio topo de chacara			
medio topo de chacara			
medio topo de chacara			
tres quartos de chacara			

/f.393v/

	Casados Años	*Hijos Años*	*serviº que a fecho cada yanacona*
482	Anton Puma Condori veinte e dos 22 Catalina Cusi Chinbo veinte—20	Pº Pumacondori dos años 2	a que le sirve ocho años de ortelano
481	Xpobal Chuqui Condori de Caxatanbo naçio en este valle v^{te} 20 Mª Yacosuyo—19		a que le sirve seys meses de ortelano
	Her^{do} Pomari Caxatanbo quarenta 40 Maria YacoChinbo 40		a que le sirve ocho meses de ortelano
vieja	Ysabel Coca sesenta aºs 60		
de Geronimo Costilla	Juan Quispi Yunga çinq^{ta} e çinco—55 Catalina Cuslaco çinquenta e çinco 55	Juan Guapa Chisqui siete años—7	a que le sirve diez y seis años de ortelano
de doña Paula	Pº Molasi Yunga quarenta y quatro 44 Elvira Suyo çinq^{ta} 50	Fran^{co} Sulluc ocho—8	a que le sirve treynta años en el beneficio de la madera y a su marido
de Gª de Melo	Fran^{co} Gualpa Chunbibilca quarenta e ocho 48 Catalina Paico quarenta—40	Alº Chacaguaiua ocho 8 Fran^{co} Bita qtrº 4 Ynes Guaruchique 7	a que le sirve treinta e dos años en el beneficio de las chacaras
	Juan Atausi Chunbibilca v^{te} e quatro—24 Françisca Mallei—30	Juan Cuyucho uno—1	a que le sirve desde muchacho de ortelano
	Garçia Chunbibilca diez y ocho—18 Maria Carua diez y seis—16		a que le sirve de ortelano y de beneficio de las chacaras seys años

/f.394/

lo que le paga por el servicio	*lo que paga de dotrina*	*lo que paga de tassa*	*tiene chacaras de comunydad*
tres quartos de chacara			
tres quartos de chacara			
un quarto de chacara			
un topo de chacara			
medio topo de chacara			
un topo de chacara			
un topo de chacara			
un quarto de topo de chacara			

/f.394v/

	Casados Años	*Hijos Años*	*servi^{o} que a fecho cada yanacona*
	Al^{o} Cume Guaire Guanca naçio en este valle çinq^{ta} y ocho 58 Ysabel Chinbo Urma çinquenta 50	P^{o} Canchari diez y ocho 18 Pablo Machaco diez y seis 16 Ysabel Upiay doze 12	a que sirve v^{te} años de ortelano y de benefiçiarle las chacaras
	Ju^{o} Casa Condur Tarma quarenta e ocho 48 Maria Pita quarenta e ocho—48	Sebastian Miapo doze 12 Martin Yzma çinco—5 Ju^{o} Bautista Mino q^{tro}—4 Ju^{o} Sulca uno—1 Ysabel Lacca ocho—8	a que sirve v^{te} e quatro años de ortelano y en las chacaras
	Ju^{o} Bautista Bilca Guanca treinta e ocho—38 Ynes Tanbo quarenta 40	Ysabel Manao nueve—9	a que le sirve de ortelano y benefiçialle las chacaras quatro años
	Ju^{o} Sulca Guaman Guaillas naçio en este valle v^{te} 20 Maria Pilco v^{te} e q^{tro} 24	Her^{do} Puscaca tres 3 Juan Chiquilli dos 2	a que le sirve siete años en lo que los demas
485	Fran^{co} Sulca Condori Tarma v^{te} e çinco 25 Madalena Cochacho v^{te} e quatro—24	Costança Piay tres 3	a que le sirve nueve años de ortelano
	Diego Quispe Guailas naçio en este valle v^{te} e quatro 24 Ynes Guaman Carica v^{te} e dos—22	Agustin Bilcapaucar çinco 5	a que le sirve ocho años en lo que los demas
	Diego Mama çinquenta e çinco 55	P^{o} Amaya quinze 15 Diego Oya seis—6 Juan Chimbo uno 1	
	Melchor Guamari mascadora v^{te} e seis 26 Maria Siquima veinte e ocho 28	Juachacha q^{tro} 4 Fran^{ca} Ruray siete 7	a que le sirve ocho años de ortelano
	Fran^{co} Tanra Ancara çinquenta e quatro 54 Juana Quisma—48	Leonor Chucha siete—7	a que le sirve çinco años de ortelano

/f.395/

lo que le paga por el servicio	*lo que paga de dotrina*	*lo que paga de tassa*	*tiene chacaras de comunidad*
un topo de chacara			
medio topo de chacara			
tres quartos de topo			
tres quartos de topo			
un topo de chacara			
tres quartos de chacara			
un topo de chacara			
un topo de chacara			

/f.395v/

	Casados Años	*Hijos Años*	*servi^o que a fecho cada yanacona*
	Juan Anba de Sora treinta—30 Juana Carua quar^ta 40		a que le sirve quatro años de ortelano
	Juan Condori Collagua çinq^ta y ocho—58 Ysabel Ynquillai 60		a que le sirve diez y seis años de ortelano
	Ynes Carua quarenta e ocho 48	Garçia Gualguari quarenta e ocho 48 +105+	a que le sirve diez y seis años de ortelano
yanaconas de Al^o de Loaysa	Lucas Anu Pumacanche quarenta e dos 42 Luysa Quipi quarenta 40	P^o Lasco diez y seis 16 Ju^o Poco Malqui q^tro—4 Marcos Puma tres 3 Fran^co Cauta dos—2 Madalena Leco uno—1	a que le sirve diez y nueve años de ortelano
tullido	Martin Guaman Quichua çinq^ta años—50 Maria Chinbo Ocllo çinquenta e seis 56		a que le sirve v^te a^os de ortelano
	Antonio Paucarmysa v^te e quatro 24 Beatriz Chunbi treinta e seis 36	Juan Ti dos 2 Ynes Yalpa quatro—4	a que le sirve tres años de ortelano
	Juan Guaman Tomaylla Conde v^te e ocho a^os 28 Felipe Sumaycolque v^te e çinco—25	Fran^ca Llaqui uno 1 Teresa Puma tres—3	a que le sirve dos años de ortelano
	Anton Aromi Aymara v^te—20 Juana Yachi v^te e seis 26		a que le sirve diez años de ortelano
yanaconas de Fran^co de Villafuerte yn^o de tassa	Gregorio Guaita Chunbibilca veinte e seis—26 +106+ Ynes Cayo treinta e dos—32	Diego Chuqui Guaita quinze 15 Garçia Guaita q^tro 4	a que le sirve catorze años de ortelano

/f.396/

lo que le paga por el servicio	*lo que paga de dotrina*	*lo que paga de tassa*	*tiene chacaras de comunidad*
un topo de chacara			
un topo de chacara			
un topo de chacara			
un topo de chacara			
un topo de chacara			
tres quartos de chacara			
tres quartos de chacara			
tres quartos de chacara			
Topo y medio de chacara			

/f.396v/

	Casados Años	*Hijos Años*	*servi^o que a fecho cada yanacona*
82	Diego Pumacanche çinquenta e quatro 54 Catalina Canco quarenta y seis 46	Maria Condor Poma siete—7 Di^o Alara çinco 5 Cat^a Parpa quatro 4 Ana Carua uno—1	a que le sirve treinta años de ortelano
34	Andres Condur Chunbibilca v^te e ocho 28 Ynes Yunpa 25	Juana Ycuchi seys—6	a que sirve dos años de ortelano
177 yanaconas de P^o de Bustinça	Martin Rimaco Ancara çinquenta e çinco 55 Ysabel Chunbi quarenta—40	Diego Guayapa diez y seis 16	a que sirve treze años de ortelano
20	Al^o Condor Guanca çinq^ta 50 Fran^ca Zibichinbo quarenta e ocho—48	Diego Malqui diez y ocho—18 Ana Zira doze 12	a que sirve treze años de ortelano
	Fran^co Tapotay de Pomatambo treinta 30 Ynes Coca Chinbo veinte e çinco 25	Maria Yaurima seis—6 Juan Cayoma tres 3 Leonor Cusilo—1	a que le sirve nueve años de ortelano y chacarero
huyose porque mato a un yn^o 229	Xpobal Mayta Yupangui de Cuzco naçio en este valle v^te e seis 26 Ana Toto v^te e quatro 24	Domingo Quino yupangui siete 7 Angelina Yupo çinco—5	a que sirve doze años de ortelano
	Alonso Caquia Yanaguara v^te e quatro 24		a diez años que le sirve de ortelano en lo que los demas
viejas	Ysabel Ñusta quarenta e seis 46	Alonso Rimache siete 7	a que le sirve ocho años de ortelano
	Barbola Mayoguai quarenta e çinco 45	Maria Chinbo onze—11	a que le sirve doze años de ortelano

/f.397/

lo que le paga por el servicio	lo que paga de dotrina	lo que paga de tassa	tiene chacaras de comunidad
un topo y un quarto de chacara			
un topo de chacara			
un topo de chacara			
un topo de chacara			
un topo de chacara			
un quarto de chacara			
un topo topo de chacara			
un quarto de topo de chacara			

/f.397v/

	Casados Años	*Hijos Años*	*servi^{o} que a fecho cada yanacona*
	Ana Macachinbi veinte—20	Leonor Ricaycancha uno 1	a que le sirve doze años en lo que los demas
	Catalina Chinbo Urma çinq^{ta}—50		a que le sirve diez años en lo que los demas
	Ynes Sumay Chinbo sesenta a^{o}s 60		a que le sirve treinta años de ortelano
	Ynes Chinbo çinq^{ta} e çinco 55	Alonso Ataupuman coxibado veinte 20	
	Ysabel Mita quarenta—40	Alonso Rimache seis—6	
viejas de Al^{o} de Loaysa	Maria Chisque quarenta i seis	Juan Topa çinco—5 Diego Coro dos—2	a diez años que le sirve en lo que le manda
178 yanaconas de Ju^{o} de Salas vz^{o}	Martin Callupa de Guanuco treinta e ocho 38 Ynes Coca—39		a que le sirve nuebe años de ortelano y chacarero
	Juan Llaviaca de Guanuco naçio en el Cuzco treinta e q^{tro} a^{o}s 34 Fran^{ca} Guanpa—18	Fran^{co} Malqui siete—7 Ju^{o} Alca seys—6 Fran^{co} Yuri çinco—5 Ysabel Alca tres—3 Ju^{o} Sipa dos—2	a que le sirve seis meses de ortelano
	Diego Auracunsanana naçio en este valle ses^{a} 60 Ysabel Cancha quarenta—40	Andres Aucallalley uno—1 Ynes Bispa seis—6 Beatriz Ylla Chuqui çinco 5	a v^{te} e seis años que le sirve de ortelano y chacarero

/f.398/

lo que le paga por el servicio	*lo que paga de dotrina*	*lo que paga de tassa*	*tiene chacaras de comunydad*
un topo de chacara			
un topo de chacara			
un quarto de topo			
tres quartos de chacara			
un topo de chacara			
un topo de chacara			

/f.398v/

	Casados Años	*Hijos Años*	*servi^{o} que a fecho cada yanacona*
	Alonso Ataucusi veinte e çinco—25 Ysabel Suma Yuquilla veinte e çinco 25	Maria Mita q^{tro} 4 Juan Pauco uno—1	
	Diego Cure de Masca quarenta y seis 46		a que le sirve diez años de ortelano
viejo	Myguel Quisto çinquenta e seis 56		
viejas	Ysabel Paico Ynguilla çinq^{ta}—50	P^{o} Cusi Carua ocho 8 Catalina Coa çinco 5	a que le sirve catorze años en el beneficio de las chacaras
	Catalina Chinbo Ynguilla çinq^{ta} 50		
yanaconas de Ju^{o} de Berrio	Martin Quispe de ora quarenta e ocho 48 Ysabel Paico quarenta y çinco 45	Fran^{co} Malqui diez y seis—16 Diego Anca q[ua]tro 4	a que le sirve v^{te} e tres años de ortelano
manco	Sebastian Collagua Condori quarenta e dos 42 Leonor Cana quar^{ta} e çinco 45	Al^{o} Suiue nueve 9 Domingo Chanca seys—6 Luzia Avia Guarme 3	a que le sirve doze años de ortelano
De Bustinça	P^{o} Curi naçio en este valle diez y ocho—18		a que le sirve ocho a^{o}s de ortelano
yanaconas de Diego de Truxillo	Diego Quispe Yauyo çinquenta e çinco—55 Ana Carua quarenta e ocho—48	Di^{o} Guaranca q^{tro} 4 Luzia Tauba seis—6 Madalena Saiba Chunbi nueve—9	a que le sirve diez y siete años de ortelano

/f.399/

lo que le paga por el servicio	*lo que paga de dotrina*	*lo que paga de tassa*	*tiene chacaras de comunydad*
un topo de chacara			
m^{o} topo de chacara			
un topo de chacara			
un topo de chacara			
m^{o} topo de chacara			
un topo de chacara			

/f.399v/

	Casados Años	*Hijos Años*	*servi^o que a fecho cada yanacona*
	Alonso Ataucuxi veinte e çinco—25 Ysabel Suma Yuquilla v[te] e çinco 25	Maria Myta q[tro] 4 Juan Pauco uno 1	
	Diego Curo de Masca quarenta e seis 46		a que le sirve diez años de ortelano
viejo	Myguel Quisto çinquenta e seis 56		
viejas	Ysabel Paico Ynquilla çinq[ta]—50	P[o] Cusi Carua ocho—8 Catalina Coa çinco 5	a que le sirve catorze años en el beneficio de las chacaras
	Catalina Chinbo Ynguilla çinq[ta] 50		
184 yanaconas de Ju[o] de Berrio	Martin Quispi de ora quarenta e ocho 48 Ysabel Paico quarenta e çinco—45	Fran[ca] Malqui diez y seis—16 Diego Sanca quatro—4	a que le sirve v[te] e tres años de ortelano
manco	Sebastian Condori Collagua quarenta e dos 42 Leonor Cana—45	Al[o] Yanc nueue 9 Domingo Chanca seis—6 Luzia Abeguarme tres—3	a que le sirve doze años de ortelano
de Bustinça	P[o] Curi naçio en este valle diez y ocho 18		a que le sirve ocho años de ortelano
yanaconas de Diego de Truxillo	Diego Quispe Yauyo çinquenta e çinco—55 Ana Carua quar[ta] e ocho 48	Diego Guaranca quatro—4 Luçia Tarua seis—6 Madalena Saiba Chunbi nueve—9	a que le sirve diez y siete años de ortelano

/f.400/

lo que le paga por el servicio	*lo que paga de dotrina*	*lo que paga de tassa*	*tiene chacaras de comunidad*
un topo de chacara			
medio topo de chacara			
un quarto de topo de chacara			
Un topo de chacara			
medio topo de chacara			
un topo de chacara			

/f.400v/

	Casados Años	*Hijos Años*	*servi^{o} que a fecho cada yanacona*
	Al^{o} Carua Quilla v^{te} e quatro naçio en este valle—24 Ana Carua diez e ocho 18	Petronilla Nyna Carua dos 2	a que le sirve diez años de ortelano
	P^{o} Paco Uri naçio en este valle veinte e dos 22 Ana Casa Carua diez y ocho—18		a que le sirve çinco años de ortelano
	Ynes Tarpo veinte e ocho—28 Ynes Cuya ses^{a}—60	G^{o} Macho v^{te} 20	a diez años que le sirve en lo que los demas
yanaconas de Bachicao	Sebastian Unapaucar treinta—30 +224+ Maria Chinbo treinta—30	Maria Topo dos 2	
37	Andres Quispe veinte e tres 23 Catalina Aca Umai veinte e dos—22	Juana Silti tres 3	
38	Agustin Sulca Yauyo çinq^{ta} e çinco 55 Juana Carua çinq^{ta} 50	Agustin Sulca veinte e dos 22 Ynes Tarpo diez y seis 16	a que sirve quinze años de ortelano
yanaconas de don Felipe Saire Topa Ynga	~~Agustin sulca yauyo~~ Her^{do} Billi Colla naçio en este valle treinta e ocho—38 +110+ Fran^{ca} Poco Tiquilla—48		a que sirve siete años en el benef^{o} de las chacaras
89	Fran^{co} Manco Guayacondo naçio en este valle quarenta 40 Ysabel Guachacu Tipa treinta—30		a que le sirve diez años de benefiçialle las chacaras
533	Lor^{co} Quispe Guaman naçio en este valle veinte—20 Luçia Toto diez e ocho 18	Beatriz Cancharma dos—2	A que le sirve siete a^{o}s en el beneficio de las chacaras

/f.401/

lo que le paga por el servicio	*lo que paga por la dotrina*	*lo que paga de tassa*	*tiene chacaras de comunydad*
un topo de chacara			
un topo de chacara			
un topo de chacara			
medio topo de chacara			
medio topo de chacara			
m^{o} topo de chacara			
medio topo de chacara			
un quarto de topo de chacara			

/f.401v/

	Casados Años	*Hijos Años*	*servi^o^ que a fecho cada yanacona*
179	Marcos Chilque Yupangui del Cuzco treinta—30 Luysa Chinbo—32	Martin Topa doze 12 Ju^o^ Muyo quatro—4 Di^o^ Muyan Tupa tres 3 Ynes Aca ocho—8	a que le sirve siete años en lo que los demas
553	Agustin Paco naçio en este valle çinq^ta^ e seis—56 Juana Paico Ocllo çinquenta e çinco 55		a que le sirve v^te^ años en el beneficio de las chacaras
166	Martin Llaoay de Atauillo treinta—30 Ju^a^ Ypranpa quarenta e çinco—45		a que le sirve diez e ocho años en el beneficio de las chacaras
viejas	Ysabel Urcomar de treinta años 30	Ynes Bispa Coca de catorze—14	a que le sirve v^te^ años en el beneficio de las chacaras
	Juana Cuya de çinquenta e seis 56		a que le sirve seis años en el beneficio de las chacaras
	Leonor Cunpla veinte e quatro 24		a que le sirve seis años en el beneficio de las chacaras
	Ysabel Sulca Poco de çinq^ta^—50		a que le sirve siete años en el benefiçialle las chacaras
	Juana Cua ses^a^ 60	Diego Paris Mango seis 6 Ysabel Puco seis—6	
de don Her^do^ Ylla Topa	Martin Condori Aymara çinquenta—50 Maria Chinbo Coca treinta e quatro 34	Juan Pachusqui çinco—5 Ysabel Chanbi Chusqui seis—6 Costança Alca Chusque 4 Bicente Anpa tres—3	a diez años que le sirve en el beneficio de las chacaras de mayz

/f.402/

lo que le paga por el servicio	*lo que paga de dotrina*	*lo que paga de tassa*	*tiene chacaras de comunydad*
medio topo de chacara			
medio topo de chacara			
un quarto de topo de chacara			
un quarto de topo de chacara			
un quarto de topo de chacara			
medio topo de chacara			
un quarto de topo de chacara			
topo y m^o^ de chacara		cada año quatro çestos de coca al dho don Hernando	

/f.402v/

	Casados Años	*Hijos Años*	*servi° que a fecho cada yanacona*
213	Pedro Uma de Chanca veinte e seis—26 Juana Toto Ocllo treinta—30		a que le sirve tres años en el benef° de las chacaras de maiz y dalle leña
	Alonso Condori Quichua çinq[ta]—50 Maria Ynguillai treinta—30	Ysabel Lasto Chunbi diez 10 Al° Usca ocho—8 Maria Coca Mulla tres 3 Juan Chialla dos—2	
40	Alonso Marca Guanca treinta—30 Catalina Mania Carua treinta—30	Catalina Upa diez 10 Ju[a] Quispe seis—6 Domingo Mita tres 3	a que le sirve dos años en el benef° de la chacara y dalle leña y maiz
	Madalena Mancaia veinte e ocho—28	Alonso Chipana ocho—8 Catalina Guay tres 3	a que le sirve dos años en la chacara de mita de yerva
	Elvira Chinbo ses[a] 60	P° Tinlabai ocho a°s 8	a que le sirve nueve años en lo que los demas
	Madalena Nuno Palta çinquenta e quatro no pareçe 54	P° Timlabai ocho a°s 8 [*sic*]	a que le sirve nueve años en lo que los demas
	Ynes Curachu ses[a] no pareçe—60	P° Tinlabayo ocho años 8	a que le sirve nueve años
82 260	Diego Laime diez y seis años—16 Martin Ysuansiba ocho su hermano no pareçe—8		a que le sirve quatro años en benefiçiar las chacaras de maiz
	Ysabel Langui quarenta y seis no pareçe—46		a que le sirve v[te] años en lo que los demas

/f.403/

lo que le paga por el servicio	*lo que paga de dotrina*	*lo que paga de tassa*	*tiene chacaras de comunydad*
topo y m° de chacara			
m° topo de chacara			
dos topos de chacara de que come			
un topo de chacara	quatro tomines de dotrina		
tres quartos de topo	quatro tomines de dotrina		
un topo de chacara de que come			
Un topo de chacara			
medio topo de chacara			

/f.403v/

	Casados Años	*Hijos Años*	*servi^o que a fecho cada yanacona*
135	Juan Toto çinq[ta] e seis 56 Ysabel Llassa çinquenta e quatro 54		sirve a mas de diez años en este valle donde manda
de don Felipe Sotapone	Juan Condori v[te] e çinco—25 +130+ Catalina Cuyllo quarenta—40		naçio en este valle
136	Juan Paucar Cusi Anochi treinta e q[tro] 34 Ynes Ynguillai—30	Juan Llamapongo quatro 4 Fran[co] Ponga Yunga uno 1	Maria Coca Llatan seis 6
107	Garçia Chara quarenta—40 Ynes Guaca quarenta—40	Martin Chara diez—10 Al[o] Supanta ocho—8 Luis Labando seis—6 M[a] Pacondor Puquio çinco 5 Ju[a] Condo Chinbo quatro 4	a quinze a[o]s que salio de su tierra
214	P[o] Chinco treinta 30	Andres Yaro Chuco Tiquilla çinco—5	
63	Baltasar Angas sesenta—60	P[o] Michay ocho 8 Maria Tiquilla diez y ocho—18	
215 viejo de don Her[do] caçique de Calca	P[o] Rimache çinq[ta] e seis 56 Fran[co] Cotiquilla Yaure veinte e quatro—24 +99+	Gonçalo Quispi çinco—5	
	Catalina Tiquilla çinquenta—50 Ysabel Silla treinta—30	Leonor Amanca diez—10 Vicente Ananpa q[tro] 4 Ysabel Chunbichisque diez 10 Costança Altachisque seis 6	
	Ynes Maca quarenta 40	Domingo Oyba mudo diez—10 Lazaro Macori q[tro] 4 Juana Cascachunbi seis 6	

/f.404/

lo que le paga por el servicio	*lo que paga de dotrina*	*lo que paga de tassa*	*tiene chacaras de comunydad*
	m[o] peso de dotrina	un pesso pa[ra] la tassa	un topo de chacara

/f.404v/

	Viejas Años	*Hijos Años*	*servi^{o} que a fecho cada yanacona*
		Baltasar Topa seis 6	
	Ynes Anachi quarenta—40	Juana Tonocho tres años—3	
	Madalena Pama quarenta—40	Ysabel Silla v^{te}	
	Juan Teco Canco sesenta—60	Ynes Cuya ses^{a} 60	Maria Catana çinquenta 50
	Leonor Mormo sesenta—60	Juana Cocanbo sesenta—60	Costança Ayro sesenta 60
		Grauiel Pasto çinco—5	Xpobal Tanlai diez y ocho 18
de Mª Pasna	Al^{o} Anco v^{te}—20 Juan Achuquibul de çinq^{ta} e çinco—55		a que le sirve quinze años en el beneficio de las chacaras
de Carvajal	Andres Lau v^{te} e quatro—24 Fran^{ca} Pasna v^{te}—20	Ynes Luchaguara siete—7 Ana Lurima çinco 5 luzia Ano Guare tres 3	
	Al^{o} Unpiri ses^{a}—60 Leonor Chacara sesenta años 60	Elvira Conama quarenta—40	Juan Cocha su hijo catorze 14
41	Al^{o} Tincas çinq^{ta}—50		

/f.405/

lo que le paga por el servicio	*lo que paga de dotrina*	*lo que paga de tassa*	*tiene chacaras de comunydad*
Leonor Chapo çinquenta 50	Juana Chapo Coca setenta 70	Ysabel Sisa sesenta 60	Barbola Toto sesenta—60
Juana Chopo veinte			
un topo de chacara			

/f.405v/ El Yll^{tre} señor frei P^{o} Gutierrez Flores de la orden y cavalleria de Alcantara visitador general por su magestad y por el Exmo señor don Françisco de Toledo bisorrei destos reinos del Piru en su real nonbre en los valles de Yucay Amaybanba Quiquixana y su distrito aviendo bisitado los y^{o}s yanaconas que poblo en el pueblo de San Benito de Alcantara hizo dellos el resumen siguiente—

lxx j yndios casados de diez y ocho años a çinquenta para poder tributar setenta e uno—

x iij yndios solteros de diez y ocho años a çinquenta para poder tributar treze—

lxxx iiij son los y^{o}s yanaconas que bibe en este pueblo de San Benito de Alcantara ochenta e quatro y^{o}s tributarios entre casados y solteros—

yndios de doze años a diez y ocho doze	x ij
yn^{o}s de doze a^{o}s abaxo nobenta e q^{tro}	xc iiij
y^{o}s viejos casados de çinquenta años arriba diez y nueve	x viiij
viejos solteros de çinquenta años arriba tres	iij
tullidos y enfermos tres	iij
un tonto	j
un guerfana	j
mugeres viudas y solteras de diez y ocho a^{o}s a çinq^{ta} diez y nueue	xix

/f.406/ moças de doze a diez y ocho çinco 5
muchachos de doze años abaxo setenta e siete lxx vij
viejas de çinquenta años arriba treinta e ocho xxx viij
una huerfana j

Es toda la gente que biue en este pueblo de los y^{o}s yanaconas entre casados y solteros de todas hedades quatroçientos y quarenta y siete personas y para que conste a su Exª se hizo el dho resumen cccc xl vij

El liçençiado frei Pedro Gutierrez Flores ante mi P^{o} Diaz Baldeon escrivano—

/f.406v/ En quinze de henero de myll e qui^{o}s e setenta e dos años se bi (sigue en el folio siguiente) y se pueblan en este pu^{o} de San Fran^{co} de Maras

	Casados Años	*Hijos Años*	*serviçio*
42	Andres Caime natural de Quichua de quar^{ta} 40 Ynes Chinbo Cuyo 40	Alonso Guaman Ylla quatro	a que sirve quinze años de labrador
30	Anton Quispe v^{te} e çinco es Colla naçio en este valle—25		a que le sirve diez años de porquero
216	P^{o} Yauqui Paucar veinte e dos es Yauyo—		a que sirve onze años de cauallerizo
43	Agustin Guaranca Chanca ses^{a} 60		tienele en su casa y dalle de comer
	Ynes Chincaya treinta e ocho 38	Alonso Tra ocho 8 Angelina Acoma tres 3	A que le sirve quatro a^{o}s en el beneficio de las chacaras
	Juana Aca Coca sesenta—60	Ysabel Sumay veinte e dos	
viejas	Juana Chinbo setenta—70	Ynes Poco sesenta 60	Catalina Guanpa set^{a} 70
yanaconas de don Xpobal Uca Poma	Pedro Paucar v^{te} e dos—22 Catalina Nysa Carua v^{te} e ocho—28	Ana Paico tres—3	a que le sirve dos años de labrador

/f.407/ sitaron los y^{o}s yanaconas de don Sancho Usca Paucar caçique son los siguientes—

paga de servicio	*paga de tasa*	*paga de dotrina*	*chacaras de tassa*
			un topo de maiz un topo de trigo dos canchas de papas otras dos de oca
quatro canchas de papas al lado dos fanegas de maiz y tres bestidos			topo y m^{o} de chacara de mayz e un topo de trigo
una camiseta seis fanegas de maiz seis bellones de lana			un topo de maiz un topo de trigo tres canchas de papas tres de oca
una camiseta			
Isavel Guanpa de ochenta			m^{o} topo de maiz m^{o} topo de trigo dos canchas de papas dos de oca
huerfanos	Domingo Yapo un año		
un topo de maiz dos topos de trigo dos canchas de papas una cancha de oca			

/f.407v/

	Casados Años	*Hijos Años*	*servicio que a fecho cada yanaconas*
180	Martin Tacoxi Conde treinta—30 Juana Puma quarenta 40		a que le sirve un año de benefiçialle las chacaras
44	Andres Masquis diez y ocho—18 de Xaquixaguana Maria Llaino v^{te}—20		a que le sirve ocho a^{o}s de labrador
217	P^{o} Cabana Cana sesenta—60 Juana Puco çinq^{ta} y ocho—58		a que le sirve diez y ocho años
viudas viejas	Ynes Chinbo Urma çinquenta y ocho 58		sirve a un hijo suyo ques yanacona del suso dho
	Madalena Coca Ynquilla ses^{a} 60		sirve a otro hijo suyo
	Leonor Chinbo sesenta—60	P^{o} Guanca setenta 70	
		Juana Poma doze—12	
	Diego Yapo Anos naçio en este termino 15	Juan Pachas su hermano ocho—8 Ju^{a} Pasna su her^{a}	sirve desde niño de porquero

/f.408/

paga de servicio	*paga de dotrina*	*paga de tassa*	*chacaras de tasa*
m^{o} topo de maiz y un topo de trigo una cancha de papas			
un topo de maiz y un topo de trigo quatro canchas de papas			
un quarto de topo de maiz otro tanto de trigo una cancha de papas			
m^{o} topo de chacara de maiz dos topos de trigo dos canchas de papas dos de oca			
medio topo de chacara un topo de chacara de trigo			

/f.408v/

	de don Alonso Cusi Paucar		
45	Alonso Canas Yanas Yanagara çinq[ta]—50	Barbola Quiapuquio tres—3 Maria Poco Carua uno—1	a que sirve siete años de labrador
de don Al[o] Titu Atauche 377	Domyngo Apasa Colla treinta e seis—36 Angelina Xaquipi treinta—30		a que le sirve quinze años
46	Andres Caxabilca treinta e dos—32 Ju[a] Cona Chinbo treinta e çinco—35	P[o] Collagua çinco—5 Diego Chuspi dos 2	a que le sirve de diez años
de don Her[do] Chui Topa	P[o] Asto quar[ta] 40 +218+ Leonor Curimayguai sesenta—60		a que le sirve quinze años
	Juan Paucar Atabillo treinta—30 Leonor Suyo treinta 30	Juana Pasna Chinbo tres—3	a çinco años que le sirve
139	Juan Carnaluna diez y ocho—18 es Guanca— Catalina Caxa—20	Juana Yauri Chinbo dos—2	a çinco años que le sirve
47	Andres Guaman Pullaca diez e ocho de Tanbo—18 Luzia Yaro Mallao veinte—20		a diez años que le sirve
146	Luys Topa Yupangui Ynga naçio en Chivches veinte—20 Ynes Chinbollo—26		a que sirve de seis años
de don Carlos Ynga 181	Myguel Guaranga treinta e seis Yauyo 36 Ynes Carua Tiquilla treinta e dos—32	Juan Luna Chigua siete 7 Al[o] Minchui tres 3	a que le sirve de quinze años

/f.409/

Gonçalo Suyo Cache quarenta Ganca	Fran[co] Paucar seis—6	a mas de quinze años que le sirve
Elvira Quispe Yauyo quarenta—40	Ynes Asto Mallao v[te] 20	sirve en lo que le mandan
Ynes Arcarna setenta 70	Martin Atau Guama doze—12	sirve en lo que le mandan
Xpobal Yauri Chagua Yauyo diez y ocho	Leonor Yaucha dos—2	
Pablo Guacara treinta e ocho de Xaquixaguana 38 Martin Suyo v[te] e ocho 28	Diego Binynilla quatro—4 Ana Tanchuco siete—7	a mas de quinze años que le sirve
Lucas Toa Cañar treynta e seis 36 Ynes Caxa 30	Ysabel Sasaychuco uno 1	a mas de quinze años que le sirve
P[o] Labacaca treinta cañar 30 Maria Yucho v[te] e seis 26	Alonso Quispe seis—6	a mas de quynze años que le sirve
P[o] Quispe Cuchus quarenta 40 Beatriz Chinbo Coca quarenta e dos 42	Catalina Coca Quipe ocho—8 Luzia Querarinque 6 Agustin Tica q[tro] 4	a que le sirve mas de quynze años
Xpobal Paucartico cin[qta] 50 P[o] Mollo Cañar ochenta 80		Elvira Caxa ochenta

/f.409v/ Resumen de los y[o]s yanaconas questan en la corona real que biuen en el pueblo de San Fr[co] de Maras

xvij yndios casados de diez y ocho años a çinquenta para poder tributar diez y siete.
Iiij solteros de diez y ocho a çinquenta años para poder tributar quatro.
XXI son los y[o]s yanaconas que an de pagar tributo a su m[t] y biben en este pueblo veinte e uno

v	moços de doze años a diez y ocho uno	i
v	muchachos de doze años abaxo diez y seis	xvi
v	viejos casados de çinquenta arriba uno	i

v	viejos solteros quatro	iiij
v	mugeres de diez y ocho a^{o}s a çinq^{ta} siete	vij
v	moças de doze años a diez y ocho una	i
v	muchachas de doze a^{o}s abajo doze	xij
v	viejas y solteras de çinquenta años arriba honze	xj
v	un huerfano	i

Biven en este pueblo de san Françisco de Maras de los y^{o}s yanaconas que a el se rreduxeron v^{te} e un y^{o}s trbutarios y son entre todos grandes y pequeños con las mugeres de los casados nobenta e tres almas. El liç^{do} frei P^{o} Gutierrez Flores ante mi P^{o} Diaz Valdeon scri^{no} xc iij

v todos estos y^{o}s yanaconas que se rreduxeron en los pueblos del valle de Yucai y en san Fran^{co} de Maras puso su Exª en la corona real de su m^{t} y los taso para que pagasen tribu^{o} a su real m^{t} como consta por el auto y tasa que dellos hizo questa en poder de los ofiçiales reales. P^{o} Diaz Valdeon escrivano.

v yo Alvaro Ruiz de Nabamuel escrivano de camara de su magestad en su audiençia real de los //
/f.410/ Reies doy fee que este treslado se saco de la bisita original que queda y esta en poder de Ant^{o} Bap^{a} de Salazar que para la sacar me entrego originalmente con la qual se corrigio y conçerto y se saco de pedimi^{to} del liçençiado Alvaro de Caravajal fiscal de su m^{t} en los rreies en v^{te} de marzo de myll e qui^{o}s e setenta e ocho años va testado /qu/ onze / siete/ tassa/ un topo de chacara enmendado/ ten/ mas entre rr^{o}s seis al liçençiado/ Albaro Ruiz de Nabamuel.

Don Felipe por la graçia de dios rrei de Castilla de Leon de Aragon de las dos Çeçilias de Jerusalen de Navarra de Granada de Toledo de Balençia de Galiçia de Mallorcas Sevilla de Cerdeña de Cordoba de Corçega de Murçia de Jaen de los Algarves de Algeçira de Gibraltar de las yslas de Canaria de las Yndias yslas y tierra firme del mar Oceano Conde de Flandes e de Tirol etc. A vos nuestro corregidor y alcaldes ordinarios y otras qualesquier nuestras justicias asi de la ciudad del Cuzco como de todas las demas ciudades villas e lugares deste reino y cada uno e qualquier dellos en vros lugares e juridiçiones a quien esta nra carta fuere mostrada salud e gracia. Sepades que pleyto e causa se sigue e trata en la nra corte e chançilleria por por nro mandado reside en la ciudad de los Reies de los nuestros reinos del Piru entre partes de la una doña Beatriz Coya muger legitima del cap^{t} Martin Garçia de Loyola y Juan de Arrandolaça su procurador en su nombre con el liç^{do} Alvaro de Caravajal nro fiscal en la dha nra audi^{a} sobre el despojo de los y^{o}s del repartimi^{o} de Yucai de su encomienda que por yanaconas no tributarios se pusieron en nra corona real y las demas causas y razones en el proceso del dho pleito contenidas en el qual aviendo dho y alegado las ptes de su justicia fuere recevida la causa a prueva con ter^{no} de noventa dias y otras prorrogaciones y se despacho nuestra carta e provision real //
/f.410v/ a pedimento del dho fiscal para hazer sus provanças y agora en ocho dias del mes de noviembre deste presente año de setenta y siete el dho nro fiscal por peticion nos hizo relacion que aviendo enviado la dha nuestra carta receptoria y los recaudos neçesarios para hazer provança en la ciudad del Cuzco al nuestro corregidor de la dha ciudad por caso futuyto [*sic*] lo por negociacion de la parte contr^{a} o colacion de los que la llevaron la dha receptoria y recaudos no se avian recevido por el dho corregidor hasta el mes de otubre proximo pasado que hera pasado ya el ter^{no} provatorio que se avian dado como pareçia por cierta carta mensiva de don Graviel Paniagua de Loaysa nro corregidor de la dha ciudad por lo qual no se avia podido hazer la dha provança en tiempo e nra real hazienda y fisco hera danificada por el convenir que se hiciese la dha provança por no aver otra instancia y averse de enviar al nro real consejo de las Yndias conforme a lo por nos mandado atento a lo qual nos pidio y suplico que por via de prorrogacion o quarto plazo o por la via que mejor oviese lugar de dr^{o} le mandasemos dar otros noventa dias de termino para hazer la dha provança y para que lo suso dho huviese efecto siendo necesario pidio restitucion yn yntregun contra el apsso o transcurso del dho termino e juro en forma no le pedir de malicia sino por convenir asi a nro dr^{o} real e que no se perdiese por falta de la dha provança sobre que pidio justicia e hizo presentacion de la dha carta mesiva del dho corregidor de lo qual se mando dar treslado a la parte contr^{a} por el qual fue respondido y alegado contra ello y conclusa la causa en este articulo y visto en la dha nra audiencia por el dho nro presidente e oydores della por auto por ellos proveido en diez y nueve de noviembre deste presente año conçedieron al dho fiscal la dha restitucion del dho ter^{no} de los noventa dias por su parte pedido los quales corriesen desde el dho dia diez y nueve de noviembre del //
/f.411/ dho año y de pedim^{to} y suplicacion del dho nro fiscal por los dhos nro presidente e oydores fue acordado deviamos mandar esta nra carta para vos en la dha razon e nos tovimoslo por bien por que vos mandamos si ante vos pareciere la parte del dho nro fiscal dentro de los dhos noventa dias que se cuenten desde los dhos diez y nueve de noviembre del dho año hagais venir y parecer ante nos a todas las personas que por t^{gos} dixere se entiende aprovechar la parte del dho nro fiscal contando que no pasen de doze t^{o}s y asi parecidos debaxo de juram^{to} que ante todas cosas dellos e de cada uno dellos recibireis los preguntareis por el conocim^{to} de las partes y por las preguntas generales de la lei y por las del interrogatorio que ante vos sera presentado firmado del secretario de la dha nuestra audiencia y al testigo que dixere que save la preg^{ta} le preguntareis como y por que la save y al que dixere que la cree como y porque la cree y al que la oyo dezir a quien y como y quando de manera que den razon suficiente de sus dhos y depusiciones y lo que los dhos tg^{os} dixeren y depusieren firmada de vro nombre y del scriv^{o} nombrada por pte del dho nro fiscal como haga fee se lo dareis y entregareis pa que lo presente ante nos en el dho p^{to} y causa en guarda de su justicia lo qual asi hazed e cumplid aviendo sido primeramente notificada esta nra carta e citado para lo en ella contenido a la parte de la dha doña Beatriz Coya para que si quisiere se halle presente al ver presentar jurar y conocer los dhos tg^{os} e que nombre scriv^{o} ante quien la dha provança pase y se haga y le nombrado dentro de tres dias mandamos la dha provança se haga ante el scriv^{o} solo nombrado por parte del dho nro fiscal y no se haga en de al so pena de la nra md y de qvios p^{o}s para la nra

camara. Dada en los Reies a veinte dias del mes de noviembre de myll e qvios y setenta y siete años. don Francisco de Toledo el lic^{do} Sanchez Paredes. El lic^{do} Ramirez de Cartagena el lic^{do} Recalde. Yo Alvaro Ruiz de Navamuel escribano de camara de su m^{t} catolica fize escrevir por su mandado con acuerdo de su presidente e oydores registrada. Juan de Murga chanciller. Lor^{ço} de Aliaga.

En la ciudad de los Reies en veinte e un dias del mes de noviembre de myll e qvios y setenta y siete años //
/f.411v/ yo Blas Hernandez escrivano publico e de cab^{o} desta ciudad ley e notifique esta carta e provision real de su m^{t} a Juan de Arrandolaca pr^{or} de la dha doña Beatriz Coya en su persona y le apercivi para todo lo en ella contenido y le apercivi para que nombrase por su parte escrivano ante quien pase la provança que por esta real provision se manda tg^{os} Domingo de Destre y Melchor Casta residentes en esta dha ciudad. Blas Hernandez escrivano publico y del cabildo.

En los Reies en veinte e un dias del mes de noviembre de myll e qvios y setenta y siete años en presencia de mi Alonso Ramos Cervantes escribano de su m^{t} y tg^{os} yuso escriptos parecio el señor licenciado Alvaro de Carvajal fiscal de su m^{t} en esta real audiencia que reside en esta dha ciudad e dixo que dava su poder cumplido que de dr^{o} se requiere a Sancho Verdugo alguazil mayor de la ciudad del Cuzco e Antonio Rodriguez y Gregorio Lopez de Unzueta oficiales de la real hazienda de su m^{t} de la dha ciudad e a qualquier dellos para que por el y en su nombre puedan presentar esta carta y provision real de su m^{t} receutoria ante qualesquier justicias e juezes e pedir cumplimi^{to} della en su cumplimi^{to} presentar tg^{os} y escriptos e hazer qualesquier pedimi^{o}s e requerimi^{o}s que sean nezesarios para lo que dho es e fha la dha provança la puedan sacar y enbiarsela a esta real audiençia que quan cumplido poder a e tiene e para lo que dho es se requiere otro tal y ese mesmo les dio con sus yncidencias y dependencias y con libre e general administracion para lo de suso referido y lo otorgo en esta forma siendo tg^{os} el licenciado Pedro de Bizcarra e Albaro Rodriguez Monsilla y Melchor Castañeda residentes en esta dha ciudad e lo firmo el lic^{do} Alvaro de Carvajal e yo el dho Alonso Ramos Cervantes scriv^{o} de su magestad en todos los sus reinos lo fize escrivir e fize my signo en testim^{o} de verdad. Alonso Ramos Cervantes.

/al margen: Ynterrog^{o} del fiscal/ Por las preguntas siguientes sean preg^{dos} los testigos que presentaren por el licenciado Alv^{o} de Caravajal fiscal de su m^{t} en la causa con doña //
/f.412/ /al margen: interrog^{o} del fiscal probança del fiscal/ Beatriz Coya sobre los y^{o}s yanaconas naborias questan reducidos e poblados en los pueblos de San Benito de Alcantara Santiago de Oropesa San Bernardo San Fran^{co} de Maras terminos del tr^{no} del Cuzco puestos en cabeça de su magestad.

Primeram^{te} si conocen a las partes y si tienen noticia de los dhos pueblos y de quando se reduxeron y poblaron por el padre fray P^{o} Gutierez visitador general que fue de los terminos de la ciudad del Cuzco.

Yten si saven e conocen quel dho lic^{do} fray P^{o} Gutierez visitador por comision del señor visorey los termin^{o}s de la dha ciudad del Cuzco hallando en la dha visita muchos y^{o}s yanaconas anavorias que no tributavan ni estavan encomendados en persona alguna constandole ser ansi por averiguaciones e ynformaciones bastantes los junto e reduxo y poblo en la forma sig^{te} en el pueblo de Santiago de Oropesa ciento e ochenta y^{o}s tributarios sin otros muchachos viejos y enfermos y huerfanos y viudas y solteras y en el pu^{o} de San Bernardo ciento y sesenta e quatro tributarios sin otros muchachos y enfermos como esta dho y en el pueblo de San Benito de Alcantara ochenta e quatro tributarios demas de los dhos muchachos viejos y enfermos y en el pueblo de San Francisco de Maras veinte e un y^{o}s tributarios sin los dhos enfermos y muchachos todo en ter^{no} de la dha ciudad del Cuzco digan lo que saven.

Yten si saven e conocen que todos los dhos y^{o}s yanaconas que asi el dho lic^{do} frei P^{o} junto y poblo en los dhos pueblos al tiempo quel dho licenciado frei P^{o} los visito y antes dende que los españoles entraron en este reino heran yanaconas o naborias y no estavan encomendados en persona alguna ni tributavan a persona alguna y en tal posesion de yanaconas y como tales esentos de tributo estavan y heran avidos e tenidos y asi hera publico y notorio y los t^{o}s los saven por la noticia que dello tenian y si otra cosa fuera o si tributaran a alguna persona los t^{o}s lo supieran ser menos digan los t^{o}s lo que cerca dello saven y creen y como lo saben

/f.412v/ Yten si saven que por ser los dhos ansi y estar dello ynformado el señor bisorey don Francisco de Toledo puso los dhos y^{o}s en cabeça de su magestad y los taso y les dio tasa de lo que avian de tributar en conformidad de una cedula de su m^{t} que manda que a los y^{o}s yanaconas o navorias se les heche tributo pa su real hazienda digan lo que cerca desto saven y entienden.

Yten si saven e conocen que todo lo suso dho es pu^{co} y notorio y pu^{ca} voz y fama el lic^{do} Alvaro de Carvajal. Albaro Ruiz de Nabamuel.

En la ciudad del Cuzco a treinta dias del mes de diziembre de myll e qvios y setenta y siete años ante el Yll^{e} señor Fran^{co} de Valverde juez e justicia mayor en esta dha ciudad y su jur^{on} por su m^{t} y por ante mi el scriv^{o} pu^{co} ynfraescripto parecieron presentes los señores juezes e oficiales reales de la real hazienda de su magestad presentaron esta provision real de su m^{t} de receptoria emanada de la real audiencia de los Reies con el ynterr^{o} de preg^{tas} que presentaron e pidieron al señor juez mande examinar los t^{o}s que en este negocio presentaren e pidieron justicia. Pero Diaz Baldeon escrivano publico.

E por el señor juez visto mando que presenten los t^{o}s de que se entienden aprovechar y se exsaminaran por las preg^{tas} del ynterr^{o} que tienen presentado dentro del termino contenido en la real provision. Fran^{co} de Valverde. P^{o} Diaz Valdeon escribano publico.

En la ciudad del Cuzco a quinze dias del mes de henero de myll e qvios y setenta y ocho años ante el Yll^{e} señor don Gabriel Paniagua de Loaysa cavallero de la orden de Calatrava corregidor e justicia mayor por su magestad en esta ciudad del Cuzco e su jur^{on} etc. E por ante mi el scriv^{o} pu^{co} ynfraescripto los señores juezes y oficiales reales de la real haz^{da} desta ciudad presentaron //
/f.413/ esta pregunta añadida ques como se sigue. Pedro Diaz Valdeon escribano publico.

Muy poderoso señor el lic^{do} Alvaro de Carvajal vro fiscal en la causa con doña Beatriz Coya y Juan de Arrandolaça su pr^{or} sobre los yanaconas poblados en el valle de Yucai y termi^{o}s de la ciudad del Cuzco sup^{co} a vra Al^{a} que los t^{o}s presentados por parte de vro fisco demas de las preguntas del ynterr^{o} que presentado tengo sean preguntados los preguntas siguientes.

Yten si saven y conocen que los y^{o}s yanaconas que se reduxeron en los dhos pueblos que el dho lic^{do} frey Pedro Gutierez poblo dellos en el dho valle de Yucai muchos de los dhos y^{o}s fueron y^{o}s que los españoles y otras personas pusieron e tenian en huertas y otras haziendas que tenian en el dho valle de Yucai trayendolos de otras partes fuera del dho valle para el benef^{o} dellas y se quedaron alli digan lo que saven declarando especificada y particularmente lo que cerca desto saven.

Otro si a vra alteza sup^{co} mande que por ellas se exsaminen los testigos que se presentaren en la ciudad del Cuzco o otras partes por parte de vro fysco don se a enviado receptoria y para ello se me de un traslado autoriçado della pa lo qual es. El licenciado Alvaro de Carvajal.

En la ciudad de los Reies en cinco dias del mes de diciembre de mill e qvios y setenta y siete años ante los señores presidente e oydores en audi^{a} de relaciones se presento esta peticion y pregunta.

Y por los dhos señores vista la ovieron por presentada y mandaron que los t^{o}s digan por las dhas preguntas y se le de el treslado que pide enmendado por este fue Alvaro Ruiz de Navamuel.

E pidieron al señor corregidor mande los t^{o}s que en este caso presentaren se exsaminen por ella e pidieron justicia P^{o} Diaz Valdeon escriv^{o} pu^{co}

/f.413v/ E por el señor corregidor bisto m^{do} que los t^{o}s que en este negocio se presentaren se exsaminen por la dha pregunta P^{o} Diaz Valdeon escriv^{o} pu^{co}.

En la ciudad del Cuzco a treze dias del mes de henero de myll e qvios y setenta y ocho años ante el Yll^{e} señor don Gabriel Paniagua de Loaysa cavall^{o} de la orden de Calatrava corregidor e justicia mayor por su m^{t} en esta dha ciudad e su jur^{on} etc. E por ante mi el escriv^{o} pu^{co} ynfraescripto los señores juezes y oficiales reales de la real hazienda presentaron por t^{o}s en esta causa a Garçia de Melo y Damian de la Bandera y a Juan Lopez de Arrieta y a Juan de Salas de Valdes y a Diego de Mercado vz^{o}s e moradores en esta dha ciudad de los quales e de cada uno dellos el señor coreg^{dor} tomo juram^{to} en forma jurando por dios e por Santa Maria su madre e por la señal de la cruz que como buenos cristianos guardando sus conciencias diran verdad en este negocio de lo supieren y les fuere preg^{do} y si asi lo hizieren dios les ayude y lo contr^{o} se lo demande e cada uno dellos dixo si juro e amen t^{o}s Juan de Castañeda e Ju^{o} Bautista. Pedro Diaz Valdeon escriv^{o} publico.

En la ciudad del Cuzco a v^{te} e nueve dias del mes de henero de myll e qvios y setenta e ocho a^{o}s los dhos señores juezes y oficiales reales e por ante mi el dho escriv^{o} presentaron por t^{o}s en esta causa a Diego Descobar del qual fue tomado juram^{to} en forma segun que los demas t^{o}s e prometio de dezir verdad so pena de perjuro t^{o}s. Juan Bautista y Pedro Suarez Carvajal. Pedro Diaz Valdeon escriv^{o} pu^{co}.

En la ciudad del Cuzco a treinta e un dias del mes de henero de myll e qvios e setenta e ocho años antel dho señor corregidor e por ante mi el dho escriv^{o} los señores juezes y oficiales reales presentaron por t^{o} en esta causa al governador Martin Hurtado de Arbieto y a Juan de Cellorigo vz^{o}s desta ciudad del Cuzco de los quales e de cada uno dellos el señor corregidor tomo juram^{to} en forma segun //
/f.414/ que de los demas t^{o}s y prometieron de dezir verdad so pena de perjuros. t^{o}s Diego de Mercado y el lic^{do} Alonso Perez. P^{o} Diaz Valdeon escriv^{o} pu^{co}.

En la ciudad del Cuzco a cinco dias del mes de hebr^{o} de mill e qvios e setenta e ocho a^{o}s ante el señor corr^{dor} e por ante mi el dho escriv^{o} los dhos señores juezes e oficiales reales presentaron por t^{o}s en esta causa a Pablo de Carvajal y a don Fran^{co} de Auina vz^{o}s desta ciudad y a Xpobal Holgado y a P^{o} Guerero mayordomo desta ciudad de los quales e de cada uno dellos el señor corregidor tomo juram^{to} en forma segun que de los demas t^{o}s e prometieron de dezir verdad so pena de perjuros. t^{o}s el lic^{do} Alonso Perez y Nuno de Mendoça alcaldes ordinarios en esta dha ciudad. P^{o} Diaz Baldeon escriv^{o} publico.

E lo que cada uno de los t^{o}s dixeron secreta y apartadam^{te} es como se sigue. P^{o} Diaz Valdeon escriv^{o} publico.

Provança del fiscal en lo de Loyola.

T^{o} El dho tesorero Garçia de Melo vz^{o} desta ciudad presentado por pte del señor fiscal aviendo jurado e preguntado dixo lo siguiente.

i A la primera pregunta dixo que conoce a doña Beatriz y al cap^{t} Loyola su marido y no conoze al señor fiscal.

De las generales dixo ques de hedad de sesenta y ocho años poco mas o menos q que no concure en ning^{a} de las generales.

ij a la pregunta dos dixo que save e vio que el lic^{do} frey P^{o} Gutierez visito a los y^{o}s del valle de Yucai e Maras e otros questan en rio arriba e rio abaxo e la dha visita hizo por comision de su Exª como la preg^{ta} lo dize y en lo demas contenido en la dha pregunta se remite a la poblazon que el dho visitador hizo de los pueblos contenidos en ella.

iij A la pregunta tres dixo queste t^{o} tiene dho su dho en este pleito por parte de la dha doña Beatriz Coya y del dho cap^{t} Loyola su marido donde dixo lo que savia deste caso al qual se remitio e que no save otra cosa mas de lo que alli tiene dho lo qual dixo que hera verdad so cargo del dho juram^{to} y lo firmo. Melo ante my P^{o} Diaz Valdeon escriv^{o} publico.

/f.414v/ Testigo Damian de la Bandera vz^{o} desta ciudad e juez de naturales en ella aviendo jurado y preguntado dixo lo siguiente.

i A la primera pregunta dixo que conoce a las ptes ecepto al señor fiscal que no le conoce.

De las generales dixo ques de hedad de mas de cinq^{ta} e cinco años e que no concure en ninguna dellas.

ij A la pregunta dos dixo que lo que della save es queste t^{o} en tiempo del marques de Cañete virey que fue destos reinos que dios aya este t^{o} por comision suya visito los y^{o}s del dho valle de Yucay e otros muchos en esta provincia del Cuzco y al tiempo que bisito los del dho valle de Yucai hallo en el muchos anaconas [*sic*] que sirvian a diversas personas españoles e y^{o}s los quales no estavan tasados con los y^{o}s del dho valle ni pagavan tributo a persona alguna mas de servir a quien se avian allegado por lo qual entiende este t^{o} que con justa razon el visitador frei P^{o} Gutierez los visito por anaconas y su Exª los puso en cabeça de su magestad e les mando pagar tributo como al presente lo pagan e esto save desta pregunta.

iij A la preg^{ta} tres dixo lo que dho tiene en la preg^{ta} antes desta.

iiij a la pregunta quatro dixo que dize lo que dho tiene en la pregunta dos e questo es la verdad so cargo del dho juramento y lo firmo. Damian de la Bandera ante mi P^{o} Diaz Valdeon escriv^{o} publico.

T^{o} el dho Juan Lopez de Arrieta residente en esta gran ciudad del Cuzco t^{o} presentado por pate del dho fiscal y siendo preguntado al tenor de las dhas preguntas dixo e depuso lo siguiente.

i A la primera pregunta dixo que conoce a las partes e que conoce algunos de los yanaconas que residen en el valle de Yucai e que tiene noticia del valle de Yucai e pueblos que en el se reduçieron por el licenciado frai P^{o} Gutierez Flores por aver estado en ellos y del dho pueblo de Maras.

De las generales dixo ques de hedad de quarenta años poco mas o menos e que no es pariente //
/f.415/ de las partes ni le ba interese en este caso ni concure en el ninguna de las preguntas generales de la ley.

ij A la segunda pregunta dixo que save y es pu^{co} y notorio quel dho licenciado frei P^{o} Gutierez fue visitador e bisito el pu^{o} y valle de Yucai e pueblos que la preg^{ta} dize e que en los dhos pueblos hallo muchos y^{o}s yanaconas que no heran tributarios a su m^{t} ni a otro persona alguna los quales estavan en guertas y estancias de españoles a quien servian e que se reduçieron a pueblos por orden e mando del dho visitador como la pregunta dize e que no save la cantidad de y^{o}s que ansi hallo y bisito de los dhos yanaconas ni los que los reduzieron a cada pueblo e que se remite a la visita e reduzion que delos dhos y^{o}s yanaconas se hizo por do parecera.

iij A la preg^{ta} tres dixo que dize lo que dho tiene en este su dho de suso e que se refiere.

iiij a la pregunta quatro dixo que save y es notorio que su Exª del señor bisorey despues que por el dho lic^{do} frai P^{o} Gutierez fue visitado el dho valle de Yucai e los dhos y^{o}s yanaconas e fho tributo a los dhos yanaconas y los puso en la corona real por queste t^{o} a bisto el auto por do su Exª hecho el dho tributo y los dhos y^{o}s a que se refiere y questo responde a esta pregunta.

v A la final pregunta dixo que lo que dho tiene en este su dho es la verdad y lo que paso y en ello se afirmo y firmolo de su nombre.

Añadida

A la pregunta añadida dixo ques pu^{co} y notorio que muchos de los dhos yanaconas que el dho lic^{do} frai P^{o} Gutierez visito en el dho valle de Yucai son y^{o}s advenediços no naturales del dho valle porque son traidos e puestos en las dhas estancias y huertas por los españoles dueños dellas traiendolos de fuera pte y ansi este t^{o} tiene en el dho valle una guerta y tierras donde los yanaconas que alli tiene los a llevado y puesto en la dha guerta de otra pte fuera del dho valle de Yucai e questo es la verdad y lo que save y en ello se afirmaba y afirmo y firmolo de su nombre. Juan Lopez de Arrieta ante mi P^{o} Diaz Valdeon escribano publico.

/f.415v/ t^{o} El dho Juan de Salas vz^{o} desta ciudad aviendo jurado y preguntado dixo lo siguiente.

i A la primera pregunta dixo que conoce a las ptes ecepto que no conoce al señor fiscal.

De las generales dixo ques de hedad de mas de sesenta años e que no concure en ning^{a} de las generales.

ij A la preg^{ta} dos dixo que save e vio que el dho licenciado frai P^{o} Gutierez visito el valle de Yucai por comision de su Exª e vio quexarse a algunos encomenderos de que y^{o}s de sus encomiendas lo avia fho yanaconas e los poblo en los pueblos parecera por los padrones que hizo y esto save desta pregunta.

iij A la preg^{ta} tres dixo que muchos de los yanaconas que avia en este valle de Yucai heran de personas particulares que avian venido al valle de otras encomiendas e servian a quien les parecia sin tributar queste t^{o} viese ni supiese.

iiij A la preg^{ta} quatro dixo que por yanaconas los puso su Exª en la cabeça de su m^{t} y al presente por esta causa los y^{o}s que se visitaron en el valle de Yucai por anaconas pagan tributo a su magestad.

Añadida. A la preg^{ta} añadida dixo que asi como la preg^{ta} lo dize por que en las huertas que ay en la quebrada de Urcos del valle de Yucai de los vz^{o}s desta ciudad save este t^{o} que los anaconas que en ellas avia heran de los vz^{o}s e algunos dellos venidos de otras partes al valle y todos pagan tribu^{o} y esto es la verdad y lo que deste caso save so cargo del dho juram^{to} y lo firmo. Juan de Salas ante mi P^{o} Diaz Valdeon scriv^{o} pu^{co}.

t^{o} El dho Diego de Mercado aviendo jurado y preguntado dixo lo siguiente.

i A la primera preg^{ta} dixo que conoce a las partes e que no conoce al señor fiscal.

De las generales dixo ques de hedad de mas de cinq^{ta} años e que no concure en ninguna dellas.

ij A la preg^{ta} dos dixo que save que el dho frai Pedro Gutierez visitador del partido de los dhos pueblos reduxo en ellos mucha cantidad de y^{o}s que llaman //
/f.416/ yanaconas que servian a muchas personas particulares que tienen huertas estancias y haziendas en el dho valle de Yucai donde son los dhos pueblos los quales nunca jamas vio este t^{o} ni entendio que pagasen tribu^{o} a la dha doña Beatriz ni a otra p^{a}s alguna porque veia este t^{o} que los dhos españoles davan a los dhos y^{o}s llamados yanaconas tierras de donde se sustentasen e coxiesen comida y de bestir y otras cosas por el servi^{o} que les hazian los quales reduxo a los dhos pueblos como dize la preg^{ta} que la quantia de quantos fueron este t^{o} no lo save mas de que tres de los dhos yanaconas reducidos servian a este testigo y los tuvo en su servi^{o} mas tiempo de ocho años los quales heran de un Ynga que se llamava Paucar Topa y despues servian a una hija suya sin pagar tasa como dho es a persona alguna y esto responde.

iij A la pregunta tres dixo que dize lo que dho tiene en la pregunta antes desta que todos los anaconas que asi estan reducidos en los dhos quatro pueblos que servia a españoles e Yngas que tenian las dhas estancias e huertas del dho valle a quien davan tierras y los sustentavan save este t^{o} como dho tiene que no pagavan tribu^{o} ni tasa a la dha doña Beatriz questos dhos yanaconas son muy conocidos e se podian sacar por la dha visita estos tales no fueron visitados en visita alguna por de la encomienda de la dha doña Beatriz Coya por ser los mas dellos advenediços y traidos de muchas partes deste reino por los dhos españoles de diferentes repartimientos e nacion asi como Chunbibilcas e Aimaraes e Quito e Yungas e Yngas e Cañares e otras ptes para efeto de servirse dellos y dalles de comer y bestir y sustentalle como dho es y estos tales jamas tributaron a la dha doña Beatriz Coya pero que save este t^{o} que en las dhas reducciones del dho valle otros muchos yanaconas e y^{o}s que estavan en posesion de no tributar a la dha Coya y heran yanaconas hijos de los naturales de los dhos pu^{o}s de la encomienda de la dha Coya y servian a caciques //
/f.416v/ y mayordomos de la dha Coya y de sus antecesores de la dha encomienda y los mandavan los dhos caciques asi como don Fran^{co} Chilche a mas de setenta o ochenta y^{o}s que los llamava yanaconas y los sustentavan de sus tierras y otros caciques como dho tiene tenian otros muchos e questos tales entiende este t^{o} que aunque no estavan tasados que heran de la dha encomienda e naturales del dho valle de Yucai los quales asi mysmo son muy conoçidos y se pueden sacar por la bisita general que dellos se hizo y esto save desta pregunta porque a bisto muchos dellos en el dho valle y tratado con ellos y save ser y pasar asi como dho tiene.

iiij A la pregunta quatro dijo que save este testigo que por auerse visitado los dhos yanaconas en la bisita general que hizo el frey Pedro Gutierez por y^{o}s que no avian sido tasados por y^{o}s bacos y los puso en cabeça de su m^{t} el señor bisorey y los taso como dize la pregunta e asi a visto que los oficiales de la real hazienda desta çiudad cobran el tribu^{o} dellos y estan en posesion de lo cobrar demas de tres años a esta parte y esto save desta pregunta—

v A la pregunta añadida dijo que dize lo que dho tiene en la pregunta antes desta y/ que se afirma e ratifica y es la verdad para el juram^{to} que tiene fecho y lo firmo con su nonbre Diego de Mercado ante mi P^{o} Diaz Valdeon escri^{o} publico.

v t^{o} El dho Diego Descobar aviendo jurado y preguntado dijo lo siguiente—

j A la primera preg^{ta} dijo que conoze a las partes

De las generales dijo ques de hedad de mas de treinta e seis a^{o}s e que no concure en ninguna de las generales—

/f.417/ ij A la preg^{ta} dos dijo que tiene notiçia de los dhos pu^{o}s por que los a bisto y save que hizo la visita y reduzion dellos el liçençiado frai Pedro Gutierez visitador general que fue del valle de Yucai y esto save desta pregunta.

iij A la preg^{ta} tres dijo queste t^{o} a bisto que en el dho valle de Yucai los mas de los y^{o}s ortelanos de vz^{o}s y otras personas son y^{o}s de los repartimi^{o}s questan fuera del dho valle y esto save desta preg^{ta}.

iiij A la preg^{ta} quatro dijo que tiene notiçia que su Exª los puso en caveça de su mag^{t} como la preg^{ta} lo dize.

v A la preg^{ta} añadida dijo que dize lo que dho tiene y esto es la verdad so cargo del dho juramento y lo firmo Diego descobar ante mi P^{o} Diaz Valdeon escrivano publico.

v t^{o} El dho Juan de Cellorigo vz^{o} desta çiudad aviendo jurado y preguntado dijo lo siguiente.

j A la primera preg^{ta} dijo que conoçe a las ptes eçepto al señor fiscal y ques de hedad de mas de treinta años e que no concure en ninguna de las generales.

ij A la pregunta dos dijo que save e vio que el dho liçençiado frei Pedro Gutierez visito ~~d~~el valle de Yucai por comision de su Exª e hizo lo que la preg^{ta} dize como en ella se contiene.

iij A la preg^{ta} tres dijo que los y^{o}s yanaconas que servian en las huertas que los llevaron los dueños de las haziendas al valle de Yucai y estos no son naturales del valle de Yucai sino advenedizos que los llevaron de otras partes e se sirvian dellos como anaconas sin pagar tributo a ninguna persona y asi fueron visitados por tales yanaconas y en la visita que hizo el liç^{do} Gutierez se puede ver muy claro quales son y demas destos yanaconas avia otros yanaconas muchos naturales //
/f.417v/ del dho valle servian a los caçiques e prinçipales de los y^{o}s del repartimi^{to} de Yucai y a otras personas como por la visita pareçera a que se remite y esto save desta pregunta.

Y algunos dellos an servido por yanaconas desde el tiempo de los Yngas y este titulo tenian por dezir que hera recamara del Ynga el valle de Yucai.

iiij A la pregunta quatro dixo que se remite a los autos que sobre ello hizo su Exª.

añadida A la pregunta añadida dixo que dize lo que dho tiene en la pregunta tres e que esto es verdad e lo que deste casso save so cargo del dho juramento y lo firmo Juan de Cellorigo ante mi Pedro Diaz Baldeon escrivano pu^{co}.

v t^{o} El governador Martin Hurtado de Arbieto aviendo jurado y preguntado dijo lo siguiente.

j A la primera pregunta dijo que conoçe a las partes y que no conoçe al señor fiscal.

De las generales dijo ques de hedad de mas de çinquenta años e que no concure en nynguna de las generales.

ij A la pregunta dos dixo que save e vio quel liç^{do} frei P^{o} Gutierez bisito los y^{o}s del valle de Yucai y los poblo como la preg^{ta} lo dize.

iij A la preg^{ta} tres dixo que save e vio que en el valle de Yucai avia muchos yanaconas que tenia don Fran^{co} Chilche e otros caçiques que se servian dellos y fuera destos yanaconas avia otros yanaconas que tenian cargo de las chacaras e huertas y todos ellos los puso en cabeça de su m^{t} como a personas que no tributaban y esto save de todas las preguntas y de la añadida dijo ques verdad //
/f.418/ so cargo del dho juramento y lo firmo Martin Hurtado de Arvieto ante mi P^{o} Diaz Valdeon escri^{o} publico.

v t^{o} EL dho Xpobal Holgado residente en el valle de Yucai aviendo jurado y siendo preguntado por el dho ynterrogatorio dixo lo siguiente

j A la primera pregunta dixo que conoçe/ a las partes e que no conoze al señor fiscal e ques de hedad de mas de sesenta años e que no concure en ninguna dellas.

ij A la pregunta dos dixo que save e vio que el liçençiado frei P^{o} Gutierez visito por comision de su Exª los y^{o}s del valle de Yucay y entrellos visito muchos y^{o}s o yanaconas y los poblo en los pu^{o}s contenidos en la pregunta por la forma y orden que en ella se declara y esto save desta pregunta.

iij A la pregunta tres dijo que save e vio/ que los caçiques y prinçipales del valle de Yucay tenian muchos y^{o}s de que se sirvian/ como yanaconas e avia otros españoles que tenian y^{o}s poblados en el dho valle que se sirvian dellos como yanaconas y este t^{o} no save de donde heran sacados ni si ayudavan a tributar o no y esto save desta preg^{ta}.

iiij A la pregunta quatro dixo que se remite a lo que su Exª hizo sobre este negoçi.

v A la pregunta añadida dixo que save y es verdad que algunos yanaconas estavan poblados en las huertas de los vz^{o}s desta çiudad y heran //
/f.418v/ advenediços que no heran naturales del valle e quantos e quienes este t^{o} no lo save y esto que dho tiene dixo que hera verdad y lo que deste caso save so cargo del dho juram^{to} y no fyrmo por que dixo que no savia y se afirmo e ratifico en lo que tiene dho ante mi P^{o} Dias Valdeon escri^{o} publico.

t^{o} El dho Pablo de Carvajal vz^{o} desta çiudad aviendo jurado y siendo preguntado dixo lo sig^{te}.

j A la primera pregunta dixo que conoçe a las partes e que no conoçe al señor fiscal y ques de hedad de mas de çinquenta años y que no concure en ninguna de las generales

ij A la pregunta dos dixo que save e vio que el liç^{do} frei P^{o} Gutierez visito el valle de Yucay por mandado de su Exª e reduxo los y^{o}s a pueblos formados como la preg^{ta} lo dize y en el dho valle visito muchos y^{o}s yanaconas y los reduxo y poblo en los dhos pueblos unos que tenian amos y otros que les tenian sin estar encomendados en persona alguna los que tenian amos y asi mismo bisito por yanaconas los y^{o}s ortelanos de las huertas de Yucai y esto save desta pregunta.

iij A la pregunta tres dixo que en el dho valle de Yucai y en esta çiudad y en muchas ptes deste reino y en todo el save y entiende e vio que avia muchos y^{o}s yanaconas que servian a españoles y a otras personas y otros andauan bagamundos sin pagar tasa ni tribu^{o} ni estar encomendados en persona alguna y los que asi avia en valle de Yucai y en esta çiudad heran lo mismo y los pusieron todos en la corona real y mando su Exª que tributasen a su m^{t} y este a pagado por los yanaconas que tiene en la huerta de Yucai y por //
/f.419/ los que tiene en esta çiudad el tributo y esto save desta pregunta.

iiij A la pregunta quatro dixo ques asi como la pregunta lo dize y declara y este t^{o} vio el auto que sobre este negoçio hizo su Exª en poder de los ofiçiales reales y por esto save lo que la pregunta dize.

añadida A la pregunta añadida dixo que dize lo que dho tiene e questo es la verdad so cargo del dho juram^{to} y lo firmo Pablo de Carvajal ante mi P^{o} Diaz Valdeon escri^{o} publico.

t^{o} El dho P^{o} Guerero vz^{o} e mayordomo desta çiudad aviendo jurado e siendo preguntado dixo lo siguiente

j A la primera pregunta dixo que conoçe a las partes e que no conoçe al señor fiscal y ques de hedad de mas de çinquenta a^{o}s y que no concure en ninguna de las generales.

ij A la pregunta dos dixo que save e vio este t^{o} que el liçençiado frei Pedro Gutierez por comision de su Exª visito el valle de Yucai e reduxo e poblo los y^{o}s del asi los mitimas como naturales y demas yanaconas que avia de particulares a los pueblos que la preg^{ta} dize y por la forma e horden que en ella se declara y esto save desta pregunta.

iij A la pregunta tres dixo que la mayor pte de los y^{o}s yanaconas que avia en el valle de Yucai heran de los mitimas y otros y^{o}s yanaconas ortelanos heran de personas particulares que los avian llevado a sus haziendas y estos no tributavan sino como personas libres servian a sus amos y no acudian con tribu^{o} ni tasa y los y^{o}s mitimas questavan en su lugar de yanaconas muchos dellos //
/f.419v/ servian a caçiques y prinçipales del dho valle como y^{o}s mitimas e oy en dia entiende este t^{o} lo hazen asi y esto save desta pregunta.

iiij A la pregunta quatro dixo que save y es verdad que su Exª puso todos los dhos yanaconas en cabeça de su magestad y asi tributan de la bisita general aca a su m^{t} y esto save y a visto desta pregunta.

añadida A la pregunta añadida dixo que dize lo que dho tiene en las preguntas rectro escriptas y lo que dho tiene es la verdad y lo que save deste caso so cargo del dho juram^{to} y lo firmo P^{o} Guerero ante mi P^{o} Diaz Valdeon escri^{o} pu^{co}.

t^{o} El dho don Fran^{co} de Acuña vz^{o} e regidor perpetuo desta çiudad aviendo jurado e siendo preguntado dixo lo siguiente.

j A la primera pregunta dixo que conoçe a las partes y que no conoçe al señor fiscal y ques de hedad de mas de çinq^{ta} años e que no concure en ninguna de las generales.

ij A la pregunta dos dixo que save e vio este t^{o} que el liç^{do} frei P^{o} Gutierez por comision de su Exª visito los y^{o}s del valle de Yucay y los reduxo y poblo asi los y^{o}s mitimas del dho valle como naturales e yanaconas que avia en el de personas particulares a pu^{o}s formados que son los contenidos en esta preg^{ta} y esto save e vio desta pregunta.

iij A la pregunta tres dixo que save e vio este t^{o} que los y^{o}s yanaconas que servian en el valle de Yucai a personas particulares de ortelanos y chacareros para el benef^{o} de sus haziendas estos no tributavan sino que como yanaconas y personas libres estavan en el dho valle sirviendo cada uno a su amo en lo //

/f.420/ que le mandava y los amos les davan chacaras y lo nezes^{o} para su sustento e quantos heran destos y^{o}s que asi serviana españoles este t^{o} no lo save y save que asi mismo los caçiques a y^{o}s prinçipales del dho valle de Yucai se servian de muchos y^{o}s mitimas so color desta que eran yanaconas si tributavan con alg^{a} cosa o no no lo save y esto save e vio desta preg^{ta}

iiij A la pregunta quatro dixo ques asi como la pregunta lo dize y declara porqueste t^{o} la visto que de la visita general aca todos los y^{o}s yanaconas tributan a su m^{t} y este t^{o} paga tribu^{o} por tres yanaconas que tiene en el valle de Yucai y esto save desta preg^{ta}

añadida A la pregunta añadida ques verdad lo contenido en la dha pregunta porque asi lo a visto este t^{o} ser y pasar como en la preg^{ta} se declara porque los y^{o}s yanaconas que sirven en las huertas y chacaras que los españoles tienen en el valle de Yucai todos o la mayor pte dellos son y^{o}s que los españoles los adquirieron y llevaron de otras ptes al dho valle y la cantidad destos y^{o}s este t^{o} no lo save quantos son y esto que dho tiene dixo que hera verdad y lo que deste caso save so cargo del dho juram^{to} y lo firmo don Fran^{co} de Acuña ante mi P^{o} Diaz Valdeon escrivano publico.

E fecha la dha provança los señores juezes ofiçiales de la real haz^{da} pidieron al señor coreg^{or} se la mande dar en pu^{ca} forma y en manera que haga fee para la presentar en la real audi^{a} de los Reies donde pende la dha causa y pidieron justiçia P^{o} Diaz Valdeon escr^{o} pu^{co}

E por el señor corregidor visto mando a mi el dho escrivano les de un treslado de la dha //
/f.420v/ provança e para el efeto que lo piden y lo firmo t^{o}s Sancho Verdugo e Hernando Rramirez e Gabriel Paniagua de Loaysa yo P^{o} Diaz Valdeon escrivano de su m^{t} pu^{co} del numero de la çiudad del Cuzco fui presente e fize aqui mi signo en tertimonio de verdad pero Diaz Valdeon escri^{o}

v En la causa de doña Beatriz Coya muger del cap^{t} Martin Garçia de Loyola y Juan de Arrandolaça su pr^{dor} con el liç^{do} Alvaro de Carvajal fiscal de su m^{t} sobre los y^{o}s yanaconas.

v /al margen: autos de remiss^{on} al consejo/ En la çiudad de los Reies en ocho Dias del mes de abril de mill e qui^{o}s e setenta e ocho años los señores presidente e oydores desta real audiençia vista la dha causa la remitieron a su m^{t} e señores de su real consejo de las Yndias e mandaron quel proçeso del dho pleito se enbie originalm^{te} al dho real consejo en la forma hordinaria quedando un treslado del en poder del secretario de la causa e mandaron çitar las dhas ptes en forma pa que bayan o enbien en seguimi^{to} della con señalamiento de los estrados reales del dho real consejo e que si antes quel dho pleito se registre el dho fiscal presentare sus provanças e le reçivan y enbien con el dho pleito originalmente quedando asi mesmo un treslado dellas en poder del dho secretario e asi lo proveyeron e rubricaron.

v Pronunçiose este auto estando haziendo audiençia pu^{ca} los señores presidente y oydores en el dho dia mes y año en el contenido pres^{te} Juan de Arrandolaça pr^{dor} de la dha doña Beatriz a quien se notefico y asi mismo estava presente el liç^{do} Carvajal fiscal Molina

v Por las preguntas siguientes sean preg^{dos} los t^{o}s que se presentaren por el liç^{do} Alvaro de Carvajal fiscal de su m^{t} en la causa con doña Beatriz Coya sobre los yanaconas o naborias questan //
/f.421/ reduçidos y poblados en los pu^{o}s de San Benito de Alcantara Santiago de Oropesa San Bernardo San Fran^{co} de Maras ter^{nos} de la çiudad del Cuzco puestos en cabeça de su m^{t}.

v Primeramente si conoçen a las partes y si tienen notiçia de los dhos pu^{o}s y de quando se reduxeron y poblaron por el liçençiado frei P^{o} Gutierez visitador que fue de los ter^{nos} de la dha çiudad del Cuzco.

v Yten si saven etc. que el dho liç^{do} frei P^{o} Gutierez visitador visitando por comision del señor visorei los ter^{nos} de la dha çiudad del Cuzco ha llando en la dha visita muchos y^{o}s yanaconas o naborias que no tributauan ni estavan en comendados en persona alguna costandole ser asi por aueriguaçiones e ynformaçiones bastantes los junto y reduxo y poblo en la forma siguiente: En el pueblo de Santiago de Oropesa çiento y ochenta y^{o}s tributarios sin otros muchachos viejos y enfermos y huerfanos y buidas y solteras y en el pueblo de san Bernardo çiento y sesentay quatro tributarios sin otros muchachos y enfermos como esta dho y en el pu^{o} de San Benito de Alcantara ochenta y quatro tributarios demas de los dhos muchachos viejos y enfermos y en el pueblo de San Fra^{nco} de Maras veinte e un y^{o}s tributarios sin los dhos enfermos y muchachos todo en ter^{no} de la dha çiudad del Cuzco digan lo que saven.

v Yten si saven etc. que todos los dhos y^{o}s yanaconas que asi el dho liç^{do} frei P^{o} junto e poblo en los dhos pu^{o}s los visito y antes dende que los españoles entraron en este reino heran yanaconas o naborias y no estavan encomendados en persona alguna ni tributavan a persona alguna y en tal //
/f.421v/ posesion de yanaconas y como tales y exsemptos de tributo estavan y heran abidos y tenidos y asi hera pu^{co} y notorio y los te^{o}s lo saven por la notiçia que dello tenian y si otra cossa fuera o si tributaron a alguna persona los t^{o}s lo supieran y no pudiera ser menos digan lo çerca dellos saven y creen e como lo saven.

iiij Yten si saven que por ser lo suso dho asi y estar dello ynformado el señor bisorei don Françisco de Toledo puso los dhos y^{o}s en caueça de su m^{t} y los taso y les dio tasa de lo que avian de tributar en conformidad de vna çedula de su m^{t} que manda que a los y^{o}s yanaconas o naborias se les heche tribu^{o} para su real hazienda digan lo que çerca desto saven y entienden v Yten si saven etc. que todo lo suso dho es pu^{co} e notorio e pu^{ca} boz e fama va esscripto en la margen/ como tales el liç^{do} Carvajal

En los Reies en v^{te} e uno de junio de mill e qui^{o}s y sententa y siete a^{o}s ante los señores presidente y oydores en audi^{a} la pres^{to} el liç^{do} Albaro de Carvajal fiscal de su magestad y los dhos señores visto le ouieron por presentado en quanto es pertinente que los t^{o}s digan por el Nabamuel.

v muy poderoso señor el liç^{do} Alvaro de Carvajal vro fiscal en la causa con doña Beatriz Coya y Juan de arrandolaça su pr^{or} sobre los yanaconas poblados en el valle de Yucai ter^{no} de la çiudad del Cuzco sup^{co} a Vra Al^{a} que los t^{o}s presentados por parte de vro fisco demas de las preguntas del ynterr^{o} que presentado tengo sean preg^{dos} por la pregunta siguiente.

v Yten si saven e conocen que los y^{o}s yanaconas que se reduxeron en los dhos pueblos quel dho liç^{do} frei P^{o} Gutierez poblo dellos en el dho valle de Yucai e muchoss de los dhos y^{o}s son y fueron y^{o}s que los españoles y otras personas pusieron y tenian en huertas y otras haziendas que tenian en el dho //
/f.422/ /al margen: Arriba mas t^{o}s del fiscal/ valle de Yucai trayendolos de otras ptes fuera del dho valle para el benef^{o} dellas y se quedaron alli digan lo que saven declarando espeçificada y particularmente lo que çerca desto saven.

v otro si a Vra Al^{a} sup^{co} mande que por ella se exsaminen los t^{o}s que se presentaren en la çiudad del Cuzco o otras partes por parte de v^{ro} fisco donde sea enbiado reçeutoria y para ello se me den treslado autoriçado dello para lo quel etc. el liçençiado Alvaro de Carvajal.

v En la çiudad de los Reies en çinco Dias del mes de dizienbre de mill e qui^{o}s e set^{a} y siete años ante los señores presidente e oydores en audiençia de relaçiones se presento esta pet^{on} y preguntas.

v y por los dhos señores vista la ovieron por presentada e mandaron que los t^{o}s digan por las dhas preguntas y se le de el treslado que pide Nabamuel.

v En los Reies catorze dias del mes de henero de mill e qui^{o}s e setenta y ocho años Melchor del Castillo soliçitador del fisco pa en la causa quel fiscal de su mag^{t} trata con doña Beatriz Coya sobre los anaconas poblados en Yucai presento por testigo a Martin Garçia de Licona y a Lazaro Martin y a Juan de la Banda mulato y a don Ju^{o} Calla Petia yndio estantes en esta çiudad de los quales y de cada vno dellos yo el escrivano y reçeutor yuso escrito tome y reciui juramento en forma de dr^{o} y ellos lo hiçieron segun se requiere por dios e por la señal de la cruz y prometieron de dezir verdad ante mi Rodrigo de Bivero escrivano de su m^{t}

v t^{o} el dho Martin Garçia de Licona estante al pres^{te} en esta çiudad de los Reies testigo presentado por el dho Melchor del Castillo soliçitador del fisco el qual aviendo jurado //
/f.422v/ e siendo preguntado por las preg^{tas} del dho ynterr^{o} e generales de la ley dijo lo sig^{te}.

j A la primera pregunta dixo que conoçe a las partes y tiene notiçia de los pueblos que la preg^{ta} dize e conoçe a algunos de los anaconas questan reduçidos e poblados en algunos de los dhos pueblos en espeçial en el mismo pueblos de Yucay.

Y preguntado por las preguntas generales dixo ques de hedad de çinquenta e seis años poco mas o menos e que no le toca ninguna de las preguntas generales que le fueron fechos.

ij A la segunda pregunta dijo que este t^{o} save e vido que el dho frei P^{o} Gutierez bisito los dhos pu^{o}s por orden de su Exª y en lo demas se remite a la bisita y a lo que en virtud dello hizo y esto responde a esta pregunta.

iij A la terzera pregunta dijo queste t^{o} save que los dhos yanaconas muchos dellos estavan en anparo de sus encomenderos que les hazian algun servi^{o} y que tribu^{o} no save ni entendio que pagasen ninguno en plata sino algunas bezes se ocupan en llevarles leña e yerva a sus encomenderos e otros servi^{o}s manuales y esto save e responde a esta preg^{ta}.

iiij A la quarta pregunta dixo que se remite a la çedula real y a lo que en virtud della su Exª tiene proveido e ordenado y esto save desta pregunta.

añadida preg^{do} por la pregunta añadida dixo que algunos españoles que tienen chacaras e casas en el dho valle de Yucai an tenido algunos y^{o}s anaconas e que no save este testigo donde los truxeron eçepto çiertos anaconas que don Diego Saire e doña Maria Coya su muger quando salieron de Bilcabanba a dar obediençia a su m^{t} truxeron a los queste testigo oyo dezir muchos y^{o}s e yndias //
/f.423/ que quedaron algunos dellos en el dho valle de Yucai y la dha doña Maria les dio casas en que biviesen y tierras donde senbrasen y benefiçiavan las chacaras de la dha doña Maria y tenian cargo dellas y algunos de los dhos yanaconas estan agora y an estado en el Cuzco y residen en el Cuzco porque este t^{o} los conoçe y esto save desta pregunta e que lo que tiene dho es lo que save y la verdad pa el juramento que hizo y firmolo de su nonbre Martin Garçia de Licona ante mi Rodrigo de Bivero escr^{o} de su majestad.

v t^{o} el dho Juan de la Banda testifo pres^{do} por el dho Melchor del Castillo soliçitador del fisco el qual aviendo jurado e siendo preguntado por las preguntas del dho ynterr^{o} y generales de la ley dixo lo siguiente.

j A la primera pregunta dixo que conoçe al fiscal de su magestad y tiene notiçia de los pueblos quel liç^{do} frei P^{o} Gutierez hizo reduçir en el valle de Yucai y conoçe algunos anaconas de los que en el biven.

Y preguntado por las preguntas generales dixo ques de hedad de mas de quarenta y un años y que no le toca ninguna de las preguntas generales que le fueron fhas.

ij A la segunda pregunta dixo que save quel dho frei P^{o} Gutierez hizo la dha visita y que todos los que se reduxeron a los dhos pueblos por anaconas no pagavan tasa a ninguna persona porque andauan exsentos y fuera de sus repartimi^{o}s y que en la cantidad se remite a la dha visita y esto save desta pregunta porque lo vio ser e pagar ansi en esta //
/f.423v/ y en otras reduçiones que se hizieron en la comarca del Cuzco de anaconas.

iij A la terzera pregunta dixo que dize lo que dho tiene en la pregunta antes desta a que se refiere y esto save desta pregunta.

iiij A la quarta pregunta dixo que se remite al proveymiento que su Exª hizo de los dhos y^{o}s y esto save desta pregunta.

añadida preguntado por la pregunta añadida dixo que los y^{o}s en la bisita que les hiçieron lo abian declarado al qual este t^{o} se remite y lo demas no save y que lo que tiene dho es lo que save y la verdad para el juram^{to} que hizo e firmolo de su nonbre Ju^{o} de la Vanda ante my R^{o} de Bivero escri^{o} de su mag^{t}.

t^{o} el dho Lazaro Martin estante al presente en esta çiudad de los Reies testigo presentado por el dho Melchor del Castillo soliçitador del fisco el qual aviendo jurado y siendo preguntado por las preguntas del dho ynterr^{o} e generales de la lei dixo lo siguiente.

j A la primera pregunta dixo que conoçe a las partes y tiene notiçia de los pueblos yanaconas que la pregunta dize.

Preg^{do} por las preguntas generales dijo ques de hedad de quarenta e çinco años poco mas o menos e que no le toca ninguna de las preg^{tas} generales que le fueron fechas.

ij A la segunda pregunta dijo queste t^{o} save que siendo el dho frei P^{o} Gutierrez visitador por mandado del señor bisorei don Fran^{co} de Toledo visito el valle de Yucai e sus anexos y hallo en la dha visita muchos y^{o}s anaconas que no estavan encomendados en persona ninguna por los governadores que an sido en este reino sino que algunos dellos tenian y^{o}s señores deçendientes de Guaina Capa e de- //
/f.424/ mas Yngas señores que fueron deste reino e los tenian en estançias e tierras porquel dho valle de Yucai hera recreaçion y regalo de los Yngas y que ansi muchos dellos tenian sus caserias y estançias por ser de tan buen tenple y muchos españoles vz^{o}s e moradores de la dha çiudad del Cuzco ansimysmo tenian e tienen alli sus huertas y estançias e anaconas en ellas de partes diferentes deste reino e aun este t^{o} en una estançia que alli tiene tiene çinco o seis anaconas destos y bisto por el dho visitador questos anaconas que alli estavan no tenian encomenderos particulares sino amos que los tenian alli en las dhas tierras a lo queste t^{o} a entendido lo devio de comunicar con el dho señor bisorei e los puso en cabeça de su m^{t} y le pagan tasa y asi este t^{o} paga por los que tiene lo que les cabe e que en quanto a los y^{o}s que ay en cada pueblo de los dhos anaconas este t^{o} no lo save e que sobre ello se remite a la bisita e reduçion dellos y esto save desta pregunta.

iij A la terzera pregunta dixo que dize lo que dho tiene en la pregunta antes desta a que se refiere y esto save desta pregunta.

iiij A la quarta pregunta dixo queste t^{o} save que los dhos anaconas pagan tasa como dho ti^{e} e que lo demas que dize la pregunta lo a oydo dezir por cossa publica e notoria lo contenido en esta pregunta y esto responde a esta preg^{ta}.

v A la quinta pregunta dixo ques ansi lo que la pregunta dize como lo tiene dho e declarado en la segunda pregunta a que se refiere e questo responde a esta pregunta y que lo que tiene dho es lo que sabe //
/f.424v/ y la verdad para el juramento que hizo y firmolo de su nonbre Lazaro Martin ante mi Rodrigo de Bivero escri^{o} de su majestad.

Exmo señor
v El liç^{do} Alvaro de Carvajal ffiscal de su mag^{d} digo que para presentar en çiertos pleytos que se tratan en esta real audiençia contra el fisco real y para otras cosas convenyentes al real serviçio de su mag^{d} tengo neçesidad se me de un treslado de la çedula real de su mag^{d} por la qual manda se pongan en su real corona todos los yanaconas que oviere en este reyno y de la çedula por la qual su mag^{d} manda no se encomienden nyngunos yndios a persona alguna por dexaçion que ellos ayan hecho a V Ex^{a} pido y suplico mande se me de un treslado dellas para el dho heffeto para lo qual etc. el liçen^{do} Alvaro de Carvaxal.

v En veynte y quatro de mayo la presento el dho en el acuerdo de justiçia su Ex^{a} dixo que Antonio Baptista de Salazar de al ffiscal de su mag^{d} la declaraçion de su magestad de todos los yndios que an de pagar tributo en este reyno e ansimesmo le de la declaraçion que su magestad a hecho de no se encomyenden yndios por renunçiaçion ny dexacion.

v En la çiudad de los Reyes en veynte y çinco dias del mes de junio de myll y qui^{o}s y setenta y siete años de pedimiento del liçen^{do} Alvaro de Carvajal fiscal de su mag^{d} notiffique la pet^{on} de suso y lo a ella proveydo por el Exmo señor don Françisco de Toledo visorrey deste reyno a Antonyo Baptista de Salazar en su persona en fee de lo qual lo ffirme de my nombre Fran^{co} de Alcozer escrivano de su mag^{d}.

v muy p^{o} s^{or} el liç^{do} Alvaro de Caravajal vro fiscal en la causa con doña Beatriz Coya sobre los yanaconas del valle //
/f.425/ de Yucay hago present^{on} ante vra Alt^{a} del auto en que vro vissorey puso todos los yanaconas del ter^{no} de la çiudad del Cuzco en vra real corona el qual me fue enbiado agora nuevamente por vros of^{e}s de la çiudad del Cuzco.

v A vra Alt^{a} pido y suplico lo aya por present^{on} e mande que se ponga en el processo e haga en la dha causa segun de que tengo pedido e just^{a} lo qual pido e pa ello es.

v En los Reyes en diez y siete Dias del mes de julio de myll e qui^{o}s y setenta y ocho años ante los señores pres^{e} e oydores desta real audiençia e chançilleria de su mg^{t} estando en audiençia publica el liç^{do} Alvaro de Caravajal fiscal de su mag^{t} presento esta petiçion e lo contenido.

v E visto por los dhos señores lo ovieron por presentado y mandaron que se ponga en el proceso y dar treslado a la otra pte e que responda pa la prim^{a} audiençia Navamuel

v En la çiudad del Cuzco en onze Dias del mes de agosto de myll e qui^{o}s y setenta y dos años el muy Ex^{te} señor don Fran^{co} de T^{do} vissorey governador y capitan general destos reynos del Piru por su mag^{t} etc. dijo que por quanto su mag^{t} por sus reales çedulas y un capitulo de ynstruçion de los que dio a su Exª tiene proveido y mandado que aviendo de ynponerse tributo a los yn^{o}s yanaconas deste reyno que no estan encomendados se pongan en su corona real //
/f.425v/ y el tributo que diere sea pa su caxa real e que aviendo su Exª salido de la ciudad de los Reyes a visitar el reyno por su persona e proveido visitadores que por las provinzias hagan la dha visita y en la que en esta ciudad del Cuzco se a fho de los yn^{o}s de todas las parroquias della e y^{o}s que sirven a españoles e que andan vagamundos sean hallado mucha cantidad de y^{o}s de los quales algunos son los que llaman yanaconas y otros naturales desta dha ciudad que llaman Cuzcos que nynguno dellos pagavan tributo a su mag^{t} ny a otra ps^{a} que los tuviese en encomyenda e por que conforme a dr^{o} ninguno de los dhos yn^{o}s son exsentos de pagar los tributos debidos a su mag^{t} por razon del soberano señorio que tiene en estos reinos por mantenerlos en paz y en just^{a} y darles la dotrina del santo evangelio y este dr^{o} se puede prescrivir por dilacion alguna de tpo y atento a las necesidades notorias de su mag^{t} y algunos particulares que en este reyno ay que forçosamente se avian de cumplir de su real caxa y que por andar los //
/f.426/ dhos y^{o}s sin reconoçer caçiques y sin estar reduzidos a pueblos ny tener oblig^{on} de pagar tributos andauan bagamundos y ociosos e por eso mas llenos de vizios y sospechosos de ydolatrias y supertiziones la que su mag^{t} tiene mandado por las dhas çedulas e ynstruçiones los dhos yanaconas se reduzgan a pueblos y tributen a su real caxa y los demas y^{o}s que llaman cuzqueños no ai razon que les escuse de pagar tributo e quando alg^{a} tubieron que tal no tienen no merezan gozar della por la sospecha que contra ellos se a tenido de aver sido causa del levantamiento de Titu Cusi Yupangui Topa Amaro su her^{no} y Quispi Tito su hijo de toda la provinzia de Vilcabamba y de otras culpas notables que se contienen en el proçeso criminal que contra don Carlos y don F^{e} su hermano y don Al^{o} Tito Atauchi y don Agustin Condemayta y don D^{o} Cayo y otros y^{o}s naturales desta çiudad y fuera della se trata antel dotor Grauiel de Loarte alcalde de corte por su mag^{t} por comision de su Exª por todas las dhas causas e por reduzir los dhos y^{o}s a mas puliçia de la que hasta aqui an tenido e porque este mas a proposito para poderles enseñar la dotrina evangelica e no tengan lugar de andar ociosos ni vagamundos su Exª a mandado reduzir todos los dhos y^{o}s a parroquias haziendo y fundando algunas de nuevo y abriendo calles e reduziendo a mejor forma las que antes estavan hechas y les a dado y nombrado caçiques a cada una en la forma que se cont^{e} en los titulos de sus caçicazgos que se les a mandado dar e que queriendo cumplir en lo que resta lo que su mag^{t} tiene hordenado e proveer lo que a su natural servi^{o} conviene ponia e puso en la real corona de su mag^{t} todos los y^{o}s yanaconas questan visitados y se visitaren y adel^{te} pareçieren y se descubrieren en esta çiudad y en las perroquias de nra s^{a} de Belen y el hospital de Santana San Xpoval San Blas San Sebastian Santiago San Ger^{mo} y en todas las rancherias y casas de vz^{o}s y moradores desta çiudad labranças y estancias valle de Yucai y Pisa y Calca y los andes de la coca y en todos los demas de los ter^{nos} e juri^{on} desta dha çiudad agora bivan con españoles o anden vagamundos o bivan por si o en otra qualquier manera e pte questen que no estuvieren encomendados pa que se les reparta los tributos que justamente pareçiere que puedan pagar moderandolos quanto sea posible y en qu^{to} a los y^{o}s cuzqueños que como esta dho hasta aqui no an pagado tributo no obstante que su Exª pudiera encomendarlos a las p^{a}s que le pareçiera benemeritos usando del poder general que su mag^{t} t^{e} pa encomendar y^{o}s por no tener horden particular en que aunque tratase desta mat^{a} de y^{o}s teniendo atenzion a las muchas e grandes necesidades que su mag^{t} tiene asi en estos reynos como en los demas sus reynos y señorios //
/f.426v/ la qual su mag^{t} ti^{e} hordenado que pa cumplir alguna parte de las dhas neçesidades se vayan teniendo en su corona algunos repartimientos que estuvieren vacos o vacaren su Exª mandava y m^{do} a los dhos yn^{o}s cuzqueños que no esten encomendados por sus parroquias como estan poblados y mandados poblar en ellas se les reparta el tributo que buenam^{te} pueden pagar con la mayor moderaçion que sea posible los quales dhos tributos por diez años primeros siguientes y hasta que de otra pte se provea donde se cumpla lo que de yuso yra declarado despues que se le rep^{ta} aplicava y aplico desde agora para la obra de la fortaleza que tiene acordado de hazer en esta çiudad del Cuzco e pa el sal^{o} del alcalde que nombrare e pusiere e sal^{o} de artillero y muniziones y provisiones de la dha fortaleza e gastos de la visita general que se va haziendo e por la orden e forma que su Exª lo mandara destribuyr y asentar y con esta condiçion e pa este efeto ponia e puso e yncorporava e yncorporo los dhos yn^{o}s cuzqueños en la corona real de Castilla y reservava y reservo en si de tasar y moderar los tributos que los dhos yanaconas e yn^{o}s cuzqueños an de pagar aviendo visto los pareceres que sobre ello daran los visitadores eclesiasticos y seglar de la çiudad e parroquias y de las demas partes suso dhas que ynformandose de p^{a}s que lo puedan saber y entender y asi dixo que lo proveia y proveyo esto conque de lo que montaren los dhos tributos se de a los dhos

yanaconas e yn^{o}s cuzqueños por q^{ta} de su mag^{t} y de las dhas obras la dotrina neces^{a} que por agora dexara hordenado su Exª que aya en las dhas parroquias con pareçer del perlado y adel^{e} se hordenare por los visorreyes governadores que por tpo fueren y mandaua y m^{do} a los oficiales reales de su mag^{t} desta çiudad que luego que con este auto sean requeridos tomen y aprehendan la posesion de los dhos yanaconas e yn^{o}s cuzqueños en nombre de su mag^{t} y tengan q^{ta} de cobrar los tributos dellos conforme a las tasas que se hizieren y meter y metan en la caxa real por qu^{ta} de su mag^{t} los tributos de los dhos yanaconas y se hagan cargo dellos de los dhos y^{o}s cuzqueños los tengan por qu^{ta} aparte pa cumplir lo que arriba esta declarado pa que se situen conforme a la destribuz^{on} que su Exª mandara hazer lo qual ansi hagan y cumplan so pena de un mil p^{o}s de oro pa la camara y fisco de su mag^{t} demas que se cobrara de sus personas y bienes todo el daño e ynteres e que por su descuido viniere a su mag^{t} y a las dhas obras y ansi lo proveyo e firmolo va entre renglones y gastos de la visita general que se va haziendo vala y de las demas parte suso dhas don Fran^{co} de T^{do} ante mi Alvaro Ruiz de Navamuel.
E yo Joan Lopes de Arrieta escri^{o} de su mag^{t} presente fui al ver corregir este treslado con el auto que original de su Exª que queda en poder de los señores oficiales //
/f.427/ reales desta çiudad del Cuzco y va çierto y verdadero que por ende fyze my signo en testimonio de verdad Joan Lopez de Arrieta.

Yo Alvaro Ruiz de Navamuel escri^{o} de su mag^{t} en su real audi^{a} de los Reyes y de la governacion desstos reynos en cumplimiento de lo mandado por los dhos presidente e oidores desta real audiençia y de pedimi^{to} de la pte del cap^{t} Martin Garçia de Loyola y doña Beatriz Coya su muger hize sacar este tres^{do} del proçeso original que en esta real audi^{a} sea tratado entre los suso dhos con el fiscal de su mag^{t} sobre los yn^{o}s yanaconas del valle de Yucay segun que de suso se haze minsion con el qual dho original se corrigio en la çiudad de los Reyes en veynte e dos dias del mes de otubre de myll e qui^{o}s y setenta y ocho años va tes^{do} que sacan/ x/ e pal dho en io/ guarden ansi/ que se vales/ yra/ este/ edos no vala. Entre renglones y otros de los naturales deste valle/ que guardando el conzierto/ y suso/ y doña/ ante mi/ e tributos en/ ante/ miguel si vala/ en m^{do}/ y ocho/ ciudad del dho/ doze/ sidente/ exsesiones/ y tres/ hijos/ hansi/ mi Cl/ fue leido Vilca/ Fran^{co} hispi y ocho. Vala
Y fize aqui mi signo en testimonio de verdad

Alvaro Ruiz de Nabamuel

/f.427v/ tasasen

v tasanse las treçientas y quarenta y tres ffojas que estan escritas en este proçeso como pare el en treçientas y veinte que a medio peso cada una corrientes /margen: clxj p^{o}s/ confforme al arançel monta çiento y sesenta p^{o}s corrientes.

v las veynte y tres ffojas restantes se le quitan por falta de partes y renglones Blas Hernandez

v çitaçion
En la çiudad de los Reyes en veynte y dos Dias del mes de otubre de mill e qui^{o}s y setenta y ocho años yo Fran^{co} de Alcozer escrivano de su mag^{d} y su rezeptor del numero desta real audi^{a} de los Reyes doy fee que zite a Joan de Arrandolaza pr^{dor} del cap^{t} Martin Garçia de Loyola e doña Beatriz Coya conforme al auto desta real audi^{a} proveido en ocho dias del mes de abril deste pres^{te} año para que vaya o envie en seguimiento del dho pleito y causa ante su mag^{d} y señores de su real consejo de Yndias como por el dho auto se m^{da} y le cite e apercibi para todas ynstançias conforme al dho auto en su persona el qual dixo que lo oyo. t^{o}s Lucas Gasco est^{e} en esta çiudad.

Fran^{co} de Alcoçer
escri^{o} de su mag^{d}

v E despues de lo suso dho en la dha çiudad de los /margen: çit^{on} al fiscal/ Reyes en este dho dia mes y año dhos yo el dho Fran^{co} Alcozer escri^{o} reçeptor suso dho doy fee conforme al dho auto cite para todo señalado al liç^{do} Alvaro de Carvajal fiscal de su mag^{d} desta real audi^{a} en su persona y le ley el dho auto vervo ad verbum y le aperçevi conforme añ dho auto para que vaya o envie al seguimeitn del dho pleito para todas ynstancias el qual dixo que pide que se le lleve este pleito antes que se enbie porque lo quiere ver y corregir t^{o}s el liç^{do} Vizcarra e Juan Guillermo moradores en la dha çiudad
Fran^{co} de Alcoçer
escri^{o} de su mag^{d}

/f.428/ Yo Gironimo de Andrada escriv^{o} de su mag^{t} y de mynas e registros en esta çiudad de los Reies doy ffee a los que la pres^{te} vieren como por el registro de oro y plata y de otras cosas que ante mi hizo y otorgo Joanes de Urrutia maestre del navio nonbrado Todos Santos para el reyno de tierra firme este presente año de myll e qui^{o}s y set^{ta} e ocho a^{o}s entre las demas partidas quel dho maestre recivio recibio [*sic*] la del tenor sig^{te}.

v En la çiudad de los Reies a veynte e tres Dias del mes de otubre de mill e qui^{o}s e set^{ta} e ocho años ante mi el escriv^{o} e testigos desta partida pareçio pres^{te} al dho maestre y otorgo que recivio de Gironimo de Bustam^{te} en nonbre del secretario Alvaro Ruiz de Navamuel e lleve en su poder en avio un proceso çerrado y sellado enbuelto en un ençerado con //
/f.428v/ un sobre escrito que dize proceso y lleva remytido al real consejo de las Yndias de la real audiençia de los Reies entre el cap^{tan} Martin Garçia de Loyola e doña Beatriz Coya con el fiscal de su magestad sobre los yndios yanaconas del balle de Yucay va originalm^{te} del qual

dho proçeso el dho m^{e} /maestre/ se dio por contento y entreg^{do} a su voluntad por quanto lo reçivio realmente e con effeto en presençia del escriv^{o} pu^{co} e testigos desta p^{da} de que yo el escriv^{o} doy ffee e se obligo que llevandole dios en salvam^{to} y al dho su navio lo dara y entregara en la çiudad de Panama del reino de tierra firme a los ofiçiales de la real ha- //
/f.429/ zienda de su magestad dho reino para que lo enbien registrado en el registro del rey a los reynos despaña al dho real c^{o} de las Yndias en el primer navio que de alli saliere e para el cumplimi^{to} desta p^{da} el dho maestre obligo su pers^{a} e bienes avidos e por aver y lo firmo de su nombre siendo testigos Fran^{co} Rendon e Fran^{co} de la Pala e Ju^{o} de Çoto. Juanes de Urrutia. Ante my Ger^{mo}de Andrada escriv^{o} de su mag^{d}

segun que todo lo suso dho consta e parece por el dho reg^{o} e p^{da} orig^{al} questa en mi poder e p^{a} que dello conste de pedimi^{to} del secret^{o} Navamuel di el pres^{te} ques ffecho en los Reies a seis de nov^{e} de myll e qui^{o}s y set^{a} e ocho a^{o}s. va t^{do} pu^{co} no vala.
En fee dello fize aqui este my signo en testimonio del berdad

Geronimo de Andrada
escri^{o} de su mag^{t}

/f.429v/ /en blanco/

/f.430/ muy p^{o} s^{or}

Martin Garçia de Loyola por mi procu^{or} digo que el proçeso que se trato en esta real audiençia con vro fiscal sobre los yanaconas del balle de Yucay se envio a los reynos de Castilla original por m^{do} y orden desta real audiençia y aunque alla se a buscado no aparesçido asta hoy de que my justiçia resçibe mucha dilacion.

pido y sup^{co} a V^{a} Alt^{a} mande al secretario me de un tr^{do} del en pu^{ca} forma çitando pa ello al fiscal y para ello es. Martin Garçia de Loyola

/f.430v/ En los Reyes en ocho de abril de myll e qui^{o}s y ochenta e çinco a^{o}s ante los pres^{e} e oydores en audi^{a} publica se leyo esta peticion.

y los dhos sr^{es} visto mandaron que se le de lo que pide

Jhoan de Montoya

/f.431/ muy p^{o} señor

pide se haga de nuevo auto de remission attentas las causas que alega

Juan Sanchez de los Rios en n^{e} de Martin Garcia de Loyola y doña Beatriz Coya su muger en el pleito con vro fiscal sobre los y^{o}s de su repartimi^{to} que por orden de vro vissorey Don Fran^{co} de Toledo se pusieron en vra corona real diziendo ser yanaconas digo que aunque el auto original se envio a vro real consejo el treslado que quedo en poder del secretario Nabamuel el que con los demas demas papeles a subcedido al s^{or} Montoya no ay ny se halla el dho treslado auto de remision de vro presidente y oydores desta real ciudad al dho real consejo a donde se entiende que en el original que se llebo al real consejo tanpoco no fue auto de remysion que podria ser que se pusiese dada y obre si dilaçion y para atajarlo conviene se aga formalm^{te} auto de remysion y se cite de nuebo vro fiscal se me de testimonio dello pa enviarlo al real consejo

Por tanto sin perjuicio del dr^{o} de mys ptes y no oblig^{do}los a diligencia demasiada pido y sup^{co} a V. Al^{a} m^{de} //
/f.431v/ hazer el dho auto de remysion y se notifique al dho vro fiscal en forma pa lo enbie que segun yra de la causa y si me de testim^{to} de todo esto pa lo enbiar al dho real consejo pa que se ponga en el dho proceso que alla se envio y pa ello es.

Vasquez Fajardo

En la ciudad de los Reies en cinco dias del mes de julio de mill e qui^{o}s y ochenta e cinco años ante los señores presidente e oydores en audi^{a} pu^{ca} se presento esta petiçion e por los dhos señores vista mandaron traer los autos. Montoya

Que se aga el auto /ilegible/ y se cite al fiscal.

/f.432/ En la çiudad de los Reyes en veynte y dos Dias de mes de henero de mill/ e quinientos y ochente y seis a^{o}s ante mi el presente escrivano de Camara el comendador Martin Garçia de Loyola por si y en non^{e} de doña Beatriz Coya su mujer p^{o} la ynformacion questa ofrescido a dar de la muerte de P^{o} Dias Baldeon e don Fran^{co} Chilche presento por t^{o}s a Hernan Sanchez residente en la çiudad del Cuzco y al pres^{te} en esta ante el qual aviendo jurado segun forma el dr^{o} y siendo siendo preguntado dixo que sabe y es verdad que el dho Pero Dias Baldeon e don Fran^{co} Chilche son muertos e pasados desta preste vida lo qual sabe porque como residente en la dha çiudad del Cuzco sabe que el dho Pero Dias Baldeon murio de un susto hechando mano a una espada sin poderla sacar y el dho don Fran^{co} Chilco [*sic*] muchos años ques muerto y esto es la verdad y lo que save pa el juramento que fecho tiene y dixo ser de hedad de mas de sesenta a^{o}s y no le tocan las generales y lo firmo de su nombre y en el dho su dho se afirmo e ratifico.

Hernan Sanchez.
Ante mi Jhoan de Montoya

/f.432v/ t^{o} Luego el dho dia mes y año contenido de veynte y dos de henero de mill e qui^{o}s y ochenta y seis a^{o}s pa la dha ynformacion ante el pres^{te} escrivano de Camara el dho Martin Garcia de Loyola pres^{to} por t^{o} a Miguel Merino vezino de la ciudad del Cuzco y residente en esta corte el qual aviendo jurado segun forma de derecho y siendo preguntado dixo que sabe que el dho Pero Dias Baldeon y don Fran^{co} Chilco son muertos e passados desta pres^{te} vida preguntado como lo sabe dixo que este t^{o} se hallo en la ciudad del Cuzco al tienpo y quando el dho Pedro Dias Baldeon murio que abra tiempo de tres años y medio poco mas o menos y murio de subito queriendo echar mano al espada y el don Fran^{co} Chilco a muchos a^{o}s ques muerto y pasado desta pres^{te} vida y que lo que dho tiene es la verdad e lo que sabe y passa por el juram^{to} que hizo en el qual se afirmo y ratifico y firmo de su n^{e} y dixo ser de hedad de veynte y dos a^{o}s y no le tocan las generales en que son cuñados e por eso dejara de dezir la verdad t^{o}s no lo no bala

Miguel Merino
Ante my Jhoan de Montoya

/f.433/ En la ciudad de los tteyes en veynte y dos Dias del mes de henero de mill e qui^{o}s y ochenta y seis a^{o}s ante mi el pres^{te} escri^{o} de Camara pa la dha ynformaçion el dho Martin Garcia de Loyola pres^{to} por t^{o}s a Jhoan de Porras residente en la ciudad del Cuzco y al pres^{te} en esta ante el que aviendo jurado segun forma de dr^{o} y siendo preguntado dixo que conoçe este t^{o} a Pero Dias Baldeon ya era tienpo de quatro a^{o}s poco mas o menos que murio en la dha ciudad del Cuzco abintestado queriendo hechar mando al espada y este t^{o} le vido muerto y publico e notorio la verdad de lo que dho tiene y en ello se affirmo y ratifico y firmo de su nombre y dixo ser de hedad de quarenta a^{o}s y que no le toco en las generales

Jhoan de Porras
Ante my Jhoan de Montoya

/f.433v/ /en blanco/

/f.434/ Yo Joan de Montoya escrivano de Camara desta real audiencia que por mandado de su mag^{d} reside en esta çiudad de los Reyes doy ffe questando los señores presidente e oydores desta real audiençia en audi^{a} publica en ocho dias del mes de noviembre de mill y quinientos e ochenta y çinco años Joan Sanchez de los Rios en nombre de Martin Garçia de Loyola y de doña Beatriz Coya su muger por petiçion que presento pido y suplico se le diese conpulsorio para que el secretario Joan Gutierez de Molina le diese un traslado de las provisiones y çedulas de su magestad en que manda traer de paz a Mango Ynga y las mercedes que les mando hazer porque viniesen de paz e ansi mismo una carta quel conde de Nieva y comisarios avian escrito a su magestad sobre el sacar de paz al Ynga a pedimi^{to} de Joan Sierra de Leguiçamo lo qual queria para presentar en el p^{to} que trata en esta real audiençia con el liçençiado Alvaro de Carvajal ffiscal de su mag^{d} sobre los yanaconas y por los dhos señores se le mando dar el conpulsorio que pide citado el dho ffiscal el qual pa el dho heffeto cite en su persona y para que dello conste de pedimiento del dho Martin Garcia de Loyola //
/f.434v/ di el presente en la ciudad de los Reyes en treze Dias del mes de noviembre de mill e quinientos y ochenta e çinco años Joan de Montoya.

v En cumplimiento de lo que yo Joan Gutierez de Molina escri^{o} de camara de su magestad en la audiençia e chançilleria real que reside en esta çiudad de los Reyes del Piru doy ffee que en el libro que en mi poder esta donde se asientan e ponen las çedulas cartas y provisiones que su magestad enbia a este reino etc. una çedula que trata çerca de lo contenido en el dho conpulsorio sobre que biniendo de paz el hijo de Mango Ynga e los otros caçiques e yndios que con el andavan alçados fuesen perdonados y asimismo doy fee que entre los protocolos papeles y escrituras questan en el dho officio e me fueron entregados esta una provança de serviçios fechos en la dha real audiençia ante Françisco de Caravajal escriv^{o} de camara que fue della a pedimiento de Juan Sierra de Leguiçamo vezino que fue de la çiudad del Cuzco //
/f.435/ en la qual dha provança de serviçios esta una carta e parecer que el conde de Nieva y la dha real audi^{a} dio çerca de la dha provança que su thenor del dho paresçer y çedula real es como se sigue.

El Prinçipe

Don Antonio de Mendoça visorrey governador de las provinçias del Piru y presidente de la audi^{a} real que en ella reside con la partes mando enbiar una provision de su magestad que contiene que viniendo de paz el hijo de Mango Ynga e los otros caçiques e yndios que con el andan alzados sean perdonados y se promete que no seran enagenados de la corona real ellos ni los pueblos donde poblaren y que se les haga todo buen tratamiento y que las casas e chacaras que tenia el dho Mango Ynga su padre al tiempo que se alço le sean bueltas y restituidas y otras cossas como por ella vereis y por tener como teneis vos la cosa presente e acordado de se le remytir para que si viere del que es bien usar della lo hagais y asi os encargo e mando que la beais e useis della como vieredes //
/f.435v/ que conviene segun el estado y calidad de los tiempos y cosas de lo que en ello hiziere y del nos dareis avisso fecha en la villa de Madrid a diez e nueve dias del mes de março de mill e quinientos e çinquenta e dos a^{o}s yo el prinçipe por mandado de su alteza Joan de Samano.

v la qual dha çedula real yo Fran^{co} de Carvajal escrivano de camara de su magestad en la su real audiençia y chançilleria que reside en la çiudad de los Reyes e de la gobernaçion de la Nueva Cast^{a} hize sacar e tresladar de la çedula original de su mag^{d} cuyo treslado presente en la dha ciudad de los Reyes en veynte e ocho Dias del mes de setienbre de myll e quinientos y sesenta e dos años a las espaldas de la qual avia çinco rubricas de los señores del consejo real de su mag[d] e fueron t[o]s al ber corregir con la dha original Diego Gonçales de Espinossa e Joan de Salas e Di[o] Gumyel. Françisco de Caravajal

v E. C. R. M[t] Joan Sierra de Leguisamo pidio en esta real audiençia se resçiviese ynformaçion conforme a la real hordenança de como era nieto de Guayna Capac cuyos fueron estos reynos del Piru e hijo de conquistador dellos y de como avia sido parte para sacar de paz al Ynga su //
/f.436/ primo her[no] la qual se hizo ques la que con esta se enbia paresce por ella que es hijo natural de Mansio Sierra de Leguisamo vezino de la çiudad del Cuzco uno de los primeros descubridores e conquistadores destos reynos y de doña Beatriz Yupangui hija del dho Guayna Capa e que fue parte para sacar o traer de paz al Ynga su primo her[no] nyeto ligitimo del dho Guayna Capa su aguelo por cuya causa an sesado muchos saltos e robos e fuerzas e muertes en los capitanes del dho Ynga hazian e ques cassado en esta tierra e hijodalgo que tiene en encomienda un pueblo que se llama Pisac que renta hasta quatrozientos pesos e que por no tener mas renta esta en mucha neçecidad por ser los gastos desta tierra muy eçesivos atento a las dhas causas nos paresçe que cabra bien en el qualquier md que via md fuere servido de le hazer los repartimyentos que señala para en que vra mag[d] le haga merçed son los que tuvieron en encomienda el liç[do] de la Gama y Joan de Saavedra despues que los señalo sean encomendado ya que no abra lugar de se cumplir en ellos la merçed que pide de los Reyes a honze Dias del mes de dizienbre de myll e quini[o]s e sesenta e un años el conde de Nieva el //
/f.436v/ dotor Bravo de Saravia el liç[do] Saabedra el liç[do] don Alvaro Ponce de Leon el liç[do] Salazar de Villasante ante mi Fran[co] de Carvajal.

v El qual dho treslado corregi y conserte con los dhos originales de donde fue sacado y doy fe e que va çierto y berdadero en la çiudad de los Reyes a quinze dias dias [*sic*] del mes de novienbre de myll e qui[o]s e ochenta y çinco años t[o]s que fueron presentes al ber corregir y consertar Pedro de Ayllon e Lorenço de Nogales Alonso Bicente residentes en esta çiudad.

Jhoan de Montoya

/f.437/ Don Hurtado de Mendoça marques de Cañete guarda mayor de la çiudad de cuenca visorrey e capitan general en estos reynos e provinçias del Piru por su magestad etc. por quanto su mag[d] por sus provisiones y cartas reales tiene mandado que se procure por las buenas maneras que ser pudieren traer de paz y a su obidiençia y serviçio real al Ynga para que viniesen el y los naturales que con el andubiesen en conosçimiento de nuestro santa fee y la resçibiesen para su saluaçion y en cumplimy[to] dello luego como llegue a estos dhos reynos por que cesasen los grandes daños e ynconvinientes que a causa de andar alçado y de guerra en los Andes Sayri Topa Mango Capac Yupangui Ynga hijo de Mango Ynga y nieto de Guaina Capac señor natural que fue destos dhos reynos por los muchos saltos muertes y rrobos que hordinariamente se hazian por sus capitanes y gente en los caminos reales a españoles y naturales e la cantidad de naturales que llevaua y recogia a los dhos andes donde andava de los que estan paçificos y debajo de la obidiençia de su magestad e el desasosiego e ynquietud que con el dho Ynga tenian los naturales de los repartimientos de yndios que siruen a los vezinos de las çiudades del Cuzco e Guamanga provei que religiosos y mensageros fuesen a hablarle de parte de su magestad y de la mia en su real nombre para que viniese de paz y a su real obidiençia y serviçio y le embie perdones de las muertes despañoles y naturales que oviese hecho y de otras qualesquier crimines y delitos que quiese cometido ofresçiendole que viniendo de paz e a lo suso dho dentro de çierto termino que le fue señalado le harian merçedes en su real nombre de los repartimientos de yndios de Yucai que tubo encomendado don Françisco Piçarro menor //
/f.437v/ hijo del marques don Fran[co] Piçarro difunto y de Xaquixaguana Guaylla Quipa e Pucara que estubo encomendado en Françisco Hernandez Giron vezino del Cuzco difunto que estan vacos con todo lo a ellos subjeto y que demas de lo suso dho le serian hechas otras merçedes de tierras y solares y otras cosas contenidas en las provisiones que dello se mandaron dar y enbiaron lo qual aviendo lo tratado los dhos religiosos e mensajeros con el dho Ynga lo açeto y salio y bino de paz y entro en esta çiudad de los Reyes y corte bispera de la fiesta de los Reyes deste presente año de quinientos çinquenta e ocho y dio a su magestad y a mi en su real nombre la obidiençia debida y prometio de sienpre servirle como su bueno y leal vasallo debe y es obligado hazer y porque abiendo fecho lo suso dho es justo que se tenga quenta con su persona y se le cunplan las dhas merçedes para con que se sustente y su muger casa e familia y de nuebo se le hagan otras porque se afiçione y obligue mas al serviçio de su magestad y tenga voluntad de se conbentir y conbierta a nra santa fee catolica para que se salve y obligue y anime a los demas naturales destos dhos reinos a que hagan lo mismo que es lo que prinçipalmente su magestad a pretendido y pretende y por lo que ynporta a la quietud y so siego destos dhos reynos por la presentes su real nonbre y por virtud de su real poder que para ello tengo su tenor del qual es el que se sigue.

Don Carlos por la divina clemençia enperador senper Augusto rei de Alemania doña Joana su madre y el mismo don Carlos por la misma graçia reyes de Castilla //
/f.438/ de Leon de Aragon de las dos Seçilias de Jerusalen de Nabarra de Granada de Toledo de Balençia de Galiçia de Mallorcas de Sebilla de Cerdeña de Cordova de Corçega de Murçia de Jaen de los Algarves de Algeçira de Gibraltar de las yslas de Canaria de las Yndias yslas e tierra firme del mar oceano conde de Flandes e de Tirol etc. A todos los conçejos regidores caballeros escuderos ofiçiales y omes buenos de todas las çiudades villas e lugares de las provinçias de la nueba Castilla llamada Piru y de la Nueba Toledo y de las otras provinçias e yslas sujetas y conprehendidas en el distrito e juridiçion de la mia audi[a] y chançilleria real de las dhas provinçias del Piru y a otras qualesquier personas eclesiasticas y seglares de qual quier estado condiçion preminençia o dinidad que sean o ser puedan vezinos estantes y abitantes en las dhas provinçias y en cada una dellas a quien toca e atañe y puede tocar y atañer lo en esta nra carta contenido y a cada uno e qualquier de bos salud y graçia sepades que nos abiendo entendido las alteraçiones e cosas acaesçidas en

esas dhas provinçias del Piru despues de Fran^{co} Hernandez Xiron con otros muchos que con el se juntaron se alçaron con la çiudad del Cuzco y prendieron a Gil Ramirez Davalos nro corregidor que hera //
/f.438v/ en la dha çiudad y deseando como deseemos que hesas provinçias se pongan en toda paz sosiego e quietud para que en ellas se haga el serviçio de dios de nro señor y su santa fee catolica sea abmentada y para este hefeto y que nos seamos servidos y esas dhas provinçias vayan en todo creçimi^{to} y nobleçimi^{to} y los pobladores dellas bivan en todo contentami^{to} abemos acordado de enbiar a ellas una persona de autoridad y confiança para que entienda en ello y por el gran conçepto que thenemos de la persona de don Hurtado de Mendoça marques de Cañete le abemos elegido y señalado por nro visorrei desa tierra y por presidente de la audiençia real que en ella reside para que haga e administre justiçia ygual a todos nros subditos e basallos y para que ansi mismo entienda en hazer y hordenar todo lo que conbenga para el sosiego quietud y nobleçimi^{to} desa tierra como dho es por la presente de nro propio motuo e deliberada boluntad elegimos constituimos y señalamos para ello al dho marques de Cañete y le demos e otorgamos todo nro poder cumplido libre e llenero y bastante con libre e general administraçion segun e tan cunplidamente que lo nos sabemos y de fecho y de dr^{o} mas y mejor puede y debe valer para que por nos y en nro nonbre e como nras mismas personas pueda entender y //
/f.439/ entienda en la paçificaçion y sosiego de hesas dhas provinçias y administraçiones de justiçia en ellas e provea en todas las cosas que ocurrieren asi conçernientes a la dha administraçion y execuçion de la nra justiçia como de la buena governaçion y defensa de esas dhas prouinçias y obescimi^{to} dellas e gratificaçion de los pobladores nros subditos y basallos que los an ydo a poblar y bien e buen tratami^{to} y conservaçion de los naturales dellas y buen recaudo de nra hazienda y en todas las otras cosas y casos y negoçios de qualquier calidad e condiçion que sean y se ofrescan lo que le paresçiere o biere que conbiene y se debe hazer y provea en nro nonbre y como nos mismos lo podramos hazer y proveer todos los ofiçios y cargos ansi de justiçia y de governaçion como de otra qual quier manera de esas dhas provinçias y de cada una dellas que conforme a dr^{o} nos podemos y debemos proveer y hazer en nro nonbre graçias e merçedes de qualesquier thenençias alcaidias regimi^{tos} e escrivanias y otros qualesquier ofiçios y cosas de qualquier calidad que sean asi por renunçiaçion como por vacaçion y en otra qualquier manera y pa que siendo menester para defension de esas provinçias y bien y utilidad dellas pueda perçebir de guerra e llamar y conbocar a las //
/f.439v/ çiudades e billas e otros pueblos y quelos perlados gobernadores justiçias caballeros y otras personas de esas provinçias y estantes en ellas para que bengan donde fuere neçesario con la gente que por el les fuere mandado y sobre ello hazer todas las otras provisiones e mrd^{es} que al caso conbengan y le paresçiere y finalmente pueda hazer y prover y provea todo aquello que nosotros mismos podriamos hazer y proveer de qual quier calidad y condiçion que sea o ser pueda en esas dhas provinçias por que los mandamos todo e a cada vno de bos como dho es que lo que asi por el dho marques de Cañete fuere proveido hordenado e mandado en quales quier casos e cosas que sean o ser puedan en esas prouinçias lo guardeis e cumplais y executeis e hagais guardar e cunplir y executar y la obedezcais e acateis como a persona que tiene nras vezes y que representa nras personas reales e hagais e cumplais sus merd^{es} segun y de la manera que el dijere y mandare de nra parte por escrito e por palabra y fuere contenido en las dhas sus cartas e provisiones e mandami^{tos} sin poner en ello escusa ni dilaçion alguna e sin dar a ello otro entendimi^{to} ni ynterpretaçion ni declaraçion y sin nos mas requerir ni consultar ni esperar sobre ello otro mio mandado //
/f.440/ bien asi como si por nras mismas personas o por nras cartas firmadas de nros nonbres lo dixesemos e ordenasemos e mandasemos lo qual vos mandamos que asi hagais e cumplais so pena de caer en mal caso y de las otras penas en que caen y incurren los que no obedesçen las cartas e mrd^{es} de sus Reyes e señores naturales e so las penas que por el os fueren puestas canos por la presente le damos y conçedemos e otorgamos para ello y para todo lo a ello conçerniente en qual quier manera nro poder cumplido e bastante con todas sus ynsidençias y dependençias ymergençias anexidades y conexidades y queremos queste dho poder tenga tanta fuerça como si fuera fecho e otorgado en cortes generales e dezimos e otorgamos que todo quanto el dho marques de Cañete en nro nonbre iziere ordenare e mandare conforme a este dho poder en esas dhas provinçias que lo abremos e avemos por firme y estable e baledero para sienpre jamas de los qual mandamos dar la presente firmada de mi el rey y sellada con nro sello dada en la villa de Bruselas a diez dias del mes de março de mill e qui^{o}s e çinquenta e çinco años yo el rey yo Françisco de Heraso secretario de sus çesarea y catolicas magestades la fize scrivir //
/f.440v/ por su mandado registrada qecha de Luyando chançiller Martin de Ramoyn el marques el l^{do} Tello de Sandoval el l^{do} don Joan Sarmiento el dotor Vasquez el l^{do} Villagomez

v hago mrd al dho Saire Topa Mango Capac Yupangui Ynga de los dhos repartimi^{tos} de yndios de Yucai y Jaquijaguana Guaillaquipa y Pucara que son en terminos de la çiudad del Cuzco y estan bacos por muerte de los dhos don Françisco Piçarro menor y Françisco Hernandez Xiron con todos los pueblos y estançias y sus tr^{os} caçiques prinçipales e yndios dellos ayllos sujetos y perteneçientes segun e como los tenian e poseyan e tubieron y poseyeron y gozaron de el los suso dhos y cada uno dellos para que los tenga e posea aya y goze y cobre todos los tributos que son u fueren obligados a dar y dieren dende primero deste presente mes de henero y año de mill e qui^{o}s e çinquenta y ocho años en adelante conforme a las tasas que estan hechos v se hizieren y para que por su fin e muerte suçedan perpetuamente en el dho repartim^{to} de yndios sus hijos desçendientes y suçesores que tubiere como se puede y debe susçeder en los mayorasgos que se hazen con liçençia de su magestad en los reinos despaña y con las condiçiones y apellido y armas //
/f.441/ quel dho Ynga quisiere e hordenare que para ello le doy liçençia e facultad porque baya en acreçintami^{to} su honrra linaje y estado de sus hijos y deçendientes desçendiendo como desçiende de linaje de los Yngas e prinçipales destos dhos reinos del Piru y porque aya memoria e renombre de quien tubo prinçipio desta mrd y porque permanezca y mejor se afiçione al serviçio de dios nro s^{or} y ensalçar nra santa fee catolica y a servir a su magestad para honra y defensa de su linaje casa y estado con que por si ni por ynterpositas personas ne se sirua de serviçio personal/ de los dhos yndios en su casa ni en otras obras e grangerias so las penas conthenidas en las provisiones y çedulas reales que açerca della estan dadas y con que los trate bien y procure su conseruaçion y multiplicaçion y tenga cuidado de que en el dho repartimi^{to} aya clerigos o religiosos que dotrinen a los naturales en las cosas de nra santa fee catholica y por la presente mando al liçençiado Muñoz corregidor de la dha çiudad del Cuzco que luego que por parte del dho Sayre Topa Mango Ynga Capac Yupangui Ynga fuere pedida posesion del dho repartimi^{to} de yndios se la de y metido el y las demas justiçias de su magestad le anpa- //

/f.441v/ ren y defiendan en ella y no consientan que della sea despojado sin primero ser oydo e bençido por fuero e juiçio lo qual asi hagan y cunplan so pena de cada dos mill pesos de oro para la Camara e fisco de su magestad

Fecho en los Reyes a treze Dias del mes de henero de mill e quinientos e çinquenta e ocho años el marques por mandado de su Exª Joan Muños Ricon

v En la gran çiudad del Cuzco cabeça destos reinos e provinçias del Piru a veinte e un Dias del mes de março año del naçimi^to^ de nro salvador Jesu Xpo de mill e quinientos e çinquenta e ocho años ante el mui magnifico señor liç^do^ Ju^o^ Baptista Muñoz corregidor e justiçia mayor en la dha çiudad y su juridiçion por su magestad y en presençia de mi Françisco de Barrientos escrivano del numero de la dha/ çiudad e de los testigos de yusso escritos paresçio presente doña Beatriz Mango Capac Yupangui muger de Diego Hernandez vezino de la dha çiudad en nonbre de Saire Topa Mango Capac Yupangui e por virtud del poder que del tiene de que hizo presentaçion signado descrivano de su magestad e en el dho nonbre presento //
/f.442/ esta provision e çedula de encomienda del muy excelente señor marques de Cañete visorrey destos reynos e pidio e requirio al dho señor corregidor que conforme a ella en el dho nonbre le de la posesion corporal autual belcasi de los caçiques e yndios de los dhos repartimi^tos^ de que por su magestad e su Exª del dho señor visorrey en su real nonbre fue y le an hecho merçed al dho Saire Topa Mango Capa Yupangui Ynga la qual dha posesion le de en don Françisco Chilche caçique prinçipal del repartimi^to^ de Yucai e don Pedro e don Lucas prinçipales del dho repartimi^to^ y en don Xpoval Chotas e don Diego Caguatay caçiques prinçipales de Xaquijaguana e don Alonso Cullina caçique de Quilloa que presentes estavan repartimi^tos^ encomendados por su excelençia en nonbre de su magestad en al dho Saire Topa Mango Capa Yupangui Ynga su parte como por la dha provision/ de su exçelençia constaba e paresçia sobre que pidio justicia.

v El dho señor corregidor thomo en sus manos la dha provision de su exçelençia e la obedesçio con el acatamiento debido y en //
/f.442v/ quanto al cunplimi^to^ della dixo questaba presto de hazer e cunplir lo que por ella le hera mandado y haziendolo y cunpliendolo tomo por las manos a los dhos don Françisco Chilche caçique prinçipal de Yucai e don Pedro e don Lucas prinçipales del dho repartimi^to^ e don Xpoval Chotas e don Diego Caguatay caçiques e prinçipales de Xaquijaguana e don Alonso Cullena caçique de Quilloa y en señal de posesion los entrego por las manos a la dha doña Beatriz Mango Capa Yupangui en nonbre del dho Saire Topa Mango Capa Yupangui su parte en nonbre de los demas caçiques prinçipales e yndios naturales de los dhos repartimi^tos^ e pueblos dellos y luego la dha doña Beatriz Capa Yupangui en el dho nonbre tomo por las manos a los dhos caçiques e prinçipales de los dhos pueblos de suso nonbrados en señal de posesion propiedad e señorio como sujetos y basallos del dho Saire Topa Mango Capa Yupangui Ynga su parte conforme a la dha provision de su exçelençia la qual dha posesion dixo que tomaba e tomo en el dho nonbre en los dhos caçiques e prinçipales se suso nonbrados por ellos y en boz y en nonbre de //
/f.443/ los demas prinçipales yndios e yndias a ellos sujetos e de como tomaba e tomo la dha posesion quieta e paçificamente sin contradiçion de persona alguna que yo el dho escrivano viese ni oyese de que yo doy e hago fee que paso asi sin contradiçion alguna la dha doña beatris en el dho nombre lo pidio por testimonio signado para en guarda de su derecho y el dho s^r^ corregidor se lo mando dar lo qual todo segun e como de suso se contiene la dha doña Beatriz dixo e le fue dado a entender por lengua de yndio siendo presentes por testigos a lo que dho es Gaspar de Sotelo alcalde hordinario de la dha çiudad e Diego de Truxillo e Miguel Sanchez e Antonio de Marchena vesinos de la dha çiudad y el dho señor corregidor lo firmo aqui de su nonbre el liç^do^ Muñoz paso ante mi Françisco de Barrientos.

v En la gran çiudad del Cuzco cabeça destos reinos del Piru en veinte e nuebe Dias del mes de otubre de mill e qui^os^ y setenta e dos años ante el Yll^e^ señor dotor Gabriel de Loarte del consejo de su magestad y su alcalde de corte en estos reinos e justiçia mayor en esta dha çiudad y su jur^on^ etc. y por ante mi Joan de Castañeda escrivano de su magestad y publico de la //
/f.443v/ dha çiudad paresçio el capitan Martin Garçia Oñez y Loyola caballero de la horden de Calatrava como marido y conjunta persona de doña Beatriz Coya presento unas provisiones e çedula del Excelentisimo señor don Françisco de Toledo visorey destos reinos firmada de su nombre y refrendado de Alvaro Ruiz de Nabamuel su secretario a lo que por ella pareçe que su thenor coregido con su original es como se sigue.

/al margen: Provision pa dar posesion a Martin Garcia de Loyola y doña Beatriz su mujer de los indios del valle de Yucay/

Don Francisco de Toledo mayordomo de su magestad su bisorey gobernador e capitan general destos reinos e provinçias del Piru e tierra firme etc. A vos la justiçia mayor e juez de residencia de la ciudad del Cuzco y alcaldes ordinarios e otras quales quier justiçias de la dha ciudad y a los visitadores del valle de Yucai de Xaquixaguana Quipa e Pucara e a cada uno e qualesquier a quien esta mi provision fuere mostrada sabed que el capitan Martin Garçia Oñez y Loyola caballero de la horden de Calatrava me hizo relacion diziendo que como hera notorio el se abia casado con doña Beatriz Coya hija de don Diego Saire Topa Ynga el qual tubo e poseyo para el y sus herederos y susçesores por mrd que le hizo el marques de Cañete visorey que fue destos reinos en termino de la ciudad del Cuzco de los caciques e y^os^ del valle de Xaquixaguana que son caciques del pueblo de Cazca don Diego Guamantica //
/f.444/ del pueblo de Cuzco don Martin Guaman del pueblo de Anta Marcos Atao Pongo del pueblo de Equeco Baltasar Cuxiauca del pueblo de Tambo don Juan Urcosupa los quales dhos caciques e yndios estan de presente mandados reducir al pueblo de Nuestra Señora del Valle y en el dho valle de Xaquixaguana del pueblo de Pomaguanca de que es cacique don Françisco Yupangui del pueblo de Çurite Felipe Pazlla del pueblo de Lavangui Baltasar Turba Guaman del pueblo de Chiguan Quilisca y don Geronimo Atao Rimache del pu^o^ de Guarocondo don Felipe Pomacaua del pu^o^ de Lacrama don Joan Cauas todos los quales ansimismo se reducen en el dho valle e pueblo de San Nicolas y del pueblo de Quillua y don Alonso Colina del pu^o^ de Caquia Xaquixaguana de ques cacique don Diego Topa del pueblo de Coya Mateo Rimache del pueblo de Paulo don Joan Pata Yupangui del pueblo de Tangarpacta don Hernando Gualpa

Topa del pu^{o} de Pataguailla y a don Garçia principal del pueblo de Tocxa don Juan Paria Tanta del pueblo de Paulo Guaillacaba Baltasar Conocopa del pueblo de Chuquibanba don Antonio Pomachi los quales pueblos e yndios estan al presente mandado reducir al pueblo de Alcatura en el valle de Pisa y del valle de Yucai de que son caciques princi- //
/f.444v/ pales don Françisco Chilche y don Garçia Quispi Capi y del pueblo de Guayllabamba en el dho valle don Garçia Toma que estan mandados reduzir en los pueblos del dho valle y en el pueblo de Maras cacique don Diego Poma Cuxi sujeto al dho don Françisco Chilche y del valle de Guaylla de que son caciques don Baltasar Caua y don Diego Challi que se reduzen al dho valle y de Quipa e Pucara de que es cacique don Hernando Taca que se reduze al dho pueblo de Pucara con todos los indios caciques e principales estancias y ovejeros a ellos sujetos como parece por la mrd y tasas de que se hizo demostracion que dellos le fue fecha por donde parece ser yncluso los dhos caciques e yndios de los pueblos e lugares suso dhos en la mrd que el dho marques de Cañete hizo al dho don Diego Saire Topa Ynga y en la posesion que se le dio por el l^{do} Muñoz siendo corregidor de la dha ciudad del Cuzco en la dha ciudad del Cuzco que por la verificacion que los visitadores que he mandado poner en los partidos de los dhos yndios me a dado hallando en la dha posesion a la dha doña Beatriz hija y suscesora del dho don Diego Saire Topa y que la dha doña Beatriz Coya habia suscedido en el señorio de la mrd que el dho marques de Cañete hizo de los dhos pueblos e yndios al dho su padre como su hija //
/f.445/ mayor legitima y por aberse casado el me pedia e supliçava le hiziese mrd de le mandar dar la posesion dellos e de sus caciques e yndios en que asi sucedio de la dha doña Beatriz como dho es fueron del dho don Diego Saire Topa Mango Capa Yupangui su padre e por nos visto lo suso dho y a tento a que el dho capitan Loyola es casado con la dha doña Beatriz Coya acorde dar y di la presente por la qual vos mando que luego que por ella fueredes requerido vos o qualquier de bos por parte del dho capitan Martin Garcia de Oñez y Loyola le deis cedeis e meteis en la posesipon de los pueblos caciques e y^{os} a ellos sujetos que la dha doña Beatriz tiene e posee por la mrd que dellos se hizo al dho don Diego Saire Topa Ynga su padre para que los tenga e posea segun e de la manera que en la dha mrd se contiene la qual dha posesion dareis conforme a lo que dho es como a marido de la dha doña Beatriz Coya sin consentir ni dar lugar que en ello se le pueda poner ni ponga ynpedimiento alguno y asi dada la dha posesion mando que sea anparado y defendido en ella y no sea desposeido sin ser primero oydo e por fuero e dr^{o} vençido y los unos e los otros no dexeis de lo ansi cumplir por alguna manera so pena de cada mill pesos de oro para la camara de su mag^{t}. Fecho en el tambo de Chicacupi terminos de la ciudad del Cuzco a veinte e un dias del //
/f.445v/ mes de otubre de mill e quinientos y setenta e dos años. don Françisco de Toledo por mandado de su Exª Alvaro Ruiz de Nabamuel.

/al margen: Posesion/ Y por virtud de la dha provision çedula que de suso va yncorporada y conforme a ella pidio a su mrd del dho señor dotor Loarte le de la posesion real corporal jure domine velcasi de los caciques e principales e yndios qye de yuso yran declarados en boz y en nombre de los demas principales e yndiosh pueblos y estancias y obejeros y mitimaes anejos e concernientes a los dhos repartimi^{os} que los dhos caciques e pueblos son los siguientes.

Valle de Yucay

v Don Françisco Chilche y don Garçia Quispi Capi y don Garçia Thoma caciques y principales del balle de Yucai y sus sujetos.

Valle de Xaquix[a]

v Don Martin Atao Poma cacique del pu^{o} de Çanco.
v Marcos Atao Pongo cacique del pu^{o} de Anta.
v Don Françisco Guamantica principal del pueblo de Cazca de que es cacique principal don Di^{o} Guamantica.
v Don Luis Supa principal del pueblo de Equeco de que es cacique principal Cusi Aucar.
v Don Juan Aucapoma principal del pu^{o} de Tanboqui de ques cacique don Ju^{o} Urcosupa.
v Alonso Roca principal del pueblo de Pomaguanca de ques cacique don Fran^{co} Yupangui.
v Martin Arcasa principal del pueblo de Sorite de ques cacique Felipe Paylla.
/f.446/ v Don Hernando Tunba Guaraca cacique del pueblo de Lavangui.
v Don Pedro Cavatuco cacique del pu^{o} de Chiguan Quiliscache de ques cacique principal don Gr^{mo} Atao Rimache.
v Don Joan Cuyo Tupa cacique del pu^{o} de Pomaguanca.
v Sebastian Quipocamayo del pu^{o} de Lacrama de ques cacique don Ju^{o} Cana.

Balle de Pissa

v Don Alonso Colina cacique del pu^{o} de Quillay.
v Don Diego Topa cacique del pueblo de Caquia Xaquijaguana.
v Mateo Rimache cacique del pu^{o} de Coya Cuzco.
v Don Ju^{o} Pata Yupangui cacique del pueblo de Paulo.
v Agustin Guaman Oyarico del pu^{o} de Tancarpata de ques cacique don Hernando Gualpa Topa.
v Don Garçia Punaparo cacique del pueblo de Pata Guailla.
v Baltasar Corocopa cacique del pu^{o} de Chuquibamba.
v Don Baltasar Rimache cacique del pueblo de Hanan Coya.
v Don Juan Maullo cacique del pu^{o} de Tucxa.

Quipa y Pucara

v Don Di^{o} Vica principal de Quipa y Pucara ques en el Collao.

De los quales dhos caciques principales e yndios de suso declarados que son de los de Yucai y Pisa y Xaquixaguana //
/f.446/ y pueblos de Quipa y Pucara que de presente estan en esta dha ciudad de los que a de tomar la dha posesion conforme a la dha cedula e mrd que dellos esta fha en don Diego Saire Topa Ynga padre de la dha doña Beatriz Coya su muger como su heredera en los dhos repartimi[os] pidio se le de la posesion dellos como dho tiene e justicia y lo firmo testigos Rodrigo de Esquivel y Amador de Cabrera y Joan Fernandez Coronel. Martin Garçia de Loyola ante mi Joan de Castañeda escrivano publico.

/Al margen: posesion/ E por su mrd del dho señor dotor Loarte vista la dha cedula e provision de suso declarada que originalmente le fue mostrada y el dho pedimiento estando en las casas de su morada y en ella el dho capitan Loyola e los caciques e principales e yndios suso referidos por la horden e forma que se conti[e] en su pedimiento en cumplimiento de lo que su Excelencia del dho señor visorey mando tomo por la mano al dho capitan Martin Garçia de Loyola e le dio y entrego en señal de posesion a los dhos caciques e principales e yndios a los quales el suso dho tomo por la mano en señal de berdadera posesione a los caciques e principales les mando sentar en sus duhos y a los demas en el suelo y que se levantasen los quales le obedescieron como a su amo y señor y les quito las mantas e se las torno a dar //
/f.447/ e hizo otros autos de posesion jure domine la qual aprehendio en los suso dhos y en cada uno dellos por los pueblos estancias obejeros y mitimaes a ellos anejos e concernientes segun e como en la dha çedula e provision mas largo de declara y la dha posesion aprehendio quieta e pacificamente sin contradicion alguna en la qual su mrd del dho señor dotor Loarte dixo que le amparaba e anparo para que della no sea despojado en manera alguna hasta primero ser vencido por fuero e derecho y el dho capitan Loyola pidio por testimonio y se dio a entender lo suso dho a los dhos caciques por ynterpretacion de Pedro Dominguez yndio ynterprete publico siendo t[o]s los dhos Rodrigo de Esquivel e Amador de Cabrera y Ju[o] Fernandez Coronel. El doctor Loarte ante mi Joan de Castañeda escrivano publico.

En la ciudad del Cuzco del Piru a veinte y seis dias del mes de nobienbre de mill e quinientos e setenta e dos años Alonso de Valdes en nombre del capitan Martin Garçia de Loyola e doña Beatriz Coya su muger e por virtud de su poder parescio ante el muy magnifico señor P[o] de Valdes alcalde hordinario en esta ciudad y su jur[on] por su magestad y pidio su mrd le mande dar la posesion real corporal juro domine vel casi del repartimiento de Gualla de la encomienda de los suso dhos conforme a la çedula //
/f.447v/ e provision de su Excelencia de suso e para ello hizo presentacion del poder que de los suso dhos tiene ques como se sigue.

/al margen: Poder de Martin de Loyola y de su mujer/ Sepan quantos esta carta vieren como yo Martin Garçia de Loyola comendador del abito de Calatrava vezino desta gran ciudad del Cuzco y capitan de la guardia del Exmo señor don Françisco de Toledo virey destos reinos e yo doña Beatriz Coya su legitima mujer con licencia y espreso consentimiento que pido e demando al dho señor capitan mi marido para otorgar esta escritura como en ella fuere conthenido la qual dha licencia yo el dho capitan le doy e concedo quan firme e bastante de dr[o] se requiere y me obligo de la aber por firme y lo que por virtud della fuere fho e otorgado en esta escritura su obligacion que p[a] ello hago de mi persona e bienes avidos e por aber e usando della e anbos a dos juntos e ynsolidum otorgamos e conoçemos que damos e otorgamos nro poder cumplido qual de derecho se requiere a Alonso de Valdes y a Joan Fernandez Coronel a anbos a dos juntamente e cada uno dellos ynsolidum especialmente para que nos y en nro nombre tenga en beneficio la administracion los tributos e yndios de nra encomienda e los defiendan e amparen como mas y mejor convenga a los dhos indios //
/f.448/ e les pongan dotrina suficiente e paguen lo que se debiere pagar a los sacerdotes que los dotrinare e los pongan en buena pulicia e sigan e los defiendan en todos sus pleitos e causas que tubieren asi y de la manera que nosotros lo podriamos hazer y para que puedan recabar e cobren de los dhos yn[o]s de nra encomienda todos los tributos e haziendas que son y fueren obligados a nos dar e pagar de tasa en cada un año e lo que paresciere debernos de las mitas pasadas y de resto de quentas y en otra qualquier manera y de otras qualesquier personas quales quier maravedies e pesos de oro plata joyas esclavos ganados mercaderias e otras cosas qualesquier que nos deban e devieren por escrituras y recaudos y en otra qualesquier manera y del rescibo dellos den e otorguen sus cartas de p[o] finiquito e lasto y cançelacion y los demas autos que conbengan e balgan como si nos e cada uno de nos las diesemos e otorgasemos e p[a] que pidan e tomen quenta a los dhos yn[o]s e otras qualesquier personas que nos las deban dar en qualquier manera y les hagan cargos y resciban descargos y las adicionen e nombren terceros contadores y arbitradores y les den y señalen tr[no] e facultad p[a] ello e hagan alcançes e los resçiban e cobren y den e otorguen carta de pago y finiquito dello segun de suso se conti[e] y siendo necesario renuncien //
/f.448v/ la excecion y leyes del entrego paga e prueva della y del engaño como en ella se contiene e para que puedan vender nros bienes y tributos e arendar qualesquier casas e chacaras y otros bienes raizes por el precio e precios que les pareciere de contado o de fiado al tiempo que quisieren e rescibir el precio dello obligandonos a la hebision e saneami[o] de lo que ansi vendieren e arendaren en la forma que les fuere pedido y bien visto y para que puedan pagar e paguen de nros bienes y haziendas a qualesquier personas las deudas que paresciere deberles por escritura conocimi[os] y quenta corriente y en otra manera y resciban los recaudos de pago e finiquito que conbengan e si yo el dho capitan Martin Garçia de Loyola enbiare a los dhos Alonso de Valdes y Ju[o] Fernandez Coronel algunas cartas e memorias firmadas de mi nombre las cumplan qualquier dellos e hagan e compren e vendan e paguen e conçierten lo que por ella le dixere como conbenga y bieren ser necesarios y para que puedan rescebir y salariar qualesquier mayordomos e criados que entiendan en el beneficio e aumento de nras haziendas el fruto de las quales resciban e cobren e vendan e benefiçien como lo demas de suso contenido y les tomen quentas e salarien letrados e procuradores e solicitadores para nros pleitos e causas e los despidan e a los dhos criados e a los //
/f.449/ que de presente tenemos yles señalen e nombren salarios y se los den e paguen de nros bienes e resciban medicos e çirujanos y los salarien e paguen segun dho es e para que hagan otorguen y hefetuen con qualesquier personas qualesquier compañias e conçiertos transacciones sueltas quitas quiebras en poca o en mucha cantidad y por el precio e tpo y en la forma e manera que les paresçiere y pongan de nra parte los puestos y posturas y condiciones neçesarias y que les parescieren y den y paguen de contado lo que concertaren e fiado a los plazos que en las escrituras fuere contenido e para que puedan comprar e compren de qualesquier personas qualesquier bienes y haziendas muebles y raizes ropa mercadurias esclabos e otras cosas quales paresçiere de contado o fiado y lo paguen e nos

obliguen a que los daremos e pagaremos a los plazos que se concertaren y sobre todo lo suso dho e cada cosa e parte dello hagan e otorguen las escrituras de pago finiquito cançelacion obligaçion poderes transaciones conciertos ventas compromisos arendamientos salarios y demas escrituras que sean neçesarias con las fuerças e vinculos obligaciones renunciaciones sumisiones poder a las justicias e demas firmeças que para su validacion se requieran que asi e de la manera que ellos las //

/f.449v/ hizieren e otorgaren las otorgamos aprovamos corroboramos e confirmamos como en ellas fuere contenido las quales abemos aqui por insertas y especificadas y las cumpliremos e pagaremos e para que parezcan ante qualesquier juez y tribunal e presenten e pidan qualesquier çedulas e provisiones e las que yo les enviare y diere y pidan cumplimiento dellas y thome y aprehendan posesion de los yndios de nra encomienda conforme a la provision e provisiones que para ello tenemos e la amparen e defiendan e contradigan e usen de hefeto de las dhas provisiones como y donde convengan y sobre lo suso dho e cada cosa e parte dello siendo necesario parezcan en jui^{o} y en el el y fuera del pidan demanden respondan nieguen conozcan contradigan aleguen satisfagan juren prueben tachen presenten recusen e abonen y se aparten de las reçusaçiones pidan e hagan execuciones prisiones ventas de bienes y remates dellos y presenten qualesquier escrituras e otros recaudos y usen dellos en juiçio e fuera del e hagan todos los demas autos e deligencias judiciales y esta judiciales que conbengan e nosostros hariamos quel poder que para todo lo que dho es es neçesario y se requiere se lo damos y otorgamos con sus insidencias e dependencias e conexidades e libre e general administracion e con facultad que lo puedan sostituir //

/f.450/ e revocarlos e poner otros de nuebo a los quales e a ellos relebamos en forma de derecho e para lo ansi cumplir e lo que por virtud del fuere fho oblig^{o}s nras personas e bienes abidos e por aber e damos poder a qualesquier juezes e justicias de qualesquier partes ante quien esta carta paresciere para que por todo rigor de dr^{o} e via ex^{a} nos compelan e apremien a lo ansi cumplir como por sentencia definitiva pasada en cosa juzgada y renunçiamos qualesquier leyes fueros e derechos en nro fabor e las que dizque renunciacion de leyes fha en general no vala e yo la dha doña Beatriz renuncio las leyes de los emperadores Justiniano e Beliano y el senatus consulto e leyes de Toro fuero e partidas e leyes segundas nucias e todo auxilio e remedio de buen baron e las demas que son en favor de las mugeres de cuyo efeto e remedio fue avisada por el pres^{te} escrivano e asi las renuncio e otorgamos esta carta en el Cuzco en treinta e un dias del mes de otubre de mill e qui^{o}s e setenta e dos años testigos Juan de Çianca e Françisco P^{e}z pro^{or} e Domingo de Garro e lo firmaron los otorgantes a los quales yo el escrivano conozco. Martin Garçia de Loyola doña Beatriz Coya ante mi Gr^{mo} de Quesada scriv^{o} pu^{co}.

/f.450v/ Yo Geronimo de Quesada escrivano publico del numero del Cuzco ante quien paso lo suso dho lo fize escribir y aqui mi signo. Gr^{mo} de Quesada escrivano publico.

E por su mrd del dho señor alcalde visto el dho pedimiento mando que parezcan ante su mrd los caciques e principales del dho reparti^{o} de Gualla y questa presto de le dar la posesion dellos y de los yndios a ellos sujetos en el dho nombre e asi lo proveyo Pedro de Valdes ante mi Joan de Castañeda escrivano publico.

<u>Posesion.</u> E luego el dho Alonso de Valdes traxo antel dho señor alcalde a don Luis Uyua e Fran^{co} Caba e Baltasar Hicay y Ju^{o} Guaman caciques principales del dho repartimiento sujetos a don Diego Challi principal de la parcialidad de Hurin Gualla y a don Alonso Say principal de la parcialidad de Hurin Gualla en los quales dhos principales en nombre de todo el repartimiento pidio se le de la posesion real corporal jure domine belcasi y el dho s^{or} alcalde conforme a la dha çedula de su Exª y en cumplimiento dello tomo por la mano a los dhos principales e los dio y entrego al dho Alonso de Valdes el qual en señal de la dha posesion los tomo por la mano e les quito las mantas e las torno a dar en señal de tributo que an de dar al dho su amo en cuyo nombre tomo la dha posesion la qual aprehendio pacificam^{te} sin contradicion alg^{a} y el dho señor alcalde le amparo y defendio en ella para que no sea desposeido sin primero ser vencido por fuero e dr^{o} //

/f.451/ e lo pidio por testimonio siendo tg^{os} el l^{do} Garçia Arr^{o}s e Françisco Perez e Ju^{o} Alvarez por quien se dio a entender la dha posesion a los dhos principales. Pedro de Valdes por ynterprete e testigo Joan Alvarez ante mi Juan de Castañeda escrivano publico.

E yo Joan de Castañeda escrivano de su magestad e publico de la gran ciudad del Cuzco presente fui a lo suso dho en lo que de mi se hace mencion e lo demas fize escrebir segun por ello pareze en siete fojas con esta e aqui mi signo en testimonio de verdad. Ju^{o} de Castañeda escrivano publico.

En la ciudad del Cuzco del Piru en diez y nueve dias del mes de otubre de mill e qui^{o}s e setenta e quatro años Alonso de Valdes residente en esta dha ciudad pr^{or} de Martin Garçia de Loyola caballero de la horden de Calatrava e doña Beatriz de Mendoça Coya su muger y en su nombre dixo que sostituya y sostituyo el dho poder en Alonso de Urena e Françisco Perez procuradores residentes en esta dha ciudad para en n^{e} del dho Martin Garçia de Loyola e de la dha doña Beatriz su muger presente estos recaudos ante su señoria Yl^{ma} en el pleito matrimonial de Xpoval Maldonado y hagan qualesquier pedim^{os} requerimientos citaciones p^{o}testaciones enbargos secuestros presentaciones de t^{o}s p^{o}vanças escritos y escrituras y todos los demas recaudos que a lo suso dho conbengan y en efeto hagan e autuen todos los demas autos //

/f.451v/ e deligenicias judiciales y estra judiciales que necesarios sean de hazer con libre e general administracion que el poder ques necesario para todo lo suso dho e seguir el dho p^{to} matrimonial tal se le doy y sostituyo en forma de derecho e les relievo segun yo soy relebado e obligo los bienes a mi obligados y otorgue sostitucion en forma siendo t^{o}s Ju^{o} Alvarez y G^{o} de Mora y don Garçia residentes en la dha ciudad y el dho otorgante lo firmo a quien doy fee que conozco. Al^{o} de Valdes ante mi Martin de Yaben escrivano.

En la ciudad del Cuzco a diez dias del mes de março de mill e quinientos y ochenta y nueve años yo Gaspar de Prado scriv^{o} del rey nuestro s^{or} e pu^{co} desta dha ciudad por ausencia de Antonio Sanchez svano publico del numero desta dha ciudad saque e fize sacar este traslado de su original que quedo en poder del dho comendador Martin Garçia de Loyola va cierto e verdadero coregido e concertado siendo t^os Joan Perez e Antonio Muriel e Diego Ruiz residentes en la dha ciudad va testado que dezia Hernando vala. Y lo fize screvir y aqui mi signo.

Gaspar de Prado. /rubrica/

/f.452/ En la ciudad de los Reyes en ocho dias del mes de noviembre de mill e quinientos y ochenta e cinco años estando los señores pres^te y oydores desta real audi^a haciendo audiencia pu^ca e por ante mi Juan de Montoya escrivano de camara desta real audiencia Juan Sanchez de los Rios en nombre de Martin Garcia de Loyola y doña Beatriz Coya su muger pres^to la peticion siguiente.

Muy poderoso señor Juan Sanchez de los Rios en nombre de Martin Garcia de Loyola e de doña Beatriz Coya su muger en la causa con vuestro fiscal sobre los yndios que les quitaron diciendo ser yanaconas digo que para presentar ne esta causa tengo nezesidad de las escrituras siguientes.

Las provisiones e zedulas de buestra real persona en que mando traer de paz a Mango Ynga y a Sayre Topa Ynga y las mercedes que les mando p^a que viniesen de paz.

Yten la zedula de buestra real persona en que mando que el marques de Cañete cumpliese y ejecutase las cedulas y provisiones que avia dado dirigidos a don Ant^o de Mendoza e a los demas visoReyes.

Yten un testimonio de la platica que //
/f.452v/ frai Pedro Gutierez dijo a los yn^os del balle de Yucay quando empezo a hazer la visita del y desia y en la dha visitaçion hecha a la dha doña Beatriz Coya o al alguna persona por ella e de los capitulos de la instruccion primero y catorce y setenta y siete en que don Françisco vuestro visorey daba el horden que se avia de tener en declarar por yndios tributarios o no a los yndios forasteros o yanaconas.

Yten que se saque de la corona destos reinos de las Yndias que conpuso Diego Hernandez el capitulo quarto libro tercero en que trata del horigen y suçesion de los Yngas del capitulo quinto del dho libro en que trata del horden quel dho marques tubo en sacar al dho Saire Topa Ynga de paz e lo que con el hizo con las proviçiones de buestra alteza para ynprimir.

Y de una carta quel Conde de Nieva y los comisarios escrivieron a V. Real persona sobre el sacar de paz el Ynga a pedimiento de Juan Sierra de Liguisamo.

A V. Alt^a pido y sup^co mande a los escrivanos de Camara en cuyo poder estan los procesos y zedulas de yuso contenidas me den un traslado de todo ello en publica forma sacado con çitacion de vuestro fiscal para lo presentar en esta causa sobre que pido justicia e para ello es. Juan //
/f.453/ Sanchez de los Rios. Martin Garçia de Loyola.

Presentada la dha peticion e por los dhos señores vista mandaron que se le den los dhos traslados que pide e que fuese çitado para ello el licenciado Albaro de Carabaxal fiscal de su magestad al qual estando pres^te se cito en forma Montoya.

En cumplimi^to de lo qual yo Alvaro de Montoya scriv^o de camara desta real audi^a doy fee que en un libro de cedulas las questa en el dho of^o donde se asientan e ponen las çedulas e probisiones reales de su mag^d y otras çedulas e titulos esta una çedula del emperador don Carlos nro s^or ques la que por la dha peticion se pide y demanda la qual segun como esta en el dho libro hize sacar e saque ques del tenor siguiente.

/f.453v/ Don Ph^e por la gracia de dios rey de Castilla de Leon de Aragon de las Çiçilias de Jerusalem de Nabarra de Granada de Toledo de Valencia de Galicia de Mallorca de Sevilla de Zerdenia de Cordova de Corcega de Murcia de Xaen de los Algarves de Algezira de Gibraltar duque de Milan conde de Flandes e de Tirol etc. Por quanto por p^te de vos Di^o Fernandez vecino de la ciudad de Palencia nos fue fecha relacion diciendo que vos aviades descrito e compuesto el alzamiento e tirania de Fran^co Hernandez //
/f.454/ Giron en las Yndias ansimismo la rebelion de Gonzalo Pizarro e su castigo la qual se avia visto por los de nuestro consejo de las Yndias e os aviamos dado lizencia para los poder ymprimir e vender en ellas por lo qual nos pedistes e suplicastes os diesemos lizencia p^a lo poder ymprimir e vender en estos nuestros reinos o como la nuestra md fuese e visto en el nuestro que las deligencias contenidas en vuestra pet^on e lizencia que os dimos para que los dhos libros se ynprimiesen e vendiesen en las que fue acordado que deviamos mandar esta nuestra carta para bos en la dha razon e nos tuvimoslo por bien por la qual bos damos lizencia e facultad para que en estos nuestros reinos por esta bez podais hazer ynprimir los dhos libros que de yuso de haze mincion son que por ello cay- //
/f.454v/ gais ni yncurrais en pena alguna e mandamos que la dha ynprision se haga por los originales que van los dos firmados al cabo de el dotor Fran^co de Villafane y el otro del dotor Aguilera de el nuestro consejo se las Yndias e que despues de ynpresos no se puedan vender ni vendan sin que primero se traiga al nuestro consexo juntam^te con los dhos originales para que se bean si la dha ynpresion esta conforme a ellos e se tase ante todas cosas el precio que se ovieren de vender cada volumen so pena de caer e incurrir en las penas contenidas en la dha prematica e leyes de nuestros reinos e mas de la nuestra md y de diez mill maravedies p^a la nuestra cam^a. dada en Madrid a diez y nueve dias del mes de hebrero de myll e quinientos y setenta e nueve años. Dcard segunt. El dotor Diego Gasca el licenciado Morilla el //

/f.455/ el licenciado Atienza el D. Suarez de Toledo don Antonio de Padilla.

El REY

Por quanto por parte de vos Diego Hernandez vz^{no} de la ciudad de Palencia nos fue fecha relacion que bos avia describir el alzamiento e tirania de Fran^{co} Hernandez Giron en las Yndias e ansimismo la rebelion de Gonçalo Pizarro e su castigo lo qual se a visto por los de nuestro consejo de las Yndias e os aviamos dado lizencia para los poder ymprimir e vender en ellas suplicandonos vos diesemos lizencia para los poder ynprimir e vender los dho libros en estos nuestros reinos e que otra nenguna persona sin vuestro poder lo pudiese hazer o como la nuestra md fuese visto en el nuestro consejo las diligencias contenidas en vuestra pet^{on} //
/f.455v/ e licencia que os dimos p^{a} que los dhos libros ynprimiesen e vendiesen en las Yndias lo avemos tenido por bien por ende damos liz^{a} e facultad a vos el dho Diego Fernandez para que bos o la persona que vuestro poder especial para ello oviere e no otra alguna podais hazer e ynprimir e vender los dhos libros que de suso haze mincion en estos nuestros reinos e señorios de Castilla siendo primeramente tasado por los del nuestro consejo el precio porque se a de vender cada volumen e poniendo el traslado desta nuestra zedula con la dha tasacion al principio de los dhos libros por tiempo y espacio de diez años cumplidos primeros siguientes que se quentan desde el dia de esta nuestra zedula en adelante so pena que qualquiera pers^{a} o personas que sin tener para ello vuestro poder los ynprimiesen o vendiesen o hiziesen ynprimir o vender //
/f.456/ pierdan toda la ynpresion que hicieren o vendieren e los moldes e aparexos de ella e mas yncurran en pena de cinquenta mil maravedies por cada vez que lo contrario hicieren la qual dha pena sea a la tr^{a} parte para la persona que lo acusare e la otra tercia parte para el juez que lo sentenciare e la otra terzera parte para la nuestra camara e fisco. E mandamos a los del nuestro consexo e a otra qualesquier justicias de nuestros reinos e señorios que guarden y cumplan y ejecuten e hagan guardar cumplir y executar esta nuestra zedula e lo en ella contenido. Fecha en el Pardo a seis dias del mes de março de mill e qui^{o}s e sesenta y nueve años. yo el Rey. Por mandado de su magestad Ant^{o} de Derasa.

EL REY

/al margen: <u>sobre el alzamiento de G^{o} Pizarro</u>/ Por quanto por parte de vos Diego Fernandez vecino de Palençia me a sido fecha relacion //
/f.456v/ que bos aveis fecho un libro yntitulado Ystoria del alzamiento y tirania de Gonzalo Pizarro con el suceso de la Nueva España sobre la ex^{on} de las nuevas leyes en que abeis pasado muncho trabaxo ocupacion e gastos e por quel dho libro era mui util e provechoso me suplicastes os diese lizençia e facultad para que bos o quien vuestro poder oviese le pudiesedes ynprimir e llevar a vender a las nuestras Yndias isla e tierra firme de mar ozeano o en otra persona alguna pa tiempo de diez años so graves penas como la mi merced fuese y por quel dho libro fue visto y exsaminado por los del nuestro consejo de las Yndias e lo tenido por bien por ende por la presente doy lizencia a vos el dho Diego Fernandez p^{a} que por tiempo de diez años primeros siguientes que corran y se quenten desde el dia de la fecha desta nuestra zedula en ade- //
/f.457/ lante podais vos e las personas que tienen vuestro poder ynprimir el dho libro e venderle en las nuestras Yndias yslas e tierra firme de mar ozeano e mando e defiendo que durante el dho tiempo de los dhos diez años otras algunas personas de qualquier estado condiçion que sea eclesiasticas e seglares no sea nos dados de ynprimir ni hazer que se ymprima el dho libro ni lo vender en las dhas nuestras Yndias salvo vos el dho Diego Fernandez e las personas que para ello vuestro poder tuviere so pena que qualquiera otra persona o personas que sin tener p^{a} ello vuestro poder durante el dho tiempo lo ynprimiere o hicieren ynprimir e bender en las dhas nuestras Yndias pierdan por el mismo caso y hecho la ynpreçion que hicieren e los moldes e aparejos con que lo hicieren e los //
/f.457v/ libros que ynprimieren siendo inpresos e hechos e demas desto yncurran cada uno dellos en pena de zinq^{ta} mill m^{e}s cada bez que lo contrario hicieren las quales dhas penas e se repartan en esta manera la mitad para nuestra camara e la otra mitad para bos el dho Diego Fernandez la qual dha md bos hazemos con tanto que antes que comenzeis a hazer e vender el dho libro se hagan por vuestra p^{te} las deligencias que la prematica agora nuebam^{te} dispone e con que ayais de vender e vendais cada pliego de molde en la dha Nueba España e Nueva Galicia e Guatimala e provinçias de Honduras Yucatan e Cocumel e tierra firme y Nicaragua Venezuela e Cartagena Cabo de la Vela Ysla Española San Juan y Cuba diez maravedis. Y en el nuevo reino de Granada e prov^{a} de Popayan a doze maravedis y en las provincias del Piru //
/f.458/ quinze maravedis y en las de Chile diez y ocho que es el precio porque esta tasado por el dho nuestro consejo de las Ynd^{a}s e mandamos a los de nuestro consexo pres^{tes} e oydores de las nuestras audiencias reales de las dhas nuestras Yndias yslas e tierra firme del mar ozeano y a todos los otros juezes e justicias de todas las ciudades villas e lugares dellas ansi a los que agora son como a los que seran de aqui adelante que guarden y cumplan e hagan guardar e cumplir esta nuestra zedula e lo en ella contenido e contra el tenor e forma dellas no bayan ni pasen ni consientan yr ni pasar en tiempo alguno ni por alguna manera so pena de la nuestra md e de cinquenta mill mr^{e}s para la nuestra camara a cada uno que lo contrario hiciere. Fecha en Madrid a onze de abril de mill e qui^{o}s e sesenta e ocho años //
/f.458v/ yo el Rey por m^{do} de su magestad Fran^{co} de Heraso.

EL REY

Por quanto por p^{te} de bos Diego Hernandez vecino de la ciudad de Palencia me a sido fha relacion questando vos en las provincias del Piru suzedio la tirania de Fran^{co} Hernandez Giron e desde principio de la guerra hasta el fin os hallastes en ella debajo del estandarte real quel marques de Cañete nuestro visorey que fue de las dhas provincias constandole de vuestra avilidad y noticia que teniades de lo suzedido en la dha guerra y en otras cosas dependientes de ella os avia hordenado que lo escriviesedes e ansi lo aviades hecho e teniades escrito un libro que se llama e yntitula La Historia del Piru en que abeis pasado muncho trabaxo ocupacion e gas- //
/f.459/ tos e me suplicastes os diese licencia e facultad para que vos o qualquier que vuestro poder oviere le pudiesedes ynprimir e llevar a vender a las nuestras Yndias yslas e tierra firme del mar oceano y no en otra persona alguna por tiempo de diez años so graves penas o como la nuestra md fuese y exsaminado por los del nuestro consejo de las Yndias e lo contenido por vien por ende por la pres^{te} doy

lizencia e facultad a vos el dho Diego Hernandez para que por tiempo de diez años primeros siguientes que corran e se quenten desde la fha desta mi zedula en adelante podais vos e las personas que tuvieren vuestro poder ynprimir el dho libro e venderle en las nuestras Yndias islas e tierra //
/f.459v/ firme del mar ozeano e m[do] e defiendo que durante el dho tiempo de los dhos diez años otras lagunas ni nengunas personas de qualquier estado e condicion que sean eclesiasticas o seglares no sean osados de ynprimir ni hazer que se ynpriman el dho libro ni los vender en las dhas nuestras Yndias salvo bos el dho Diego Hernandez e las personas que p[a] ello el dho nuestro poder tuvieren so pena que qualquier otra persona o personas que sin tener para ello vuestro poder durante el dho tiempo lo ynprimiere o hiciere ynprimir e bender en las dhas nuestras Yndias pierdan por el mesmo caso y hecho la ynpresion que hicieren e los moldes e aparejos con que lo hicieren e los libros que ynprimieren çiendo ynpresos y hechos e demas desto yncurran cada uno dellos en pena //
/f.460/ de zinquenta mill mr[e]s cada bez que lo contrario hicieren las quales dhas penas se repartan en esta manera la mitad para la nuestra camara e la otra mitad para bos el dho D[o] Hernandez la qual dha md vos hazemos con tanto que antes que comenzeis a vender el dho libro se haga por vuestra parte las deligencias que la prematica agora nuevamente hechas dispone con que ayais de bender e bendais cada pliego de molde del dho libro en la Nueva España e Nueva Galicia e Guatemala e prov[a] de Honduras y Yucatan e Cocumel e tierra firme y Nicaragua Venezuela e Cartagena Cabo de la Vela e Ysla Española e San Juan y Cuba diez maravedis y en el nuevo reino de Granada e provi[a] de Popayan doze mr[e]s y en las provi[as] del Piru quinze mr[e]s y en las //
/f.460v/ provincias de Chile diez y ocho maravedis que es el precio en que esta tasado por el dho nuestro consejo de las Yndias e mandamos a los de nuestro consexo pres[tes] e oydores de las nuestras audiencias reales de las dhas nuestras Yndias yslas e tierra firme del mar ozeano y a todos los otros juezes e justi[a]s de todas las ciudades villas e lugares dellas ansi a los que agora son como a los que seran de aqui adelante que guarden y cumplan e hagan guardar e cumplir esta nuestra zedula e lo en ella contenido e contra el tenor e forma dellas no bayan ni pasen ni consientan yr ni pasar en tiempo alguno ni por alguna manera so pena de la nuestra merzed e de cinquenta mill maravedies para la nuestra camara a ca- //
/f.461/ da uno que lo contrario hiciere. Fecha en Madrid a dos de febrero de mill e qui[o]s e sesenta e ocho años. Yo el Rey por mandado de su magestad Françisco de Heraso.

Capitulo Quarto como el Linga [*sic*] Saire Topa Yupangue salio e vino a dar la ovediencia al rey

Quando el virey don Hurtado de Mendoza enbio al lizenciado Muñoz por corregidor al Cuzco le envio con el a doña Beatriz Mango Capa Yupangue casada con Diego //
/f.461v/ Hernandez natural de Talavera hija de Guaina Cava tia de Saire Topa Yupangue para que ella hiciese saber a Saire Topa su sobrino como el avia venido a estos reinos nombrado por su magestad para en su nombre hazerle merzedes e para el bien de todos los naturales. En el Cuzco do ella residia no avia quedado señor ombre ni muger prencipal como ella e por esta razon el marques le es envio y encargo muncho e rogo afectuosamente que enviase mensaje a su sobrino //
/f.462/ ofreciendo gratificacion por ello por que entendio que Saire Topa no se confiava ni daba credito a otra persona alguna. Visto que ubo doña Beatriz la carta despacho un prencipal cacique tio del Inga para que fuese con algunos yndios con el mandado el qual se partio y por causa que los pasos estaban cortados e las puentes hiço como mejor pudo sus puentes de suerte que aunque con trabaxo pasaron e llegados aunque con dificultad a Vilcapanpa dio su mandado a Ynga e todos sus capitanes porque a la saçon aun no avia rezevido la borla del señor e hasta entonzes fue antigua costumbre de los Yngas no tener berdadero mando e las cosas de la governacion y de guerra se consultavan por el consejo que tenian de principales e antiguos caciques aviendo puesta Risca que ansi se llamaba el yndio que envio doña Beatriz hecho su envaxada fue acordado por el consexo de los antiguos y capitanes que aquel principal y sus yndios se quedasen alli que su p[te] fuese //
/f.462v/ otro principal llamado Cussi con otros quatros yndios al ciudad del Cuzco a tratar sobre el negocio e para informarse vien de la doña Beatriz de lo que pasaba y entender is en ello avia alguna cautela e dieron comysion para que entendiendo no aver engaño hablase al lizenciado Muñoz del Cuzco para que les enviase a Juan Sierra hijo de Mançio Sierra conquistador e de doña Beatriz porque del se tenia mas confianza que de otr algu[o] e se ynformarian mejor e mandaron qu no viniesen sin el porque a no venir dijeron que entenderian que los querian engañar e negado Cussi al Cuzco con sus yndios e aviendo hecho su envasada dioseles relacion deste caso e mostraron quedar satisfechos e otorgoseles amorosamente llebar consigo a Juan Sierra y estando ya de partida tuvieron por nueva cierta como el virey avia despachado de lIma para el efeto que fuese por Guamanga al asiento de Vilcapanpa un padre dominico nombrado frai Melchor //
/f.463/ de los Reyes a Juan de Betanços vecino del Cuzco gran lengua e ynterprete los quales enviaba para tratar con el Linga e sus capitanes trato de concordia y paz y llebaban una provi[on] real de perdon de todo lo pasado con el Linga Saire Topa y viniese a la ovidencia de su magestad y el padre y otro compañero suyo y Vetanços no hallando paso por Guamanga para poder entrar por ser aspera e dificultosa la entrada e aber en medio rios caudalosos tomaron la vuelta de Andahuaylas creyendo que harian por alli mejor pasage empero tanvien hallaron la mesma dificultad de lo qual ansimismo tuvo noticia el lizen[do] Muñoz y escrivioles se viniesen luego al Cuzco porque alli se daria orden e ynstruçion de lo que se devia hazer venido pues al Cuzco trataron el lizenciado Muñoz e la doña Beatriz que se fuesen delante de los enbaxadores con su hijo Juan Sierra al Linga //
/f.463v/ y que quedasen siempre atras y en parte segura el fraile y Betanços e ansi siendo deste acuerdo partieron del Cuzco tres dias antes el fraile y Vetanços diciendo aguardarian en el camino enpero quiriendo ganar la onra de primeros enbaxadores se adelantaron hasta do esta la puente que llaman de Chuquichaca donde comienza la juridiçion del Ynga e pasada la puente con harto trabaxo los yndios de guerra que alli estavan por guarda del paso los tomaron e detuvieron sin les hazer otro daño salbo que no les quisieron dejar pasar adelante ni bolver atras e ansi estuvieron detenidos hasta otros dia que llego Juan Sierra con los envaxadores y con otros diez yndios que por mandado del Linga avian salido en busca de los enbajadores e con otros diez yndios e mando que Juan Sierra entrase con ellos seguramente e no otra persona alguna finalm[te] que Betanços e los frailes quedaron detenidos //

/f.464/ e Juan Sierra e los envaxadores pasaron adelante pero avian andado vien poco quando tan vien fueron detenidos hasta dar mandado al Linga de su venida saviendo /el/ Ynga que Ju^{o} Sierra venia e siendo ynform^{do} quel fraile y Betanços benian por enbaxadores del virey envio un capitan con doscientos yndios de guerra armados conrivdes [*sic*] que son yndios guereros que se comen unos a otros en guerra para que diesen al cap^{an} que era su general el mandado y enbajada que traia llegado el general les dio la vienvenida e no quiso oirlos hasta la venida quel venido Juan Sierra solo le reprendio por venir acompañado de cristianos. Juan Sierra se desculpo diciendo que aquello avia sido por consejo e mandado del coreg^{or} del Cuzco y de su tia doña Beatriz y dioles a envasada que para el Ynga traia e les declaro e leyo las cartas de su madre y del corrge^{or} e la quel virey avia escrito //

/f.464v/ a doña Beatriz quel virey avia dado a Juan Sierra su embajador hicieron venia en aquel lugar a Vetanços e a los frailes e les pidieron la misma razon que Juan Sierra por ver si en algo diferian ellos mostraron la provision el perdon e les dieron la envasada que traian junto con un presente que el virey envia al Linga de ciertas piezas de terciopelo y damasco e dos copas de p^{ta} doradas y otras cosas hecho esto el general e capitanes mandaron a dos yndios que a todo avian sido presentes e fuese luego a dar relacion al Inga el qual aviendolo vien entendido dio por respuesta que luego se volviesen de alli sin les hazer ningun daño con sus cartas e provision y presente porque el no queria cosa alguna mas de que el virey hiciese su voluntad por que el tanvien haria la suya como hasta alli lo avia fecho estando ya de partida Juan Sierra e los demas llegaron otros yn^{o}s con mandado que todos entrasen //

/f.465/ y dar a Ynga e a sus capitanes la envaxada que traian en t^{do} y a no mas de quatro leguas del Inga llego mandado que Juan Sierra fuese solo con los recaudos e que a los demas aviasen de lo necesario para su comida e para su partida otro dia Ju^{o} Sierra se partio para el Ynga y estando a dos leguas de adonde estava le vino mandado que se detuviese alli dos dias e por otra parte fueron mensajeros pa que Betanzos e los frailes se volvieron pasados los dos dias el Ynga envio por Juan Sierra e venido ante el le recivio con muncho amor e como a deudo principal suyo e Juan Sierra le dio y esplico lo mexor que pudo su envaxada e recaudos el Ynga mostro holgarse muncho con la enbaxada enpero dixo que el solo no era parte para efetuarlo a causa que no hera señor jurado ni tenia poder para ello por no aber reçivido la vorla que es como la corona entre los Reyes por no tener edad //

/f.465v/ cumplida e que era necesario que enviase la envaxada a sus capitanes e aviendolo hecho se mando por ellos que frai Melchor de los Reyes viniese a explicar la envaxada del virey el qual gratamente oydo e bien recivido el pres^{te} que traia e dieron los capitanes por respuesta quel fraile e Juan Sierra aguardasen por la respuesta hasta que ellos entrasen en su consulta e despues de aberlo entre si consultado se resumieron que ellos avian de mirar tal neg^{o} despacio e consultar sus guacas para la resolucion y que en el ynter Juan Sierra y el fraile con dos capitanes suyos fuesen a Lima e besasen las manos al virey de parte del Inga e tratasen le hiciese merzedes pues los reinos naturalmente le perteneçian por herencia y suzesion e ansi partieron de aquel asiento e vinieron para Andahuaylas //

/f.466/ a la ciudad de los Reyes y entraron en la ciudad por junio dia del señor San P^{o} los yndios capitanes dieron su enbaxada al virey e fueron bien rezevidos e ospedados estuvieron en Lima estos dos capitanes ocho dias y en este tiempo se vieron munchas veces con el virey sobre dar corte en las mercedes e cosas que al Inga se le avian de dar para salir de paz e dar la ovidiencia al rey y el virey lo consulto con el arçovispo e oydores e acordo de darle para sus gastos e que como señor se pudiese sustentar diez y siete mil castellanos de renta para el e sus hijos con encomienda de los yndios de el repartimiento de Fran^{co} Hernandez con el valle tanvien de Yuca yndios del repartimi^{to} de don Fran^{co} Pizarro hijo del marques e mas unas tierras encima de la fortaleza del Cuzco para hazer su morada e casa e de sus yndios con este acuerdo e //

/f.466v/ determinacion se hiço y libro provision en forma e se le dio a Juan Sierra para que el solo fuese con los capitanes e con cierto presente al Inga y en la provision se contenia que el Ynga saliese de sus pueblos do residia dentro de seis meses que contaban desde la data de la provision que fue a cinco de julio y ya quando alego Juan Sierra el Ynga recibido la borla e mostro holgarse en etremo con los despachos del virey a esta sazon avia llegado Diego Hernandez marido de doña Beatriz a verse con el Ynga e tratar con el e sus capitanes estos negocios estuvieron alli algunos dias Diego Hernandez e Juan Sierra esperando resulucion porque la resolucion los capitanes ponian gran dificultad sobre la salida y entraron sobre ello munchas bezes en sus acuerdos e consultas hasta el dia de Nuestra Selora de setiembre de mill //

/f.467/ e quinientos e cinquenta e siete años que todos fueron de acuerdo de hazer sacrificio segun su costumbre para pedir respuesta al sol y a la tierra e a las demas guacas que tienen e ansi por la mañana aviendo mandado este dia que todos ayunasen mientras la pregunta durase e que no se hiciese fuego algu^{o} todos los capitanes se suvieron a una sierra alta y el Ynga con ellos con sus trompetas llevando consigo y antes si los sacerdotes a los quales se tiene gran respeto e guarda toda ovidiencia pidieron pues los sacerdotes con sus cirimonias al sol tierra e guacas declarasen sin aquella salida que avian consultado saldria bien lo qual hecho e mirados sus agujeros dijeron los sacerdotes que tenian respuesta del sol e de la tierras e tamvien de su guacas que la sa- //

/f.467v/ lida seria benturosa e vien afortunada porque a todas sus preguntas avian respondido con si lo qual avia sido contrario en las demandas que otras bezes avia pedido sobre salir a otros gobernadores que con ellos lo avian procurado. Hecho esto luego sonaron las trompetas para baxar la sierra viniendo todos con grande alegria como ovieron baxado llamaron todos los capitanes a Juan Sierra e preguntaron que donde avia dho el virey quel Inga e sus capitanes le fuesen a dar la ovediencia en nombre del rei lo qual referido por Juan Sierra pareçia que aun los capitanes todavia mostraban alguna tivieça y entendido por el Inga los hablo e dixo ansi en alta boz "vien sabeis como el cielo y la tierra e nuestras guacas nos aconsejan la salida por tanto no me digais que de miedo como pusilanimo me salgo ni que //

/f.468v/ pero aveis de considerar que el sol quiere que yo salga por ser cosa que me cumple y por que me bea aumentado en señorio para que alla fuera pueda ser remedio de mi sangre y de todos vosotros por lo qual os digo que yo quiero salir bien que supiese me costase por ello la vida por eso todos los que bien me quisieredes y mi servicio me seguid en esta empresa e los que no os quedar por que yo os prometo que antes de muncho tiempo os arepintais e que yo tome la enmienda por ello haziendo castigo en vosotros dhas estas palabras todos sus capitanes se le humillaron delante e digeron que en todo le querian ser ovidientes e hazer su voluntad e que viese quando queria salir porque todos irian sirviendole en el viaje luego aquellos ocho dias hicieron grandes fiestas e borracheras con gran regocixo puesto que algunos de los capitanes mas anzianos estaban tristes por la salida pasados los //

/f.469/ ochos dias que fue a siete de otubre salio /el/ Ynga con tresçientos yndios e con todos los principales capitanes desando su asiento como antes estaba con la misma guarnicion que tenia a cinco de noviembre llego a Andaguailas donde donde hizo alto e de alli envio a Juan Sierra pa que en su nombre fuese a besar las manos al virey e le hiciera saber como hera salido en cumplimiento de lo que se le mandaba entro pues a Lima vispera de los Reyes a cinco de henero en unas andas que llevaban sus yndios fue luego a vesar las manos al virey que estava aguardando en las casas de su morada reziviole el virey amorosam[te] levantandose a el e sentandole a par de si y en las platicas con que se rezivieron e despues pasaron hasta que se despidio fue del virey y de los oydores //

/f.469v/ juzgado el Linga por cuerdo e de buen juizio e que mostraba bien ser descendiente de aquellos señores Yngas que tan prudentes y valerosos fueron cuyo principio e descendencia diremos con algunas particularidades e çirimonias pa que mexor se entienda como este benia a suceder en el Piru por señor natural que no dexara de dar gusto a los que tienen not[a] de aquellas provincias o la desean tener.

Capitu[o] del origen e principio que los Yngas tuvieron e de su dezendencia

Ynga quiere dezir tanto como señor y ansi al primero que comenzo a conquistar e sujetar los Yngas le llamaron Ynga pareciendoles que era mas valiente e para mas que los otros o que hacian mas que nengu[o] entre ellos avia fecho. El primer Ynga se llamo Mango Capa Ynga de quien prozeden todos los demas que avido en el Piru //

/f.470/ quiere dezir e aun lo afirman los yndios que no se le conoçio padre ni madre mas de que salio de unas piedras questan zerca del Cuzco este Mango Capa fue valiente e comenzo a conquistar alguna gente de la que por alli cerca avia e pusoles debaxo de servidumbre tuvo una mujer llamada Mama Guaco de la qual tubo un hijo que se nombro Sinche Roca Ynga tubo ansimesmo munchos hijos de esta y de otras mugeres pero entre los Yngas no tenian quenta sus vasallos e criados mas de con la mujer primera e con el primer hijo y eredero aunque algunas bezes se tuvo quenta entre ellos con otros hijos hermanos del heredero por esto era porque algunos dellos eran balientes e sus padres hazian quenta dellos pero no se haçia quenta como del principal e suzesor en el mando

/f.470v/ de Sinche Roca Ynga segundo

Sinche Roca Ynga fue valiente y començo a ser mas conocido que su padre y entendiose mas e sujeto mas yn[o]s alrededor del Cuzco tubo una muger que se llamo Mama Cura desta dize que tuvo cinco o seis hijos no tienen noticia de los nombres [dellos] mas de los dos del uno porque fue baliente el qual se llamo Cuxi Guananchiri y el otro fue le heredero que se nombro Llocu Quepangue Ynga [*sic*]

De Lluco Pangue Ynga terzero

Lluco Pangue Ynga no conquisto ni gano cosa alguna de nuebo mas de sustentar lo que su p[e] avia ganado e ponerlo en mas sujecion este no tubo hijo alguno hasta que fue mui viejo e siendo ya tan viejo que casi les parezia a los yndios tener hijos ni virtud para engendrar un criado suyo hallandose muy corrido de que su amo no uviese tenido hijos e viendo que trata- //

/f.471/ ban dellos dicen que un dia le tomo en brazos e le llebo a donde estaba su muger la se nombraba Mama Anabarque e hizo que tuviese parte con ella y a zeso del qual quedo preñada e pario un hijo que se nombro Mayta Capa Ynga e no tubo otro hijo alguno de su madre ni de otras mugeres que tubo.

De Maita Capa Ynga quarto

Maita Capa Ynga fue baliente sujeto e conquisto todos los yndios que estaban alrededor de Cuzco e a lo mismos del Cuzco que nunca sus antezesores avian podido sujetar por que eran balientes e se defendian este los subjeto aunque se le defendieron muncho fue el primero que mando en el Cuzco tubo una muger llamada Mama Yacchi de la qual tubo un hijo que llamo Capac Yupangue Ynga dicen que tubo otros hijos ansi desta mu/jer/- //

/f.471v/ como de otras no tienen memoria.

De Capa Yupangue Ynga quinto

Capa Yupangue Ynga no acrezento ni gano cosa nueba mas de sustentar lo que avia ganado su padre tubo este por muger una que fue llamada Mama Cagua de qual tubo un hijo que se llamo Ynga Ruca Ynga y ansimismo tubo desta e de otras mugeres hijos pero no se acuerdan ni tienen not[a] de los nombres.

De Inga Ruca Ynga sesto

Ynga Ruca Ynga hizo lo mesmo que su padre que no acrezento ni gano cosa en nuevo mas de sustentar lo que su p[e] le dexo este tubo por muger a Mama Micay de la qual tubo un hijo llamado Yaguar Guac [*sic*] Ynga Yupangue y otros dos el uno se nombro Apomaita y el otro Vilcaquiri este Yaguar Guac Yn- //

/f.472/ ga Yupangue siendo de tres meses fue hurtado en el Cuzco e de ai dos meses dicen que parezio en poder de un cazique mui principal que tenia sus tierras en Xaquixaguana e por alli alrededor ansimismo afirman que en este tiempo que tubo hurtado le quisieron matar e platicando si le matarian o no dicen que entre otras bezes que lloro como los demas niños lo suelen hazer lloro una bez sangre e visto por los yndios que el niño echava sangre por los ojos dexaron de matarle diçiendo que aquella era gran señal y que aquel niño avia de ser gran señor y que qerian ver el fin que abria al fin [no] le mataron y en este medio tiempo abia un tio suyo llamado Guailla Cancara el qual era baliente entendio y supo donde estaba el muchacho e tornolo a hurtar e traxolo al Cuzco por chasquis despues que este Ynga crezio //

/f.472v/ fue baliente e tubo en concierto e sujecion todo lo que sus antezesores ganaron y el ansimismo acrezento otros dos pueblos. Tubo este Ynga una muger entre las demas llamada Mama Chiquia de la qual tubo seis hijos el primero Viracocha Ynga el segundo Apocama el terzero Apumaroti el quarto Ynga Maita el quinto Paguac Guallica Mayta el sesto Chima Chauyc tubo tambien de otras mugeres munchos e acuerdanse destos porque fueron balientes y comian e bebian con sus padres e tenpian quenta con ellos e como el padre la tenia tenianla ansimismo basallos del.

De Biracocha Ynga setimo

Biracocha Ynga conquisto cinco pueblos fue baliente y tubo una muger que se llamo Mama Yunto Cayan de la qual tubo cinco hijos los quales se nombraron el primero que fue he- //

/f.473/ redero Pachacuti Ynga el segundo Ynga Urcon Ynga el tercero Ynga Maita el quarto Cunayura Chali Curopangue el quinto Capa Yupangue.

De Pachacoti Ynga otabo

Pachacoti Ynga fue baliente mas que sus antezesores por que conquisto e sujeto munchos caciques e señores por vasallos e munchos indios debaxo de su mando e señorio este fue el que comenzo la fortaleza del Cuzco y lo que en ella hizo fue trazarla e hacer sacar los cimientos que es obra de las mas señaladas del Piru tubo este una muger que se llamo Mama Anabarque de la qual tubo cinco hijos el primero que fue señor y heredero se nombro Topa Ynga Yupangue el segundo Amaro Topa Ynga el tercero Capac Guari el quarto Chinche Roca Ynga el quinto Guayllipa Tupa sin estos tubo otros munchos //

/f.473v/ de diferentes mugeres.

De Topa Ynga Yupangue Ynga nono.

Topa Ynga Yupangue fue gran señor y mui baliente entendiose y sujeto mas tierras que todos sus pasados porque como tenia su padre tanta gente tierras y vasallos debaxo de su mando y era tan rico este suzedio en ello. puso luego deligencia en conquistar por todas partes e ansi conquisto toda la tierra hasta Chile y Quito e a todos tubo en gran conçierto e razon y en qualquier p^{te} que mandase cosa alguna se hacia e cumplia luego con gran presteza deligencia e solicitud este vista la obra que su padre dexo comenzada en la fortaleza del Cuzco prosiguiola como vio ser cosa tan señalada e hiço tanto en ella que quando murio la dexo casi toda hecha hizo este ansimismo los caminos que ban del Cuzco a las Charcas e a Chile los que //

/f.474/ ban a Quito ansi por los llanos como por la sierra que llevan tan señalada dio orden como por todos estos caminos ubiese chasques o postas para saber con brevedad todo lo que pasase y uviese en Chile y en Quito y en todo lo demas de toda la tierra e savialo con tanta brevedad que en quinze dias e menos venian desde Chile e dende Quito al Cuzco e ansimismo le llebaban el pescado fresco en tres dias desde la costa al Cuzco que son ciento e v^{te} leguas ques cierto era muncho por aberlo de correr a pie a causa que hasta que hasta que [*sic*] los cristianos llegaron xamas los indios tuvieron ni bieron caballos ni mulas ni otras bestias domesticos e silbestres. Tuvo Topa Ynga Yupangue por mujer a Mama Ocllo de la qual tubo tres hijos al prencipal //

/f.474v/ y heredero nombraron Guaina Capa Ynga al segundo Auqui Topa Ynga al terzero Auqui Toma tubo desta muger e de otras munchos hijos e tantos que creen y tiene por cierto fueron mas de çiento y çinquenta no tienen noticia dellos por lo questa dho.

De Guaina Capa Ynga dezimo

Suzedio luego Guaina Capa Ynga el qual si su padre fue baliente el fe muncho mas e paso delante de loque su p^{e} gano e conquisto llego hasta los Pastos e sujeto los Guancavilcas y Cayambe Ruparupa y Conchuco y abaxo lo que su padre avia dexado por acavar en la fortaleza del Cuzco aunque faltava bien poco paso en mas con çierto orden y razon todo el reino fue Guaina Caba casado o tubo por muger a Coya Pilco Baco la qual fue primera y la señora de //

/f.475/ esta no tubo hijo ninguno enpero tubo otras munchas mugeres y dellas munchos hijos que fueron tantos y mas que los de su p^{e} de los quales pornemos qui [*sic*] algunos de los que fueron mas balientes y señores por que destos ai mem^{a} y se tubo e tiene el dpia de oy quenta tubo el primero y el señor a Guascar Ynga e su m^{e} sera bao [*sic*] e lo tubo a Mango Ynga Yupangue y fue llamada su madre Mama Runto Coya tubo a Tabalipa y a Ninan Cuyuchi y a Guanca Auqui y Auqui Catungui a Uquicon o Nunocura Cangui Auqui Atau Rimachi Quivisca Chauqui Auqui Choquixuaman Auqui Tancuchi Guairi Tito Guanca Tupa Paulo Tito a Utay Chipicchu Tito y a Yngiltupa e a otros munchos.

De Guascar Ynga y Atahualpa yngas un dezimo y duo dezimo

/f.475v/ Entre Guascar Ynga y su hermano Atabalipa ubo munchas diferencias sobre mandar el reyno y quien avia de ser señor estando Guascar Ynga en el Cuzco y su hermano Atabalipa en Caxamarca envio Atabalipa dos capitanes suyos mui principales que se nombraban el uno Calcuchiman y el otro Quizquiz los quales heran balientes e llevaron muncho numero de gente e yban de proposito de prender a Guascar Ynga por que ansi se avia conzertado e les avia m^{do} para el efeto que siendo Guascar preso quedase Atabalipa por señor e hiciese de Guascar lo que por vien tuviese fueron por el camyno conquistando caziques e yndios poniendolo todo debaxo el mando y servidumbre de Atabalipa e como Guascar tubo noticia desto e de lo que benian haçiendo aderezose luego e //

/f.476/ salio del Cuzco e vinose para Quipaipan que es una legua del Cuzco donde se la dio la batalla e aunque Guascar tenia muncha gente al fin fue vencido e preso e murio muncha gente de ambas partes e fueron tanta que se dize por cosa çierta serian mas de çiento e cinquenta mil yndios despues que entraron con la vitoria en el Cuzco mataron muncha gente onbres mugeres y niños por que todos aquellos que se declaravan por servidores de Guascar los mataban e buscaron todos los hijos que Guascar tenia e los mataron e ansi mismo las mugeres que deçian estar del preñadas e una muger de Guascar que se llamaba Mama Barca e puso tan buena deligenzia que se escapo con una hija del Guascar llamada Coya Cuxi Barcae que agora es muuger de //

/f.476v/ Saire Topa Ynga que es de quien abemos fho mincion prencipalm^{te} en esta ystoria hecho esto e poniendo estos dos capitanes de Atabalipa el Cuzco e toda la gente en conçierto e razon debaxo el mando de Atabalipa volvieronse para su señor e llevando preso a Guascar y

tratabanle tan mal que le davan a beber orines por el camino e a comer cosas muy çuçias e sabandixas en este comedio entro en la tierra don Fran^{co} Pizarro con los demas cristianos e prendieron a este Atabalipa en Caxamalca e siendo preso preguntaronles munchas cosas y entre ellas si avia otro señor en aquella tierra sino el qual respondio que si y que tenia otro hermano llamado Guascar preguntaronle que a donde estaba y el visto que le preguntaban tanto por su hermano parezio que le hacian mas caso de Guascar que no del e que le dexa- //
/f.477/ rian por señor e por esto enbio por chasquis a sus capitanes que le matasen los quales cumpliendo el m^{do} mataron a Guascar en Andamarca y Atabalipa murio en Caxamarca.

De Mango Ynga p^{e} de Xaire Topa Ynga

Muertos Atabalipa e Guascar sucedio en el estado MangoYnga su hermano e tubo por hijo eredero a Xaire Topa Ynga que es este de quien tratamos el qual caso con Coya Cussi Vanca hija de Guascar e quando tomo la borla antes que saliese de su tierra para benir a Lima se mudo el nombre en Mango Capa Pacchacuti Yupangue e ansi todos los nombres se an de entender ser todo uno e queda declarado como este Xaire Topa venia a suzeder en los reinos del Piru.

Al tiempo de la visita algunos yndios que se ha- //
/f.477v/ llaron en el repartimiento alegaron para no ser visitados en el que son de otros repartimientos en que a poco que vinieron a lo qual haran favor los caziques por servirse dellos e porque no se tasen averiguarlas que tanto tiempo a que estan en el repartimi^{to} e aviendo menos tiempo de diez años tomareis mem^{a} dellos e de sus mugeres e hijos que tuvieren con sus heredades e dareis aviso dello al encomendero e caziques de donde fueren e a los visitadores de su repartimi^{to} para que alla sean visitados e tasados pero si ovieren estado en el tal repartimi^{to} diez años e mas besitarloseys en el e se contarse ansi en la visita por yndios del dho repartimi^{to} para que en el tributen e sirvan como los demas yndios naturales.

Por este nos ynformareis que yanaconas ay fuera de los repartimintos en pueblos despañoles en otras //
/f.478/ partes e a quien sirven e que tanto salieron de los repartimientos e si pagan tributo quien lo cobra y en que cantidad y si se juntaron con el cuerpo del tributo o lo toman los caciques para si lo qual hareis de los yndios que de diez años a esta parte ovieren salido del dho repartimi^{to} e no mas.

Don Carlos por la divina clemencia enperador senper agusto rei de Alemania y doña Juana su madre y el mismo don Carlos por la gr^{a} de dios rey de Castilla de Leon de Aragon de las dos Çicilias de Jerusalem de Nabarra de Granada de Toledo de Balenzia de Galicia de Mallorca de Sevilla de Zerdenia de Cordova de Corcega de Murcia de Jaen de los Algarves de Algezira de Gibraltar de las yslas de Canaria de las Yndias Yslas e tierra firme del mar oceano conde de Flandes y de Tirol a bos Blasco Nuñez Vela //
/f.478v/ nuestro visorrey e gobernador de las provincias del Piru e pres^{te} de la nuestra audienzia e chancilleria nos que en ella avemos mandado proveher salud e graçia. Sepades que nos emos sido ynformados quen la dha provi^{a} anda alzado el Ynga e otros munchos yndios questan huidos por las sierras e montes a causa de los malos tratamientos que le an sido hechos por los españoles que en ella an residido e otros que de su voluntad sin les aber hecho mal ni daño alguno estan en ellos e por que nos deseamos que los dhos yndios vengan de paz en conocimiento de nuestra santa fe catolica e que sean traidos a los pueblos donde solian vivir que alli residan e se les pueda enseñar la dotrina cristiana vos mandamos que por todas las buenas maneras que pudieredes sin guerra ny muerte ni robos de los yndios e guardando las leyes por nos fhas para el govierno de esas partes e vuen tratamiento de los naturales dellas procureys //
/f.479/ como el dho Ynga e todos sus subjetos e otros qualesquier yndios que en la dha provinçia anduvieren alzados se reduzgan a nuestro servicio e si para ello fuere nezesario otorgalles algunas libertades e franquezas de toda manera de tributos lo podais hazer e hagais por el tiempo e de la forma que os pareziere e perdonarles qualesquier delitos de rebelion que lo uvieren cometido aunque sea contra nos e nuestro servi^{o} e asimismo procureis que los perlados de esas provincias e los religiosos que en ellos estuvieren trabajen en reducir los pueblos e los de yndios que estan rebelados e no uvieren venido a obedienzia nuestra por la via e dotrina que a ellos les pareciere consultandolo prim^{a}m^{te} con bos e si los dhos perlados e religiosos por su yndustria e ttrabaxo reducieren algunos pueblos o indios //
/f.479v/ les deis las esenziones e libertades que a bos os pareciere por quatro a^{o}s e por el mas tiempo que bos vieredes que conviene e sobre ello como a perlado emos mandado dar al obispo del Cuzco la zedula que bereis e para hazer e cumplir lo suso dho por esta nuestra carta bos damos poder cumplido con todas sus ynçidencias anexidades e cunegidades [*sic*]. Dada en la villa de Valladolid a v^{te} e ocho dias del mes de set^{e} de mill e qui^{o}s e quarenta y tres años. yo el Prinzipe. Yo Juan de Samano secretario de cesarea e catolicas magestades lo fize escribir por mandado de su alteza e p^{o}s con chen [*sic*] el dotor Bernal el licenciado Greg^{o} Lopez el lizen^{do} Salmiron registrada Ochoa de Luyando por chanciller Blas de Saavedra.

En los Reyes a v^{te} e tres de set^{e} de myll e qui^{o}s e cinquenta e un años fue sacado correg^{do} e conzertado este tr^{do} //
/f.480/ de la dha provision original e ba cierto e verdadero de que doy fe t^{gos} a lo ver sacar corregir e conzertar Juan de Padilla escriv^{o} e Juan Fernadez e Di^{o} de Ocampo estantes en esta ciudad.

El REY

Lizen^{do} de la Gasca del nuestro consejo de la santa y general ynquisicion sabed que al tiempo que nos mandamos yr a las provinçias del Piru a Blas Nuñez Bela por nuestro visorrey e governador dellas se le dieron algunas provisiones. Zedulas e yntrucciones de lo que avia de hazer en las dhas provinzias e despues aca se le an enviado otras tocantes a nuestro servi^{o} como al vien de aquella tierra e naturales della e a personas particulares e bos m^{do} que llegado que ayais a las dhas provinzias beais las zedulas e provisiones que ansi nos ovieremos mandado //

/f.480v/ e se ovieren cometido al dho Blasco Nuñez Bela y useis dellas ejecutando las que os pareziere convenir e debeis executar e sobre la ex^{on} de las otras que os pareciere que no se executen hasta tanto que nos lo consulteis e nos mandemos proveer lo que convenga sonre ello que para ello por esta mi zedula bos doy poder cump^{do} con todas sus inçidenzias e dependençias emergencias anexidades e conesidades. Fecha en la villa de Benelo a diez e seis dias del mes de hebrero de myll e quinientos e quarenta e seis años yo el Rey. Por m^{do} de su majestad Fran^{co} de Heraso. Y en las espaldas de la dha zedulas estaban hechas çinco rubricas.

En los Reyes a v^{te} e tres dias del mes de set^{e} de myll e quinientos e cinquenta e un años yo P^{o} de Abendaño escrivano de cam^{a} de la audi^{a} real que reside en esta çiudad hize sacar este traslado con la zedula //
/f.481/ original e se corrigio e conzerto testigos Juan de Padilla e Ju^{o} Flores e Diego de Ocampo estantes en esta ciudad.

El PRINCIPE

Ynga. Yo e sido ynformado que por algunos malos tratamientos que los españoles nuestros subditos e naturales hicieron a Mango Ynga Yupangue buestro p^{e} se alzo e anduvo alzado haciendo algunos daños e que muerto el quedastes bos e andais tambien alzado e destraido del servi^{o} del emperdaro my s^{or} e traeis en vuestra compañia munchos caziques e yndios capitanes de buestro padre de que nos a desplacido ansi por el daño que bos dello abreis r^{do} como del estorbo que a causa dello a avido e ay para que bos e los naturales desa tierra que con bos andan no ayais benido en conocimi^{to} de nuestra s^{ta} fe cat^{ca} e por que agora se nos a fho relacion que bos teneis //
/f.481v/ voluntad de ser cristiano e benir al servi^{o} e obedienzia de su magestad se os envia una proviçion de su majestad sellada con su sello en que se vos perdona lo pasado como por ella vereis y enviamos a mandar a don Ant^{o} de Mendoza nuestro visorrey de esa tierra que viniendo vos e los caçiques e yndios que con bos andan de paz os haga buen tratami^{to} e os favorezca e os haga volver las casas e chacaras que tenia vuestro padre al tiempo que se alzo yo vos ruego y encargo que luego questa veapis os vengais donde el dho visorrey estuviere que el os reçivira e hara buen tratami^{to} como se lo emos mandado. De Madrid a iez y nueve de março de myll e quinientos e cinquenta e dos años. Yo el Principe por m^{do} de su Al^{a} Ju^{o} de Samano.

Yo Fran^{co} Lopez escriv^{o} de su magestad e de cam^{a} en la audi^{a} e chancilleria real //
/f.482/ desta ciudad de los Reyes hize sacar este traslado de la dha zedula de su mag^{d} original questaba en un cofre donde estan las provisiones de la dha real audi^{a} en vte e un dias del mes de mayo de mill e quinientos e sesenta e un a^{o}s y en testim^{o} de verdad fize aqui mi signo. Fran^{co} Lopez.

EL REY

Lo que vos don Hurtado de Mendoza marques de Cañete nuestro visorrey e governador del Piru e pres^{te} de la audiencia real que reside en la ciudad de los Reyes aveis de hazer en servi^{o} de Dios nuestro señor e nuestro e bien de aquella tierra por virtud de los poderes e comision de que llebais e desta nuestra ynstrucciones es lo sig^{te}.

Yten si por caso algunas //
/f.482v/ personas en las dhas provincias del Piru estuvieren ynovidientes a nuestro servi^{o} e permanezieren en ello e por vuenos medios no pudieren ser atraidos a ovidienzia en tal caso podreis hazelles guerra segun e como e de la manera que os pareziere.

Todo lo qual os encargamos que hagais con la deligencia e cuidado que bos confiamos e que guardeis e cunplais lo cont^{do} en esta nuestra ynstrucion porque ansi conviene a nuestro servi^{o}. fecha en la villa de Bruselas a diez dias del mes de março de myll e qui^{o}s e cinq^{ta} e zinco a^{o}s. yo el Rey. Por m^{do} de su mag^{d} Fran^{co} de Eraso.

EL REY

Don Hurtado de Mendoza marques de Cañete pariente nuestro visorrey de las provincias del Piru y pres^{te} de la audi^{a} real que en ella reside sabed que al tiempo que nos mandamos yr a las dhas provinçias del Piru a don Ant^{o} de //
/f.483/ Mendoza nuestro visorrey e governador que fue dellas se le dieron algunas provisiones zedulas e ynstrucciones de lo que avia de hazer en las dhas provinçias e despues se le enviaron otras ansi tocantes a nuestro servicio como al vien de aquella tierra e naturales della e a personas particulares. Yo os mando que llegado que seais a las dhas provinçias veais las zedulas e provisiones que ansi nos ovieremos mandado dar e se ovieren cometido al dho don Antonio de Mendoza huseis dellas executando las que os pareziere convenir e debeis executar e sobreseyendo en la ex^{on} de las otras que os pareziere que no convienen que se executen hasta tanto que nos lo consulteis e nos mandemos proveer sobre ello lo que convenga que para ello por esta mi zedula bos doy poder cump^{do} con todas //
/f.483v/ sus yncidencias e dependencias emergencias anejidades e conejidades. Fecha en Bruselas a diez dias del mes de março de myll e quinientos e cinquenta e cinco a^{o}s. yo el Rey. Por mandado de su magestad Fran^{co} de Eraso y en las espaldas tenia cinco rubricas y señales.

Fecho sacado corregido e conzertado fue este traslado de la dha cedula original de su magestad en la ciudad de los Reyes a veinte e dos dias del mes de abril de myll e qui^{o}s e cinquenta y ocho a^{o}s siendo presentes por t^{o}s Alonso Hernandez e Baltasar Perez e Pero Alonso e por ende fize aqui mio signo atras en testimonio de verdad. Juan de Padilla escriv^{o} pu^{co}.

Concuerda con el original fue sacado.

Jhoan de Montoya (rubrica)

/f.484/ En la ciudad de los Reyes en doze dias del mes de noviembre de mill e quinientos e ochenta e cinco a^{o}s estando los señores pres^{te} e oydores desta real audiencia en audi^{a} pu^{ca} pres^{to} esta peticion el cont^{do} en ella.

Muy poderoso señor Martin Garcia de Loyola por mi procurador digo que para en prueva de mi derecho en el p^{to} que trato con buestro fiscal sobre los yndios de Yucay tengo nezesidad de quel secret^{o} de camara ante quien pasa saque del proceso viejo de los otros yndios los dhos de P^{o} Diaz Baldeon e don Fran^{co} Chilche difunto con sus ratificaciones y se me reciba ynform^{on} como lo suso dho son difuntos.

A V. Al^{a} sup^{co} asi lo provea e mande ya ya [*sic*] las dhas declaraçiones por presentadas e pido just^{a} etc. Martin Garcia de Loyola.

E por los dhos s^{e}s vista mandaron que se le de con notificacion de la p^{te} contr^{a} y estando pres^{te} //
/f.484v/ el lizenciado Albaro de Caravajal fiscal de su magestad fue citado para ello en forma. Juan de Montoya.

En cumplimiento de lo qual yo Juan de Montoya scri^{o} de camara desta real audi^{a} doy fee que en un pleyto que en esta real audi^{a} paso e se trato entre el fiscal de su mag^{d} de la una parte con Martin Garcia de Loyola e doña Beatriz Coya su muger sobre los yanaconas que esta remytido al real consejo de las Yndias estan los dhos de P^{o} Diaz Baldeon y don Fran^{co} Chilche difunto que son los que por la dha p^{on} se piden e demandan con las ratificaciones de los dhos testigos de los quales hize sacar e saque un treslado segun e como estan en el dho proceso del dho pleyto que se le sigue.

/f.485/ El dho don Fran^{co} Chilche cacique principal de los y^{o}s del valle de Yucay repartimiento y encomienda aviendo jurado y preguntado por las preguntas del dho ynterrogat^{o} dixo lo sig^{te}.

j A la primera preg^{ta} dixo que conoze a las partes y tiene noticia de todos los yndios contenidos en esta pregunta e mem^{a} e no conoze al señor fiscal.

De las generales dixo que es de hedad de mas de ochenta aos e que no concurre a ningu^{a} de las generales e que dira verdad en el negocio.

2 A la preg^{ta} dos dixo queste test^{o} es cacique principal de los yndios del valle de Yucay de este repartimyento y encomienda y aviendole leido y dado a entender todos los yndios contenidos en la dha mem^{a} dixo que los conoze a todos ellos e save que son todos yndios deste repartimy^{to} y encomienda porque vinieron los yndios mitimas sus antepasados y antezesores destos por yanaconas de los Yngas a este valle de Yucay y ansi fueron to- //
/f.485v/ dos encomendados en don Di^{o} Saire Topa Ynga padre de la dha doña Beatriz y esto sabe de la dha pregunta.

3 A la preg^{ta} tres dixo que save e vio este t^{o} que los dhos don Diego Saire Topa Ynga e doña Mª Coya su mujer fueron casados e belados segun horden de la santa madre yglesia y como tales marido y mujer les vio este testigo hazer vida maridable durante su matrimonio uvieron por su hixa legitima a la dha doña Beatriz Coya mujer del dho capitan Martin Gar^{a} de Loyola y por tal su hija legitima la an tenido e tiene este t^{o} y es avida e tenida y comunm^{te} reputada en este reino.

4 A la pregunta quatro dixo ques verdad lo contenido en esta pregunta porque este t^{o} save e vio que no tuvieron mas hijos ni hija que a la dha doña Beatriz Coya la qual suzedio en los bienes y haziendas del dho su p^{e} y en el repartimi^{to} de yndios que tenia el dho don Di^{o} Saire Topa que son los yndios deste valle de Yucay e los demas que tiene en encomienda en el titulo de mayo- //
/f.486/ razgo que dellos tiene y si otra cosa fuera este t^{o} lo supiera e oviera visto.

5 A la pregunta cinco dixo que save e vio que los yndios deste valle ansi los contenidos en la dha memoria como los demas que al pres^{te} estan visitados por desta encomienda e avia en el dho valle todos ellos los tuvo e poseyo el marques don Fran^{co} Pizarro y estuvieron subjetos a este t^{o} como cazique prenzipal que era de todos ellos y asi suçedieron en la encomienda del dho Gonzalo Pizarro su hijo y lo mismo en tiempo que tributaron a su magestad por estar bacos y despues fueron encomendados por el marques de Cañete visorrey que fue destos reinos en el dho don Di^{o} Saire Topa Ynga e P^{o} Alonso Carrasco e Juan de Berrio visitaron a todos los yndios contenidos en la dha mem^{a} por yndios tributarios deste repartimi^{to} //
/f.486v/ con los demas que en el avia al tiempo que se visitaron y esto sabe e vio desta preg^{ta} e todos ellos tributaban por tributo e tasa en las cosas que la preg^{ta} dize porque haçian las sementeras e chacaras de coca e serviçio personal que en aquella sazon se acostumbrava a dar e hazer.

vi A la preg^{ta} seis dixo que es mui notorio lo contenido en esta pregunta e que fue e paso como en ella se dize.

vij A la siete preg^{ta} dixo que es verdad lo contenido en la preg^{ta} porque en tiempo del dho marques don Fran^{co} Pizarro los yndios deste repartimi^{to} no pagavan su tributo sino es lo que la preg^{ta} dize y esto fue hasta que el presidente Gasca los taso.

viij A la pregunta ocho dixo que dize lo que dho tiene.

ix A la pregunta nueve dixo que la causa por donde se divi- //

/f.487/ dieron los yn^{o}s deste repartimiento y se convertieron de yndios de encomyenda en y^{o}s yanaconas fue por la diferenzia que ubo entre este t^{o} y el dho don Garcia Quispicapi porque como estavan diferentes el uno con el otro por aver dividido e partido entre ellos el cacicazgo cada uno sacava los yn^{o}s del dho repartimiento que querian e los escondian e se servian dellos como de yn^{o}s yanaconas siendo todos yndios tributarios deste repartimy^{to} y encomienda dando e pagando tasa todos ellos como tributarios que heran de esta encomy^{da}.

x A la preg^{ta} diez dixo que es verdad que como por las razones que dho tiene en la pregunta antes desta se avia exsentado munchos yndios deste repartimi^{to} y encomienda y estaban ya puesto como por yanaconas el dho Diego Escudero como cura deste repartimiento hizo division entre ellos //
/f.487v/ poniendo unos por yanaconas como se los nombraron los principales e declara en esta preg^{ta}.

xj A la preg^{ta} honze dixo que save y es verdad quel lizenciado frai P^{o} Gutierrez visitador que fue deste valle hizo la visita de los dhos yanaconas segun como se declara en esta preg^{ta} e todos a efeto de que pagasen tributo a su magestad e no al dho encomendero e ansi quito de este repartimiento veinti cinco yndios que Gar^{a} de Melo avia adjudicado a este repartimyento quando los visito que los quito a este t^{o} que los tenia por yndios yanaconas a causa de visitallos por el padron del dho Di^{o} Escudero a buelta de otros yanaconas que a este t^{o} quedaron de la visita del dho Garcia de Melo sin hazer distincion de unos ni de otros sino todo por adquirir en esta visita muncho num^{o} de yanaconas y esto sabe e vio desta preg^{ta}.

xij A las doze preguntas dixo que la causa que fue visitar los dhos yndios por yanaconas e no por yndios tributarios //
/f.488/ de este repartimyento y encomienda como lo son fue por sacarlos del padron quel dho Diego Escudero tenia fecho e ansi por sacarlos el dho visitador de alli se bisitaron por yanaconas e no por yn^{o}s tributarios.

xiij A la preg^{ta} treze dixo que save y es verdad que la dha doña Beatriz Coya y el cap^{an} Martin Gar^{a} de Loyola su marido an sido desposeidos de los dhos y^{o}s individamente a causa de no aver tenido quien los recogiese e mirase por ellos en lo qual an sido muy agraviados porque se les quito el tributo que habia de haber de los dhos yn^{o}s siendo suyos dellos.

xiiij A la pregunta catorze dixo que lo que dho tiene por lengua de los dhos ynterpretes es la verdad so cargo del dho juram^{to} y tornandoselo a dar a entender se afirmo y ratifico en ella por ser verdad so cargo del dho juram^{to} e lo firmaron los dhos ynterpretes y este t^{o} don Fran^{co} Chilche Hernando de Morales //
/f.488v/ Martin Palacios ante mi Pedro Diaz Valdeon escrivano.

El dho Fran^{co} Chilche cacique principal de los yndios del valle de Yucay aviendo jurado en esta ciudad del Cuzco y siendo preguntado por las preguntas del dho ynterrog^{o} dixo lo sig^{te}.

A la prim^{a} preg^{ta} dixo que conoze a las partes por ser como es cazique prenzipal de los yn^{o}s del dha balle de Yucai.

De las generales dixo ques de hedad de mas de ochenta años e que no concurre en ninguna de las generales e que dira verdad en este neg^{o}.

Ij A la preg^{ta} dos y a las demas del ynterrogatorio dixo queste t^{o} tiene dho en esta causa en veinte e tres dias del mes de hebrero de mill e quinientos e set^{a} e siete años donde dixo e declaro todo lo que savia e siendole leydo e dado a entender por los dhos ynterpretes dixo que ansi como le fue leydo e dado a entender lo dixo e de- //
/f.489/ claro y en ello se afirmo e ratifico por ser verdad so cargo del dho juramento e lo firmaron con los dhos ynterpretes. Hernando de Morales Martin Quispe Topa ante mi P^{o} Diaz Baldeon escrivano.

El dho P^{o} Dias Baldeon escrivano pu^{co} desta ciudad presentado por el dho Domingo Lopez de Larinaga para la dha provanza el qual aviendo jurado e siendole preguntado dixo lo sg^{te}

A la prim^{a} pregunta dixo que conoze a las partes.

De las generales dixo ques de hedad de cinq^{ta} años e que no concurre en ningu^{a} dellas.

A la preg^{ta} dos dixo queste t^{o} verifico en la visita general que antes se hizo de los yndios del dho valle que munchos de los yn^{o}s contenidos en el dho memorial pagaban tributo a la dha doña Beatriz Coya e lo avian dado a los demas encomenderos y es de creer e tener por cosa mui cierta que //
/f.489v/ sino fueran todos de la dha encomienda que no pagavan tributo los dhos encomenderos e si se vesitaron por yanaconas fue por el p^{e} Di^{o} Escudero que los dotrinava por tenerlos yntitulados en lugar de yanaconas e como su Ex^{a} avia mandado que todos los yndios yanaconas se empadronasen por si entendiendo que en ello se hacia servi^{o} se hiço ansi e si uviera al tiempo que se empadronaron quien procurara por ellos por parte de su encomendero se verificava bastantemente ser de la dha encomienda y entonces por de cierta pregunta e a las demas preguntas del dho ynterrogat^{o} dixo e dixo que es verdad so cargo del juram^{to} que hizo e lo firmo. P^{o} Diaz Baldeon escriv^{o}.

E para que conste di el presente en los Reyes en diez y seis dias del mes de nobiembre de myll e qui^{o}s y ochenta e cinco años.

Jhoan de Montoya.

/f.490/ En la ciudad de los Reyes en quinze dias del mes de nobiembre de mill e quinientos y ochenta y cinco años estando los señores presidente e oydores desta real audiencia en audiencia publica Martin Garcia de Loyola presento la peticion siguiente.

Muy poderoso señor. Martin Garcia de Loyola por mi procurador en el pleyto con vro fisca sobre los yndios que doña Beatriz Coya mi muger e yo estamos despojados en el valle de Yucay diciendo que son yanaconas digo que al derecho de mi parte conbiene presentar un testimonio del dia en que se bautizo la dha doña Beatriz mi muger la qual esta presentada en el pleyto matrimonil que tratamos Xpoval Maldonado e yo ante Fran^{co} de Alarcon notario apostolico residente en esta ciudad.

A Vra Alteza suplico mande dar su compulsorio para que me den un traslado autorizado e para ello es.

Otro si digo que en el pleyto viejo de los demas yndios de que estamos la dha mi muger e yo desposeidos que con el dho vro fiscal tratamos en vro real consejo //
/f.490v/ de Yndias esta un auto proveydo por don Fran^{co} de Toledo visorrey que fue destros reinos en que por el puso los dichos yndios sobre que agora se trata pleyto en vra corona real sin aver notificado a la dicha mi muger ni a su curador.

A Vra Al^{a} pido y sup^{co} mande de que se ponga en este proceso un treslado del dicho auto y de como no consta averse notificado a la dicha mi muger ni a su curador. Martin Garcia de Loyola.

E por los dichos señores vista mandaron que se le con citacion de la otra parte y estando presente el licenciado Alvaro de Caravajal fiscal de su mag^{d} fue citado para ello en forma. Juan de Montoya.

En cumplimiento de lo qual yo Jhoan de Montoya escrivano de camara desta real audi^{a} que por mandado de su mag^{d} reside en esta ciudad de los Reyes doy fe que en el pleyto e causa que en esta real audi^{a} se a tratado entre el fiscal de su mg^{d} con doña Beatriz Coya y Martin Garcia de Loyola sobre los yanaconas de Yucay y sobre las demas causas e raçones //
/f.491/ en el proceso del dho pleyto contenidas esta el auto que don Fran^{co} de Toledo visorrey que fue destos reynos proveyo cerca de los dhos yanaconas ques el que por la dha p^{on} se pide y demanda del qual hize sacar e saque un treslado del tenor sig^{te}

v En la çiudad del Cuzco en onze Dias del mes de agosto de myll e qui^{o}s y setenta y dos años el muy Ex^{te} señor don Fran^{co} de T^{do} vissorey governador y capitan general destos reynos del Piru por su mag^{t} etc. dijo que por quanto su mag^{t} por sus reales çedulas y un capitulo de ynstruçion de los que dio a su Exª tiene proveido y mandado que aviendo de ynponerse tributo a los yndios yanaconas deste reyno que no estan encomendados se pongan en su corona real y el tributo que diere sea pa su caxa real e que aviendo //
/f.491v/ su Exª salido de la ciudad de los Reyes a visitar el reyno por su persona e proveido visitadores que por las provinzias hagan la dha visita y en la que en esta ciudad del Cuzco se a fho de los yndios de todas las parroquias della e yndios que sirven a españoles e que andan vagamundos sean hallado mucha cantidad de yndios de los quales algunos son los que llaman yanaconas y otros naturales desta dha ciudad que llaman Cuzcos que nynguno dellos pagavan tributo a su mag^{d} ny a otra ps^{a} que los tuviese en encomyenda e por que conforme a derecho ningu^{o} de los dhos yndios son exsentos de pagar los tributos debidos a su mag^{d} por razon del soberano señorio que tiene en estos reinos por mantenerlos en paz y en justicia y darles la dotrina del santo evangelio y este derecho se puede prescrivir por dilacion alguna de tiempo y atento a las necesidades notorias de su mag^{d} y algunos particulares que en este reyno ay que forçosamente se avian de cumplir de su real caxa y a que por andar //
/f.492/ los dhos y^{o}s sin reconoçer caçiques y sin estar reduzidos a pueblos ny tener oblig^{on} de pagar tributos andauan bagamundos y ociosos e por eso mas llenos de vizios y sospechosos de ydolatrias y supertiziones la que su mag^{t} tiene mandado por las dhas çedulas e ynstruçiones los dhos yanaconas se reduzgan a pueblos y tributen a su real caxa y los demas y^{o}s que llaman cuzqueños no ai razon que les escuse de pagar tributo e quando alg^{a} tubieron que tal no tienen no merezan gozar della por la sospecha que contra ellos se a tenido de aver sido causa del levantamiento de Titu Cusi Yupangui Topa Amaro su her^{no} y Quispi Tito su hijo de toda la provinzia de Vilcabamba y de otras culpas notables que se contienen en el proçeso criminal que contra don Carlos y don F^{e} su hermano y don Al^{o} Tito Atauchi y don Agustin Condemayta y don D^{o} Cayo y otros y^{o}s naturales desta çiudad y fuera della se trata antel doctor Gabieliel de Loarte alcalde de corte por su mag^{d} //
/f.492v/ por comision de su Exª por todas las dhas causas e por reduzir los dhos y^{o}s a mas puliçia de la que hasta aqui an tenido e porque este mas a proposito para poderles enseñar la dotrina evangelica e no tengan lugar de andar ociosos ni vagamundos su Exª a mandado reduzir todos los dhos y^{o}s a parroquias haziendo y fundando algunas de nuevo y abriendo calles e reduziendo a mejor forma las que antes estavan hechas y les a dado y nombrado caçiques a cada una en la forma que se cont^{e} en los titulos de sus caçicazgos que se les a mandado dar e que queriendo cumplir en lo que resta lo que su mag^{t} tiene hordenado e proveer lo que a su natural servi^{o} conviene ponia e puso en la real corona de su mag^{t} todos los y^{o}s yanaconas questan visitados y se visitaren y adel^{te} pareçieren y se descubrieren en esta çiudad y en las perroquias de nra s^{a} de Belen y el hospital de Santana San Xpoval San Blas San Sebastian Santiago San Ger^{mo} //
/f.493/ y en todas las rancherias y casas de vz^{o}s y moradores desta çiudad labranças y estancias valle de Yucai y Pisa y Calca y los andes de la coca y en todos los demas de los ter^{nos} e juri^{on} desta dha çiudad agora bivan con españoles o anden vagamundos o bivan por si o en otra qualquier manera e pte questen que no estuvieren encomendados pa que se les reparta los tributos que justamente pareçiere que puedan pagar moderandolos quanto sea posible y en qu^{to} a los y^{o}s cuzqueños que como esta dho hasta aqui no an pagado tributo no obstante que su Exª pudiera encomendarlos a las p^{a}s que le pareçiera benemeritos usando del poder general que su mag^{t} t^{e} pa encomendar y^{o}s por no tener horden particular en que aunque tratase desta mat^{a} de y^{o}s teniendo atenzion a las muchas e grandes necesidades que su mag^{t} tiene asi en estos reynos como en los demas sus reynos y señorios ya que su mag^{d} ti^{e} hordenado que pa cumplir alguna parte de las dhas neçesidades se vayan poniendo en su corona //

/f.493v/ algunos repartimientos que estuvieren vacos o vacaren su Exª mandava y m^{do} a los dhos ynºs cuzqueños que no esten encomendados por sus parroquias como estan poblados y mandados poblar en ellas se les reparta el tributo que buenam^{te} pueden pagar con la mayor moderaçion que sea posible los quales dhos tributos por diez años primeros siguientes y hasta que de otra pte se provea donde se cumpla lo que de yuso yra declarado despues que se le rep^{ta} aplicava y aplico desde agora para la obra de la fortaleza que tiene acordado de hazer en esta çiudad del Cuzco e pa el salº del alcalde que nombrare e pusiere e salº de artillero y muniziones y provisiones de la dha fortaleza e gastos de la visita general que se va haziendo e por la orden e forma que su Exª lo mandara destribuyr y asentar y con esta condiçion e pa este efeto ponia e puso e yncorporava e yncorporo los dhos ynºs cuzqueños en la corona real de Castilla y reservava y reservo en si de tasar y moderar los tributos que los dhos yanaconas e ynºs cuzqueños an de pagar aviendo visto los pareceres que //
/f.494/ sobre ello daran los visitadores eclesiasticos y seglar de la çiudad e parroquias y de las demas partes suso dhas que ynformandose de pªs que lo puedan saber y entender y asi dixo que lo proveia y proveyo esto conque de lo que montaren los dhos tributos se de a los dhos yanaconas e ynºs cuzqueños por q^{ta} de su mag^{t} y de las dhas obras la dotrina necesª que por agora dexara hordenado su Exª que aya en las dhas parroquias con pareçer del perlado y adel^{e} se hordenare por los visorreyes governadores que por tpo fueren y mandaua y m^{do} a los ofiçiales reales de su mag^{t} desta çiudad que luego que con este auto sean requeridos tomen y aprehendan la posesion de los dhos yanaconas e ynºs cuzqueños en nombre de su mag^{t} y tengan q^{ta} de cobrar los tributos dellos conforme a las tasas que se hizieren y meter y metan en la caxa real por qu^{ta} de su mag^{t} los tributos de los dhos yanaconas y se hagan cargo dellos de los dhos yºs cuzqueños los tengan por qu^{ta} aparte pa cumplir lo que arriba esta declarado para que se //
/f.494v/ situen conforme a la distribucion que su Exª mandara hazer lo qual ansi hagan y cumplan so pena de un mil pºs de oro pa la camara y fisco de su mag^{t} demas que se cobrara de sus personas y bienes todo el daño e ynteres e que por su descuido viniere a su mag^{t} y a las dhas obras y ansi lo proveyo e firmolo va entre renglones y gastos de la visita general que se va haziendo vala y de las demas parte suso dhas don Fran^{co} de T^{do} ante mi Alvaro Ruiz de Navamuel. E yo Joan Lopes de Arrieta escriº de su mag^{t} presente fui al ver corregir este treslado con el auto que original de su Exª que queda en poder de los señores oficiales reales desta çiudad del Cuzco y va çierto y verdadero que por ende fyze my signo en testimonio de verdad Joan Lopez de Arrieta.

Yo Alvaro Ruiz de Navamuel escriº de su mag^{t} en su real audiª de los Reyes y de la governacion desstos reynos en cumplimiento de lo mandado por los dhos presidente e oidores desta real audiençia y de pedimi^{to} de la pte del cap^{t} Martin Garçia de Loyola y doña Beatriz Coya su muger hize sacar este tres^{do} del proçeso original //
/f.495/ que en esta real audiª sea tratado entre los suso dhos con el fiscal de su mag^{t} sobre los ynºs yanaconas del valle de Yucay segun que de suso se haze minsion con el qual dho original se corrigio en la çiudad de los Reyes en veynte e dos dias del mes de otubre de myll e quiºs y setenta y ocho años va tes^{do} que sacan/ x/ e pal dho en io/ guarden ansi/ que se vales/ yra/ este/ edos no vala. Entre renglones y otros de los naturales deste valle/ que guardando el conzierto/ y suso/ y doña/ ante mi/ e tributos en/ ante/ miguel si vala/ en m^{do}/ y ocho/ ciudad del dho/ doze/ sidente/ exsesiones/ y tres/ hijos/ hansi/ mi Cl/ fue leido Vilca/ Fran^{co} hispi y ocho. vala e fize aqui mi signo en testimonio de verdad. Alvaro Ruiz de Nabamuel

Segun mas largamente consta e pareze por el dho proceso e autos a que me refiero e para que dello conste di el presente en los Reyes en diez y ocho dias del mes de nobiembre de myll e quiºs y ochenta y cinco aºs.

Jhoan de Montoya

/f.495v/ /en blanco/

/f.496/ En la ciudad de los Reyes a veintidos dias del mes de n^{be} de mill e quinientos e ochenta e cinco años ante los señores pres^{te} e oydores desta real audiencia por ante mi Jhoan de Montoya escrivº de camª desta real audiª Juan Sanchez de los Rios en n^{e} de doña Beatriz Coya pres^{to} la peticion siguiente.

Mui poderoso señor Jhoan S^{e}s de los Rios en nombre de doña Beatriz Coya en el p^{to} con buestro fiscal digo que al drº de mi parte conviene que se me saque e ponga en este proceso los recaudos siguientes.

Un traslado de la tasa que vuestro visorrey don Fran^{co} de Toledo hizo de los indios sobre ques este pleito

Un traslado de dos capitulos del libro llamado Republica del Mundo que son el primº e quinze capitulos del titulo llamados repu^{ca} de los yndios oçidentales con la lizencia de V Alª que para imprimir el dho libro ubo.

Yten un traslado del capitulo dos de unlibro intitulado el descubrimiento e conquista del Piru hecha por Agustin de Zarate contador de V. Alª ympreso con la //
/f.496v/ de V Alª

A V Alª pido e suplico mande al secretario que saque los dhos recaudos con cit^{on} de vuestro fiscal e los ponga que desde luego yo en n^{e} de mi parte hago presentacion dellos para en prueva de su justª la qual pido e para ello es. El lizenciado Falcon.

E por los dhos señores vista mandaron que se le de. Juan de Montoya.

En cumplimiento de lo qual yo Juº de Montoya doy fe que en los libros yntitulados republica del mundo y otro yntitulado descubrimiento y conquista del estan los capitulos contenidos en la dha p^{on} que para el dho efeto el dho Martin Garcia de Loyola exsibio ante los sres

pr^{e} e oydores y el capitulo de la tasa echa de los yndios del ques este pleyto por don Fran^{co} de Toledo ques //
/f.497/ asimesmo esibio el dho Martin Garcia de Loyola del qual y del autoridad de los dhos libros que se esibieron y de los capitulos dellos
que piden por la dha peticion hize sacar e saque un treslado ques del tenor siguiente.

EL REY

Por quanto por parte de bos frai Geronimo Roman fraile profeso de la horden de San Agustin nos fue fecha relacion diciendo que bos
aviades hecho un libro yntitulado Las Republicas del Mundo el qual era mui util e provechoso suplicandonos os mandasemos dar
lizencia para el poder ymprimir e previlegio por el //
/f.497v/ tiempo que fuesemos servido o como la nuestra md fuese lo qual visto por los del nuestro consexo e como por su mandado se hicieron
las deligencias qe la prematica por nos fecha sobre la ynpresion de los libros dispone por os hacer vien e md fue acordado que deviamos
mandar dar esta nuestra zedula para bos en la dha razon e yo tubelo por bien e por la presente os damos poder e facultad p^{a} que por
tiempo de diez años prim^{os} siguientes que corren e se quentan desde el dia de la fecha desta nuestra zedula bos o la persona que buestro
poder oviere podais ynprimir e bender el dho libro de suso se hase m^{on} e por la pres^{te} damos poder e facultad a qualquier ynpreso destos
nuestros reinos que bos nombrare del para que por esta vez lo puedan ynprimir con que despues de ynpreso antes que se benda lo traigais
al nuestro consejo para que corrixa con el original //
/f.498/ que ba rubricado e firmado al cavo de Gonzalo Pumarejo nuestro escrivano de camara de los que residen en el nuestro consexo e se os
tase el precio que por cada un volumen oviere del de aber e mandamos que durante el dho tiempo persona alguna sin buestra lizencia
no lo pueda ynprimir ni vender so pena que que lo ynprimiere e vendiere aya perdido e pierda todo e qualquier libros e moldes que del
estuviere e bendiere en estos nuestros reinos e mandamos a los del nuestro consexo pres^{te} e oydores de las nuestras audiencias e corte
e chancillerias e a todos los corregidores asistentes governadores alcaldes mayores e hordinarios e otros juezes e justiçias qualesquier
de todas las ciudades villas e lugares de los nuestros reinos e señorios ansi los que agora son como a los que seran de aqui adelante que
vos guarden e cunplan esta nuestra zedula e md que ansi bos hazemos e contra el tenor //
/f.498v/ e forma della bos no ayan ni consientan yr ni pasar por manera alguna so pena de la nuestra md e de diez mill mr^{e}s pa la nuestra camara
dada en el Pardo a v^{te} e cinco de hen^{o} de myll e qui^{o}s e setenta e quatro años yo el Rey. Por mandado de su mag^{d} Antonio de Heraso.

Del descubrimiento de las Indias Oçidentales de la qual trata esta republica capitulo primero

No escrivire yo aqui la larga ni con particular horden de las cosas de las Yndias e Piru por quel argumento desta hobra no camina a esto
mi intento es solo e con toda brevedad mostrar el tiempo que se hallo este nuebo mundo de quien tengo de contar tantas y tanuarias
cosas porque para lo demas ya ay munchos onbres que lan escrito largam^{te} ansi como P^{o} Martin o Nicolas Fernandez de Oviedo e Fran^{co}
Lopez de Gomara e otros //
/f.499/ cuyas ystorias andan en publico de manera que si aqui no soy largo no soy obligado a serlo e quando lo fuera hera salir de los limites que
promete mi obra. Dos balerosos capitanes produjo Europa para gloria de nuestra España por medio de los quales se hallaron que visto un
nuebo mundo cuya grandeza ni fue hallada de los antiguos ni los que cada dia ban descubriendo no la saben que cuando tenga fin el principio
de tan gran inpresa tubo principio de Cristoval Colon e de Fernando Cortes el uno ytaliano y el otro español pero diremos es Cristonal Colon
que pareze que Dios lo guardo con especial cuidado para que le llebase el premio de su fortuna prospera e los españoles hallasen a donde
entender sus animos e cudicia fue escrito al Colon natural de los pueblos lugares que oy se llama la costa de Genova //
/f.499v/ unos dizen que fue de un aldea llamada Cugure o de Querui aldea de Genova pero la berdad es que era de un lugar llamado Aruiello
lugar aspero e olvidado junto a Saona no fue ilustre ni famoso en letras mas tubo natural inclinacion a seguir la navegacion e con esta
hambre e cudicia anduvo por diversas partes de lebante con los tratantes de Genova que andavan todo el mundo e andandose desde su
moçedad a estos andubo todos los puertos e islas e riberas del mar Mediterraneo e como fuese mui dado a la geografia todo su yngenio
enpleo en contemplar todas las tierras e provincias que se contienen en el glovo de la tierra con hervor [*sic*] e fatiga tan perpetua que por
astrologia aprendio maravillosamente la medida de los tropicos e de la equinocia e de los climas e todo el uso de la ca/rta/ de navegar
e de la aguja por lo qual juega a maestro de hazer cartas e anpliabalas y entendialas mucho mas //
/f.500/ que los antiguos e siempre hacia en ellas mayor la tierra dando manifiesta pruebas de que avia tierras escondidas e que por pereza de
los onbres no se descubrian y ansi daba un nuevo mundo a los codiciosos de saber e de riquezas esto alcanzo el con la leccion de Platon
e Seneca e otros munchos griegos e latinos los quales dexaron rastros e indicios para considerar semexantes cosas acrecenta muncho
sus esperanzas el ver que poco antes un frances llamado Betancos o Betancurt abia conquistado las Canarias e que los portugueses
hallaron Isperideba [*sic*] delante del Cavo Verde e que la armada del ynfante don Enrique de Portugal avia pasado el ultimo cavo de
Etiopia llamado cabo de Buena Esperanza puesto debaxo del polo Antartico delante del circulo de Capricornio avia envidia este ginoves
osado e pasavales que //
/f.500v/ los ginoveses que en antigua reputacion de disciplina nabal excedian a todas las naciones perdiesen una e casi entran grande por la qual
podian hazerse famosos en todos los siglos e mas ricos que ningun rey por cogele la empresa otras naciones mirando pues todas las cosas
con diferentes ymaginaciones aunque con constante espiritu procuro de poner en efeto lo que tanta esperanza le daba e vacilando a donde
va halla munchos difcultades en parte por ser hombre pobre e poco conocido e tanbien por que queria persuadir a una cosa tan grande que
aun despues de hallada e salido con ella avia de parezer yncreible aun a los que la viesen mas con todo eso quiso provar ventura e llegando
al rei de Portugal a pedille favor hallolo tan ocupado en la guerra de Africa y en la empresa que traçava en Oriente que le pa- //
/f.501/ recia cosa demasiada al rey de Castilla no se atrevio acometerle semejante hecho por que nadaba muy encendido en la guerra de Granada
e pretendia destruir de todo punto la seta [*sic*] de Mahoma de toda España pues hera señor de casi toda ella tenia Cristobal Colon un
hermano llamado Bartolome que aunque no tan industrioso todavia el era compañero e ovedeziales por que traia creido que no yna
cristobal Colon fuera de camino e ansi Cristobal le enviaba al de Inglaterra que hera Enrico Setimo rey el mas rico de todos los de
Europa en dinero pero aunque lo prometia el Bartolome muchos provechos no le quiso dar algun favor el rey e m^{do} se pues desamparado

fuese al rei don Alonso Quinto de Portugal pero no hallo el recaudo que esperava porque avia en aquel reino un ovispo de Viseo a la saçon gran hombre en el arte del //

/f.501v/ marear e puso tantas dificultades en el hecho e tan poca çerteça en lo que Colon prometia que se ubo de volver a Cast^{a} a los reyes catolicos para quienes avia de ser esta ynpresa tan grande estava a la saçon el rey con su corte y exercito sobre Granada e tratando con unos e otros aconsexabanle que hablase a los duques de Medina Cidonia e Medinacelo para que el uno con dinero el otro con el puerto le ayudasen pero sus animos no caminaban a cosas que traian tanta ventura e ansi guiado por dios divinalm^{te} determino de poner las esperanzas deste hecho en los reyes catolicos e dando e tomando e hallando muchas dificultades e inconvenientes pidio con animo confiado que se le diese aquella ynpresa prometiendo a uno tanto como lo que despues dio e los reyes catolicos principalm^{te} la reina doña Isabel que tenia un animo exselso y real y le dio grandes esperanzas //

/f.502/ e mirandose todas las cosas con muncho acuerdo despues de haber entendido una perseverancia tan grande le proveyeron de gente naos e provision e poder sobre todo como el que llebaba la ynpresa a su cargo munchos murmuraron deste hecho pareciendoles que no era solo este neg^{o} peligroso mas cosa desatinada e por grande pecado arriscar a las inconstantes ondas del mar oceano las naos y españoles por satisfazer la voluntad de un hombre no conocido e que dava esperanzas mayores de lo que podian creer los hombres e de cosas que de todo pareçia inciertas llevaria consigo ciento e v^{te} onbres entre soldados e marineros y encomendado a dios este negocio se arroxo en la mar munchos dias anduvo nabegando sin hallar rastro de lo que deseaba e avia prometido e aunque yba muy confiado los compañeros yban desesperados porque no sola- //

/f.502v/ mente no beian tierra mas tampoco hallaban señales dello e lo que mas sentian era que les yba faltando el mantenimiento miraba aquel valeroso ombre los animos de todos enflaquecidos e que en ninguno beia coraçon codicioso de gloria e ansi andaba su espiritu ynquieto y en ondas mas crueles que las del mar por que allende que no los podia animar con alguna çierta esperanza beiales ynquietos e ovedecian el mal e querialos matar pero este hablo con animo osado e les amenaço con la yra del rey porque si hacian cosa contra el m^{do} del principe avian de ser castigados seberamente esto hiço detener los animos dellos españoles e con el tenian gran respeto de alli adelante no pasaron despues de este alboroto e motin munchos dias en que vieron tierra con lo qual se alegraron sus animos en gran manera e comenzaron a dar gracias a dios e al tercero dia tomaron tierra que fue a los treze //

/f.503/ de otubre del año de mil e quatrocientos e nobenta e dos fue la primera tierra y una ysla de los Lucayos llamada Guanahani que cae entre La Florida e Cuba e alli se tomo posesion de las Yndias e por los reyes catolicos e de ai fueron costeando las demas yslas gran espanto rezivieron aquellas gentes barbaras de ver nuestra gente con tan diverzo traje del suyo e ansi admirados huian a los montes pero los nuestros queriendo tomar tiento e rastro a la tierra fueron en su seguimi^{o} e no pudiendo alcanzar hombres prendieron una muger a la comenzaron a halagar con dadivas porque dieron pan e vino e otras cosas de comer e vistieronla porque benia desnuda e mostrandole por señas que no le harian mal a ella ni a nadie le pidieron que llamase a los que huian ella aviando rezevido aquel genero de umanidad fue a llamar los que huian e diciendoles lo que con ella hicieron los hiço venir a todos a la costa e Colon viendolos tan barbaros los //

/f.503v/ comenzo a cariciar e atraer con muncho amor e pidioles mantenimientos por su dineros e viendo como le traian pan gallipavos e otros mantenimientos de la tierra atraxo con amorosos meneos por que este fue el primer ynterprete que tuvieron aquellas dos gentes tan diferentes en ley y costumbres y ellos conociendo el buen tratamiento que les hacia començaron a perder el miedo y a servirlos conoçio Colon que aquella gente tenia oro porque para sus hornamentos e gala usaban de zarzillos de oro e de otras joyas que aunque mal labradas ellos la tenian por cosa grande tambien conocio de que cosas carezian e viendolos ydolatras persuadiolos en pago de los mantenimientos que le traian a que creyesen en Cristo e adoraron la cruz e viendo tan principios determino volver a España con la nueba del mundo nuebo e dexados en aquellas yslas treinta e ocho españoles con su cap^{an} ^{dio} la vuelta con el resto trayendo //

/f.504/ para testimy^{o} de cosas tan grandes diez yndios quarenta papagaios munchos gallipabos conejos mui distintos de los nuestros que los llaman Urias traxo el pan de aquella gente que eran de unas raizes dhas vatatas tanvien traxo de las especias que ellos usaban que se llamaba axi e nosotros llamamos pimienta de las Yndias e algun maiz que es su trigo tanvien traxo oro para que ansi viesen todos el zebo que avia de pescar a munchos e llebarlos a ver nuebas tierras con este presente no mui grande pero de grandes esperanzas llego a España e fue a besar las manos de los reyes catolicos que a la sazon estavan en Varcelona fue grande el regocixo que aquellos principes rezivieron por ver cosas tan particulares y estaban atentos a las relaciones que dava Cristobal Colon e por que en todo heran cristianisimos hicieron bautizar los yndios e fueron ellos los padrinos e porque supieron que aquellas gentes se comian unas a otras hi- //

/f.504v/ cieron boto de quitar la ydolatria e aquellas costumbres tan crueles al Colon lo mandaronlo asentar delante de si contra la costumbre de los reyes de España que no permitian que nadie este asentado en presencia del rey e luego dandole titulo de Almirante de las Nuebas Yndias lo mandaron volver a la ynpresa llebando mas gente e aparato e porque era aquel neg^{o} grande y arduo e no podian los reyes apoderarse de ninguna tierra ajenas sino se les dava la investidura con dr^{o} ligitimo pidieron al papa Alejandro Sesto que a la dha sazon gobernaba la yglesia que atento que se avia hallado ciertas gentes ydolatras e que se comyan unas a otras su santidad les concediese el conquistarlas por que recibiesen la fe e dexasen los ydolos e aquella ferocidad e por el papa la santa demanda conzedio una bula lena de muncha dotrina e santidad en la qual daba ynstruccion de como se an de aver con aquellas gentes e ansi fueron conquistando con las harmas espirituales e temporales //

/f.505/ aquel nuevo mundo siendo Cristobal Colon el principio de tan grande empresa y despues salidos de las yslas hallaron tierra llana e tendidas provinçias potentisimos reyes grandes riquezas de oro plata e piedras preciosas a quien se debe dar despues de Cristobal Colon gracias de tanta cosa a Hernando Cortes cristianisimo varon capitan fortunado soldado valiente el veras señor el qual gano a Mexico e hiço pedricar [*sic*] con gran zelo la palabra del evangelio sin tener amviciom ni cudizia de las riquezas ni de mandar contentandose con solo que en n^{e} de Cristo fuese pregonado e con hazer hechos dinos de ynmortal gloria destas gentes que se hallaron tan barbaras tan sin dios e tan poseidas del demonio quiero escrivir e mostrar a los venideros su religion e sacrificios que quien quisiere leer atentamente podra conocer quan poderoso fue el demonio entre aquellas gentes //

/f.505v/ aqui cura sus costumbres en los matrimonios e mortuorios no quedara cirimonias que toque a la religion que no se halle aqui tanbien vera el govierno ele y el por donde juzgavan sus causas munchas costumbres que sera para abergonzarnos la potencia de sus reyes e

su magestad en fin todo aquello que toca a una republica mostraremos y esto con muncha fidelidad e çerteza porquestas cosas quanto menos autores ay dellas tanto con mayor obligacion estoy obligado a dar las limpias de sospecha e porque el letor sepa de donde saque tantas cosas en una palabra referire las diligenzias que yze para cosa tan particular primeramente ube a las manos las mas relaciones que se enviaron a los catolicos reyes y al emperador don Carlos V de feliz recordacion vi munchas cartas de Fernando Torres e de los Pizarros comunique con hombres doctos en las cosas de aquellas Yndias ube //
/f.506/ papeles del santo varon don frai obispo de Chiapa sin esto e leido todas las ystorias que andan escritas o ynpresas e con esta diligenzia me pareze que puede a darse segura esta republica delante de los mui deligentes e los que quisieren añadir podran lo hazer e reprehender mexor si fueren mexores sus testimonios e lo que se dize de Indias e se dize del Piru porque donde dejo comienzo mi republica tubo principio todo como se bera a la clara.

de la caida del rei[o] del Piru con todos los reyes que aquella gente tuvo hasta que se incorporo en la corona de los Reyes de España como lo vemos oy.

El undezimo rey Ynga del Piru fue Guaina Caba este principe en su bejez tuvo noticia de nuestros españoles que avian llegado por mar a las costas de sus reinos y el saviendolo quiso ynformarse de que gente hera e que queria e respondiendo Fran[co] //
/f.506v/ Pizarro que querian oro y el les envio cierta cantidad de ello pero quando los yndios volvieron con el horo a la costa ya los españoles heran partidos en este medio murio el Linga e segun se dize aviso a sus hijos que tuviesen paz e amistad con los barbudos hombres blancos si estos si esto fue ansi o no yo no lo tengo de determinar aqui por que no escrivio la ystoria destas gentes mas su cayda este rey dexo dos hijos en los quales dividio su grande y estendido reino el uno e mayor de ellos se llamaba Guascar el segundo Atapalipa mas como el mandar no sufre compañero ni ygual luego Guascar quiso hazer guerra al menos hermano porque dezia quel reino era suyo o a lo mesnos ciertas provinçias que a el importaba muncho e ansi como lo penso ansi lo puso por obra e juntando infinitas gentes peleo con Atapalipa e le prendio e vencio su ejercito e teniendolo preso mientras los ejercitos celebraban la vi- //
/f.507/ toria con grandes comidas e bebidas le rompio una pared gruesisima con unas grandes barras de p[ta] e cobre que le dio una muger en ansi huyo e llegado que fue a sus tierras junto sus gentes e capitanes e hiçoles una hordenada platica en la les pinto un gran milagro quel sol avia fho con el e fue que se avia tornado culebra e lo saco por un agujero muy estrecho e que le avia prometido la vitoria si savria pelear e ansi les pinto como avia sido maltratado y afrentado e puesto en prision esto les dixo e con tan buen semblante e demostracion de tristeza que todos se conmovieron a piedad e a furor para vengar las injurias de su rey e va Atapalipa de su natural e baliente y animoso e sobre manera liberal ques lo que sale e ponerle fuera y animo a los guerreros de manera que con lo que les dixo e con la buena opinion que tenian del prometieron de servirle fielmente visto por Atapalipa quan fieles hallaba sus vasallos juntos grandes //
/f.507v/ exercitos por que lo podia hazer façilisamente e teniendo capitanes balerosos e de yndustria fue en busca de su her[no] e mas enemigo e presentandole batalla el otro que no la rehuyo el Atapalipa salio al cavo venzedor e pelearon otras dos e tres vezes e vencio tanbien de manera que Guascar llebaba cada dia lo peor Atapalipa con todo eso no se aseguraba hasta ver en su poder al enemigo y ansi rehiço de nuebo el ejercito y envio a sus capitanes que peleasen de nuebo e que muerto o preso no volviesen sin el e ansi fue que le prendieron e trajeron en presencia de Atapalipa y el lo mato e asi se aseguro del her[no] e no miro que tenia otros crueles enemigos e mayorrs que su hermano al tiempo que andaban en estas contiendas llegaron Fran[co] Pizarro e otros su hermano e despues fueron tres que se llamaron Gonzalo e Fran[co] Pizarro los mas malos ombres que salieron de otra alguna nacion e mas del honra ganaron los Reyes de España //
/f.508/ lo qual ellos y sus conpañeros que lo que les interesa de tan grandes reinos por que por ellos se a dho munchas cosas entre grandes letrados e onmbres de conçiencia pero dexado esto aparte como llegase Fran[co] Pizarro a este tiempo al Piru vino a ver a Atapalipa e luego comenzaron los nuestros a mostrar gran soberbia contra un poderosisimo rei e a tenerle tan poco respeto que llego con la boca del cavallo un mal español junto con las del rei e levantandose una sediçion breve bino a ser un cruel guerra e aprender el rei sin mas ni mas e porque llegase la maldad a lo ultimo echaronle en una cadena quando el Ynga Atapalipa se vio ansi como hera de gran corazon e novilisimo sintio aquella afrenta muncho y dixo que lo tratasen vien e prometio un gran rescate e porque no lo cumplio como ellos quisieran como si a ello fuera obligado se procedio contra el por todo rigor //
/f.508v/ e le amenazaron e trataron mal e al fin fue muerto pero la causa el vien que se sepa pues tratamos de la caida de un potentisimo reino sin escrivir ystoria ordenada e larga e fue desta manera un esclavo llamado Felipillo que hera ynterprete de nuestra gente para con ellos enamorose de una de las mugeres del rei Atapalipa como mala queriendo anteponer un esclavo al gran rei dixo que se casaria con el si matavan al rei o moria el traidor del esclavo preso de la pasion determino de lebantar un falso testimonio al rey Atapalipa e pudolo hazer facilmente por ser el la lengua entre aquella gente y la nuestra e fue que dixo que avia oydo tratar a los yn[o]s entre si que matasen a los cristianos e que el rey Atapalipa juntaba de secreto grandes exercitos esto comenzo luego a tratarse entre pocos e despues se supo por todo el ejercito cristiano por lo qual creyendo ser ansi unos decian que matasen a Atapalipa //
/f.509/ porque ansi se asegurasen otros deçian que lo enviasen a España como si fuera basallo del rei por que era caer en mal caso matar tan grande rey aunque tuviese culpa en fin los avarientos cubdiciosos del oro daban priesa a que muriese por que decian que mientras muriese Atapalipa nunca gozarian del oro e riquezas que avia en aquella tierra el traidor del Pizarro por codiçia e por tener mexor ocasion de ganar la tierra y estar mpas seguro determino matarle e pa esto formo prozeso contra el como si le oviera señalado por juez el papa o el emperador p[a] conocer desa causa e acusaron de la muerte de Guascar su hermano que tambien como esta visto era rey de la tierra e probaron que tambien avia querido matar los españoles mas esta cosa averiguada fue que mentian todos porque la quel siervo Felipillo ynbento la maldad como siervo porque al tiempo //
/f.509v/ que los yndios eran ynterrogados si savian algo respondian ellos que no y es como ynterprete decia lo que queria e se le antoxaba e lo bueno era que nunca se proçedio contra el delante de los españoles sino a solas con aquellos que Pizarro queria el Atapalipa nego siempre diciendo que no cavia en razon tratar cosas que no podia salir con ella por las munchas guardas e prisiones que le tenian puestas amenaço a Felipillo e recusole e pidio que no le creyesen mas no le aprovecho nada y ansi lo sentenciaron a muerte y el oyendo la sentencia se quexo muncho de Fran[co] Pizarro que aviendole prometido de soltarle por rescate lo mataba rogandole lo enviase a España

e que no ensangrentase sus manos e fama en quien xamas le ofendio e avia hecho rico quando lo llevaban ajusticiar pidio el bautismo por consexo de los que le yban ayudando y consolando porque de otra manera estaba sent[do] a quemar vivo en un palo como a mal- //

/f.510/ hechor señor tu que miras de las alturas todas las cosas mira agora que exsemplo nos pusiste delante de los ojos de las maldades que los ombres cometen tu les daras el castigo que merezen murio Atapalipa con esfuerço de principe e mando se llevara sepultar a la ciudad de Quito donde estaban los demas principes donde el venia hera este principe vien dispuesto savio valiente e mui pulido a su modo castigolo dios porque mato a su hermano pero mexor titulo tubo para matarlo que no Fran[co] Pizarro en matarlo a el porque lo mesmo hiciera Guascar de Atapalipa que Atapalipa hiço de Guascar pero Fran[co] Pizarro no tenia juridicion sobre el ni el papa Alexandro ni el rey don Fernando ni el emperador oviera mandado que entrasen ansi en la tierra agena pero dios castigo tan gran pecado pues el papa ni el emperador no quisieron poner rem[o] por que un fraile de Santo Domingo //

/f.510v/ llamado frai Vizente de Balverde que altero a los españoles para que matasen los yn[o]s porque avia arroxado Atapalipa la biblia o su brebario dios lo castigo ygnominosamente porque a palos lo mataron siendo ya obispo los mesmos yn[o]s de la ysla de Puna el Fran[co] Pizarro ya murio en las manos de sus enemigos y españoles a Ju[o] Pizarro mataron los yndios en el Cuzco el Fernando Pizarro dicen que no tubo culpa en la muerte deste rey a lo menos dios lo a castigado en tantas cosas que no creo que le tendra envidia a nadie asi castigo dios a los demas el Gonzalo Piçarro murio como traydor e ansi acavo la prenzipal gente desta casa e no es menester otro mayor testimy[o] del castigo que dios dio a esta gente sino las palabras que dixo un P[o] de Alvarado que hera de los mesmos malos estando a la muerte e fue ansi que como lo oviese rebatido un caballo que benia rodando por una questa abaxo curandolo despues e viendo que se moria preguntabanle que que [*sic*] le dolia respondio siempre el alma //

/f.511/ este pues fue el fin de aquel reino e monarquia la qual como otro tiempo la de los Asirios se paso a los Medos asi se paso la del Piru a los españoles los reyes que yo hallo son estos: Ayar Mango 1 Çinchi Roga Ynga 2 Lluchi Yupangue 3 Yndimaitoacapac 4 Capac Yupangue 5 Ynga Roca Ynga 6 Yaguar Guacac Ynga 7 Viracocha Ynga 8 Pachacuti Capac Ynga Yupangue 9 Tupa Ynga Yupangue 10 Guaina Capa 11 Guascar y Atapalipa 12.

Despues que fue muerto el Guascar como dize reino en la prision el Atapalipa e despues que le fue dado garrote infamemente como a hombre comun por dorar el pecado que avia cometido Fran[co] Pizarro dio el reino como si el fuera señor a Mango hermano de Atapalipa e fue el trezeno rey de los yndios del Piru acabose este e yncorporose el reino en la corona real de los reinos de España e suzedio en el reino el rei don Carlos rei de España y emperador de Alemania y fue el 14 rey del Piru y el 15 es el cristianisimo es el rey don Felipe II de los ansi llamados //

/f.511v/ cuya vida nuestro señor prospere por largos años porque si verdaderamente alguno a tenido algun vuen dr[o] al reino a sido el por el gran cuidado que tiene de que se predique el santo evangelio e de que se envien ombres de mucha santidad por perlados e juezes retos y en fin bemos que ya no ay quien se atreva a usar de tiranias ni robos porque luego son castigados e poesto bemos que los yndios cuia es la tierra justamente e no nuestra son vien tratados e favorecidos de su rei e señor natural.

EL REY

/al margen: Lizenzia de Agustin de Zarate/ Por quanto por parte de bos Agustin de Zarate nos fue fha relacion diciendo quel año de quarenta e tres yendo por nuestro mandado por contador general de las provi[as] del Piru vistas las novedades que alli avia suzedido aviades hecho un libro dello del descubrimiento de aquella tierra hasta quel lizenciado Gasca ovispo que fue del Palençia avia venido a estos reinos en que //

/f.512/ se declaraban en partes convenientes las cosas naturales que en aquella tierra se hallaban con su graduacion e cosmografia e por que avia falta dellos e no se hallaban nos suplicastes le mandasemos dar lizen[a] para poder ynprimir e privilegio por diez años para que otro nenguno lo pudiese ynprimir o como la nuestra md fuese lo qual visto por los del nuestro q[o] por quanto en el dho libro se hizo la deligenzia que la prematica agora nuebamente sobre lo suso dho fha dispone fue acordado que deviamos mandar esta nuestra carta e zedula para que bos en la dha razon e yo tubelo por bien por la qual vos damos lizençia e facultad para que bos o la persona que para ello vuestro poder oviere e no otra persona alguna podais hazer ynprimir e vender el dho libro que de suso se nace mincion en estos nuestros reinos por tiempo y espacio de diez años cum- //

/f.512v/ plidos primeros siguientes que corren y se quentan desde el dia de la data desta nuestra zedula so pena que qualquiera persona que sin tener para ello buestro poder lo ynprimiere o vendiere con los moldes e aparexos della e mas en pena de cinquenta mill mr[e]s por cada bez que lo contrario hizieren la mitad de la qual pena sea para la nuestra camara e fisco e la otra mitad para bos el dho contador Agustin de Zarate e todas las bezes que se oviere de ynprimir el dho libro durante el tiempo de los dhos diez años se traiga al nuestro consexo juntam[te] con el original que en el fue visto que ba rubricada cada plana e firmada al fin del de Al[o] de Ballexo nuestro escribano de cam[a] e uno de los que en el nuestro consexo residen para que se vea si la dha ynpresion esta conforme al original e se os de lizencia para que lo podais vender e se tase el precio en que se a de vender cada volumen //

/f.513/ so pena de caer e yncurrir en las penas contenidas en la dha prematica e leyes de nuestros reinos e mandamos a los del nuestro q[o] e otras qualesquier nuestras justicias destos nuestros reinos que guarden e cumplan y ejecuten e hagan guardar cumplir y executar esta nuestra zedula e todo lo en ella cont[do]. Fecha en San Lorenzo el Rol. A onze dias del mes de set[e] de myll e quinientos e setenta e seis años. yo el rey y por mandado de su magestad Martin Gastelu.

Capitulo doze del estado que estavan las guerras del Piru al tiempo que los españoles llegaron a ellas

Aunque el intento principal desta ystoria sea contar las cosas en ella suzedidas a los españoles que la conquistaron entonzes e despues aca del descubrimiento pero porque esto no se podria a vien entender sin tocar algo del estado //

/f.513v/ en que los negocios de los yndios que la gobernaban estaban en aquella sazon e tanvien pa que se vea claramente como fue permision divina que los españoles llegasen a esta conquista al tiempo que la tierra estava dividida en dos parcialidades e que era imposible o a lo menos muy dificultuoso poderla ganar de esta manera dize en suma los terminos en que hallaron la tierra en aquella coyuntura pa que aya mas claridad en la ystoria. Guaina Caba despues de aver sujetado a su ynperio gran num[o] de provincias por espacio de quinientas leguas contando desde el Cuzco hasta el ocidente determino yr en persona a conquistar la provi[a] del Quito en cuyas entradas se acavaba su señorio e ansi saco su ejercito e fue e hiço la conquista e por se la calidad de la tierra muy apazible a su condicion residio alli muncho tiempo desando en el Cuzco algunos hijos e hixas suyos especialmente su hijo mayor llamado Guascar Ynga y a Mango Ynga y a Paulo Ynga e a otros munchos y en Quito tomo nueba mujer hixa del señor de la tierra //

/f.514/ e della ubo un hixo llamado Atabaliba a quien el quiso muncho e dexandole debaxo de tutores en Quito torno a visitar la tierra del Cuzco y en esta vuelta le hicieron el camino tan trabaxoso de la sierra de questa a hecha relacion despues de aber estado en el Cuzco algunos años determino de volverse a Quito ansi porque le hera mas agradable aquella tierra como por el deseo de ver a Atavaliba su hijo a quien el queria mas que a los otros e ansi volvio a Quito por el camino que emos dho de los llanos donde vivio e tuvo su asiento lo restante de la vida hasta que murio e mando que aquella provi[a] de Quito quel avia conquistado quedase para Atavaliba pues avia sido de sus abuelos muerto Guaina Caba Atabaliba se apodero de su ejercito e de las riquezas que consigo traia aunque las principales como mas pesados la avia dexado en su recamara en el Cuzco en poder de su hijo mayor al qual Atabaliba envio envaxadores haciendole saber la muerte de su padre e dandole ovidençia //

/f.514v/ suplicandole que le dexase aquella provincia de Quito pues su padre la avia ganado y era fuera de su estado e mayorazgo e sobre todo que avia sido de su madre e abuelo Guascar le respondio quel se viniese al Cuzco y le entregase el exercito e que le daria tierra donde se mantuviese muy onrradamente pero que a Quito no se le podia dar por ser el fin de su tierra e que de alli avia de hazer sus entradas contras los enemigos e tener gente como en frontera y que sino venia que iria sobre el sin quel fuese primero e le ternia por enemigo Atavaliba tuvo su consexo con dos capitanes de su padre mui esforzados e cursados en la guerra el uno llamado Quizquiz y el otro Cilicuchima los quales le aconsexaron que no esperase a que su hermano viniese sobre el sino quel fuese primero pues con el exercito que tenia era parte para señorearse de todas las provincias por do pasase y yr cada dia acrezentandole //

/f.515/ de manera que su hermano tuviese por bien de confe/de/rarse con el tomando su consejo saliose de Quito e fuese apoderando de la tierra poco a poco e tanvien Guascar envio un governador e cap[an] suyo con cierta gente a la ligera e llegando a gran priesa a una provinçia que se dize Tumibamba ques mas de cien leguas de Quito e savido como Atavaliva avia ya salido con su exersito despacho una posta al Cuzco haciendo saber lo que pasaba a Guascar para que le enviase dos mil hombres de los capitanes e gente pratica en la guerra por que con ellos juntaria treinta mil hombres de una provi[a] que se llama Los Cañares gente mui belicosa que estaba por leyes lo hiço ansi e despachados los dos mil hombres a gran priesa se juntaron con ellos los caziques de Tumibamba y los Chaparras e Pastas e Cañares questaban en aquella comarca e savido por //

/f.515v/ Atabaliva salieron contra ellos e pelearon tres dias muriendo muncha gente de anbas partes hasta que desbaratados los de Quito Atabaliba fue preso sobre la puente del rio de Tumibamba y estando haciendo la gente de Guascar grandes fiestas e borracheras por la vitoria Atabaliba con una barra de cobre que una muger le dio rompio una mui gruesa pared del tambo de Tumibamba e se fue huyendo a Quito ques veinticinco leguas de alli e torno a juntar su gente e haçiendoles entender que su p[e] le avia convertido en culebra e hecho salir por un pequeño agujero e le avia prometido la vitoria si tornasen a pelear los animo tanto que volvio sobre sus enemigos e peleo con ellos e los vencio e desbarato aviendo muerto muncha gente de anbas partes en estas dos batallas tanto que hasta oy duran los corrales e monto/nes/ //

/f.516/ que ali estavan de huesos de los hombres continuando e siguiendo Atabaliba la vitoria determino ir sobre su hermano e llegando a la provincia de los Cañares mato sesenta mill ombres dellos porque le avian sido contrarios e metio a fuego e sangre e asolo la poblacion de Tumibamba situada en un llano ribera de tres grandes rios la qual era muy grande e alli fue conquistando la tierra e de los que se defendian no dexaba ombre vivo e los que salian de paz lo juntava consigo e desta manera yban multiplicando su exersito e ydo a Tumbes quiso conquistar por mar la ysla de la Puna que arriba esta dho mas el cacique salio con munchas balsas y se le defendio e porque Atabaliba pareçio que aquella conquista requeria mas espacio e supo que su hermano Guascar venia sobre el con su exercito continuo su camino hacia el Cuzco e quedandosele en Caxamarca envio delante sus dos ca- //

/f.516v/ pitanes con hasta tres o quatro myll ombres que fue a descubrir el campo a la ligera e llegado cerca del exercito de Guascar por no ser sentidos se desviaron del camino por un ataxo por el qual acaso se avia apartado tambien el mesmo Guascar con seteçientos ombres de sus principales por salir del ruido del exercito e topandole pelearon e le prendieron e teniendole preso benia ya todo el exercito sobre ellos e los cercaron por todas partes donde no dexaran ninguno bivo porque avia mas de treynta para uno si los capitanes de Atabaliba no dijeran a Guascar viendo benir su gente que los mandase volver sino que luego le cortarian la cabeza e luego Guascar con temor de la muerte y con que le dixeron que su hermano no queria del otra cosa sino que le dexase en la tierra de Quito reconociendole por señor mando a su gente de que no pasase de alli //

/f.517/ sino que luego se volviesen al Cuzco y ellos lo hiçieron e savida tan buena ventura como acaso suzedio por Atabaliba envio a mandar a sus capitanes que le traxesen a su hermano preso alli a Caxamalca donde el esperaba y en esta coyuntura llego el governador don Fran[co] Pizarro con los españoles que llebaba a la tierra del Piru e tubo lugar de hazer la conquista que en el libro siguiente se dira porque el exercito de Guascar era desbaratado e huido el de Atabaliba estaba la mayor parte del pedido por la nueva vitoria.

/al margen: Tasa y tributo que mando pagar a su magestad el virrey don Fran[co] de T[do] yndios que saco por yanaconas en el valle de Yucay el dotor P[o] Gutierrez/

Don Francisco de Toledo mayordomo de su mag[d] su visorrey governador e cap[an] general destos reynos e provinçias del Piru e tierra firme e presidente de la real audiencia e chancilleria que reside en la ciudad de los Reyes. A vos los caziques principales que soys e fueredes del pueblo de Santiago de Oropesa e del pueblo de San Bernardo que agora nuevamente se an señalado //

/f.517v/ e reducido por el liçenciado frai Pº Gutierrez del avito de Alcantara y visitador general por mi nombrado en el valle de Yucai e a los caciques de pachacas principales e ynºs de los dhos pueblos a quien lo quede y uso en esta mi provi^{on} sera contenido toca y atañe y a guardar y cumplir y a cada uno y qualesquier de vos save que aviendo bisto la visita numeracion y averiguacion de los yndios que el dho visitador hallo en el dho valle de Yucay que no estavan encomendados a ningun encomendero ni an pagado ni pagan tributo parece por la dha visita y fe que dellas se dio que los dhos yndios que no pagaban tributo ni estavan encomendados hallo y reduxo en el dho pueblo de San Benito de Alcantara setenta e cinco yndios casados de diez y ocho años hasta cinquenta e ocho yndios solteros de los dhos diez y ocho hasta cinquenta años y en el pueblo de Santiago de Oropesa ciento y sesenta y ocho yndios casados de diez y ocho hasta cinquenta años y catorce yºs solteros //
/f.518/ de las dhas hedades y en el dho pueblo de San Bernardo ciento y treinta y seis yndios casados de la dha hedad de diez y ocho hasta cinquenta años y ocho ynºs solteros de las dhas hedades y en el pueblo de San Fran^{co} de Maras poblo y reduxo otros nueve yndios de las dhas hedades los quales dexo subjetos a vos el dho cacique principal del pueblo de San Bernardo que son por todos los dhos yndios que ansi se reduxeron a los dhos pueblos por la forma y orden que dha es quatrocientos y diez y ocho yºs tributarios de los que como esta dho no estavan encomendados ni pagavan tributo y aviendo visto ansimismo el parecer que el dho visitador dio de los tribuºs que debriades y podriades pagar a su magestad en cada un año en cuya cabeza e corona por un auto mio estais puestos y por la presente os pongo siendo nezesario aplicando como aplico los tributos provision y bastimento del castellano e personas que //
/f.518v/ an de quedar en esta ciudad y asistir en la fortaleza della para que mejor se pueda conservar y sustentar en el servicio de su magestad segun que de yuso yra declarado e ynformandome de personas celosas de vuestro bien y teniendo consideracion a que nuevamente se os manda pagar este tributo y a los gastos y trabajos que abeis tenido en la reduçion de los dhos pueblos ydeficios de la yglesia me a parecido de proveer y mandar como por la presente proveo y mando que desde el dia que os fuere notificado esta mi provision en adelante pagueis vos el dho cacique y los dhos buestros pachacas prencipales e yndios de los dhos pueblos que como dho es no estan encomendados a persona alguna ni aveis pagado tributo hasta agora en cada un año de seis y seis meses la mitad a su magestad y a sus oficiales reales que residen en la ciudad del Cuzco para los efetos susodhos en que por la presente aplico los tributos que aveis de pagar mil e docientos e cinq^{ta} y quatro pºs //
/f.519/ de plata ensayada e m^{da} de valor cada uno de quatrocientos y cinquenta m^{e}s que sale razonado por cabezas cada yndio tributario de la dha hedad de los dhos quatrocientos y diez y ocho yndios que ansi quedan reducidos y poblados en los dhos pueblos a tres pºs de plata ens^{da} e m^{da} aunque respeto de lo que pagan los demas yndios a sus encomenderos y de los rescates oficios y aprovechamientos que por estar tan cerca de la ciudad del Cuzco teneis e de beneficiº quede yncorporaros en la corona real se echase podriades pagar mucho mas los quales dhos tributos vos los dhos caziques aveis de cobrar cada uno por lo que les toca repartiendolo ygualm^{te} e sin agravio de ninguno de los dhos yndios e pagarlo a los dhos oficiales reales para los dhos efetos a los plazos susodhos en la forma y horden siguiente:

/f.519v/ v Doscientas hanegas de trigo puestas en la dha ciudad del Cuzco en poder de los dhos oficiales reales y tasadas y moderadas a dos pºs de p^{ta} corriente que es el precio a que comunmente valen en la dha ciudad suman y montan quatrocientos pesos de p^{ta} corriente y entre tanto que no tuvieren tierras pa dar el dho trigo la paguen en plata al dho precio pa que los dhos oficiales reales les compren de harina para la dha fortaleza y no se pueda gastar en otra cosa.

v Doscientas hanegas de maiz puestas ansimismo en la dha ciudad del Cuzco en poder de los dhos oficiales reales que tasados y moderados a los dhos dos pºs de p^{ta} corriente cada una ques al precio a que comunmente valen en esta dha ciudad montan otros quatrocientos pºs de p^{ta} corriente.

v Quatrocientas cargas de leña del topo de la ciudad //
/f.520/ del Cuzco que tasados y moderados a tomin cada una ques el precio a que comunmente balen montan cinquenta y seis pºs y dos tomines de plata corriente.

v Que todo lo suso dho suma y monta ochocientos y cinquenta y seis pºs y dos tomines de la dha plata corriente.

Y lo demas restante pagado todo lo susodho en el dho trigo maiz y leña a cumplimiento de los dhos mil e doscientos e cinquenta y quatro pesos de la dha plata ensaiada e marcada lo aveys de dar y pagar a los dhos oficiales reales en la dha plata ensayada so pena de privacion de vros cacicazgos si ansi no lo hicieredes y cumplieredes y cobrado y repartiendo a los yºs mas tribuºs de los que conforme a lo que dho es les cupiere y siendo nos o qualquier de nos negligente en la cobranza y pago de los dhos tributos a los plazos se ponia en vro lugar otro cacique que mexor lo cobre e haga confor- //
/f.520v/ me a lo que dexo ordenado a los dhos oficiales reales en la ynstruccion que les mande dar y an de ser ansimesmo a vro cargo tener quenta que no se derramen los dhos yºs de los pueblos por que aunque alegueis que se os ayan ydo y muerto no se os aya de recevir descuento alguno pues en lugar de los que se mueren yran entrando otros en la dha hedad de diez y ocho aºs y pagaran tasa que agora son menores y no se les reparte tribuº y de los que en adelante fueren naciendo ni tampoco se vos ha de pedir mas tribuº de lo que aqui se os manda pagar a que de los dhos yºs menores de los diez y ocho años baian entrando en edad de tributar mas de los fueren saliendo y tampoco por razon de los ausentes se os a de descontar nada pues esta a vro cargo el recoxerlos y conservarlos por la obligacion de vros oficios y porque la conciencia de su m^{t} se descargue de la obligacion que tiene de daros dotrina mando a los dhos oficiales reales que de los dhos tributos que asi aveis de dar y pagar en plata en cada un año den y paguen por los tercios del como fueren cobrando de vosotros al sazerdote o sazerdotes que estan pre- //
/f.521/ sentados o adelante se presentaren a los cargos y dotrinas de los dhos pueblos para que os administren los sacramentos de la santa yglesia y enseñe y dotrine en las cosas de nuestra santa fee catolica el salario que rata por cantidad cupiere y se deviere pagar por razon

de los dhos quatrocientos y diez y ocho yndios del salario questuviere señalado o señalare en las dotrinas de los dhos pueblos y porque mejor se puedan cobrar los dhos tribu^{o}s y conservar y recoxer los y^{o}s en los dhos pueblos mando al dho visitador os entreguen a vos los dhos caciques principales un treslado autentico de la numeracion de todos los y^{o}s que de los dhos pueblos se hiciere ansi varones como hembras por sus ayllos y cacicazgos y principales y mando al correg^{or} y alcaldes hordinarios y otras justicias qualesquier de la dha ciudad del Cuzco y de otras qualesquier villas e lugares destos nuestros reinos //

/f.521v/ ante quien pidieredes cumplimi^{to} de justicia que os entreguen y hagan dar y restituir los y^{o}s contenidos en la dha numeracion y los hijos y nietos que adelante tuvieren que se ausentaren y ovieren ausentado de los dhos pueblos haziendo os acudir con los tribu^{o}s que por esta tasa se mandan pagar a cada indio del tiempo que huvieren estado ausentes y los unos ni los otros no deseeis ni deseen de lo ansi cumplir y hazer so las dhas penas puestas a vos los dhos caciques principales y de cada mill pesos de oro para la camara de su majestad. Fecha en la ciudad del Cuzco a veinte dias del mes de setiembre de myll e qui^{o}s y setenta y dos años. don Francisco de Toledo por mandado de su Exª Albaro Ruiz de Navamuel.

En la ciudad del Cuzco a veinte y siete dias del mes de setiembre de mill e qui^{o}s e set^{a} e dos años yo el dho secret^{o} notifique esta tasa e provi^{on} de su Exª a Miguel Sanchez contador de la real hazienda //

/f.522/ desta ciudad y al fator Juan Perez de Prado en sus personas y dello doy fee. t^{gos} Felipe de Leon y Ger^{mo} Diez y lo firmaron Miguel Sanchez Juan Perez de Prado. Alvaro Ruiz de Navamuel.

Segun mas largamente consta e pareze por la dha tasa e libros a que me refiero e para que dello conste di el presente en los Reyes a beinte y siete de nobiembre de myll e qui^{o}s y ochenta e cinco a^{o}s.

Jhoan de Montoya (rubrica)

/f.522v–f.524v/ /en blanco/

/f.525/ Don Phelipe por la gracia de Dios rey de Castilla de Leon de Aragon de las dos Çicilias de Jherusalem de Portugal de Navarra de Granada de Toledo de Valencia de Galicia de Mallorca de Sevilla de Çerdeña de Cordova de Corcega de Murcia de Jaen de los Algarves de Algeçira de Gibraltar de las yslas de Canaria de las Yndias orientales y occidentales yslas e tierra firme del mar oceano archiduque de Austria duque de Borgoña Bravante y Milan conde de Ausburg de Flandes y de Tirol y de Barcelona señor de Vizcaya y de Molina etc. Por quanto esta proveydo y mandado por nuestra persona real que en cada un año se le embie toda su real hazienda destos nuestros reynos del Piru a los despaña para cuyo efecto sea fecho armada de navios y galeras con los peltrechos y demas cosas nesçesarias para ello y para que la dha nuestra real hazienda y la de particulares se lleve con mas seguridad a causa de averse dho que algunos piratas yngleses an entrado en este mar del sur por el estrecho de Magallanes a robar y hazer otros daños a nuestros subditos y naturales conviene nombrar para la buena administracion y govierno de la dha armada capitan general que la lleve a su cargo que sea persona de calidad y confiança y celoso de nuestro real servicio confiando de vos Martin Garcia de Loyola cavallero de la horden de Calatrava nuestro governador y capitan general de la provincia del Rio de la Plata que sois tal persona visto por el nuestro presidente e oydores de la audiencia y chancilleria real que reside en la ciudad de los Reyes de los dhos nuestros reinos del Piru governadores dellos fue acordado que os deviamos nombrar como por la presente os nombramos y proveemos //

/f.525v/ por nuestro capitan general de la dha armada de navios y galeras queste año ande yr al reino de tierra firme con la plata de nuestra real hazienda y de particulares que destos reynos se envia y de los demas que con ella fueren y nos tovimoslo por bien por la qual vos mandamos que como tal nuestro capitan general de la dha armada asi en yda al dho reyno de tierra firme como en la buelta conviniendo venyr en conserva y aviendo de venir divididos en el navio en que vuestra persona viniere useis y podais usar el dho oficio y cargo de tal nuestro capitan general en todas las cosas y casos a el anexas y concernientes y que el almirante y capitanes alferez sargentos y demas oficiales y soldados maestros y pilotos marineros y pasajeros y otras qualesquier personas que fueren en la dha armada y bolvieren en ella os tengan respeten acaten y obedescan como a tal cap^{t} general y cumplan vuestros mandamientos y guarden la orden que les dieredes asi en lo que toca a la navegacion como en las ocasiones de guerra so las penas que para ello les pusieredes las quales desde luego nos las avemos por puestas y por condenados en ellas a los que los contrario hizieren y os damos poder y comision para las executar que asi todos de la dha armada como todas las justicias cavalleros escuderos oficiales y homes buenos de los puertos y partes y lugares donde tomaredes tierra os ayan y tengan por tal nuestro capitan general de la dha armada y os guarden y hagan guardar todas las honrras gracias merçedes franquezas prerrogativas e ynmunidades que por razon del dho oficio se os han y deven ser guardadas bien asi como se guarden a los demas capitanes generales de los nuestras armadas reales y que en el uso y exercicio del dho cargo no os pongan ni consientan poner embargo ny contrario alguno antes os den todo el favor //

/f.526/ e ayuda que en nuestro n^{e} les pidieredes y menester hubieredes asi de gente armas y municiones pertrechos y bastimentos y otras qualesquier cosas nescesarias para la dha armada y jornada y ellos las tengan pagandoles por ello loque fuere justo y si algunos pleytos asi civiles como criminales durante el tiempo de la dha navegacion subcedieren en la dha armada entre los capitanes soldados y demas personas que en ella fueren podais conosçer dellas y de los delitos que hizieren y librar los pleytos y debates y castigarlos segun orden y usança de guerra que para todo ello y para la buelta recoxer la artilleria armas municiones y pertrechos en los navios que os paresçiere y elegir el que conviniere en que venga vuestra persona y nombrar los oficiales de la dha armada que faltaren y para todo lo demas a ello anexo y dependiente os damos poder y facultad qual en tal caso se requiere en forma y aveis de hazer pleyto omenaje de que bien y fielmente usareis el dho oficio y cargo de tal capitan general y para el efecto que se os da y comete y que defendereis la dha armada y navios y galeras y lo que en ella fuere y en su defensa peleareis con todos los hombres del mundo que contra la dha armada salieren y que sino fuere a nos o a los dhos nuestro presidente y oydores o visorrey no entregareis la dha armada ni cosa della y que guardareis la ynstrucion que por ellos os sera entregada y los unos ni los otros no fagades ni fagan en de al por alguna manera so pena de la nuestra mrd y de cada dos mil pesos de oro para la nuestra camara. Dada en los Reyes a veinte quatro dias del mes de abril de mill e quinientos y ochenta e quatro años. va enmendado pidi vala. El liçenciado de Monzon el dotor Alonso Criado de Castilla. Yo Juan Ramos de Gauna escrivano de camara de su magestad catolica la fize escrevir por su mandado con acuerdo de su pres^te^ y oydores registrada Juan de Cagastiçaval chanciller //

/f.526v/ en el puerto e Callao de la ciudad de los Reyes del Piru a veinte e ocho dias del mes de abril de mill e quinientos y ochenta y quatro años estando en en monasterio de Buena Guia el muy Yll^e^ señor Martin Garcia de Loyola cavallero de la horden de Calatrava e governador del Rio de la Plata e capitan general del armada real que va a tierra firme en cumplimiento de lo proveido en esta real conduta hizo el juramento e pleyto omenaje en forma contenido en la dha real conduta en manos del muy Yll^e^ señor doctos Castilla del consejo de su magestad oydor desta real audiencia que por comision della esta en el dho puerto en el despacho de la dha armada como mas largo consta e queda en mi registro a que me refiero ante mi Joan Gutierrez de Molina.

Yo Alonso Ramos Çervantes escrivano de su magestad y mayor de minas y registros en esta ciudad de los Reyes del Piru doy fee y certifico a los señores que el presente vieren como en mi presencia y de los t^o^s que a ello fueron presentes en virtud de una real provision de su mag^d^ desta real audiencia el general Pedro de Arana alço e quito el pleyto omenaje que el comendador Martin Garcia de Loyola hizo del armada que se le entrego de que fue por general al reyno de tierra firme conforme a esta provision real y hizo entrego de lo que fue a su cargo como tal general y para que dello conste di la presente de pedimiento del dho comendador Martin Garcia de Loyola ques fho en los Reyes en veinte y nueve dias del mes de abril de mil e quinientos y ochenta y cinco años y fueron t^o^s al quitar el dho pleyto omenaje el doctor Diego de Salinas y Julian Bravo y Garcia R^o^s Medrano estantes en esta corte en fee de lo qual fize aqui mio signo a tal en testimonio de verdad. Alonso Ramos Cervantes.

En la ciudad del Cuzco a diez dias del mes de março de mill e quinientos y ochenta y nueve años yo Gaspar de Prado escrivano del rey nuestro señor e publico desta dha ciudad por ausencia de Antonio Sanchez scriv^o^ publico del numero della saque e fize sacar este traslado de su original que quedo en poder del comendador Martin Garcia de Loyola e va cierto e verdadero corregido //

/f.527/ y concertado con su original siendo presentes por testigos Antonio Muriel y Diego Ruiz e Joan Perez residentes en la dha ciudad e m^do^ de. Y lo fize screvir y aqui mi signo.

Gaspar de Prado (rubrica)

/f.528/ Don Phelipe por la gracia de Dios rey de Castilla de Leon de Aragon de las dos Çicilias de Jherusalem de Portugal de Navarra de Granada de Toledo de Valencia de Galicia de Mallorca de Sevilla de Çerdeña de Cordova de Corcega de Murcia de Jaen de los Algarves de Algeçira de Gibraltar de las yslas de Canaria de las Yndias orientales y occidentales yslas e tierra firme del mar oceano archiduque de Austria duque de Borgoña Bravante y Milan conde de Ausburg de Flandes y de Tirol y de Barcelona señor de Vizcaya y de Molina etc.

Don Phelipe por la gracia de Dios rey de Castilla de Leon de Aragon de las dos Çicilias de Jherusalem de Portugal de Navarra de Granada de Toledo de Valencia de Galicia de Mallorca de Sevilla de Çerdeña de Cordova de Corcega de Murcia de Jaen de los Algarves de Algeçira de Gibraltar de las yslas de Canaria de las Yndias orientales y occidentales yslas e tierra firme del mar oceano archiduque de Austria duque de Borgoña Bravante y Milan conde de Ausburg de Flandes y de Tirol y de Barcelona señor de Vizcaya y de Molina etc. Por quanto a nuestro servicio y buena administracion de nuestas justicia conbiene nombrar corregidor de la ciudad de Guamanga y su jurisdiccion y de la Villa Rica de Oropesa y minas de asogue y asiento de Huancavelica y alcalde m^or^ de las dichas minas para que aya buena corresponsion en la labor y beneficio de las dichas minas y en los yndios que ban a ellas y para escusar los ynconvinientes y competencia que ha avido por estar el dicho corregimiento en dos personas de que ha resultado daño y menoscavo a nra hazienda a parecido que este en una persona y que Gomez de Chavez y Rodrigo de Cantos de Andrada que hasta agora han usado el dicho oficio de corregidores en la dicha ciudad y villa se vengan a esta corte a entender en las cosas que se les mandaren tocantes a nro servicio y que se les tome residencia del tiempo que han usado los dichos oficios y porque bos Martin Garcia de Loyola cavallero del havito de Calatrava soys persona en quien concurren las partes y calidades necesarias para el uso del dicho oficio y que de los que se os han encargado por los nros visorreyes y governadores de los nros reynos del Piru asi en la paz como en la guerra haveis dado buena quenta y de vras residencias a constado la cristiandad y limpieça con que los haveis servido y el mucho acrecentamiento que con vra ynteligencia y buena yndustria havepiz causado a nra hazienda y el zelo que de vos conocemos que teneis de lo continuar y porque entendemos que a nro servicio y al bien de los vezinos naturales y pobladores de la dicha ciudad y villa y al reparo conservacion y aumento de las dichas minas que estan tan arruynadas y perdidas como es notorio conbiene proveer semejante persona por el daño yrreparable que de lo contrario se podra esperar a la dicha nra hazienda y a todo el dicho reyno acatando las dichas causas y otros justos respetos y consideraciones que a ello nos mueben Visto por don Fernando de Torres y Portugal nuestro pariente visorrey governador y capitan general de los dichos nros reynos y provincias del Piru fue acordado que os devamos nombrar y proveer como por la presente os nombramos y proveemos por nro corregidor y justicia mayor y juez de residencia de la dicha ciudad de Guamanga y Villa Rica de Oropesa y alcalde mayor y de las minas de Huancavelica y su juridicion para que como tal por tiempo de un año mas o menos lo que fuere nra voluntad podais traer y traygais vara de nra justicia y conocer y conozcais de qualesquier causas y negocios asi civiles como criminales de qualesquier calidad y condicion que sean de que conforme a las leyes y prematicas de nros reynos uso y costumbre dellos pueden y deven //

/f.528v/ conocer los dichos corregidores alcaldes mayores de minas y juezes de residencia y si algunos pleitos estubieren por fenecer de los que han pasado ante los dhos Gomez de Chavez y Rodrigo Cantos de Andrada corregidores que han sido de la dicha ciudad y villa o ante los alcaldes ordinarios que son de la dicha ciudad o ante otros corregidores e alcaldes que antes han sido della los podais tomar en el punto y estado en que estubieren y los fenecer y acavar sentenciar y determinar bien asi como si ante vos se enpeçasen de nuevo y las senten^as^ que dieredes y pronunciaredes que segun derecho obiere lugar apelacion la otorgareis a las partes que la ynterpusieren si fuere en tiempo y en forma para que la puedan proseguir ante quien y con derecho devan y de las que no oviere lugar apelacion las hareis executar y executeis como de derecho podais y devais y hazer y hagais todas las otras cosas e casos al dicho oficio anexos y concernientes e que convinieren a nro servicio y execucion de nuestra real justicia y mandamos al cavildo justicia y regimiento de la dicha ciudad de Guamanga que juntos en el dicho cavildo segun lo han de uso y costumbre luego que con esta nra carta fueren requeridos sin esperar para ello otra nueba provision ni mandamiento segunda ni tercera jusion [*sic*] tomen y reciban de bos el dicho Martin Garcia de Loyola el juramento solenidad y fianças que en tal caso se requieren y debeis hazer antes que seais recivido al dicho oficio lo qual ansi por vos fecho bos reciban ayan y tengan por tal nro corregidor justicia mayor e juez de residencia de la dicha ciudad de Guamanga y de la dicha Villa Rica de Oropesa y alcalde mayor de minas del dicho asiento de Huancavelica y usen y execran con vos el dicho oficio en todos los casos y cosas a el anexas y pertenecientes y que ellos y todos los demas cavalleros escuderos oficiales homes buenos de la dicha ciudad villa asiento e minas bos obedezcan y respeten y acaten por tal correg^{or} y justicia mayor e juez de residencia e alcalde mayor e hagan y cumplan vros mandamientos e vengan a vros conocimientos so las penas que para ello les pusieredes de nra parte las quales nos se las podemos y havemos por puestas y por condenados en ellas lo contrario haziendo y os damos poder y facultad para que las podais executar en las personas y bienes de los que rebeldes e ynobedientes fueren y mandamos que os acudan y hagan recudir con los salarios derechos y aprovechamientos al dicho oficio devidos y pertenecientes y os guarden y hagan guardar todas las honras gracias mercedes franquezas y libertades preminencias exempciones e ynmunidades que por razon del dho oficio deveys aver y gozar y os deven de ser guardadas de todo bien y cumplidamente en guisa que bos no mengue ni falte en de cosa alguna e que en ello ni en parte dello vos no pongan ni consientan poner enbargo ni contrario alguno e a nos por la presente bos recivimos y havemos por recevido al dicho oficio uso y exercicio del y os damos poder y facultad para lo usar y exercer caso que por ellos o alguno dellos a el no seais recevido y otro si os damos comision para que si vieredes que conbiene a nro servi^{o} y execucion de nra real justicia que algunas personas de las que estan o adelante estubieren en la dicha ciudad de Guamanga y Villa Rica de Oropesa y minas de Huancavelica y sus terminos e juridicion salgan dellas y se venga a presentar ante nos en la nuestra //

/f.529/ audiencia real que reside en la ciudad de lo Reyes de los dichos nros reynos del Piru y ante el dicho nro visorrey e gobernador les podais compeler a ello y enbiar la causa porque lo hareis e porque esta mandado por ordenanças e ynstrucciones de los nros visorreyes que han sido de los dichos reynos del Peru que los indios naturales dello no se carguen vos mandamos tengais mucho cuidado de que se cumpla asi e que se les haga buen tratamiento a los de vra juridicion e que sean doctrinados en las cosas de nra santa fee catolica e no lo consentireis ni dareis lugar que ningun encomendero por si ni por ynterpositas personas se sirva dellos ni de ningun servicio personal ni les lleven mas tributos de los que estan obligados a pagar conforme a las tasas hechas y que se hizieren ni los saque de su natural ni puedan hazer comutacion de unas cosas en otras de aquellas que estuvieren puestas en la tasa ni les hagan otras fuerças ni agravios y que en los casos que esta permitido alquilense a personas que no sean encomenderos les hagais pagar el jornal que esta acordado o se acordare que se ha de dar a los dichos yndios en sus propias manos teniendo particular cuydado de los que sirven en los tambos de Acos Picoy Parcos y Asangaro y otros de vra juridicion e de que aya en ellos las cosas necesarias para el buen aviamiento de los caminantes pagandoles su justo valor e que se guarde y cumpla lo que los visitadores dexaron proveido e ordenado y si algunas personas contra lo suso dho fueren o vinieren procedereis contra ellos con mucho rigor conforme a nras cedulas e provisiones e no dareis a los dhos yndios carta ni mandamientos de amparo comos hasta aqui se han dado por los derechos que pagavan antes les hareis justicia en los casos que fueren agraviados brevemente sin les llevar derechos y no consentireis que se los lleve ningun escrivano letrado ni procurador alguazil ni carcelero ni otra ninguna persona ni dadivas ni presentes en mucha ni en poca cantidad a ningunos caciques ni principales ni comunidad ni yndios particulares por ninguna causa ni razon que sea de autos peticiones mandamientos escrituras proçesos ni carcelerias mas de los que se permiten en el aranzel que nuebamente se a fecho por la dicha nra audiencia so pena de lo pagar con el quatro tanto e porque nra real persona esta proveydo y mandado que las personas que estubieren en estos reynos e fueren casados en los de España y otras partes vayan a hazer vida con sus mugeres o las traigan consigo terneis muy particular cuidado de ynquirir y saver que pers^{as} de las suso dichas ay en la dicha ciudad y asiento y minas de Huancavelica y V^{a} de Oropesa y en sus terminos y juridicion para proveer como se haga y cumpla lo que su mag^{d} tiene ordenado e mandado proveyendo que las tales personas sin escusa ni dilacion alguna y si les dar prorrogacion ni licencia para residir en la dicha ciudad de Guamanga asiento e minas de Huancavelica y sus terminos se presenten ante nos en la dicha nra audiencia o ante el dicho nro visorrey dentro del termino que les dieredes dando fianças bastantes de lo que hazer asi donde no enbiarlos e yr presos a su costa executando en ellos y en las personas y bienes de sus fiadores las penas de las obligaciones y fianças que ubieren fecho las quales hareis meter //

/529v/ en nuestra real caxa e terneis muy particular cuidado en no consentir que en vro distrito ni juridicion aya ni anden bagamundos ni jugadores publicos e que entre los yndios no anden negros mulatos ni mestizos por los daños e agravios que les hazen e mal exemplo que les dan e no consentireis que por ninguna causa ni razon que sea el cavildo de la dicha ciudad enbie juez de comision fuera della ni bos lo enbiareis sino que quando algo acaeciere en vro distrito e juridicion vais en persona o proveays quien vaya sin que lleveis ni lleve ningun salario y aveis de estar advertido que no aveis de tener tratos ni grangerias ni minas en vro distrito por bos ni por ynterpositas personas ni ocupar en lo suso dicho ningunos yndios de vra juridicion con jornal ni sin el so pena de privacion de oficio e que no sereis mas proveydo en semejantes cargos de perdimiento de todos los bienes que asi truxeredes en los dichos tratos e grangerias ni os servireis de los yndios e yndias en vra casa si no fuere de los que llevaredes señalados por orden del dicho nro visorrey que estos podreis alquilar dandoles el jornal que les fuere tasado y asimismo vos mandamos que al principio de cada un año tomeis quenta a los oficiales de nra real hazienda de la dicha ciudad de Guamanga de lo que nos pertenece y otras cosas que fueren a su cargo e dentro de tercero dia cobrareis dellos los alcances que les hizieredes e los metereis luego en nra real caxa procediendo en ello con todo rigor enbiando un treslado de las dichas quentas y alcances que hizieredes ante el dicho nro visorrey las quales tomareis por la orden que hasta agora se han tomado y si en la dicha ciudad o V^{a} no oviere mas de dos oficiales tomareis vos una de las tres llaves que havemos mandado aya en cada caxa de nra real hazienda e no la aveis de poder entregar ni entregueis a ninguna persona sino fuere estando enfermo o ausente que en tal caso los podreis entregar a vro teniente y asimismo tomareis quenta a todos los tutores y curadores de menores que uviere en la dicha ciudad o villa y asiento de Guacavelica de los bienes que de los tales fueron a su cargo y dareis orden como los dichos bienes sean beneficiados y aprovechados y empleados en cosas que les sea util e provechoso a los dichos menores y cobrareis los alcances de los dichos tutores e curadores e hareis que se empleen en las cosas que dicho es lo qual cumplireis dentro de tres meses como llegaredes a la dicha ciudad e villa sin embargo de que no ayan espirado ni fenecido las dichas tutelas y curadorias y de lo que en ello hizieredes avisareis al dicho nro visorrey y demas de lo suso dicho aveis de tener muy particular cuydado de hazer cumplir y executar los asientos que el dicho nro visorrey en nro nombre ha tomado o tomare con los fatores e mineros del dicho asiento e minas de Huancavelica e que tengan de respeto e de ordinario la cantidad de pesos de oro que son obligados a tener para la paga de los jornales de los yndios que ban a trabajar en las dichas //

/f.530/ minas y si no los tubieren executareis en ellos las penas que estan puestas y asistireis a la paga de los dichos jornales que se ha de hazer a los dichos yndios cada semana porque ha de ser en vra presencia y ante el escrivano de cavildo que ha de dar fee de como no queda ningun yndio por pagar y si quedaren algunos lo qual no aveis de consentir se dira porque causa y vos les hareis pagar como se contiene en el dicho asiento de los dichos fatores y cada mes enbiareis testimonio al dicho nro visorrey de lo que en esto se haze so pena de cient pesos de oro la mitad para la nra camara y la otra mitad para el hospital del dicho asiento y denunciador por iguales partes en la queal dicha pena bos doy por condenado lo contrario haziendo e para que tengais mas cuidado de hazer lo que se os manda en esta provision al tiempo que se os entregen jurareis y os obligareis que terneis en vro poder vereis y leereis muchas vezes y guardareis y cumplireis y hareis guardar y cumplir a todo vro leal poder los capitulos de corregidores que con esta se os entregaran y asimismo las ordenanças provisiones e cedulas que por nos o por los nros visorreyes y governadores que han sido de los dichos reynos del Peru estan hechas e se hizieren para la dicha ciudad de Guamanga y Villa Rica de Oropesa y minas de Huancavelica y sus terminos y los asientos de los dichos mineros y fatores sin eçeder de la ynstrucion que por el dho nro visorrey se os diere en manera alguna e porque ynporta mucho al beneficio y aumento de nuestra hazienda e quintos reales que aya persona en la dicha villa de Oropesa y minas de Huancavelica que con nra autoridad haga guardar y cumplir las ordenanças e yntruciones que estan hechas y se hizieren para las dichas minas y los asientos que se an tomado y tomaren con los dichos mineros e fatores de los azogues os mandamos que asistais todo lo mas del tiempo que pudieredes en la dicha villa e minas y os damos comision y facultad para que nombreis teniente que resida en la dicha ciudad de Guamanga y en vro lugar y en nro nombre administre justicia en ella el qual ha de ser letrado e que concurra en el las partes y calidades que para usar el dicho oficio se requieren e para hazer el dicho nombramiento los aveis de comunicar con el dicho nro visorrey para que el vea si es persona qual conviene y lo confirme y por el travajo e ocupacion que aveis de tener en el uso y exercicio de los dichos oficios ayais y lleveis tres mil y dozientos pesos de plata ensayada y marcada los quales mandamos bos sean dados y pagados en cada un año de los que usaredes los dichos oficios desde el dia que os presentaredes en el //

/f.530v/ cavildo de la dicha ciudad de Guamanga de nra caxa real de la dicha ciudad y villa de Huancavelica de seis en seis meses en cada paga la mitad con tanto que de los dichos tres mil y duzientos pesos se de y pague al dicho vro teniente que ha de residir en la dicha ciudad de Guamanga seiscientos pesos de plata corriente por razon de la ocupacion e travajo que ha de tener en el dicho oficio que con vras cartas de pago e traslado autorizado desta nra provision que se ha se asentar en los libros reales mandamos se le reciban y pasen en quenta a los oficiales reales de la dicha ciudad y villa lo que asi bos dieren y pagaren los quales meternan en si de tercio postrero del año en que se os oviere de tomar residencia e no os lo daran ni pagaran hasta tanto que la dicha residencia se aya visto y determinado por la dicha nra audiencia y en ella se provea lo que del dicho tercio se ha de hazer so pena a los dichos oficiales que lo contrario hizieren que lo pagaran otra vez por sus personas y bienes y los unos ni los otros no fagades ende al por alguna manera so pena de la nra merced y de quinientos pesos de oro para la nra camara. Dada en los Reyes a diez y siete dias del mes de abril de mill e qui^{o}s y ochenta y seis años. El Conde del Villar. Yo Melchor Perez de Mariduena escrivano mayor de la governacion del Piru por su mag^{d} catolica lo fize escrivir por su mandado con acuerdo de su visorrey registrada. Juan de Gastiçaval chanciller Juan de Aliaga.

En la ciudad del Cuzco a diez dias del mes de março de mill e quinientos y ochenta y nueve años yo Gaspar de Prado scriv^{o} del rey nro s^{or} pu^{co} de la dha ciudad por ausencia de Antonio Sanchez scriv^{o} pu^{co} del num^{o} dellos saque e hize sacar este traslado de su original el va çierto e verdad^{ro} corregido y concertado con el dho original que ques en poder del comendador Martin Garcia de Loyola t^{o}s Antonio Muriel y Joan Perez e Diego Ruiz residentes en la dha ciudad. Y lo fize screvir y aqui mi signo

Gaspar de Prado (rubrica)

/f.531/ En la ciudad del Cuzco en ocho dias del mes de março de mill /roto/ ochenta e nueve años ante Luis de Espinosa teniente corregidor por /roto/ de Porras y Santillan correg^{or} e justicia m^{or} en esta dha ciudad y su jur^{on} por /roto/ rey nuestro señor e por ante mi Gaspar de Prado escribano del rey /roto/ señor pu^{co} y del numero de la dha ciudad se presento la peticion siguiente.

Martin Garcia de Loyola digo que a mi me conviene sacar un t^{do} de una sentencia que Garcia de Paredes dio en la resid^{a} que me tomo de corre^{or} de Guamanga y Guancavelica questa en el proceso que con el hago pres^{on} signado de Juan Bascones scriv^{o} pu^{co} del as^{to} de Guancavelica.

A V. M. sup^{co} se haga y se me de un tr^{do} o dos demas que aga /ilegible/ y pido justicia.

Martin Garcia de Loyola.

El dho teniente m^{do} se le un treslado o mas de la dha sentencia como lo pide por esta peticion.

E yo el dho Gaspar de Prado scrivano en cumplimiento de lo proveydo por el dho teniente saque e hize sacar de un proceso quel dho comendador Martin Garcia de Loyola trajo ante mi el scrivº un traslado de la dha sentencia que en la dha peticion se haze minsion con la pronunciacion y notificacion que dize ansi //

/f.531v/ El pleyto y causa de residencia que por comy[on] del rey nro señor sea causado contra Martin Garcia de Loyola del avito y cavallero de Calatrava corregidor que a sido en esta Villa Rica de Oropesa minas de Guancavelica y de la ciudad de Guamanga y su distrito visto el presente proceso y los descargos fechos por el dho comendador Martin Garcia de Loyola y los demas autos del y lo que ver conbino. Fallo que devo de absolver y absuelbo dar y doy por libre y quieto al dho Martin Garcia de Loyola de los cargos contra el fecho en esta causa y de todo lo demas contra el en este proceso contenido y declaro aver el suso dho usado y exercido el dho ofº de corregidor bien justa y rectam[te] como fiel ministro del rey nro señor y como tal en el tiempo que exercio el dho oficio aber acrecentado y aumentado la real hazienda de su mag[d] en mucha cantidad de pesos de oro por su buena solicitud yndustria y cuidado que tubo en la labor y beneficio de las minas de azogue desta villa de Guancabelica y averlos puesto en estado que este presente año la real hazienda terna dellas muchos aprovechamientos como paresce por los autos deste dho proceso por todo lo qual le declaro por tal bueno recto y fiel juez ministro de su mag[d] y que merece quel rey nuestro señor y su visorrey en su real nombre y sus ministros le hagan mucha mrd y le provean en oficios muy ynportantes y de calidad y cantidad porque en ellos servira a su mag[d] como fiel ansi lo declaro pronuncio y mando sin costas. Garcia de Paredes. En la villa de Oropesa a diez y nueve dias del mes de agosto de mill e quiºs y ochenta e siete años el capitan Garcia de Paredes corregidor y juez de residencia desta villa dio y pronuncio la sentencia de atras contenida y la mando notificar a las partes. tºs Diego Ruiz Pardo Diego Holguin residentes en esta dha villa ante mi Alonso Lopez escrivano.

La dha sentencia como en ella se contiene al dho Martin Garcia de Loyola en su persona y dello doy fee siendo tºs presentes Pedro Cavallero Miguel Merino de Llicana Fran[co] de Yrarraçaval residentes en la dha villa ante mi Alonso Lopez escrivano e yo Fran[co] de Bascones escrivano de su mag[d] y publico desta Villa Rica de Oropesa lo fize escrevir e fize mio signo en testimonio de verdad. Francisco de Bascones escrivano publico el qual dho traslado va cierto e verdadero corregido y concertado con su original que quedo en poder del dho com[or] Loyola en el Cuzco a diez dias del mes de março de mill e quiºs y ochenta y nueve aºs siendo tºs Joan Perez Antº Muriel y Diº Ruiz e M[co] Villadon y Fize mi signo.

Gaspar de Prado (rubrica)

/f.532/ La parte de doña Beatriz Coya presento ynterrogatº en el pleito con el fiscal

Por las preguntas siguientes se exsaminen los testigos que se presentaren por parte de Martin Garcia de Loyola caballero de la orden de Calatrava y doña Beatriz Coya su mujer en el pleito que trata con el fiscal de su mag[d] sobre los doscientos y treynta e un yndios del valle de Yucay de que el visitador frey Pedro Gutierrez desposeyo a la dha doña Beatriz e frutos dellos.

/1/ Primeramente si conocen a las partes y si conoscieron a don Diego Sayre Topa y a doña Maria Coya su mujer nieto de Guayna Capac señor que fue destos reynos y si tienen noticia de los dhos doscientos y treynta y un yndios de que el dho visitador desposeyo a la dha doña Beatriz que son de mas y allende de los otros trecientos y treynta yndios sobre que trata otro pleyto.

/2/ Si saven que Sayre Topa Mango Capac Yupangui fue hijo de Mango Ynga y nieto del dho Gayna Capac y por fin y muerte de su padre y demas hermanos que tubo se averiguo por don Francisco Piçarro governador que fue destos reynos que el dho Mango Ynga era el legitimo subcesor destos reynos y a quien derechamente le pertenescian y como a tal le dio la borla de que usavan los señores deste reyno.

/3/ Si saven que el dho Sayre Topa fue el hijo mayor y primogenito del dho Mango Ynga y por tal fue avido y tenido y subcedio al dho su padre en todos sus bienes y demas cosas que tubo y le pertenescen por su muerte los yndios de Vilcabamba y demas provincias a ellas subjetas que estavan debaxo del dominio del dho Mango Ynga obedecieron por su señor natural al dho Sayre Topa y como a tal le dieron la dha borla e ynsignia de rey de que usaban los señores deste reyno.

/4/ Si saven que aviendo el dho Mango Ynga dado la ovidiencia a su mag[d] estando en la ciudad del Cuzco esperando la mrd que su mag[d] le avia de hazer algunos spañoles poco temerosos de dios y menos celosos del serviº de su mag[d] hizieron muchos malos tratamientos al dha Ynga tratandole mal de palabra y obras especialmente que un spañol le dio una bofetada y otros le tomaron sus mugeres y ubo español que por menospreciarle le meo en el rostro.

/5/ Si saven que el dho Mango Ynga por causa de los dhos malos tratamientos //
/f.532v/ se retiro a la provincia de Vilcabamba con mas de veinte mil yndios de guerra estando en ella y governando en aquella sazon estos reynos el lic[do] Gasca procuro con mucha ynstancia sacarle de paz y para este efecto le ymbio provision en nombre de su mag[d] de muchos ofrecimientos y mercedes que se le harian en su real nombre si saliese a dar la obidiencia y vasallaje a su mag[d].

6. Si saven que visto por el dho Mango Ynga los malos tratamientos que havia rescibido y que estaba desposeydo y no se podia sustentar en el Peru conforme a su calidad y señorio y que en Vilcabamba tenia mucho numero de yndios asi de los que con el se avian entrado como de otras provincias que le estaban subjetos no quiso salir de paz antes se estubo en la dha provincia señoreando y governando los yndios della como su señor natural.

7. Si saven que todo el tiempo que el dho Mango Ynga bibio sus capitanes ynquietavan y robaban y salteavan los pueblos de yndios convecinos de las dhas provincias de Vilcabamba y a los spañoles y otras personas que caminavan desde la ciudad de Guamanga al Cuzco.

8. Si saven que aviendo subcedido el dho Sayre Topa al dho su padre y estando en el señorio de la dha provincia de Vilcabamba continuo los dhos robos e ynquietudes por sus capitanes en tal manera que perturbaba la paz y quietud destos reynos y la conbersion de los naturales y no se podian andar los caminos.

9. Si saven que entendido por su mag[d] del emperador don Carlos nro señor lo suso dho y los muchos ynconvenientes que dello se seguian y esperavan seguir por cartas y provisiones encargo a los visorreyes don Antonio de Mendoza y a otros governadores que procurasen atraer de paz a su ovidiencia y servi[o] al dho Ynga y le escrivio sus cartas perdonandole los daños y robos que avia hecho y le ofrecio las tierras que avian sido de su padre que valen mas de cinquenta mill pesos de renta en cada un año y otras mercedes.

10 Si saven que aviendo fallescido el dho vizorrey don Antonio de Mendoça antes de poner en efecto y execucion lo contenido en las dhas cedulas y provisiones le subçedio en el govierno destos rey[o]s el marques de Cañete el qual tubo cedula de su mag[d] para //
/f.533/ cumplir lo que estava cometido al dho don Antonio de Mendoça su antecesor.

11 Si saven que luego que el dho marques llego a este reyno pareciendole que el mas ynportante servi[o] que podia hazer a su mag[d] era sacar de paz y traer a su real obidiencia al dho Sayre Topa scrivio a doña Beatriz Mango Capac su tia para que persuadiese al dho su sobrino a que saliese de paz y diese la obidiencia a su mag[d].

12. Si saven que la dha doña Beatriz en cumplimiento de lo suso dho ymbio a Juan Sierra Legiçamo su hijo y primo del dho Sayre Topa a tratar con el la dha salida y el dho Juan Sierra lo hizo y lo trato con el dho Sayre Topa el qual le dio muestras de la voluntad que tenia de dar la obidiencia a su mag[d] si el dho marques en su real nombre le hiziese mercedes pa la sustentacion de su persona casa y estado y de los muchos deudos que tenia.

13. Si saven que el dho Juan Sierra de Leguiçamo venio a la ciudad de los Reyes y dio quenta al dho marques de lo suso dho y el dho marques con parescer de don Geronimo de Loaysa arçobispo destos rey[o]s y de los oydores desta real audiencia acordo de ymbiar a fray Melchor de los Reyes y a fray Pedro de Arona religiosos principales de la orden de Santo Domingo para que tratasen con el dho Sayre Topa la dha salida.

14. Si saven que el dho Marques para mober el animo del dho Sayre topa y que tubiese efecto su salida le escrivio rogandole con mucho encarecimi[o] que saliese a este rey[o] de paz y que su mag[d] le daria un estado y señorio con que se pudiese sustentar y en el entretanto el en nombre de su mag[d] le haria muchas mercedes y le ymbio un presente de mucha ynportancia.

15. Si saven que los dhos religiosos y con ellos el dho Ju[o] Sierra de Leguiçamo entraron a la dha provincia de Vilcabamba a rogar y persuader al dho Ynga lo suso dho y le ofrecieron que el dho marques en nombre de su mag[d] le daria diez y ocho mil pesos ensayados de renta en cada un año para se entretener y sustentar en el entretanto que su mag[d] le dava el dho estado y señorio y entendido por //
/f.533v/ el dho Ynga determino de ymbiar como ymbio sus capitanes y embaxada al dho marques para que resumidamente asentase con ellos lo que con el se avia de guardar y cumplir y que mercedes se le avian de hazer.

16. Si saven que los dhos capitanes dieron la dha embaxada al dho marques el qual en nombre de su mag[d] y aprobando el ofrecimi[o] y asiento que avian tomado los dhos frailes en su nombre con el dho Sayre Topa dixo a los dhos capitanes y asento con ellos que lo acetaron en nombre del dho Ynga de le dar para el y para sus hijos y descendientes perpetuamente para siempre jamas por bia de mayorazgo en el entretanto que como dho es su mag[d] le diese el dho estado y señorio el repartimi[o] que tubo en encomienda Fran[co] Hernandez Giron y el valle de Yucay que tubo en encomienda don Fran[co] Piçarro hijo del marques don Francisco Pizarro questavan vacos con todo lo a ello subjeto segun que los suso dhos lo avian poseydo con que saliese dentro de seis meses a dar la ovidiencia a su mag[d]

17. Si saven que a la sazon que se hizo el dho ofrecimi[o] al dho Sayre Topa valian los tributos de los dhos repartimientos mas de veinte mil pesos en cada un año los quales el dho marques ofrecio en nombre de su mag[d] que valdrian de renta los dhos tributos y se le sustentarian para siempre jamas hasta que su mag[d] le hiziese otras mayores mercedes.

18 Si saven que los dhos capitanes bolbieron a la dha provincia de Vilcabamba con la razon del dho concierto y ofrecimi[o] y aviendola dado al dho Sayre Topa se dispuso a salir y salio a este dho rey[o] con su muger y capitanes y se presento ante le dho marques en esta ciudad dentro de los dhos seis meses.

19. Si saven que entendiendo el dho Ynga que se cumpliria con el lo tratado y concertado dexo en la dha provincia de Vilcabamba mas de veinte mil yndios que le estaban subjetos y tributavan asi naturales de la dha provincia de Vilcabamba como del Capacati y Manaries y Momori y Pilcoçones y otros muchos que los tributos y renta dellos le valian en cada un año mucha mayor suma y cantidad que la que se ofrecio a le sustentar el dho marques y de que le dio titulo

/f.534/ 20. Si saven que entendido por el dho marques la salida del dho Ynga y que llegava a esta ciudad la vispera de los Reyes del año de cinquenta y ocho mando salir a rescivir al dho Ynga a toda la ciudad con el estandarte que sacan aquel dia y el mesmo marques lo rescivio en las casas reales y le hizo ospedar y le puso casa destado mostrando grandisimo contentami^o^ con su llegada y estimandola por el mayor servi^o^ que a su mag^d^ podia hazer en este rey^o^ como diversas vezes lo dixo el dho marques.

21. Si saven que el dho marques cumpliendo en nombre de su mag^d^ el trato y concierto que tenia puesto con el dho Ynga y visto que el dho Ynga de su parte avia cumplido le dio provision titulo y encomienda de los dhos repartimi^o^s y tomo la posesion dellos y los tubo y gozo en su vida como los avian gozado y tenido sus antecesores libres de toda pension.

22. Si saven que el dho marques dio titulo de adelantado del dho valle de Yucay al dho Sayre Topa como paresçe por el titulo con lo qual el dho Ynga se bautiço y dio la ovidiencia y vasallaje a su mag^d^.

23. si saven que con los yndios que dexo el dho Ynga la dha provincia se poblo en nombre de su mag^d^ la ciudad de San Fran^co^ de la Bitoria en que ay governador y muchos vecinos ricos a sido una ciudad de mucha importancia para la sustentacion de la ciudad del Cuzco y para la paz y quietud destos rey^o^s.

24. Si saven y entienden los testigos que si el dho Ynga por algun camino entendiera que lo se la avia ofrecido no se le avia de cumplir y sustentar no saliera de paz de la dha provincia y para sacalle quando por vien no quisiera fuera muy dificultuoso y no se puediere hazer sin grandisimo gasto y costa asi de parte de su mag^d^ como de los vezinos e yndios deste rey^o^.

25. Si saven y entienden los testigos ques muy justo y devido y conviene para el descargo de la real conciencia de su mag^d^ que se guarden al dho Sayre Topa y a sus hijos y descendientes lo que con el se asento y capitulo y se le de el estado y señorio que se le prometio y no se le a dado y se le hagan otras muy mayores mercedes en las tierras de sus pasados en recompensa de tantos //
/f.534v/ millones de oro y plata perlas esmeraldas y otras muchas cosas que su mag^d^ y sus vasallos de la corona de Castilla an tenido y tienen y tendran deste rey^o^.

26. Si saven que el dho Sayre Topa quando se bautiço tomo por nombre don Diego y se caso ligitimamente segun orden de la santa madre iglesia de Roma con doña Maria Cusiguarcay su hermana con quien estava antes casado conforme a la costumbre de los Yngas qe eran y se casaban con sus hermanos y los que nacian de semejante matrimonio llamavan Capa Ynga que quiere dezir solo señor con la qual estubo casado y bibieron y hizieron bida maridable como marido y muger.

27. Si saven que doña Beatriz Coya muger legitima de Martin Garcia de Loyola cavallero del abito de Calatrava es hija legitima y natural del dho don Diego Sayre Topa y de doña Maria Cusiguarcay y su unica heredera y no tiene ni dexo otra alguna ni hijo varon.

28. Si saven que por fin y muerte del dho don Diego Sayre Topa la dha doña Beatriz Coya subcedio en todos los vienes derechos y aciones y encomienda y demas cosas que tubo y poseyo y pertenescen al dho su padre y por la costumbre que se tenia de subceder en el señorio el que hera hijo de hermano y her^na^ el llamarse solo Ynga y señor subcedio en todo ello la dha doña Beatriz como tal hija ligitima de dos hermanos.

29. Si saven que por el año de setenta y uno y setenta y dos que fue la tpo que don Fran^co^ de Toledo visoreyy que fue destos reynos cometio al doctor fre P^o^ Gutierrez la visita del valle de Yucay y otros pueblos del repartimi^o^ de la dha doña Beatriz era menor y estava debajo de la tutoria y curadoria de Tilano de Anaya por poder que para ello tenia de don Diego Titu Cusi Yupangui su tio y curador principal questava en la provincia de Vilcabamba.

30. Si saven que al tiempo que el dho doctor fre P^o^ Gutierrez començo la visita del dho valle de Yucay el dho Tilano de Anaya estava ausente de la ciudad del Cuzco y del dho repartimi^o^ en las montañas de Vilcabamba donde avia ydo por mandado del dho visorrey a procurar sacar de paz al dho Titu Cusi y donde le mataron.

/f.535/ 31. Si saven que el dho doctor frey Pedro Gutierrez hizo la visita del dho valle sin citar ni llamar a la dha doña Beatriz ni a su curador ni estar persona de su parte presente a la dha visita y numeracion de yndios como por ella pareze que pido se muestre a los testigos o que se refieran a ella.

32. Si saven que quando el dho frey Pedro Gutierrez fue a hazer la visita del dho repartimiento y la platica que se hizo a los dhos yndios entre otras cosas les dio a entender que los yndios que fuesen yanaconas no avian de tributar y entendido por ellos que avian de ser reservados de tributo y sus caciques que quedando reservados se podian servir dellos no embargante que eran yndios tributarios dixeron al dho visitador que eran yanaconas.

33. Si saven que para hazer el dho visitador la numeracion que hizo y para declarar en ella por yanaconas los yndios del dcho repartimi^o^ que eran tributarios no hizo ningun genero de averiguacion mas de solo tomar el padron que Diego Escudero cura del dho repartimi^o^ tenia hecho y por el dho padron sin mas averiguacion hizo la dha visita.

34. Si saven que los dozientos y treinta y un yndios sobre que es este pleyto son distintos e separados de los otros trezientos y treinta y dos sobre que la dha doña Beatriz tiene mobido pleyto al fiscal como pareçe por las m^{a}s que pido se muestre a los testigos.

35. Si saven que Guayna Capac Ynga señor que fue destos rey^{o}s tubo su recamara en el valle de Yucay y los yndios del asi naturales como los mitimaes le servian y a sus mugeres e hijos de yanaconas beneficiandole sus chacaras y haziendo otras cosas como lo hazian todos los yndios deste rey^{o} los quales todos solo tributavan en servicios personales y no en otra cosa.

36. Si saven que al tiempo que los españoles conquistaron la ciudad del Cuzco el marques don Fran^{co} Piçarro tomo para si y para su servi^{o} todo el valle de Yucay e yndios del asi naturales como mitimaes y los dhos yndios sirvieron al dho marques pagandole el tributo en //
/f.535v/ servicios personales beneficiandole las chacaras de coca que tenia en los Andes llamadas Tono Yanavire Paucarbamba Yanatay y otras digan lo que saven.

37. Si saven que en el dho tpo los yndios deste rey^{o} no tenian ni pagavan tasa conocida y que en lugar de tributar davan a sus encomenderos servi^{o} personal como lo tenian de costumbre en tiempo del Ynga para sus chacaras y casa y otras cosas y esto era comunmente en todos los yndios deste rey^{o} y ese mismo tributo pagavan los yndios naturales y mitimaes del valle de Yucay que pagavan los otros sin pagar diferentes tributos unos que otros ni otros que otros.

38. Si saven que por muerte del dho marques don Fran^{co} Piçarro subcedieron en el dho repartimi^{o} e yndios del dho valle de Yucay don Fran^{co} Piçarro su hijo y por ausencia y muerte se pusieron los dhos yndios en cabeza de su mag^{d} y en el un tpo y en el otro los dhos yndios pagavan el tributo en servi^{o} personal beneficiando las chacaras que antes veneficiaban y acudiendo con el fruto dellas y con los demas servi^{os} y cosas que solian dar al dho marques en el un tiempo al dho don Fran^{co} y en el otro a los oficiales reales.

39. Si saven que por virtud del asiento que el dho marques de Cañete tomo con el dho don Diego Sayre Topa de que se ha hecho mencion el suso dho en su vida tubo y poseyo el dho repartimi^{o} de Yucay e yndios del asi mitimays como naturales y se sirvio dellos como los demas sus antecesores y por aver ya en este tiempo tasa cobraba la tasa dellos segun el repartimi^{o} que para la pagar hazian los caciques del dho valle y por su muerte doña Beatriz su hija subcedio en el dho repartimi^{o} ella e sus tutores criados y mayordomos cobraron la tasa del dho repartimi^{o} hasta la ultima visita.

40. Si saven que los yndios contenidos en la memoria en esta causa presentada que pido se muestre y lea a los testigos son naturales y mitimaes del dho valle y son de los yndios que siempre acudieron //
/f.536/ a pagar el dho tributo y tasa y los que no son ellos mesmos son hijos de yndios tributarios del dho repartimi^{o} y fueron subjetos a don Fran^{co} Chilche y don Garcia Quispi Capi caciques principales del.

41. Si saven que la causa de estar declarado por la visita que unos yndios pagavan un tributo y otros no unas mas y otros menos no es por ser mas libres de tributo los unos que los otros sino por que los caciques a cuyo cargo estava hazer la distribucion de la gruesa de la tasa antes de la ultima visita por sus fines hechaban a un indio mas tributo que a otro sin aver mas causa para la uno que para lo otro y a unos yndios reservaban de todo punto y a otros cargavan lo que aquellos reservados avian de pagar sin mas consideracion de su voluntad y fines.

42. Si saven que don Garcia Quispicapi cacique principal de los yndios naturales del dho valle y don Fran^{co} Chilche cacique principal de los yndios mitimaes del q^{do} hazia el repartimi^{o} de la gruesa de la tasa reservaba a muchos de los yndios contenidos en la dha memoria a unos por ser hermanos y padres deudos de yndias con quien ellos estavan amancebados y casados y a otros por servirse dellos en sus chacaras y otras granjerias dellos y sus hijos mugeres y hermanos.

43. Si saven que por las razones contenidas en las preguntas antes desta los dhos caciques y otros yndios del dho repartimi^{o} llamavan y siempre an llamado a los dhos yndios reservados por los dhos caciques yanaconas y este es el nombre que comunmente tienen todos los yndios que sirven a otros como lo hazian estos a los dhos caciques y a sus mugeres e hijos y hermanos aunque sean yndios tributarios como estos lo son.

44. Si saven que por auto del visorrey don Fran^{co} de T^{do} la dha doña Beatriz fue desposeyda de los dhos yndios sin ser oyda ni vencida ni hazer pleito con ella ni con sus curadores ni con otra persona alguna en su nombre ni el auto que sobre ello se probeyo se le notifico a ninguno dellas sino como menor e yndefensa fue desposeyda de los dhos yndios.

/f.536v/ 45. Si saven que por razon de aver quitado al dho repartimi^{o} los dhos yndios y los demas que se le quitaron sobre que esta mobido otro pleyto y por aver rebasado los tributos que antiguam^{te} pagavan los dhos yndios los tributos del dho repartimi^{o} an benido a menos de tal manera que no lo cobra el dia de oy la dha doña Beatriz cinco mil pesos de todos los tributos de los repartimi^{o}s que le encomendo el marques de Cañete.

46. Si saven que Martin Garcia de Loyola marido de la dha doña Beatriz cavallero notorio de la orden de Calatrava y una de las personas principales deste rey^{o} de mucha discrecion y entendimi^{o} y tal a quien su mag^{d} por su real provision tiene encomendada la governacion de las provincias del Rio de la Plata.

47. Si saven que por la satisfaccion que tubo el visorrey don Fran^{co} de Toledo de la persona y discrecion del dho Martin Garcia de Loyola le cometio la visita de la ciudad del Cuzco y la de la ciudad de la Plata y la revista de la Villa Imperial de Potosi y el corregimi^{o} de la provincia de los Charcas y exercito los dhos oficios con el cuydado y diligencia que de su satisfaccion se tuvo.

48. Si saven que el dho visorrey eligio al dho Martin Garcia de Loyola por uno de los capitanes que fueron a la jornada de Vilcabamba donde sirvio a su mag^{d} a su costa tan aventajadamente que todas las faciones de importancia que en ellas se hizieron hasta la prision del Ynga y de sus capitanes mas principales las hizo el dho Martin Garcia de Loyola con su compañia.

49. Si saven que por el dho visorrey fue elexido por su teniente general de todo el distrito de la audiencia de los Charcas donde exerciendo el dho cargo hizo justicia de Rengifo y de Borrero personas que trataron de alborotar la dha provincia contra el servi^{o} de su mag^{d} y ultimam^{te} fue nombrado por la real audiencia de los Reyes por general de la mar //
/f.537/ del Sur en tiempo de noticia de corsarios y fue al rey^{o} de tierra firme con la mas gruesa armada que se ha hecho en la mar del Sur donde se llevo a su mag^{d} y particulares mas de tres millones de plata todo a su costa y mision con gran gasto de su haz^{da} y riesgo de su persona.

50. Si saven que le dho visorrey entre otras cosas que cometio al dho Martin Garcia de Loyola por su entendimi^{o} fue el asistir a los acuerdos de haz^{da} real de las provincias de los Charcas mandando a los oficiales reales della que no hiziesen ninguno de importancia sin su asistencia por el mucho fruto que espero que dello se seguiria a la haz^{da} y quintos reales.

51. Si saven que el dho Martin Garcia de Loyola en el tpo que tubo a su cargo la dha provincia de los Charcas acrecento a la haz^{da} real mas cantidad de un millon de ducados porque en el arrendami^{o} de los azogues del año de setenta y nueve acrecento mas de novecientos mil pesos porque no hallandose persona que quisiere tomar el dho arrendami^{to} por el orden de los arrendamientos pasados el dho Martin Garcia de Loyola en el arrendami^{to} del dho año y capitulaciones que en el hizo causo el dho acrecentami^{to} y en consumir la plata corriente que avia en la dha provincia y hazella fundir y quintar y que cesase como ceso de todo punto negocio que se avia pretendido por los visorreyes pasados y por todos los corregidores mucha instancia y no se avia podido hazer antes se sigue de ynteres a la haz^{da} real mas cantidad de cinquenta mil pesos.

52. Si saven que demas de los dhos aprovechamientos que se siguieron en razon de lo contenido en la pregunta antes desta por yndustria y medio del dho Martin Garcia de Loyola se acrecento en la casa de moneda de Potosi dos hornacas sin costa ninguna de su mag^{d} que demas de lo que vale en senoraje //
/f.537v/ que pertenece costaran a su mag^{d} si a su costase huvieran de hazer mas de dize mil pesos.

53. Si saven que el dho Martin Garcia de Loyola acudiendo al servi^{o} de su mag^{d} todo el tpo que tubo a su cargo la dha provincia de los Charcas despues de aver en fin de cada un año recogido y enbiado a su mag^{d} toda su haz^{da} real de cada un año para que se pudiese prevaler en sus grandes necesidades de mas hz^{da} de lo suya procuraba de inbiar y enbiaba mas de cien mil pesos en cada un año que recogia y pedia prestados a los vezinos de la dha provincia y amigos suyos en que hazia muy particular servi^{o} e importante a su mag^{d}.

54. Si saven y entienden los testigos que el dho Martin Garcia de Loyola en todo lo que se ha ofrecido a tenido muy gran lealtad al servi^{o} de su mag^{d} y es muy celoso de su real servi^{o} y tiene tanta calidad y descricion y suficiencia persona y autoridad que podra servir a su mag^{d} en qualquier cosa de ymportancia que le encomiende tambien como el que mejor lo pudiera hazer en este rey^{o} y es avil y capaz y cave en el qualquiera gran mrd que su mag^{d} le haga y no esta gratificado de sus servi^{os}.

Si saven que todo lo suso dho es publico y not^{o}. ba testado veinte no bala y entre renglones diez/ Cusiguaman su hermana/bala.

El ll^{do} Falcon (rubrica) Jhoan Sanchez.

En la ciudad de los Reyes en v^{te} e cinco dias del mes de otubre de mill e qui^{o}s y ochenta e cinco años ante los señores presidente e oydores //
/f.538/ desta real audi^{a} estando en audiencia publica se presento este ynterrogatorio y por los dhos señores vista le ovieron por presentada en quanto es pertinente y mandaron que los t^{o}s se exsaminen por el estado y ubo.

Montoya (rubrica)

/f.538v/ P^{o} de Arona en 13 de noviembre 1585 a^{o}s juro y dixo.
Garci Gonzales Rubin en 3 de marzo 1586.
Bartolome Diaz en dho dia.
Fran^{co} Heraudez Palacio en 4 de abril.
P^{o} R^{o} Osorio el dho dia.
Fran^{co} de Yllescas el dho dia.
Fran^{co} de Camargo el dho dia.

En cinco de abril. Ju^{o} Sanchez de los Rios pro^{or} de Loyola.
Julian de Arellano. R^{o} de Bustillo en 4 de julio de 1587.

El capitan Fran^{co} de Caceres.
Di^{o} de Ocampo.
Diego de Agüero.
Sancho de Rivera.
Martin de Ampuero.
Fran^{co} Ampuero.

En 6 de abril.
Don P^{o} de Cordova Guzman.
Lorenço de Arrova.
Al^{o} Ylto de Molina.
San Juan de Balustre y
Ju^{o} Alvarez Maldonado.
Juan de Meudra.
Alvaro Lopez Barriales.
Al^{o} Lopez Barriales.
Fran^{co} Gutierrez caballeria.
Marcos Cano.
Ju^{o} de Bispina
Don Lugo de Garzo.

/f.539/ En la ciudad de los Reyes en tres dias del mes de novi^{e} de mill quinientos y ochenta y cinco años ante mi el presente secretario de camara parecio presente Martin Garcia de Loyola cavallero del avito de Calatrava e presento por t^{go} para la provança que haze en el pleyto y causa que en esta real audiencia trata con el lic^{do} Alvaro de Caravajal fiscal de su mag^{d} sobre los yanaconas del valle de Yucay al padre fray Pedro de Arona de la horden de Santo Domingo el qual juro en forma de dr^{o} por la horden de San Pedro y San Pablo y prometio de decir verdad de lo que supiere y le fuere preguntado en este caso para ques presentado por t^{go} el qual a la conclusion del dho juramento dixo si juro y amen siendo t^{gos} Franco Garcia y Di^{o} de Leytona.

Ante mi Jhoan de Montoya.

En la ciudad de los Reyes en tres dias del mes de novi^{e} de mill quinientos y ochenta y siete [*sic*] a^{o}s el dho capitan Martin Garcia de Loyola para en la dha provança presento por t^{go} a Garci Gonçales Rubin del qual tome el devido juramento en forma devida de dr^{o} //
/f.539v/ por dios y por Santa Maria so cargo del qual prometio de dezir verdad de lo que supiere y le fuere preguntado siendo tg^{os} Fran^{co} Garcia y P^{o} Gonçales.

Ante mi Jhoan Montoya.

En la ciudad de los Reyes en el dho dia tres de março del dho año el dho capitan Martin Garcia de Loyola para en la dha provança presento por t^{o} a Bartolome Dias de Pineda del qual tome y recibi juramento en forma devida de dr^{o} so cargo del qual prometio de dezir verdad segun deste e mas y dello doy fee.

Ante mi Jhoan Montoya.

En la ciudad de los Reyes en quatro dias del mes de abril del dho año de mill y qui^{o}s y ochenta y siete a^{o}s el dho capitan Martin Garcia de Loyola para la dha provança presento por tg^{o} a Fran^{co} Hernandez de Palacios del qual tome e recibi juramento en forma de dr^{o} segun que es e de demas so cargo del qual prometio de dezir verdad en lo que fuere preguntado.

Ante mi Jhoan Montoya.

/f.540/ En la ciudad de los Reyes el dho quatro de abril del dho año el dho capitan Martin Garcia de Loyola para la dha provança presento por tg^{o} a Pedro Rios Osorio del qual tome e recibi juramento en forma devida de dr^{o} so cargo del qual prometio de dezir verdad de lo que supiere y fuere preguntado y dello doy fee.

Ante mi Jhoan Montoya.

En la ciudad de los Reyes en dicho dia quatro de abril del dho año de ochenta y cinco el dho capitan Martin Garcia de Loyola pa la dha informacion presento por tg^{o} a Fran^{co} de Yllescas del qual tome e recibi juramento en forma devida de dr^{o} segun que es este e mas so cargo del qual prometio de dezir verdad de lo que supiere y fuere preguntado y dello doy fee.

Ante mi Jhoan de Montoya.

El dicho dia quatro de abril del dho año el dho capitan Martin Garcia de Loyola para la dha informacion presento por tg^{o} a Fran^{co} de Camargo del qual tome e recibi juram^{to} en forma devida de dr^{o} segun queste e mas so cargo del qual prometio de dezir verdad de lo que supiere e le fuere preguntado y dello doy fee.

Ante mi Jhoan de Montoya.

/f.540v/ En cinco dias del mes de abril del dho año de ochenta y seis a^{o}s el dho capitan Martin Garcia de Loyola pa la dha informacion presento por tg^{o} a Julian de Arencano del qual tome e recibi juramento en forma devida de dr^{o} so cargo del qual prometio de dezir verdad de lo que supiere y fuere preguntado y dello doy fee.

Ante mi Jhoan de Montoya.

El dicho dia cinco de abril del dho año de ochenta y seis el dho capitan Martin Garcia de Loyola pa la dha informacion presento por tg^{o} al capitan Fran^{co} de Caceres del qual tome e recibi juramento en forma devida de dr^{o} segun que es este e mas so cargo del qual prometio de dezir verdad de lo que supiere y fuere preguntado y dello doy fee. Va testado de nas no bala.

Ante mi Jhoan de Montoya.

El dicho dia cinco de abril de ochenta y seis el dho capitan Martin Garcia de Loyola pa la dha informacion presento por tg^{o} al capitan Di^{o} de Ocampo del qual tome e recibi juramento en forma devida de dr^{o} segun que los demas so cargo del qual prometio de dezir verdad de lo que supiere y fuere preguntado y dello doy fee.

Ante mi Jhoan de Montoya.

/f.541/ El dicho dia cinco de abril de ochenta y /roto/ el dho capitan Martin Garcia de Loyola pa la dha informacion presento por tg^{o} a Diego de Aguero del qual tome e recibi juramento en forma devida de dr^{o} segun que a los demas so cargo del qual tome e recibi juramento y debaxo del dho jurmanento prometio de dezir verdad de lo que supiere y fuere preguntado y dello doy fee.

Ante mi Jhoan de Montoya.

En el dho dia cinco de abril para la dha informacion el dho capitan Martin Garcia de Loyola presento por tg^{o} a Sancho de Ribera del qual tome y recibi juramento en forma devida de dr^{o} so cargo del qual prometio de dezir verdad de lo que supiere y fuere preguntado y dello doy fee.

Ante mi Jhoan de Montoya.

En la ciudad de los Reyes el dho dia cinco de abril del dho año para la informacion presento por tg^{o} el dho capitan Martin Garcia de Loyola a Martin de Ampuero vz^{o} y regidor desta ciudad del qual tome e recibi juramento en forma de dr^{o} so cargo del qual prometio de dezir verdad de lo que supiere y le fuere preguntado. tg^{o} Fran^{co} Garcia e dello doy fe.

Ante mi Jhoan de Montoya.

/f.541v/ En la dha ciudad de los Reyes en el dho dia cinco de abril del dho año el dicho capitan Martin Garcia de Loyola para la dha informacion presento por tg^{o} a Fran^{co} de Ampuero del qual tome e recibi juramento en forma devida de dr^{o} so cargo del qual prometio de dezir verdad de lo que supiere y le fuere preguntado. tg^{o} el dho y dello doy fee.

Ante mi Jhoan de Montoya.

En la dha ciudad de los Reyes en seis dias del mes de abril del dho año de mill e qui^{o}s y ochenta y siete a^{o}s el dho capitan Martin Garcia de Loyola para la dha informacion presento por tg^{o} a don Pedro de Cordova Guzman cavallero del avito de Santiago del qual tome y recibi juramento en forma de dr^{o} so cargo del qual prometio de dezir verdad de lo que supiere y le fuere preguntado tg^{o} Fran^{co} Garcia y D^{o} de Castilla.

Ante mi Jhoan de Montoya.

En la ciudad de los Reyes el dho dia seis de abril del dho año el dho cap^{an} Martin Garcia de Loyola para la dha informacion presento por tg^{o} a Lorenço de Arrona del qual tome e r^{e} juramento en forma de dr^{o} so cargo del qual prometio de dezir verdad de lo que supiere y le fuere preguntado tg^{os} los dhos.

Ante mi Jhoan de Montoya.

/f.542/ En la dha ciudad de los Reyes en seis de abril del dho año de ochenta y seis el dho capitan Martin Garcia de Loyola para la dha informacion presento por tg^{o} a Al^{o} Nieto de Molina del qual tome e recibi juram^{to} en forma de dr^{o} so cargo del qual prometio de decir verdad de lo que supiere y fuere preguntado tg^{os} los dhos.

Ante mi Jhoan de Montoya

En la dha ciudad de los Reyes el dho dia el dho capitan Martin Garcia de Loyola para la dha informacion presento por tg^{o} a San Joanes Belaustegui del qual tome e recibi juram^{to} en forma devida de dr^{o} so cargo del qual prometio de decir verdad de lo que supiere y fuese preguntado tg^{os} los dhos.

Ante mi Jhoan de Montoya

En la dha ciudad de los Reyes el dho dia para la dha informacion presento por tg^{o} el dho capitan Martin Garcia de Loyola a Joan Albarez Maldonado del qual tome e recibi juramento en forma devida de dr^{o} segun que los demas el qual aviendo jurado prometio de decir verdad de lo que supiere y fuese preguntado tg^{os} los dhos.

Ante mi Jhoan de Montoya

/f.542v/ En la dha ciudad de los Reyes en el dho dia seis de abril del dicho año de mill e qui^{o}s y ochenta y seis años el dho capitan Martin Garcia de Loyola para la dha informacion presento por tg^{o} a Joan de Mendia y a Pero Lopez Barriales y a Alonso Lopez Barriales e Fran^{co} Gutierrez Cavalleria y Marco Çolano y Joan de Espina e Domingo de Garro de los quales tome e recibi juramento en forma devida de derecho so cargo del qual cada uno de por si prometieron de decir verdad de lo que supieren y les fuese preguntado tg^{os} los dichos Fran^{co} Garcia y D^{o} de Castillo.

Ante mi Jhoan de Montoya

En la dha ciudad de los Reyes en quatro dias del mes de julio de mill e quinientos y ochenta y siete años Joan Sanchez de los Rios como procurador del cap^{an} Martin Garcia de Loyola para en la dha provança presento por tg^{o} a Rodrigo de Bustillo del qual tome e recibi juramento en forma devida de dr^{o} so cargo del qual prometio de decir verdad de lo que supiere y le fuese preguntado. Tg^{os} los dhos.

Ante mi Jhoan de Montoya

/s.f.1/ Yndice

De los Autos Ynstrumentos y Diligencias de este Libro 2° de la Genealogia Ascendencia y Descendencia de D^{n} Diego Sairitupac Mango Capac Yupangui Ynga

Desde

Antes y Despues de la Feliz Conquista y Pacificacion del Reyno del Peru

Hasta

El dia 31 de Julio de 1741 en que termino

Çontiene

Todas las Actuaciones echas en el 1° Quaderno de los autos que se refieren desde 19 de Julio de 1585 hasta el 4 de Julio de 1587 de foxas 1^{a} hasta foxas 542 escritas porque de foxas 543 hasta foxas 553 estan rayadas en blanco

A foxas 1^{a} Escrito de demanda de Martin Garcia pidiendo que en atencion a las justas consideraciones que expuso se sirviese la Real Audiencia //
/s.f.1v/ de Lima declarar por de ningun valor ni efecto la numeracion echa de los 231 yndios de los pueblos del Valle de Yucay por el visitador fr. Pedro Gutierrez Flores que el señor Virrey Toledo mando incorporar en la corona real sin haber oido a la Coya Dª Beatriz q quien pertenecian como propios del Mayorazgo fundado a su padre D^{n} Diego Sairitupac y que en su consequencia se le restituyesen con todos los frutos que produgesen hasta la Real entrega cuyo numero de yndios era distinto de los que se contenian en otro pleito de igual naturaleza que estaba siguiendo contra el señor fiscal en la misma Real Audiencia de cuya solicitud se le dio traslado en 19 de julio de 1585.

A foxas 3. Nomina o razon de los 231 yndios con sus nombres apellidos y edades.

A foxas 5. Escrito del señor fiscal de la Real Audiencia de Lima licenciado Albaro de Carabajal pidiendo en lo principal se declarase no haver lugar a dicha demanda ni deberse proceder sobre ella y por otro si pidio se llebase a la vista el proceso que seguia dicho //
/s.f.2/ Loyola sobre otros yndios para que se viese con la citada demanda y que se le diese un testimonio de el estado que tubiese.

A foxas 6. Escrito de dicho Loyola respondiendo a la declinatoria del Sor Fiscal pidiendo se despreciase y se mandase segun y como tenia a lo que en 3 de septiembre de 1585 se mando que el señor fiscal respondiese derechamente a la citada demanda.

A foxas 7. Escrito del señor Fiscal suplicando del referido auto respecto que los autos de igual naturaleza seguidos por parte del dicho Loyola sobre el mismo asunto estaban remitidos a el Real y Supremo Consejo de las Yndias para donde si era necesario suplicaba de nuebo por el fisco y sin embargo por auto de 13 de septiembre de 1585 se confirmo el de foxas 6 buelta mandando que el señor fiscal respondiese derechamente no obstante la suplicacion que interpuso.

A foxas 8. Escrito por parte de D[a] Beatriz insistien- //
/s.f.2v/ do se llebase a debido efecto lo mandado respecto a que las demandas de los yndios que tenian puestas eran dibersas.

A foxas 8 buelta. Auto de 24 de septiembre mandando que dentro de 90 dias las partes presentasen las escrituras y testigos de que intentasen aprobecharse y que los testigos no fuesen mas de 12 con apercibimiento que pasado dicho termino sin admitirle otra probanza se remitirian a S. M. y su Real y Supremo Consejo de las Yndias dichos autos conforme a ordenanza.

A foxas 9. Escrito de Martin Garcia pidiendo que el relator Vizcarra cotejase los procesos y pusiese certificacion de que eran distintos de que se dio traslado al señor fiscal.

A foxas 10. Escrito de Yd. Pidiendo se pusiese con los autos el documento que presentaba y se llebasen para proveer.

A foxas 11. Testimonio dado por Alonso de Valencia escribano del numero de la ciudad de Lima en 5 de enero de 1583 de la Real //
/s.f.3/ cedula expedida por S. M. en Lisboa a 13 de nobiembre de 1581 por la que nombro a Martin Garcia de Loyola caballero del orden de Calatrava por governador y capitan general de las provincias del Rio de la Plata cuyo empleo estaba vacante por muerte del adelantado Juan Ortiz de Zarate.

A foxas 13. Escrito del señor fiscal suplicando en lo principal del auto de prueba de foxas 8 buelta para que se rebocase y no se oyese en la causa a la parte de D[a] Beatriz por los motivos que expuso y por un otro si pidio se acumulasen a estos los otros autos seguidos por parte de la Coya D[a] Beatriz sobre los mismos yndios de que se dio traslado.

A foxas 15. Escrito por parte de la Coya D[a] Beatriz presentando con el los yntrumentos que refiere en 15 de nobiembre de 1585.

A foxas 16. Testimonio de la Real Probision librada por el licenciado La Gasca presidente y gobernador que fue de los reynos y provincias del Peru en 18 de agosto de 1548 por la //
/s.f.3v/ que perdono a Sairitupac hijo de Mango Ynga Yupangui señor natural que fue de dichos reynos los delitos que hubiese cometido como saliere con sus mugeres e hijos a dar la obediencia al señor Emperador Carlos 5[0] y que ademas de ser bien tratado se le harian diferentes mercedes y bolberian los vienes tierras y casas que fueron de dicho su padre en los terminos que declara.

A foxas 19. Real Provision original librada por la Real Audiencia del Peru a 9 de nobiembre de 1554 por la que se hicieron a dicho Sairitupac las mismas propuestas que contiene la que libro el señor Licenciado La Gasca y que tambien se le darian yndios en Abancay para que el Ynga poblase y formase un estado con que se pudiese mantener y a su familia en los terminos que se declara.

/al margen: Mayorazgo de Sayritupac/
A foxas 20. Testimonio dado por Sancho Ortiz de Orue escribano publico y del cabildo del //
/s.f.4/ Cuzco en 10 de enero de 1560 de la probision librada por el señor virrey Marques de Cañete en 13 de enero de 1558 en virtud de poder del señor emperador Carlos 5[0] firmado en Bruselas a 10 de marzo de 1555 por la que fundo mayorazgo perpetuo como los que se instituyen en Castilla con facultad real sobre los repartimientos de Yucay Jaquijaguna y demas que se expresan en fabor de D[n] Diego Sairitupac sus hijos descendientes y subcesores concediendole facultad para que tomase el apellido y armas que quisiese a cuya fundacion acompañan las posesiones que en virtud de poder de dicho D[n] Diego tomo de los repartimientos su tia legitima D[a] Beatriz Mango Capac Yupangui.

/al margen: Perdon y ofrecim[to] de mercedes/
A foxas 30. Real Probision librada por el señor Marques de Cañete en Lima a 1[o] de enero de 1557 por la que perdono a dicho Sairitupac y le ofrecio hacer en virtud de los poderes que tenia del señor emperador Carlos //
/s.f.4v/ 5[o] las mismas mercedes que expresan las reales provisiones de foxas 16 y foxas 19.

/al margen: Titulo de Adelantado/

A foxas 32. Real probision librada por el señor virrey Marques de Cañete en 12 de enero de 1558 por la que en virtud de los poderes que tenia del señor emperador Carlos 5º hizo merced a d^{n} Diego Sairitupac del titulo de adelantado mayor de Yucay y demas pueblos en donde estaban los repartimientos del Mayorazgo perpetuo a que se contrahe la fundacion de foxas 20.

/al margen: Rebocaz^{on} de la posesion de Gomez Arias/
A foxas 35. Probision original librada por el señor virrey Marques de Cañete en 2 de febrero de 1558 por la que declaro por nula la merced de 20 pesos que gozaba de pension Gomez Arias de Abila sobre los yndios que poseyo Francisco Hernandez Giron y que en su consequencia los gozase libremente D^{n} Diego Sairitupac como propio del mayorazgo que le habia fundado en los terminos que se declara

/s.f.5/ **A foxas 37.** Escrito de Martin Garcia de Loyola pidiendo se le diesen los testimonios que expresa de diferentes reales provisiones y otros documentos los que con efecto se le mandaron dar en 8 de nobiembre de 1558 con citacion del señor fiscal a quien se le notifico.

A foxas 38. Escrito de yd. Pidiendo testimonio de la partida de bautismo de la Coya Dª Beatriz que estaba presentada en el pleito matrimonial que seguia dicho Loyola con Christobal de Maldonado ante el notario apostolico Francisco de Alarcon residente en Lima y que tambien se le diese testimonio del auto por el qual el señor virrey Toledo puso en la corona real los yndios sobre que se seguian estos autos cuyos testimonios se le manda dar con citacion del señor fiscal.

A foxas 39. Escrito pidiendo se le diese testimonio de los documentos presentados //
/s.f.5v/ en el pleito viejo el que se le mando dar con citacion del señor fiscal.

A foxas 40. Escrito de yd. Pidiendo testimonio de la tasa que señalo el señor virrey Toledo debian pagar los yndios sobre que se seguian estos y los otros autos.

Yd. de los capitulos 1º y 15 de el libro titulado Republica del Mundo con la licencia en cuya virtud se imprimio.

Yd. Testimonio del libro titulado Descubrimiento y Conquista del Peru escrito por Agustin de Zarate cuyos testimonios se le mandaron dar.

A foxas 41. Escrito de yd. pidiendo se hiciese como tenia solicitado en su primer escrito.

A foxas 42. Auto de la real audiencia pronunciado en 6 de diciembre de 1585 por el qual se confirmo el de foxas 8 buelta sin embargo de la suplica interpuesta por el señor fiscal a quien se le notifico

/s.f.6/ **A foxas 43.** Escrito de la Coya Dª Beatriz pidiendo 3 meses mas de termino para la presentacion de sus documentos los que se concedieron comunes y se notifico.

A foxas 44. Testimonio de la platica que hizo en el valle de Yucay a 26 de julio de 1572 el visitador Fr. Pedro Gutierrez Flores a los yndios de los repartimientos de la Coya Dª Beatriz a fin de que tributasen para el rey y que con efecto los empadrono sin citar ni oir a la referida Dª Beatriz.

A foxas 46. Escrito de Martin Garcia pidiendo se le diese testimonio de la merced de 1500 pesos anuales que le hizo por sus serbicios el señor virrey D^{n} Francisco de Toledo por dos vidas.

A foxas 47. Escrito del señor fiscal pidiendo apremio por los autos contra Juan Sanchez de los Rios.

A foxas 48. Escrito del procurador Juan Sanchez de los Rios pidiendo a nombre de la Coya Dª Beatriz testimonio del titulo de adelantado y del mayorazgo fundado a su padre D^{n} //
/s.f.6v/ Diego Sairitupac.

A foxas 49. Escrito de Martin Garcia de Loyola presentando un testimonio.

/al margen: Merced a Loyola por la prision del Ynga D^{n} Phelipe sus herm^{s} una hija y sobrinos de que no hacen mencion las Historias del Peru/

A foxas 50. Testimonio dado por Melchor Perez de Mandueña escribano de S. M. y mayor de la governacion y guerra de la ciudad de Lima en 18 de abril de 1586 de la probision librada por el señor virrey D^{n} Francisco de Toledo en la Villa de Potosi en 10 de febrero de 1573 refrendada de su secretario Albaro Ruiz de Nabamuel por la que hizo merced a Martin Garcia de Loyola de 1500 pesos de plata ensayada anualmente por dos vidas que fueron la suya y la de su hija o hijo que tubiese en los primeros yndios que se bacasen de aquella fecha en adelante a cuyo fin reboco las ordenes que tenia dadas para que todas la encomiendas se cobrasen de cuenta de S. M. en atencion a los meritos y servicios de diho Loyola y a los que dice contrajo con la prision que hizo en el //

/s.f.7/ pueblo de Panquin provincia de Vilcabamba del Ynga Tupac Amaro de dos hermanos de este y de una hija suya y de quatro sobrinos con su capitan general Cusipaucar en virtud de la licencia que le concedio Martin Urtado de Arbieto capitan general gobernador y poblador de dicha probincia en los terminos que expresa.

A foxas 58. Escrito del señor fiscal respondiendo en lo principal a 3 peticiones de la parte de la Coya D[a] Beatriz insistiendo en que se denegase su solicitud como tenia alegado y por el primer otro si puso demanda de mutua reconbencion sobrel a nulidad de los repartimientos en que el Marques de Cañete fundo el mayorazgo a el Ynga D[n] Diego Sairitupac y que los debia devolver su hija la Coya D[a] Beatriz con los frutos que habia percibido y por el segundo otro si pidio se le diese testimonio de la merced de 1500 pesos que el señor virrey Toledo hizo al nominado Martin Garcia Loyola.

/s.f.7v/ **A foxas 60.** Escrito del señor fiscal pidiendo se le diese testimonio del pleito viejo seguido por la Coya D[a] Beatriz y su marido por que sobre los mismos yndios era el presente.

A foxas 61. Escrito por parte de Loyola pidiendo se lo notificase en persona lo proveydo.

A foxas 62. Auto de la Real Audiencia pronunciado en 16 de agosto de 1586 mandando que le testimonio del pleito que se remitio a España se acumulase a el presente de consentimiento de Martin Garcia de Loyola a quien se le notificase y a la Coya su muger la demanda de mutua reconbencion que les habia puesto el señor fiscal por el primer otro si del citado pedimento de foxas 58.

A foxas 63. Escrito de la parte de la Coya D[a] Beatriz y su marido respondiendo a la citada demanda mutua pidiendo que en atencion a los motibos que alegan se declarase no haber lugar a dicha demanda imponiendo perpetuo silen- //
/s.f.8/ cio a el señor fiscal.

A foxas 64. Escrito del señor fiscal pidiendo conclusion de la causa.

A foxas 65. Auto de la Real Audiencia pronunciado en 21 de nobiembre de 1596 mandando que las partes alegasen y presentasen los documentos que tubiesen por conveniente dentro de 90 dias a que se recibio la causa a prueba sobre la demanda de mutua reconvencion y que pasados se remitiese a S. M. en el Real y Supremo Consejo de las Yndias.

A foxas 66. Poder que otorgaron en la Villa de Oropesa en 14 de diciembre de 1586 el comendador Martin Garcia de Loyola y su muger la Coya D[a] Beatriz ante Francisco de Bascones escribano publico de la dicha villa en fabor de Juan Sanchez de los Rios y otros procuradores de la Real Audiencia de Lima para el seguimiento de estos autos en todas instancias.

A foxas 67. Escrito del señor fiscal presentando la //
/s.f.8v/ Real probision de emplazamiento que se notifico en persona a Martin Garcia de Loyola y a su muger.

A foxas 68. Real provision librada en 19 de noviembre de 1586 a pedimento del señor fiscal para hacer saber a Martin Garcia de Loyola y a su muger la Coya D[a] Beatriz la mutua y nueba demanda que les puso sobre los yndios de su mayorazgo.

A foxas 70 71. Dos escritos de la parte de D[a] Beatriz pidiendo se prorrogase el termino de esta causa por 6 meses mas.

A foxas 72. Escrito del señor fiscal pidiendo testimonio de la tasa de los tributos de los yndios que tenian los repartimientos de la Coya D[a] Beatriz y de la merced que el s[or] virrey Toledo hizo a el referido Loyola.

A foxas 73. Escrito de la parte de la Coya D[a] Beatriz pidiendo3 meses mas de termino.

A foxas 74. Escrito del señor fiscal contradiciendo dicho termino.

A foxas 75. Escrito de la parte de D[a] Beatriz in- //
/s.f.9/ sistiendo en la concesion de dicho termino.

A foxas 76. Otro escrito de Yd. Acusando rebeldia al señor fiscal.

A foxas 72. Auto de la Real Audiencia pronunciado en 3 de nobiembre de 1587 mandando que el termino de los 90 dias concedidos para la prueba corriesen desde la notificacion de este auto por no haberse echo de aquel escrito.

A foxas 78. Escrito de Martin Garcia de Loyola pidiendo se hiciese en todo segun y como tenia solicitado en sus anteriores pedimentos por los fundamentos que alego en este.

A foxas 80. Escrito de Yd. Pidiendo se le diese testimonio de las reales cedulas y provisiones que cita.

A foxas 81. Escrito de Yd. Pidiendo se librase compulsorio para que se diese testimonio de los que habian rentado los repartimientos de la Coya Dª Beatriz en el tiempo que expresa.

/s.f.9v/ **A foxas 82.** Escrito del señor fiscal pidiendo que el escribano de Camara le entregase el testimonio de la causa que fue remitida al Real y Supremo Consejo de las Indias.

/al margen: Autos en testimº seguido por los prim^{os} yndios incorporados a la Real Corona pª que su tributo fuese de la R^{l} Haz^{da}/

De foxas 83 hasta foxas 427. Testimonio dado por Albaro Ruiz de Nabamuel escribano de S. M. y de la governacion de los Reynos del Peru en la ciudad de Lima a 22 de octubre de 1578 de los autos originales seguidos por el capitan Martin Garcia de Loyola y la Coya Dª Beatriz su muger con el señor fiscal de S. M. sobre los yndios yanaconas del valle de Yucay cuyo testimonio comprende los pedimentos providencias y demas ynstrumentos sig^{tes}.

En dicha foxa 83. Escrito de apelacion interpuesta por Martin Garcia de Loyola en la Real Audiencia de Lima en 20 de julio de 1574 de las probidencias dadas por el visitador de los yndios del valle de Yucay presentando testimonio de los autos que expresa cuyo recurso se admitio y man- //
/s.f.10/ do que la parte pidiese en su vista lo que le conbiniese.

En dicha foxa escrito de Loyola presentado con un ynterrogatorio en 11 de enero de 1574 ante el señor Dr Gabriel de Loarte alcalde del crimen de la Real Audiencia de Lima y corregidor del Cuzco pidiendo que a su tenor se recibiese informacion ad perpetuan para los fines que le conbenia a su muger Dª Clara Coya (sic alguien tacho el nombre Clara con lapiz y puso Beatriz).

A foxas 83 buelta. Despacho del virrey D^{n} Francisco de Toledo librado en la ciudad de la Plata hoy Chuquisaca a 2 de diciembre de 1573 mandando se recibiese dicha ynformacion.

/al margen: Yndios del primero p^{to}/

De dicha foxa hasta la 89 razon de los nombres apellidos y edades de los yndios del valle de Yucay que se incorporaron a la Corona con el pretexto de que eran tributarios y sobre que fue el primer pleito con el señor fiscal.

De foxas 89 hasta foxas 92. Exposicion de //
/s.f.10v/ los echos en que Martin Garcia de Loyola fundo la propiedad y posesion que tenia su muger la Coya Dª Beatriz de los expresados yndios.

/al margen: Ynterrogatorio de la Coya/

A foxas 92 ynterrogatorio de dicho Loyola comprehensibo de 19 preguntas para que a su tenor se recibiese la citada ynformacion acerca de los puntos que refiere y son: Que el valle de Yucay en tiempos de Guaina Capac fue recamara suya por lo que los yndios de el solo serbian para los destinos que les ordenaba como labrar sus haciendas y demas relatibo a su serbicio y palacio. Que al tiempo de la conquista por los españoles tomo para si D^{n} Francisco Pizarro todo el valle de Yucay haciendo que sus yndios le labrasen cocales maizales y le diesen leña y otras cosas para el serbicio de su casa. Que al tiempo que a los españoles se les encomendaron los yndios del Peru no les pa- //
/s.f.11/ gaban tributo y que solo contribuian con el serbicio personal trabajandoles sus haciendas y que los mismo hacian los de Yucay con dicho Pizarro. Que el mismo servicio hacian los yndios de Yucay a Gonzalo Pizarro hijo del marques D^{n} Francisco que por muerte del dicho Gonzalo los oficiales r^{s} del Cuzco se sirbieron de los yndios de Yucay en los terminos insinuados. Que el marques de Cañete virrey del Peru dio a D^{n} Diego Sairitupa hijo de Mango Ynga y nieto de Guaina Capac dicho valle de Yucay con titulo de mayorazgo perpetuo en el que por su muerte subcedio Dª Beatriz Coya su hija legitima y unibersal heredera muger de dicho Loyola. Que por disposicion del marques don Francisco Pizarro fue cazique principal de Yucay D^{n} Francisco Chilichi [*sic*] para que cuidase de que los yndios trabajasen a beneficio de los encomenderos. Que D^{n} Garcia Quispicapi pleito a dicho Chilichi sobre el cazi- //
/s.f.11v/ casgo de Yucay el que transaron siendo D^{n} Francisco cazique de los yndios mitimaes y advenedizos y D^{n} Garcia de los naturales. Que el visitador Damian de la Bandera mando que los yndios de Yucay tributasen a sus encomenderos. Que dichos yndios aunque eran guardas del cuerpo de Guaina Capac tributaban y serbian a los encomenderos. Que el tesorero Garcia de Melo visitador de dicho valle mando que dhos yndios tributasen en plata y no en coca. Que el visitador frey Diego Escudero puso por yanaconas a los yndios tributarios de dicho valle que le dixeron los caciques. Que lo mismo practico el licenciado frey Gregorio [*sic*] Gutierrez Flores sin mas aberiguacion ni motivo que haberlo echo frey Diego Escudero su antecesor. Que los yndios de dicho valle declararon voluntariamente eran tributarios y no yanaconas y que como tales habian pagado lo que debian a su encomendero //
/s.f.12/ Sairitupac y a su hija legitima que le subcedio en el mayorazgo.

/al margen: Ynformaz^{on} ad perpetuan de la Coya al tenor del ynterrogatorio de f^{s} 92/

De foxas 96 buelta hasta foxas 168 buelta se halla la ynformacion ad perpetuam dada por parte de Dª Beatriz Clara Coya al tenor de dicho ynterrogatorio con numero de 17 testigos ante Pedro Diaz Baldeon escribano de S. M. publico y del numero del Cuzco y dos ynterpretes en

11 de enero de 1574 por la que consta hera cierto publico y notorio todo lo contenido y articulado en dichas preguntas en cuya informaz^{on} que fue aprobada en 1° de abril de dicho año por el referido señor corregidor del Cuzco D^{n} Gabriel de Loarte declararon:

1. D^{n} Pedro Cochachi cazique de S^{n} Sebast^{n} de 61 a^{s}
2. Sebastian Tenazuela de 70 a^{s}
3. D^{n} Diego Casatambo de 80 a^{s}
4. Martin Yupangui de 60 a^{s}
5. Martin Yana de 60 a^{s}
6. Lucas Chico de 70 a^{s}
7. Martin Caritopa 70 a^{s}

/s.f.12v/
8. D^{n} Garcia Paucar de 60 a^{s}
9. Miguel Chirisuca 60 a^{s}
10. Martin Condemayta de 60 a^{s}
11. Martin Sauni 88 a^{s}
12. Diego Escudero cura de Yucay de 50 a^{s}
13. Marcos Cayogualpa de 80 a^{s}
14. Alonso Chauca de 80 a^{s}
15. Pedro Chinancila de 85 a^{s}
16. Juan Bautista Vilcana de 90 a^{s}
17. Hernando Coacalla de 61 a^{s}

A foxas 169. Escrito de la parte de D^{a} Beatriz pidiendo se le diese un testim^{o} de dicha ynformacion aprobandola en forma lo que asi se mando en 1° de abril de 1574 por dicho corregidor ante el citado escribano en que dio el referido testimonio.

A foxas 169 buelta. Escrito de la parte de Dª Beatriz pidiendo se recibiese ynformacion de que en la visita que hizo de los yndios del valle de Yucay se padecio el equivoco de empadronar mas de 250 yndios pertenecientes al mayorazgo de //
/s.f.13/ la suso dicha que fundo a D^{n} Diego Sairitupac en virtud de poder del señor Carlos 5° el virrey Marques de Cañete lo que se habia practicado en perjuicio de aquella por su menor hedad y no tener antes que se casase con Martin Garcia Onza de Loyola quien mirase por ella de que le resultaba un notorio despojo y el perjuicio que se dejaba considerar por el menoscabo de su renta para cuya manifestacion presento una razon de 241 yndios con sus nombres y apellidos protextando exibir otra con los de sus mugeres e hijos para el mayor esclarecimiemto de su justicia y que contra ella se visitaron y empadronaron por el comendador frey Pedro Gutierrez Flores poniendolos en la corona real.

A foxas 170 buelta. Razon de los nombres y apellidos de dichos yndios.

A foxas 172 buelta. Poder de Martin Garcia de Loyola comendador del orden de Calatrava y de D^{a} Beatriz Coya su mu- //
/s.f.13v/ ger otorgado en el Cuzco en 31 de octubre de 1572 ante Geronimo de Quesada escribano del numero de aquella ciudad en fabor de Alonso Valdes y Juan Fernandez Coronel para la administracion de las encomiendas y rentas de su mayorazgo y generalmente para todos sus pleitos y causas.

/al margen: Mayorazgo antiguo o primero/

A foxas 176. Probision del Marques de Cañete virrey del Peru librada en virtud del poder que esta inserto del señor emperador Carlos 5° en fabor de D^{n} Diego Sairitupac igual a la que se halla a foxas 20 de estos autos que se omite extractar por no duplicar una misma cosa previniendose que las diligencias sobre que se fundo dicho mayorazgo llegan hasta la foxa 183 buelta.

A foxas 183 buelta. Escrito de los caziques D^{n} Garcia Quispicaci y D^{n} Francisco Chilichi contradiciendo se pusiesen los yndios //
/s.f.15/ del valle de Yucay por tributarios de S. M. en atencion a ser de la encomienda y mayorazgo perpetuo de D^{a} Beatriz hija legitima y heredera de D^{n} Diego Sairitupac.

A foxas 184. Escrito de Alonso Baldes apoderado de dicha Dª Beatriz haciendo la misma contradiccion y pidiendo se amparase a su parte en la posesion en que estaba de dichos yndios restituyendola inmediatamente lo que se hubiese cobrado de ellos y de lo contrario apelo para la Real Audiencia de Lima protextando los daños y perjuicios.

A foxas 185. Auto proveido en el valle de Yucay a 20 de enero de 1572 por frey Pedro Gutierrez Flores de la orden y caballeria de Alcantara visitador general del Peru por nombramiento y titulo del virrey D^{n} Fran^{co} de Toledo su fecha en el Cuzco a 30 de julio de 1571 por cuyo auto consta la exhortacion que hizo a los yndios de dicho valle para que se allanasen //
/s.f.15v/ a pagar tributo a S. M. y con efecto sin citar a la parte de D^{a} Beatriz verifico dicho empadronamiento.

/al margen. Padron/

De foxas 190 buelta hasta foxas 230. Razon de dichos yndios con sus nombres y apellidos y edades la de sus mugeres e hijos lo que pagaban de serbicio de doctrina y de tasa con los topos de tierras que tenian para sus sementeras.

A foxas 230 buelta. Escrito de Dª Beatriz exponiendo el agrabio que se le hizo de poner los yndios de su mayorazgo por tributarios de la Real Corona y concluyo pidiendo se le admitiese la apelacion que interponia de las probidencias dadas por el visitador frey Pedro Gutierrez Flores.

A foxas 231 buelta. Escrito de la parte de Dª Beatriz formalizando dicha apelacion y expresando los agrabios que se la habian inferido con el empadronam^{to} //
/s.f.16/ de tributarios a la Real Corona a los yndios de las encomiendas perpetuas de su mayorazgo y concluyo pidiendo que restituyendoselos ante todas cosas se declarase por nulo violento y atentado dicho empadronamiento y que en su consequencia se la amparase en la posesion en que se hallaba para lo qual se recibiese la causa a prueba.

/al margen. Yncorporaz^{n} a la corona de los yndios de Dª Beatriz. 481/

A foxas despacho librado por el virrey D^{n} Francisco de Toledo en la ciudad del Cuzco a 20 de septiembre de 1572 mandando que los 418 yndios del valle de Yucay que se havian empadronado pagasen de tributo a S. M. en cada año 1254 pesos de plata ensayada y marcada de 450 maravedies cada uno en el valor de las fanegas de maiz y trigo que refiere lo que se notifico en 30 del dicho mes y año a los caziques principales de //
/s.f.16v/ dichos yndios.

A foxas 237 buelta. Auto del alcalde de corte y corregidor del Cuzco D^{n} Gabriel de Loarte remitiendo a la Real Audiencia de Lima los autos y diligencias anteriores para su determinacion y vistas en ella en 3 de agosto de 1576 se dio traslado al señor fiscal de los agravios expresados por parte de dicha Dª Beatriz en su escrito de foxas 231.

A foxas 237 b^{ta}. Escrito del señor fiscal respondiendo a el de agrabios de Dª Beatriz pidiendo no se devia admitir su pretension ni en la Real Audiencia se podia conocer de ella y que asi se remitiese conforme a la probision de Malinas al tribunal correspondiente que era el Real y Supremo Consejo de las Yndias.

A foxas 238. Auto de la Real Audiencia proveido en 21 de agosto de 1576 teniendo por conclusa esta causa.

/s.f.17/ A foxas Yd. Auto de la Real Audiencia en 28 de septiembre de dicho año mandando que Dª Beatriz usase y siguiese su justicia donde le conbiniese.

A foxas 238 buelta. Escrito de primera demanda de Dª Beatriz sobre los citados yndios pidiendo su restitucion y la posesion en que de ellos estaba a cuyo fin se rebocase todo lo fecho y actuado en los autos de que se dio traslado al s^{or} fiscal en 16 de octubre de 1576.

A foxas 239 buelta. Escrito del señor fiscal pidiendo se despreciase dicha demanda imponiendo perpetuo silencio a la parte de Dª Beatriz de que se la dio traslado.

A foxas 240. Escrito de Dª Beatriz pidiendo se recibiese la causa a prueba con el termino ordinario conforme a la ordenanza de Malinas.

A foxas 240 buelta. Otro escrito por parte de Dª //
/s.f.17v/ Beatriz insistiendo en lo mismo.

A foxas 241 buelta. Auto de la Real Audiencia probeido en 11 de diciembre de 1576 recibiendo la causa a prueba con termino de 90 dias que se notifico a la parte y al señor fiscal.

A foxas 245 buelta. Auto de la Real Audiencia en vista de varios pedimentos de Dª Beatriz y del señor fiscal mandando que este dentro de 10 dias presentase los documentos que tubiese relatibos a dicha causa y que no lo haciendo corriese el termino de prueba.

A foxas 246. Escrito del señor fiscal pidiendo en lo principal que el escribano de camara Albaro Ruiz de Nabamuel le diese testimonio de la visita y numeracion que hizo de los yndios del valle de Yucay frey Pedro Gutierrez y por un otro si pidio se librase provision para que //
/s.f.18/ los oficiales reales del Cuzco le diesen certificacion del auto en que el virrey Toledo incorporo en la corona dichos yndios lo que asi se mando.

A foxas 247. Escrito de Dª Beatriz pidiendo se hiciese publicacion de probanzas en lo que consintio el señor fiscal pidiendo se remitiese la causa al Real y Supremo Consejo para su determinacion lo que asi se mando por auto de 11 de octubre de 1577.

Probanza por parte de la Coya Dª Beatriz

A foxas 247 buelta. Real probision librada por la R^{l} Audiencia de Lima en 20 de diciembre de 1576 para hacer probanza a el tenor del ynterrogatorio presentado por parte de Dª Beatriz en la citada causa que se halla inserto y contiene 14 preguntas reducidas a que los yndios de su encomienda del valle de Yucay de que habia sido despojada eran 331 cuyos nombres y apellidos se expresan en la ra- //
/s.f.18v/ zon que presento y se halla de foxas 252 hasta foxas 256 numerados a su margen de numero 223 hasta 561 que dichos yndios los posehia Dª Beatriz por tributarios pertenecientes a el mayorazgo perpetuo en que subzedio por muerte de D^{n} Diego Sairitupac su padre legitimo a quien se le fundo el virrey Marques de Cañete en virtud de poder del señor Carlos 5º que Dª Beatriz era hija legitima del citado D^{n} Diego y de su muger y hermana legitima Dª Maria Manrique Cusiguarcay de cuyo matrimonio nacio el año de 1558. Que dichos sus padres no tubieron otro hijo ni hija legitima mas que Dª Beatriz su unica y universal heredera. Que antes que dichos yndios se diesen por titulo de mayorazgo perpetuo a Sairutupac los poseyeron el Marques Francisco Pizarro y su hijo Gonzalo a quienes como a Dª Beatriz y a su padre pagaban tributo y labraban sus semen- //
/s.f.19/ teras y haciendas de coca que eran Cono [*sic*] Paucarbamba y demas que tenian por ser el modo con que en aquel tiempo pagaban el tributo. Que antes que Pizarro entrase en el Peru poseyo el Ynga Guaina Capac los yndios de dicho valle y con sus mugeres e hijos le beneficiaban sus haciendas que era el tributo que le daban sirviendo ademas con sus personas en lo que les mandaba. Que el tesorero Garcia de Melo en la visita que hizo mando que dichos yndios pagasen el tributo en plata. Que el visitador frey Pedro Gutierrez Flores empadrono por yanaconas los 331 yndios de dicho valle no lo siendo imitando a su antecesor el padre Diego Escudero sin atender a que eran tributarios y del mayorazgo de Dª Beatriz con cuyo motibo fue despojada de la posesion en que se hallaba causandole irreparable perdida.

A foxas 241 buelta. Obedecimiento del corregidor del Cuzco D^{n} Gabriel Paniagua de Loaisa //
/s.f.19v/ en 16 de febrero de 1577 mandando que la parte de Dª Beatriz diese la prueba que se manda por la Real Probision de foxas 247 buelta.

/al margen: Yndios 331/

De foxas 252 hasta foxas 256. Razon de los 331 yndios de que Dª Beatriz fue despojada con sus nombres y apellidos.

A foxas 257. Poder de Martin Garcia Onza de Loyola a favor del reverendo padre fray Domingo de Loyola provincial del orden de predicadores para sus pleitos y negocios y recaudos sus rentas otorgado en la ciudad de Arequipa a 22 de enero de 1574 ante Juan de Vera escribano del numero de ella.

/al margen: Maiorazgo antiguo o primero/

De foxas 261 hasta foxas 271. Provision librada por el virrey Marques de Cañete en 13 de enero de 1558 en virtud de poder del señor Carlos 5º a fabor de Sairitupac igual a la de foxas 20 y a la de foxas 176 con el poder de dicho Sairutupac y posesiones que tomo de los yndios de su //
/s.f. 20/ mayorazgo que llegan hasta la foxa 271.

Probanza por parte de la Coya Dª Beatriz en segunda ynstancia

De foxas 271 buelta hasta foxas 309. Probanza echas por parte de dicha Dª Beatriz en la referida causa al tenor del ynterrogatorio inserto en la real provision de foxas 247 buelta cuyos 23 testigos exponen de afirmatiba y ciencia cierta el contenido de las preguntas habiendose ratificado los que vivian de la ynformacion de foxas 96 y por los que habian muerto se puso la respectiva diligencia que se halla a foxas 309 buelta los testigos fueron.

1. Garcia de Melo thesorero de edad de 67a^{s}
2. D^{n} Fran^{co} Chilichi cazique de Yucay de 80 a^{s}
3. Marcos Puri de 60 a^{s}
4. Hernando Bachicao de 43 a^{s}
5. Pedro Bustinza de 38 a^{s}
6. Alonso Bermudez de 50 a^{s}
7. D^{n} Pedro Cochachi de 61 a^{s}
/s.f.20v/ 8. Juan Bautista Vilcana de 90 a^{s}
9. D^{n} Diego Casatambo de 80 a^{s}
10. Martin Yupangui de 60 a^{s}
11. Martin Yana de 60 a^{s}
12. Hernando Coacaya de 61 a^{s}
13. Lucas Chico de 70 a^{s}
14. Martin Sauni de 88 a^{s}
15. D^{n} Garcia Paucar de 60 a^{s}
16. Miguel Chirisuca de 60 a^{s}

17. Marcos Cayo Gualpa de 80 a^{s}
18. Alonso Chauca de 80 a^{s}
19. D^{n} Diego Escudero de 50 a^{s}
20. Martin Cutipa de 70 a^{s}

Todos los que fueron notificados.

A foxas 310. Escrito del señor fiscal pidiendo restitucion del termino de prueba que se concedio por el auto de foxas 312 de consentimiento de la parte de Dª Beatriz.

A foxas 312 buelta. Escrito de la parte de la suso dicha pidiendo se enbiasen los autos a el Real y Supremo Consejo para su determinacion.

/s.f.21/ **A foxas 313**. Escrito del señor fiscal oponiendose a dicha solicitud.

/al margen Padron Gral del valle de Yucay/

De foxas 315 hasta foxas 410. Testimonio dado por Albaro Ruiz de Nabamuel escribano de camara de la Real Audiencia de Lima en 20 de marzo de 1578 de los autos originales de la visita y numeracion y empadronamiento que hizo de los 2323 yndios de los quatro pueblos del valle de Yucay nombrados Guayllabamba Urubamba Maraz y Yucay conocidos por Santiago S^{n} Bernardo S^{n} Benito y S^{n} Francisco pertenecientes al mayorazgo de D^{a} Beatriz cuya numeracion practico el comendador frey Pedro Gutierrez Flores del orden de Calatrava por comision del virrey D^{n} Francisco Toledo en 20 de enero de 1572 expresando en ella sus nombres apellidos edades clase de serbicio que hacian p^{a} la paga del tributo con sus mugeres e hijos que tenian de cuyos 2323 yndios solam^{te} los 449 pagaban dho tributo y fueron //
/s.f.21v/ los mismos que dicho virrey incorporo en la corona de S. M. mandando que pagasen tributo a la Real Hacienda en los terminos que se refiere.

A foxas 410. Provision receptoria librada por la R^{l} Audiencia de Lima a 20 de nobiembre de 1577 a pedimento del señor fiscal de ella p^{a} hacer probanza en dicha causa a el tenor del ynterrogatorio que presento cuyas preguntas se reducen a: Que los yndios del valle de Yucay no estaban encomendados a persona alguna y que los reduxo y poblo el visitador frey Pedro Gutierrez Flores en el pueblo de Santiago de Oropesa 180 tributarios en el de S^{n} Bernardo 164 en el de S^{n} Benito de Alcantara 84 en el de S^{n} Francisco de Maras 21 y en todos ellos muchos viejos y muchachos. Que dichos yndios desde antes que los españoles entraran en el Peru eran yanaconas y despues no estaban encomendados a persona //
/s.f.22/ alguna y que por lo mismo el virrey Toledo los incorporo en la corona real mandando que pagasen tributo a S. M.

De foxas 414 hasta foxas 420. Probanza del señor fiscal en que declararon al tenor del ynterrogatorio el thesorero Garcia de Melo Damian de la Bandera Juan Lopez de Arrieta Juan de Salas Diego de Mercado Diego de Escobar Juan de Cillorigo el governador Martin Hurtado y Arbieto Christobal Delgado Pablo de Carabajal Pedro Guerrero y Francisco de Acuña quienes no conbienen en el tenor de las preguntas pues afirman que los yndios del valle de Yucay estuvieron encomendados desde que los españoles entraron en el Peru en diferentes personas.

A foxas 420. Auto de la Real Audiencia de Lima probeido en 8 de abril de 1578 mandando que estos autos que empezaron desde la foxa 83 se remitiesen originales a el R^{l} y Supremo Consejo en la forma ordinaria //
/s.f.22v/ citadas las partes quedando un testimonio en la escribania de camara y que si el fiscal presentase antes su prueba tambien se remita original.

/al margen: Prueba del s^{r} fiscal/

De foxas 422 hasta foxas 426. Prueba dada en la ciudad de Lima por el señor fiscal con Martin Garcia de Licona Juan de la Banda y Lazaro Muñoz al tenor de su ynterrogatorio y solo dicen que el visitador Flores empadrono los yndios del valle de Yucay y que el virrey Toledo mando pagasen tributo a S. M.

A foxas 425. Escrito del señor fiscal presentando dicha prueba y pidiendo que la causa se tuviese por conclusa de que se dio traslado a la parte de Dª Beatriz.

/al margen: Yncorporaz^{on} de los yndios en la R^{l} Corona/

A dicha foja auto del virrey Toledo proveido en el Cuzco a 11 de agosto de 1572 poniendo los yndios del valle de Yucay en la Real Corona mandando que pagasen tributo a S. M. en la forma que //
/s.f.23/ refiere con lo qual concluye dicho testimonio en la foxa 427 a cuya buelta se hallan las citaciones echas a las partes de Dª Beatriz y al señor fiscal.

/al margen: r^{vo} de los autos orig^{s} y su remision al consejo/

A foxas 428. Testimonio dado por Geronimo de Adrada escribano de S. M. de minas y registros de la ciudad de Lima a 6 de nobiembre de 1578 de la partida de registro que en 23 de octubre de dicho año otorgo Juan de Urrutia maestre de nabio nombrado Todos los Santos que del puerto del Callao salia para el reyno de Tierra Firme de los autos originales seguidos entre el capitan Martin Garcia de Loyola como marido de la Coya Dª Beatriz y el s^or fiscal sobre los yndios yanaconas del valle de Yucay que estaban cerrados en un encerado y sellados rotulados para el Real Consejo de Yndias cuyo pliego se obligo a entregar el citado maestre a los oficiales reales de la ciudad de Panama //
/s.f.23v/ para su remision al dicho Real y Supremo Consejo.

A foxas 430. Escrito de Martin Garcia de Loyola presentado a la Real Audiencia en 8 de abril de 1585 pidiendo que respecto de no haber llegado al consejo los autos originales que se citan en la partida de registro de foxas 428 y cuyo testimonio empieza en la foxa 83 y acaba en la 427 se le diese otro de dhos autos para evitar el perjuicio que se le seguia lo que asi se mando.

A foxas 431. Escrito de la parte de Martin Garcia de Loyola pidiendo que la R^l Audiencia proveyese nuevo auto de remision de la segunda causa seguida con el señor fiscal sobre los yndios yanaconas del valle de Yucay propios del mayorazgo de la Coya Dª Beatriz lo que asi se mando en 15 de julio de 1585.

/s.f.24/ **A foxas 432**. Declaraciones de Hernando Sanchez Miguel Merino y Juan de Porras echas en la ciudad de Lima en 22 de enero de 1586 ante Juan de Montoya escribano de camara de aquella real audiencia por la que consta habian muerto el escribano publico y del numero del Cuzco Pedro Diaz Baldeon y el cazique D^n Francisco Chiliche por cuyo motibo no se habian ratificado en las declaraciones que hicieron en los citados autos.

A foxas 434. Testimonio dado por Juan Gutierrez de Molina escribano de camara de la real audiencia de Lima en 15 de noviembre de 1585 de la real cedula expedida por el señor D^n Felipe 2º siendo principe en Madrid a 19 de marzo de 1552 dirigida al virrey del Peru D^n Antonio de Mendoza para que como estaba resuelto pusiese todos los medios oportunos a fin //
/s.f.24v/ de que el Ynga Sairitupac saliese a dar obediencia a S. M. y que verificado se le hiciesen las mercedes que expresan las reales cedulas que se citan.

/al margen. Mayorazgo antiguo primero/

De foxas 437 hasta foxas 451. Testimonio dado por Gaspar de Prado escribano de S. M. y del numero de la ciudad del Cuzco en 10 de marzo de 1589 de la probision librada por el marques de Cañete virrey que fue del Peru en 13 de enero de 1558 en virtud de poder especial del señor emperador Carlos 5º dado en Bruselas a 10 de marzo de 1555 por la que fundo mayorazgo perpetuo como los que instituyen en Castilla con facultad real a favor de D^n Diego Sairitupac sus hijos y descendientes igual a la que esta a foxas 20 de estos autos. Asimismo comprenhende la provision expedida por el virrey Francisco de Toledo en el //
/s.f.25/ /al margen: posesion del primer mayorazgo dada a Dª Beatriz/ tambo de Chicacupi jurisdiccion del Cuzco en 21 de octubre de 1572 por la que mando que en atencion a haber muerto el referido D^n Diego se diese la posesion de los repartimientos sobre que estaba fundado dicho mayorazgo a Martin Garcia de Loyola como marido y conjunta persona de la Coya Dª Beatriz hija legitima unica heredera del expresado D^n Diego cuya posesion tomo en los caziques de los valles de Yucay Jaquijaguna Pisac Quipi y Pucara en 26 de noviembre de dicho año. Tambien se halla insertos el poder que otorgaron los citados Martin Garcia y su muger en 31 de octubre del mismo año ante Geronimo de Quesada essno de numero del Cuzco en favor de Alonso de Baldes y Juan Fernandez Coronel para que administrasen las rentas de los repartimientos de dicho //
/s.f.25v/ mayorazgo y demas bienes que les pertenecian.

De foxas 452 hasta foxas 483. Testimonio dado por Juan de Montoya essno de Camara de la Real Audiencia de Lima a pedimento de Martin Garcia de Loyola en 22 de abril de 1585 en el que se hallan insertos los instrumentos siguientes.

A foxas 453 buelta. La real cedula expedida en Madrid a 9 de febrero de 1569 concediendo licencia a Diego Fernandez vecino de la ciudad de Palencia para que pudiese imprimir la Historia de los Alzamientos y Sublevaciones que hicieron en los reynos del Peru Francisco Hernandez Giron y Gonzalo Pizarro con los echos ocurridos hasta su castigo.

A foxas 455 hasta foxas 461. 3 reales zedulas expedidas en el Pardo a 6 de marzo de 1569 en Madrid a 11 de abril de 1568 y en 2 de febrero de 1568 y en 2 de febrero de 1568 concediendo no //
/s.f.26/ solo licencia para imprimir dicha historia sino es tambien para que se vendiese en los reynos de España e Yndias

/al margen. Hechos q^e precedieron para que Sairitupac diese la oved^a a S. M. C. en manos del virrey Marques de Cañete en 5 de en^o de 1558/

A foxas 461 empieza el testimonio del capitulo 4º relativo a que el Ynga Sairitupac Yupangui salio de las montañas de Vilcabamba y paso a la ciudad de Lima y dio obediencia a el Marques de Cañete virrey del Peru en nombre del señor emperador Carlos 5º a persuasion de su tia la Coya Dª Beatriz Mango Capac Yupangui casada con Diego Hernandez natural de Talavera en cuyo capitulo se expresa por menos todos los echos ocurridos en la salida de dho Sairitupac y que por ella se le ofrecieron mantener su casa y familia 17 mil Castellanos de

oro de renta anual con los repartimientos que poseyeron Francisco Hernandez Giron y Francisco Pizarro menor las tierras de encima de la fortaleza del Cuzco y demas que se refiere y //
/s.f.26v/ concluye el citado capitulo con la exortacion que el Ynga hizo a sus capitanes e yndios para que tubiesen a bien su salida a vivir con los españoles por los motibos que les expuso.

/al margen: Yngas o reyes del Peru desde la fundaz[on] del Ymperio hasta Sairitupac/

A foxas 469 buelta. Empieza el capitulo del origen que tubieron los Yngas reyes del Peru y de su descendencia desde el primero que lo fue Mango Capac hasta mango Ynga el segundo padre del referido Sairitupac.

A foxas 478. Real cedula del señor emperador Carlos 5º firmada del señor Felipe 2º siendo principe en Valladolid a 28 de septiembre de 1543 dirigida al virrey Blasco Nuñez Vela para que pusiese todos los medios correspondientes a fin de que el Ynga saliese a dar la obediencia bajo de las mercedes que se le ofrecieron.

A foxas 480. Otra Real Cedula del señor D[n] //
/s.f.27/ Felipe 2º expedida en Madrid a 19 de marzo de 1552 dirigida al Ynga Sairitupac sobre que diese la obediencia a S. M. y mercedes que por ello se le harian.

A foxas 482. Real instruccion dada por el señor emperador Carlos 5º al Marques de Cañete virrey del Peru su fecha en Bruselas a 10 de marzo de 1555 del modo con que debia manejarse acerca de la reduccion del Ynga y mercedes que por ello le haria.

A foxas 482 buelta. Real cedula dada en Bruselas a 10 de marzo de 1555 para que el Marques de Cañete virrey del Peru llebase a debido efecto las que se habian dirigido a sus antecesores acerca de la reduccion del Ynga Sairitupac.

A foxas 488. Testimonio dado por Juan de Montoya essno de Camara de la Real Audiencia de Lima en 16 de nobiembre de 1585 en el que estan insertas las declaraciones de Pedro Dias Baldeon essno publico del //
/s.f.27v/ Cuzco y el cacique D[n] Francisco Chilichi acerca del despojo que se hizo de los yndios de su mayorazgo a la Coya D[a] Beatriz con los demas que se refiere.

/al margen: Yncorporaz[on] a la Corona de los yndios de D[a] Beatriz/

A foxas 490. Testimonio dado por dicho escribano de camara en 18 de nobiembre de 1585 del auto proveido en 11 de agosto de 1572 por el virrey D[n] Francisco de Toledo mandando poner en la corona real los yndios de los repartimientos pertenecientes al mayorazgo que gozaba la Coya D[a] Beatriz como hija unica y unibersal heredera de D[n] Diego Sairitupac.

De foxas 496 hasta foxas 522. Testimonio dado por Juan de Montoya escribano de camara de la Real Audiencia de Lima en 27 de nobiembre de 1585 que contiene los instrumentos siguientes:

A foxas 497. Real cedula expedida en el Pardo a 25 de enero de 1564 por la que se concedio licencia y facultad a fr. Geronimo Roman del orden de S[n] Agustin para //
/s.f.28/ que pudiese imprimir la obra que havia escrito titulada Republica del Mundo.

A foxas 498 buelta. Capitulo 1º que trata del Descubrimiento de los Indias Occidentales en los terminos que refiere.

/al margen. Origen de los Yngas desde la fundaz[on] del Peru h[ta] su conquista/

A foxas 506. Capitulo de la caida del Rey del Peru con expresion de todos los Reyes que tubo aquel reyno hasta que se incorporo en la corona real de España.

A foxas 511 buelta. Real cedula expedida en S[n] Lorenzo a 11 de septiembre de 1566 concediendo licencia a Agustin de Zarate para que imprimiese la obra que el año de 1543 habia compuesto titulada Descubrimiento y Conquista del Peru hasta que el licenciado La Gasca governador de el regreso a España y fue electo obispo de Palencia.

A foxas 513. Capitulo 12 de dicha Historia relatibo a el estado que que estaban las guerras que tenian los peruanos a el tiempo que los españoles llegaron a este reyno.

A foxas 517. Auto proveido por el virrey D[n] Fran[co] //
/s.f.28v/ /al margen. Incorporaz[on] a la corona de los 413 yndios de la Coya D[a] Beatriz/ de Toledo en la ciudad del Cuzco a 20 de septiembre de 1572 declarando que los 413 yndios que el visitador Pedro Gutierrez saco del valle de Yucay y pueblos nombrados S[n] Benito de Alcantara Santiago de Oropesa S[n] Bernardo y S[n] Francisco de Maras pertenecian a la corona real y en su consecuencia mando que el tributo y tasa que antes pagaban se cobrase por cuenta de la Real Hacienda y se enterase en las r[s] caxas de dicha ciudad.

A foxas 524. Titulo de capitan general de la armada que salio del puerto del Callao reyno del Peru para el de Tierra Firme expedido en 24 de abril de 1584 en fabor de Martin Garcia Onza de Loyola caballero del orden de Calatrava gobernador y capitan general del Rio de la Plata para que condujese los caudales y tesoros de S. M. y executase lo demas correspondiente al rl servicio.

A foxas 528. Real titulo expedido en 16 de abril de 1586 en fabor de Martin Garcia Oñaz de //
/s.f.29/ Loyola del orden de Calatrava para que sirbiese el Corregimiento de la ciudad de Guamanga y el de la Villa rica de Oropesa y Minas de Huancavelica en atencion a los meritos y serbicios que por menor se refieren a cuya continuacion se halla un testimonio dado por Gaspar de Prado Escribano del numero del Cuzco en 10 de Marzo de 1589 de que no le resulto cargo alguno a dicho Loyola en el tiempo que sirbio los referidos empleos.

/al margen. Interrogatorio Original de la Coya Da. Beatriz/

De foxas 532 hasta foxas 537. Interrogatorio original presentado en el segundo pleito por Martin Garcia de Loyola como marido de la Coya Da. Beatriz con el Señoro Fiscal sobre los 231 Yndios que el Visitador Fr. Pedro Gutierrez del Orden de Alcantara saco del Valle de Yucay despojando de su posesion a la suso dicha; cuyo Interrogatorio comprende 54 preguntas reducidas a que Dn. Diego Sairitupac y Da. Maria Cusi Guarcay su hermana y mujer legitima fueron hijos de Mango //
/s.f.29v/ /al margen: Indios del Primer Pleito 231 y del 2º - 330. Total 561/ Ynga Yupangui el segundo y nietos de Guainacapac Señores que fueron del Peru: si tenian noticias de los 231 Yndios de que el dciho visitador despojo a la referida Da. Beatriz los guales eran distintos de los otros 330 sobre que asimismo estaba pendiente otro pleito con el referido Señor Fiscal: que el citado Dn. Diego Sairitupac Mango Capac Yupangui Ynga fue hijo legitimo del citado Mango Ynga el segundo y nieto de GuainaCapac y que por fin y muerte de su padre y demas hermanos que tubo se justifico por Dn. Francisco Pizarro Gobernador que fue de aquellos Reynos que dicho Mango Ynga hera el legitimo subzesor de ellos y a quien derechamente pertenecian y como a tal le dio la Borla que usaban los Señores Yngas sus antecesores: que dicho Sairitupac fue el hijo primogenito y mayor del citado Mango Ynga y por tal fue habido y tenido y subcedido en todos sus vienes y demas cosas que le pertenecian //
/s.f.30/ y por consiguiente fue obedecido como tal Rey usando de las Insignias que le correspondian: Que dciho Mango Ynga el segundo habiendo dado la obediencia a la Majestad Catolica de España estando esperando en el Cuzco la merced que por tan generosa accion se le haria algunos españoles le hicieron muchos malos tratamientos de palabra y de obra hasta darle una bofetada y tomarle sus mujeres de modo que hubo Español que por menospreciarle le manoseo el rostro: Que por dichos malos tratamientos el citado Ynga se retiro a la probincia de Bilcabamba con mas de 20 D (20 mil) indios de Guerra y estando en ella llego al Peru el Licenciado La Gasca el que en virtud de las Reales cedulas del Señor Carlos 5º le embio Real Probision haciendole muchas mercedes con tal que diese la obediencia a la Corona de Castilla y la jurase Vasallaje //
/s.f.30v/ que obstante de estos ofrecimientos no quiso salir de Vilcabamba dicho Ynga resentido de los referidos malos tratamientos y que por consiguiente mandaba muchas provincias y a los indios de ellas como su Rey y Señor natural: que en todo el tiempo que vibio sus capitanes y genete de Guerra salteaban los pueblos convecinos de Vilcabamba: Que Sairitupac executo lo mismo luego que murio su padre y fue aclamado Señor del Peru: Que con noticia que tubo el Señor Emperador Carlos 5º de todo lo referido mando que los Virreyes Dn. Antonio Mandoza y otros procuradores traer de paz a dicho Ynga ofreciendole perdon de todo y las tierras que habian sido de su padre que balian mas de 50 D (50 mil) pesos de renta en cada un añoy que tambien se le harian otras mercedes: Que por muerte del Virrey Mendoza sin poner en exe- //
/s.f.31/ cucion lo mandado por el Señor Carlos 5º se le cometio su observancia al Marques de Cañete el que escribio a Da. Beatriz Mango Capac tia de Sairitupac para que le persuadiese saliese de paz y diese la obediencia a S. M: que Da. Beatriz en desempeño de la confianza del Virrey embio a Juan de Sierra de Leguizamo su hijo y como tal Primo de Sairitupac a que tratase con este el asunto de dicha salida: Que Sairitupac ofrecio salir y dar la obediencia si se le hiciesen mercedes y señalasen rentas suficientes con que poder mantener su casa y familia con el decoro y distincion que le correspondia teniendo presente los muchos parientes que tenia: Que el referido Sierra paso a la ciudad de Lima a dar cuenta de la respuesta del Ynga a el Virrey el que con dictamen del Arzobispado Dn. Geronimo de Loaiza y de los Oidores de la Real Audiencia acordo que fuesen Fr. Melchor de //
/s.f.31v/ Los Reyes y Fr. Pedro de Arroyo del Orden de Santo Domingo para que con el Ynga tratasen de su salida para lo que le escribio el Virrey con muchas encarecimientos ofreciendole en nombre de S.M un Estado y Señorio con que se mantuviese y que en el interin le haria muchas mercedes ademas del regalo muy importante que le embio: Que dichos Religiosos con el referido Sierra fueron a Vilcabamba a dicho efecto ofreciendo a el Ynga que el Virrey en nombre de S.M. le daria 18 D (18 mil) pesos ensayados de renta anual en el interin que S.M. le daba dicho Estado y Señorio; en cuya vista embio dicho Sairitupac sus capitanes y Embajadores para que se asentase con ellos por el Marques lo que se le habia de guardar y mercedes que se le harian: Que en su vista el Virrey aprobo el ofrecimiento que habian echo los Religiosos y Sierra; el que aceptaron dichos //
/s.f.32/ Embajadores con la calidad de que todo fuese perpetuo para los hijos y descendientes del Ynga por via de Mayorazgo en el entretanto que S.M. le daba dicho Estado y Señorio y el repartimiento que tubo Francisco Hernandez Giron y el Valle de Yucay con todo lo a el sugeto como le poseyo Francisco Pizarro menor con cuya calidad prometio salir a dar la obediencia dentro de seis meses: que los citados repartimientos y tributos que pagaban los indios de ellos valian mas de 20 D (20 mil) ducados de renta en cada un año y que el Virrey en nombre de S.M. ofrecio a el Ynga le serian perpetuos y que el Rey le haria mayores mercedes; en cuya vista salio el Ynga con su Mujer y Familia y se presento a el Virrey dentro de los seis meses dejando en Vilcabamba mas de 20 D (20 mil) Yndios que le estaban sujetos y pagaban tributos como tambien los de las provincias de Capacatti Mañarias Momori y Pilcocones cuyos tributos y rentas valian en cada un año //

/s.f.32v/ mayor cantidad que la que el Virrey le dio en la fundacion de Mayorazgo que le hizo: Que el dia 5 de Enero del año de 1558 verifico su entrada en Lima dicho Sairitupac habiendole recibido el Virrey en las casas Reales estimando esta accion por el mayor servicio que pudo hacer a S. M. como publicamente lo decia dicho Virrey: Que en vista de haber cumplido el Ynga con lo que ofrecio el Virrey libro probicion con titulo de Mayorazgo perpetuo de dichos repartimientos de que aquel tomo posesion y los poseyo hasta que murio como los habian gozado sus antecesores libres de toda pension: Que ademas se dio a el Ynga titulo de Adelantado del Valle de Yucay con lo qual se baptizo y dio la obediencia y vasallaje a S. M: Que con los Indios que dejo se poblo la ciudad de San Francisco de la Victoria: Que si el Ynga por algun medio hubiese entendido que //

/s.f.33/ no se le habia de cumplir lo que se le ofrecio no hubiera salido y que aunque por armas se intentase lo executase servia muy dificultoso y con grandisimo gasto asi de parte de S. M. como de los vecinos e Indios de todo el Reyno: Que era justo y debido que para descargo de la Real conciencia se cumpliese todo lo que se le ofrecio a dicho Ynga y a sus hijos y descendientes dandoseles el Estado y Señorio que se les prometio haciendoles mayores mercedes en las tierras de sus antecepasados en recompensa de tantos millones de oro y plata perlas Esmeraldas y otras muchas cosas que los vasallos de la corona de castilla han sacado del Reyno del Peru: Que dicho Ynga quando se bautizo tomo el nombre de Diego y se caso infacte Eclesice con Da. Maria Cusi Guarcay su hermana con quien antes lo estaba segun las leyes Peruanas y que los que nacian de sus matrimonio se llama //

/s.f.33v/ ban Capac Ynga que quiere decir solo Señory asi vivio dicho Dn Diego con la referida su hermana y mujer legitima hasta que murio dejando solo por su hija legitima a la Coya Da. Beatriz que caso con Martin Garcia de Loyola Caballero del abito de Calatrava la que subsedio en todos los bienes mayorazgo derechos y acciones que tubo su padre: Que el año de 571 y 572 en que el Virrey Dn Francisco Toledo cometio al Doctor Fr. Pedro Gutierrez la visita del Valle de Yucay y otros pueblos de los repartimientos del mayorazgo de Da. Beatriz era este menor y estaba bajo de la tutela de Atilano de Anaya por poder que para ello tenia de su tio Dn. Diego Tito Cusi Yupangui su curador principal que estaba en la Provincia de Vilcabamba /al margen: A este Diego llaman Garcilaso Calancha y otros historiadores del Peru Felipe sin duda equivocadamente por que no vieron estos autos y sus recomendables pruebas/ que el referido Anaya fue muerto en Vilcabamba quando fue a tratar de paz con dicho Tito Cusi. Que el citado visitador hizo la visita de dicho Valle sin citacion ni noticia de Da. Beatriz ni de otra persona en su nom- //

/s.f.34/ bre diciendo a los Indios que los que fuesen Yanaconas no pagarian tributos y que asi todos dixeron que lo eran sin que los justificase en modo alguno arreglandose al Padron que le dio Diego Escudero cura de dicho Repartimiento: Que los 231 Yndios sobre que se seguia este pleito eran distintos y separados de los otros 332 sobre que tambien estaba pendiente otra causa de igual naturaleza con el Fiscal de S. M. segun resultaba de las minutas respectivas. Que Guainacapac fue Rey del Peru y tubo su recamara en el valle de Yucay y los Indios de el asi naturales como mitimas le serbian y a sus mujeres e Hijos beneficiandoles sus haciendas y haciendo el serbicio personal con que pagaban el tributo y no en otra cosa: Que luego que los españoles entraron en el Peru el Marques Dn Francisco Pizarro tomo para si dicho valle pagandole el tributo en servicio personal beneficiandole las haciendas //

/s.f.34v/ de coca que tenia llamadas Touo Yanabire Paucarbamba Yanatay y otras: Que en dicho tiempo los indios del Peru tenian tasa conocida y que en lugar de tributo daban a sus encomenderos el servicio personal como en tiempo del Ynga: Que por muerte de el Marques Dn. Francisco Pizarro subcedio en dicho Repartimiento su hijo menor: Que en virtud del asiento que el marques de cañete tomo con Dn. Diego Sairitupac poseyo este dicho Valle como sus antecesores y que por su muerte recayo en Da. Beatriz su hija y le poseyo hasta la ultima visita: Que los Indios contenidos en la memoria de esta causa eran naturales y mitimaes de dicho valle y son lo que siempre acudieron a pagar el tributo y tasa y que los que no son los antiguos son hijos de Indios tributarios de dicho repartimiento sujetos a Dn. Francisco Chilichi y Dn. Garcia Quispica //

/s.f.35/ pi Caciques principales de dicho Valle: Que el nombre de estar declarado que unos Indios pagaban un tributo y otros otro; unos mas y otros menos era por que los Caziques por sus fines particulares asi lo hacian: Que si dichos Caciques reservaban algunos Indios era por que unos eran hermanos Padres y Deudos de Indias con quien ellos estaban casados y amancebados y por que se serbian de ellos para sus grangerias y trabajo de sus chacaras: Que por dichas razones a los indios reservados por los Caziques llamaban Yanaconas aunque este era el nombre que tenian comunmente los que serbian a los Caziques aunque fuesen como eran tributarios: Que por auto del Virrey Toledo fue despojado de dichos indios la Coya Da. Beatriz sin que hubiese precedido pleito ni diligencia alguna ni se la notificase dicho despojo: Que por haber quitado a la suso dicha dichos indios y //

/s.f.35v/ los demas sobre que estaba pendiente otro pleito y por haber rebajado los tributos del estado repartimiento se minoro la renta de Da. Beatriz de tal suerte que se hallaba reducida a menos de cinco mil pesos la de los repartimientos sobre que el marques de Cañete fundo el estado Mayorazgo: Que Martin Garcia de Loyola Marido de Da. Beatriz era caballero notorio del orden de Calatrava Gobernador y Capitan General de las provincias del Rio de la Plata visitador de las ciudad del Cuzco Chuquisaca y Villa de Potosi y Corregidor de la Provincia de los Charcas cuyos empleos desempeño a satisfaccion del Virrey Dn. Francisco Toledo el que le nombro por uno de los

Capitanes que fueron a la Jornada de Vilcabamba donde sirbio a su costa hasta que se consiguio la prision del Ynga (que fue Dn. Felipe Tupac Amaro) y de sus Capitanes: Que a dicho //

/s.f.36/ Loyola nombro el Virrey Toledo por su Teniente General del distrito de la Real Audiencia de los Charcas que alborotaban con sublevaciones Rengifo y Borrero a quienes ahorco con cuyo castigo consiguio la quietud publica y que ultimamente fue nombrado por la Real Audiencia de Lima por General de la Mar del Sur llebando al Reyno de tierra Firme mas de tres millones pertenecientes a S. M. y a particulares en tiempo de Corsarios con gran riesgo de su persona y gastto de su hacienda: Que dicho Virrey mando que el estando Loyola por su entendimiento asistiese a los acuerdos de la Real hacienda de la provincia de los Charcas en la que aumento el Real Haber en mas de un millon de ducados anual; y en el año de 579 aumento 900 D (900 mil) pesos en el Ramo de los Azogues y la casa de Moneda de Potosi sin costo alguno de S. M.: Que para que S.M socorriese las urgencias que tenia le embio dicho Loyola mas de 100 D (100 mil) pesos en cada un año lo que //

/s.f.36v/ pedia prestado a sus amigos y vecinos de los Charcas ademas de lo que remitia de su hacienda: Que dicho Loyola siempre habia sido muy leal y celoso del Real Servicio por lo que y por su calidad discrecion suficiencia y autoridad de su persona podria serbir a S. M. en cosas de la mayor importancia tambien como el mejor; aunque no estaba gratificado de sus servicios como era publico y notorio cuyo Interrogatorio se presento en la Real Audiencia de Lima en 25 de Octubre de 1585 y a su tenor se mandaron examinar los testigos que fuesen presentados que fueron los Siguientes...

1. Fr. Pedro de Arona del Orden de Santo Domingo de 56 años............................
2. Garcia Gonzales..
3. Bartolome Diaz de Pineda de 70 años ....
4. Francisco Hernandez Palacio de 70 años ....
5. Pedro Godinez Osorio de 65 año ....
6. Francisco de Illescas de 80 años ....
7. Francisco Camargo de 40 años ....
8. Julian de Arincano de 48 años ....

/s.f.37/ 9. El Capitan Francisco de caceres de 55 años ....
10. Diego de Ocampo de 58 años ....
11. Diego de Agüero de 42 años ....
12. Sancho de Ribera de 40 años ....
13. Martin de Ampuero de 45 años ....
14. Francisco de Ampuero de 41 años ....
15. Don Pedro de Cordoba Guzman de 60 años ....
16. Lorenzo de Arona de 35 años ....
17. Alonso Nieto de Molina de 38 años ....
18. San Juan Velaustegui de 34 años ....
19. Juan Nuñez Albares Maldonado de 40 años ....
20. Juan de Mendiaz de 27 años ....
21. Pedro Lopez Barreales de 25 años ....
22. Alonso Lopez Barreales de 25 años ....
23. Francisco Gutierrez Caballeria de 45 años ....
24. Marcos Cano de 33 años ....
25. Juan de Espina de 50 años ....
26. Domingo de Jarro de 44 años ....
27. Rodrigo Bustillos de 80 años ....

Cuyos 27 testigos fueron juramentados en la Ciudad de Lima desde 13 de Noviembre de 1585 hasta 4 de Julio de 1587 por Juan de Montoya escribano de Camara de la Real Audiencia de dicha ciudad como //

/s.f.37v/ resulta de las diligencias originales **de foxas 539 hasta foxas 542** con que concluye el quaderno 1° de dichos autos por que **de foxas 543 hasta foxas 553** estan en blanco y rayadas; y remitiendome a lo que expondre al final del indice del Libro 4° de los instrumentos relatibos a el estado y Mayorazgo de Oropesa que se enuncian en este 2° lo firmo en la Villa de Madrid a 28 de Junio de 1795.

Dn Vicente Jose Garcia (Rubrica)

Frequent Abbreviations

acatami^{to}	acatamiento
acrecentami^{o}	acrecimiento
adel^{te}	adelante
admi^{on}	administración
ag^{to}	agosto
alçamy^{to}	alzamiento
Al^{o}	Alonso
Alt^{a}/Al^{a}	Alteza
Alv^{o}/Alvr^{o}	Alvaro
Ant^{o}	Antonio
a^{o}s	años
apelas^{on}	apelación
apercibimi^{o}	apercibimiento
aprovechamy^{o}	aprovechamiento
arrendami^{to}	arrendamiento
as^{to}	asiento
audi^{a}	audiencia
Bap^{a}	Bautista
bast^{e}	bastante
benef^{o}	beneficio
b^{e}s	bienes
Br^{me}	Bartolomé
Cab^{o}	Cabildo
cam^{a}	cámara
cap^{on}	capitulación
cap^{t}	capitán
Cast^{a}	Castilla
Cat^{a}	Catalina
cat^{ca}	católica
cinq^{ta}	cincuenta
cit^{on}	citación
c^{o}	consejo
com^{or}	comendador
conocimi^{to}/conoscimy^{o}	conocimiento
cont^{dos}	contenidos
contr^{a}/contr^{o}	contraria/o
correg^{or}	corregidor
crecimi^{to}	crecimiento
cump^{do}	cumplido
cumplimi^{to}	cumplimiento
dem^{da}	demanda
dha/dho	dicha/dicho
di^{e}	diciembre
dif^{o}s	difuntos
D^{o}/Di^{o}	Diego
doç^{os}	doscientos
D^{or}	Doctor
dr^{o}	derecho
ef^{to}	efecto
emplaçami^{to}	emplazamiento
encomy^{da}	encomienda
enp^{or}	emperador
ens^{da}	ensayada
escri^{o}	escribano
Exª	Excelencia
Exmo	Excelentísimo
ex^{on}/ex^{o}n	ejecución
ex^{te}	excelente

febr^{o}	febrero
Ff^{e}	Felipe
Franca/Fran^{co}	Francisca/ Francisco
Fr^{co}	Francisco
Gen^{al}	general
G^{o}	Gonzalo
g^{or}	gobernador
Greg^{o}	Gregorio
Gr^{mo}/Jer^{mo}	Gerónimo
hazi^{da}	hacienda
hebr^{o}	febrero
hen^{o}	enero
Her^{do}	Hernando
her^{no}	hermano
horden^{o}	ordenamiento
interro^{o}	interrogatorio
jui^{o}	juicio
juntam^{te}	juntamente
Ju^{o}/Ju^{a}	Juan/Juana
juram^{to}	juramento
jur^{on}	jurisdicción
just^{a}	justicia
largam^{te}	largamente
l^{do}/ll^{do}/licen^{do}	Licenciado
Lor^{ço}	Lorenzo
lugarteni^{e}	lugarteniente
M^{a}	María
Mal^{do}	Maldonado
mag^{co}	magnifico
mag^{t}/m^{t}/mag^{d}	magestad
Marq^{sa}	Marquesa
mayorm^{te}	mayormente
m^{de}/m^{do}	mande/mandó
m^{o}	medio
mem^{a}	memoria
m^{e}s/mr^{e}s	maravedis
M^{or}	Melchior
m^{or}/my^{or}	mayor
m^{o}s	menos
mrd	merced
nacimi^{to}	nacimiento
n^{e}	nombre
neces^{o}/nezes^{o}	necesario
neg^{o}	negocio
ning^{a}	ninguna
n^{o}/nobr^{e}	noviembre
noblecimi^{to}	noblecimiento
nombrami^{to}	nombramiento
not^{a}	noticia
not^{o}	notificó
notr^{o}	notorio
nov^{ta}	noventa
nro/nra	nuestro/nuestra
nuevam^{te}	nuevamente
num^{o}	numero
oblig^{on}	obligación
of^{o}	oficio
ofrecimi^{o}	ofrecimiento
orig^{al}	original
originalm^{te}	originalmente
oct^{e}/otr^{e}	octubre
p^{a}/pa	para
pacificaz^{on}	pacificación
p^{da}	pedida
p^{e}	padre
pedim^{to}/pedimy^{to}	pedimiento
perjui^{o}	perjuicio
pers^{a}	persona
pet^{on}/p^{on}	petición
P^{e}z	Pérez
P^{o}	Pedro
p^{o}	poderoso, puso
poss^{on}	posesión
preg^{do}	preguntado
preg^{ta}	pregunta
principalm^{te}	primcipalmente
prim^{a}	primera
pres^{dos}	presentados
presen^{on}/pres^{cion}	presentación
procu^{or}/pr^{or}	procurador
prorrog^{on}	prorrogación
prov^{a}	provincia
provis^{on}	provisión
pr^{te}	presente
ps^{o}	pesos
ps^{tes}	presentes
p^{ta}	plata
pte/p^{te}	parte
p^{to}	pleito
pu^{co}/pu^{ca}	público/a
pu^{o}	pueblo
q^{e}/q’	que
qr^{to}	cuarto
q^{tro}	cuatro
qui^{o}s	quinientos
qu^{ta}	cuarenta, cuenta
rectam^{te}	rectamente
regimi^{to}	regimiento
rei^{o}/rey^{o}	reino
remiss^{on}	remisión
repartimi^{to}	repartimiento
repu^{ca}	republica
requerimi^{o}	requerimiento
resid^{a}	residencia
R^{l}	Real
R^{o}	Rodrigo
sal^{o}	salario
Scriv^{o}	escribano

secret^{o}	secretario
seg^{da}/seg^{do}	segunda/segundo
servi^{o}	servicio
S^{e}s	Sanchez
ses^{a}	sesenta
set^{a}	setenta
set^{e}	setiembre
sig^{te}	siguiente
s^{r}/s^{ra}	señor/señora
S^{s}/ss^{es}	Señores
s^{ta}	santa
sup^{co}/supp^{co}	suplico
supp^{on}	suplicación
T^{do}	Toledo
ter^{no}	termino
testim^{o}	testimonio
tg^{o}/ts^{o}	testigo
ti^{e}	tiene
tpo	tiempo
tratami^{to}	tratamiento
tr^{do}	treslado
trib^{o}	tributo
tr^{no}	termino
tr^{o}	tercero
ultimam^{te}	ultimamente
V	Vuestra
V.M.	Vuestra Majestad
verdaderam^{te}	verdaderamente
vic^{o}	vicario
vra/vro	vuestra/o
v^{te}	veinte
vz^{o}/vez^{no}	vecino
Xaquix^{a}	Xaquixaguana
xpiano	cristiano
Xpoval/Xp^{o}bal	Cristóbal
ygualm^{te}	igualmente
Yll^{e}	Ilustre
Ympedimi^{to}	impedimento
ynfor^{on}	información
Yn^{a}s	Indias
yn^{o}s/y^{o}s	indios/as
ynport^{a}	importancia
ynterr^{o}	interrogatorio

Appendix A

Spanish and Andean Elites in the Yucay Valley in 1571

R. Alan Covey

Among the documents published in the present collection are copies of the *reducción* visits made in the Yucay Valley by Pedro Gutiérrez Flores in 1571. During these visits, Gutiérrez Flores produced a household-level survey of retainer families in four communities in the valley, recording the names and ages of husband and wife, the names and ages of children, and information on service and tribute payment. These data alone provide unparalleled glimpses into demography and household organization in the early Colonial period (see Covey and Elson 2007). The occasional designation of householder ethnicity and the identification of a retainer's master or mistress yield additional important information on migration patterns and the organization of retainer labor on lands formerly belonging to the Inka nobility. The following is a list of individuals with *yanakuna* in the Yucay Valley in 1571, with information about their identities. Masters and mistresses have been divided between Inka individuals, Cañaris and other Andeans, and Spaniards, with a final section for unclear or unknown entries.

Inkas

don Diego Acamaqui. A local elite named Acamaqui was conquered by Inca Viracocha. His town of Pacaycacha (Paqukancha?) was in the valley of Pisaq. A man named Camiqui (and Acamaque) was "cacique and señor natural" of the "natives" (*naturales*) in the Yucay Valley around 1550, and is described as an *orejón* (Sarmiento de Gamboa 1965[1572: ch. 25]; Villanueva 1971:42, 52). A prominent hill and *huaca* overlooking the Yucay Valley is called Ayamaqui (Dead Hand) (e.g., ADC Colegio Ciencias, L. 12, C. 31 [1785]).

don Juan Ayranbo [Ailambo]. *Kuraka* in charge of Tito Atauche's *yanakuna*. He declared that the lands worked by *yanakuna* in his charge were formerly worked by the guards of Huayna Capac's mummy. There is a town near Cajamarca called Ailambo.

Pedro de Bustinza [Bustincia]. Son of Beatriz Huayllas Ñusta (daughter of Huayna Capac and a princess from Huaylas) and the *conquistador* Pedro (or Martín) de Bustinza. He acted as *curador* of Beatriz Coya's estate while she was young, and accompanied the expedition that captured Tupa Amaro (AGN Real Audiencia, Causas Civiles, L. 13, C. 66 [1573]; Garcilaso de la Vega 1965[1609: bk. 9, ch. 37]; Guaman Poma 1980[1615: f. 467]; Hemming 1970:235, 239; Rostworowski 1962).

don Felipe Cari Topa. Is named as an Inka captain who supported the Spanish cause during the uprising of 1536 and was baptized along with Paullu Inca (*khipukamayuqkuna* 1974[1542/1609]). He later served in Cusco as a native *alcalde* in 1560. He was served by don Diego Gualpa Rimache, a Wanka from Xauxa. A Juan Cari Topa went to Yucay in 1550 to verify land tenure there (Espinoza Soriano 1974[1571]:192; González Pujana 1982; Villanueva 1971).

don Francisco Cayo Topa. Probably the son of Diego Cayo Topa, either an illegitimate son of Paullu or a descendant of Pachacutic. Don Diego Cayo appeared before Toledo as a descendant of Pachacutic, son of a man who served as *segunda persona* to Huayna Capac. A García Cayo Topa is named as an Inka captain who supported the Spanish cause and was baptized with Paullu Inca (*khipukamayuqkuna* 1974[1542/1609]). He claimed in 1585 to be a descendant of Tupa Inca Yupanqui and a member of Ayllu Cayao, and traced descent from a man by the same name who owned lands in Yucay before 1550. Francisco Cayo Topa led 1500 Cusco natives in the expedition against Tupa Amaro. He appears to have been an informant for Murúa's history (Heffernan 1995:75, n. 7; Hemming 1970:427; Rowe 1985:222; Sarmiento de Gamboa 1965[1572]; Stirling 1999; Toledo 1940[1571d]:167-73; Villanueva 1971:36-37).

don Hernando Chui Topa. Unclear. A Francisco Chui Topa appeared as a descendant of Tupa Inca Yupanqui in 1585 (Ayllu Cayao).

The Chuyes were an ethnic group from Bolivia, conquered by Tupa Inka, and the title of Chuy Tupa might have been conferred on one of his sons (Sarmiento de Gamboa 1965[1572: ch. 41]; Rowe 1985:222).

don Pedro Cochachi. *Cacique* of Ayllu Machi, reduced by Bandera into Yucay in 1558. He stated in Toledo's *informaciones* that he was from Chuquipata and served Beatriz Coya (Toledo 1940[1571c]:101-4; Villanueva 1971).

doña Beatriz Clara Coya. Daughter of Sayri Tupa and María Cusi Guarcay, heir of the Yucay estate (Hemming 1970; Rostworowski 1970).

doña María Cusi Guarcay. Daughter of Manco Inca, full sister of Sayri Tupa. The two received papal dispensation to marry. Garcilaso says she was the daughter of Huascar and a woman named Mama Guarcay (Garcilaso de la Vega 1965[1609: bk. 9, ch. 37]; Hemming 1970; Guaman Poma 1980[1615: f. 443]).

don Alonso Cusi Paucar. Possibly the son of Cusi Paucar, who along with Gualpa Roca was *principal* of Ayllu Cachi in 1558 (Villanueva 1971).

doña María Diez de Betanzos. Daughter of Angelina Añas Yupanki (a daughter of Huayna Capac) and Juan de Betanzos. She was raised in the Santa Clara monastery (Hemming 1970; Burns 1999).

Gualpa Roca [Rucana]. Cobo (1964[1653: bk. 12, ch. 19]) identifies Gualpa Roca as a military captain of Huascar's during the Inka civil war. Along with Cusi Paucar, he was listed as the *principal* of Ayllu Cachi in the town of Cachi in 1558. He had fields in the Yucay area that are referred to in a document of Angelina Yupanqui. A don Carlos Gualpa Roca is mentioned in the Betancur collection documents (Rostworowski 1962; Villanueva 1971).

Guari Tito. A brother or half-brother of Manco Inca, said to have been present at the Coricancha when he was sworn in as ruler. His son may be don Pedro Guari Tito, who is mentioned in 1573 as the brother of don Felipe Saire Topa and a descendant of Huayna Capac (although Hemming lists Pedro Guaritito as a son of Paullu). An Inka prince called Huaritico was killed by Atawallpa's troops while aiding the Spaniards as they traveled from Cajamarca. Niles notes that Guaman Poma identifies a Uaritito whose father was Huayna Capac and whose mother was a woman named Anahuarque (Hemming 1970:92; Niles 1999:112; Rostworowski 1970:254, 1963).

don Antonio Nari Gualpa. Possibly the same as a don Antonio Mariguacca who claimed to manage Beatriz Coya's *repartimiento* in Yucay (Toledo 1940[1571b]:71-74).

don Marcos Puri. Possibly the same person as a Marcos Hampire who claimed to be a *kuraka* of Guaro in Yucay in 1571. In the first household survey, he is said to be from Moyobamba. He stated that his grandfather had been appointed to the post by Tupa Inca Yupanqui. He had one hundred *yanakuna* and had stopped giving tribute during the conflict between Chilche and Quispecapi (Toledo 1940[1571c]:108-12).

don García Quispe Capi. A descendant of the Inka *cacique principal* in Yucay, who claimed all *naturales* in the Yucay Valley as his own grant. He, Francisco Chilche, and García Taina are mentioned as the *principales* of Yucay at the time of the 1572 *reducción* (f. 2, 90, 93v, 99v, 445v; Rostworowski 1962; Villanueva 1971:51).

don Jerónimo Quispe Capi. Probably the son of don García Quispicapi, who as the descendant of the Inka *cacique principal* had claimed all *naturales* in the Yucay Valley as his own grant (f. 2, 90, 93v, 99v).

doña María Ramírez. The wife of Juan Sierra de Leguizamo. It is unlikely that she was Inka, as she lived in Lima when she married. Her husband died in 1571, so it is likely that her access to tributary labor in the Yucay Valley was due to his descent from Huayna Capac (he was the son of the *coya* doña Beatriz Huayllas Ñusta, Sayri Tupa's aunt, and Mancio Sierra de Leguizamo) (Stirling 1999).

don Juan Sona. He was part of a group of Inkas baptized with Paullu (*khipukamayuqkuna* 1974[1542/1609]). In 1561, he testified in Juan Sierra de Leguizamo's *probanza de méritos*, stating that he (Sona) was *cacique principal* of the Inka elite (*orejones*). Testified in 1571 that he was a son of Tupa Yupanqui, and said to be a member of the lineage of Tupa Inca Yupanqui. Was served in the 1570s by Alonso Quella, the Chupaychu *kuraka* of Sauanmarca. Served in Cusco as a native *alcalde* in 1560 (González Pujana 1982; Stirling 1999:174; Toledo 1940[1571a]:61-64, 1940[1571d]:141-49).

don Felipe Saire Topa. Same as Felipe Cari Topa? In 1573, don Phelipe Sayre Topa Ynga was *principal* of the parish of San Cristóbal, and the thirty-four-year-old claimed descent from Huayna Capac (Rostworowski 1963).

don García Taina [Toma]. *Cacique principal* of Urcos (Urquillos). Was head of Ayllu Cuzco in the town at the time of Bandera's *reducción* (Rostworowski 1990; Villanueva 1971).

don Alonso Titu Atauche. The son of Titu Atauche, a son of Huayna Capac who was killed either during the civil war following Huayna Capac's death or during the Spanish invasion. He also presented himself as a representative of Huascar's and Tupa Inca Yupanqui's lineages. He had led soldiers against Girón's rebels, and was granted royal favors for his loyalty. In 1558, he was head of Ayllu Yanacona in Yucay, and, in 1571, was *alcalde* of Cusco, living in San Crostóbal. In 1570, he claimed to be about forty years old. He appeared in numerous legal proceedings in the later sixteenth century (Espinoza Soriano 1974[1571]:195-96; Hemming 1970:341-42; González Pujana 1982; Oliva 1895[1598: bk. 1, ch. 4]; Toledo 1940[1571d]:167-73; Rostworowski 1962, 1963; Rowe 1985; Sarmiento de Gamboa 1965[1572: ch. 69, 70]; Villanueva 1971).

don Alonso Topa Cusi Gualpa Ynga. An elite who appears to have served doña Ana Quispe. He was twenty-five in the first household survey. It is possible that he was related to the short-lived ruler Huascar, whose full name was Tupa Cusi Huallpa Inti Illapa (Sarmiento de Gamboa 1965[1572: ch. 60]). He was among the Inka population of the Yucay valley receiving lands in the repartition of 1595 (ADC Urubamba, L. 1, C. 3 [1595].

don Alonso Topa Rimache. Possibly related to a Topa Rimache who was a close relative of Manco Inca (Rostworowski 1970:256).

Francisco Villafuerte. A Francisco de Villafuerte was among the original citizens of Cusco, but this individual is referred to as "*indio de tasa.*" Since he is said to have married a Spanish woman, it is likely that this person took his name when baptised (Garcilaso de la Vega 1965[1609: bk. 9, ch. 30]; Lohmann Villena 1986:166).

don Felipe Ylla Topa. Probably the father or son of Hernando Ylla Topa.

don Hernando Ylla Topa. *Cacique principal* of Calca in 1577 (e.g., ADC Corregimiento, L. 1, C. 7 [1568]; Espinoza Soriano 1977[1577]).

don Carlos Ynga. Son of Paullu. He was given an *encomienda* after his father's death that included Pichigua, Yauri, Mohina, and Guayobamba (Hemming 1970; Calvete de Estrella 1964[1565-1567]; Cook 1975:130, 131, 202; Toledo 1940[1571d]).

don García Ynguil Topa. A descendant of Huayna Capac. Niles notes that Guaman Poma identifies an Inquiltopa whose father was Huayna Capac and whose mother was a Cañari woman. He was tortured by Loarte to reveal supposed connections between Cusco and Vilcabamba (Hemming 1970:454; Niles 1999:112; Sarmiento de Gamboa 1965[1572: ch. 62]).

Cañaris and Other Andeans

don Lucas Andabisnai. Unknown.

Cristobal Apassa. Possibly a Lupaqa? The chief Lupaqa leader in 1538 was Cariapaxa, and Cari was an inherited title. Garci Diez's *visita* lists several people with Apassa as a complete or partial last name. One chronicler states that Huayna Capac entrusted one of his daughters to the care of Cariapassa.

don Francisco Zaraunanta Chilche. Head of the Yucay Cañaris. Ran the *repartimiento* of Francisco Pizarro, and owned trees in the Chicon quebrada, where he had tributary laborers. He was chosen as *alcalde* of Carmenga (and Santa Ana?) in 1560. He states his age as seventy in 1570 (Garcilaso de la Vega 1965[1609]; Heffernan 1995; Hemming 1970; González Pujana 1982; Rostworowski 1963; Toledo 1940[1571c]:99-101).

don Hernando Guartanaula. Son of Chilche. He was *cacique principal* in Yucay in 1577 (Espinoza Soriano 1977[1577]; Heffernan 1995).

Juan Bautista Tulpulla. Son of Chilche.

Pedro Miguel. Served as *alguacil* to Francisco Chilche in 1560. Acted as interpreter to Francisco Chilche in a land case in 1573, and is described as *interprete general* in 1570, at which time he claimed to be twenty-five years old (González Pujana 1982; Rostworowski 1962, 1963).

don Francisco Pacanaula. Unknown.

don Luis Quisna [Quino]. *Principal* of Ayllu Guaro in the town of Cachi in 1558. Sarmiento mentions that Huayna Capac conquered an Ecuadorian leader named Quisna, perhaps the father of don Luis (Villanueva 1971).

don Alonso Ucusicha. Ecuadorian elite brought to Cusco by Guanca Auqui? A Cañar named Uarsucha is said to have been killed during Gonzalo Pizarro's rebellion (Betanzos 1999[1551-1557]; Villanueva 1971:39, 52).

doña Ynes. Wife of Francisco Chilche.

Spaniards

Hernando Bachicao. A Bachicao presented documents on his services in Cusco in 1539, and had a house in Cusco. He came from Nicaragua to Peru with horses and weapons to aid in suppressing the Inka uprising and was awarded a coat of arms in 1540 (AGI Patronato 93, N. 9, R. 8 [1539]; AGI Gobierno, Lima 566, L. 4, f. 111v [1540]). He later aided Gonzalo Pizarro's uprising in a trip to Panama where he seized weapons and ammunition (Gutiérrez de Santa Clara 1963-1964[ca. 1600]. He was captured and hanged by Carbajal at Juli, and his estate was condemned to a loss of goods and native service after the rebellion (Fernández 1963[1571: bk. II, ch. 80]). The Bachicao that appears in a 1570 document states his age as thirty-six, so he must be the son of the original one (Garcilaso de la Vega 1965[1609: bk. 7, ch. 9]; Guaman Poma 1980[1615: f. 420]; Lohmann Villena 1986:119; Rostworowski 1963; Zárate 1995[1555]).

Damián de la Bandera. Conducted a *visita* in the 1550s that led to limited reductions in some areas. He produced some chronicle information (Bandera 1965[1557]; Guaman Poma 1980[1615: f. 409]; Villanueva 1971). Francisco de Toledo appointed him as *corregidor* of Potosí and Charcas.

[Gabriel] Bermúdez [Vermudes]. Granted a *solar* in Yucay that had belonged to Mama Ocllo. He supported the royal cause during Gonzalo Pizarro's rebellion (Guaman Poma 1980[1615: f. 422]; González Pujana 1982:70; Zárate 1995[1555: bk. 6, ch. 16]).

Juan de Berrio. *Encomendero* who received holdings in Arapa, Lauray Ulpo, Coyango, and Guancarlara from Gasca. In 1536, he was named *capitán general* by Pizarro, and he was a witness to Pizarro's 1537 will. During the siege of Cusco, he was sent to Panama to raise troops to bring back, but apparently did not return until the rebellion had been suppressed (AGI Patronato 90B, N. 1, R. 55 [1572]). In 1539, he was a citizen in San Joan de la Frontera (Huamanga), but had holdings in Los Reyes as well and a house in Cusco. During the uprisings of the younger Almagro, Gonzalo Pizarro, and Hernández Girón, he supported the Crown cause (AGI Gobierno, Lima 1, N. 102 [1592]). He later served as *regidor* of the Cusco *cabildo*, and as *alcalde ordinario*. He was given lands in the Urquillos canyon following Bandera's visit around 1550 (AGI Lima 208, N. 2 [1586]; Cook 1975:87, 139, 180, 193; Fernández 1963[1571]; Garcilaso de la Vega 1965[1609: bk. 7, ch. 9]; González Pujana 1982; Hemming 1970:219-20; Lohmann Villena 1986:97, 124, 269, 270, 305, 342, 368; Ocampo 1999[1610]; Rostworowski 1962; Villanueva 1971:13).

Juan de Beres. Unknown.

Pablo de Carvajal. *Encomendero* who received rents from Olachea. He also had a *repartimiento* in Canas that included Cinto, Ansa, Bayba, and Lurucache. He was elected *alcalde* of Cusco in 1550 and was listed as a citizen of the city in 1560 (Cook 1975:113; González Pujana 1982; Ocampo 1999[1610]; Mendiburu 1902:237; Miranda [1578-1583] in Maurtua 1906:198).

Miguel Codicula. Unknown.

Geronimo Costilla. Wealthy *encomendero* and member of Cusco *cabildo*. He had arrived in Peru in 1535 and accompanied Almagro on his expedition to Chile. He was made *corregidor* in 1566, and was *justicia mayor* in 1573, and a knight of the order of Santiago. His holdings included Asillo, Culcora (Corcora), and Marasaca, as well as the town of Coceana (Burns 1999:47-61; Cook 1975:89, 194; Garcilaso de la Vega 1965[1609: bk. 7, ch. 9]; Hemming 1970:342-43; González Pujana 1982; Ocampo 1999[1610]; Rostworowski 1962, 1963; Toledo 1940[1571b]:92-95, 1940[1571d]:158-67; Zárate 1995[1555]).

Juan Enriquez. A Juan Enriquez was present in Peru in the late 1530s (Lohmann Villena 1986:188, 193).

Alonso de Loaysa. Was on a list of merchants granted permission in 1534 to travel to Peru with Almagro or Hernando Pizarro bearing 50,000 maravedies of merchandise (AGI Gobierno, Lima 565, L. 2, f. 31v [1534]). In 1541, he was a citizen of La Plata, and had received a town called Cochabilica, but he is listed as a *vecino* in the Cusco *cabildo* documents. He received a grant from Gasca following the Gonzalo Pizarro uprising that included Collana Aymara, Cupirpongo, Tambococha, and Amantuy. In Gasca's 1549 *tasa*, he had 870 tributaries in the province of Aymaraes. *Encomendero* who in 1557 claimed lands in Tiobamba and Amantuy that had formerly belonged to Tupa Inca Yupanqui. He was related to the archbishop of Lima and the archbishop of Seville (Cook 1975:116, 162; Garcilaso de la Vega 1965[1609: bk. 7, ch. 9]; González Pujana 1982; Lohmann Villena 1986:143; Ocampo 1999[1610]; Rostworowski 1962).

Diego López de Ayala. A priest with this name was a citizen of Cusco in the second half of the sixteenth century (AGI Gobierno, Lima 205, N. 4 [1561]).

Gonzalo Martín. A Gonzalo Martín is mentioned in a 1539 *provisión* dealing with the inheritance of *encomiendas* by widows and children (AGI Gobierno, Lima 565, L. 3, f. 156v [1539]). A Lope Martín, possibly his son, was given lands in the Urquillos canyon following Bandera's visit around 1550 (Villanueva 1971:13). This individual also served as a *regidor* of Cusco in the sixteenth century (AGI Indiferente 527, L. 1, f. 16 [1596]). His son was Antonio Pereira (AGI Gobierno, Lima 1, N. 147 [1595]; AGI Gobierno, Lima 1, N. 169 [1596]).

García de Melo. Crown official who served as treasurer of the royal *hacienda* in Cusco. He had served the Crown against Gonzalo Pizarro and Francisco Hernández Girón, losing a hand at the battle of Chupas (Cieza de León 1881[ca. 1550: ch. 78]). He had tributary labor in the town of Umay (Oma) in the Sacred Valley, and may have received part of Tupa Inka's Tiobamba lands. In the 1560s, he was sent to Vilcabamba to arrange a marriage alliance between Beatriz Coya and Quispe Titu, the son of Titu Cusi Yupanqui—part of a royal plan to convince Titu Cusi Yupanqui to leave Vilcabamba. In 1573, he was a judge of a comission and visitor to the Yucay Valley. He states his age as sixty in 1570 (Garcilaso de la Vega 1965[1609: bk. 7, ch. 9]; Hemming 1970; Toledo 1940[1571d]:158-67; Rostworowski 1962, 1963).

Martín de Meneses. *Encomendero* of Cotagucia (Cotahuasi), member of Cusco *cabildo*. In 1559, he sought possession of lands that had belonged to Huascar, near Paullu and Coya. He was part of the expedition to capture Tupa Amaro, and supposedly captured the golden image of Punchao (Cook 1975:129; Garcilaso de la Vega 1965[1609: bk. 7, ch. 9]; Hemming 1970; González Pujana 1982; Ocampo 1999[1610]; Rostworowski 1962). He returned to Spain and was granted a license to remain there with his son in 1587 (AGI Indiferente 2096, N. 178 [1587]).

Diego de Mercado. Early citizen of Peru and supporter of Almagro (Enríquez de Guzmán 1886[1543: ch. 55]), who was to receive the natives of Eredia if he returned to Spain (Lohmann Villena 1986:50, 87, 343; see AGI Patronato 110, R. 9 [1563]). A cleric named Diego de Mercado possessed an *encomienda* in the Titicaca Basin in the time of Toledo.

Cristobal de Ojeda. Unknown.

Juan Ortiz. A family crest was granted in 1540 to a Juan de Ortiz, who had come to Peru from Guatemala to aid in fighting against the Inka rebellion (AGI Patronato 169, N. 1, A1540, R. 1 [1540]). Pizarro instructed in 1535 that Juan Ortiz was to receive the natives of Beltran de Castro if he returned to Spain. Guaman Poma says that he rebelled against the Crown in the 1550s and was punished. A Diego Ortiz had labor tribute in towns called Xanxapo and Guamallata in the Cusco region in the 1570s (Cook 1975; Guaman Poma 1980[1615: f. 467]; González Pujana 1982:87; Toledo 1940[1571d]:158-67; Zárate 1995[1555]). A Juan Ortiz de Zárate is mentioned in several early Colonial sources.

Juan de Pancorbo [Celiorigo]. Original citizen of Cusco, he distinguished himself in the siege of Cusco. His son (also Juan de Pancorvo) received honors for the father's services (AGI Lima 566, L. 4, f. 195v [1541]; AGI Lima 566, L. 4, f. 202v [1541]) and held an *encomienda* that included Ayavire, Cupi, Olachea, Yparo, and Colono. He served as *alcalde ordinario* in 1559. A Cuyo elite from his *encomienda* appeared before Toledo in 1571. He ratified Sarmiento's history and provided testimony on the Inka past to Toledo, and appeared in a number of legal proceedings (Cook 1975:100, 113, 114, 288; Garcilaso de la Vega 1965[1609: bk. 7, ch. 10, 11]; González Pujana 1982; Lohmann Villena 1986:166; Ocampo 1999[1610]; Rostworowski 1962; Toledo 1940[1571b]:74-78; Trujillo 1985[1571]).

Juan de Salas [de Valdés]. *Encomendero* who held Taraco. He was an *alguacil* of Cusco in 1553. Also a member of the Cusco *cabildo*, and brother of the archbishop of Seville (AGI Lima 208, N. 1 [1586]; Cook 1975:92; Espinoza Soriano 1974[1553]:181-83; Garcilaso de la Vega 1965[1609: bk. 7, ch. 9]; González Pujana 1982; Ocampo 1999[1610]).

Diego Sanchez. Unknown.

Alonso de Tapia. Was on a list of merchants granted permission in 1534 to travel to Peru with Almagro or Hernando Pizarro bearing 50,000 maravedies of merchandise (AGI Gobierno, Lima 565, L. 2, f. 31v [1534]). An Alonso de Tapia was named *veedor* of Paria in 1537 (AGI Indiferente 416, L. 3, f. 95 [1537]) and granted a regiment in the Marañón Valley in 1538 (AGI Indiferente 416, L. 3, f. 38 [1538]).

Diego de Trujillo. Original conqueror and chronicler, whose grant included Lares and Matinga. He served on the Cusco *cabildo* and was *corregidor*. His testimony was sufficient to reallocate lands in the Yucay Valley. He appeared in a number of early legal proceedings, and wrote an account of the conquest (Cook 1975:204-5; Garcilaso de la Vega 1965[1609: bk. 7, ch. 9]; González Pujana 1982; Rostworowski 1962; Lockhart 1972; Trujillo 1985[1571]).

Unknown Masters/Mistresses and Those Known from Other Sources

Coya Cusi Rimay. A wife of Huayna Capac with Yucay lands (Villanueva 1971:52).

Inca Roca. Uncle of Huayna Capac, had Yucay lands (Villanueva 1971:52).

doña Inés. Daughter of Huayna Capac, granted ten topos in Yucay in 1560 (González Pujana 1982).

doña Beatriz Manco Capac Coya [Huayllas Ñusta]. Daughter of Huayna Capac, claimed a plot of *ají* in Yucay in 1573 (AGN Real Audiencia, Causas Civiles, L. 13, C. 66 [1573]; Rostworowski 1962).

doña Beatriz Cucul. Unknown.

Mama Ocllo. Mother of Huayna Capac, had lands in Yucay, probably for mummy (Villanueva 1971:52).

Manco Inca. Had a house near Chaoca in the Yucay Valley (Villanueva 1971:40, 53).

doña Juana Marcachimbo. A woman with lands and a house in Yucay around 1550 (Villanueva 1971:39).

Lucas Moreno. Unknown.

doña María Pasna. Unknown.

doña Paula. Unknown.

doña Ana Quispe. Unknown.

Raba Ocllo. A wife of Huayna Capac with Yucay lands (Villanueva 1971:52).

Don Felipe Sotapone. Unknown.

doña Menzia Toto. A doña Mencia Tocto Ocllo is described as a native of Calca in a repartition of lands in the Guayllabamba area in 1595 (ADC Urubamba, L. 1, C. 7 [1595]).

don Cristobal Uca Poma. Unknown.

don Cristóbal Vilca Topa. Unknown.

References Cited

Unpublished Archival Documents

Archivo Departamental del Cusco (ADC)

1785 ADC Colegio Ciencias, L. 12, C. 31. Autos ejecutivos iniciados por esta comisión contra las haciendas de Cacya, Quillabamba, Pastelero, Chuncarbamba, Tiobamba, en la doctrina de Maras.

1568 ADC Corregimiento, L. 1, C. 7. Autos de información de testigos que presenta don Gonzalo Rodríguez, en nombre de Hernando Illa y demás caciques principales de los indios de Calca, encomendados en don Arias Maldonado, sobre que en la mita de las chácaras de coca de Toayma y Quisquín, han muerto mucha cantidad de indios.

1569 ADC Urubamba, L. 2, f. 7-8v. Expediente sobre tierras de Paucarchaca.

1594 ADC Urubamba, L. 1, f. 1-2v. Repartición de tierras, Valle de Urubamba—Pichingoto y San Francisco de Maras.

1595 ADC Urubamba, L. 1, C. 3. Repartición de las tierras del Valle de Yucay entre el Cacique, el aillo Yngas del Cuzco los viejos y viejas huérfanos y viudas.

1595 ADC Urubamba, L. 1, C. 7. Disposiciones del Juez medidor de tierras del valle de Yucay.

1931 ADC Protocolo Notarial Basilio Cevallos. Testamento de Don Ángel Vega Enriquez. Cuzco 31 de agosto de 1931.

Archivo General de Indias (Sevilla) (AGI)

1534 AGI Gobierno, Lima 565, L. 2, f. 31v. Mandamiento del Consejo de Indias a los oficiales de la Casa de Contratación, para que dejen pasar a la provincia del Perú, en los navios de Diego Almagro o de Hernando Pizarro, a Alonso de Tapia, Alonso de Loaysa, Juan Méndez, Diego de Orellana, Juan de Valverde, Baltasar García, y Pero Días Conde, con tal que cada uno lleve 50,000 maravedies de mercaderías.

1537 AGI Indiferente 416, L. 3, f. 95. Real Provisión a Alonso de Tapia nombrándolo veedor de la provincia de Paria.

1537 AGI Patronato 90A, N. 1, R. 9. Legitimación de dos hijos de Francisco Pizarro.

1538 AGI Indiferente 416, L. 3, f. 38. Real Provisión a Alonso de Tapia haciéndole merced de un regimiento del pueblo donde residiere el gobernador y justicias del Río Marañón.

1539 AGI Gobierno, Lima 565, L. 3, f. 156v. Real Provisión de D. Carlos al gobernador de la provincia del Perú, por la que le manda que a la encomienda que tiene Gonzalo Martín, vecino de la provincia del Perú, aplique la carta acordada sobre la tasación de los indios y sucesión en la mujer e hijos de los encomenderos.

1539 AGI Patronato 93, N. 9, R. 8. Méritos y servicios de Hernando Bachicao.

1540 AGI Gobierno, Lima 566, L. 4, f. 111v. Nota de haberse despachado un privilegio de armas para Hernando de Bachicao, vecino de la ciudad del Cuzco, por el que se le concede el uso del escudo que se detalla en el documento.

1540 AGI Patronato 169, N. 1, A1540, R. 1. Concesión escudo de armas a Juan de Ortiz.

1541 AGI Lima 566, L. 4, f. 195v. Nota de haberse despachado una legitimación para honras y heredar en Indias a favor de Juan de Pancorbo, hijo de Juan de Pancorbo, con la condición de que no pueda suceder [a su padre] en los indios.

1541 AGI Lima 566, L. 4, f. 202v. Real provisión de D. Carlos al gobernador de la provincia del Perú por la que le manda que guarde para Juan de Pancorbo, vecino del Cuzco, la provisión dada sobre la tasación de las encomiendas y su sucesión en las mujeres e hijos de los encomenderos.

1551 AGI Patronato 90B, N. 1, R. 51. Provisión de la Audiencia de Lima sobre enviar dos hijos de Francisco Pizarro a España.

1561 AGI Gobierno, Lima 205, N. 4. Informaciones de oficio y parte, de Diego López de Ayala, presbítero, vecino de Cuzco.

1561 AGI Patronato 29, R. 16. Descripción de la ciudad de La Plata, Cuzco, y otros pueblos.

1563 AGI Patronato 110, R. 9. Méritos y servicios de Diego de Mercado.

1566-1568 AGI Justicia 657, N. 2. El fiscal contra Arias y Cristóbal Maldonado sobre el casamiento clandestino de doña Beatriz de Mendoza.

1572 AGI Indiferente 426, L. 25, f. 161r-161v. Real cédula mandando que ante el Consejo de Indias se revise un pleito criminal pendiente en grado de apelación entre el fiscal de dicho Consejo y Arias y Cristóbal Maldonado, sobre un delito contra Beatriz de Mendoza, hija de Saire Topa Ynga.

1572 AGI Patronato 90B, N. 1, R. 55. Informaciones de los méritos y servicios del Marqués don Francisco Pizarro, descubridor y conquistador que fue de los reinos del Perú.

1572 AGI Patronato 118, R. 9. Méritos y servicios de Martín García Oñaz de Loyola.

1576 AGI Lima 1, N. 3. Merced a Martín García de Loyola de 1000 pesos de rentas.

1578 AGI Patronato 3, N. 25. Validación matrimonio Cristóbal Maldonado y Beatriz Coya.

1586 AGI Lima 208, N. 1. Informaciones de oficio y parte, Juan de Salas de Valdés (El Mozo).

1586 AGI Lima 208, N. 2. Informaciones de oficio y parte, Juan de Berrio.

1587 AGI Indiferente 2096, N. 178. Expediente de prórroga de licencia para permanecer en España, a favor del Capitán Martín de Meneses, vecino del Cuzco, con su hijo Dionisio de Meneses.

1592 AGI Gobierno, Lima 1, N. 102. Sobre hacer merced a don Miguel de Berrio Manrique de 1,000 pesos de renta en indios vacos del Perú por dos vidas.

1595 AGI Gobierno, Lima 1, N. 147. Sobre hacer merced a don Antonio Pereira de un regimiento en la ciudad del Cuzco que vacó por muerte de su padre, don Lope Martín.

1596 AGI Gobierno, Lima 1, N. 169. Sobre hacer merced de 800 pesos de renta por dos vidas en indios vacos a don Antonio Pereyra en consideración a los servicios de su padre, el capitán Lope Martín.

1596 AGI Indiferente 527, L. 1, f. 16. Real Provisión a Don Antonio Pereira, dándole título de regidor del Cuzco, en Perú, en lugar del capitán Lope Martín.

1563-1761 AGI Lima 472. Expediente de D. Juan de Bustamante Carlos Inca sobre la sucesión en el estado de Oropesa y peticiones, testimonios sobre privilegios y mercedes concedidos a los descendientes de los Incas.

Archivo General de la Nación (Lima) (AGN)

1557 AGN Títulos de Propiedad, L. 1, C. 3. Títulos de las haciendas y tierras de Amantuy, junto al pueblo de Maras, Obispado del Cuzco, las mismas que pertenecieron a Doña Mariana de la Cuba Centeno.

1573 AGN Real Audiencia, Causas Civiles, L. 13, C. 66. Autos seguidos por Martín García de Licona, en grado de apelación, nulidad y agravio de ciertas sentencias dadas contra él por el Teniente de Corregidor de la ciudad del Cuzco capitán Francisco de Grado . . .

1586 AGN Superior Gobierno, L. 1, C. 10. Testimonio de las diligencias que se practicaron en el pueblo de Maras, en el Cuzco, por el Licenciado Dn. Gallen de Torres, Teniente de la Corregidor de la ciudad del Cuzco, sobre la propiedad de unas tierras que fueron pastos y moyas del Inca, las cuales pretendía los Padres de la Compañía de Jesús de esa ciudad.

1616 AGN Real Audiencia, Causas Civiles, L. 39, C. 150. Testimonio de los autos seguidos por D. Tomás Alvarez sobre el mejor derecho a la herencia de doña Felipa de Orué.

Published Sources

Alcina Franch, José (editor)
1976 *Arqueología de Chinchero*. Madrid: Ministerio de Asuntos Exteriores, Dirección General de Relaciones Culturales, Junta para la Protección de Monumentos y Bienes Culturales en el Exterior.

Amado González, Donato
2004 Ángel Vega Enríquez: Un gestor de la historia cuzqueña. *Revista del Archivo Regional del Cusco* 73-87.

Bandera, Damian de la
1965[1557] Relación general de la disposición y calidad de la Provincia de Guamanga. In *Relaciones Geográficas de Indias*

(Perú). Vol. I, edited by M. Jiménez de la Espada, pp. 176-80. Madrid: Ediciones Atlas.

Bauer, Brian S.
1992 *The Development of the Inca State*. Austin: University of Texas Press.
1999 The early ceramics of the Inca Heartland. *Fieldiana*. Anthropology, New Series, 31. Chicago: Field Museum of Natural History.
2004 *Ancient Cuzco: Heartland of the Inca*. Austin: University of Texas Press.
2007 *Kasapata and the Archaic Period of the Cuzco Valley*. Los Angeles: Cotsen Institute of Archaeology Press.

Bauer, Brian S., and R. Alan Covey
2002 Processes of state formation in the Inca Heartland (Cuzco, Peru). *American Anthropologist* 104(3):846-64.

Bauer, Brian S., and Bradford Jones
2003 The Early Intermediate and Middle Horizon ceramic styles of the Cuzco Valley. *Fieldiana*. Anthropology, New Series, 34. Chicago: Field Museum of Natural History.

Bélisle, Véronique, R. Alan Covey, and Carlos Delgado González
2007 Early Intermediate Period and Middle Horizon Interaction in the Xaquixaguana Plain. Presented at the 72nd Meeting of the Society for American Archaeology, Austin.

Betanzos, Juan de
1999[1551-1557] *Suma y narración de los incas*. Cuzco: Universidad Nacional de San Antonio Abad del Cusco.

Burns, Kathryn
1999 *Colonial Habits: Convents and the Spiritual Economy of Cuzco, Peru*. Durham, NC: Duke University Press.

Cahill, David
2004 First among Incas: the *Marquesado de Oropesa* litigation (1741-1780) en route to the Great Rebellion. *Jarbuch für Geschichte Lateinamerikas* 41:137-66.
2006 A liminal nobility: the Incas in the middle ground of Late Colonial Peru. In *New World, First Nations: Native Peoples of Mesoamerica and the Andes under Colonial Rule*, edited by David Cahill and Blanca Tovías, pp. 169-95. Portland, OR: Sussex Academic Press.

Calvete de Estrella, Juan Cristóbal
1964[1565-1567] *Rebelión de Pizarro en el Perú y vida de D. Pedro Gasca*. Biblioteca de Autores Españoles, vols. 167-68. Madrid: Atlas.

Chávez, Karen Mohr
1980 The archaeology of Marcavalle, an Early Horizon site in the Valley of Cuzco, Peru: Part I. *Baessler-Archiv*, neue Folge, 28(2):203-329.
1981a The archaeology of Marcavalle, an Early Horizon site in the Valley of Cuzco, Peru: Part II. *Baessler-Archiv*, neue Folge, 29(1):107-205.
1981b The archaeology of Marcavalle, an Early Horizon site in the Valley of Cuzco, Peru: Part III. *Baessler-Archiv*, neue Folge, 29(1):241-386.

Cieza de León, Pedro
1881[ca. 1550] *Guerra de Chupas*. Colección de Documentos para la Historia de España, 76. Madrid: Miguel Ginesta.

Cobo, Bernabé
1964[1653] *Obras del P. Bernabé Cobo de la Compañía de Jesús*. Vol. 2, edited by P. Francisco Mateos. Biblioteca de Autores Españoles, vol. 92. Madrid: Ediciones Atlas.

Cook, Noble David (editor)
1975 *Tasa de la visita general de Francisco de Toledo*. Lima: Universidad Nacional Mayor de San Marcos.

Covey, R. Alan
2003 A processual study of Inka state formation. *Journal of Anthropological Archaeology* 22(4):333-57.
2006a *How the Incas Built Their Heartland: State Formation and the Innovation of Imperial Strategies in the Sacred Valley, Peru*. Ann Arbor: University of Michigan Press.
2006b Chronology, succession, and sovereignty: the politics of Inka historiography and its modern interpretation. *Comparative Studies in Society and History* 48(1):166-99.

Covey, R. Alan, and Christina M. Elson
2007 Ethnicity, demography, and estate management in sixteenth-century Yucay (Cusco, Peru). *Ethnohistory* 54(2):303-35.

Covey, R. Alan, and Karina Yager
2005 Herding Practices in Cusco, Peru: Evaluating the Inka-Colonial Transition. Presented at the 70th meeting of the Society for American Archaeology, Salt Lake City, Utah.

Covey, R. Alan, and Nicholas Griffis
n.d. Archaic Period Settlement Patterns on the Xaquixaguana Plain. Manuscript in possession of the author.

Covey, R. Alan, Véronique Bélisle, and Allison R. Davis
2006 Variations in Late Intermediate Period Group Interaction in the Cusco Region (Peru). Presented at the 71st meeting of the Society for American Archaeology, San Juan, Puerto Rico.

Davis, Allison R., and R. Alan Covey
2007 An Early "Vertical Archipelago"? Patterns of Landscape Use on the Xaquixaguana Plain (2200 BC-AD 200). Presented at the 72nd meeting of the Society for American Archaeology, Austin, Texas.

Enríquez de Guzmán, Alonso
1886[1543] *Libro de la vida y costumbres de don Alonso de Enríquez, caballero noble desbaratado*. Colección de Documentos para la Historia de España, 85. Madrid: Miguel Ginesta.

Espinal, Manuel de
1959[1539] Relación hecha por el Tesorero Manuel de Espinal al Emperador. In *Cartas del Perú (1524-1543)*, edited by Raúl Porras Barrenechea. Colección de Documentos Inéditos para la Historia del Perú, 3, pp. 344-67. Lima: Sociedad de Bibliófilos Peruanos.

Espinoza Soriano, Waldemar
1974[1571] El habitat de la etnía Pinagua, siglos XV y XVI. *Revista del Museo Nacional* 40:157-220.

1977[1577] Los cuatro suyus del Cuzco, siglos XV y XVI. *Bulletin de l'Institut Français des Études Andines* 6(3-4):109-22.

Farrington, Ian S.
1984 Medidas de tierra en el Valle de Yucay, Cuzco. *Gaceta arqueológica andina* 3(11):10-11.
1995 The mummy, palace, and estate of Inka Huayna Capac at Quispeguanca. *Tawantinsuyu* 1:55-65.

Fernández, Diego "El Palentino"
1963[1571] Primera, y segunda parte de la Historia del Perú. In *Crónicas del Perú*. Vols. 1-2. Biblioteca de Autores Españoles, vols. 164-65, edited by Juan Pérez de Tudela Bueso. Madrid: Atlas.

Gade, Daniel W.
1975 *Plants, Man and the Land in the Vilcanota Valley of Peru*. The Hague: Dr. W. Junk B.V.

Garcilaso de la Vega, "El Inca"
1965[1609] Los comentarios reales de los incas. In *Obras Completas*. Biblioteca de Autores Españoles, vols. 132-35, edited by Carmelo Sáenz de Santa María. Madrid: Atlas.

Garrett, David T.
2005 *Shadows of Empire: The Indian Nobility of Cusco, 1750-1825*. New York: Cambridge University Press.

González Pujana, Laura (editor)
1982 *El libro del Cabildo de la ciudad del Cuzco*. Lima: Instituto Riva-Aguero.

Guaman Poma de Ayala, Felipe
1980[1615] *El primer nueva corónica y buen gobierno*, edited by John V. Murra and Rolena Adorno. Mexico City: Siglo Veintiuno.

Gutiérrez de Santa Clara, Pedro
1963-1964[ca. 1600] *Quinquenarios o Historia de las guerras civiles del Perú y de otros sucesos de las Indias*. Biblioteca de Autores Españoles, vols. 165-67. Madrid: Ediciones Atlas.

Heffernan, Ken
1995 Paullu, Tocto Usica, and Chilche in the royal lands of Limatambo and Quispeguanca. *Tawantinsuyu* 1:66-85.

Hemming, John
1970 *The Conquest of the Incas*. New York: Harcourt, Brace, Jovanovich.

Huaycochea Núñez de la Torre, Flor de María
1994 *Qolqas, bancos de reserva andinos: Almacenes inkas, arqueología de qolqas*. Cusco: Universidad Nacional de San Antonio Abad del Cusco.

Julien, Catherine J.
2001 Inca estates and the Encomienda: Hernando Pizarro's holdings in Cusco. *Andean Past* 6:229-75.

khipukamayuqkuna (Callapiña, Supno, and others)
1974[1542/1609] *Relación de la descendencia, gobierno y conquista de los incas*. Lima: Editorial Jurídica.

Lockhart, James
1972 *The Men of Cajamarca: A Social and Biographical Study of the First Conquerors of Peru*. Austin: University of Texas Press.

Lohmann Villena, Guillermo
1986 *Francisco Pizarro: Testimonio—Documentos oficiales, cartas y escritos varios*. Monumenta Hispano-Indiana, 5 Centenario del Descubrimiento de América, 3. Madrid: Consejo Superior de Investigaciones Científicas, Centro de Estudios Históricos, Departamento de Historia de América Fernández de Oviedo.

McEwan, Gordon F., Arminda Gibaja, and Melissa Chatfield
1995 Archaeology of the Choquepukio Site: an investigation of the origin of the Inca civilisation in the Valley of Cuzco, Peru. A report on the 1994 field season. *Tawantinsuyu* 1:11-17.

Mendiburu, Manuel de
1902 *Apuntes históricos del Perú y noticias cronológicas del Cuzco*. Lima: Imprenta del Estado.

Miranda, Cristóbal de
1906[1578-1583] Relación de los oficios que se proveen en el Reino del Perú, de las personas que los confieren y de los salarios asignados á ellos. In *Juicio de límites entre el Perú y Bolivia*. Vol. 1, edited by Victor M. Maurtua, pp. 151-280. Barcelona: Imprente Henrich y Comp.

Murúa, Martín de
1987[1590-1611] *Historia general del Perú*. Madrid: Historia 16.

Nair, Stella E.
2003 Of Remembrance and Forgetting: The Architecture of Chinchero, Peru from Thupa' Inka to the Spanish Occupation. PhD dissertation, School of Architecture, University of California, Berkeley.

Niles, Susan A.
1999 *The Shape of Inca History: Narrative and Architecture in an Andean Empire*. Iowa City: University of Iowa Press.

Ocampo, Báltasar de
1999[1610] Account of the province of Vilcabamba and a narrative of the execution of the Inca Tupac Amaru. In *History of the Incas*, translated and edited by Clements Markham, pp. 203-47. Mineola, NY: Dover Publications, Inc.

Oliva, Juan Anello
1895[1598] *Historia del Reino y Provincias del Perú*. Lima: Imprenta y Librería de S. Pedro.

Rivera Serna, Raúl (editor)
1965[1534] *Libro primero de cabildos de la Ciudad del Cuzco*. Lima: Universidad Mayor de San Marcos.

Rostworowski, María
1962 Nuevos datos sobre tenencia de tierras reales en el Incario. *Revista del Museo Nacional* 31:130-59.
1963 Dos manuscritos inéditos con datos sobre Manco II, tierras personales de los Incas y mitimaes. *Nueva Corónica* 1: 223-39. Departamento de Historia, Facultad de Letras, Universidad Nacional Mayor de San Marcos.

1970 El repartamiento de doña Beatriz Coya en el valle de Yucay. *Historia y Cultura* 4:153-267. Lima, Peru.

1990 La visita de Urcos de 1562. Un kipu pueblerino. *Historia y Cultura* 20:295-317.

Rowe, John H.

1982 Genealogía y rebelión en el siglo XVIII: algunos antecedentes de la sublevación de José Gabriel Thupa Amaru. *Histórica* 6:65-85.

1985 Probanza de los incas nietos de conquistadores. *Histórica* 9(2):193-245.

1990 Machu Picchu a la luz de documentos del siglo XVI. *Histórica* 14(1):139-54.

1997 Las tierras reales de los incas. In *Arqueología, antropología e historia en los Andes: Homenaje a María Rostworowski*, edited by Rafael Varón Gabai and Javier Flores Espinoza, pp. 277-87. Lima: Instituto de Estudios Peruanos.

Sarmiento de Gamboa

1965[1572] *Historia de los incas: Segunda parte de la historia general llamada índica, la cual por mandado del excelentísimo señor don Francisco de Toledo, virrey, gobernador y capitán general de los reinos del Perú y mayordomo de la casa real de Castilla, compuso el capitán Pedro Sarmiento de Gamboa*. Biblioteca de Autores Españoles, vol. 135. Madrid: Ediciones Atlas.

Stern, Steve J.

1987 The age of Andean insurrection, 1742-1782: a reappraisal. In *Resistance, Rebellion, and Consciousness in the Andean Peasant World, 18th to 20th Centuries*, edited by Steve J. Stern, pp. 34-93. Madison: University of Wisconsin Press.

Stirling, Stuart

1999 *The Last Conquistador*. New York: Sutton.

Titu Cusi Yupanqui, Diego de Castro

1992[1570] *Instrucción al Licenciado don Lope García de Castro (1570)*, edited by Liliana Regalado de Hurtado. Lima: Pontificia Universidad Católica del Perú.

Toledo, Francisco de

1940[1571a] Cuatro informaciones levantadas por orden del Virrey Don Francisco de Toledo . . . Hechas en Tambo de Vilcas en 27 de Enero, en Tambo de Pina en 31 de Enero, en Limatambo en 6 y 7 de Febrero y en Tambo de Mayo en 10 de febrero de 1571. In *Don Francisco de Toledo, supremo organizador del Perú: Su vida, su obra (1515-1582). Tomo II: Sus informaciones sobre los incas (1570-1572)*, edited by Roberto Levillier, pp. 47-64. Buenos Aires: Espasa-Calpe.

1940[1571b] Información hecha en el Cuzco por orden del Virrey Toledo . . . Cuzco, 13-18 Marzo 1571. In *Don Francisco de Toledo, supremo organizador del Perú: Su vida, su obra (1515-1582). Tomo II: Sus informaciones sobre los incas (1570-1572)*, edited by Roberto Levillier, pp. 65-98. Buenos Aires: Espasa-Calpe.

1940[1571c] Información hecha por orden del Virrey Don Francisco de Toledo . . . Yucay, Marzo 19-Julio 2 de 1571. In *Don Francisco de Toledo, supremo organizador del Perú: Su vida, su obra (1515-1582). Tomo II: Sus informaciones sobre los incas (1570-1572)*, edited by Roberto Levillier, pp. 99-121. Buenos Aires: Espasa-Calpe.

1940[1571d] Información comenzada en el Valle de Yucay . . . Junio 2-Septiembre 6 de 1571. In *Don Francisco de Toledo, supremo organizador del Perú: Su vida, su obra (1515-1582). Tomo II: Sus informaciones sobre los incas (1570-1572)*, edited by Roberto Levillier, pp. 122-77. Buenos Aires: Espasa-Calpe.

Trujillo, Diego de

1985[1571] Relación del descubrimiento del reino del Perú que hizo Diego de Trujillo en compañía del Gobernador don Francisco de Pizarro y otros capitanes, desde que llegaron a Panamá en año de 1530, en que refiere todas derrotas y sucesos, hasta 15 de abril de 1571. In *Francisco de Xérez: Verdadera relación de la conquista del Perú*, edited by Concepción Bravo, pp. 191-206. Madrid: Historia 16.

Valcárcel, Carlos Daniel

1970 Genealogía y persona de Túpac Amaru. *Revista del Instituto Peruano de Investigaciones Genealógicas* 25:59-68.

Valencia Zegarra, Alfredo I.

1982 Complejo arqueológico de Yucay. In *Arqueología de Cuzco*, edited by Italo Oberti, pp. 65-81. Cuzco: INC.

Varón Gabai, Rafael

1997 *Francisco Pizarro and His Brothers: The Illusion of Power in Sixteenth-Century Peru*, translated by Javier Flores Espinosa. Norman: University of Oklahoma Press.

1998 Las encomiendas de Hernando Pizarro. In *Actas del IV Congreso Internacional de Etnohistoria*. Vol. 2, pp. 535-49. Lima: Pontificia Universidad Católica del Perú.

Villanueva Urteaga, Horacio

1971 Documentos sobre Yucay, siglo XVI. *Revista del Archivo Histórico del Cuzco* 13:1-148.

Villar, Conde de [Torres y Portugal, don Francisco]

1906[1589] Carta del virrey Conde de Villar á S. M. dando noticia del estado de la provincia de Vilcabamba, y de la residencia intentada al Gobernador Martín Hurtado de Arbieto (12 de mayo de 1589). In *Juicio de límites entre el Perú y Bolivia*. Vol. 7, edited by Victor Maurtua, pp. 181-88. Barcelona: Imprenta de Henrich y Comp.

Zapata Rodríguez, Julinho

1998 Los cerros sagrados: panorama del período Formativo en la cuenca del Vilcanota, Cuzco. *Boletín de Arqueología PUCP* 2:307-36.

Zárate, Agustín de

1995[1555] *Historia del descubrimiento y conquista del Perú*, edited by Franklin Pease and Teodoro Hampe Martínez. Lima: Pontificia Universidad Católica del Perú.